THE OXFORD HANDBOOK OF

THE AZTECS

THE OXFORD HANDBOOK OF

THE AZTECS

Edited by
DEBORAH L. NICHOLS
and
ENRIQUE RODRÍGUEZ-ALEGRÍA

Oxford University Press is a department of the University of Oxford. It furthers
the University's objective of excellence in research, scholarship, and education
by publishing worldwide. Oxford is a registered trade mark of Oxford University
Press in the UK and certain other countries.

Published in the United States of America by Oxford University Press
198 Madison Avenue, New York, NY 10016, United States of America.

© Oxford University Press 2017

First issued as an Oxford University Press paperback, 2020

All rights reserved. No part of this publication may be reproduced, stored in
a retrieval system, or transmitted, in any form or by any means, without the
prior permission in writing of Oxford University Press, or as expressly permitted
by law, by license, or under terms agreed with the appropriate reproduction
rights organization. Inquiries concerning reproduction outside the scope of the
above should be sent to the Rights Department, Oxford University Press, at the
address above.

You must not circulate this work in any other form
and you must impose this same condition on any acquirer.

Library of Congress Cataloging-in-Publication Data
Names: Nichols, Deborah L., editor. | Rodríguez-Alegría, Enrique, editor.
Title: The Oxford handbook of the Aztecs / edited by Deborah L. Nichols and
Enrique Rodríguez-Alegría.
Description: New York, NY : Oxford University Press, 2016. |
Series: Oxford handbooks | Includes bibliographical references and index.
Identifiers: LCCN 2016010926 (print) | LCCN 2016011519 (ebook) |
ISBN 9780199341962 (hardback) | ISBN 9780197503591 (paperback) |
| ISBN 9780190634179 (eBook) | ISBN 9780199341979 (eBook) | ISBN 9780190634162 (eBook)
Subjects: LCSH: Aztecs.
Classification: LCC F1219.73 .O94 2016 (print) | LCC F1219.73 (ebook) | DDC 972—dc23
LC record available at https://lccn.loc.gov/2016010926

1 3 5 7 9 8 6 4 2
Printed by Sheridan Books, Inc., United States of America

Contents

List of Figures   xi
List of Tables   xxv
List of Contributors   xxvii

    Introduction—Aztec Studies: Trends and Themes   1
    Enrique Rodríguez-Alegría and Deborah L. Nichols

PART I ARCHAEOLOGY OF THE AZTECS

1. Ancient Stone Sculptures: In Search of the Mexica Past   21
Eduardo Matos Moctezuma

2. The Historical Sources: Codices and Chronicles   29
Juan José Batalla Rosado

3. Museums and the Conservation of Mexica Cultural Heritage   41
María de Lourdes Gallardo Parrodi

PART II HISTORICAL CHANGE

4. Comments on Cultural Continuities Between Tula and the Mexica   53
Luis M. Gamboa Cabezas and Robert H. Cobean

5. Aztec Settlement History   73
L. J. Gorenflo and Christopher P. Garraty

6. The Creation, Rise, and Decline of Mexica Power   93
Enrique Florescano

7. The Measure, Meaning, and Transformation of Aztec Time and Calendars   107
Anthony F. Aveni

8. Aztec Pictography and Painted Histories 117
   Elizabeth Hill Boone

9. The Languages of the Aztec Empire 129
   Jane H. Hill

10. Aztec State-Making, Politics, and Empires: The Triple Alliance 143
    Lane F. Fargher, Richard E. Blanton, and
    Verenice Y. Heredia Espinoza

11. Nahua Thought and the Conquest 161
    Michel R. Oudijk and María Castañeda de la Paz

PART III LANDSCAPES AND PLACES

12. Aztec Agricultural Production in a Historical Ecological Perspective 175
    Emily McClung de Tapia and Diana Martínez Yrizar

13. Population History in Precolumbian and Colonial Times 189
    Lourdes Márquez Morfín and Rebecca Storey

14. Aztec Urbanism: Cities and Towns 201
    Michael E. Smith

15. Tenochtitlan 219
    José Luis de Rojas

16. Aztec Palaces and Gardens, Intertwined Evolution 229
    Susan Toby Evans

17. Households in the Aztec Empire 247
    Kristin De Lucia

PART IV ECONOMIC AND SOCIAL RELATIONS IN THE AZTEC EMPIRE

18. Aztec Agricultural Strategies: Intensification, Landesque Capital,
    and the Sociopolitics of Production 263
    Christopher T. Morehart

19. The Structure of Aztec Commerce: Markets and Merchants 281
    Kenneth Hirth and Deborah L. Nichols

PART IV-A AZTEC MANUFACTURING

20. Aztec Use of Lake Resources in the Basin of Mexico — 301
    JOHN K. MILLHAUSER

21. Aztec Metallurgy — 319
    DOROTHY HOSLER

22. Aztec Obsidian Industries — 329
    ALEJANDRO PASTRANA AND DAVID M. CARBALLO

23. Aztec Lapidaries — 343
    CYNTHIA L. OTIS CHARLTON AND ALEJANDRO PASTRANA

24. Pottery and the Potter's Craft in the Aztec Heartland — 355
    LEAH D. MINC

25. Pregnant in the Dancing Place: Myths and Methods of Textile Production and Use — 375
    GEOFFREY MCCAFFERTY AND SHARISSE MCCAFFERTY

PART IV-B SOCIAL RELATIONS

26. Gender and Aztec Life Cycles — 387
    CAROLINE DODDS PENNOCK

27. The Human Body in the Mexica Worldview — 399
    ALFREDO LÓPEZ AUSTIN

28. Nahua Ethnicity — 411
    JAMES M. TAGGART

29. Inequality and Social Class in Aztec Society — 423
    MICHAEL E. SMITH AND FREDERIC HICKS

PART V AZTEC PROVINCES, FRIENDS, AND FOES

30. Structure of the Triple Alliance Empire — 439
    FRANCES F. BERDAN

31. Mexica War: New Research Perspectives — 451
    MARCO ANTONIO CERVERA OBREGÓN

32. Aztec Provinces of the Central Highlands 463
Maëlle Sergheraert

33. Aztec Provinces of the Southern Highlands 473
Gerardo Gutiérrez

34. Aztec Provinces of the Gulf Lowlands 495
Marcie L. Venter

35. Tututepec: A Mixtec Imperial Capital in Southern Oaxaca 509
Marc N. Levine

36. Cholula in Aztec Times 523
Patricia Plunket and Gabriela Uruñuela

37. The Independent Republic of Tlaxcallan 535
Lane F. Fargher, Richard E. Blanton, and
Verenice Y. Heredia Espinoza

38. The Tarascan (Purépecha) Empire 543
Anna S. Cohen and Christopher T. Fisher

39. Aztec Empire in Comparative Perspective 557
R. Alan Covey and Amanda S. Aland

PART VI RITUAL, BELIEF, AND RELIGION

40. Humans and Gods in the Mexica Universe 571
Guilhem Olivier

41. Aztec Art, Time, and Cosmovisión 585
William L. Barnes

42. The Aztec Ritual Landscape 595
León García Garagarza

43. State Ritual and Religion in the Sacred Precinct of Tenochtitlan 605
Alfredo López Austin and Leonardo López Luján

44. Aztec Domestic Ritual 623
Lisa Overholtzer

PART VII AZTECS AFTER THE CONQUEST

45. Post-Conquest Rural Aztec Archaeology 643
    PATRICIA FOURNIER G. AND CYNTHIA L. OTIS CHARLTON

46. A City Transformed: From Tenochtitlan to Mexico City in the Sixteenth Century 661
    ENRIQUE RODRÍGUEZ-ALEGRÍA

47. The Aztecs and the Catholic Church 675
    LOUISE M. BURKHART

48. Aztec Art after the Conquest and in Museums Abroad 689
    RAY HERNÁNDEZ-DURÁN

49. The Aztecs and Their Descendants in the Contemporary World 707
    ALAN R. SANDSTROM

Index 721

PART VII AZTECS AFTER THE CONQUEST

List of Figures

0.1 Panel, "Coming of Quetzalcoatl," of the mural, "The Epic of American Civilization," painted by José Clement Orozoco. Commissioned by the Trustees of Dartmouth College. Reproduced with permission of the Hood Museum of Art, Dartmouth College.   2

0.2 Map of the Triple Alliance Empire. Redrawn by Maëlle Sergheraert (this volume) and Kristin Sullivan after Berdan et al. (1996:Figure II.1).   4

0.3 The Basin of Mexico. Drawn by Kristin Sullivan.   5

1.1 The "Sun Stone" or "Aztec Calendar." Courtesy of the Templo Mayor-Instituto Nacional de Antropología e Historia, Mexico.   22

1.2 Coyolxauhqui. Courtesy of the Templo Mayor-Instituto Nacional de Antropología e Historia, Mexico.   22

1.3 Tlaltecuhtli. Courtesy of the Templo Mayor-Instituto Nacional de Antropología e Historia, Mexico.   26

3.1 Archaeological zone of the Templo Mayor. Photograph by author.   43

3.2 *In situ* conservation of the Mictlantecuhtli sculpture. Área de Conservación del MTM. Photograph by author.   44

3.3 Conservation of monumental ceramic merlon in front of the *calmecac*. Photograph by José Vázquez.   46

3.4 A headdress made of paper, rubber, wood, and agave fibers and a polychrome painted wooden mask from Offering 102 following conservation. Photograph by Estudio Michel Zabé.   47

4.1 Ceremonial precinct of Tula Grande. Arrows indicate Aztec structures built over Toltec ruins (Proyecto Tula digital collection). Redrawn by Luis Gamboa, edited by Kristin Sullivan.   54

4.2 The Burnt Palace showing the location of an Aztec tomb with Aztec III pottery (Proyecto Tula digital collection). Redrawn by Luis Gamboa, edited by Kristin Sullivan.   55

4.3 Late Postclassic anthropomorphic stone sculpture with serpent body (Museo Jorge R. Acosta, Acervo digital Proyecto Tula).   57

4.4 Aztec flint knife found in a stone box near Tula's *tzompantli* (Museo Jorge R. Acosta, Proyecto Tula digital collection).   58

4.5 (a) Aztec III Black-on-Orange bowl (Museo Jorge R. Acosta, Proyecto Tula digital collection). (b) Aztec III Black-on-Orange *molcajete* (ceramic grater) (Museo Jorge R. Acosta, Proyecto Tula digital collection). (c) Aztec III Black-on-Orange bowl (Museo Jorge R. Acosta, Proyecto Tula digital collection). 61

4.6 (a) & (b) Aztec III Black-on-Red bowl (Museo Jorge R. Acosta, Proyecto Tula digital collection). (c) Aztec III Black-on-Red copa (cup) (Museo Jorge R. Acosta, Proyecto Tula digital collection). 62

4.7a (a) Aztec IV Black-on-Orange *molcajete* (grater). (Museo Jorge R. Acosta, Proyecto Tula digital collection). (b) Aztec IV Black-on-Orange bowl. (Museo Jorge R. Acosta, Proyecto Tula digital collection). 62

5.1 The Basin of Mexico, showing major physical geographic features, archaeological survey regions, and key localities mentioned in text. Drawn by L. J. Gorenflo. 74

5.2 Illustrations of Aztec I–IV decorated Black-on-Orange pottery sherds and associated chronology (Aztec I illustrations provided by Destiny Crider; Aztec II–IV illustrations modified from Hodge and Minc 1991). Drawn by Kristen Sullivan and L. J. Gorenflo. 76

5.3 Settlement patterns in the Basin of Mexico, based on archaeological surveys, dating to the Late Aztec (a), Early Aztec (b), and Late Toltec (c) periods of occupation. Drawn by L. J. Gorenflo. 79

5.4 Summaries of Late Aztec and Late Toltec settlement based on survey data: number of sites by environmental zone (a); estimated population by environmental zone (b); number of sites by site type (c); and estimated population by site type (d). Drawn by L. J. Gorenflo. 81

6.1 The Mexicas emerge from Aztlan, represented by six houses next to a pyramid. To the right, an individual in a canoe symbolizes the exit from Aztlan, while the glyph 1 *Tecpatl* represents the year. To the far right is an altar to Huitzilopochtli inside of a bent mountain. From *Tira de la peregrinación* (*Codex Boturini*). Photograph from Kinsborough, II, Figure 1. Public domain. 95

6.2 The Basin of Mexico ca. A.D. 1400. After Gibson. 1964. Redrawn by author and Kristin Sullivan. 97

6.3 The *tlatoque* (rulers) of Mexico-Tenochtitlan. On the right: Acamapichtli, Huitzilihuitl, Chimalpopoca, Itzcoatl, Axayacatl, and Motecuhzoma Ilhuicamina. On the left: Tizoc, Ahuitzotl, Moteuczoma II, and Cuauhtemoc. From Sahagún, *Primeros Memoriales*, Fol. 51. Courtesy of the University of Oklahoma Press. 99

6.4 Extent of the Mexica empire ca. A.D. 1500, showing the areas conquered by each *tlahtoani*. Redrawn by Kristin Sullivan from public domain. 101

6.5	Mexica political organization ca. A.D. 1500. Prepared by author and edited by Kristin Sullivan.	102
6.6	1524 Map of Tenochtitlan. Courtesy of the Newberry Library.	103
7.1	The Aztec Day Signs: (a) *Cipactli* (Alligator), (b) *Ehecatl* (Wind), (c) *Calli* (House), (d) *Cuetzpalin* (Lizard), (e) *Coatl* (Snake), (f) *Miquiztli* (Death), (g) *Mazatl* (Deer), (h) *Tochtli* (Rabbit), (i) *Atl* (Water), (j) *Itzcuintli* (Dog), (k) *Ozomatli* (Monkey), (l) *Malinalli* (Grass), (m) *Acatl* (Reed), (n) *Ocelotl* (Jaguar), (o) *Cuauhtli* (Eagle), (p) *Cozcacuauhtli* (Buzzard), (q) *Ollin* (Movement), (r) *Tecpatl* (Flint), (s) *Quiahuitl* (Rain), (t) *Xochitl* (Flower). (Caso 1971:Figure 1).	108
7.2	The center of the celebrated Aztec Sun Stone, which depicts the five creations. (Aveni 1989:Figure 1).	111
7.3	Human history, the testimony of people, and natural history; the testimony of things are conflated in the Aztec interpretation of history. (Quiñones Keber, *Codex Telleriano Remensis*, f.42r.).	112
7.4	The Aztec map of Tenochtítlan. (Berdan and Anawalt, *Codex Mendoza* p.1r.). Reproduced with permission.	113
7.5	A contrast of early and late post-Conquest calendar wheels reveals the gradual intrusion of Western into indigenous temporal concepts: (a) the Calendar Wheel of Motolinía (1549) includes, in addition to *tonalpohualli* dates, an accompanying text listing corresponding *xihuitl* dates. (Calendar Wheel of Motolinia 1903; *Memoriales de Toribio de Motolinía*. G. Pimentel (ed.) Mexico); (b) the calendar wheel of *Gemelli* (1697) falsely emphasizes lunar months. (Gemelli-Careri Wheel, 1697; Berthe 1968:144).	115
8.1	Pictographic expressions: (a) the water goddess Chalchihuitlicue (*Codex Borbonicus* 5); (b) death of Motecuzoma and the accession of Axayacatl in the year 2 Flint (Tira de Tepechpan 12); (c) place sign of Coatepec (*Codex Boturini* 5); (d) place sign of Colhuacan (*Codex Boturini* 20). Drawing of (a) by Heather Hurst, drawings of (b)–(d) by John Montgomery.	119
8.2	Mapa Sigüenza. Reproduced with permission, Conaculta, Instituto Nacional de Antropología e Historia, Mexico.	122
8.3	Founding of Tenochtitlan in the *Codex Mendoza*, folio 2r. Photograph courtesy of the Bodleian Library, Oxford University.	123
8.4	Annals history of the *Codex Mexicanus*, pp. 71–72. Reproduction courtesy of the Bibliotheque nationale France.	125
12.1	Postclassic settlement in the Basin of Mexico (Sanders 1981).	183
12.2	Estimated extension of post-Aztec period *chinampa* cultivation in the southern Basin of Mexico (Luna Golya 2014). With permission of Luna Golya.	183

12.3	Composite aerial view of Ejido San Gregorio Atlapulco showing remnant *chinampa* plots (prepared by Guillermo Acosta Ochoa and Victor García, April 2014). With permission of Acosta Ochoa and García.	184
12.4	Characteristic flora of canals surrounding Ejido San Gregorio Atlapulco (photo Emily McClung de Tapia).	184
12.5	Excavation of a relict chinampa in Ejido San Gregorio Atlapulco (photo Emily McClung de Tapia).	185
13.1	Hypothetical population pyramid for Tlatilco. Used with permission and calculations done by Patricia Hernandez E. and Lourdes Márquez.	190
13.2	Population pyramid modeled for skeletal sample from the *chinamperos* of San Gregorio Atlapulco-Xochimilco, Late Postclassic period. Used with permission and calculations done by Patricia Hernandez E. and Lourdes Márquez Morfín.	192
13.3	Estimates and pattern of depopulation during the Colonial period in Greater Tenochtitlan. Source: Aguirre Beltrán 1946; Márquez Morfín 1993.	192
14.1	Epicenters of the Toltec capital Tula and Coatetelco, an *altepetl* capital in Morelos. A: modified from Mastache et al. (2002:92); B: map by Michael E. Smith.	202
14.2	Map of the locations of the best-documented Aztec cities. Map by Juliana Novic.	203
14.3	The main pyramid of Tenayuca. Photograph by Michael E. Smith.	203
14.4	Circular temple at Huexotla. Photograph by Michael E. Smith.	204
14.5	Central plaza at Ixtapaluca, looking north from the main pyramid. Photograph by Michael E. Smith.	205
14.6	Structure 1, a neighborhood temple at Calixtlahuaca. Photograph by Maëlle Sergheraert, Calixtlahuaca Archaeological Project.	209
15.1	The Valley of Mexico (Toussaint et al. 1938:155).	220
15.2	Tenochtitlan: First published in the *Relación* of the Anonymous Conqueror (Toussaint et al. 1938: 48).	221
16.1	The Nahuatl glyph for *tecpan* (noble house) as a stylized house in profile, surmounted by the ruler's copil headdress and featuring a lintel adorned with row of pierced disks (*chalchihuitl*), ancient symbols of preciousness. Drawing by S. T. Evans.	234
16.2.	Quinatzin's palace, a detail from the Oztoticpac lands map (1540s; see also Cline 1966). Library of Congress, Geography and Map Division.	236
16.3	Cihuatecpan's *tecpan* (noble house) development can be traced through three stages: the 1370s, the 1430s, and the post-Conquest sixteenth century. Drawing by S. T. Evans.	237

16.4	The plan of Nezahualcoyotl's palace in Texcoco featured a main courtyard overseen by the ruler's dais room, as depicted in the Mapa Quinatzin (1959 [ca. 1542]). Drawing by S. T. Evans.	240
17.1	Colonial-period house complex from Culhuacan, 1581 (after Lockhart 1992:Figure 3.4). Drawing by Santiago Juarez.	248
17.2	Examples of houses as depicted in the *Florentine Codex* (Sahagún 1950–1982). Courtesy University of Utah Press.	249
17.3	Example of house groups from El Canal, Tula (after Healan 1993:Figure 2). Drawing by Santiago Juarez.	252
17.4	Structure 1, an Aztec I period house at Xaltocan. Figure by Kristin DeLucia.	255
18.1	Low stone alignments of contour terrace system on Cerro Ahumada, in the northern Basin of Mexico. Photograph by author.	266
18.2	Canal embankment of Cuauhitlan River (Doolittle 1990, reproduced with permission).	268
18.3	Contemporary chinampa planted in maize at Xochimilco. Photograph by author.	268
18.4	Storage maize bin (*troje*) for tribute as depicted in the *Codex Mendoza* (Berdan and Anawalt 1992), reproduced with permission.	270
19.1	A Tarascan Marketplace. Illustration from the *Relacion de Michoacan*. Reproduced with permission.	283
19.2	Major Aztec cities and towns in the Basin of Mexico. Cities with *pochteca* merchants are shown in caps. Redrawn by Kristin Sullivan.	288
19.3	Map of Otumba and its workshops. Drawn by Kristin Sullivan.	289
20.1	Map of the Basin of Mexico showing locations described in the text. Map by author.	302
20.2	Assorted uses of products made from reeds: (top) merchants with a stool, carrying pack, and tall basket; (middle) baskets arrayed in preparation for a feast; (bottom) a noble woman on high-backed seat and *petate* (mat). *Florentine Codex*, Book 9:Figures 26 and 27, Book 10:Figure 76, © University of Utah Press.	305
20.3	Fishing and hunting in the lakes: (top) a fisherman using a net and canoe, (bottom) a hunter collecting birds from a net. *Florentine Codex*, Book 10:Figure 133, Book 11:Figure 187, © University of Utah Press.	307
20.4	Fragments of Texcoco Fabric Marked pottery from San Bartolomé Salinas, Estado de Mexico. Photograph by author.	308
20.5	Map of Middle and Late Postclassic salt-making sites in the Basin of Mexico during the Postclassic. Map by author.	309

22.1	Central Mexican obsidian sources and select population centers controlled by Triple Alliance cities. Note the corridor of sites leading to Sierra de Las Navajas that moved to Tenochca control. Drawn by authors.	331
22.2	Toponymns associated with obsidian (redrawn from the *Codex Mendocino*). Drawn by authors.	332
22.3	Depictions from the *Florentine Codex* of (a) obsidian scraper, blade, blade-core, crutch for removing prismatic blades, and a European razor for comparison with the blades; (b) classes of obsidian recognized by the Aztecs including green *tolteca itzli*. (Sahagún 1963:778–779).	333
22.4	Camp structures and workshop deposits in the Sierra de Las Navajas. Photo by Alejandro Pastrana.	336
22.5	Replica *machuahuitl* (obsidian-lined broad-sword). Photo by Alejandro Pastrana.	337
23.1	Reproduction of an obsidian ritual scepter and mirror. Objects and photo by Alejandro Pastrana.	347
23.2	Preforms for ritual scepters from a Sierra de las Navajas workshop. Drawing by Alejandro Pastrana.	348
23.3	Preforms for obsidian mirrors from a Sierra de las Navajas workshop. Drawing by Alejandro Pastrana.	349
23.4	Unfinished obsidian lapidary objects and tool from the Otumba lapidary workshop. Photo by Cynthia Otis Charlton.	350
23.5	Chert tools and artifacts from the Otumba lapidary workshop. Photo by Cynthia Otis Charlton.	351
24.1	Aztec Black/Orange types. Prepared by author.	357
24.2	Early Aztec and Late Aztec Red ware bowls. Prepared by author.	360
24.3	Comparison of Early Aztec (upper) and Late Aztec (lower) ceramic pastes from Orange ware (left) and Red ware (right). False color image of petrographic thin-sections showing size distribution and frequency of inclusions. Prepared by author.	361
24.4	Electron microprobe analysis indicating the composition of pigments used on Aztec Red wares. Prepared by author.	362
24.5	The clay worker (after Sahagún 1950–1982, Book 10:plate 136).	363
24.6	Comparison of normalized compositional profiles for Black/Orange and Red ware ceramics by production area (Chalco, Tenochtitlan-Ixtapalapa, and Texcoco). Note that Black/Orange ceramics are consistently higher in the rare earth elements.	367
25.1	Supported spinning with wooden spindle and disc whorl in a spinning bowl (Charney 1887). Redrawn by Kristin Sullivan.	377

25.2	Weaving tools as symbolic offerings for girl's bathing ritual (Sahagún 1950–1982). Redrawn by Kristin Sullivan.	379
25.3	Goddess Cihuacoatl with weaving batten (*Codex Magliabechino* 1983:folio 45. Redrawn by Kristin Sullivan).	380
25.4	Decorated spindle whorls from Cholula. Photograph by author.	381
26.1	Bathing and naming of a child from the Codex Mendoza (Berdan and Anawalt 1992). Reproduced with permission of Frances F. Berdan.	390
26.2	First folio of the parallel upbringing of children from the Codex Mendoza (Berdan and Anawalt 1992). With permission of Frances F. Berdan.	391
26.3	Female manuscript painter, *la pintora*, *Codex Telleriano-Remensis* (Quiñones Keber 1995). With permission, Bibliothèque nationale de France.	392
26.4	Sculpture of a *cihuateotl*. With permission @ British Museum.	395
27.1	The cosmos is divided into two time-space realms. The divine is the realm of the gods and supernatural forces and is composed of subtle substance. The profane realm is inhabited by beings (composed of dense substance) as well as the gods and supernatural forces. Thresholds between the realms permit communication. Drawn by author and Kristin Sullivan.	400
27.2	The body is composed of dense and subtle substance. The different souls are composed of subtle substance. Formative souls are necessary for human existence. In contrast, humans can survive without the different contingent souls. Prepared by author and redrawn by Kristin Sullivan.	402
27.3	Each god can separate into two or more different gods, and two or more different gods can join together to form a single god. These two processes are known as fission and fusion. The gods can also separate into multiple gods, which can join together again. These two processes are known as division and reintegration. Prepared by author and redrawn by Kristin Sullivan.	403
27.4	The god Quetzalcoatl can fission to form two different gods: Tlahuizcalpantecuhtli and Ehecatl. Tlahuizcalpantecuhtli and Ehecatl can fuse together to form the god Quetzalcoatl. Prepared by author and redrawn by Kristin Sullivan.	404
27.5	Parton gods belong to distinct hierarchies, presiding over the different *calpollis*, cities, ethnicities, and of all humankind. Prepared by author and redrawn by Kristin Sullivan.	405
28.1	Nahuat woman. Photo by author.	416
28.2	Nahuat men. Photo by author.	417
29.1	Palaces of Aztec nobles. The Texcoco and Tizatlan examples are from codices, and their size is unknown; the others are archaeological plans. See Smith (2008:ch. 4) for discussion and citations. Graphic by Michael E. Smith.	425

29.2	Urban commoner residence at Yautepec, Morelos. The dimensions of this structure (unit 517) are approximately 7 m × 5 m. Photograph by Michael E. Smith.	427
29.3	Labor and goods (left), often incorrectly called "tribute," paid by commoners to two nobles (right). Each box shows the number of laborers from a named community; to their right are bundles of cotton cloth (money). The nobles are identified by their name glyph. Redrawn from the *Codex Kingsborough*, lám. 5A (Valle 1995).	432
30.1	The Triple Alliance capitals and their domains in the Basin of Mexico. Map drawn by Jennifer B. Lozano.	441
30.2	*Pochteca* cities in the Basin of Mexico. Map drawn by Jennifer B. Lozano.	445
30.3	The Triple Alliance or Aztec Empire, 1519. Map drawn by Jennifer B. Lozano.	447
31.1	Experimental reconstruction of a *macuahuitl* by Marco Cervera and Marco Antonio de la Cruz. (Photo: Marco Antonio Cervera File).	453
31.2	Experimental reconstruction of a *teputopilli* by Marco Cervera and Marco Antonio de la Cruz. (Photo: Marco Antonio Cervera File).	454
31.3	Nezahualcoyotl as a soldier, with weapons that include a *macuahuitl* and *chimalli*. He carries a small drum on his back to transmit orders on the battle field. *Codex Ixtlilxóchitl*, Folio 106r.	458
31.4	Resin replica of a Mexica soldier, dressed as *Tzitzimitl*. First hyperrealistic reconstruction developed in Mexico for artistic and scientific purposes by *Caronte Lab* in consultation with Marco Cervera. (Photo: Marco Antonio Cervera File)	459
32.1	Map of the Aztec Empire. Based on Berdan et al. (1996:Fig. 11.1); redrawn by Marion Forest, Maëlle Sergheraert, and Kristin Sullivan.	464
32.2	Conquest of Xiquipilco by Tenochtitlan. *Codex Teleriano-Remensis*, folio 37v; redrawn by Maëlle Sergheraert.	465
32.3	Imperial taxes paid by the Huaxtepec Province. *Codex Mendoza*, folio 24v-25r; from Berdan and Anawalt (1992:4:54–55). Reproduced with permission.	466
33.1	Map of the southern highlands of Mexico showing areas that were Aztec provinces and other independent political entities. Map by author.	474
33.2	Language group distributions at the time of the Aztec Empire (after Barlow 1949). The area shown includes the modern states of Guerrero and Oaxaca, Map by author.	481
33.3	The union of Lord Couixcal and Matlatli Oçomaxoch from the Lienzo de Tlapa. By permission of Biblioteca Nacional de Antropología e Historia, Mexico.	482

33.4	Regions reported as under the control of the Aztecs but that do not appear in the *Codex Mendoza*. These regions were organized into 12 "strategic" provinces by Berdan et al. (1996). Map by author.	484
33.5	Map showing the deviations in shape and area of the interpretations of the Tlapan province (Barlow [1949] versus Berdan et al. [1996]). Note that the two graphic interpretations do not match the actual extent of the Tlapan province according to the *Cartas de Religiosos* (1904). Map by author.	485
33.6	Map showing the military campaigns of Aztec emperors in the southern highlands. Map by author.	486
34.1	Mesoamerican Gulf Lowlands showing conventional divisions and imperial provinces (Divisions within the Gulf Lowlands following Daneels 2012:25.1 and Stark and Arnold 1997:Figure 1; provincial boundaries adapted from Berdan et al. 1996:Figure II-1; Carrasco 1999; Gerhard 1993; Killion and Urcid 2001:Figure 9). Prepared by Marcie Venter.	496
35.1	Map of Oaxaca highlighting estimated boundaries of Tututepec Empire. (Based on Smith 1973:Map 4; Spores 1993:Figure 1). Drawn by author.	510
35.2	Tututepec Monument 6. Photograph by author.	511
35.3	*Codex Nuttall*, pages 45 (right) and 46 (left); (A) indicates the toponym for Tututepec or Yucu Dzaa ("Hill of the Bird"); while (B) shows Lord 8 Deer conducting a ballcourt ritual with a "Toltec" official; and (C) indicates a series of seven conquered place names pierced by spears. Copyright Dover Publications, used with permission.	512
35.4	Ceramic spindle whorls used for spinning cotton from household excavations at Tututepec. Photograph by author.	515
35.5	Mixteca-Puebla polychrome pottery bowl with tripod supports from household excavations at Tututepec. Photograph by author.	517
36.1	Map of the Puebla-Tlaxcala. Drawing by Patricia Plunket.	524
36.2	Map of Tollan Cholollan. Redrawn by Gabriela Uruñuela from the *Historia Tolteca-Chichimeca* ca. 1550:26v–27r.	526
36.3	Codex-style polychrome vessel from Cholula. Drawing by Gabriela Uruñuela.	528
37.1	Map Showing the geopolitical position of Tlaxcallan in the Postclassic Mesoamerican world. Prepared by Lane F. Fargher, Kristin Sullivan, and David Romero.	536
38.1	Map of the Tarascan Empire showing major archaeological sites within the Lake Pátzcuaro Basin, Michoacán, Mexico. Drawing by author.	544
38.2	Rattle for a Purépecha thunderstick composed of multiple bells around a central ring. From the cemetery at the site of Angamuco, Michoacán,	

	Mexico, Late Postclassic. Drawing by Daniel Salazar Lama for the LORE-LPB project.	545
38.3	Purépecha stirrup spouted vessel possibly for cacao. From the cemetery at the site of Angamuco, Michoacán, Mexico, Photo copyright of the LORE-LPB project, used with permission.	546
38.4	Traditional *yacata*-style pyramid composed of a rectilinear and circular element, from the site of Angamuco, Michoacán, Mexico. (A) Shows a plan view of this feature as a 5cm contour map; (B) shows a perspective view of this same feature using the same contour map overlain on a hillshade. All features derived from a .25 cm digital elevation model created from high resolution LiDAR data. Prepared by author	547
39.1	Imperial territory sizes and populations. Prepared by R. Alan Covey.	558
40.1	The 13 layers of heaven and the nine layers of the underworld based on beliefs from the Postclassic-period Central Highlands (*Códice Vaticano-Latino 3738* 1996:fol. 1v-2r). Reproduced with permission.	572
40.2	A *tonalpouhque* ("He who possesses the count of days") uses a codex to show a woman on the day ("10 Rabbit") on which her child will be baptized (Sahagún 1959–1982:I, Book 4: fol. 34 v°). Reproduced with permission.	574
40.3	Quetzalcoatl, with a mouth mask identifying him in his manifestation as Ehecatl, god of wind (*Codex Telleriano-Remensis* 1995:fol. 8 v°). Reproduced with permission.	576
40.4	Sacrifice of the young man representing the god Tezcatlipoca during the 20-day *Toxcatl* festival (Sahagún 1959–198:I, Book 2:fol. 30 v°) Reproduced with permission.	578
40.5	Tezcatlipoca, god of destiny, surrounded by the signs of the divinatory calendar (*Códice Fejérváry-Mayer* 1994:44). Reproduced with permission.	580
41.1	Images of goldsmiths at work. From the *Florentine Codex* 9, f52. Reproduced with permission.	587
41.2	The Aztec Calendar Stone, or Stone of the Sun. Drawing courtesy of Emily Umberger.	588
41.3	The Coyolxauhqui Stone. Drawing courtesy of Emily Umberger.	590
42.1	Aerial Projection of Lake Texcoco from the West. Image used with permission of Thomas Filsinger.	602
43.1	The Sacred Precinct of Mexico-Tenochtitlan according to Sahagún (1993: fol. 269r). Drawing by Fernando Carrizosa, courtesy of the Templo Mayor Project.	606
43.2	The Sacred Precinct of Mexico-Tenochtitlan according to Cortés (1994: second letter). Drawing by Fernando Carrizosa, courtesy of the Templo Mayor Project.	607

43.3 The archaeological zone of the Templo Mayor, Mexico City. Drawing by Leonardo López Luján, Saburo Sugiyama, and Michelle De Anda, courtesy of the Templo Mayor Project. 609

43.4 The archaeological zone of the Templo Mayor, Mexico City. Photograph by Leonardo López Luján, courtesy of the Templo Mayor Project. 609

43.5 Hypothetical reconstruction of the Templo Mayor. (A) sculptures of the goddess Coatlicue, (B) standard bearers, (C) geometric sacrificial stone, (D) Chacmool sacrificial stone, (E) Coyolxauhqui monolith, (F) Tlaltecuhtli monolith and Offering 126. Drawing by Tenoch Medina, courtesy of the Templo Mayor Project. 610

43.6 Templo Mayor Offering 126 was discovered under the monolith of the earth goddess Tlaltecuhtli. Photograph by Jesús López, courtesy of the Templo Mayor Project. 613

44.1 Long-handled censer recovered from Xaltocan house. Drawing by Viveros Sánchez. 624

44.2 Aztec rattle figurines and figurine mold. Drawings by Juan Joel Viveros Sánchez (left, center) and Tom Quinn (right). 627

44.3 Calendrical design motifs on household feasting pottery from Xaltocan: (a) Quadripartite design; (b) Cipactli motif; (c) spiral or oscillating motion motif. Drawings by Juan Joel Viveros Sánchez. 630

44.4 Disposal of household goods for the New Fire ceremony, Sahagún 1950–1982, Book 7:Figure 19 Florence, The Biblioteca Medicea Laurenziana, ms. Med. Palat. 220, f. 21r. Reproduced with permission of MiBACT. Further reproduction by any means is prohibited. 631

44.5 Household musical instruments recovered from Xaltocan house: (a) flute and flower from end of flute, (b) whistle, (c) rattle, (d) bone rasp or *omechicahuaztli*. Photograph by the author. 633

45.1 Map of central Mexico with locations mentioned in the text (base map adapted from Detenal 1:250,000 series 1970/1977: Cynthia Otis Charlton). 644

45.2 Aztec IV Black-on-Orange *molcajetes* from the Alameda district in Mexico City (upper row) and the Sierra de las Navajas obsidian source (lower rows). Adapted from Charlton et al. 2007:443–444. 648

45.3 Colonial Red wares. Top row: plate from Tlatelolco (adapted from Charlton et al. 2007:449). Bottom row: molded zoomorphic support from a tripod plate and a decorated spinning bowl from the Santa Inés site. Photos by Patricia Fournier G. 650

45.4 Colonial figurines from the Otumba site. Illustrations by Cynthia Otis Charlton. 651

45.5 Colonial high-backed scraper from the Sierra de las Navajas obsidian source. Adapted from Pastrana and Fournier 1998:491. 653

46.1 Some of the house lots excavated by the Programa de Arqueología
Urbana in the historic center of Mexico City. Drawn by the author, based
on maps published in Matos Moctezuma 1999:12, 2003:9). 663
1. Metropolitan Cathedral and Tabernacle.
2. Centro Cultural de España.
3. Donceles #97.
4. Plaza Manuel Gamio.
5. Guatemala #38.
6. Palacio del Marqués del Apartado.
7. Luis González Obregón #25.
8. Palacio Nacional.
9. Moneda #11.
10. Argentina #15, Librería Porrúa.
11. Licenciado Verdad #2-8.
12. Justo Sierra #33.
13. Correo Mayor #11.

46.2 Colonial Column Base with Tlaltecuhtli, ca. 1525–1537, stone. Courtesy
Instituto Nacional de Antropología e Historia, Museo Nacional de
Antropología, Mexico City. 666

47.1 Franciscan friars burn temples in the city of Tlaxcala, driving out gods
whom the indigenous artist, working later in the sixteenth century,
depicts as devils. Drawing in Diego Muñoz Camargo's *Descripçion de
la çiudad y prouincia de Tlaxcala*, f. 240v. Courtesy of the University of
Glasgow Library, Special Collections. 676

47.2 A Franciscan friar joins a Nahua couple in marriage. The groom wears
a traditional indigenous man's cloak; his adoption of European style
hat, shoes, and pants suggests he is of high social rank. Woodcut in Fray
Alonso de Molina, *Confessionario mayor, en lengua mexicana y castellana*
(Antonio de Espinosa, Mexico, 1565:f. 57r). Courtesy of the John Carter
Brown Library at Brown University. 677

47.3 The sixteenth-century church at Tepoztlán, Morelos. Photograph by the
author. 679

47.4 The Ten Commandments and the Seven Deadly Sins, adapted into the
Nahuatl language in one of the earliest surviving Nahuatl books. Fray
Pedro de Gante, *Doctrina christiana en lengua mexicana* (Mexico, 1547:f.
12v-13r). Courtesy of the John Carter Brown Library at Brown University. 681

47.5 The Hail Mary prayer in a pictographic catechism from 1714. A Nahua
notary named don Lucas Mateo painted the images and wrote out the
accompanying text of the prayer in Nahuatl. The kneeling figures in red
cloaks represent indigenous men praising Mary and Jesus. (*Doctrina
cristiana*, Egerton Ms. 2898, British Museum, f. 2v-3r). Courtesy Trustees
of the British Museum. 685

48.1 Unidentified artist, Colonial column base with Tlaltecuhtli, ca. 1525–37, stone. Courtesy of Instituto Nacional de Antropología e Historia, Museo Nacional de Antropología, Mexico City.   691

48.2 Unidentified artist, "The Founding of Tenochtitlan," Frontispiece: *Codex Mendoza*, ca. 1541, ink and watercolor on paper. Bodleian Library, Oxford University, Oxford. (Berdan and Anawalt, *Codex Mendoza* p.1r.). Reproduced with permission.   692

48.3 School of San José de los Naturales, "The Mass of St. Gregory," 1539, feathers on wood with paint. Musée des Jacobins, Auch, France. Reproduced with permission.   693

48.4 Unidentified Artist, "Calendar Stone," ca. 1502–1520, stone. Photograph by William T. Gassaway. Courtesy of Instituto Nacional de Antropología e Historia, Museo Nacional de Antropología, Mexico City.   695

48.5 Agostino Aglio, "Mexican Exhibition at the Egyptian Hall, Piccadilly," 1824–1825, drawing and lithograph. With permission of Getty Research Institute, Los Angeles.   697

List of Tables

9.1	Languages of the Aztec Empire and the Independent *Señorios* © *Author*	131
13.1	Ethnic Groups by Percentage in Mexico City in 1790. © *Author*	197
13.2	Some Survivorship Estimates for Eighteenth-Century Samples from Colonial Mexico City © *Author*	197
14.1	Sizes of Aztec Cities in the Late Aztec Period. © *Author*	207
16.1	Aztec Palaces and Parks: Late Postclassic Period, Central Highlands of Mexico. © *Author*	230
19.1	Types of Producer-Sellers in Large Daily Aztec Marketplaces. © *Author*	285
19.2	Levels of Commercial Involvement in Aztec Society © *Author*	293
29.1	Types of *Calpixque* (Tax Collectors) © *Author*	429
29.2	Wealth Differences among Social Categories © *Author*	431
33.1	Aztec Provinces of the Southern Highlands © *Author*	475

List of Contributors

Amanda S. Aland (Southern Methodist University)

Anthony F. Aveni (Colgate University)

William L. Barnes (University of St. Thomas)

Juan José Batalla Rosado (Universidad Complutense de Madrid)

Frances F. Berdan (California State University, San Bernardino)

Richard E. Blanton (Purdue University)

Elizabeth Hill Boone (Tulane University)

Louise M. Burkhart (University at Albany, State University of New York)

David M. Carballo (Boston University)

María Castañeda de la Paz (Universidad Nacional Autonoma de México)

Marco Antonio Cervera Obregón (Universidad Anáhuac México)

Robert H. Cobean (Instituto Nacional de Antropología e Historia)

Anna S. Cohen (University of Washington)

R. Alan Covey (University of Texas at Austin)

Kristin De Lucia (Colgate University)

Caroline Dodds Pennock (University of Sheffield)

Susan Toby Evans (Pennsylvania State University)

Lane F. Fargher (Departamento de Ecología Humana, Cinvestav del IPN—Unidad Mérida)

Christopher T. Fisher (Colorado State University)

Enrique Florescano (Instituto Nacional de Antropología e Historia)

Patricia Fournier G. (Escuela Nacional de Antropología e Historia)

María de Lourdes Gallardo Parrodi (Instituto Nacional de Antropología e Historia)

Luis M. Gamboa Cabezas (Instituto Nacional de Antropología e Historia)

León García Garagarza (University of California, Santa Barbara)

Christopher P. Garraty (Logan Simpson)

L. J. Gorenflo (Pennsylvania State University)

Gerardo Gutiérrez (University of Colorado Boulder)

Verenice Y. Heredia Espinoza (Centro de Estudios Arqueológicos, El Colegio de Michoacán)

Ray Hernández-Durán (University of New Mexico)

Frederic Hicks (University of Louisville, deceased)

Jane H. Hill (University of Arizona)

Kenneth Hirth (Pennsylvania State University)

Dorothy Hosler (Massachusetts Institute of Technology)

Marc N. Levine (Sam Noble Museum of Natural History, University of Oklahoma)

Alfredo López Austin (Universidad Nacional Autonoma de México)

Leonardo López Luján (Instituto Nacional de Antropología e Historia, Museo del Templo Mayor)

Lourdes Márquez Morfín (Escuela Nacional de Antropología e Historia)

Diana Martínez Yrizar (Universidad Nacional Autonoma de México)

Eduardo Matos Moctezuma (Instituto Nacional de Antropología e Historia)

Geoffrey McCafferty (University of Calgary)

Sharisse McCafferty (University of Calgary)

Emily McClung de Tapia (Universidad Nacional Autonoma de México)

John K. Millhauser (North Carolina State University)

Leah D. Minc (Oregon State University)

Christopher T. Morehart (Arizona State University)

Deborah L. Nichols (Dartmouth College)

Guilhem Olivier (Universidad Nacional Autonoma de México)

Cynthia L. Otis Charlton (Independent Scholar)

Michel R. Oudijk (Universidad Nacional Autonoma de México)

Lisa Overholtzer (McGill University)

Alejandro Pastrana (Instituto Nacional de Antropología e Historia)

Patricia Plunket (Universidad de las Americas Puebla)

Enrique Rodríguez-Alegría (University of Texas at Austin)

José Luis de Rojas (Universidad Complutense de Madrid)

Alan R. Sandstrom (Indiana University—Purdue University Fort Wayne)

Maëlle Sergheraert (Agence Nationale de la Recherché)

Michael E. Smith (Arizona State University)

Rebecca Storey (University of Houston)

James M. Taggart (Franklin and Marshall College)

Gabriela Uruñuela (Universidad de las Americas Puebla)

Marcie L. Venter (Murray State University)

THE OXFORD HANDBOOK OF
THE AZTECS

INTRODUCTION

Aztec Studies: Trends and Themes

ENRIQUE RODRÍGUEZ-ALEGRÍA
AND DEBORAH L. NICHOLS

THE Aztecs are among the most famous and most researched of all ancient civilizations. They have captured the imagination of the public and scholars alike for having one of the largest empires in the Americas; for their military might, great cities, art, and monumental architecture; and, perhaps most important, their program of ritual sacrifice. Claims of descent from the Aztecs are mobilized today by the Mexican government, by sports teams, and by many people living in Mexico and the United States (Sandstrom this volume). Today, themes related to the Aztecs, the Spanish Conquest, and Aztec heritage appear in artwork in Mexico and the United States (Carrasco 2008; Zamudio-Taylor 2001) and in some of the finest murals by celebrated artists such as Diego Rivera, José Clemente Orozco, and David Alfaro Siqueiros (Figure 0.1). International museum exhibits attract crowds of visitors to see Aztec art and artifacts (e.g., Brumfiel and Feinman 2008; López Luján and McEwan 2010). Much scholarly research and government funding is devoted to the Aztecs every year, yet many aspects of this ancient civilization are still unknown.

This handbook presents important developments in Aztec studies of the past half century, along with recent trends in Aztec scholarship. The chapters in the handbook show how Aztec scholars have taken advantage of the many lines of evidence available to them. This includes archaeological material, monuments and other works of art, architecture, and historical sources of both indigenous and European authorship in alphabetic as well as pictorial form. In spite of the rich evidence, we have much to learn about Aztec civilization, and the debates even include the meaning of the term *Aztec*.

FIGURE 0.1 Panel, "Coming of Quetzalcoatl," of the mural, "The Epic of American Civilization," painted by José Clement Orozoco. Commissioned by the Trustees of Dartmouth College. Reproduced with permission of the Hood Museum of Art, Dartmouth College.

THE MEANING OF *AZTEC*

Central Mexico was ethnically diverse in the early sixteenth century. Indigenous histories attribute that diversity to migrations reflecting shifting city-state politics and the importance of place as a primary dimension of ethnic identify (Berdan 2008:108; Taggert this volume). The term *Aztec*, meaning "people from Aztlan," remains controversial in the scholarly literature, yet it is the term most widely used by the public in Mexico and elsewhere in the world. *Aztlán* means "place of the herons" or "place of whiteness," and it refers to a probably mythic place north of central Mexico. It appears in ethnohistoric sources as the place where various groups began their migration before settling in central Mexico (León Portilla 2000; Matos Moctezuma 2012:19–20). In that sense, the term is general and could refer to any of the groups of people tracing their origins to Aztlan. Aztec does not refer to a specific ethnic group, and it was not used emically by indigenous groups (Berdan 2008:113). The primary sources do not use the term *Aztec Empire* (Barlow 1945). According to León Portilla (2000), *Aztec* has been most commonly employed in the English-speaking world since 1810, probably in an effort to distinguish between the ancient Aztecs and the modern Mexicans, given that the other commonly used term is *Mexica*.

Mexica is an ethnic name adopted by a group who migrated from Aztlán. Ethnohistorical sources state that Huitzilopochtli, patron god of a group that emigrated from Aztlán, appeared and explained to a group of Nahuatl speakers that they would call themselves Mexica from that day on, probably after one of their leaders called "Mexi." Huitzilopochtli gave them feathers for their ears, bows, arrows, and nets and ordered the sacrifice of three people (Matos 2012:20). Thus the new ethnonym was accompanied by some of the material goods that distinguished "civilized" people (especially bows and arrows) from others. Huitzilopochtli became their patron deity and guided their journey to settle in Tenochtitlan and Tlatelolco in the Basin of Mexico (Escalante Gonzalbo 1995; Florescano this volume; León Portilla 2000). *Tenochca* is a more specific term that refers to the people of Tenochtitlan (Umberger 1996). Both *Mexica* and *Tenochca* are prehispanic terms. Additional ethnic groups included the Acolhua, Tolteca, Matlatzinca, Culhua, Otomí, Teochichimeca, Tepeneca, Ocuilteca, Totonaque, and others that appear in ethnohistoric sources (Berdan 2008:118–120).

Nahua is an important and relevant term used by many scholars to refer to indigenous people after the Spanish Conquest. This linguistic label means "Nahuatl speaker," and people sometimes referred to themselves as Nahua (Lockhart 1992:1). The term introduces different problems, because people outside the Basin of Mexico, including in Guerrero and Tlaxcala, a rival confederation of the Triple Alliance, also spoke Nahuatl, along with people on the Gulf Coast and other parts of Mexico and central America. Further, in the Late Postclassic (A.D. 1350–1519), although about half of the people in the Basin of Mexico were considered Nahuas (specifically, Nahuatl speakers; see Hill this volume), others were Otomis, Mazahuas, and Matlazincas (Escalante Gonzalbo 1995).

Berdan (2008:113) has argued that "naming was no simple or static matter," and the difficulties in arriving at a stable term to refer to the Aztecs is an example. The use of terminology changed historically during the Late Postclassic, and it has changed among modern scholars. Readers will find some variation in the terms authors employ in this handbook, but, in general, different authors use *Aztecs* to refer to people incorporated into the empire of the Triple Alliance in the Late Postclassic period. An empire of such broad geographic extent (Fig. 0.2) subsumed much cultural, linguistic, and social variation, and the term *Aztec Empire* should not obscure that. Scholars often use more specific identifiers, such as Mexica or Tenochca, when appropriate, and they generally employ the term *Nahuas* to refer to indigenous people in central Mexico (Fig. 0.3) after the Spanish Conquest, as Lockhart (1992) proposed. All of these terms introduce their own problems, whether because they are vague, subsume too much variation, are imposed labels, or are problematic for some other reason. We have not found a solution that all can agree on and thus accept the varied viewpoints of authors. We use the term *Aztec* because today it is widely recognized by both scholars and the international public.

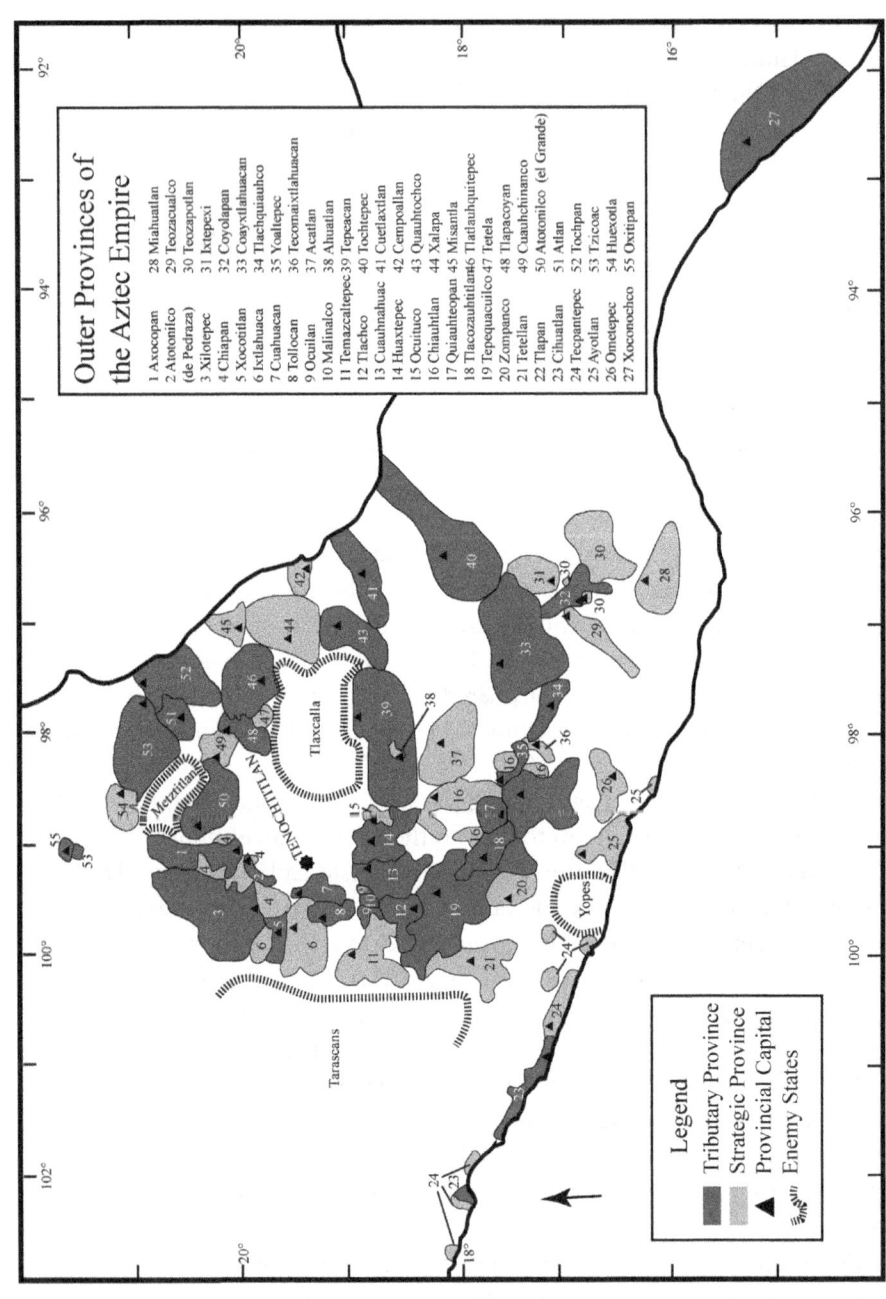

FIGURE 0.2 Map of the Triple Alliance Empire. Redrawn by Maëlle Sergheraert (this volume) and Kristin Sullivan after Berdan et al. (1996:Figure II.1).

FIGURE 0.3 The Basin of Mexico. Drawn by Kristin Sullivan.

Protoethnographies, Ecology, and Practice

Scholarship on the Aztecs in the past 50 years has developed in a variety of institutional contexts and diverse theoretical orientations, reflecting broader trends in Mesoamerican studies (Nichols and Pool 2012). Regardless of current theoretical orientations, most, if not all, scholarship about the Aztecs owes a great deal to the rich documentary record produced in the sixteenth century. Especially important sources are the proto-ethnographies written by Fray Bernardino de Sahagún (1950–1982, 1993) in the sixteenth century, historical chronicles of other Spanish conquistadors and colonizers, and the many sources written and painted by indigenous scribes and intellectuals (Batalla this volume; Boone this volume). Indigenous scholarship includes texts in Spanish, Latin, Nahuatl, Otomi, and other languages, as well as pictorial sources (Boone this volume). These sources form the core of most research on the Aztecs, regardless of the theoretical orientation. Newer facsimiles and editions of texts have stimulated new research and expanded geographic coverage (e.g., Batalla this volume; Boone this volume; Gutiérrez and Brito 2014; Williams and Hicks 2010; see also Lee and Brokaw 2010:7–8).

Incredible monumental finds in Mexico City, including the Great Coatlicue and the Aztec Calendar Stone, among others, have spurred an interest in Aztec archaeology and art history since the early nineteenth century (Matos Moctezuma this volume; Matos Moctezuma and López Luján 2012). The initial interest in Aztec antiquities was born out of an aesthetic admiration for the material remains, intellectual curiosity, and nationalist ideas (Keene 1971). A combination of these ideas and monumental findings helped create the institutions that have provided the context for research on the Aztecs, including the Museo Nacional de Antropología, the Instituto Nacional de Antropologia e Historia, the Escuela Nacional de Antropología e Historia, and the Templo Mayor Museum, among others. Scholars studying the Aztecs in these institutions have expanded their research programs well beyond the goals of nationalist culture history, developing theoretical perspectives and methodologies that include processualism or scientific archaeology, cultural ecology, Marxism, culture history, and theoretical holism firmly rooted in four-fields anthropology (Gándara 2012; Robles García 2012). The Templo Mayor project deserves special mention. For more than three decades it has directed research that combines excavation, cutting-edge conservation techniques, ethnohistory, and scientific research to provide an unparalleled view of the religion, architecture, and art of the Mexica (Gallardo this volume; López Luján and López Austin this volume).

The theoretical and methodological pluralism of scholars in Mexico has resulted in a series of contributions to Aztec studies that could benefit scholars interested in the past anywhere in the world. Among their major contributions we list the preservation of cultural patrimony, multidisciplinary research methods, the formulation of chronologies, an understanding of Aztec art and its role in society, and attention to the interplay of cosmology and different aspects of Aztec society. The work of Mexican scholars exemplifies the engagement of scholarship with the general public and a concern for how archaeology can improve the quality of life for people today (Robles García 2012:48). Their museum exhibits, educational programs for children, and publications, especially articles in the widely available *Arqueología Mexicana* journal, make some of the best scholarship on the Aztecs available to wide audiences in Mexico and beyond. Foreign-led projects, most often by scholars based in academic institutions in the United States, have had a major impact in Aztec studies as well.

Benjamin Keen (1971:567) attributed the recognition of the Aztec Empire in the mid-twentieth century as "one of the world's great civilizations" in part to important archaeological findings in urban capitals and to neo-evolutionary theories of the mid-twentieth century. Trigger (2003) included the Aztecs in his important comparative study of early civilizations, but Scheidel (2015) recently pointed out they and other civilizations of the Americas still do not receive enough attention in comparative studies. He attributes their omission to the way many comparative studies are chronologically framed and the fact that, before the late 1400s, states and cities developed in the Americas apart from interactions with Eurasia.

In mid-twentieth-century neo-evolutionary theory, landscape archaeology and cultural ecology inspired the Basin of Mexico settlement pattern survey that brought a regional perspective to Aztec archaeology and also encouraged the development of household archaeology, historic archaeology, and ethnoarchaeology (Gorenflo and Garraty this volume; Nichols 2004; Nichols and Evans 2009; Sanders et al. 1979). The surveys showed that the population of the Basin of Mexico, the core of the Aztec Empire, grew very rapidly during the thirteenth and fourteenth centuries, resulting in a population four times larger than in any previous period (Sanders et al. 1979:161). Growth took place in urban centers but also in rural areas, resulting in the highest density rural population in central Mexico of the prehispanic era.

Key to sustaining this demographic growth was a complex economic system that has been the focus of significant research, both documentary and archaeological, in recent decades. We thus devote a section of this handbook to Aztec technology and economy. The lakes provided an important artery of transportation and also a source of raw materials such as reeds and important foods. The presence of the lakes partly offset the lack of large, domesticated herbivores and facilitated the relatively high degree of urbanism even with limited transportation technology (Parsons 2008; Millhauser this volume). Intensive agriculture in central Mexico incorporated adaptations to both too little water (e.g., irrigation) and too much water (*chinampas* or drained fields; see Morehart, this volume). *Chinampa* development along the southern lakes was critically important to sustaining the growth of Tenochtitlan. People and land were bound in multiple ways—economically, socially, and culturally. McClung and Martinez (this volume) see historical ecology as offering a way to navigate between systems and agency-centered approaches. Morehart and Frederic (2014), for example, found that a combination of environmental and social factors led to the collapse of Xaltocan's *chinampa* system near the end of the fourteenth century.

Interest and debates about the political economy and ecology of Aztec hydraulic agriculture have been long-standing (Sanders et al.1979; Scarborough 2003). Luna (2014:54) shows in his analysis of aerial imagery how the expansion of *chinampas*, or drained fields, depended on system-wide controls of water levels of the southern lakes that involved construction of monumental hydraulic works in the mid-1400s. The scale of these works and the rapidity of the enlargement of the *chinampa* system convince Luna that this entailed central management. At the same time, the variability in *chinampa* construction observed by Frederick (2007) implies local control. This suggests situational state intervention for large construction projects and management of lake levels with tenant farmers and local corporate groups responsible for *chinampa* construction and maintenance.

A theoretical shift began in the 1970s from systems-centered perspectives of neo-evolution and cultural ecology to emphasize humans as agents shaping society and history in interaction with each other (in alliances, conflict, factions, social classes, and many other social groups and forms of interaction), as well as with the environment (McClung and Martinez this volume). In recent decades, scholars have applied and contributed to the development of diverse theoretical strands, including theories of agency and practice, collective action, feminism, Marxism, political economy, urbanism, and world systems, to explain the historical and social dynamics of the Aztecs and other Middle and Late Postclassic societies (Gándara 2012). Most, if not all, of the pioneers of these approaches to Aztec archaeology were mentored by scholars working under cultural ecology and processual theoretical orientations. In spite of the important theoretical shifts and the increasing interest in human agency, the current generation of scholars have always benefitted from the data and substantive contributions of the previous generation. In that sense, rather than a clean break from previous scholarship, their scholarship represents a development of knowledge, and it is testament to the rigor and solid contributions of previous generations of scholars.

A main contribution of this generation of archaeologists includes attention to variation across the Aztec Empire (e.g. Berdan et al. 1996; Blanton et al. this volume; De Lucia this volume; Garraty 2010; Garraty and Ohnersorgen 2009; Fargher et al. this volume; Fisher this volume, Gutiérrez this volume, 2013; Hodge and Smith 1994; Levine this volume; Plunket and Uruñuela this volume, 2005; Smith 2008; Smith and Berdan 2003; Venter this volume). Another major focus is on Aztec social relations in studies of gender, age, households, different social classes, and factions (Berdan 2014; Brumfiel 1991, 1992; De Lucia 2010; Overholtzer this volume; Pennock this volume Smith and Hicks this volume). The current generation of researchers has continued, and even increased, the efforts of previous generations to integrate research on the Aztecs with broadly relevant social theories, (e.g., Blanton et al. this volume; Blanton and Fargher 2008; De Lucia 2010; Garraty 2010; Smith this volume). Culture history remains an important focus of Aztec archaeology and ethnohistory in Mexico (Florescano this volume; Gándara 2012) Scholars have also sought to engage with the public through national and international museum exhibits (Brumfiel and Feinman 2008; Brumfiel and Millhauser 2014; Solis 2004a, 2004b; McEwan and López Luján 2009; Pohl and Lyons 2010).

Since the 1970s, a major contribution of art historians has been the integration of Aztec monuments into specific historical moments through the careful analysis of texts and formal aspects of the art (e.g. Townsend 1979). Scholars have shown that the monumental artwork of the Aztecs did not merely consist of ahistorical representations of deities and religious concepts but was also involved in particular historical moments and often made for political purposes. For example, Umberger (2007, 2012:821) suggests that the Coyolxauhqui stone in front of the Templo Mayor is not just a depiction of an element of the charter myth of the Mexica but also commemorated the Mexica victory in the war against Tlatelolco through a series of metaphors that portrayed Tlatelolcas as feminine and failed rulers. The study of monumental art has enhanced knowledge obtained from historical documents, making its own contributions to Aztec scholarship (Barnes this volume; Matos Moctezuma and Lopez Luján 2012; Townsend 1979; Umberger 1996, 2012).

Another major development in Aztec studies began in earnest in the 1990s. Called the "New Conquest History" (Restall 2012), its roots can be traced to previous decades, including seminal works by Gibson (1964) and Lockhart (1992). The New Conquest History has challenged histories that focus narrowly on Spanish conquistadors. It questions the Spanish as the sole protagonists of the Conquest and of Colonial Mexico and the overreliance on conquistadors' descriptions of Aztec society and the Conquest, including the victory of the Spaniards. Scholars have thus reexamined documents written by the Spanish. They also have studied a wealth of documents written in indigenous languages and pictorials drawn by indigenous people (e.g. Diel 2008; Mundy 2015; Wood 2003) to understand different versions of events, processes, and the perceptions and ideas of different people, whether Spanish, indigenous, or African.

Their contributions have shown that many indigenous people did not see themselves as conquered and defeated by the Spanish (Oudjik and Castañeda this volume; Restall 2003); that indigenous people and Africans were important participants, even protagonists, in the long process of the Conquest (Matthew and Oudjik 2007); that colonial Nahuas saw continuity in their colonial history well into the Aztec and pre-Aztec past (e.g., Diel 2008, Mundy 2015); and that there was much continuity in the daily life, politics, and economic life of indigenous people before and after the Spanish Conquest (Gibson 1964; Lockhart 1992). For decades, archaeologists and art historians also have studied the topic of change and continuity in daily life before and after 1521 (e.g., Boone and Cummins 1998; Charlton 1968, 1976; Charlton et al. 2005; Fournier and Charlton this volume; Pastrana 2007; Rodríguez-Alegría 2008).

THE FUTURE OF AZTEC STUDIES

We anticipate that the application of archaeological science and the pursuit of interdisciplinary science studies will continue to increase. Debates about sociopolitics and commerce and their roles in shaping the Aztec's other premodern economies drove much productive research during the late twentieth and early twenty-first centuries (Berdan 2014; Hodge and Smith 1994). Expanded applications of geochemical sourcing methods provided a means for archaeologists to track and model market exchange of household goods not detailed by chroniclers. These studies have been extended both back in time into the Early Postclassic and earlier and also into the Early Colonial period, to provincial areas of the Aztec Empire (Garraty 2013; Nichols et al. 2002; Rodríguez-Alegría et al. 2013; Skoglund et al. 2006), and across the boundaries of the Aztec Empire and neighboring states (Millhauser et al. 2015). The ceramic database for neutron activation analysis (NAA) for archaeological ceramics from the Basin of Mexico is now the largest in Mesoamerica, and it is heavily weighted with Aztec ceramics (Nichols et al. 2013). Combining NAA with other sourcing methods and attribute-based stylistic analysis can improve the resolution of composition groups and allow a finer-grained analysis of the market trade (Crider et al. 2017; Garraty 2013; Stoner et al. 2015).

Ethnohistorians have expanded their research about the Aztec economy to capture more of its geographic and cultural breadth (Berdan 2014). Few today would question the importance of commerce in the Aztec economy. Most goods continued to be made in household workshops that often engage in multicrafting to produce the large amounts of goods that move through the market and tax/tribute systems (Hirth and Nichols this volume; Nichols 2013) despite limited transportation technology (Garraty 2006:209). This research has contributed to broader theories of market development, although no Aztec marketplace has been excavated (Blanton and Fargher 2008; Garraty 2010; Hirth 2013). Comparative research is leading to new theories and new understandings of Aztec imperialism and Postclassic state formation and urbanization (Blanton et al. this volume; Covey and Aland this volume; Smith this volume). From a comparative perspective, Smith (2015) makes a strong case that the fiscal payments conventionally referred to as tribute for the Aztecs meet the criteria of taxes in their regularity. Moreover, Smith feels that use of the term *tribute* harkens back to the substantivist-formalist debates of the 1960s and 1970s that obscured understanding ancient/historic economies such as the Aztecs. Berdan (2014), on the other hand, feels that *tribute* better conveys the ritualized aspect of these payments and their expression of domination and subordination. The application of collective action theory by Blanton and Fargher (2008) is also advancing comparative studies of the Aztecs and organizational differences between their imperial state and the Tlaxcallans/Tarascans and other world regions (Fargher et al. this volume; Fisher this volume).

Demography remains a long-standing matter of debate among Aztec scholars. It is relevant to issues related to agricultural production, urban provisioning, imperial power, and post-Conquest demographic collapse, among others. The overall size of the populations in the core of the Aztec Empire, and in many of the major cities, including Tenochtitlan, is periodically debated using a combination of historical and archaeological evidence (Evans 2013: 49; Gorenflo and Garraty this volume; Storey and Morfín this volume), and future work may result in a better understanding of the size, composition, and histories of populations in the Aztec Empire. Isotopic and DNA analysis will contribute much to our understanding of the effects of disease, work, and the changing political conditions on populations in prehispanic and colonial Mexico (e.g., Mata-Míguez et al. 2012). The relatively small number of human remains from most Aztec provincial and rural sites has hindered biogenetic studies that can also provide important details about social relations. Given the number of Aztec houses that have been excavated, this is puzzling; perhaps there are prehispanic cemeteries that have yet to be discovered? The pioneering residue analyses of Luis Barba and his colleagues (1996) at the Templo Mayor to document rituals warrant broader application, as does the microarchaeology approach of De Lucia (2013) to households.

Research that focuses on the colonial period will remain a strength in Aztec studies, and we anticipate that the use of different lines of evidence, not just historical documents, will increase in the following decades. The use of material evidence, including archaeological material and works of art, will increase as scholars recognize the importance of all kinds of evidence to discover different aspects of the lives of colonial Nahuas, Spaniards, Africans, and *castas* (Fournier and Charlton this volume; Rodríguez-Alegría this volume). In the years ahead, scholars will intensify their attention to indigenous material culture and power in the Colonial period, including in places that have been traditionally associated with the Spanish, such as Mexico City. Scholars have shown not only continuity in household material culture but also the construction of public architecture associated with indigenous rulership in Mexico City in the Colonial period (Mundy 2015). As researchers find empirical and theoretical support for understanding the dynamics of indigenous power, politics, and social stratification in colonial Mexico City, this will add complexity to previous models that emphasized Spanish rule. It is likely that a model that emphasizes parallel structures of power and governance, one Spanish and one indigenous, will emerge, or that the complexity of power and governance in Colonial Mexico and its consequences for social and cultural life will be even greater than we can imagine now.

Finally, we anticipate that scholars will enhance their efforts in collaborating with contemporary populations that think of the Aztecs as an important part of their heritage (Sandstrom this volume). Collaborations will likely include consulting with descendant communities to understand their questions, assess the impact of knowledge production on their lives, and identify the ways that scholarly research may benefit those communities. Intellectual work by colonial and contemporary Nahuas is capturing the interest of contemporary scholars (McDonough 2014), and we believe such an interest will increase in years ahead. The revived interest in communicating and collaborating with contemporary communities can only make our work on the Aztec Empire more relevant and more useful to society. Public debates about the Aztecs often address stereotypes and overemphasize Aztec sacrifice, morality, cannibalism, and warfare. The scholarship we present in this volume, and scholarship in the decades ahead, will continue to add nuance to those debates and counterbalance the tendency to provide normative depictions of Aztec society by showing the rich variety of the social and cultural lives of the many people who formed the Aztec world.

Acknowledgments

We thank the Claire Garber Goodman Fund and the William J. Bryant 1925 Professor of Anthropology, Dartmouth College, and the University of Texas for their support of this handbook. Kristin Sullivan translated articles from Spanish and guided the preparation of many of the maps and drawings; we deeply appreciate her contributions and commitment to the project. Linda Gregonis skillfylly prepared the index. Research in Mexico is conducted under the auspices of the Instituto Nacional de Antropología e Historia, which is responsible for stewarding the nation's patrimony. The National Science Foundation along with the National Endowment for the Humanities, has supported our research in Mexico and the work of many other US authors contributing to the handbook. We thank the editors of Oxford University Press, including Stefan Vranka, and Sasirekka Gopalakrishnan and the Newgen staff for bringing this project to fruition.

References Cited

Barba, Luis, A. Ortiz. K. F. Link López Luján, and L. Lazos
1996 Chemical Analyses of Residues in Floors and the Reconstruction of Ritual Activities at the Templo Mayor, Mexico. *Archaeological Chemistry* 625:139–156.
Barlow, R. H.
1945 Some Remarks on the Term "Aztec Empire." *The Americas* 1(3):345–349.
Berdan Frances F.
2007 *The Technology of Ancient Mesoamerican Mosaics: An Experimental Investigation of Alternative Super Glues*. Report to FAMSI. Electronic document http://www.famsi.org/reports/06015/, accessed 6 April 2015.
2008 Concepts of Ethnicity and Class in Aztec-Period Mexico. In *Ethnic Identity in Nahua Mesoamerica*, edited by Frances F. Berdan, John K. Chance, Alan R. Sandstrom, Barbara L. Stark, James Taggart, and Emily Umberger, pp. 105–132. University of Utah Press, Salt Lake City.
2014 *Aztec Archaeology and Ethnohistory*. Cambridge University Press, Cambridge, UK.
Berdan, Frances F., Richard E. Blanton, Elizabeth Hill Boone, Mary G. Hodge, Michael E. Smith, and Emily Umberger (editors)
1996 *Aztec Imperial Strategies*. Dumbarton Oaks Research and Library Collection, Washington, DC.
Blanton, Richard E., and Lane F. Fargher
2008 *Collective Action in the Formation of Pre-Modern States*. Springer, New York.
Boone, Elizabeth Hill, and Tom Cummins (editors)
1998 *Native Traditions in the Post-Conquest World*. Dumbarton Oaks Research and Library Collection, Washington, DC.
Brumfiel, Elizabeth M.
1991 Weaving and Cooking: Women's Production in Aztec Mexico. In *Engendering Archaeology: Women and Prehistory*, edited by Joan M. Gero and Margaret W. Conkey, pp. 224–251. Basil Blackwell, Oxford.
1992 Distinguished Lecture in Archaeology: Breaking and Entering the Ecosystem—Gender, Class, and Faction Steal the Show. *American Anthropologist* 94:551–567.

Brumfiel, Elizabeth M., and Gary Feinman (editors)
2008 *The Aztec World*. Abrams, New York.
Brumfiel, Elizabeth M., and John Millhauser
2014 Representing Tenochtitlan: Understanding Urban Life by Collecting Material Culture. *Museum Anthropology* 37(1):6–16.
Carrasco, David
2008 Imagining a Place for Aztlan: Chicanismo and the Aztecs in Art and Resistance. In *The Aztec World*, edited by Elizabeth M. Brumfiel and Gary Feinman, pp. 225–240. Abrams, New York.
Charlton, Thomas H.
1968 Post-Conquest Aztec Ceramics: Implications for Archaeological Interpretation. *The Florida Anthropologist* 21:96–101.
1976 Contemporary Mexican Ceramics: A View from the Past. *Man* 11(4):517–525.
Charlton, Thomas H., Cynthia L. Otis Charlton, and Patricia Fournier García
2005 The Basin of Mexico A.D. 1450–1620: Archaeological Dimensions. In *The Postclassic to Spanish-Era Transition in Mesoamerica: Archaeological Perspectives*, edited by Susan Kepecs and Rani T. Alexander, pp. 49–64. University of New Mexico Press, Albuquerque.
Crider, Destiny, Deborah L. Nichols, and Christopher Garraty
2017 A Geospatial Approach to the Development of Postclassic Markets: Ceramic Production and Exchange from the Epiclassic through Late Postclassic in the Basin of Mexico. In *Mesoamerican Research in Honor of Dan Healan*. Middle American Research Institute Papers. Tulane University, New Orleans, forthcoming.
De Lucia, Kristin
2010 A Child's House: Social Memory, Identity, and the Construction of Childhood in Early Postclassic Mexican Households. *American Anthropologist* 112(4):607–624.
2013 Domestic Economies and Regional Transition: Household Multicrafting and Exploitation in Pre-Aztec Central Mexico. *Journal of Anthropological Archaeology* 32:353–367.
Diel, Lori Boornazian
2008 *The Tira de Pepechpan: Negotiating Place under Aztec and Spanish Rule*. University of Texas Press, Austin.
Escalante Gonzalbo, Pablo
1995 Sociedad y costumbres nahuas antes de la conquista. *Arqueología Mexicana* 15:14–19.
Evans, Susan T.
2013 *Ancient Mexico and Central America: Archaeology and Culture History*. Thames & Hudson.
Frederick, Charles
2007 Chinampa Cultivation in the Basin of Mexico: Observations on the Evolution of Form and Function. In *Seeking a Richer Harvest: The Archaeology of Subsistence Intensification, Innovation, and Change*, edited by Tina Thurston and Christopher T. Fisher, pp. 107–124. Springer, New York.
Gándara, Manuel
2012 A Short History of Theory in Mesoamerican Archaeology. In *The Oxford Handbook of Mesoamerican Archaeology*, edited by Deborah L. Nichols and Christopher A. Pool, pp. 31–46. Oxford University Press, Oxford.
Garraty, Christopher P.
2006 *The Politics of Commerce: Aztec Pottery Production and Exchange in the Basin of Mexico, A.D. 1200–1650*. Ph.D. dissertation, School of Human Evolution and Social Change, Arizona State University, Tempe.

2010 Investigating Market Exchange in Ancient Societies: A Theoretical Review. In *Archaeological Approaches to Market Exchange in Ancient Societies,* edited by Christopher P. Garraty and Barbara L. Stark, pp. 3–32. University of Arizona Press, Tucson.
2013 Market Development and Expansion under Aztec and Spanish Rule in Cerro Portezuelo. *Ancient Mesoamerica* 24:151–176.

Garraty, Christopher P., and Michael A. Ohnersorgen
2009 Negotiating the Imperial Landscape: The Geopolitics of Aztec Control in the Outer Provinces of the Empire. In *The Archaeology of Meaningful Places,* edited by Brenda J. Bower and Maria Nieves Zedeño, pp. 107–131. University of Utah Press, Salt Lake City.

Gibson, Charles
1964 *The Aztecs Under Spanish Rule.* Stanford University Press, Palo Alto, CA.

Gutiérrez, Gerardo
2013 Negotiating Aztec Tributary Demands in the Tribute Record of Tlapa. *In Merchants, Markets, Exchange in the Pre-Columbian World,* edited by Kenneth G. Hirth and Joanne Pillsbury, pp. 141–168. Dumbarton Oaks Research Library and Collection, Washington, DC.

Gutiérrez, Gerardo, and Baltazar Brito
2014 *El Códice Azoyú 2: politica y erritorio en el Señorio de Tlapa-Tlachinollan siglos XIV–XVI.* Instituto Nacional de Antropología e Historia, México, D.F.

Hirth, Kenneth G.
2013 The Merchant's World: Commercial Diversity and the Economics of Interregional Exchange in Highland Mesoamerica. In *Merchants, Markets, Exchange in the Pre-Columbian World,* edited by Kenneth G. Hirth, and Joanne Pillsbury, pp. 85–112. Dumbarton Oaks Research Library and Collection, Washington, DC.

Hodge, Mary and Michael Smith
1994 *Economies and Polities in the Aztec Realm.* Institute for Mesoamerican Studies, State University of New York, Albany.

Keen, Benjamin
1971 *The Aztec Image in Western Thought.* Rutgers University Press, New Brunswick, NJ.

Lee, Jongsoo, and Galen Brokaw
2014 Texcocan Studies: Past and Present. In *Texcoco: Prehispanic and Colonial Perspectives,* edited by Jonsoo Lee and Galen Brokaw, pp. 1–14. University Press of Colorado, Boulder.

León Portilla, Miguel
2000 Los Aztecas: Disquisiciones sobre un gentilicio. *Estudios de Cultura Náhuatl* 30:307–313.

Lockhart, James
1992 *The Nahuas after the Conquest.* Stanford University Press, Stanford, CA.

López Luján, Leonardo, and Colin McEwan (editors)
2010 *Moctezuma II: tiempo y Destino de un Gobernante.* Instituto Nacional de Antropología e Historia, México, D.F.

Luna Goyla, Gregory G.
2014 *The Aztec Agricultural Waterscape of Lake Xochimilco: A GIS Analysis of Lakebed Chinampas and Settlement.* Ph.D. dissertation, Department of Anthropology, Pennsylvania State University, University Park.

McDonough, Kelly
2014 *The Learned Ones: Nahua Intellectuals in Postconquest Mexico.* University of Arizona Press, Tucson.

McEwan, Colin, and Leonardo López Luján
2009 *Moctezuma: Aztec Ruler.* British Museum Press, London.

Mata-Míguez, Jaime, Lisa Overholtzer, Enrique Rodríguez-Alegría, and Deborah A. Bolnick

2012 The Genetic Impact of Aztec Imperialism: Ancient Mitochondrial DNA Evidence from Xaltocan, Mexico. *American Journal of Physical Anthropology* 149(4):504–516.

Matos Moctezuma, Eduardo

2012 La Sociedad Mexica. In *Escultura Monumental Mexica*, edited by Eduardo Matos Moctezuma and Leonardo López Lujá, pp. 19–69. Fundación Conmemoraciones and Fondo de Cultura Económica, Mexico City.

Matos Moctezuma, Eduardo, and Leonardo López Luján

2012 *Escultura Monumental Mexica*. Fundación Conmemoraciones and Fondo de Cultura Económica, Mexico City.

Matthew, Laura E., and Michel R. Oudijk (editors)

2007 *Indian Conquistadors: Indigenous Allies in the Conquest of Mesoamerica*. University of Oklahoma Press, Norman.

Millhauser, John, Lane F. Fargher, Verenice Y. Heredia Espinoza, and Richard E. Blanton

2015 The Geopolitics of Obsidian Supply in Postclassic Tlaxcallan: A portable X-Ray fluorescence Study. *Journal of Archaeological Science*. 58:133–146.

Morehart, Christopher T., and Charles Frederick

2014 The Chronology and Collapse of Pre-Aztec Raised Field (Chinampa) Agriculture in the Northern Basin of Mexico. *Antiquity* 88:531–548.

Mundy, Barbara E.

2015 *The Death of Aztec Tenochtitlan, the Life of Mexico City*. University of Texas Press, Austin.

Nichols, Deborah L.

2004 Rural and Urban Landscapes of the Aztec State. In *Mesoamerican Archaeology: Theory and Practice*, edited by Rosemary Joyce and Julia Hendon, pp. 265–295. Blackwell, Oxford.

2013 Merchants and Merchandise. In *Merchants, Markets, Exchange in the Pre-Columbian World*, edited by Kenneth G. Hirth and Joanne Pillsbury, pp. 49–84. Dumbarton Oaks Research Library and Collection, Washington, DC. Nichols, Deborah L., Elizabeth M. Brumfiel, Hector Neff, Mary Hodge, Thomas H. Charlton, and Michael D. Glascock

2002 Neutrons, Markets, Cities, and Empires: A 1000-Year Perspective on Ceramic Production and Distribution in the Postclassic Basin of Mexico. *Journal of Anthropological Archaeology* 21:25–82. Nichols, Deborah L., and Susan T. Evans

2009 Aztec Studies. *Ancient Mesoamerica* 20:265–270. Nichols, Deborah L., Hector Neff, and George L. Cowgill

2013 Cerro Portezuelo: An Overview. *Ancient Mesoamerica* 24:47–71.

Nichols, Deborah L., and Christopher A. Pool

2012 Mesoamerican Archaeology: Recent Trends. In *Oxford Handbook of Mesoamerican Archaeology*, edited by Deborah L. Nichols and Christopher A. Pool, pp. 1–28. Oxford University Press, New York.

Parsons, Jeffrey R.

2008 Environment and Rural Economy. In *The Aztec World*, edited by Elizabeth M. Brumfiel and Gary M. Feinman, pp. 23–52. Abrams, New York.

Pastrana, Alejandro

2007 *La Distribución de la Obsidiana de la Triple Alianza en la Cuenca de México*. Colección Científica, Serie Arqueología. Universidad Nacional Autónoma de México, Mexico City.

Plunket, Patricia, and Gabriela Uruñuela

2005 Recent Research in Puebla Prehistory. *Journal of Archaeological Research* 13:89–127.

Pohl, John, M. D., and Lyons, Claire L.

2010 *The Aztec Pantheon and the Art of Empire*. J. Paul Getty Museum, Los Angeles.

Restall, Matthew
2003 *Seven Myths of the Spanish Conquest*. Oxford, New York.
2012 The New Conquest History. *History Compass* 10(2):151–160.
Robles García, Nelly M.
2012 Mexico's National Archaeology Programs. A Short History of Theory in Mesoamerican Archaeology. In *The Oxford Handbook of Mesoamerican Archaeology*, edited by Deborah L. Nichols and Christopher A. Pool, pp. 47–54. Oxford, New York.
Rodríguez-Alegría, Enrique
2008 Narratives of Conquest, Colonialism, and Cutting-Edge Technology. *American Anthropologist* 110(1):33–41.
Rodríguez-Alegría, Enrique, John J. Millhauser, and Wesley D. Stoner
2013 Trade, Tribute, and Neutron Activation: The Colonial Political Economy of Xaltocan, Mexico. *Journal of Anthropological Archaeology* 32:397–414.
Sahagún, Fray Bernardino de
1950–1982 *Florentine Codex: A History of the Things of New Spain*. 13 vols. Edited and translated by Arthur J. O. Anderson and Charles E. Dibble. School of American Research, Santa Fe, NM, and University of Utah, Salt Lake City.
1993 *Primeros Memoriales*. University of Oklahoma Press, Norman.
Sanders, William T., Jeffrey R. Parsons, and Robert S. Santley
1979 *The Basin of Mexico: Ecological Processes in the Evolution of a Civilization*. Academic Press, New York.
Scarborough, Vernon L.
2003 *The Flow of Power: Ancient Water Systems and Landscapes*. School of American Research, Santa Fe, NM.
Scheidel, Walter
2015 *Rome, Tenochtitlan, and Beyond: Comparing Empires Across Time and Space*. Princeton/Stanford Working Papers in Classics. Princeton University, Princeton, NJ, and Stanford University, Stanford, CA.
Skoglund, Thanet, Barbara L. Stark, Hector Neff, and Michael D. Glascock
2006 Compositional and Stylistic Analysis of Aztec-Era Ceramics: Provincial Strategies at the Edge of Empire, South-Central Veracruz. *Latin American Antiquity* 17:541–559.
Smith, Michael E.
2008 *Aztec City-State Capitals*. University Press of Florida, Gainesville.
2015 The Aztec Empire. In *Fiscal Regimes and the Political Economy of Premodern States*, edited by Andrew Monson and Walter Scheidel, pp. 71–114. Cambridge University Press, Cambridge, UK.
Smith, Michael E., and Frances F. Berdan (editors)
2003 *The Postclassic Mesoamerican World*. University of Utah Press, Salt Lake City.
Solis, Felipe
2004a *The Aztec Empire*. Guggenheim Museum, New York.
2004b *National Museum of Anthropology, Mexico City*. Abrams, New York.
Stoner, Wes, and Deborah L. Nichols, Bridget Alex, and Destiny Crider
2015 The Emergence of Early-Middle Formative Exchange Patterns in Mesoamerica: A View from Altica in the Teotihuacan Valley. *Journal of Anthropological Archaeology* 39:19–35.
Townsend, Richard
1979 State and Cosmos in the Art of Tenochtitlan. *Studies in Pre-Columbian Art and Archaeology*, Vol. 20. Dumbarton Oaks Research and Library Collection, Washington, DC.

Trigger, Bruce
2003 *Understanding Early Civilizations: A Comparative Study.* Cambridge University Press, New York.

Umberger, Emily
1996 Art and Imperial Strategy in Tenochtitlan. In *Aztec Imperial Strategies,* edited by Frances F. Berdan, Richard E. Blanton, Elizabeth Hill Boone, Mary G. Hodge, Michael E. Smith, and Emily Umberger, pp. 85–106. Dumbarton Oaks Research and Library Collection, Washington, DC.
2007 The Metaphorical Underpinnings of Aztec History: The Case of the 1473 Civil War. *Ancient Mesoamerica* 18:11–29.
2012 Art in the Aztec Empire. In *The Oxford Handbook of Mesoamerican Archaeology,* edited by Deborah L. Nichols and Christopher A. Pool, pp. 819–829. Oxford University Press, Oxford.

Venter, Marcie
2012 A Reassessment of the Extent of the Eastern Aztec Empire in the Mesoamerican Gulf Lowlands. *Ancient Mesoamerica* 23(2):235–250.

Williams, Barbara J., and Frederic Hicks
2010 *Codice Vergara: edicion fascimilar con comentario: pintura indigen.* Universidad Autónoma de México, México, D.F.

Wood, Stephanie
2003 *Transcending Conquest: Nahua Views of Spanish Colonial Mexico.* University of Oklahoma Press, Norman.

Zamudio-Taylor, Victor
2001 Inventing Tradition, Negotiating Modernism. In *The Road to Aztlan: Art from a Mythic Homeland,* edited by V. M. Fields and V. Zamudio-Taylor, pp. 38–77. Los Angeles County Museum of Art, Los Angeles.

PART I

ARCHAEOLOGY OF THE AZTECS

CHAPTER 1

ANCIENT STONE SCULPTURES
In Search of the Mexica Past

EDUARDO MATOS MOCTEZUMA

On August 13, 1790, a huge stone sculpture representing the goddess Coatlicue ("she who wears the skirt of serpents" in Nahuatl) was unearthed in the *Zócalo*, Mexico City's main plaza (León y Gama 1832, Part. I:10). On December 17 of that year, the monumental "Sun Stone," also known as the "Aztec Calendar," was discovered (Figure 1.1).

The following year, another monumental sculpture—the "Stone of Tizoc"—was located near the Catedral Metropolitana de la Ciudad de México (Mexico City's Metropolitan Cathedral) (León y Gama 1832, Part II:46). All three monoliths were unearthed during works commissioned by Viceroy Revillagigedo with the goal of leveling the city's main plaza and installing drains.

The sculpture of Coatlicue—at the time known as Teoyaomiqui—represents a decapitated deity, with two streams of blood gushing from her severed neck; the streams of blood take the form of two serpents that come together at the top, taking the place of her head (León y Gama 1832). This goddess is the focus of one of the most important Mexica myths recounting how Coatlicue became pregnant with Huitzilopochtli—god of the sun and war—while doing penance on Coatepec Hill. According to the myth, Huitzilopochtli was born to battle his siblings because some of Coatlicue's other children—the *centzon huitznahua*, or "400 (innumerable) southerners (constellations)"—were outraged over their mother's mysterious pregnancy. They convinced their sister Coyolxauhqui, the moon deity, to go to Coatepec Hill and kill their mother in revenge. Huitzilopochtli was born full-grown and fully armed; he immediately began attacking his siblings, overcoming them and taking Coyolxauhqui prisoner. He decapitated his sister and threw her body off the top of the hill; her body rolled to the bottom of the hill, where it lay beheaded and dismembered (Figure 1.2).

The Sun Stone is the best example of the Mexica concept of time. Tonatiuh, the sun god, is depicted in the center, surrounded by four quadrangles corresponding to the four previous Suns, or eras (León y Gama 1832, Part I:93–95, Figure 1.1). In the Mexica concept

FIGURE 1.1 The "Sun Stone" or "Aztec Calendar." Courtesy of the Templo Mayor-Instituto Nacional de Antropología e Historia, Mexico.

FIGURE 1.2 Coyolxauhqui. Courtesy of the Templo Mayor-Instituto Nacional de Antropología e Historia, Mexico.

of time, these four Suns preceded the current one and represented attempts by the deities to create and sustain humans, each ending cataclysmically. The gods came together in Teotihuacan and created the Fifth Sun; once it was set in motion, they once again created humans and, this time, provided them with corn. Quetzalcoatl was the god who created this marvel of sustenance and thus began the new Sun. On the monolith, these four Suns are encircled by images of the 20 days composing each month. Another circle surrounds it, and four triangular rays of sunlight emerge from both circles. Finally, two fire serpents surround the sculpture, carrying the sun across the sky from east to west.

The content of the third stone monument is distinct. At the top, we see the sun surrounded by images depicting the victories of Tizoc, a Mexica *tlahtoani* or emperor who ruled from A.D. 1481–1486. The monument portrays a very important ceremony: a lopsided battle between a heavily armed Mexica warrior and an enemy prisoner of war forced to defend himself with blunt weapons. Ultimately, the vanquished prisoner of war is sacrificed (Matos Moctezuma and López Luján 2012).

The discovery of these stone sculptures during the eighteenth century marked the inauguration of Mexica archeology. The first study of these important pieces was undertaken by Antonio de Leon y Gama (1832), who published his book *Descripción histórica y cronológica de las dos piedras* in 1792. The work included the first two monuments, and in 1832 a second edition was released, including all three sculptures as well as others uncovered during construction work undertaken by the viceroy Revillagigedo. In 1803 Baron Alexander von Humboldt arrived in Mexico from South America, interested in learning more about these sculptures and their content. He described his impressions in his book *Vistas de las Cordilleras y Monumentos de los pueblos indígenas de América* (Humboldt 1995). Humboldt saw to it that the Coatlicue sculpture was exhumed from the university courtyard, where it had been buried by monks from the Real y Pontificia Universidad de México (Royal and Pontifical University of Mexico) who feared that the sculptures might lead to idolatry. The sculpture's reappearance was brief; the baron left as soon as he had seen the sculpture, and the monks reburied it shortly thereafter. It would be some time before the sculpture's permanent unveiling.

New objects continued to be uncovered during the nineteenth century, including one piece of particular interest: a diorite sculpture of the goddess Coyolxauhqui. The sculpture represents the goddess after being decapitated by her brother Huitzilopochtli; her eyes are half-closed and in place of her neck is the *atlachinolli*, or symbol of war. The discovery occurred in 1830 at the Convent of the Conception, and the abbess donated the sculpture to the Museo Nacional de Antropología (National Anthropology Museum). The museum was founded in 1825, and these and other important artifacts became part of the archaeological collection. Mexico achieved independence from Spain in 1821 and to the emerging country the prehispanic world represented an indigenous past destroyed by the Spaniards. Hence Mexico's flag and coat of arms both depict Tenochtitlan with an eagle perched on a cactus devouring a snake.

Some of the most important studies on the ancient world have been presented by researchers at the Museo Nacional de Antropología (National Anthropology Museum), which was founded in 1825 by a decree from President Guadalupe Victoria. In 1877 the

Anales del Museo Nacional (Proceedings of the National Museum) included the most recent research by eminent scholars specializing in the Mexica (Mendoza 1877). During the presidency of Porfirio Díaz, archaeologist Leopoldo Batres founded the Inspección de Monumentos (Monuments Inspectorate) in 1884 and in 1900 directed excavations behind Mexico City's Metropolitan Cathedral, publishing most of the excavated materials in his book *Exploraciones en la calle de las Escalerillas* (Batres 1902, 1979). In 1901 Jesús Galindo y Villa (1979) announced the discovery of two important sculptures carved from volcanic stone and unearthed beneath the Palacio del Marqués del Apartado (Palace of the Marquis del Apartado): a feline over 2 m long currently exhibited in the Sala Mexica (Mexica Hall) of the National Anthropology Museum and a serpent's head currently on display at the Museo del Templo Mayor (Templo Mayor Museum). Further excavations in 1985 revealed yet another important sculpture, a stone eagle uncovered in the building's patio. Together, these sculptures form a triad composed of the eagle, feline, and serpent. In 1914 Manuel Gamio discovered the southwest corner of Tenochtitlan's Templo Mayor at the intersection of Calles Santa Teresa and Seminario, near the main plaza (Gamio 1920–1921). We now know that the segment encountered in 1914 represents Construction Phase III, dating to ca. A.D. 1430. The site remains open to the public, but it would be another 60 years before further work would be undertaken at this important site.

In the early morning of February 21, 1978, workers from Luz y Fuerza del Centro, the now-defunct Mexican Light & Power Company, were working at the corner of Calles República de Guatemala and República de Argentina (formerly Calles Santa Teresa y Relox) near the Metropolitan Cathedral in the heart of Mexico City. They encountered a large stone that prevented them from advancing and soon realized that the monolithic stone was engraved. Work came to a halt and archaeologists from the Instituto Nacional de Antropología e Historia (National Institute of Anthropology and History) inspected the find. Excavation of the monolith started on March 20 in the same year in which I initiated the Proyecto Templo Mayor (Templo Mayor Project) as project director (Matos 1982, 1988). Working in an urban setting involves certain peculiarities that must be taken into consideration. First, there is constant pressure from the press, who inquire incessantly about what has been uncovered. Second, the city's historical and modern buildings were built on top of the prehispanic monument, seriously complicating excavation efforts. Upon further analysis, some buildings from the twentieth century were deemed to have little architectural value, permitting their demolition in order to continue with the excavation. Thus it was possible to uncover the remains of the principal Mexica temple, the Templo Mayor, which represented the fundamental core of the Mexica worldview. With its main façade oriented toward the west, the structure consisted of four sloped terraces and two stairways leading to two shrines at the top. One shrine was dedicated to the sun and war god Huitzilopochtli. The other shrine was for venerating Tlaloc, the god of water and rain, who was associated with agricultural production. Together they represented the basis of the Mexica economy: agriculture and tribute extracted from groups conquered through military expansion.

The temple was gradually enlarged; excavations have revealed up to seven construction stages or enlargements, as well as a number of partial enlargements of specific areas (Matos 1982, 1988). When the Spaniards arrived, the Templo Mayor measured 82 m on each side and towered 45 m overhead. Following the final victory of Hernán Cortés' forces, which included indigenous allies who were enemies of the Mexicas, the temples were destroyed and their building blocks were used to build new houses and churches in the colony. Those who had supported the Spanish captain during the Conquest were rewarded with houses built on the ruins of the Templo Mayor Houses. Cortés tried to erase all vestiges of the main temple and was successful to the point that during the twentieth century we still did not know where this important building might be located until it was accidentally uncovered. Manuel Gamio's (1920) excavations preceded those conducted as part of the Proyecto Templo Mayor, creating an impressive database consisting of thousands of artifacts uncovered inside the Templo Mayor and nearby shrines.

A museum located next to the excavated portions of the temple offers visitors the opportunity to view many of the archaeological pieces uncovered during excavations. Visitors to the archaeological site can view the architectural remains of the Templo Mayor, including the building's various construction phases, as well as other shrines like the "Red Temple," where traces of the paint that once decorated the structure's walls are still visible today. To the north of the Templo Mayor, the Mexicas conducted important ceremonies and rituals in the "House of the Eagles," where excavations have uncovered ceramic sculptures of Mictlantecuhtli, Lord of the Underworld, and two sculptures of Eagle Warriors.

One of the most surprising finds occurred on October 2, 2006, when the monumental sculpture of the earth goddess Tlaltecuhtli (Figure 1.3) was uncovered during excavations conducted as part of the Programa de Arqueología Urbana (Urban Archaeology Program), which I initiated in 1991 in order to recover data from the Mexica ceremonial site (Matos and López Luján 2007, 2012).

The monolithic stone sculpture measures 4.16 m × 3.58 m, with an average width of 32 cm. The goddess is shown in a squatting position in preparation for childbirth; a stream of blood originating from her womb trickles out of her mouth. Her arms are raised and huge claws emerge from her hands; on her right claw is the glyph "10 Rabbit," or A.D. 1502, marking the death of the Mexica ruler Ahuitzotl, who reigned between A.D. 1486 and 1502. This *tlahtoani* was succeeded by Motecuhzoma II until the latter's unfortunate death in A.D. 1520; two possibilities have been presented regarding who executed him. The Spanish version states that while the emperor tried to calm the masses surrounding Axayacatl's palace where the Spaniards were staying, the Mexicas themselves stoned their *tlahtoani* who eventually died from his wounds. The indigenous version, in contrast, states that it was the Spaniards who killed him. I lean more toward the latter idea, since Motecuhzoma had already been deposed as *tlahtoani* and Cuitlahuac had been chosen to replace him as ruler of Tenochtitlan. Therefore, Motecuhzoma was powerless against his own people and was no longer useful to the Spaniards; on the contrary, he was now a hindrance to the conquerors. The fate of Motecuhzoma—"The

FIGURE 1.3 Tlaltecuhtli. Courtesy of the Templo Mayor-Instituto Nacional de Antropología e Historia, Mexico.

Bereaved," as Alfonso Reyes (1964b) refers to him in his book *Visión de Anahuác*—had been sealed.

We return once again to Tlaltecuhtli. This deity devoured the dead and then gave birth to their souls, directing them toward their particular destiny, which was based on their manner of death. Warriors killed in combat or sacrifice were destined to accompany the sun from its appearance in the east until noon. Women who died during childbirth accompanied the sun from noon until sunset, since childbirth was considered combat and thus women who died while giving birth were seen as warriors. The eastern portion of the universe was the male half, while the west conceived of as feminine. Those whose death was related to water (drowning, edema, etc.) went to Tlaloc's paradise, Tlalocan, while those who died in other ways went to Mictlan. According to some historical sources, the Cuauhxicalco—where the ashes of some Mexica rulers were interred—was located in front of the Templo Mayor (Reyes 1964b, 1964b). Thus both Leonardo Lopez Lujan and I argue that this sculpture was the headstone of Ahuitzotl, who ruled Tenochtitlan from A.D. 1486–1502 (Matos and López Luján 2007, 2012). Excavations around and underneath the piece have yielded an enormous number of artifacts, most associated with mortuary rites. The piece is currently on display in the Templo Mayor Museum, along with thousands of other artifacts associated with this deity.

On 2015 our excavations located the *tzompantli* or skull rack. Before that, we had found the *Cuauhxicalco*, a building where some of the Aztec kings had been buried, including Axayacatl, Tizoc, and Ahuitzotl. We also found part of the ball court. These architectural remains are located west of the Templo Mayor.

Upon completion of excavations and analysis of the recovered materials, we hope to be able to respond in greater detail to the myriad questions raised so far. Downtown Mexico City, of course, is actually one city superimposed upon another; thus it is no surprise that objects from Tenochtitlan are constantly being uncovered. As Alfonso Reyes states in his *Visión de Anahuác*:

> Ecstatic before the cactus and the eagle and serpent—happy emblem of our countryside—they heard the voice of the prophetic bird, promising them refuge among the hospitable lakers. From huts of mud a city rose, peopled again and again by the incursions of mythological warriors who came from the Seven Caves, cradle of the seven tribes that dwell in our land. From the city an empire grew, and the roar of a giant civilization, like that of Babylon or Egypt, still reverberated, though diminishing, in the woeful days of the feeble Moteuczoma. And it was then that, in an hour we well may envy, Cortés and his men ("dust, sweat, and iron"), the snow-crusted volcanoes behind them now, stood wonderstruck on the rim of that circle of resonance and light, spaciously ringed about by mountains.
>
> At their feet, in a shimmering crystal mirage, lay the painted city, all its streets emanating from the temple, radiating from the corners of the pyramid [Reyes 1964a:83–84].

References Cited

Batres, Leopoldo
1902 *Exploraciones arqueológicas en la Calle de las Escalerillas*. Tip. y Let. "La Europea," J. Aguilar Vera y Compañía, Mexico City.
1979 Exploraciones en las calles de las Escalerillas. In *Trabajos arqueológicos en el centro de la ciudad de México* (Antología), coordinated by Eduardo Matos Moctezuma, pp. 61–90. Instituto Nacional de Antropología e Historia, Mexico, City.
Galindo y Villa, Jesús
1979 Escalinata descubierta en el nuevo edificio de la Secretaría de Justicia e Instrucción Pública. In *Trabajos arqueológicos en el centro de la ciudad de México* (Antología), coordinated by Eduardo Matos Moctezuma, pp. 91–94. Instituto Nacional de Antropología e Historia, Mexico City.
Gamio, Manuel
1920–1921 Vestigios del Templo Mayor de Tenochtitlan descubiertos recientemente. *Ethos* 1(8–12):205–207.
Humboldt, Alexander von
1995 *Vistas de las Cordilleras y monumentos de los pueblos indígenas de América*. Editorial Siglo XXI, Mexico City.

León y Gama, Antonio
1832 *Descripción histórica y cronológica de las dos Piedras*. Alejandro Valdéz, Mexico City. Electronic document, https://books.google.com.mx/books?id=-D0PAAAAQAAJ, accessed August 7, 2015.

Matos Moctezuma, Eduardo
1982 *El Templo Mayor: excavaciones y estudios*. Instituto Nacional de Antropología e Historia, Mexico City.
1988 *The Great Temple of the Aztecs*. Thames and Hudson, London.

Matos Moctezuma, Eduardo, and Leonardo López Luján
2007 La diosa Tlaltecuhtli de la Casa de las Ajaracas y el rey Ahuítzotl. *Arqueología Mexicana* 83:22–29.
2012 *Escultura Monumental Mexica*. Fondo de Cultura Económica, Mexico City.

Mendoza, Gumesindo (editor)
1877 *Anales del Museo Nacional de México* 1(1):1–288. Electronic document, http://www.mna.inah.gob.mx/anales.html, accessed August 7, 2015.

Reyes, Alfonso
1964a *Mexico in a Nutshell and Other Essays*. Translated by C. Ramsdell. University of California Press, Berkeley and Los Angeles.
1964b *Visión de Anáhuac*, FCE, Mexico City.

CHAPTER 2

THE HISTORICAL SOURCES
Codices and Chronicles

JUAN JOSÉ BATALLA ROSADO

HISTORICAL documents describing Aztec culture are abundant and rich in information on the cultural development of the group that dominated much of present-day Mexico City prior to the arrival of the Spanish. Given the sheer number of sources, I focus here on the most important documents from the sixteenth century in terms of the quality of the data presented, evaluating the veracity of the sources whenever possible.

I divide these historical documents into two types: codices and chronicles. The former includes works with pictorial content made using the prehispanic technique of presenting information through images and glyphs. Nearly all of them were painted after the Conquest and at the request of the Spanish; thus space was left on each page so written descriptions of the illustrated scenes could be added. Thus these documents offer two types of data: pictorial ("indigenous book") and textual ("European written book") (see Batalla 2002b:7–8). In addition, I include among the "codices" those works that have traditionally been considered as such, although they are, in fact, European "illustrated works." In contrast, the chronicles include books written by Spanish soldiers, priests, civilians, and descendants of the Aztecs.

CODICES

Many codices or "painted books," which offer extensive information on Aztec culture, have survived to the present day (Batalla 2011b). A detailed description can be found in Reyes and Oudijk (2013) where documents are listed in alphabetical order along with an extensive bibliography. I also make reference to the most recent editions, as they include images, as well as the authors who have studied these documents. Moreover, when I discuss a particular codex, I indicate in parenthesis where the entire document can be found online so that readers can consult the contents directly. Finally, I only discuss codices we are certain come from the Aztec area. Thus, despite their importance, I do not include documents from nearby areas, like the so-called Borgia Group, among other sources.

I present the different documents based on the type of information they contain (Batalla 2011b:218–221; Glass 1975:28). The main categories are religion, history, society, and economy. In many cases, all of these data are interspersed throughout a given document.

The existence of a hieroglyphic writing system in ancient Mesoamerica allowed indigenous groups to record information they wanted to transmit over time. The Spanish were so taken aback by the existence of these "painted books" or "books of symbols" that priests and administrative officials allowed their production to continue into Colonial times, particularly during the sixteenth century. The missionaries used these documents to learn about indigenous religion in order to monitor idolatrous practices. Moreover, from the administrative point of view, the books helped the Spanish learn about and understand the history, way of life, and, above all, economy of the Aztecs, so they could successfully levy taxes (see Batalla 2011b:203–214).

Regarding Aztec religion, the first document that should be mentioned is the *Codex Borbonicus* (1974). The reasons for this are clear. It is, in my opinion (Batalla 1994a, 1994b, 2011a), the only Aztec codex with religious content that is prehispanic in origin. Painted on *amate* paper, with a folding screen layout, it originally contained a total of 40 pages. It now contains just 36, because both the first and last two pages have been lost (Anders et al. 1991). Its content describes the calendars used by the Aztecs. These included the *tonalpohualli*, or 260-day cycle (Anders et al. 1991:2–20), indicating the patron deities of each trecena (13-day period), the 13 lords of the day, the 9 lords of the night, and the 13 prophetic birds; the *xiuhmolpilli*, or 52-year cycle (Anders et al. 1991:21–22), which identified the gods that presided over each year; the *xiuhpohualli*, or 365-day cycle (Anders, et al. 1991:23–36), which showed the patron gods of each of the 18 months of 20 days, as well as the major rituals and festivals held throughout the year; and a new, somewhat anomalous *xiuhmolpilli* (see Batalla 2011a), discussed on pp. 37–38 of the Codex Borbonicus (1974). Despite the difficulties in dating and the presence of the last cycle of years, Batalla (2011a) is one of the most important existing sources on Aztec religion. Furthermore, it is a wonderful example of how prehispanic books were produced.

After the Conquest, European religious authorities saw these books as "the work of the devil" and thus burned them. This represented a serious loss in terms of our knowledge of Aztec culture. However, with the arrival of more open-minded friars, a very interesting phenomenon occurred: Aztec painters, or *tlacuiloque*, were asked to once again produce books with religious content. In addition, they were generally asked to leave enough space on the pages for written descriptions of the painted scenes, such that any Westerner could understand the contents as well. Thus were born the Colonial codices, in which written texts slowly replaced painted images. Two sets of manuscripts exemplify this type of document: the Magliabechiano Group and the Huitzilopochtli Group, both from the second half of the sixteenth century.

The former is named after one of the documents that comprises it, the *Codex Magliabechiano* (1970), although the documents included in this set were not copied from the original. In fact, the source that gave rise to all of these texts was the indigenous book known as the *Codex Tudela* or the *Codex del Museo de América* (Batalla 2002b:159–165, 2010). This, then, is a clear example of the European tradition of manuscript copying in the Americas—in this case, transmitting two different types of information: the copies of the paintings in the group and the translation of the texts describing the images. Thus after the pictorial information from the *Codex Tudela* was copied into the *Libro de figuras* (since lost), the images were discussed separately, resulting in similar European written books but with clear differences in terms of the information they contained.

The *Codex Tudela* (Batalla 2002b) not only describes the different calendars but also includes considerable information on rituals dedicated to the god of death (Mictantecuhtli) and the gods of *pulque*, the ritual vestments associated with each deity, and so on (Batalla 2002b:167–435). Therefore, it is also a major source of knowledge on Aztec religion, which is complemented by the descriptive texts in the *Codex Magliabechiano* (Anders and Jansen 1996b; Batalla 2010).

The Huitzilopochtli Group (Glass and Robertson 1975:136–139) consists of two manuscripts: the *Codex Telleriano-Remensis* (1899) and the *Codex Ríos* or *Vaticano A* (1990). The latter is considered a copy of the former, thus both are translations of the same original text that has since been lost: the *Codex Huitzilopochtli*. However, codicological studies suggests that at least some portions of each document may derive from different sources (Batalla 2006, n.d.). Both describe the Aztec calendar, but the *Codex Ríos* contains a wider variety of novel information on religion. Of particular interest in this codex are the sections devoted to the vertical universe, the five eras or cosmogonic suns, the sacred history of deities, and other features of Aztec religion (Anders and Jansen 1996a). What makes the *Codex Telleriano-Remensis* unique are the parts describing the calendars, and, in particular, the historical information provided (Quiñones 1995).

Thanks to these and other documents, such as the *Tonalamatl de Aubin* (1981) and the five *Borgia Group* documents (*Codex Borgia* 1976). today's researchers have access to indigenous pictorial sources that enable us to better understand Aztec religious beliefs. This is of particular importance considering that the religious system is one of the cultural traits that defines the Mesoamerican culture area.

In terms of Aztec history, we only have Colonial codices, which are limited to the information offered to the Colonial chroniclers by their Aztec informants. That is, when the Aztec recounted their history, they painted themselves as "victors" up until the Spanish Conquest. Therefore it is necessary to conduct a comprehensive review of each source to understand how true to life they actually are. Some examples are the systematic "elimination" of information regarding the administration that had previously subjected them, the Tepanec Empire (see Santamarina 2006); data relating to "dark" events in their Motecuhzoma II, the Aztecs or the Spanish (with each, of course, blaming the other). The overall impression is neither side was especially interested in exposing the truth (see Batalla 2011c).

Also, when studying the history of the Aztecs, we must consider the portions of the codices describing the period of migration from Aztlan or Chicomoztoc (the Seven Caves) to the Valley of Mexico as part of their sacred history. This sacred history was rewritten to show the Aztecs as the victors following their defeat of the Tepanec Empire and their rise to power, creating the Era of the Fifth Sun and thus transforming themselves into the "chosen" people. Thus, at the time of the Spanish Conquest, the available historical evidence reflected the interests of the ruling class—who never presented themselves as "defeated"—as they told their history to serve their own interests.

Many existing historical manuscripts describe Aztec history up until the Conquest, including the *Tira de la Peregrinación* (2007), the *Codex Mendoza* (Berdan and Anawalt 1992), the *Codex Telleriano-Remensis* (1899), the *Codex Aubin* or *Codex de 1576* (1963), and the *Codex Mexicanus* (1952). The first describes the Aztec migration as the people "chosen" by their patron deity, Huitzilopochtli, from A.D. 1168 until they reach Chapultepec in the Valley of Mexico in A.D. 1335. The second discusses (folios 1–16) the founding of Tenochtitlan and the conquests carried out by all of the Aztec rulers, or *tlatoque*. The remaining three sources also discuss Aztec history following their departure from Aztlan through to the arrival of the Spanish and continue well into Colonial times.

In terms of the "daily life" of the Aztecs, one work in particular stands out: the third part of the *Codex Mendoza* (Berdan and Anawalt 1992). Without a doubt, this is the most important pictographic work on the subject. Thus, in folios 56–71, the codex describes Aztec life, from birth to 70 years old. Moreover, it is a well-organized codex in terms of its presentation, which also includes abundant textual descriptions of the paintings.

Finally, the *Matrícula de tributos* (1980), which, in my opinion, was produced in Prehispanic times (Batalla 2007a, 2007b), is among the prehispanic codices describing the Aztec economy, listing all of the goods delivered to the Aztec Empire by the groups they conquered. Moreover, it was also copied in the second part of the *Codex Mendoza* (folios 17–55), to which considerable textual information was later added. The *Matrícula de tributos* was also mentioned during Colonial times in the blank spaces between the Nahuatl paintings and the Castilian text. Furthermore, since many of the goods collected as tribute during prehispanic times were later collected during Colonial times as well (corn, cacao, peppers, cotton, loads of wood, containers, blankets, etc.), Colonial codices, like the *Codex de tributos de Coyoacán* (Batalla 2002a), the *Codex Osuna* (1973), and the *Codex Kingsborough* (1993) provide invaluable information on the Aztec economy.

Among what are considered Mesoamerican codices and chronicles, two authors are especially important for their knowledge on the Aztecs: Fray Bernardino de Sahagún and Fray Diego Duran. Fray Bernardino de Sahagún (1499–1590) is considered the father of ethnography; his *magnum opus* is a sort of "encyclopedia" on the Aztecs. Around the middle of the sixteenth century, he began compiling information about their culture by asking Aztec informants a series of questions, which would eventually form part of his *Historia general de las cosas de Nueva España*. To this end, he first presented information in the *Codex Matritenses* (ca. 1559–1561), which includes a wealth of information in both Nahuatl and Castilian. Moreover, his *Primeros memoriales* (1993) includes pictorial representations. He dedicated considerable time to the three-volume *Codex Florentino* (1950–1982), which includes texts in Nahuatl and Castilian along with several illustrations, making it more like a European picture book. Finally, based on this document, he wrote his *Historia general* in Castilian. Despite the abundant literature on these three works, no researcher has yet undertaken a critique of these sources. Fray Bernardino de Sahagún conducted his research among indigenous people who were either owned by, or descendants of, the upper class of Aztec society; thus, in my opinion, the information collected reflects the "official version" of the Aztec Empire. Regardless of whether this is the case, it remains the main source of information on the Aztecs, with Aztec culture discussed in several chapters.

Meanwhile, Fray Diego Duran (1581) wrote the *Historia de las Indias de Nueva España e islas de Tierra Firme*, between 1579 and 1581, which is also a typical European illustrated work. Divided into three parts, it presents the history of the Aztecs, from their departure from Aztlan to the rise of their empire, describing in detail what happened during the reign of each *tlahtoani*. The work also discusses the deities and ceremonies held in their honor before finally turning to the calendar system. Yet again we have content that requires very critical consideration, as it is clearly biased in favor of the Aztecs since the informants, as was the case with Sahagún's informants, were either the property of, or descended from, Aztec nobles.

Chronicles

The chronicles include a number of documents that describe the Aztec Empire at the time of Spanish contact (Esteve 1992:154–314; Gibson and Glass 1975:322–400). If the information contained in the codices is examined critically, the chronicles pose an even greater "risk" in that each chronicler had his own personal and cultural interests. When considering Hernan Cortes' *Cartas de relación* (2003), for example, it must be noted that he carried out his conquest of Mexico illegally, an offense punishable by death. Therefore, the manuscripts he submitted to the king does little but justify his own illegal actions. However, his second and third *Cartas* offer some credible information regarding Aztec society and its economy at the time of contact. All of this information, however, must be tempered by the realization that at times he may have exaggerated or lied.

Yet another important work, the *Historia verdadera de la Conquista de la Nueva España*, was written more than 50 years after the Conquest by soldier Bernal Diaz del Castillo (1960). Traditionally considered one of the primary sources on Aztec culture from 1519 to 1521, Michel Graulich (1996, 2006) argues that Bernal Diaz came to Tenochtitlan after Cortes' defeat of Panfilo de Narvaez in Veracruz. Furthermore, according to Christian Duverger's (2013) recent analysis, the author was Cortes himself, although his idea could be presented with greater conviction. While the debate continues regarding the "authorship" and "participation" of Bernal Diaz, we should use the information contained in this document with care. It is unlikely the story was simply "made up"; most likely it was based on experiences recounted by peers. Moreover, if Cortes did indeed write it, at least we know he participated in the Conquest from the beginning.

Among the other soldiers accompanying Hernan Cortes, several stand out, including Andrés de Tapia (1866), Bernardino Vázquez de Tapia (1970), and Francisco de Aguilar (1977). These chroniclers wrote descriptions of the Conquest of Mexico, providing information on Aztec life based on their firsthand observations.

Several friars also penned chronicles about the Aztecs, including the *Memoriales* and the *Historia de los Indios de la Nueva España* by Fray Toribio de Benavente (2009, 2014), the *Historia de las Indias y conquista de México* by Francisco López de Gómara (2014), the *Historia natural y moral de las Indias* by José de Acosta (1894), and *Monarquía indiana* (1975–1983) by Fray Juan de Torquemada, originally published in 1615.

Among the works of European authors who were not soldiers or priests, the *Antigüedades de la Nueva España*, (1986) by military physician Francisco Hernández, and the *Relación de las cosas notables de la Nueva España*, by Judge Alonso de Zorita (1999), describe Aztec society and religion.

Also important are the works of authors who were descendants of Aztec nobility, although most of their education was entirely European and they present a highly idealized view of their birthplace. Such works include Hernando Alvarado Tezozomoc's *Crónica Mexicana* (in Spanish, 1878) and *Crónica Mexicayotl* (originally in Nahuatl, Spanish translation [1949]). Both focus on Tenochtitlan, and the author appears to be the only pure indigenous descendant of *tlatoque* who did not receive a European education. In Texcoco, Juan Bautista Pomar's *Relación de Texcoco* (1991) and Fernando de Alva Ixtlilxochitl's *Relaciones históricas* (1891) and *Historia de la nación chichimeca* (2010) stand out. Regarding Chalco, Francisco de San Anton Muñón Chimalpahin's *Relaciones originales de Chalco Amaquemecan* (1965) is an important source, as is Diego Muñoz Camargo's *Descripción de la ciudad y provincia de Tlaxcala* (1981) for Tlaxcala. Of course all of these works emphasize the importance of the groups from which the authors descended, and the authors are biased. The *Codex Chimalpopoca* (1992) is also noteworthy, as it includes the *Anales de Cuauhtitlán* and the *Leyenda de los soles*, which describe Aztec history and religion, respectively.

Finally, among the many other chronicles documenting Aztec culture I review two of the utmost importance: the *Relaciones geográficas del siglo XVI* (Ovando y Godoy 1982–1988) and the *Vocabularios* (Molina 1571).

First, the *Relaciones geográficas del siglo XVI* (Ovando y Godoy 1982–1988), written between 1579 and 1585, was the result of several surveys of the Indies by Juan de Ovando y Godoy. The first consisted of 37 questions (1569), the second 200 (1570), and the third 135 (1573). However, due to the low response rate, Lopez de Velasco condensed these surveys into a 50-question "report," which was sent with printed instructions on how to respond. Importantly, questions 9, 13, 14, and 15 focus on the history of prehispanic settlement and society in the area. The response from civilians was very uneven, but today these data offer insight into life in Prehispanic and Colonial times. Regarding the Aztec, the most important are those documents relating to Mexico and Tlaxcala, including works by Juan Bautista Pomar (1991) and Diego Muñoz Camargo (1981), although it appears that the work of Alonso de Zorita (1999) could also derive from this questionnaire.

Second, the *Vocabularios* (Molina 1571) are also a source of knowledge on indigenous cultures. For the our purposes, the *Vocabulario en lengua castellana y mexicana* by Fray Alonso de Molina (1571) is important for the study of Aztec culture, as the analysis of the Nahuatl language offers considerable data on their daily lives. For example, for those who doubt the existence of an Aztec writing system, the list of sixteenth-century Nahuatl words listed in this document proves that no words were foreign loans, reflecting their independent origins.

REFERENCES CITED

Acosta, José de
1894 *Historia natural y moral de las indias*. R. Anglés Impr., Madrid. Electronic document, https://archive.org/details/historianatural02acosrich, accessed August 9, 2015.
Aguilar, Francisco de
1977 *Relación breve de la conquista de la Nueva España*. Edited by Jorge Gurría Lacroix. Universidad Nacional Autónoma de México, Mexico City.
Alva Ixtlilxochitl, Fernando de
1891 *Obras Históricas*. Edited by Alfredo Chavero. Oficina Tipográfica de la Secretaría de Fomento, Mexico City. Electronic document, https://archive.org/details/obrashistricas-d00ixtlgoog, accessed August 15, 2015.
2010 *Historia de la nación Chichimeca*. Linkgua Digital, Barcelona.
Alvarado Tezozomoc, Hernando
1878 *Cronica Mexicana*. Edited by Jose M. Vigil. Imprenta y Litografía de Ireno Paz, Mexico City. Electronic document, https://archive.org/details/cronicamexicana00alvaiala, accessed August 10, 2015.
1949 *Crónica Mexicayotl*. Translated by Adrián León. Publicaciones del Instituto de Historia Vol. 1, No. 10. Impresora Universitaria, Mexico City.
Anders, Ferdinand, and Maarten Jansen
1996a *Libro de la Vida: texto explicativo del llamado Códice Magliabechiano*. Contribuciones de Jessica Davilar and Anuschka vant Hooft. Fondo de Cultura Económica, Mexico City, and Akademische Druck-u. Verlagsanstalt, Graz.
1996b *Religión, costumbres e historia de los antiguos mexicanos: libro explicativo del llamado Códice Vaticano A*. Fondo de Cultura Económica, Mexico City, and Akademische Druck-u. Verlagsanstalt, Graz.
Anders, Ferdinand, Maarten Jansen, and Luis Reyes García
1991 *El libro del Ciuacoatl: homenaje para el año del Fuego Nuevo: libro explicativo del llamado Códice Borbónico*. Fondo de Cultura Económica, Mexico City, and Akademische Druck-u. Verlagsanstalt, Graz.
Batalla Rosado, Juan José
1994a Datación del Códice Borbónico a partir del análisis iconográfico de la representación de la sangre. *Revista Española de Antropología Americana* 24:47–74.
1994b Teorías sobre el origen colonial del Códice Borbónico. *Cuadernos Prehispánicos* 15:5–42.

2002a *Códice tributos de Coyoacán*. Editorial Brokarte, Madrid.
2002b *El Códice Tudela y el Grupo Magliabechiano: la tradición medieval europea de copia de códices en América*. Ministerio de Educación Cultura y Deportes, Agencia Española de Cooperación Internacional, and Testimonio Compañía Editorial, Madrid.
2006 Estudio codicológico de la sección del xiuhpohualli del Códice Telleriano-Remensis. *Revista Española de Antropología Americana* 36(2):69–87.
2007a Matrícula de Tributos y Códice Mendoza: la autoría de un mismo maestro de pintores para los folios 6r a 11v del primero y la totalidad del segundo. *Anales del Museo de América* 15:9–20.
2007b The Scribes Who Painted the Matrícula de Tributos and the Codex Mendoza. *Ancient Mesoamerica* 18:31–51.
2010 La importancia del *Códice Tudela* y la escasa validez del *Códice Magliabechiano* para el estudio de la religión azteca: el mal llamado Grupo Magliabechiano. *Anales del Museo de América* 18:7–27.
2011a El *Códice Borbónico*: reflexiones sobre la problemática relativa a su confección física y contenido. In *La quête du serpent à plumas: arts et religions de l'Amérique précolombienne. Hommage à Michel Graulich*, edited by N. Ragot, S. Peperstraete, and G. Olivier, pp. 197–211. Brepols, Turnhout, Belgium.
2011b La importancia de la escritura en Mesoamérica: Los códices o libros pintados. In *Mitificadotes del pasado falsarios de la Historia*, edited by José Antonio Munita, pp. 203–254. Servicio Editorial de la Universidad del País Vasco, Bilbao, Spain.
2011c La muerte de Motecuhzoma II: entre todos lo mataron y él solito se murió. *Arqueología Mexicana* 112:48–53.
n.d. Estudio codicológico del *Códice Vaticano A o Ríos*. Unpublished manuscript.
Benavente, Toribo de
2009 *Memoriales*. Edited by Nancy Joe Dyer. Colegio de México, Mexico City.
2014 *Historia de los indios de la Nueva España*. Edited by Mercedes Serna Arnaiz and Bernat Castany Predo. Centro para la Edición de los Clásicos Españoles, Real Academia Española, Madrid.
Berdan, Frances F., and Patricia R. Anawalt
1992 *The Codex Mendoza*. 4 vols. University of California Press, Los Angeles. *Codex Aubin*
1963 *Historia de la nación Mexicana: reproducción a todo color del Códice de 1576 (Aubin)*. Ediciones José Poruna Turenzes, Madrid. Electronic document, http://www.britishmuseum.org/research/collection_online/collection_object_details.aspx?objectId=3008812&partId=1, accessed August 6, 2015.
Codex Borbonicus
1974 *Codex Borbonicus, Bibliotheque de l'Assemblee nationale, Paris (Y 120): vollstandige Faksimile-Ausg. des Codex im Originalformat*. Akademische Druck-u. Verlagsanstalt, Graz. Electronic document, http://www.famsi.org/research/graz/borbonicus/thumbs_0.html and http://www.assemblee-nationale.fr/histoire/7gfborbonicus.asp, accessed August 4, 2015.
Codex Borgia
1976 *Bibiothéque de Assemblée Nationale Paris. Commentaries by K. A. Nowtny Messicano Selecti*, Vol. 58. Akademische Druck-u. Verlagsanstalt, Graz. Electronic document, http://www.famsi.org/research/graz/borgia/index.html, accessed August 4, 2015.

Codice Chimalpopoca
1992 *Códice Chimalpopoca, Anales de Cuauhtitlán y Leyenda de los Soles.* Translated by Primo Feliciano Velázquez. Universidad Nacional Autónoma de México, Mexico City.

Codex Kingsborough
1993 *Memorial de los indios de Tepetlaoztoc o Códice Kingsborough, a cuatrociientos cuarenta años.* Instituto Nacional de Antropología e Historia, Mexico City. Electronic document, http://www.britishmuseum.org/research/collection_online/collection_object_details.aspx?assetId=2609 29001&objectId=662793&partId=1, accessed August 3, 2015.

Codex Magliabechiano
1970 *Codex Magliabechiano C1 XIII.3 (B.R. 232), Biblioteca Nazionale Centrale di Firenze.* Edited by Ferdinand Anders. Akademische Druck-u. Verlagsanstalt, Graz. Electronic document, http://www.famsi.org/research/graz/magliabechiano/, accessed August 4, 2015.

Codex Mexicanus
1952 Codex Mexicanus: Bibliothèque Nationale de Paris, Nos. 23–24. *Journal de la Société des Américanistes* 41(1). Electronic document, http://amoxcalli.org.mx/codice.php?id=083 and http://gallica.bnf.fr/ark:/12148/btv1b55005834g, accessed August 5, 2015.

Codex Osuna
1973 *Pintura del Gobernador, Alcaldes y Regidores de México.* 2 vols., edited by Vicenta Cortés Alonso. Ministerio de Educación y Ciencia, Madrid. Electronic document, http://www.wdl.org/en/item/7324/, accessed August 4, 2015.

Codex Telleriano-Remensis
1899 *Codex Telleriano-Remensis: Manuscrit mexicain du cabinet de Ch.-M Le Tellier, Archevèque de Reims a la Bibliothèque Nationale (Ms. Mexicain No. 385).* Facsimile reproduction by the Duke of Loubat, with commentary and translations by E.-T. Hamy. Angers. Imp. Burdin, Section Orientale de l'imp. et Cie, Paris. Electronic document, http://www.famsi.org/research/loubat/Telleriano-Remensis/thumbs0.html and http://gallica.bnf.fr/ark:/12148/btv1b8458267s/f1.image, accessed August 4, 2015.

Codex Vaticanus
1900 *Il Manoscritto Messicano Vaticano 3738 detto il Codice Rios.* Facsimile reproduction by the Duke of Loubat for the Vatican Library. Stabilimento Danesi, Rome. Electronic document, http://www.famsi.org/research/graz/vaticanus3738/, accessed August 4, 2015.

Cortés, Hernán
2003 *Cartas de Relación.* Edited by Mario Hernández Sánchez-Barba. S. L. Dastin, Madrid.

Díaz del Castillo, Bernal
1960 *Historia Verdadera de la Conquista de la Nueva España.* Edited by Joaquín Ramírez Cabañas. Editorial Porrúa, Mexico City.

Duran, Fray Diego
1581 Historia de las indias de nueva españa e islas de la tierra firme. Manuscript on file, Biblioteca Nacional de España, Madrid. Electronic document, http://bdh-rd.bne.es/viewer.vm?id=0000169486&page=1, accessed August 3, 2015.

Duverger, Christian
2013 *Crónica de la eternidad. ¿Quién escribió la Historia Verdadera de la Conquista de Nueva España?* Ed. Taurus, Madrid.

Esteve Barba, Francisco
1992 *Historiografía Indiana.* Editorial Gredos S.A., Madrid.

Gibson, Charles, and John B. Glass
1975 A Census of Middle American Prose Manuscripts in the Native Historical Tradition. In *Handbook of Middle American Indians*, Vol. 15, Robert Wauchope, general editor, pp. 322–400. University of Texas Press, Austin.

Glass, John B.
1975 A Survey of Native Middle American Pictorial Manuscripts. *Handbook of Middle American Indians*, Vol. 14, Robert Wauchope, general editor, pp. 3–80. University of Texas Press, Austin.

Glass, John B., and Donald Robertson
1975 A Census of Native Middle American Pictorial Manuscripts. In *Handbook of Middle American Indians*, Vol. 14, Robert Wauchope, general editor, pp. 81–252. University of Texas Press, Austin.

Graulich, Michel
1996 La mera verdad resiste a mi rudeza: forgeries et mesonges dans l'Historia verdadera de la conquista de la Nueva España de Bernal Díaz del Castillo. *Journal de la Société des Américanistes* 82:63–95.
2006 ¿Bernal Díaz del Castillo: testigo de la Conquista? In *Escrituras Silenciadas en la época de Cervantes*, edited by Manuel Casado, Antonio Castillo, Paulina Numhauser, and Emilio Sola, pp. 333–353. Universidad de Alcalá, Alcalá de Henares.

Hernández, Francisco
1986 *Antigüedades de la Nueva España*. Edited by Asención de León-Portilla. Crónicas de América Vol. 28, Historia 16, Madrid.

López de Gomara, Francisco
2014 *Historia General de las Indias*. Linkgua, S.L., Barcelona.

Matricula de Tributos
1980 *Matricula de Tributos, Museo de Antropología, México (Col. 35–52): vollstandige Faksimile-Ausg. des Codex im Originalformat*. Commentary by Frances Berdan and Jacqueline de Durand-Forest. Akademische Druck-u. Verlagsanstalt, Graz. Electronic document, http://www.wdl.org/en/item/3248/, accessed August 4, 2015.

Molina, Alonso de
1571 *Vocabulario en lengua castellana y mexicana*. Casa de Antonio de Spinosa, Mexico City. Electronic document, https://archive.org/details/vocabularioenlenoomoli, accessed August 15, 2015.

Muñon Chimalpahin, Francisco de San Antón
1965 *Relaciones originales de Chalco Amequamecan*. Translated by Silvia Rendŏn. Fondo de Cultura Económica, Mexico City.

Muñoz Camargo, Diego
1981 *Descripción de la ciudad y provincia de Tlaxcala de las Indias y del Mar Océano para el buen gobierno y ennoblecimiento dellas*. Edited by René Acuña. Universidad Nacional Autónoma de México, Mexico City.

Ovando y Godoy, Juan de
1982–1988 *Relaciones Geográficas del siglo XVI*. 10 vols. Edited by René Acuña. Universidad Nacional Autónoma de México, Mexico City.

Pomar, Juan Bautista
1991 Relación de Tezcoco. In *Relaciones de la Nueva España*, edited by Germán Vázquez, pp. 21–99. Crónicas de América No. 65. Historia 16, Madrid.

Quiñones Keber, Eloise
1995 *Codex Telleriano-Remensis: Ritual, Divination, and History in a Pictorial Aztec Manuscript*. University of Texas Press, Austin.

Reyes Coria, Sergio, and Michael R. Oudijk
2013 Wiki-Filología. Electronic document, http://132.248.101.214/wikfil/index.php/Portada, accessed August 3, 2015.

Sahagún, Fray Bernardino de
1950–1982 *Florentine Codex: General History of the Things of New Spain*. 14 vols. Translated and edited by A. Anderson and C. Dibble. School of American Research, Santa Fe, NM, and University of Utah, Salt Lake City. Electronic document, http://www.wdl.org/en/item/10096/, accessed August 4, 2015.

1993 *Primeros Memoriales by Fray Bernardino de Sahagún*. Edited by Ferdinand Anders. Facsimile edition. University of Oklahoma Press, Norman.

Santamarina Novillo, Carlos
2006 *El sistema de dominación azteca: el Imperio Tepaneca*. Fundación Universitaria Española, Madrid.

Tapia, Andrés de
1866 Relación de algunas cosas de las que acaecieron al muy ilustre señor Don Hernando Cortés, Marqués del Valle, desde que se determinó a ir a descubrir tierra en la tierra firme del mar océano. In *Collección de Documentos para la Historia de México, Tomo Segundo*, edited by Joaquin García Icazbalceta, pp. 554–594. Librería de J. M. Andiade, Mexico City. Electronic document, https://books.google.com.mx/books?id=VcoCAAAAYAAJ, accessed August 8, 2015.

Tira de la Peregrinación (Codex Boturini)
2007 Edición Especial 26 de *Arqueología Mexicana*. Editorial Raíces, Mexico.

Tonalmatal de Aubin
1981 *Reproducción facsímil de la edición de 1900–1901*. Estudio introductorio de Carmen Aguilera. Gobierno de Tlaxcala, Mexico.

Torquemada, Juan de
1975–1983 *Monarquía indiana*. 7 vols. Edited by Miguel León-Portilla. Universidad Nacional Autónoma de México, Mexico City. Electronic document, http://www.historicas.unam.mx/publicaciones/publicadigital/monarquia/, accessed August 9, 2015.

Vázquez de Tapia, Bernardino
1970 *Relación de méritos y servicios del conquistador Bernardino Vázquez de Tapia, vecino y regidor de esta gran ciudad de Tenustitlan, México*. Edited by Jorge Gurria Lacroix. Universidad Nacional Autónoma de México, Mexico City. Electronic document, http://ru.ffyl.unam.mx:8080/bitstream/1039, 1/1387/1/Relaci%C3%B3n%20de%20m%C3%A9ritos%20y%20servicios.pdf, accessed August 8, 2015.

Zorita, Alonso de
1999 *Relación de Nueva España. Relación de algunas de las muchas cosas notables que hay en la Nueva España y de su conquista y pasificación y de la conversión de los naturales de ella*. 2 vols. Edited by Ethelia Ruiz Medrano, Wiebke Ahrndt, and José Mariano Leyva. Consejo Nacional para la Cultura y las Artes, Mexico City.

CHAPTER 3

MUSEUMS AND THE CONSERVATION OF MEXICA CULTURAL HERITAGE

MARÍA DE LOURDES GALLARDO PARRODI

WHAT IS ARCHAEOLOGICAL CONSERVATION?

LIKE many other disciplines, the conservation of archaeological materials has undergone an important phase of development in recent years. The primary goal of archaeological conservation—beyond recovering the aesthetics of a certain artifact—is to conserve the item in the best possible condition. The discipline's methodology involves limiting the use of substances different from those originally used to produce the artifact with the goal of recovering as much information as possible regarding the cultural dynamics to which the object was subjected over time. These procedures can be applied to isolated pieces or entire collections; the latter is more common as archaeological fieldwork typically involves recovering groups of objects.

While conservation is now common practice for archaeological projects, sites, and museums, the early treatment of prehispanic artifacts was different. The conservation project developed by the Templo Mayor Museum exemplifies how modern conservation techniques are applied to archaeological remains.

In Mexico, the assessment and treatment of artifacts as cultural heritage did not become formalized until after Independence; by then, important prehispanic artifacts had already been subjected to more than 300 years of systematic destruction and looting. One of the first steps toward formalizing the field occurred in 1822 when Agustín de Iturbide established the Conservatorio de Antigüedades (Conservatory of Antiquities) and the Gabinete de Historia Natural (Department of Natural History) at the Universidad Nacional Autónoma de México (National Autonomous University of Mexico) in order to assemble the prehispanic artifacts that had survived the Conquest and Colonial period. Three years later, this initiative would lead to the creation of the Museo Nacional (National Museum), where the first regulations regarding the protection, management, and exhibition of Mexico's cultural heritage were proposed. Some of these provisions would later be put into action at the museum's new location on Calle Moneda (Morales 1994:29–45). Located in the main hall and patio, the Monoliths Gallery showcased the most representative pieces in the collection, including nearly all of the large stone sculptures from the Mexica culture (see Matos this volume). In 1964—nearly a century later—the archaeological collections were relocated to the newly inaugurated Museo Nacional de Antropología (National Museum of Anthropology) in Chapultepec Park (Solís 2004:15). Several of the pieces from the Monoliths Gallery were put on display in the Mexica Hall, complementing the existing collection with an extensive set of objects of varying size manufactured in stone, clay, bone, shell, obsidian, and metal. At that time, these were the materials most commonly recovered from the excavation of archaeological contexts; they were also thought to be the only items to have survived their discard and burial. Although the inorganic nature of these objects affords them greater resistance, we now know that an artifact's composition is not the only factor determining its preservation. Importantly, little or nothing was known of the original contexts of these artifacts.

The documentary sources from the sixteenth and seventeenth centuries offer contradictory information. However, several textual sources agree that the Mexica used a variety of raw materials to produce different goods; the variety of these goods can be appreciated in the lengthy descriptions of the offerings placed around Tenochtitlan's main structures (e.g., Chimalpahín 2012; Durán 1967; Motolinía 2007; Sahagún 2006). In addition to stone, pottery, bone, shell, metal, and obsidian, these chroniclers report that objects were also commonly made from plant fibers, flowers, fruits, seeds, and other perishable materials. However, until a few years ago, artifacts of this nature were only very rarely recovered from archaeological contexts. Fortunately, this situation has changed; today, it is increasingly more common for such objects to be retrieved during excavation and preserved for future generations.

The Templo Mayor Project

In Mexico, and particularly regarding Mexica artifact collections, one of the turning points in terms of the formalization of archaeological conservation was the commencement of the Templo Mayor Project in 1978 (Matos 1979:20). Since its inception, this unprecedented project has involved the participation of conservators and other specialists from the very moment of discovery. The establishment of the Department of Conservation permitted conservators to design and implement the most suitable procedures to treat each object individually, beginning with their discovery in context, their careful extraction, the application of conservation processes in the laboratory, and the display or long-term storage of the artifacts. The interdisciplinary nature of this project greatly facilitated recording and recovering materials that otherwise might have been lost and has allowed the project to fulfill one of its primary goals: the recovery of Mexica artifacts from their original archaeological contexts. The most intense stage of excavation occurred from 1978 to 1993. During this time, conservators, archaeologists, and other project members worked collaboratively to solve different problems ranging from treating architectural remains consisting of stone and mortar with mural painting applied over a smoothed mud or plaster surface to the intervention of numerous offerings, including skull masks with shell, obsidian, and flint inlays; bones from a variety of animals; richly decorated stone figurines; sawfish rostrums; turquoise mosaic discs; copper bells; flint knives with inlay decoration; maguey spines; stone sculptures decorated with polychrome painting; and gold beads, among many other items.

As a direct result of the project, the Templo Mayor Museum was founded in 1987 (Matos 1997). At that time, the Department of Conservation was founded and became one of the many departments housed in the new building, which was built on the east side of the archaeological site.

With the transfer of the collection to the museum, the three main areas under the purview of the Department of Conservation were defined: the collections exhibited in the eight permanent halls and curated in storage, the architectural structures and elements of the site, and objects recently excavated from the site. The cultural heritage from the Templo Mayor, including the archaeological zone itself (Figure 3.1), encompasses all three areas.

With the diversification of conservation tasks, new techniques have been developed and unprecedented materials have been employed successfully to treat specific cases, ultimately leading to the establishment of intervention protocols for the growing collection. The permanence and continuity of the project have also provided the opportunity to study the dynamics of deterioration and evaluate the effectiveness of the procedures and substances used over the short, medium, and long term.

It is precisely this growing and diverse collection that has determined the direction of the actions related to its conservation and management. In this case, and unlike at other museums, the collection is constantly increasing due to two factors. First, the archaeological project is still in force, with the eighth season of excavation currently underway at the site. Second, the continuity of archaeological investigation at the site has led to the development of the Programa de Arqueología Urbana (Urban Archaeology Program),

FIGURE 3.1 Archaeological zone of the Templo Mayor. Photograph by author.

focused on exploring the prehispanic ruins under the Colonial and modern buildings that surround the archaeological zone (Barrera 2006). A substantial number of objects have been recovered by the Programa de Arqueología Urbana; most artifacts date to prehispanic times, but some also come from post-Conquest contexts (Rodríguez-Alegría this volume). As a result, the collection has tripled and now exceeds 40,000 items with 1,392 pieces exhibited in the permanent halls and 20,000 artifacts from recent excavations currently under investigation (Fernando Carrizosa Montfort, personal communication, November 2013; personal communication), nearly four times the size of the collection in 1983 (Velázquez 1997:41). This significant increase is directly related to improvements in excavation and conservation techniques, as well as technological advances, which have permitted us to identify and rescue more finds.

During the past 36 years, the redefinition of conservation treatments has also led to a gradual shift toward implementing preventive conservation measures in order to comprehensively address the specific challenge present by each item. Thus the conservation actions for the collection are focused on (a) understanding the behavior of different agents and dynamics of deterioration based on initial diagnoses and follow-up evaluations (Figure 3.2), (b) recording and maintaining the macro- and micro-environmental conditions of different objects, (c) recording and monitoring the specific processes and

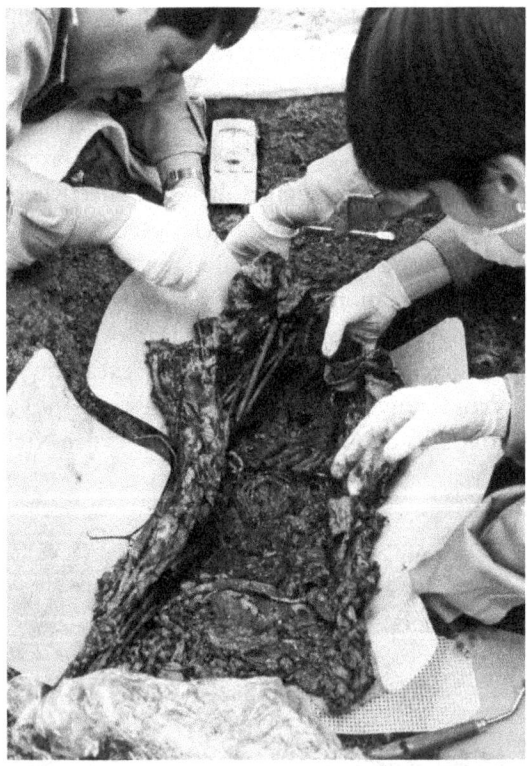

FIGURE 3.2 *In situ* conservation of the Mictlantecuhtli sculpture. Área de Conservación del MTM. Photograph by author.

materials applied to artifacts, (d) prioritizing and applying specific treatments, and (e) establishing general conservation guidelines and recommendations for the museum as part of the comprehensive management of the collection. Most of the department's permanent programs are dedicated to meeting these objectives.

Collections on Display and in Storage

Four programs have been implemented to care for this category of Mexica cultural heritage, including the periodic inspection and cleaning of the pieces exhibited outside of display cases; of particular interest are 48 sculptures and other large-format items. A second program is focused on the conservation and movement of monumental sculptures; the program focuses on large-format items like stone or ceramic sculptures and architectural elements with the aim of carrying out treatment to stabilize and protect each piece in situ in order to then transport them to the museum. Emblematic examples of the work carried out as part of this program include the monoliths representing the Mexica goddesses of the moon and earth, Coyolxauhqui and Tlaltecuhtli, respectively. Although discovered 28 years apart, both pieces benefitted from the knowledge and experience of various specialists who proposed the most appropriate conservation systems. As a result of the characteristics of the collection, a third program was developed focusing on the design and installation of conservation supports for pieces that, based on their raw materials and/or formal characteristics, require internal or external reinforcement. Representative cases of these supports can be appreciated in the articulated structures designed to provide internal support to parts of the monumental ceramic sculptures representing two eagle warriors and the two effigies of the god Mictlantecuhtli, as well as the monumental ceramic merlons recovered from Tenochtitlan's *Calmecac* (school for the sons of Mexica nobility; Figure 3.3) (Gallardo et al. 2013). In conjunction with other departments, the fourth conservation program provides ongoing conservation maintenance for the items on display as well as the cultural heritage safeguarded in museum storage. This program also permits the long-term evaluation of different conservation techniques and provides the opportunity to apply other, more appropriate treatments when necessary. This very important program has permitted us to review and update conservation procedures and materials, which in some cases has even resulted in new interpretations of artifacts. An example is the *Pinctada mazatlanica* shell pendants deposited in circles as part of the offering in Chamber II; prior to re-evaluation, they had been interpreted as part of a necklace (see Gallardo [2010] for a complete description of the conservation techniques applied to this offering).

The Archaeological Zone

The Templo Mayor has been exposed to ambient conditions for more than 30 years; thus conserving the architectural elements represents an important challenge. Due to

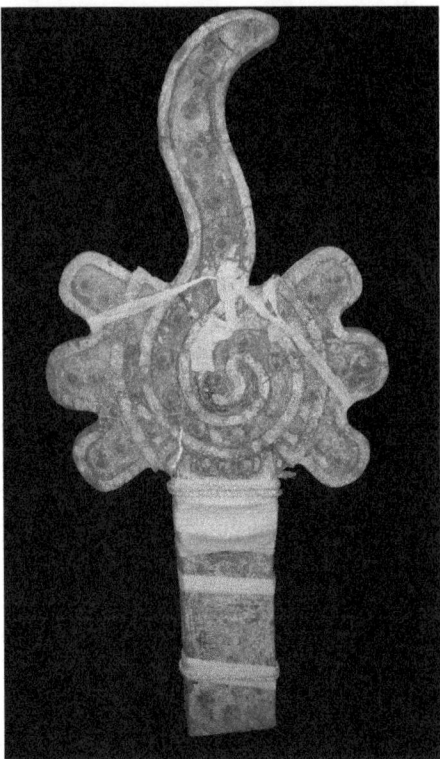

FIGURE 3.3 Conservation of monumental ceramic merlon in front of the *calmecac*. Photograph by José Vázquez.

its particular location, the architectural remains have suffered very specific changes and deterioration caused by natural and human agents; the characteristic indications left behind are periodically reported and an attempt is made to control the damage as much as possible. Currently, the primary challenges are related to the differential settlement of the subsoil, water table desiccation, pollution, and weathering. The permanent comprehensive conservation project was established to address these challenges at the archaeological zone, with the goal of performing maintenance tasks such as cleaning, maintaining the exhibits on both floors of the museum, consolidating structural cracks, and treating the plaster and polychrome paint decorating the different constructive stages throughout the archaeological site. The project has also generated some specific conservation interventions that have been developed as part of the regular inspections.

As mentioned earlier, one of the procedures implemented from the very beginning of the project has been the involvement of conservators from the moment an object is discovered. The long-term project has permitted the accrual of extensive conservation experience that complements this ongoing collaboration. Currently, conservation efforts are focused on designing prospective conservation systems and assessing the risks associated with each intervention. Over the course of the project, conservators have been involved in delimiting artifacts in context, recording and maintaining ambient conditions, offering support to archaeologists excavating and extracting delicate artifacts, implementing stabilization treatments, and preparing special packaging to protect specific pieces during transport.

A relatively recent example of the effectiveness of these procedures involves the materials recovered in 2000 from the Casa de las Ajaracas and the Casa de las Campanas, sites where a variety of artifacts were recovered from nine different offerings. Of particular interest is a large concentration of objects made of organic materials, including anthropomorphic figurines made of rubber; polychrome painted copal figurines in extravagant attire and adorned with flags made of paper and sticks; snails with remnants of periostracum (the protein coating that forms the outer layer of their shells); traces of skin, seeds, cactus spines, sticks, leaves, flowers, carved and painted wood; a container made from a dried gourd; and ceremonial garments woven using vegetable fibers like cotton and maguey and adorned with feathers and paper ornaments (Figure 3.4). Given the representativeness of some of the items discovered in those offerings, the conservation

FIGURE 3.4 A headdress made of paper, rubber, wood, and agave fibers and a polychrome painted wooden mask from Offering 102 following conservation. Photograph by Estudio Michel Zabé.

procedures were specifically designed to achieve two parallel and complementary objectives: (a) the recovery of as much information as possible from the systematic observation of the pieces and (b) the application of primarily preventative conservation procedures starting with the comprehensive assessment and prioritization of intervention actions (Gallardo 2006:565–555). Today, 14 years after its discovery, a representative selection of these valuable objects is on display in Hall 6; the remainder has been safeguarded in the museum's storage facilities where it is constantly monitored.

The Department of Conservation is currently focused on the conservation of the portable and nonportable artifacts around Plaza Gamio, where work is currently underway on a construction project to enlarge the museum and add a new lobby.

Final Considerations

In recent years, advances in the conservation of archaeological materials have been considerable. These advances have simultaneously offered invaluable ongoing academic training to conservation students as well as students in other fields, such as archeology and anthropology. Interdisciplinary research and the incorporation of practical lessons learned throughout this period have been important to this development in terms of integrating the results provided by specific research programs. Mexican and international projects, including interdisciplinary collaboration, have united disciplines such as chemistry, biology, physics, anthropology, and history. This cross-disciplinary cooperation has provided a more nuanced understanding of the archaeological remains and the opportunity to update specific aspects such as those relating to the nature of different raw materials, deterioration processes, the behavior of different conservation treatments and substances, and project management. The conservation program developed within this project has been publishing results since its earliest stages. Conservation work continues today, building on previous experiences as well as the documentation and review of the conservation techniques and materials applied to the collection and the establishment and development of particular systems that have been extrapolated from other similar cases encountered during this and other projects.

Finally, although conservation work has been planned and executed by specialists in the field, any and all success should be attributed to the participation of and permanent coordination with other areas involved in achieving better management of the Mexica cultural heritage recovered from the Templo Mayor.

References Cited

Barrera Rivera, Álvaro
2006 El Programa de Arqueología Urbana del Museo del Templo Mayor. In *Arqueología e historia en el Centro de Mexico. Homenaje a Eduardo Matos Moctezuma*, edited by Leonardo

López Luján, David Carrasco, and Lourdes Cué, pp. 265-272. Instituto Nacional de Antropología e Historia, Mexico City.

Chimalpahin, Domingo

2012 *Tres crónicas mexicanas: textos recopilados por Domingo Chimalpahin*. Edited by Rafael Tena. Cien de Mexico, Conaculta, Mexico City.

Durán, Fray Diego

1967 *Historia de las Indias de Nueva España e islas de tierra firme*. Edited by Angel M. Garibay. Editorial Porrúa, Mexico City.

Gallardo Parrodi, María de Lourdes

2006 La conservación de las ofrendas de la Casa de las Ajaracas y de la Casa de las Campanas. In *Arqueología e historia en el Centro de Mexico: homenaje a Eduardo Matos Moctezuma*, edited by Leonardo López Luján, David Carrasco, and Lourdes Cué, pp. 555-565. Instituto Nacional de Antropología e Historia, Mexico City.

2010 Los círculos de concha de la cámara II. In *Ecos del pasado: los moluscos arqueológicos de México*, edited by María de Lourdes Suárez and Adrián Velázquez, pp. 205-218. Instituto Nacional de Antropología e Historia, Mexico City.

Gallardo Parrodi, María de Lourdes, José Vázquez, Ximena Rojas, Carlos del Olmo, and María Barajas

2013 La conservación preventiva en el Museo del Templo Mayor. *Gaceta de Museos* 56:12-15.

Matos Moctezuma, Eduardo

1979 *Trabajos arqueológicos en el centro de la ciudad de México*. Instituto Nacional de Antropología e Historia, Mexico City.

Matos Moctezuma, Eduardo (editor)

1997 *Museo del Templo Mayor: 10 años*. Instituto Nacional de Antropología e Historia, Mexico City.

Morales Moreno, Luis Gerardo

1994 *Orígenes de la museología mexicana. Fuentes para el estudio del Museo Nacional 1780-1940*. Universidad Iberoamericana A.C., Mexico City.

Motolinía, Fray Toribio

2007 *Historia de los indios de la Nueva España: relación de ritos antiguos, idolatrías y sacrificios de los indios de Nueva España y de la maravillosa conversión que dios en ellos ha obrado*. Editorial Porrúa, Mexico City.

Sahagún, Fray Bernardino de

2006 *Historia General de las cosas de Nueva España*. Edited by Ángel M. Garibay. Editorial Porrúa, Mexico City.

Solís Olguín, Felipe (editor)

2004 *Museo Nacional de Antropología. Libro Guía*. Instituto Nacional de Antropología e Historia, Mexico City.

Velázquez, Adrián

1999 *El simbolismo de los objetos de concha del Templo Mayor de Tenochtitlán*. Instituto Nacional de Antropología e Historia, Mexico City.

PART II
HISTORICAL CHANGE

CHAPTER 4

COMMENTS ON CULTURAL CONTINUITIES BETWEEN TULA AND THE MEXICA

LUIS M. GAMBOA CABEZAS
AND ROBERT H. COBEAN

Before the Mexica

In *his General History of New Spain*, Fray Bernardino de Sahagún mentions a certain Ce Acatl Topiltizin Quetzalcóatl, who ruled the great city of Tollan Xicocotitlan (Sahagún 2000:949–950). Sahagún recounts a legend that describes a magnificent city with monumental structures incorporating unique sculptural elements, like columns and the so-called Atlantes, or Atlantean figures.

Archaeologist Jorge R. Acosta directed early excavation and consolidation projects of these monumental structures at Tula, revealing the archaeological site that corresponds to the impressive city mentioned by Sahagún and others. Thanks in large part to Acosta's archaeological project, the monuments are currently open to the public. Moreover, many structures and artifacts postdate the Toltec occupation, reflecting the importance of the city even after its initial abandonment. Interestingly, sources like the *Ruinas de la Antigua Tollan* (García Cubas 2003) and *Les anciennes villes du Noveau Monde* (Charnay 1998 [1885]) do not mention any post-Toltec occupations at the site.

The majority of the excavations in and around the monumental core were directed by archaeologist Jorge R. Acosta, who led an 18-season project from 1940 to 1960. His earliest findings were published in the article "Exploraciones en Tula, Hidalgo, 1940" (Acosta 1940), which appeared in the Sociedad Mexicana de Antropología's *Revista Mexicana de Estudios Antropológicos*. The monuments excavated by Acosta include Pyramid B (also known as the Pyramid of the Atlantean Figures or the Temple of Tlahuizcalpantecuhtli, the Lord of the Dawn) and the *coatepantli* ("serpent wall") that surrounds it; the

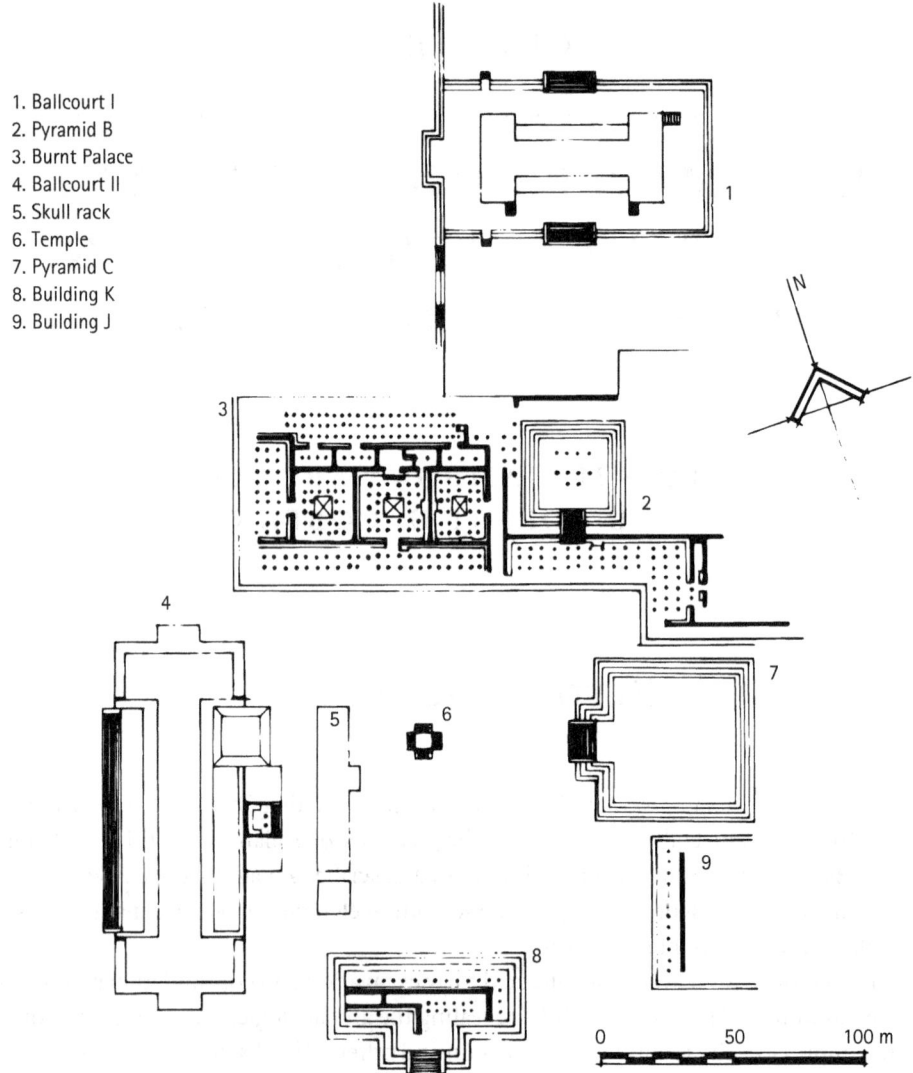

FIGURE 4.1 Ceremonial precinct of Tula Grande. Arrows indicate Aztec structures built over Toltec ruins (Proyecto Tula digital collection). Redrawn by Luis Gamboa, edited by Kristin Sullivan.

ballcourt; the Burnt Palace; Pyramid C; and El Corral, with its unique semirectangular, semicircular foundation (Figures 4.1, 4.2).

The first roundtable on Tula and the Toltecs was convened in 1941 for the Sociedad Mexicana de Antropología (Leon-Portilla 1980). Acosta's archaeological research and an ethnohistorical study conducted by Jiménez Moreno were presented during the conference, leading the experts in attendance to identify Tula, Hidalgo as the mysterious location mentioned by Sahagún and others (Jiménez Moreno 1941). This designation is also supported by the local setting, which includes the Tula River and Cerro El

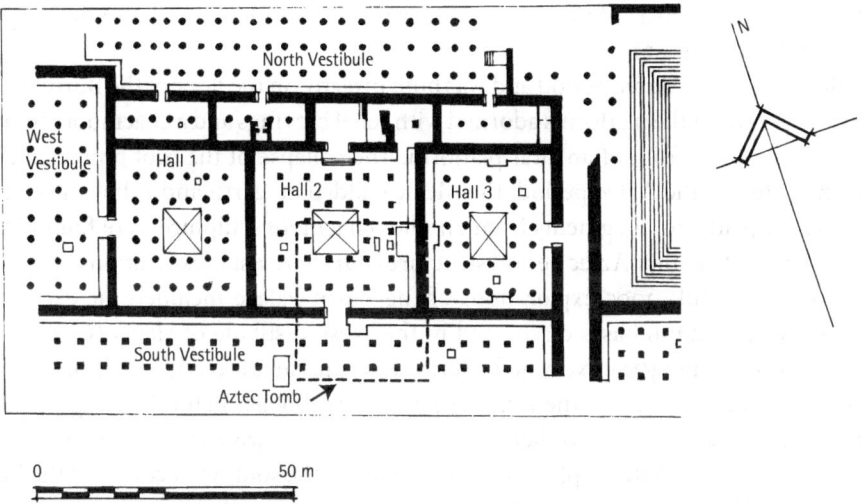

FIGURE 4.2 The Burnt Palace showing the location of an Aztec tomb with Aztec III pottery (Proyecto Tula digital collection). Redrawn by Luis Gamboa, edited by Kristin Sullivan.

Tesoro (El Tesoro Hill). Previously, researchers had suspected a number of important Mexican archaeological sites, including Teotihuacan, Xochicalco, and Chichen Itza, could be Tula.

THE CULTURAL SEQUENCE OF TULA

Based on stratigraphic excavations and the cultural sequence derived from the excavated ceramic assemblages, Acosta proposed the first chronology for Tula, which fell chronologically between the Classic period city of Teotihuacan and the Late Postclassic period Mexica occupation of the Basin of Mexico. Moreover, the early occupation of Tula could be divided further into two phases. The Epiclassic period occupation is represented archaeologically by the Coyotlatelco ceramic complex. Subsequently, the Early Postclassic period Tollan phase is indicated archaeologically by the appearance of brush pattern–painted Toltec orange pottery and Macana red-on-brown painted bowls; during this phase, the Toltec Empire expanded its territory beyond the local area. While Acosta was primarily concerned with the Toltec occupation of the site, he also reported evidence that the Mexica later used the site as well (Cobean et al. 2012; Healan 2011).

Archaeologically, the long-term Mexica occupation of Tula is reflected in the presence of Aztec II (A.D. 1200–1400/1450), III (A.D. 1300/1350–1521), and IV (Final Late Postclassic–Early Colonial period) pottery as well as post-Toltec structures built on top of the ruins of the abandoned Toltec capital. At the Burnt Palace, a later structure covering portions of Halls 2 and 3 is evident today. Remnants of these later walls overlaying Toltec are architectural elements; they were excavated during Acosta's tenth field season

(Acosta 1957), when part of the later structure was dismantled in order to fully explore Halls 1 and 2 (Figure 4.2).

Hall 2 dates to the Aztec period and was built directly on the floor of the Burnt Palace, preserving some of the platforms adorned with relief carvings and a chacmool sculpture that were found in front of an altar platform. The collapse of the roof protected these elements. During the Aztec period, the Mexica added an earth and rubble fill to raise the level the platform. Fragments from another chacmool sculpture were found in the construction fill of other Aztec period structures during Acosta's excavations in Hall 2.

The Proyecto Tula 2005 explorations of the Burnt Palace included the excavation of some of the column bases discovered in the West Vestibule of Hall 3 (Cobean and Gamboa 2005). Among the excavated offerings were prismatic blades made of transparent green obsidian dating to the Aztec II phase, possibly left behind during the renovation of these spaces prior to their later reoccupation. Two Aztec period altars with pottery dating to the Aztec II phase were identified in the southwest corner of the Burnt Palace's West Vestibule. The centrally located double staircase that provides access to the West Vestibule was also dated to the Aztec II phase (Gamboa 2005).

What Acosta (1956) called the Tumba Azteca ("Aztec Tomb"; Diehl 1989:27) in the South Vestibule of the Burnt Palace provides further evidence of the post-Toltec occupation of Tula; the burial included human remains and an offering with Aztec II phase ceramics. Regardless of the Toltec period function of the Burnt Palace prior to its abandonment, it was reoccupied during the Aztec II phase when offerings were placed in the center of the earlier Toltec structures and new structures were built over them. Regarding the fiery destruction of the palace, Acosta noted that: "the adobe blocks making up the walls became high-fired bricks as a result of the intense heat of the conflagration. The evidence indicates that the destruction of the Toltec capital was intentional and carried out by the people who produced 'Tenayuca,' or Aztec II, pottery" (translated from Acosta 1956–1957:75). Large amounts of Aztec II pottery were found in several sectors of Tula Grande by Acosta, and one of the most rigorous published analyses of Aztec II ceramics was written by Acosta's friend Jose Luis Franco (1945) based on sherds of this type from Tula.

Acosta (1958) directed excavations at Pyramid C from 1946 to 1960. During the sixth to ninth seasons of his project, the excavations revealed information regarding the appearance of the facade during the final Toltec construction phase. The project also recovered offerings from later contexts dating to the Late Postclassic (Aztec III phase), which were probably associated with Aztec period structures. These offerings included the important discovery of a flint blade and a jade pendant and bead, all of which were covered by fragments of braziers (Acosta 1956:Figure 13).

Whole vessels and a stone sculpture of a coiled snake with an anthropomorphic face (Acosta 1956:49, Plate 7) were also discovered (Figure 4.3). Three other offerings included Aztec period pottery: (a) a group of three orange vessels, (b) a pastillaje (appliqué) decorated brazier, and (c) two vessels with jade beads, alabaster, and snails deposited inside. Regarding the offerings, Acosta (1956:86) stated that "the three offerings are more or less contemporary and were buried well after those interred prior to the initial Toltec construction … [these three later offerings] include Aztec III ceramics."

FIGURE 4.3 Late Postclassic anthropomorphic stone sculpture with serpent body (Museo Jorge R. Acosta, Acervo digital Proyecto Tula).

Moreover, large quantities of ceramic braziers with images of Tlazolteotl and the "weeping" Tlaloc were recovered during the exploration of a Mexica platform in the northwest corner of Pyramid C (Acosta 1956:109–110, Plates 51 and 52). Above the Aztec period platform was a human head sculpture depicting a prince wearing a xiuhuizolli or diadem. In the northwest corner of Pyramid B, Acosta also discovered a dual altar that had inside an offering of Aztec III pottery and a possible fragment of an Aztec III phase chacmool sculpture.

At Ballcourt I, Aztec period rooms were identified in the southeastern portion and the lower panels of the foundation. There are indications of *temazcales* (sweat baths). The square *temazcales* have interior–exterior ventilation and a circular fire pit. The form is similar to the *temazcal* described in the *Codex Magliabechiano* (Boone 1983:Folio 77); in the state of Mexico similar *temazcales* dating to the Aztec III phase have been reported at Acozac, Ixtapaluca, and in the Casa de Morelos at Ecatepec, both in the state of Mexico (García et al. 2003).

Eduardo Matos Moctezuma directed the Proyecto Tula 1968 excavations of Ballcourt II, a structure located in the western part of the main plaza at Tula Grande; opposite is a large platform identified as a *tzompantli* ("skull rack") (Matos 1974, 1976).

Ballcourt II measures ca. 114 m long, making it one of the largest excavated ballcourts; the size and orientation are similar to the Great Ballcourt at Chichen Itza. Some post-Toltec architectural elements were also uncovered, including a *temazcal* located roughly midfield on the exterior of the ballcourt's east wall. Some Aztec period residential compounds were identified at the southeast end of the ballcourt; these later structures were superimposed on the earlier ballcourt and consist of a series of corridors communicating small rooms; several tlecuiles (braziers) were uncovered in different open areas. In some cases, it is necessary to take a step up to access interior rooms, suggesting that the floors of the rooms were built on fill.

The *tzompantli* is located within the main plaza. Human skulls, bones, and teeth as well as an offering that consisted of a series of sacrificial knives were recovered during excavation of the upper staircase on the east side. The form, raw materials, and decoration of the knives are similar to examples from Aztec period contexts, allowing them to be dated to post-Toltec times (Figure 4.4).

Matos' Proyecto Tula 1968 also included a surface survey in order to define the extent, form, and complexity of the city, including its occupational history, residential neighborhoods, and craft production areas. The research culminated in the development of a chronology for the region, including Prehispanic, Colonial, and Modern occupations. Interestingly, several sectors of the city have evidence for post-Toltec occupation, including El Cielito, La Malinche, El Salitre, El Llano, and Tultengo; some of these areas are associated with the production of prismatic blades. Archaeologist Juan Yadeun (1975) generated obsidian distribution maps that highlight the correlation between stone tool production areas and the Aztec period occupation of the site. Archaeologists Agustín Peña and María del Carmen Rodríguez (1976) directed excavations at residential compounds in the Dani neighborhood in the west of the ancient city; they note that the compounds were first occupied during the Toltec period and then again during the later Aztec period.

The Aztec period occupation is densest to the east of what was the Toltec capital, where Toltec buildings were reoccupied. Examples have been excavated at Viviero and Nopalera; a chipped stone workshop was discovered at the latter. Other examples were excavated in 2001 as part of the Proyecto de Rescate Arqueológico Boulevard

FIGURE 4.4 Aztec flint knife found in a stone box near Tula's *tzompantli* (Museo Jorge R. Acosta, Proyecto Tula digital collection).

Tula-Iturbe (Quiles; Juglans 2001); one altar housed a burial consisting of two funerary urns, one of which represents a jaguar. The structure was dated to the Aztec II phase.

Southwest of the Tula Archaeological Zone, petroglyphs have been located on Cerro La Malinche (Coayahualco). They were first reported in 1873 by engineer García Cubas (1874), who noted they were located on the east side overlooking Cerro El Tesoro (Toltacatepetl). During a tour of the area in 1938, Wilberto Jiménez Moreno and Agustín Villagrán described and drew the petroglyphs (Jiménez Moreno 1941); they mention two dates corresponding to 8-*técpatl* ("flint or obsidian knife") and 4-*ácatl* ("reed"). They related these dates to events during the Toltec period using the Anales de Cuautitlán (1945); by adding two cycles of 52 years to 8-*técpatl*, they obtained the year A.D. 980, which corresponds to the year Ce Acatl Topiltizin Quetzalcóatl established himself in Tula.

Scholars have more recently argued that the rock art at Cerro La Malinche most likely dates to the Late Postclassic and commemorates the rise to power of the Mexica (Navarrete and Crespo 1971). The rocks used to carve the petroglyphs have an irregular substrate, with numerous protrusions and depressions, and the Aztecs are known to have selected such irregular rocks for carving in other places in Tula, Amecameca, Texcotzingo, Chapultepec, and south of Mexico City. Other stylistic and iconographic aspects of the art support its dating to the Aztec period.

The carving of Ce Acatl Topitlztin Quetzalcoatl is accompanied by a feathered serpent that is adorned with obsidian or flint knives. The knives are similar to those portrayed in the Aztec "Teocalli of Sacred Warfare." The date 1-*ácatl* accompanies the feathered serpent and is rendered in an Aztec, not Toltec, style. The main figure in the petroglyph appears seated on a mat, wearing a loin cloth and sandals and using a maguey spine to pierce his earlobe. The maguey spine is similar to other Aztec representations of autosacrifice (Navarrete and Crespo 1971). The face and torso of the figure were purposefully erased.

The carving of another figure, Centeotl (a maize deity), has a headdress with six short, rounded feathers and another seven feathers in the vertical position. The figure is decorated with chalchihuites (precious stones), in the manner typically represented in Aztec monuments. The chalchihuitl glyphs are well-known in Aztec iconography (Navarrete and Crespo 1971).

Two other date glyphs are part of the carving, in addition to the 1-*ácatl* date mentioned earlier. Meyer (1939) argues that the dates 8-*técpatl* and 4-*ácatl* that accompany the glyphs at Cerro La Malinche correspond to major events during the Toltec era. Meyer proposes that the former was Toltec, as it can be correlated with five dates prior to A.D. 1116. We interpret the dates 8-*técpatl* and 4-*ácatl* as referencing A.D. 1396 and A.D. 1431, respectively. In light of this chronological placement, the dates commemorate when Acamapichtli founded the Mexica royal dynasty. Acamapichtli's enthronement is detailed pictographically in the *Codex Azcatitlán* (1995), one of the few historical sources to narrate the transition from teuctli (lord) to the highest authority, huey *tlahtoani* ("emperor"). Thus this event marks the end of Toltec power and the rise of the Mexica.

The Late Postclassic in the Tula Region

The post-Toltec structures built on the ruins of Tula were occupied as long as 300 years. Within the Toltec monumental zone, these Late Postclassic structures include temples and altars dedicated to ritual activities. Outside this zone are residential compounds with evidence of specialized craft production, including Aztec III pottery production, and the manufacture of chipped stone tools. It is difficult to identify the post-Toltec groups occupying Tula based solely on the pottery they used because Aztec III and IV pottery was produced in several locations during the Late Postclassic, including Tenochtitlan, Texcoco, Chalco, and the western part of the Iztapalapa peninsula (Hodge and Minc 1991).

Vaillant (1938, 1956) dated the black-on-orange pottery to the Aztec period, between A.D. 1247 and A.D. 1519; the former corresponds to the construction of the Tenayuca Pyramid. Thus, considering the 52-year calendar cycle, Acosta (1958) was able to further divide the Aztec period into three phases: Aztec I (A.D. 1247–1299), Aztec II (A.D. 1299–1403), and Aztec III (A.D. 1403–1507). Vaillant (1956) also proposed that the Aztec IV phase spanned the years between A.D. 1507 and the arrival of the Spaniards in A.D. 1519.

Fieldwork in the Basin of Mexico directed by William T. Sanders, Jeffrey R. Parsons and Robert S. Santley (Sanders et al. 1979) permitted more accurate dating of the Aztec I phase, pushing its start back to A.D. 1150 and the fall of Tula. Likewise, with the additional contextual data recovered during their archaeological project, it was possible to combine the Aztec I and II phases, as well as Aztec phases III and IV. They proposed this change as they interpreted Aztec I and II as temporally contemporary but geographically distinct, with the former being used south of Mexico City and the latter being used to the north. They found Aztec III pottery to be in continuous use up until the arrival of the Spaniards, while Aztec IV pottery continued to be used post-Conquest.

Based on these data, William T. Sanders (Sanders et al. 1979) proposed an Early Aztec period (A.D. 1150–1350), which could be divided into the Culhuacan (Aztec I) and Tenayuca (Aztec II) phases. Likewise, the Late Aztec period (A.D. 1350–1521) can be divided into the Mexica (Aztec III) and Tlatelolco (Aztec IV) phases. Since then, several investigations have relied on these phase designations when discussing the Late Postclassic period (Blanton 1972; Parsons 1971; García García 1987; Vega 1978). The process of establishing the chronology for the Basin of Mexico by identifying temporal changes in ceramic complexes served as a model for developing the ceramic chronology for Tula, Hidalgo. Robert H. Cobean (1990) refined the Tula chronology by applying a type-variety approach in defining the phases of the Toltec ceramic complex. The main sources used to define the Late Classic and Early Postclassic ceramic complexes at Tula include Acosta's (1956, 1958) excavation, James Stoutamire's (1974, 1975) survey of Tula's urban area, the University of Missouri excavations of Tollan phase residences in the northeast portion of the urban area (Healan 1977), test pits excavated at Tula Chico as part of the Instituto Nacional de Antropología e Historia and University of Missouri projects (Matos 1974; Cobean 1982), and Guadalupe Mastache and Ana María Crespo's (1974, 1982) survey of the Tula region.

Cobean (1990) proposes three phases for the Late Postclassic period in Tula: Fuego (A.D. 1150–1350), distinguished by the use of ceramics similar to those from the Aztec II–III phases in the Basin of Mexico (Figure 4.5); Palacio (A.D. 1350–1520), identified by ceramic materials similar to Aztec III and some Aztec IV types in the Basin of Mexico (Figure 4.6); and Tesoro (A.D. 1520), with ceramics similar to Aztec IV and Colonial pottery from the Basin of Mexico (Cobean 1990:27) (Figure 4.7). Excavations of the residential compounds outside Tula's monumental core have recovered ceramic materials from earlier phases, an interesting topic that warrants further investigation.

Some investigators argue that the Fuego phase (A.D. 1150–1350) represents the transition between Aztec II–III pottery and Aztec III ceramics (Cobean 1990:27). For other researchers in the Basin of Mexico, Fuego phase pottery is contemporary with Aztec II (García, Raul 2004); at sites like Huexotla, Texcoco, and Tezoyuca, the zacate (grass)

FIGURE 4.5 (a) Aztec III Black-on-Orange bowl (Museo Jorge R. Acosta, Proyecto Tula digital collection). (b) Aztec III Black-on-Orange *molcajete* (ceramic grater) (Museo Jorge R. Acosta, Proyecto Tula digital collection). (c) Aztec III Black-on-Orange bowl (Museo Jorge R. Acosta, Proyecto Tula digital collection).

FIGURE 4.6 (a) & (b) Aztec III Black-on-Red bowl (Museo Jorge R. Acosta, Proyecto Tula digital collection). (c) Aztec III Black-on-Red *copa* (cup) (Museo Jorge R. Acosta, Proyecto Tula digital collection).

FIGURE 4.7 (a) Aztec IV Black-on-Orange *molcajete* (grater). (Museo Jorge R. Acosta, Proyecto Tula digital collection). (b) Aztec IV Black-on-Orange bowl. (Museo Jorge R. Acosta, Proyecto Tula digital collection).

design has a closed border characteristic of Aztec II–III pottery. In other cases, the closed-border zacate design is identified as Aztec III pottery (García García 1987). Thus Fuego phase (A.D. 1150–1350) pottery poses a chronological challenge as the phase may represent Aztec II pottery influenced by the Texcoco region of the Basin of Mexico; Aztec II–III pottery actually belongs to the transition between Azteca II and III, or, at Tula, the so-called transition materials may actually correspond to the early Azteca III phase.

Historical References Regarding the Post-Toltec Occupation of Tula

Considered in conjunction with the historical sources, the Aztec II pottery style is a chronological indicator of the period when Azcapotzalco (the Tepaneca Empire), through Mexica mercenaries, exercised political and economic hegemony in the region known as the Teotlalpan. In the fourteenth century A.D., the Acolhua empire controlled the eastern Basin of Mexico and surrounding areas; in 1325, Mexico-Tenochtitlan was founded by the Aztecs, a group that arrived late to the region (Barlow 1994a:201; 1994b:304). At the time, the western Basin of Mexico was politically subordinate to the Azcapotzalco city-state: The Aztecs acted as mercenaries and at other times formed armies sent to subject groups rebelling against Tepanec rule (Graulich 1988:10).

From A.D. 1372 to 1391, Acamapichtli governed Mexico-Tenochtitlan as the first *tlahtoani* recognized by Azcapotzalco (Chimalpain 1998:223); thus they conquered the Chinampeca of Xochimilco, Cuitlahuac, Mizquic, and other areas. In A.D. 1375, the Tepanecs and Mexicas initiated a campaign against Chalco, and by the end of the fourteenth century the Tepanec Empire had overthrown the Acolhuas (A.D. 1395). This campaign set the pattern for Tepanec-Mexica relations, with the latter acting on behalf of the former as far as foreign policy was concerned. Then, in A.D. 1398, the Mexica executed a military expedition against Coatlinchan. From A.D. 1414–1418 the Tepanecs and Mexicas waged war against Acolhuacan (Texcoco). Thus we have a much clearer picture of the relationship between Azcapotzalco and the Mexicas in the late fourteenth and early fifteenth centuries (Santamarina 2005:610).

By this time Tula was under Tepanec rule, and the presence of a settlement just south of Tula Grande with Aztec II ceramics indicates the existence of possible Mexica settlements, dating to the time when they acted as Tepanec mercenaries. Moreover, they may well have been settlers sent by Azcapotzalco to ensure a firmer hold on its colonies, like Tula.

Around El Salitre and the east bank of the Tula River, archaeological investigations of the architectural remains have yielded information regarding where Aztec period ceramics were used for both daily utilitarian purposes and as funeral urns (ritual ceramics). While this does not clear up the confusion regarding ethnic origin, to some extent it does clarify the political affiliation of the people inhabiting the Aztec period settlement at Tula, at least during the fourteenth century.

During this time of Tula contact, the territorial hegemony included settlements at Atenco, Mixquiahuala, Tazayulan, Acolco, Huapalcalco, and Oztlalpan, the latter pertaining to the Tepanec ruler of Cuautitlan. The tribute collected in Tula was brought to Atotonilco de Tula. People in most communities spoke Otomi; only Tepexic and Xippacoyan had Nahuatl affiliations and their own *tlahtoani*. The communities of Michimaloya, Nextlalpan, Tepetitlan, and Xochitlan sent tribute to Jilotepec (Smith 1993).

Conclusion

Tula Under Spanish Rule

The archaeological site of Tula was not like Teotihuacan, an important earlier Mesoamerican city that expanded its territorial boundaries and influenced contemporary cultures. Tula's transcendence prompted later cultures to reference important people from that time, including Ce Acatl Topiltzin Quetzalcóatl, and reproduce spatial layouts or elements charged with symbolism. The city thus became a sacred city, as occurred at many similar locations throughout Mesoamerica at other times. Even after the abandonment of the Toltec period settlement, Tula persisted through the Mexica, as a means of legitimating power and hegemony in order to gain respect from contemporary groups.

After the Spanish conquest, this pattern of legitimizing power based on kinship led indigenous groups from Tula and other regions of Teotlalpan to declare a descendant of Emperor Moteuczoma Xocoyotzin, Pedro Moteuczoma, as an *encomendero*. This in turn led to a *mayorazgo* (entailed estate) appointment from A.D. 1528–1606 (Gerhard 1986:341). However, recent research by Ramirez Calva (2005) has demonstrated that not all descendants of the indigenous nobility enjoyed privilege and power. Some lived modestly; their wealth was the memory of their family's past greatness.

The endless quest to integrate previously fragmented territories was replaced by the *encomienda* system, which permitted some indigenous nobility a means to achieve political and economic benefits from the Spanish crown. Prior to the conquest, Moteuczoma Xocoyotzin had organized the empire into various provinces, creating a strong centralized government that was regulated through a tributary system. When he came to power, a large number of subjected *altepetl* (city-states) were being heavily taxed.

Through the *encomienda*, the Spanish sought immediate justification to legitimize their possession of lands previously held by indigenous nobles as a right of descent. Tlacahuepantzin Yohualicahuacatzin, later known as Pedro Moteuczoma, was considered the heir to various estates in the Teotlalpan that included the modern municipalities of Mixquiahuala, Tecozautla, Tula, Tlahuelilpan, and Tlaxcopan (Gerhard, 1986:304–309; Lopez, 2005:79, Map 5).

Having received *the mayordomía* (stewardship), Tlacahuepantzin Yohualicahuacatzin was allotted a territory belonging to the Toltec lineage and given the right to benefit from the goods produced there. Reality, however, was different; he died in A.D. 1570, still unable to take possession of some estates that were being used by the Spanish Crown to extract taxes. Arguing that it was his right to do so, in A.D. 1564 one of his sons, Martín Moteuczoma, requested that the court turn over the earnings from the estates held in the Royal Treasury. However, since he was not the legitimate son of Pedro Moctezuma, his petition was denied (Ramirez Calva 2005).

Pedro Moteuczoma legitimate son, Diego Luis de Moteuczoma Ihuitemotzin, was taken to Spain by King Felipe II, where he married Francisca de la Cueva y Valenzuela. From that moment on, all the Ihuitemotzin descendants would originate in Spain, including Pedro Tesifón de Moteuczoma (Chipman 2010). Today we know more about Pedro Moteuczoma's sister, Isabel de Moteuczoma (Gerhard 1986:190). Only two of his brothers survived the fall of Tenochtitlan: Nezahualtecolotl and Tlacahuapan. Cuauhtemoc, through Axayacatl and Totlehuicotl, ordered that several of them be put to death on "The Night of Sorrows": Chimalpopoca, Xoxopehualoc, and Tzihuacoyotllos were found dead in an irrigation canal in Tenochtitlan. Ilhuitl Temoc died in the first smallpox epidemic; we know nothing of Cuauhtlecohuatzin and Acamapichtli. Pedro Moteuczoma died having never received any of the profits from the 12 estates he held through the encomienda; he was buried in the Church of Santo Domingo in Mexico City (Ramirez Calva 2005).

The Toltec Heritage

It is important to conclude this chapter by taking into account the great significance of the Toltec culture for the Mexica. Much of Aztec ideology and religion has Toltec origins (Leon-Portilla 1980; López Luján and López Austin 2009; Matos Moctezuma 2009; Nicholson 2001). Many of the key types of architecture and sculpture in Aztec cities first appeared at Tula several centuries earlier. Many of these shared monuments have not been analyzed systematically yet. The best synthesis is by Leonardo López Luján and Alfredo López Austin (2009). Commonly cited monuments shared by the Toltec and Aztec include atlantean warrior columns, chacmools, skull rack platforms (*tzompantli*), serpent walls (*coatepantli*), benches with warrior processions, standard bearer statues, balastrades with serpent heads, and I-shaped ballcourts with proportions similar to the ballcourts at Tula. Long colonnaded halls and rectangular colonnaded rooms, which Beatriz Braniff and Marie-Areti Hers (1998) call *salas claustros,* are important components of Toltec and Aztec sites that may have originated in the Classic period architecture of the Tolteca Chichimeca in the northern Mesoamerican periphery (Cobean and Mastache 2001:239; Healan 1989; Jiménez and Cobean 2016; Mastache et al. 2015; Nicholson 1971).

Many sculptures of Mexica emperors possess archaic Toltec-style costume elements such as butterfly pectorals and stepped helmets. These archaic features are present in the Tizoc stone, the commemorative stone for Axayacatl, and the Cuauhxicalli for Motecuhzoma I (Nicholson 1971; Pérez Castro et al. 1989; Wicke 1976). These monuments usually involve celebrations of the emperors' victories in war, and that they are depicted as Toltec warriors probably constitutes a direct association of the Aztec kings with their glorious Toltec past (Mastache et al. 2015:104). The Aztecs wanted to be identified directly with the Toltec of Tula, and the Mexica had massive programs of destruction, dismantling and looting buildings and offerings at Tula to bring the sculptures, ceramics, and other Toltec materials to Tenochtitlan, Tlatelolco, and other cities in the Basin of Mexico.

López Luján and López Austin (2009) also describe destruction at Tula to obtain sacred objects for the Aztec state. For the fifteenth century there is a written account in the *Historia de los Mexicanos por sus Pinturas* of the king of Tlatelolco sending an expedition to Tula to obtain Toltec sculptures for the templo mayor of Tlatelolco. In his investigations of the House of Eagles in the Templo Mayor of Tenochtitlan, López Luján (2006) recovered 201 personages sculptured on benches using Toltec-style costumes. Nearby in the foundations of the residence of the Marquis del Apartado, a basalt chacmool in pure Toltec style (and surely from Tula) was recovered by the Templo Mayor project (López Luján and López Austin 2009:Figure 13).

The offerings of Tenochtitlan, Tlatelolco, Tula, Chichen Itza, and other key Postclassic Mesoamerican centers need more comparative analyses, although the enormous volume of offerings recovered in Tenochtitlan make this a gigantic task. An interesting problem that involves ideology, iconography, and elite long-distance trade is the importance of turquoise during the Postclassic. In a recent profound investigation, Karl Taube (2012) has shown that turquoise does not appear in Mesoamerica until the beginning of the Postclassic (ca. 900 A.D.). During the Early Postclassic, objects decorated with turquoise mosaics became key components of elite costumes and elite offerings. The turquoise mosaic discs (tezcacuitlapilli) of Tula and Chichen Itza possessed both of these functions. Taube (2012:126) shows that, by the Late Postclassic, turquoise had become "the most esteemed form of royal regalia" with the royal crown (xiuhuitzoli) of the Aztec emperors made of turquoise.

References Cited

Acosta, Jorge R.
1940 Exploraciones en Tula, Hidalgo. *Revista Mexicana de Estudios Antropológicos, Sociedad Mexicana de Antropología* 4:172–194.
1956 Resumen de las exploraciones arqueológicas en Tula, Hidalgo, durante 1950. *Anales Instituto Nacional de Antropología e Historia* 8:37–115.
1957 Resumen de los informes de las exploraciones arqueológicasen Tula, Hidalgo durante las IX y X temporadas, 1953–1954. *Anales Instituto Nacional de Antropología e Historia* 9:119–169.

1958 Interpretaciones de algunos de los datos obtenidos en Tula relativos a la época Tolteca. *Revista Mexicana de Estudios Antropológicos* 14:75–110.

Anales de Cuauhtitlan

1945 *Códice Chimalpopoca*. Translated by Primo Fleciano Velázquez. Universidad Nacional Autónoma de Mexico, Mexico City.

Barlow, Robert H.

1994a El Códice Azcatitlan. In *Fuentes y estudio sobre el México Indígena Obras de Robert H. Barlow*, Vol. 5: *Primera parte*, edited by Jesús Monjarás-Ruiz, Elena Limón, and María de la Cruz Paillés H., pp. 179–276. Instituto Nacional De Antropología e Historia, Mexico City.

1994b Una nueva Lamina del Mapa de Quinatzin. In *Fuentes y estudio sobre el México Indígena Obras de Robert H. Barlow*, Vol. 5: *Primera parte*, edited by Jesús Monjarás-Ruiz, Elena Limón, and María de la Cruz Paillés H., pp. 277–314. Instituto Nacional e Antropología E Historia, Mexico City.

Blanton, Richard

1972 *Prehispanic Settlement Patterns of the Ixtapalapa Peninsula, Mexico*. Occasional Papers in Anthropology No. 6. Penn State University, Department of Anthropology, University Park, PA.

Boone, Elizabeth H.

1983 *The Codex Magliabechiano and the Lost Prototype of the Magliabechiano Group* (issued together with reprint of *The Book of the Life of the Ancient Mexicans* by Zelia Nuttall [1903], part 2 in two-volume set edición). University of California Press, Berkeley.

Braniff, Beatriz, and Marie-Areti Hers

1998 Herencias Chichimecas. *Arqueologia* 19:55–80.

Charnay, Désiré

1998 [1885] *Les anciennes villes du nouveau monde*. Hachette, Paris.

Chimalpain Cuauhtlehuanitzin, Domingo

1998 *Las ocho relaciones y el memorial de Colhuacan*. Consejo Nacional para la Cultura y las Artes, Mexico City.

Chipman, Donald E.

2010 *Moteuczoma's Children: Aztec Royalty under Spanish Rule, 1520–1700*. University of Texas Press, Austin.

Cobean, Robert H.

1982 *Investigaciones Recientes en Tula Chico*. Estudios sobre la Antigua Ciudad de Tula, INAH, *Col. Científica*, No.121, pp. 37–122, Mexico City.

1990 *La cerámica de Tula*. Hidalgo, Instituto Nacional de Antropología e Historia, Mexico City.

Cobean, Robert H., and Luis Manuel Gamboa Cabezas

2005 *Programa de Investigación Conservación y Mantenimiento de la Zona Arqueológica de Tula*. Consejo de Arqueología, Instituto Nacional de Antropología e Historia, Mexico City.

Cobean, Robert H., Elizabeth Jiménez García, and Alba Guadalupe Mastache Flores

2012 *Tula*. Fondo de Cultura Economica, El Colegio de Mexico. Mexico City.

Cobean, Robert H., and Alba Guadalupe Mastache

2001 Toltec. In *The Oxford Encyclopedia of Mesoamerican Cultures*, Vol. 3. Edited by David Carrasco, pp. 239–241. Oxford University Press, New York.

Codex Azcatitlan

1995 *Códice Azcatitlan*. 2 vols. Translated by Leonardo López Luján, Bibliothèque Nationale de France, Société des Américanistes, Paris

Diehl, Richard A.
1989 Previous Investigations at Tula. In *Tula of the Toltecs: Excavations and Survey*, edited by Dan M. Healan, pp. 13–33. University of Iowa Press, Iowa City.

Franco, Jose Luis
1945 Comentarios sobre tipología y filogenia de la decoración negra sobre color natural del barro en la cerámica Azteca II. *Revista Mexicana de Estudios Antropológicos, Sociedad Mexicana de Antropología* 7:163–186.

Gamboa Cabezas, Luis Manuel
2005 *Informe de la investigación y conservacion del Palacio Quemado, Tula de Allende, Hidalgo.* Centro Instituto Nacional de Antropología e Historia, Archivo Técnico, Mexico City.

García Chávez, Raúl E.
2004 *De Tula a Azcapotzalco. Caracterización arqueológica de los Altepetl de la Cuenca de México del Posclásico Temprano y Medio, a través del estudio cerámico regional.* Ph.D. dissertation, National Autonomous University of Mexico, Mexico City.

García Chávez, Raúl., Luis M. Gamboa Cabezas, and Verónica Saldaña Velez
2003 *Informe final del Salvamento Arqueológico Circuito Exterior Mexiquense: tramo Ecatepec Peñón.* Archivo Técnico del INAH. Consejo de Arqueología, Mexico City.

García Cubas, Antonio
2003 Escritos diversos de 1870 a 1874 / Antonio García Cubas. Alicante. Biblioteca Virtual Miguel de Cervantes. Electronic document http://www.cervantesvirtual.com/nd/ark:/59851/bmck07d3 Access May 23, 2016.

García García, María Teresa
1987 *Huexotla: un sitio del Acolhuacan.* Colección Científica 65. Instituto Nacional de Antropología e Historia, Mexico City.

Gerhard, Peter
1986 *Geografia Historica de la Nueva España 1519–1821.* Universidad Nacional Autonoma de Mexico, Mexico City.

Graulich, Michel
1988 *Quetzalcóatl y el espejismo de Tollan.* Instituut voor Amerikanistiek, Antwerpen, Belgium. Electronic document, http://www.sup-infor.com/etudes/etudes.htm, accessed December 6, 2015.

Healan, Dan M.
1977 Archaeological Implications of Daily Life in Ancient Tollan, Hidalgo, Mexico, *World Archaeology* 9:140–156.
1989 House, Household and Neighbourhood in a Postclassic City. In *Households and Communities*, edited by S. Mac Eachern, D. Archer, and R. Gavin, pp. 416–429. University of Calgary, Calgary.
2011 The Archaeology of Tula, Hidalgo, Mexico. *Journal of Archaeological Research* 2(0):53–115.

Healan, Dan M. (editor)
1989 *Tula of the Toltecs: Excavations and Survey.* University of Iowa Press, Iowa City.

Healan, D. M., and J. W. Stoutamire
1989 Surface Survey of the Tula Urban Zone. In *Tula of the Toltec's: Excavations and Survey*, edited by Dan M. Healan, pp. 203–236. University of Iowa Press, Iowa City.

Hodge, Mary, and Leah Minc
1991 *Aztec-Period Ceramic Distribution and Exchange Systems.* Report to the National Science Foundation, Arlington, VA.

Jiménez Moreno, W.
1941 Tula y los toltecas según las fuentes históricas. *Revista Mexicana de Estudios Antropológicos, Sociedad Mexicana de Antropología* 5:79–83.
Jiménez García, Elizabeth, and Robert H. Cobean
2016 Ritual Processions in Ancient Tollan: The Legacy in Stone. In *Processions in the Ancient Americas*, edited by Susan Toby Evans. Occasional Papers in Anthropology No. 33. Department of Anthropology, Pennsylvania State University, University Park, PA, in press.
Leon-Portilla, Miguel
1980 *Toltecayotl: aspectos de la Cultura Nahuatl.* Fondo de Cultura Economica, Mexico City.
López Aguilar, Fernando
2005 *Símbolos del Tiempo.* Consejo Estatal para las Culturas y las Artes del Estado de Hidalgo, Mexico City.
López Luján, Leonardo
2006 *La Casa de las Aguilas: un Ejemplo de la Arquitectura Religiosa de Tenochtitlan.* 2 vols. Fondo de Cultura Economica, Mexico City.
López Luján, Leonardo, and Alfredo López Austin
2009 The Mexica in Tula and Tula in Mexico-Tenochtitlan. In *The Art of Urbanism*, edited by William L. Fash and Leonardo López Luján, pp. 384–422. Dumbarton Oaks Research Library and Collection, Washington, DC.
Mastache, Alba Guadalupe, Robert H. Cobean, and Dan M. Healan
2015 *Ancient Tollan: Tula and the Toltec Heartland.* 2nd ed. University Press of Colorado, Boulder.
Mastache, Guadalupe, and Ana María Crespo
1974 *La ocupación prehispánica en el área de Tula, Hgo.* Proyecto Tula, Colección científica. Instituto Nacional de Antropología e Historia, Mexico City
1982 Análisis sobre la traza General de Tula, Hgo. In *Estudios sobre la Antigua Ciudad de Tula*, pp. 11–36. Colección Científica 121. Instituto Nacional de Antropología e Historia, Mexico, D.F.
Matos Moctezuma, Eduardo
1974 *Proyecto Tula (1ª parte).* Colección Científica 15. Instituto Nacional de Antropología e Historia, Mexico City.
1976 *Proyecto Tula (2ª parte).* Colección Científica 33. Instituto Nacional de Antropología e Historia, Mexico City.
2009 Configuration of the Sacred Precinct of Mexico-Tenochtitlan. In *The Art of Urbanism*, edited by William L. Fash and Leonardo Lóprez Luján, pp. 423–442. Dumbarton Oaks Research Library and Collection, Washington, DC.
Meyer, Enrique
1939 Noticia sobre los petroglifos de Tula, Hgo. *Revista Mexicana de Estudios Antropológicos* 3(2):122–128.
Navarrete, Carlos, and Ana María Crespo
1971 Un Atlante Mexica y algunas consideraciones sobre los relieves del cerro La Malinche, Hidalgo. *Estudios de Cultura Náhuatl* 9:11–15.
Nicholson, Henry B.
1971 Major Sculpture in Pre-Hispanic Central Mexico. In *Handbook of Middle American Indians*, Vol. 10, edited by Gordon F. Ekholm and Ignacio Bernal, pp. 92–134. University of Texas Press, Austin.
2001 *Topiltzin Quetzalcoatl: The Once and Future Lord of the Toltecs.* University Press of Colorado, Boulder.

Parsons, Jeffrey R.
1971 *Prehistoric Settlement Patterns in the Texcoco Region, Mexico.* Memoirs No. 3. Museum of Anthropology, University of Michigan, Ann Arbor.

Peña, Augustin, and Carmen Rodriguez
1976 Excavaciones en Daini, Tula, Hgo. *Proyecto Tula, parte 2.* Edited by Eduardo Matos Moctezuma, pp. 85–90. Colección Científica 33. Instituto Naciona de Antropologíe e Historia, Mexico City.

Perez Castro, Guillermo, Pedro Sanchez Nava, Maria Estefan, Judith Padilla y Yedra, and Antonio Gudiño Garfias
1989 El Cuauhxicalli de Moctezuma l. *Arqueologia* 5:131–151.

Quiles, Juglans
2001 *Proyecto de Rescate Arqueológico Boulevard Tula-Iturbe.* Centro Instituto Nacional de Antropología e Historia, Mexico City

Ramirtez Calva, Verenice Cipatli
2005 *Caciques y cacicazgos indígenas en la región de Tollan, siglos XVI–XVII.* Ph.D. dissertation, El Colegio de Michoacán A. C., Zamora, Michoacán, Mexico.

Sahagún, Fray Bernardino de
2000 Libro Decimo Capitulo XXIX. In *Historia General de las Cosas de la Nueva España*, pp. 949–950. Consejo Nacional para la Cultura y las Artes, Mexico City
2000 *Historia general de las cosas de la Nueva España*, Introducción, paleografía y notas de Alfredo López Austin y Josefina García Quintana, Consejo Nacional para la Cultura y las Artes, 3 vols.

Sanders William T., Jeffrey R. Parsons, and Robert S. Santley
1979 *The Basin of Mexico: Ecological Processes in the Evolution of a Civilization.* Academic Press, New York.

Santamarina Novillo, Carlos
2005 *El sistema de dominación azteca: el Imperio tepaneca.* Ph.D. dissertation, Departamento de Historia de América II Universidad Complutense de Madrid, Facultad de Geografía e Historia, Madrid.

Smith, Michael E.
1993 The Strategic Provinces. In *Aztec Imperial Strategies*, edited by Frances F. Berdan, Richard E. Blanton, Elizabeth Hill Boone, Mary G. Hodge, Michael E. Smith, and Emily Umberger, pp. 137–150. Dumbarton Oaks Research Library and Collection, Washington, DC.

Stoutamire, James
1974 Archaeological Survey of the Tula Urban Zone. In *Studies of Ancient Tollan: A Report of the University of Missouri Tula Archaeological Project*, edited by Richard A. Diehl, pp. 25–31. University of Missouri, Columbia.
1975 *Trend Surface Analysis of Survey Data from Tula, Hidalgo, Mexico.* Ph.D. dissertation, Department of Anthropology, University of Missouri, Columbia.

Taube, Karl A.
2012 The Symbolism of Turquoise in Ancient Mesoamerica. In *Turquoise in Mexico and North America: Science, Conservation, Culture and Collections*, edited by J. C. H. King, pp. 117–134. British Museum, London.

Vaillant, George C.
1938 A Correlation of Archaeological and Historical Sequences in the Valley of Mexico. *American Anthtopologist* 40:535–573.
1956 *The Aztecs of Mexico.* Pelican Books, Suffolk, UK.

Vega Sosa, Constanza
1978. Datos para una cronología relativa en el área del recinto sagrado de Mexico-Tenochtitlan. *Boletín del Instituto Nacional de Antropologia* 24:72–79.

Wicke, Charles R.
1976 Once More around the Tizoc Stone. *Actas del XLI Congreso Internacional de Americanistas* 2:209–222.

Yadeun, Juan
1975 *El Estado y la Ciudad: el Caso de Tula, Hidalgo.* Instituto Nacional de Antropología e Historia, Mexico City.

CHAPTER 5

AZTEC SETTLEMENT HISTORY

L. J. GORENFLO AND CHRISTOPHER P. GARRATY

Introduction

THE Aztecs were what anthropologists call a *complex society*, a type of sociocultural system characterized primarily by centralized leadership but containing hierarchical social and economic elements as well (Wright 1977, 2006; see also Fried 1967; Service 1971). Certain features of such societies translate into the geographic arrangement of people. At the community scale, many settlements in complex societies include different areas that correspond to various activities—a zone of administrative buildings, an area of manufacturing workshops, a neighborhood of merchants, and so on. At the regional scale, in turn, complex societies usually comprise multiple settlements spatially organized in hierarchies, where different communities host activities that contribute to the functioning whole of a regional settlement system. In such settlement hierarchies, one community might occur near a particular resource to promote its exploitation and distribution to other settlements in the system, while another might contain large buildings used for administrative functions for governing smaller communities. This chapter examines the Aztecs at a regional scale, examining how regional settlement (primarily Late Aztec) emerged, its similarities and differences with settlement from preceding periods, and how the Aztec settlement pattern provides important insights on key aspects of the prehistoric complex society that created it.

This chapter focuses on the Basin of Mexico. This region contained the core of the Aztec Empire, also known as the Triple Alliance, including its capitals at Tenochtitlan, Texcoco, and Tlacopan (Figure 5.1). In addition, it is the best-known part of the vast Aztec imperial landscape (Berdan et al. 1996) in terms of regional settlement, thanks in part to more than a decade of archaeological settlement pattern surveys that discovered and described thousands of prehispanic sites, though also to a remarkably rich written record on the Aztecs, both predating and immediately following the Spanish Conquest

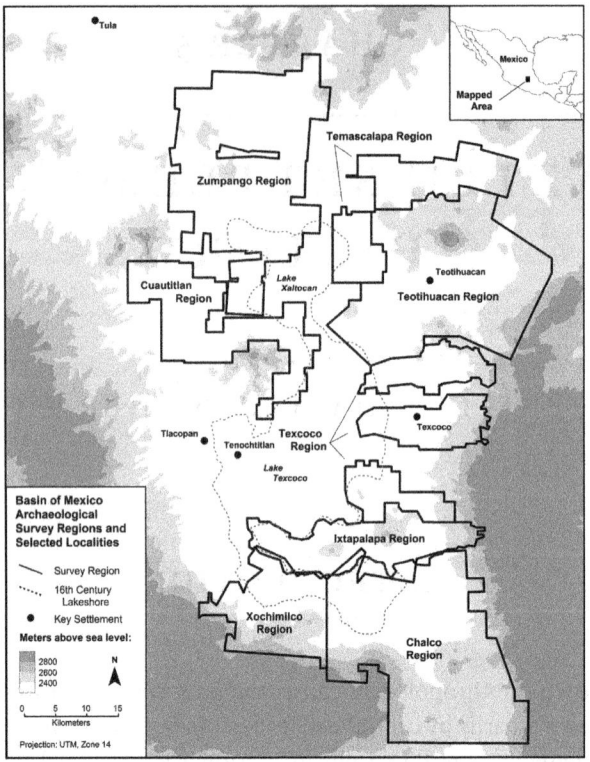

FIGURE 5.1 The Basin of Mexico, showing major physical geographic features, archaeological survey regions, and key localities mentioned in text. Drawn by L. J. Gorenflo.

(the *ethnohistoric* record; Sanders et al. 1979). These two data sources complement one another, with the ethnohistoric record helping to interpret archaeological remains and archaeological survey data providing coverage of geographic areas and social groups not adequately discussed in ethnohistoric sources.

Aztec Regional Settlement and Chronology: Methods, Data, and Interpretation

Making sense of Aztec regional organization in the Basin of Mexico requires an understanding of the region's physical geography. The basin comprises a closed physiographic area covering about 7,000 km² near the southern end of Mexico's central plateau. Volcanic activity during the Late Tertiary period of geologic history created a basin defined by large volcanic mountain ranges to the west, south, and east and a low series of hills to the north. Erosion over succeeding millennia further sculpted the basin as it deposited thick layers of sediment in low-lying areas (Frederick et al. 2005; González and Fuentes 1980; Lugo 1984; Maldonado-Koerdell 1964; Mooser et al. 1956). A series of interconnected shallow lakes eventually formed from water that collected in the lowest parts of this closed hydrologic unit (Bradbury 1989; Caballero and Ortega 1998; Lozano and Ortega 1998; Lozano et al. 1993; Palerm 1973). The result was a complex environmental setting characterized by dramatic physical features—highly varying topography and a central lake system—that provided both challenges to and opportunities for the prehistoric peoples who eventually occupied the region.

Changing elevations, highly variable annual precipitation that decreases from about 1,100 mm in the southwest to about 500 mm in the northeast, and assorted geophysical characteristics (e.g., slope, hydrology, and soil) created a series of environmental zones in the Basin of Mexico. Archaeologists interested in prehistoric human adaptation to this region defined 10 such zones: lakebed, island, saline lakeshore, deep soil alluvium, thin soil alluvium, upland alluvium, lower piedmont, middle piedmont, upper piedmont, and sierra (Sanders et al. 1979). Although varying environmental settings undoubtedly influenced human settlement in the basin, impacts on the natural environment during the Colonial occupation and subsequent periods greatly altered the natural setting (Córdova 1997; Kovar 1970; O'Hara et al. 1993; Rzedowski 1977, 1978, 2001; Simpson 1952). Despite efforts to identify key characteristics of the basin environment, our understanding remains incomplete, although variables such as elevation, rainfall, soil, and proximity to the central lake system certainly would have affected how the Aztecs settled and used the region.

Between 1960 and 1975, archaeologists employing knowledge of key ceramics (primarily) as chronological markers conducted intensive surveys of eight areas in the Basin of Mexico to define prehispanic settlement patterns in the region (Sanders 1981; Sanders et al. 1979). Survey crews walked across each area, guided by landscape features visible on 1:5,000 aerial photographs, and recorded evidence of prehistoric remains that they encountered—mainly scatters of artifacts (especially decorated potsherds) and mounds signifying the remnants of buildings. Localities judged to contain sufficient surface evidence were designated as archaeological sites, with areal extent, density of artifact scatters, and special features (e.g., mounds, concentrations of stone rubble) recorded. Subsequent analysis of these data enabled estimation of population for most sites. The presence of particular types of architecture, such as public buildings, and certain categories of artifacts, such as remains from stone tool and salt production, led to the assignment of specialized site function, although researchers interpreted most sites as farming communities. The result of these surveys was an extraordinarily rich database consisting of archaeological sites for several periods of prehistoric occupation between 1500 B.C. and A.D. 1519, providing a basis for studying past regional organization. Archaeologists surveyed the entire Basin of Mexico with two major exceptions: a small area in the northcentral part of the region and a large area in the southwestern basin occupied by modern Mexico City (the latter area, unfortunately, also encompassing locations of the Triple Alliance capitals of Tenochtitlan and Tlacopan, along with several other prominent Aztec centers; see Figure 5.1).

Potsherds collected from the surface provided the principal evidence for determining the ages of sites and site components recorded during the surveys. Archaeologists working in the basin developed a chronological sequence for pottery based on recognizable changes in certain decorative styles and attributes, such as the thickness of painted lines, the arrangement of decoration on the vessel surface, and the presence or absence of specific elements such as lines, dots, spirals, and circles. Based on this evidence, they assigned Aztec-era occupations in the Basin of Mexico to either the Early Aztec (ca. A.D. 1200–1350) or Late Aztec period (ca. A.D. 1350–1520). Several of the most important ceramic markers for Aztec occupations were first identified by Franz Boas and Manuel Gamio (1921), Eduardo Noguera (1935), and George Vaillant (1938), who defined four successive styles of Black-on-Orange pottery (Aztec I–IV) that archaeologists continue to use as a basis for site chronologies (Figure 5.2).

Despite decades of reliance on these pottery types, recent research indicates a need for caution when using them as temporal markers. For example, the Basin of Mexico

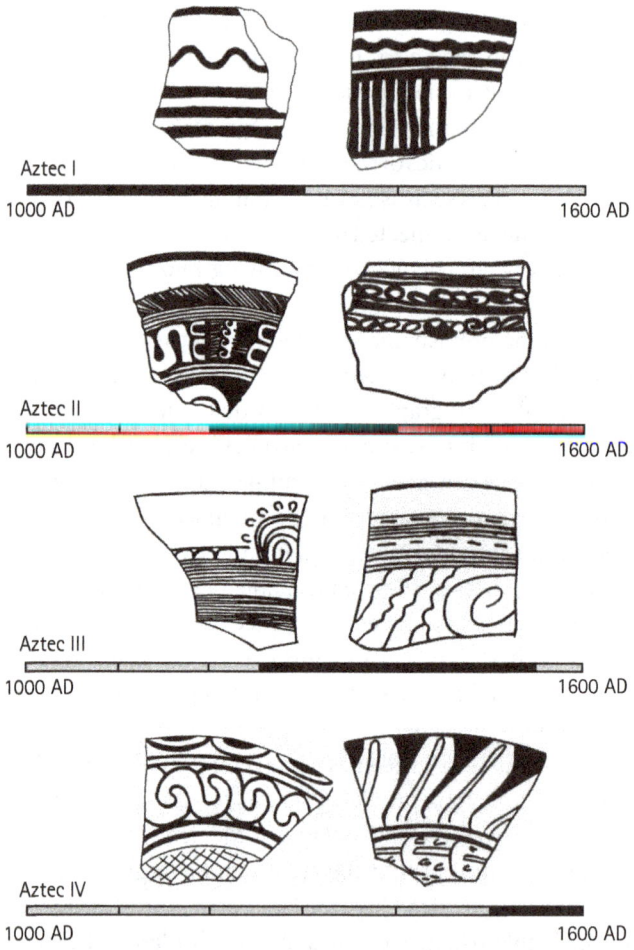

FIGURE 5.2 Illustrations of Aztec I–IV decorated Black-on-Orange pottery sherds and associated chronology (Aztec I illustrations provided by Destiny Crider; Aztec II–IV illustrations modified from Hodge and Minc 1991). Drawn by Kristen Sullivan and L. J. Gorenflo.

survey team defined Early Aztec settlements based on the presence of Aztec I- and Aztec II-style decorated potsherds. However, the distribution of Aztec I Black-on-Orange pottery is largely limited to the southern part of the basin (Brumfiel 2005; Parsons and Gorenflo 2016), and it was used over the course of possibly four centuries (A.D. 900s–1200s), overlapping with both the preceding Toltec-era Mazapan tradition and the later Aztec II tradition (Parsons et al. 1996). Both of these complicating factors limit its utility as a temporal marker for Early Aztec. Aztec II Black-on-Orange was widely used throughout the basin and serves as the foremost pottery type for defining Early Aztec occupation. However, its span of manufacture appears to have been fairly limited to the late A.D. 1200s through early to mid-1400s, and thus the distribution of Aztec II pottery provides little insight into settlement during the first century or so of the Early Aztec period (Parsons and Gorenflo 2016). The distributions of Aztec I and II styles generally provide a reasonable basis for defining settlement patterns during the centuries immediately preceding the Aztec Empire, though our understanding of Early Aztec regional organization will remain limited until further research refines the geography and chronology of the key ceramic markers.

Archaeologists use Aztec III and Aztec IV Black-on-Orange pottery to identify Late Aztec occupations. Aztec III Black-on-Orange pottery production began in the mid-A.D. 1300s (Hare and Smith 1996; Nichols and Charlton 1996) and overlapped with Aztec II for one-half century or more (Charlton 2000; García Chávez 2004). Production continued for possibly a century or more after the Spanish conquest in 1521. Despite these complications, its presence generally is considered a reliable indicator of occupation during the Late Aztec period and the Aztec Imperial era (Charlton 2000). Aztec III-style potsherds are extensively distributed and abundant in all areas of the basin and neighboring valleys. Outside the basin, their presence provides a useful indicator of Aztec imperial incursions throughout much of western Mesoamerica (Garraty and Ohnersorgen 2009; Silverstein 2001; Smith 1990); inside the basin, their abundance represents a very high density of Late Aztec occupation, with nearly continuous scatters of pottery in some areas making definition of discrete Aztec communities extremely difficult (Parsons and Gorenflo 2016; Sanders et al. 1979). The Basin of Mexico survey teams also used Aztec IV Black on-Orange to identify Late Aztec period occupations. However, this style likely began immediately prior to or soon after the Spanish Conquest (Parsons 1966) and overlapped with Aztec III styles for possibly a century or more (Charlton 1968, 1972; Charlton et al. 2005). Reliance on Aztec IV Black-on-Orange pottery as a temporal marker introduces the possibility that a small portion of the sites defined as Late Aztec by the survey team actually might have been inhabited after the Spanish Conquest. The size of the indigenous population declined substantially after the Conquest, with an estimated population loss as high as 90 percent of pre-Conquest levels (Gibson 1964). This massive depopulation likely reduced the amount of post-Conquest Aztec IV ceramics deposited and hence errors in assigning Colonial occupations to the Late Aztec period. In addition, given the settlement continuity during the decades immediately following the conquest (e.g., Hassig 1985; Lockhart 1985, 1992), it is likely that most sites with Colonial-era potsherds were occupied continuously from the Late Aztec period. Thus, we assume that using Aztec IV ceramics to define Late Aztec period sites probably does not compromise our interpretations of Late Aztec settlement patterns.

Archaeological surveys of the Basin of Mexico discovered remains of more than 3,900 sites dating between 1500 B.C. and A.D. 1519, with more than 1,550 of them assigned to the Late Aztec occupation (i.e., containing some combination of Aztec III- and Aztec IV-style decorated potsherds; Parsons et al. 1983; Gorenflo and Sanders 2007) (Figure 5.3a). The Late Aztec settlement pattern contrasts sharply with its precursors, Early Aztec and Late Toltec (ca. A.D. 950–1350) occupations (Figures 5.3b and 5.3c). The most dramatic characteristics of Late Aztec settlement are the sheer number of sites and their broad geographic distribution throughout the basin. For much of the earlier occupations, including Early Aztec, settlement tended to emphasize the southern portion of the basin, possibly because higher rainfall in the south reduced risk for the agriculture activities that formed the foundation of prehistoric economies in the region (Gorenflo 2006, 2015; Sanders et al. 1979). Although settlement in the Late Toltec period occurred in the northern basin, likely influenced by proximity to the Toltec capital at Tula, the expansion of Late Aztec settlement in the northern basin is particularly notable. High population throughout the basin during the Late Aztec period may represent expansion into more arid regions as people sought new farming or resource-extraction opportunities in previously unsettled areas ("Hirth and Nichols, this volume." (p. 8)).

Estimated population based on Late Aztec survey data was nearly 360,000 for the Basin of Mexico (Gorenflo 2015), though this estimate excludes the massive urban center of Tenochtitlan and its hinterland, which, as noted earlier, were not accessible for survey (see Figure 5.1). The unsurveyed area around Mexico City may have accounted for at least this many people, if not more, resulting in a total basin population estimated at or near 1 million (Sanders et al. 1979; also see Calnek 2003; Sanders 2003). By comparison, the Late Toltec population estimate for all surveyed areas is less than 85,000, and although population figures are unavailable for the Early Aztec occupation because of an absence of data on occupational density, an examination of Figure 5.3b indicates many fewer settlements and much lower intensity of settlement than during the Late Aztec period.

One can also assess the Late Aztec settlement pattern in terms of environmental zones occupied and site types, again focusing exclusively on data from archaeological surveys (with certain environmental zones from the 10 originally combined by archaeologists combined to facilitate discussion). Examining settlement by environmental zone indicates considerable importance of the lower piedmont—the lower slopes of mountains surrounding the basin—which contained more than 900 Late Aztec sites, nearly 60% of the total recorded during survey (Figure 5.4a). Lakebed/islands, lakeshore plain, alluvium, and upper piedmont each contained in excess of 135 sites, totaling 40% of surveyed sites from that period. The proportional distribution of Early Aztec and Late Toltec sites by environmental zone was generally similar to that during the Late Aztec period, with Early Aztec having a smaller percentage of sites in the alluvium and Late Toltec having relatively fewer sites in the lakebed/islands and upper piedmont zones.

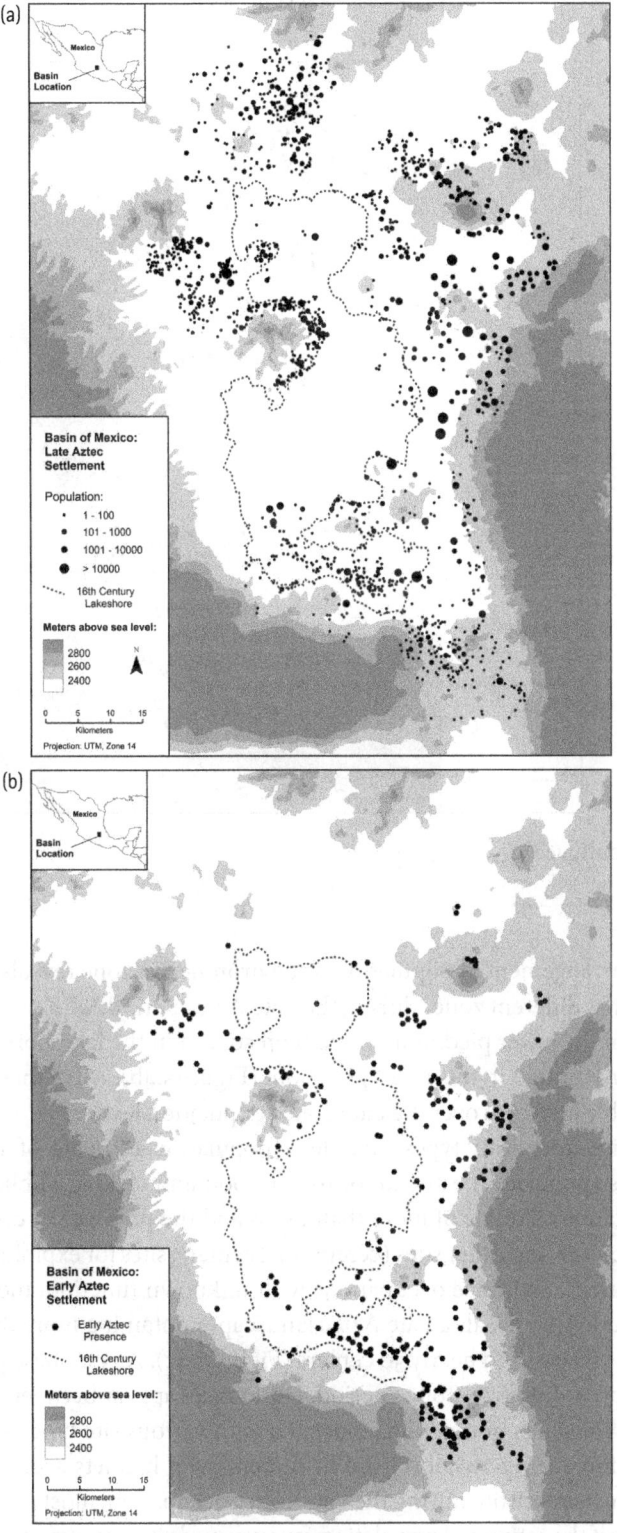

FIGURE 5.3 Settlement patterns in the Basin of Mexico, based on archaeological surveys, dating to the Late Aztec (a), Early Aztec (b), and Late Toltec (c) periods of occupation. Drawn by L. J. Gorenflo.

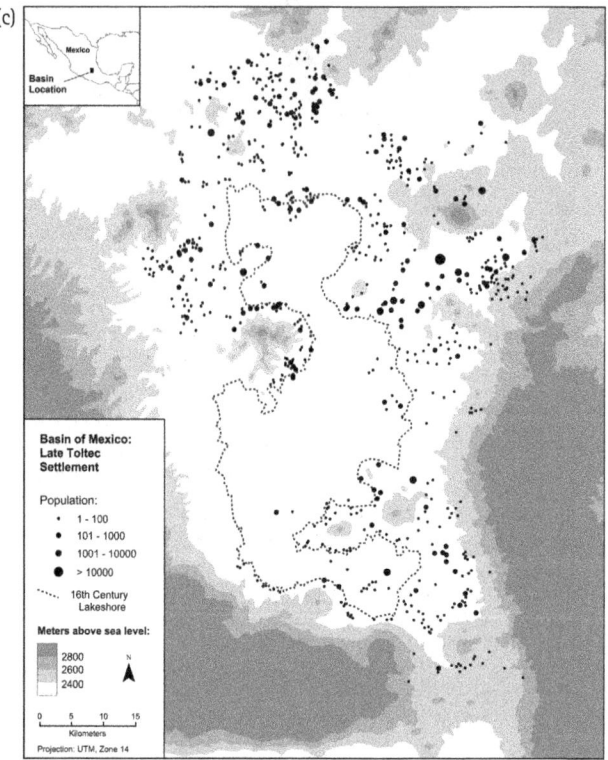

FIGURE 5.3 (continued)

However, the arrangement of population by environmental zone reveals the magnitude of reliance on the different zones during the Late Aztec period, with more than 190,000 people living in the lower piedmont, more than 50,000 in the lakeshore plain and alluvium, and nearly 24,000 in the upper piedmont (Figure 5.4b). All of these figures represent considerable increases over the Late Toltec population levels.

Grouping sites into four types—hamlets (population estimate of 100 persons or fewer), villages (population estimate of 101 to 1,000 and lacking public architecture), centers (population estimate of more than 1,000 and the presence of distinct administrative architecture), and other sites (ceremonial centers, sites for exploitation of specific localized resources, and trace occupations with unknown function, most lacking permanent population)—reveals a Late Aztec landscape containing more than 1,000 hamlets, about 300 villages, and nearly 30 centers (Figure 5.4c). Again, these proportions are similar to the preceding Late Toltec period. Differences appear between these two periods when one considers population associated with various site types: during the Late Aztec occupation, nearly 208,000 lived in centers, with hamlets accounting for fewer than 30,000; in comparison, during the Late Toltec occupation, most people lived in villages (nearly half the estimated population for surveyed sites, or almost 40,000 people),

AZTEC SETTLEMENT HISTORY   81

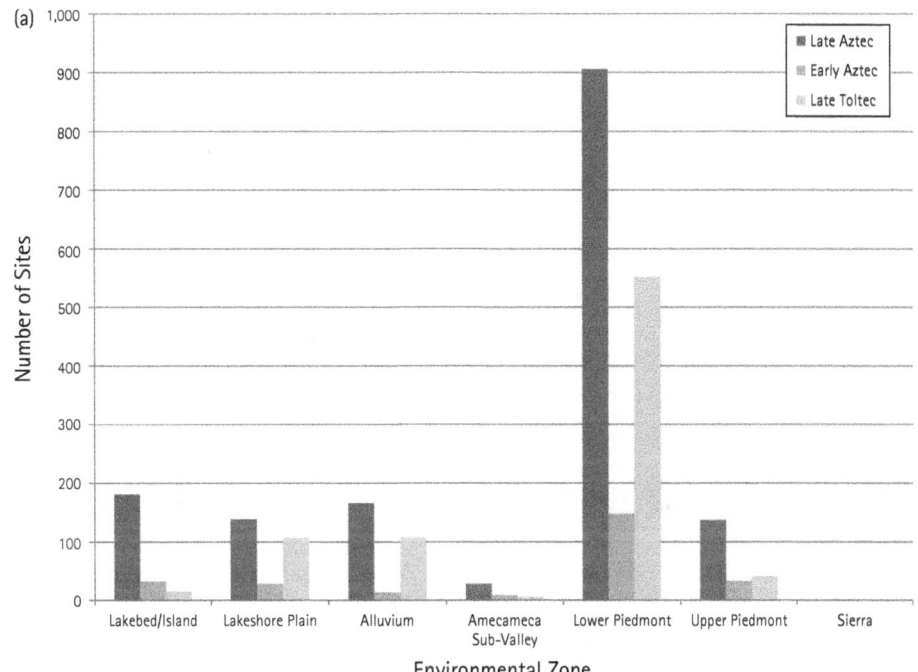

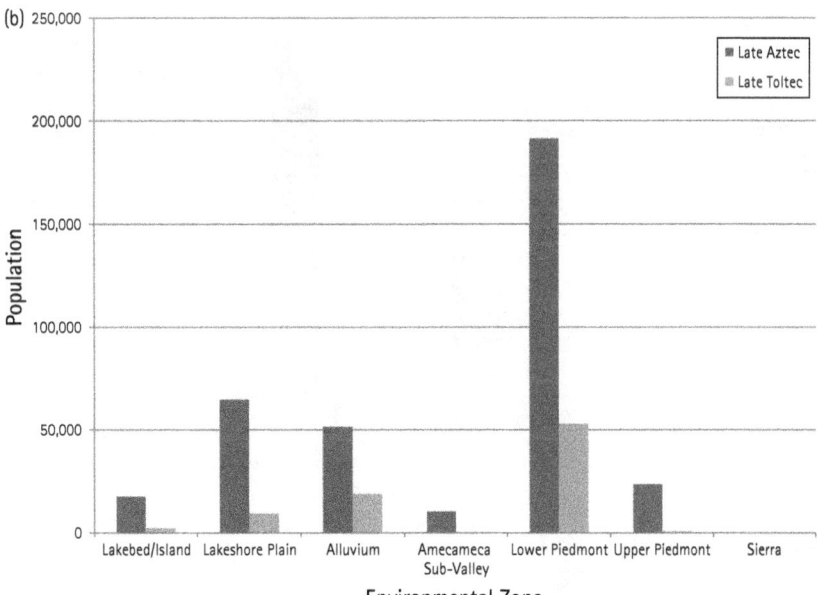

FIGURE 5.4 Summaries of Late Aztec and Late Toltec settlement based on survey data: number of sites by environmental zone (a); estimated population by environmental zone (b); number of sites by site type (c); and estimated population by site type (d). Drawn by L. J. Gorenflo.

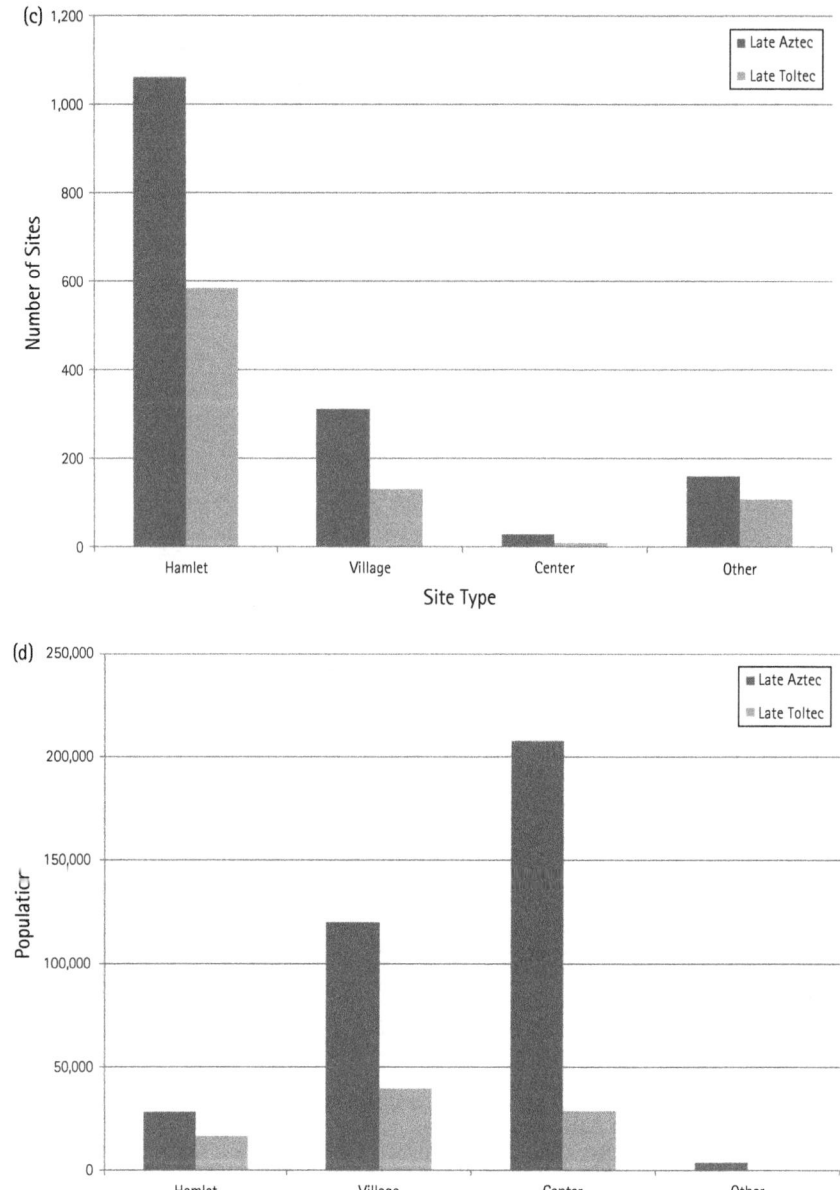

FIGURE 5.4 (continued)

with administrative sites playing a much smaller role in terms of regional demographics (Figure 5.4d).

The increase in total population during the Late Aztec occupation to previously unknown levels, as well as the geographic expansion of populations to most environmental zones in the basin, introduced a new set of challenges. One gains an appreciation of these challenges when considering the difficulty of growing crops amid limited rainfall in the northern basin and the likely broad reliance on irrigated agriculture throughout much of the region. Evidence for irrigation in the basin extends back to the Middle Formative occupation (ca. 1000–650 B.C.; Nichols 1980), and research at the prehispanic urban center of Teotihuacan in the northeastern basin has revealed the presence of irrigation canals that played a central role in supplying food to its enormous population (Cabrera 2005; Nichols 1987; Nichols and Frederick 1993; Nichols et al. 1991). Ethnohistoric sources discuss water control during the Aztec period (Cortés 1986; Diaz del Castillo 1956; Doolittle 1990; Palerm 1955, 1973; Sanders et al. 1979; see also "Hirth and Nichols, this volume; Smith, this volume". (p. 10)). Although many of those sources emphasize the central lake system and the impressive collection of dykes and causeways used to control water levels, evidence of irrigation systems was also documented. Archaeological evidence for widespread irrigation during the Late Aztec period largely is indirect, indicated by large sites that occur in northern portions of the basin where reliable production of crops other than xerophytic varieties would likely have been impossible (see Figure 5.3a). For example, eight Late Aztec sites with estimated populations of 10,000 or more occur in areas where average annual rainfall is 700 mm or less (Gorenflo 2015). Assuming that maize was the most important crop, permanent or rainfall irrigation would have been necessary to avoid crop failure, even during years of normal rainfall. It is likely that increased control of water was crucial to population growth and geographic expansion, the exception being particularly arid northern parts of the region, where low rainfall, absence of surface water, relatively flat local topography, or some combination of these factors precluded irrigation and required production of other crops or pursuit of other economic activities.

Further evidence of selective geographic expansion of Late Aztec settlement is the considerable increase in occupation within the ancient lake system and close to its shore. Settlement within the lake, on natural or artificial islands (built up by salt-making), exceeded 60 persons/km^2 in the areas surveyed, more than four times the density found in any previous period (Gorenflo 2015). Population within 1 km of the lakeshore approached 140 persons/km^2, more than three times the highest previous density. Ethnohistoric evidence indicates that the Aztecs relied heavily on lake resources in the Basin of Mexico, likely in part to help meet subsistence demands of the enormous population by exploiting additional resources and in part because a regional market system facilitated the distribution of specialized resources (Hassig 1985). Fish, salt, insect larvae, and waterfowl all would have been important to the prehispanic population (Berres 2000; Parsons 2001, 2006; Parsons and Morett 2004), as would the potential to travel by canoe, which greatly increased the efficiency of transporting goods by water in a region that lacked beasts of burden during prehistoric times (Gibson 1964; Hassig 1985; Sanders and Santley 1983).

As discussed earlier, the survey data document Late Aztec settlement throughout much of the Basin of Mexico. As is often the case, however, although archaeological data provide important insights on past sociocultural organization, many key details remain elusive. Fortunately, the ethnohistoric record for this region is quite rich, and it provides important information to help us understand broader patterns in Aztec regional settlement. By the time the Aztec Empire had developed to the level encountered by Spanish invaders in 1519, it had become highly reliant on tribute to support the large number of urban residents who produced no food for themselves (Parsons 1976; Sanders and Evans 2001; Sanders et al. 1979). Documentary evidence describes a vast network of tribute flowing mainly into Tenochtitlan from settlements throughout the basin and beyond (Barlow 1949; Berdan and Anawalt 1997; Carrasco 1999). Organized hierarchically, the tribute system rested on a foundation of city-states (Bray 1972; Carrasco 1999; Evans 2001; Gibson 1964; Hicks 1982, 1992; Hodge 1984), represented by the nearly 30 larger sites in Figure 5.3a (called "centers" earlier), though featuring another 15 to 20 (including Tenochtitlan and Tlacopan) that were not surveyed but are known from ethnohistoric sources (Sanders et al. 1979). Prior to the Aztec period, tribute flows in the basin appear to have been local, involving the hinterlands of larger communities (Hassig 1985). The expansion to new areas of the basin is consistent with the need to extract more resources to support increasing demand at the top of the sociopolitical hierarchy. Some of these resources would have taken the form of nonfood items, provided by communities close to key resources or with particular specializations (Charlton and Otis Charlton 1994; Charlton et al. 2000; Evans 2001; Nichols et al. 2000). But food likely rose to paramount importance, and one sees changes in regional settlement that supports this.

One piece of evidence for subsistence-oriented settlement is the presence of sites in areas used much less intensively during prior occupations of the basin. As noted, many Late Aztec communities occurred in areas with inadequate rainfall to support production of most crops, likely requiring increased water control. Settlement expansion into the more arid north may have been predicated on agricultural production of plants that did not require much water, notably maguey, possibly made more feasible by integration into a regional exchange system that enabled those communities to obtain other nonlocal resources to supplement local production (Evans 1990, 2001; Gorenflo and Sanders 2016; Parsons and Parsons 1990). Increased settlement near the lake system would have enabled increased exploitation of lacustrine resources; the enormous expansion of salt production in lakes Xaltocan and Texcoco during the Late Aztec period underscores increased reliance on the lakes (Parsons 2001; Sanders and Gorenflo 2007). Once again, a regional market system would have provided communities near the lake system access to food staples, pottery, stone tools, and other domestic necessities (Hassig 1985). However, probably the most important outcome of increased habitation in and around the lake system was the opportunity to develop *chinampa* agriculture to a much greater extent than had previously occurred. Chinampa is a type of intensive agriculture conducted in artificial fields created within the shallow lakes (Armillas 1971). Constant restoration of nutrients through frequent addition of new soil from the lake bottom, coupled with a steady supply of water from the lakes, enabled continuous cropping and multiple crops per year. Although chimampa agriculture occurred in the Basin of Mexico prior to the Late Aztec period, it peaked during this occupation, covering extensive areas in the southern basin estimated between

9,000 and 10,000 ha and yielding up to 4 million tons of maize annually (Armillas 1971; Parsons 1976; Sanders 1957).

Conclusions

Examining the regional settlement history and chronology in the Basin of Mexico associated with the Late Aztec occupation provides a sense of the emergence and workings of this complex society. Settlements occurred throughout the area, arranged in a hierarchy organized around city-states with responsibilities for local administration and resource extraction. The large population occupied a broad range of environmental settings throughout the basin, often in areas little used previously. Certainly this reflects the need to support a larger population than prior occupations, including considerable numbers of nonfood producers residing in the local city-states and, especially, Tenochtitlan. But it also reflects what had become *possible* through specialized adaptation to particular areas and the opportunity to exchange resources in a regional market system. Such an understanding is consistent with our understanding of complex societies in general—individual communities were parts of a broader, hierarchically organized regional system in which different places exploited nearby resources and distributed them to other places in return for items or resources they could not obtain themselves. Ethnohistoric accounts of marketplaces in the Basin of Mexico about the time of the Spanish Conquest list a remarkable array of items available from many parts of Mesoamerica, let alone the basin (Barlow 1949; Cortés 1986; Diaz del Castillo 1956; Gibson 1964; Hassig 1985). In examining the archaeologically documented Late Aztec settlement pattern in the Basin of Mexico, we see the basis for such a system in terms of where communities were located, the resources they likely exploited, and actions needed to meet the challenges inherent in integrating these resources within a larger regional system. Preceding Late Toltec and Early Aztec settlement, patterns show hints of these characteristics, the roots of what would become a fully integrated regional system during the Late Aztec period.

This chapter has focused largely on archaeological settlement patterns and what they tell us about Late Aztec regional organization and the sociocultural system underlying it. Archaeological data have limitations, often lacking the detail essential to understanding many intricacies of sociocultural systems. And yet they can complement other types of data, in many cases providing insights not covered in written sources, or providing evidence for aspects of a sociocultural system unavailable elsewhere. Archaeological settlement patterns help round out an understanding about the Aztec people who lived in the communities discovered by archaeological survey. In combination with other evidence, these data help develop an image of a prehistoric complex society adapted to a range of natural settings through a capacity to modify the natural environment and develop specific strategies for exploitation, where separate places played roles in a broader system of specialization and exchange in a region whose individual parts were coordinated economically, politically, and socially.

Acknowledgments

Jeff Parsons read and commented on an earlier version of this chapter. Kris Sullivan helped draft Figure 5.2. Destiny Crider and Leah Minc kindly provided permission to print, respectively, the Aztec I and Aztec II, III, and IV potsherd illustrations in Figure 5.2.

References Cited

Armillas, Pedro
1971 Gardens on Swamps. *Science* 174:653–661.
Barlow, Robert H.
1949 *The Extent of the Empire of the Culhua Mexica*. Ibero-America 28. University of California Press, Berkeley.
Berdan, Frances F., and Patricia R. Anawalt
1997 *The Essential Codex Mendoza*. University of California Press, Berkeley.
Berdan, Frances F., Richard E. Blanton, Elizabeth Hill Boone, Mary G. Hodge, Michael E. Smith, and Emily Umberger (editors)
1996 *Aztec Imperial Strategies*. Dumbarton Oaks Research Library and Collection, Washington, DC.
Berres, T.
2000 Climatic Change and Lacustrine Resources at the Period of Initial Aztec Development. *Ancient Mesoamerica* 11:27–38.
Boas, Franz, and Manuel Gamio
1921 Album de colecciones arqueológicas. Museo Nacional de Arqueología, História y Etnografía, Mexico City.
Bradbury, J. P.
1989 Late Quaternary Lacustrine Paleo environments in the Cuenca de Mexico. *Quaternary Science Reviews* 8:75–100.
Bray, Warwick
1972 The City-State in Central Mexico at the Time of the Spanish Conquest. *Journal of Latin American Studies* 4:161–185.
Brumfiel, Elizabeth M.
2005 Ceramic Chronology at Xaltocan. In *Production and Power at Postclassic Xaltocan*, edited by Elizabeth M. Brumfiel, pp. 117–152. University of Pittsburgh Department of Anthropology and Instituto Nacional de Antropología e Historia, Pittsburgh, PA, and Mexico City.
Caballero, M. E., and B. Ortega
1998 Lake Levels since 40 000 Years Ago at Chalco Lake, Near Mexico City. *Quaternary Research* 50:69–79.
Cabrera, Rueben
2005 Nuevas evidencias arqueológicas del manejo de agua en Teotihuacan. El Campo y la Ciudad. In *Arquitectura y urbanismo: pasado y presente de los espacios en Teotihuacan*, edited by M. E. Ruiz-Gallut and J. Torres-Peralta, pp. 121–161. Memoria de la Tercera Mesa Redonda de Teotihuacan. Instituto Nacional de Antropología e Historia, Mexico City.

Calnek, Edward
2003 Tenochtitlan-Tlatelolco. The Natural History of a City. In *Urbanism in Mesoamerica/ Urbanismo en Mesoamérica*, edited by William T. Sanders, Alba G. Mastache, and Robert H. Cobean, pp. 149–201. Instituto Nacional de Anthropología e Historia, Mexico City, and Department of Anthropology, Pennsylvania State University, University Park.

Carrasco, Pedro
1999 *The Tenochca Empire of Ancient Mexico: The Triple Alliance of Tenochtitlan, Tetzcoco, and Tlacopan*. University of Oklahoma Press, Norman.

Charlton, Thomas H.
1968 Post-Conquest Aztec Ceramics: Implications for Archaeological Interpretation. *The Florida Anthropologist* 21:96–101.
1972 *Post-Conquest Developments in the Teotihuacan Valley, Mexico*. Report No. 5. Office of the State Archaeologist, Des Moines, IA.
2000 The Aztecs and Their Contemporaries: The Central and Eastern Mexican Highlands. In *Cambridge History of New World Peoples, Vol. II: Mesoamerica, Part 1*, edited by R. E. W. Adams and Murdo J. MacLeod, pp. 500–557. Cambridge University Press, Cambridge, UK.

Charlton, Thomas H., and Cynthia Otis Charlton
1994 Aztec Craft Production in Otumba, 1470–1570: Reflections of a Changing World. In *Chipping Away on Earth*, edited by E. Quinones Keber, pp. 241–251. Labyrinthos, Lancaster, CA.

Charlton, Thomas H., Cynthia Otis Charlton, and Patricia Fournier G.
2005 The Basin of Mexico A.D. 1450–1620: Archaeological Dimensions. In *The Postclassic to Spanish-Era Transition in Mesoamerica: Archaeological Perspectives*, edited by Susan Kepecs and Rani T. Alexander, pp. 49–63. University of New Mexico Press, Albuquerque.

Charlton, Thomas H., Deborah L. Nichols, and Cynthia. L. Otis Charlton
2000 Otumba and Its Neighbors: Ex Oriente Lux. *Ancient Mesoamerica* 11:247–265.

Córdova, Carlos E.
1997 *Landscape Transformation in Aztec and Spanish Colonial Texcoco, Mexico*. Ph.D. dissertation, University of Texas, Austin. University Microfilms, Ann Arbor.

Cortés, Hernan
1986 *Letters from Mexico*. Translated and edited by A. Pagden. Yale University Press, New Haven, CT.

Diaz del Castillo, Bernal
1956 *The Discovery and Conquest of Mexico*. Translated by A. P. Maudslay. Ferrar, Strauss, and Cudahy, New York.

Doolittle, William E.
1990 *Canal Irrigation in Prehistoric Mexico: The Sequence of Technological Change*. University of Texas Press, Austin.

Evans, Susan T.
1990 The Productivity of Maguey Terrace Agriculture in Central Mexico during the Aztec Period. *Latin American Antiquity* 1:117–132.
2001 Aztec-Period Political Organization in the Teotihuacan Valley: Otumba as a City-State. *Ancient Mesoamerica* 12:89–100.

Frederick, Charles D., B. Winsborough, and Virginia S. Popper
2005 Geoarchaeological Investigations in the Northern Basin of Mexico. In *Production and Power at Postclassic Xaltocan*, edited by Elizabeth M. Brumfiel, pp. 71–115. University of Pittsburgh/Instituto Nacional de Antropología e Historia, Mexico City.

Fried, Morton H.
1967 *The Evolution of Political Society*. Random House, New York.

García Chávez, Raul
2004 *De Tula a Azcatpotzalco: caracterización arqueológica de los altepetl de la Cuenca de México, a través del estudio cerámico regional*. Ph.D. dissertation, Universidad Nacional Autónoma de México, Mexico City.

Garraty, Christopher P., and Michael A. Ohnersorgen
2009 Negotiating the Imperial Landscape: The Geopolitics of Aztec Control in the Outer Provinces of the Empire. In *The Archaeology of Meaningful Places*, edited by B. Bowser and N. Zedeño, pp. 107–131. University of Utah Press, Salt Lake City.

Gibson, Charles
1964 *The Aztecs under Spanish Rule. A History of the Indians of the Valley of Mexico, 1519–1810*. Stanford University Press, Stanford, CA.

González, L., and M. Fuentes
1980 El Holoceno de la Porción Central de la Cuenca de México. In *Memorias del III Coloquio sobre Paleobotánica y Palinología*, edited by F. Sánchez, pp. 113–132. Instituto Nacional de Antropología e Historia, Mexico City.

Gorenflo, L. J.
2006 The Evolution of Regional Demography and Settlement in the Prehispanic Basin of Mexico. In *Population and Preindustrial Cities: A Cross-Cultural Perspective*, edited by Glenn R. Storey, pp. 295–314. University of Alabama Press, Tuscaloosa.
2015 Compilation and Analysis of Pre-Columbian Settlement Data in the Basin of Mexico. *Ancient Mesoamerica* 26:197–212.

Gorenflo, L. J., and William T. Sanders
2007 *Archaeological Settlement Pattern Data from the Cuautitlan, Temascalapa, and Teotihuacan Regions, Mexico*. Occasional Papers in Anthropology No. 30. Department of Anthropology, Pennsylvania State University, University Park.
2016 *Prehispanic Settlement Patterns in the Temascalapa Region, Mexico*. Occasional Papers in Anthropology. Department of Anthropology, Pennsylvania State University, University Park, in press.

Hare, Timothy S., and Michael E. Smith
1996 New Postclassic Chronology for Yautepec, Morelos. *Ancient Mesoamerica* 7:281–297.

Hassig, Ross
1985 *Trade, Tribute, and Transportation. The Sixteenth Century Political Economy of the Valley of Mexico*. University of Oklahoma Press, Norman.

Hicks, Frederick
1982 Tetzcoco in the Early 16th Century: The State, the City, and the Calpolli. *American Ethnologist* 9:230–249.
1992 Subject States and Tribute Provinces: The Aztec Empire in the Northern Valley of Mexico. *Ancient Mesoamerica* 3:1–10.

Hodge, Mary G.
1984 *Aztec City-States*. Memoir 18, Museum of Anthropology, University of Michigan, Ann Arbor.

Kovar, Anton
1970 The Physical and Biological Environment of the Basin of Mexico. In *The Natural Environment, Contemporary Occupation and 16th Century Population of the Valley*, edited by William T. Sanders, Anton T. Kovar, Thomas H. Charlton, and Richard A. Diehl,

pp. 13–68. Teotihuacan Valley Project Final Report Vol. 1. Occasional Papers in Anthropology. Department of Anthropology. Pennsylvania State University, University Park.

Lockhart, James

1985 Some Nahua Concepts in Postconquest Guise. *History of European Ideas* 6:465–482.

1992 *The Nahuas after the Conquest: A Social and Cultural History of the Indians of Central Mexico, Sixteenth through Eighteenth Centuries*. Stanford University Press, Stanford, CA.

Lozano, M. S., and B. Ortega

1998 Late Quaternary Environmental Changes of the Central Part of the Basin of Mexico: Correlation between Chalco and Texcoco Basins. *Review of Palaeobotany and Palynology* 99:77–93.

Lozano, M.S., B. Ortega, M. Caballero, and J. Urrutia

1993 Late Pleistocene and Holocene Environments of Chalco Lake, Central Mexico, *Quaternary Research* 40:332–342.

Lugo, H. J.

1984 Geomorfología del sur de la Cuenca de México. *Instituto de Geografía, Seria Varia Tomo 1, Número 9*. Universidad Nacional Autónoma de México, Mexico City.

Maldonado-Koerdell, M.

1964 Geohistory and Paleogeography of Middle America. In *Handbook of Middle American Indians*, Vol. 1, edited by Robert Waucope, pp. 3–32. University of Texas Press, Austin.

Mooser, F., S. E. White, and José L. Lorenzo

1956 *La Cuenca de México: consideraciones geológicas y arqueológicas*. Dirección de Prehistoria, Instituto Nacional de Antropología e Historia, Mexico City.

Nichols, Deborah L.

1980 *Prehispanic Settlement and Land Use in the Northwestern Basin of Mexico, the Cuautitlan Region*. Ph.D. dissertation, Department of Anthropology, Pennsylvania State University, University Park.

1987 Prehispanic Irrigation at Teotihuacan, New Evidence: The Tlajinga Canals. In *Teotihuacan: nuevos datos, nuevas síntesis, nuevos problemas*, edited by E. McClung de Tapia and E. C. Rattray, pp. 133–160. Instituto de Investigaciones Antropológicas, Universidad Nacional Autónoma de México, Mexico City.

Nichols, Deborah L., and Thomas H. Charlton

1996 The Postclassic Occupation of Otumba: A Chronological Assessment. *Ancient Mesoamerica* 7:231–244.

Nichols, Deborah L., and Charles D. Frederick

1993 Irrigation Canals and Chinampas: Recent Research in the Northern Basin of Mexico. *Research in Economic Anthropology* Suppl. 7:123–150.

Nichols, Deborah L., Mary J. McLaughlin, and Maura Benton

2000 Production Intensification and Regional Specialization: Maguey Fibers and Textiles in the Aztec City-State of Otumba. *Ancient Mesoamerica* 11:267–291.

Nichols, Deborah L., Michael Spence, and Mark Borland

1991 Watering the Fields of Teotihuacan: Early Irrigation at the Ancient City. *Ancient Mesoamerica* 2:119–129.

Noguera, Eduardo

1935 La cerámica de Tenayuca y las excavaciones estratigráficas. In *Tenayuca*, pp. 141–201. Secretaria de Educación Pública, Departamento de Monumentos, Mexico City.

O'Hara, S. L., F. A. Street-Perrott, and T. P. Burt
1993 Accelerated Soil Erosion Around a Mexican Highland Lake Caused by Prehispanic Agriculture. *Nature* 362:48–51.

Palerm, Angel
1955 The Agricultural Bases of Urban Civilization in Mesoamerica. In *Irrigation Civilizations: A Comparative Study*, edited by Julien H. Steward, pp. 28–42. Social Science Monographs I. Pan American Union, Washington, DC.
1973 *Obras hidráulicas prehispánicas en el sistema lacustre del Valle de México*. Instituto Nacional de Antropología, Centro de Investigaciones Superiores, Mexico City.

Parsons, Jeffery R.
1966 *The Aztec Ceramic Sequence in the Teotihuacan Valley, Mexico*. Ph.D. dissertation, Department of Anthropology, University of Michigan, Ann Arbor.
1976 The Role of Chinampa Agriculture in the Food Supply of Aztec Tenochtitlan. In *Cultural Change and Continuity: Essays in Honor of James Bennett Griffin*, edited by Charles Cleland, pp. 233–262. Academic Press, New York.
2001 *The Last Saltmakers of Nexquipayac, Mexico: An Archaeological Ethnography*. Anthropological Papers No. 92. University of Michigan Museum of Anthropology, Ann Arbor.
2006 *The Last Pescadores of Chimalhuacan, Mexico: An Archaeological Ethnography*. Anthropological Papers No. 96. University of Michigan Museum of Anthropology, Ann Arbor.

Parsons, Jeffery R., Elizabeth M. Brumfiel, and Mary G. Hodge
1996 Developmental Implications of Earlier Dates for Early Aztec in the Basin of Mexico. *Ancient Mesoamerica* 7:217–230.

Parsons, Jeffery R., and L. J. Gorenflo
2016 Why Is Aztec II Black-on-Orange Pottery So Scarce in the Zumpango Region? A Regional Perspective from the Basin of Mexico on Tula's Collapse and its Aftermath. In *Homenaje a Alba Guadalupe Mastache Flores*, edited by A. Martinez, L. Martos, and R. Cobean. Instituto Nacional de Antropología e Historia, Mexico City, Mexico, in press.

Parsons, Jeffery R., Keith W. Kintigh, and Susan A. Gregg
1983 *Archaeological Settlement Pattern Data from the Chalco, Xochimilco, Ixtapalapa, Texcoco, and Zumpango Regions, Mexico*. Technical Report 14. University of Michigan Museum of Anthropology, Ann Arbor.

Parsons, Jeffery R., and Luis Morett
2004 Recursos acuáticos en la subsistencia Azteca: cazadores, pescadores, y recolectores. *Arqueología Mexicana* 12(8):38–43.

Parsons, Jeffery R., and Mary H. Parsons
1990 *Maguey Utilization in Highland Central Mexico: An Archaeological Ethnography*. Anthropological Papers No. 82. University of Michigan Museum of Anthropology, Ann Arbor.

Rzedowski, J.
1977 Flora y vegetación. In *Memoria de las obras del sistema de drenaje profundo del Distrito Federal*, Vol. I, edited by Roberto Ríos Elizondo, pp. 85–134. Departamento del Distrito Federal, Mexico City.
1978 *Vegetación de México*, Editorial Limusa, Mexico City.
2001 Principal comunidades vegetales. In *Flora fanerogámica del Valle de México*, edited by G. Calderón de Rzedowski and J. Rzedowski, pp. 32–38. CONABIO, Instituto de Ecología, A.C., Xalapa, Mexico.

Sanders, William T.

1957 *Tierra y Agua (Soil and Water)*. Ph.D. dissertation, Department of Anthropology, Harvard University, Cambridge, MA.

1981 Ecological Adaptation in the Basin of Mexico: 21,000 B.C. to the Present. In *Archaeology*, edited by Jeremy A. Sabloff, pp. 147–187. Supplement to the Handbook of Middle American Indians Vol. 1. University of Texas Press, Austin.

2003 The Population of Tenochtitlan-Tlatelolco. In *Urbanism in Mesoamerica/Urbanismo en Mesoamérica*, edited by William T. Sanders, Alba G. Mastache, and Robert H. Cobean, pp. 203–216. Instituto Nacional de Antropología e Historia, Mexico City, and Department of Anthropology, Pennsylvania State University, University Park.

Sanders, William T., and Susan T. Evans

2001 The Teotihuacan Valley and Temascalapa Region during the Aztec Period. In *The Aztec Period Occupation of the Valley*, edited by Susan T. Evans and William T. Sanders, pp. 931–1074. Teotihuacan Valley Project Final Report Vol. 5. Occasional Papers in Anthropology No. 25, Part 3—Syntheses and General Bibliography. Department of Anthropology, Pennsylvania State University, University Park.

Sanders, William T., and L. J. Gorenflo

2007 *Prehispanic Settlement Patterns in the Cuautitlan Region, Mexico*. Occasional Papers in Anthropology No. 29. Department of Anthropology, Pennsylvania State University, University Park.

Sanders, William T., Jeffery R. Parsons, and Robert S. Santley

1979 *The Basin of Mexico: Ecological Processes in the Evolution of a Civilization*. Academic Press, New York.

Sanders, William T., and Robert S. Santley

1983 A Tale of Three Cities: Energetics and Urbanization in Prehispanic Central Mexico. In *Prehistoric Settlement Patterns: Essays in Honor of Gordon R. Willey*, edited by Evon Z. Vogt and Richard M. Leventhal, pp. 243–292. University of New Mexico Press, Albuquerque.

Service, Elman R.

1971 *Prehistoric Social Organization*. 2nd ed. Random House, New York.

Silverstein, Jay

2001 Aztec Imperialism at Oztuma, Guerrero. *Ancient Mesoamerica* 12:31–48.

Simpson, Leslie B.

1952 *Exploitation of Land in Central Mexico in the Sixteenth Century*. Ibero-Americana 36. University of California Press, Berkeley.

Smith, Michael E.

1990 Long-Distance Trade under the Aztec Empire: The Archaeological Evidence. *Ancient Mesoamerica* 1:153–169.

Valliant, George

1938 A Correlation of Archaeological and Historical Sequences in the Valley of Mexico. *American Anthropologist* 40:535–573.

Wright, Henry T.

1977 Recent Research on the Origin of the State. *Annual Review of Anthropology* 6:379–397.

2006 Early State Dynamics as Political Experiment. *Journal of Anthropological Research* 62:305–319.

CHAPTER 6

THE CREATION, RISE, AND DECLINE OF MEXICA POWER

ENRIQUE FLORESCANO

In the Valley of Mexico, the Aztecs, or Mexicas as they called themselves, founded the most well-known precolumbian city and state in the Americas. As discussed in this chapter, this origin myth is an original narrative, recounting a trajectory punctuated by spectacular events, as seen through the idealized lens of nostalgia. Not by chance, the historical context of this story is rooted in Mesoamerica's oldest cosmological, political, ethnic, and ideological traditions.

I examine this narrative using the three types of sources available to us today: indigenous cartographic accounts, hieroglyphic texts translated by experts both past and present, and interpretations offered by chroniclers and historians. These sources recount how the Mexicas arrived from northwestern Mesoamerica accompanied by other clans, with whom they shared ethnic and cultural ties and whose migration was also led by a god or priest. The story dates back to A.D. 900, a period that witnessed the collapse of the great kingdoms of the Maya area, followed by those of Tajin and Xochicalco. In A.D. 1000, Tula and Chichen Itza emerged as two major political capitals; both exerted their considerable influence throughout Mesoamerica, particularly the former, the Toltec capital. While both began to experience a decline around A.D. 1200, Cholula held strong as a large commercial and religious center. This period was characterized by successive waves of migration from the north, including that of the Mexicas. Between A.D. 900 and 1200, Mesoamerica experienced profound political and social upheaval that spawned new forms of settlement, exchange, wars, alliances, and social organization in the Central and Southern Highlands, as well as other parts of Mesoamerica.

What was unique about these organizations? First and foremost, the political organization was unprecedented; instead of being based on the power of the ancient hereditary nobility, [Middle and Late] Postclassic (A.D. 1100–1521) seigniories and states were ruled by military leaders and conquerors who established their polities through conquest and by forging alliances with the heads of ancient lineages. For the northern clans—Matlatzincas, Xochimilcas, Chalcas, Tepanecas, Acolhuas, Chichimecas, Huejotzincas, and Malinalcas as well as the Aztecs and other ethnic groups—the migration process involved forming marriage alliances with the existing noble families in central Mesoamerica, leaving behind their lives as nomadic hunters to become sedentary agriculturalists and founding *seigniories* (lords) and states based on prestigious Toltec values. Polities were created from military prestige and conquest, which gradually eroded the foundations of the traditional institutions of the ancient nobility and the autonomy of the peasants organized in *calpolli s*. Some of these migrants claimed to have come from the legendary cave of origin, Chicomoztoc (seven caves), while the Mexicas asserted that they came from Aztlan.

The Arduous Mexica Migration

A characteristic of the northern migrant groups is that they all chronicled their journey, emphasizing their ethnicity and their settlement of the predestined final stop of their migration. The Mexicas followed this pattern as well, yet they also claimed to be the last to arrive in the fertile lands of the Valley of Mexico which, surrounded by a more than 2,000 km^2 lake system, represented an extraordinarily rich natural environment. In contrast to the Mixtecs and other earlier groups who proudly claimed to originate from the very land they governed, Postclassic tales are stories of migration. "Migration," according to Elizabeth Boone (2010:184–185), "is a crucial feature of all Nahua accounts of the past, and there were multiple migrations, not just one. Each village had its own distinctive migration and arrival, and each story underscores the independent nature of these journeys." Federico Navarrete Linares (2011) offers an insightful discussion of the migrations of other ethnic groups.

Painted maps of the Mexica migration, like the *Sigüenza Map*, offer synthetic narratives of the exodus from the island of Aztlan to the founding of Mexico-Tenochtitlan, describing the principal sites visited along the way (Aztlan, Coatepec, and Chapultepec) as well as the founding of Tenochtitlan. The textual sources elaborate on the different stops on the migration and recount the episodes that highlighted the predestined and monumental nature of the migration that would culminate in the founding of a powerful state. These sources chronicle how seven *calpolli s* ("corporate kinship groups") left Aztlan guided by four leaders, known as *teomamaque*, or "god carriers," who communicated with their patron god Huitzilopochtli (Figure 6.1). Under these auspices, the Aztecs left the island and went to Colhuacan by canoe, where texts and maps portray Huitzilopochtli, carried on the backs of the *teomamaque*, showing them the way. Their political leaders and priests, representing different *calpolli s*, occasionally met as a council and participated in decision-making during the trip.

Several important events occurred during the journey from Colhuacan to Chicomoztoc, the place of the seven caves where the Chichimecas were said to originate. The Aztecs, named after Aztlan, broke their ties with the other groups or clans that

FIGURE 6.1 The Mexicas emerge from Aztlan, represented by six houses next to a pyramid. To the right, an individual in a canoe symbolizes the exit from Aztlan, while the glyph *1 Tecpatl* represents the year. To the far right is an altar to Huitzilopochtli inside of a bent mountain. From *Tira de la peregrinación* (*Codex Boturini*). Photograph from Kinsborough, II, Figure 1. Public domain.

accompanied them and decided to continue their journey as an independent political and ethnic group. In Chicomoztoc, they performed the first human sacrifice and were given the bow, arrow, and shield characteristic of the Chichimec conquerors and a new name. According to the *Codex Aubin* (Lehmann et al. 1981) and other sources:

> And then, [Huitzilopochtli] changed their name from the Aztecs:
> He said to them:
> "From this point on, you are no longer the Aztecs, you are the Mexica."
> Thus, he persuaded them, and they took the name Mexica.

During the process that forged the individuality of the Mexicas, the group again fragmented when they reached Lake Patzcuaro, where, according to Fray Diego Durán (1995:30), some migrants decided to settle on the lakeshore. In response, Huitzilopochtli ordered his followers to abandon them there under false pretenses, which they did immediately. Shortly thereafter, Huitzilopochtli ordered them to abandon his sister, Malinalxochitl, who was said to practice witchcraft and be a threat to the god's followers.

Continuing on their arduous path, the Mexicas arrived at Coatepec (Serpent Hill), where yet another notable event occurred. Huitzilopochtli instructed them to build a dam to create an artificial lake, a replica of the lagoon that was destined to be their final stop. Corn, pumpkins, beans, and a variety of useful plants immediately began to grow along the lakeshore, which also provided plentiful lacustrine fauna. However, when Coyolxauhqui and her group of followers requested that the journey end there and that they settle in that miraculous place, Huitzilopochtli denied their request and suddenly appeared armed from head to toe, transformed into an unrelenting warrior who, with incredible force, destroyed the *centzonhuitznahuaque* and killed Coyolxauhqui, slitting her throat, eating her heart, and hurling her body down the stairs of the temple in Coatepec. Based on one interpretation of this mythical episode, at this point Huitzilopochtli ceased to be an effigy carried by the *teomamaque*. He became, instead, an anthropomorphic god, fierce and implacable against all who interfered with his chosen people's journey to their promised land.

After this episode, indelibly embedded in Mexica memory, they arrived in the valley, circumscribed by high mountains, which would later bear their name (Figure 6.2). At this point, substantive changes are noted in the narrative.

This stage is described in the most detail, occupying more than twice the space dedicated to the previous stories. It also marks a shift from recounting miracles and supernatural acts to focusing on the ethnic, social, political, cultural, and religious ties between the Mexicas and the valley's historical inhabitants. It is also the period in which the migrating group experienced the most qualitative changes. The Mexicas visited various places (Zumpango, Xaltocan, Ecatepec, Cohuatitlan, Tecpayocan, Popotlan, on the northern and western shores of Lake Texcoco), engaged in a number of wars, were expelled, suffered illnesses, and faced other difficulties, including becoming subordinate to the Tepanecs, whose capital was Atzcapotzalco and whom the Mexicas served as mercenaries. As a result, the Mexicas dispersed to different regions of the lake. Mexica sources agree that Chapultepec (Grasshopper) Hill was the most important stop on their journey. There, according to various sources, the Mexicas tried to crown Huitzilihuitl as their first *tlahtoani*. However, this attempt ended in disaster. Other chronicles identify this as the place where the Mexicas sacrificed and killed Copil, son of Malinalxochitl (Huitzilopochtli's sister), who, to avenge his mother, roused other towns along the lakeshore against the invading Mexicas.

In addition to the death of many Mexicas, this defeat also resulted in their expulsion from Chapultepec, followed by their dispersion to different regions of the valley; the capture, humiliation, and sacrifice of Huitzilihuitl and his family; the confinement of the group to hostile regions, like Atizapan; and their humiliating transformation into Colhua vassals. The people of Huitzilopochtli were nearly annihilated. The *Tira de la peregrinación*, or *Códice Boturini* (1944), reports that those who survived served and paid taxes to Colhuacan.

For decades the people of Huitzilopochtli were destined to be slaves, tax payers, and armed mercenaries ready for war under the tutelage of Colhuacan and Tepanec power. For many years, the Mexicas were oppressed people, but at the same time they inserted themselves into the center of a volatile political and social setting that then drove the great transformation of the Valley of Mexico. Colhuacan, the *altepetl*[1]

FIGURE 6.2 The Basin of Mexico ca. A.D. 1400. After Gibson. 1964. Redrawn by author and Kristin Sullivan.

that embraced them as tax payers and mercenaries, was the largest cultural center in the region. This was the capital that, in the ninth and tenth centuries, combined Teotihuacan's legacy with the birthplace of Ce Acatl Topiltzin Quetzalcoatl, the legendary Toltec *tlahtoani* who united the northern peoples (Chichimecas and Otomis) and founded Tula, the kingdom that for more than a century imposed its rule in central and southern Mesoamerica.

Their journey, stay in Colhuacan, and relationship with Atzcapotzalco, the largest military force in the region, radically changed the Mexicas and they became skilled in the art of war and eager learners of the myriad forms of building alliances and the art of political intrigue. Despite being produced long after the events they narrate, the codices and chronicles that recount their migratory journey take into account the profound social, political, and cultural transformations the migrants experienced.

In Colhuacan, the Mexicas learned about political and religious institutions, libraries and schools, rituals, ceremonies, and arts, all infused with ancient Toltec wisdom. Their arrival at the lakes region tied them to the most concentrated, competitive, and volatile political scenes of the time, an experience they voraciously absorbed. According to historian Rudolf van Zantwijk (1985:97–107, Chap. 9), this tradition begat Mexica political institutions (the *altepetl, tlahtoani,* and the hierarchical division into nobles and commoners), thus fortifying the idea that the legitimacy of their rulers resided in their direct sanguine link to the lineage of Topiltzin Quetzalcoatl.

After their expulsion from Chapultepec, the Mexicas took refuge in Tizapan, under Colhua protection, and, while there, further assimilated aspects of Toltec culture. Following the ancient Mesoamerican pattern, their first strategy was to marry women of Toltec descent and ensure political and military alliances with their protectors. One of their initial requests to the king of Colhuacan was that they "be given entry and employment in their city, and consent to form marital bonds." Thus the "Mexicas first gained entry to *Colhuacan*, socializing, freely entering into contracts with each other, and marrying into Colhua families, thus becoming their siblings and relatives" (Alvarado Tezozómoc 1987:28; Tena 2004:69).

Subordinate to Colhuacan, the Mexicas accompanied the kingdom's military leaders on campaigns in Xochimilco, Mizquic, and Cuitlahuac, ensuring Tepanec dominion in the southern lakes region (*Codex Azcatitlan* 1995:86–90, 104; Hassig 1998:132). In their chronicles, the Mexicas stated that their first *tlahtoani*, Acamapichtli (1375–1395), was of noble Colhuacan descent and that his ancestors had married into the families of Toltec rulers. Under Acamapichtli's command, the Mexicas adopted a centralized government, with the tlahtoani as the apex, developed a regime notable for its military leadership, and overcame rivalries between calpolli leaders.[2] Later, Huitzilihuitl (1395–1417) followed suit, under the command of the lords of Atzcapotzalco, in the region of Texcoco, where he led campaigns to strengthen Tepanec control. Atzcapotzalco was the first political organization of the Valley of Mexico to lay the foundations for a strong and complex state (Carrasco 1996:73–92). Their diverse matrimonial, commercial, political, military, and cultural ties with the Tepanecs and Colhuas formed the basis for Mexica influence in this region.

The Founding of Mexico City-Tenochtitlan

Mexica accounts of their rise to power depict the founding of Mexico-Tenochtitlan as the ultimate, glorious achievement of a valiant people. These accounts, however, are an idealization, crafted years later, when they became the supreme power in the Valley of Mexico. In fact, in 1325 or 1345, when the city was founded, Tenochtitlan was a small town, devoid of glory or fame. The earliest tlatoque (sing. *tlahtoani*, he who speaks)—Acamapichtli (1375–1395), Huitzilihuitl (1396–1417), and Chimalpopoca (1417–1426) (Figure 6.3)—were all subject to the lords of Atzcapotzalco, to whom the Mexicas paid tribute.

Only when the Mexicas defeated the Tepanecs in 1428 did the founding of Tenochtitlan come to symbolize the successful completion of the chosen people's long march, their chosen land, and their predestined future greatness (Alvarado Tezozómoc 1949; Florescano 2009:407–409).

FIGURE 6.3 The *tlatoque* (rulers) of Mexico-Tenochtitlan. On the right: Acamapichtli, Huitzilihuitl, Chimalpopoca, Itzcoatl, Axayacatl, and Motecuhzoma Ilhuicamina. On the left: Tizoc, Ahuitzotl, Moteuczoma II, and Cuauhtemoc. From Sahagún, *Primeros Memoriales*, Fol. 51. Courtesy of the University of Oklahoma Press.

Historians acknowledge that the instigator of that great historical change was Itzcoatl (Obsidian Serpent, 1427–1460), the fourth Mexica *tlahtoani*. Three circumstances prompted this shift. First, in the war waged by Tezozomoc against Texcoco, the alliance between Mexica warriors and the powerful Tepanec *tlahtoani* was instrumental in defeating Ixtlilxochitl's army from Texcoco. This victory provided them with tax payers, land, and a political presence on the eastern and western shores of the lagoon. Second, in 1428, upon the death of Tezozomoc, the designated heir was ordered killed by Maxtla, his younger brother. This usurpation divided the kingdom of Atzcapotzalco and led to its demise. Third, Itzcoatl, already famous for his military conquests and political savvy, took the opportunity to ally himself with Nezahualcoyotl. The latter was the son of the unfortunate Ixtlilxochitl, who had been killed by Tezozomoc, and aspired to the throne of Texcoco. With this ally and Tlacopan and other *altepetl* eager to break free of Tepanec tyranny, Itzcoatl formed the so-called Triple Alliance (*Excan tlahtoloyan*, government of the three tlatoque city-states, a term proposed by Herrera Meza, López Austin, and Martínez Baracs, following Chimalpahin).

This form of political organization was not new, having been mentioned in 856 and later, in 1047, when the Mexicas joined the Colhuacan, Coatlinchan, and Atzcapotzalco tlatoque (Chimalpahin 1998). The political and military alliances among the tlatoque of Tenochtitlan, Texcoco, and Tlacopan created a force to be reckoned with. Based on the study by Pedro Carrasco (1996), the three ancient *altepetl* that formed this partnership retained their own form of government as well as their territorial autonomy. However, they joined forces to form an imperial entity, endowed with such military, political, and economic prowess that they forever changed the sociopolitical organization of the valley and much of Mesoamerica (Figure 6.4).

Motecuhzoma Ilhuicamina (1440–1469) successfully consolidated power into a single state, strengthening partnerships and initiating the great territorial expansion and campaigns to amass tax payers and subject states in different regions. The relationship between the three partner polities, although solid, was not without disagreements and conflicts.

These changes also paved the way for new relationships with the *calpolli s* (corporate neighborhoods of people united through kinship and land ownership and with their own authorities). The common people, villagers or *macehualtin* (sing. *macehualli*), paid tribute to the nobility, the privileged group, and were required to work on public projects, fight in wars, and participate in public ceremonies. This was the main principal underlying Mesoamerican and Nahua social organization. Nobles or leaders, known as *pipillin* (sing. *pilli*), occupied the top positions in the government, priesthood, and military.

Alvarado Tezozómoc (1949) identifies the 15 sectors or *calpolli s* that divided the city. In turn, these were grouped into four districts: Moyotlan, Teopan, Atzacualco, and Cuepopan. According to the *Crónica mexicáyotl* (Alvarado Tezozómoc 1949:74), each of these districts formed an autonomous political unit, "capable" of building "at will" and organizing *calpolli s* under their own authority.

The creation and development of the Triple Alliance, or *Gobierno de los Tres Tlatoques*, involved a new way of distributing governmental functions, military obligations, and the resources amassed as the tribute paid by conquered peoples (Figure 6.4). The ultimate

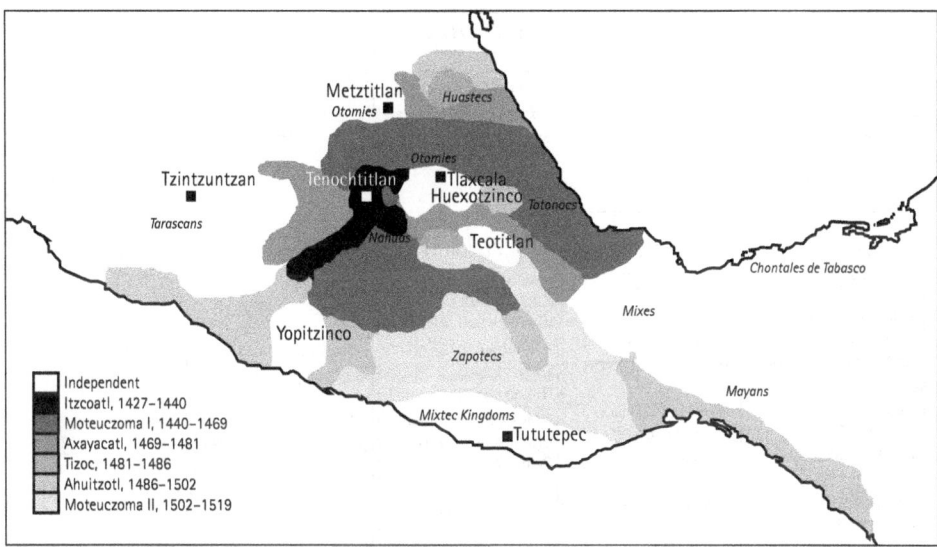

FIGURE 6.4 Extent of the Mexica empire ca. A.D. 1500, showing the areas conquered by each *tlahtoani*. Redrawn by Kristin Sullivan from public domain.

political leader and focal point of major decisions was the *huey tlahtoani* of Tenochtitlan. The military contingents of the three tlatoque organized a campaign, with tasks assigned to each contingent, each led by their own captain, based on their particular strengths. The elite corps (jaguars, eagles, coyotes, and Otomis) were charged with undertaking the most important military campaigns. At the end of the battle, prisoners were rationed among the three tlatoques, although most were taken to Tenochtitlan to be sacrificed in terrifying ceremonies performed in the city's temples (Escalante 2010:159–160).

The political reforms introduced by Itzcoatl and the influential Cihuacoatl Tlacaelel repressed the participation of the *calpolli* and district leaders in favor of forming a Supreme Council. Later, with Tlacaelel's encouragement, Moteuczoma Ilhuicamina reorganized the structure of the state, as described in Alvarado Tezozómoc (1949:64–65):

> [Tlacaelel] created nearly as many committees as exist in Spain. He established different town councils which were audiences composed of court judges and deputies; he also designated other subordinates as magistrates, mayors, lieutenants, sheriffs, and assistants, with an admirable order under which, ultimately, they were each subordinate to another in such a way as to not impede or interfere with their myriad tasks. The Council of the four princes who accompanied the king [the so-called Supreme Council] was the highest authority.
>
> The very king was selected based on Tlacaelel's advice and maneuvering. Tlacaelel maintained the harmony of both the palace and the court, selecting countless officers to serve as stewards, governors, porters, butlers, pages, and footmen as well as the tribute collectors, treasurers, and tax officers [in charge of collecting taxes] throughout the empire.

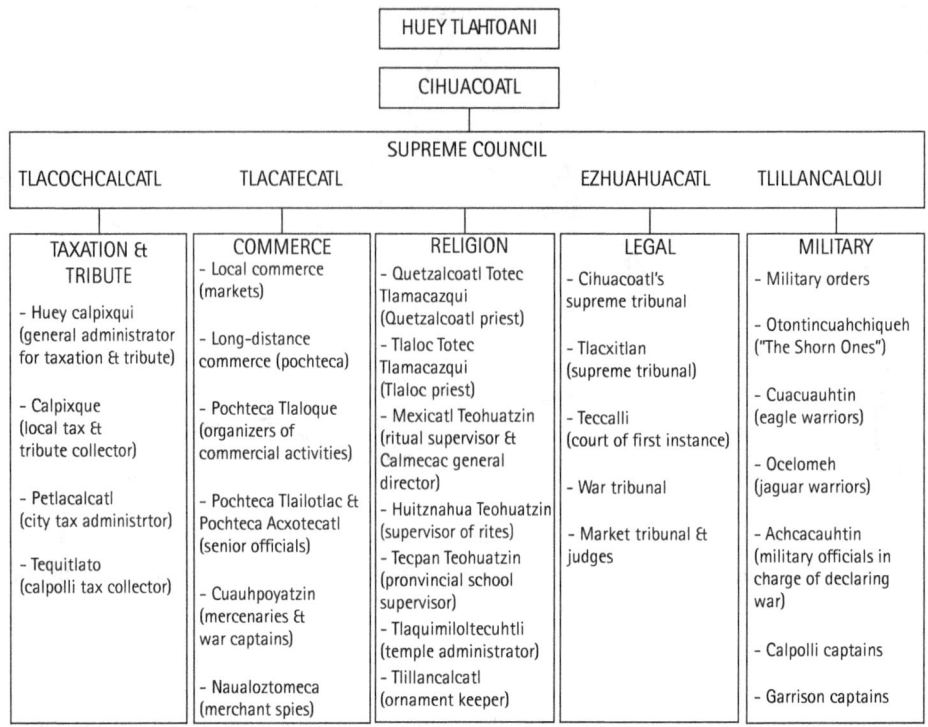

FIGURE 6.5 Mexica political organization ca. A.D. 1500. Prepared by author and edited by Kristin Sullivan.

He established the same order and selected as many ministers to fill the ecclesiastic hierarchy as well. There were as many high ministers as there were minor ones [...] one out of every five people dedicated their time to the law and worship of the gods [Figure 6.5]

Power, the City, and the Toltec Legacy

Mexica power was based on their extraordinary talent for war, their leaders' cunning, and their voracious ability to seamlessly meld their conquest ideology with the civilized characteristics of their Toltec ancestors. They incorporated into the worship of Huitzilopochtli-Tonatiuh the sacrifice-based religion of Teotihuacan, where, according to myth, the creation of the Fifth Sun took place. The ancient myth of the creation of the cosmos and the complex worldview of the Classic period also contributed to the mythology, calendar, divinatory almanacs, seasonal renewal rites, theogony, and cosmogony of the Mexicas.

With the same sensitivity they displayed in recognizing their Chichimec ancestry, they threw themselves into the task of making Toltec culture an inseparable aspect of being Tenochca. Following in the footsteps of their illustrious ancestors, the Mexicas built another Tollan and in the center erected a great temple, the architecture and symbolism of which was a compendium of their immemorial worldview and an expression of Tenochca power. Like its predecessors, the Templo Mayor mimicked the primordial mountain and represented the forces germinating from the water and seeds of mother earth. It was the abode of Tlaltecuhtli and Coatlicue, deities of the earth and fertility, and of Tlaloc and Chalchiuhtlicue, the gods of lightning and thunder who watered the fields. The shrine of Tlaloc, in the northern portion of the Templo Mayor, emphasizes the telluric qualities of that worldview, although the entire building was adorned with offerings and symbols reflecting the generative forces of the earth and water. The Templo Mayor, the sacred mountain, was the land itself, the source of fertility and the incessant cycle of life and death, the place of human origin, the house of the patron god, and the source of power, authority, and order (López Austin and López Luján 2009).

The military had made Tenochtitlan the political capital of the empire and, with the Templo Mayor, had managed to transform it into a great religious center and symbol of Mexica power. The city center was accentuated by more than 78 buildings; each distinct edifice zealously guarded sculptures, paintings, and precious objects. Moctezuma Ilhuihcamina, Axayacatl (1469–1481), Tizoc (1481–1486), and Moteuczoma II each strove to embellish the city periodically. The city itself, as the political capital and center of the world, was a system of plazas, roads, markets, palaces, gardens, temples, and monuments created with high-quality raw materials, designed by renowned architects, and adorned with beautiful and harmonious symbols (Figure 6.6). It was a cosmopolitan metropolis, populated by people of distinct ethnicities and professions from diverse regions.

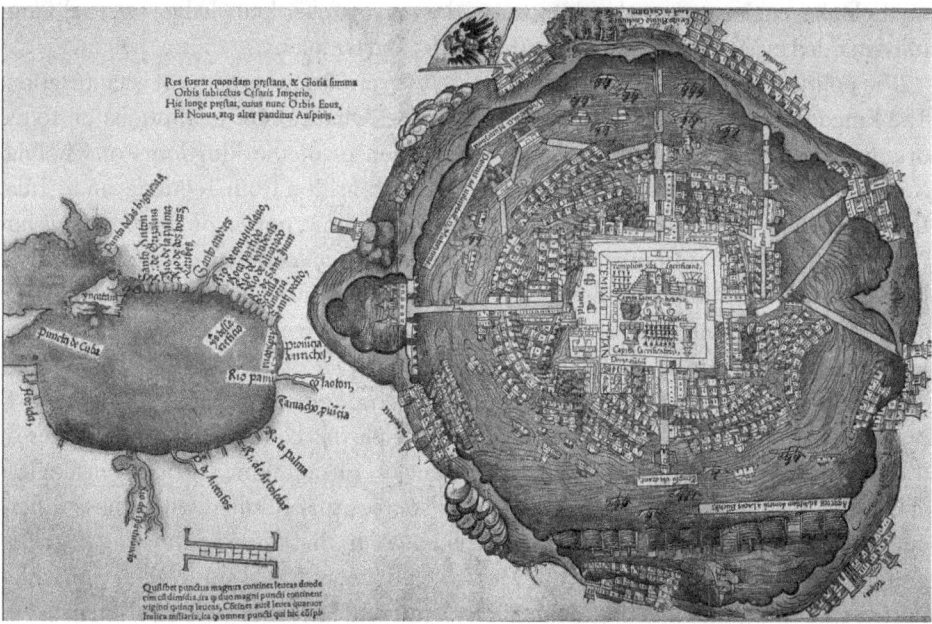

FIGURE 6.6   1524 Map of Tenochtitlan. Courtesy of the Newberry Library.

The city was located in the navel of the earth, on the island of Tenochtitlan, linked to the four cardinal points and vertically integrated into three distinct levels. The Templo Mayor summarized these qualities as a mass rising from the underworld, anchored to the ground yet rising to reach the sky, projected into the four corners of the cosmos (Figure 6.6). Its construction was paid for using the taxes collected from the empire's subjects. Offerings, representing the various seas, the diversity of plants from contrasting ecological niches, the equally rich variety of wildlife, goods obtained from remote provinces, combined with the treasures of the ancient Olmec and Toltec cultures, the many gods of the conquered peoples, and the works of art of different ethnicities accumulated inside and around the Templo Mayor. It was an *imago mundi* (a mirror of the cosmos), and the Huey *tlahtoani* was the universal sovereign.

This cosmic conception of the kingdom, the capital, and its ruler was not invented by the Mexicas. Rather it was developed by earlier kingdoms in Olmec and Mayan territories (800–350 B.C.) and transformed and enriched over time, in particular during the height of Tollan-Teotihuacan (A.D. 100–550). Teotihuacan was the first state, under the regime of *tlahtoani* as supreme ruler, to build an economy, an army, and religious institutions that operated as state agencies (i.e., were governed by their own principles and ordinances but were under the authority of the supreme ruler).

From the moment they elected their first *tlahtoani*, the Mexicas accelerated their assimilation of Toltec institutions and cultural heritage. Chronicles and archaeological evidence indicate that, between 1470 and 1500, the Toltec cultural heritage was firmly entrenched in Tenochtitlan and formed the core of Mexica identity. The calendar, astronomical and scientific knowledge, laws and political institutions, the anthology of literature, the extensive catalog of the arts, the accumulation of historical traditions, the galaxy of their gods and mythologies, engineering and architecture—the sum of Toltec knowledge—were all carefully guarded in Mexica schools, libraries, palaces, and temples.

The political organization of the state drove the continuous process of acculturation. The kingdom and the Mexica Empire (the Triple Alliance) are institutions of Toltec origin, enriched and transformed by the experiences of the kingdoms of Cholula, Xochicalco, Tula, Colhuacan, and Texcoco. In the transition from Teotihuacan to Tula, the Toltec state witnessed a reduction in the hegemonic power of the *tlahtoani* but retained the ancient administrative organization: tax collection and management of markets and domestic and foreign trade; recruitment, training, and organization of the army; the rectory of temples and religious cults; and the messages elaborated by these institutions (see Figure 6.5).

In her *Relatos en rojo y negro*, Elizabeth Boone (2010) presents an analysis of the various written and painted sources that recount the past as conceived by the peoples of Mesoamerica. She examines the annals, chronicles, cartographic stories, genealogical and dynastic histories, and numerous hybrid sources that resulted when these different narrative forms were combined. There is no doubt that these contrasting historiographic styles were evaluated by the Mexica tlatoque and tailored to their particular purposes. During the time of growth and splendor, the libraries of Tenochtitlan accumulated the extensive panoply of the history books then in use as well as the knowledge to interpret and reproduce them. However, among all these memorable legacies, the Mexicas adopted the political and ideological tradition of Tollan-Teotihuacan in order to build their ideal state and civilized life and thus prolonged and gave new life to the prestigious Toltec heritage. Fortified by that legacy, the Mexica people created a new state, an impressive example of Mesoamerican sociopolitical and economic organization. Their talents and creations were well summarized in the final words with which Jacques Soustelle (1956:243) closes his book on the ancient Mexicas:

> From time to time, in the infinity of time and in the midst of the enormous indifference of the world, some human groups give rise to something that exceeds a society: they create a civilization. They are the creators of cultures. And the Indians of Anahuac, at the foot of volcanoes, on the banks of the lagoons, may be counted among them.

The most poignant paradox of the building of this great empire is that the despotic force relentlessly imposed by the leaders of the Triple Alliance on their seigniories and conquered regions became the most powerful reagent compelling these people to join forces with the Spanish armies, converting the formidable "Indian conquerors" into their victims, and ultimately leading to the fall of Mexico-Tenochtitlan.

1. The basic political-territorial unit in central Mexico —the *altepetl* (town or city) — comprised, on the one hand, one or more compact civic and ceremonial centers, with temples and palaces to house the ruling class and, on the other hand, a number of rural settlements where tax-paying farmers resided. The *altepetl* was a political unit governed by a tlahtoani; as such it was a tlatocayotl, a government of the tlahtoani, a kingdom (Carrasco 1996:565).

2. According to Hassig (1998:125), "the Aztecs adopted the tlahtoani system because it was militarily superior to their own decentralized system, and they chose a foreign ruler to provide legitimacy and overcome the competing interests of the various calpolli leaders, which prohibited the elevation of an internal candidate."

References Cited

Alvarado Tezozómoc, Hernando
1949 *Crónica mexicáyotl*. Translated by Adrián León. Imprenta Universitaria, Mexico City.
1987 *Crónica mexicana. Códice Ramírez*. Porrúa, Mexico City.
Boone, Elizabeth Hill
1994 Aztec Pictorial Histories: Records Without Words. In *Writing Without Words: Alternative Literacies in Mesoamerica and the Andes*, edited by Elizabeth Hill Boone and Walter Mignolo, pp. 50–76. Duke University Press, Durham, NC.
2010 *Relatos en rojo y negro: historias pictóricas de aztecas y mixtecos*. Fondo de Cultura Económica, Mexico City. [1st edition in English, 2000].
Carrasco, Pedro
1996 *Estructura político-territorial del Imperio Tenochca*. Fondo de Cultura Económica, Mexico City.

Chimalpahin, Domingo
1998 *Las ocho relaciones y el memorial de Colhuacan*, 2 vols. Translation by Rafael Tena. Conaculta, Mexico City.

Codex Azcatitlan
1995 *Codex Azcatitlan*. Bibliotheque nationale de France, Paris.

Códice Boturini
1944 *Tira de la Peregrinación*. Librería Anticuaria, Mexico.

Durán, Fray Diego
1995 *Historia de las Indias de Nueva España e Islas de Tierra Firme*, 2 vols. Introductory study by Rosa Camelo and José Rubén Romero. Conaculta, Mexico City.

Escalante Gonzalbo, Pablo
2010 El posclásico en Mesoamérica. In *Nueva historia general de México*, pp. 119–168. El Colegio de México, Mexico City.

Florescano, Enrique
2009 *Los orígenes del poder en Mesoamérica*. Fondo de Cultura Económica, Mexico City.

Hassig, Ross
1998 *Aztec Warfare: Imperial Expansion and Political Control*. University of Oklahoma Press, Norman.

Lehmann, Walter, and Gerdt Kutscher (editors)
1981 *Geschichte der Azteken: Codex Aubin und verwandte Dokumente*. Gebr. Mann, Berlin.

López Austin, Alfredo, and Leonardo López Luján
2009 *Monte Sagrado-Templo Mayor*. National Autonomous University of Mexico, Mexico City.

Navarrete Linares, Federico
2011 *Los orígenes de los pueblos indígenas del valle de México: los altépetl y sus historias*. National Autonomous University of Mexico, Mexico City.

Soustelle, Jacques
1956 *La vida cotidiana de los aztecas*. Fondo de Cultura Económica, Mexico City.

Tena, Rafael (translator)
2004 *Anales de Tlatelolco*. Conaculta, Mexico City.

Zantwijk, Rudolph van
1985 *The Aztec Arrangement: The Social History of Pre-Spanish Mexico*. University of Oklahoma Press, Norman.

CHAPTER 7

THE MEASURE, MEANING, AND TRANSFORMATION OF AZTEC TIME AND CALENDARS

ANTHONY F. AVENI

The Aztec calendar, largely kept by priests of the noble class, though understood on a practical basis by commoners, shared a number of characteristics with timekeeping systems spread across Mesoamerica, among them the adoption of commensurate cycles built around 13 × 20 = 260 (*tonalpohualli*) and 18 × 20 + 5 = 365 (*xihuitl*) day counts. These meshed together to form a larger cycle of 18,980 (= 73 × 260 = 52 × 365) days (called the Calendar Round in popular parlance) at the overturn of which a New Fire ceremony of the cyclic renewal of time was celebrated. The mechanics of the calendar are explored in the first part of this chapter. The second part deals with the Aztec ideology of time, which rests principally on solar worship and is directed toward the ritual celebration of seasonal festivals connected with subsistence as well. During the post-1428 expansionist period, calendrics were further directed toward the legitimization and pursuit of war. The last part of the chapter charts the syncretic effect of the manipulation and reorganization of time affected by the Hispanic intrusion.

MECHANICS OF THE CALENDAR

All Mesoamerican calendars share in the principle of commensuration, a process whereby resonances are sought among small temporal cycles, which are then built up to form larger ones. The component cycles are derived in large part from natural rhythms. The most fundamental cycle is the *tonalpohualli*, or "count of days" in Nahuatl, which is made up of "months" of 20 named days, called *veintena* by the Spaniards, which surely derived from the number of fingers and toes on the human body, and 13 coefficients (*trecena*), the number of layers of heaven. The same cycle of 13 and 20 recurs every 260 days. Recognized as early as A.D. 30 in the southern Maya lowlands, this cycle and its components were found to resonate with a host of natural rhythms. This likely led to its widespread pan-Mesoamerican adoption and central importance. For example, 260 days is a good approximation of the human gestation period and the average interval of the appearance of the planet Venus as evening or morning star. It also resonates with the most fundamental cycle of the recurrence of eclipses in the ratio of two to three (cf. Aveni [2001] for a detailed discussion). Moreover, the division of the *tonalpohualli* into four and five parts without a remainder is in accord, respectively, with the Mesoamerican cosmological notion of a four-sided universe consisting of five regions (including the center). The 20 days are rendered pictorially, while coefficients are represented by dots. (In Aztec arithmetical notation there are no bars such as one finds in the Maya corpus.) Day names are depicted in Figure 7.1; see Caso (1971:334–336) for a list of deities associated with the numbers. In the codices, *tonalpohualli* dates consist largely of prognostications about good or bad luck and ritual prescriptions applied thereto, while on the carved monuments they are connected mostly with dynastic matters.

The *xihuitl* consists of 18 months, or *meztli*, which is the same as the Nahuatl word for "moon," each consisting of 20 days, to which five days, the *nemontemi*, so-called worthless or unlucky days, were added at the end of the last month to make a close approximation of the tropical year of 365.2422 days, by modern reckoning. Like appended intervals at the end that approximate the seasonal count in the calendars of other cultures, these days were not counted and they bore no calendrical name. Each of the 18 named months was dedicated to a feast connected to the tulelary deity of that month (see Caso [1971:341]

FIGURE 7.1 The Aztec Day Signs: (a) *Cipactli* (Alligator), (b) *Ehecatl* (Wind), (c) *Calli* (House), (d) *Cuetzpalin* (Lizard), (e) *Coatl* (Snake), (f) *Miquiztli* (Death), (g) *Mazatl* (Deer), (h) *Tochtli* (Rabbit), (i) *Atl* (Water), (j) *Itzcuintli* (Dog), (k) *Ozomatli* (Monkey), (l) *Malinalli* (Grass), (m) *Acatl* (Reed), (n) *Ocelotl* (Jaguar), (o) *Cuauhtli* (Eagle), (p) *Cozcacuauhtli* (Buzzard), (q) *Ollin* (Movement), (r) *Tecpatl* (Flint), (s) *Quiahuitl* (Rain), (t) *Xochitl* (Flower). (Caso 1971:Figure 1).

for a list; cf. also Broda 1971). These feasts were tuned, at least at the time of Hispanic contact, to appropriate times of the seasonal year (e.g., the anticipated arrival of the rainy season, planting, harvesting, and so on) and to the appropriate sacrifice in debt payment to the gods being offered that month. For example, *Atlcahualo*, which falls two months before the start of the rainy season, was the time to sacrifice the most youthful of celebrants, the young children, whose tears are a reminder of the rain that initiates the life cycle of maize. At the end of a Calendar Round cycle, the chronicler Sahagún says that all fires were extinguished, household items discarded, and houses swept clean. On this occasion priests led a procession to Uixachtecatl (Star Hill) from the top of which participants watched the Pleiades star group pass the overhead position, a sign that the world would not be destroyed by the *tzitzimime*, or demons who threatened to descend from heaven to devour people. Then in a cyclic ritual of purification, fire was kindled in the breast of a sacrificial victim and dispersed to the citizens to take back to their houses.

We know that the *tonalpohualli* was not fixed in the seasonal year, though the order of the months in various accounts was the same; however, there has been considerable debate on the issue of when the Aztec year began in real time, whether they intercalated time to keep the *xihuitl* in tune with the tropical year, what the first day of the year was, and how the Aztec and Christian calendars were correlated. Each of these are dealt with in turn.

The problem of which month began the year is complicated by the likelihood that not all people in the area around Tenochtítlan, from which chroniclers extracted information at different times, necessarily kept the same calendar. For example, the months of Atlcahualo, the choice of the early chroniclers, as well as Tlacaxipeualiztli, and Izcalli, have variously been so designated (cf. Caso 1971:343–344); Prem (2008:207) gives a table of candidate sources.

The first day of a given year is termed its Year Bearer. Because division by 20 into 365 yields a remainder of 5, only 4 of the 20 day names, five days apart in the sequence shown in in Figure 7.1, would qualify. Moreover, because 365 divided by 13 yields a remainder of 1, the 13-base number sequence in successive Year Bearer advances by 1; thus a sample sequence of first days of successive New Years might be named 1 Tochtli (Rabbit), 2 Acatl (Reed), 3 Tecpatl (Flint), 4 Calli (House), and 5 Tochtli.

How Year Bearers match years in the Christian calendar relates to the correlation question. Reliable Aztec sources tell us that the Hispanic siege of Tenochtítlan ended with the surrender of Cuauhtemoc to Cortez on day 1 Coatl (Snake) in the *tonalpohualli*, (e) in Figure 7.1, and the second day of the month of Xocotlhuetzi in the *xihuitl* and that it happened in a 3 House year. Straightforward computation equates this indigenous Calendar Round date with 13 August (Julian) 1521 (A reliable online conversion calculator can be found at www.azteccalendar.com.) This correlation was first proposed by Caso, who published it in 1939 and after whom it was so named. One implication of the Caso correlation, which remains the most widely accepted version to date, at least for Tenochtítlan, is that the Aztec years were named not by the first day of the first month on which they began but rather by the last day of the last month of that year. Such nomenclature is consistent with the emphasis placed on temporal completion throughout

Mesoamerica. Caso's correlation is also in agreement with other events recounted by the chroniclers during the period 1519–1521, when the Spaniards invaded the capital. The most recently updated list of events, along with an assessment of their reliability, is given by Prem (2008:234, Table 91). See also Milbrath (2013:5–10) for a discussion of the positioning of the Year Bearer and possible conflicting data.

The intercalation or "leap year" problem poses the question: How did the Aztecs reckon the position of the seasonal year in relation to the *xihuitl*? While it was the case that seasonally celebrated festivals in the months of the *xihuitl* fit natural and agrarian events at the time of the conquest, they would be expected to fall out of line with the occurrence of those events. The slippage between *xihuitl* and seasonal years would amount to approximately one day every four years ($4 \times 365.2422 - 0.9688 = 4 \times 365$ days), 13 days after 52 years, and a full Aztec month after 83; the two forms of reckoning the year would recycle over 1508 *xihuitl*. Extrapolating the slippage backward, the foundation date of Tenochtítlan, 2 House 1325, turns out, using the Caso correlation, to fall on 14 March, two days after the vernal equinox, a time that is accorded particular attention in the Aztec foundation myth (cf. Aveni et al. 1988). There is little evidence that the Aztecs employed a leap-year correction, that is, the regular insertion of a fixed period of time to take up the slack. This disagrees with what some chroniclers, who were deeply immersed in their own European ways of reckoning time, have to say. (It is worth noting that the much-debated Gregorian leap-year reform of the calendar in Europe took place in 1582.) The Maya, about whose calendrical operations we know a good deal more, tracked where days of the *xihuitl* fell in the seasonal year by reference to fixed points in the 260-day count. Tena (1987) is among a minority of scholars who favor a leap-year hypothesis, but see Prem (2008:89–97) for a critique (cf. also Milbrath 2013:114, no. 17).

Time, History, and Ideology

Two defining characteristics of the cosmic component of the Aztec ideology of time deal with the way the universe was partitioned and the strong emphasis placed on the sun and solar worship. Aztec cosmology, like that of most cultures of ancient Mesoamerica, was based on a quadripartite taxonomy, with various attributes of the real world each assigned their proper place in a counterclockwise-ordered space-time. Thus the eastern *side* of space (there were no cardinal *points*, as in the West) was associated with the eagle and the Year Bearer Acatl; its designated color usually was yellow. North corresponded to jaguar, Tecpatl, and red; west went with serpent, Calli, and white; and south was represented by rabbit, Tochtli, and blue.

Time was said to have begun, Sahagún tells us, when the gods sacrificed themselves by diving into a celestial bonfire over the eastern horizon of Teotihuácan. This sacred act first set the sun, in the personage of the god Tonatiuh, in motion. It also set the mandate for blood sacrifice, necessary to keep it on its course, the ultimate debt payment for the present creation. But this was not the first world: there had been four previous cycles of creation, or "suns." In the sun of Jaguar giant people were said to have roamed the world, but their imperfections led the gods to destroy their creation by sending jaguars to eat them. In the second creation, the "sun of wind," hurricanes were sent to purge the world but not before some of its inhabitants were transformed into monkeys. Aptly termed the "sun of fire-rain," the third creation was destroyed by a volcanic eruption, some of its survivors having been changed into turkeys. The fourth sun was that of water; it was done in by a great flood. The present world, the "sun of earthquake" or "movement" after the Year Bearer Ollin (Motion), will ultimately meet its designated fate lest victims participate actively in seeking its continuation via sacrifice. These creations are vividly displayed at the center of which appears the celebrated Aztec sun stone (Figure 7.2), where each creation Year Bearer glyph accompanied by the coefficient four is embedded in a carved 4 Motion glyph at the center appears the effigy of Tonatiuh, with lolling flint-knifed tongue, the instrument of heart extraction.

Along the vertical dimension, the cosmos consisted of the 13 layers of heaven, while 9 levels below comprised the underworld, counting level 1 in each instance as the one in which we live. There was a daily rotation of assigned patron deities, known as the

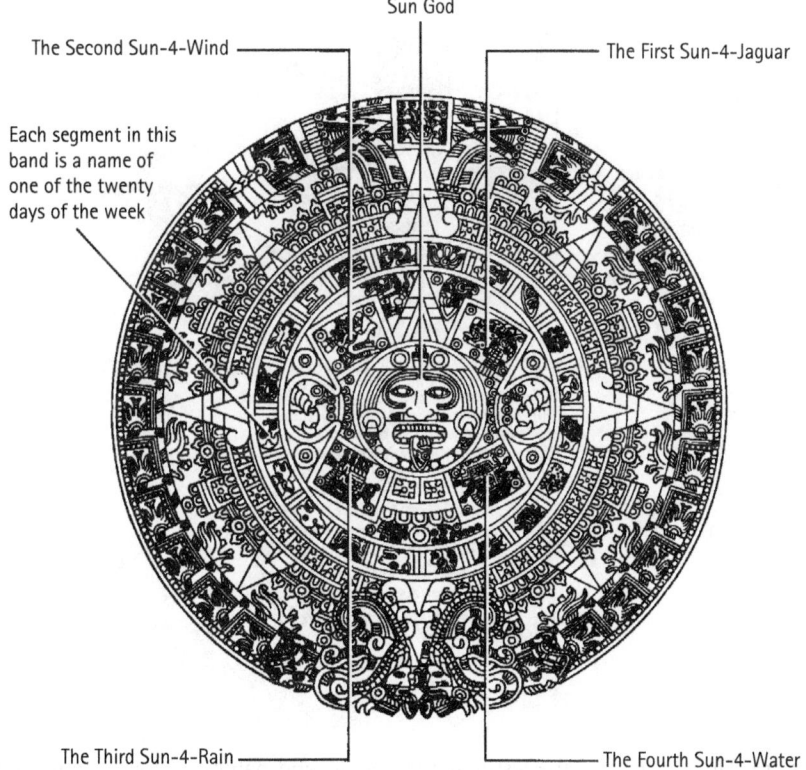

FIGURE 7.2 The center of the celebrated Aztec Sun Stone, which depicts the five creations. (Aveni 1989:Figure 1.)

Day Lords and Lords of the Night, along with their attributes and prognostications from each realm.

Even the most casual examination of the Aztecs' pictorial histories reveals that, quite unlike the modern West but perhaps not so different from the idea of history in the Western prescientific revolution, human and natural events are conflated. In the codices, pictorial scenes designated by Year Bearers depict battles, conquests, famines, and feasts, alongside eclipses, "smoking stars" (meteors or comets), earthquakes, and floods (one example is shown in Figure 7.3).

Aztec chronology also exhibits a tendency to relate early historical events to more recent ones by officially recording them as having occurred in years in the Calendar Round that contain the same name: so-called like-in-kind events (Umberger 1981). There is good evidence that this sort of revisionist history took place once the imperialist expansion was underway with the Aztec victory over Atzcapotzalco in the year 1 Flint 1428. Thus 1 Flint records the beginning of the Aztec migration from Aztlan, the ancient homeland; the birth of Huitzilopochtli, their tutelary god of both the sun and war; their arrival at the site of their future capital city on an island in Lake Texcoco in the Valley of Mexico; and so on. Many like-in-kind events were pegged to celestial phenomena,

FIGURE 7.3 Human history, the testimony of people, and natural history; the testimony of things are conflated in the Aztec interpretation of history. (Quiñones Keber, *Codex Telleriano Remensis*, f.42r.).

especially eclipses, which are recorded with unusual frequency after 1428 (cf. Aveni and Calnek, 1999; Prem 2008:253–256). Hassig (2001, cf. esp. 58–63) gives greater primacy to the forces of political motivation over religious beliefs in the reconstruction of Aztec history. He argues that the Aztecs thought of the large-scale structure of time as linear and that the rulers manipulated it as a means of controlling their widely dispersed tribute state they had recently created. Once the conquest terminated Aztec control, the calendar was broken up, and only the lesser cycles survived.

Like other cosmologically based drawings from central Mexico, such as of the *Codex Fejérváry-Mayer* (1971:1), the early post-Conquest map of Tenochtítlan that appears on f.1r of the *Codex Mendoza* (Berdan and Anawalt 1997) vividly displays the quadripartite fusion of Aztec space-time (Figure 7.4).

Clearly rectangular in form, it displays the eagle-cactus foundation symbol at the center, surrounded by a four-sided stream of blue water, with similar streams radiating outward from the center to the intercardinals. Ancestral rulers are pictured and named within the blue borders; below and outside them important battle/conquest scenes are shown. Also, as in the *Codex Fejérváry-Mayer*, time flows in a (partial) rectangular border along the outer periphery. The 52-year count proceeds counterclockwise from 2 House (1325) at the upper left corner, to 3 Rabbit, and so on, ending at 13 Reed, top center.

FIGURE 7.4 The Aztec map of Tenochtítlan. (Berdan and Anawalt, *Codex Mendoza* p.1r.). Reproduced with permission.

The Templo Mayor and Tenochtítlan's quadripartite layout are among the few archaeologically definable features in Mesoamerica for which there is also ethnohistorical documentation. The orientation of the Templo Mayor may have been associated with the mythic starting point of the calendar as well as with calendar reform. One clue is provided in a quote by Motolinía, taken to imply that the alignment of the building was intended to frame the rising equinox sun between the temples of Tlaloc and Huitzilopochtli located on its summit (see Aveni et al. [1988] for a full discussion of the link between the calendar, astronomical function, the foundation myth, and the layout of the ceremonial center). Ties between the calendar and the peripheral landscape include the highest point on the eastern horizon where Mount Tlaloc, or Tlalocan, is located.

From the standpoint of ideology, one can think of such arrangements as accommodations between symbolic structures in the mythic landscape revealed in stories about the Aztec gods and the actual arrangement and location of their counterparts in the land and skyscape visible to all in the capital. Such an accommodation is not unlike that between the old theocratic mountain-rain-fertility cult of Tlaloc and the more recently established sun-war cult of Huitzilopochtli, manifested by the juxtaposition of the two representative structures at the top of the Templo Mayor.

The Changing Shape of Time After the Conquest

Practically every pictorial representation of the calendar in precolumbian central Mexico and even in the Maya written corpus displays the indigenous quadripartite form (cf. e.g., Boone 2007; Milbrath 2013), but, after the Conquest, the chroniclers, strongly wedded to ways of understanding and expressing the calendar they had been taught, reconfigured what they saw in a circular format. The degree of embeddedness of the Old World convention of the circle as a way of organizing and conveying knowledge at the time of Hispanic contact cannot be overstated. The persistent imagery of wheels that grind out time and the perfectly round shape of the Platonic and Aristotelian universe reminds one both of the gearwork on the inside and the face on the outside of a mechanical clock. The form of the circle was further ingrained in the Renaissance mind in a much wider framework. Circular diagrams known as *rotae* served in many European books of knowledge and entered the Hispanic *reportorios* as a means of lending order to the activities of the seasons, the fixing of the houses, and signs of the zodiac—even the ages of mankind. The arrangement of matter in the cosmos found expression as well in circular shells and orbs in the Copernican heliocentric models of the universe, the sea change from one to the other having taken place shortly after the time of contact.

For the chroniclers, circular diagrams became the preferred form of teaching and learning about the shape of Mesoamerican time. Such forms were both representational and computational; the intruders were concerned largely with the mechanics

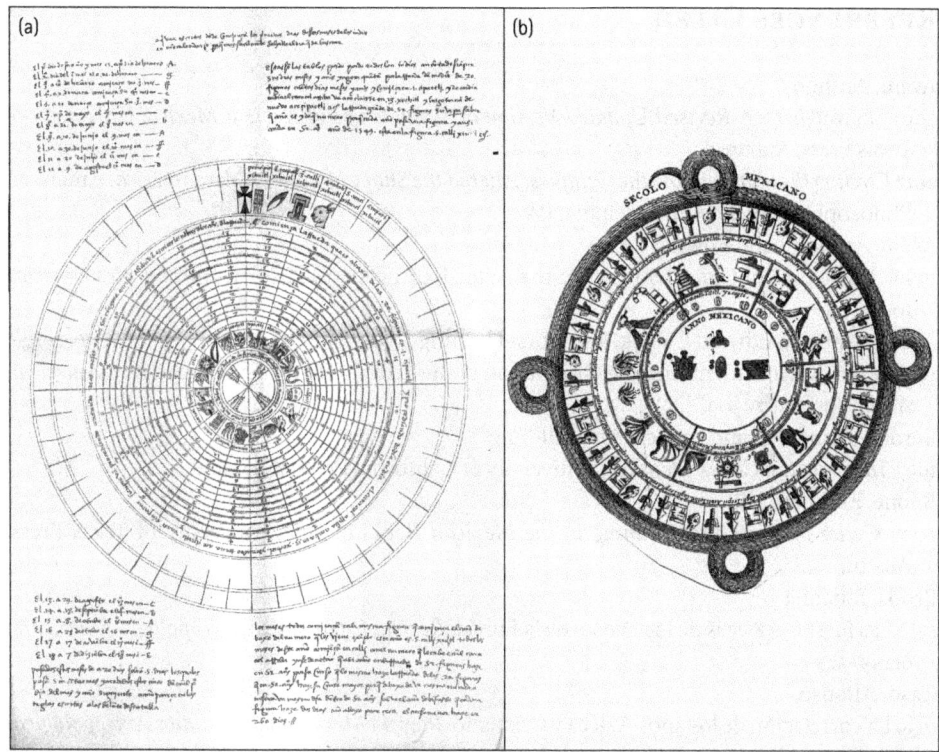

FIGURE 7.5 A contrast of early and late post-Conquest calendar wheels reveals the gradual intrusion of Western into indigenous temporal concepts: (a) the Calendar Wheel of Motolinía (1549) includes, in addition to *tonalpohualli* dates, an accompanying text listing corresponding *xihuitl* dates. (Calendar Wheel of Motolinía 1903; *Memoriales de Toribio de Motolinía*. G. Pimentel (ed.) Mexico); (b) the calendar wheel of *Gemelli* (1697) falsely emphasizes lunar months. (Gemelli-Careri Wheel, 1697; Berthe 1968:144).

and hardly at all with the indigenous meaning of Mesoamerican time. Details of the gradual forced overlay of the European circular paradigm on indigenous temporality are clearly reflected in a number of colonial calendar wheels (Aveni 2012). See Figure 7.5 for a contrasting pair of calendar wheels, one early (1549) and the other late (1697).

These are among some 10 known examples used to express the 365-day festival calendar in the form of a circle depicting 18 months of 20 days plus an additional 5 days, which likened the *xihuitl* to the liturgical seasonal round in which festival dates (such as All Saint's Day) were pinned down more precisely to specific dates of the year. So too was the trecena, or 13 count, forced to resemble the hours on the face of the ubiquitous European clock or the base12 format of the Western zodiac. Other European concepts that intruded on native forms of expressing space and time included the Greek elements, the wind compass, the synodic lunar month, the Olympiad, the Jubilee Year, and, not surprisingly given the concurrent (late sixteenth century) European calendar reform, the concept of leap years.

References Cited

Aveni, Anthony
2001 *Skywatchers: A Revised Updated Version of Skywatchers of Ancient Mexico*. University of Texas Press, Austin.
2012 *Circling the Square: How the Conquest Altered the Shape of Time in Mesoamerica*. American Philosophical Society, Philadelphia, PA.

Aveni, Anthony, and Edward Calne
1999. Astronomical Considerations in the Aztec Expression of History. *Ancient Mesoamerica* 10:87–98.

Aveni, Anthony, Edward Calnek, and Horst Hartung
1988 Myth, Environment, and the Orientation of the Templo Mayor of Tenochtitlan. *American Antiquity* 53:287–309.

Berdan, Frances F., and Patricia Anawalt
1997 *The Essential Codex Mendoza*. University of California Press, Berkeley.

Boone, Elizabeth Hill
2007 *Cycles of Time and Meaning in the Mexican Books of Fate*. University of Texas Press, Austin.

Broda, Johanna
1971 Las Fiestas Aztecas de los Dioses de la Lluvia. *Revista Española de Antropología Americana* 6:245–327.

Caso, Alfonso
1939 La correlación de los años Azteca y Cristiano. *Revista Mexicana de Estudios Antropológicos* 3(1):11–45.
1971 Calendrical Systems of Central Mexico. In *Archaeology of Northern Mesoamerica*, Part 1, edited by Gordon Ekholm and Ignacio Bernal, pp. 333–348. Handbook of Middle American Indians, Vol. 10, Robert Wauchope, general editor. University of Texas Press, Austin.

Codex Fejerváry-Mayer
1971 *Codices Selecti XXVI*. Akademiche Druck-und Verlagsanstalt, Graz.

Hassig, Ross
2001 *Time History and Belief in Aztec and Colonial Mexico*. University of Texas Press, Austin.

Milbrath, Susan
2013 *Heavenly History: Ancient Mexican Astronomy in the Codex Borgia*. University of Texas Press, Austin.

Prem, Hanns
2008 *Manual de la Cronología Mexicana*. Centro de Investigaciones y Estudios Superiores en Antropología Social, Mexico City.

Tena, Rafael
1987 *El Calendario Mexica y la Cronografía*. Instituto Nacional Antropología y Historia, Mexico City.

Umberger, Emily
1981 The Structure of Aztec History. Archaeoastronomy. *The Bulletin of the Center for Archaeoastronomy* 4(4):10–18.

CHAPTER 8

AZTEC PICTOGRAPHY AND PAINTED HISTORIES

ELIZABETH HILL BOONE

The Aztecs recorded knowledge and the historical events of their past by means of a pictographic system that relied on precisely arranged figures and symbols. They referred to it as *tlacuilolli*, which after the Conquest the Spanish translated to mean both "writing" and "painting" (Molina 1970:58, 96, 2nd pag. 16). Indeed, Aztec pictography was as much a pictorial system as it was a script. Its effectiveness was measured according to its accuracy in recording concepts and facts, but its perfection was judged in terms of its poetics, balance, and graphic execution. Pictography filled the cultural category that for the Aztecs embraced both writing and painting.

The Franciscan friar Motolinia and the Jesuit José de Acosta were among those who recognized early the recording capabilities of pictography (Motolinia 1951:74–75; Acosta 2003:334–335, 340). They noted that although the Amerindians did not employ alphabetic letters and words, the Aztecs recorded histories and communicated knowledge graphically in books, that, to quote Motolinia, "were written in symbols and pictures. This is their way of writing" (Motolinia 1951:74). Although Motolinia decried the books that recorded divinatory and religious information as the work of the devil, he celebrated the veracity and accuracy of Aztec annals histories.

Painted books, which are now referred to as "codices," were central to Aztec life. Rulers commissioned histories to record the significant events of their past, histories that supported their rights to power and their relationships with the allied and enemy polities around them (Alva Ixtlilxochitl 1985:1:285–286, 527; Boone 2000; Motolinia 1971:5, 9). Imperial officials kept painted tribute rolls that detailed the kinds and amounts of goods that were regularly owed and received from near and distant provinces (Cortés 1986:109; Díaz del Castillo 1977:1:273). Judicial clerks recorded the details of court cases, and local authorities maintained census and property records, specifying private lands and the use of communal lands (Alva Ixtlilxochitl 1985:1:286, 527; Boone 1998:150–155; Zorita 1963:110). Travelers relied on maps to follow routes of safe passage (Cortés 1986:94, 192, 340, 344). Philosophers and priests looked to cosmogonies, divinatory manuals, and books of sacred discourse to understand the structures and relationships of the physical and spiritual worlds (León-Portilla 1963); the priests also consulted books for precise prescriptions for ritual observance (Boone 2007:157–169). Everyone, from rulers to commoners, had their fates read at crucial times in their lives by calendar priests skilled in translating the mysteries of the divinatory books (*tonalamatl*, "day book") (Boone 2005:14–15; 2007; Sahagún 1953–1982, Book 4). Data in the painted books recorded the deep and recent past, the obligations and actualities of the present, and the expectations and forces that shaped the future.

The divinatory manuals (books of the fates) were the books most often seen by ordinary people, who sought to know prognostications at birth and marriage and for important activities, such as travel and the sowing and harvesting of fields. Such books were probably held in both large and small temples and in the homes of calendar priests, to whom people went for consultation. *Calpolli* heads also kept their own records of land use and taxes. Most practical documents and the histories, however, were maintained in administrative and royal libraries, such as the great libraries of Texcoco and Tenochtitlan (Alva Ixtlilxochitl 1985:1:286; Díaz del Castillo 1977:1:143, 273; Pomar 1986:46).

As objects, Aztec books took the form of rolled strips (*tiras*), screenfolds (folded *tiras*), and panels. Most were composed of deer hide or the pounded fibers of maguey or fig tree bark (*amatl*) that were feathered and glued together. The panels and long strips could then be folded back and forth into individual pages, and their hard surfaces were sized with a white gesso support for the painted content. Wooden or stiffened hide covers protected the interior content. The Aztecs also used great cotton sheets (*lienzos*) for maps and cartographic histories, as did their neighbors in Puebla and Oaxaca. The size of books varied. The largest Aztec book is the *Codex Borbonicus* (1974), a screenfold divinatory and festival book of *amatl* that has pages measuring c. 40 cm^2 and stretches for 14 m when fully extended. In contrast, the *Tira de Tepechpan* (Diel 2008), an annals history also of *amate*, has pages only 21 cm high and extends for a little over 6 m (Glass with Robertson 1975:97, 205).

Those who owned and controlled the content of the books were the *tlamatinime* (wise men, wise women, or sages), a class of individuals that included women as well as men (Sahagún 1953–1982, Book 6:29–30). The painters (*tlacuiloque*) partially overlapped as a class with the *tlamatinime*, for *tlamatinime* could themselves be the painters of the books, but not all painters were necessarily *tlamatinime*. All, however, were trained in the *calmecac*, the elite school for advanced learning in the arts and sciences. The Aztecs looked to the *tlamatinime* as the guides for correct living; they provided intellectual, moral, and religious leadership. They included astronomers, astrologers, cosmographers, historians, religious practitioners, poets, and orators; most prominently, the Spanish chroniclers record that they were owners of books (Sahagún 1953–1982, Book 10:29–30, 10.190–191; León-Portilla 1963:18–19; 1986:86, 138–141; Boone 2005).

Mexican Pictography

The pictography practiced in central and southern Mexico in the Postclassic period is a figural semasiographic system, or a system of figural images that record things, actions, and concepts but do not usually use spoken language as their primary referent. The images are highly motivated in the linguistic sense that they usually have a visual relationship to what they depict, but they are not illusionistically realistic in describing optically perceived form (Figure 8.1).

Instead, they are flat, stable, and stationary renderings that should be read as graphic abstractions of entities, qualities, events, times, locations, and sometimes sounds. Most signs are based on human and animal forms, sometimes fused or with interchangeable parts and represented in a manner that displays the most characteristic features of the form and allows it to hold the most information. Thus most forms (heads, torsos, limbs, and extremities) are rendered in profile, and accouterments that would cover the chest are rotated to appear frontally on the image. The complex pictographic image is also accretive and agglutinative—as is the Nahuatl language—composed of multiple visual elements added to a core.

An example of a complex glyphic expression is the supernatural Chalchiuhtlicue (She of the Jade Skirt), the goddess of groundwater, when she is rendered as the patron of a 13-day week in a divinatory almanac (Figure 8.1a). She is configured in the conventional pose—knees up, feet staggered forward, and arms outstretched forward—of such

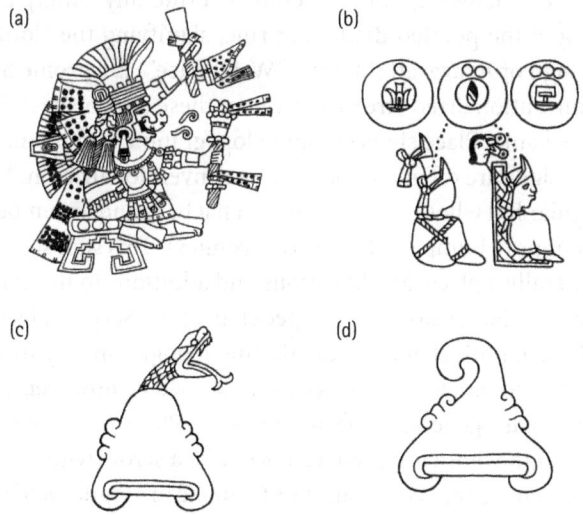

FIGURE 8.1 Pictographic expressions: (a) the water goddess Chalchihuitlicue (*Codex Borbonicus* 5); (b) death of Motecuzoma and the accession of Axayacatl in the year 2 Flint (*Tira de Tepechpan* 12); (c) place sign of Coatepec (*Codex Boturini* 5); (d) place sign of Colhuacan (*Codex Boturini* 20). Drawing of (a) by Heather Hurst, drawings of (b)–(d) by John Montgomery.

supernatural patrons and is here seated on a stool that conveys authority. The presentation of her human form is anatomically impossible, however, for she is depicted with two right feet, two left hands, and arms that are merely extensions of the body mass. Her form is not to be read as an organic, corporeal body but instead as an armature for the display of her multiple physical attributes and accouterments. These accouterments, all rotated to present their characteristics and components clearly, are packed on the form to signify the realms and forces controlled by this supernatural.

A less densely layered but equally complex set of images is used to signify the death of an Aztec-Mexica ruler and the accession of his successor. The multipart glyphic expression is composed of two seated males, their knees drawn up in the conventional seated-man's pose, and their forms attached by dotted lines to one year date (2 Flint) in a series of such year dates (Figure 8.1b). The deceased ruler is presented as a wrapped and bound corpse bundle that wears the pointed diadem of rulership. His successor is presented as alive, with facial features and open eyes, sitting on a reed throne, and wearing a white cloak and the same diadem of rulership. Both figures (the dead Motecuhzoma and the living Axayacatl) are named by individual glyphic affixes. Conventionally, the glyphic record of the death of one ruler usually requires a record of his successor's ascent, with the two images united in time by their attachment to the same year sign. They both face in the direction in which the year signs progress, with the deceased behind (and thereby earlier) than the successor. When pictorial histories include only the accessions, the preceding deaths are thereby inferred.

Glyphic appellatives that record the names of persons, ethnicities, and places often function glottographically to record sound. They are usually composed of graphic forms that represent entities logographically, but some contain forms that function in a purely phonetic manner. The name sign of Motecuhzoma (literally "Angly Lord"), for example, is a rendering of the pointed diadem of rule, signifying the "lord" (*teuctli*) in his name. The name sign of Axayacatl (literally "Water Face") is a profile head to which are appended two conventionalized streams of water, these streams yielding the initial "a" (*atl* [water]) of his name. Place signs combine logographic and phonetic elements in a similar way. Place signs are often composed of a conventionalized hill sign: a form like a rounded, triangular hill whose sides curl over a flat base and are embellished with distinctive "earth" bumps (a bump flanked by two volutes). This sign signifies a hill (*tepetl*) but also more generally a place. Modifications and additions to this basic form provide the name of the places. For example, Coatepec (Hill of the Serpent) has a serpent (*coatl*) on top of the hill sign, both elements functioning logographically to yield "coa-tepec" (Figure 8.1c). Pure phoneticism does occasionally occur, however. For example, the place sign of Colhuacan (generally referred to as the Place of Those with Ancestors) is composed of a hill sign whose top is curved over like a scroll, with the curve signifying "curve" (*coltic*) and cuing the "col" sound of Colhuacan (Figure 8.1d). Phoneticism in pictography is limited to appellatives, for which the sound of a spoken name is sought.

The syntax of pictography is spatial and highly variable depending on the genre of the document. In some historical records and divinatory almanacs, clusters of images are organized sequentially along registers. These registers can read left to right, right to left, up to down, down to up, or in a back-and-forth boustrophedon. Cartographic histories and some other kinds of almanacs are arranged as diagrams, in which relationships between images are dependent on their relative placement within the larger field. Pictography has no single or universal grammar or syntax; instead, the content of the book generally determines the arrangement of its signifying imagery.

Painted Histories

Spanish chroniclers noted that the Aztecs produced a wide range of painted histories (Alva Ixtlilxochitl 1985:1:527; Motlinia 1951:74–75, 1971:5, 9). These included cosmogonies, histories of peoples and polities, genealogies, and biographies (see also Batalla this volume). Land documents that specified ownership or use also sometimes contained historical data on the individuals involved. Some histories reached deep into the past; others recounted major events up to the then present. Many did both. Unfortunately, all the Aztec histories that were painted before the Conquest have been lost. Thus our knowledge of the historical genres rests on the descriptions of the chroniclers and on the histories that were painted after the Conquest. Of these early colonial histories, dozens have survived, and many clearly reflect the pre-Conquest tradition.

These surviving histories largely pertain to the *altepetl* or community kingdom as a corporate entity, rather than to the lives of individual rulers. Rulers appear in Aztec pictorial histories at the times of their installation and death and when they are personal agents of war, but, with the exception of several histories from Texcoco (*Codex Xolotl* [Dibble 1980], *Mapa Tlotzin* [1849], and *Mapa Quinatzin* [1891]), there is usually no information about their families and genealogies (Boone 2000:186–194; Douglas 2010:135–158). This general silence about genealogy distinguishes Aztec histories from the histories of the Mixtec, Zapotec, and other neighbors to the south (Boone 2000:241–243). We find the reason for this in nature of Aztec royal succession. Aztec rulers were chosen from a pool of eligible men of the royal family, and although sons could follow their fathers, it was often that rule passed to an uncle, brother, or cousin (Durán 1994:58; Zorita 1963:89–93). Lacking a system of primogeniture descent, which the Mixtecs and their neighbors had, Aztec historians were less concerned about details of genealogy such as exact parentage and birth order. Instead, the focus of Aztec history was on the *altepetl* itself.

Surviving Aztec histories treat two broad historical themes: the long migration from a place of origin or ancestral homeland to the place where they established their capital and the subsequent development and expansion of the polity. The founding of the capital stands as the historical and visual bridge between the two. Although some extant histories pertain only to the migration (e.g., *Codex Boturini* [1964–1967], *Mapa Sigüenza* [Castañeda de la Paz 2006]), and a few fragments recount events only after the capital is founded (e.g., *Codex Moctezuma* [Glass 1964:69, 1975:170–171], *Codex Saville* [Cuevas 1929]), most treat both (Boone 2000:162–237).

Accounts of the migration often take a cartographic form, for the essential story of the migration is the movement of people across the land. The journey is usually presented as a circuit or itinerary that follows a sequence of locations identified by their place names; footprints mark the journey itself. The migration then ends with the arrival at the predestined place, where the capital is founded. Such is the *Mapa Sigüenza*, a sheet of *amate* paper that traces the migration of the Mexica Aztecs from Aztlan to the new capital of Tenochtitlan (Boone 2000:162–177; Castañeda de la Paz 2006) (Figure 8.2).

The right side of the sheet and the top third of the left side are devoted to the itinerary of the journey, beginning at Aztlan in the upper right and following a path of footprints from place to place until the path (and implicitly the people) reach the Valley of Mexico on the left side. The Valley of Mexico is itself presented as a map, with place signs located in geographic relation to each other, the lake characterized as a swamp cut through by canals and dotted with rushes and reeds, and the place sign of Tenochtitlan in the center.

Almost all painted histories feature the migration as a principal aspect of Aztec self-definition, and each polity distinguished its own migration from that of others. The Mexica Aztec accounts recorded that other communities also left Aztlan but stress the different times of departure and the different routes they traveled. It was important that

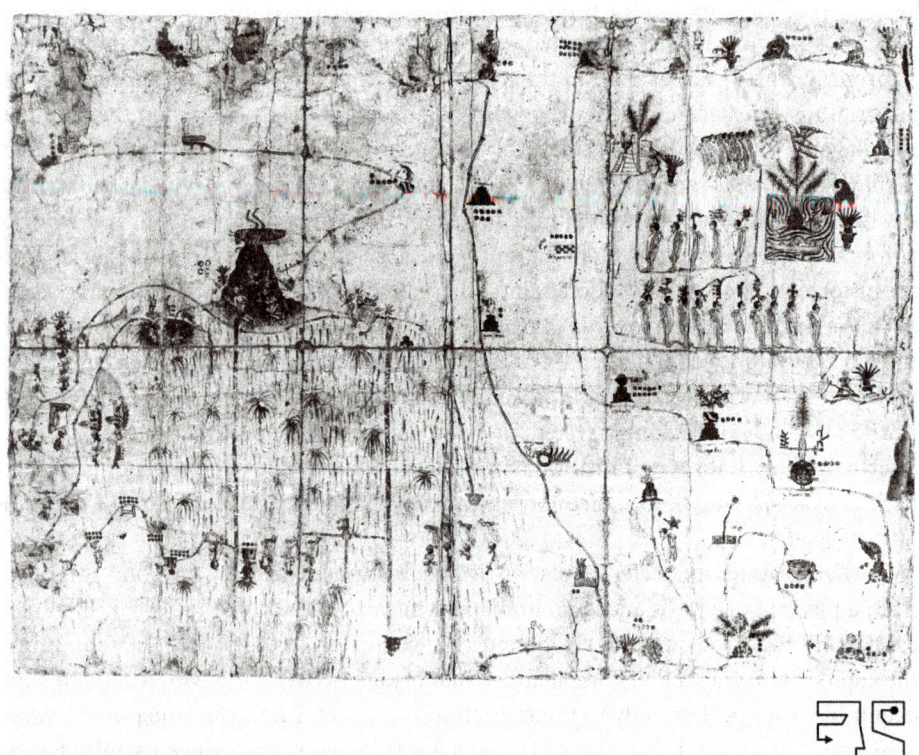

FIGURE 8.2 Mapa Sigüenza. Reproduced with permission, Conaculta, Instituto Nacional de Antropología e Historia, Mexico.

each community have its own, separate migration; this proved its ancient autonomy, which, in the Colonial period, allowed polities to maintain their independence and *altepetl* status (Lockhart 1992:15–16).

The founding of the polity itself after the migration is usually presented as a major event prominently featured in the painted books. The *Codex Mendoza*, which was painted on European paper to show the Spanish king the rulers, military history, extent, tribute, and lifeways of his newly conquered land, devotes an entire page to the founding of Tenochtitlan (Berdan and Anawalt 1992) (Figure 8.3).

The large place sign of Tenochtitlan (a nopal cactus above a conventionalized stone) in the center on which a great eagle sits dominates the page. Since the sighting of the eagle on the cactus was the sign that the Mexica Aztecs should establish their capital there, the presence of this eagle transforms the place sign into an event glyph for the founding itself. The location of this event is described visually as a marshy island, surrounded by blue waters and cut through by canals. Within the space of the island, the 10 leaders who guided their people are indicated; they are seated on low mats of authority, characterized as warriors by the bound tuft of upright hair, and individually identified by their name glyphs. The principal leader, Tenoch, just to the left of the foundation glyph, is

FIGURE 8.3 Founding of Tenochtitlan in the *Codex Mendoza*, folio 2r. Photograph courtesy of the Bodleian Library, Oxford University.

differentiated as a priest by his long hair, black face paint, and blood red patch next to his ear; he is further characterized as the foremost ruler of this group by his speech scroll, which signifies his role as *tlahtoani*, or speaker, and the woven reed mat on which he sits. Below this presentation of the founding are statements that the Mexica Aztecs conquered the polities of Colhuacan (left) and Tenayuca (right). Conquest is conventionally signified by the burning temples with their roofs askew and the two armed Mexica warriors grabbing their captives by the hair. The historian locates the founding and these conquests in time by framing them in a band of year signs that read from 2 House (1325, the traditional date of the founding) in the upper left to 13 Reed 50 years later.

Following statements of Tenochtitlan's founding, Mexica histories continue to present events that are important to the status and well-being of the polity. Generally, they are structured as annals, which the Aztecs called *xiuhpolhualli* (year count, year relations), *xiuhamatl* (year paper, year book), and *xiuhtlacuilolli* (year writing) (Lockhart 1992:376). In these annals histories, the historical account is organized not according to geography or space, as in the cartographic histories, but according to time. In them, a band of sequent year signs provides the armature to which the historical events are tied. These events are recorded beside the appropriate year and are often graphically linked to the year by a line.

Information in the annals is that which was important to the polity as a whole, for these are stories of the *altepetl* (community kingdom) rather than dynastic or personal histories. Events include the deaths and accessions of the rulers, conquests, significant building programs, extraordinary celebrations (such as the dedication of the Templo Mayor of Tenochtitlan in 1486 and the periodic New Fire Ceremony), and significant climatic and natural phenomena (e.g., drought, pestilence, earthquakes, floods, and eclipses). Rulers appear in the annals when they accede to the throne and when they die, but their births, marriages, and offspring are not usually included. Conquests are presented as statements of fact rather than the results of individual action on the part of a ruler (Boone 2000:197–237).

The events themselves are rendered glyphically and conventionally, in order to fit within the space adjacent to the relevant year sign. The *Codex Mexicanus* is typical of such annals, as exemplified in the two-page section that covers events of the years 4 Reed through 2 Rabbit (Boone 2000:67–69; Mengin 1952:455–456) (Figure 8.4).

Progressing left to right, the historian notes that the ruler Tizoc, conventionally enthroned and crowned and identified by his chalk-leg name sign, takes office in 4 Reed and begins to renovate the Templo Mayor of Tenochtitlan. Two years later the Mexica are defeated by the Matlatzinca, who are identified phonetically by name sign of a hunting basket (*matlatl*) and an image of a lower body (*tzintli*). In the following year, Tizoc dies and his successor Ahuitzotl (Water Beast) takes office; the Templo Mayor is then dedicated in 8 Reed. The years 10 House through 13 Flint are each marked by calamity: an earthquake, a hailstorm so severe it killed fish, a plague of locusts, and a drought. Each of these events is signified precisely and economically and is placed next to and tied to its relevant year. Because the Aztec Mexica annals are local histories, it is assumed that most events pertain to the place whose history it is; place signs are rarely included,

FIGURE 8.4 Annals history of the *Codex Mexicanus*, pp. 71–72. Reproduction courtesy of the Bibliotheque nationale France.

except when an event occurs in another location, as in the case of the conquest of or by enemy polities.

Some annals histories cover both the migratory past as well as the time after the founding, as the Mexica empire grew (e.g., *Codex Aubin* [Lehmann and Kutscher 1981], *Codex Mexicanus, Tira de Tepechpan*). A number also record the Spanish Conquest and continue to document Aztec life under Spanish domination. They present the Conquest as a series of events occurring over several years. The *Codex Mexicanus* and the *Tira de Tepechpan*, for example, record the arrival of Spaniards and Christianity, the smallpox epidemic, the death of Aztec rulers, and the burning of the Templo Mayor. The indigenous historians simply introduce the new set of actors and new events as glyphic statements, which effectively become part of the ongoing native story. There is no great rupture and little sense that the precolumbian era has come to an end. Instead, the Colonial annals document a gradual process of adjustment and accommodation until they break off at the time of their composition toward the end of the century.

Despite the Spanish Conquest and the introduction of alphabetic writing and a new administrative order, indigenous rulers continued to value their painted histories well into the Colonial period. They and Spanish authorities continued to recognize these traditional documents as authentic accounts of the past, which could be and were wielded in legal battles to retain and gain lands, titles, and privileges. It was the pictorial nature of the painted histories, more so than the details of their stories, that attested to their antiquity and thus their validity as containers of knowledge about the indigenous past.

References Cited

Acosta, José de
2003 *Natural and Moral History of the Indies*. Edited by Jane F. Mangan. Translated by Frances López-Morillas. Duke University Press, Durham, NC.
Alva Ixtlilxochitl, Fernando de
1985 *Obras históricas*, 3rd ed. 2 vols. Edited by Edmundo O'Gorman. Universidad Nacional Autónoma de México, Mexico, D.F.

Berdan, Frances F., and Patricia Rieff Anawalt
1992 *The Codex Mendoza*. 4 vols. University of California Press, Berkeley.
Boone, Elizabeth Hill
1998 Pictorial Documents and Visual Thinking and Postconquest Mexico. In *Native Traditions in the Postconquest World*, edited by Elizabeth Hill Boone and Thomas Cummins, pp. 149–199. Dumbarton Oaks Research Library and Collection, Washington, DC.
2000 *Stories in Red and Black: Pictorial Histories of the Aztecs and Mixtecs*. University of Texas Press, Austin.
2005 In Tlamatinime: The Wise Men and Women of Aztec Mexico. In *Painted Books and Indigenous Knowledge in Mesoamerica: Manuscript Studies in Honor of Mary Elizabeth Smith*, edited by Elizabeth Hill Boone, pp. 9–25. Middle American Research Institute, Tulane University, New Orleans.
2007 *Cycles of Time and Meaning in the Mexican Books of Fate*. University of Texas Press, Austin.
Castañeda de la Paz, María
2006 *Pintura de la peregrinación de los Culhuaque-Mexitin (El Mapa de Sigüenza)*. El Colegio Mexiquense and Instituto Nacional de Antropología e Historia, Zinacantepec and Mexico, D.F.
Codex Borbonicus
1974 *Codex Borbonicus, Bibliotheque de l'Assemblee nationale, Paris (Y 120): vollstandige Faksimile-Ausg. des Codex im Originalformat*. Akademische Druck-u. Verlagsanstalt, Graz.
Codex Boturini
1964–1967 Explicación del Códice Boturini o Tira de la Peregrinación. In *Antiguedatdes de México, basadas en la recopilación de Lord Kingsborough*, Vol. 2, edited by José Corona Núñez, pp. 7–29. Secretaria de Hacienda y Crédito Público, Mexico City.
Codex Mexicanus
1952 *Codex Mexicanus*, Bibliothèque Nationale de Paris, Nos. 23–24. *Journal de la Société des Américanistes* 41(2), Supplement.
Cortés, Hernan
1986 *Hernan Cortés, Letters from Mexico*. Translated and edited by Anthony Pagden. Yale University Press, New Haven, CT.
Cuevas, Mariano
1929 *Codex Saville*: America's Oldest Book. *Historical Records and Studies* 19:7–20, folding plate facing p. 24.
Díaz del Castillo, Bernal
1977 *Historia verdadera de la conquista de la Nueva España*. 2 vols. Edited by Joaquín Ramírez Cabañas. Editorial Porrúa, Mexico. D.F.
Dibble, Charles E. (editor)
1980 *Códice Xolotl*. Universidad Nacional Autónoma de México, Mexico City.
Diel, Lori Boornazian
2008 *Tira de Tepechpan: Negotiating Place under Aztec and Spanish Rule*. University of Texas Press, Austin.
Douglas, Eduardo de J.
2010 *In the Palace of Nezahualcoyotl: Painting Manuscripts, Writing the Pre-Hispanic Past in Early Colonial Period Tetzcoco, Mexico*. University of Texas Press, Austin.
Durán, Diego
1994 *The History of the Indies of New Spain*. Translated and edited by Doris Heyden. University of Oklahoma Press, Norman.

Glass, John B.
1964 *Catálogo de la colección de códices*. Museo Nacional de Antropología, Instituto Nacional de Antropología e Historia, Mexico City.

Glass, John B., with Donald Robertson
1975 A Census of Native Middle American Pictorial Manuscripts. In *Handbook of Middle American Indians*, Vol. 14, edited by Robert Wauchope and Howard F. Cline, pp. 81–252. University of Texas Press, Austin.

Lehmann, Walter, and Gerdt Kutscher (translators and editors)
1981 *Geschichte der Azteken: Codex Aubin und verwandte Dokumente*. Gebr. Mann, Berlin.

León-Portilla, Miguel
1963 *Aztec Thought and Culture*. University of Oklahoma Press, Norman.

León-Portilla, Miguel (translator and editor)
1986 *Colóquios y doctrina cristiana: los diálogos de 1524 según el texto de Fray Bernardino de Sahagún y sus colaboradores indígenas*. Universidad Nacional Autónoma de México and Fundación de Investigaciones Sociales, Mexico. D.F.

Lockhart, James
1992 *Nahuas After the Conquest: A Social and Cultural History of the Indians of Central Mexico, Sixteenth Through Eighteenth Centuries*. Stanford University Press, Stanford, CA.

Mengin, Ernst
1952 Commentaire du Codex Mexicanus Nos. 23–24 de la Bibliothèque Nationale de Paris. *Journal de la Société des Américanistes* 41(2):387–498.

Molina, Alonso
1970 *Vocabulario en lengua castellana y mexicana y mexicana y castellana*. Edited by Miguel León-Portilla. Editorial Porrúa, México, D.F.

Motolinia
1951 *Motolinia's History of the Indies*. Edited and translated by Francis Borgia Steck. Academy of American Franciscan History, Washington, DC.
1971 *Memoriales o libro de las cosas de Nueva España y de los naturales de ella*. Edited by Edmundo O'Gorman. Instituto de Investigaciones Históricas, Universidad Nacional Autónoma de México, Mexico, D.F.

Pomar, Juan Bautista
1986 Relación de la ciudad and provincia de Tezcoco. In *Relaciones geográficas del siglo XVI*, Vol. 8, edited by René Acuña, pp. 21–113. Universidad Nacional Autónoma de México, Mexico, D.F.

Quinatzin, Mapa
1891 Cour Chichimeque et Histoire de Tezcuco. In *Documents pour servir à l'histoire du Mexique: catalogue raisonné de la collection de M.E. Eugène Goupil (ancienne collectin J. M. A. Aubin)*, Vol. 1, edited by Eugène Boban, pp. 219–242, pls. 211–212. Ernest Leroux, Paris.

Sahagún, Bernardino de
1953–1982 *Florentine Codex: The General History of the Things of New Spain*. Translated and edited by Arthur J. O. Anderson and Charles E. Dibble. 12 books in 13 vols. School of American Research, Santa Fe, NM, and University of Utah, Salt Lake City.

Tlotzin, Mapa
1849 *Mappe Tlotzin: histoire du royaume d'Acolhuacan ou de Texcuco (Peinture nonchronologique)*. Lith. de Jules Desportes, Paris.

Zorita, Alonso de
1963 *The Lords of New Spain: The Brief and Summary Relation of the Lords of New Spain*. Translated and edited by Benjamin Keen. Rutgers University Press, New Brunswick, NJ.

CHAPTER 9

THE LANGUAGES OF THE AZTEC EMPIRE

JANE H. HILL

THE Aztec Empire included speakers of at least 40 languages belonging to five distinct language families: Uto-Aztecan, Otomanguean, Totonacan, Mixe-Zoquean, and Mayan. Brown et al. (2011) argue that Totonacan and Mixe-Zoquean can be combined into a single family (Totozoquean). Mora-Marin (2016) suggests a common ancestor for Mayan and Mixe-Zoquean, noting that this hypothesis does not necessarily contradict the Totozoquean hypothesis. Cuitlatec and Tarascan are isolates with no known linguistic relatives. Several languages lack any documentation of existence other than the name listed in the Colonial-era sources, so they cannot be classified. Harvey (1972) reviews the documentation (and lack thereof) for these unknown languages. In addition, classification is often uncertain when the language name in the sources is one of the several Nahuatl-language insults for people regarded as less civilized than the Mexica. These include, at least, *chochon* (or *chohchol*), *chontalli, tenitl*, and *pinōtl*, all with implications of rudeness, rusticity, and stupidity, and foreignness, as well as *popoloca*, a verb meaning "to mumble, babble, speak incoherently, speak a barbarous language." These epithets could probably be applied to any non-Nahuatl language; thus "Chontal" is recorded for an unknown language of Guerrero; for Tequistlatec, a Hokan language of Oaxaca; and for a Mayan language of the Cholan subgroup. "Popoloca" appears in the sources in reference to Chocho, an Otomanguean language; Sierra Popoloca, a Zoquean language; and for what was probably the Otomanguean language Pame. The "Tenime" included the Olmeca, Uixtoti, Mixteca, and Tlapaneca, all so named "because they spoke a barbarous tongue" (Sahagún 1950–1982, Book X:188) *Chīchīmēcah* (a plural) is both an ethnonym and a political assertion, which by the time of the empire was contrasted with *Tōltēcah* in a complex system of meanings elucidated by Berdan (2008:114–115), where *Chichimeca* referred both to uncivilized ancestors (in contrast with the deep history of civilization among the *Tolteca*) but also to a proud history of warlike conquerors. However, *Chīchīmēcah* was also used as a label for speakers of Pamean languages and perhaps varieties of Otomi. Another problem is that designations like "Mixtec" and "Zapotec" collapse under a single label what were surely diverse languages of the large Mixtecan and Zapotecan subfamilies of Oto-Manguean.

Table 9.1 lists the languages of the provinces of the empire. At the end of the table I list also the languages that have been identified for the independent states that were surrounded by provinces of the empire. The order of the list reflects the order of dominance of the language, where this is recorded. The middle column in Table 9.1 gives the genetic affiliation of the language; I list this only the first time the language name appears. Where a language cannot be classified, it is listed as "unknown." Although Nahuatl, the dominant language of the Triple Alliance states, is not always listed, it must have been spoken in all provinces, if only by small communities of traders or imperial officials and by local bilingual elites.

The languages of the central provinces are given as listed by Berdan and Anawalt (1992:Table 10.1). The languages of the outer provinces (divided into "tributary" and "strategic" types) are listed following the organization and numbering proposed by Smith and Berdan (1996). Where other sources note additional languages, I have checked these against the discussion in Gerhard (1992) and included them if they seem plausible. Additional sources are cited when they are more detailed or comprehensive. Information on the languages of the empire comes from ethnohistoric sources (especially the *Relaciones Geográficas* [Harvey 1972]) dating from decades after its fall and should be approached with caution, considering the massive demographic collapse and rearrangement of populations during the Colonial period, as well as population movements during the empire itself. However, these data support the suggestion made by Berdan (1996) that language affiliation played a minimal role in the political-geographical organization of the empire. Berdan (1996:121) notes a single exception, the possibility that the boundary between Ocuilan (9) and Malinalco (10) was motivated by language differences.

While the cities of the Triple Alliance *āltēpeh* themselves were Nahuatl dominant, speakers of many other languages must have lived there. Gerhard (1992:247) notes that Matlatzinca was an important second language at Azcapotzalco. Both Mexico City and Tetzcoco had sizeable communities of Otomi speakers (Gerhard 1992:180, 311), and "other languages must have been heard" (Gerhard 1992:180).

The ancestral language of the various Nahua-speaking peoples, Proto-Aztecan, a member of the Uto-Aztecan family of languages, clearly arose in Mesoamerica. As pointed out by Beekman and Christensen (2003) and Beekman (2010), while Nahuatl speakers did enter the Valley of Mexico from the north and northwest, their claims of a recent hunter-gatherer origin should not be taken literally. Most of the typological features suggested for the "Mesoamerican linguistic area" (Campbell et al. 1986) can be reconstructed for Proto-Aztecan. Loan words datable to that language show that its speakers were in contact with Totonacans, Huastecans, Zoqueans, and Zapotecans (Kaufman 2001; Kaufman and Justeson 2007; Wichmann 1998). Words for "zapote," "avocado," and "silk-cotton tree" can be reconstructed for the proto-language, locating its community of speakers firmly within the tropics, and a reconstructed suite of vocabulary for the cultivation of

Table 9.1 Languages of the Aztec Empire and the Independent Señorios

Province/Señorio	Language	Classification	Source
Tlatelolco (Central)	Nahuatl	Uto-Aztecan	B&A:33
Petlacalco (Central)	Nahuatl		B&A:35
	Otomi	Otomanguean (Otopamean)	
Acolhuacan (Central)	Nahuatl		B&A:39
	Otomi		
	"Populuca" (Pame?)	Otomanguean (Oto-Pamean)	
Hueypuchtla (Central)	Otomi		B&A:55
	Nahuatl		
	Chichimec (Pame)		
Chalco (Central)	Nahuatl		B&A:97
Cuauhtitlan (Central)	Nahuatl		B&A:48
	Otomi		
1. Axocopan (Tributary)	Otomi		S&B:266
	Nahuatl		
	"Chichimec" (Pame)		
2. Atotonilco de Pedraza (Tributary)	Otomi		S&B:266
	Mazahua	Otomanguean (Oto-Pamean)	
3. Xilotepec (Tributary)	Otomi		S&B:266
	Mazahua		
	Pame		
4. Chiapan (Strategic)	Nahuatl		S&B:267
	Otomi		
5. Xocotitlan (Tributary)	Mazahua		S&B:267
	Matlatzinca	Otomanguean (Oto-Pamean)	
	Otomi		
6. Ixtlahuaca (Strategic)	Nahuatl		S&B:267
	Mazahua		
	Matlatzinca		
	Otomi		
7. Cuahuacan (Tributary)	Nahuatl		S&B:268
	Otomi		
	Matlatzinca		

(*continued*)

Table 9.1 (Continued)

Province/Señorio	Language	Classification	Source
8. Tollocan (Tributary)	Matlatzinca Mazahua Otomi Nahuatl		S&B:268
9. Ocuilan (Tributary)	Matlatzinca		S&B:269
	Ocuilteco	Otomanguean (Oto-Pamean)	
10. Malinalco (Tributary)	Nahuatl		S&B:269
11. Temazcaltepec (Strategic)	Nahuatl Matlatzinca Mazahua		S&B:269
12. Tlachco (Tributary)	Chontal de Guerrero	Unclassified	S&B 270
	Nahuatl		
	Mazatec	Otomanguean (Popolocan)	
	Matlatzinca		
	Tarascan	Isolate	Barlow 1992 [1949]:31
13. Quauhnahuac (Tributary)	Nahuatl		S&B:270
14. Huaxtepec (Tributary)	Nahuatl		S&B:271
	Mixtec ("pockets")	Otomanguean (Mixtecan-Amuzgoan)	
	Chocho-Popoloca ("pockets")	Otomanguean (Popolocan)	
15. Ocuituco (Stratetic)	Nahuatl		S&B:273
16. Chiauhtlan (Strategic)	Nahuatl		S&B:273
17. Quiauhteopan (Tributary)	Nahuatl Mixtec		S&B:273
	Tlapanec	Otomanguean (Tlapanec/ Mangue)	
	Matlame	Unknown	
18. Tlacozauhtitlan (Tributary)	Cohuixca (Nahuatl)	Uto-Aztecan	S&B:274
	Tuxteco	Unknown	
	Tlapanec Matlame		

(*continued*)

Table 9.1 (Continued)

Province/Señorio	Language	Classification	Source
19. Tepequacuilco (Tributary)	Chontal de Guerrero	Unknown	S&B:274
	Cohuixca (Nahuatl)		
	Cuitlatec (G:152)	Isolate	
	Tuxteco Matlame Itzucan (G:152) Nahuatl (Barlow 1992 [1949]:26) Mazateco ("pockets") G:152		
20. Zompanco (Strategic)	Cohuixca Tuxteco (G:316) Matlatzinca (G 316)		S&B:275
21. Tetellan (Strategic)	Cuitlatec Tepuzteco Chontal de Guerrero		S&B:276
22. Tlapan (Tributary)	Tlapanec Nahuatl Mixtec		S&B:276
23. Cihuatlan (Tributary)	Tepuzteco		B&A:84, Litvak-King 1971:61
	Tolimeco, Chumbío, Panteca	All unknown	
	Cuitlatec (G:393)		
	Zacatula	"Idioma por si" (probably Nahuatl)	Barlow 1992 [1949]:19
	"Mexicana corrupta" (Cohuixca?) (Brand 1943:51)		
24. Tecpantepec (Strategic)	Cuitlatec Tepuzteco Nahuatl Minor Cihuatlan lgs.		S&B:277
	Yope (Tlapanec)		Brand 1943:49
25. Ayotlan (Strategic)	Nahuatl Tlapaneca Yope (Tlapanec)		S&B:278
	Zinteca	Unknown	
	Quahuteca	Unknown	
26. Ometepec (Strategic)	Nahuatl		S&B:278
	Ayacastec	Unknown	

(*continued*)

Table 9.1 (Continued)

Province/Señorio	Language	Classification	Source
	Amuzgo	Otomanguean (Mixtecan-Amuzgoan)	
	Tlapanec		
27. Xoconochco (Tributary)	Huehuetlatecan	Mixe-Zoquean	B&A:117, Gasco 2003:286
	Tapachultec	Mixe-Zoquean	
	Chiapanec/Mangue	Otomanguean (Tlapanec-Mangue)	
	Mam	Mayan	
	Nahuatl (central and Chiapas Nahuatl or "Waliwi")		
28. Miahuatlan (Strategic)	Zapotec	Otomanguean (Zapotecan)	S&B:279
29. Teozacualco (Strategic)	Zapotec Mixtec		S&B:279
	Chatino	Otomanguean (Zapotecan)	
30. Teozapotlan (Strategic)	Zapotec Mixtec		S&B:280
31. Ixtepexi (Strategic)	Zapotec "Corrupt" Nahuatl		S&B:280
	Chinantec	Otomanguean (Oto-Chinantecan)	
32. Coyolapan (Tributary)	Zapotec Mixtec Nahuatl		S&B:281
33. Coayxtlahuacan (Tributary)	Mixtec Chocho-Popolocan		S&B:282
	Cuicatec	Otomanguean (Mixtecan)	
	Chinantec		
34. Tlachquiauco (Tributary)	Mixtec		S&B:282
	Trique	Otomanguean (Mixtecan)	

(*continued*)

Table 9.1 (Continued)

Province/Señorio	Language	Classification	Source
35. Yoaltepec (Tributary)	Mixtec "Mexicano rústico" (Barlow 1992 [1949]:152)		S&B:283
36. Tecomaixtlahuac (Strategic)	Mixtec Nahuatl Amuzgo		S&B 283
37. Acatlan (Strategic)	Mixtec "a local version of Nahuatl" Nahuatl (Central)		S&B:283-84
38. Ahuatlan (Strategic)	Nahuatl		S&B:284
39. Tepeacac (Tributary)	Nahuatl Chocho-Popoloca Otomi Mixtec (G:281)		S&B:284
40. Tochtepec (Tributary)	Nahuatl Chinantec Mazatec		B&A:113, S&B 285
	Popoloca	Mixe-Zoquean	
41. Cuetlaxtlan (Tributary)	"Archaic" (G 340) Nahuatl		S&B:286
	"Pinomeh"	Unknown (Totonac? Mixtec?)	
42. Cempoallan (Strategic)	Totonac	Totonacan	S&B:286
	Nahuatl		
43. Quauhtochco (Tributary)	Nahuatl		S&B:287
44. Xalapa (Strategic)	Nahuatl Totonac		S&B:287
45. Misantla (Strategic)	Totonac Nahuatl		S&B:288
46. Tlatlauhquitepec (Tributary)	Totonac Nahuatl		S&B:288
47. Tetela (Strategic)	Nahuatl Totonac		S&B:289
48. Tlapacoyan (Tributary)	Nahuatl Totonac		S&B:289
49. Cuauhchinanco (Strategic)	Totonac Nahuatl Otomi		S&B:290

(*continued*)

Table 9.1 (Continued)

Province/Señorio	Language	Classification	Source
50. Atotonilco El Grande (Tributary)	Otomi		S&B:290
	Tepehua	Totonacan	
	Nahuatl		
51. Atlan (Tributary)	Nahuatl Otomi Tepehua		S&B:291
	Huaxtec	Mayan	
	Totonac (2 varieties)		
52. Tochpan (Tributary)	Huastec Totonac Nahuatl		S&B:291
53. Tzicoac (Tributary)	Huastec Tepehua Nahuatl		S&B:292
54. Huexotla (Strategic)	Tepehua Nahuatl		S&B 293
55. Oxitipan (Tributary)	Huastec		S&B:293
Teotitlan del Camino (Probably tributary but not listed in S&B)	Nahuatl Mazatec Cuicatec		G:305-6
	Ixcatecan	Otomanguean (Popolocan)	
Metztitlan (Independent)	Nahuatl Otomi		Barlow 1992 [1949]:81
Tlaxcallan (Independent)	Nahuatl ("rustic") Otomi "Pinomes"		Davies 1968:92
Yopitzinco (Independent)	Yope (Tlapanec)		Barlow 1992 [1949]:156
Totoltepec	Chatino Amuzgo Mixtec Zapotec Nahuatl Pochutec Nahua		Spores 1993:169
	Chontal (Tequistlatec)	Hokan ?	

Note: B&A = Berdan and Anawalt (1992); G = Gerhard (1992); S&B = Smith and Berdan (1996).

maize, beans, gourds, chile, and cotton suggests that they were almost certainly cultivators. Current debates concern whether Nahuatl speakers were a substantial presence in the Basin of Mexico prior to the Epiclassic period, and especially, whether they were an important presence at Teotihuacan (Cowgill 1992; Dakin 2010a; Dakin and Wichmann 2000; Davletshin 2012; Kaufman and Justeson 2007; Taube 2000; Whittaker 2012; Wichmann 2010). Nahuatl words in Maya inscriptions can be identified as early as the late fifth century A.D. (Macri 2005; Macri and Looper 2003).

By around 400 A.D, Pochutec, the most divergent Nahua variety (I avoid the word "dialect" because of its negative implications in Mexican Spanish usage), recorded from the municipio of San Pedro Pochutla on the Pacific Coast in Southern Oaxaca in the early twentieth century, was probably already distinctive (Kaufman 2001). The remaining varieties, comprising "General Aztec" must have begun to divide by that date into western and eastern regional varieties (Canger 1988; Canger and Dakin 1985; Dakin 2010). At an early date, speakers of Nahuatl were established southwest of the Basin of Mexico, where Von Mentz (2012) has identified a cluster of toponyms with the archaic place-name suffix *ma/-man*, like Oztuma, Toliman, Colima, and Tecoman, reaching to the Pacific Coast and perhaps reflecting Classic period trade routes. Influence on lowland Mayan languages, from speakers of eastern varieties of Nahuatl who included the people known as Toltecs, shows up in a diverse suite of loan words (Justeson et al. 1985) and extended to elite contexts such as the *Dresden Codex*, which includes three Nahuatl-language deity names (Whittaker 1986). By the thirteenth century, varieties of Nahuatl were spoken from Durango, Nayarit, Jalisco, Colima, and Michoacan in the west, across central Mexico to the Gulf Coast from the Huasteca to the Isthmus of Tehuantepec, and south to Central America. Attestation of these noncentral varieties in the Colonial records often labels them as "corrupt," "rustic," or "unpolished," but they were recognized as related to the prestigious central variants.

Canger (1988) argues that the varieties of central Nahuatl from which the speech of the Mexica and the other peoples of the Triple Alliance states is descended were formed when speakers of a western variety that she labels the "Aztlan migrants" arrived in Tlaxcala, Puebla, and the Basin of Mexico. This intrusion split off the Nahuatl of Guerrero (called "Cohuixca" in the Colonial period) from its eastern relatives. The Aztlan migrations also brought westerners into contact with speakers of eastern varieties, giving rise to a mixed variety that Dakin (2010b:180) calls "a kind of koine."

Harvey (1972:313–314) claims that "we can have little doubt that over 90 percent of the population in the region in which the Triple Alliance held sway was Nahua-speaking." While this very high number is not really justified by the evidence, recent work by Dakin (1981, 2010b) has uncovered linguistic evidence of a very widespread use of the language prior to Colonial times. The evidence attests to a variety of the Basin of Mexico koine that Dakin (1981, 2010b) labels the "Nahuatl lingua franca." This lingua franca is clearly precolonial, since it lacks the late innovations that took place in Tenochtitlan and Texcoco and are found in the "Classical Nahuatl" of the early Spanish documents (Dakin 1981, 2010b; Flores 2010; Whittaker 1988). Traces of the lingua franca can be identified in colonial Nahuatl texts from as far south as Guatemala; such traces are rare in the west, where the Tarascan frontier would have stopped its spread. Colonial documents from the old imperial periphery are often palimpsests of language change, reflecting successive waves of Nahua linguistic influence. For instance, a 1565 petition from Soconusco (Anderson et al. 1976:190–195) includes traces of the old local eastern varieties in occasional replacement of *tla- by /ta-/, traces of the imperial lingua franca (as in the preterite verb ōcalaqui "he entered," with the lingua franca proclitic ō-, a Western feature that survived in central varieties but without the later innovation of truncation seen in the Classical and notarial form ōcalac), alongside a consistent use of a very late innovation that spread from Tenochtitlan and Texcoco as preferred usage in the notarial Nahuatl of the Colonial era (the first-person reflexive prefix to-, which replaced conservative mo-).

Umberger (1996:141) identified hints in early sources that the Acolhua may have pursued linguistic "Nahuatlization," along with the imposition of the worship of Huitzilopochtli, among their subject peoples. However, it is unlikely that the spread of Nahuatl as a lingua franca during the Aztec Empire occurred as the result of deliberate imposition. Valiñas (2010:149) finds no evidence for Aztec policies of language planning or language officialization, and such policies would have been inconsistent with the imperial strategy of using indirect methods of domination whenever possible (Hassig 1988). However, there is no question that the Aztecs regarded their own language as superior; the dismissive views of Sahagún's informants toward other languages are richly recorded in the famous passages about foreign peoples in Book X of the *Florentine Codex*. Evidence that Nahuatl was not only superior but simply prototypical and taken for granted is found in the use of the symbol of a talking mouth in the trunk of the tree in the place name glyph for Cuauhnahuac (*cuauh-*, "tree(s)," *nāhuac*, "among"), where the symbol must be read as *nāhua*, not *tlahtoa*, "to speak." Furthermore, the word for "to interpret" is *nāhuatlahtoa*, as if "interpretation" could go only one direction. The only clear evidence of even semiofficial use of foreign languages is the practice by the *ōztōmēcah*, the "vanguard traders," of learning foreign languages so that they could pass unnoticed as spies (Sahagun 1950–1982, Book IX:21–22). The widespread use of Nahuatl in the empire probably resulted partly from elite emulation of the prestigious language of imperial officials but also, I suspect, from instrumentally motivated acquisition of a useful lingua franca by many ordinary people who had access to linguistic models in the form of Nahuatl speakers present among them as traders, colonists, and garrisoned troops.

References Cited

Anderson, Arthur J. O., Frances Berdan, and James Lockhart
1976 *Beyond the Codices: The Nahua View of Colonial Mexico*. UCLA Latin American Studies Series Vol. 27. University of California Press, Berkeley.
Barlow, Robert H.
1992 [1949] *La extensión del imperio de los Culhua Mexica*. Edited by Jesus Monjarás-Ruiz, Elena Limón, and María de la Cruz Paillés H. Translated by Jesus Monjarás-Ruiz. Obras de Robert H. Barlow Vol. 4. INAH/UDLA, México, D.F.

Beekman, Christopher
2010 Comment on Kaufman and Justeson, "The History of the Word for Cacao in Ancient Mesoamerica." *Ancient Mesoamerica* 21:415–418.
Beekman, Christopher, and Alexander F. Christensen
2003 Controlling for Doubt and Uncertainty Through Multiple Lines of Evidence: A New Look at the Mesoamerican Nahua Migrations. *Journal of Archaeological Method and Theory* 10:111–164.
Berdan, Frances F.
1996 The Tributary Provinces. In *Aztec Imperial Strategies*, edited by Frances F. Berdan, Richard E. Blanton, Elizabeth Hill Boone, Mary G. Hodge, Michael E. Smith, and Emily Umberger, pp. 115–135. Dumbarton Oaks Research Library and Collection, Washington, DC.
2008 Concepts of Ethnicity and Class in Aztec-Period Mexico. In *Ethnic Identity in Nahua Mesoamerica: The View from Archaeology, Art History, Ethnohistory, and Contemporary Ethnography*, edited by Frances F. Berdan, John K. Chance, Alan R. Sandstrom, Barbara L. Stark, James M. Taggart, and Emily Umberger, pp. 105–132. University of Utah Press, Salt Lake City.
Berdan, Frances F., and Patricia Rieff Anawalt
1992 *The Codex Mendoza*, Vol. II: *Description, Bibliography, Index*. University of California Press, Berkeley.
Brand, Donald D.
1943 An Historical Sketch of Geography and Anthropology in the Tarascan Region: Part I. *New Mexico Anthropologist* 6–7(2):37–108.
Brown, Cecil, David Beck, Grzegorz Kondrak, James K. Watters, and Søren Wichmann
2011 Totozoquean. *International Journal of American Linguistics* 22:323–372.
Campbell, Lyle, Terrence Kaufman, and Thomas C. Smith-Stark
1986 Mesoamerica as a Linguistic Area. *Language* 62:530–570.
Canger, Una
1988 Nahuatl Dialectology: A Survey and Some Suggestions. *International Journal of American Linguistics* 54:28–72.
Canger, Una, and Karen Dakin
1985 An Inconspicuous Basic Split in Nahuatl. *International Journal of American Linguistics* 51:358–361.
Cowgill, George
1992 Teotihuacan Glyphs and Imagery in the Light of Some Early Colonial Texts. In *Art, Ideology, and the City of Teotihuacan*, edited by Janet Catherine Berlo, pp. 231–246. Dumbarton Oaks Research Library and Collection, Washington, DC.
Dakin, Karen
1981 Characteristics of a Nahuatl Lingua Franca. In *Nahuatl Studies in Memory of Fernando Horcasitas*, edited by Frances Karttunen, pp. 55–68. Texas Linguistic Forum 18. Department of Linguistics, University of Texas, Austin.
2010a Comment on Kaufman and Justeson, "The History of the Word for Cacao in Ancient Mesoamerica." *Ancient Mesoamerica* 21:420–424.
2010b Lenguas francas y lenguas locales en la epoca prehispanica. In *Historia Sociolingüística de México*, Vol. I: *México prehispánico y colonial*, edited by Rebeca Barriga Villanueva and Pedro Martín Butragueño, pp. 161–184. El Colegio de México, Mexico City.
Dakin, Karen, and Søren Wichmann
2000 Cacao and Chocolate, A Uto-Aztecan Perspective. *Ancient Mesoamerica* 11:55–75.

Davies, Claude Nigel Byam
1968 *Los Señorios Independientes del Imperio Azteca*. Serie Historia 19. Instituto Nacional de Antropología e Historia, Mexico City.

Davletshin, Albert
2012 La lengua de los así llamados teotihuacanos e interpretaciones protonahuas para sus glosas en las inscripciones jeroglíficas mayas. In *Teotihuacan: medios de comunicación y poder en la ciudad de los dioses*, edited by Nikolai Grube and Ingrid Kummels, in press.

Flores Farfán, José Antonio
2010 Hacia una historia sociolingüística mesoamericana: explorando el náhuatl clásico. In *Historia Sociolingüística de México*, Vol. 1: *Mexico Prehispánico y Colonial*, edited by Rebeca Barriga Villanueva and Pedro Martín Butragueño, pp. 185–205. El Colegio de Mexico, Mexico City.

Gasco, Janine
2003 The polities of Xoconochco. In *The Postclassic Mesoamerican World*, edited by Michael E. Smith and Frances F. Berdan, pp. 50–54. University of Utah Press, Salt Lake City.

Gerhard, Peter
1992 *A Guide to the Historical Geography of New Spain*. Rev. ed. University of Oklahoma Press, Norman.

Harvey, H. R.
1972 The *Relaciones Geográficas*, 1579–1586: Native Languages. In *Handbook of Middle American Indians*, Vol. 12: *Guide to Ethnohistorical Sources, Part One*, edited by Howard F. Cline, pp. 279–323. University of Texas Press, Austin.

Hassig, Ross
1988 *Aztec Warfare: Imperial Expansion and Political Control*. University of Oklahoma Press, Norman.

Justeson, John S., William M. Norman, Lyle Campbell, and Terrence Kaufman
1985 *The Foreign Impact on Lowland Mayan Language and Script*. Middle American Research Institute Publication 53. Tulane University, New Orleans.

Kaufman, Terrence
2001 The History of the Nawa Language Group from Earliest Times to the Sixteenth Century: Some Initial Results. Electronic document, http//www.albany.edu/anthro/maldp/Nawa.pdf.

Kaufman, Terrence, and John Justeson
2007 The History of the Word for Cacao in Ancient Mesoamerica. *Ancient Mesoamerica* 18:193–237.

Litvak King, Jaime
1971 *Cihuatlán y Tepecoacilco, provincias tributarias de México en el siglo XVI*. Instituto de Investigaciones Históricas, National Autonomous University of Mexico, Mexico City.

Macri, Martha
2005 Nahua Loan Words from the Early Classic Period: Words for Cacao Preparation on a Río Azul Ceramic Vessel. *Ancient Mesoamerica* 16:321–326.

Macri, Martha, and Mathew G. Looper
2003 Nahua in Ancient Mesoamerica: Evidence from Maya Inscriptions. *Ancient Mesoamerica* 14:285–297.

Mora-Marin, David F.
2016. Testing the Proto-Mayan-Mije-Sokean hypothesis. *International Journal of American Linguistics* 82:125–180.

Sahagún, Fray Bernardino de
1950–1982 *Florentine Codex: General History of the Things of New Spain*. Translated and edited by Arthur J. O. Anderson and Charles E. Dibble. School of American Research, Santa Fe, NM, and University of Utah Press, Salt Lake City.

Smith, Michael E., and Frances F. Berdan
1996 Appendix 4: Province Descriptions. In *Aztec Imperial Strategies*, edited by Frances F. Berdan, Richard E. Blanton, Elizabeth Hill Boone, Mary G. Hodge, Michael E. Smith, and Emily Umberger, pp. 265–349. Dumbarton Oaks Research Library and Collection, Washington, DC.

Spores, Ronald
1993 Tututepec. *Ancient Mesoamerica* 4:167–175.

Taube, Karl
2000 *The Writing System of Ancient Teotihuacan*. Ancient America I. Center for Ancient American Studies, Washington, DC.

Umberger, Emily
1996 Aztec Presence and Material Remains in the Outer Provinces. In *Aztec Imperial Strategies*, edited by Frances F. Berdan, Richard E. Blanton, Elizabeth Hill Boone, Mary G. Hodge, Michael E. Smith, and Emily Umberger, pp. 151–179. Dumbarton Oaks Research Library and Collection, Washington, DC.

Valiñas, Leopoldo
2010 Historia lingüística: migraciones y asentamientos. Relaciones entre pueblos y lenguas. In *Historia sociolingüística de México*, Vol. I: *México prehispánico y colonial*, edited by Rebeca Barriga Villanueva and Pedro Martín Butragueño, pp. 97–160. El Colegio de México, Mexico City.

Von Mentz, Brigida
2012 Multilingüismo, nahuatización, y toponímia: apuntes etnohistóricos a partir del norte de Guerrero y del comercio a larga distancia. Paper presented at the annual meeting of the Friends of Uto-Aztecan, Cholula, Puebla, August 9–12.

Whittaker, Gordon
1986 The Mexican Names of Three Venus Gods in the Dresden Codex. *Mexicon* 8:56–60.
1988 Aztec Dialectology and the Nahuatl of the Friars. In *The Work of Bernardino de Sahagun, Pioneer Ethnographer of Sixteenth-Century Aztec Mexico*, edited by J. J. Klor de Alva, H. B. Nicholson, and E. Quinones Keber, pp. 321–339. Institute for Mesoamerican Studies, State University of New York, Albany.
2012 The Names of Teotihuacan. *Mexicon* 34(3):55–58.

Wichmann, Søren
1998 A Conservative Look at Diffusion Involving Mixe-Zoquean Languages. In *Archaeology and Language II: Correlating Archaeological and Linguistic Hypotheses*, edited by Roger Blench and Matthew Spriggs, pp. 297–323. Routledge, London.
2010 Comment on Kaufman and Justeson, "The History of the Word for Cacao in Ancient Mesoamerica." *Ancient Mesoamerica* 21:437–441.

CHAPTER 10

AZTEC STATE-MAKING, POLITICS, AND EMPIRES
The Triple Alliance

LANE F. FARGHER, RICHARD E. BLANTON,
AND VERENICE Y. HEREDIA ESPINOZA

The transition from the Classic to Postclassic (ca. A.D. 650–950) in central Mexico brought profound changes in political structure, economy, technology, and culture. This important archaeological sequence poses many interesting questions and has engaged the energies and talents of an army of archaeologists and ethnohistorians, in part owing to the fact that by studying it we gain a window onto those social and cultural processes that have shaped premodern complex societies. Additionally, researchers recognize the region's significant impact on the development of the Mexican nation-state and before that on the history of many prehispanic Mesoamerican peoples.

To understand the origins of the Postclassic society is challenging in no small part owing to the fact that, in spite of years of research by devoted and capable archaeologists, there are still many aspects of Classic period Teotihuacan that we do not understand. In addition, the transitional period after Teotihuacan's collapse (which occurred ca. A.D. 550/650) has proven to be an exceedingly complex one, involving probable phases of inter- and intraregional migration, multiple ethnic groups and historical figures, a changing suite of dominant centers and the polities and alliances between them, and changing ceramic styles and regional commercial systems. Recent research at Postclassic Teotihuacan itself (Garraty 2000) and other centers with Classic to Postclassic histories such as Cerro Portezuelo (Nichols 2013; Nichols et al. 2013), coupled with work to refine ceramic sequences (e.g., Crider 2011), augment earlier information from excavations and survey archaeology to provide a wealth of empirical information, which is summarized in other chapters of this book but still leaves many unanswered questions.

Complementing archaeological work, central Mexico is endowed with an abundance of Postclassic ethnohistoric documents that provide emic accounts of the histories of

Nahuatl-speaking peoples and their struggles to build polities and eventually to establish the Aztec Empire. Based on the aboriginal texts, historians document how fierce Chichimec warriors arrived in Central Mexico in the twelfth century (Carrasco Pizana 1971b; Davies 1980; Smith 1984), eventually adopting an agricultural, sedentary, urban, and literate lifestyle from their Toltec predecessors, while the marriages of leading Chichimec families to Toltec nobility granted them legitimate political authority in their local domains. Migration histories have tended to dominate many discussions of Aztec political history, but this literature provides limited theoretical insights on how state-building and imperial ambitions could be realized. Although some authors have pointed to evidence for historical authenticity of mythic-historical accounts (e.g., Beekman and Christensen 2003; see descriptions in Berdan 2005:2, 3, 7 and Smith 1984), we doubt their value for developing social and cultural theories of change.

Side-by-side with ethnohistoric work, anthropologists have proposed institutional theories that address change in comparative and theoretical senses. Institutional research tries to get at how the "rules of the game" influenced social behavior and how these rules changed over time. Institutional analysis investigates change at varying spatial scales of household, community, market, polity, and world economy, asking questions such as: What were the basic building blocks of society at the household and community level, and how were they constituted? What was recognized as legitimate governance, and how did it vary in space and change through time? How were economies socially and culturally constructed?

Two main kinds of institutional theory-building have been applied in relation to the Central Mexican Postclassic period (A.D. 950–1521). One is a strongly cultural-ecological approach (e.g., Sanders et al. 1979) that identifies population growth and resource stress as key engines of social change. Individuals or groups able to manipulate water management systems and economic redistribution, and were successful at warfare, were able to exercise political and economic power, following the kinds of arguments made by cultural materialists such as Carneiro (1970), Flannery (1972, 1999), Haas (1982), Wittfogel (1957), and Wolf (1999). Sanders and Price (1968:186–187, 192–193) provide a clear example of the theory's main argument: a framework with a clear historical link to Marx's discredited Asiatic Mode of Production concept (e.g., Isaac 1993), which tends to see premodern states as powerful autocracies ruled by god-kings.

Data resulting from the massive archaeological surveys that were stimulated by this research design, however, did not lend support to the cultural ecological arguments (e.g., Blanton et al. 1993:ch. 4; Brumfiel 1976, 1983). The theory also failed to account for the growth of a vast regional-scale Postclassic commercial system whose territorial reach far exceeded the scale of the constituent local polities, very much unlike the prior Teotihuacan system. Ecological theory also failed to account for the fact that the political formations of the Postclassic departed in many instances from the "Asiatic type", and, in fact, were quite variable and, we think, more productively explained in terms of collective action theory than Asiatic theory (Blanton and Fargher 2008; Fargher and Blanton 2012; Fargher et al. 2011). For example, some states, including Tlaxcallan and the core polities of the Aztec imperial system, made use of power sharing and extensive controls over political officials, while states in parts of eastern Puebla tilted more in the direction of despotic governance (Fargher et al. 2011).

Along these lines, Blanton and his colleagues (1993:212–217) offered an alternative to the ecological theory. This more regional-specific theory posited that, following Teotihuacan's collapse, groups strategized to maintain acceptable levels of social functioning in the absence of a unitary governing structure, and in the process they developed new institutions that placed more emphasis on the construction of viable and self-regulating market systems (Blanton et al. 1993). This theory, like the ecological theory, failed to predict cross-polity variation but has the advantage that it provided a window onto a key aspect of Postclassic social formations that differed strongly from the Teotihuacan system. This change entailed the emergence of a highly organized regional-scale system of marketplaces and the corresponding rise of a powerful paragovernmental institution, the Pochteca organization, that provided regulatory governance, apart from the state, not only in the conduct of foreign trade but also in the daily management of the major marketplaces of central Mexico. In what follows, we elaborate on Blanton et al.'s theory by describing in more detail the nature of the Postclassic Basin polities, which we place within the framework of the history and ideas about market evolution.

Aztec State Formation Phase I: The Altepetl

Structure of the Altepetl

The fundamental unit of Aztec political organization during the Postclassic period was the *altepetl*, the native independent state found in the Basin of Mexico and Morelos. Its structure is best described as consisting of four elements: a dynastic ruler (*tlahtoani*), a patron deity, a market, and multiple ranked social groups, the *tlaxilacaltin* (García Sánchez 2005:84; Hodge 1991, 1996; Lockhart 1992:14–16, 185; Monzón Estrada 1949:57; Schroeder 1991:144–145, 1994, Smith 2003:148, 2008:89; van Zantwijk 1985; Williams 1991). The *tlahtoani* (speaker) was the chief administrative official who "... symbolized the unity of the altepetl, acted as the voice of that altepetl in relations with other *altepetl*, and was the focal point for political integration of the constituent tlaxilacaltin" (Fargher et al. 2011:307); he lived in a sumptuous palace (*tecpan*), which was the seat for the *altepetl*'s administrative activities that included policing, judging, and tax collection (Calnek 1976:295; Carrasco Pizana 1971b:365; Offner 1983:169–170; Sanders and Price 1968:153; Smith 2003:148). While the *altepetl* always had these main features, there was variation in organizational specifics in different locations. For example, in those *altepetl* that featured a relatively heterarchical or collective structure, the heads of the constituent *tlaxilacaltin* formed a ruling council that deliberated on important decisions with the *tlahtoani* and elected the *tlahtoani*'s successor from among his male relatives (Davies

1987:108–109; Durán 1994:75–76, 264; Schroeder 1991, 1994:264–266; Smith 2003:149; van Zantwijk 1985:97).

All free individuals, including commoners (*macehualtin*), nobles (*pipiltin*), and even the *tlahtoani*, were members of one of the *altepetl's tlaxilacaltin*. Tlaxilcaltin were highly complex corporate groups ruled by a hereditary noble head (*teuctlitlatoani*) and, in some cases, a council of elders (Lockhart 1992:16; Monzón Estrada 1949:47; Offner 1983:169; see also Zorita 1963:105–109). They were specialized and carried out specific functions, such as land management, tax collection, and policing (Lockhart 1992:17; Williams 1991; Williams and Harvey 1997). In the case of *tlaxilacalli* lands, elders, together with the aid of *altepelt* officials called *tlalhuehuetque* (land elders), oversaw the measurement of land and the preparation of indigenous pictorial cadastral registers, decided on the distribution of land, approved sales, and settled conflicts over ownership (Lockhart 1992:142–163; Williams 1984, 1991:201, 204). They also invested heavily in physical infrastructure, constructing a plaza with a *tecpan*, a temple dedicated to the *tlaxilacalli's* patron deity, and (in some cases) a *tepochcalli* (school) at the center of the *tlaxilacalli* (Calnek 1976:297; Carrasco Pizana 1971a:33; Lockhart 1992:142–163; Reyes García 1996:44; Smith 2008:90, 119, Figure 6.1; Williams 1991:201, 204; van Zantwijk 1985:25).

The diverse specializations and autonomous functions of each *tlaxilacaltin* had the additional social function of partitioning duties and responsibilities in such a way that *tlaxilacaltin* had to cooperate in order for the *altepetl* to function (Lockhart 1992; van Zantwijk 1985:25). Such cooperation would have been pivotal for integrating members of the different *tlaxilacaltin* and to minimize intra-*altepetl* conflict. Social integration was also reinforced through participation in large-scale rituals conducted in the central plaza and associated central temple.

Evolution of the Altepetl

Continuity from Teotihuacan, we suggest, is an important factor to consider to better understand the origins of the Postclassic *altepetl*. We think it is important to note that ethnohistoric descriptions of migrating Chichimecs reveal highly sophisticated corporate groups like the *tlaxilacalli* that we would not expect to find in the context of desert-adapted hunter-gatherers (see van Zantwijk 1985). Other cultural features described in these same documents are consistent with *tlaxilacalli*, including a ruling household and patron deity. We propose that the relatively complex institutions evident in ethnohistoric documents can be accounted for by tracing them to much early developments in Teotihuacan. Specifically, a close examination of Teotihuacan apartment compounds and ethnohistorically described *tlaxilacalli* reveals interesting similarities between the two:

1. The materialization of both involved a communal or public space (e.g., principal courtyard or plaza) (Calnek 1976:297; Carrasco Pizana 1971a:33; Jarquín Pacheco and Martínez Vargas 1982; Manzanilla 1996:233; Séjourné 1966; Sempowski 1994; Smith 2008).

2. In both, a central temple or shrine in the public space functioned to reinforce a shared group identity involving the veneration of a patron deity or group ancestors (Calnek 1976:297; Carrasco Pizana 1971a:33; Manzanilla 1996; Séjourné 1966; Sempowski 1994; Smith 2008; Storey 1991). Interestingly, archaeological research suggests that venerated ancestors were exhumed and carried as relics (bundles) when corporate groups migrated out of Teotihuacan, and Postclassic/Colonial codices depict migrating Nahua *tlaxilacaltin* carrying bundles that contained their deities or deified ancestors (Manzanilla 2002:62; van Zantwijk 1985:38, Figure 3.1, 103, Figure 5.2). Ethnohistoric sources indicate that *tlaxilacalli* members developed a shared religious identity around their patron deity and participated in *tlaxilacalli*-wide rituals (Lockart 1992:142–163, 203–204; Reyes García 1996:44; Smith 2003:229–233, 2008:170–172).
3. In both cases, group members often shared an occupational specialization (Alva Ixtlilxochitl 1965, Vol. 2; Evans 1990:120–121; Gómez Chávez 1996; Manzanilla 1996; Millon 1973; Monzón Estrada 1949; Nichols 1994:182–184; Smith 2003:94–98; Spence 1981; Storey and Widmer 1999; cf. Brumfiel 1980, 1986; Carrasco Pizana 1971b).
4. Both were internally stratified, with commoners and elites belonging to the same corporate group (Carrasco Pizana 1976; Lockhart 1992:16; Manzanilla 1996; Monzón Estrada 1949:51, 63; Sempowski 1994; Storey 1991; van Zantwijk 1985:16–17; Williams 1991:200, 206).
5. Finally, although neither was a clan or other type of kinship organization, both showed residential stability over generations and, thus, strong biological relationships among some group members residing in separate households (Manzanilla 1996; Spence 1974; van Zantwijk 1985:16).

While we argue that a *tlaxilacalli*-scale organizational unit represented to some degree a carryover from the Teotihuacan apartment compound, still Epiclassic (A.D. 650–950) to Postclassic (A.D. 950–1521) social and cultural change was not entirely a continuation of the larger Teotihuacan system; for example, no city was ever constructed as a duplicate of Teotihuacan with its orthogonal street plan, although Tula displays some similarities in this regard (Mastache et al. 2002:Figure 6.9), and the eventual Aztec capital, Tenochtitlan, also features a partially orthogonal (gridded) street Plan. Postclassic social formations maintained the essential features of basal-level multifamily organization, while new social arrangements, which were unlike Teotihuacan's, forged these smaller units into towns, cities, polities, and alliances of multiple polities. Although many aspects of Teotihuacan social organization remain a mystery, we would suggest Postclassic change is found principally in the elaboration of two institutions that served to integrate local-scale units into larger cohesive social wholes, namely inherited leadership in the form of the office of *tlahtoani* and its associated royal and palace symbolism, on the one hand, and a growing degree of regional-scale market integration on the other.

The emergence of a royal lineage associated with the governance of society may have been a significant departure from the Teotihuacan political order; if a royal line were present at Teotihuacan, it was not materialized as it was by the end of the Postclassic period, with its well-developed symbolism and clear evidence for palaces. However, the Postclassic origins of royal rule and other Postclassic institutions are not clear. Tula, Hidalgo (ca. A.D. 950–1150), is cited in the ethnohistoric sources as an ancient center of Toltec royalty in a period preceding the Aztec Empire, but it is still not definite that the Early Postclassic city had a palace or palaces (although see Báez Urincho 2007). Tula might have been a locus of change, however, in another key respect. Although it is not possible to claim that the important Postclassic deity Tezcatlipoca was invented at Tula, still, it is the case that the first representation of this god is found on Pyramid B there, associated with a frieze depicting a procession of merchants and thus with Tula's "business narrative" as interpreted by Kristan-Graham (1993). (We discuss the role of Tezcatlipoca adoration below.)

We suggest that the characteristic form of Postclassic state-building occurred hand-in-hand with a growing commercial economy. While it is likely (but not demonstrated) that Teotihuacan's Great Compound was the city's central marketplace, local-scale marketplaces in or outside the main center have not been securely identified, and the larger question of the role of commercialization in Teotihuacan's economy remains largely unanswered (Carballo 2013). By contrast, we see markets as having played a key role in the social transformation leading to the Aztec state and the *altepetl* structure. Interestingly, as we described, each *altepetl* featured its own distinct marketplace, which members of the various constituent *tlaxilacalli* patronized. *Altepetl* marketplaces point to a novel form of social cohesiveness operating at the polity scale, and markets were also institutions with the capacity to provide social linkages at regional scales, as some well-situated marketplaces prospered and served not only as regional organizational nodes but also could become important sources of revenue for the emerging governing institutions (e.g., Blanton 1996).

Any turn to an emphasis on commercial integration poses potential benefits to polity members but also new forms of organizational challenge. Markets are a domain of human social intercourse replete with potential cooperation problems that require institution-building to enhance the degree of trust that markets will be safe and that all participants will be treated fairly and equally irrespective of gender, status, or ethnic affiliation (Blanton 2013; Blanton with Fargher 2016). Local-scale markets are not organizationally problematic because most market participants know each other. "Open" markets that can attract a more diverse clientele beyond the local population and thus are able to serve the interests of market participants and the governing elite (as sources of revenue) require more institutional development for effective market management, including the maintenance of fair practices, public safety, and effective and fair adjudication of market disputes. In this connection it is interesting to note that in historically and ethnographically documented "open" marketplaces, market managers often "piggyback" markets onto religiously important places, facilities, and figures so as to gain the benefits of religious notions in their construction of a trustworthy and thus, hopefully, prosperous marketplace (Blanton 2013).

The spatial and social organization of the *altepetl* fits very nicely with this market-building scenario. The focus of the *altepetl* was an open and accessible but formal space, the plaza, where markets and *altepetl*-wide rituals and festivals occurred, bounded by the *altepetl's* central temple and *tecpan* (Fargher et al. 2011:309–312; Smith 2008). Although this central complex was often located within the territory of one *tlaxilacalli*, it was socially and physically accessible to all *altepetl* residents (Lockhart 1992:105), and major markets served large territories beyond the *altepetl*. The construction of the *altepetl's* central pyramid along one side of the central plaza gave the marketplace the status of sacred ground. In this way state-builders fashioned an inclusive and collective political structure around power sharing among a *tlahtoani* and a governing council consisting of the heads of the constituent *tlaxilacaltin* to offer impartiality in (market) governance, as well as legal recognition of property rights (Fargher and Heredia Espinoza 2012; Fargher et al. 2011).

Aztec State Formation Phase II: Confederacies and Empires

Confederacies

Open markets thrive when consumers have destination choices regarding price, selection, and location; when they trust they will receive equal treatment in commodity transactions and in adjudication; and when they trust that market activities can occur in safe venues. Moreover, we can safely postulate that political architects would have been highly interested in promoting market expansion because it would have provided increased state revenues (see Anderson et al. 1976; Blanton 1996:78; Hicks 1987). We suggest the open market process drives institutional change, one of which, we suggest, is the establishment of confederacies of states that would have the effect of reducing disruptive interpolity conflict and dissolving ethnic and political boundaries to enhance the potential for free movement between multiple market destinations.

It is interesting to note that the immediate post-Teotihuacan Epiclassic period (A.D. 650–950) featured a high level of both political and economic fragmentation at the regional scale (summarized in Nichols et al. 2013:59–60, 63). Beginning during the Early Postclassic period (A.D. 950–1150), however, the fragmented pattern began to change, as is evident by an increase in ceramic exchange at the regional scale, and the process of region-wide economic integration was even more notable by the Late Postclassic (A.D. 1350–1521; see Blanton 1996). It was during the same period of growing regional-scale economic activity, probably sometime during Aztec II (ca. A.D. 1150–1350) and Early Aztec III (ca. A.D. 1350–1428; see Nichols and Rodríquez-Alegría [this volume] for a discussion of ceramic types and chronology), that confederacies (*tlayacatl*) resulted in heterarchical political structures in the southern Basin. In the case of Culhuacan, Xochimilco, and Cuitlahuac, previously independent *altepetl* ostensibly fused into larger *tlayacatl* ruled by multiple *tlatoque*, who resided in the *tlayacatl's* capital (Hodge

1996:32; Smith 2003:44). According to ethnohistoric information, each *tlahtoani* administered an individual domain, which probably corresponded with each formerly independent *altepetl* (Hodge 1996:32). Although all of these *tlatoque* are named as rulers, one apparently led the *tlayacatl* in diplomacy and warfare (Hodge 1996:32). In the case of Chalco, the situation was yet more complicated. This "confederacy" consisted of four loosely allied *tlayacatin*, each with its own capital, Tlalmanalco, Amaquemecan, Tenanco, and Chimalhuacan (Lockhart 1992:23–24; see Chimalpahin [Schroeder 1994] for details). In turn, each of these four *tlayacatin* were tightly bound units each ruled by multiple *tlatoque* (Lockhart 1992:24). The ethnohistoric record provides only limited details regarding the decisions that resulted in the formation of these *tlayacatin*; however, violent conflicts among disparate "ethnic groups" are referenced repeatedly throughout the chronicles (e.g., *Codice Xolotl* [Dibble 1951]; Alva Ixtlilxochitl 1965). Thus, an interest in reducing interpolity conflict was probably a significant concern in the development of *tlayacatl* (Hodge 1984).

Pre-Imperial Empires: Tepaneca and Acolhua

During this same period (Aztec II—Early Aztec III: ca. A.D. 1150–1428), political evolution along the eastern and western edges of Lake Texcoco took a decidedly different course. In these subregions, larger hierarchical or "imperial" polities were primarily constructed through conquest, but marriage alliances were also important. On the eastern side of the lake, Coatlinchan-Huexotla emerged as the head of the Acolhua domain (Parsons 1971:218). However, by Aztec III (ca. A.D. 1350–1521), population growth had filled in the landscape and additional centers emerged, stimulating a struggle for control of the Acolhua domain. According to the chroniclers, Nezahualcoyotl, the *tlahtoani* of Texcoco, ultimately triumphed (van Zantwijk 1985). After consolidating Acolhuacan, he expanded his political control over much of the eastern Basin through conquest. In general, he left the political structure of the conquered *altepetl* intact and required only tribute payments; but in other cases, he did intervene in the political process and appointed *tlatoque* (Hodge 1996:34; Offner 1983).

The western Basin or Tepaneca domain experienced an even more tumultuous and violent history. One of the first important states was Xaltocan, an Otomi capital, which was defeated by Cuauhtitlan in 1395 and abandoned, after a protracted conflict (see *Anales de Cuauhtitlan* 2011). Further south, in about 1347, Azcapotzalco began consolidating the Tepaneca domain with a crucial victory over Culhuacan. Afterward, it began attacking Chalco, (a reoccupied) Xaltocan, Cuauhtitlan, and Tepozotlan (Gibson 1964:16). By the early fifteenth century, through a combination of decisive military victories and astute marriage alliances, the *tlahtoani* of Azcapotzalco, Tezozomoc, emerged as the suzerain of the Tepaneca domain. Once this subregion had been consolidated, he attacked and conquered Texcoco (Acolhualcan), bringing the Basin under a single government for the first time since Teotihuacan's collapse (van Zantwijk 1985:106). The defeated ruler of Texcoco (Nezahualcoyotl) was forced into exile for a brief period before his mother and aunts prevailed upon Tezozomoc to let him return to his palace in Texcoco (van Zantwijk 1985:107). In the Tepaneca domain, conquered *altepetl* were also left intact and forced to pay tribute to Tezozomoc and his allies, who were granted administrative and tribute rights (e.g., the rulers of Tlatelolco, Tenochtitlan, Coatlichan, Otumba, Acolman and Chalco; van Zantwijk 1985:106).

Overall, the period from the Middle Postclassic (A,D. 1150–1350) through the early Late Postclassic (A,D, 1350–1428) saw population growth and the consolidation of small independent *altepetl* into "subregional" political blocks primarily through either "confederation" (cooperation) or conquest (coercion); however, in the more exclusionary states marriage alliances were used to motivate cooperation among powerful dynasties. Archaeological data indicate that together with this consolidation, market integration expanded within the major domains (Tepaneca, Acolhua, and Lake Xochimilco-Chalco subregion; Blanton 1996; Minc 2006; Nichols et al. 2002).

Aztec Triple Alliance: Tenochtitlan-Texcoco-Tlacopan

Three Tenochca-Mexica relatives, Itzcoatl, Motecuhzoma, and Tlacaelel[1] and their Acolhua cousin, Nezahualcoyotl, masterminded the formation of one of the largest and most important empires in the Prehispanic history of Mesoamerica: the Aztec Triple Alliance (see van Zantwijk 1985:ch. 5). In 1426 Tezozomoc died, and a succession dispute erupted among his heirs. In this dispute, Maxtla, a son of Tezozomoc who was interested in centralizing power and reducing the growing military and political power of Tenochtitlan, defeated the heir apparent. Then, sometime between 1427 and 1428, Itzcoatl, Motecuhzoma, and Tlacaelel, concerned with Maxtla's attempts to directly control Tenochtitlan politically, and Nezahualcoyotl, who wanted to free Acolhuacan, devised the blueprint for their alliance. They first gained control of the Tenochca state; Itzcoatl became the new *tlahtoani*, Motecuhzoma became the chief military official, and Tlacaelel became the *cihuacoatl* (chief of internal administration) of Tenochtitlan. Then, together with Nezahualcoyotl and Tlacopan, and a host of allies, they attacked Azcapotzalco. When the dust settled, Tenochtitlan and Texcoco (Tlacopan's participation was essentially symbolic and Tenochtitlan quickly asserted control over its "territory") essentially controlled the Basin of Mexico, except for the Xochimilco-Chalco region, which had to be laboriously reconquered. Importantly, it is clear from this historical description that Nezahualcoyotl was a key figure in the development of the empire (van Zantwijk 1985:107, 109). Thus, Tenochtitlan and Texcoco were partners. They neither functioned independently nor was their relationship antagonistic; in addition, the Aztec Triple Alliance is clearly real and not a fictional entity conjured up post hoc as some authors have suggested (Gillespie 1998). It is best described as a federacy, which is defined as a political formation in which separate states (the Tenochca-Mexica and Acolhua states in this case) united under a single sovereign power (the *tlatocan* in this case), but each retained management of its local affairs (Fargher and Blanton 2007:869). This organization coupled with imperial expansion created highly complex and hard to understand strategies for the distribution of tribute and federacy-wide policy (see Berdan et al. 1996).

Although it is difficult to discern from the documents, Tlacaelel was apparently the chief architect in the development of a new kind of government following the defeat of Azcapotzalco and the establishment of the Aztec Triple Alliance as the dominant power in the Basin of Mexico. The strategies employed by Tlacaelel to build the Triple Alliance state included (see Fargher and Blanton 2007:869–871 for bibliographic details):

1. The promotion of a corporate ideology based in the philosophy of the mythic history of Tollan, which was first symbolically represented at Tula, Hidalgo. This philosophy featured a duality between a concept of noble privilege associated with Quetzalcoatl and an egalitarian notion that challenged noble privilege associated with Huemac and his god Tezcatlipoca. The egalitarian ideal emphasized the importance of evaluating individuals based on merit rather than on ascripted status (Fargher et al. 2010).
2. The polity was implemented through a combination of hierarchy, manifested in the bureaucratization of the political administration, and heterarchy, expressed through the integration of functionally diverse social groups based on patterns of structural oppositions and complementarity (van Zantwijk's [1985] "Aztec Arrangement"). An important feature of this system was the development of ritual cycles, "carried out in symbolically charged precincts" (van Zantwijk 1985: 213–216, 261) set apart from rulers' palaces (Blanton et al. 1996:11).
3. The establishment of a moral code that set clear limitations on the ruler's treatment of constituents and how imperial revenues could be handled, as well as specifying the ruler's obligations to the body politic (Davies 1987:103, 124). This moral code also included an emphasis on equal justice regardless of social class or position (a code that was strictly enforced through a codified civil and criminal code, a sophisticated court system, and effective policing).
4. The vesting of governing authority in a combination of councils and a hierarchy of bureaucratic officials. The supreme ruling authority was a council called the *tlatocan* (imperial council). The inner *tlatocan* consisted of the three *tlatoque* of Tenochtitlan (the *hueyi* or great *tlahtoani*), Texcoco, and Tlacopan; the *cihuacoatl* of Tenochtitlan; and the four prime ministers (one of whom was a commoner; van Zantwijk 1985:111, 112, 117; see also Durán 1994). The outer *tlatocan* included these officials plus "all of the lords of the empire," which probably refers to the chief bureaucratic officials and *tlaxilacalli* heads (Durán 1994: 208, 209, 253; van Zantwijk 1985: 117–119; see Offner 1983 for Texcoco: Table 6.1). The *tlatocan* had the power to monitor, castigate, or remove any official including the *hueyi tlahtoani*, which it apparently did on three different occasions (Davies 1987:110; Durán 1994:307, 371; van Zantwijk 1985:88). It also intervened in the selection of the new *hueyi tlahtoani* and elected this official from among the eligible princes. There were additional councils at lower levels in the hierarchy, including the

council of the *cihuacoatl* and the council of Acolhuacan (Davies 1987:117; Offner 1983:56–57, 60, 83, 155, 157, 161; van Zantwijk 1985:120–122).

5. The bureaucratization of political administration through a shift to the appointment of officials based in part on merit and training in the *calmecac* (special schools), specialization of duties and responsibilities, heading departments with both a commoner and an élite official, appointments for short periods (one or two years) in low-level positions, frequent and effective evaluation of bureaucratic performance, and the use of an *appanage*[2] system to remunerate officials (Fargher and Blanton 2007:871). Bureaucratic departments were created, including a centralized tax collection service (*calpixcacalli*), a hierarchical judicial system with professional judges, a state police department, and tribunals to hear complaints against the state and its officials.

6. The extensive distribution of public goods, especially in Tenochtitlan-Tlatelolco but also to some degree in areas outside the capital. State-funded public goods included the construction and maintenance of roads, bridges, and causeways; the construction of the dike of Nezahualcoyotl, aqueducts, and parks (in Tenochtitlan-Tlatelolco); the construction of large-scale drainage canals and dikes in the southern *chinampa* zone; and public security (Armillas 1948, 1971; Cortés 1986:103; Davies 1987:117, 137, 153; Durán 1994:110–111, 210, 365; Offner 1983; Parsons 1991:40; Parsons et al. 1985:88; Sanders and Price 1968:153, 177; van Zantwijk 1985:121, 276, 283; Zorita 1994: 111–112, 157, 160).

This governing strategy was implemented around A.D. 1430 and remained relatively unchanged until about A.D. 1515. In the final years before the Spanish Conquest, the highly collective system designed by Tlacaelel came under threat as Motecuhzoma Xocoyotzin promoted an elitist policy and expelled commoners from the upper levels of the bureaucracy (see Durán 1994). At about the same time, a succession dispute erupted in Acolhuacan that seriously undermined the power of this state and later contributed to the success of the Spanish in recruiting allies in the eastern Basin. Interestingly, a thorough reading of the Chronicle X (Durán 1994) leaves the reader with the impression that from the native point of view the Spanish Conquest was a punishment set upon the Aztec (especially Motecuhzoma as the *hueyi tlahtoani*) by the gods for abandoning the egalitarian vision of Huemac.

Notes

1. Tlacaelel is an enigmatic figure in Aztec ethnohistory. Given the length of time that he was physically active in politics and warfare (until age 120), this name probably represents a composite of two or three generations of individuals that held the office of *cihuacoatl* and took the same name, creating a faceless or symbolic quality to this political position. Such a symbolic aspect is consistent in many ways with the political policies advanced by Tlacaelel. To address this issue to some degree, the individual described

here is identified as the first of the name (Tlacaelel I) (Davies 1987:49–50; van Zantwijk 1985:187–188).

2. Officials were assigned income produced by a set amount of land held by the imperial government and cultivated through the tax-collecting bureaucracy; they received only the produce of these lands and never directly controlled them or regarded them as personal or family property as in the case of a benefice or prebend.

References Cited

Alva Ixtlilxochitl, Fernando de
1965 *Obras históricas*, Vol. 2. Edited by Alfredo Chavero. Editorial Nacional, Mexico City.

Anales de Cuauhtitlan
2011 *Anales de Cuauhtitlan*. Paleography and Translation by Rafael Tena. Dirección General de Publicaciones del Consejo Nacional para la Cultura y las Artes, Mexico City.

Anderson, Arthur J., Frances Berdan, and James Lockhart
1976 *Beyond the Codices: The Nahua View of Colonial Mexico*. University of California Press, Berkeley.

Armillas, Pedro
1948 A Sequence of Cultural Development in Meso-America. In *A Reappraisal of Peruvian Archaeology*, edited by Wendell C. Bennet, pp. 105–111. Society for American Archaeology Memoirs, Washington, DC.
1971 Gardens in Swamps. *Science* 174:653–661.

Báez Urincho, Fernando
2007 El Edificio 4: palacio del Rey Tolteca. *Arqueología Mexicana* 15(85):51–54.

Beekman, Christopher S., and Alexander F. Christensen
2003 Controlling for Doubt and Uncertainty Through Multiple Lines of Evidence: A New Look at the Mesoamerican Nahua Migrations. *Journal of Archaeological Method and Theory* 10(2):111–164.

Berdan, Frances F.
2005 *The Aztecs of Central Mexico: An Imperial Society*. Wadsworth, Belmont, CA.

Berdan, Frances F., Richard E. Blanton, Elizabeth Hill Boone, Mary G. Hodge, Michael E. Smith, and Emily Umberger (editors)
1996 *Aztec Imperial Strategies*. Dumbarton Oaks Research Library and Collection, Washington, DC.

Blanton, Richard E.
1996 The Basin of Mexico Market System and the Growth of Empire. In *Aztec Imperial Strategies*, edited by Frances F. Berdan, Richard E. Blanton, Elizabeth Hill Boone, Mary G. Hodge, Michael E. Smith, and Emily Umberger, pp. 47–84. Dumbarton Oaks Research Library and Collection, Washington, DC.
2013 Cooperation and the Moral Economy of the Marketplace. In *Merchants, Markets, and Exchange in the Pre-Columbian World*, edited by Kenneth G. Hirth and Joanne Pillsbury, pp. 23–48. Dumbarton Oaks Research Library and Collection, Washington, DC.

Blanton, Richard E., and Lane F. Fargher
2008 *Collective Action in the Formation of Pre-Modern States*. Springer, New York.

Blanton, Richard E., with Lane F. Fargher
2016 *How Humans Cooperate: Confronting the Challenges of Collective Action*. The University Press of Colorado, Boulder.

Blanton, Richard E., Gary M. Feinman, Stephen A. Kowalewski, and Peter N. Peregrine
1996 A Dual-Processual Theory for the Evolution of Mesoamerican Civilization. *Current Anthropology* 37(1):1–14, 65–68.

Blanton, Richard E., Stephen A. Kowalewski, Gary M. Feinman, and Laura M. Finsten
1993 *Ancient Mesoamerica: A Comparison of Change in Three Regions*, 2nd ed. Cambridge University Press, New York.

Brumfiel, Elizabeth M.
1976 *Specialization and Exchange at the Late Postclassic (Aztec) Community of Huexotla, Mexico*. PhD dissertation, Department of Anthropology, University of Michigan, Ann Arbor.

1980 Specialization, Market Exchange, and the Aztec State: A View from Huexotla. *Current Anthropology* 21(4):459–478.

1983 Aztec State Making: Ecology, Structure, and the Origin of the State. *American Anthropologist* 85:261–284.

1986 The Division of Labor at Xico: The Chipped Stone Industry. In *Economic Aspects of Prehispanic Highland Mexico*, edited by Barry L. Isaac, pp. 245–279. Research in Economic Anthropology Supplement 2. JAI Press, Greenwich, CT.

Calnek, Edward E.
1976 The Internal Structure of Tenochtitlan. In *The Valley of Mexico: Studies in Pre-Hispanic Ecology and Society*, edited by Eric R. Wolf, pp. 287–302. University of New Mexico Press, Albuquerque.

Carballo, David M.
2013 The Social Organization of Craft Production and Interregional Exchange at Teotihuacan. In *Merchants, Markets, and Exchange in the Pre-Columbian World*, edited by Kenneth G. Hirth and Joanne Pillsbury, pp. 113–140. Dumbarton Oaks Research Library and Collection, Washington, DC.

Carneiro, Robert
1970 A Theory of Origin of the State. *Science* 169:733–738.

Carrasco Pizana, Pedro
1971a Los barrios antiguos de Cholula. *Estudios y Documentos de la Región de Puebla-Tlaxcala* 3:9–88.

1971b Social Organization of Ancient Mexico. In *Handbook of Middle American Indians*, Vol. 10, edited by Gordon F. Ekholm and Ignacio Bernal, pp. 349–375. Archaeology of Northern Mesoamerica. University of Texas Press, Austin.

1976 Los linajes nobles de México antiguo. In *Estratificación Social en la Mesoamérica Prehispánica*, edited by Carrasco Pizana P. and Johanna Broda, pp. 19–36. Centro de Investigaciones Superiores, Instituto Nacional de Antropología e Historia, Mexico City.

Cortés, Hernán
1986 *Letters from Mexico*. Translated by Anthony Pagden. Yale University Press, New Haven, CT.

Crider, Destiny
2011 Epiclassic and Early Postclassic Interaction in Central Mexico as Evidenced by Decorated Pottery. Ph.D. dissertation, School of Human Evolution and Social Change, Arizona State University, Tempe.

Davies, Nigel
1980 *The Toltec Heritage: From the Fall of Tula to the Rise of Tenochtitlán*. University of Oklahoma Press, Norman.
1987 *The Aztec Empire: the Toltec Resurgence*. University of Oklahoma Press, Norman.
Dibble, Charles E. (editor)
1951 *Códice Xolotl*. Universidad Nacional Autónoma de México, Instituto de Historia, Mexico City.
Durán, Diego
1994 *The History of the Indies of New Spain*. Translated by Doris Heyden. University of Oklahoma Press, Norman.
Evans, Susan T.
1990 The Productivity of Maguey Terrace Agriculture in Central Mexico During the Aztec Period. *Latin American Antiquity* 1(2):117–132.
Fargher, Lane F., and Richard Blanton
2007 Revenue, Voice and Public Goods in Three Pre-Modern States. *Comparative Studies in Society and History* 49:848–882.
2012 Segmentación y acción colectiva: un acercamiento cultural comparativo sobre la voz y el poder compartido en los estados premodernos. In *El poder compartido. Ensayos sobre la arqueología de organizaciones políticas segmentarias y oligárquicas*, edited by Annick Daneels and Geraldo Gutiérrez Mendoza, pp. 205–235. CIESAS, Mexico City., and El Colegio de Michoacán, Zamora.
Fargher, Lane F., Richard Blanton, and Verenice Y. Heredia Espinosa
2010 Egalitarian Ideology and Political Power in Pre-Hispanic Central Mexico: The Case of Tlaxcallan. *Latin American Antiquity* 21: 227–251.
Fargher, L. F., and Verenice Y. Heredia Espinoza
2012 Ripping up the Stilts: Problematizing Romantic, Ethnocentric Legacies in Mesoamerican Archaeology. Paper presented at the 77th annual meeting of the Society for American Archaeology, Memphis.
Fargher, Lane F., Verenice Y. Heredia Espinoza, and Richard E. Blanton
2011 Alternative Pathways to Power in Late Postclassic Highland Mesoamerica. *Journal of Anthropological Archaeology* 30:306–326.
Flannery, Kent V.
1972 The Cultural Evolution of Civilizations. *Annual Review of Ecology and Systematics* 3:399–426.
1999 Process and Agency in Early State Formation. *Cambridge Archaeological Journal* 9:3–21.
García Sánchez, Magdalena A.
2005 Los que se quedan: las familias de los difuntos en la región de Ocotelulco, Tlaxcala, 1572–1673. Un estudio etnohistórico con base en testamentos indígenas. Ph.D. dissertation, CIESAS, Mexico City.
Garraty, Christopher P.
2000 Ceramic Indices of Aztec Eliteness. *Ancient Mesoamerica* 11:323–340.
Gibson, Charles
1964 *The Aztecs under Spanish Rule: A History of the Indians of the Valley of Mexico, 1519–1810*. Stanford University Press, Stanford, CA.
Gillespie, Susan D.
1998 The Aztec Triple Alliance—A Postconquest Tradition. In *Native Traditions in the Postconquest World*, edited by Elizabeth Hill Boone and Tom Cummins. Dumbarton Oaks Research Library and Collection, Washington, DC.

Gómez-Chávez, Sergio
1996 Unidades de producción artesanal y de residencia en Teotihuacán. Primeros resultados de las exploraciones del frente 3 del Proyecto La Ventilla 1992-94. *Revista Mexicana de Estudios Antropológicos* 42:31-49.

Haas, Jonathan
1982 *The Evolution of the Prehistoric State*. Columbia University Press, New York.

Hicks, Frederic
1987 First Steps toward a Market-Integrated Economy in Aztec Mexico. In *Early State Dynamics*, edited by Henri Claessen and Pieter van de Velde, pp. 91-107. E. J. Brill, Leiden.

Hodge, Mary G.
1984 *Aztec City-States*. Museum of Anthropology, University of Michigan, Ann Arbor.
1991 Land and Lordship in the Valley of Mexico: The Politics of Aztec Provincial Administration. In *Land and Politics in the Valley of Mexico: A Two Thousand-Year Perspective*, edited by Herbert R. Harvey, pp. 113-139. University of New Mexico Press, Albuquerque.
1996 Political Organization of the Central Provinces. In *Aztec Imperial Strategies*, edited by Frances F. Berdan, Richard E. Blanton, Elizabeth H. Boone, Mary G. Hodge, Michael E. Smith, and Emily Umberger, pp. 17-45. Dumbarton Oaks Research Library and Collection, Washington, DC.

Isaac, Barry L.
1993 AMP, HH & OD: Some Comments. In *Economic Aspects of Water Management in the Prehispanic New World*, edited by Vernon L. Scarborough and Barry L. Isaac, pp. 429-471. JAI Press, Greenwich, CT.

Jarquín Pacheco, Ana María, and Enrique Martínez Vargas
1982 Las excavaciones en el Conjunto 1D. In *Memoria del proyecto arqueológico Teotihuacán*, coordinated by Rubén Cabrera, Rodríguez García, and Noel Morelos, pp. 80-82. Arqueología, Colección Científica 132. Instituto Nacional de Antropología e Historia, Mexico City.

Kristan-Graham, Cynthia
1993 The Business of Narrative at Tula: An Analysis of the Vestibule Frieze, Trade, and Ritual. *Latin American Antiquity* 4(1):3-21.

Lockhart, James
1992 *The Nahuas after Conquest: A Social and Cultural History of the Indians of Central Mexico, Sixteenth through Eighteenth Centuries*. Stanford University Press, Stanford, CA.

Manzanilla, Linda
1996 Corporate Groups and Domestic Activities at Teotihuacan. *Latin American Antiquity* 7:228-246.
2002 Houses and Ancestors, Altars and Relics: Mortuary Patterns at Teotihuacan, Central Mexico. In *The Space and Place of Death*, edited by Helaine Silverman and David B. Small, pp. 55-66. Archaeological Papers of the American Anthropological Association 11. Washington, DC.

Mastache de Escobar, Alba Guadalupe, Robert H. Cobean, and Dan M. Healan
2002 *Ancient Tollan: Tula and the Toltec Heartland*. University Press of Colorado, Boulder.

Millon, Rene
1973 *Urbanization at Teotihuacan, Mexico*, Vol. 1: *The Teotihuacan Map, Part 1: Text*. University of Texas Press, Austin.

Minc, Leah D.
2006 Monitoring Regional Market Systems in Prehistory: Models, Methods, and Metrics. *Journal of Anthropological Archaeology* 25(1):82-116.

Monzón Estrada, Arturo
1949 *El Calpulli en la organización social de los tenochca*. Instituto Nacional Indigenista, Mexico City.

Nichols, Deborah L.
1994 The Organization of Provincial Craft Production and the Aztec City State of Otumba. In *Economics and Politics in the Aztec Realm*, edited by Mary G. Hodge and Michael Smith, pp. 175–194. Institute of Mesoamerican Studies, State University of New York, Albany, and University of Texas Press, Austin.
2013 Merchants and Merchandise: The Archaeology of Aztec Commerce at Otumba, Mexico. In *Merchants, Markets, and Exchange in the Pre-Columbian World*, edited by Kenneth G. Hirth and Joanne Pillsbury, pp. 49–84. Dumbarton Oaks Research Library and Collection, Washington, DC.

Nichols, Deborah, Elizabeth Brumfiel, Hector Neff, Mary Hodge, Thomas H. Charlton, and Michael D. Glascock
2002 Neutrons, Markets, Cities and Empires: A 1000-Year Perspective on Ceramic Production and Distribution in the Postclassic Basin of Mexico. *Journal of Anthropological Archaeology* 21:25–82.

Nichols, Deborah, Hector Neff, and George L. Cowgill
2013 Cerro Portezuelo: States and Hinterlands in the Pre-Hispanic Basin of Mexico. *Ancient Mesoamerica* 4(1):47–71.

Offner, Jerome A.
1983 *Law and Politics in Aztec Texcoco*. Cambridge University Press, Cambridge, UK.

Parsons, Jeffrey R.
1971 *Prehistoric Settlement Patterns in the Texcoco Region, Mexico*. University of Michigan, Museum of Anthropology, Ann Arbor.
1991 Political Implications of Prehispanic Chinampa Agriculture in the Valley of Mexico. In *Land and Politics in the Valley of Mexico: A Two Thousand Year Perspective*, edited by Herbert R. Harvey, pp. 17–42. University of New Mexico Press, Albuquerque.

Parsons, Jeffrey R., Mary Parsons, Virginia Popper, and Mary Taft
1985 Chinampa Agriculture and Aztec Urbanization in the Valley of Mexico. In *Prehistoric Intensive Agriculture in the Tropics*, edited by Ian Farrington, pp. 49–96. BAR International Series, BAR, Oxford.

Reyes García, Luis
1996 El término calpulli en documentos del siglo XVI. In *Documentos nauas de la ciudad de México del siglo XVI*, edited by L. Reyes García, pp. 21–68. CIESAS and Archivo General de la Nación, Mexico City.

Sanders, William T., Jeffrey Parsons, and Robert S. Santley
1979 *The Basin of Mexico: Ecological Processes in the Evolution of a Civilization*. Academic Press, New York.

Sanders, William T., and Barbara J. Price
1968 *Mesoamerica: The Evolution of a Civilization*. Random House, New York.

Schroeder, Susan
1991 Indigenous Sociopolitical Organization in Chimalpahin. In *Land and Politics in the Valley of Mexico: A Two Thousand-year Perspective*, edited by Herbert R. Harvey, pp. 141–162. University of New Mexico Press, Albuquerque.
1994 *Chimalpahin y los reinos de Chalco*. Translated by Joaquín F. Zaballa Omaña. El Colegio Mexiquense and Ayuntamiento Constitucional de Chalco, Zinacantepec.

Séjourné, Laurette
1966 *Arquitectura y pintura en Teotihuacán*. Siglo Veintiuno Editore, Mexico City.

Sempowski, Martha L.
1994 Part I: Mortuary Practices at Teotihuacan. In *Mortuary Practices and Skeletal Remains at Teotihuacan,* edited by Martha L. Sempowski and Michael W. Spence, pp. 1–314. Urbanization at Teotihuacan, Mexico 3. University of Utah Press, Salt Lake City.

Smith, Michael E.
1984 The Aztlan Migrations of the Nahuatl Chronicles: Myth or History? *Ethnohistory* 31(3):153–186.
2003 *The Aztecs,* 2nd ed. Blackwell, Malden, MA.
2008 *Aztec City-State Capitals.* University Press of Florida, Gainesville.

Spence, Michael W.
1974 Residential Practices and the Distribution of Skeletal Traits in Teotihuacan, Mexico. *Man* 9(2):262–273.
1981 Obsidian Production and the State in Teotihuacan. *American Antiquity* 46(4):769–788.

Storey, Rebecca
1991 Residential Compound Organization and the Evolution of the Teotihuacán State. *Ancient Mesoamerica* 2(1):107–118.

Storey, Rebecca, and Randolph J. Widmer
1999 The Burials of Tlajinga 33. In *Prácticas funerarias en la ciudad de los dioses: Los enterramientos humanos de la antigua Teotihuacán,* edited by Linda Manzanilla and Carlos Serrano, pp. 203–218. Universidad Nacional Autónoma de México, Instituto de Investigaciones Antropológicas, Mexico City.

van Zantwijk, Rudolf A. M.
1985 *The Aztec Arrangement: The Social History of Pre-Spanish Mexico.* University of Oklahoma Press, Norman.

Williams, Barbara J.
1984 Mexican Pictorial Cadastral Registers: An Analysis of the Códice de Santa María Asunción and the Codex Vergara. In *Explorations in Ethnohistory: Indians of Central Mexico in the Sixteenth Century,* edited by Herbert R. Harvey and Hanns J. Prem, pp. 103–125. University of New Mexico Press, Albuquerque.
1991 The Lands and Political Organization of a Rural Tlaxilacalli in Tepetlaoztoc, c. A.D. 1540. In *Land and Politics in the Valley of Mexico: A Two Thousand-Year Perspective,* edited by Herbert R. Harvey, pp. 187–208. University of New Mexico Press, Albuquerque.

Williams, Barbara J., and Herbert R. Harvey
1997 *The Códice de Santa María Asunción. Facsimile and Commentary: Households and Lands in Sixteenth-Century Tepetlaoztoc.* University of Utah Press, Salt Lake City.

Wittfogel, Karl A.
1957 *Oriental Despotism: A Comparative Study in Total Power.* Yale University Press, New Haven, CT.

Wolf, Eric R.
1999 *Envisioning Power: Ideologies of Dominance and Crisis.* University of California Press, Berkeley.

Zorita, Alonso de
1963 *Life and Labor in Ancient Mexico: The Brief and Summary Relation of the Lords of New Spain.* Translated by Benjamin Keen. Rutgers University Press, New Brunswick, NJ.
1994 *Life and Labor in Ancient Mexico: The Brief and Summary Relation of the Lords of New Spain.* Translated by Benjamin Keen. University of Oklahoma Press, Norman.

CHAPTER 11

NAHUA THOUGHT AND THE CONQUEST

MICHEL R. OUDIJK AND
MARÍA CASTAÑEDA DE LA PAZ

Sources

ONE of the serious problems for the historiographical re-evaluation of the Conquest period is the available sources. On the one hand we have the Spanish sources, beginning as early as 1519, which set the tone for an account of the triumphant undertaking of Spanish conquistadors. In fact, Hernán Cortés was writing as the events of the Conquest were taking place. It is an extraordinary kind of travelogue, where the author, as it were, washes the blood from his hands in order to describe the marvelous world that only a couple of months before did not even exist in the minds of his readers. This was followed by wave upon wave of authors describing the same events from the same point of view. On the other hand we have the indigenous sources, none of which were published until well into the twentieth century and most of which were written at least 50 years after the Conquest in an indigenous language, unintelligible to the layman and most academic readers, or, if in Spanish, in a tedious and repetitive administrative language.

It is therefore not too surprising that indigenous voices about their participation in the Conquest were not heard. Furthermore, until fairly recently historians were not particularly interested in hearing these indigenous voices. After all, history was forged by white European men and was written by their equally white descendants. While the latter is still very much true, what has particularly changed is the sensibility of scholars toward the indigenous role in its own history, which can be observed in the use and treatment of the sources over time.

Whereas the classic works by the conquerors (Cortés 1993; Díaz del Castillo 1992 [1568]; López de Gómara 1979 [1553]) were the main sources throughout the Colonial period and the nineteenth century, the twentieth and particularly the twenty-first century saw this change radically. The great British tradition of historiography continued in Hugh Thomas's *The Conquest of Mexico* (1993); the author, like the colonial historians and the great William H. Prescott (1913), still used the conquerors as his framework but added an enormous amount of archival work (although almost exclusively on Spanish participants). There was now also a wide array of scholars continually published indigenous, mainly Nahuatl, sources, that showed the other side of the coin, which not always or necessarily contradicted the Spanish side.

These indigenous sources can be divided into pictographic and alphabetic sources. In the first group there are many references to the Conquest and the indigenous participation in it. However, most of these are extremely brief or simply confirm information that is already known from other sources. Furthermore, considering the size of the corpus, academic attention has been sporadic, focused on particular documents, and, with notable exceptions, descriptive and not very profound. Thus few of these have been considered useful for revising the existing views and ideas on the Conquest. In fact, the *Lienzo de Tlaxcala* has most often been used as an example to confirm the authenticity of the information in Hispanic sources.

The translation and analysis of the alphabetic corpus has been growing steadily since the 1940s with Ángel María Garibay (1979 [1965], 1987 [1953], 2000) and his successor Miguel León-Portilla (1961, 1992 [1959], 2011), and particularly since the 1970s with James Lockhart (1991, 1992, 1993) and his followers in the United States (Haskett 2005; Horn 1997; Restall 1995, 1998; Terraciano 2001; Wood 2003) and Luis Reyes García (1977, 1988, 1996, 2001) and his followers in Mexico (Medina Lima 1995; Medina González 1998; Rojas Rabiela et al. 1999–2004). These studies show that indigenous peoples played an important role in colonial society, without losing their identity, which made it possible to adapt to the new situation. However, the focus of this field was not the Conquest but rather the Colonial society from the second half of the sixteenth century until Independence. While not its initial objective, with time this field has shown to be the breeding ground for the subsequent revisionist current.

As mentioned, this widening indigenous corpus certainly made scholars aware that there were other voices on the Conquest besides the Spanish. Many of them argued against the homogeneous Spanish pose and confronted it with the indigenous colonial experience, but they never radically broke with the Hispanic traditional historiography. This happened with what has been denominated the "New Conquest History" (see Restall [2012] for a more detailed discussion of this and its previous currents). The most important aspect of this new current was that it placed the existing ideas about the Conquest upside-down through the study of indigenous archival documents, primarily written in Spanish, that had been sent to the Spanish authorities in order to obtain privileges and exemptions from tribute payments. In these documents the indigenous claimants presented themselves as conquerors without whom the Conquest and colonization of Mesoamerica would have been impossible.

This new set of archival texts consists of such items as indigenous proofs of merit or communal claims for privileges, which often are back-to-back with similar texts of Spanish conquerors. In these documents indigenous conquerors made two basic claims: (a) they became allies of the Spaniards right from the start and therewith joined the military conquest of Mesoamerica or parts of it, and (b) shortly after they became allies, they were baptized and had been faithful Christians ever since. These claims were supported by innumerable amounts of testimonies from indigenous and Spanish witnesses, leaving little doubt as to their legitimacy or veracity.

Interestingly, and based on this paradigm shift, the information from traditional sources, such as Cortés's letters, to Nahuatl historical sources has now begun to be reevaluated and reanalyzed in regard to how these fit into this new historical scheme. For example, the numbers of indigenous participants in the Conquest given in the Spanish sources now can be compared with the aforementioned indigenous proofs of merit, and they suddenly start to make more sense. Also, the somewhat strange lack of indigenous resistance in the Mixteca Alta mentioned in the Spanish sources is explained by the conquests in that region by Don Gonzalo Mazatzin Moteuczoma. Finally, the complaints by Díaz del Castillo (1992 [1568]) about how López de Gómara (1979 [1553]) ignored the contributions of the other conquistadors besides Cortés can now be considered ironic as Díaz del Castillo did the very same thing with the indigenous conquistadors.

Through this change in analysis of indigenous and Spanish texts, we have been able to construct a series of categories that prove that the indigenous participation in the Conquest was structural and essential to the point where it was more of a continuation of prehispanic sociohistorical processes than a Spanish undertaking. These categories are the numbers of indigenous participants, the ubiquity of indigenous allies throughout Mesoamerica, the crucial role of noncombatant auxiliaries, and the Conquest imitating existing pre-Conquest patterns of military expansion (Oudijk and Restall 2007, 2008). These categories have been dealt with elsewhere (Altman 2010; Matthew 2012; Mathew and Oudijk 2007; Oudijk 2012; Yannakakis 2008). However, much remains to be done.

In this chapter we focus on another category and how it played out in the Nahuatl-speaking regions. Our particular interest here is how Mesoamerican thought determined the response of certain Nahua lords toward the Spanish arrival and the consequent Conquest period.

Nahua Thought and the Conquest

One of the most intriguing and controversial aspects of the Early Conquest period is the manner in which the emperor Moteuczoma Xocoyotzin received Hernán Cortés and the relationship that existed between the protagonists. Moteuczoma's response to the arrival of Cortés on the coast of present-day Veracruz seems particularly ambivalent (Cortés, 1993:105–159, first letter). On the one hand, he seemed to resist by having his subject towns fight against the Spanish and indigenous allied army, while on the other hand his messages were friendly and he sent expensive gifts to Cortés. At several stops along the way toward the city of Tenochtitlan, Moteuczoma had his ambassadors tell Cortés not to continue because he and his army would suffer inconveniences in the city. Moteuczoma also promised to pay Cortés tribute of gold, silver, slaves, and cotton cloth if he did not continue on his journey. However, when the army continued and arrived in the city, Moteuczoma received Cortés with all the prowess of an emperor and hosted the allied army in a lavish palace, while he himself returned to his own.

Cortés reproduced a long speech by Moteuczoma where he referred to a Toltec account, according to which after the fall of Tula its people dispersed, founding new towns all over central Mexico. They brought with them the cult of Quetzalcoatl, which was thus established in the region. The account relates that during their migration the people of Tula, the Toltecs, were guided by a lord who had left them only to return at a later moment. But when he came back, his people no longer accepted his command and so he decided to leave again. The arrival of Cortés was regarded as that of this lord's ambassador, who should be accepted as the new ruler.

Six days after Cortés and his people arrived in Tenochtitlan, an extraordinary set of events was set in motion that was to determine the fate of the ruler and his people. Cortés received word about Qualpopoca, a ruler from a kingdom on the Gulf Coast and subject to Tenochtitlan, who had killed two Spaniards by the order of Moteuczoma. Cortés went to Moteuczoma's palace and demanded he bring this ruler to Tenochtitlan in order to establish whether the Mexica ruler was responsible. Furthermore, while waiting for Qualpopoca to be brought to the city, Moteuczoma was to stay in Cortés's palace, clearly as a captive. For some reason Moteuczoma agreed to this treatment.

This situation continued for two or three weeks until Qualpopoca arrived in Tenochtitlan and was interrogated. Although he denied that Moteuczoma had ordered him to kill the Spaniards, he was sentenced to death by burning. Qualpopoca then confessed that the Tenochca ruler was behind the deaths. Cortés put Moteuczoma in shackles, intending to leave him there if only for one day. For other Nahua rulers this was the breaking point. Cacamatzin of Texcoco openly declared that he no longer supported Moteuczoma nor recognized the Spanish king.[1] Moteuczoma then betrayed him and had him imprisoned. This episode ended with another extraordinary event, when Moteuczoma gave the *translatio imperii*; with another speech he handed over his empire to the king of Spain, again alluding to the same Toltec account as when he received Cortés in Tenochtitlan.

This stream of events is described by Cortés in his first letter, and there is much debate about it. Most important are the two speeches made by Moteuczoma. Some have suggested that these are mere inventions by Cortés, while others claim that they were made but that their contents as represented by Cortés were invented (Elliot 1967; Frankl 1966; Gillespie 1989; Wagner 2004). However, recently, Nicholson (2001) analyzed the sources again and came to the conclusion that there is no reason to doubt either the existence of the speeches or their contents, an opinion followed by Graulich (1994) and that we also agree on.

One important argument against the validity of Cortés's account of these speeches that has not been dealt with sufficiently is that he misconstrued the meaning of Moteuczoma's words and did not understand them to be normal Mesoamerican discourse of hospitality (Elliot 1967:30). Indeed, these kinds of speeches were very flowery and full of meanings that could be misunderstood. If Moteuczoma did not hand over his kingdom, how can we explain the fact that he sentenced Qualpopoca, a subject ruler of Tenochtitlan, but while in Tlaxcala he had refused to do so because "I was in their land, and that they punished him as they were accustomed to, and that I did not want to interfere in punishing one of theirs, being in their land"? So in Tlaxcala Cortés followed the rules of Indian law, respecting the local traditions, while in Tenochtitlan he applied Spanish law (Luque Talaván, personal communication, October 9, 2013). Cortés dispensing justice thus meant he considered himself to be the authority, and Moteuczoma recognized this as he did not do anything against it. Of course Cortés putting shackles on Moteuczoma should remove all possible doubt about the meaning of the Tenochca ruler's speeches.

There are five other reasons to believe Cortés's account is trustworthy: (a) the story of a Mesoamerican lord arriving, leaving, coming back, and leaving again is fairly complex and has no relationship to any European story; (b) its structure is perfectly Mesoamerican and particularly related to migration accounts, as Cortés's was; (c) in none of his letters or other archival material did Cortés ever suggest he had used the claim of being a Mesoamerican god in order to gain military or political power;[2] (d) three other Spaniards report Moteuczoma's speeches; and (e) Cortés included a question about the speeches and their contents in his *residencia* and six witnesses confirmed them.

Accepting Moteuczoma's speeches means accepting the startling idea of the Tenochca ruler handing over his kingdom based on his beliefs. What ruler in his right mind would give up all his power? It is simply incomprehensible for a modern audience. However, does questioning this not say more about us than about the Mexica? After all, we have to accept that people can think fundamentally differently from us and, therefore, do things fundamentally differently from the way we do them, if only at times.

If we do accept the idea that Moteuczoma believed Cortés to be an emissary of the legitimate ruler, it would explain the otherwise unexplainable actions of the Mexica lord. Through his ambassadors he offered to become a vassal of the Spanish king, but he continuously deterred the allied army from entering Tenochtitlan. Of course once Cortés was in the city, there would be no way Moteuczoma could have continued to rule legitimately. By then, Moteuczoma was following his demands, from being sequestered in Cortés's residence, to having Cortés accuse him of lying, to dispensing justice over one of his subject lords, to Cortés putting Moteuczoma in shackles and arresting the Texcocan ruler, a partner of the Triple Alliance. How else can this be explained if not by Moteuczomas deeply grounded belief in Charles V's legitimate right to the throne of Tenochtitlan?

Moteuczoma's views and beliefs were not necessarily shared by all Mesoamericans or Nahuas but rather were those of this particular ruler and, likely, a particular group of people at a particular moment in time. Already at the massacre of Cholula there was evidence of discord, as Moteuczoma claimed that he was not responsible for the hostilities toward the Spanish but rather attributed them to local factions. These may have just been words, but they were recorded by Cortés. Once Moteuczoma was put into shackles,

Cacamatzin of Texcoco chose to no longer follow the Tenochca ruler and openly defied Cortés and the Spanish king. Surely this decision was not the first disagreement with the politics of welcoming Cortés. In fact, even in Tlaxcala we see opposing factions in regard to how to treat Cortés and his allies; first the Tlaxcalans fought Cortés and his allies, and finally the Tlaxcalans joined them. This same discord seems to have been playing out between Moteuczoma and his allies, but apparently his political and military power was such that it allowed Cortés to march on Tenochtitlan and rule there until Moteuczoma was discredited and had lost his allies.

Continuation of Nahua Thought

Moteuczomas actions and reactions to the arrival of Cortés had profound consequences for the Conquest period and have therefore been commented on numerous times. Of course in the case of Moteuczoma one can hardly speak about a "continuation of indigenous thought" as it concerned the actual moment of contact. However, the ideas and beliefs that made up his worldview continued in others and were to determine their actions and how the colonial society took shape.

An intriguing Nahua cultural aspect is the idea of a lord "washing himself as a ruler" (*motlatocapaca*). It formed part of the old rituals of enthronization that validated the ruler in his new position. This practice consisted of going to war in order to capture prisoners and sacrifice them before the patron god (see Durán 1995 [1581] Book I, ch. XL:361–371; Sahagún 2000 [1570] Book II:773–775; Torquemada 1975–1983 [1615] Book II, ch. LV:238; also Olivier 2008:263–291, although he does not discuss *motlatocapaca*). It was registered in relation to the ascension of Maxtla to the throne of Azcapotzalco in 1426 when he "in order to validate his kingdom began a war" (Anales de Tlatelolco 2004 [c. 1555]:89). It seems thus no coincidence that the first colonial indigenous governors of Tenochtitlan immediately went to war. Such is the case of Don Pablo Xochiquentzin, who in the very year of being elected governor, in 1532, joined Nuño de Guzmán with his armies to Nueva Galicia. However, contrary to prehispanic circumstances, don Pablo had to stay away from the throne a long three years. Similarly, upon being named governor of Tenochtitlan, Don Diego de San Franciso Tehuetzquititzin left with viceroy Don Antonio de Mendoza to "wash himself as lord" in the war of Mixton (Tezozomoc 1992 [1598]:171–172).

Shortly after the war, and similar to their Spanish counterparts, these indigenous conquistadors began to seek the privilege of obtaining coats of arms. Their readiness to apply for these emblems was probably due to their familiarity with them, as they had their prehispanic equivalents. In Nahuatl such emblems were called *tlahuiztli*, which referred to coats or insignias of war consisting of shields or *chimalli*, the war garment and headdress or *yaotlatqui*, and the so-called *tlamamalli*, a kind of wooden back rack decorated with feathers, paper, and other rich materials (Anawalt 1981; Asselbergs 2004; Castañeda de la Paz 2009; Olko 2005). The famed conqueror Bernal Díaz del Castillo (1992 [1568]:176) had already compared these insignias with those of Spanish dukes and counts.

As in Europe, in New Spain these emblems became prestigious symbols of the nobility and warriors. While over time the traditional *tlahuiztli* were reserved for public feasts, the indigenous symbols were combined with European ones and incorporated into the otherwise European coats of arms that in turn were also called *tlahuiztli*. Normally, such symbols were related to war, ethnic background, or lineage, but they were often also of a religious nature. Whereas some were clearly Christian, others were Mesoamerican. Thus the blazon of Coyoacan contains Dominican crosses on ancient *chimallis* and the ornaments of the god Otontecuhtli as decoration of the coyote's headdress that holds the shield, while the coat of arms of Tlacopan shows the *chimalli* of Xipe Totec, the prehispanic flayed god (Castañeda de la Paz and Luque Talaván 2010a, 2010b).

Surely while the indigenous rulers had the objective to "wash themselves as rulers" and validate their new position after they had ascended to their respective thrones, the Spaniards interpreted their participation in wars as a collaboration, a sign that they were vassals to the king of Spain and had incorporated into colonial society. Motivated as such, these rulers soon continued their ancient traditions with their *tlahuiztli*, be it in hybrid formats, whereby they constructed a complex society where old and new, indigenous and Spanish, melted together into one.

Conclusion

From this discussion we can conclude that the belief systems of the indigenous rulers who were confronted with the arrival of the Spaniards were crucial for how they responded and eventually how the Conquest period developed. While in many of the indigenous actions and reactions we see a clear pragmatism, there are other aspects that are much more difficult to understand. Giving up one's kingdom for what one truly believes can be quite difficult to understand if it is not accepted that such beliefs can exist. But is letting one's child die of a disease for which a medicine exists because one believes it is God's will so much different? If Moteuczoma truly believed that Cortés was sent by the legitimate ruler of Tenochtitlan, why would he not give up his throne? Strong beliefs and convictions of individuals and peoples have many times determined the path of history, and the Conquest of Mesoamerica is no exception to this rule.

Notes

1. See question 6 of the residencia against Pedro de Alvarado (1847, 2008) for other reasons that could explain Cacamatzin's rejection of Spanish hegemony.
2. These speeches are fundamental in the discussion about whether the Nahuas thought Cortés, and the Spaniards, were gods and, particularly, whether Cortés was Quetzalcoatl. Notwithstanding the importance of these issues, for our purposes here we need only to determine whether the contents of the first letter of Cortés are accurate.

References Cited

Altman, Ida
2010 *The War of Mexico's West: Indians and Spaniards in New Galicia, 1524–1550.* University of Mexico Press, Albuquerque.

Alvarado, Pedro de
1847 *Proceso de residencia contra Pedro de Alvarado.* Edited by José Fernando Ramírez. Valdés y Redondas, Mexico.
2008 *Juicio a un conquistador. Pedro de Alvarado.* 2 vols. Edited by José María Vallejo García-Hevia. Marcial Pons Historia, Madrid.

Anales de Tlatelolco
2004 [c. 1555] *Anales de Tlatelolco.* Translated by Rafael Tena. Conaculta, Cien de México, Mexico.

Anawalt, Patricia Rieff
1981 *Indian Clothing Before Cortes. Mesoamerican Costumes from the Codices.* University of Oklahoma Press, Norman.

Asselbergs, Florine
2004 *Conquered Conquistadors. The Lienzo de Quauhquechollan: A Nahua View of the conquest of Guatemala.* Research School CNWS, Leiden University, Leiden.

Castañeda de la Paz, Maria
2009 Central Mexican Indigenous Coats of Arms and the Conquest of Mesoamerica. *Ethnohistory* 56(1):125–161.

Castañeda de la Paz, Maria, and Miguel Luque Talaván
2010a Heráldica Indígena: iconografía tipo códice en los escudos de armas tepanecas. *Arqueología Mexicana* 105:70–75.
2010b Privileges of the "Others": The Coats of Arms Granted to Indigenous Conquistadors. In *The International Emblem: From Incunabula to the Internet: Selected Proceedings from the Eighth International Conference of the Society for Emblem Studies, 28th July–1st August, Winchester College 2008*, edited by Simon McKeown, pp. 283–316. Cambridge Scholars Publishing, Newcastle-upon-Tyne, UK.

Cortés, Hernán
1993 *Cartas de relación.* Clásico Castalia, Madrid [1st letter 1520].

Díaz del Castillo, Bernal
1992 [1568] *Historia de la conquista de Nueva España.* Editorial Porrúa, Mexico.

Durán, Fray Diego
1995 [1581] *Historia de las Indias de Nueva España e Islas de Tierra Firme.* Conaculta, Cien de México, Mexico.

Elliott, John H.
1967 The Mental World of Hernán Cortés. *Transactions of the Royal Historical Society* 17:41–58.

Frankl, Victor
1966 Die Cartas de Relación des Hernán Cortés und der Mythos der Wiederkehr des Quetzalcoatl. *Adeva Mitteilungen* 10:7–17.

Garibay, Ángel María
1979 [1965] *Teogonía e historia de los mexicanos: tres opúsculos del siglo XVI.* Editorial Porrúa, Mexico.
1987 [1953] *Historia de la literatura náhuatl.* 2 vols. Editorial Porrúa, Mexico.

2000 *Cantares Mexicanos: manuscrito de la Biblioteca Nacional de México.* Universidad Nacional Autónoma de México, Mexico City.

Gillespie, Susan D.

1989 *The Aztec Kings: The Construction of Rulership in Mexica History.* University of Arizona Press, Tucson.

Graulich, Michel

1994 *Moteuczoma ou l'apogée et la chute de l'empire aztèque.* Fayard, Lille.

Haskett, Robert

2005 *Visions of Paradise: Primordial Titles and Mesoamerican History in Cuernavaca.* University of Oklahoma Press, Norman.

Horn, Rebecca

1997 *Postconquest Coyoacan. Nahua-Spanish Relations in Central Mexico, 1519–1650.* Stanford University Press, Stanford, CA.

León-Portilla, Miguel

1961 *Los antiguos mexicanos: a través de sus crónicas y cantares.* Fondo de Cultura Económica, Mexico City.

1992 [1959] *Visión de los vencidos: relaciones indígenas de la conquista.* Universidad Nacional Autónoma de México, Mexico City.

2011 *Cantares Mexicanos.* 3 vols., Instituto de Investigaciones Bibliográficas, Universidad Nacional Autónoma de México, Mexico City.

Lockhart, James

1991 *Nahuas and Spaniards: Postconquest Central Mexican History and Philology.* Stanford University Press, Stanford, CA.

1992 *The Nahuas after the Conquest: A Social and Cultural History of the Indians of Central Mexico, Sixteenth Through Eighteenth Centuries.* Stanford University Press, Stanford, CA.

1993 *We People Here: Nahuatl Accounts of the Conquest of Mexico.* UCLA Center for Medieval and Renaissance Studies, University of California, Los Angeles.

López de Gómara, Francisco

1979 [1553] *Historia general de las Indias y vida de Hernán Cortés.* Biblioteca Ayacucho, Caracas.

Matthew, Laura E.

2012 *Memories of Conquest: Becoming Mexicano in Colonial Guatemala.* University of North Carolina Press, Chapel Hill.

Matthew, Laura E., and Michel R. Oudijk

2007 *Indian Conquistadors: Indigenous Allies on the Conquest of Mesoamerica.* University of Oklahoma Press, Norman.

Medina González, Xochitl

1998 *Histoire mexicaine depuis 1221 jusqu'en 1594: manuscrito num. 40 del Fondo de Manuscritos Mexicanos, Biblioteca Nacional de Francia.* Instituto Nacional de Antropología e Historia, Mexico City.

Medina Lima, Constantino

1995 *Libro de los guardianes y gobernadores de Cuauhtinchan (1519–1640).* Secretaría de Educación Pública/CIESAS, Mexico City.

Nicholson, H. B.

2001 *The "Return of Quetzalcoatl": Did It Play a Role in the Conquest of Mexico?* Labyrinthos, Lancaster, CA.

Olivier, Guilhem
2008 Le cerf et le roi: modèle sacrificiel et rite d'intronisation dans l'ancien Mexique. *Journal de la Société des Américanistes* 94:191–230.

Olko, Justyna
2005 *Turquoise Diadems and Staffs of Office: Elite Costume and Insignia of Power in Aztec and Early Colonial Mexico.* Ośrodek Badań nad Tradycją Antyczną and Polsce I w Europie Środkowo-Wschodniej, Warsaw.

Oudijk, Michel R.
2012 The Conquest of Mexico. In *The Oxford Handbook of Mesoamerican Archaeology*, edited by Deborah L. Nichols and Christopher A. Pool, pp. 459–470. Oxford University Press, New York.

Oudijk, Michel R., and Matthew Restall
2007 Mesoamerican Conquistadors in the Sixteenth Century. In *Indian Conquistadors: Indigenous Allies on the Conquest of Mesoamerica*, edited by Laura E. Matthew and Michael R. Oudijk, pp. 28–64. University of Oklahoma Press, Norman.
2008 *La conquista indígena de Mesoamérica: el caso de don Gonzalo Mazatzin Moctezuma.* Secretaría de Cultura del Estado de Puebla, Puebla.

Prescott, William H.
1913 *The Conquest of Mexico.* J. M. Dent & Sons, London.

Restall, Matthew
1995 *Life and Death in a Maya Community: The Ixil Testaments of the 1760s.* Labyrinthos, Lancaster, CA.
1998 *Maya Conquistador.* Beacon Press, Boston.
2012 The New Conquest History. *History Compass* 10(2):151–160.

Reyes García, Luis
1977 *Cuauhtinchan del Siglo XII al XVI: formación y desarollo histórico de un senorío prehispánico.* Franz Steiner Verlag, Wiesbaden.
1988 *Documentos sobre tierras y senoríos en Cuauhtinchan.* CIESAS/Fondo de Cultura Económica, Mexico City.
1996 *Documentos nauas de la ciudad de México del siglo XVI.* CIESAS/Archivo General de la Nación, Mexico City.
2001 *Como te confundes? Acaso no somos conquistados? Anales de Juan Bautista.* CIESAS, Mexico City.

Teresa Rojas Rabiela, Elsa Leticia Rea López, and Constantino Medina Lima (editors: vols. 1–3); Teresa Rojas Rabiela and Elsa Leticia Rea López (editors: vols. 4 and 5)
1999–2004 *Vidas y bienes olvidados: testamentos indigenas novohispanos.* 5 vols. CIESAS/Secretaría de Educación Pública/Archivo General de la Nación, Mexico City.

Sahagún, Fray Bernardino de
2000 [c. 1570] *Historia general de las cosas de Nueva España.* 3 vols. Conaculta, Cien de México, Mexico City.

Terraciano, Kevin
2001 *The Mixtecs of Colonial Oaxaca: Ñudzahui History, Sixteenth Trough Eighteenth Centuries.* Stanford University Press, Stanford, CA.

Tezozomoc, Fernando Alvarado
1992 [1598] *Crónica Mexicayotl.* Instituto de Investigaciones Históricas, Universidad Nacional Autónoma de México, Mexico City.

Thomas, Hugh
1993 *La conquista de México: el derrumbamiento del gran imperio de Moctezuma.* Planeta, Barcelona.
Torquemada, Fray Juan de
1975–1983 [1615] *Monarquía indiana.* 6 vols. Instituto de Investigaciones Históricas, Universidad Nacional Autónoma de México, Mexico City.
Wagner, Henry R.
1944 *The Rise of Fernando Cortés.* Cortes Society, Berkeley, CA.
Wood, Stephanie
2003 *Transcending Conquest: Nahua Views of Spanish Colonial Mexico.* University of Oklahoma Press, Norman.
Yannakakis, Yanna
2008 *The Art of Being In-Between: Native Intermediaries, Indian Identity, and Local Rule in Colonial Oaxaca.* Duke University Press, Durham, NC.

PART III
LANDSCAPES AND PLACES

CHAPTER 12

AZTEC AGRICULTURAL PRODUCTION IN A HISTORICAL ECOLOGICAL PERSPECTIVE

EMILY MCCLUNG DE TAPIA
AND DIANA MARTÍNEZ YRIZAR

ECOLOGICAL perspectives in archaeology have evolved and vied for attention since the mid-twentieth century, ostensibly beginning with cultural ecology as originally proposed by Steward (1955). In Mesoamerican archaeology, although MacNeish's work in Tamaulipas (1958) and the Tehuacan Valley (1967) was greatly influenced by Steward's views, the formal cultural ecological framework for research was initially proposed and implemented by William T. Sanders (1957, 1965; Sanders and Price 1968) and applied in the Basin of México (Sanders 1981; Sanders et al. 1979). In our experience, cultural ecology purported as a theoretical orientation still crops up from time to time, particularly in research proposals by Mexican scholars, and it is interesting to note that few authors have really taken the time to evaluate Steward's postulates for what they represent: a methodological tool to better examine how individual human beings and communities adapt to and interact with their environment through technology and how environment affects the interaction between communities (McClung de Tapia 1984) rather than a specific theoretical orientation. Ecological thinking and interest in systems' frameworks that sought to go beyond the functional relationships espoused in Sanders' position were put forward by Flannery (1972). However, over the ensuing decades, Mesoamerican archaeologists seem to have found themselves somewhat at a loss to find suitable ways to recognize, describe, and understand the complexity of relationships between humans and their biophysical surroundings.

It is beyond the scope of this chapter to discuss and critique the ecological approaches employed in Mesoamerican archaeology over the past six decades. More detailed considerations of these ideas may be found in McClung de Tapia (1984, 2010, 2012a), and Crumley (1994) broadly summarizes the different lines represented by ecological approaches in general. Rather, our goal here is to explore how more recent perspectives, particularly historical ecology and its close "associates," landscape ecology and resilience theory, provide elements for the development of more productive hypotheses with respect to human behavior and its role in the transformations of human landscapes. Balée (2006) outlines the intellectual context within which historical ecology developed as a response to the inadequacies of cultural ecology. Historical ecology brings to the arena a long-term perspective. In addition, it seeks to develop understandings of causation as interactive or dialectical forces rather than deterministic factors in change over time.

We do not favor an ecosystem approach in which humans are seen strictly as one of many biological taxa (ecological communities interacting with their abiotic environment) because humans obviously bring something more to the functioning of ecosystems due to their ability to consciously propose and further specific objectives through the transmission of information and development of appropriate technology mediated by culture. On the other hand, it is counterproductive to imagine human communities outside of and unconnected to the biophysical surroundings. Some recent discussions of historical ecology emphasize the fundamental role of human agency (Balée 2006) and individuals in this relationship (Whitehead 1998), stressing the importance of human decision-making and its potential long-term consequences on the environment. While this is clearly feasible in the ethnographic study of traditional management of resources by communities, in the case of archaeological investigations, a more materialistic view is inevitable, particularly insofar as the evidence for cultural continuity through time is rarely straightforward. Furthermore, putting "persons, not organic systems, at the center of changing ecological relationships through time" (Whitehead 1998:31) is unrealistic with respect to a considerable portion of Mesoamerican history for which written documents are essentially absent.

What is historical ecology? Crumley (1994:6) suggests that landscapes represent the "material manifestation" of the relationships between humans and their environment, defining historical ecology as the study of past ecosystems through evidence of change in landscapes through time. The subtle interplay between archaeology, geography, ethnology, and ethnohistory within a regional perspective provides the temporal and spatial parameters within which to identify

1. extant environmental and cultural evidence for the region in question;
2. the range of current practices likely to be impacted by environmental change;
3. traditional and innovative adaptive strategies appropriate to the region, to the culture(s) affected, and to the nature and magnitude of anticipated change; and
4. the means by which such adaptations may be fostered [Crumley 1994:8].

The emphasis on adaptation is not lost in this perspective, and the role of long-term adaptation is seen as an indicator of how human groups have fared through time in relation to their environments, particularly when faced with "natural" events (e.g., meteorological or geological phenomena) and the consequences of past decisions.

Balée (2006:76) summarized the program of historical ecology as a concern "with the interactions through time between societies and environments and the consequences of these interactions for understanding the formation of contemporary and past cultures and landscapes." Here much of the concern is expressed in terms of management of the environment or landscape and the impact of human decision-making; focusing on human adaptations to the environment neglects the engagement of societies with their landscapes.

Landscape is clearly the key component of both perspectives, although we recall Whitehead's (1998) counter-argument that individual praxis rather than society should be the initial level of analysis. This author further argues that although development of appropriate field methodologies for historical ecology may be feasible, historical anthropology already provides the necessary framework within which to consider the issues and topics, the implication being that this approach represents a methodological tool rather than a theoretical focus—similar to that which Steward (1955) originally attributed to cultural ecology.

Landscape Ecology and Resilience Theory (McClung 2010, 2012a, 2012b) are scarcely present in mainstream Mesoamerican archaeology, although these approaches, together with historical ecology, appear to offer a broader range of conceptual tools to support the development of integrative methodologies. In resilience theory in particular, adaptation is once more given a central role in order to focus on the strategies that humans develop to facilitate their survival.

Although it may be argued that these approaches do not differ significantly from earlier functionalist and systems' perspectives, their methodologies provide new ways of constructing arguments to better explain complex situations and relationships as well as tools for the application of lessons learned from history to new and future situations. Thus the integration of historical information, including archaeological data, can contribute to the construction of potential scenarios with which modern actors can recognize possible emergent properties of systems and make appropriate decisions based on past experiences.

Redman (2005) and others point out the unique role of archaeology in providing time depth—*longue durée* perspectives. In Mesoamerican archaeology, this direction of thinking has yet to develop into a significant line of research, although it has been implicit to some extent in regional settlement pattern studies.

Legacies are relevant to the understanding of how past ecologies move to present ones and to the future. While it is improbable that most past strategies would be operable under future conditions, they represent case studies of how human groups responded to particular circumstances and the material manifestations of these circumstances on the landscape. By "legacy," we mean the continual interplay between natural and anthropogenic factors playing against one another through time (Fisher et al. 2009). Although manifestations in the landscape, such as deforestation, soil erosion, desertification, and biodiversity loss, are frequently evoked as causes for concomitant changes in socioeconomic and political organizations (structures), they cannot be understood outside of an extensive temporal framework. Social and environmental aspects of societies must be examined together.

Human–environmental relations over time are driven by complex phenomena that go beyond population changes, climate change, or dramatic natural events; the dynamic relationship between human action, unintended consequences, and natural change must be examined, and new questions and methodologies are contributing to this effort (Dearing et al. 2010).

Redman et al. (2009:17) argue that land use is traditionally viewed as human impact, without concern for the social dynamics that motivate humans to alter the landscape in different ways—the deep-time perspective. Such a perspective allows us to recognize ultimate rather than proximate causes affecting the collapse of socioecological systems. The history of human–environment interactions, attainable through the archaeological record, permits analysis of human responses and strategies developed over time to meet short-term needs. The long-term consequences of short-term strategies cannot be foreseen and may lead to the collapse of extant systems and future resilience of both environmental and social systems.

The anthropological interpretation of archaeological evidence, together with an integrated approach toward contributions from other disciplines, promotes a broad understanding of the linked dynamics of social and ecological systems across a range of organizational scales: individual households, hamlets, villages, cities, and larger agglomerations (Redman et al. 2009:18). Finally, while it is clear that human management of the landscape may result in the stabilization of ecosystem functions over time, when the social structures within which these strategies arise are sufficiently altered or collapse, the consequences for socionatural systems may be drastic. Although external factors such as conquest and colonization may be germane to such consequences—as in the case of the collapse of the Aztec Empire—other factors, both internal and external, clearly come into play.

Aztec Technology and Agricultural Systems: Created Landscapes, Sacred Landscapes

The Late Postclassic–Colonial transition period in the Basin of Mexico is particularly interesting because of the availability of historical documents that record indigenous lifeways in the early sixteenth century through the eyes of colonial representatives as well as native documents that refer to historical events and personages from that period together with earlier times. References to Aztec lifeways and worldview are interspersed throughout detailed descriptions, providing a window into the ways in which economic factors such as landscape management and agricultural productivity were mediated by ideological manifestations largely reflecting social and political control.

Observations concerning the technological aspects and productivity of Aztec agricultural systems and their modern counterparts in the Basin of Mexico have been amply described in the anthropological and geographical literature, including terraces, chinampas, other irrigation systems, and massive hydraulic works (Armillas 1971; Coe 1964; Charlton 1970; Doolittle 1990; Killian 1992; McClung de Tapia 1990, 2000; Rojas Rabiela 1988; Sanders 1957). In addition, recent works detailing and analyzing Aztec sacred geography and ceremonial celebrations associated with specific times of the year and related economic activities described by Fray Bernadino de Sahagún and Fray Diego Durán are available (Arnold 1991; Broda 1971, 1991, 2004; Carrasco 1991). Based on these interpretations of ceremonial landscapes, we focus on specific aspects of the relationship between the sacred landscape and the created landscape, manifest in terraces and chinampa systems, in an attempt to bring together some aspects of Aztec worldview and the mundane realities of sustaining human population through technology—the creation of agroecosystems.

It is popular to perceive the prehispanic indigenous societies in Mesoamerica as essential "ecological Indians" (cf. Krech 1999; Denevan 1992, 2011), committed to a respect for nature and the careful management of available resources and at the same time having little impact on the landscape. However, several decades of controversy in the scientific literature demonstrate that human impact was a significant factor on large extensions of the landscape in the Americas at the time of European arrival (Denevan 1992, 2011). However, that is not to deny that human impact varied from place to place, and, furthermore, it does not exclude the evidence for notions of respect and restraint in the exploitation of the environment inherent in the worldviews of indigenous peoples. We examine some aspects of this argument to try to gain a meaningful perspective concerning the way in which Aztec farmers were able to balance ideology and symbolic manifestations with the intensive exploitation of the landscape to meet their own needs as well as compliance with tribute demands in labor and goods. In addition, we consider the legacy of these practices in the context of modern extant chinampas in the area of San Gregorio Atlapulco, Xochimilco, and the social–political–economic challenges faced by these traditional productive systems.

AZTEC WORLDVIEW AND LANDSCAPE MANAGEMENT

Although Mesoamerica, and particularly central México, underwent significant transformations as a result of European arrival and settlement, ethnohistorical and historical documents relate certain aspects of Aztec worldview, providing the framework within which modification of the landscape in the form of intensive transformative agricultural systems can be understood (López Austin 2013; López Austin and López Luján 2009). It is difficult to summarize the complex relationships between deities and humans in the Aztec cosmos. In the greatly reduced discussion that follows, we attempt to link some fundamental facets of Aztec worldview with the material aspect of exploitative activities and their manifestations in the landscape. An initial question is: How can intensive environmental-altering agricultural techniques be justified within a sacred landscape?

López Austin and López Luján (2009) point out that the origin of work stems from the gods' creation of *Oxomoco*, a man whose predetermined role was to work the land, and *Cipactónal*, a woman dedicated to spinning and weaving. From this initial couple, the *macehuales* were descended with the obligation to engage in work. Within a framework of reciprocity that pervaded all aspects of the relations between supernatural beings, humans, animals, ancestors, and geographical places, equilibrium was established and maintained through the fulfillment of their respective obligations by each of these participants.

Supernatural beings are represented by two broad categories: supernatural forces and deities. The former are impersonal whereas the latter possess personalities rather similar to humans and exercise their will through actions affecting the perceptible world. The cosmos represents the dynamic interchange between the supernatural and natural.

The deities fulfill their obligations through intervention in the metaphorical cycles of nature: they "'bear' the year, the day and night, the heavens and the earth, the souls and bodies of men and women, and provide men with the means to guarantee their survival" (López Austin and López Luján 2009:178). Human beings, on the other hand, maintain a privileged reciprocity with the deities derived from their unique faculties, giving humans a share in the responsibility for the correct functioning of cosmic processes. Thus humans must offer the products of their work as sustenance for the deities, in the form of the essences of nature, blood, and body.

The functions of humans are performed collectively and from the articulation of work and the distribution of work roles as defined in remote time by *el Dueño*, the overall patron of the Sacred Mountain, responsible for the distribution of particular roles and the establishment of the corresponding hierarchy from which social distinctions are derived. Patron deities of each office bequeath that role to their respective group; the specific activities of each group are integral components of the reciprocal relationship with the patron. *El Dueño* delegates obligations to maintain order to human representatives who serve as intermediaries in the transmission of the gods' wishes to their subjects.

The Sacred Mountain is a symbol for the obtainment of sustenance. Its position in the *axis mundi* of the Aztec world is central; the cardinal directions emanate from it. From the springs of the Sacred Mountain flows the water that feeds rivers and streams, which ultimately travel to the sea, thus the connection with a subterranean vault of Tlalocan, referred to by Sahagún's informants (López Austin and López Luján 2009:53). The forces behind germination and growth were believed to spring from the interior of the Sacred Mountain to penetrate through plants, animals, and human beings.

The reciprocal arrangement between human beings and *el Dueño* consisted, then, of a pact. In order to receive the gift of sustenance, viewed as a sort of temporal loan, earthly beneficiaries accepted the obligation to serve as peons in the cosmic order following death. If the contract was not fulfilled or the debtor wished to elude the obligation of suitable payment at a given time, human sacrificial victims could be offered as substitution in the other world until the debt could be liquidated.

Broda (1991:84), for example, emphasizes the structural role of child sacrifices in order to procure water, rain, maize, and fertility in general, as acts of reciprocity according to the principle of *do ut des* (give as you receive) in which a "pay ahead" policy is established on the basis of which beneficial natural phenomena were being negotiated. Commoners understood these sacrifices as fulfilling their part of a contractual agreement with Tlaloc, god of rain, earth, and vegetation, the embodiment of the landscape (Arnold 1991:219).

Broda (2004) distinguishes three groups of festivals and their concomitant ceremonies in honor of the deities affiliated with rain and maize, manifest in the annual agricultural cycle and all intimately related to mountains and to water believed to be present within them. The cycle corresponding to the beginning of the Aztec year, during the dry season, was marked by child sacrifices carried out in the mountains surrounding the Basin of Mexico to propitiate rain. The cycle associated with planting, growth, and maturation of maize took place beginning with the transition between the dry season and the rainy season and during the rains. The harvest and beginning of the subsequent dry season was marked by celebration of the dead in the mountains and the return to child sacrifices associated with the petition of rains. During each of these periods complex state-sponsored rituals as well as more popular manifestations were systematically carried out. Ritualized political relations expressed in Aztec calendar festivals represent reciprocal interactions within the structure of a deeply stratified society rather than exchanges between equals (Broda 1991:101). The role of these ceremonies served to reinforce the position and function of each social group within the larger structure of Aztec society, each component concentrating on the appropriate realization of their respective obligations, thus maintaining cosmic harmony through these transactions and, consequently, guaranteeing prosperity for all. Offerings were a medium through which communication could be established with the appropriate deities, not only to bridge communication between humans and the deities but also to guarantee the deities' necessity of collaboration on the part of humans. The annual celebratory cycle was not geared toward recognizing and giving thanks for the termination of significant events but rather to propitiate the success of events to come.

Chinampas in the Sacred Landscape

Well-developed social organization, coordination of activities, and intensive labor compensated for the lack of sophisticated agricultural instruments: tools were geared toward individual activities and plants were given individual attention for the most part. Although this is characteristic of planting, tending, and harvesting in terrace systems and temporal plots in alluvial plains, it is especially notable in the techniques developed in chinampa cultivation, where single plants were transplanted following germination (Armillas 1971; Coe 1964; Rojas 1988).

Chinampa cultivation represented the ultimate manifestation of intensive labor and production, as well as an extreme incursion into the sacred landscape, especially insofar as it extended into the lake itself and created "land" where there was none. Although it is not entirely clear to what extent chinampa cultivation represented a "bottom-up" or "top-down" management regime during the Aztec period in the southern Basin of Mexico (Morehart and Frederick 2014), the labor-intensive nature of this form of agricultural production undoubtedly required structured organization. The justification for this intensive exploitation in the sacred waters emanating from the Sacred Mountain can be found in the pact between gods and humans—not only the human requirement for sustenance but the fulfillment of the gods' needs as well. The need to obtain sustenance from the sacred landscape, embedded within the complex ritual cycle, mitigated the potential imbalance in the cosmic equilibrium that such exploitation might provoke; ecological instability was mitigated through structured systematic agricultural techniques undertaken in the guise of fulfilling humans' obligation to work the land to provide for the gods and for themselves in a perpetual cycle of production. Cost-benefit analysis as applied in some ecological studies misses the point in this context: while costs are inordinately high, the potential benefits are extraordinary.

The legacy of intensive agricultural production is visible today in the remnants of the chinampa system of the southeastern Basin of Mexico, particularly in the area of San Gregorio Atlapulco (Figures 12.1, 12.2, 12.3), where, ironically, Sanders (1957) described the techniques and concomitant organization surrounding chinampa production in the 1950s. Current geoarchaeological survey and excavation in the area (Figures 12.4, 12.5) highlights the continual loss of this productive system as stakeholders of Ejido San Gregorio Atlapulco, now part of a Natural Protected Area that includes the Ejido Xochimilco, confront the will to preserve traditional cultivation practices and the aquatic environment with modernization and the introduction of a modern irrigation system in adjacent lands (Dirección General de la Comisión de Recursos Naturales 2006). Historical ecology offers a viable framework within which to situate the future of this and other chinampa zones in the southeastern Basin of Mexico. The current interdisciplinary focus of research in San Gregorio builds on the legacy from prehispanic through historic and modern periods to preserve what remains as a relic of the past, challenged by the realities of preserving traditional agricultural practices in expanding urban communities (Figures 12.1–12.3).

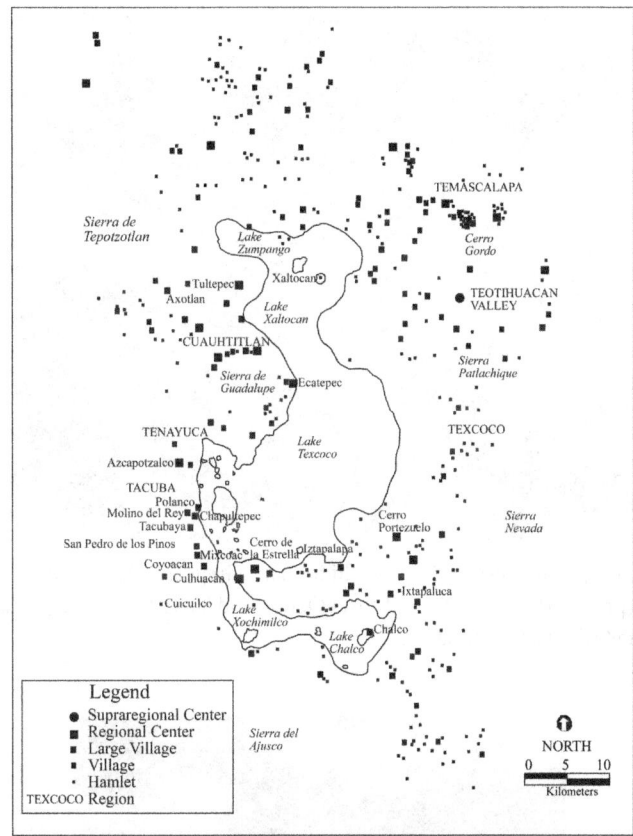

FIGURE 12.1 Postclassic settlement in the Basin of Mexico (Sanders 1981).

FIGURE 12.2 Estimated extension of post-Aztec period *chinampa* cultivation in the southern Basin of Mexico (Luna Golya 2014). With permission of Luna Golya.

FIGURE 12.3 Composite aerial view of Ejido San Gregorio Atlapulco showing remnant *chinampa* plots (prepared by Guillermo Acosta Ochoa and Victor García, April 2014). With permission of Acosta Ochoa and García.

FIGURE 12.4 Characteristic flora of canals surrounding Ejido San Gregorio Atlapulco (photo Emily McClung de Tapia).

FIGURE 12.5 Excavation of a relict chinampa in Ejido San Gregorio Atlapulco (photo Emily McClung de Tapia).

Acknowledgments

Current archaeological investigation in Ejido San Gregorio Atlapulco is financed by DGAPA-UNAM, PAPIIT, grant no. IG400513, awarded to Emily McClung de Tapia and Guillermo Acosta Ochoa.

References Cited

Armillas, Pedro
1971 Gardens on Swamps. *Science* 174(4010):653–661.
Arnold, Philip P.
1991 Eating Landscape: Human Sacrifice and Sustenance in Aztec Mexico. In *Aztec Ceremonial Landscapes*, edited by David Carrasco, pp. 219–232. University Press of Colorado, Niwot.
Balée, William
2006 The Research Program of Historical Ecology. *Annual Review of Anthropology* 35:75–98.
Broda, Johanna
1971 Las fiestas Aztecas de los dioses de la lluvia. *Revista Española de Antropología Americana* 6:245–327.
1991 The Sacred Landscape of Aztec Calendar Festivals: Myth, Nature and Society. In *Aztec Ceremonial Landscapes*, edited by David Carrasco, pp. 74–120. University Press of Colorado, Niwot.

2004 Cíclos agrícolas en la cosmovisión prehispánica: el ritual Mexica. In *Historia y vida ceremonial en las comunidades Mesoamericanas: los ritos agrícolas*, edited by Johanna Broda and Catharine Good Eshelman, pp. 35–60. Instituto Nacional de Antropología e Historia/ Universidad Nacional Autónoma de México, Mexico City.

Carrasco, David (editor)

1991 *Aztec Ceremonial Landscapes*. University Press of Colorado, Niwot.

Charlton, Thomas H.

1970 Contemporary Agriculture of the Valley. In *The Natural Environment, Contemporary Occupation and 16th Century Population of the Valley*. The Teotihuacan Valley Project. Final Report, Vol. I, edited by William T. Sanders, Anton Kovar, Thomas Charlton, and Richard A. Diehl, pp. 253–383. Occasional Papers in Anthropology No. 3. Department of Anthropology, Pennsylvania State University, University Park.

Coe, Michael

1964 The Chinampas of Mexico. *Scientific American* 211(1):90–98.

Crumley, Carole L. (editor)

1994 *Historical Ecology: Cultural Knowledge and Changing Landscapes*. School of American Research, Santa Fe, NM.

Dearing, John A., Ademola K. Braimoh, Anette Reenberg, Billie L. Turner, and Sander van der Leeuw

2010 Complex Land Systems: The Need for Long Time Perspectives to Assess Their Future. *Ecology and Society* 15(4). http://www.ecologyandsociety.org/vol15/iss4/art21/.

Denevan, William M.

1992 The Pristine Myth: The Landscape of the Americas in 1492. *Annals of the Association of American Geographers* 82(3):369–385.

2011 The Pristine Myth Revisited. *The Geographical Review* 101(4):576–591.

Dirección General de la Comisión de Recursos Naturales

2006 *Programa de Manejo del Area Natural Protegida "Ejidos de Xochimilco y San Gregorio Atlapulco."* Secretaria de Medio Ambiente, México, D.F.

Doolittle, William E.

1990 *Canal Irrigation in Prehistoric Mexico: The Sequence of Technological Change*. University of Texas Press, Austin.

Fisher, Christopher T., J. Brett Hill, and Gary M. Feinman

2009 Introduction: Environmental Studies for Twenty-First-Century Conservation. In *The Archaeology of Environmental Change*, edited by Christopher T. Fisher, J. Brett Hill, and Gary M. Feinman, pp. 1–14. University of Arizona Press, Tucson.

Flannery, Kent V.

1972 The Cultural Evolution of Civilizations. *Annual Review of Ecology and Systematics* 3:399–426.

Killion, Thomas W. (editor)

1992 *Gardens of Prehistory: The Archaeology of Settlement Agriculture in Greater Mesoamerica*. University of Alabama Press, Tuscaloosa.

Krech, Shepard III

1999 *The Ecological Indian: Myth and History*. W. W. Norton, New York

López Austin, Alfredo

2013 Ofrenda y comunicación en la tradición religiosa Mesoamericana. In *De hombres y dioses*, edited by Xavier Noguez and Alfredo López Austin. pp. 187–202. El Colegio Mexiquense, A.C., Gobierno del Estado de México, El Colegio de Michoacan, A.C., Zinacantepec, Estado de México.

López Austin, Alfredo, and Leonardo López Luján
2009 *Monte sagrado—Templo Mayor.* Instituto de Investigaciones Antropológicas, Universidad Nacional Autónoma de México, Mexico City.

Luna Golya, Gregory Gerard
2014 Modeling the Aztec Agricultural Waterscape of Lake Xochimilco: A GIS Analysis of Lakebed Chinampas and Settlement. PhD dissertation, Department of Anthropology, Pennsylvania State University, University Park.

MacNeish, Richard S.
1958 Preliminary Archaeological Investigations in the Sierra de Tamaulipas, Mexico. *Transactions of the American Philosophic Society* 48(6):1–210.
1967 A Summary of the Subsistence. In *The Prehistory of the Tehuacan Valley*, Vol. 1, edited by Douglas Byers, pp. 290–309. University of Texas Press, Austin.

McClung de Tapia, Emily
1990 Ecología, agricultura y ganadería durante la Colonia. In *Medicina Novohispana siglo XVI*, Vol. II: *historia de la medicina en México*, edited by Gonzalo Aguirre Beltrán and Roberto Moreno de los Arcos, pp. 60–77. Academia Nacional de Medicina/Facultad de Medicina, Universidad Nacional Autónoma de México, Mexico City.
1984 *Cultura y ecología en Mesoamérica*, 2nd ed. Dirección General de Publicaciones, Universidad Nacional Autónoma de México, Mexico City.
2000 Prehispanic Agricultural Systems in the Basin of Mexico. In *Imperfect Balance: Landscape Transformations in the Precolumbian Americas*, edited by David Lentz, pp. 121–146. Columbia University Press, New York.
2010 Reflexiones en torno al paisaje prehispánico: reconstrucción del paleoambiente del Valle de Teotihuacan. In *VI Coloquio Bosch Gimpera*, edited by E. Ortiz, pp. 245–265. Instituto de Investigaciones Antropológicas, Universidad Nacional Autónoma de México, Mexico City.
2012a Ecological Approaches to Archaeological Research in Central Mexico: New Directions, In *Oxford Handbook of Mesoamerican Archaeology*, edited by Deborah L. Nichols and Christopher Poole, pp. 567–578. Oxford University Press, New York.
2012b Silent Hazards—Invisible Risks: Prehispanic Erosion in the Teotihuacan Valley, Central Mexico. In *Living with the Dangers of Sudden Environmental Change: Understanding Hazards, Mitigating Impacts, Avoiding Disasters*, edited by Jago Cooper and Payson Sheets, pp. 139–161. University Press of Colorado, Niwot.

Morehart, Christopher T., and Charles Frederick
2014 The Chronology and Collapse of Pre-Aztec Raised Field (Chinampa) Agriculture in the Northern Basin of Mexico. *Antiquity* 88:531–548.

Redman, Charles L.
2005 Resilience Theory in Archaeology. *American Anthropologist* 107:70–77.

Redman, Charles L., Margaret C. Nelson, and Anne P. Kinzig
2009 The Resilience of Socioecological Landscapes: Lessons from the Hohokam. In *The Archaeology of Environmental Change*, edited by Christopher T., J. Brett Hill, and Gary M. Feinman, pp. 14–39. University of Arizona Press, Tucson.

Rojas Rabiela, Teresa
1988 *Las siembras de ayer: la agricultura indígena del siglo XVI*. Secretaria de Educación Pública/Centro de Investigaciones y Estudios Superiores de Antropología Social, Mexico.

Sanders, William T.
1957 Tierra y Agua (Soil and Water). A Study of the Ecological Factors in the Development of Meso-American Civilization. PhD dissertation, Department of Anthropology. Harvard University, Cambridge, MA.

1965 *The Cultural Ecology of the Teotihuacan Valley: A Preliminary Report of the Results of the Teotihuacan Valley Project.* Department of Anthropology, Pennsylvania State University, University Park.

1981 *Ecological Adaptation in the Basin of Mexico: 23,000 B.C. to the Present.* Supplement to the Handbook of Middle American Indians Vol. 1, edited by Jeremy A. Sabloff, pp. 147–197. University of Texas Press, Austin.

Sanders, William T., Jeffrey R. Parsons, and Robert S. Santley

1979 *The Basin of México: Ecological Processes in the Evolution of a Civilization.* Academic Press, New York.

Sanders, William T., and Barbara J. Price

1968 *Mesoamerica: The Evolution of a Civilization.* Random House, New York.

Steward, Julian H.

1955 *The Theory of Culture Change: The Methodology of Multilinear Evolution.* University of Illinois Press, Urbana.

Whitehead, Neil L.

1998 Ecological History and Historical Ecology: Diachronic Modeling versus Historical Explanation. In *Advances in Historical Ecology*, edited by William Balée, pp. 30–41. Columbia University Press, New York.

CHAPTER 13

POPULATION HISTORY IN PRECOLUMBIAN AND COLONIAL TIMES

LOURDES MÁRQUEZ MORFÍN
AND REBECCA STOREY

The Basin of Mexico has been central to both the precolumbian and postcolumbian history for Mesoamerica and is one of the locations generally credited with being a "cradle of civilization." It also has been the locus of the largest cities and the densest populations during its history, including contemporary Mexico City. The Basin of Mexico is important because it was the center of the Triple Alliance and its capital city of Tenochtitlan. As population size and density are associated with complex societies, the growth and decline of population at various times mirrored the political fortunes of the societies and people who settled the region.

Modern researchers are fortunate that there are multiple sources of information about the region's population history, something that is not possible for all of Mesoamerica. For the precolumbian period, there are archaeological settlement surveys, skeletal samples, and some ethnohistorical information. For the Colonial period, one can add written records and censuses. All of these, unfortunately, require some assumptions to be useful for reconstructing population history. For example, there is not a single population number given in any written document for the precolumbian period. In the Colonial period there are numbers, but they do not cover all areas of interest, nor was a total population estimate the goal of a census. For the Late Postclassic (A.D. 1350–1519), the period just before Spanish Conquest, and the ensuing Early Colonial Period, the question of the population size is of great interest but also the focus of much debate. We begin with the Pre-Columbian period, discuss the controversy of the Aztec population at the time at the Spanish Conquest, and then proceed to the Colonial period. The archaeological, ethnohistorical, and census evidence forms the basic population estimates, while the skeletal samples can give estimates of fertility and mortality that provide complementary information based on the archaeological estimates of population growth.

The Precolumbian Population

Precolumbian Estimates of Population before the Aztec Periods

Population information prior to the Late Postclassic is based on archaeological survey, which depends on accurate delineation of settlement size and reasonable estimates of population density. These are based on various assumptions and are subject to errors that are not easily quantified. While there may be problems with the numbers, the trend seems to be well supported by the archaeological evidence. The Basin of Mexico was apparently first settled around 1500 B.C. when hamlets and small villages appeared (Sanders et al. 1979). The adoption of agriculture and emergence of sedentism was a process that took several millennia in Mesoamerica (Pool 2012), and it appears that the Basin of Mexico was not among the earliest to experience these trends. The population grew steadily and relatively quickly during these early years, doubling in size about every 200 years (Sanders et al. 1979). The large village of Tlatilco (1300 to 900 B.C.) had an extensive skeletal sample (Márquez Morfín 2006) that reveals a young population with a modest positive growth rate, estimated at a mean family size of 2.9 children (Figure 13.1).

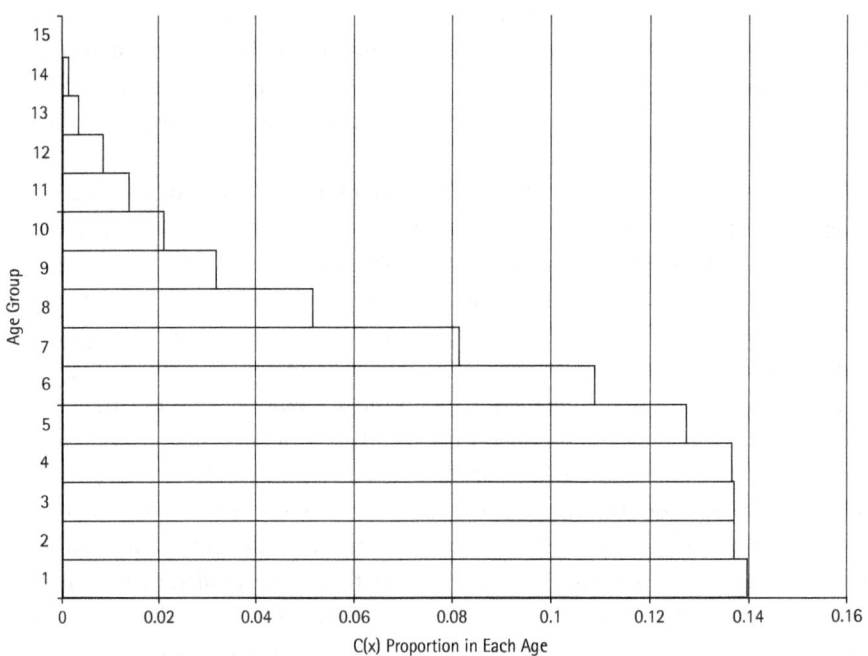

FIGURE 13.1 Hypothetical population pyramid for Tlatilco. Used with permission and calculations done by Patricia Hernandez E. and Lourdes Márquez.

The Basin of Mexico first came to prominence in the Terminal Formative and Classic period (ca. 100 to 600 A.D.), with the rise to prominence of Teotihuacan, the earliest city. An intensive survey of the settlement found over 2,000 apartment compounds, which was the basic residence type, and evidence of urban planning (Millon 1973). Besides being the largest and probably densest city in the Americas at the time, the city had tremendous influence in much of Mesoamerica, even as far as the Maya area, as shown by archaeological research in recent decades (Braswell 2003). Teotihuacan collapsed quickly in the seventh century A.D., and people left the city. Other centers, such as Tula, Cholula, and Xochicalco around the peripheries of the Basin of Mexico, came to prominence in succeeding centuries, while it is debated whether Teotihuacan remained the largest site in the Basin (Parsons and Sugiura 2012). The Basin of Mexico survey found that the population decreased and it became a backwater until perhaps the thirteenth and early fourteenth centuries (Sanders et al. 1979). At this time, centers that would become important in the history of the Triple Alliance started to come to prominence.

Aztec Population Estimates in the Basin of Mexico and Central Mexico

One of the interesting demographic patterns in precolumbian Mesoamerica is the amazing increase in population numbers in the Basin of Mexico that characterizes the last couple of centuries before the arrival of the Spaniards (Sanders et al. 1979). This includes the centers of the Triple Alliance (Tenochtitlan, Texcoco, and Tlacopan), which were relatively unimportant before the development of the most complex and largest empire of the precolumbian. Population growth is documented by a change from 398 sites dated to between A.D. 1150–1350 to 1,636 identified sites dated from A.D. 1350–1519 (Sanders et al. 1979:185), an increase of 400 percent. However, putting actual numbers to this trend is purely a question of applying assumptions and manipulation of data, as there is no way to verify the population size (Henige 1998). The effect of this growth can be seen in the Late Postclassic skeletal sample from San Gregorio Atlapulco-Xochimilco (Hernández 2006; Bullock et al. 2013; Figure 13.2), where a modeled high growth rate of 2.5 percent per year reveals a very young population with a large average family size of five children, especially when compared with the Tlatilco population pyramid (see Figure 13.1).

The size of Tenochtitlan is obviously a key to understanding the number of people present in the late precolumbian times before Spanish contact. As the capital of the Triple Alliance, it was clearly the largest city in the Basin of Mexico and in precolumbian Mesoamerica, but that may be all that most will agree about it. Much of it is buried beneath Mexico City, and little archaeological excavation has been possible. Maps from the Early Colonial period are frankly ambiguous, as are the population estimates made by Spaniards of the time. The most popular estimate is Calnek's (1974) figure of a residential density of 12,000 per km, which, if applied to Tenochtitlan's whole area (12 to 15 km^2) would result in a population of about 150,000 to 200,000 (Figure 13.3).

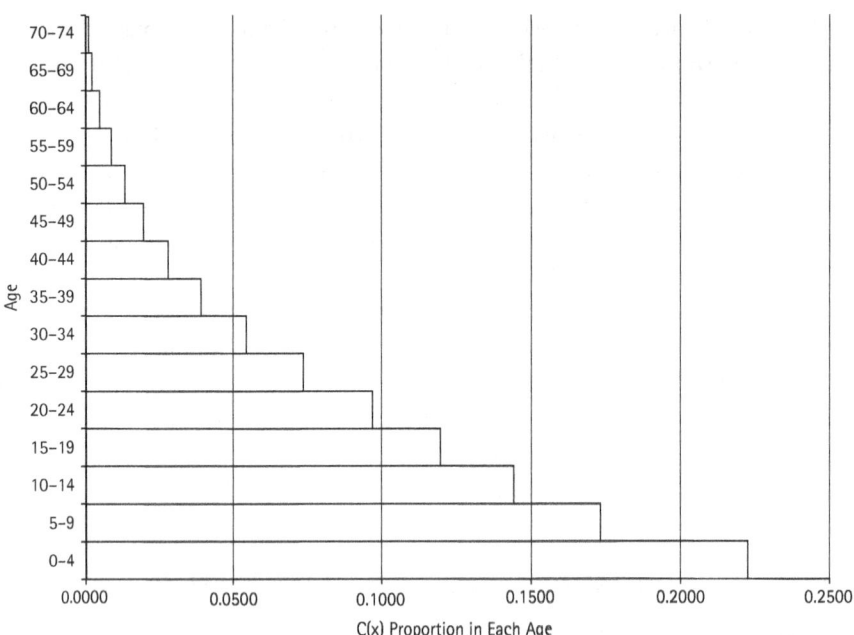

FIGURE 13.2 Population pyramid modeled for skeletal sample from the *chinamperos* of San Gregorio Atlapulco-Xochimilco, Late Postclassic period. Used with permission and calculations done by Patricia Hernandez E. and Lourdes Márquez Morfín.

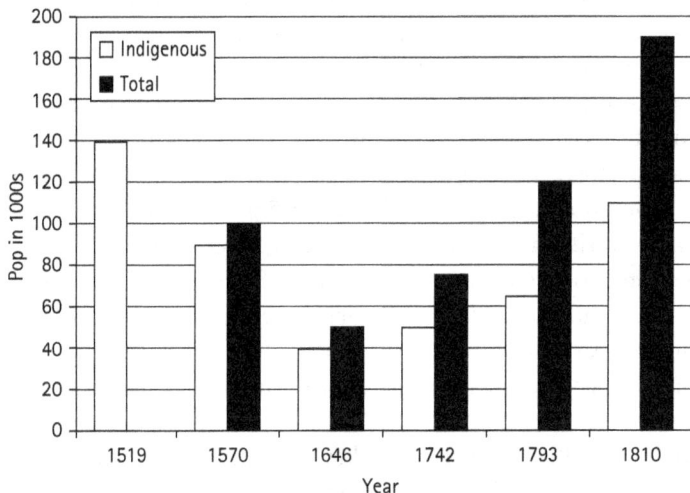

FIGURE 13.3 Estimates and pattern of depopulation during the Colonial period in Greater Tenochtitlan. Source: Aguirre Beltrán 1946; Márquez Morfín 1993.

Smith (2008:152) uses 212,500, and Rojas (2012:52–53, this volume) has recently argued that 300,000 would be reasonable, based on contact period documents and estimates of space per individual. This density, 20,000 to 25,000 per km^2, is only slightly less than that of Manhattan (27,000 per km^2, the most densely settled city in the modern

United States), and Rojas's assumption that cities with multiple-story buildings are suitable as comparable cases is incorrect, given that Tenochtitlan was largely a single-story city (Evans 2013:549). Evans suggests that Tenochtitlan's population was fewer than 100,000. This is a reasonable estimate if Calnek's residential density is applied appropriately, to residential areas only. Tenochtitlan had many plazas and many special-purpose nonresidential buildings, including temples; there were streets, causeways, canals, greenswards, and parks. The area devoted to residences may have been 50 to 60 percent of the total area of 12 to 15 km^2, resulting in an estimated range of population of 72,000 to 108,000. However, there is no way to verify the number. What can be said is that the impressive size of Tenochtitlan is matched by the number of centers and hamlets present in the Basin of Mexico during the last two centuries of the precolumbian era.

However, there is both interest and controversy over the size of the contact population in the Basin of Mexico and the Triple Alliance Empire. It really is a "numbers" game, which is influenced by the philosophy and intuitions of individual researchers (Henige 1998; Rabell 1993). Unfortunately, while numbers have been produced, there is no way at this point in our scholarship to even be sure how close they are to the "truth." Earlier in the twentieth century, the estimates for Mexico at contact were 3.2 million (Kroeber 1934) and Rosenblat (1954) at 4.5 million. Then in the 1960s, the estimates jumped to 25 million (Borah and Cook 1963) and Dobyns (1966) at 30 million to 37.5 million in central Mexico alone. While more recent estimates for Mexico are less at 16 million (Whitmore 1992) and 17.2 million (Denevan 1992), these are definitely higher than the earlier estimates. What changed? Whether one believes the precolumbian populations were few or many seems to be affected by opinions on how complex or "civilized" precolumbian societies were and how devastating European conquest and colonization were (Alchon 2003). Mesoamerica definitely had large-scale, complex, hierarchical societies, so that some dense populations and significant numbers of people would have been present.

Estimates have been made using two sources of information: archaeological settlement surveys and censuses from the Colonial period. Both methods resulting in similar estimates has been seen as providing some conformation for the numbers. Central Mexico has been the focus of research on precontact population estimates. The most famous is Borah and Cook's (1963) estimate of over 25 million, which some have accepted but which has also been severely criticized. Using pre-Conquest tribute lists (compiled in the Colonial period) and other documents, they calculated the number of tributaries in central Mexico. For total population, they multiplied the number of tributaries by a probable average family size (4.5) and then added an estimate of the proportion of population exempted from tribute (35 to 40 percent). However, the relationship between Aztec tribute and population is rather tenuous, as there is no evidence that such tribute was based on the number of taxpayers in a province; it was levied on conquered rulers, and how they collected it is unknown (Sanders 1976). The exempt proportion also seems inflated. As "High Counters," Borah and Cook piled assumption on assumption, and their estimate was more often cited than any evidence warranted (Henige 1998).

Sanders (1976; Sanders et al. 1979) criticized Borah and Cook (1963) but also offered his own calculations based on documentary and archaeological evidence, especially for the Basin of Mexico. He begins with numbers for 1568, the first reliable census evidence, and then calculates a depopulation ratio back to 1519 to arrive at an estimate of 1.0 million to 1.2 million for the Basin of Mexico and 2.6 million to 3.1 million for the Basin and the adjacent areas of Puebla, Tlaxcala, Morelos, and Hidalgo (Sanders 1976:129). He also considers archaeological evidence from archaeological settlement pattern surveys of the Basin of Mexico (Sanders et al. 1979). Archaeologists have recorded 1,636 sites for the Late Postclassic period. Using artifact density and size of settlements, Sanders calculated a population of 1 million to 1.2 million at contact, very similar to his documentary estimate but much less than Borah and Cook.

Whitmore (1992) also tried to calculate the Basin of Mexico's population in 1519 with a computer simulation model based on censuses in 1530s and 1560s, while estimating fertility, mortality, and migration from epidemiological models of morbidity and mortality for newly introduced diseases. He ran the simulation multiple times, varying the demographic and epidemiological parameters, and then compared estimates with the historical data and what seemed probable. He derived an estimate of 1.5 million for the Basin in 1519, close to Sanders (1976), and 16 million for Mexico (64 percent of Borah and Cook 1963).

The Conquest and Colonial Periods

The Depopulation Controversy in the Basin of Mexico and Central Mexico

The underlying reason for controversy about the size of the 1519 population is the question of the magnitude of the depopulation in the Early Colonial period. Throughout the sixteenth century, the Spanish noted the loss of the native population, which they depended on for labor and taxes. The historical consensus is that the conquest and colonization of Mesoamerica was made possible by the introduction of new epidemic diseases to "virgin-soil" populations (e.g., Crosby 1972). Although precolumbian Mesoamerica certainly was not free of disease or famines (Alchon 2003; Márquez 2012), the appearance of smallpox, measles, influenza, and other infectious diseases wreaked havoc on native people and their societies who had no experience, and thus no immunity, against them. In such virgin-soil epidemics, all ages become ill and mortality is high, historically, around 30 to 40 percent for smallpox and 10 to 20 percent for measles (Whitmore 1992). Some feel that the mortality in Mesoamerica would be higher, because everyone would be ill and nurses and cooks would be lacking. There also were the disruptions caused by the Spanish (Dobyns 1993).

The first Old World disease introduced to Mesoamerica was smallpox, in 1520, during the Conquest; this is documented by various eyewitness accounts. The outbreak significantly hampered the defense of Tenochtitlan (Hassig 2006; McCaa 1995), and various sources and researchers claim that half the population of the Basin died during this epidemic (e.g., Dobyns 1993). McCaa (1995) investigated the sources and found that the mortality is not recoverable, whether it was 10 or 50 percent, but it was a significant epidemic and more serious than any in Europe at that time. He projected a probable 30 percent loss, similar to historical examples. The sixteenth-century accounts also point to epidemics in 1545–1546 and 1576–1577 as more deadly, but it is hard to diagnose (McCaa 1995; Prem 1991) let alone document the mortality rate.

The real controversy about the role of disease is not that new diseases were introduced but how widespread and serious their effects were. The precontact High Counters mentioned earlier favor very high depopulation ratios on what was a large and dense population. The depopulation ratio, which Dobyns (1993) had placed at 90 to 95 percent for the Americas based partly on central Mexico, indicates a terrible demographic catastrophe. Whitmore's (1992) simulations for the Basin of Mexico try to test what might be plausible depopulation patterns using epidemiological and demographic modeling. His various simulations were compared with historical estimates and showed that a depopulation ratio of near 90 percent is most likely almost a century after the Conquest, with higher ones being unrealistic.

Perhaps what is distinctive about the Mesoamerican case, and the Americas generally, is the extent of population loss and the long time it took to begin to recover. After the introduction of a new disease, a population starts to recover as soon as the epidemic is passed, but here, with the introduction of so many new diseases within a century, the population never could rebound significantly until a couple of centuries had passed (Whitmore 1992). Add the disruptions caused by the Spanish forcing native labor to extract resources, the loss of native lands to the Spaniards, and lower economic opportunities for survivors, and we find that the Nahuas and others, in essence, lost most of their social, political, and economic institutions, a further hindrance to demographic recovery (Alchon 2003).

Most researchers have simplistically used preconceptions of large, or sometimes small, populations to guide their choice of sources and numeric multipliers, too often unquestioningly using previous estimates of High Counters (Henige 1998). The very high estimates of precontact population and very high depopulation ratios have fallen out of favor. To argue about whether the precise figure was 66 or 75 percent, or even 95 percent, is less important than grasping the tragedy of the post-Conquest demographic history of Mesoamerica (Henige 1998; Alchon 2003).

The Recovery and Colonial Period Population

As the Spanish Colonial period began in the sixteenth century, Tenochtitlan became Mexico City and the Basin part of New Spain. The demography was affected by the depopulation of the natives as well as continued migration into the city, although documents about the people during this century are rare (Márquez 1994). In the first century of the Colonial period, indigenous numbers dropped dramatically, and in the following centuries, the numbers of Spanish, mestizos, and blacks increased (Márquez 1993). Evidence shows that natives were displaced mostly to the peripheries and suburbs of the city, while Spaniards became the dominant ethnic group in the central areas. Also, the population of the city became predominantly female, as they were in demand as servants, nannies, and prostitutes, for a sex ratio of 78 males to 100 females. Migration into the city in search of work also influenced the demographic structure. Sanders' (1976:130) estimates that population in the Basin of Mexico in 1568 (the earliest reliable census information available today) was 404,000 to 407,000 with 109,000 in Greater Mexico City. This indicates that significant depopulation of the native population and significant migration into the city had taken place.

In the sixteenth century, the demographic crisis was more widespread and severe, caused by the smallpox epidemic of 1520–1521, the *cocoliztli* (disease not yet definitely identified) epidemic of 1545–1548, and the *matlazahuatl* epidemic (likely typhus) in 1576. Another important factor was the imbalance in food production, which caused shortages and famine, which also had a negative impact on the population. There also seems to have been a decline in the birth rate among indigenous groups; a disinterest in conceptions and births was probably caused by both ill health and inadequate food. The decline of the indigenous population is not easy to quantify because of intense population movement, due to displacement, relocation, and disappearance of settlements, in some cases by depopulation and in others by the new laws regulating settlements.

The drastic decrease of the population is an accepted fact, but the debate persists as to the amount that occurred as well as the timing of the nadir of the population. Figure 13.3 presents the best information for the Colonial period. The differences in the numbers are very sharp in the first half of the sixteenth century and decrease as we approach the middle of the next century. The nadir of the population is usually placed at around 1650, and there is increase at the end of that century and the beginning of the next. The growth of the nonindigenous population as a proportion of the total population also increases with the rebound to reach its highest proportion by the end of the Colonial period.

For communities of the Valley of Mexico, Gibson (1964) estimates the low was reached in the mid-seventeenth century. There was a severe decrease in the sixteenth century, followed by an increase in the late seventeenth and eighteenth centuries. However, the recovery rate was higher in the southern valley than the north, especially in the eighteenth century. The indigenous population numbers for colonial Mexico City indicate a decrease from before 1560 until the mid-seventeenth century and an increase thereafter. The eighteenth century saw a growth in population, despite a demographic crisis due to *matlazahuatl* (typhus) in 1737 (Gibson 1964). Thus most information indicates that the change to growth occurred after 1650.

There is better information from the eighteenth century, toward the end of the Colonial period. A census by Viceroy Revillagigedo in 1790 (published in 1793, cited in Márquez 1993) listed 112,926 inhabitants of the city. If compared with Sanders' (1976) estimate, it shows that there may have been little growth in the city for two hundred years. Along with the census, there was also a breakdown by ethnic group (Table 13.1),

Table 13.1 Ethnic Groups by Percentage in Mexico City in 1790

	Total (%)	Spanish (%)	Indios (%)	Mulattos (%)	Mestizos (%)	Others (%)
	100.0	48.08	24.43	6.77	18.47	2.22
Men	43.41	20.36	10.72	2.82	7.47	2.02
Women	56.58	27.71	13.71	3.94	11.0	0.20

Source: Márquez Morfín (1994).

Table 13.2 Some Survivorship Estimates for Eighteenth-Century Samples from Colonial Mexico City

Series	$E_{(0)}$	$E_{(15)}$	Average Age	Average Age[a]
Metropolitan Cathedral	24.3	21.6	30.8	34.8
Parroquia de la Soledad	26.2	26.3	33.5	63.5
Hospital de San José	–	15.7	–	29.1

[a] Of those age 15+.
Source: Hernández and Márquez (2008).

although such identities were in flux as people could change their ethnic group or others could impose it. The pattern of mostly Spaniard and female residents, identified earlier in the Colonial period, is still characteristic of the city.

Between 1790 and 1811, the city grew to 168,846 and to 179, 830 by 1820 (Márquez 1994). This is robust growth between these first two censuses, whereas it may be that little growth occurred in the two previous centuries, indicating that perhaps the city took longer to "turn the corner" than the rest of central Mexico. This would fit with the problems of preindustrial cities, which had such poor health and life conditions for much of the population that even maintaining population numbers was difficult (DeVries 1984).

There is some support for this in the few skeletal samples available for the eighteenth century (Table 13.2). The sample from the Cathedral is of Spaniards and some mestizos, probably of good social status. There were 750 individuals, with good representation of all ages except newborns. However, the life expectancy was low at birth (E_0) and not much better at age 15. Even the average age of adults was only about 35 years. Some of these individuals were victims of epidemics and infections, so the overall environment was unhealthy. The Soledad parish sample was of mestizo and indigenous individuals of poor status, but an almost complete lack of young individuals makes their average ages look better. More informative is the still low average adult life expectancy. The poorest segment of the city was at the hospital for new indigenous migrants who had the lowest survivorships, indicating how difficult the city health environment was for new, poor residents.

By the end of the Colonial period, central Mexico was probably growing again. As is usual in regional histories, there are demographic ups and downs. This region is notable for its precolumbian pattern, with tremendous growth in the last two centuries before Spanish contact. Also notable were the severe effects of colonization, including newly introduced diseases, causing probably one of the greatest demographic disasters in human history. The trends are evident, but the actual numbers are unknown. It is hoped that future research will provide more concrete information.

REFERENCES CITED

Aguirre Beltrán, Gonzalo
1946 *La población negra de México, 1519–1810, Estudio etnohistórico*. Fondo de Cultura Económica, México, Mexico City.

Alchon, Suzanne A.
2003 *A Pest in the Land: New World Epidemics in a Global Perspective*. University of New Mexico Press, Albuquerque.

Borah, Woodrow W., and Sherbourne F. Cook
1963 *The Aboriginal Population of Central Mexico on the Eve of the Spanish Conquest*. University of California Press, Berkeley.

Braswell, Geoffrey E. (editor)
2003 *The Maya and Teotihuacan: Reinterpreting Early Classic Interaction*. University of Texas Press, Austin.

Bullock, Meggan, Lourdes Márquez, Patricia Hernández, and Fernando Ruíz
2013 Paleodemographic Age-at-Death Distributions of Two Mexican Skeletal Collections: A Comparison of Transition Analysis and Traditional Aging Methods. *American Journal of PhysicalAnthropology* 152:67–78.

Calnek, Edward E.
1974 Conjunto urbano y modelo residencial en Tenochtitlan. In *Ensayos sobre el desarrollo urbano de México*, edited by Woodrow Borah, pp. 11–65. Secretaría de Educación Pública, Mexico City.

Crosby, Alfred W.
1972 *The Columbian Exchange: Biological and Cultural Consequences of 1492*. Greenwood, Westport, CT.

Denevan, William M.
1992 *The Native Population of the Americas in 1492*, 2nd ed. University of Wisconsin Press, Madison.

De Rojas, Jose Luis
2012 *Tenochtitlan: Capital of the Aztec Empire*. University Press of Florida, Gainesville.

De Vries, Jan
1984 *European Urbanization, 1500–1800*. Harvard University Press, Cambridge, MA.

Dobyns, Henry F.
1966 Estimating Aboriginal American Population: An Appraisal of Techniques with a New Hemispheric Estimate. *Current Anthropology* 7:395–416, 425–349.

1993 Disease Transfer at Contact. *Annual Review of Anthropology* 22:273–291.

Evans, Susan T.

2013 *Ancient Mexico and Central America: Archaeology and Culture History*, 3rd ed. Thames & Hudson, London.

Gibson, Charles F.

1964 *The Aztecs under Spanish Rule: A History of the Indians of the Valley of Mexico, 1519–1810*. Stanford University Press, Stanford, CA.

Hassig, Ross

2006 *Mexico and the Spanish Conquest*, 2nd ed. University of Oklahoma Press, Norman.

Henige, David P.

1998 *Numbers from Nowhere: The American Indian Contact Population Debate*. University of Oklahoma Press, Norman.

Hernández, Patricia

2006 Entre flores y chinampas: la salud de los entiguos habitantes de xochimilco. In *Salud y sociedad en el México prehispánico y colonial*, edited by L. Márquez Morfín and E. P. Hernández, pp. 327–366. Conaculta, Instituto Nacional de Antropología e Historia, Mexico City.

Hernández, Patricia, and Lourdes Márquez

2008 Vivir en la época colonial: avatares de los vecinos de la antigua Ciudad de México. Paper presented at the XI Reunión Nacional de Investigación Demográfica en México, Mérida, Mexico.

Kroeber, Alfred L.

1934 Native American Population. *American Anthropologist* 36:1–25.

Márquez Morfin, Lourdes

1993 La evolución cuantitativa de la población novohispana siglos XVI–XVIII. In *El poblamiento de México: una visión histórico-demográfica*, edited by Ana Arenzana, pp. 33–63. Consejo Nacional de Población, Mexico City.

1994 *La desigualdad ante la muerte en la Ciudad de México: el Tifo y el Cólera*. Siglo Veintiuno Editores, Mexico City.

2006 La transición de la salud en Tlatilco y el surgimiento del estado en Cuicuilco. In *Salud y sociedad en el México prehispánico y colonial*, edited by Lourdes Márquez Morfín and Patricia Hernández Espinosa, pp. 151–210. Conaculta, Instituto Nacional de Antropología e Historia, Mexico City.

2012 Vida urbana y salud en la Mesoamérica Prehispánica. *Boletín de Antropología* 26(43):215–238.

McCaa, Robert

1995 Spanish and Nahuatl Views on Smallpox and Demographic Catastrophe in Mexico. *Journal of Interdisciplinary History* 25:397–431.

Millon, Rene

1973 *Urbanization at Teotihuacan, Mexico*, Vol. 1: *The Teotihuacan Map. Part One: The Text*. University of Texas Press, Austin.

Parsons, Jeffrey R., and Yoko Sugiura Y.

2012 Teotihuacan and the Epiclassic in Central Mexico. In *The Oxford Handbook of Mesoamerican Archaeology*, edited by Deborah L. Nichols and Christopher A. Pool, pp. 309–323. Oxford University Press, Oxford.

Pool, Christopher A.

2012 The Formation of Complex Societies in Mesoamerica. In *The Oxford Handbook of Mesoamerican Archaeology*, edited by Deborah L. Nichols and Christopher A. Pool, pp. 169–187. Oxford University Press, Oxford.

Prem, Hans J.
1991 Disease Outbreaks in Central Mexico during the Sixteenth Century. In *"Secret Judgments of God": Old World Disease in Colonial Spanish America*, edited by N. David Cook and W. G. Lovell, pp. 20–48. University of Oklahoma Press, Norman.

Rabell, Cecilia
1993 El descenso de la población indígena durante el siglo XVI y las cuentas del gran capitán. In *La población de México*, Vol. 2, pp. 18–37. Consejo Nacional de Población, México, D.F.

Rosenblat, Ángel
1954 *La población indígena y el mestizaje en América*. Editorial Nova, Buenos Aires.

Sanders, William T.
1976 The Population of the Central Mexican Symbiotic Region, the Basin of Mexico, and the Teotihuacan Valley in the Sixteenth Century. In *The Native Population of the Americas in 1492*, edited by W. M. Denevan, pp. 85–151. University of Wisconsin Press, Madison.

Sanders, William T., Jeffrey Parsons, and Robert S. Santley
1979 *The Basin of Mexico: Ecological Processes in the Evolution of a Civilization*. Academic Press, New York.

Smith, Michael E.
2008 *Aztec City-State Capitals*. University of Florida Presses, Gainesville.

Whitmore, Thomas M.
1992 *Disease and Death in Early Colonial Mexico: Simulating Amerindian Depopulation*. Westview Press, Boulder, CO.

CHAPTER 14

AZTEC URBANISM

Cities and Towns

MICHAEL E. SMITH

The huge Mexica capital Tenochtitlan (Rojas 2012) drew the attention and admiration of the Spanish conquerors and chroniclers, and today Tenochtitlan sometimes seems synonymous with the concept of Aztec urbanism. Yet this hyperurbanized metropolis was an anomaly, the least-typical city in the entire Aztec Empire. The Aztec landscape was divided politically into several hundred *altepetl*, or city-states, and the modest capitals of these small polities were the predominant form of Aztec city (Smith 2008). As in other city-state cultures throughout history (Hansen 2000), the capitals cannot be understood outside of their political and administrative context.

Most Aztec *altepetl* and their capitals were founded in the Early Aztec period in the wake of the Aztlan migrations (Smith 2006). The forms and functions of these cities synthesized two historical traditions: (a) millennia-old Mesoamerican urban patterns and (b) innovations created by the Aztec kings and their architects. Mesoamerican cities—from the Olmec period on—exhibit several fundamental principles of urban planning (Smith 2007). First, most cities had a standard set of civic buildings: temple-pyramids, smaller shrines, ballcourts, and royal palaces. Second, these buildings were arranged carefully around formal rectangular plazas. Third, most of the civic architecture was concentrated in an epicenter, and large cities often had smaller, subsidiary ceremonial zones. And fourth, commoners and lower-ranking elites built their houses in neighborhoods around the epicenter without planning or direction from the king or central administration. In most Mesoamerican cities, residential density was low (in comparison with Old World cities) because major areas were dedicated to cultivation as gardens or infields (Isendahl and Smith 2013).

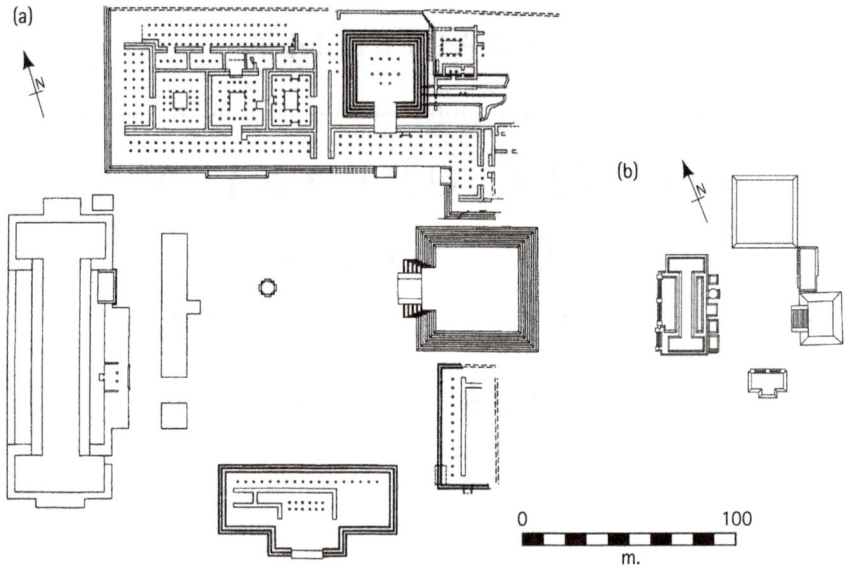

FIGURE 14.1 Epicenters of the Toltec capital Tula and Coatetelco, an *altepetl* capital in Morelos. A: modified from Mastache et al. (2002:92); B: map by Michael E. Smith.

When Aztec kings established their dynasties, they looked back to the kings of Tula (Mastache et al. 2002) as their sacred ancestors and the source of legitimacy. They even invented a whole mythology of the greatness of the Toltecs and the wealth of Tula. It is hardly surprising, then, that some Aztec kings adopted the epicenter layout of Tula as a template for laying out their own cities. Key elements include the use of a single large public plaza with the largest pyramid on the eastern side, a royal palace and ballcourt on other sides of the plaza (Smith 2006, 2008:ch. 3), and an overall high level of symmetry and formality of layout (Smith, 2007). The city of Coatetelco, in Morelos, was clearly modeled after Tula, although on a smaller scale (Figure 14.1). Locations of the major cities discussed in this chapter are shown in Figure 14.2.

A Sample of Aztec Cities

Almost all of the capitals of *altepetl* at the time of the Spanish Conquest were founded during the Middle Postclassic period. The founding of a city was an important ceremonial event that established both the legitimate dynasty of the rulers and the city as an urban place (Smith 2006). The most powerful *altepetl* of the Middle Postclassic period was *Tenayuca*. According to historical accounts, Tenayuca was founded by

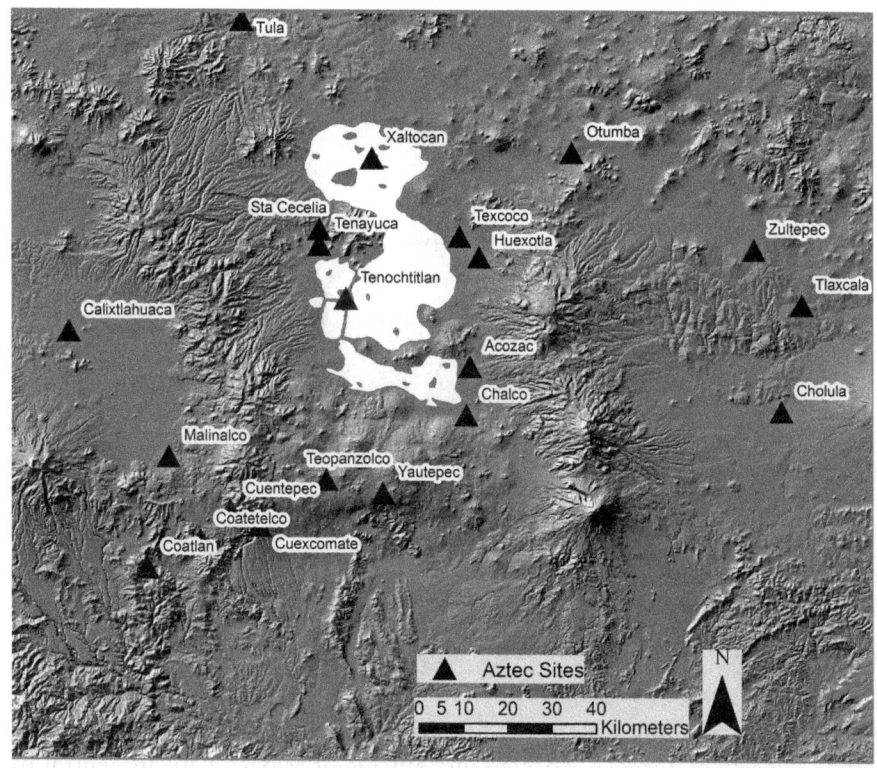

FIGURE 14.2 Map of the locations of the best-documented Aztec cities. Map by Juliana Novic.

FIGURE 14.3 The main pyramid of Tenayuca. Photograph by Michael E. Smith.

FIGURE 14.4 Circular temple at Huexotla. Photograph by Michael E. Smith.

the semi-legendary king Xolotl, the first of the Nahuatl kings and founder of the Acolhua dynasty of Texcoco. Located just outside of Mexico City, its central pyramid was the focus of one of the first major excavations after the Mexican Revolution (Anonymous 1935). This pyramid had two stairways, leading to two temples on top (Figure 14.3).

There is more information about cities in the Late Aztec period. Three cities that survive today as government archaeological zones—Huexotla, Ixtapaluca, and Calixtlahuaca—give an idea of the nature of cities in Late Aztec times. *Huexotla* was an important city affiliated with the Acolhua kingdom; the king of Huexotla was a subject of Nezahualcoyotl and the other kings of Texcoco. More than 100 years ago, Leopoldo Batres excavated several buildings, including a platform with large rooms known today as *La Comunidad*, and a circular temple dedicated to Ehecatl, the god of wind (Figure 14.4). In the 1970s, Elizabeth Brumfiel carried out an archaeological study of the social and economic organization of the ancient city (Batres 1904; Brumfiel 1980; García García 1987).

Ixtapaluca was another *altepetl* whose king was subject to Texcoco. Part of the site was excavated in the 1970s as a salvage project. A housing development, the Unidad Deportiva y Residencial Campestre Acozac, was planned for the hilltop that contained the ruins of the ancient city. When the construction activities for this project destroyed several ancient buildings, the work was stopped and excavations began. The major structures were excavated and restored, and visitors can see them today (Figure 14.5). The large structure in the middle was probably a palace, but half of the building

FIGURE 14.5 Central plaza at Ixtapaluca, looking north from the main pyramid. Photograph by Michael E. Smith.

was destroyed by construction activity before the work was stopped (Blanton 1972; Brüggemann 1976).

Calixtlahuaca is an archaeological zone just north of the city of Toluca. Formerly called Matlatzinco, the city was the capital of the Toluca Valley before its conquest by the Mexica emperor Axayacatl in 1478. José García Payón first excavated at the site in the 1930s and restored the major buildings. The site contains the best-preserved examples of an Aztec royal palace and a circular Ehecatl temple. More recent fieldwork at the site (Smith et al. 2009; Smith et al. 2013) revealed an urban area of 2.64^2 km that covered the sides of an extinct volcanic crater, Cerro Tenismo. The entire hillside was terraced, with houses and agricultural plots on most terraces.

URBANIZATION

As the capitals of *altepetl* and as distinctive places on the landscape, Aztec cities were of fundamental importance in Aztec society. Yet in his influential synthesis of early Colonial Nahuatl-language documents, James Lockhart (1992:19) downplayed the size and importance of these cities, claiming that "a dominant central city was not really compatible with the principles of *altepetl* organization. The notion of a city separate from the *altepetl* did not enter into the vocabulary in the form of any distinct word." Lockhart (1993:19–20) did not even accept the label "city" as appropriate for these settlements, which he saw as merely places where several calpolli intersected in a nonurban settlement. Lockhart's account contains serious errors and distortions, and because his ideas have now entered the secondary literature (e.g., Hirth 2008), some comment is called for.

Lockhart's claim that Nahuatl lacked a "distinct word" for city was countered by Pedro Carrasco (1999:16–20), who discusses several such terms. The problem is that the absence of terms for "city" in the particular (Colonial period) documents analyzed by Lockhart was transformed into a claim for the lack of such a word in the Nahuatl language. More serious, however, is Lockhart's claim that *altepetl* centers were not distinctive places on the landscape. This claim is contradicted by three kinds of evidence. First, *altepetl* capitals were much larger than other settlements. Second, they contained distinctive monumental civic architecture not found in smaller settlements. Third, they were the setting for urban functions—activities and institutions that had a powerful effect on hinterland communities—and such urban functions were lacking in smaller communities. A foreign visitor would have had no difficulty at all in identifying the capital city of an *altepetl*.

The sources of Lockhart's errors are not hard to find. First, although the *altepetl* continued functioning into the Colonial period, its status shrank from an independent polity to a local administrative unit. The *altepetl* in Lockhart's documents was not a state polity. It no longer sponsored warfare, and it no longer administered a state religion. Its leader, still known as a *tlahtoani*, was no longer a king; he was a low-level bureaucrat. The urban functions of the *altepetl* capital were terminated. So while Lockhart was correct in claiming that *altepetl* centers were not important *in a particular group of colonial period documents*, his inferences cannot be applied to Aztec cities without serious distortion. The second source of his errors is his failure to consider the archaeological record.

In comparison with the hyper-urbanized Tenochtitlan, Aztec *altepetl* capitals were considerably smaller (Table 14.1). The median city covered 209 hectares in area, with a median population of 7,250. The median population density was 50 persons per hectare (5,000 persons per square kilometer). But these capital cities were an order of magnitude larger than other settlements within the *altepetl*. According to data assembled by Mary Hodge (1997) and others—presented in Smith (2008:152)—the median size of the second-largest settlement in an *altepetl* of the Basin of Mexico was 7 percent of the size of the capital city. In other words, these cities were much larger than any other settlement in their *altepetl*. The following sections document the distinctiveness of *altepetl* capitals in their civic architecture and urban functions, demonstrating the inadequacy of Lockhart's view of these settlements. In one respect, however, Aztec cities did resemble smaller settlements: commoner life was quite similar in rural and urban settings.

Table 14.1 Sizes of Aztec Cities in the Late Aztec Period.

City	Area (ha.)		Population	
	City	Epicenter	No.	Density
State of Mexico				
Amecameca	400		10,000	25
Calixtlahuaca	285		–	–
Cerro Tlaloc			–	–
Chalco	250		12,500	50
Chiautla	115		600	40
Chi malhuacan	260		12,000	45
Coatepec	85		2,500	35
Coatlinchan	210		11,000	25
Cuitlahuac	90		4,500	50
Culhuacan	65		4,400	70
Huexotla	300		17,100	57
Ixtapalapa	28		2,800	100
Ixtapaluca	90	15.0	1,400	16
Malinalco	–	–	–	–
Mixquic	45		2,300	50
Otumba	220		10,700	49
Sta. Cecelia Acatitlan			–	–
Tenayuca			–	–
Tepetlaoztoc	450		13,500	30
Texcoco	450		24,100	54
Tlalmanalco	80		4,000	50
Xaltocan	26		1,300	50
Xochimilco	214		10,700	50
Federal District				
Azcapotzalco	–	–	–	–
Tlacopan	–	–	–	–

(continued)

Table 14.1 (Continued)

City	Area (ha.)		Population	
	City	Epicenter	No.	Density
Tenochtitlan	1,350	16.9	212,500	157
Tlatelolco	–	–	–	–
Other states				
Cholula (Puebla)	–	–	–	–
Zultepec (Tlaxcala)	–	8.0	–	–
Coatetelco (Morelos)	–	1.1	–	–
Coatlan (Morelos)	15	1.0	800	53
Cuexcomate (Morelos)	15	1.2	800	53
Teopanzolco (Morelos)	–	1.9	–	–
Tepozteco (Morelos)	–	–	–	–
Yautepec (Morelos)	209	–	15,100	72
Median size	209	1.9	7,250	50

Note: Data from: Smith (2008).

PUBLIC ARCHITECTURE

The monumental buildings in *altepetl* capitals were constructed of stone. Most temples consisted of small rooms located on top of step pyramids. The rooms, which housed images of the gods and other items of religious cult and ceremony, were reached by a stairway on one side of the pyramid. The pyramids and platforms were filled with rough stone rubble. The exteriors of buildings were covered with lime plaster, which was often painted red. In this section I describe the major building types; this discussion is based on Smith (2008:ch. 4).

Pyramids with Two Temples

The pyramid with two temples on top, each with its own stairway up the side of the pyramid, was a popular style in the Early Aztec period; surviving examples include Tenayuca (Figure 14.1), Santa Cecilia Acatitlan, and Teopanzolco. In the Late

Aztec period, most pyramids had only a single temple (see later discussion). But at Tenochtitlan, Tlatelolco, and Texcoco, this ancient style was revived, perhaps as a deliberate reference to the great ancient city of Tenayuca. The best-known Aztec-period temple is the Templo Mayor of Tenochtitlan, a pyramid with two temples. There is considerable information, from both archaeology and ethnohistory, about the symbolism, rituals, and religious significance of the Templo Mayor (see López Austin and López Luján, this volume). The extent to which these interpretations can be applied to other temples is unknown.

Pyramids with a Single Temple

The rectangular pyramid with a single temple on top was the most common form at Aztec-period cities (Figure 14.1B). The largest temple in a city was usually dedicated to the patron god of the *altepetl*. Excavations at a pyramid with a single temple at Calixtlahuaca (structure 4) uncovered offerings of vessels with the face of Tlaloc, leading to the interpretation that this temple was dedicated to Tlaloc. But this is an exception to the usual situation at capitals of *altepetl*, where the identity of the patron god is uncertain. These pyramids ranged in size from small to very large. Most cities had numerous temples of this form in addition to their large, central temple, often serving as neighborhood temples (see Figure 14.6).

FIGURE 14.6 Structure 1, a neighborhood temple at Calixtlahuaca. Photograph by Maëlle Sergheraert, Calixtlahuaca Archaeological Project.

Circular Temples

Unlike the rectangular pyramids, which could be dedicated to a wide range of gods, circular pyramids (Figure 14.4) were always dedicated to Ehecatl, god of wind and avatar of Quetzalcoatl (Pollock 1936). This association is known from numerous depictions in the ritual codices and accounts in written sources. In a few cases, sculptures of Ehecatl have been excavated as offerings in circular pyramids, as at temple 3 at Calixtlahuaca or a small circular pyramid excavated in the metro in Mexico City; the latter structure is visible to the public today in the Pino Suárez metro station.

Ball Courts

Ball courts were important features at all Aztec-period cities, and the pictorial codices have many images of ballcourts at capitals of *altepetl* (Nicholson and Quiñones Keber 1991). Only a few ballcourts have been excavated at Aztec-period sites, however. The site of Coatetelco in Morelos (Figure 14.1B) has the most completely excavated Aztec ballcourt (Arana Álvarez 1984), and part of a ballcourt under the Sacred Cathedral in Mexico City was excavated by the Programa de Arqueología Urbana (Matos Moctezuma 2001).

Small Altars

Small platforms or altars were important features at Mesoamerican cities for many centuries. But in the Aztec period urban designers started building many small platforms in prominent locations. These altars became one of the most distinctive features of urban planning at cities in this period (Smith 2008:108–113). The photograph of Ixtapaluca (Figure 14.5) shows two of these features in the foreground. Although excavations of small altars and ethnohistorical documents provide some clues about their use and significance, they remain poorly understood. Some were bases for racks of skulls from sacrificial victims; others were shrines dedicated to themes of female fertility and curing associated with the *tzitzimime* deities (Klein 2000); and others were altars for offerings to the god Tezcatlipoca (Olivier 2003). For individual shrines, it is difficult to distinguish between these or other possible uses. Nevertheless, the large number of these altars and their central locations in cities indicate that they were a crucial component of the urban townscape.

Palaces

Each *altepetl* capital had a royal palace. It was the residence of the *tlahtoani* and his family; the center of government, where advisors and high nobles gathered for meetings; a meeting place; and an economic facility where goods were stored and artisans produced fine objects for the *tlahtoani*. There are a number of depictions of royal palaces in the codices, and several have been excavated (see Evans, this volume). Although each example was unique in its size and form, all Aztec palaces shared key principles of design (Evans 2004; Smith 2008:115–119).

Palaces were built around an open courtyard with a single opening to the outside. Opposite the opening was a platform that served as a shrine for offerings and ritual activities. On the sides of the palaces were rooms built on low platforms. These rooms included both residential facilities and important chambers for the *tlahtoani* and his government. Nobles below the level of the *tlahtoani* built palaces that were smaller than the royal palace but with similar principles of design.

Other Public Buildings

Other public buildings in Aztec cities included schools and buildings where warriors gathered. Two kinds of schools are described in written documents: the *calmecac* and the *telpochcalli* (Calnek 1988). Houses where elite warriors gathered are described in some written sources, and one example—the Eagle Warriors House—has been excavated adjacent to the Templo Mayor of Tenochtitlan (López Luján 2006).

Urban Functions and Regional Context

The capitals of *altepetl* were urban centers where a variety of activities were concentrated. Activities and institutions that occur in cities but affect a larger part of the landscape are called "urban functions." The major urban functions of these cities can be described as political, religious, and economic.

The status of Aztec cities as capitals of *altepetl* is an example of a *political urban function*. The *tlahtoani* (ruler) resided in the capital city, but his influence extended to the entire *altepetl*. This political role was the most important urban function of these cities. The royal palace—the center of political and administrative activities—was usually the largest building within an *altepetl* (largest in area, but not in height), highlighting the centrality of the king.

The territorial organization of the *altepetl* followed principles very different from those of modern nation-states. In the contemporary world, a polity or state is defined by territory and borders. Membership is defined by location: people living within the borders are citizens and those outside are not. The *altepetl*, however, was structured differently. Instead of having borders that were marked and defended, membership in the *altepetl* was defined by personal relationships (Tomaszewski and Smith 2011). All people who were subject to a *tlahtoani* were members of his *altepetl*. Sometimes people subject to a given *tlahtoani* lived interspersed with those subject to a rival *tlahtoani* (Gibson 1964:44–47). This principle shows the importance of the *tlahtoani* in the organization of the *altepetl*. It also illustrates why the political function was the most important function of these cities: the *tlahtoani* lived in the capital, and the capital existed in order to support and promote the reign of the *tlahtoani* (Smith 2008).

The tlatoque claimed supernatural support for their rule, and many of the sacrifices and ceremonies at the city's central pyramid helped reinforce their power and legitimacy. As *religious urban functions*, rituals within the city affected the entire *altepetl*. People from outside the city came into town to participate in ceremonies, and the offerings that priests made to the gods were done in the name of the entire *altepetl*. The link between religion and politics in the *altepetl* was so strong that it is difficult today for us to separate the two fields.

The capitals of *altepetl* were also centers of economic activity, but *economic urban functions* were far more variable than the political and religious functions discussed earlier. All cities had a marketplace where goods from near and far could be purchased. Most markets met once a week (the week was five days in the Aztec period), and the larger cities had markets that met every day (Smith 2012:ch. 5).

Archaeologists have found that there was much variation among cities in the extent of craft production. At one end of the scale was Otumba, a craft center in the Teotihuacan Valley with numerous workshops for the production of obsidian tools, maguey textiles, ceramic objects, and other items (Nichols et al. 2000). At the other end of the scale, Brumfiel (1980) found no evidence of craft production at Huexotla other than the domestic production of textiles, a fundamental activity within all families. Other urban sites where craft production has been studied by archaeologists (e.g., Calixtlahuaca, Xaltocan, and Yautepec) have more workshops than Huexotla but fewer than Otumba.

Urban Life

Whereas the realms of public architecture and urban functions sharply distinguished *altepetl* capitals from smaller settlements, the nature of urban life was remarkably similar in urban and rural contexts.

Urban Households

Excavations of houses have provided much new information about the lives of both commoners and nobles in Aztec cities (see De Lucia, this volume). Two types of commoner house have been identified. In Tenochtitlan and other cities in the Basin of Mexico, houses were complex structures with several rooms (Evans 1988; Alcántara Gallegos 2004). In Morelos and the Toluca Valley, on the other hand, most commoner houses were small, one-room structures (Smith et al. 1989; Smith et al. 1999; Smith et al. 2013).

In Morelos, comparisons of urban and rural domestic contexts revealed many similarities (Smith 2012:chs. 3, 6). Commoner houses were identical in rural and urban settings; both areas had small, adobe-brick houses. The population densities were quite similar (60 persons/ha in urban Yautepec and 50 persons/ha in the rural town of Cuexcomate), suggesting the presence of cultivation within both rural and urban settlements (Isendahl and Smith 2013). While each region had its own suite of decorated serving vessels, the assemblages of ceramic forms were identical in rural and urban settings. Rural and urban households had ready access to imported goods, from obsidian to ceramic vessels to bronze objects (Nichols 2004). In Aztec central Mexico, rural and urban life were not terribly different.

Neighborhoods

The *calpolli* was a group of commoners who lived near one another and shared some basic economic and social characteristics, including service to a noble who owned the land people farmed (see Smith and Hicks, this volume). In many cities, the calpolli operated as a neighborhood. The members lived in a cluster, spatially separated from the residents of other neighborhoods. Each calpolli had a patron god, whose image was kept in a temple that served the neighborhood (Figure 14.6). Most calpolli in cities also had a telpochcalli (school) and a small market. In Tenochtitlan and Otumba, some calpolli were specialized economically.

Popular Participation

While people probably spent most of their time in their own neighborhoods and fields, a variety of events brought people from different neighborhoods together, often in the central area of their city. Attending the market was the most common such event. Public religious ceremonies were another opportunity for popular participation in the life of the city. The 18 monthly ceremonies typically lasted for several days and included many different types of activity. Some of these, including processions and dances, were settings for widespread popular participation.

People also had obligations to the *tlahtoani* and the *altepetl* that were organized on a public basis. For example, most urban residents had to provide goods or labor service to the palace. This was organized on a rotating basis; when it was a family's turn, its members went to the palace to run errands or do other tasks (Hicks 1984). Large public construction projects—temples, palaces, dams, and canals for irrigation—were organized by a form of labor service known as *coatequitl*. Officials organized the workers in each neighborhood into groups of 20 laborers, who had to work for a certain number of days each year (Rojas Rabiela 1979).

Aztec Cities Today

Most *altepetl* capitals were transformed into colonial cities, leaving few remains for archaeologists to study. Those cities whose ruins remain intact today as archaeological zones have a particularly important role. Sites such as Huexotla, Otumba, Xaltocan, Calixtlahuaca, and others are places where archaeologists continue to learn about these ancient cities that once dominated the landscape of central Mexico. These are also places where the public can see ancient remains and learn first-hand about these ancient cities. They contain tangible evidence of the history and heritage of both individual communities and the Mexican nation.

For these reasons, it is important to protect these places from further destruction. Governments at all levels—national, state, and municipal—play crucial roles in the protection of archaeological zones. The members of local communities have perhaps the most important role in protecting sites from illegal looting and destruction. These archaeological sites are places where scholarship and heritage come together for the benefit of both realms.

References Cited

Alcántara Gallegos, Alejandro
2004 Los barrios de Tenochtitlan: topografía, organización interna y tipología de sus predios. In *Historia de la vida cotidiana en México*, Vol. I: *Mesoamérica y los ámbitos indígenas de la Nueva España*, edited by Pablo Escalante Gonzalbo, pp. 167–198. El Colegio de México and Fondo de Cultura Económica, Mexico City.

Anonymous
1935 *Tenayuca: estudio arqueológico de la pirámide de este lugar, hecho por el Departamento de Monumentos de la Secretaría de Educación Pública*. Talleres Gráficos del Museo Nacional de Antropología, Historia y Etnografía, Mexico City.

Arana Álvarez, Raúl M.
1984 El juego de pelota en Coatetelco, Morelos. In *Investigaciones recientes en el área maya, XVII Mesa Redonda, Sociedad Mexicana de Antropología*, Vol. 4, pp. 191–204. Sociedad Mexicana de Antropología, Mexico City.

Batres, Leopoldo
1904 *Mis exploraciones en Huexotla, Texcoco y Montículo de "El Gavilán."* J. I. Guerro, Mexico City.

Blanton, Richard E.
1972 *Prehistoric Settlement Patterns of the Ixtapalapa Region, Mexico*. Occasional Papers in Anthropology Vol. 6. Department of Anthropology, Pennsylvania State University, University Park.

Brüggemann, Jürgen Kurt (editor)
1976 *Estudios estratigráficos en el sitio arqueológico de acozac, 1973, y estudios estratigráficos en el ajusco, 1974*. Departamento de Monumentos Prehispánicos, Serie Arqueología Vol. 3. Instituto Nacional de Antropología e Historia, Mexico City.

Brumfiel, Elizabeth M.
1980 Specialization, Market Exchange, and the Aztec State: A View From Huexotla. *Current Anthropology* 21:459–478.

Calnek, Edward E.
1988 The Calmecac and Telpochcalli in Pre-Conquest Tenochtitlan. In *The Work of Bernardino de Sahagún: Pioneer Ethnographer of Sixteenth-Century Aztec Mexico*, edited by Jorge Klor de Alva, H. B. Nicholson, and Eloise Quiñones Keber, pp. 169–177. Institute for Mesoamerican Studies, Albany, NY.

Carrasco, Pedro
1999 *The Tenochca Empire of Ancient Mexico: The Triple Alliance of Tenochtitlan, Tetzcoco, and Tlacopan*. University of Oklahoma Press, Norman.

Evans, Susan T.
1988 *Excavations at Cihuatecpan, an Aztec Village in the Teotihuacan Valley*. Vanderbilt University Publications in Anthropology Vol. 36. Department of Anthropology, Vanderbilt University, Nashville.
2004 Aztec Palaces and Other Elite Residential Architecture. In *Palaces of the Ancient New World*, edited by Susan T. Evans and Joanne Pillsbury, pp. 7–58. Dumbarton Oaks Library and Collection, Washington, DC.

García García, María Teresa
1987 *Huexotla: un sitio del Acolhuacan*. Colección Científica Vol. 165. Instituto Nacional de Antropología e Historia, Mexico City.

Gibson, Charles
1964 *The Aztecs Under Spanish Rule: A History of the Indians of the Valley of Mexico, 1519–1810*. Stanford University Press, Stanford, CA.

Hansen, Mogens Herman (editor)
2000 *A Comparative Study of Thirty City-State Cultures*. Royal Danish Academy of Sciences and Letters, Copenhagen.

Hicks, Frederic
1984 Rotational Labor and Urban Development in Prehispanic Tetzcoco. In *Explorations in Ethnohistory: Indians of Central Mexico in the Sixteenth Century*, edited by Herbert R. Harvey and Hanns J. Prem, pp. 147–174. University of New Mexico Press, Albuquerque.

Hirth, Kenneth G.
2008 Incidental Urbanism: The Structure of the Prehispanic City in Central Mexico. In *The Ancient City: New Perspectives on Urbanism in the Old and New World*, edited by Joyce Marcus and Jeremy Sabloff, pp. 273–298. SAR Press, Santa Fe, NM.

Hodge, Mary G.
1997 When Is a City-State? Archaeological Measures of Aztec City-States and Aztec City-State Systems. In *The Archaeology of City-States: Cross-Cultural Approaches*, edited by Deborah L. Nichols and Thomas H. Charlton, pp. 209–228. Smithsonian Institution Press, Washington, DC.

Isendahl, Christian, and Michael E. Smith
2013 Sustainable Agrarian Urbanism: The Low-Density Cities of the Mayas and Aztecs. *Cities* 31:132–143.

Klein, Cecelia F.
2000 The Devil and the Skirt: An Iconographic Inquiry into the Pre-Hispanic Nature of the Tzitzimime. *Ancient Mesoamerica* 11:1–26.

Lockhart, James
1992 *The Nahuas After the Conquest: A Social and Cultural History of the Indians of Central Mexico, Sixteenth Through Eighteenth Centuries*. Stanford University Press, Stanford, CA.

López Luján, Leonardo
2006 *La Casa de las Águilas: un ejemplo de arquitectura religiosa de Tenochtitlan.* 2 vols. Fonda de Cultura Económica, Conaculta, and Instituto Nacional de Antropología e Historia, Mexico City.

Mastache, Alba Guadalupe, Robert H. Cobean, and Dan M. Healan
2002 *Ancient Tollan: Tula and the Toltec Heartland.* University Press of Colorado, Boulder.

Matos Moctezuma, Eduardo
2001 The Ballcourt in Tenochtitlan. In *The Sport of Life and Death: The Mesoamerican Ballgame*, edited by E. Michael Whittington, pp. 88–95. Thames & Hudson, New York.

Nichols, Deborah L.
2004 The Rural and Urban Landscapes of the Aztec State. In *Mesoamerican Archaeology: Theory and Practice*, edited by Julia A. Hendon and Rosemary Joyce, pp. 265–295. Blackwell, Oxford.

Nichols, Deborah L., Mary Jane McLaughlin, and Maura Benton
2000 Production Intensification and Regional Specialization: Maguey Fibers and Textiles in the Aztec City-State of Otumba. *Ancient Mesoamerica* 11:267–292.

Nicholson, H. B., and Eloise Quiñones Keber
1991 Ballcourt Images in Central Mexican Native Traditional Pictorial Manuscripts. In *The Mesoamerican Ballgame: Papers Presented at the International Colloquium, "The Mesoamerican Ballgame, 2000 BC–AD 2000,"* edited by Gerard W. van Bussell, Paul L. F. van Dongen, and Ted J. J. Leyenaar, pp. 119–133. Rijksmuseum voor Volkenkunde, Leiden.

Olivier, Guilhem
2003 *Mockeries and Metamorphoses of an Aztec God: Tezcatlipoca, "Lord of the Smoking Mirror."* Translated by Michel Bisson. University Press of Colorado, Boulder.

Pollock, Harry E. D.
1936 *Round Structures of Aboriginal Middle America.* Publications Vol. 471. Carnegie Institution of Washington, Washington, DC.

Rojas, José Luis de
2012 *Tenochtitlan: Capital of the Aztec Empire.* University Press of Florida, Gainesville.

Rojas Rabiela, Teresa
1979 La organización del trabajo para las obras públicas: el coatequitl y las cuadrillas de trabajadores. In *El trabajo y los trabajadores en la historia de México*, edited by Elsa Cecilia Frost, Michel C. Meyer, and Josefina Zoraido Vázquez, pp. 41–66. El Colegio de México, Mexico City.

Smith, Michael E.
2006 La fundación de los capitales de las ciudades-estado aztecas: la recreación ideológico de Tollan. In *Nuevas ciudades, nuevas patrias: Fundación y relocalización de ciudades en Mesoamérica y el Mediterráneo antiguo*, edited by María Josefa Iglesias Ponce de León, Rogelio Valencia Rivera, and Andrés Ciudad Ruiz, pp. 257–290. Sociedad Española de Estudios Mayas, Madrid.
2007 Form and Meaning in the Earliest Cities: A New Approach to Ancient Urban Planning. *Journal of Planning History* 6(1):3–47.
2008 *Aztec City-State Capitals.* University Press of Florida, Gainesville.
2012 *The Aztecs*, 3rd ed. Blackwell, Oxford.

Smith, Michael E., P. Aguirre, C. Heath-Smith, K. Hirst, S. O'Mack, and T. J. Price
1989 Architectural Patterns at Three Aztec-Period Sites in Morelos, Mexico. *Journal of Field Archaeology* 16:185–203.

Smith, Michael E., Aleksander Borejsza, Angela Huster, Charles D. Frederick, Isabel Rodríguez López, and Cynthia Heath-Smith
2013 Aztec-Period Houses and Terraces at Calixtlahuaca: The Changing Morphology of a Mesoamerican Hilltop Urban Center. *Journal of Field Archaeology* 38(3):227–243.

Smith, Michael E., Cynthia Heath-Smith, and Lisa Montiel
1999 Excavations of Aztec Urban Houses at Yautepec, Mexico. *Latin American Antiquity* 10:133–150.

Smith, Michael E., Juliana Novic, Angela Huster, and Peter C. Kroefges
2009 Reconocimiento superficial y mapeo en Calixtlahuaca. *Expresión Antropológica* 36:39–55.

Tomaszewski, Brian M., and Michael E. Smith
2011 Politics, Territory, and Historical Change in Postclassic Matlatzinco (Toluca Valley, central Mexico). *Journal of Historical Geography* 37:22–39.

CHAPTER 15

TENOCHTITLAN

JOSÉ LUIS DE ROJAS

Sources recount that when the Mexicas arrived in the Valley of Mexico and discovered the place marked by an eagle perched on a prickly pear cactus, the island that would become Tenochtitlan was deserted and barren. Thus the Lord of Azcapotzalco, whose kingdom included the island, did not oppose the founding of the city. Tenochtitlan began as a small village clustered around the temple dedicated to Huitzilopochtli. Most sources cite A.D. 1325 as the year Tenochtitlan became the capital of a mighty empire. We know little about the city's appearance and development until shortly before the Spanish Conquest. The lack of access to fresh water was resolved by constructing the Chapultepec aqueduct and using other water sources. In addition, the island's location in the middle of a lake necessitated the construction of roads and bridges. Although there is much we do not know, it is clear that the situation changed drastically following the triumphant rebellion against Azcapotzalco and the founding of the Triple Alliance around A.D. 1430. Control of the mainland and freedom from subjugation to a higher authority, which might hinder or obstruct the construction of necessary public works, allowed the city to grow. The city was also enriched by the expansion of the empire and the wealth and people the process attracted. The immigration of many people allowed Tenochtitlan to reach its impressive population. This resulted in the intermingling of people speaking different languages and practicing different customs; thus Tenochtitlan was a city unlike any other in that respect (Figure 15.1)

THE SIZE OF THE CITY

Both the extent and the size of the population are hotly debated. The available data (see Rojas 2012b) suggest the city measured ca. 13–15 km^2. This extensive area was made possible by reclaiming land from the lakes, building artificial islands, and connecting them with channels and bridges in an engineering feat that would become one of the city's highlights: streets alongside canals, streets that served as canals, and packed earth

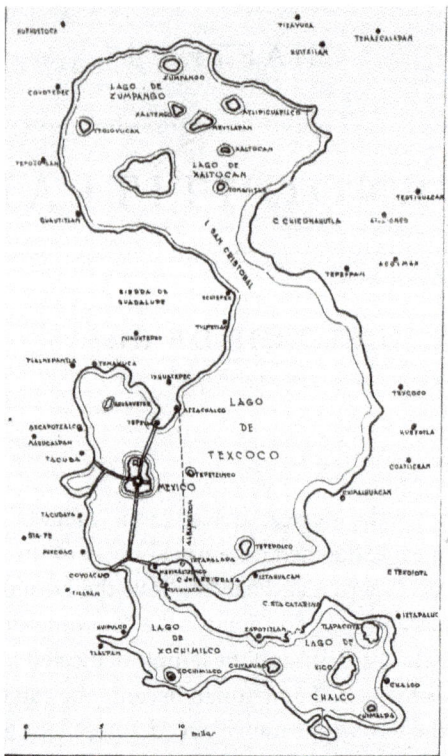

FIGURE 15.1 The Valley of Mexico (Toussaint et al. 1938:155).

streets. Moreover, the canals permitted the movement of people and goods within the city by canoe (Figure 15.2).

When the Spanish arrived, the population of Tenochtitlan is estimated to have been between 60,000 and 1 million inhabitants, although some sources offer population estimates of up to 150,000 to 200,000 and even 300,000, inhabitants. The latter is based on estimates provided by the chroniclers, while the former is based on a density of ca. 12,000–13,000 inhabitants per km². While it is virtually impossible to calculate the exact population, using surface data on residences, family composition, and modes of space use, I estimate the city could have housed up to 300,000 inhabitants (Rojas 1986, 2012b). This estimate is consistent with population figures and data on the number of people engaging in different professions (Rojas 1987, 2012b:145, Table 7.1).

The Appearance of the City

The codices and maps describe Tenochtitlan as a network of streets converging on the city center, where both the temple and the palace of the *Huey Tlahtoani* (supreme ruler)

FIGURE 15.2 Tenochtitlan: First published in the *Relación* of the Anonymous Conqueror (Toussaint et al. 1938: 48).

were located. The residences of the lords, all of whom had a dwelling in Tenochtitlan, were also located around the city center (Cortés 2001:107, Second Letter). As mentioned earlier, there were three types of streets: land based, water based, and a combination of the two, each dotted with bridges at key access points. As was the case with the roads leading into the city from the mainland, many of these bridges could be removed and reinstalled with ease. The houses were low, usually just one story—only the great lords could build upper floors—and quite variable in size. For example, Calnek (1974) identified commoner residences with an area of ca. 30–40 m^2 (minimum 10 m^2), all of which had *chinampas* (land to cultivate) measuring 4 to 1,300 m^2, with occupancy varying from 3 to 30 people. The houses were grouped around a courtyard, often with a shared kitchen and steam bath (*temazcal*). Homes were made of adobe and had flat roofs. Water tanks and granaries were also common (Calnek 1974:31–32). Cervantes de Salazar (1971) highlights the cleanliness of the streets and canals, which were maintained daily by "over a thousand men."

Communication was achieved through the movement of boats via the canals and lakes and of people via the three causeways that connected Tenochtitlan to the mainland: one in the north to Tepeyac Hill; another to the west linking with the city of Tlacopan, one of the three capitals of the empire; and a third to the south, which split into two, leading to Coyoacan and Iztapalapa. To the east Texcoco, the second largest city in the empire and one of the three allies, was not connected by a road, as the distance was greater. Moreover, the waters of Lake Texcoco were separated by a dam known as the dike of Nezahualcoyotl, although some authors, such as Armillas (1987), question whether it ever existed. If we believe the Spanish chroniclers, eight riders on horseback could circulate simultaneously on these avenues, which were transected at intervals to permit the flow of water and allow the movement of canoes. These openings were covered with planks that could be removed and reinstalled at will; in fact, during the Spanish siege of the city they were used as a means of defense. Along the road to Tlacopan was the Chapultepec aqueduct, the main source of water for the city. To ensure a constant supply of water, it was constructed of two parallel pipes; thus one could supply water while the other was being cleaned. Canoes were used to transport water from the aqueduct to points throughout the city for sale; indeed, water carriers were always of strategic importance in ancient cities. The aqueduct also needed constant surveillance, as the lack of water sources within the city was one of its major weaknesses.

The city was divided into four quarters and over one hundred neighborhoods. Each of these districts had local leaders, a temple, and a learning center known as the *telpochcalli* where children were trained for their future professions. In the center, as previously mentioned, were the main buildings. The temple precinct housed 78 structures (Sahagún 1951:165), including a *tzompantli* (skull rack), a ball court, the circular temple dedicated to Quetzalcoatl, and the Templo Mayor, which was described by the chroniclers and where excavations began in 1978 (López and López this volume). This structure was several stories high with a double staircase on its western side leading to two temples at the top: the north dedicated to Tlaloc, the god of water, and the south to Huitzilopochtli, the patron god of the Mexica, identified as a warrior god. In front of the temple was a *techcatl* (sacrificial stone) on which victims were positioned in order to extract their still-beating heart and offer it to the gods. Excavations have shown that the temple was expanded several times, in both area and height, as each *tlahtoani* gained greater prominence in Mesoamerica. In fact, excavations have recovered objects from different parts of the empire, as well as structures and items in earlier styles, such as that of Teotihuacan or Tula, leading to interesting questions about the Mesoamerican concept of time and space.

In addition to expanding the temple, each ruler also built his own palace. The most well-known ruler was Motecuhzoma Xocoyotzin, *tlahtoani* when the Spanish arrived. The palace was not only the residence of the Supreme Lord and his extended family (polygamy permitted a huge number of wives, as marriage between ruling families was an expression of the political structure) but also the administrative center. The precinct was the locus of activity and the center of city life; it housed the different judicial offices, the military council, stores, the house of songs, administrative offices, and the prison. Also noteworthy was Motecuhzoma's zoo, where both domesticated and wild animals were kept and bred. Particularly striking was the house of snakes, given the great diversity of these animals in Mesoamerica, and the house of birds, where birds were cared for and their feathers harvested for used in one of the most impressive Mexican artisanal crafts.

In addition, there was a house where deformed individuals of both sexes were kept, including albinos, dwarfs, and hunchbacks. Francisco Hernández (1946:97) argued that "they were not born that way," an idea that was used rather skillfully by Gary Jennings (1980) in his novel *Aztec*.

LIFE IN THE CITY

The nerve center of Tenochtitlan was the market. For ancient inhabitants and modern researchers alike, what was bought and sold is an important barometer for understanding the needs of the inhabitants and even determining their occupations. People bought a variety of foods—plants and animals, raw and cooked—suggesting that they did not produce their own food but rather had other means of supporting themselves, including selling items in the market. A variety of raw materials were also sold, including wood, stone, thread, dyes; tools and construction supplies; jewelry and ornaments; clothing for men and women; ointments and perfumes; alcoholic beverages, such as *pulque*, and nonalcoholic beverages, like cacao; "tubes filled with smoke" for smoking; and services: pharmacists, barbers, houses where "food and drink are offered for a price"; water carriers; artisans such as carpenters and potters, as well as porters, that is, young men hired to perform services, like the *tlameme* (shippers). Although the layout of Tenochtitlan permitted some items to be transported via canoe, the fundamental mode of transportation in Mesoamerica was a person carrying a frame (*huacalli*) held in place by a strap (*mecapalli*) secured across the forehead. Daily, thousands of people transported the large quantities of goods entering and leaving Tenochtitlan and moved items within the city itself. The larger the population, the more goods would have to be moved and the more porters there must have been to do so. If we include distance in the calculation, the figures are off the charts (Rojas and Batalla 2008). A large percentage of the population of the city dedicated themselves to trade and transportation.

In the market, some exchange might have occurred through bartering, but the evidence for different types of money suggests yet another form of exchange. Money establishes equivalence, even if it does not circulate. Cacao beans were used as low-denomination coins, while cotton cloth was used as hard currency (Millon 1957; Rojas 1998). Thus the prices of various items are mentioned in the codices in terms of either cacao beans or cotton cloth. For example, slaves were valued in cotton cloth, while maize was priced in terms of cacao beans.

In addition to transportation, all of these goods had to be stored somewhere, at the site of origin, during travel, and at the destination; unfortunately, the study of Mesoamerican storage systems is still in its infancy (Bortot et al. 2012). We know from ancient sources that grain was stored in the palace for emergencies. In fact, the *tlahtoani*'s granary could keep grain fresh for 20 years. These reserves were used in extreme cases, like the Great Famine of 1450–1454.

Since they did not produce their own food, it is clear that the majority of the inhabitants of Tenochtitlan did not work as farmers, although those with *chinampas* could have gardens for flowers or to cultivate corn. Tenochtitlan, being the city it was, kept its inhabitants busy doing other things. One of the most important of these activities was the construction and maintenance of the city: houses, temples, palaces, roads, aqueducts, and bridges all had to be built, maintained, and repaired. Simply keeping the city and aqueduct clean would have required a large number of people. We also know of the existence of bricklayers, carpenters, sculptors, stonemasons, and other tradesmen.

There were many different types of artisans, as reflected by the list of products sold in the market. There were those who produced luxury items, such as jewelry of various metals and stones; those who made clothing; and the famous feather workers (*amanteca* in Nahuatl), who decorated textiles and costumes adorned with figures of colored feathers, particularly quetzal feathers. Others made everyday items such as mats and seats, and all kinds of containers were made from gourds or squash. Also manufactured were looms; tools to carry loads, such as *mecapales*, which could be wrapped around the forehead to help carry heavy loads; and *huacales*, the frames for carrying loads. Important, too, were those who made obsidian blades.

The services sector, however, employed the largest number of people in a wide variety of tasks. First and foremost were those who provided everything necessary for life in the city, which must have involved several thousand people, among them producers, merchants, and shippers. Although they have received little attention to date, we must also consider the warehouses used to store different goods (Smith 2012; Rojas 2012a). The administration of these warehouses and their operation was overseen by the palace (Torquemada 1975–1983:4:331–4.332). Also under palace administration were the employees in charge of city maintenance, including janitorial and public works, such as those who collected the night soil and other waste generated by the residents of Tenochtitlan as mentioned by Bernal Díaz del Castillo (1800:144). Teachers were also called to the palace to receive instructions. The palace and the city both had a guard service. Administrators, or *calpixque*, met at the *petlacalco* and were supervised by the *huey calpixqui*, or chief administrator, who collected and managed taxes and kept the books for the *huey tlahtoani*. The justice system, which included judges, lawyers, process servers, executioners, officers, and numerous *tlahcuiloque* or scribes, was also based in the palace. Although few prehispanic codices survive today, we know that everything was written down and archived.

Many people were also religious specialists. According to Cervantes de Salazar (1971:1:333), more than 5,000 people lived in the precinct of the Templo Mayor, including a variety of priests and their support staff (e.g., chefs). There were many different types of priests, as this was a true career in which specialists were initiated as apprentice priests when they were young boys. They then ascended to higher positions based on their capabilities, support, and luck. The priests were in charge of scheduling and leading the many festivities for the pantheon of gods on the specific dates designated in the ritual calendar. Some priests specialized in consulting calendars to identify the positive or negative omens associated with dates selected for commercial expeditions, war, marriage, child-naming ceremonies, and other events. Every neighborhood had at least one temple, and each had to be staffed by priests. There were also priestesses, although their roles are less well known.

Also tied to the Templo Mayor and surrounding neighborhoods were those responsible for educating children, both in the *telpochcalli*, schools in each district that offered more general instruction, as well as the more specialized *calmecac* schools, which were reserved for the sons of priests and nobles who learned, among other things, how to read and write.

Attention must also be paid to the medical practitioners who specialized in diseases, fractures, wounds, healing herbs, and prayers. Their rank was related to the types of diseases and, in particular, the types of patients they treated. Midwives were also important. Presumably there were also qualified dentists, given the evidence suggested by the prevalence of dental deformation in ancient Mesoamerica.

Steam was also used for medical purposes. Sweat lodges must have been ubiquitous, although they are not well-represented archaeologically, and those responsible for supplying sufficient wood and water (dissatisfied customers might leave without paying should the fire be extinguished) also worked there.

We must also consider those responsible for leading funeral services; these rites lasted for several days and required the participation of specialists as well as mourners.

Although they are rarely mentioned in the sources, we should also consider the places where visitors could stay and freshen up, as Díaz del Castillo mentions (1975:175). Staff at such places could work part- or full-time.

Of course the great lords, with the *huey tlahtoani* at the top, also had staff at home, creating yet another sector that must have employed numerous people.

Finally, the prostitutes and their world became topics of interest to Fray Bernardino de Sahagún (e.g., 1969, Book 6:ch. 19, 1961, Book 10:ch. 15). In Book 10 (Sahagún 1961), he introduces us to an extensive assortment of people of "ill repute": thugs, thieves, swindlers, sodomites, traitors, and others.

LIFE IN THE CITY

Nighttime and daytime punctuated the rhythm of life in the city. Activities were determined by one's social status, occupation, age, and gender. One important distinction was between those who worked from home and those who had to travel to their place of work. Aside from that, each day would have been very similar to any other. The rhythm of life only changed during important festivals, complete with food, drink, and dancing. Of course a variety of rites of passage affecting smaller groups also disrupted the daily pattern, including the birth of a child, naming ceremonies, the starting and finishing of school, the selection of a mate, marriage, and the death of close relatives. In the professions involving frequent travel, the departure and return of family members would also be celebrated. Moreover, in the case of warriors or merchants, who spent long periods away from home, households were organized in such a way that extended family members likely helped each other. The residence pattern, as we have seen, reflects the coexistence of several couples and a number of people in the same house, and it was customary for children to learn the craft practiced by their parents.

TENOCHTITLAN, CAPITAL OF AN EMPIRE

Thus the city lived for itself and for its mission: the seat of government of a great empire. The growth of the city was tied to the empire, and its triumphs and setbacks also affected the capital. As more lords came under the control of the *huey tlahtoani* of Tenochtitlan, more palaces were built in the city. In the Mexica imperial model, as has been the case in many historical examples, the residences of local rulers or their representatives—often children or close relatives, ranging from guest to hostage status, as well as family members resulting from marriage alliances—were located within the city. Tenochtitlan can only be understood as part of the empire and vice versa. Our understanding of them both will help us interpret similar, less well-documented cases.

REFERENCES CITED

Armillas, Pedro
1987 *La aventura intelectual de Pedro Armillas*. Edited by José Luis de Rojas and Jorge Durand. El Colegio de Michoacán, Zamora, Michoacán, Mexico.

Bortot, Séverine, Dominique Michelet, and Véronique Darras (editors)
2012 *Almacenamiento prehispánico del Norte de México al Altiplano Central*. Laboratoire Archéologie des Amériques, Université Paris Pantheon-Sorbonne, Universidad Autónoma de San Luis Potosí, and Centro de Estudios Mexicanos y Mesoamericanos, Mexico City.

Calnek, Edward
1974 Conjunto urbano y modelo residencial en Tenochtitlan. In *Ensayos sobre el desarrollo urbano de México*, by Woodrow Borah, Edward E. Calnek, Keith Davies, Luis Unikel, and Alejandra Moreno Toscano, pp. 11–59. Secretaría de Educación Pública, Mexico City.

Cervantes de Salazar, Francisco
1971 *Crónica de la Nueva España*. 2 vols. BAE, Madrid.

Cortés, Hernán
2001 *Letters from Mexico*. Translated by Anthony Pagden. Yale University Press, New Haven, CT.

Díaz del Castillo, Bernal
1800 *The True History of the Conquest of Mexico*. Translated by Michael Keating. J. Wright, London.
1975 *Historia verdadera de la conquista de la Nueva España*. Espasa-Calpe, Madrid.

Hernández, Francisco
1946 *Antigüedades de la Nueva España*. Ed. Pedro Robredo, Mexico City.

Jennings, Gary
1980 *Aztec*. Tom Dorherty Associates, New York.

Millon, René
1957 *When Money Grew on Trees. A Study of Cacao in Ancient Mesoamerica*. Ph.D. dissertation, Columbia University, New York. University Microfilms, Ann Arbor.

Rojas, José Luis de
1986 *México-Tenochtitlan. Economía y sociedad en el siglo XVI*. El Colegio de Michoacán, Crónica de la ciudad de México, and Fondo de Cultura Económica, Mexico City.
1987 Reflexiones sobre algunas cuantificaciones referentes a la ciudad de Tenochtitlan en 1519. *Relaciones* 32:5–39.
1998 *La moneda indígena y sus usos en la Nueva España en el siglo XVI*. CIESAS, Mexico City.
2012a El almacenamiento en el imperio mexica: una necesidad evidente en busca de evidencias. In *Almacenamiento prehispánico del Norte de México al Altiplano Central*, edited by Séverine Bortot, Dominique Michelet, and Véronique Darras, pp. 173–178. Laboratoire Archéologie des Amériques, Université Paris Pantheon-Sorbonne, Universidad Autónoma de San Luis Potosí, and Centro de Estudios Mexicanos y Mesoamericanos, Mexico City.
2012b *Tenochtitlan: Capital of the Aztec Empire*. University Press of Florida, Gainesville.

Rojas, José Luis de, and Juan José Batalla
2008 Los números ocultos del *Códice Mendoza* y la *Matrícula de Tributos*. *Revista Española de Antropología Americana* 38(2):199–206.

Sahagún, Fray Bernardino de
1951 *The Florentine Codex: Book 2*. Translated by Arthur J. O. Anderson and Charles E. Dibble. University of Utah Press, Salt Lake City.
1961 *The Florentine Codex: Book 10*. Translated by Arthur J. O. Anderson and Charles E. Dibble. University of Utah Press, Salt Lake City.
1969 *The Florentine Codex: Book 6*. Translated by Arthur J. O. Anderson and Charles E. Dibble. University of Utah Press, Salt Lake City.

Smith, Michael E.

2012 El almacenamiento en la economía azteca: una perspectiva comparativa. In *Almacenamiento prehispánico del Norte de México al Altiplano Central*, edited by Séverine Bortot, Dominique Michelet, and Véronique Darras, pp. 203–220. Laboratoire Archéologie des Amériques, Université Paris Pantheon-Sorbonne, Universidad Autónoma de San Luis Potosí, and Centro de Estudios Mexicanos y Mesoamericanos, Mexico City.

Tousaint, Manuel, Federico Gómez de Orozco, and Justino Fernández

1938 *Planos de la ciudad de México en los siglos XVI y XVII*. Instituto de Investigaciones Estéticas, Universidad Nacional Autónoma de México, Mexico City.

Torquemada, Fray Juan

1975–1983 *Monarquía Indiana*. 6 vols. Universidad Nacional Autónoma de México, Mexico City.

CHAPTER 16

AZTEC PALACES AND GARDENS, INTERTWINED EVOLUTION

SUSAN TOBY EVANS

MONUMENTAL residences and gardens are diagnostics of ancient agrarian civilizations, and Aztec royal dynasties used them to express their power and connections, both spiritual and secular. Rulers rivaled each other in projects of building and garden design, and as the Aztec Empire matured, the types of palaces and gardens became more numerous and elaborate. The most basic form was the administrative palace (*tecpan calli*), and by 1519 there were about five hundred of these in the Basin of Mexico, the heartland of the empire.[1] Pleasure palaces were found in dynastic parks, horticultural gardens, orchards, and game reserves (Table 16.1).

The *tecpan* was the essential political arena, and as the Aztec Empire evolved, they proliferated: critical passages in Aztec history are marked by palace construction and garden development, sending clear messages of increasing wealth and political power. Pleasure palaces and pleasure gardens multiplied, some of them combining an inspiring setting with such practical functions as producing crops and fruit, plant-based medicines, and decorative cuttings as well as nursery-grown plants.

Aztec gardens are known mostly from post-Conquest descriptions by indigenous and Spanish observers who noted their size, elegance, variety, and beauty. Hernan Cortés (1986 [1526]:196) and Bernal Díaz del Castillo (1956 [1560s]:375) called Aztec gardens the best in the world. Garden layout and features, including plant material, are described in glowing but sketchy terms—there are no complete plans of Aztec gardens or monumental parks. Therefore, our ability to reconstruct the interplay of Aztec palaces and gardens is hampered by limited information, but in considering palaces we must acknowledge the importance of the landscaped setting, including palace courtyards with trees and decorative foliage garlands. Extensive landscaping throughout Tenochtitlan, especially along the canals, gave the city itself a park-like appearance.

Table 16.1 Aztec Palaces and Parks: Late Postclassic Period, Central Highlands of Mexico[a]

Site name	Type and name	Lord's title/name	Domain or province, 1519
Acatetelco (Atenco, El Contador)	Park: pleasure garden, hydrological, horticultural	*huetlahtoani* of Texcoco	Acolhua
Acozac (Ixtapaluca Viejo)	Palace: administrative tecpan	*calpixqui*	Acolhua
Acxotlan	Palace: administrative tecpan	*tlahtoani*	Chalca
Amecameca	Palace: administrative tecpan	*tlahtoani*	Chalca
Amecameca	Palace: pleasure palace	*tlahtoani*	Chalca
Azcapotzalco	Palace: administrative tecpan	*tlahtoani*	Tepaneca
Calixtlahuaca	Palace: administrative tecpan	*tlahtoani*	Toluca
Calpulalpan	Park: horticultural	*huetlahtoani* of Texcoco	Acolhua
Chalco	Palace: mansion (?)	*tlahtoani*	Chalca
Chalco Atenco	Palace: administrative tecpan	*tlahtoani*	Chalca
Chapultepec	Park: dynastic, hydrological, horticultural/botanical	*huetlahtoani* of Tenochtitlan	Mexica Tenochtitlan
Chiconautla	Palace: administrative tecpan (?)	*tlahtoani*	Acolhua
Chimalhuacan Atenco	Palace: administrative tecpan	*tlahtoani*	Acolhua
Chimalhuacan Chalco	Palace: pleasure palace	*tlahtoani* or other noble	
Cihuatecpan	Palace: administrative tecpan	village head	Acolhua Otumba
Cozcaquauhco	Park: game reserve	*huetlahtoani* of Texcoco	Acolhua
Cuauhtitlan	Palace: administrative tecpan	*tlahtoani*	Tepaneca
Cuauhyacac	Park: game reserve	*huetlahtoani* of Texcoco	Acolhua
Cuetlachatitlan	Park: game reserve	*huetlahtoani* of Texcoco	Acolhua
Cuexcomate	Palace: administrative tecpan	village head	Huaxtepec
Culhuacan	Palace: administrative tecpan	*tlahtoani*	Culhuaque
Huaxtepec	Park: dynastic, hydrological, horticultural/botanical	*huetlahtoani* of Tenochtitlan	Huaxtepec
Huexotla	Palace: pleasure palace	*tlahtoani*	Acolhua
Ixtapalapa	Palace: administrative tecpan	*tlahtoani*	Ixtapalapa
Mazaapan	Park: horticultural	*huetlahtoani* of Texcoco	Acolhua
Mazantzintamalco	Park: horticultural	*huetlahtoani* of Tenochtitlan	Mexica Tenochtitlan

(*continued*)

Table 16.1 (Continued)

Site name	Type and name	Lord's title/name	Domain or province, 1519
Otumba	Palace: administrative tecpan	*tlahtoani*	Acolhua
Otumba	Palace: mansion	noble (FC Ixtlilxochitl)	Acolhua
Tenayuca	Palace: administrative tecpan	*tlahtoani*	Tepanec
Tenochtitlan	Palace: administrative	Cihuacoatl (e.g., Tlacaelel)	Mexica Tenochtitlan
Tenochtitlan	Palace: mansion	noble lord (Cuauhtemoc)	Mexica Tenochtitlan
Tenochtitlan	Palace: mansions, diplomatic	foreign lords	Mexica Tenochtitlan
Tenochtitlan	Palace: tecpan, imperial, ("Motecuhzoma II's new tecpan")	*huetlahtoani* of Tenochtitlan, Motecuhzoma II	Mexica Tenochtitlan
Tenochtitlan	Palace: tecpan, imperial, old ("Axayácatl's" or "Motecuhzoma II's old tecpan")	*huetlahtoani* of Tenochtitlan, Ahuítzotl and before	Mexica Tenochtitlan
Tenochtitlan	Park (?): zoo of fierce beasts	*huetlahtoani* of Tenochtitlan	Mexica Tenochtitlan
Tenochtitlan	Park: pleasure garden "Ahuehuetlan" ("Domus ad voluptare D. Mutesuma"	*huetlahtoani* of Tenochtitlan	Mexica Tenochtitlan
Tenochtitlan	Park: pleasure garden "Viridazul D. Mutesuma"	*huetlahtoani* of Tenochtitlan	Mexica Tenochtitlan
Tenochtitlan	Park: pleasure garden, zoo-aviary, new "place of whiteness"	*huetlahtoani* of Tenochtitlan	Mexica Tenochtitlan
Teotihuacan	Palace: mansion	noble lord (FC Ixtlilxochitl)	Acolhua
Tepepulco	Park: game reserve	*huetlahtoani* of Tenochtitlan	Mexica Tenochtitlan
Tepetzingo	Park: game reserve	*huetlahtoani* of Texcoco	Acolhua Texcoco
Texcoco	Palace: administrative tecpan, "Quinatzin's palace"	*tlahtoani* of Texcoco (Quinatzin)	Acolhua Texcoco
Texcoco	Palace: administrative tecpan, imperial, "Nezahualcoyotl's palace"	*huetlahtoani* of Texcoco (Nezahualcoyotl)	Acolhua Texcoco
Texcoco	Palace: administrative tecpan, imperial, "Nezahualpilli's palace"	*huetlahtoani* of Texcoco (Nezahualpilli)	Acolhua Texcoco
Texcoco	Palace: mansion	noble lord (Axoquentzin)	Acolhua Texcoco

(*continued*)

Table 16.1 (Continued)

Site name	Type and name	Lord's title/name	Domain or province, 1519
Texcoco	Palace: mansion	noble lord (Iztacquautzin)	Acolhua Texcoco
Texcoco	Palace: mansion or tecpan	noble lord, later *huetlahtoani* (Cacama)	Acolhua Texcoco
Texcoco	Palace: mansion or tecpan "Cillan" or "Zilan"	*huetlahtoani* of Texcoco or other noble	Acolhua Texcoco
Texcoco	Palace: mansion, "Tecpilpan"	noble lord (FC Ixtlilxochitl)	Acolhua Texcoco
Texcoco	Palaces: mansions, over 400	noble lords	Acolhua Texcoco
Texcoco	Park: zoo/aviary complex	noble lords	Acolhua Texcoco
Texcotzingo	Park: dynastic, hydrological, horticultural/botanical	*huetlahtoani* of Texcoco	Acolhua Texcoco
Tlatelolco	Palace: administrative tecpan	military governor	Mexica Tenochtitlan
Tulancingo	Palace: administrative tecpan	military governor	Triple Alliance
Tzinacanoztoc	Park: game reserve	*huetlahtoani* of Texcoco	Acolhua
Xaltocan	Palace: administrative tecpan	*tlahtoani* or *calpixqui*	Tepaneca
Yautepec	Palace: administrative tecpan	*tlahtoani*	Huaxtepec
Yehualican	Park: horticultural	*huetlahtoani* of Texcoco	Acolhua

[a]As known from archaeological and ethnohistorical evidence and based on compilations in Evans (2000:210, 2004:11–13).

1986 *México-Tenochtitlan. Economía y sociedad en el siglo XVI*. El Colegio de Michoacán, Crónica de la ciudad de México, and Fondo de Cultura Económica, Mexico City.

1987 Reflexiones sobre algunas cuantificaciones referentes a la ciudad de Tenochtitlan en 1519. *Relaciones* 32:5–39.

1998 *La moneda indígena y sus usos en la Nueva España en el siglo XVI*. CIESAS, Mexico City.

2012a El almacenamiento en el imperio mexica: una necesidad evidente en busca de evidencias. In *Almacenamiento prehispánico del Norte de México al Altiplano Central*, edited by Séverine Bortot, Dominique Michelet, and Véronique Darras, pp. 173–178. Laboratoire Archéologie des Amériques, Université Paris Pantheon-Sorbonne, Universidad Autónoma de San Luis Potosí, and Centro de Estudios Mexicanos y Mesoamericanos, Mexico City.

2012b *Tenochtitlan: Capital of the Aztec Empire*. University Press of Florida, Gainesville.

Rojas, José Luis de, and Juan José Batalla

words had English cognates: "palaces" and "gardens." The related, Latin-derived European words for "palace" originated not from a root word pertaining to rulership but from the location of the palaces of early Roman emperors, the Palatine Hill, whose name may be an ancient reference to the sky. In etymological contrast, the related words "garden" (English) and *jardín* (Spanish) are derived from proto-Germanic root words for "yard," meaning a bounded property and thus having a functional referent relevant to present usage.

Relevant Nahuatl terms are at once more literal and more metaphorical. There are several different compound words for "palace," depending on the status of the resident lord,[2] but the most common term for the ruler's administrative residence is *tecpan-calli* (or *tecpan*), with the combined Nahuatl words for "lord-place house" revealing the building's function as grounded in the concept of rulership. To simplify Sahagún's (1961 [1569]:270) informants' 250-word description, *tecpan*

> means the house of the ruler ... where the rulers ... the householders, assemble. It is a good place ... a place of honor ... a fearful place ... There is glory ... there are haughtiness, presumption, pride, arrogance ... It is a place where one is intoxicated, flattered, perverted.... It is a center of knowledge, of wisdom. It is ... well made, the product of carved stone ... plastered ... a red house.

The precious status of the *tecpan* is expressed in the *chalchihuitl* disks in the *tecpan* glyph (Figure 16.1), and the theme of preciousness also infused Nahuatl words pertaining to gardens. Many such words began with *xochitl*, the Nahuatl word and the word root usually translated as "flower," which also conveyed the sense of something precious and fine.[3] Nahuatl terms that refer to professional gardeners and descriptions of flowers and other plants often feature the *xochi-* root and emphasize elite prerogatives and aesthetics as well as economics in this aspect of Aztec horticulture.

Administrative *Tecpans* and Their Gardens: Form Followed Function

Today in Mexico the term *tecpan* is used interchangeably with *comunidad* (community building), where records are kept, officials dictate or negotiate policy, and community members congregate to discuss matters of mutual concern (Haskett 1991). The persistence of this term at the local level contrasts with Spanish terms and administrative protocols in use at major capitals beginning in the Colonial period. The location of the subcontinent's most important palace remained unchanged, but with its post-Conquest rebuilding its title shifted and it is now known as the Palacio Nacional of Mexico.

Understanding the *tecpan* is essential for understanding the Aztec political system, because its architecture expressed its function as a nexus of local authority and as a level in the empire's hierarchy of political power. Local authority was expressed

FIGURE 16.1 The Nahuatl glyph for *tecpan* (noble house) as a stylized house in profile, surmounted by the ruler's copil headdress and featuring a lintel adorned with row of pierced disks (*chalchihuitl*), ancient symbols of preciousness. Drawing by S. T. Evans.

in the *tecpan*'s plan, a telescoping linkage of the town's public plaza with the *tecpan*'s main courtyard. The plaza provided space for rituals and meetings that drew crowds larger (and less privileged) than could convene in the *tecpan*'s courtyard; the *tecpan* roof became a speaking platform to address those assembled in the plaza, as it did when Motecuhzoma II tried to calm the Aztecs after the Toxcatl massacre in 1520. However, the lord's usual place within the *tecpan* was a dais room raised above the level of the main courtyard. Other, adjacent rooms were used for smaller meetings and deliberation and for storage of tribute goods, weaponry, musical instruments, and costumes. Beyond these more public areas were family quarters, smaller open courtyards surrounded by residential suites.

The size and complexity of a *tecpan* reflected its community's position in the hierarchy of the Aztec political system. A chain of command extended from the heads of the empire in their *huetecpan*s ("exalted" or "revered" *tecpans*), down through vassal lords ruling from one or more palaces in each city-state, to local village leaders who in their own *tecpans* organized the peasant tribute upon which the Aztec Empire's wealth was ultimately based. At all levels, *tecpan* courtyards were settings for debate, or at least for extended and flowery commentary. City-state rulers were "speakers"

(Nah. *tlatoque*, sing. *tlahtoani*), a title reflecting the high value placed on skilled rhetoric, which was seen as proof of personal quality and education. Aztec political organization was not a participatory democracy, but the hierarchical system of governance emphasizing public eloquence permitted public opinion to rise through the ranks; cogent arguments, elegantly expressed, was remembered and considered and could perhaps influence policy.

Classic and Early Postclassic Period Palaces

The *tecpan* had its roots in Epiclassic Tula and contemporaneous Coyotlatelco sites in the Basin of Mexico. After Teotihuacan declined in the mid-sixth century A.D., no great center arose in the Late Classic Basin of Mexico, but instead surviving local populations and Coyotlatelco culture immigrants lived in clusters of villages around small regional centers, where the first architectural locus of social control may have been the temple shrine for the group's patron or protector. This shrine served as a residence for the group's early leaders, probably the god-bearer family who safeguarded the sacred bundle, until a separate *tecpan* was built (*Annals of Cuauhtitlan* 1992:72).

The Tula region just northwest of the Basin of Mexico was a major stopping place for migrants to the Basin of Mexico. The great Toltec capital Tula had an impressive civic-ceremonial center with a variety of so-called palaces, their spatial features suggesting the importance of processions and gatherings. Colonnaded buildings adjacent to the two major temple-pyramids may have served administrative purposes; at the south end of Tula's ceremonial complex is the Palacio Tolteca, excavated in the nineteenth century and with a plan of rooms around a large courtyard.

The Tenochca were among the many migrant ethnic groups who lived at Tula. Their records indicate 19 years of residence, probably working in semiskilled service jobs and observing closely how the Toltecs administered their domain, marshaling military and mercantile cadres to bring far-flung resources under their control. Tula influenced the Basin of Mexico through their allies such as Culhuacan; the Culhuaque mimicked Toltec patterns of administration. Culhuacan's dynasts carried the sacred Quetzalcoatl-derived bloodline, which the Tenochca sought repeatedly to establish their own royal rulers.

Middle Postclassic Period Palaces and Gardens

The *tecpan* system of the Basin of Mexico grew, along with its population, from ca. 1200 to 1519. Several hundred thousand people became nearly a million, and small towns grew into cities of varying size and diversity. Dispersed villages spread over the shallows of the freshwater lakes as chinampa houselots were developed and extended along the terraced piedmont above the alluvial plain with the expansion of maguey farming communities. The growing population, a rich source of labor, food, and goods, required careful administration to channel these resources through the political system. As a result, administrative *tecpans* proliferated, and the hinterlands around city-states were valuable prizes in the competition between capitals. Tepanec Azcapotzalco seized neighboring Tenayuca, forcing refugees to move across the lake to establish the Acolhua domain at Texcoco and extend domination over eastern Basin city-states. The Texcoco palace for their ruler, Quinatzin, was still in use two hundred years later; in the sixteenth century, its fine orchards and still-functioning buildings were the spoils in a lawsuit between descendants of Quinatzin and the Spanish Colonial authorities (Cline 1966) (Figure 16.2).

Azcapotzalco's most aggressive vassal, Tenochtitlan, was established in Tepanec territory in the early 1300s. Fifty years later, Tenochtitlan became a dynastic *altépetl* in its own right. This might mark the establishment of "Axayácatl's palace" (also known as Motecuhzoma II's Old Palace). It eventually covered ca. 180 m × 190 m and faced the Templo Mayor across a broad expanse of what would become the temple precinct but which at that time may have been Tenochtitlan's plaza. Palace development and the formalization of an adjacent plaza were important advances in Tenochca urbanization.

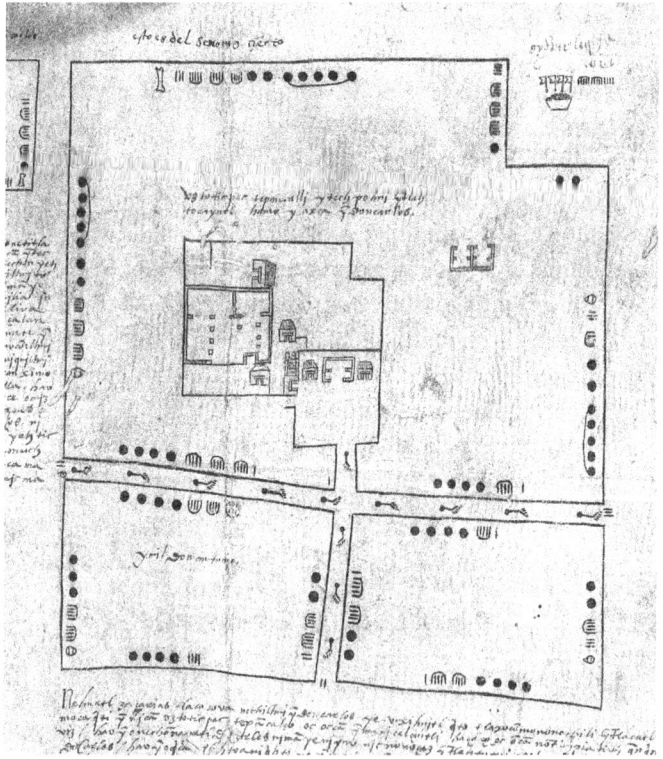

FIGURE 16.2 Quinatzin's palace, a detail from the Oztoticpac lands map (1540s; see also Cline 1966). Library of Congress, Geography and Map Division.

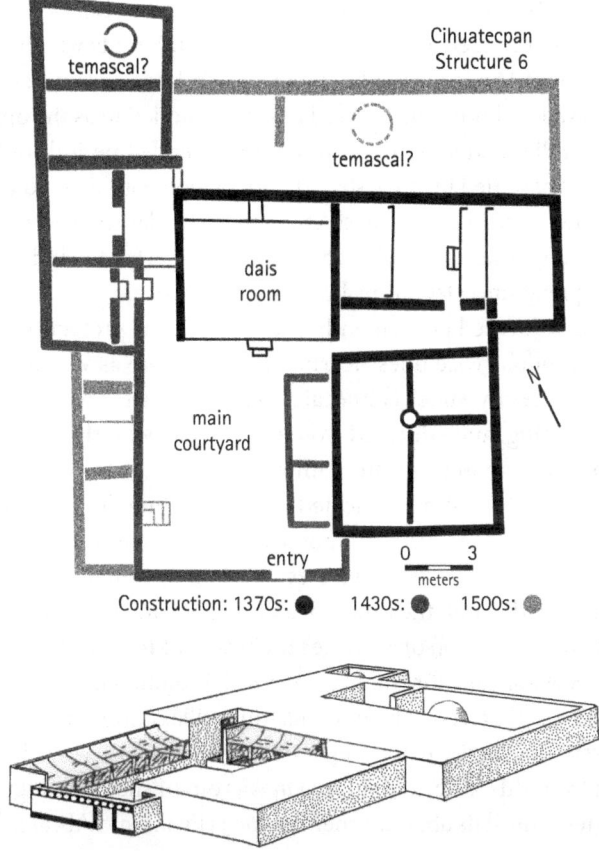

FIGURE 16.3 Cihuatecpan's *tecpan* (noble house) development can be traced through three stages: the 1370s, the 1430s, and the post-Conquest sixteenth century. Drawing by S. T. Evans.

Across the lake, the Acolhua scrambled to consolidate their city-state confederation in the face of Tepanec aggression. By 1519, the Basin's maguey-farming villages had clusters of civic-ceremonial buildings, including *tecpans*, and limited archaeological evidence suggests that *tecpan* development may have begun in the later 1300s, at about the same time that Tenochtitlan's dynasty was established. Rural *tecpan* development asserted the authority of local city-states throughout the countryside, taking advantage of two demographic increases: that of the tribute-paying villagers and that of the *altépetl* dynasty—elite polygyny resulted in large cohorts of offspring requiring positions in some suitable profession (Figure 16.3).

The *Tecpan* and Specialized Knowledge

The establishment of local village *tecpans* was useful politically and economically but also demonstrated the *tecpan*'s role in the dissemination of privileged knowledge. The

Aztecs lived and died by their calendars, land maps, and other ritual and historical records (Boone 2007:22–24). It is likely that the small bands of migrants who founded Toltec era hamlets in the Basin of Mexico looked to their own god-bearer families for prognostication and advice based on knowledge passed down and added to as the opportunity arose. The god-bearer families had scant opportunity for extended periods of formal training, but during episodes of settled life they shared information with their counterparts among the locals. Mesoamericans in general and Aztecs in particular were ever curious about the spiritual powers in any landscape, object, or deity. Migrants felt the influence of each local repertoire of interpretation, celebration, litanies, and practices.

When these groups settled permanently and received the protection of the local city-state rulers, each group's "wise ones" learned the local lore as well as coming into the intellectual orbit of the city-state's calmécac. "Wise ones" were women and men—both received special training, and educated women were particularly important to the process of overseeing birth-giving and fate-naming.

Villages grew to need full-time educated resident ruling families to keep calendars and other books of all kinds, to lead ceremonies and adjudicate disputes, and to organize tributes and service cadres. *Tecpans* were established for village head families, which were probably created through the union of a daughter (or, less likely, a son) of the altepetl ruling family with the scion of a village's highest-ranking family.

This scenario may account for the *tecpan* at the Acolhua village Cihuatecpan (Nah. "woman-lord-place"). This typical maguey-farming village grew from a cluster of houses in the Late Classic/Epiclassic, extending by the 1370s over several hundred terraced hectares. Dating from this time, a small *tecpan* was established (see Figure 16.3). It grew in several increments until its abandonment in 1603 (Evans and Abrams 1988:118–181).

Pleasure Palaces and Control of Water Sources

The Tepanec takeover of the Acolhua domain in 1418 forced into exile the dynastic heir Nezahualcoyotl, who would become the greatest palace and park developer in Aztec history. A few years later, Nezahualcoyotl returned to the Basin of Mexico in the custody of his cousins, the rulers of Tenochtitlan. In the 1420s he designed for them a dynastic park at Chapultepec ("Grasshopper Hill"), 5 km west-southwest of Tenochtitlan (Torre 1988).

Chapultepec was critical to Tenochca history, and a dynastic park there formalized their identity as a growing power and their rights to the freshwater springs, essential to their city's future growth. Nezahualcoyotl designed baths at the springs, as well as an aqueduct to carry water to Tenochtitlan. At the same time, he could see, from the summit of Chapultepec, his family's retreat, the hill of Texcotzingo, 40 km to the east-northeast, and in the sightline between the two dynastic hill-parks fell Tenochtitlan and Texcoco (30 km further, across Lake Texcoco). The duality and symmetry of *altepetl* and parks, along this sightline, would have inspired Nezahualcoyotl to consider his dynasty's future as a balanced partner to that of Tenochtitlan as well as considering Texcotzingo's design. Development of dynastic parks with their iconographic statements and clear demonstrations of economic power and elite status rivalry is one aspect of the cultural evolution of archaic agrarian states. The Aztecs present Mesoamerica's clearest example of this global phenomenon.

In Chapultepec we see the interplay between politics, economic resources, and ideology. Tenochca appropriation of Chapultepec's springs provoked Tepanec retribution, prompting the Tepanec War of the early 1430s, which delivered Azcapotzalco's conquest states to Tenochca control. However, even though Azcapotzalco was demoted to a third-rate political power, the town retained its market and elite artisans, and its palace remained the place of "the court and the kings of the Tepanecs" (Durán 1994 [1581]:61).

CONSOLIDATION THROUGH PALACE REPURPOSING AND EXPANSION

Nezahualcoyotl acceded to rule at Texcoco in the early 1430s and began to build his vast city palace, eventually nearly 1 km^2 and encompassing Texcoco's market plaza (Mapa Quinatzin 1959 [ca. 1542]) (Figure 16.4). Nezahualcoyotl affirmed the loyalty of some vassals and replaced treacherous ones with stewards (*calpixque*), such as at Acozac, where the tecpan, 45 m × 45 m, was framed by a plaza, ballcourt, and temples (Contreras Sanchez 1976; Evans 2004:30, Figure 12).

Several other Acolhua altepetl *tecpans* are known from archaeological evidence. Chimalhuacan Atenco's tecpan may have measured 50 m × 30–40 m (Garcia et al. 1998). Chiconautla's presumed *tecpan* is of unknown total size; the excavated east terrace residential wing is roughly 30 m × 48 m (Vaillant and Sanders 2000:786). Political retrenchment in the Acolhua domain at the village level is seen at Cihuatecpan; in the 1430s the tecpan expanded to encompass a large formal main courtyard with red-painted walls and a northwest wing consisting of habitation rooms and a service yard with a structure interpreted as a sweat bath.

THE MATURE EMPIRE AND ITS PALACES AND PARKS

Throughout the last half of the fifteenth century, the wealth of the Aztec Empire underwrote increasingly complex iconographic and construction projects at *tecpans* and parks. Texcotzingo's temple was dedicated in 1467, and the park was Nezahualcoyotl's soaring monument to the scope of the Acolhua domain. An aqueduct 8 km long brought water from higher mountains and routed it through fountains and baths as it moved downslope to irrigate fields above Texcoco (Medina 1997). Microenvironments shielded tender plants from the high-altitude chill, and those that could not survive

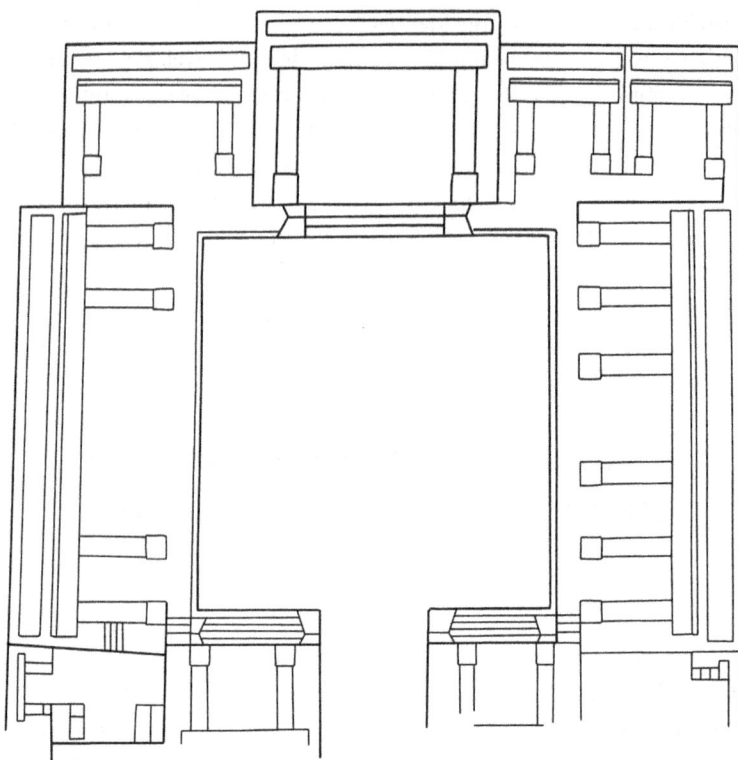

FIGURE 16.4 The plan of Nezahualcoyotl's palace in Texcoco featured a main courtyard overseen by the ruler's dais room, as depicted in the Mapa Quinatzin (1959 [ca. 1542]). Drawing by S. T. Evans.

were depicted in bas relief, creating a living and artistic representation of the botany of empire. Such Aztec designs may have inspired Europeans to develop botanic gardens, which appeared in the 1540s.

As the Tenochca saw Texcotzingo become a massive sculpted shrine to the Acolhua domain, their own Chapultepec park proved insufficient to display their own status to their Texcocan cousins. Motecuhzoma I acquired a huge property in Morelos, Huaxtepec. The tropical climate and many springs were a setting for "the most beautiful and refreshing gardens ever seen" (Cortés 1986 [1526]:196), planted with rare exotics from newly conquered provinces in the Gulf lowlands and embellished with palaces and sculpture.

The imperial capitals also developed urban pleasure parks, another site type for which Aztec culture provides our strongest Mesoamerican evidence. Tenochtitlan had several of these pleasure parks, most notably the Tenochca zoo-aviary complex west of the civic-ceremonial precinct, which was accessible from the *tecpans* via the Acequia Royal, as that canal came to be known. There, palace buildings stored tribute in goods and in beings—animals and humans, particularly albinos—and in this park the Tenochca created a new Aztlan ("place of whiteness") where the ruler and nobles could contemplate a *teixíptla* of their homeland. There also was another zoo facility behind the Templo Mayor for fierce wild beasts; they may have eaten the unused parts of sacrificial victims.

In Tenochtitlan, Axayacatl's *tecpan* was rebuilt as required by flood damages (e.g., 1449 and 1475) or opportunity (the 1460s conquest of Chalcan cities and attendant influx of wealth in materials and service). In Texcoco in 1481, Quinatzin's and Nezahualcoyotl's palaces remained in use while Nezahualpílli built his own palace. It was smaller than Nezahualcoyotl's but more luxurious, with more baths, gardens, and rooftop observatories (Alva Ixtlilxochitl 1985 [1600–1640]: II.150). Motolinia (1951 [1541]:267) noted that it featured "many gardens and a very large pond which they used to enter in boats through a canal below the ground." This permitted direct canoe transport to the lake and thus to Tenochtitlan and its palaces. Torquemada (1975–1983 [1615]:4.186) reported that "within his gardens still remain palaces built for the king's women."

In 1499 Tenochtitlan was once again flooded, and rebuilding included a new palace that filled a huge square lot (ca. 200 m × 200 m) just east of the city plaza (the Zócalo). This was Motecuhzoma II's New Palace, and it straddled the Acequia Real as it ran west to the animal and albino sanctuary and east to Lake Texcoco, connecting with canals to the north and south.

Besides serving as recreational facilities, gardens were devoted to horticultural study and production (Musset 1986). The Tenochca rulers established a pleasure palace on the island of Mazantzintamalco, at the junction of the Tenochtitlan-Tacuba causeway and the Chapultepec aqueduct, which was an important strategic location. This property was visited by the ruler for ceremonies honoring agricultural fertility, and it may have been the estate identified by Cervántes de Salazar (1875 [1554]:267) in the 1550s as belonging to Cortés. The Acolhua park at Acatetelco featured a huge square reservoir surrounded by lines of cypress trees (*ahuehuetl*, arboreal avatar of rulership). Acolhua palaces at Calpulalpan and Yehualican included gardens planted with medicinal herbs. All of these properties were infused with sacred meaning and served as special locations for rituals.

These properties were status perquisites and status symbols, affordable only for the wealthiest. There are few references to *altépetl* lords owning pleasure palaces, and the barrio or village head might know them from visits at the invitation of wealthier and more powerful kin. Ironically, almost all commoner families had experience in palaces of the *altépetl* or imperial capital, because labor service rotas would regularly require them to work in and around palaces and gardens.

Aztec Palaces and Gardens under Spanish Rule

After the conquest of Tenochtitlan in 1521, the Spaniards rebuilt the capital as their own but followed important features of the Aztec plan: the Catholic cathedral was in the Templo Mayor ritual precinct; the plaza was retained, named the Zócalo (from the Arabic word for "market"); and Motecuhzoma's New Palace became, first, the site of Cortés's residence and then the site of the Viceroy's. Chapultepec was admired by several conquistadores, but the Spanish crown claimed it for the viceroys. Huaxtepec was a treasure house of valuable plants, visited by the great Spanish natural historian Francisco Hernández (2000 [ca. 1570s]); the beautiful setting insured the continuation of its function as a "pleasure palace" into the present day, as it now serves as a public recreational facility. Tenochtitlan's old zoo-aviary, the new "place of whiteness," was granted to the Franciscan religious order, perhaps in honor of St. Francis's concern for animal welfare.

Franciscans were quick to understand the *tecpan*'s function as an arena for public speaking. Pedro de Gante lived in Nezahualcoyotl's *tecpan* for three years and used the *tecpan* plan in designing schools for elite youth to facilitate their acculturation to Spanish colonial administration (Maza 1972). The *tecpan* also influenced the design of the Colonial church; the natives were unused to rituals in enclosed spaces, so churches were dwarfed by huge atria, with courtyards attached to the churches as *tecpan* courtyards had been to the dais rooms of local lords (Motolinía 1951 [1541]).

Archbishop Zumarraga also understood the power of architectural and landscape design. He ordered the destruction of Texcotzingo's iconographic sculptures as potent works of the devil, too far from Tenochtitlan/Mexico City to be closely monitored. Nezahualcoyotl's magnificent landscape-as-text was mostly erased, but the Aztec legacy of parks and palaces lives on in Chapultepec and many other places.

Notes

1. General descriptions presented in this article are documented in Evans (1998, 2000, 2001, 2004, 2005a, 2005b, 2006, 2007, 2008, 2010).
2. In this essay, "lord" is gender-neutral. Aztec titles of political office—and of places where political or economic authority resided—varied greatly. Sahagún's (1963 [1569]:269–274) informants present terms for palaces and other buildings in Book 11. For the Chalco region of the Basin of Mexico, for example, this variety in office titles has been well-documented (see Schroeder 1991).
3. For example, *xochitia* = "to utter witticisms and bon mots; to make people laugh" (Karttunen 1983:328).

References Cited

Alva Ixtlilxóchitl, Fernando de
1985 [1600–1640] *Obras Históricas*, 4th ed. 2 vols. Edited by Edmundo O'Gorman, ed. Universidad Nacional Autónoma de México, Mexico City.
Anales de Cuauhtitlán

1992 [ca. 1570] *Anales de Cuauhtitlán*. In *History and Mythology of the Aztecs: The Codex Chimalpopóca, Annals of Cuauhtitlan* and *Legend of the Suns*, translated by John Bierhorst, pp. 17–138. University of Arizona Press, Tucson.

Boone, Elizabeth Hill
2007 *Cycles of Time and Meaning in the Mexican Books of Fate*. University of Texas Press, Austin.

Cervántes de Salazar, Francisco
1875 [1554] *México en 1554: tres diálogos latinos*. Translated by J. Garcia Icazbalceta. Antigua Librería de Andrade y Morales, Mexico City.

Cline, Howard F.
1966 The Oztoticpac Lands Map of Texcoco 1540. *The Quarterly Journal of the Library of Congress* 23:76–115.

Contreras Sanchez, Eduardo
1976 La zona arqueológica de Acozac, México; temporada 1973–1974. *Boletín* 16(n.s.):19–26.

Cortés, Hernán
1986 [1519–1526] *Letters from Mexico*. Translated and edited by Anthony Pagden. Yale University Press, New Haven, CT.

Díaz del Castillo, Bernal
1956 [1560s] *The Discovery and Conquest of Mexico*. Edited by Genaro García. Translated by A. P. Maudslay. Farrar, Straus, and Cudahy, New York.

Durán, Fray Diego
1994 [1581] *The History of the Indies of New Spain*. Translated by Doris Heyden. University of Oklahoma Press, Norman.

Evans, Susan Toby
1998 Sexual Politics in the Aztec Palace. *RES: Anthropology and Aesthetics* 33:165–183.
2000 Aztec Royal Pleasure Parks. *Studies in the History of Gardens and Designed Landscapes* 20:206–228.
2001 Aztec Noble Courts. In *Royal Courts of the Ancient Maya*, Vol. 1, edited by Takeshi Inomata and Stephen Houston, pp. 237–273. Westview Press, Boulder, CO.
2004 Aztec Palaces. In *Palaces of the Ancient New World*, edited by Susan Toby Evans and Joanne Pillsbury, pp. 7–58. Dumbarton Oaks Research Library and Collection, Washington, DC.
2005a The Aztec Palace under Spanish Rule: Disk Motifs in the *Mapa de México de 1550* (Uppsala Map or Mapa de Santa Cruz). In *The Postclassic to Spanish-Era Transition in Mesoamerica*, edited by Susan Kepecs and Rani T. Alexander, pp. 13–34. University of New Mexico Press, Albuquerque.
2005b Green Evolution: Landscape Design and Culture Change in Ancient Mesoamerica. *Anales de Antropología* 39:99–110.
2006 Antecedents of the Aztec Palace: Palaces and Political Power in Classic and Postclassic Mexico. In *Palaces and Power in the Americas*, edited by Jessica Joyce Christie and Patricia Joan Sarro, pp. 285–310. University of Texas Press, Austin.
2007 Precious Beauty: The Aesthetic and Economic Value of Aztec Gardens. In *Botanical Progress, Horticultural Innovation and Cultural Change*, edited by Michel Conan and W. John Kress, pp. 81–101. Dumbarton Oaks Library and Collection, Washington DC.
2008 Concubines and Cloth: Women and Weaving in Aztec Palaces and in Colonial Mexico. In *Servants of the Dynasty: Palace Women in World History*, edited by Anne Walthall, pp. 215–231. University of California Press, Berkeley.

2010 Garden of the Aztec Philosopher King. In *Gardening*, edited by Dan O'Brien, pp. 207–219. Blackwell-Wiley, London.

Evans, Susan Toby, and Elliot M. Abrams

1988 Archaeology at the Aztec Period Village of Cihuatecpan, Mexico: Methods and Results of the 1984 Field Season. In *Excavations at Cihuatecpan*, edited by S. T. Evans, pp. 50–234. Vanderbilt University Publications in Anthropology No. 36. Vanderbilt University, Nashville.

García, Raúl, Felipe Ramírez, Lorena Gámez, and Luis Córdoba

1998 *Chimalhuacan: rescate de una historia*. Municipio de Chimalhuacan and Instituto Nacional de Antropología e Historia, Mexico City.

Haskett, Robert

1991 *Indigenous Rulers: An Ethnohistory of Town Government in Colonial Cuernavaca*. University of New Mexico Press, Albuquerque.

Hernández, Francisco

2000 [ca. 1570s] *The Mexican Treasury: The Writings of Dr. Francisco Hernández*. Edited by Simon Varey. Translated by Rafael Chabrán, Cynthia L. Chamberlin, and Simon Varey. Stanford University Press, Stanford, CA.

Karttunen, Frances

1983 *An Analytical Dictionary of Nahuatl*. University of Texas Press, Austin.

Mapa Quinatzin

1959 [ca. 1542] Mapa Quinatzin. In *Mexican Manuscript Painting of the Early Colonial Period*, by Donald Robertson, Plates 13, 46–47, pp. 135–140. Yale University Press, New Haven, CT.

Maza, Francisco de la

1972 Fray Pedro de Gante y la capilla abierta de San José de los Naturales. *Artes de México* 150:33–38, 104–107.

Medina, Miguel

1997 *Arte y Estética de el Tetzcotzinco: arquitectura de paisaje en la époco de Netzahualcóyotl*. Universidad Nacional Autónoma de México, Mexico City.

Motolinía (Fray Toribio de Benavente)

1951 [1541] *History of the Indians of New Spain*. Translated and edited by F. B. Steck. Academy of American Franciscan History, Washington. DC.

Musset, Alain

1986 Les jardins préhispaniques. *Trace* 10:59–73.

Sahagún, Fray Bernardino de

1961 [1569] *The People: Book 10 of the Florentine Codex*. Translated by C. E. Dibble and A. J. O. Anderson. School of American Research, Santa Fe, NM, and University of Utah, Salt Lake City.

1963 [1569] *Earthly Things: Book 11 of the Florentine Codex*. Translated by A. J. O. Anderson and C. E. Dibble. School of American Research, Santa Fe, NM, and University of Utah, Salt Lake City.

Schroeder, Susan

1991 *Chimalpahin and the Kingdoms of Chalco*. University of Arizona Press, Tucson.

Torquemada, Juan de

1975–1983 [1615] *Monarquia indiana*. 6 vols. Universidad Nacional Autónoma de México, Instituto de Investigaciones Históricas, Mexico City.

Torre, Mario de la (editor)

1988 *Chapultepec: historia y presencia*. Smurfit Cartón y Papel de México, Mexico City.

Vaillant, George C., and William T. Sanders
2000 Excavations at Chiconautla. In *The Teotihuacan Valley Project Final Report,* Vol. 5: *The Aztec Period Occupation of the Valley* Part 2, edited by William T. Sanders and Susan Toby Evans, pp. 757–787. Occasional Papers in Anthropology 26. Department of Anthropology, Pennsylvania State University, University Park.

CHAPTER 17

HOUSEHOLDS IN THE AZTEC EMPIRE

KRISTIN DE LUCIA

It is in the practice of everyday life that broader patterns of change and stability take meaning (de Certeau 1984; Robin 2013). While regional and site-wide analyses of change lend important insight into broad patterns of Aztec commerce, politics, and demographic shifts, it is the detailed study of everyday life that tells us what people were doing on a daily basis and how they attributed meaning to those actions. Moreover, broader social, political, and economic relations operate through the locus of everyday life, and it is ultimately through daily practice that change is generated (de Certeau 1984; Robin 2013). Many of the activities of daily life take place within or around houses. So it is here, at the household level, that we can explore how the practices of ordinary Aztecs intersected with the macro-levels of social, political, and economic organization. Because Aztec studies have focused so extensively on the study of elites—their temples, palaces, and monuments—the study of households offers us a window into the lives of the less visible but vast majority of the population: the commoners.

Households provide the basic structure for agricultural, subsistence, craft, ritual, and commercial activity while also serving as the fundamental social unit (Ashmore and Wilk 1988; Wilk and Rathje 1982; Yanagisako 1979). Archaeologists can use the remains of physical dwellings and the activities that took place within them to reconstruct the organization of their associated social units and to study the daily practices that become mapped out through the use of space. The study of Aztec households is informed by both a rich ethnohistoric data set in addition to well-preserved archaeological remains. Although houses in the Aztec capital of Tenochtitlan are covered over by modern-day Mexico City, household archaeology conducted in the surrounding regions has been instrumental to understanding the lives of Aztec commoners (Carballo 2011). By integrating each of these various lines of evidence, we can begin to bring to life the actual people who lived, worked, played, and worshipped during the most remarkable period in central Mexican history.

Ethnohistorical Evidence

Although both indigenous and Spanish histories focus extensively on dominant narratives of warfare, elite histories, and religious ideologies, ethnohistorians have been able to extract an impressive array of information on ordinary households in Aztec society. Documentary evidence suggests that in Late Postclassic (A.D. 1350–1521) Mexico, most people lived in multigenerational or joint households, characterized by bilateral kinship, although nuclear family and individual households were also present (Kellogg 1986; McCaa 2003). Household size was variable; for example, Harvey (1985) estimates that mean household sizes were between 5.3 and 6.2 people in the eastern Basin of Mexico during Aztec times, while Calnek (1972) suggested that household size ranged from 10 to 15 persons in urban Tenochtitlan's *chinampa* zone.

Multifamily residences, or house compounds, with rooms opening onto a common patio were the norm (Calnek 1974; Kellogg 1993, 1986; Lockhart 1992; McCaa 2003). Descriptions of these compounds suggest that there were most commonly three structures (or *calli*) arranged around a central patio with each *calli* inhabited by an individual nuclear family (Figure 17.1).

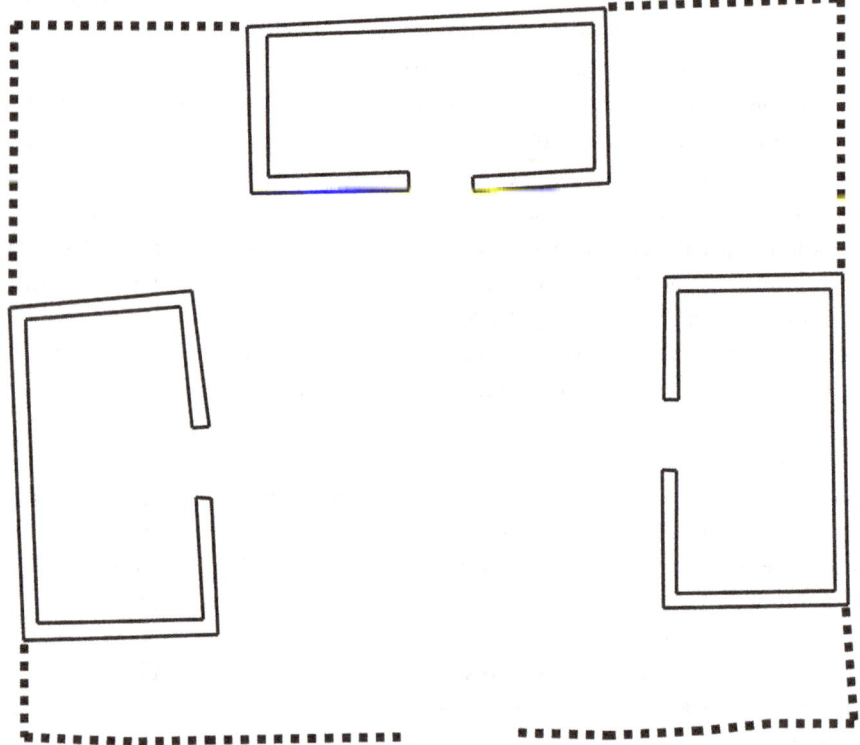

FIGURE 17.1 Colonial-period house complex from Culhuacan, 1581 (after Lockhart 1992:Figure 3.4). Drawing by Santiago Juarez.

The buildings were often oriented according to the cardinal directions, which were important elements of central Mexican cosmology (Lockhart 1992). The *cihuacalli* or "woman's room" is described as one of the largest rooms in a compound and may have been a common area where a wide range of daily activities took place, particularly those tasks commonly performed by women such as cooking (Calnek 1974; Kellogg 1993, 1995; Lockhart 1992). In some cases, each *calli* had its own storage room or structure revealing a certain degree of separation between households within a compound. House compounds were likely closed off from the outside by walls or impermanent fences such as reed fences, trees, or rows of magueys, which are still used today to mark boundaries. Thus James Lockhart (1992:64) describes the Aztec household as "inward-turned," and some scholars argue that even within individual houses, space may have been further divided according to gender with men and women remaining in separate spaces (Calnek 1974:46). Household compounds were organized into wards or *calpolli*, which were corporate landholding groups with a collective responsibility to pay tribute (Carrasco 1971, 1976; Hare 2000).

Aztec houses varied widely in style and size, and commoner houses were built with adobe bricks, stone, or wood and often had straw roofs (Figure 17.2).

FIGURE 17.2 Examples of houses as depicted in the *Florentine Codex* (Sahagún 1950–1982). Courtesy University of Utah Press.

The Franciscan friar Benardino de Sahagún (1950–1982, Book 11:269–275) describes various types of houses ranging from the palaces of nobles to the huts of commoners. According to Sahagún (1950–1982, Book 11:270–272), commoner houses were built of plain adobe or wood and were described as "squat, crude, unfit, unfinished, small and not finished; humble." Palaces were beautifully decorated, plastered and painted with bright colors and sculptures, and encrusted with mosaics; they tended to be larger, sometimes with two stories. Rooms could be expanded, added, or removed as families grew, and walls were often constructed when relations became strained between household members, physically representing the social division (Kellogg 1986). Thus while the multihousehold compound was the most common organization for Aztec houses, household organization was ultimately fluid and reflected the changing nature of social relations.

The Aztec house was not just a dwelling but a place where identity was constituted. The Nahuatl words for the English word "family," in fact, all make reference to the residential structure or dwelling unit (Calnek 1974). For example, the most common term for "relative" is *huanyolque* or "those who live with one" (Lockhart 1992:72). According to Lockhart (1992:59), linguistic evidence suggests that all of the words for family "emphasize the setting in which a joint life takes place, not the origin of the relationship between those living together." The fundamental unit of social organization in ancient Mexico was thus the household, which was defined by common residence rather than family or relatedness. As common identity derived from the physical residence of household members, the archaeological study of houses (see later discussion) is thus a socially relevant unit of analysis.

Significant changes in household and community organization took place following the Spanish Conquest. Kellogg (1993) found that there was a shift from multifamily dwellings in the prehistoric period toward single nuclear family units following the Conquest. This type of shift would have had profound consequences for daily social interactions and social relations as families became gradually more isolated. One such consequence was that "women were increasingly restricted to domestic contexts and were cut off from many traditional sources of extrafamilial power and authority" (Kellogg 1993:220). Historic accounts, therefore, may overemphasize divisions between the sexes and the importance of the nuclear family in Aztec society. Moreover, as noted by Carrasco (1971), we cannot assume that prehispanic social organization would have been uniform across ethnic, class, or regional groups, let alone throughout time. Thus while achieving an understanding of household organization at the time of Spanish Conquest can be informative, to understand broader patterns of variation and change in household organization we must include archaeology.

Archaeological Evidence

Household archaeology does not merely serve as a complement to documentary evidence but can offer new insight into the day-to-day activities and interactions of ordinary commoners since these aspects of daily life are frequently ignored in historic accounts. The physical arrangement of space provides insight into social interactions while the distribution of artifacts across household space aids in our understanding of how activities were organized. In addition, archaeological evidence can offer something that documents cannot—it can tell us how households changed through time. The following discussion thus focuses on the archaeology of households throughout the Postclassic period (A.D. 900–1500).

Although there is a wide range of variation, the most common house form encountered archaeologically in Postclassic central Mexico is the multiroom, multifamily residence. Typically smaller than the apartment compounds that characterized Classic period Teotihuacan, multifamily compounds likely reflect the persistence of a corporate form of social organization. For example, in the Tula region just outside of the Basin of Mexico, multifamily residences are commonly associated with the Early Postclassic period (A.D. 900–1200). Multifamily residences or compounds at Tula were arranged around a central patio but were physically connected (Healan 1989; Paredes Gudiño 1986). These compounds were remodeled over time and sometimes expanded to incorporate new household units. Each household was associated with its own cooking area, which is indicated by the presence of a stone-lined hearth or *tlecuil* and cooking implements, such as groundstone tools and ceramic cooking jars (Paredes Gudiño 1986). Similar forms of household organization with connecting houses and patios have also been identified at the Early Postclassic sites of Tlalpizáhuac near Chalco (Ahumada 1998) and at Xaltocan, in the northern Basin of Mexico (see later discussion).

People were commonly buried under room floors and in shared patio spaces. The presence of human burials under compound floors highlights the importance of the structure to the maintenance of the identity of the social group (De Lucia 2010a). Further, osteological analyses of the burials from Tlalpizáhuac, a community that exploited lake resources, indicate that men and women had similar patterns of arthritis and thus had overlapping daily activities (Cisneros and Sánchez 2002). At Xaltocan, another community that exploited lake resources, household space was divided by function, with rooms for sleeping, entertaining, and productive actives, but space does not appear to have been divided along gender lines as production activity areas were overlapping (De Lucia 2011). Such shared activity spaces or overlapping patterns of arthritis indicate that in multifamily compounds social roles were collaborative and intersecting. Thus tightly clustered compounds with shared walls, patios, and activities would have required daily interaction and cooperation between household members, likely reflecting a corporate social structure and shared identity that was reinforced through the burial of household members under house floors.

At Tula there was a second type of house organization, the house group (Healan 1989). House groups are represented by the El Canal site at Tula (Figure 17.3), where three or more multiroom houses were arranged around a single patio (Healan 1989, 1993).

The houses had doorways that opened onto the patio but were not internally connected. Houses were tightly clustered and closed to the outside, so that in some cases they resembled compounds, making them distinct from the "patio groups" that characterize the Maya area. Patios contained altars where ritual activities and daily interactions

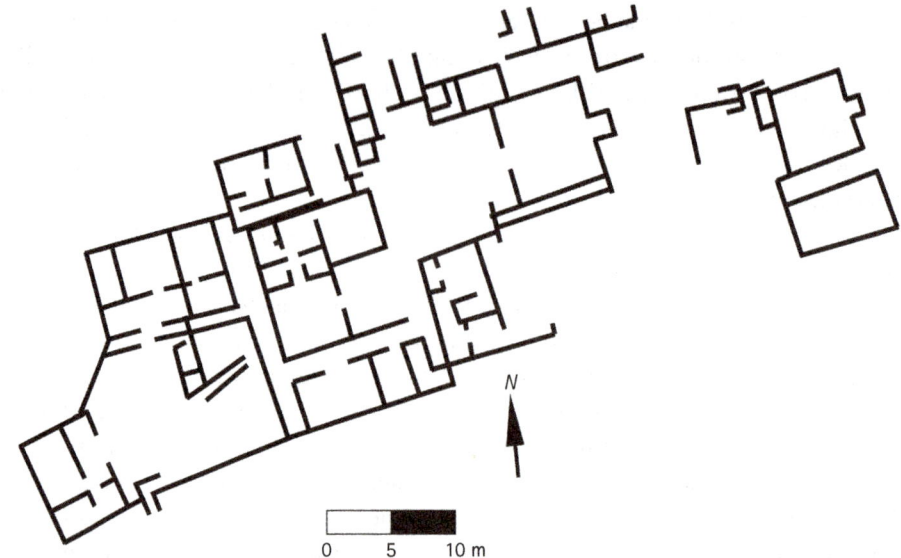

FIGURE 17.3 Example of house groups from El Canal, Tula (after Healan 1993:Figure 2). Drawing by Santiago Juarez.

took place, and burials were located under house floors. A similar house group was also excavated at Tepetitlán, a rural settlement to the north of Tula (Cobean and Mastache 1999). At Tepetitlán interhousehold interaction is suggested by the fact that house groups had common symbolic elements that linked them together (Mastache and Cobean 1999; Mastache et al. 2002). The central location of altars, the presence of centrally located burials, and the use of patios for collective ritual and domestic tasks suggest that house groups also shared social bonds (Healan 1993).

In contrast, at Cholula to the southeast of the Basin of Mexico, an Early Postclassic domestic structure, UA-1 Structure 1, had only four rooms and was associated with two porch areas, a sweat bath (*temazcal*), a well, burials, and painted plaster floors and façades (McCafferty 2007; McCafferty and McCafferty 2006). The house opened onto a patio and was surrounded by an exterior wall. As only one structure was excavated, it is unclear if it was part of a patio group, but it clearly did not have a compound organization, nor does it conform to the closely spaced house groups of Tula. At the site of Tetla, to the southeast of the Basin of Mexico in Morelos, archaeologists excavated another four room house dating to A.D. 1230 + /−75 (Norr 1987). Although small, the house had painted plastered floors and plastered adobe walls. Activities were more segregated as weaving and food preparation were concentrated in a single room while a separate room held a shrine and was the location for lithic production (Norr 1987). The houses excavated at Cholula and Tetla thus both represent forms of household organization distinct from those described earlier and may reflect a lesser degree of gender collaboration.

The Late Postclassic (A.D. 1350–1519) rural houses in Morelos at the sites of Cuexcomate and Capilco demonstrate yet another pattern. These sites had simple one-room houses often in groups of three or four arranged around a central patio (Smith 1992, 2008:164). The walls of houses were constructed with simple adobe bricks and lacked elaborate painted plaster floors. Given the small size of the houses, it is likely that each house was occupied by a nuclear family group. Craft production took place at low levels primarily for immediate household use, although there is evidence that some patio groups specialized in the production of bark paper (Smith 1992:381). The placement of burials in and around the house was rare; only 5 out of 44 houses excavated had burials. This pattern contrasts with the conjoined houses typical of the Basin of Mexico and the multiroom houses seen at Cholula and Tetla. Smith (2008:166) suggests that the semitropical climate in Morelos may account for the variation in house size, as people would have conducted the majority of their daily activities outdoors in a climate that is warm year-round (see also Evans 1993:179). In contrast, in the highlands of the Basin of Mexico, more activities were conducted indoors, thus requiring multiple rooms and larger living spaces. These differences may also be a product of social organization, where identity was less tied to common residence as indicated by the lack of subfloor burials.

Household organization was malleable and varied according to locally specific economic and social contexts. At the island site of Mexicaltzingo in the southern Basin of Mexico, individual houses were constructed on small artificial islands and raised platforms in a manner similar to *chinampa* fields. During the Aztec II period (A.D. 1200–1300) in Mexicaltzingo, commoner houses were simple one-room structures with compact clay floors and associated patios, canals, and *chinampa* fields (Avila López 2006). Unlike the sites previously discussed, these houses were not organized into patio groups, likely so that they could be in close proximity to their *chinampa* fields. Elite residences were larger and had plastered walls, floors, benches, and large walls to isolate the residence from the outside. Elite structures typically had four rooms, including a kitchen and habitation rooms, as well as a roofed portico supported by pillars, outdoor patio, private piers, and access canals (Avila López 2006:283). In contrast, at Cihuatecpan, an Aztec period rural village located in the foothills of the eastern Basin of Mexico, all houses engaged in maguey farming, and archaeological investigations revealed that house size ranged varied from at least 2 to as many as 21 rooms, with larger houses representing joint or elite households (Evans 1993; Evans et al. 1988). All residential structures included several contiguous habitation rooms arranged around a central common patio or work area, following the multifamily complex pattern. Household labor was likely collaborative and all household members would have been involved in processing maguey and making products for exchange and tribute.

In sum, there were almost as many forms of household organization as there are sites in central Mexico. The Postclassic period was characterized by rapid change, with the rise of powerful city-states, the expansion of the market system, and the eventual political integration brought by Triple Alliance rule. Because few sites had continuous occupation from the Early through the Late Postclassic periods, it is difficult to assess the impact of these changes on households. The site of Xaltocan in the northern Basin of Mexico discussed next thus provides a unique case study, as it was occupied continuously from the Early Postclassic through modern times.

Household Production and Social Change in Xaltocan

In Aztec society, craft production activities typically took place within domestic contexts rather than within specialized workshops. In the city-state of Otumba, for example, archaeologists uncovered evidence of household-based craft production. Full-time, household-based craft production in the urban core of Otumba included core-blade workshops, lapidary workshops, groundstone workshops, figurine workshops, censer workshops, and locations for the manufacture of spindle whorls (Charlton et al. 1991; Otis Charlton et al. 1993). Craft-producing households tended to be aggregated in *barrios* or wards with other households producing similar goods (Otis Charlton et al. 1993). The production of goods for exchange was not limited to luxury artisans but was also regionally specific, as households strategically exploited local resources and employed diverse economic strategies as they articulated with broader political economies.

Xaltocan, an island community in the northern Basin of Mexico, was occupied continuously throughout the Postclassic period and has stratified archaeological deposits that allow for studies of change through time. Xaltocan was located on an artificially constructed island, and its inhabitants engaged in *chinampa* agriculture and exploited lake resources for local and regional exchange (Brumfiel 2005; De Lucia 2013; Frederick et al. 2005; Morehart and Eisenberg 2010). Xaltocan was founded ca. A.D. 900 and became an important pre-Aztec regional center. Household excavations at Xaltocan have offered new insight into household production, organization, and change from the Early Postclassic through Colonial periods (Brumfiel 2005, 2010; De Lucia 2010b, 2011, 2013; De Lucia and Brumfiel 2004; De Lucia and Overholtzer 2014; Overholtzer 2012).

As Xaltocan was an island site, its inhabitants were involved in the extraction and processing of lake resources. Methodological advances using micro-analyses have enabled the identification of activity areas as well as previously unidentified production activities. For example, through an analysis of residues and microartifacts deposited on room floors, I was able to identify the processing of fish along with other activities associated with lake exploitation (De Lucia 2011, 2013). In addition to processing fish, the inhabitants of Structure 1 also wove mats, made bone tools, and produced ceramic vessels and thus can be characterized as multicrafting households (De Lucia 2013). Like the inhabitants of Cihuatecpan and Otumba, the residents of Xaltocan exploited their local environment to produce goods that could be sold in the marketplace. While all households had evidence of low-intensity production activities, each household also produced different specialized goods.

During the earliest period of occupation at Xaltocan, associated with Aztec I-style ceramics (A.D. 900–1200), houses were multiroom, multifamily adobe structures with earthen floors and outdoor patios and middens (Figure 17.4).

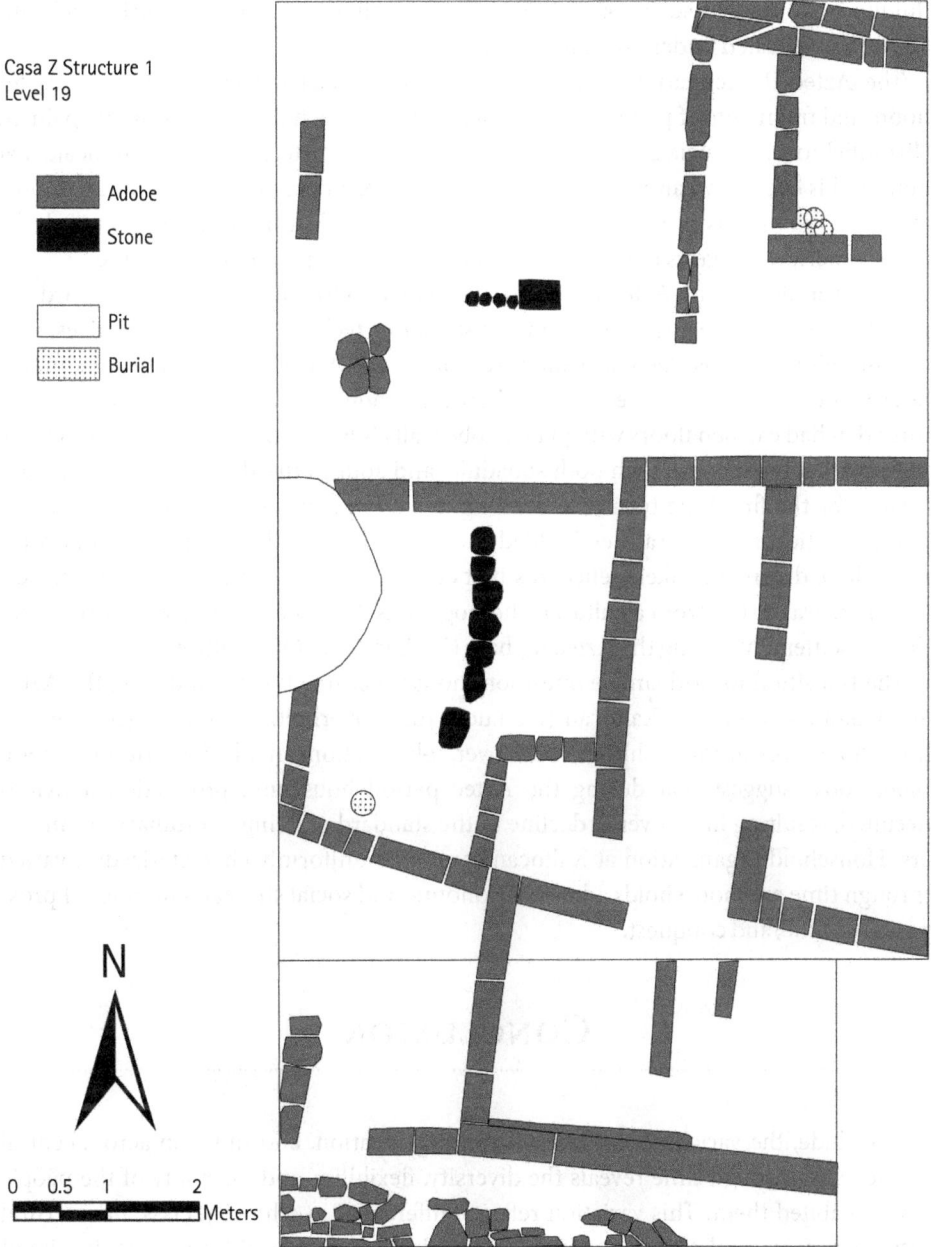

FIGURE 17.4 Structure 1, an Aztec I period house at Xaltocan. Figure by Kristin DeLucia.

Rooms were divided functionally, with family and social space largely divided from work areas. Outdoor patios served multiple functions as they were used for both ritual and domestic tasks (De Lucia 2011). The adobe structures were associated with multiple stratified floors and multiple renovations that reconfigured room space, reflecting fluidity in household social organization through time. Additionally, burials, all subadults, were located under house floors (De Lucia 2010a).

The Aztec II occupation (A.D. 1200–1350) was associated with a shift to plaster floors and fragments of painted plaster suggest that these houses were brightly painted (Brumfiel 2010; De Lucia 2011). The improved construction techniques may indicate that households became wealthier during this period as Xaltocan rose to become an important center in the Basin. The reuse of the same adobe walls from the Aztec I through the Aztec II periods suggests that there was continuity of occupation through time.

However, during the Aztec II period, new houses were also established toward the periphery of the site using different construction techniques, burial practices, and consumption patterns (De Lucia and Overholtzer 2014). Unlike the multiroom, multihousehold dwellings described previously, the new houses were simple one-room structures that had earthen floors with plain adobe walls (Overholtzer 2012). Burial practices were markedly different, with both subadults and adults buried outside of houses and infants for the first time buried in cooking jars (De Lucia and Overholtzer 2014). As burial practices are culturally embedded and closely entwined with identity and worldview, these differences likely reflect distinct cultural identities. Thus these data suggest that there was a shift from a culturally homogenous Aztec I community toward a more diverse settlement during the Aztec II phase (De Lucia and Overholtzer 2014).

The transition toward simple one-room houses became the norm during the Aztec and Colonial periods in Xaltocan (De Lucia 2012; Overholtzer 2012), suggesting that household organization shifted. Moreover, observations made by Brumfiel (1991, 1996, 2005) suggest that during the Aztec period household production activities declined, resulting in an overall decline in the standard of living of ordinary commoners. Household organization at Xaltocan cannot be uniformly characterized; it varied through time and households adjusted economic and social strategies in times of prosperity, decline, and conquest.

Conclusion

To conclude, the variability in house form, organization, and function across central Mexico and through time reveals the diversity, flexibility, and ingenuity of the people who inhabited them. This variation reflects differences in ethnicity, class, urban/rural residence, ecological context, economic organization, and local history. At the site of Xaltocan, households each specialized in the production of different types of goods derived from nearby resources, thereby contributing to Xaltocan's growth and success as an important political power. However, in Xaltocan, as across the region, those strategies shifted under domination and in times of economic decline. Household archaeology thus yields a dynamic history of social organization and change, diversity, and continuity throughout central Mexican history.

References Cited

Ahumada, Alejandro Tovalín
1998 *Desarrollo arquitectónico del sitio arqueológico de Tlalpizáhuac*. Instituto Nacional de Antropología e Historia, Mexico City.

Ashmore, Wendy, and Richard R. Wilk
1988 Household and Community in the Mesoamerican Past. In *Household and Community in the Mesoamerican Past*, edited by R. R. Wilk and W. Ashmore, pp. 1–27. University of New Mexico Press, Albuquerque.

Avila López, Raúl
2006 *Mexicaltzingo: arqueología de un reino culhua-mexica*, Vol. 1. Instituto Nacional de Antropología e Historia, Mexico City.

Brumfiel, Elizabeth M.
1991 Weaving and Cooking: Women's Production in Aztec Mexico. In *Engendering Archaeology: Women and Prehistory*, edited by J. M. Gero and M. W. Conkey, pp. 224–251. Blackwell, Oxford.
1996 The Quality of Tribute Cloth: The Place of Evidence in Archaeological Argument. *American Antiquity* 61(3):453–462.
2005 *Production and Power at Postclassic Xaltocan*. Instituto Nacional de Antropología e Historia, Mexico City and University of Pittsburgh, Pittsburgh, PA.
2010 *Estrategias de las Unidades Domésticas en Xaltocan Postclásico*. Informe Final al Instituto Nacional de Antropología e Historia, Mexico City and Northwestern University, Evanston, IL.

Calnek, Edward E.
1972 Settlement Pattern and Chinampa Agriculture at Tenochtitlan. *American Antiquity* 37:104–115.
1974 Conjunto urbano y modelo residencial en Tenochtitlan. In *Esayos sobre el desarrollo urbano de México*, edited by E. E. Calnek, W. Borah, A. M. Toscano, K. A. Davies, and L. Unikel, pp. 11–65. SepSetentas, Mexico City.

Carballo, David M.
2011 Advances in the Household Archaeology of Highland Mesoamerica. *Journal of Archaeological Research* 19:133–189.

Carrasco, Pedro
1971 Social Organization of Ancient Mexico. In *Archaeology of Northern Mesoamerica: Part One*, edited by G. F. Ekholm and I. Bernal, pp. 349–375. Handbook of Middle American Indians, Vol. 10. University of Texas Press, Austin.
1976 The Joint Family in Ancient Mexico: The Case of Molotla. In *Essays on Mexican Kinship*, edited by H. G. Nutini, P. Carrasco, and J. M. Taggart, pp. 45–64. University of Pittsburgh Press, Pittsburgh, PA.

Charlton, Thomas H., Deborah Nichols, and Cynthia Otis Charlton
1991 Aztec Craft Production and Specialization: Archaeological Evidence from the City-State of Otumba, Mexico. *World Archaeology* 23(1):98–114.

Cisneros, Héctor Favila, and Soledad Garcia Sánchez
2002 Un Acercamiento al Estudio de las Costumbres Funerarias del Sitio Arqueológico de Tlalpizáhuac en el Posclásico Temprano (950–1200 d.C.) *Expresión Antropológica* 16:36–51.

Cobean, Robert H., and Alba Guadalupe Mastache

1999 *Tepetitlán, un espacio doméstico rural en el área de Tula*. Instituto Nacional de Antropología e Historia, Mexico City and University of Pittsburgh, Pittsburgh, PA.

de Certeau, M.

1984 *The Practices of Everyday Life*. University of California Press, Berkeley.

De Lucia, Kristin

2010a A Child's House: Social Memory, Identity, and the Construction of Childhood in Early Postclassic Mexican Households. *American Anthropologist* 112(4):607-624.

2010b Informe Preliminar de los Entierros en el Cementerio Aztec II. In *Estrategias de las Unidades Domésticas en Xaltocan Postclásico*, edited by E. M. Brumfiel, pp. 110-119. Informe Final al Instituto Nacional de Antropología e Historia, México, D.F, and Northwestern University, Evanston, IL.

2011 Domestic Economies and Regional Transition: Household Production and Consumption in Early Postclassic Mexico. Ph.D. dissertation, Northwestern University, Evanston, IL.

2012 Producción y consumo en los conjuntos residenciales de Xaltocan, México durante el Posclásico temprano: trabajo de campo de la temporada 2008: Final Field Report. On file at the Consejo de Arqueología, Instituto Nacional de Antropología e Historia, Mexico City.

2013 Domestic Economies and Regional Transition: Household Multicrafting and Lake Exploitation in Pre-Aztec Central Mexico. *Journal of Anthropological Archaeology* 32:353-367.

De Lucia, Kristin, and Elizabeth M. Brumfiel (editors)

2004 *Space and Social Organization at Postclassic Xaltocan, Mexico*. 2003 Annual Report. Instituto Nacional de Antropología e História, Mexico City.

De Lucia, Kristin, and Lisa Overholzter

2014 Everyday Action and the Rise and Decline of Ancient Polities: Household Strategy and Political Change in Postclassic Xaltocan, Mexico. *Ancient Mesoamerica* 25(2):441-458.

Evans, Susan T.

1993 Aztec Household Organization and Village Administration. In *Prehispanic Domestic Units in Western Mesoamerica: Studies of the Household, Compound, and Residence*, edited by R. S. Stantley and K. G. Hirth, pp. 173-189. CRC Press, Boca Raton, FL.

Evans, Susan Toby, Elliot Marc Abrams, and Bruce Gregory McCoy

1988 *Excavations at Cihuatecpan, an Aztec Village in the Teotihuacan Valley*. Vanderbilt University, Nashville, TN.

Frederick, Charles D., Barbara Winsborough, and Virginia S. Popper

2005 Geoarchaeological Investigations in the Northern Basin of Mexico. In *Production and Power at Postclassic Xaltocan*, edited by E. M. Brumfiel, pp. 71-115. Instituto Nacional de Antropología e Historia, Mexico City and University of Pittsburgh, Pittsburgh, PA.

Hare, Timothy S.

2000 Between the Household and the Empire: Structural Relationships within and among Aztec Communities and Polities. In *The Archaeology of Communities: A New World Perspective*, edited by M. A. Canuto and J. Yaeger, pp. 78-101. Routledge, London.

Harvey, Herbert R.

1985 Household and Family Structure in Early Colonial Tepetlaoztoc: An Analysis of the Códice Santa María Asunción. *Estudios de Cultural Náhuatl* 18:275-294.

Healan, Dan M.

1989 House, Household and Neighbourhood in a Postclassic City. In *Households and Communities: Proceedings of the Twenty-First Annual Conference of the Archaeological*

Association of the University of Calgary, edited by S. MacEachern, D. J. W. Archer, and R. D. Garvin, pp. 416–429. University of Calgary, Calgary.

1993 Urbanism at Tula from the Perspective of Residential Archaeology. In *Prehispanic Domestic Units in Western Mesoamerica*, edited by R. S. Stantley and K. G. Hirth, pp. 105–119. CRC Press, Boca Raton, FL.

Kellogg, Susan M.

1986 Kinship and Social Organization in Early Colonial Tenochtitlan. In *Supplement to the Handbook of Middle American Indians: Ethnohistory*, Vol. 4, edited by R. Spores, pp. 103–121. University of Texas Press, Austin.

1993 The Social Organization of Households among the Tenochca Mexico Before and After Conquest. In *Prehispanic Domestic Units in Western Mesoamerica: Studies of the Household, Compound, and Residence*, edited by R. S. Stantley and K. G. Hirth, pp. 207–224. CRC Press, Boca Raton, FL.

1995 The Woman's Room: Some Aspects of Gender Relations in Tenochtitlan in the Late Pre-Hispanic Period. *Ethnohistory* 42:563–576.

Lockhart, James

1992 *The Nahuas After the Conquest: A Social and Cultural History of the Indians of Central Mexico, Sixteenth Through Eighteeth Centuries*. Stanford University Press, Stanford, CA.

Mastache, Alba Guadalupe, and Robert H. Cobean

1999 Activity Areas. In *Tepetitlán, Un Espacio Doméstico Rural en el área de Tula*, edited by R. H. Cobean and A. G. Mastache, pp. 239–293. Instituto Nacional de Antropología e Historia, Mexico City and University of Pittsburgh, Pittsburgh, PA.

Mastache, Alba Guadalupe, Robert H. Cobean, and Dan M. Healan

2002 *Ancient Tollan: Tula and the Toltec Heartland*. University Press of Colorado, Boulder.

McCaa, Robert

2003 The Nahua Calli of Ancient Mexico: Household, Family and Gender. *Continuity and Change* 18(1):23–48.

McCafferty, Geoffrey G.

2007 Altar Egos: Domestic Ritual and Social Identity in Postclassic Cholula, Mexico. In *Commoner Ritual and Ideology in Ancient Mesoamerica*, edited by N. Gonlin and J. C. Lohse, pp. 213–250. University Press of Colorado, Boulder.

McCafferty, Geoffrey G., and Sharisse D. McCafferty

2006 Boys and Girls Interrupted: Mortuary Evidence of Children from Postclassic Cholula, Puebla. In *The Social Experience of Childhood in Ancient Mesoamerica*, edited by T. Ardren and S. R. Hutson, pp. 25–52. University Press of Colorado, Boulder.

Morehart, Christopher T., and Dan T. A. Eisenberg

2010 Prosperity, Power and Change: Modeling Maize at Postclassic Xaltocan, Mexico. *Journal of Anthropological Archaeology* 29:94–112.

Norr, Lynette

1987 The Excavation of a Postclassic House at Tetla. In *Ancient Chalcatzingo*, edited by D. C. Grove, pp. 400–409. University of Texas Press, Austin.

Otis Charlton, Cynthia, Thomas H. Charlton, and Deborah L. Nichols

1993 Aztec Household-Based Craft Production: Archaeological Evidence from the City-State of Otumba, Mexico. In *Prehispanic Domestic Units in Western Mesoamerica*, edited by R. S. Santley and K. G. Hirth, pp. 147–171. CRC Press, Boca Raton, FL.

Overholtzer, Lisa

2012 Empires and Everyday Material Practices: A Household Archaeology of Aztec and Spanish Imperialism at Xaltocan, Mexico. Ph.D. dissertation. Northwestern University, Evanston, IL.

Paredes Gudiño, Blanca

1986 La unidad habitacional en la cuenca de México: periodo Postclasico. In *Unidades Habitacionales Mesoamericanas y Sus Areas de Actividad*, edited by L. Manzanilla, pp. 221–256. Universidad Nacional Autonoma de Mexico Imprenta Universitaria, Mexico City.

Robin, Cynthia

2013 *Everyday Life Matters: Maya Farmers at Chan*. University Press of Florida, Gainsville.

Sahagún, Fray Bernardino de

1950–1982 *Florentine Codex: General History of the Things of New Spain*. 12 vols. Translated by Arthur J. O. Anderson and Charles E. Dibble. University of Utah Press, Salt Lake City.

Smith, Michael E.

1992 *Archaeological Research at Aztec-Period Rural Sites in Morelos, Mexico*, Vol. 1. University of Pittsburgh, Pittsburgh, PA.

2008 *Aztec City-State Capitals*. University Press of Florida, Gainesville.

Wilk, Richard R., and William L. Rathje

1982 Household Archaeology. *American Behavioral Scientist* 25(6):617–639.

Yanagisako, Sylvia Junko

1979 Family and Household: The Analysis of Domestic Groups. *Annual Review of Anthropology* 8:161–205.

PART IV

ECONOMIC AND SOCIAL RELATIONS IN THE AZTEC EMPIRE

CHAPTER 18

AZTEC AGRICULTURAL STRATEGIES

Intensification, Landesque Capital, and the Sociopolitics of Production

CHRISTOPHER T. MOREHART

INTRODUCTION

IT is impossible to understand the nature of the Aztec Empire—its development, expansion, and conquest—without considering agriculture. Like most state societies, the demographic and political economic structure of the Aztec Empire was built on an agricultural base. The Aztec landscape was composed of a mosaic of agricultural strategies, which had the capacity of supporting thousands of individuals in both rural and urban settings. Beyond subsistence, agriculture was tied to multilayered political and social economies: produce was paid as tribute to local lords and imperial officials. Land was a political currency of conquest. Market exchange of agricultural products enabled a complex division of labor. Several species of domesticated plants, with spiritual and cosmological dimensions, were required for household, community, and state-sponsored rituals. The lives of Aztec farmers also exhibited fine-grained understandings of the cycles that shaped plants, soil, water, and seasons—a body of traditional ecological knowledge that was passed on to subsequent generations.

This chapter focuses on major themes and processes that have attracted the interests of scholars of indigenous agriculture—both contemporary and Colonial—since the Spanish Conquest. Although at times this discussion is descriptive, the nature of Aztec farming was strategic, rather than static. Viewing farming as a strategy helps to convey how agricultural production occurred not simply to meet the demographic needs of households and communities. Instead, these strategies, uniquely adapted to the material constraints of a diverse macroregional landscape, allowed farmers to meet multiple obligations, to teach children about the world, and to survive as both biological and social beings.

Agricultural Intensification and Landesque Capital

Before any discussion of the range of agricultural landscapes among the Aztecs, I reflect on two concepts that capture human investment in land: intensification and landesque capital. *Intensification* is a relative process that expresses an increase in key variables of production, and several definitions exist (Boserup 1965; Brookfield 1972, 1984; Geertz 1963; Morrison 1994; Turner and Brush 1987). Intensification can represent an increase in the number of plants cultivated or the total product harvested from a unit of land. Alternatively, intensification expresses not the amount of crops produced but the amount of energy or labor invested (Boserup 1965). These are not entirely parallel processes. Increasing labor might result in more produced overall but at the cost of increased per capita investment, a potentially diminishing trajectory that can cause total production to decline. Brookfield (1972) noted feedback between these phenomena and argued that once a threshold to lower overall returns was reached, people raised that threshold by intensifying. Population, production, and labor, thus, mutually influenced how farmers make decisions. As we will see with the Aztec case, the political demands of production and competing economic opportunity costs (i.e., market exchange) also must be considered (Brookfield 1972). Together, these variables capture key elements in farming households' repertoire of behavior that enable them to reproduce themselves and adapt to change (Chayanov 1966; Netting 1993; Wolf 1966).

Investing in land alters it, often in very dramatic ways. The idea of *landesque capital* captures the unique nature of capital as a factor of production specifically in an agricultural economy (Blaikie and Brookfield 1987; Fisher 2005; Håkansson and Widgren 2014; Kirch 1994; Sen 1959). Landesque capital represents investments in land with the potential to persist beyond their original input, which has intended and unintended consequences. Investments can enhance or stabilize production, promote sustainability, reduce future labor inputs, and shape how agriculturalists plan short-term and long-term goals (Morehart 2010:71). Researchers typically recognize landesque capital in the form of elaborate landscape modifications (terraces, canals, irrigation systems), which not only persist as a form of heritable property but often present remnants for archaeological study (Whitmore and Turner 2001). Beyond these more obvious examples, more micro-level modifications also constitute landesque capital (Brookfield 2001), as when farmers incorporate organic amendments into the soil (Wilken 1987:46–95). Nonetheless, landesque capital changes the relationship between energy inputs and productive potential, with some examples seemingly immune to the effects of diminishing marginal returns despite progressive (involutionary) investments (see Geertz 1963).

Agricultural Landscapes

Passing from the Gulf of Mexico en route to the central highlands, the Spanish conquerors were fascinated by the agricultural landscapes they encountered. According to Cortés (1986:75), "there are so many people living in these parts that not one foot of land is uncultivated." A diversity of agricultural landscapes was closely attuned to the physical characteristics of the environment. In the Basin of Mexico, a hydraulically closed plateau between 2500 and 2700 m above sea level, the major ecozones consist of (a) freshwater, brackish, and saline lakes and lagoons, (b) the deep alluvium at the base of (c) the foothills that characterize the piedmont, and (d) the rugged sierra (Sanders et al. 1979). Temperature and precipitation also varied. The southern Basin was warmer and wetter than the drier and colder northern Basin, where seasonal frosts could threaten crops (Logan and Sandres 1976; Nichols 1987; Parsons 2008; Sanders et al. 1979).

Aztec agricultural systems reflect adaptations to these environmental constraints, particularly slope, soil, water, and the specific crops cultivated. Aztec farmers cultivated a wide range of plant species, including maize (*Zea mays*), beans (*Phaseolus* spp.), squash (*Cucurbita* spp.), chiles (*Capsicum* spp.), maguey (*Agave* spp.), nopal (*Opuntia* spp.), amaranth (*Amarantus* spp.), tomato (*Physalis* spp.), chenopods (*Chenopodium* spp.), chia (*Salvia hispanica*), and many others (Clavijero 1958; Sahagún 1963; Torres 1985). Aztec farmers maintained a complex folk classification system of soils and land types of various qualities (Rojas Rabiela 1985; Sahagún 1963; Sanders et al. 1979; Williams 1979). They engaged in rain-fed, shifting cultivation; built terrace systems; created canals and channels to drain land along rivers and lakes; and built formal plots elevated above lake levels.

Highly intensive strategies appear to have been the most common strategy, especially with high populations during the height of the Aztec Empire. In a synthesis of Colonial sources on indigenous farming, for example, Rojas Rabiela (1985:154) only "found three cases of seasonal farming in the highlands of central Mexico with explicit mention of periods of rest and rotation." Technologically, Aztec farmers made few innovations to greatly augment their labor (laboresque capital [see Sen 1959]). To till the soil, they used fire-hardened digging sticks (*coa*) and foot hoes (*uictli*). In those cases where human labor was used to irrigate, either in household gardens or raised fields, jars were employed to pot irrigate plants, a long stick with a cloth bag attached (*zoquimaitl*) was used to collect water or canal muck, or simple canoe paddles were used to splash crops (Rojas Rabiela 1985; Sanders 1957; Santamaría 1912; West and Armillas 1950; Wilken 1987). Despite the simple forms of laboresque capital, they made long-lasting innovations in the creation of landesque capital.

Terrace agriculture was one of the most widespread types of landesque capital investments in the Aztec landscape. Terracing represents efforts to combat erosion by building up stone, soil, or planting particular plants, such as maguey, that stabilize the earth (Borejsza et al. 2008; Donkin 1979; Evans 1990; Parsons and Parsons 1990; Pérez et al. 2012; Sanders et al. 1979:243; Smith and Price 1994; Turner 1983; Wilkin 1987). Terraces not only served agricultural purposes but, in many areas of Mesoamerica, permitted the creation of residential areas (Smith et al. 2013; Feinman 2006; Pérez Pérez et al. 2012; Pérez Rodríguez 2006; Wyatt 2012). Vestiges of terrace systems can be seen lining many hills in the Basin and surrounding uplands today (Figure 18.1). Farmers likely cultivated some hill slopes with more extensive techniques reliant exclusively on rainfall, a technique called *tlacolol* in Nahuatl or *temporal* in Spanish (Rojas Rabiela 1985; Sanders 1957; Sanders et al. 1979:324; Smith 2003:66). However, terracing was more common. As Sanders et al. (1979:243) observed, "there is reason to believe that most of the sloping terrain in the central and northern portions of the Basin was covered by complex and carefully constructed terrace systems in 1519."

Several types of terrace systems existed. Terraces consisting of low earthen berms planted in maguey plants are known as *metepantle* (Borejsza et al. 2008; Evans 1990; González Jácome 2003:121; Smith et al. 2013; Wilkin 1987:107; Whitmore and Turner 2001). In a study of terrace systems in Morelos, Smith and Price (1994) delineated two types: cross-channel terraces and contour terraces (see also Smith and Heath-Smith 1994). Contour systems were constructed by piling stones to create walls behind which soil accumulated, resulting in narrow planting surfaces that follow the contours of hill slopes (see Figure 18.1). At Calixtlahuaca, in the Toluca valley, contour systems consisted of more elaborate bench terraces capable of supporting gardens and houses (Smith et al. 2013). Cross-channel, or check dam, terraces consisted of stone walls built across and perpendicular to water courses flowing through ravines or valley depressions. Silt and sediment amassed behind the walls

FIGURE 18.1 Low stone alignments of contour terrace system on Cerro Ahumada, in the northern Basin of Mexico. Photograph by author.

as water flowed through the streams. Over time, soil accumulation and newly constructed walls could lead to very large field platforms over 2 m in height (Smith 2012:68).

As the evidence for cross-channel terraces suggests, many Aztec agricultural landscapes were adaptions to major hydrological systems (Doolittle 1990; Palerm 1973; Rojas Rabiela 1974; Whitmore and Turner 2001). Irrigation allowed cultivators to prepare for the planting season in advance of seasonal rains, significantly reducing risks (Doolittle 1990; Nichols 1987; Sanders et al. 1979:252), and to greatly augment moisture. Combined with terracing or raised fields, irrigation systems also enabled previously unusable land to be either cultivated or intensified (Morehart 2010:88). The sixteenth-century Spanish priest Bernardino de Sahagún (1963:252) vividly described how land and water was modified to create irrigated land (*atlalli*): "Its name is [so] called from atl [water] and tlalli [earth]. This is the irrigated field. It is a watered garden, one which can be irrigated; it is irrigable; [land] which becomes wet, becomes mud. It is good, fine, precious; a source of food; esteemed; a place of fertility."

Palerm (1973:20–22) proposed a simple typology to characterize the diverse agrohydraulic systems in the Basin of Mexico. His first type consisted of small irrigation systems that originated from permanent springs, typically at the foot of large mountains. Major canals from the springs were integrated into networks of smaller canals and dams to deliver water to fields, many of which were terraced. Such small, spring-fed systems were very common in the Teotihuacan valley and the Texcoco region (Armillas et al. 1956; Palerm 1973; Wolf and Palerm 1955). Many of these systems were adaptations to seasonal floods, especially in the alluvial plains where shallow water channels and deep soils exist (Sander et al. 1979:253).

Palerm's second type consisted of major irrigation systems that relied on permanent or semipermanent rivers. These systems often had enormous canals and embankments that diverted water to fields, expanding arable land. Most of these systems were located in the lakeshore plain or alluvial bottomlands of the Basin of Mexico, areas most intensively occupied and built on from the Colonial period until today. Thus most no longer exist for archaeological study (Palerm 1973:21). The Cuauhtitlan River in the northwest Basin provides a well-known example with vestiges that still exist (Doolittle 1990) (Figure 18.2). In the early to mid-fifteenth century the entire course of the river was diverted via a large canal from the Xaltocan lake basin to the Tepotzotlan River, which drained into Lake Zumpango (Bierhorst 1992:103; Doolittle 1990; Palerm 1973:147; Strauss 1974:148).

Palerm's final agrohydraulic types were lacustrine-based systems. Chinampa systems are the most well-known example of this strategy. *Chinampas*, a word that derives from the Nahuatl term *chinamitl*, meaning an area enclosed by hedges (Molina 1944:21), consist of long, raised plots constructed above water levels and separated by narrow canals (Ávila Lopez 1991, 2006; Crossley 1999; Frederick 2007; Morehart 2012; Palerm 1973; Parsons 1976; Rojas Rabiela 1991; Sanders 1957; Santamaría 1912; West and Armillas 1950). Unlike many agricultural strategies, which constitute adaptations to limited water, chinampas are a response to too much water. Chinampas, many still in cultivation today (Figure 18.3), represent a classic example of agricultural intensification. The relationship between field and canal creates a unique micro-environment

FIGURE 18.2 Canal embankment of Cuauhitlan River (Doolittle 1990, reproduced with permission).

FIGURE 18.3 Contemporary chinampa planted in maize at Xochimilco. Photograph by author.

that permits subirrigation and protects crops from season frosts. They also can absorb considerable labor. For example, *chinamperos* commonly first plant in seed beds (*almácigos*), and healthy seedlings are then transplanted to the parcel—a practice that greatly increases energy investment. Chinampas are highly productive and can be kept in continuous cultivation, given the fertility of canal muck. Armillas (1971) and Parsons (1976) argued that the chinampas of the southern Basin could have supported over half the population of the Aztec capital of Tenochtitlan. Hence, they represent a unique configuration between land and labor that keeps production above the margin even with intensive investment. Chinampas existed in several locations in the Basin of Mexico, though they are better known around Lakes Xochimilco and Chalco (Armillas 1971; Ávila Lopez 1991, 2006; Frederick 2007; Morehart 2012; Parsons et al. 1982; Sanders 1957; West and Armillas 1950). They not only were present in the rural hinterland but also within cities, including Tenochtitlan (Calnek 1972).

The Social and Political Economy of Production

Sahagún (1961:41) wrote that "the good farmer" not only was hardworking and knowledgeable but also "bound to the soil." Both landed and landless peasants lived in the area (Hicks 1976; Parsons 1976), and those without lands or ties to local corporate groups had more mobility (Hicks 1984, see also Smith and Hicks this volume). However, the concept of landesque capital sheds light on how landed peasants became bound to the soil. With increased investment in land, agriculturalists' mobility declines as people are less likely to abandon their fields. As Geertz (1963:100) observed, "once the radical intensification of agriculture is accomplished, it is difficult to retreat from it." Being bound to the land is not just about economic investment; it is also a social and cultural issue, as patterns of inheritance, political obligations, or localized systems of ecological knowledge attest (Morehart 2010). This unintended consequence of landesque capital increases producers' susceptibility to control and exploitation by local or nonlocal power-holders (Childe 1951; Erickson 1993; Earle 1997; Gilman 1981).

The notion of binding, thus, helps archaeologists better clarify the relationship between the state and the agricultural producer, a configuration that is too often simplified in discussions of state control versus the autonomy of the farming household. Although the Aztec state sponsored major hydraulic engineering projects that directly affected agricultural systems (Doolittle 1990; Palerm 1973), most systems did not require a high degree of administration and were managed either by the household or by a community of users (Morehart 2010; Sanders and Price 1968; Smith et al. 2013; Smith and Price 1994). Yet recognizing that landesque capital binds producers to place—via complex and nested systems of investment, entitlement, and conveyance—elucidates how political institutions can come to influence local farmers even in agricultural landscapes lacking systemic integration or administration (Earle 1997:72).

In 1544, *encomendero* Jerónimo López wrote to Carlos, king of Spain, that during the time of Motecuhzoma "all the towns and provinces of his kingdom were forced to plant and there were overseers in his time to see if they were planted" (Paso y Troncoso 1939:169). Aztec communities paid taxes, which were collected by imperial officials specifically charged with this task (Hicks 1992). Most tribute was assessed at the provincial level and included a variety of goods and subsistence items. In the *Codex Mendoza*, which illustrates the range of tribute items, maize grain and flour, chia seeds, and beans were the most common agricultural products (Anderson and Barlow 1943; Berdan and Anawalt 1992) (Figure 18.4).

Subject towns farther from the imperial capital paid less in foodstuffs and more in wealth items (Drennan 1984; Hassig 1985). At the imperial level, tribute was paid up to twice a year, but payments to local, subimperial lords were more frequent and possibly more onerous (Offner 1981; Guzmán 1938; Smith 2008:191).

In addition to tribute, agricultural products were important elements of the Aztec market system (Morehart and Eisenberg 2010). A class of farmer-merchants likely existed. Sahagún (1961:65–66) states that farmers themselves sold their products in the marketplace: "The seller of maize grains [is] a worker of the fields, a worker of the land, or a retailer." In addition to maize grain, farmer-merchants exchanged other seeds, such as beans, squash, and amaranth; sold flour; and traded processed foods, such as tamales and tortillas (Rojas 2012; Sahagún 1961). The diversity of agricultural and other products in the market at Tlatelolco was so great that conquistador Bernal Díaz del Castillo (1956:216) remarked, "Why do I waste so many words in recounting what they sell in the great market?—for I shall never finish if I tell it all in detail." The influence of market exchange on agricultural production was shaped by the structure of the imperial

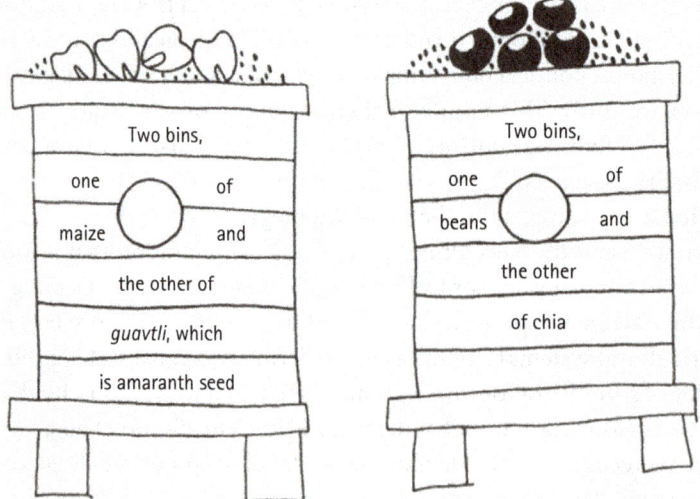

FIGURE 18.4 Storage maize bin (*troje*) for tribute as depicted in the *Codex Mendoza* (Berdan and Anawalt 1992), reproduced with permission.

political economy. Aztec officials were paid in tribute items, which they then traded on the market for subsistence goods (Berdan 1975; Calnek 1978). Flooding the market with such items may have lowered the exchange value of crafts produced in some communities, creating new conditions of economic dependency with imperial incorporation. Brumfiel (1980), for example, argued that this process led to a reduction of craft production and an increase in agricultural specialists in Late Postclassic Huexotla in the Texcoco region (cf. Charlton et al. 1991).

Although imperial officials and rulers were more interested in farmers' output than managing their daily affairs, land was directly caught up into the imperial political economy in complex ways. In general, land was balanced between patterns of individual usufruct and inheritance versus the corporate rules by which they were managed (Gibson 1964; Harvey 1984; Lockhart 1992; Zorita 1994). The large number of land terms that existed demonstrates that the state was not a monolithic entity but was comprised of multiple institutional structures that shaped the flow of wealth, the distribution of power, and the conveyance of resources. For the Aztecs, land was political currency awarded to nobles and allies. Many of these lands became noble estates, referred to as *pillalli* and worked by commoners for their likely absentee landlords (Calnek 1975; Lockhart 1992; Parsons 1976). Other lands were specifically set aside to support governmental offices and institutions. Thus rulers maintained their own patrimonial lands, known as *tlatocatlalli* (ruler's land) or *teuctalli* (lord's land). Institutions likewise were associated with tracts of land, such as the *teotlalli* (temple land), *tecpantlalli* (palace land), and *milchimalli* (army land) (Lockhart 1992:156). Lands also were categorized by the quality (rather than quantity) of labor. For instance, a category of tribute land, *tequitcatlalli* or *tequitcamilli*, existed, derived from the Nahuatl verb *tequiti*, "to perform tribute duty, pay tribute" (Lockhart 1992:157; see also Hicks 1982).

Although these lands were associated with specific imperial institutions, they were nonetheless worked by commoners who had to integrate labor on "state" land with other tribute assessments (Gibson 1964; Hicks 1984; Hodge 1996; Morehart and Eisenberg 2010). Most state lands were worked communally as tribute labor (Gibson 1964:258), and the local heads of community-based corporate groups, referred to in historic records as either *capolli* or *tlaxiclalli*, seemed to have organized workers for this purpose (Hicks 1982; Lockhart 1992:142; Zorita 1994:105). But such corporate groups could also maintain land (e.g., *calpollalli*), awarded by a local lord (Carrasco 1976; Hicks 1982; Lockhart 1992; Smith and Novic 2012). However, such "community" lands were inalienable in that the corporate group awarded tracts to its members, which they could pass on to heirs but not to nonmembers.

Farmers maintained considerable autonomy over their agricultural practices. Although they found themselves in a structure of entitlements that influenced conveyance, they worked their plots individually and could bequeath holdings to heirs. Gibson (1964:267) noted that though "calpullalli might be identified as 'common' land, it was not worked in common but was subdivided into individual plots." Most farmers, in other words, were basically smallholders (Netting 1993). Individual plots were the principal source of produce at the household level, and many families maintained lands distinctively associated with, and often spatially adjacent to, the household (Gibson 1964:267; Lockhart 1992:150; Sahagún 1963:252; Smith et al. 2013; Williams and Harvey 1997). Moreover, the *macehualtin* were not a monolithic class of commoners. Some had more and better land than others, reflecting economic and social differences (Anderson et al. 1976; Harvey 1984; Williams 1984; Williams and Harvey 1997).

Understanding pre-European land tenure systems among the Aztecs is complicated, and translating tenure into something archaeologically visible is difficult. The diversity of tenure terms was not correlated to the specific kinds of lands or landesque capital investments. Farmers, landlords, and the state maintained land in distinctive ecological settings with different structural properties (Anderson et al. 1976; Cline 1986; Lockhart 1992:150–151). The status and significance of particular corporate groups, such as the *calpolli*, has plagued historical research for decades (e.g., Harvey 1984; Hicks 1982; Offner 1984). In a consideration of the range of tenure terms that appear in historical sources, Lockhart (1992:156) cautions, "I propose that these categories were not mutually exclusive, that they were controversial, that terminology varies with time, region, and even speaker . . . we cannot simply take the chronicles at face value." This situation presents a challenge for archaeologists seeking to associate specific land use practices with particular forms of tenure, management, and governance. Nevertheless, the archaeological evidence of diverse agricultural landscapes combined with the multifaceted nature of tenure sheds light on the range of social, political, and ecological regimes that influenced farming strategies.

Conclusion

The mosaic of agricultural landscapes that the Spanish observed when they first arrived in central Mexico resulted from complex strategies as farmers confronted and navigated broader organizational regimes. This consideration of farming elucidates one of the most important aspects of the vast majority of the Aztec population. Although most archaeological research has centered on communities or households, agricultural landscapes represent the bulk of archaeological sites, though their detection is becoming increasingly difficult with modern development and urban expansion. These seemingly uninhabited spaces were important loci where farmers spent the majority of their days, investing in land, producing food, and instructing children. This element of the Aztec past is overlooked when contemporary imaginations center exclusively on warfare, human sacrifice, or the art and monumental architecture of high culture and urban life. A consideration of farming reveals that such romantic themes of the ancient Aztecs were only possibly via the lives and labors of agriculturalists themselves.

References Cited

Anderson, Eugene, and Robert H. Barlow
1943 The Maize Tribute of Mocteczuma's Empire. *Annals of the Missouri Botanical Garden* 30:413–420.

Anderson, Arthur, Frances F. Berdan, and James Lockhart (editors)
1976 *Beyond the Codices: The Nahua View of Colonial Mexico*. University of California Press, Berkeley.

Armillas, Pedro
1971 Gardens on Swamps. *Science* 175:653–661.

Armillas, Pedro, Angel Palerm, and Eric Wolf
1956 A Small Irrigation System in the Valley of Teotihuacan. *American Antiquity* 21:396–399.

Avila López, Raúl
1991 *Chinampas de Iztapalapa, D. F.* Instituto Nacional de Antropología e Historia, Mexico, D.F.
2006 *Mexicaltzingo: arqueologia de un Reino Culhua-Mexica*. 2 vols. Conaculta, Mexico, D.F.

Berdan, Frances F.
1975 *Trade, Tribute and Market in the Aztec Empire*. Ph.D. dissertation, University of Texas, Austin.

Berdan, Frances F., and P. R. Anawalt (editors)
1992 *The Codex Mendoza*. 4 vols. University of California Press, Berkeley.

Bierhorst, John
1992 *History and Mythology of the Aztecs: The Codex Chimalpopoca*. University of Arizona Press, Tuscon.

Blaikie, Pierre, and Harold C. Brookfield
1987 *Land Degradation and Society*. Methuen, London.

Borejsza, Aleksander, Isabel Rodríguez López, Charles Frederick, and Mark D. Bateman
2008 Agricultural Slope Management and Soil erosion at La Laguna, Tlaxcala, Mexico. *Journal of Archaeological Science* 35:1854–1866.

Boserup, Ester
1965 *The Conditions of Agricultural Growth: The Economics of Agrarian Change under Population Growth*. Aldine, New Brunswick, NJ.

Brookfield, Harold C.
1972 Intensification and Disintensification in Pacific Agriculture: A Theoretical Approach. *Pacific Viewpoint* 13:30–48.
1984 Intensification Revisited. *Pacific Viewpoint* 25:15–44.
2001 Intensification, and Alternative Approaches to Agricultural Change. *Asia Pacific Viewpoint* 42:181–192.

Brumfiel, Elizabeth M.
1980 Specialization, Market Exchange, and the Aztec State: A View of Huexotla. *Current Anthropology* 21:459–478.

Brush, Stephen B., and Billie L. Turner
1987 The Nature of Farming Systems and Views on Their Change. In *Comparative Farming Systems* edited by B. L. Turner and S. B. Brush, pp. 11–48. Guilford Press, New York.

Calnek, Edward E.
1972 Settlement Pattern and Chinampa Agriculture at Tenochtitlan. *American Antiquity* 37:104–115.

1975 Organización de los Sistemas de Abastecimiento Urbano de Alimentos: el Caso de Tenochtitlan. In *Las Ciudades de América Latina y sus Áreas de Influencia a través de la Historia*, edited by Jorge E. Hardoy and René P. Schaedel, pp. 41–60. Ediciones S.I.A.P., Buenos Aires, Argentina.

Carrasco, Pedro

1976 The Joint Family in Ancient Mexico: The Case of Molotla. In *Essays on Mexican Kinship*, edited by Hugo Nutini, Pedro Carrasco, and James M. Taggert, pp. 45–64. University of Pittsburgh Press, Pittsburgh, PA.

Charlton, Thomas, Deborah Nichols, and Cynthia Otis-Charlton

1991 Aztec Craft Production and Specialization: Archaeological Evidence from the City-State of Otumba, Mexico. *World Archaeology* 23:98–114.

Chayanov, Aelxander V.

1966 On the Theory of Non-Capitalist Economic Systems. In *The Theory of Peasant Economy by A. V. Chayanov*, edited by D. Thorner, B. Kerblay, and R. E. F. Smith, pp. 1–28. University of Wisconsin Press, Madison.

Childe, V. Gordon

1951 *Man Makes Himself*. Mentor Books, New York.

Clavijero, Francisco J.

1958 *Historia Antigua de México*, Vol. I. Editorial Porrua, Mexico, D.F.

Cline, Sarah L.

1986 *Colonial Culhuacan, 1580–1600: A Social History of an Aztec Town*. University of New Mexico Press, Albuquerque.

Cortes, Hernán

1986 *Letters from Mexico*. Translated by A. Pagden. Yale University Press, New Haven, CT.

Crossley, Philip

1999 *Sub-Irrigation and Temperature Amelioration in Chinampa Agriculture*. Ph.D. dissertation, University of Texas, Austin.

Díaz del Castillo, Bernal

1956 *The Discovery and Conquest of Mexico:1517–1521*. Farrar, Straus, and Cudahy, New York.

Donkin, R. A.

1979 *Agricultural Terracing in the Aboriginal New World*. University of Arizona Press, Tuscon.

Doolittle, William E.

1990 *Canal Irrigation in Prehistoric Mexico: The Sequence of Technological Change*. University of Texas Press, Austin.

Drennan, Robert D.

1984 Long-Distance Transport Costs in Pre-Hispanic Mesoamerica. *American Anthropologist* 86:105–112.

Earle, Timothy

1997 *How Chiefs Come to Power: The Political Economy in Prehistory*. Stanford University Press, Stanford, CA.

Erickson, Clark

1993 The Social Organization of Prehispanic Raised Field Agriculture in the Lake Titicaca Basin. In *Economic Aspects of Water Management in the Prehispanic New World*, edited by Vernon L. Scarborough and Barry L. Isaac, pp. 369–426. JAI Press, Greenwich, CT.

Evans, Susan T.

1990 The Productivity of Maguey Terrace Agriculture in Central Mexico during the Aztec Period. *Latin American Antiquity* 1:117–132.

Feinman, Gary M.
2006 The Economic Underpinnings of Prehispanic Zapotec Civilization: Small-Scale Production, Economic Interdependence. In *Agricultural Strategies*, edited by Joyce Marcus and Charles Stanish, pp. 255–280. Cotsen Institute of Archaeology, Los Angeles.

Fisher, Christopher
2005 Abandoning the Garden: Demographic and Landscape Change in the Lake Pátzcuaro Basin, Mexico. *American Anthropologist* 107:87–95.

Frederick, Charles
2007 Chinampa Cultivation in the Basin of Mexico: Observations on the Evolution of Form and Function. In *Seeking a Richer Harvest: The Archaeology of Subsistence Intensification, Innovation and Change*, edited by T. L. Thurston and C. T. Fisher, pp. 107–124. Springer Scientific, New York.

Geertz, Clifford
1963 *Agricultural Involution: The Process of Ecological Change in Indonesia*. University of California Press, Berkeley.

Gibson, Charles
1964 *The Aztecs under Spanish Rule: A History of the Valley of Mexico, 1519–1810*. Stanford University Press, Stanford, CA.

Gilman, Antonio
1981 The Development of Social Stratification in Bronze Age Europe. *Current Anthropology* 22:1–24.

González Jácome, Alba
2003 *Cultura y Agricultura: transformaciones en el Agro-Mexicano*. Universidad Iberoamericano, Mexico, D.F.

Guzmán, Eulalia
1938 Un Manuscrito de la Colección Boturini que Trata de los Antiguos Señores de Teotihuacan. *Ethnos* 3:89–103.

Håkansson, Thomas, N. and Mats Widgren (editors)
2014 *Landesque Capital: The Historical Ecology of Enduring Landscape Modifications*. Left Coast Press, Walnut Creek, CA.

Harvey, H. R.
1984 Aspects of Land Tenure in Ancient Mexico. In *Explorations in Ethnohistory: Indians of Central Mexico in the Sixteenth Century*, edited by H. R. Harvey and Hanns J. Prem, pp. 83–102. University of New Mexico Press, Albuquerque.

Hassig, Ross
1985 *Trade, Tribute, and Transportation: The Sixteenth-Century Political Economy of the Valley of Mexico*. University of Oklahoma Press, Norman.

Hicks, Frederic
1982 Tetzcoco in the Early 16th Century: The State, the City, and the Calpolli. *American Ethnologist* 9:230–249.
1984 Rotational Labor and Urban Development in Prehispanic Tetzcoco. In *Explorations in Ethnohistory: Indians of Central Mexico in the Sixteenth Century*, edited by H. R. Harvey and H. J. Prem, pp. 147–176. University of New Mexico, Albuquerque.
1992 Subject States and Tribute Provinces: Aztec Empire in the Northern Valley of Mexico. *Ancient Mesoamerica* 3:1–10.

Hodge, Mary G.
1996 Political Organization of the Central Provinces. In *Aztec Imperial Strategies*, edited by Frances F. Berdan, Richard Blanton, Elizabeth H. Boone, Mary G. Hodge, Michael E.

Smith, and Emily Umberger, pp. 17–45. Dumbarton Oaks Research Library and Collection, Washington, DC.

Kirch, Patrick V.

1994 *The Wet and the Dry: Irrigation and Agricultural Intensification in Polynesia*. University of Chicago Press, Chicago.

Lockhart, James

1992 *The Nahuas after Conquest: A Social and Cultural History of the Indians of Central Mexico, Sixteenth through Eighteenth Centuries*. Stanford University Press, Stanford, CA.

Logan, Michael, and William T. Sanders

1976 The Model. In *The Valley of Mexico: Studies in Pre-Hispanic Ecology and Society*, edited by E. Wolf, pp. 31–58. University of New Mexico Press, Albuquerque.

Molina, Alonso

1944 *Vocabularo en Lengua Castellan y Mexicana*. Ediciones Cultura Hispanica IV. Colección de Incunables Americanos, Madrid.

Morehart, Christopher T.

2010 The Archaeology of Farmscapes: Production, Place, and the Materiality of Landscape at Xaltocan, Mexico. Unpublished Ph.D. dissertation, Northwestern University, Evanston, IL.

2012 Mapping Ancient Chinampa Landscapes in the Basin of Mexico: A Remote Sensing and GIS Approach. *Journal of Archaeological Science* 39:2541–2551.

Morehart, Christopher T., and Daniel T. A. Eisenberg

2010 Prosperity, Power, and Change: Modeling Maize at Postclassic Xaltocan, Mexico. *Journal of Anthropological Archaeology* 29:94–112.

Morrison, Kathleen D.

1994 The Intensification of Production: Archaeological Approaches. *Journal of Archeological Method and Theory* 1:111–159.

Netting, Robert M.

1993 *Smallholders, Householders: Farm Families and the Ecology of Intensive, Sustainable Agriculture*. Stanford University Press, Stanford, CA.

Nichols, Deborah

1987 Risk and Agricultural Intensification during the Formative Period in the Northern Basin of Mexico. *American Anthropologist* 89:596–616.

Offner, Jerome A.

1981 On the Inapplicability of "Oriental Despotism" and the "Asiatic Mode of Production" to the Aztecs of Texcoco. *American Antiquity* 46:43–61.

1984 Household Organization in the Texcocan Heartland. In *Explorations in Ethnohistory: Indians of Central Mexico in the Sixteenth Century*, edited by H. R. Harvey and H. J. Prem, pp. 127–146. University of New Mexico Press, Albuquerque.

Palerm, Ángel

1973 *Obras Hidráulicas prehispánicas en el Sistema Lacustre del Valle de México*. Instituto Nacional de Antropología e Historia, Mexico, D.F.

Parsons, Jeffrey R.

1976 The Role of Chinampa Agriculture in the Food Supply of Aztec Tenochtitlan. In *Cultural Change and Continuity: Essays in Honor of James B. Griffin*, edited by Charles Cleland, pp. 233–257. Academic Press, New York.

2008 *Prehispanic Settlement Patterns in the Northwestern Valley of Mexico: The Zumpango Region*, with contributions by Larry J. Gorenflo, Mary H. Parsons, and David J. Wilson. Memoirs No. 45, Museum of Anthropology, University of Michigan, Ann Arbor.

Parsons, Jeffrey, Elizabeth M. Brumfiel, and David J. Wilson
1982 *Prehispanic Settlement Patterns in the Southern Valley of Mexico: The Chalco-Xochimilco Region*. Memoirs of the Museum of Anthropology 14. Museum of Anthropology University of Michigan, Ann Arbor.

Parsons, Jeffrey R., and Mary Parsons
1990 *Maguey Utilization in Highland Central Mexico: An Archaeological Ethnography*. Museum of Anthropology, University of Michigan, Ann Arbor.

Paso y Troncoso, Francisco del
1939 *Epistolario de Nueva España, 1505–1818*, Vol. IV: *1540–1546*. Antigua Librería Robredo, Mexico.

Pérez-Pérez, Julia, Emily McClung de Tapia, Luis Barba-Pingarrón, Jorge E. Gama-Castro, and Armando Peralta-Higuera
2012 Remote Sensing Detection of Potential Sites in a Prehispanic Domestic Agricultural Terrace System in cerro San Lucas, Teotihuacan, Mexico. *Boletín de la Sociedad Geológica Mexicana* 64:109–118.

Pérez Rodríguez, Veronica
2006 States and Households: The Social Organization of Terrace Agriculture in Postclassic Mixteca Alta, Oaxaca, Mexico. *Latin American Antiquity* 17:3–22.

Rojas, Jose Luís
2012 *Tenochtitlan: Capital of the Aztec Empire*. University Press of Florida, Gainesville.

Rojas Rabiela, Teresa (editor)
1974 *Nuevas Noticias sobre las Obras Hidráulicas Prehispánicas y Coloniales en el Valle de México*. Instituto Nacional de Antropología e Historia, Mexico, D.F.

Rojas Rabiela, Teresa
1985 La Tecnología Agrícola Mesoamericana en el Siglo XVI. In *Historia de la Agricultura Epoca Prehispánica, Siglo XVI*, edited by T. Rojas Rabiela, pp. 129–232. Instituto Nacional de Antropología e Historia, Mexico, D.F.
1991 Ecological and Agricultural Changes in the Chinampas of Xochimilco-Chalco. In *Land and Politics in the Valley of Mexico*, edited by H. R. Harvey, pp. 275–290. University of New Mexico Press, Albuquerque.

Sahagún, Fray Bernardino de
1961 *Florentine Codex, General History of the Things of New Spain: Book 10, The People*. Monographs of the School of American Research, Santa Fe, NM.
1963 *Florentine Codex, General History of the Things of New Spain: Book 11, Earthly Things*. Monographs of the School of American Research, Santa Fe, NM.

Sanders, William T.
1957 *Tierra y Agua (Soil and Water): A Study of the Ecological Factors in the Development of Meso-American Civilizations*. Ph.D. dissertation, Harvard University, Cambridge, MA.

Sanders, William T., Jeffrey R. Parsons, and Robert S. Santley
1979 *Basin of Mexico: Ecological Processes in the Evolution of a Civilization*. Academic Press, New York.

Sanders, William T., and Barbara J. Price
1968 *Mesoamerica: The Evolution of a Civilization*. Random House, New York.

Santamaría, Miguel
1912 *Las Chinampas del Distrito Federal*. La Secretaria de Fomento, Mexico, D.F.

Sen, Amartya K.
1959 The Choice of Agricultural Techniques in Underdeveloped Countries. *Economic Development and Cultural Change* 7:279–285.

Smith, Michael
2008 *Aztec City State Capitals*. University of Florida Press, Gainesville.
2012 *The Aztecs*, 3rd ed. Blackwell, Malden, MA.
Smith, Michael E., Aleksander Borejsza, Angela Huster, Charles Frederick, Isabel Rodríguez López, and Cynthia Heath-Smith
2013 Aztec Period Houses and Terraces at Calixtlahuaca: The Changing Morphology of a Mesoamerican Hilltop Urban Center. *Journal of Field Archaeology* 38:227–243.
Smith Michael E., and Cynthia Heath-Smith
1994 Rural Economy in Late Postclassic Morelos: An Archaeological Study. In *Economies and Polities in the Aztec Realm*, edited by Mary G. Hodge and Michael E. Smith, pp. 349–376. Institute for Mesoamerican Studies, Albany, NY.
Smith, Michael E., and Juliana Novic
2012 Neighborhoods and Districts in Ancient Mesoamerica. In *The Neighborhood as a Social and Spatial Unit in Mesoamerican Cities*, edited by Marie Charlotte Arnauld, Linda Manzanilla and Michael E. Smith, pp. 1–26. University of Arizona Press, Tucson.
Smith, Michael E., and Jeffrey T. Price
1994 Aztec Period Agricultural Terraces in Morelos, Mexico: Evidence for Household-Level Agricultural Intensification. *Journal of Field Archaeology* 21:169–179.
Strauss, Raphael A. K.
1974 El Área Septentrional del Valle de México: problemas Agrohidráulicos Prehispánicos y Coloniales. In *Nuevas Noticias sobre las Obras Hidráulicas Prehispánicas y Coloniales en el Valle De México*, edited by T. Rojas Rabiela, pp. 135–174. Instituto Nacional de Antropología e Historia, Mexico, D.F.
Torres, Barbara
1985 Las Plantas Utiles en el México Antiguo Según las Fuentes del Siglo XVI. In *Historia de la Agricultura Epoca Prehispánica, Siglo XVI*, edited by T. Rojas Rabiela, pp. 53–128. Instituto Nacional de Antropología e Historia, Mexico, D.F.
Turner, Billie L.
1983 *Once Beneath the Forest: Prehistoric Terracing in the Río Bec Region of the Maya Lowlands*. Westview Press, Boulder, CO.
West, Robert, and Pedro Armillas
1950 Las Chinampas De México, Poesía y Realidad de los Jardines Flotantes. *Cuadernos Americanos* 50:165–182.
Whitmore, Thomas M., and Billie L. Turner
2001 *Cultivated Landscapes of Middle America on the Eve of Conquest*. Oxford University Press, Oxford.
Wilken, Gene C.
1987 *Good Farmers: Traditional Agricultural Resource Management in Mexico and Central America*. University of California Press, Berkeley.
Williams, Barbara J.
1979 Mexico: Aztec Soil Classification and Land Tenure. In Actes du XLII Congrès International des Américanistes. Congrès du Centenaire, Paris 1976, Paris, Société des Américanistes. Vol. 9B, pp. 165–175.
1984 Mexican Pictorial Cadastral Registers. In *Explorations in Ethnohistory: Indians of Central Mexico in the Sixteenth Century*, edited by H. R. Harvey and H. J. Prem, pp. 103–126. University of New Mexico Press, Albuquerque.

Williams, Barbara J., and H. R. Harvey
1997 *The Códice de Santa María Asunción: Households and Lands in Sixteenth-Century Tepetlaoztoc*. University of Utah Press, Salt Lake City.

Wolf, Eric R.
1966 *Peasants*. Prentice-Hall, Englewood Cliffs, NJ.

Wolf, Eric R., and Ángel Palerm
1955 Irrigation in the Old Acolhua Domain, Mexico. *Southwestern Journal of Anthropology* 2:265–281.

Wyatt, Andrew
2012 Agricultural Practices at Chan: Farming and Political Economy in an Ancient Maya Community. In *Chan: An Ancient Maya Farming Community*, edited by C. Robin, pp. 71–88. University Press of Florida, Gainesville.

Zorita, Alonso de
1994 *Life and Labor in Ancient Mexico: The Brief and Summary Relation of the Lords of New Spain*. Translated by B. Keen. University of Oklahoma Press, Norman.

CHAPTER 19

THE STRUCTURE OF AZTEC COMMERCE

Markets and Merchants

KENNETH HIRTH AND DEBORAH L. NICHOLS

COMMERCE as defined by Merriam-Webster (1968, 1990) is the "exchange or buying and selling of commodities on a large scale involving transportation from place to place . . . as between cities or countries." It refers to economic activity organized to make a profit whether at the level of an individual enterprise or a whole industry or nation. While it is possible to talk about the commercial dealings of individual firms or businesses, *commerce* generally refers to the broad sweep of economic activities within society and the many diversified forms that they may take.

Any discussion of Aztec commerce needs to fit the term to its proper cultural frame of reference. Aztec commerce refers to the organization and scale of exchange in a precapitalist and preindustrial New World society. The Aztec economy was precapitalist in that it lacked an active market for both land and labor (Isaac 2013). While commodities were bought and sold using several forms of currency, land and labor rarely were; instead, they were accessed through the social relations of group affiliation and/or political control. The Aztecs also had a preindustrial economy where most production was small-scale and organized at the level of individual households. Where production existed above the household, it usually was organized as socially conscripted corvee labor.

Given its precapitalist and preindustrial organization, it is pertinent to ask whether the term *commerce* is even appropriate for discussing Aztec economic activity. After all, the scale and distance over which goods moved was sharply constrained by one of the ancient world's worst transportation systems. The Aztec world lacked beasts of burden, wheeled vehicles, and paved roads and had few navigable rivers and very limited maritime trade. Staple and luxury goods moved primarily by human porters (*tlameme*) who used tumplines to carry loads in baskets or on special traveling frames. Regardless of these constraints, the Aztecs still had an active commercial economy carried out at different scales by a large number of people.

Commerce as defined here refers to the negotiated purchase or balanced exchange of goods by economic entrepreneurs for purpose of improving their economic well-being. According to Smith (2004:78–79), ancient commercialized economies are characterized by the presence of price-making markets and institutions that facilitate their formation through the use of money, marketplaces, credit, and banking. Intrinsic to commerce is the search for profit, and this was clearly the case, judging from the Aztecs' rich commercial vocabulary (Christiansen and Hirth 2013). The Nahuatl word for "profit" was *tlaixtlapana*, which literally means to produce an increase through face-to-face negotiation.[1] Profit among the Aztecs covered everything from procuring food and staple resources, to meeting household subsistence needs and accumulating large quantities of imperishable wealth (i.e. textiles, jade, etc.).

This study examines the structure of Aztec commerce from the broadest possible perspective. It is concerned with identifying the range of economic exchanges that moved goods over both long and short distances. It begins by examining the importance of the marketplace that was both the central place of Aztec commerce and the institution that enabled the development of economic specialization within society. Because Aztec commerce was diverse, this is followed by a discussion of the individuals involved in trade and the scale over which they bought, sold, and transported their goods. This discussion draws information not only from ethnohistoric sources but also from archaeological data from the important Aztec commercial community of Otumba.

The Marketplace: The Place of Commerce

Trade and exchange were common occurrences among the Aztec. No household was completely self-sufficient for all the goods and resources it needed or desired. Households exchanged food and other goods they produced for the resources that they could not procure themselves. The result was a lively commercial economy with individuals involved in exchange at many different levels, ranging from intermittent target marketers intent on obtaining a few items throughout the year to full-time merchants involved in regional and long-distance trade. The distance over which commodities moved varied with their degree of bulkiness and the goals of the individuals moving them. We know that Aztec women traveled short distances to sell lake products collected by their husbands at marketplaces in the Basin of Mexico (Duran 1994). Conversely, long-distance merchants ranged as far south as Xoconusco near the Guatemalan border (Gasco and Berdan 2003) to bring back cacao and other high-value luxury goods (Duran 1994; Voorhies 1989:33). The important point is that people at all levels of society were involved in commercial exchange to mobilize the commodities that they needed or desired. What varied was their level of involvement and the degree to which it constituted a major strategy used to meet household subsistence needs.

The marketplace was the center of Aztec commerce. It was the hub of economic life, and, like markets elsewhere in the ancient world, it was where large numbers of people came together to barter or buy goods from one another. Exchanges within the marketplace were immediate, balanced, and based on establishing price through negotiation (Berdan 1989; Plattner 1989a, 1989b). Markets were held daily in large cities like Tlaltelolco, Texcoco, and Tenochtitlan (Figure 19.1).

In smaller cities and rural towns, markets were convened on rotating schedules of 5-, 9-, 13-, and 20-day cycles (Hassig 1982). This produced an integrated system of large and small marketplaces that provided ready access to a wide range of commodities on a predictable schedule. As a result, the majority of the population in central Mexico was within a single day's walk of a market that could meet their provisioning needs.

It was a law among the Aztecs that economic transactions be conducted in the marketplace. This enabled supervision of economic transactions as well as the collection of tax from sellers that covered the cost of market operations. The marketplace was where most economic transactions took place, but its success and popularity was not because it was the legislated point for trade—rather, it was due to the tremendous economic benefits it provided the individuals who frequented it. Markets fulfilled three important functions not just for the Aztecs but for all precolumbian societies that had them.

A primary benefit of the marketplace was that it made household provisioning very efficient. Commoner households were the primary users of the marketplace. It gave individual households access to a great diversity of goods and enabled them to satisfy multiple provisioning needs in a single trip. Sellers bore the burden of assembling goods for sale in the marketplace with buyers incurring only the take-home costs of the items purchased. Moreover, markets allowed households to provision themselves through their own efforts with a minimum of institutional control or interference.

FIGURE 19.1 A Tarascan Marketplace. Illustration from the *Relacion de Michoacan*. Reproduced with permission.

Second, the marketplace stimulated a great deal of independent economic activity within commoner households. Particularly important was the development of intermittent craft production and resource collection that enabled households to sell the fruits of their labors for supplementary income (Hirth 2010). Women engaged in a range of activities to supplement household income that included weaving and selling craft goods, prepared foods, fruit, and a range of other natural resources and staple foods. The ability of everyone to sell in the marketplace stimulated the development of a rich and diversified craft economy that rivaled continental Europe at the time of the Conquest.

Third, the economic pull of the marketplace made it a natural collection point for goods within Aztec society. Small-scale producers brought surpluses for sale when needed, as did the representatives of elite estates. Retailers bought food surpluses in the marketplace and resold them in both small and large quantities. The resource mobilization function of the marketplace provided an important conversion function within Aztec society that linked state tribute networks, elite estates, professional merchants, and small-scale peasant farmers in an interconnected network of resource flows (Carrasco 1978). The ability of the marketplace to facilitate the conversion of resources into alternative products allowed the Aztec system of wealth finance to operate with minimal state involvement or supervisory cost (cf. Blanton and Feinman 1984; D'Altroy and Earle 1985). The marketplace promoted a system of diversified commerce by enabling individual merchants and craftspeople to convert the commodities they produced or obtained through trade into alternative goods.

The marketplace was also an adaptation to the high costs of transportation by shifting the primary cost of movement to sellers. While buyers could make multiple purchases in a single a trip to a marketplace, professional merchants might travel hundreds of kilometers to procure the goods they sold. The proliferation of markets across the highlands allowed buyers at all levels of society to remain relatively stationary in comparison to sellers. Moreover, holding markets on different days in combination with the 5-, 9-, and 13-day rotations allowed professional merchants to travel efficiently from one marketplace to another with a minimum amount of time lost in between (Bromly et al. 1975; Symanski and Weber 1974). Although sellers were limited in the loads they could carry, it was profitability and not energetics that encouraged or discouraged commercial trade (Hirth 2013).

THE AGENTS OF COMMERCE

A good understanding of Aztec commerce can be acquired by examining the range of individuals involved to differing degrees in trade and exchange. Six groups of economic practitioners are apparent in the ethnohistoric and archaeological record. These include a broad array of producer-sellers, craftsmen, retail merchants, itinerant craftsmen, long-distance *pochteca* merchants, and simple peddlers. These were recognized as meaningful analytical categories by the Aztecs themselves and illustrate the variation found in the individuals involved, the distances over which they operated, and how they were organized to engage in trade.

The foundation of Aztec commerce was the producer-seller from commoner households that sold a range of food, natural resources, and craft goods in the marketplace (Hirth 2013:90). They are identified in the ethnohistoric literature by the Nahuatl suffix of *-chiuqui* and numerically were the most common category of vendors found in the marketplace. Their involvement in commercial activities was often intermittent rather than full-time. The range of their commercial operations was generally small, confined to their own community or limited to the region within a single day's journey to markets in neighboring towns. Table 19.1 summarizes the numbers of producer-sellers regularly found in the large daily Aztec marketplaces in the Basin of Mexico such as that of Tlaltelolco.

Craftsmen were one important group of producer-sellers. While some craftsmen sold the goods they produced, many others did not, preferring instead to practice their craft and entrust their goods to peddlers or retail vendors (see later discussion). The available evidence suggests that most craftsmen did not practice their trade on a full-time basis. Either they combined crafting with agriculture on an intermittent basis or engaged in a form of multicrafting by practicing several related or complementary trades (Hirth 2009a, 2009c). Most craft specialists worked in their homes, fabricating both utilitarian and wealth goods on the patios of their houses or in small associated workshops or work areas. Likewise, most craft work was organized using household labor except that organized for the specialized production of wealth or status goods used by the state.

Most craftsmen used regionally available raw materials in their craft and did not travel far from home. An interesting exception to this practice was itinerant obsidian craftsmen who traveled from marketplace to marketplace where they produced and sold prismatic blades (Hirth 2009b). Obsidian was an indispensable commodity for the Aztecs providing all of their usable cutting edge. The high demand for obsidian blades

Table 19.1 Types of Producer-Sellers in Large Daily Aztec Marketplaces

Types of Producer-Sellers	No.	%
Food producers	16	14.3
Processed food sellers	15	13.4
Foragers and collectors	16	14.3
Craftsmen	54	48.0
Service providers	11	10.0
Total producer-sellers	112	100.0

Source: Hirth (2013:Table 4.1).

and the difficulty in producing them led to itinerant crafting where obsidian craftsmen (*itznamacac*) produced razor-sharp blades on demand in the marketplace for individuals to purchase (Sahagún 1961). Like other producer-sellers, they were organized at the household level but established contacts with other craftsmen in quarry areas through which they obtained raw material and possibly even apprenticed their children to improve their skills (Hirth 2009b).

While craftsmen could take their goods to the marketplace, many chose to sell them to intermediate retailers. The retail merchant was referred to by the indigenous Nahuatl term of *tlanecuilo*. These merchants tended to specialize in classes of related goods such as ceramics, gourd containers, textiles, and other items (Hirth 2013; Nichols 2013). Most retailers appear to have been involved in commerce on a full-time basis. Furthermore, these merchants were often mobile, with the distance they traveled being a function of the class of goods sold. They included regional retailers who circulated from local marketplace to marketplace as well as those who procured, transported, and sold commodities like salt and raw cotton between regions (Berdan 1980). Some *tlanecuilo* merchants also operated permanent booths or stalls in large daily marketplaces where they likely stored goods from day to day.

The best-known Aztec merchants are the full-time, long-distance professional merchants known as *pochteca* and *oztomeca* (Sahagún 1959). These merchants operated over very long distances both inside and outside the Aztec Empire. The focus of their trade was on lightweight and high-value goods such as feathers, textiles, and cacao. While their economic ventures were organized primarily to enrich themselves, they also played an important role in the operation of Aztec political economy. They served as economic agents for Aztec kings such as Ahuitzotl, utilizing alliance relationships with distant groups to trade goods in their names. It is likely that they did the same for other elite members of society. Long-distance merchants also provided an important military service for the Aztec state; the *oztomeca* traveled incognito in hostile areas to collect intelligence about groups who were Aztec enemies.

The success of long-distance *pochteca* merchants was largely due to their internal corporate organization. Long-distance trade was most successful when it involved cooperation between knowledgeable and disciplined individuals who regularly worked together. *Pochteca* merchants were organized as hereditary *calpultin* (see Smith and Hicks this volume) with endogamous marriage, their own *calpolli* temple, and a graded social hierarchy of offices that provided governance over its members (van Zantwijk 1970). This form of organization had several benefits. First, it provided the social cohesiveness and cooperation between individuals needed to make long-distance trade both safe and profitable. Second, *pochteca* merchants were wealthy members of the commoner class and faced the constant envy of elite members of society. The corporate structure of the merchant *calpolli* together with the economic and political services that they provided the Aztec state helped to insulate *pochteca* from envious elite who might otherwise extort them as individuals.

Peddlers who were known among the Aztec as the *tlacôcoalnamacac* were the last group involved in Aztec commerce (Sahagún 1961:91). These were small-scale mobile merchants who probably operated in much the same way that peddlers have operated in many societies throughout time (Plattner 1975). They sold a range of utilitarian items and circulated between small marketplaces as well as sold directly to households in thinly populated areas that lacked marketplaces. Peddlers traveled as individuals or in father-and-son tandems and could operate on either a full- or part-time basis depending on the seasonality of demand for different goods. In mountainous regions, peddlers could have exchanged goods for regional specialty items like herbal medicines, roots, and *amole* soap for resale in markets or in other regions.

COMMERCE IN ACTION: THE COMMUNITY OF OTUMBA

Contact period sources indicate that 13 communities in the Basin of Mexico contained enclaves of long distant *pochteca* merchants at the time of the Spanish Conquest[2] (Figure 19.2). While most of these communities lie beneath modern communities, the town of Otumba located in the northeastern edge of the Basin of Mexico was well enough preserved to permit intensive archaeological investigations in the late 1980s (Charlton et al. 1991, 2008; Nichols 1994, 2013). These investigations have been invaluable because while early scholars viewed the merchants who lived there as long-distance commercial specialists (Acosta Saignes 1945), archaeological research reveals a more complete picture of the economic composition of Aztec commercial communities.

The prehispanic town of Otumba grew during the Late Postclassic (A.D. 1350–1519) to 220 ha with an estimated population of 3,600 to 5,500 people and became an important regional center of commerce with a marketplace, diverse craft industries, and merchants (Charlton et al. 1991; Nichols 1994, 2013:57–59; Nichols and Charlton 1996; Otis Charlton and Charlton 2011; Sanders and Evans 2001:997). The town was the political capital of the largest *altepetl* (city-state) in the Teotihuacan Valley and included a nucleated core of about 40 ha with a main temple, elite residences, and a large plaza that could have served as the marketplace (Figure 19.3). A large dispersed residential zone comprised the rest of town where most commoners lived, some in neighborhoods organized by craft specialties.

Archaeologists have documented at least seven craft industries at Otumba: (a) obsidian core-blade; (b) lapidary production; (c) ground basalt tools; (d) maguey fibers; (e) ceramic figurines, musical instruments, spindle whorls, stamps, and earspools; (f) red ware pottery, and (g) long-handled ritual censers (Charlton et al. 1991, 2008; Nichols 2013:59–64; Otis Charlton and Charlton 2011). All the goods were made in residential workshops, as was typical of prehispanic Mesoamerica.

Commoners dominated the craft industries, but two obsidian core-blade workshops are present in the nucleated core (Figure 19.3). Elites were also associated with ritual

FIGURE 19.2 Major Aztec cities and towns in the Basin of Mexico. Cities with *pochteca* merchants are shown in caps. Redrawn by Kristin Sullivan.

censer production as molds for making censers were concentrated on the southwestern side of the nucleated core, perhaps representing a neighborhood of censer-makers whose production was oriented for the town and hinterland villages (Otis Charlton and Charlton 2011:242). Most craft specialists lived in the dispersed residential zone, some within their own neighborhoods with workshops in and around their houses.

In the southeastern part of the town was a large neighborhood of potters who massproduced figurines in molds and made various other ceramic goods (Charlton et al.

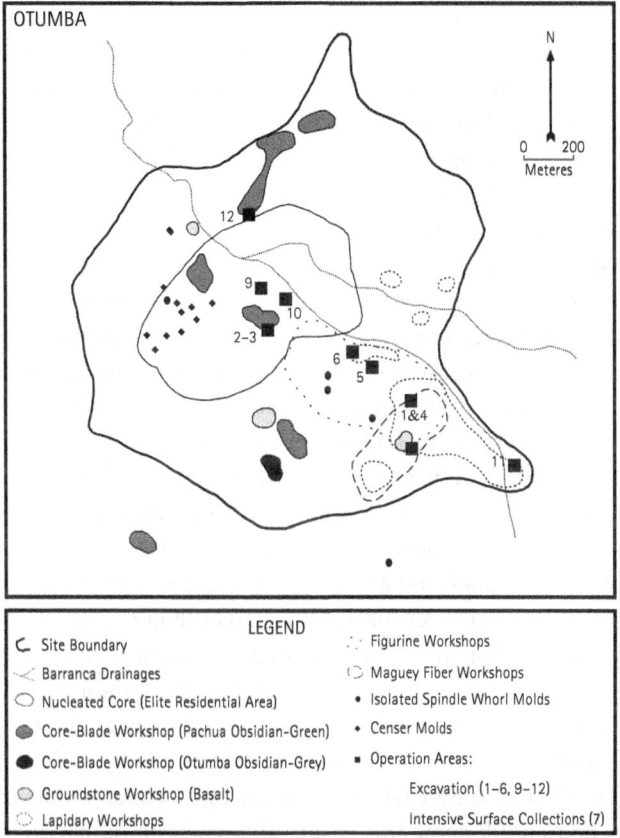

FIGURE 19.3 Map of Otumba and its workshops. Drawn by Kristin Sullivan.

2008; Otis Charlton and Charlton 2011). Nearby was a neighborhood of lapidaries, while another neighborhood was involved in processing maguey fiber (Nichols et al. 2000; Otis Charlton 1994; Otis Charlton et al. 1993). *Calpolli* organization, as suggested by these neighborhoods, would have facilitated mobilizing labor for certain manufacturing activities, such as processing of maguey, and/or training novice workers in crafts that required high skill as in the case of lapidaries. The neighborhoods of specialists at Otumba duplicated a pattern reported for the imperial cities that were also major centers of commerce. Texcoco reportedly had separate craft "barrios," for featherworkers, lapidaries, painters, and metalworkers, among others (Alva Ixtlilxóchitl 1965 [1891–1892], 1975–1977:1:444; 11:101). Sahagún (1950–1969, Book 9:18–20) describes barrios of featherworkers and merchants in Tenochtitlan. Rulers of both Texcoco and Tenochtitlan brought selected craft specialists to their imperial cities, and it is reported that Nezahuacoyotl, the famous ruler of Texcoco situated each specialty in their own "barrio." Thus some specialists, such as the lapidaries, might have been located at Otumba since it was a Texcoco dependency during Nezahuacoyotl's reign (Hicks 1982:241–242; Otis Charlton and Charlton 2011:235).

The intensity of craft specialization varied among the commodities made at Otumba—most workshops produced high-consumption and low- to moderate-value goods such as figurines and pottery and likely were intermittent or part-time producer-sellers. Cynthia Otis Charlton (1993, 1994) believes that the lapidaries who made high-value, low-consumption items, such as jewelry, worked continuously or full-time and held an intermediate social status within the town.

Commodities made by specialists also varied in terms of the scale of commerce. At one end of the spectrum was a local Red Ware pottery referred to as Otumba Polished Tan (Neff et al. 2000; Otis Charlton and Charlton 2011). Potters mostly likely sold Otumba Polished Tan bowls and jars in the town's regional marketplace to consumers from the town and nearby rural villagers. This inference is based on the very limited recovery of Otumba Polished Tan outside the Otumba *altepetl* (Nichols 2013:Table 3.5).

The potters who made Otumba Polished Tan pottery also produced a high volume of molded figurines (and molds) that had a wider market area (Otis Charlton and Charlton 2011:241). Both finished figurines and molds likely were traded by regional merchants, as well as by the potters as producer-sellers. Otumba has the only known figurine workshop in the Teotihuacan Valley, and figurines (and musical instruments) of the type (and chemical composition) made at Otumba are found both in towns and villages throughout the valley (Otis Charlton and Charlton 2011:245–249) and outside the region as far as southern Texcoco (Nichols 2013:71; Nichols et al. 2013). Spindle whorls, like figurines, were mass-produced in molds in both the pottery and maguey fiber workshops; these likely were sold by their makers, as well as by peddlers and regional merchants, as spindle whorls are mostly distributed in their home chemical composition group.

Nearly every household, rural and urban, elite and commoner in the Teotihuacan Valley spun thread and wove both maguey and cotton (Evans 1990; Nichols et al. 2009). The maguey-processing workshops at Otumba are the first such fiber workshops found at an Aztec site (Nichols et al. 2000). The presence of workshops at Otumba suggests production for export through the market, as well as for tribute, and would have involved regional merchants and perhaps also *pochteca* (Evans 1990). Parsons and Parsons' (1990:229) studies of maguey fiber processing suggest that a higher volume of production for export may have involved some supra-household integration of tasks.

Neither basalt nor obsidian core-blade workshops were clustered in neighborhoods; rather these workshops were dispersed, each likely representing single household work areas. The basalt specialists made common household tools, *manos, metates,* mortars, and maguey scrapers and also specialized tools for lapidaries. They supplied residents of the town and hinterland villages and perhaps sold polishers directly to lapidaries. The manufacturing activities of Otumba's ground stone makers, lapidaries, and core-blade producers were interconnected as lapidaries used basalt grinding tools to transform exhausted obsidian cores of green Pachuca obsidian into earspools and gray obsidian cores into lip plugs, labrets, and other items.

Otumba is the only city-state in the Basin of Mexico with its own obsidian source—the Otumba source supplied gray obsidian that was widely used for military and hunting weapons, maguey scrapers, jewelry, and sometimes prismatic blades (Charlton and

Spence 1983; Parry 2001, 2002). Otumba obsidian dominates one core-blade workshop, but the other workshops obtained most of their blade-making material in the form of macro-cores from the Pachuca source 50 km to the north. Blades were common household items and also were used as craft tools, as one concentration of used obsidian blades and refuse at Otumba indicates (Parry 2001, 2002). Core-blade workshops supplied residents of the town and rural villages—the nearby town of Teotihuacan also had core-blade workshops, so the Otumba workshops were not sole regional manufacturers (Spence 1985). The presence of two household-based core-blade workshops in the town's nucleated core is a bit puzzling as documentary sources indicate that blade-making was a low-status occupation and there is no evidence that blade-making was an elite administered activity (Parry 2001, 2002).

Blade-makers would have worked intermittently, and some from Otumba might have traveled to other marketplaces in the Teotihuacan Valley or sold finished goods directly to *pochteca*. Obsidian knives were one of several commodities produced at Otumba that *pochteca* took with them to trade; other items Otumba could have supplied to *pochteca* included obsidian razors and jewelry, and rock crystal ear plugs, cochineal, and textiles (Sahagún 1950–1982, Book 9:17–18).

Perhaps with the exception of highly skilled lapidaries, craft specialists at Otumba were producer-sellers who also farmed. Combining craft production and farming and multicrafting were common household strategies in the Aztec economy because of the high cost of overland transportation, One example comes from a maguey fiber workshop at Otumba that also made both cotton and maguey spindle whorl molds and spindle whorls, basalt scrapers to process maguey, as well as doing some lapidary working (Nichols et al. 2000:278). This workshop also consumed a relatively large number of blades. Farming intensified during the Late Postclassic period. Floodwater irrigation canals watered the alluvial plain and hillsides were terraced. Farming incorporated local ecological specialties and had a commercial dimension. In addition to maize, households cultivated nopal cacti and maguey, which grew well in the northeastern Basin of Mexico and were important both as foods and raw materials. The body of insects (*Dactylopius coccus*) that grow on nopals were ground to produce cochineal, a valued dye for textiles, and also used for cosmetics and as paint in codices and other materials (Donkin 1977). Cochineal appears on Aztec tribute lists from the Teotihuacan Valley (Evans 2001:95). Maguey supplied fibers, as well as serving as an important source of food.

Examples of multicrafting combined with farming are also known from other Aztec towns (DeLucia 2013). Although craft production was concentrated at Otumba, it was not confined to the urban center. Workshops in rural villages manufactured bifacial tools, including scrapers and projectile points, from obsidian mined and processed by villages at the Otumba source (Charlton and Spence 1983:45; Evans 1998; Parry 2001, 2002). Documentary sources also note the sale of turkeys at the weekly market, which reflects another dimension of commercial activity by local households (Blanton and Hodge 1996:244–245).

Independent households integrated by the marketplace formed the backbone of both farming and craft specialization at Otumba. Markets and merchants also supplied goods and raw materials to Otumba. For example, nearly every urban and rural Otumba household had some Texcoco Fabric Mark pottery used to transport salt. Salt sellers traveled from "market to market" with salt produced in village workshops along the shores of Lake Texcoco (Sahagún 1961:85). Households in rural and urban Otumba obtained Aztec decorated and plain ware pottery manufactured not only in the Teotihuacan Valley but also from further away in the Basin of Mexico, in the Texcoco, Tenochtitlan, and Cuauhtitlan areas. Merchants also would have brought goods from the western Basin of Mexico across Late Texcoco to the lakeshore town of Chiconautla at the mouth of the Teotihuacan Valley (Nichols et al. 2009).

Otumba lay on a long-standing trade corridor between the Basin of Mexico and the Gulf Coast. The presence of *pochteca* at Otumba set it apart from other city-state centers in the Teotihuacan Valley. In Tenochtitlan, *pochteca* had close relations with lapidaries, although merchants and lapidaries each resided in separate neighborhoods. At Otumba lapidaries, core-blade makers, fiber processors, and weavers who may also have prepared cochineal possibly sold their goods to *pochteca*, as well as in the marketplace. There are two areas in Otumba's dispersed residential zone with relatively higher concentrations of foreign pottery that are candidates for a *pochteca* neighborhood (Nichols 2013:Figure 3.18). Likewise, the adjacent site of TA-39 also contains a maguey fiber and lapidary workshop and might be an extension of the Otumba town (Charlton et al. 1991:99). It is the only site outside Otumba with such workshops, making it another candidate as the residence of *pochteca*. Recent salvage excavations at Azcapotzalco on the western side of the Basin of Mexico are providing the first archaeological details of an urban *pochteca* neighborhood (Instituto Nacional de Antropología e Historia 2012).

The archaeological investigations of Otumba and its rural villages demonstrate the important role commoners played in Aztec commerce as producer-sellers, merchants, and professional long-distance merchants and the complex ways they were integrated by the marketplace.

Discussion

The available evidence indicates a high level of commercial activity in Aztec society ranging from full-time *pochteca* merchants specializing in long-distance exchange to small-scale craftsmen and producer-sellers who sold goods intermittently throughout the year. No households produced all the goods they consumed annually. Their solution to this problem was to produce goods for exchange in the marketplace for the items that they needed. Importantly, Aztec commerce was primarily a commoner activity. The elite did not engage in commerce as they did among the Maya further to the southeast (Scholes and Roys 1968; Tokovinne and Beliaev 2013; Tozzer 1941). Aztec elite only engaged in commerce to the extent that they sold agricultural surpluses, goods, or other resources mobilized through the *tequitl* relationships from tributary dependents.

Similarly, the support for most Aztec institutions came from noncommercial *tequitl* or tribute relationship (Hirth 1996, 2012).

Table 19.2 summarizes the variation in the level of commercial involvement found in Aztec society. The level of participation ranged from full- to part-time activity, with part-time practitioners traveling shorter distances than those involved in full-time commerce. Commercial travel beyond distances of 150 km (five *jornadas* or a day's travel) seems to be the domain of full-time merchants. Individuals involved in commercial exchange at the regional level (50–150 km) include a wide range of both full- and part-time participants. Most of the individuals involved in part-time or intermittent commercial exchange normally operated at the local level, traveling distances of 50 km or less (Hirth 2013). This variation in commercial behavior is understandable given the demands of agriculture that remained the foundation of subsistence for most commoner households.

Surprisingly, full-time commercial involvement does not correlate directly with involvement in long-distance exchange. Full-time commercial participation is found among retailers who run the gamut from the stationary vendors in large daily markets to those traveling over 150 km to obtain cotton, salt, cacao, or other valuable resources. The degree of mobility and the distance traveled by economic practitioners appears to depend on the type of commodity procured and sold, the commercial strategy employed, and the degree of concentrated demand that sellers had access to.

Table 19.2 Levels of Commercial Involvement in Aztec Society

Practitioner	Commercial Involvement	Mobility	Distances Traveled	Social Status
Producer-Seller	Part-time	Low	Local	Macehualli, commoner
Craftsmen	Part-time	Low	Stationary and Local	Macehualli, commoner
Itinerant Craftsmen	Part-time	Low to Moderate	Local and Regional	Macehualli, commoner
Peddlers	Part-time and Full-time	Moderate to High	Local and Regional	Macehualli, commoner
Retailers	Full-time	Low to High	Stationary, Local, Regional, and Interregional	Macehualli, commoner
Pochteca Merchants	Full-time	High	Interregional Long Distance	Macehualli, commoner

Note: Stationary refers to no movement. Other distances are Local >50 km, Local Regional = 50–150 km, Interregional >150 km.

Marketplaces centralized demand and made the transportation of specialized goods for sale more efficient for those supplying them. It was the absence of concentrated demand that made peddling both possible and necessary in areas poorly serviced by marketplaces and led to the diversified sets of products that peddlers offered for sale.

The scale and structure of Aztec commerce was directly linked to the presence and/or absence of prehispanic marketplaces. Markets encouraged a high level of craft and provisioning specialization by bringing together demand in a centralized locale on a regular schedule. The majority of specialists who produced goods for sale operated from multigenerational households using the labor available within them. The organization of production for commercial purposes was rare to nonexistent above the level of individual households; where production existed outside the household it was organized by the state to meets its own special consumption needs. Marketplaces were supervised and regulated to ensure fair dealing and to collect a tax from the sellers to support its operation (Cortes 1962:93). The pulse and the lifeblood of the marketplace, however, were the multitudes of independent buyers and sellers who frequented it on a regular basis to provision their households with the goods they needed for their support. The marketplace was the center piece of the Aztec precapitalist and preindustrial economy, and, as the Spanish conquistadors repeatedly observed, the largest Aztec marketplaces surpassed any of the large emporia found in Europe during the sixteenth century.

Notes

1. The entymology for *tlaixtlapana* meaning profit is: *tla*, the indefinite object prefix for something, *ix* from *ixtli* referring to a person's face, and *tlapan(a)*, the verb meaning to split or divide.
2. The 13 communities that contained *pochteca* merchants were Tenochititlan, Tlaltelolco, Tlacopan, Texcoco, Huexotla, Coatlichan, Chalco, Xochimilco, Huitzilopochco-Churubusco, Mixcoac, Azcapotzalco, Cuauhtitlan, and Otumba (Sahagún 1959:48).

References Cited

Acosta Saignes, Miguel
1945 Los pochteca: ubicación de los mercaderes en la estructura social Tenochca. *Acta Antropológica* 1(1).
Alva Ixtlilxóchitl, Fernando de
1965 [1891–1892] *Obras históricas*. 2 vols. Editora Nacional, Mexico City.
Berdan, Frances
1980 Aztec Merchants and Markets: Local-Level Economic Activity in a Non-Industrial Empire. *Mexicon* 2:37–41.
1989 Trade and Markets in Precapitalist States. In *Economic Anthropology*, edited by Stuart Plattner, pp. 78–107. Stanford University Press, Stanford, CA.
Blanton, Richard, and Gary Feinman
1984 The Mesoamerican World System. *American Antiquity* 86:673–682.

Blanton, Richard E., and Mary G. Hodge
1996 Appendix 2: Data on Market Activities and Production Specializations of *Tlahtoani* Centers. In *Aztec Imperial Strategies*, Frances F. Berdan, Richard E. Blanton, Elizabeth Hill Boone, Mary G. Hodge, Michael E. Smith, and Emily Umberger, pp. 243–246. Dumbarton Oaks Research Library and Collection, Washington, DC.

Bromley, Ray, Richard Symansky, and Charles Good
1975 The Rationale of Periodic Markets. *Annals of the Association of American Geographers* 65:530–537.

Carrasco, Pedro
1978 La economía del México prehispánico. In *Economía política e ideología en el México prehispánico*, edited by Pedro Carrasco and Johanna Broda, pp. 13–74. Editorial Nueva Imagen, Mexico City.

Charlton, Thomas H., Deborah L. Nichols, and Cynthia Otis Charlton
1991 Craft Specialization within the Aztec City-State of Otumba, Mexico: The Archaeological Evidence. *World Archaeology* 23:98–114.
2008 Aztec Otumba, AD 1200–1600: Patterns of the Production, Distribution, and Consumption of Ceramic Products. In *Pottery Economics in Mesoamerica*, edited by Christopher A. Pool and George J. Bey III, pp. 237–266. University of Arizona Press, Tucson.

Charlton, Thomas H., and Michael W. Spence
1983 Obsidian Exploitation and Civilization in the Basin of Mexico. In *Mining and Mining Techniques in Ancient Mesoamerica*, edited by Phil C. Weigand and Gretchen Gwynne, pp. 7–86. Anthropology 4. Department of Anthropology State University of New York, Stony Brook.

Christensen, Mark, and Kenneth G. Hirth
2013 Appendix: A Nahuatl Economic Vocabulary. In *Merchants, Trade and Exchange in the Pre-Columbian World*, edited by Kenneth Hirth and Joanne Pillsbury, pp. 106–107. Dumbarton Oaks Library and Research Collection, Washington, DC.

Cortés, Hernando
1962 5 Letters of Cortés to the Emperor. W. W. Norton, New York.

D'Altroy, Terrence, and Timothy Earle
1985 Staple Finance, Wealth Finance, and Storage in the Inca Political Economy. *Current Anthropology* 26:187–206.

DeLucia, Kirstin
2013 Domestic Economies and Regional Transition: Household Multicrafting and Lake Exploitation in Pre-Aztec Central Mexico. *Journal of Anthropological Archaeology* 32:353–367.

Donkin, R. A,
1977 Spanish Red: An Ethnogeographical Study of Cochineal and the Opuntia Cactus. *Transactions of the American Philosophical Society New Series* 67(5):1–84.

Duran, Diego
1994 *The History of the Indies of New Spain*. Translated by D. Hayden. University of Oklahoma Press, Norman.

Evans, Susan Toby
1990 The Productivity of Maguey Terrace Agriculture in Central Mexico during the Aztec Period. *Latin American Antiquity* 1:117–132.
1998 *Excavations at Cihuatecpan: An Aztec Village in the Teotihuacan Valley*. Vanderbilt University Publications in Anthropology 36. Vanderbilt University, Nashville, TN.
2001 Aztec-Period Political Organization in the Teotihuacan Valley: Otumba as a City-State. *Ancient Mesoamerica* 12:80–100.

Gasco, Janine, and Frances Berdan
2003 International Trade Centers, in *The Postclassic Mesoamerican World*, edited by M. Smith and F. Berdan, pp. 109–116. Dumbarton Oaks Library and Research Collection, Washington, DC.

Hassig, Ross
1982 Periodic Markets in Pre-Columbian Mexico. *American Antiquity* 47:346–355.

Hicks, Frederic
1982 Tetzcoco in the Early 16th Century: The State, the City, and the Capolli. *American Ethnologist* 9:230–249.

Hirth, Kenneth
1996 Political Economy and Archaeology: Perspectives on Exchange and Production. *Journal of Archaeological Research* 4:203–239.

2009a Craft Production, Household Diversification, and Domestic Economy in Prehispanic Mesoamerica, In *Housework: Craft Production and Domestic Economy in Ancient Mesoamerica*, edited by K. Hirth, pp. 13–32. Archaeological Publications of the American Anthropological Society No. 19. Wiley, Hoboken, NJ.

2009b Craft Production in the Mesoamerican Marketplace. *Ancient Mesoamerica* 20:89–102.

2009c *Housework: Craft Production and Domestic Economy in Ancient Mesoamerica*. Archaeological Publications of the American Anthropological Society No. 19. Wiley, Hoboken, NJ.

2010 Finding the Mark in the Marketplace: The Organization, Development and Archaeological Identification of Market Systems. In *Archaeological Approaches to Market Exchange in Pre-Capitalistic Societies*, edited by Christopher Garraty and Barbara Stark, pp. 227–247. University Press of Colorado, Boulder.

2012 Markets, Merchants, and Systems of Exchange. In *Oxford Handbook on Mesoamerican Archaeology*, edited by Deborah L. Nichols and Christopher A. Pool, pp. 639–652. Oxford University Press, New York.

2013 The Merchant's World: Commercial Diversity and the Economics of Interregional Exchange in Highland Mesoamerica. In *Merchants, Trade and Exchange in the Pre-Columbian World*, edited by Kenneth Hirth and Joanne Pillsbury, pp. 85–112. Dumbarton Oaks Library and Research Collection, Washington, DC.

Instituto Nacional de Antropología e Historia
2012 Hallen en Azcapotzalco vestigos de barrio Tepaneca. Electronic document http://www.inah.gob.mx/index.php/boletines/17-arqueologia/6006-hallan-en-azcapotzalco-vestigios-de-barrio-tecpaneca, accessed August 13, 2013.

Isaac, Barry
2013 Discussion. In *Merchants, Markets and Exchange in the Pre-Columbian World*, edited by Kenneth Hirth and J. Pillsbury, pp. 85–112. Dumbarton Oaks Research Library and Collection, Washington, DC.

Merriam-Webster Inc.
1968 *Webster's New World Dictionary of the American Language*. The Southwestern Company, Nashville, TN.

1990 *Webster's Ninth New Collegiate Dictionary*. Merriam-Webster, Springfield, MA.

Neff, Hector, Michael D. Glascock, Thomas H. Charlton, Cynthia Otis Charlton, and Deborah L. Nichols
2000 Provenience Investigations of Ceramics and Obsidian from Otumba. *Ancient Mesoamerica* 11:207–322.

Nichols, Deborah L.
1994 The Organization of Provincial Craft Production and the Aztec City-State Otumba. In *Economies and Polities in the Aztec Realm*, edited by Mary G. Hodge and Michael E. Smith, pp. 175–194. Studies on Culture and Society 6. Institute for Mesoamerican Studies, State University of New York, Albany, and University of Texas Press, Austin.
2013 Merchants and Merchandise: The Archaeology of Aztec Commerce at Otumba, Mexico. In *Merchants, Trade and Exchange in the Pre-Columbian World*, edited by Kenneth Hirth and Joanne Pillsbury, pp. 49–83. Dumbarton Oaks Library and Research Collection, Washington, DC.

Nichols, Deborah L., and Thomas H. Charlton
1996 The Postclassic Occupation at Otumba: A Chronological Assessment. *Ancient Mesoamerica* 7:231–244.

Nichols, Deborah L., Christina Elson, Leslie G. Cecil, Nina Neivens de Estrada, Michael D. Glascock, and Paula Mikkelsen
2009 Chiconautla, Mexico: A Crossroads of Aztec Trade and Politics. *Latin American Antiquity* 20:443–472.

Nichols, Deborah L., Mary Jane McLaughlin, and Maura Benton
2000 Production Intensification and Regional Specialization: Maguey Fibers and Textiles in the Aztec City-State of Otumba. *Ancient Mesoamerica* 11:267–292.

Nichols, Deborah L., Hector Neff, and George L. Cowgill
2013 Cerro Portezuelo: States and Hinterlands in the Prehispanic Basin of Mexico. *Ancient Mesoamerica* 24:47–71.

Otis Charlton, Cynthis
1993 Obsidian as Jewelry: Lapidary Production in Aztec Otumba: *Ancient Mesoamerica* 4:231–243.
1994 Plebeians and Patricians: Contrasting Patterns of Production and Distribution in the Aztec Figurine and Lapidary Industries. In *Economics and Politics in the Aztec Realm*, edited by Mary G. Hodge and Michael E. Smith, pp. 195–220. Institute for Mesoamerican Studies, State University of New York, Albany, and University of Texas Press, Austin.

Otis Charlton, Cynthia L., and Thomas H. Charlton
2011 Sociocultural Evolution and Craft Specialization: The Case of the Household-Based Fired Clay Industries of Otompan. In *Producción artesanal y especializada en Mesoamerica: Áreas de actividad y procesos productivos*, edited by Linda R. Manzanilla and Kenneth G. Hirth, pp. 227–260. Instituto Nacional de Antropología e Historia and Universidad Nacional de Autónoma de México, Instituto de Investigaciones Antropológicas, Mexico City.

Otis Charlton, Cynthia, Thomas H. Charlton, and Deborah L. Nichols
1993 Aztec Household-Based Craft Production: Archaeological Evidence from the City-State of Otumba, Mexico. In *Prehispanic Domestic Units in Western Mesoamerica: Studies in Household, Compound, and Residence*, edited by Robert S. Santley and Kenneth. G. Hirth, pp. 147–172. CRC Press, Boca Raton, FL.

Parry, William J.
2001 Production and Exchange of Obsidian Tools in Late Aztec City-States. *Ancient Mesoamerica* 12:101–111.
2002 Aztec Blade Production Strategies in the Eastern Basin of Mexico. In *Pathways to Prismatic Blades: A Study in Mesoamerican Obsidian Core-Blade Technology*, edited by Kenneth G. Hirth and Bradford Andrews, pp. 39–48. Cotsen Institute of Archaeology, University of California, Los Angeles.

Parsons, Jeffrey R., and Mary H. Parsons
1990 *Otomí Maguey Utilization: An Ethnoarchaeological Perspective*. Museum of Anthropology Papers 82. University of Michigan, Ann Arbor.

Plattner, Stuart
1975 The Economics of Peddling. In *Formal Methods in Economic Anthropology*, edited by Stuart Plattner pp. 55–76. American Anthropological Association, Washington, DC.
1989a Economic Behavior in Markets. In *Economic Anthropology*, edited by Stuart Plattner, pp. 209–221. Stanford University Press, Stanford, CA.
1989b Markets and Marketplaces. In *Economic Anthropology*, edited by Stuart Plattner, pp. 171–208. Stanford University Press, Stanford, CA.

Sahagún, Fray Bernardino de
1959 *Florentine Codex: General History of the Things of New Spain. Book 9, The Merchants*. Translated by A. Anderson and C. Dibble. University of Utah Press, Salt Lake City.
1961 *Florentine Codex: General History of the Things of New Spain. Book 10, The People*. Translated by A. Anderson and C. Dibble. University of Utah Press, Salt Lake City.

Sanders, William T., and Susan Toby Evans
2001 The Teotihuacan Valley and the Temascalapa Region during the Aztec Period. In *The Aztec Period Occupation of the Valley Part 3, Synthesis and General Bibliography*, edited by William T. Sanders and Susan Toby Evans, pp. 932–1078. Department of Anthropology, Pennsylvania State University, University Park.

Scholes, Frances, and Ralph Roys
1968 *The Maya Chontal Indians of Acalan-Tixchel*. University of Oklahoma Press, Norman.

Smith, Michael
2004 The Archaeology of Ancient State Economies. *Annual Review of Anthropology* 33:73–102.

Spence, Michael W.
1985 Specialized Production in Rural Aztec Society: Obsidian Workshops of the Teotihuacan Valley. In *Contributions to the Archaeology and Ethnohistory of Greater Mesoamerica*, edited by William J. Folan, pp. 76–125. Southern Illinois University Press, Carbondale.

Symanski, Richard, and M. J. Webber
1974 Complex Periodic Market Cycles. *Annals of the Association of American Geographers* 64:203–213.

Tokovinne, Alexandre, and Dmitri Beliaev
2013 People of the Road: Traders and Travelers in Ancient Maya Words and Images. In *Merchants, Trade and Exchange in the Pre-Columbian World*, edited by Kenneth Hirth and Joanne Pillsbury, pp. 169–200. Dumbarton Oaks Library and Research Collection, Washington, DC.

Tozzer, Alfred
1941 *Landa's Relación de las Cosas de Yucatan: A Translation*. Peabody Museum of American Archaeology and Ethnology 18. Harvard University, Cambridge, MA.

van Zantwijk, Rudolf
1970 Las organizaciones social-económica y religiosa de los mercaderes gremiales Aztecas. *Boletin de Estúdios Latino-Americanos* 10:1–20.

Voorhies, Barbara
1989 Whither the King's Traders? Reevaluating Fifteenth-Century Xoconochco as a Port of Trade. In *Ancient Trade and Tribute: Economies of the Soconusco Region of Mesoamerica*, edited by Barbara Voorhies, pp. 21–47. University of Utah Press, Salt Lake City.

PART IV-A
AZTEC MANUFACTURING

CHAPTER 20

AZTEC USE OF LAKE RESOURCES IN THE BASIN OF MEXICO

JOHN K. MILLHAUSER

The Basin of Mexico was the political, demographic, and economic core of the Aztec Empire. Its landscape of lakes and marshes shaped settlement patterns, the flow of resources, and the subsistence base (Hirth and Nichols this volume; McClung de Tapia and Martínez this volume; Rojas this volume). Importantly, the lakes supported a highly productive agricultural system of canals and raised beds, called *chinampas*, which was integral to the growth and sustenance of Aztec cities and to the maintenance of the region's political economy (Armillas 1971; Morehart 2012, this volume; Palerm 1973; Sanders et al. 1979). But these lakes and marshes also provided a variety of flora, fauna, and minerals that were crucial sources of food and raw materials (Parsons 1996, 2005; Rojas Rabiela 1998; Sanders et al. 1979:291–292). Jeffrey Parsons (1994, 1996, 2001, 2005, 2006, 2008, 2010) has vigorously argued that these nonagricultural resources were critical to the growing, and increasingly urban, population of the Postclassic Basin of Mexico.

This chapter focuses on the lakes' nonagricultural resources—waterfowl, fish, other edible plants and animals, reeds, and salt—and on the "aquatic specialists" (Parsons 2005:58) whose livelihoods depended on them. Based on the dramatic increase in the number, sizes, and locations of settlements at the margins of the lakes, Parsons (2005:51) has argued that aquatic resources were "so important as to attract large numbers of people engaged full-time in their extraction, processing, and distribution during the Middle and Late Postclassic, if not earlier." While Parsons has focused on nonagricultural flora, fauna, and minerals as subsistence goods, I expand his model to include their roles in culture and commerce. For example, edible plants, animals, and minerals were as important for a rich and varied precolumbian cuisine as they were for nutrition—Europeans did not invent the taste bud. Similarly, durable goods made from aquatic resources—such as reed mats, baskets, and seats—were ubiquitous in Aztec homes, temples, palaces, and markets. Incorporating these commercial and cultural values enhances our understanding of the Aztec economy and the particular roles of these resources.

The Ecological Context

The Basin of Mexico is an internal-drainage basin that lacks a natural outlet for water. Today, after nearly 400 years of efforts to drain the lakes, its floor is almost completely dry—but in precolumbian times it was filled by shallow, interconnected lakes and marshes (Figure 20.1). In the north, Lakes Xaltocan and Zumpango were brackish. During the summer rainy season, they were replenished by fresh water and drained into Lake Texcoco, but during the winter dry season they shrank and became more saline. To the south, permanent springs, perennial streams, and abundant precipitation fed the fresh waters of Lakes Chalco and Xochimilco, which also drained into Lake Texcoco. At the center, Lake Texcoco was the largest, lowest, and most saline of the lakes. The resources of this lacustrine bottomland complemented those of the drier piedmont

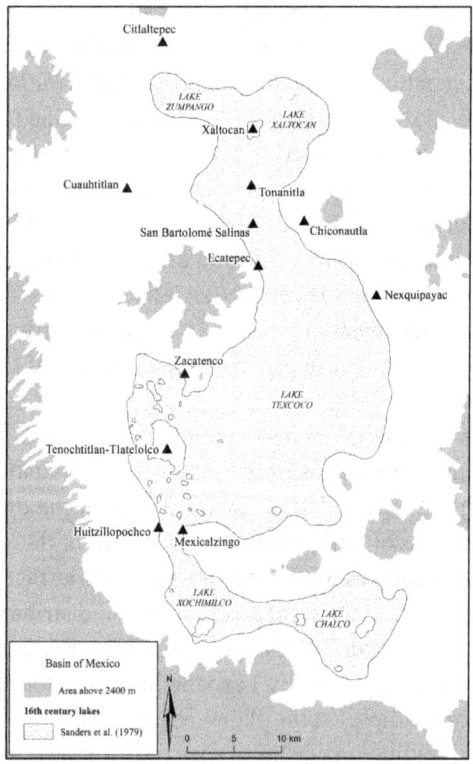

FIGURE 20.1 Map of the Basin of Mexico showing locations described in the text. Map by author.

slopes, where maguey and cacti thrived, as well as upland forests, where game and firewood were plentiful (Figure 20.1). This variable environment supported intraregional specialization and exchange (Blanton 1976; Sanders and Price 1968:190–191).

Beginning as early as the thirteenth and culminating in the fifteenth century, the massive expansion and intensification of chinampas transformed Lakes Chalco and Xochimilco (Armillas 1971; Brumfiel 1991; Parsons 1991). By the Late Postclassic (A.D. 1430–1521), much of the arable land in the basin had been converted to agricultural production (Palerm and Wolf 1957; Sanders et al. 1979:176–177), although the chinampas of the northern saline lakes declined (Morehart and Frederick 2014). Over this same time, the saline lakes came to support larger and more numerous settlements. Access to water-borne transportation and the markets of Tenochtitlan-Tlatelolco attracted new populations (Hassig 1985), but neither urbanism nor agriculture explains all of the lakeshore settlements (Parsons 2008:55).

Increasing demand for nonagricultural lake products was an important factor that may have motivated some people to work, and to settle, among the lakes. Greater demand for these products was a general consequence of population growth and urbanization. Yet, population growth was a double-edged sword as it also created demand for more agricultural products. Many tribute-paying households and communities responded to growing demands for labor and staple foods by emphasizing agricultural production over other activities (Brumfiel 1980, 1983, 1986, 1987, 2005; Hicks 1984, 1987). If many households and communities focused more energy on farming, this would have created the need, or the opportunity, for others to emphasize collecting, processing, or producing nonagricultural resources. But aquatic resources were not evenly distributed, and growing cities and large-scale irrigation and drainage projects progressively restricted access to these resources (Sanders et al. 1979:293). As more land was farmed, what remained may have been agriculturally marginal—and thus the choice to diversify or intensify the exploitation of aquatic resources may have been more one of necessity rather than opportunity.

Evidence of Aquatic Specialization

Documentary sources help us to reconstruct the circulation of lake products and the scale and diversity of demand. Of particular value are sixteenth-century written and pictorial sources that describe the natural environment and pre-Conquest way of life in the Basin of Mexico. Ethnographic and ethnoarchaeological studies of contemporary hunters, fishers, basket-weavers, mat-makers, and saltmakers in the basin and the central highlands provide key insights into the scheduling and division of labor and resource sharing. Archaeological evidence of consumption and circulation of lake products is limited by poor preservation. Yet archaeological sources are essential for investigating regional variation, household production, and changes over time. Such sources include regional settlement surveys, investigations of resource extraction zones and chinampas, systematic surface collections of settlements, and excavations of households and work areas. These complementary sources reveal industries practiced on a small scale and a flexible schedule that were also widespread sources of income, identity, and political agency for households and communities alike.

Demand, Circulation, and Consumption

The bountiful lakes, marshes, and swamps of the valley floor provided wild foods that were fundamental to the Aztec diet (Rojas Rabiela 1998; Sahagún 1950–1982). Lake dwellers hunted ducks, geese, and other migratory and resident waterfowl and collected their eggs. They also fished and collected fish eggs. They hunted for eels, turtles, frogs, tadpoles, and salamanders and collected edible water plants, crustaceans, and mollusks, as well as aquatic insects and their eggs and larvae. Importantly, foods such as insect eggs and algae that, by contemporary standards, might be seen as buffer foods to be eaten during times of scarcity and hardship were likely to have been broadly consumed staples (Ortiz de Montellano 1978; Parsons 1996, 2005, 2006, 2008; Santley and Rose 1979).

Subsistence concerns were central, but not singular, in shaping the demand for wild plants and animals. The demand for diverse ingredients was as much about flavors and textures as it was about calories (Coe 1994; Pilcher 1998). Edible resources served other needs as well. Ducks and geese provided plumes, down, and other feathers used in a diverse array of textile and featherwork (Anawalt 1981:12; Díaz del Castillo 1956:101; Durán 1994:203–204; McCafferty and McCafferty this volume). Many plants that flourished among the shallow lakes were also integral to Aztec medicinal and ritual practices (Cruz 1940; Espinosa Pineda 1996; Ortiz de Montellano 1990; Rojas Rabiela 1985).

The Aztec recognized a variety of commercially important species of reeds, sedges, and bulrushes that are today categorized under the name *tule* (Orozco y Berra 1864:162–163). Woven goods made of tules included baskets, mats, seats, footwear, and fire fans, which were ubiquitous items in Aztec households (Figure 20.2) (Durán 1971:427; Sanders et al. 1979:293; Weitlaner Johnson 1971). Baskets served as containers for transporting bulk goods, household storage, steaming or warming food, and displaying goods in the market. Woven mats (*petates*) were used as floor coverings in homes, temples, palaces, public buildings, outdoor work areas, and markets. They were also used as sleeping mats, temporary shelters for soldiers (Durán 1994:153), game boards (*patolli*) (Durán 1971:246), and packaging for bulk goods. Woven furniture consisted of low stools (*icpalli*) and seats with high backs (*tzonicpalli*), the latter being reserved for high-status individuals. Other noteworthy uses of tules included construction materials (Sahagún 1950–1982:11:191–195, 273), hunting aids (Apenes 1943a; Parsons 2006; Sugiura 1998; Williams 2009), the shafts of arrows and darts (Durán 1994:167), lapidary tools (Sahagún 1950–1982:10:87; Vaillant 1950:145), tobacco pipes (Sahagún 1950–1982:10:88), blood-letters (Durán 1971:246, 266, 451), loose floor coverings used in domestic and public rituals (Berdan and Anawalt 1992:2:147; Durán 1971:103, 453), tempering material

FIGURE 20.2 Assorted uses of products made from reeds: (top) merchants with a stool, carrying pack, and tall basket; (middle) baskets arrayed in preparation for a feast; (bottom) a noble woman on high-backed seat and *petate* (mat). *Florentine Codex*, Book 9:Figures 26 and 27, Book 10:Figure 76, © University of Utah Press.

in pottery (Sahagún 1950–1982:10:83, 11:256–257), and armatures for headdresses and ephemeral statuary (Durán 1971:428).

Lakes Texcoco, Xaltocan, and Zumpango also supplied an assortment of salts found in their water, soils, and plants. In the sixteenth century, Nahuatl speakers recognized two kinds of salt: *tequesquitl*, a mixture of salt, soda, and saltpeter, and *iztatl*, which was the refined, white salt we know as table salt (Millhauser 2012:159–172; Siméon 1977). They were used as sources of dietary sodium, condiments, and food preservatives; medicines; dyeing, bleaching, and tanning agents; media of exchange; and religious offerings (Ewald 1985; Ewald et al. 1994; Parsons 2001; Sahagún 1950–1982:9:48, 10:147–150, 153, 155, 162, 178, 183). Today, the most common of these salts is called *tequesquite*, which refers to a variety of saline crystals, crusts, and powders that form at the edges of swamps and lagoons during the dry season (Flores 1918; Parsons 2006). Iztatl could be produced from the tequesquite-rich soils of the Basin of Mexico through a process of fractional evaporation (Apenes 1944; Parsons 2001), but it was also available through various marine and inland sources (Blanton et al. 2005; Kepecs 2003; Mendizábal 1929; Williams 2010).

Markets were the primary conduits through which these goods flowed (Blanton 1976, 1996). Rarely are aquatic resources mentioned as part of either imperial tribute or the trade in luxury goods that streamed into the capital cities (Berdan 1987, 1996; Smith 1990, 2003). Cuauhtitlan was the only province that paid a part of its tribute in reed mats and seats, in addition to local birds, fish, flowers, and vegetables (Ixtlilxóchitl 1965:1:319; Berdan and Anawalt 1992:2:48, 70). However, many aquatic resources circulated through local and regional tribute and patronage systems (Hicks 1974, 1984, 1991), although documentary sources provide little information to estimate the volume of these flows.

Nevertheless, given the nature of the demand for these lacustrine goods, the scale of consumption was hardly insignificant. Beyond their immediate use to satisfy subsistence needs, many of the lakes' resources were part of the supply chains that supported other crafts, from valuable and elaborate seats and feathered costumes to utilitarian goods like prepared foods and salted fish. Some of these resources also left the region as packaging as well as consumable goods in the context of long-distance trade. For example, merchants who traveled to the distant province of Tehuantepec carried among their trade goods insect eggs and barbecued ducks from the lakes (Durán 1994:349). Individually, the resources of the lakes were not of great value, but the volume and tempo of demand may have been great enough to support aquatic specialists.

Procurement, Processing, and Production

Cycles of agricultural production would have influenced many household decisions about scheduling and the division of labor in the Basin of Mexico, especially during the summer months. Exploiting some resources, like hunting for migratory waterfowl and collecting salt, was best accomplished during the winter months and thus fit well with farmers' schedules. However, imperial demands for labor in military campaigns and public works also occurred during the winter months, so as not to interfere with agricultural production (Hassig 1988). Archaeological evidence from Xaltocan, for example, shows that hunting, fishing, and saltmaking decreased during the Late Postclassic, presumably because households diverted more of their summer labor to farming and more of their winter labor to household maintenance (Brumfiel 2005:365; see also Overholtzer 2012). It is difficult, however, to make a blanket statement about seasonal limitations and when people could make the best use of the lakes. For example, access to naturally forming tequesquite crusts would have been limited to the dry season, but saltmaking could have been practiced year-round with the use of covered storage facilities and fire to evaporate brine and dry cakes of salt (Parsons 2006).

The great variety of ways to exploit the lakes' resources could have led to heterogeneity and seasonal variation rather than dedication to a particular occupation (Hirth 2009). But documentary sources suggest that some people specialized in the exploitation of the lakes' resources. For example, Sahagún (1950–1982:10:61, 69, 80, 84–86, 93) identified a variety of specialist vendors in the marketplace: three who sold foodstuffs acquired from the lakes, one of local bird feathers, five of goods made from reeds, and two of salt. In each case, at least some of these merchants were described as hunters or fishers, matmakers and basket-weavers, or saltmakers who procured or produced what they sold (see also Berdan 1986:289, 296). Producing a surplus for sale in the market did not necessarily require a large scale of production, but it would have required time, knowledge, and access to spatially limited resources.

Hunting, fishing, or collecting wild resources rarely required more than several people, a canoe, nets and lines, minimal tools, and access to the appropriate territory (Blanco Padilla 1994; Parsons 2006; Serra et al. 1982). Sixteenth-century images of hunting and fishing depict a variety of such activities involving only one or two people at a time (Figure 20.3) (Arroyo 2008; Berdan and Anawalt 1992:3:127; Graulich and Barlow 1995; Linné 1937; Rojas Rabiela 1998). Similarly, basket-weaving and mat-making were likely organized at the scale of the household and required few tools besides knives, stone anvils and hammers to flatten reeds, and awls to produce a tight weave (Orozco y Berra 1864:163; Parsons 2006:Table 7.15; Sugiura 1998; Sugiura and Serra 1983; Ugent 2000; Williams 2009). Thus hunters, fishers, and reed-processors were limited less by

FIGURE 20.3 Fishing and hunting in the lakes: (top) a fisherman using a net and canoe, (bottom) a hunter collecting birds from a net. *Florentine Codex*, Book 10:Figure 133, Book 11:Figure 187, © University of Utah Press.

the need for specialized tools or large labor pools and more by access to hunting, fishing, and collecting grounds and the time to collect and process what they culled.

Material markers of these kinds of tasks have been found in extraction zones and domestic contexts in the Basin of Mexico dating to the Preclassic and Early Postclassic (De Lucia 2013; McClung de Tapia et al. 1986; Morehart 2010; Niederberger 1976; Parsons and Morett 2004; Serra et al. 1982; Serra Puche 1986, 1988) but are less apparent in Late Postclassic contexts. The absence of data in this case may reflect the limits of our samples—few of the Late Postclassic settlements along the lakeshore have been systematically investigated. Those that have, however, reveal that saltmaking, among other tasks, was an important and intensively practiced activity.

The labor and materials involved in making salt varied greatly depending on the desired end product. Collecting seasonally available tequesquite crusts would have been a low-intensity activity. However, observations of saltmaking in the Basin of Mexico from the sixteenth to the twentieth centuries suggest that many saltmakers collected and mixed saline soils, leached salty brine from the soil, and boiled the brine to produce different kinds and qualities of salt (Apenes 1944; Castellón Huerta 2008; Cortés 1971:83; De Leon 2009; Gibson 1964:338; Parsons 1994, 1996, 2001; Sahagún 1950–1982:10:84, 11:257; Williams 1999).

Material evidence of Postclassic leaching and boiling includes dense concentrations of a distinctive pottery, named Texcoco Fabric Marked (Figure 20.4), for the impressions of textiles on the pots' exterior surfaces, as well as large mounds of saline soil, called *tlateles*, left over from the leaching process (Apenes 1943b, 1944; Charlton 1969; Millhauser 2012; Noguera 1975; Parsons 1994, 2001). Tlateles range in size from a few meters across to over 100 meters long and several meters high. Texcoco Fabric Marked pottery was likely used to boil brine or to mold and package cakes of salt (Baños Ramos 1980; Baños Ramos and Sanchez 1998; Parsons 2001; Sánchez Vázquez 1984, 1987; Talavera Barnard 1979; Tolstoy 1958). Some of this pottery was also used to transport salt, perhaps during the rainy season, because small quantities of it are found at sites far from the main salt-producing zones. Based on where tlateles and high concentrations of Texcoco Fabric Marked pottery are found and the ages of these sites, intensive

FIGURE 20.4 Fragments of Texcoco Fabric Marked pottery from San Bartolomé Salinas, Estado de Mexico. Photograph by author.

saltmaking spread from the outskirts of urban centers to dispersed lakeshore settlements and work sites during the Middle and Late Postclassic (Figure 20.5) (Millhauser 2012:299, 332–337; Sanders et al. 1979:171–175; Tolstoy 1958:52–53). Thus the growing demand for salt may have made living and working in agriculturally marginal lands a viable option.

Leaching and boiling were intensive and costly activities that required fuel, access to the right soils, abundant water, and specialized pottery. Excavations at saltmaking sites

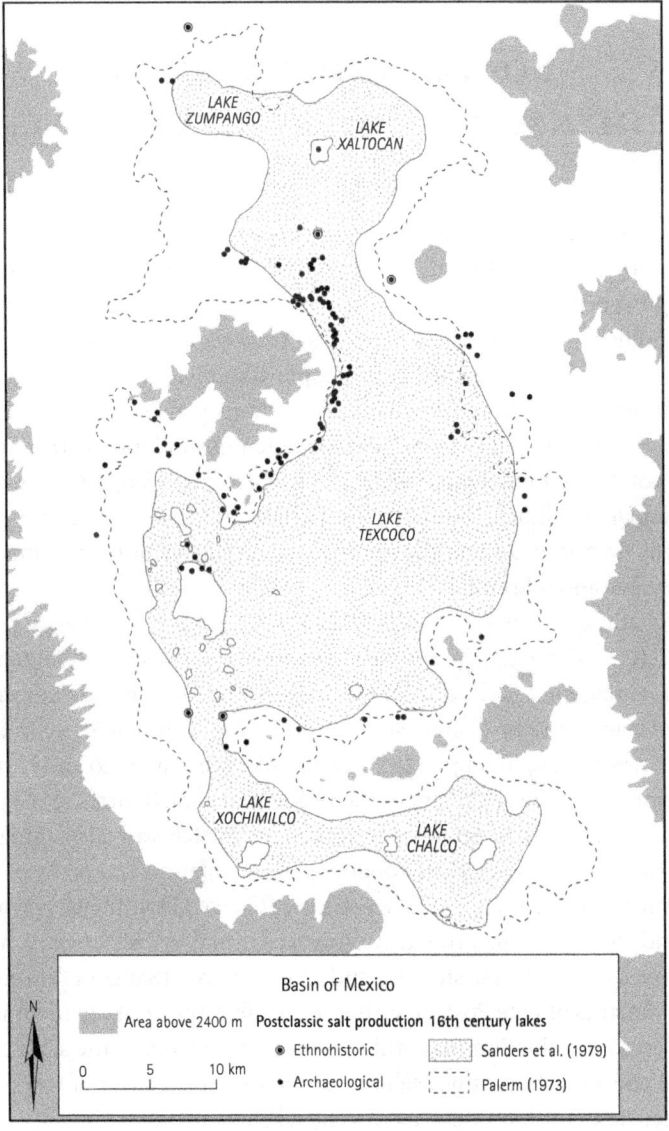

FIGURE 20.5 Map of Middle and Late Postclassic salt-making sites in the Basin of Mexico during the Postclassic. Map by author.

like Zacatenco (Sánchez-Vazquez 1984, 1987) and San Bartolomé Salinas (Millhauser 2012) have revealed ovens, tanks for evaporating or decanting brine, and canals that demonstrate significant investments of capital by saltmakers. Furthermore, chemical and mineralogical studies of Texcoco Fabric Marked pottery suggest that it was produced locally, perhaps by saltmakers themselves, which indicates an even greater investment of resources (Millhauser 2012; Minc 1999). Although ethnographic accounts suggest that the labor involved in these tasks was likely to have been organized at the scale of the household (De Leon 2009; Parsons 2001; Williams 1999), settlement patterns show that saltmakers congregated in discrete lakeshore communities.

Social and Political Dimensions: Community Matters

Exploiting aquatic resources brought producers together as communities by sharing territories, following local rhythms of production, and participating in exchange networks. Sahagún (1950–1982: 1:37, 45, 73–74; 2:91; 11:31, 33, 36, 65) makes several references to hunters and fishers as "water folk" and to saltmakers as men and women who "lived where there was salt," "salt people," and "people who dwelt in the salt marshes." These were not just labels applied by outsiders—membership also involved shared religious practices, implying a shared sense of identity. Each group had a patron deity: hunters and fishers worshipped Opochtli, mat-makers worshiped Nappa teuctli, and saltmakers worshiped Uixtocciuatl (Berdan 2005:35; Sahagún 1950–1982:1:37, 45, 73–74; 2:91). These patterns do not mean that the groups were exclusive or static—merely that they were recognizable and relevant.

Among aquatic specialists, saltmakers especially appear to have congregated at or within discrete settlements. The sixteenth-century *Relaciones Geográficas* identify Chiconautla, Citlaltepec, Xaltocan, Nexquipayac, and Ecatepec as communities that were primary centers of pre-Conquest salt production (Acuña 1982–1987:6:152–153, 237, 7:203–203, 244, 250, 8.104, 112, 145–146). At cities like Mexicalzingo and Huichilipochco, saltmakers worked on the periphery of the residential zone (Cortés 1971:83). Outside of large settlements, more than 60 percent of the Late Postclassic saltmaking sites identified in regional surveys had evidence of domestic occupation and many of the rest were located within 50 to 500 meters of a settlement (Chávez Dominguez 1979; Millhauser 2012:199; Sanders et al. 1979:173). Excavations at saltmaking settlements have revealed multiple domestic structures, storage, and ritual spaces (Sánchez-Vazquez 1984), as well as the hallmarks of Late Postclassic domestic life, from cooking to household ritual (Millhauser 2012). Production may still have been organized at the scale of the household, but the concentration of households doing the same kinds of work was likely to have generated new communities as well as novel challenges.

The concentration of aquatic specialists around the lakes must have challenged existing systems for distributing land and mediating conflict. Sixteenth-century documents record individual and community ownership of territory dedicated to bird-hunting, fishing, and algae-collecting—as well as prolonged and bitter disputes over them (Gibson 1964:339–342; Hernández 1959:408–409). Where resources overlapped, accommodations had to be made. In the town of Tonanitla, for example, local authorities curtailed fishing near reed beds to prevent disturbances to nesting ducks (Castillo y Piña 1947:292). We know little about aspects of Aztec law, land tenure, and community organization as they pertained to nonagricultural land, but the sites where people lived and worked around the lakes provide some of the best remaining evidence that they resolved whatever new challenges they created or encountered.

Conclusion

Investigating evidence of the use of aquatic resources adds to a growing literature on rural Aztec economies that were regionally varied and interdependent (Charlton et al. 1991; Garraty 2006; Hodge and Minc 1991; Millhauser et al. 2011; Minc 1999; Nichols 1994; Parsons 2001, 2006; Parsons and Parsons 1990; Rodríguez-Alegría et al. 2013). Without a doubt, the nonagricultural resources of the lakes were crucial to the subsistence base of the Postclassic Basin of Mexico, but they also played fundamental roles in cuisine and commerce. Parsons' (2005, 2008) notion of the aquatic specialist does more than refine our understanding of the Aztec economy. It challenges us to think about how increasing scales of resource extraction and new settlements created value, opportunities for cooperation, possibilities for conflict, ecological change, and other unintended consequences.

Fruitful avenues of future research into the use of aquatic resources could include investigations of resource exploitation outside of settlements and especially in areas of low agricultural potential; contextual analyses of artifacts, microartifacts, and residues related to the processing of aquatic resources; more broadly comparative studies of faunal and botanical data; and investigations of skeletal markers of occupational specialization. Continuing to study variability and consistency among households, as well as moving the scope of work to encompass settlements, neighborhoods, and enclaves, will also help us recognize and appreciate the complex ways in which people negotiated access to aquatic resources in a landscape of changing value and opportunity.

References Cited

Acuña, René (editor)
1982–1987 *Relaciones Geográficas del Siglo XVI*. 10 vols. Universidad Nacional Autónoma de México, Mexico City.
Anawalt, Patricia R.
1981 *Indian Clothing before Cortés: Mesoamerican Costumes from the Codices*. University of Oklahoma Press, Norman.

Apenes, Ola
1943a The Pond in Our Backyard. *Mexican Life* 19:15-18.
1943b The "Tlateles" of Lake Texcoco. *American Antiquity* 9(1):29-32.
1944 The Primitive Salt Production of Lake Texcoco, Mexico. *Ethnos* 1:35-40.
Armillas, Pedro
1971 Gardens on Swamps. *Science* 175(4010):653-661.
Arroyo, Salvador G.
2008 La caja de agua del Colegio de la Santa Cruz de Tlatelolco. *Arqueología Mexicana* 15(89):62-65.
Baños Ramos, Eneida
1980 *La industria salinera en Xocotitlan, Cuenca de México*. Unpublished licenciatura thesis, Escuela Nacional de Antropología e Historia, Mexico City.
Baños Ramos, Eneida, and María de Jesus Sánchez V.
1998 La industria salinera prehispánica en la cuenca de México. In *La sal en México II*, edited by J. C. Reyes G, pp. 65-84. Gobierno del Estado de Colima, Secretaría de Cultura, and Universidad de Colima, Colima, Mexico.
Barlow, Robert H., and Michel Graulich
1995 *Codex Azcatitlan*. 2 vols. Bibliotheque nationale de France, Société des Américanistes, Paris.
Berdan, Frances F.
1986 Enterprise and Empire in Aztec and Early Colonial Mexico. In *Economic aspects of prehispanic highland Mexico*, edited by Barry L. Isaac, pp. 281-302. JAI Press, Greenwich, CT.
1987 The Economics of Aztec Luxury Trade and Tribute. In *The Aztec Templo Mayor: A Symposium at Dumbarton Oaks, 8th and 9th October 1983*, edited by Elizabeth Hill Boone, pp. 161-184. Dumbarton Oaks Research Library and Collection, Washington, DC.
1996 The Tributary Provinces. In *Aztec Imperial Strategies*, edited by Frances F. Berdan, Richard E. Blanton, Elizabeth Hill Boone, Mary G. Hodge, Michael E. Smith, and Emily Umberger, pp. 115-135. Dumbarton Oaks Research Library and Collection, Washington, DC.
2005 *The Aztecs of Central Mexico: An Imperial Society*. Thomson Wadsworth, Belmont, CA.
Berdan, Frances F., and Patricia R. Anawalt (editors)
1992 *The Codex Mendoza*. 4 vols. University of California Press, Berkeley.
Blanco Padilla, Alicia
1994 El tejido de malla en el Postclásico de la cuenca de México: una propuesta de actividad prehispánica. In *De fragmentos y tiempos: Arqueología de salvamento en la Ciudad de México*, edited by Subdirección de Salvamento Arqueológico, pp. 105-118. Instituto Nacional de Antropología e Historia, Tecamachalco, Mexico.
Blanton, Richard E.
1976 The Role of Symbiosis in Adaptation and Sociocultural Change in the Valley of Mexico. In *The Valley of Mexico: Studies in Pre-Hispanic Ecology and Society*, edited by Eric R. Wolf, pp. 181-201. University of New Mexico Press, Albuquerque.
1996 The Basin of Mexico Market System and the Growth of Empire. In *Aztec Imperial Strategies*, edited by Frances F. Berdan, Richard E. Blanton, Elizabeth Hill Boone, Mary G. Hodge, Michael E. Smith, and Emily Umberger, pp. 47-84. Dumbarton Oaks Research Library and Collection, Washington, DC.
Blanton, Richard E., Lane F. Fargher, and Verenice Heredia Espinoza
2005 The Mesoamerican World of Goods and Its Transformations. In *Settlement, Subsistence, and Social Complexity: Essays Honoring the Legacy of Jeffrey R. Parsons*, edited by Richard E. Blanton, pp. 260-294. Cotsen Institute of Archaeology, University of California, Los Angeles.

Brumfiel, Elizabeth M.
1980 Specialization, Market Exchange, and the Aztec State: A View from Huexotla. *Current Anthropology* 21:459–478.
1983 Aztec State Making: Ecology, Structure, and the Origin of the State. *American Anthropologist* 85(2):261–284.
1986 The Division of Labor at Xico: The Chipped Stone Industry. In *Economic Aspects of Prehispanic Highland Mexico*, edited by Barry L. Isaac, pp. 245–280. Research in Economic Anthropology Supplement 2. JAI Press, Greenwich, CT.
1987 Elite and Utilitarian Crafts in the Aztec State. In *Specialization, Exchange, and Complex Societies*, edited by Elizabeth M. Brumfiel and Timothy K. Earle, pp. 102–118. Cambridge University Press, Cambridge, UK.
1991 Agricultural Development and Class Stratification in the Southern Valley of Mexico. In *Land and Politics in the Valley of Mexico*, edited by Herbert R. Harvey, pp. 43–62. University of New Mexico Press, Albuquerque.
2005 Conclusions: Production and Power at Postclassic Xaltocan. In *Production and Power at Postclassic Xaltocan*, edited by Elizabeth M. Brumfiel, pp. 349–368. University of Pittsburgh, Pittsburgh, PA, and Instituto Nacional de Antropología e Historia, Mexico City.

Castellón Huerta, Blas
2008 Etnografía, arquelogía, decisiones técnicas y complejidad social: la producción de sal antigua y moderna en el centro de México. In *Perspectivas de la Investigación Arqueológica III*, edited by Fernando López Aguilar, Walburga Wiesheu, and Patricia Fournier, pp. 171–200. Instituto Nacional de Antropología e Historia, Escuela Nacional de Antropología e Historia, Mexico City.

Castillo y Piña, José
1947 *Siluetas del Estado de Méjico*. E. Rebollar, Mixcoac, Mexico.

Charlton, Thomas H.
1969 Texcoco Fabric-Marked Pottery, Tlateles, and Salt-Making. *American Antiquity* 34(1):73–76.

Charlton, Thomas H., Deborah L. Nichols, and Cynthia O. Charlton
1991 Aztec Craft Production and Specialization: Archaeological Evidence from the City-State of Otumba, Mexico. *World Archaeology* 23(1):98–114.

Chávez Dominguez, Humberto
1979 *Arqueología de superficie en San Critstóbal Ecatepec, Estado de México: Un estudio del desarrollo de las fuerzas productivas en el México Prehispánico*. Biblioteca Enciclopédica del Estado de México, Mexico City.

Coe, Sophie D.
1994 *America's First Cuisines*. University of Texas Press, Austin.

Cortés, Hernán
1971 *Letters from Mexico*. Grossman, New York.

Cruz, Martín de la
1940 *The Badianus Manuscript (Codex Barberini, Latin 241) Vatican Library; an Aztec Herbal of 1552*. Johns Hopkins University Press, Baltimore, MD.

De León, Jason P.
2009 Rethinking the Organization of Aztec Salt Production: A Domestic Perspective *Archaeological Papers of the American Anthropological Association* 19:45–57.

De Lucia, Kristin
2013 Domestic Economies and Regional Transitions: Household Multicrafting and Lake Exploitation in Pre-Aztec Central Mexico. *Journal of Anthropological Archaeology* 32:353–367.

Díaz del Castillo, Bernal
1956 *The Discovery and Conquest of Mexico, 1517–1521*. Farrar Straus and Cudahy, New York.

Durán, Fray Diego
1971 *Book of the Gods and Rites and the Ancient Calendar*. Translated by F. Horcasitas and Doris Heyden. University of Oklahoma Press, Norman.
1994 *The History of the Indies of New Spain*. Translated by Doris Heyden. University of Oklahoma Press, Norman.

Espinosa Pineda, Gabriel
1996 *El embrujo del lago: el sistema lacustre de la Cuenca de México en la cosmovisión mexica*. Universidad Nacional Autónoma de México Instituto de Investigaciones Antropológicas, Mexico City.

Ewald, Ursula
1985 *The Mexican Salt Industry, 1560–1980: A Study in Change*. Gustav Fischer Verlag, Stuttgart.

Ewald, Ursula, Enno Seele, and Javier Alcocer
1994 Tequezquite: A Story with Loose Ends (the Occurrence of Natural Soda in Mexico). *Journal of Salt History* 2:71–100.

Flores, Teodoro
1918 *El tequesquite del Lago de Texcoco*. Anales del Instituto Geológico de México No. 5. Departamento de Talleres Graficos de la Secretaria de Fomento, Mexico City.

Garraty, Christopher P.
2006 The Politics of Commerce: Aztec Pottery Production and Exchange in the Basin of Mexico, A.D. 1200–1650. Unpublished Ph.D. dissertation, Department of Anthropology, Arizona State University, Tempe.

Gibson, Charles
1964 *The Aztecs under Spanish Rule: A History of the Indians of the Valley of Mexico, 1519–1810*. Stanford University Press, Stanford, CA.

Hassig, Ross
1985 *Trade, Tribute, and Transportation. The Sixteenth-Century Political Economy of the Valley of Mexico*. University of Oklahoma Press, Norman.
1988 *Aztec Warfare: Imperial Expansion and Political Control*. University of Oklahoma Press, Norman.

Hernández, Francisco
1959 *Historia natural de Nueva España*. 2 vols. Universidad Nacional Autónoma de México, Mexico City.

Hicks, Frederic
1974 Dependent Labor in Prehistoric Mexico. *Estudios de cultura nahuatl* 11:243–266.
1984 Rotational Labor and Urban Development in Prehispanic Tetzcoco. In *Explorations in Ethnohistory: Indians of Central Mexico in the Sixteenth Century*, edited by Herbert R. Harvey and Hanns J. Prem, pp. 147–174. University of New Mexico Press, Albuquerque.
1987 First Steps toward a Market-Integrated Economy in Aztec Mexico. In *Early State Dynamics*, edited by Henri J. M. Claessen and Piet van de Velde, pp. 91–107. E. J. Brill, Leiden.
1991 Gift and Tribute: Relations of Dependency in Aztec Mexico. In *Early State Economies*, edited by Henri J. M. Claessen and Piet van de Velde, pp. 199–213. Transaction, New Brunswick, NJ.

Hirth, Kenneth G.
2009 Craft Production, Household Diversification, and Domestic Economy in Prehispanic Mesoamerica. *Archaeological Papers of the American Anthropological Association* 19:13–32.

Hodge, Mary G., and Leah D. Minc
1991 *Aztec-Period Ceramic Distribution and Exchange Systems*. Final Report Submitted to the National Science Foundation for Grant BSM-8704177.

Ixtlilxóchitl, Fernando de Alva
1965 *Obras históricas*. 2 vols. Editora Nacional, Mexico City.

Kepecs, Susan
2003 Salt Sources and Production. In *The Postclassic Mesoamerican World*, edited by Michael E. Smith and Frances F. Berdan, pp. 126–131. University of Utah Press, Salt Lake City.

Linné, Sigvald
1937 Hunting and Fishing in the Valley of Mexico in the Middle of the 16th Century. *Ethnos* 2:56–64.
1940 Bird-Nets of Lake Texcoco, Mexico Valley. *Ethnos* 5(3–4):122–130.

McClung de Tapia, Emily, Mari C. Serra Puche, and Amie E. Limón de Dyer
1986 Formative Lacustrine Adaptation: Botanical Remains from Terremote-Tlaltenco, Mexico City. *Journal of Field Archaeology* 13:99–113.

Mendizábal, Miguel O.
1929 *Influencia de la sal en la distribucion geografica de los grupos indigenas de Mexico*. Imprenta del Museo nacional de Arqueologia Historia y Etnografia, Mexico City.

Millhauser, John K.
2012 Saltmaking, Craft, and Community at Late Postclassic and Early Colonial San Bartolome Salinas, Mexico. Unpublished Ph.D. dissertation, Department of Anthropology, Northwestern University, Evanston, IL.

Millhauser, John K., Enrique Rodríguez-Alegría, and Michael D. Glascock
2011 Testing the Accuracy of Portable X-Ray Fluorescence to Study Aztec and Colonial Obsidian Supply at Xaltocan, Mexico. *Journal of Archaeological Science* 38:3141–3152.

Minc, Leah D.
1999 The Aztec Salt Trade: Insights from INAA of Texcoco Fabric-Marked Pottery. Paper presented at the 64th annual meeting of the Society for American Archaeology, Chicago.

Morehart, Christopher T.
2010 The Archaeology of Farmscapes: Production, Place, and the Materiality of Landscape at Xaltocan, Mexico. Unpublished Ph.D. dissertation, Department of Anthropology, Northwestern University, Evanston, IL.
2012 Mapping Ancient Chinampa Landscapes in the Basin of Mexico: A Remote Sensing and GIS Approach. *Journal of Archaeological Science* 39:2541–2551.

Morehart, Christopher T., and Charles Frederick
2014 The Chronology and Collapse of Pre-Aztec Raised Field (Chinampa) Agriculture in the Northern Basin of Mexico. *Antiquity* 88:531–548.

Nichols, Deborah L.
1994 The Organization of Provincial Craft Production and the Aztec City-State of Otumba. In *Economies and Polities in the Aztec Realm*, edited by Mary G. Hodge and Michael E. Smith, pp. 175–194. Institute for Mesoamerican Studies, Albany, NY.

Niederberger, Christine
1976 *Zohapilco: cinco milenios de ocupación humana en un sitio lacustre de la Cuenca de México*. Instituto Nacional de Antropología e Historia, SEP, Departamento de Prehistoria, Mexico.

Noguera, Eduardo
1975 Identificación de una Saladera. *Anales de Antropología* 12:115–117.

Orozco y Berra, Manuel
1864 *Memória para la Carta Hidrográfica del Valle de México*. Sociedad Mexicana de Geografía y Estadística, Mexico.
Ortiz de Montellano, Bernard R.
1978 Aztec Cannibalism: An Ecological Necessity? *Science* 200:611–617.
1990 *Aztec Medicine, Health, and Nutrition*. Rutgers University Press, New Brunswick, NJ.
Overholtzer, Lisa
2012 Empires and Everyday Material Practices: A Household Archaeology of Aztec and Spanish Imperialism at Xaltocan, Mexico. Unpublished Ph.D. dissertation, Department of Anthropology, Northwestern University, Evanston, IL.
Palerm, Angel
1973 *Obras hidráulicas prehispánicas en el sistema lacustre del valle de México*. Sepinah. Instituto Nacional de Antropología, México, DF.
Palerm, Angel, and Eric R. Wolf
1957 Ecological Potential and Cultural Development in Mesoamerica. *Pan American Union Social Science Monographs* 3:1–37.
Parsons, Jeffrey R.
1991 Political Implications of Prehispanic Chinampa Agriculture in the Valley of Mexico. In *Land and Politics in the Valley of Mexico*, edited by Herbert R. Harvey, pp. 17–42. University of New Mexico Press, Albuquerque.
1994 Late Postclassic Salt Production and Consumption in the Basin of Mexico: Some Insights from Nexquipayac. In *Economies and Polities in the Aztec Realm*, edited by Mary G. Hodge and Michael E. Smith, pp. 257–290. Institute for Mesoamerican Studies, Albany, NY.
1996 Tequesquite and Ahuauhtle: Rethinking the Prehispanic Productivity of Lake Texcoco-Xaltocan-Zumpango. In *Arqueología Mesoamericana: Homenaje a William T. Sanders*, edited by Alba G. Mastache, Jeffrey R. Parsons, Robert S. Santley, and Mari C. Serra Puche, pp. 439–459. Instituto Nacional de Antropología e Historia, Arqueología Mexicana, Mexico City.
2001 *The Last Saltmakers of Nexquipayac, Mexico: An Archaeological Ethnography*. Museum of Anthropology, University of Michigan, Ann Arbor.
2005 The Aquatic Component of Aztec Subsistence: Hunters, Fishers, and Collectors in an Urbanized Society. *Michigan Discussions in Anthropology* 15:49–89.
2006 *The Last Pescadores of Chimalhuacán, Mexico: An Archeological Ethnography*. Museum of Anthropology, University of Michigan, Ann Arbor.
2008 Beyond Santley and Rose (1979): The Role of Aquatic Resources in the Prehispanic Economy of the Basin of Mexico. *Journal of Archaeological Research* 64(3):351–366.
2010 The Pastoral Niche in Pre-Hispanic Mesoamerica. In *Pre-Columbian Foodways: Interdisciplinary Approaches to Food, Culture, and Markets in Ancient Mesoamerica*, edited by John. E. Staller and Michael D. Carrasco, pp. 109–136. Springer, New York.
Parsons, Jeffrey R., and Luis Morett
2004 Recursos Acuáticos en la subsistencia Azteca: cazadores, pescadores y recolectores. *Arqueología Mexicana* 12(68):38–43.
Parsons, Jeffrey R., and Mary H. Parsons
1990 *Maguey Utilization in Highland Central Mexico: An Archaeological Ethnography*. Museum of Anthropology, University of Michigan, Ann Arbor.
Pérez Espinosa, José G.

1998 La pesca en el medio lacustre y chinampero de San Luis Tlaxialtemalco. In *La cosecha del agua en la cuenca de México*, edited by Teresa Rojas Rabiela, pp. 101–116. Centro de Investigaciones y Estudios Superiores en Antropología Social, Mexico City.

Pilcher, Jeffrey M.

1998 *Que Vivan los Tamales! Food and the Making of Mexican Identity*. University of New Mexico Press, Albuquerque.

Rodríguez-Alegría, Enrique, John K. Millhauser, and Wesley D. Stoner

2013 Trade, Tribute, and Neutron Activation: The Colonial Political Economy of Xaltocan, Mexico. *Journal of Anthropological Archaeology* 32(4):397–414.

Rojas Rabiela, Teresa

1998 *La cosecha del agua en la cuenca de México*. Centro de Investigaciones y Estudios Superiores en Antropología Social, Mexico City.

Sahagún, Fray Bernadino de

1950–1982 *Florentine Codex: General History of the Things of New Spain*. 12 vols. Translated by Arthur J. O. Anderson and Charles E. Dibble. School of American Research, Santa Fe, NM, and the University of Utah Press, Salt Lake City.

Sánchez Vázquez, María de Jesus

1984 Zacatenco: una unidad productora de sal en la ribera norooccidental del Lago de Texcoco. Unpublished licenciatura thesis, Escuela Nacional de Antropología e Historia, Mexico City.

1987 Un Sitio Productor de Sal en Zacatenco, D.F. *Cuaderno de Trabajo Departamento de Salvamiento Arqueológico, Instituto Nacional de Antropología e Historia* 6:51–56.

Sanders, William T., Jeffrey R. Parsons, and Robert S. Santley

1979 *The Basin of Mexico: Ecological Processes in the Evolution of a Civilization*. Academic Press, New York.

Sanders, William T., and Barbara J. Price

1968 *Mesoamerica: The Evolution of a Civilization*. Random House, New York.

Santley, Robert S., and Eric K. Rose

1979 Diet, Nutrition, and Population Dynamics in the Basin of Mexico. *World Archaeology* 11(2):185–207.

Serra, Mari C., Luis Torres, and Alfonso Rodríguez

1982 Desfibradores: análisis microscópico de algunos implementos líticos en una aldea de pescadores y canasteros, Terremote-Tlaltenco. *Antropología y Técnica* 2:7–52.

Serra Puche, Mari C.

1986 Unidades Habitacionales del Formativo en la Cuenca de Mexico. In *Unidades Habitacionales Mesoamericanas y sus Areas de Actividad*, edited by Linda Manzanilla, pp. 161–192. Universidad Nacional Autonoma de México, Mexico City.

1988 *Los recursos lacustres de la Cuenca de México durante el formativo*. Universidad Nacional Autónoma de México, Mexico City.

Siméon, Rémi

1977 Diccionario de la lengua nahuatl o mexicana. Siglo Veintiuno, Mexico.

Smith, Michael E.

1990 Long-Distance Trade Under the Aztec Empire: The Archaeological Evidence. *Ancient Mesoamerica* 1:153–169.

2003 Key Commodities. In *The Postclassic Mesoamerican World*, edited by Michael E. Smith and Frances F. Berdan, pp. 117–125. University of Utah Press, Salt Lake City.

Sugiura, Yoko

1998 *La caza, la pesca y la recolección: etnoarqueología del modo de subsistencia lacustre en las ciénegas del Alto Lerma*. Universidad Nacional Autónoma de México Instituto de Investigaciones Antropológicas, Mexico City.

Sugiura, Yoko, and Mari C. Serra

1983 Notas sobre el modo de subsistencia lacustre. La Laguna de Santa Cruz Atizapan, Edo de Mexico. *Anales de Antropología* 20:9–26.

Talavera Barnard, Elena R.

1979 Las salinas de la Cuenca de México y la cerámica de impresión textil. Unpublished licenciatura thesis, Escuela Nacional de Antropología e Historia, Mexico City.

Tolstoy, Paul

1958 *Surface Survey of the Northern Valley of Mexico: The Classic and Post-Classic Periods*. Transactions of the American Philosophical Society 48, Part 5. American Philosophical Society, Philadelphia, PA.

Ugent, Donald

2000 The Master Basket Weavers of the Toluca Market Region (Mexico). *Economic Botany* 54(3):256–266.

Vaillant, George C.

1950 *Aztecs of Mexico: Origin, Rise, and Fall of the Aztec Nation*. Penguin Books, Baltimore, MD.

Weitlaner Johnson, Irmgard

1971 Basketry and Textiles. In *Archaeology of Northern Mesoamerica, Part One*, edited by Gordon Ekholm and Ignacio Bernal, pp. 297–321. Handbook of Middle American Indians Vol. 10, Robert Wauchope, general editor, University of Texas Press, Austin.

Williams, Eduardo

1999 The Ethnoarchaeology of Salt Production at Lake Cuitzeo, Michoacan, Mexico. *Latin American Antiquity* 10(4):400–414.

2009 The Exploitation of Aquatic Resources at Lake Cuitzeo, Michoacan, Mexico: An Ethnoarchaeological Study. *Latin American Antiquity* 20(4):607–627.

2010 Salt Production and Trade in Ancient Mesoamerica. In *Pre-Columbian Foodways: Interdisciplinary Approaches to Food, Culture, and Markets in Ancient Mesoamerica*, edited by John E. Staller and Michael Carrasco, pp. 175–190. Springer, New York.

CHAPTER 21

AZTEC METALLURGY

DOROTHY HOSLER

We do not know when the people we call Aztec first began to fashion metal objects. We do know from sixteenth-century Spanish observations that Aztec golden and silver objects attracted and confounded the invaders. Aztec metalworkers rendered an encyclopedic array of cast and worked forms with subtlety and intense focus on detail. Some Spaniards were fully cognizant of the artistry and provided precise descriptions that now furnish a fundamental data set for our work on this topic. We owe them a great debt, because scholars have estimated that 95 percent of Aztec gold, silver, and copper objects were eventually melted to bullion. Legends that had been circulating in Europe for decades about the cities of gold in the Americas were not literally the case. Nonetheless, the astonishing Aztec pleasure parks (Evans 2000), with pools, ritual stone carvings, waterfalls, and hundreds of species of Mexican flora and fauna sometimes displayed those plants and animals in metal. Although large European cities contained pleasure parks, as far as we know the penchant for replicating flora and fauna in metal, stone, and other materials is uniquely Aztec. Metal among the Aztec thus was used in public display—in gardens containing metal rocks, plants, animals, birds, butterflies, flowers, and fish—as well as for myriad other sumptuary and utilitarian items from copper.

By about A.D.1100 in Jalisco's Sayula Basin (Garcia 2007; Hosler 2012), metal workers were casting bells and hammering sheet metal into open rings and tools from copper alloys, including coppersilver, an array of bronzes, copper-tin, copper-arsenic, and sometimes copper-arsenic-tin. Crucial aspects of this technology were introduced from Ecuador, Peru, and Bolivia (Arsandeaux and Rivet 1921; Dewan and Hosler 2008; Mountjoy 1969; 1994) and from lower Central America (Caso 1965; Hosler 1988; Pendergast 1972). The required ores of arsenopyrite (arsenic mineral), cassiterite (tin mineral), and copper (malachite, cuprite minerals) exist in pockets in this area of Jalisco, although tin tends to concentrate in the states of Zacatecas. After A.D. 1200 the Tarascan State became a major center for production of castings of copper-tin, copper-arsenic, and copper-arsenic-tin and especially for production of copper-silver alloy sheet metal, to the extent that Cortez called this alloy "the metal of Michoacan."

People living in the region that roughly defines modern Oaxaca, by contrast, cast gold and copper-gold and copper-silver-gold alloys (Bray 1977; Caso 1962; Hosler 1986, 1994) into intricate and complex body ornaments. They also made small implements and tools and mushroom-shaped axe monies (Hosler 1986; Hosler et al. 1990) from copper and copper-arsenic bronze. Strong evidence exists that, by about A.D.1150 or 1200, some aspects of the metallurgical know-how responsible for the technology that developed in both western Mexico and Oaxaca had disseminated throughout Mesoamerica. At the same time, in the southeastern areas of Mesoamerica, people were casting bells and producing other items from metal (Hosler 1994, 2005). Aspects of this technology probably were related to earlier developments in lower Central America (Coggins 1984; Root, in Lothrop 1952), but at the same time evidence is strong for a local metalworking tradition (Hosler 1994, 2005) on the coast of Belize, for example. The closest sources of copper ore are in Highland Chiapas, Guatemala, and Honduras. After about A.D. 1200, people were fashioning and exchanging metal objects, though rarely in large numbers, in networks throughout Mesoamerica. The Aztec thus appropriated, integrated, and inherited hundreds of years of Mesoamerican regional metallurgical knowledge and experience.

Metal Production at Tenochtitlan and the Templo Mayor Bell Offerings

We have no archaeological data concerning where artisans cast the specular gold, silver, and copper multipiece objects or the cold-worked metal objects so interesting to the sixteenth-century historians and chroniclers. Documentary evidence suggests that goldsmiths and silver workers worked in Azcatzpozalco and goldworkers in Yopico (De Rojas 1986). However, we lack archaeological evidence concerning where other elite display objects (shields, leggings, headbands, crowns, nose rings, and earrings) made from copper gold and silver and their alloys as well as nonelite objects (needles punches, tweezers, awls, axes, needles) made from copper, copper-silver, silver, and gold and their alloys were crafted. We do know from Nicklaus Schultz's work (2008) that the Aztec cast small bells for dedicatory Temple Mayor offerings using binary and ternary alloys of copper-tin, copper-arsenic, copper-lead, and copper-arsenic-tin. Schultz's comprehensive study of these offerings convincingly shows that these bells were most probably cast at workshops at Tenochtitlan, near the Temple Mayor. From semiquantitative analytical studies of a subsample (567) of nearly 4,000 bells excavated from dated offerings, Schultz also demonstrates that the Temple Mayor bells represent a particular and reduced selection of Mesoamerican bell types. He argues that their homogeneity (bell and alloy compositions) represents the work of one or very few workshops, or of individuals within one workshop, and that the homogeneity reflects direct exchange between the artisans and the individuals acquiring the bells. He maintains that this patterning makes the possibility unlikely that these bells were imported. Schulz's work also shows that the range of bell forms diminished through time so that in the final construction phase of the Temple Mayor, the bells were small, globular (and still contained the clapper) but too small to ring, and the alloy contained tin, which facilitated casting. Schultz thinks these bells served as icons.

Of the Aztec bells Schultz (2008) describes, the copper alloys used even for those that could not ring contained an alloying element in concentrations greater than 2 wt.%. Tin, lead, or arsenic in copper lowers the melting temperature of the alloy and facilitates the casting process (Tarkanian et al. 2007). We lack the experimental data to predict melting temperatures of the ternary alloys (copper-arsenic-lead, copper-arsenic-tin, etc.), but they certainly would be lower than that of copper. We also know that in bells of these designs the presence of tin, arsenic, or lead was irrelevant to their sound or pitch (Hosler 1986, 1994), so that casting quality (the ability of a metal to fill a mold) is highly likely to have been the property that these artisans sought even in the small copper-tin globular bells dating to the final construction phase of the Temple Mayor.

The information from the Templo Mayor study is a dramatic close-up on a particular production sequence for one class of metal object made for a specific social/ritual/communicative end. Metal objects used in many other cultural activities undoubtedly were produced through other production systems, or sometimes idiosyncratically. Berdan and Anawalt (2007), for example, indicate that some finished items were probably imported from Guerrero, and the conquest of those areas provides key insights into how Aztec people were able to avail themselves of critical ore minerals (copper, arsenic-bearing copper ores, gold, silver, and lead).

Ore Sources for Templo Mayor Metal

The most significant observation concerning Aztec metallurgy is that the Basin of Mexico and its immediate environs lack metallic ore minerals. The raw materials for this technology had to be obtained elsewhere; here I refer to copper, tin, silver arsenic or arsenic-bearing copper ores, lead, gold, and silver. The primary area that does contain these ore minerals is what I have called the west Mexican metalworking zone (Hosler 1986, 1994) This area includes Nayarit, Colima, Jalisco, Guerrero, Michoacan, the southern part of the state of Mexico, and the western part of the state of Guerrero. Oaxaca also contains ores of copper and other ore minerals, but they are less diverse and abundant than those in the metalworking zone. Oaxaca is rich in deposits of gold, although gold was available in other areas. The area that interests us here is the southern part of the state of Mexico, which the Aztec conquered and incorporated.

We do know that around 1428 the emperor ltzcoatl conquered territories in northeastern Guerrero as part of his plan to expand the Aztec Empire. Large and small copper deposits are common in this region (Hosler 2005). The two most significant conquered areas with respect to copper ore minerals were Quiauhteopan and Tepeqoacuilco. Tribute items in metal mentioned in the *Matricula de Tributos* (Berdan and Anawalt 2000) include copper axes, copper bells, gold, and silver. Litvak (1971) calculates that 77 percent of T-shaped axe-monies rendered as tribute came from Tepeqoacuilco. Two large copper mines, La Dicha (Litivak 1971; Salas 1980) and La Union (Salas 1984), are located within these provinces, as well as numerous smaller deposits (Litvak 1971; Hosler 1994). Interestingly, the T-shaped axes fail as tools (Hosler et al. 1990; Hosler 1986, 1994) and most likely were used for the metal itself. The T-shaped axe-monies were highly portable and easy to melt into low-arsenic copper-arsenic alloy metal (Hosler 1994). These items were stackable, were easily divisible as tribute, and probably served as an ideal base metal for metalworkers (Hosler 1986). We can thus point to axe-monies as at least one likely source for copper and low-arsenic copper-arsenic alloy metal at Tenochtitlan; other alloys, including copper-tin, high arsenic, copper-silver, or copper-lead require other explanations.

Thus the availability of copper metal in the form of axe-monies and perhaps axes only partially explains the sources of metal used by the Aztec for offerings at the Templo Mayor. During construction phase IVB (1469–1481), the numbers of bells increased notably (and these consist primarily of three types made from copper-lead, copper-tin, and copper-arsenic alloys). As Schultz and others have pointed out (Hosler 1986; Root, in Lothrop 1952), copper-lead alloy bells seem to have been cast in the Basin of Mexico by the Aztecs using a local source of lead. They are absent in the west but occur occasionally as tribute items in the Cenote of Sacrifice in Chichen Itzá and must have been imported from central Mexico. If the interpretation is correct, some copper alloy metal could have been imported from Tepeqoacuilco as ingots or axe-monies. Schultz's (2008) observation, that alloy types seem to coincide with the conquests of these regions by Ahuitzotl, is crucial because the ore minerals (arsenopyrite and cassiterite, and lead) do not exist in the Basin of Mexico, and the raw materials and/or ingots had to be imported. Not surprisingly, the Aztec conquests during the period 1428–1477 included precisely those areas where the ore minerals were available that became so crucial to Aztec metallurgy. The interesting question is where Aztec people obtained metallic metal before Ahuitzotl's expansion.

Tin is scarce in Mesoamerica and occurs mostly in Zacatecas and San Luis Potosí (Hosler 1986, 1994). This fact is what makes Schultz's (2008) studies of the many poorly cast copper-tin bronze bells so interesting. Tin alters color, but it also decreases casting temperature. These bells could not ring nor were they visible, so castability most likely explains the choice of the copper-tin alloy. T-shaped axes and axe-monies furnished the copper in the many copper alloy items recovered at the Templo Mayor. Copper-tin ores (stannite) are absent in Mexico. The closest tin (cassiterite) source was the Sierra de Tlataya in the state of Mexico where geological sources (Hosler 1994) identify a series of tin deposits. Naomí Quezada's work (1972) shows that metallic tin served as tribute to the Matlatzinca State (Hosler 1986, 1994) at least until 1477 when the Aztecs conquered the valley of Toluca and adjacent areas. The Sierra de Tlataya tin deposits may have been those that subsequently furnished tin to the Aztec province of Tamazcaltepec, which contains a large silver mine and was first conquered by Axayacatl (1470). Temazcaltepec, listed by Smith and Berdan (2003:310) as a tribute province, provided gold, copper, silver, and lead as tribute items. The inferential evidence indicates that this area also provided tin to the Aztec state. Cortez's oft-quoted statement that he sent men to Taxco to obtain tin for his bronze cannons has never made sense, because Taxco is not a tin-bearing ore deposit. He may have been referring to the greater area encompassing the southern portion of the state of Mexico, including the Sierra de Tlataya where tin deposits existed.

Aztec Metal Objects from Historical Descriptions

Spanish descriptions speaking to the skill of Aztec artisans in casting and working metal, and the meaning of some of these objects, merit repetition here. "They were able to cast a parrot whose tongue moved and whose head and wings could move. They cast a monkey with feet and hands who had in his hand a spindle whorl and it looked like the monkey was spinning, or it might have an apple which it appeared to be eating" (Rojas 1986:165). Saville (1920:165) describes a fish with one fin made from silver and the next from gold; he also describes a parrot with a moveable tongue; a necklace of 18 large pieces in the form of the head of an eagle with their pendant; two monsters of gold made in the shape of ducks (1920: 70); a frog; a tiger with two eagles and 36 beads; eight spindles with their whorls and a spinner that itself carried the spinner, all of gold; four heads of animals, two of which seem to be wolves and the other two tigers, and from which hung metal bells. Among many hundreds of other gold and gold alloy objects Saville (1920:74) mentions a corn stalk with its ears. He also describes "a gold disk, perhaps the calendar, five to seven feet in diameter and 8 inches thick that (had) certain animals or pictures stamped on it; in the center (there was) the image of a man seated on his throne." Saville (1920:35) thinks that this large gold disc was the Aztec calendar; a second disc was made from silver, and the Spaniards reported that it represented the moon. The most significant ideas appear in a description of the collection of Netzahualcoyotl, the King of Texcoco. Saville (1920:119) mentions representations in stone mosaic work and gold of every bird, fish, or animal that could not be obtained alive (i.e., for Netzahualcoyotl's pleasure garden in Texcoco) and that Motecuhzoma had replicas of all animals and plants in Mexico in his zoological gardens made from metal and from feathers.

The Spanish invaders melted most items into ingots; a small proportion turned up in inventories that Saville identified and were shipped to Spain and later melted. Their descriptions amplify and sharpen our idea of the range of metal objects fashioned by Aztec artisans. In addition to body ornaments, elaborate renditions of natural creatures, and ritual and utilitarian serving dishes, the Aztecs were especially intent on representing creatures and plants of their natural world: jaguars, birds, monkeys, fish, butterflies, beetles, snakes, lizards, worms, flowers, and ears of corn. These functioned as a kind of visual encyclopedia.

We know that among Mesoamerican people, gold and silver and their alloys worn by the rulers and elites were considered sacred and were associated with the supernatural

(Hosler 1986, 1994). Specifically regarding the Aztecs, Saville (1920: 43, emphasis added) quoted Duran (1967) in *La Historia de los Indios de Nueva España*

> speaking of a hidden chamber in Tenochtitlan accessed through a low door that consisted of a large and spacious room in the middle of which was a heap of gold jewels and precious stones . . . it [the heap of gold jewels] was the height of a man—so high that no one was seen on the other side. It was the treasure that the kings and their forefathers went on leaving . . . on the day of his death all he [the ruler] left objects of gold, stone, fathers . . . *with much care . . . it was a sacred thing . . . and of the gods* and so they were there as the treasure of the king who came to reign . . . there were many piles of vessels of gold, dishes and porringers made according to their style, from which the kings ate, especially four dishes like platters, all of gold very elaborately worked as big as a large shield.

From the descriptions alone, we can infer that the Aztecs were casting intricate and multipiece gold and probably copper-silver-gold, gold, and other alloy objects and that they were forging (hammering) metal (gold and silver) sheet into platters, vessels, shields, and dishes. Various authors describe extremely thin gold sheet sometimes covering stone objects. The likelihood is strong that most metal production was intended for Aztec elites and selected proportions were for sale in the markets at Tenochtitlan.

Metal was a sacred thing and "of the gods." The meanings of silver and gold have been treated elsewhere (Emmerich 1965; Hosler 1994) and lie outside the scope of this chapter. Apart from the bells that sounded in most Aztec rituals (Hosler 1994, from Sahagún 1950–1982), metalworkers also crafted musical instruments: the ayachitlitzi (the mist rattle board) the chichahuazi, and trumpets. In general, the Aztec and other Mesoamerican people were particularly interested in metal for those properties that made metal unique—color, reflectivity, ductility, toughness, fluidity, and resonant properties: properties that could not be replicated using other materials.

The history of ancient Mesoamerican metalworking is short. Metallurgy emerged after key state level societies had coalesced, sometime around A.D. 600–800. The technology initially took shape in the west, where major ore deposits are located. Metallurgy never was a primary factor in the development of early complex society in Mesoamerica as it was in the Near East and China, where tools, armor and, weapons had a significant impact on transport, agriculture, and war. Metallurgy could have played such a role among the Tarascans (in thinking about secondary state formation), but timing makes that unlikely. The Tarascan state did control one copper mine, and metal production constituted a major activity by the time of the Spanish invasion. Activities associated with mining, transport, and production allowed specialist occupations not unlike those related to stone-working elsewhere in Mesoamerica. Yet, at the same time, the data show that complex alloy systems and casting techniques were not invented or developed by the Tarascans but were already present in the Cuenca de Sayula in Jalisco and elsewhere by about A.D. 1150 (Garcia 2007; Hosler 1986). The array of copper alloy objects containing varying levels of alloy concentration tin or arsenic (Hosler 1986) suggests multiple workshops using different ore sources. The remarkable characteristic is that metalworkers across a broad geographical region clearly understood the relation between alloys, their properties and object design. The European invaders stumbled on the Aztec expression of one of the world's great metallurgies, the Mesoamerican, and destroyed it. We still have untapped documentary sources in Spanish, Nahuatl, and other languages that can help build broader and richer descriptions and understandings of Aztec and other Mesoamerica metallurgies. We also have ongoing archaeological research that sometimes can alter our perspective. What was destroyed are thousands of examples of human technical imagination, creativity, and art, just as if the Louvre were suddenly flooded in a great deluge.

REFERENCES CITED

Arsandeaux, H., and Paul Rivet
1921 Contribution a l'etude de la metalurgie mexicaine. *Journal de la Societé des Americanístes de Paris* 13:261–280.
Berdan, F., and Patricia Anawalt
1997 *The Essential Codex Mendoza* University of California Press, Berkeley.
Bray, Warwick
1977 Maya Metalwork and its External Connections. In *Social Process in Maya Prehistory*, edited by Norman Hammond, pp. 365–403 Academic Press, New York.
Caso, Alfonso
1965 Lapidary Work, Goldwork and Copperwork from Oaxaca. In *Handbook of Middle-American Indians*, Vol. 3, edited by William R. Wauchope, pp. 896–930. University of Texas Press, Austin.
Coggins, Clemency C.
1984 The Cenote of Sacriface: Catalogue. In *Cenote of Sacriface: Maya Treasures from the Sacred Well at Chichen Itzá*, edited by Clemency C. Goggins and Orin C. Shane. pp. 23–166. University of Texas Press, Austin.
De Rojas, Jose Luis
1986 *Mexico Tenochtitlan: economía y sociedad en el siglo XVI*. Fondo De Cultura Económica. Colegio de Michoacan, Zamora, Michoacan, Mexico.
Dewan, Leslie, and Dorothy Hosler
2008 Ancient Maritime Trade on Balsa Rafts: An Engineering Analysis. *Journal of Anthropological Research* 64(1):19–40.
Durán, Fray Diego
1967 *Historia de los indios de nueva españa*. 1st ed. Porrúa, Mexico.
Emmerich Andre
1965 *Sweat of the Sun and Tears of the Moon: Gold and Silver in Precolombian Art*. University of Washington Press, Seattle.
Evans, Susan Toby
2000 Aztec Royal Pleasure Parks: Conspicuous Consumption and Elite State Rivalry. *Studies in the History of Gardens and Designed Landscapes* 20:206–228.
García, Johann Sebastián Zaldúa

2007 *Arqueometalurgia del Occidente de México: la Cuenca de Sayula, Jalisco como punto de conjunción de tradiciones Metalúrgicas Precolombinas*. Ph.D. dissertation, Universidad Autonoma de Guadalajara. Guadalajara, Jalisco.

Hosler, Dorothy

1986 *The Origins, Technology, and Social Construction of Ancient West Mexican Metallurgy*. Ph.D. dissertation, University of California, Santa Barbara. University Microfilms, Ann Arbor.

1994 *The Sounds and Colors of Power: The Sacred Metallurgy of Ancient West Mexico*. MIT Press, Cambridge, MA.

1998 Sound, Color and Meaning in the Metallurgy of Ancient West Mexico. *Reader in Archaeological Theory: Post-Processual and Cognitive Approaches*, edited by David Whitely, pp. 103–118. Routledge, New York.

2009 West Mexican Metallurgy: Revisited and Revised. *Journal of World Prehistory* 22:185–212.

Hosler, Dorothy, Heather Lechtman, and Olaf Holm

1990 *Axe-monies and Their Relatives*. Dumbarton Oaks Research Library and Collections, Washington D.C.

Litvak, Jaime King

1971 *Cihuatlan y Tepecoacuilco: provincias tributaries de Mexico en el siglo XVI*. Universidad Nacional Autónoma de Mexico Ciudad Universitaria, Mexico City.

Maldonado, Blanca E., and Thilo Rehren

2009 Early Copper Smelting at Itzipratzizo, Mexico. *Journal of Archaeological Science* 36:1998–2006.

Mountjoy, Joseph J.

1969 Origin of West Mexican Metallurgy. *Mesoamerican Studies* 4:26–42.

Pendergast, David M.

1962 Metal Artifacts in Prehispanic Mesoamerica. *American Antiquity* 27:520–545.

Quzeada, Noemí

1972 *Los matlatzincas: epoca prehispanica y epoca colonial hasta 1650*. Instituto Nacional de Antropología e Historia, Mexico City.

Root, William C.

1952 *Metals from the Cenote of Sacrifice Chichen Itzá, Yucatan*. Edited by Samuel K. Lothrop. Memoirs of the Peabody Museum of Archaeology and Ethnology Vol. 10, No. 2. Harvard University, Cambridge, MA.

Sahagún, Fray Bernardino de

1950–1982 *Florentine Codex: General History of the Things of New Spain*. Edited and translated by A. J. O. Anderson and C. E. Dibble. School of American Research, University of Utah, Salt Lake City.

Salas, Guillermo

1980 *Carta y provincias metalogéneticas de la Republica Mexicana*. Consejo de Recursos Naturales, Mexico.

Saville, Marshall H.

1920 *The Goldsmith's Art in Ancient Mexico*. Museum of the American Indian, Heye Foundation, New York.

Schulze, Niklas

2008 *El Proceso de produccion metalurgica en su context cultural: los cascabeles de cobre del Templo Mayor de Tenochtitlan*. Ph.D. dissertation, Instituto de Investigaciones Antropológicas, Universidad Nacional Autonoma de Mexico, Mexico City.

Smith, Michael E., and Berdan, Frances F.
2003 Spatial Structure of the Mesoamerican World System. In *The Postclassic Mesoamerican World*, edited by Frances F. Berdan and Michael E. Smith, pp. 21–31. University of Utah Press, Salt Lake City.

Tarkanian, M., D. Hosler, and K. Hester
2009 Aspects of the Metallurgy of Calixtlahuaca. Paper presented at the 53rd International Congress of Americanists, Mexico City.

CHAPTER 22

AZTEC OBSIDIAN INDUSTRIES

ALEJANDRO PASTRANA
AND DAVID M. CARBALLO

The prehispanic societies of central and western Mesoamerica used obsidian in great quantities, as it was the primary material used for manufacturing domestic cutting tools and weapons and could also be fashioned into ornamental and religious items. Unlike in the Old World, utilitarian lithic industries were never supplanted by metallurgy, with the result that successive urban civilizations continued to exploit obsidian mines and leave exceedingly dense concentrations of production byproducts (or *debitage*) at quarry sites and workshops located within settlements. Aztec obsidian industries built upon millennia of earlier societies, including the Teotihuacano and Toltec, yet they significantly intensified and expanded obsidian extraction and exchange systems (Pastrana 2007; Pastrana and Domínguez 2009).

Like their predecessors, the Aztecs were attracted to the physical properties of obsidian because it is a sharp, durable stone that fractures cleanly and predictably. The reductive and sequential nature of production activities and the chemical regularity of obsidian originating from the same volcanic flows are additional properties that have attracted archaeologists, because a wide range of economic activities can be discerned from the material. These include the stages of manufacturing represented in different contexts, knapper skill level, relative intensity of production, and exchange routes and zones of cultural contact. Aztec archaeological sites contain a wide range of types of obsidian artifacts, such as bifacial knives and projectile points used as weapons, pressure blades and unifacial scrapers used in many domestic activities, and polished bodily adornments, vessels, and mirrors used as status and ritual items. As a result, multiple dimensions of Aztec society may be addressed through obsidian analysis. This summary outlines the major raw material sources, artifact types, quarrying and production activities, and structure of the domestic and institutional obsidian economies.

Obsidian Sources

The exploitation of large volumes of obsidian within central Mexico during the Postclassic period was concentrated primarily on the sources of Sierra de Las Navajas, Hidalgo; Otumba, state of Mexico; Paredón, Puebla; and Tulancingo, Hidalgo (Figure 22.1). The mines of Pico de Orizaba, Veracruz, were a fifth heavily exploited source located farther east. Of these, the Sierra de Las Navajas source (also known as the Pachuca source) was the most important to Aztec society and is the source about which we presently know the most (Pastrana and Athie 2001a, 2001b). Contemporary and historical place names that contain the Nahuatl term for obsidian, *itzli*, or variants thereof, signal the ancient availability of the material either because of a nearby flow or ready access through trade (Figure 22.2).

The Sierra de Las Navajas source comprises approximately 30 km^2 of the Sierra of Pachuca, centered on the peak of Cruz del Milagro, with a maximum elevation 3180 m above sea level. Obsidian formed in the south of a volcanic caldera from a lava effusion following the explosion of a rhyolitic dome. The source contains very high quality glassy material and exhibits the most intensive obsidian exploitation in Mesoamerica, having been worked during the Formative period, by Classic period Teotihuacanos, Early Postclassic period Toltecs, the Aztecs, and well into the Colonial period. Major tool production activities declined in the early eighteenth century, but deep mining activities continue today to produce items for the tourist industry. Obsidian from the Sierra de Las Navajas is famed particularly for its translucent green and grainier green-gold varieties, but there is also a brownish-red variety present at the source. Mining, production, and exchange activities involving Sierra de Las Navajas obsidian are detailed throughout this chapter.

The Otumba source comprises a rhyolitic dome and its flows covering an area measuring approximately 25 km^2 with two main foci: one to the northeast of the Cuello volcano and the other on the Soyaltepec volcano. Erosion within two streams, the Barranca de los Ixtetes and the Barranca del Muerto, has resulted in exposed outcrops of blocks, clasts, and nodules, and some of these rolled close to prehispanic sites such as Otumba (Otompan) and Teotihuacan. Material from the source appears to have been exploited primarily by Otumba's Postclassic occupants (Charlton et al. 1991; Parry 2001), after several centuries of more intensive exploitation by Classic period Teotihuacanos. Evidence of mining using shallow trenches and open pits 2 to 5 m deep are also visible, especially near the streams. Otumba obsidian is grayish-black, silvery-gray, and a brownish-red commonly called *meca*.

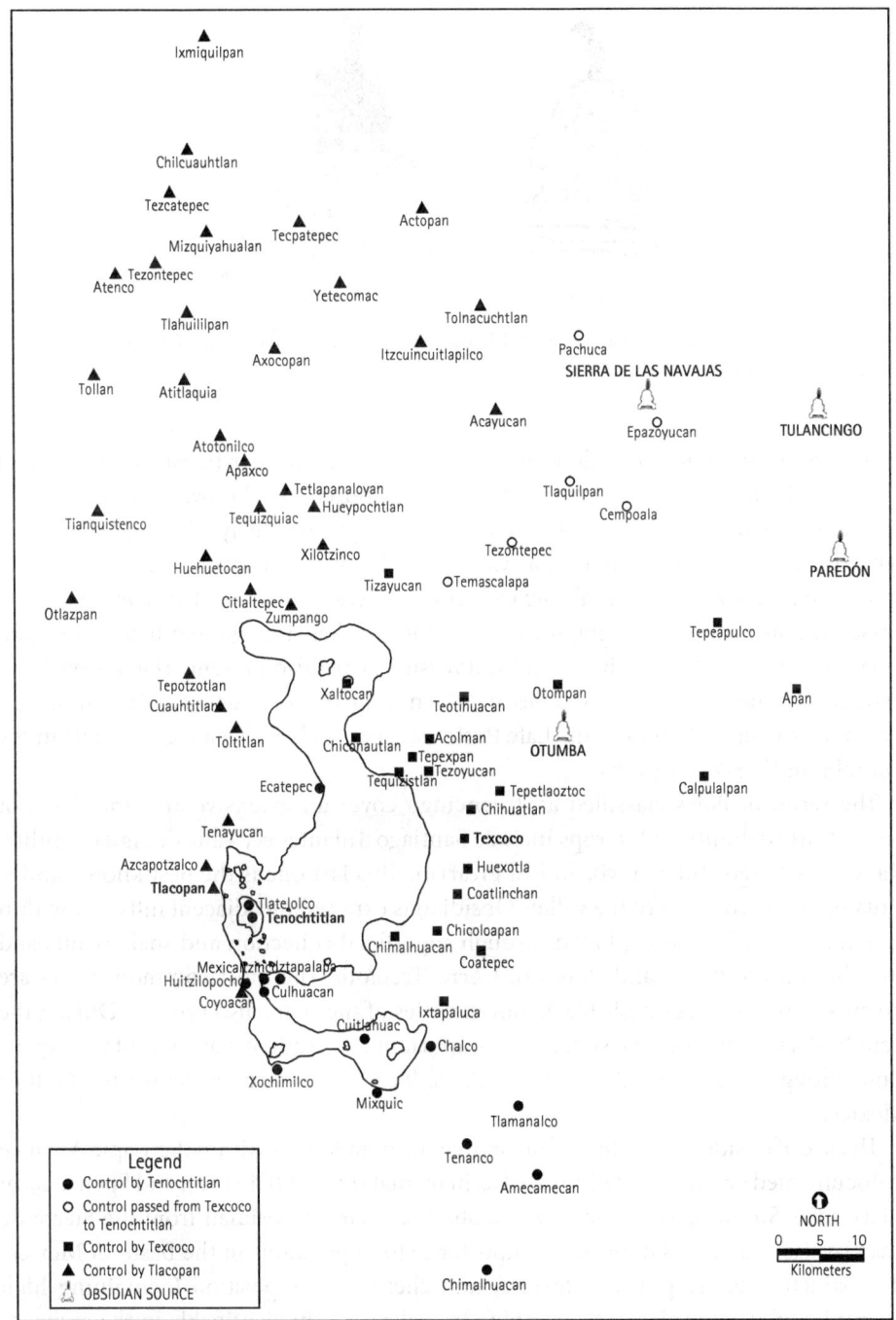

FIGURE 22.1 Central Mexican obsidian sources and select population centers controlled by Triple Alliance cities. Note the corridor of sites leading to Sierra de Las Navajas that moved to Tenochca control. Drawn by authors.

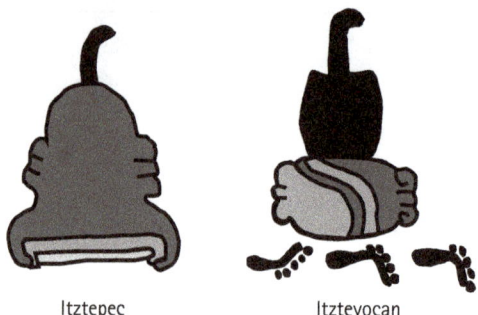

FIGURE 22.2 Toponymns associated with obsidian (redrawn from the *Codex Mendocino*). Drawn by authors.

A series of discontinuous flows extending across the border between the states of Puebla and Hidalgo are classified as the Paredón source, also known as Tecocomulco. Nodules eroded from stream walls are visible over approximately 2 km^2 of locales designated Paredón, Tres Cabezas, and Coyoaco. The obsidian can be among the most transparent or glassy of central Mexico's gray sources, though it often contains white crystalline inclusions. It is gray-black in color and has a beige hue if held to light. Small quantities of brownish-red and yellowish-red are also present. The material was extracted by the collection of nodules and the mining of blocks using shallow trenches. Paredón artifacts dating from the Late Postclassic period have been recovered from the Otumba and Texcoco regions.

The series of flows classified as Tulancingo cover an extensive area that has not been clearly delimited. Outcrops include Santiago Tulantepec, Valle de Agua Bendita, Rancho Tenango, Tulancingo, and El Pizarrín. This last one is the best known and is situated in the corridor of the valley. Obsidian is exposed on adjacent hills and within streambeds, and it was exploited through superficial collection and shallow pits and trenches on the flanks and slopes of Cerro Tecolote. The most common colors are greenish-brown and grayish-black, but varieties of meca are also present. During the Late Postclassic period, the source was important for Triple Alliance military expansion through Tulancingo due to its strategic location on a route toward the Gulf of Mexico.

The use of obsidian from these four sources by populations within the Triple Alliance is documented archaeologically as well as in textual sources (Charlton and Spence 1982; Clark 1989; Smith 1990; Spence 1985; Taube 1991). Green obsidian from the Sierra de Las Navajas source was of primary importance to populations in the Basin of Mexico. Its distinctive coloring, glassy texture, and chemical composition (containing high quantities of alkaline elements) combine to make it easily identifiable in the archaeological record. The Mexica held the material in high esteem and classified it as *tolteca itzli* ("Toltec obsidian") in the *Florentine Codex* (Figure 22.3b). Varieties of gray obsidian are more difficult to distinguish visually, yet through chemical studies and comparisons with distributions of green obsidian it is apparent that materials from the Otumba,

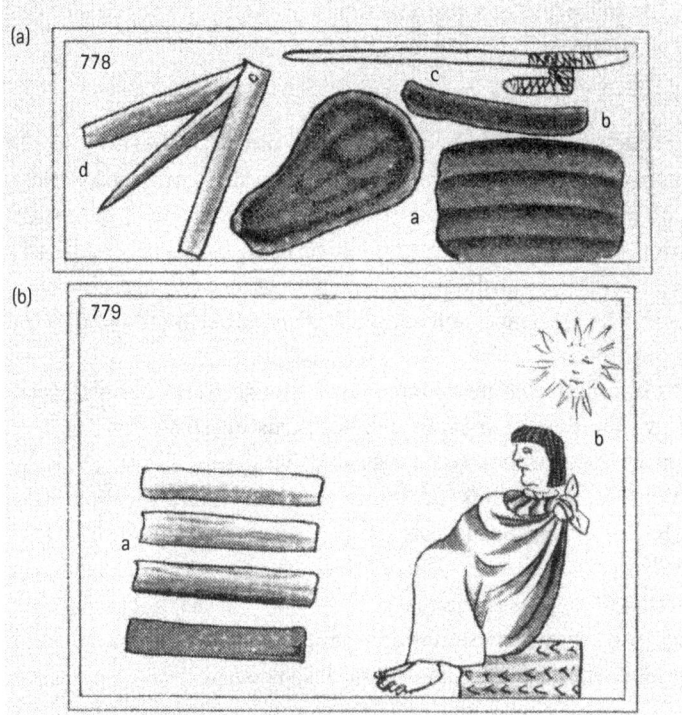

FIGURE 22.3 Depictions from the *Florentine Codex* of (a) obsidian scraper, blade, blade-core, crutch for removing prismatic blades, and a European razor for comparison with the blades; (b) classes of obsidian recognized by the Aztecs including green *tolteca itzli*. (Sahagún 1963:778–779).

Paredón, and Tulancingo sources possessed smaller, more regionally based distribution systems than did material from the Navajas source.

Obsidian Artifacts, Arms, and Symbols

The most common obsidian implements in Aztec society were prismatic blades, knives, scrapers, perforators, punches, and gravers, and these were all essential to many domestic tasks and forms of craft production (Figure 22.3a). Domestic activities using obsidian tools included food preparation, *aguamiel* (*Agave* spp. sap) extraction, and the working of organic materials including wood, vegetal fibers, bone, and hides. Since obsidian is a brittle material, the initially sharp edges of such tools dull quickly. Although the edges of certain tools could be reworked, the demand by Aztec households for new tools would have been immense and continuous. Obsidian implements were also of great importance to the military, as weapons, and for ritual and healing purposes.

We define the following groups of obsidian artifacts on the basis of their functional aspects and use contexts:

- Basic productive activities (domestic, agricultural, collection, hunting)—diverse types of knives, blades, scrapers, gravers, perforators, projectile points.
- Forms of artisanal production (basketry, feather-working, carpentry, lapidary production, decorative metallurgy)—diverse types of knives and scrapers, blades, gravers, perforators, polishers.
- Ritual activities (sacrifice, autosacrifice, dismembering, flaying)—pointed knives, gravers, perforators.
- Weapons in military contexts (arsenals, outposts, forts): knives, blades, projectile points (arrow and dart), spear points (for thrusting spears).
- Weapons in ritual contexts (offerings)—knives, projectile points, spear points.
- Adornments and symbols of status (burials, offerings, domestic contexts)—earspools, lip-plugs, beads, pendants, clubs, scepters, mirrors worn as part military dress.
- Ritual receptacles—vases and urns.
- Sculpture and effigy representations—anthropomorphic masks, animals, scepters and scepter elements in the shape of rattlesnakes.

This diversity of obsidian artifacts and use contexts demonstrate the pervasiveness of the material within Aztec society. It is probable that utilitarian central Mexican obsidian artifacts, particularly green ones, and Aztec III–IV pottery represents the spatially most widely distributed archaeological materials within the Mesoamerican culture region, extending both within and beyond the boundaries of the Triple Alliance. The extensive distribution of green obsidian from Sierra de Las Navajas and the final categories of finished implements in the previous list also speak to the highly symbolic role obsidian could play in Mesoamerican society (see also Levine and Carballo 2014). Within Aztec thought, obsidian was conceived as having formed where lightning penetrated the earth, constituting a union of the terrestrial and celestial. Several deities express manifestations of obsidian, including Itzli (obsidian personified), Itztlacoliuhqui ("Curved Obsidian Knife"), Itzpapalotl ("Obsidian Butterfly"), and Tezcatlipoca ("Smoking [obsidian] Mirror"). Based on archaeological remains discovered at the Navajas source, Ehecatl-Quetzalcoatl was also associated with obsidian, creating a divine dualism with his counterpart Tezcatlipoca. These deities cover a suite of attributes in Aztec ideology connected to war, sacrifice, justice, creativity, divination, and power (Garibay 1996). Much of the archaeological information on symbolic uses of obsidian comes from ritual deposits within the ceremonial centers of the twin cities of Tenochtitlan and Tlatelolco (Athie 2001; González Rul 1979; López Luján 1993).

Economic and Political Organization of Obsidian Industries Viewed from Sierra de Las Navajas

Since the Aztec exploitation of the Sierra de Las Navajas source has been explored in detail (Pastrana 1998), we have an informed appreciation for how the material progressed from mine to market, temple, or armory at this most important of quarries. The Aztecs practiced deep mining activities at the source, and they produced artifact preforms and macro-cores on the premises, which could be easily packaged for transporting to consumers who primarily lived 70 km away or more. Finished tools were also produced at the quarry, both for export and for use in other production activities that occurred on site. State institutions appear to have been involved in many of the production activities at Sierra de Las Navajas, but this is especially the case with the production of weaponry and ritual or status items.

Triple Alliance exploitation at the Navajas source is identifiable through its upper stratigraphic positioning; by certain technological attributes; and by Aztec ceramics in the mines, workshops, and campsites that have been mapped and excavated. Because there is not yet a clear distinction of political groups at the quarry based on ceramics, we refer to Triple Alliance exploitation rather than Tenochca, Acolhua, or Tepanec. Nevertheless, on the basis of documentary sources we are able to tease apart how different Aztec populations were involved in mining, production, and exchange. Individuals from the communities of Epazoyuca and Cempoala provided labor, provisions, and tools for mining and production operations; those from Temazcalapa, Pahuca, Tezontepec, Tetlystaca, and Tecpilpan possibly participated in transport operations, given their geographic locations (Pastrana 1998). These seven communities originally were under the domain of Texcoco, but the sixteenth-century *Relaciones Geográficas* note that they passed a least partially to Tenochtitlan beginning with the reign of Izcoatl (ca. 1428) when the Triple Alliance was formed, likely to assure the city ample access through the route between the quarry and the Basin of Mexico (Acuña 1985) (see Figure 22.1).

Aztec mining operations at the Navajas source can be observed at approximately 500 mines. These possess an average depth of approximately 18 m and appear to have been mined by groups of miners who worked 12 to 16 mines simultaneously. In between these mine clusters are the remains of one or two large workshops containing large quantities of debitage, with the camps the miners resided in located nearby (Figure 22.4). Each mine possessed an average of three access points (adits), and, given spatial limitations, approximately three miners would have fit in each adit. Our hypothetical team of nine miners associated with each mine would have worked with a support team to raise excavated deposits to the surface, which we estimate as five additional personnel. With the

FIGURE 22.4 Camp structures and workshop deposits in the Sierra de Las Navajas. Photo by Alejandro Pastrana.

additional estimate of 10 knappers working on the surface per group of miners, total group populations may have been in the vicinity of 200 individuals. Accounting for the presence of a couple of mining groups at the quarry simultaneously, with additional individuals involved in provisioning and transshipment, a maximum estimate of some 700 individuals at Sierra de Las Navajas during the height of mining season, when agricultural duties were less, seems reasonable (see also Charlton 1978; Charlton and Spence 1982; Cruz 1994; Healan 1986; Pastrana 1998; Smith 1990).

Blocks, clasts, and nodules weighing dozens of kilograms were extracted from the mines and worked at the surface workshops located near camps. Analysis of production debitage at the workshops permits the identification of discrete loci associated with particular production sequences. These include areas of cortex removal during the production of blade macro-cores and flake macro-cores, the latter commonly used to produce blanks for the later reduction into bifaces, scrapers, and other tools. Such blanks were reduced into tool preforms in other areas, and this was often the stage at which materials were shipped to consumers for final reduction at permanent settlements. However, later reduction stages are also observable at other loci, especially within or just outside of the structures of camp sites. Here, knappers produced finished utilitarian tools, weapons, and ritual items.

Demand for obsidian implements from the Navajas source would have been high from all sectors of Aztec society, but it is in weaponry production that evidence of the strongest institutional involvement on the part of the Triple Alliance is observable. The presence of spatial clustering between varied types of preforms at the quarry—for utilitarian tools, weapons, and ritual items—suggests that these artifact classes moved through different distribution channels, with the latter two the most likely to have been institutionally organized. Yet changes in exchange networks in utilitarian tools associated with imperial expansion are also discernible at places such as Xaltocan, where Millhauser (2005) detects an overall decrease in access to obsidian coupled with a relative increase in the percentage of material from the Navajas source following the subjugation of this altepetl by the Triple Alliance.

Prismatic blades were one of the major products of the quarry and had the widest distribution throughout Mesoamerica. Blade macro-cores would have often been exported from the quarry to workshops in settlements at which their platforms were pecked and ground to facilitate blade removal (Healan 2009). Finished blades were multifunctional tools that were used in all social contexts, from commoner households to state armories. The use of prismatic blades as insets within wooden weapons such as the *macuahuitl* broad-sword (Figure 22.5) and the *tepoztopilli* thrusting-spear is well documented (Hassig 1988). Wooden portions of these weapons were often made of cedar, and rows of blades, typically of Sierra de Las Navajas obsidian, were inserted using organic adhesives to provide sharp edges.

Biface preforms were excavated from several campsites at the quarry, where they were stored before circulating to other workshops for finishing into projectile points

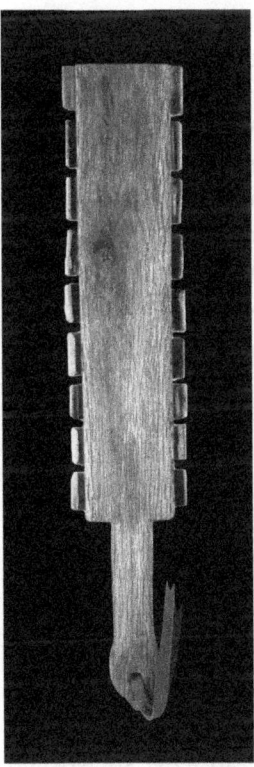

FIGURE 22.5 Replica *machuahuitl* (obsidian-lined broad-sword). Photo by Alejandro Pastrana.

and knives. Points from offerings within the ceremonial precincts of Tenochtitlan and Tlatelolco exhibit a high degree of morphological uniformity and production technique, which allows for comparison with the artifacts from the quarry and suggest the following size grades for projectile points: dart points (5–7 cm), arrowheads (2–5 cm), and miniature, ceremonial points (<2 cm). Stylistically the points grade into types designated Texcoco A and Texcoco B (García Cook 1982).

Ritual and status items have also been excavated from the Navajas camps, including large pieces exceeding 50 cm in length. Cylindrical pieces weighing several kilograms likely represent early stages in the elaboration of scepters and clubs at the larger end and vases and urns at the smaller end. Large tabular pieces exhibit properties of early stages of ceremonial bifaces, such as the emblematic scepter of Quetzalcoatl called the *xonecuilli*. Finally, circular and discoidal pieces likely represent early stages in the elaboration of mirrors, disc inlays intended for sculptures, or earspools, moving downward by size. Ritual and status items such as mirrors, lapidary items, and certain types of scepters were ground and polished following earlier bifacial reduction.

To date, the only workshops with documented evidence of the later stages of the production of ritual and status items are at Otumba, which contains evidence of the specialized production of beads, earspools, and labrets using obsidian from both the Navajas and Otumba sources (Charlton et al. 1991; Otis Charlton 1993). Yet ethnohistoric and archaeological evidence from elsewhere allows us to classify a range of types of workshops located within settlements. These include palace (*tecalli*) and neighborhood (*calpolli*) workshops specializing in the production of prismatic blades, beads, earspools, and labrets, particularly made from green obsidian; tecalli and calpolli school (*calmecac* and *telpochcalli*) workshops specialized in the production of projectile points, spear points, knives, and other weapons; and calpolli and market workshops specializing in the production of utilitarian items such as prismatic blades, knives, and scrapers.

An examination of the economic and political organization of obsidian provides an appreciation of the diversity in professions and statuses within Aztec society, viewed through a single material class. Certain forms of production, particularly those relating to military and religious institutions, can be traced as staged sequences of extraction, manufacturing, and distribution from the mines to the armories, palaces, and temples of major settlements. In the case of utilitarian goods, such as blades and scrapers, and many polished adornments, such as earspools and labrets, the economy was driven more by commercial forces and the activities of independent and state-associated (*pochteca*) merchants (Garibay 1995), who varied in their relative prestige and prosperity based on the products they fashioned and exchanged.

Conclusion

Obsidian was a critical material to Aztec society and the various groups—Tenochca, Acolhua, Tepanec—represented therein. The political and religious institutions of the

Triple Alliance had vested interests in regular access to certain obsidian implements, particularly for weapons to arm imperial soldiers and ritual and status items that were deposited as sacred offerings or used to signal status. Commoners within Aztec society would have also exerted strong demand for utilitarian items used in domestic contexts.

The Sierra de Las Navajas quarry demonstrates the staged sequences of raw material extraction, preform and artifact manufacturing, and long-distance transport to consumers. Miners, knappers, suppliers of provisions, and merchants would have all be part of these operations, swelling the population of the quarry into the hundreds during intensive periods of extraction and production. This system built on earlier traditions, and central Mexicans were constructing camps at the quarry since Teotihuacan. Yet the approximately two centuries of Aztec occupation at Sierra de Las Navajas witnessed the development of technological innovations, such as increased grinding and polishing in the production of ritual and status items. The system supplied millions of consumers with utilitarian tools, weapons, ceremonial implements, and adornments, representing the most intensive period of obsidian exploitation in Mesoamerican history and perhaps in the history of the ancient world.

References Cited

Acuña, René (editor)
1985 *Relaciones geográficas del siglo XVI: México II*. Serie Antropológica 70, Vol. I. Instituto de Investigaciones Antropológicas, Universidad Nacional Autónoma de México, Mexico City.

Athie, Ivonne
2001 La obsidiana del Templo Mayor de Tenochtitlan. Unpublished licenciate thesis, Escuela Nacional de Antropología e Historia, Mexico City.

Charlton, Thomas H.
1978 Teotihuacan, Tepeapulco and Obsidian Exploitation. *Science* 200:1227–1236.

Charlton, Thomas H., Deborah L. Nichols, and Cynthia Otis Charlton
1991 Aztec Craft Production and Specialization: Archaeological Evidence from the City-State of Otumba, Mexico. *World Archaeology* 23:98–114.

Charlton, Thomas H., and Michael W. Spence
1982 Obsidian Exploitation and Civilization in the Basin of Mexico. *Anthropology* 6(1–2):7–86.

Clark, John E.
1989 Obsidian the Primary Mesoamerican Sources. In *La obsidiana en Mesoamérica*, edited by Margarita Gaxiola G. and John E. Clark, pp. 299–330. Colección Científica 176. Instituto Nacional de Antropología e Historia, Mexico City.

Cruz, Rafael
1994 *Análisis arqueológico del yacimiento de obsidiana de Sierra de Las Navajas, Hgo*. Colección Científica 281. Instituto Nacional de Antropología e Historia, Mexico City.

García Cook, Angel
1982 *Análisis tipológico de artefactos*. Colección Científica 116. Instituto Nacional de Antropología e Historia, Mexico City.

Garibay K., Angel Ma.
1995 *Vida Económica de Tenochtitlan*, Vol. 1: *Pochtecayotl (arte de traficar)*. Universidad Nacional Autónoma de México, Mexico City.

1996 *Teogonía e historia de los mexicanos.* Sepan Cuantos No. 37. Editorial Porrúa, Mexico City.
González Rul, Francisco
1979 *La lítica de Tlatelolco.* Colección Científica 74. Instituto Nacional de Antropología e Historia, Mexico City.
Hassig, Ross
1988 *Aztec Warfare.* University of Oklahoma, Norman.
Healan, Dan M.
1986 Technological and Nontechnological Aspects of an Obsidian Workshop Excavated at Tula, Hidalgo. In *Economic Aspects of Prehispanic Highland Mexico,* edited by Barry L. Isaac, pp.133–152. Research in Economic Anthropology, Supplement 2. JAI Press, Greenwich, CT.
2009 Ground Platform Preparation and the "Banalization" of the Prismatic Blade in Western Mesoamerica. *Ancient Mesoamérica* 20:103–111.
Levine, Marc N., and David M. Carballo (editors)
2014 *Obsidian Reflections: Symbolic Dimensions of Obsidian in Mesoamerica.* University Press of Colorado, Boulder.
López Lujan, Leonardo
1993 *Las ofrendas del Templo Mayor de Tenochtitlan.* Instituto Nacional de Antropología e Historia, Mexico City.
Millhauser, John
2005 Classic and Postclassic Chipped Stone at Xaltocan. In *Production and Power at Postclassic Xaltocan,* edited by Elizabeth M. Brumfiel, pp. 267–317. Instituto Nacional de Antropología e Historia, Mexico City and University of Pittsburgh, Pittsburgh, PA.
Otis Charlton, Cynthia
1993 Obsidian as Jewelry: Lapidary Production in Aztec Otumba, Mexico. *Ancient Mesoamerica* 4:231–243.
Parry, William J.
2001 Production and Exchange of Obsidian Tools in Late Aztec City-States. *Ancient Mesoamerica* 12:101–111.
Pastrana, Alejandro
1998 *La explotación azteca de la obsidiana de la Sierra de las Navajas.* Colección Científica 383. Instituto Nacional de Antropología e Historia, Mexico City.
2007 *La distribución de obsidiana de la Triple Alianza en la Cuenca de México.* Colección Científica 519. Instituto Nacional de Antropología e Historia, Mexico City.
Pastrana, Alejandro, and Ivonne Athie
2001a Obsidian. In *The Oxford Encyclopaedia of Mesoamerican Cultures,* Vol. 2, edited by David Carrasco, pp. 399–400. Oxford University Press, Oxford.
2001b Obsidian: Properties and Sources. In *The Archaeology of Ancient Mexico and Central America: An Encyclopaedia,* edited by Susan Toby Evans and David L. Webster, pp. 546–551. Garland, New York.
Pastrana, Alejandro, and Silvia Domínguez
2009 Cambios en la estrategia de la explotación de la obsidiana de Pachuca: Teotihuacan, Tula y La Triple Alianza. *Ancient Mesoamerica* 20:129–148.
Sahagún, Fray Bernardino de
1963 *Florentine Codex: Book 11, Earthly Things, Number 14, Part XII.* Translated and edited by Arthur J. O. Anderson and Charles E. Dibble. University of Utah Press, Salt Lake City.
Smith, Michael E.
1990 Long Distance Trade under the Aztec Empire. *Ancient Mesoamerica* 1:153–169.

Spence, Michael W.
1985 Specialized Production in "Rural" Aztec Society: Obsidian Workshops of the Teotihuacan Valley. In *Contributions to the Archaeological and Ethnohistory of Greater Mesoamerica*, edited by William J. Folan, pp. 76–125. Southern Illinois University Press, Carbondale.

Taube, Karl A.
1991 Obsidian Polyhedral Cores and Prismatic Blades in the Writing and Art of Ancient Mexico. *Ancient Mesoamerica* 2:61–70.

CHAPTER 23

AZTEC LAPIDARIES

CYNTHIA L. OTIS CHARLTON
AND ALEJANDRO PASTRANA

BY the Late Postclassic (A.D. 1350–1519), the lapidary art of stone polishing was well established in Mesoamerican cultural traditions. The manipulation, beyond the purely utilitarian, of various stones, crystals, and glass of perceived high value into jewelry and other elite objects had its birth with small polished beads sometime in the Archaic period before 2000 B.C. Techniques for some of the lapidary processes appear well established by 1400 B.C., when lapidary objects such as jade jewelry appear in Olmec sites. Once established, lapidary techniques appear to have been retained and enhanced through subsequent cultures in the Mesoamerican region, and lapidary objects were an important and integral part of politics, religion, and the economy by the time of the Late Postclassic Aztec Triple Alliance.

LAPIDARY MATERIALS

Modern science classifies rocks as volcanic, sedimentary, or metamorphic by the types of minerals from which they are formed. Mineral properties depend on the chemical elements that constitute them and the geometric arrangements they exhibit. Metamorphic rocks are formed by transformation of volcanic or sedimentary rocks under great pressure and high temperatures so that their original primary crystals recrystallize to form such minerals as serpentine/jadeite and nephrite from volcanic rocks and greenish slate and marble from sedimentary and limestone rocks. It is these dense and hard surfaces that take a shiny smooth polish that make them prime lapidary material. Other materials used by lapidary artisans included quartz or rock crystal, onyx and travertine, amber, turquoise and bloodstone, as well as some such semiprecious stone as opal, rubies, and amethyst (Sahagún 1959:9:80–82). Glasses, like obsidian, are neither rocks nor minerals. Their main elements are atoms of silica and aluminum that do not have a geometric structure due to disarray from the rapid cooling of the lava where they originated. They take a high polish, giving them great value as lapidary material as well.

Aztec concepts of the materials used in lapidary work were quite different and were a mixture of properties, powers, and religious magic along an inseparable continuum of attributes connecting survival, fertility, war, sacrifice, protection, healing, creation and divination. Stone properties were considered as varied as brightness, purity, staining, attraction, sweating, density, transparency, halo, glow, and the qualities of heat or cold. Shell was also considered a form of rock (Sahagún 1963:11:201–231).

Objects produced by Aztec lapidaries included receptacles for ceremonial use; bowls and cups; small sculptures; plaques and mosaics; symbolic objects such as masks, scepters, mirrors, idols and nose pendants; and pectorals, such as the insignia of Tezcatlipoca, the god called Smoking Mirror. Jewelry included beads of various forms, round, gadrooned, tubular and a form in the shape of a duck head, and earspools and lip-plugs (Serra Puche and Solís Olguin 1994). Rock crystal as well as alabaster, marble, and other materials were fashioned into receptacles for ceremonial purposes. Rock crystal was also often used for personal adornment in the form of beads, lip-plugs, and earspools.

Of the materials worked in lapidary production, most, other than obsidian, came from areas at some distance from the Triple Alliance centers in the Basin of Mexico. Primary obsidian sources used by the lapidaries such as the Sierra de Las Navajas, Otumba, Pizarrín, and Paredon sources near the Basin and others such as Zacualtipan at a somewhat greater distance were under the direct control of the Aztecs, making that raw material widely available. Other materials had to be imported and came in by trade or as tribute. Tribute regularly delivered from Aztec-controlled provinces included finished and partially finished objects. Finished objects might arrive as strings of jade or turquoise beads, or amber and rock crystal lip plugs (Berdan 1987:163–164, 1992). The most common lapidary objects, made in a wide variety of green stone, were spherical or semispherical beads called *chalchihuites*. Chalchihuitl, as a concept, related to purity, sacredness, and fertility. The beads arrived from a number of tribute provinces (Nuttall 1901; Thouvenot 1982).

Some materials came from great distances beyond Aztec-controlled provinces. True jade/jadeite appears to have come only from a source near Rio Motagua, Guatemala (Bishop et al. 1993), while turquoise probably came from the southwestern United States. Both arrived by trade with Aztec tribute provinces that then paid it on (Berdan 1987:10). Amber came from at least three different sources in Chiapas, outside the Aztec Empire and beyond its direct trading sphere. Whether by trade or market, the amber made its way to three different Aztec tribute provinces in the area in whose tribute to Tenochtitlan it was then included (Berdan 1987:171). Opal came from Totonacapan in the far northeast of the Aztec Empire. Our understanding of how all materials arrived at the lapidary workshops is obviously incomplete. Only four types of fine stone are mentioned as tribute, for instance, but a dozen others were worked in the urban workshops (Berdan 1987:178).

Beyond the raw material used for lapidary objects, material for working the lapidary objects are also essential. Many of these such as chert for drills, planar basalt lajas for grinding and polishing, and perishable materials such as cording, bone, antler, hard wood, deer skin, and cane were available relatively nearby; some of the sophisticated array of granular sanding materials used in grinding and particularly in polishing were not. Durán (1994:417–424) describes two foreign provinces, Quetzaltepec and Tototepec, which possessed a type of polishing sand wanted by the Tenochtitlán lapidaries. The provinces refused the offer of Aztec trade and killed all the Aztec envoys, precipitating a war with the Aztecs that they lost, causing them to become tribute provinces. Presumably the polishing sand became available.

Trade, Tribute, and Lapidary Workshops

After the establishment of the Triple Alliance, the rulers sought out the most highly skilled craftsmen in the luxury trades from throughout their domain and settled them into wards or calpolli where they were supported by the ruling household and could work full-time at their profession (Hicks 1982, 1987:96). Lapidaries in particular were said to have been brought to Tenochtitlan from Xochimilco (Sahagún 1959:9:80).

Lapidaries produced for palace, for treasury, and for market (Hicks 1987:97). For the palace, lapidary goods fed the need for opulent display and support of an ever-increasing family of nobility and bureaucracy. Sent to the royal treasurer, lapidary objects were distributed according to any royal order. Some went to the priests or were commissioned specifically for honoring the gods and ceremonies (Berdan 1987:161). The rededication of an expanded Templo Mayor occasioned a great many impressive lapidary objects for the offerings (Serra Puche and Solís Olguin 1994).

A fair proportion of lapidary production went to the urban market, where it could be obtained by those needing tribute or gifting objects or was a medium of exchange. Pochteca traders not only carried valuable materials from the emperor or state to outlying areas to trade for products and exotic goods including lapidary material, but also traded their own materials, some of which they obtained in the marketplace for such commodities as jade and green stone (Hicks 1987:98–99; Sahagún 1959:9:18–19). According to Sahagún (1959:9:17–18), they carried many other things such as gold jewelry as well as crystal earspools for trade with foreign nobility, but earspools only of obsidian for the commoners, an indication, in this case perhaps, of relative values of the two commodities.

Lapidary Works

Aztec lapidary objects are most commonly found associated with caches and offerings in ritual spaces. By far the primary, or at least most abundant, lapidary objects found are jade or green stone, rock crystal, and obsidian. All have a host of embedded meaning beyond their basic identity that incorporates their origin, color, association with particular gods and ceremonies, and perceived physical attributes or qualities, some of which we do not fully understand (Heyden 1987, 1988). All of these attributes are further enhanced by transformation into the objects of lapidary production. The most elaborate of these are found in offerings from the Templo Mayor at Tenochtitlán, as revealed by extensive excavations. Unfortunately, the excavations have not been extensive enough to locate any lapidary workshops or the kind of workshops of luxury goods said to be congregated into wards or *calpolli* compounds (Hicks 1982:241–243; Ixtlilxochitl 1965:1.317; Sahagún 1959:9:83–97). The differing techniques necessary for production of objects made from these three materials probably suggests they were produced in separate workshops specific to each material type.

Green Stone Working

Jade and "green stone," of which there are many varieties, has been deeply esteemed throughout time in Mesoamerican in general and was deeply embedded in Aztec culture by the Late Postclassic (Pastrana 1991). While much jade and green stone arrived as already finished or partly finished tribute objects, there were doubtless workshops that specialized in green stone production. While no Aztec green stone workshops have been found, there is a great deal of information available from green stone workshops at Teotihuacan that is comparable and relevant (Gazzola 2005; Gómez Chávez and Gazzola 2011). Experimental work has suggested techniques used in the workshops based on the tools and debitage recovered (Velázquez Cabrera 2008a, 2008b). The nature of green stone requires a unique method of cutting, achieved by the use of a sawing technique with abrasives and string, a band of deerskin, or a flat object of something such as wood, and water. It may also be drilled with a drill or a hollow tube and incised with an abrasive and other hard stone. Tools found in the workshops include hammer stones, tools of bone, sharpening stones for the tools, and chert drills. Bits of fiber, microdebitage, and abrasive are found in cuts in the stone. Though there are no Aztec green stone workshops yet found, techniques for working stone, once developed, appear to be retained over time and cultural space.

Rock Crystal Working

Techniques for working rock crystal would differ from those used for green stone or obsidian due to its crystalline nature and impurities and planar imperfections in the original material. Though rock crystal lip plugs and earspools are mentioned as objects of tribute and part of pochteca trade materials carried out from the core of the empire, even projecting that a workshop producing rock crystal jewelry might also be working with other crystalline semiprecious stones, demand might not be so great as to keep such workshops functioning full-time unless they also produced something else.

OBSIDIAN WORKING

Obsidian lapidary workshops were probably the most numerous in that they produced not only large-scale ritual objects but also common beads, lip plugs, and earspools more often worn by lesser nobility or even some commoners and readily exchanged in the marketplace. Obsidian as a primary material was also commonly available. Some techniques from core/blade manufacture could be modified for use in obsidian lapidary working. In fact, large prepared cores for use in making ceremonial obsidian scepters and mirrors such as those found in offerings at the Templo Mayor have been found at the Sierra de Las Navajas quarries (Pastrana 2007:70–72) (Figures 23.1–23.3). One particular workshop area at Las Navajas seems to be dedicated to preparation of preforms for ritual objects (Pastrana 2007:71). Finishing work was not carried out at the quarries, however (Pastrana 2007:72), and the finishing workshops have not been located. Since volcanic glass has no internal structure, it takes well to chipping and flaking, except in places with crystalline intrusions, imperfections, and planar banding or impurities. Cutting, as

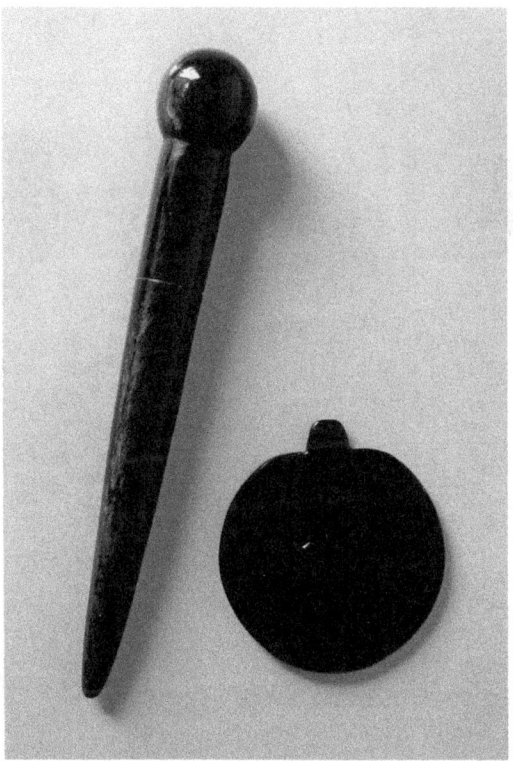

FIGURE 23.1 Reproduction of an obsidian ritual scepter and mirror. Objects and photo by Alejandro Pastrana.

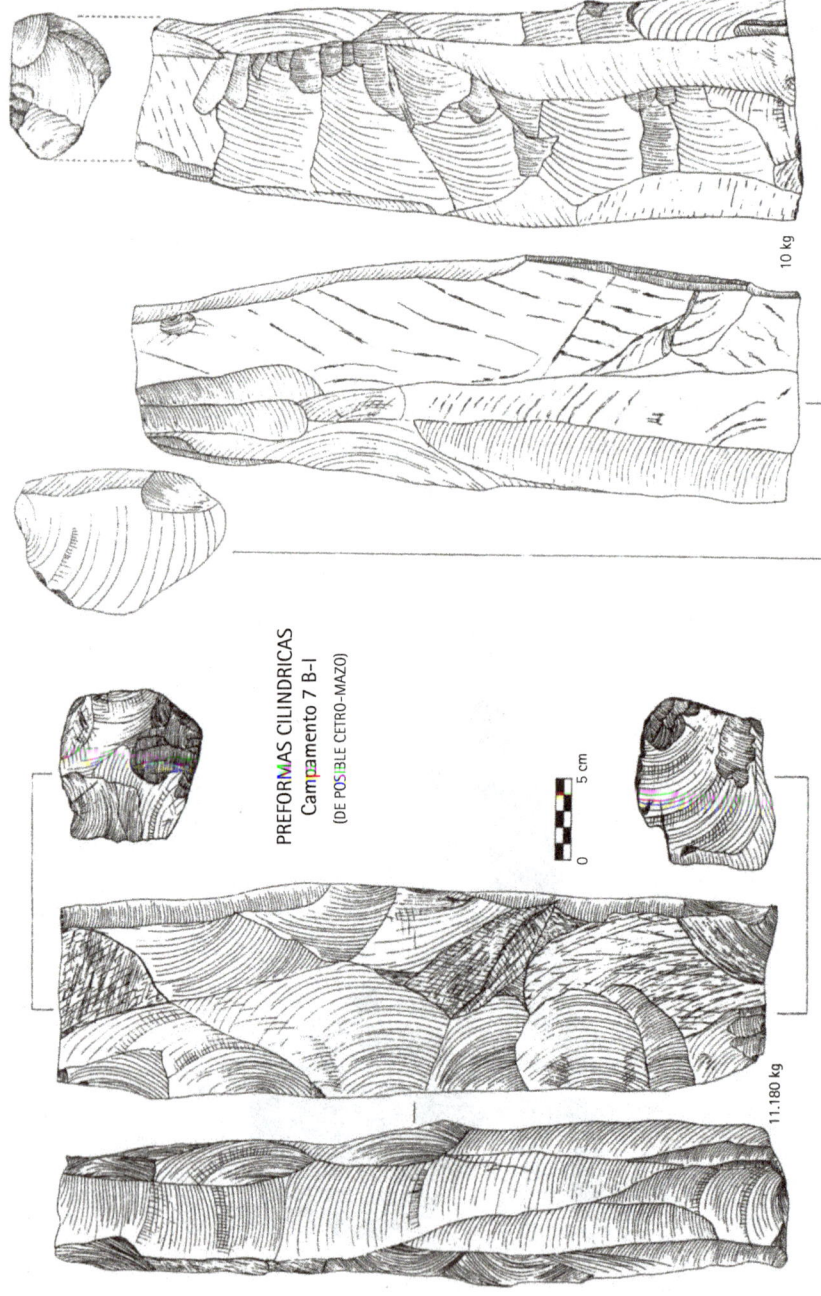

FIGURE 23.2 Preforms for ritual scepters from a Sierra de las Navajas workshop. Drawing by Alejandro Pastrana.

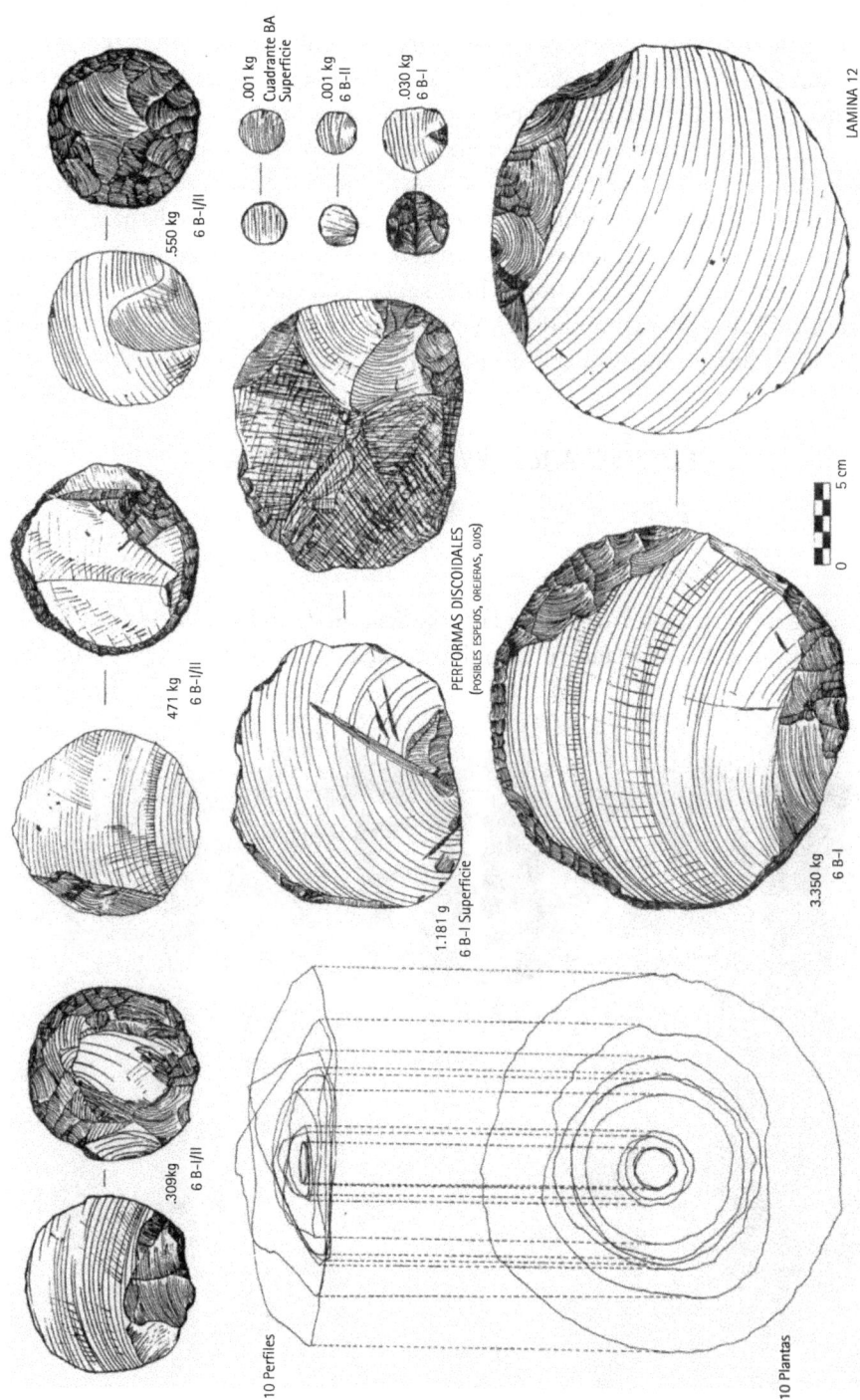

FIGURE 23-3 Preforms for obsidian mirrors from a Sierra de las Navajas workshop. Drawing by Alejandro Pastrana.

such, is unnecessary, since percussion can be used to split the raw material. Grinding and polishing, however, have not been well understood but have been the subject of a number of early suggestions (McGuire 1894; Mirambell 1968; Orchard 1927; Rau 1868; Thomsen and Thomsen 1970, 1971). Experimental studies at the Templo Mayor have shed much additional light on the processes (Athié Islas 2006; Melgar Tísoc 2011; Melgar Tísoc and Solís Ciriaco 2009). One result of the Melgar study is the finding that offerings produced from A.D. 1375–1427 showed the use of a wide variety of tools, probably indicating production at a number of separate workshops during that era. Objects produced after the establishment of the Triple Alliance (A.D. 1469–1521) showed strong tool standardization, which supports the concept of specialized artisans in a collective workshop area (Melgar Tísoc 2011:221; Melgar Tísoc and Solís Ciriaco 2009:130), probably near the palaces as suggested.

Lapidary Workshops at the Otumba City-State

The only Late Posclassic Aztec lapidary workshops found and excavated to date come from the Aztec city-state of Otumba, located on the eastern edge of the Basin

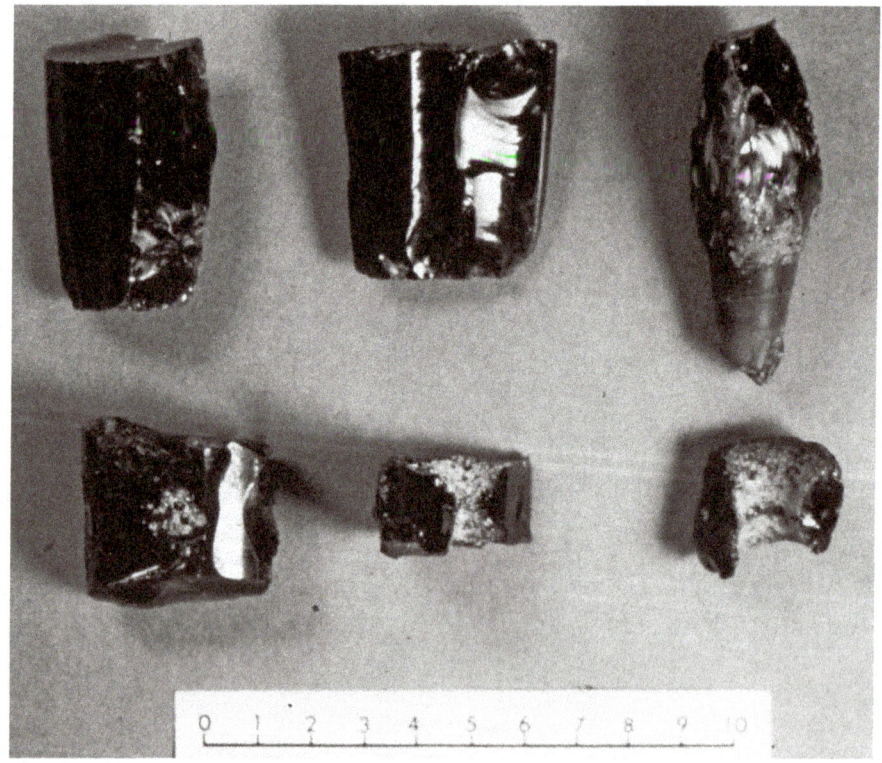

FIGURE 23.4 Unfinished obsidian lapidary objects and tool from the Otumba lapidary workshop. Photo by Cynthia Otis Charlton.

of Mexico and subject to the Triple Alliance city of Texcoco (Charlton et al. 1991; Otis Charlton et al. 1993). The objects produced in the excavated workshop were primarily obsidian jewelry, that is, round and duck head beads and sequins, lip plugs, and two varieties of earspools (Otis Charlton 1993, 1994). The workshop contrasted with the presumed Templo Mayor workshops in that the beads as well as other ornaments are smaller than those from the city and the variety and scale of production is smaller as well. The workshops were small, scattered households with no obvious physical connection to the elite core of the site. No sculptures or ritual objects were produced there, and the raw material for the pieces came not from preforms brought in from the source quarries but instead from recycled exhausted obsidian cores from the Otumba core/blade workshops (Figure 23.4). Every stage of the production process is visible in the debitage from the workshop. Tools for lapidary working included drills of obsidian and chert (Figure 23.5) and flat basalt lajas whose sides and edges had been used for grinding and polishing and sharpening other tools. Tools of bone and antler were also present. Particular grinding and polishing compounds have not been determined. Otumba's lapidary production may have been partly used for tribute and gifting locally as well as for the local and regional market located there. Pochteca traders residing at Otumba may also have accessed the products from the workshops either directly, through the local nobility, or through that local market.

FIGURE 23.5 Chert tools and artifacts from the Otumba lapidary workshop. Photo by Cynthia Otis Charlton.

Aztec lapidary production was only a small part of the ongoing culture and economy of the Triple Alliance Empire. Seen in the context of the far reach of its use and influence, however, lapidary production imparts a great deal of informational impact for the relative scarcity of its presence.

REFERENCES CITED

Athié Islas, Ivonne
2006 La obsidiana del Templo Mayor de Tenochtitlan. In *Arqueología e historia del Centro de México. Homenaje a Eduardo Matos Moctezuma*, edited by Leonardo López Luján, David Carrasco, and Lourdes Cué, pp. 539–553. Instituto Nacional de Antropología e Historia, Mexico City.

Berdan, Frances F.
1987 The Economics of Aztec Luxury Trade and Tribute. In *The Aztec Templo Mayor*, edited by Elizabeth Hill Boone, pp. 161–184. Dumbarton Oaks Research and Library Collection, Washington, DC.
1992 The Imperial Tribute Roll of the Codex Mendoza. In *The Codex Mendoza*, edited by Frances F. Berdan and Patricia Reiff Anawalt, pp. 55–79. University of California Press, Berkeley.

Bishop, Ronald L., Edward V. Sayre, and Joan Mishara
1993 Compositional and Structural Characterization of Maya and Costa Rican Jadeites. In *Pre-Columbian Jade: New Geological and Cultural Interpretations*, edited by Frederick W. Lange, pp. 30–59. University of Utah Press, Salt Lake City.

Charlton, Cynthia L. Otis
1993 Obsidian as Jewelry: Lapidary Production in Aztec Otumba, Mexico. *Ancient Mesoamerica* 4:231–243.
1994 Plebeians and Patricians: Contrasting Patterns of Production and Distribution in the Aztec Figurine and Lapidary Industries. In *Economies and Polities in the Aztec Realm*, edited by Mary G. Hodge and Michael E. Smith, pp. 195–220. Studies on Culture and Society 6, Institute for Mesoamerican Studies, State University of New York, Albany, and University of Texas Press, Austin.

Charlton, Cynthia L. Otis, Thomas H. Charlton, and Deborah L. Nichols
1993 Aztec Household-Based Craft Production: Archaeological Evidence from the City-State of Otumba, Mexico. In *Prehispanic Domestic Units in Western Mesoamerica: Studies in Household, Compound, and Residence*, edited by Robert S. Santley and Kenneth. G. Hirth, pp. 147–172. CRC Press, Boca Raton, FL.

Charlton, Thomas H., Deborah L. Nichols, and Cynthia L. Otis Charlton
1991 Craft Specialization with the Aztec City-State of Otumba, Mexico: The Archaeological Evidence. *World Archaeology* 23:98–114.

Durán, Diego
1994 *The History of the Indies of New Spain*. Translated by Doris Heyden. University of Oklahoma Press, Norman.

Gazzola, Julie
2005 La producción lapidaria en Teotihuacan: estudio de las actividades productivas en los talleres de un conjunto habitacional. In *Memoria de la Tercera Mesa Redonda de Teotihuacan, arquitectura y urbanismo: pasado y presente de los espacios en Teotihuacan*, edited by Maria

Elena Ruiz G. and Jesús Torres P., pp. 841–878. Instituto Nacional de Antropología e Historia, Mexico City.

Gómez Chávez, Sergio, and Julie Gazzola

2011 La producción lapidaria y malacológica en la mítica Tollan-Teotihuacan. In *Producción artesanal y especializada en Mesoamérica: áreas de actividad y procesos productivos*, edited by Linda R. Manzanilla and Kenneth G. Hirth, pp. 87–130. Instituto Nacional de Antropología e Historia, Universidad Nacional Autónoma de México, Mexico City.

Hicks, Frederic

1982 Tetzcoco in the Early 16th Century: The State, the City, and the Calpolli. *American Ethnologist* 9:230–249.

1987 First Steps toward a Market-Integrated Economy in Aztec Mexico. In *Early State Dynamics*, edited by H. J. M. Clausen and P. van de Velde, pp. 91–107. Studies in Human Society 2. E. J. Brill, Leiden.

Heyden, Doris

1987 Magia Negra: Texcatlipoca y obsidiana. In *Historia de la religión en Mesoamérica y áreas afines: I Coloquio*, edited by Barbra Dahlgren, pp. 83–85. Universidad Nacional Autónoma de México, Mexico City.

1988 Black Magic: Obsidian in Symbolism and Metaphor. In *Smoke and Mist: Studies in Memory of Thelma D. Sullivan*, edited by J. Kathryn Josserand and Karin Dakin, pp. 217–236. BAR International Series 402. BAR, Oxford.

Ixtlilxóchitl, Fernando de Alva

1965 *Obras históricas*. 2 vols. Editora Nacional, Mexico City.

McGuire, J. D.

1894 A Study of the Primitive Methods of Drilling. In *Report of the United States National Museum*, pp. 623–756. Smithsonian Institution, Washington, DC.

Melgar Tísoc, Emiliano Ricardo

2011 Tradiciones tecnológicas en la lapidaria de obsidiana del Templo Mayor de Tenochtitlan. In *Producción artesanal y especializada en Mesoamérica: areas de actividad y procesos productivos*, edited by Linda R. Manzanilla and Kenneth G. Hirth, pp. 207–226. Universidad Nacional Autónoma de México, Instituto de Investigaciones Antropológicas, Mexico City.

Melgar Tísoc, Emiliano Ricardo, and Reyna Beatriz Solís Ciriaco

2009 Caracterización de huellas de manufactura en objetos lapidarios de obsidiana del Templo Mayor de Tenochtitlan. *Arqueología* 42:118–134.

Mirambell, Lorena

1968 *Técnicas Lapidarias Prehispánicas*. Serie Investigaciones 14. Instituto Nacional de Antropología e Historia, Mexico.

Nuttall, Zelia

1901 Chalchihuitl in Ancient Mexico. *American Anthropologist* 3:227–238.

Orchard, William C.

1927 Obsidian Ear Ornaments. *Indian Notes* 4(3):216–221.

Pastrana, Alejandro

1991 Sobre el jade y las rocas verdes en el México prehispánico. In *Homenaje al Dr. Julio Cesar Olivé Negrete*, edited by Carlos Serrano Sánchez, pp. 195–208. Universidad Nacional Autónoma de México and Instituto Nacional de Antropología e Historia, Mexico City.

2007 *La distribución de la obsidiana de la Triple Alianza en la Cuenca de México*. Colección Científica, Serie Arqueología, Universidad Nacional Autónoma de México, Mexico City.

Rau, Charles
1868 Drilling in Stone without Metal. In *Annual Report of the Board of Regents of the Smithsonian Institution*, pp. 392–400. Government Printing Office, Washington, DC.

Sahagún, Fray Bernardino de
1950–1982 *Florentine Codex: General History of the Things of New Spain*. Edited and translated by A. J. O. Anderson and D. E. Dibble. Monograph No. 14, Parts 1–13. School of American Research, Santa Fe, NM, and the University of Utah, Salt Lake City.

Serra Puche, Mari Carmen, and Felipe Solís Olguin
1994 *Cristales y obsidiana prehispanicos*. Siglo Vientiuno Editores, S.A. de C.V., Mexico City.

Thomsen, E. G., and H. H. Thomsen
1970 Pre-Columbian Obsidian Earspools: An Investigation of Possible Manufacturing Methods. *Contributions of the University of California Archaeological Research Facility* 8:41–53.
1971 Litho-Mechanics and Archaeology. *Contributions of the University of California Archaeological Research Facility* 12:51–62.

Thouvenot, Marc
1982 *Chalchihuite, le Jade Chez les Aztéques*. Institut d'Ethnologie, Musée de l'Homme, Paris.

Velázquez Cabrera, Roberto
2008a Experimentos sobre cortes finos de rocas. Borrador consultivo, November 17, Teotihuacan, Mexico.
2008b Experimentos sobre cortes lapidarios finos como los de algunas rocas de La Ventilla, Teotihuacan. Borrador consultivo, November 12, Teotihuacan, Mexico.

CHAPTER 24

POTTERY AND THE POTTER'S CRAFT IN THE AZTEC HEARTLAND

LEAH D. MINC

CERAMICS are one of the few media permitting a realistic synthesis of chronological and economic information (Peacock 1982:1). That is, their stylistic and technical attributes form the backbone of relative chronologies, but these attributes can also reflect variability in skill, standardization, and labor investment—dimensions that can be brought to bear on questions concerning the organization and context of craft production as well as patterns of consumption. In addition, ceramics lend themselves to geochemical studies of provenance, enabling us to track their centers of production and patterns of dispersion with fair accuracy, contributing to studies of market exchange. In Aztec studies, ceramics have played a critical role in all these areas, shedding light on questions of craft specialization, market system development, and regional economic integration, as well as change through time.

AZTEC CERAMIC TYPOLOGY AND CHRONOLOGY

Ceramic typology in the Valley of Mexico has largely focused on the analysis of decorated ceramics (generally serving vessels) owing to their much greater potential for displaying chronological and regional stylistic variation. Classification of these ceramics follows a hierarchical system of (a) wares, (b) types, and (c) decorative variants and subvariants (where applicable).

Wares are distinguished on the basis of general uniformity of paste and modal surface color and finish (Parsons 1966). Three major wares are recognized: (a) Orange ware, characterized by a buff to natural paste and burnished but unslipped orange surface; (b) Red ware (also called *guinda*), identified by its red-slipped surfaces; and (c) Polychrome, distinguished by a basal white or orange slip overlain with multicolor designs executed in orange, red, brown, and/or black paint (Whalen and Parsons 1982:440–455; Hodge and Minc 1991).

Within each ware, *types* are distinguished according to basic decorative traditions, including the presence and type of paint, incising, or specific motifs. The predominant types of Orange ware are Plain Orange and the various Black-on-Orange (Black/Orange) types bearing black painted designs. Common Red ware types include Black/Red and Black-and-White/Red vessels, on which the basal red slip is overlain with black or black-and-white painted motifs, respectively, while Black/Red-Incised bears incised motifs in addition to those applied in black paint (Minc 1994). Polychrome types (e.g., Chalco, Cholula, Aztec, and Xochimilco/Churubusco) are distinguished based on surface treatment (glossy or matte), basal slip color, and organization of design field (Hodge 2008; Hodge and Minc 1991).

Aztec ceramic types are often combined with vessel forms to create single *type-shape* units. For example, the Plain Orange type encompasses the major utilitarian forms such as griddles (*comales*) and jars (*ollas*), while the most common Black/Orange vessel forms are upright-rim bowls and basins bearing exterior decoration, along with plates, tripod-support dishes, and *molcajetes* (grater bowls with slashed bases for grinding chile peppers) with interior painted designs. The most prevalent Red ware forms include small bowls, biconical goblets (often called *copas*), and plates, although larger forms such as basins are also found. Polychrome decoration is most frequently found on bowl, dish, and plate forms.

Finally, *decorative variants* are yet a more detailed category within each type-shape class. Variants are defined on the basis of specific decorative patterns such as consistencies in the choice and execution of design motifs and in the overall layout of the design (see Hodge and Minc 1991; Franco and Peterson 1957; Noguera 1930; Parsons 1966).

The Black/Orange Ceramic Sequence

While type-shape classes and stylistic variants have been defined for all three Aztec wares, the Black/Orange types form the core of Aztec ceramic typology and chronology. Based on early stratigraphic and stylistic analyses, Black/Orange ceramics were initially divided into four sequential phases (I, II, III, and IV) and assigned the phase names of Culhuacan, Tenayuca, Tenochtitlan, and Tlatelolco, respectively, after type sites of the same names where these ceramics were first encountered in great abundance (Boas 1912; Brenner 1931; Franco 1945, 1947; Franco and Peterson 1957; Gamio 1913; Griffin and Espejo 1947, 1950; Noguera 1935; O'Neill 1956–1957, 1962; Parsons 1966; Vaillant 1938, 1941). Aztec I and II (Culhuacan and Tenayuca phase) Black/Orange ceramics were attributed to the Early Aztec period (ca. A.D. 1100–1350 [Sanders et al. 1979]), while Aztec III (Tenochtitlan phase) ceramics were associated with the Late Aztec period (A.D. 1350–1520). Aztec IV (Tlatelolco phase) Black/Orange ceramics coincided with the early Spanish Colonial era. More recent analyses have focused on identifying stylistic variation within these "phases" and understanding their chronological and spatial implications.

Briefly, *Aztec I (Culhuacan) Black/Orange* was first identified as a distinctive type based on the thickness of vessel walls, poor firing, and wide-line painted decoration, including motifs of flowers and day signs (Griffin and Espejo 1947, 1950) (Figure 24.1). Bowls with stamped bases are common, as are dishes with solid, cylindrical, or effigy supports. A reanalysis of Aztec I ceramics from the southern valley revealed at least three distinctive stylistic traditions (Chalco, Mixquic, and Culhuacan) with different geographic distributions and chemical compositions (Crider 2011; Minc et al. 1994; Séjourné 1970, 1983). The three may also differ in time, with Mixquic representing the earliest Aztec ceramic tradition in the valley.

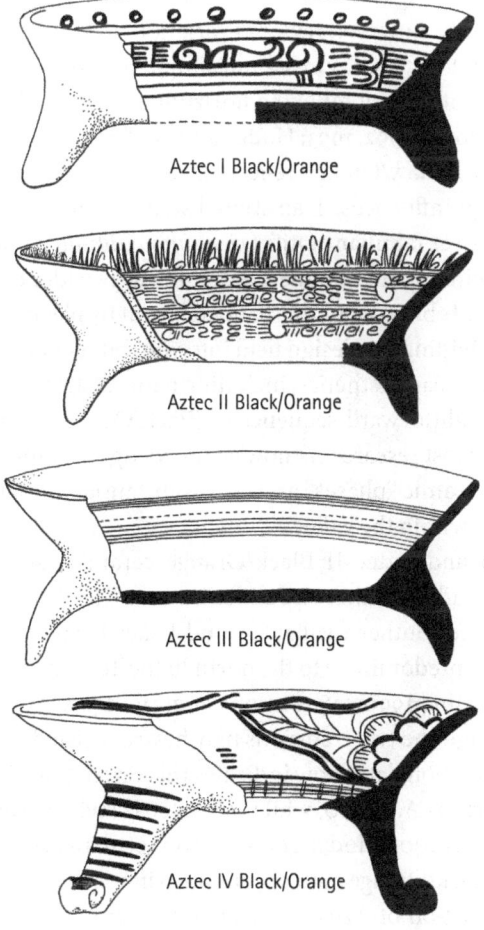

FIGURE 24.1 Aztec Black/Orange types. Prepared by author.

Aztec II (Tenayuca) Black/Orange ceramics were defined by the grass-like *zacate* element at the top of the painted panel encircling the upper vessel wall (Franco 1945; Parsons 1966:161–162). Decoration below the *zacate* element occurs in two major styles: Calligraphic designs consist of curvilinear elements such as S-curves, loops, and squiggles that resemble writing (Brenner 1931:68), while Geometric designs incorporate circle, stylized feather, and scroll motifs set off by a background of closely spaced horizontal lines (Griffin and Espejo 1950:35). Again, these distinctive styles are linked to different centers of production, with Calligraphic Black/Orange preferentially produced in the Culhuacan region and the Geometric style produced in the Texcoco region (Minc et al. 1994).

Aztec III (Tenochtitlán) Black/Orange is distinguished by a greatly simplified decorative band consisting of thin, parallel lines (or solid lines interspersed with dots or dashes) applied to the upper vessel wall with a multipoint paintbrush, which gives the appearance of standardized mass production. Decorative motifs below this band are minimal and simplified in comparison with earlier periods and include stylized scrolls, spirals, concentric circles, zig-zags, and stylized feathers. In spite of the apparent stylistic and technical uniformity, however, regional variation occurs in the choice of the motif; certain motifs (such as concentric circles and simple spirals) were clearly favored in the southern basin, while others (notably the horizontal bar motif) were more popular in the Texcoco region (Hodge 1992, 1993; Hodge and Neff 2005:Table 13.1).

Aztec IV (Tlatelolco) Black/Orange reflects a continuation of Aztec sensibilities but in contact with foreign influences. Transitional stylistic variants feature the traditional band of parallel lines over familiar motifs (*xicaliuhqui, ilhuitl*, concentric circles, or spirals), but the lines encircling the rim may be significantly wider or alternate narrow and wide lines. Later variants break with this banded layout by placing motifs in isolation on the vessel wall or by dividing the design field into vertical sections; they may also feature motifs that reflect European aesthetics, including naturalistic birds and flowers.

The seemingly straightforward sequence of Black/Orange ceramics continues to be revised and debated. Most researchers now acknowledge a significant degree of temporal overlap between ceramic "phases" as well as substantial spatial variation in the timing of ceramic change within the valley.

Currently, Aztec I and Aztec II Black/Orange ceramics are viewed as representing regional stylistic traditions that also differ in time. The Aztec I Black/Orange types are largely found in the southern valley around Lakes Chalco and Xochimilco, while Aztec II Black/Orange predominate to the north in the Texcoco and Teotihuacan survey regions (Hodge and Minc 1990:428; Parsons et al. 1982:345–351; Whalen and Parsons 1982:437–438). Although the two traditions may have coexisted for a century or more, a robust series of radiocarbon dates now indicates that Aztec I Black/Orange began much earlier, possibly as early as A.D. 900, while the Aztec II stylistic variants did not emerge until the 1100s (Brumfiel 2005; Hodge 2008; Parsons et al. 1996).

Similarly, Aztec II Black/Orange pottery continued in use through the 1300s and, in turn, overlapped the introduction of Aztec III-style pottery in ca. A.D. 1350 (Hare and Smith 1996; Nichols and Charlton 1996). In the Valley of Mexico, continuity in Aztec III Black/

Orange pottery throughout the Late Aztec period continues to frustrate attempts to distinguish periods before and after the emergence of the Triple Alliance; however, a detailed analysis of type frequencies now provides this level of chronological resolution for western Morelos, to the south of the basin (Hare and Smith 1996; Smith and Doershuk 1991).

Finally, while Aztec IV Black/Orange styles bearing European motifs were clearly a post-Conquest development, more traditional Aztec wares also persisted in the archaeological sequence until the mid-seventeenth century but with a marked decline in diversity and abundance (Charlton 1968, 1972, 1996). That is, the ceramic data do not suggest "any direct, obvious, immediate, or striking ceramic acculturation on the part of the Aztecs during the 16th century and the first half of the 17th century" (Charlton 1976:521), making it difficult to isolate the post-Conquest time period.

CHRONOLOGICAL PLACEMENT AND REGIONAL VARIATION OF OTHER DECORATED WARES

In contrast with the Black/Orange types, Red wares and Polychromes have merited relatively little attention. Red wares, in particular, have defied clear-cut chronological placement, in part because vessel form and paste change over time, while some decorative motifs show a disconcerting degree of continuity from Early Aztec into Late Aztec times. The predominant Early Aztec Red ware vessel is the simple rounded bowl with a somewhat gritty, well-oxidized buff to red-brown paste. During the Late Aztec, a distinct "Late Profile" bowl form emerged, characterized by thin, out-sloping walls, fine paste, and a pronounced dark grey to black medial core, although it did not completely replace the earlier form (Figure 24.2). Seriations of Red wares that consider vessel form and paste in addition to design motifs have now provided a basic framework for understanding chronological variation (Parsons 1966; Minc 1994), and valley-wide studies of stylistic variants have highlighted regional differences in their manufacture and distribution (Minc 1994, 2006, 2009). Similarly, detailed stratigraphic analyses at Chalco have recently clarified chronological placement of the Chalco polychrome types, while trace-element analyses are still sorting out the diversity of sources producing polychrome wares in central Mexico (Hodge 2008; Neff and Hodge 2008; Neff et al. 1994).

AZTEC CERAMIC TECHNOLOGY

Given the amount of archaeological survey and excavation undertaken in the Valley of Mexico, it is somewhat surprising that data on pottery production are so scarce. No production facility or workshop has yet been identified for the dominant Orange or Red

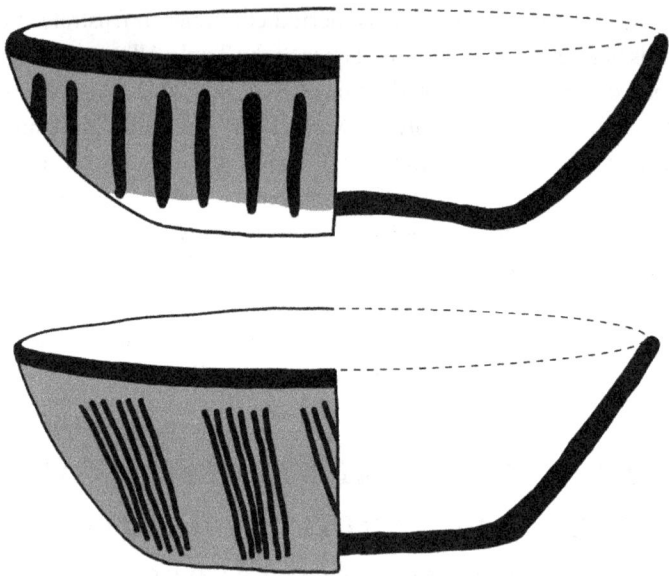

FIGURE 24.2 Early Aztec and Late Aztec Red ware bowls. Prepared by author.

ware types, although production contexts for several minor wares are known from the archaeological record (including the fabric-marked pottery used in the production of salt; see Millhauser this volume), along with evidence for manufacturing figurines and other fired clays objects (Charlton et al. 2008; Nichols 2013). We are therefore heavily reliant on early historic descriptions of pottery-making and on analyses of the vessels themselves to reconstruct the potter's craft.

Raw Material Selection

According to the *Florentine Codex*, the primary clay used in pottery production was *teçoquitl* (lit. "rock clay"), described as a firm but sticky, dark-to-blackish clay that becomes hard when fired (Sahagún 1950–1982, Book 11:252, 256). The color suggests a high organic content, such as would be found in a lacustrine setting. Clays were tempered with cattail fiber (*el floxel de las espandañas*) and prepared by trampling and kneading to produce a uniform body. Indeed, the artist of the *Florentine Codex* places both the *olla* maker and the *comal* maker in a marshy setting, in which cattail plants and bundles of cattail reeds figure prominently in the foreground. Elsewhere, however, Fray Bernardino de Sahagún (1950–1982, Book 11:257) records three different words for prepared clays, each associated with a different vessel form: *contlalli* (derived from *comitl* [olla] and *tlalli* [earth]), *comallilli* (for making *comales* or griddles), and *caxtlalli* (for making bowls). This distinction may indicate that somewhat different paste recipes were employed for different vessel forms, although all three began with the same ingredients (*teçoquitl* and cattail fiber).

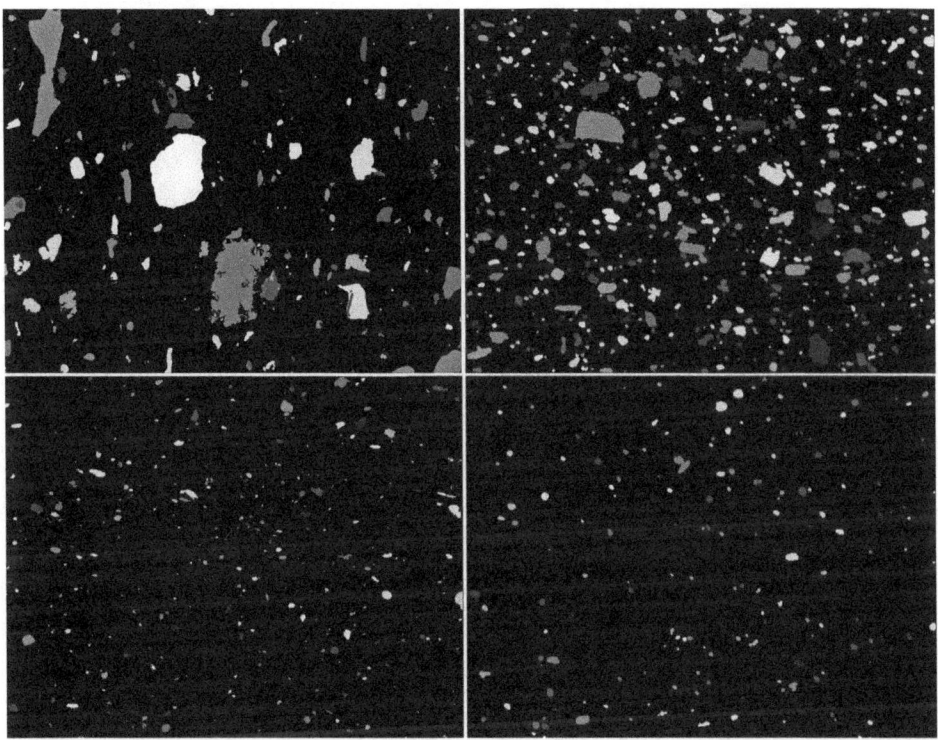

FIGURE 24.3 Comparison of Early Aztec (upper) and Late Aztec (lower) ceramic pastes from Orange ware (left) and Red ware (right). False color image of petrographic thin-sections showing size distribution and frequency of inclusions. Prepared by author.

This general picture gains support from Aztec vessels dating to the Late Aztec period. That is, pastes of both Orange and Red wares are quite fine (consistent with naturally levigated lake clays), and the occasional cast of fiber temper can be seen (Figure 24.3, lower). Further, the very dark gray to black cores found in many sherds (especially Late Profile Red ware bowls) suggest clays with a naturally high organic content. Earlier pottery, however, reveals that a broader range of clay resources were utilized. Pastes of Early Aztec Black/Orange and Red wares are substantially grittier, reflecting the use of some coarser upland (inland) clays (Figure 24.3, upper). The shift to finer paste textures through time indicates a significant change in ceramic technology or, more likely, the emergence of major centers of production in lakeside positions adjacent to fine-textured clays.

Vessel Forming and Finishing

Aztec vessels were hand-formed, probably through a combination of slab and hump-mold techniques (Branstetter-Hardesty 1978:40). In this process, the clay was first beaten into a thin slab and then draped over the base of an existing pot or mold and pressed or beaten into shape; the excess clay was then trimmed away (Foster 1955). Support for this interpretation comes from Sahagún (1950–1982) who describes the *comal* maker as one who "beats [the clay], flattens it, polishes it, smooths it" (Book 10:83), while the *caxtlalli* (bowl maker) declares "I make bowls. I make things with molds. I mold things" (Book 11:257). In our limited archaeological evidence on production, the use of molds was verified in the manufacture of fabric-marked vessels (Baños Ramos 1980; Talavera Barnard 1979) as well as simple bowls (Charlton et al. 2008).

Once formed, the surface was polished or burnished with a pebble or smooth stick. If a vessel was slipped, this step was essential to bond the slip to the vessel and create a glossy surface. Electron microprobe analysis confirms that red slips were produced with clays rich in iron oxide possibly derived from hematite (Figure 24.4), while white areas

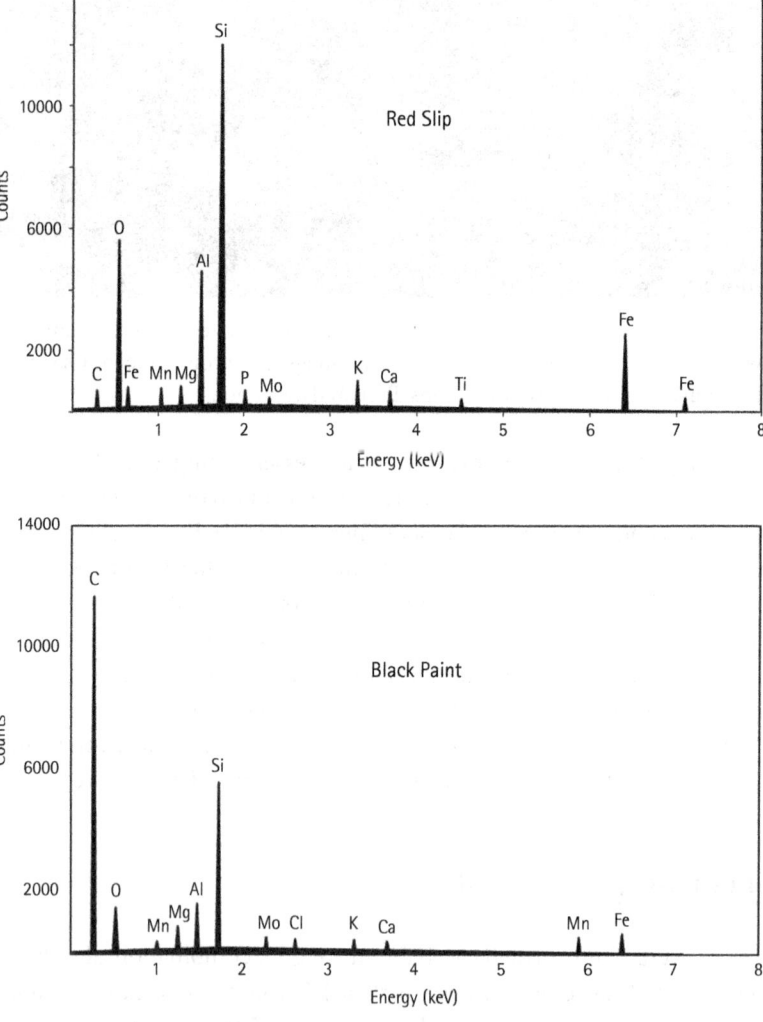

FIGURE 24.4 Electron microprobe analysis indicating the composition of pigments used on Aztec Red wares. Prepared by author.

of pigment are enriched in calcium, indicating a lime-derived substance (presumably mixed with organic binder), which adhered poorly to the surface. On multicolor Red wares and Polychromes, yellows and oranges were created by layering a thin wash of red slip over the white.

Black paint was more variable in composition and could be produced from both organic and mineral bases. On Aztec Red wares, black designs were worked in a carbon-based pigment enriched with manganese (Figure 24.4); when overfired, the carbon burned out, leaving a white "ghost" of the motif. Sahagún (1950–1982) records powdered lampblack as one substance used for making black lines (Book 11:242); graphite (possibly corresponding to Sahagún's "glistening black" *tezcatetlilli* [Book 11:243]) was an alternative black pigment utilized on Red wares and was especially popular on Late Aztec goblets bearing the *pulque* motif. In contrast, PIXE characterization of Aztec Black/Orange vessels revealed that black-painted designs on this ware were worked in a mineral (iron-manganese) paint (Crider 2013).

Firing

While no Aztec kilns are known archaeologically, Sahagún (1950–1982, Book 10:83, Book 11:257) refers twice to the potter's oven. The clay worker is shown tending a cylindrical kiln of stone or adobe, which appears to be a simple updraft kiln (Figure 24.5). Kilns of this design are known from prehispanic contexts elsewhere in

FIGURE 24.5 The clay worker (after Sahagún 1950–1982, Book 10:plate 136).

Mexico, and the technology clearly predates the Spanish Conquest (Winter and Payne 1976; Winter and Nardin 1982; Santley et al. 1989). Such kilns were roughly 1 to 1.5 m in diameter and less than 1 m in height, with an interior basal grate of adobes or large stones to support the pottery and separate it from the fuel. The kiln was loaded from the top and the contents covered with old *comales* or pieces of broken *ollas*; fuel was fed in through the front opening, which was oriented toward the prevailing wind to increase airflow. Given the absence of kiln features from the archaeological record of the Valley of Mexico, it is likely that open firing ("bonfire") or pit kilns were also commonly used. These relatively simple technologies—in which green pots are stacked and covered by a layer of brush or kindling and the whole set on fire (Foster 1955; Mindling 2010)—are still used by hundreds of potting communities across Mexico today; they are efficient and effective ways to fire pottery but may not leave a distinct or easily discernible record (Balkansky et al. 1997). Evidence that these technologies were employed by Aztec potters comes from the vessels themselves, in that the typical oxidized surfaces but gray-to-black paste cores observed in many Aztec pots are consistent with the relatively low firing temperatures (600° to 900°C) and a short burn period generated by open firing or pit kilns.

The Organization of Aztec Ceramic Production

The organization of Aztec pottery production can be examined along a number of key dimensions for assessing craft production (Brumfiel and Earle 1987; Costin 1991, 2000; Pool 1992). Briefly, *context* refers to locus of control over production activities and ownership of the resulting products (whether potters produce for an elite patron or operate independently to manufacture goods for exchange), while *distribution* characterizes the location of producers relative to each other and to the consumers they serve, at the community and regional spatial scales. The *scale* of craft production encompasses considerations of the size and output of productive enterprises, from small-scale individual or household activities to large-scale factories (Peacock 1982; Tosi 1984); in contrast, the *intensity* of production refers to the proportion of productive time devoted to that activity and ranges from part-time to full-time. Finally, *the production strategy* or *market niche* refers to the range and quality of goods produced to attract and meet consumer demand. Given that we have little direct evidence of production facilities, we are again beholden to the documentary record and to the vessels themselves to assess where Aztec potters fit on these dimensions.

The limited ethnohistoric data on ceramic production indicate that Aztec potters (like most craft producers) were commoners who worked as independent specialists to support themselves and their families by producing goods for exchange in the market (Berdan 2005:35). There is no evidence that elites attempted to directly control this utilitarian craft, although potters gave the products of their labor in tribute (Brumfiel 1998;

Hicks 1982; Hodge 1984:74; Scholes and Adams 1957:36–37). It also appears that potting was generally a male profession: the *Florentine Codex* consistently mentions or pictures individuals engaged in pottery production or related tasks as male, while the *Codice de los Alfareros* (1564) involved a legal suit brought by four male potters from Cuauhtitlán (Barlow 1951).

In the Early Colonial period, potters were distributed in both urban and rural settings, although the scale and intensity of production in these different contexts varied according to consumer demand. According to historic records, at least six cities in the Valley of Mexico were major producers of ceramics at the time of contact: Tenochtitlan-Tlatelolco, Texcoco, Cuauhtitlán, Azcapotzalco, Huitzilopochco, and Xochimilco (Barlow 1951; Branstetter-Hardesty 1978:26; Gibson 1964:350). In addition to the aforementioned, trace-element studies have now identified chemical signatures for Aztec pottery attributed to Chalco, the southern basin or Tenango area, Huexotla, Tepetlaoztoc, Xaltocan, and Otumba, suggesting that ceramic production was relatively widespread in precontact times (Charlton et al. 2008; Hodge et al. 1992, 1993; Minc 1994, 2009; Neff and Hodge 2008; Nichols et al. 2002; Nichols et al. 2009).

Within these urban centers, craft producers were concentrated in residential wards; *barrios* occupied by potters are specifically reported for Tenochtitlan-Tlatelolco (Branstetter-Hardesty 1978:26; Caso 1956:18–21), Cuauhtitlán (Barlow 1951), and Xochimilco (Gibson 1964:351). The organization of production within *barrios* is unknown. However, in the Cuauhtitlán legal case mentioned earlier, the four potters jointly presented their claim to the judge concerning a considerable debt owed for pottery produced (Barlow 1951), suggesting that small workshops employing several producers may have been the typical unit of production. While the high demand for pottery created by a relatively dense, urban population may have allowed some of these urban potters to produce full-time, it is unlikely that this led to a division of labor in the workplace. The *Florentine Codex* depicts the clay worker as participating in all steps from start to finish, even serving as a vender of the finished goods in the market place, hinting at small-scale operation in which roles were not specialized.

Archaeological evidence from the city-state center of Otumba confirms some aspects of this organizational model (Charlton et al. 2008; Nichols 2004, 2013). Survey and excavation within the residential neighborhoods revealed household-level production of multiple crafts, including fired clay objects. Much of the ceramic activity took place within the area designated as the "clay workers' barrio," a 10 to 12 ha area of clustered households engaged in the production of mold-made figurines, spindle whorls, earspools, musical instruments, and stamps, as well as simple domestic bowls of the Otumba Polished Tan type. Elsewhere in the site center, a second neighborhood of more elite households focused on the production of long-handled censers (known as the Texcoco Molded and Texcoco Filleted types).

In contrast with urban centers, the overall picture for rural pottery production is that of part-time craft specialists unevenly distributed among small communities. Our best documentary source on rural craft production is the *Matrícula de Huexotzinco*, a

1560 census listing the occupations of residents within the province east of the Valley of Mexico (Brumfiel 1987:Figure 9.2, 1998; Dyckerhoff and Prem 1976; Prem 1974). Among the 25 communities listed, 11 had pottery producers in residence, with an overall average of 1 potter for every 106 households. It is interesting to note that while the number of potters increased with the overall size of the community, the prevalence of potters decreased in communities with a high proportion of nobility, indicating that pottery was either a low-status occupation or an occupation banned from higher status communities perhaps due to the smoke produced.

Among the rural specialists listed in the Huexotzinco census, only 5 percent worked at their craft for their entire livelihood (Brumfiel 1987:104); the majority practiced subsistence agriculture for at least some portion of their support. Brumfiel (1998) has argued that continued reliance on agriculture—and the practice of passing both land and craft from father to son (Durán 1967 [1581]:II:477)—would tie craft producers to the land and create small clusters or kin groups of artisans engaged in the same craft. Archaeological evidence for other utilitarian crafts in the hinterlands confirm this general picture of part-time production within kin-based units (Nichols et al. 2000). However, the degree of participation in craft production activities appears to have varied regionally, either as a response to differences in agricultural productivity (Brumfiel 1976, 1980, 1983, 1986, 1987; Minc 1994) or as a function of distance from major urban markets (Charlton et al. 1991, 1993; Nichols 1994).

Finally, for both urban and rural settings, the degree of product specialization remains unclear. The *Florentine Codex* characterizes the clay worker or *çuquichiuhqui* as a "generalist," that is, a skilled artisan who made a large variety of ceramic forms (*ollas*, basins, braziers, bowls, ladles, and goblets), both slipped and plain earthenware (Sahagún 1950–1982, Book 10:42, 83). Certainly the diversity of objects produced within the Otumba clay workers' barrio suggests a generalist market strategy. In contrast, analyses of Aztec ceramics suggest that potters may have specialized production by ware. Archaeologists have long noted that the dominant decorated wares (Black/Orange and Red) feature distinct shape classes and ways of organizing the design field. Petrographic analyses also reveal differences in paste texture, while trace-element data indicate subtle contrasts in chemical composition between wares originating from the same region, suggestive of different clays or production loci or perhaps different clay preparation techniques (Figure 24.6). Firing technology also appears to differ by ware: Orange ware pastes tend to be well oxidized, while on Late Red wares at least, only the surface has been oxidized, leaving a dark core. If potters were indeed the generalists depicted by Sahagún, it is indeed odd that there is so little crossover in technique and style.

Further, we strongly suspect that production strategy and market niche varied by location, with urban potters producing more of the costly, high quality ceramics desired by elite customers. Texcoco was famous for its "fine" pottery (Berdan 1975:197–198; Durán 1967 [1581]:I.181–182), while the potters of Cuauhtitlán were known for their special red jars (*jarros colorados de Cuauhtitlán muy particulares*) (*Anales de Cuauhtitlán* 1945 [1975]; Gibson 1964:350–351). Trace-element analyses of Red wares confirm that

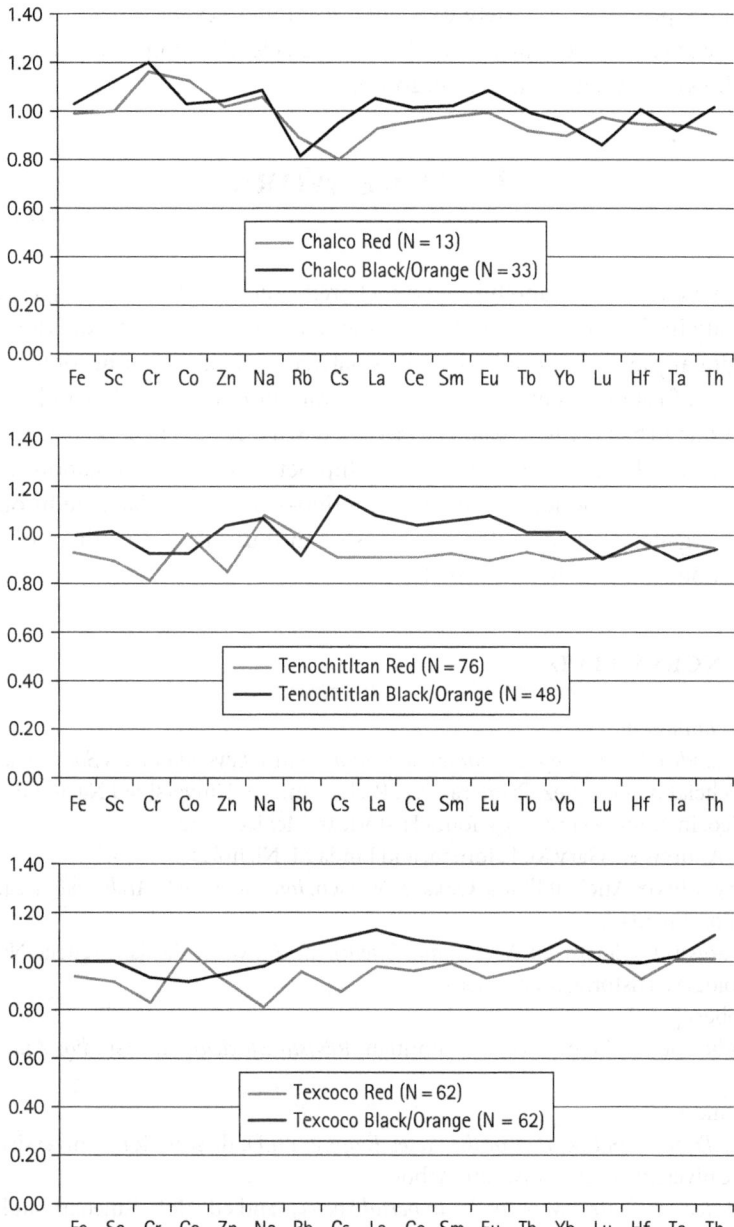

FIGURE 24.6 Comparison of normalized compositional profiles for Black/Orange and Red ware ceramics by production area (Chalco, Tenochtitlan-Ixtapalapa, and Texcoco). Note that Black/Orange ceramics are consistently higher in the rare earth elements.

urban centers produced a variety of highly decorated vessels, while rural areas surrounding Texcoco, for example, produced only vessels with simple designs (Minc 1994, 2009; Nichols et al. 2002; Nichols et al. 2009).

Future Work

The documentary sources and limited direct archaeological evidence suggest considerable diversity in the potter's craft. Aztec ceramic technology and production strategies varied regionally and temporally, as well as between urban and rural contexts. While a recent series of robust chemical analyses have monitored production and exchange of pottery among urban centers (e.g., Garraty 2013; Minc 2009; Nichols et al. 2002, 2009), rural pottery production—and the relationship between rural populations and urban centers in terms of production and consumption—are critical lacunae in our knowledge. Future generations of Aztec ceramicists can thus take heart: there is still much work to be done in clarifying these patterns.

References Cited

Anales de Cuauhtitlan
1945 [1975] *Códice Chimalpopoca: anales de Cuauhtitlan y Leyenda de los Soles.* Translated by Primo Feliciano Velázquez. Primera Serie Prehispánica 1. Universidad Nacional Autónoma de México, Instituto de Investigaciones Históricas. Mexico City.

Balkansky, Andrew K., Gary M. Feinman, and Linda M. Nicholas
1997 Pottery Kilns of Ancient Ejutla, Oaxaca, Mexico. *Journal of Field Archaeology* 24:139–160.

Baños Ramos, Eneida
1980 *La industria salinera en Xocotitlan, Cuenca de México.* Thesis, Escuela Nacional de Antropología e Historia, Mexico City.

Barlow, Robert E.
1951 El Códice de los Alfareros de Cuauhtitlan. *Revista Mexicana de Estudios Antropológicos* 12:5–8.

Berdan, Frances M. F.
1975 *Trade, Tribute, and Market in the Aztec Empire.* Ph.D. dissertation, University of Texas, Austin. University Microfilms, Ann Arbor.
2005 *The Aztecs of Central Mexico: An Imperial Society,* 2nd ed. Holt, Rinehart, and Winston, New York.

Boas, Franz
1912 *Album de Colecciones Arqueológicas Americanas.* Escuela Internacional de Arqueología y Etnología, Mexico City.

Branstetter-Hardesty, Barbara
1978 *Ceramics of Cerro Portezuelo, Mexico: An Industry in Transition.* Ph.D. dissertation, University of California, Los Angeles. University Microfilms, Ann Arbor.

Brenner, Anita
1931 *The Influence of Technique on the Decorative Style in the Domestic Pottery of Culhuacan.* Columbia University Contributions to Anthropology Vol. 13. Columbia University Press, New York.

Brumfiel, Elizabeth M. S.
1976 *Specialization and Exchange at the Late Postclassic (Aztec) Community of Huexotla, Mexico*. Ph.D. dissertation, University of Michigan. University Microfilms, Ann Arbor.
1980 Specialization, Market Exchange, and the Aztec State: A View from Huexotla. *Current Anthropology* 21:259–278.
1983 Aztec State Making: Ecology, Structure, and the Origin of the State. *American Anthropologist* 85(2):261–284.
1986 The Division of Labor at Xico: The Chipped Stone Industry. In *Economic Aspects of Prehispanic Highland Mexico*, edited by Barry L. Isaac, pp. 245–279. Research in Economic Anthropology Supplement 2. JAI Press, Greenwich, CT.
1987 Elite and Utilitarian Crafts in the Aztec State. In *Specialization, Exchange, and Complex Societies*, edited by Elizabeth M. Brumfiel and Timothy K. Earle, pp. 102–118. Cambridge University Press, New York.
1998 The Multiple Identities of Aztec Craft Specialists. *Archeological Papers of the American Anthropological Association* 8(1):145–152.
2005 Ceramic Chronology at Xaltocan. In *Production and Power at Postclassic Xaltocan*, edited by Elizabeth M. Brumfiel. University of Pittsburgh Department of Anthropology, Pittsburgh, and Instituto Nacional de Antropología e Historia, Mexico City.

Brumfiel, Elizabeth M., and Timothy K. Earle
1987 Specialization, Exchange, and Complex Societies: An Introduction. In *Specialization, Exchange, and Complex Societies*, edited by Elizabeth M. Brumfiel and Timothy K. Earle, pp. 1–9. Cambridge University Press, Cambridge, UK.

Caso, Alfonso
1956 Los Barrios Antiguos de Tenochtitlan y Tlatelolco. *Memorias de la Academia Mexicana de la Historia* 15:7–63.

Charlton, Thomas H.
1968 Post-Conquest Aztec Ceramics: Implications for Archaeological Interpretation. *Florida Anthropologist* 21:96–101.
1972 *Post-Conquest Developments in the Teotihuacán Valley, Mexico: Part I, Excavations*. University of Iowa, Iowa City.
1976 Contemporary Central Mexico Ceramics: A View from the Past. *Man* (n.s.) 11:517–525.
1996 Early Colonial Period Ceramics: Decorated Red Ware and Orange Ware Types of the Rural Otumba Aztec Ceramic Complex. In *Arqueología Mesoamericana: Homenaje a William T. Sanders*, edited by Alba Guadalupe Mastache, Jeffrey R. Parsons, Robert M. Santley, and Mari Carmen Serra Puche, pp. 461–479. Instituto Nacional de Antropología e Historia, Mexico City.

Charlton, Thomas H., Cynthia Otis Charlton, Deborah L. Nichols, and Hector Neff
2008 Aztec Otumba, AD 1200–1600: Patterns of the Production, Distribution, and Consumption of Ceramic Products. In *Pottery Economics in Mesoamerica*, edited by Christopher A. Pool and George J. Bey III, pp. 237–270. University of Arizona Press, Tucson.

Charlton, Thomas H., Deborah L. Nichols, and Cynthia Otis Charlton
1991 Aztec Craft Production and Specialization: Archaeological Evidence from the City-State of Otumba, Mexico. *World Archaeology* 23(1):98–114.
1993 Aztec Household-Based Craft Production: Archaeological Evidence from the City-State of Otumba, Mexico. In *Prehispanic Domestic Units in Western Mesoamerica*, edited by Robert S. Santley and Kenneth G. Hirth, pp. 147–172. CRC Press, Boca Raton, FL.

Costin, Cathy L.
1991 Craft Specialization: Issues in Defining, Documenting, and Explaining the Organization of Production. In *Archaeological Method and Theory*, Vol. 3, edited by M. B. Schiffer, pp. 1–56. University of Arizona Press, Tucson.

2000 The Use of Ethnoarchaeology for the Archaeological Study of Ceramic Production. *Journal of Archaeological Method and Theory* 7(4):377–402.

Crider, Destiny

2011 *Epiclassic and Early Postclassic Interaction in Central Mexico as Evidenced by Decorated Pottery*. Unpublished Ph.D. dissertation, Arizona State University.

2013 Assessing Mexican Pottery Paint Recipes Using Particle-induced X-ray Emission. *Open Journal of Archaeometry* 1(e5):20–25.

Durán, Fray Diego

1967 [1581] *Historia de las Indias de Nueva España e Islas de la Tierra Firme*. 2 vols. Editorial Porrúa, Mexico City.

Dyckerhoff, Ursula, and Hanns J. Prem

1976 La Estratificación Social en Huexotzingo. In *Estratificación social en la Mesoamérica prehispánica*, edited by Pedro Carrasco and Johanna Broda, pp. 157–177. Instituto Nacional de Antropología e Historia, Mexico City.

Foster, George M.

1955 *Contemporary Pottery Techniques in Southern and Central Mexico*. Middle American Research Institute Publication 22. Tulane University, New Orleans.

Franco C., José L.

1945 Comentarios sobre tipología y filogenía de la decoración negro sobre color natural del barro en la cerámica Azteca II. *Revista Mexicana de Estudios Antropológicos* 7:163–186.

1947 Algunos problemas relativos a la cerámica Azteca. *El México Antiguo* 7:162–208.

Franco C., José L., and Frederick A. Peterson

1957 *Motivos decorativos en la cerámica Azteca*. Serie Científica 5. Museo Nacional de Antropología, Mexico City.

Gamio, Manuel

1913 *Arqueología del Valle de México: descripción general de las colecciones que se exhiben en esta exposición, año escolar de 1911–1912*. Anexo al Informe del Presidente de la Junta Directiva de la Escuela Internacional de Arqueología y Etnología América. Tipografía y Litografía de Muller Hnos. Mexico City.

Garraty, Christopher P.

2013 Market Development and Pottery Exchange under Aztec and Spanish Rule in Cerro Portezuelo. *Ancient Mesoamerica* 24:151–176.

Garraty, Christopher P., T. Murakami, and A. Simon

2007 Thermogravimetric Analysis (TGA) of Archaeological Materials: Part II, Ceramics. *SAS Bulletin* 30:17–20.

Gibson, Charles

1964 *The Aztecs Under Spanish Rule*. Stanford University Press, Stanford, CA.

Griffin, James B., and Antonieta Espejo

1947 La Alfarería correspondiente al ultimo período de ocupación Nahua del Valle de México: I. *Tlatelolco a través de los tiempos* 9:10–26.

1950 La Alfarería Correspondiente al ultimo período de ocupación Nahua del Valle de México: II. *Tlatelolco a través de los tiempos* 11:15–66.

Hare, Timothy S., and Michael E. Smith

1996 A New Postclassic Chronology for Yautepec, Morelos. *Ancient Mesoamerica* 7:281–297.

Hicks, Frederick

1982 Tetzcoco in the Early 16th Century: The State, the City, and the Calpolli. *American Ethnologist* 9:230–249.

Hodge, Mary G.
1984 *Aztec City-States*. Memoirs No. 18. Museum of Anthropology, University of Michigan, Ann Arbor.
1992 The Geographical Structure of Aztec Imperial-Period Market Systems. *National Geographic Research and Exploration* 8:428–445.
1993 Los motivos decorativos de la cerámica y los sistemas de intercambio en la sociedad azteca. In *Entre lagos y volcanes: Chalco-Amecameca, pasado y presente*, edited by Alejandro Tortolero Villaseñor, pp. 73–102. El Colegio Mexiquense, Toluca, Mexico.
2008 *Place of Jade: State and Economy in Ancient Chalco*. University of Pittsburgh, Pittsburgh, PA, and Department of Anthropology and Instituto Nacional de Antropología e Historia, Mexico City.

Hodge, Mary G., and Leah D. Minc
1990 The Spatial Patterning of Aztec Ceramics: Implications for Prehispanic Exchange Systems in the Valley of Mexico. *Journal of Field Archaeology* 17:415–437.
1991 *Aztec-Period Ceramic Distribution and Exchange Systems*. Final Report submitted to the National Science Foundation, Grant BSM-8704177, Washington, DC.

Hodge, Mary G., and Hector Neff
2005 Xaltocan in the Economy of the Basin of Mexico: A View from Ceramic Tradewares, In *Production and Power at Postclassic Xaltocan*, edited by Elizabeth M. Brumfiel, pp. 319–348. Instituto Nacional de Antropología e Historia/University of Pittsburgh, Pittsburgh and Mexico City.

Hodge, Mary G., Hector Neff, M. James Blackman, and Leah D. Minc
1992 A Compositional Perspective on Ceramic Production in the Aztec Empire. In *Chemical Characterization of Ceramic Pastes in Archaeology*, edited by Hector Neff, pp. 203–220. Monographs in World Archaeology No. 7. Prehistory Press, Madison, WI.
1993 The Regional Structure of Black-on-Orange Ceramic Production in the Aztec Empire's Heartland. *Latin American Antiquity* 4(2):130–157.

Minc, Leah D.
1994 *Political Economy and Market Economy under Aztec Rule: A Regional Perspective Based on Decorated Ceramic Production and Distribution Systems in the Valley of Mexico*. 2 vols. Ph.D. dissertation, University of Michigan. University Microfilms International, Ann Arbor.
2006 Monitoring Regional Market Systems in Prehistory: Models, Methods, and Metrics. *Journal of Anthropological Archaeology* 25(1):82–116.
2009 Style and Substance: Evidence for Regionalization within the Aztec Market System. *Latin American Antiquity* 20(2):343–374.

Minc, Leah D., Mary G. Hodge, and M. James Blackman
1994 Stylistic and Spatial Variability in Early Aztec Ceramics: Insights into Pre-Imperial Exchange Systems. In *Economies and Polities in the Aztec Realm*, edited by Mary G. Hodge and Michael E. Smith, pp. 133–173. IMS Studies on Culture and Society Series No. 5. Institute for Mesoamerican Studies, State University of New York, Albany.

Mindling, Eric
2010 *Barro y Fuego: el Arte de la Alfarería en Oaxaca*. Editorial Arte, Oaxaca, Mexico.

Neff, Hector, Ron L. Bishop, Edward B Sisson, Michael D. Clascock, and P. R. Sisson
1994 Neutron Activation Analysis of Late Post Classic Polychrome Pottery from Central Mexico. In *Mixteca-Puebla: Discoveries and Research in Mesoamerican Art and Archaeology*, edited by H. B. Nicholson and E. Quiñones Keber, pp. 117–141. Labyrinthos, Culver City, CA.

Neff, Hector, and Mary G. Hodge
2008 Serving Vessel Production at Chalco: Evidence from Neutron Activation Analysis. In *Place of Jade: Society and Economy in Ancient Chalco*, edited by Mary G. Hodge, pp. 187–226. Latin American Archaeology Report. Department of Anthropology, University of Pittsburgh, PA, and Instituto Nacional de Antropología e Historia, Mexico City.

Nichols, Deborah L.
1994 The Organization of Provincial Craft Production in the Aztec City-State of Otumba. In *Economies and Polities in the Aztec Realm*, edited by Mary G. Hodge and Michael E. Smith, pp. 175–194. Institute for Mesoamerican Studies, State University of New York, Albany.
2004 The Rural and Urban Landscapes of the Aztec State. In *Mesoamerican Archaeology: Theory and Practice*, edited by Julia A. Hendon and Rosemary A. Joyce, pp. 265–295. Blackwell Studies in Global Archaeology No. 1, Blackwell, Malden, Massachusetts.
2013 Merchants and Markets: The Archaeology of Aztec Commerce at Otumba Mexico. In *Merchants, Trade and Exchange in the Pre-Columbian World*, edited by Kenneth G. Hirth and Joanne Pillsbury, pp. 49–83. Dumbarton Oaks Research Library and Collections, Washington D.C.

Nichols, Deborah L., Elizabeth M. Brumfiel, Hector Neff, Mary Hodge, Thomas H. Charlton, and Michael D. Glascock
2002 Neutrons, Markets, Cities, and Empires: A 1000-Year Perspective on Ceramic Production and Distribution in the Postclassic Basin of Mexico. *Journal of Anthropological Archaeology* 21:25–82.

Nichols, Deborah L., and Thomas H. Charlton
1996 The Postclassic Occupation of Otumba: A Chronological Assessment. *Ancient Mesoamerica* 7:231–244.

Nichols, Deborah L., Christina Elson, Leslie G. Cecil, Nina Neivens De Estrada, Michael D. Glascock, and Paula Mikkelsen
2009 Chiconautla, Mexico: A Crossroads of Aztec Trade and Politics. *Latin American Antiquity* 20(3):443–472.

Nichols, Deborah L., Mary Jane McLaughlin, and Maura Benton
2000 Production Intensification and Regional Specialization: Maguey Fibers and Textiles in the Aztec City-state of Otumba. *Ancient Mesoamerica* 11:267–291.

Noguera, Eduardo
1930 Decorative Aspects of Certain Types of Mexican Pottery. In *Proceedings of the XXIII International Congress of Americanists, New York, 1928*, pp. 85–92. New York, International Congress of Americanists.
1935 La Cerámica de Tenayuca y las Excavaciones Estratigráficas. In *Tenayuca*, pp. 141–201. Secretaría de Educación Pública, Departamento de Monumentos, Mexico.

O'Neill, George
1956–1957 Preliminary Report on Stratigraphic Excavations in the Southern Valley of Mexico: Chalco-Xico. *Revista Mexicana de Estudios Antropológicos* 14(2):45–51.
1962 *Postclassic Ceramic Stratigraphy at Chalco in the Valley of Mexico*. Ph.D. dissertation, Columbia University, New York.

Parsons, Jeffrey R.
1966 *The Aztec Ceramic Sequence in the Teotihuacan Valley, Mexico*. Ph.D. dissertation, University of Michigan. University Microfilms, Ann Arbor.

Parsons, Jeffrey R., Elizabeth M. Brumfiel, and Mary G. Hodge
1996 Developmental Implications of Earlier Dates for Early Aztec in the Basin of Mexico. *Ancient Mesoamerica* 7:217–230.

Parsons, Jeffrey R., Elizabeth Brumfiel, Mary H. Parsons, and David J. Wilson
1982 *Prehistoric Settlement Patterns in the Southern Valley of Mexico: The Chalco-Xochimilco Regions*. Memoirs No. 14. Museum of Anthropology, University of Michigan, Ann Arbor.

Peacock, D. P. S.
1982 *Pottery in the Roman World: An Ethnoarchaeological Approach*. Longman, London.

Pool, Christopher A.
1992 Integrating Ceramic Production and Distribution. In *Ceramic Production and Distribution: An Integrated Approach*, edited by G. J. Bey III and C. A. Pool, pp. 275–313. Westview Press, Boulder, CO.

Prem, Hanns J. (editor)
1974 *Matrícula de Huexotzinco*. Akademische Druck-u. Verlagsanstalt, Graz.

Sahagún, Fray Bernardino de
1950–1982 *Florentine Codex: A History of the Things of New Spain*. Edited and translated by Arthur J. O. Anderson and Charles E. Dibble. School of American Research, Santa Fe, NM, and University of Utah, Salt Lake City.

Sanders, William T., Jeffrey R. Parsons, and Robert S. Santley
1979 *The Basin of Mexico: Ecological Processes in the Evolution of a Civilization*. Academic Press, New York.

Santley, Robert S., Philip J. Arnold III, and Christopher A. Pool
1989 The Ceramics Production System at Matacapan, Veracruz, Mexico, *Journal of Field Archaeology* 16:107–132.

Scholes, France V., and Eleanor B. Adams (editors)
1957 *Información Sobre los Tributos que los Indios Pagaban a Moteuczoma—Año de 1554*. Documentos para la Historia de México Colonial 4, Mexico City.

Séjourné, Laurette
1970 *Arqueología del Valle de México 1: Culhuacan*. Instituto Nacional de Antropología e Historia, Mexico City.
1983 *Arqueología e Historia del Valle de México de Xochimilco a Amecameca*. Siglo Ventiuno Editores, S.A., Mexico City.

Smith, Michael E., and John F. Doershuk
1991 Late Postclassic Chronology in Western Morelos, Mexico. *Latin American Antiquity* 2(4):291–310.

Talavera Barnard, Elena
1979 *Las Salinas de la Cuenca de México y la cerámica de impresión textil*. Thesis, Escuela Nacional de Antropología e Historia, Mexico City.

Tosi, Maurizio
1984 The Notion of Craft Specialization and its Representations in the Archaeological Record of Early States in the Turanian Basin. In *Marxist Perspectives in Archaeology*, edited by M. Spriggs, pp. 22–52. Cambridge University Press, Cambridge, UK.

Vaillant, George C.
1938 A Correlation of Archaeological and Historical Sequences in the Valley of Mexico. *American Anthropologist* 40:535–573.
1941 *The Aztecs of Mexico: Origin, Rise and Fall of the Aztec Nation*. Doubleday, New York.

Whalen, Michael E., and Jeffrey R. Parsons
1982 Ceramic Markers used for Period Designations. In *Prehistoric Settlement Patterns in the Southern Valley of Mexico: The Chalco-Xochimilco Regions*, edited by Jeffrey R. Parsons, Elizabeth Brumfiel, Mary H. Parsons, and David J. Wilson, pp. 385–459. Memoirs No. 14. Museum of Anthropology, University of Michigan, Ann Arbor.

Winter, Marcus C., and Valerie Nardin
1982 Rescate Arqueológico en Loma del Trapiche, Guadalupe Hidalgo, Etla, Oaxaca. In *Estudios de Antropologia e Historia*, No. 30, pp. 1–14. Instituto Nacional de Antropologia e Historia, Centro Regional de Oaxaca, Mexico.

Winter, Marcus C., and William O. Payne
1976 Hornos para ceramica hallados en Monte Albán. *Boletin del Instituto Nacional de Antropologia e Historia* 16:37–40.

CHAPTER 25

PREGNANT IN THE DANCING PLACE

Myths and Methods of Textile Production and Use

GEOFFREY MCCAFFERTY
AND SHARISSE MCCAFFERTY

TEXTILES, including both clothing and other woven articles, were important commodities in ancient Aztec society. Although they have not preserved well in the archaeological record, textiles are abundantly depicted in pictorial manuscripts, statuary, and ceramic figurines. Additionally, Colonial period texts describe the gender associations between textile production and female identity and ideology. Ethnographic traditions among indigenous groups of the region continue these practices. Finally, archaeological spindle whorls are an abundant artifact type that are often decorated and therefore provide additional information about the functions and symbolic significance of textile production. This chapter summarizes information about Aztec textiles and their production, providing important information about the economics of this valued good as well as insights into female production and ideology.

Cotton was a common material used in Aztec textiles, and there is some ethnohistorical evidence to suggest sumptuary laws limiting cotton cloth to elite society (Duran 1994:234). On the other hand, different species of agave (*maguey*) produced fibers with distinct qualities, including some that were as fine as linen while others were used for sandals, bags, or rope. Other materials are also mentioned in early sources, including *palma*, *chichicaztli* nettles, feathers, and even fine metal wire. Some materials were more common in specific regions, such as *palma* in the Toluca region and *chichicaztli* in Oaxaca, but an active exchange network brought all of these into the markets of the Aztec capital, as suggested in the tribute lists found in the *Codex Mendoza* (1992; also Berdan 1987; Hicks 1994).

Patricia Anawalt has written the definitive descriptions of Aztec costume (1981, 1990), identifying *maxtlatl* loin-cloths and shoulder capes as characteristic male garments, while skirts and *huipil* upper-body garments were typical of females. A triangular cape known as a *quechquemitl* is also depicted on some women and goddesses, but Anawalt argues that this costume element may have been more diagnostic of warm climates such as the Gulf Coast (Anawalt 1982). It should be noted that different contexts and media portray a wider variety of costumes, including very elaborate battle dress. In general, male costume is elaborated with animal skins while females incorporate more elaborate woven and embroidered decoration (McCafferty and McCafferty 1994a).

As noted, perishable materials such as textiles have rarely preserved from the precolumbian period. Exceptions come from dry caves such as those from the Tehuacan valley where cordage and a loom-kit were discovered (Johnson de Weitlaner 1971). Another exceptional case was the La Garrafa cave in Chiapas where relatively complete examples of clothing were discovered (Landa et al. 1988), including some with painted decoration in the Mixteca-Puebla style. Lauro González-Quintero (1988) describes textile fragments recovered with burials from Tlatelolco, including one with decoration of stylized skulls with eyes and teeth. The National Museum of Anthropology in Mexico City proudly displays an elaborate *huipil* that tradition says was worn by Malintzin, the indigenous princess who helped Hernan Cortes during the Spanish Conquest (McCafferty 2009). It features a decorative embroidered *escudo* at the neck (a costume tradition that may have been adopted into Catholic religious costume during the early Colonial period), and the colored thread is made of cotton plied with feathers.

Other than the depictions of Aztec costume, the strongest evidence for textiles is found in the tools used for textile production, and spindle whorls are the most abundant of these. Spindle whorls are used on wooden spindles to spin raw fiber into thread, acting as fly-wheels to maintain inertia on the spindle (Figure 25.1).

Whorls, or *malacates*, can be made from a variety of materials (e.g., stone, seeds, wood, fruit, etc.) but in the archaeological record those made of baked clay are best preserved. Mary H. Parsons (1972) was the first scholar to recognize that different sizes and weights of spindle whorls could relate to different fibers, and since then several others have studied Aztec spindle whorls (Brumfiel 1991, 1996; Nichols et al. 2000; Smith and Hirth 1988). The general principle is that the form of the whorl will determine the speed and duration of the rotation, with whorls of greater diameter producing a longer, slower rotation than whorls of lesser diameter. A parallel from the sporting world is the rotation of a figure skater who begins with a slow rotation with arms outstretched but speeds up as he or she brings the arms in to the body.

Parsons' (1972) initial classification of Aztec whorls from the Teotihuacan survey area divided them into three categories based primarily on diameter and weight, with the smallest whorls associated with cotton production while the larger whorls were suggested as maguey whorls. This small versus large division has served as a "rule of thumb" for most subsequent analyses, although the specific sizes have varied between studies.

A more detailed method for spindle whorl analysis was developed for a large corpus from Cholula, in the adjacent Puebla/Tlaxcala valley (McCafferty and McCafferty 2000), and later expanded with collections from Central America (Beaudry-Corbett and McCafferty 2001; McCafferty and McCafferty 2008). Measurements include height,

FIGURE 25.1 Supported spinning with wooden spindle and disc whorl in a spinning bowl (Charney 1887). Redrawn by Kristin Sullivan.

weight, diameter, hole size, and a "shape" ratio of height to diameter. Using these variables, 10 different whorl "types" (plus 14 subtypes) are distinguished with different functional qualities. For example, smaller whorls with a shape ratio of greater than 0.5 would produce tightly twisted thread suitable for warping the loom using short staple cotton, while shallow whorls with a shape ratio of less than 0.25 would produce a loose thread. Sahagún's (1950–1982, Book 8:49) account of feather spinning specifies that "shallow whorls" were used for feathers, presumably plied with cotton. It is possible that these feathery threads were similar to the ones identified in Malintzin's *huipil* from the National Museum.

The relatively high frequency of smaller "cotton" whorls from the Basin of Mexico is curious, considering that it is too high and cool for cotton as a crop (Berdan 1987). Instead, maguey is much more common and was used for a variety of products besides its fiber (Parsons and Parsons 1990). Elizabeth Brumfiel (1991) used a diachronic perspective on the smaller versus larger whorls from surface survey data from the southern Basin of Mexico to suggest that maguey fiber was more commonly spun prior to the rise of the Aztec Empire but access to cotton via the international market system permitted increased use after A.D. 1350. In an even more nuanced study (Brumfiel 1996), she suggested that minor changes in whorl size may have indicated heightened tribute demands. Note that the smaller whorls would have resulted in tighter thread, which would have used less raw material while being more labor intensive; this provides another perspective on the tribute demands and concomitant responses. Cotton cloth, or *quachtlis*, were a common form of tribute payment (Hicks 1994), and skimping on the thread size and/or thread count may have represented strategic resistance to tribute demands.

Further evidence of Aztec textile production strategies was found in Otumba, where Nichols et al. (2000) recovered a high density of large whorl fragments that they interpreted as evidence of a spinning (at least) industry. While evidence for weaving is ephemeral due to the perishable nature of loom kits, spinning and weaving are generally considered to be closely related activities. Otumba, in the foothills of the Basin of Mexico, is well known for its maguey, so the many large whorls are consistent with maguey spinning. A puzzling aspect of this concentration, however, is that larger whorls were more likely used for drop-spinning, as opposed to smaller whorls that would have been used in supported spinning with the tip of the spindle resting in a small bowl (Smith and Hirth 1988). In ethnographic contexts, drop-spinning is typically done while walking about on daily rounds, so an "industry" of drop-spinners would be unlikely. Another possibility could be that this was more of a weaving cooperative where the end results of the production process were consumed.

One conclusion of these studies is that simple spindle whorls can be used to infer complex and behaviorally interesting practices. Spinning and weaving were closely related to female practice in Aztec society and also to women's gender identity. This is well-established through ethnohistorical sources, for example: "Apply thyself well, to the really womanly task, the spindle whorl, the weaving stick" (Sahagún 1950–1982, Book 6:96). In a depiction of the bathing ritual of newborns, girl children were presented with spinning and weaving tools in addition to the appropriate clothing associated with female identity (Figure 25.2). Aztec goddesses were also closely associated with spinning and weaving activities (McCafferty and McCafferty 1991; Sullivan 1982) (Figure 25.3).

Cihuacoatl, for example, is depicted holding a weaving batten, and her description from the *Primeros Memoriales* specifies her association with weaving tools (Sahagún 1993). Tlazolteotl is commonly represented with spindles and whorls in her headdress of unspun cotton (Codex Borgia 1963). The association of female deities with spinning and weaving may have historical roots back at least as far as the Teotihuacan "spider woman" (Taube 1983). It may also relate to a deep ideological opposition between chaos and order, as discussed in Cecelia Klein's (1982) "Woven Heaven, Tangled Earth."

Spinning and weaving also carry symbolic significance relating to sexuality, with the spindle embedded in the whorl seen as a metaphor for coitus (Sullivan 1982). This is described in the Aztec riddle: "What is it that they make pregnant, that they make big with child in the dancing place?" The answer was "spindles" that grew around the middle as fiber was spun into thread and wrapped around the spindle (Sahagún 1950–1982, Book 6:240). The thread was then used to weave as an act of creation that was also likened to childbirth.

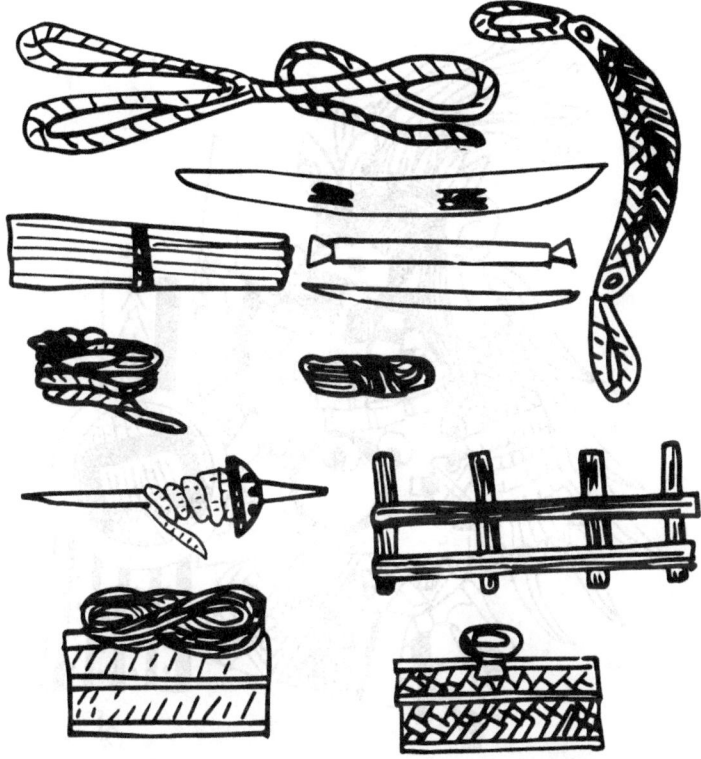

FIGURE 25.2 Weaving tools as symbolic offerings for girl's bathing ritual (Sahagún 1950–1982). Redrawn by Kristin Sullivan.

Spindle whorls were also used as part of the birthing ritual, when midwives would place a "small shield" (or *tehuehuelli*) in the hand of a woman in labor while admonishing her to "be like an eagle warrior" (Sahagún 1950–1982, Book 6:160). The *tehuehuelli* was specifically the personal shield of the patron god of war, Huitzilopochtli, and in the *Primeros Memoriales* it is depicted with decoration of feather tufts identical to many spindle whorls from Cholula. In fact, many spinning and weaving tools were metaphoric parallels to male weapons: the *tzotzopaztli* weaving batten is still referred to as a sword, or *machete*; and wooden spindles are carved to a short point and occasionally adorned with an arrowhead-like tip.

The idea of a woman in labor as a parallel to a warrior is further elaborated through the tradition that warriors who died in battle were rewarded in the afterlife by accompanying the sun on its daily journey from dawn to midday, while women who died in childbirth accompanied the sun to its daily rest in the west, the symbolic realm of women. This association is also found in the association of childbirth as a form of taking a captive: "And when the baby had arrived on earth, then the midwife shouted; she gave war cries, which meant that the little woman had fought a good battle, had become a brave warrior, had taken a captive, had captured a baby" (Sahagún 1950–1982, Book 6:167).

FIGURE 25.3 Goddess Cihuacoatl with weaving batten (*Codex Magliabechino* 1983:folio 45. Redrawn by Kristin Sullivan).

Spindle whorls played a variety of roles in the Aztec worldview. The most prominent parallel was their reference as a *temalacatl*, or stone spindle whorl. Monumental stone disks perforated in the center were used as goal markers on ball courts, as depicted in the *Codex Magliabechiano* (1983 [1903]). The famous Aztec calendar stone itself was a massive *temalacatl*, with the symbol *ollin* at its center to indicate motion. Circular stones such as this were used for a specific form of sacrifice, in which the victim was tied in the center and attacked by armed warriors while attempting to defend himself using sticks with feathers attached as if they were obsidian blades (Codex Nuttall 1975). Following the ceremony, a tall pole was inserted into the central hole, like a spindle in a whorl, and it was then wrapped in cloth banners like thread around the spindle (Duran 1971:190–191).

Actual spindle whorls were often decorated, either through incising, mold impressions, or painting. The specific designs varied regionally, probably relating to local symbolism (Figure 25.4). We have suggested that because of the strong association of spinning as a female task that the whorl decorations may provide insight into specifically feminine symbolic discourse (McCafferty and McCafferty 1991). In Cholula, for example, whorls were decorated with a variety of floral and avian patterns, in addition

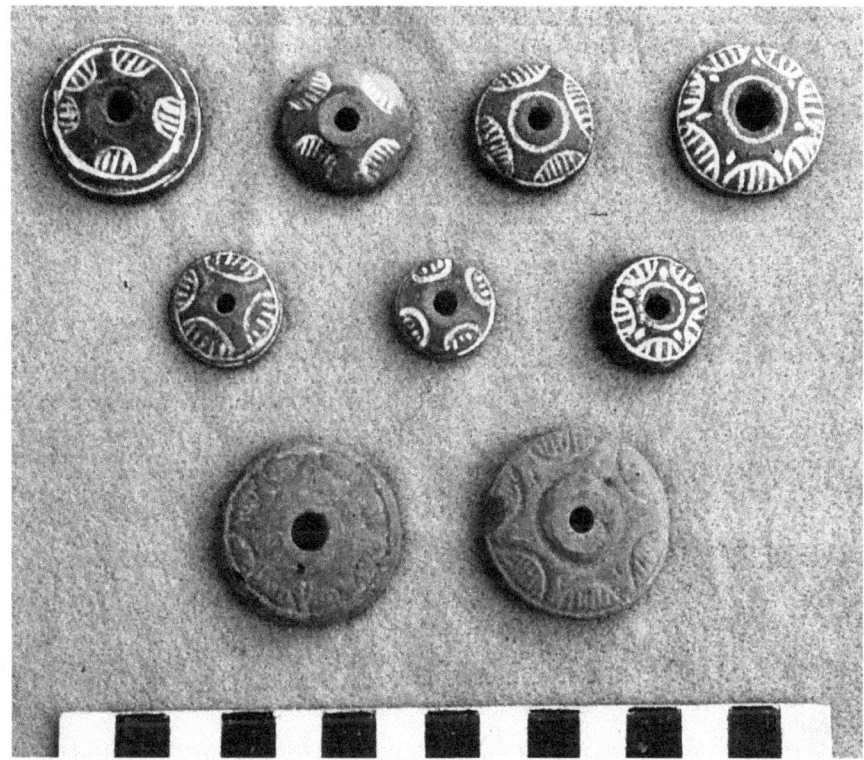

FIGURE 25.4 Decorated spindle whorls from Cholula. Photograph by author.

to geometrics. Brumfiel (2007) described the importance of solar imagery on spindle whorls from the Basin of Mexico.

Textiles were an important element in the Aztec political economy, used for exchange and even as a standard of value for tribute and barter. As a commodity that was strongly associated with female production, textile production provides one of the best windows on women's participation in Aztec economy. Furthermore, the strong symbolic linkage between textile production and female identity offers a unique perspective on gender ideology in ancient Mesoamerica.

REFERENCES CITED

Anawalt, Patricia R.
1981 *Indian Clothing Before Cortes: Mesoamerican Costumes from the Codices*. University of Oklahoma Press, Norman.
1982 Analysis of the Aztec Quechquemitl: An Exercise in Inference. In *The Art and Iconography of Late Post-Classic Central Mexico*, edited by E. H. Boone, pp. 37–72. Dumbarton Oaks Research and Library Collection, Washington, DC.
1990 The Emperor's Cloak: Aztec Pomp, Toltec Circumstance. *American Antiquity* 55:291–307.

Beaudry-Corbett, Marilyn, and Sharisse McCafferty
2001 Spindle Whorls: Household Specialization at Ceren. In *Ancient Maya Women*, edited by Traci Ardren, pp. 52–67. Altamira Press, Walnut Creek, CA.

Berdan, Frances Frei
1987 Cotton in Aztec Mexico: Production, Distribution and Uses. *Mexican Studies/Estudios Mexicanos* 3(2):235–262.

Brumfiel, Elizabeth
1991 Weaving and Cooking: Women's Production in Aztec Mexico. In *Engendering Archaeology: Women and Prehistory*, edited by J. M. Gero and M. W. Conkey, pp. 224–251. Basil Blackwell, Oxford.
1996 The Quality of Tribute Cloth: The Place of Evidence in Archaeological Argument. *American Antiquity* 61:453–462.
2007 Solar Disks and Solar Cycles: Spindle Whorls and the Dawn of Solar Art in Postclassic Mexico. *Treballs d'Arqueologia* 13:91–113.

Codex Borgia
1963 *Codice Borgia* [Facsímile]. Fondo de Cultura Economica. Mexico City.

Codex Magliabechiano
1983 [1903] *The Book of the Life of the Ancient Mexicans Containing an Account of their Rites and Superstitions* Translated by Z. Nuttall. University of California Press, Berkeley.

Codex Mendoza
1992 *The Codex Mendoza*. 4 vols. Edited by F. F. Berdan and P. R. Anawalt. University of California Press, Berkeley.

Codex Nuttall
1975 *The Codex Nuttall: A Picture Manuscript from Ancient Mexico*. The Peabody Museum Facsimile edited by Zelia Nuttall. Dover, New York.

Duran, Fray Diego
1971 *The Book of the Gods and Rites and the Ancient Calendar*. Translated by F. Horcasitas and D. Heyden. University of Oklahoma Press, Norman.
1994 *The History of the Indies of New Spain*. Translated, annotated, and with an introduction by Dors Heyden. University of Oklahoma Press, Norman, OK.

González-Quintero, Lauro
1988 Probables significados iconograficos de un textil mexica. *Arqueología* 3:207–224.

Hicks, Frederick
1994 Cloth in the Political Economy of the Aztec State. In *Economies and Polities in the Aztec Realm*, edited by M. Hodge and M. E. Smith, pp. 89–112. Institute for Mesoamerican Studies, Albany, NY.

Johnson de Weitlaner, Irmegard
1971 Basketry and Textiles. In *Handbook of Middle American Indians*, Vol. 10: *Archaeology of Northern Mesoamerica, Part 1*, edited by R. Wauchope, G. F. Ekholm, and I. Bernal, pp. 297–321. University of Texas Press, Austin.

Klein, Cecilia F.
1982 Woven Heaven, Tangled Earth: A Weaver's Paradigm of the Mesoamerican Cosmos. In *Ethnoastronomy and Archaeoastronomy in the American Tropics*, edited by A. F. Aveni and G. Urton, pp. 1–35. Annals of the New York Academy of Sciences Vol. 385. New York Academy of Sciences, New York.

Landa A., Maria Elena, Eduardo Pareyon M., Alejandro Huerta C., Emma E. Herrera G., Rosa Lorena Román T., Martha Guajardo P., Josefina Cruz R., Sara Altamirano R., and Eva Rodriguez C.
1988 *La Garrafa: cuevas de la Garrafa, Chiapas. Estudio y conservación de algunos objetos arqueológicos.* Centro Regional de Puebla. Instituto Nacional de Antropología e Historia, Mexico City.

McCafferty, Geoffrey
2009 De-Colónizing Malintzin. In *Postcolonial Perspectives in Archaeology: Proceedings from the 39th Annual Chacmool Conference*, edited by Peter Bikoulis, Dominic Lacroix, and Meaghan Peuramaki-Brown, pp. 183–192. Chacmool Archaeological Association, University of Calgary, Calgary.

McCafferty, Sharisse D., and Geoffrey G. McCafferty
1991 Spinning and Weaving as Female Gender Identity in Post-Classic Central Mexico. In *Textile Traditions of Mesoamerica and the Andes: An Anthology*, edited by M. Schevill, J. C. Berlo, and E. Dwyer, pp. 19–44. Garland, New York.
1994a The Conquered Women of Cacaxtla: Gender Identity or Gender Ideology? *Ancient Mesoamerica* 5(2):159–172.
1994b Engendering Tomb 7 at Monte Albán, Oaxaca: Respinning an Old Yarn. *Current Anthropology* 35(2):143–166.
2000 Textile Production in Postclassic Cholula, Mexico. *Ancient Mesoamerica*.11:39–54.
2006 Weaving Space: Textile Imagery and Landscape in the Mixtec Codices (with Sharisse D. McCafferty). In *Space and Spatial Analysis in Archaeology*, edited by Elizabeth C. Robertson, Jeffrey D. Seibert, Deepika C. Fernandez, and Marc U. Zender, pp. 333–341. University of Calgary Press, Calgary, AB.
2008 Spinning and Weaving Tools from Santa Isabel, Nicaragua. *Ancient Mesoamerica* 19:43–156.

Nichols, Deborah L, Mary Jane McLaughlin, and Maura Benton
2000 Production Intensification and Regional Specialization. *Ancient Mesoamerica* 11:267–291.

Parsons, Jeffrey R., and Mary H. Parsons
1990 *Maguey Utilization in Highland Central Mexico: An Archaeological Ethnography.* Anthropological Papers No. 82. Museum of Anthropology, University of Michigan, Ann Arbor.

Parsons, Mary H.
1972 Spindle Whorls from the Teotihuacan Valley, Mexico. In *Miscellaneous Studies in Mexican Prehistory*, edited by J. R. Parsons, M. W. Spence, and M. H. Parsons, pp. 45–80. Anthropological Papers of the Museum of Anthropology 45. University of Michigan, Ann Arbor.

Sahagún, Bernadino de
1950–1982 [1547–1585] *Florentine Codex: General History of the Things of New Spain.* 13 vols. Edited and translated by A. J. D. Anderson and C. E. Dibble University of Utah Press, Salt Lake City, and School of American Research, Santa Fe, NM.
1993 *Primeros Memoriales.* Civilizations of the American Indian Series 100. University of Oklahoma Press, Norman.

Smith, Michael E., and Kenneth G. Hirth
1988 The Development of Cotton Spinning Technology in Postclassic Morelos, Mexico. *Journal of Field Archaeology* 15:349–358.

Sullivan, Thelma
1982 Tlazolteotl-Ixcuina: The Great Spinner and Weaver. In *The Art and Iconography of Late Post-Classic Central Mexico*, edited by E. H. Boone, pp. 7–36. Dumbarton Oaks Research and Library Collection, Washington, DC.

Taube, Karl A.
1983 The Teotihuacan Spider Woman. *Journal of Latin American Lore* 9(2):107–189.

PART IV-B
SOCIAL RELATIONS

SOCIAL IMPLICATIONS

CHAPTER 26

GENDER AND AZTEC LIFE CYCLES

CAROLINE DODDS PENNOCK

The image of the Aztecs in the popular imagination is dominated by men. Brutal warriors, glorious kings, and bloody priests stalk across the pages of both history and fiction, reinforcing their masculinity through ruthless displays of violence, and asserting their dominance through the spectacles of warfare and sacrifice. Thanks to a strongly military public culture, often centered on the performance of "masculine" ideals and behaviors, it is easy to see why some scholars have argued that Tenochtitlan in particular was based on a social structure that "glorified the cult of male dominance" (Nash 1978:359), and for many years it was taken for granted that Aztec society was a stereotypical military patriarchy: active warrior men contrasting sharply with their domestic, subordinated wives. In reality, however, women in Aztec culture were powerful and effective figures, possessing tangible rights and responsibilities, and clearly recognized as indispensable to society's collective success.

PATRIARCHY, COMPLEMENTARITY, OR FLUIDITY?

Although popular perceptions of the Aztecs often retain a rather monolithic view of male dominance, it is now relatively rare in specialist texts (although there are some exceptions, e.g., Rodríguez-Shadow 1991). In recent years, the view of Aztec culture as a strongly patriarchal society has largely been replaced by what might be broadly seen as two alternative approaches to Aztec gender. The first, and most prevalent, approach is gender parallelism, which sees society as based on a complementary duality in which men and women possessed separate, complementary roles that were regarded as completely different but of equal value (Clendinnen 1991; Kellogg 1997). Alongside this model is a more fluid approach rooted in the belief that the Aztecs saw gender as an unstable and flexible category that required close supervision and control (Klein 2001). Whether they think it was motivated by a belief in innate gender roles or a need to control and stabilize gendered behavior, however, scholars now largely agree that male and female roles were primarily arranged into a binary system, each with its own separate spheres of responsibility and activity.

In a practical sense, Aztec gender systems appear to have combined parallelism with a degree of hierarchy, and it is probably more accurate to say that male and female roles were structurally "equivalent" rather than "equal." Men controlled most of the roles that are seen as traditional markers of influence, dominating politics, warfare, priesthood, and officialdom, but female rights were tangible in Aztec culture. Women held positions of influence not only as healers, midwives, matchmakers, teachers, and priestesses but also as leaders and administrators in their districts, as craftspeople, merchants, and marketplace overseers (responsible for good conduct of trade, pricing, assigning tributes, and provisioning the army). Power and property passed through both male and female lines to children of both genders, and all adult women were full "citizens" before the law; they were legal individuals, not dependents, entitled to appeal directly to the courts, own property, and initiate divorce proceedings. In Tenochtitlan, women also seem to have been relieved of the sole burden of childcare, which has often historically dictated female existence, and the raising of children was a shared responsibility. From an early age, both boys and girls were expected to contribute to their households, and the belief that the contribution of every citizen was vital to success permeated Aztec society and shaped their experience; everyone had their role, whether it be as ruler, worker, warrior, or mother, and all were essential. Energy and effectiveness were expected of women, just as they were expected of men.

The Problem of Sources

One of the biggest challenges for an Aztec historian lies in extricating the reality of people's gender experience from the ideal. Although this is a perennial problem for gender historians, our view is more than usually obscured by the patchy and problematic nature of the evidence. The documentary sources for Aztec culture are, of course, inherently problematic due to their post-conquest production, but on questions of gender these issues are even more pronounced. Not only did Spanish-Catholic authors tend to favor male perspectives and shape information to reflect their own expectations, but the production of texts (and even, according to some authors, the entire culture of alphabetic literacy) was also heavily male-dominated. Although there were some female informants, their perspectives were filtered through a process of recording and editing that was exclusively male. This introduces not only misunderstandings and errors (of both omission and commission) but also the deliberate possibility of "regularization": a strategic attempt by the indigenous people to promote their own cause by appealing to the values of the dominant group (Bourdieu 1977). In gendered terms, this would likely lead to a portrayal of Aztec women as conforming more closely to Judeo-Christian feminine ideals of modesty and deference.

Perhaps more than for any other subject, our view of Aztec gender is profoundly colored by the idiosyncrasies of colonial observers, not least in the sources' failure to speak to certain subjects: in a society so obsessed with blood, it is profoundly frustrating that we cannot access their attitudes toward menstruation, for example. We must remain constantly alert to the possibility of colonial imposition, misunderstanding, or omission, but, fascinatingly, despite the inevitable corruptions and misreadings, the picture of indigenous gender relationships that emerges from the sixteenth-century sources is one that remains remarkably resistant to Spanish stereotyping. Women appear as able, active, and articulate, partners and full participants in Aztec society. This impression is furthered by scrutiny of pictorial sources and material culture. In the *Florentine Codex*, for example, women are depicted engaging in a much greater diversity of ceremonial roles than are elaborated in the text (Brown 1985). Archaeology can also provide an important corrective to the focus on Tenochtitlan that typifies most of the textual evidence (Brumfiel 1991). It is reasonable to assume a significant degree of diversity across the Basin of Mexico, but it is much harder to identify institutions and practices outside of the major urban centers, where ethnohistorical and archaeological evidence is concentrated. Despite their weaknesses, any attempt to access daily life in Aztec culture will inevitably return to the colonial documents, as they are the most detailed available records for individuals' experience; however, there were variations in practice not only within the city but also beyond. Certainly the sources, often originating with informants looking back through blurred or rose-tinted glasses, tend to create an idealized and collective image of Aztec people, giving us little sense of the distinctiveness of individual experience: women behave in one way and men in another. Only rarely do exceptional or unique characters, such as the fascinating *patlaches* (hermaphrodites) or *cuiloni* (effeminates), peek out of the past to disrupt the harmonious ideal (Sigal 2007).

LIFE CYCLES

Gender was imprinted from birth in Aztec culture. For a boy, his warrior destiny was marked by the gift of model weapons and the burial of his umbilical cord on the battlefield. If the baby was a girl, a broom and weaving implements were pressed into her tiny hands and her ties to the home cemented by the interment of her umbilical cord by the grinding stone (Figure 26.1). This appears to be a powerful physical expression of the sixteenth-century *Florentine Codex*'s claim that the man was to "issue forth in war in all parts," while "the woman was to go nowhere" (Sahagún 1969, Book VI). This stark division fails to capture the complexity of Aztec life, but it does evoke very effectively the gendered binary that shaped individual and collective existence from an early age.

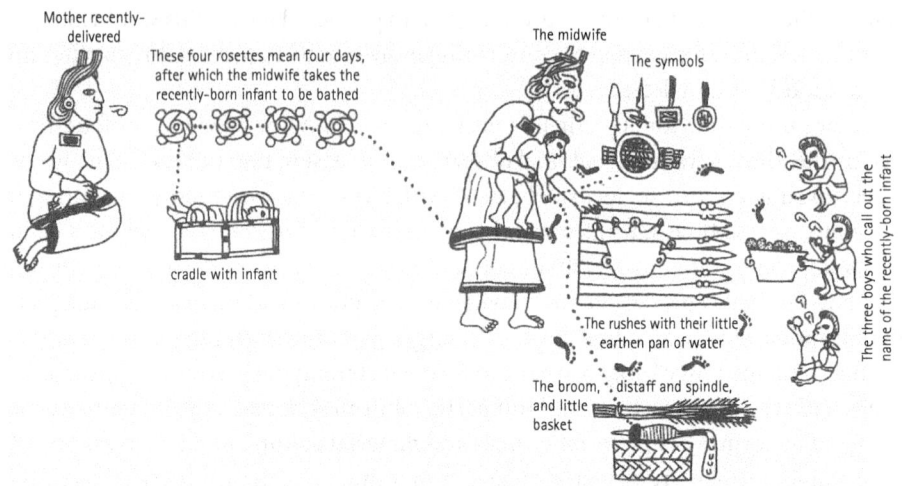

FIGURE 26.1 Bathing and naming of a child from the Codex Mendoza (Berdan and Anawalt 1992). Reproduced with permission of Frances F. Berdan.

Once a baby was weaned and no longer dependent on its mother, childcare and basic skills training also seems to have been gendered, with fathers principally responsible for their sons and mothers for their daughters (Figure 26.2) (Berdan and Anawalt 1992). This system reinforced gender roles, as well as providing a practical way to teach children the skills and responsibilities appropriate to their sex, a duality that was continued in formal education. Tenochtitlan possessed a universal education system, but young men were subject to more institutional occupational training, attending either the residential *telpochcalli* (warrior school) or *calmecac* (priestly school), while young women principally learned their trades and household responsibilities at home or in their communities. During puberty, however, boys and girls learned history, philosophy, and religion together in the *cuicacalli* (house of song), providing a rare opportunity to dance, mix, and maybe even socialize with teenagers of the opposite sex.

The age at which young men and women were seen to mature and start thinking of marriage is obscure but seems to have been younger for women, probably in their early teens. Men were expected to finish their training before moving out of the warrior house into "the company of women" in their late teens or early twenties (Sahagún 1969, Book VI; Smith 2012). Although experiences were far from uniform, marriage was the norm for the majority of Aztecs (with the exception of priests, who were required to remain celibate) and formed the basis for social structures and expectations. When a young man (or perhaps his parents) decided that he was ready to marry, his mother and father consulted family and community leaders to find an appropriate bride. Orchestrated by an elderly female matchmaker, the match was agreed between the two families, with the assumption that the wife would join the husband's household. The extent to which the couple's wishes were considered is difficult to tell, but (although dynastic considerations

FIGURE 26.2 First folio of the parallel upbringing of children from the Codex Mendoza (Berdan and Anawalt 1992). With permission of Frances F. Berdan.

presumably prevailed at the higher echelons of society) the sources imply that personal preferences were also taken into account.

Marriage marked the moment of an Aztec's entry into full adulthood and community membership, and the *calpolli* ensured that every young couple had sufficient resources to set up their own household and engage fully in the life of the district. The wife controlled the household "finances," trading in the marketplace, grinding, cooking, cleaning, and supplying the home, as well as producing the cotton cloth, which was a valuable medium of exchange. Weaving was central to Aztec women's identity as well as their economic independence. Imagery and archaeology suggest that spindle whorls and weaving battens performed for women an equivalent function to shields and swords in male culture: sites for the expression of geographical, tribal, and individual identity (McCafferty and McCafferty 1991). The husband's responsibilities clearly included military service, hunting, fishing, and farming, as well as representing his household in what we might call local politics, but the division of duties becomes much less clear-cut when we look at trades. Although artisans are most often depicted as male, some sources also suggest that women participated in skilled crafts such as writing (Figure 26.3), lapidary design, and featherwork, and these seem likely to have been family or local specialisms.

FIGURE 26.3 Female manuscript painter, *la pintora*, *Codex Telleriano-Remensis* (Quiñones Keber 1995). With permission, Bibliothèque nationale de France.

Only men were traveling merchants, but both men and women were traders, as well as marketplace overseers, healers, teachers (of their own sex), and local officials.

In a subsistence and barter economy, women's roles as producers of both food and goods for exchange were highly valued, lending them respect and concrete influence. The perception that both male and female contributions were required for productivity is borne out by the fact that marriage was the moment at which a young man was officially inscribed into the registers of the community and became liable to its full social, economic, and political obligations (Zorita 1965). Women's economic activities were vital to society and, coupled with their ability to hold property, presumably secured them a degree of independence from their husbands. Polygyny was practiced among the nobility, however, and it seems likely women were seen as less important in elite society except for their reproductive function and as a tool to cement dynastic alliances. The practical extent of polygyny (except among *tlatoque*) is unclear, however, and a distinction seems to have been made between "legal" and "primary" wives and those of lesser status, with some partners likened more to "concubines" (Read and Rosenthal 2006). The importance of women's productive function was clearly recognized at all levels, however, with the acquisition of wealth through weaving even being posited as a possible motivation for polygyny, a structure that, although traditionally seen as diminishing women's status, could also arguably provide women with practical (and even emotional) support networks (Townsend 2006). Occasional references to *cihuatlatoque* ("female rulers," sing. *cihuatlatoani*) make clear that some noblewomen were able to wield significant political authority; inheritance passed through both male and female lines, and the royal origins of the Tenochca dynasty lie with a woman, Illancueitl (Kellogg 1995).

As the most obvious example of gender complementarity, marriage demonstrates the perceived importance of both male and female activities for collective success. Even in conceiving a child, continued intercourse was believed to be necessary so that the couple could jointly "grow" the baby. (At least up to a point—beyond a certain time, "excessive" coupling would apparently produce a sticky, oversized child!) A microcosm of Aztec society, this most fundamental gendered pairing exemplifies patterns of parallelism that are seen not only in kinship but also throughout the social, political, and religious world.

Symbolism, Religion, and Myth

Gendered pairings are seen at every level of Aztec life and belief, and parallelism profoundly influenced both structures and ideals. Both gods and goddesses appear prominently in Aztec mythology, and it is common to see deities appearing in either male/female pairings or, in many cases, with both male and female aspects. The duality of the creation of the universe is seen in the supreme originating deities Ometecuhtli and Omecihuatl. One rather pragmatic explanation of this primordial couple translates their names as "Bone Lord" and "Bone Woman" in reference to the creation of humanity from bones of a previous era, but the duality of their gendered identity is made even more explicit in the argument that sees them as "Two Lord" and "Two Woman," masculine and feminine aspects of Ometeotl ("Two God" or "Lord of Duality") (León-Portilla 1999). Whichever interpretation we favor, both male and female influences were clearly regarded as indispensable in creation, as they were in destruction; at the other end of the cycle, Mictlan, the land of the dead, was ruled over by Mictlantecuhtli and Mictlancihuatl, the lord and lady of the realm of deceased souls.

In the physical realm, Tenochtitlan was headed by the "omnipotent dyad" (Schroeder 1997) of the *tlahtoani* ("he who speaks") and *cihuacoatl* ("woman snake"); although both were physically male, as the name makes explicit, the *cihuacoatl* was metaphorically female and, on ceremonial occasions, was dressed in female attire, literally personifying his eponymous goddess. Although the power dynamics between the two rulers are a little hazy (perhaps due to Spanish misunderstanding or to shifts in the latter years of empire) it seems that, much like a married couple, the *tlahtoani* and *cihuacoatl* each held discrete, gendered responsibilities. Broadly speaking, the *tlahtoani* was responsible for politically "external" matters such as warfare, diplomacy, state religion, and national politics, while the *cihuacoatl* held more "domestic" (in the political, internal, sense) responsibilities, maintaining order in the city, and acting as principal judge, as well as governing the city when the *tlahtoani* was on military campaigns (Read 2000). High political office was ordinarily reserved to men, but this symbol of female influence at the apex of authority is symptomatic of the gendered parallelism that shaped Aztec experience.

Just as a husband and wife shared the duties essential to the success of their household, so the state flourished through the corresponding endeavors of its ruling partnership: "One could see the Mexica house as a model of the cosmos, writ small, but perhaps it would be better to see the Mexica cosmos as a house writ large" (Burkhart 1997:30–31). While women maintained and controlled the "domestic" sphere (a term that, in a society of extended kin groups, should be understood as encompassing the community more widely, not limited to nuclear family units), men were more "outward-facing," taking on the "public" responsibilities such as warfare and politics. The same pattern can be observed in priestly duties, where male priests were solely responsible for human sacrificial ritual and public discourse, while *cihuatlamacazque* ("women priests") maintained and supplied the temple, as well as taking part in silent devotions in public.

This public/domestic dichotomy, as well as the dominance of men in traditional spheres of influence, perhaps tempts us to identify traditional patterns of patriarchy at work, but such assumptions are challenged by the respect for women, and their contribution, which is visible in Aztec culture and behavior. It is only by looking to the cosmological underpinnings of Aztec ideals that we can illuminate the origins of their distinctive gendered interactions.

Male and female roles were strongly shaped by the Aztecs' profound bond with the gods and their mythical past. During childbirth, women were believed to be literally possessed by the goddess Cihuacoatl (the same deity who was personified by one of the ruling dyad). One of the aspects of the Earth Goddess, whose power was so awesome that even to be in her presence was considered perilous, Cihuacoatl gave women a physical connection to the spiritual world that offered them access to forces both

FIGURE 26.4 Sculpture of a *cihuateotl*. With permission @ British Museum.

awesome and perilous. A woman who died during childbirth remained permanently imbued with the presence of the goddess, and her corpse had to be guarded from the predations of young warriors who hoped that carrying her finger or arm into battle might allow them to draw on Cihuacoatl's power. This physical embodiment of divine power also elevated the deceased woman's spirit to godly status; she became one of the Cihuateteo ("Woman Gods") (Figure 26.4) who haunted the crossroads and promised to transform into the Tzitzimime ("Devil Women") who would devour humanity at the end of the Fifth Age.

While male roles in religion were diverse and functional, rooted in the necessity to provide blood to the gods in exchange for the blood let by male deities to bring about their own birth, women's religious significance was narrowly identified and awe-inspiring. Men served the gods; women embodied them (Dodds Pennock 2008).

WARFARE

It has been argued that women's authority was gradually diminished by the increasing focus on military issues associated with the Aztecs' rise to political prominence in central Mexico. The increasing reliance on tribute and the spoils of war, both channels of wealth controlled by men, arguably marginalized women and domestic activities, establishing warfare as the principal route to social mobility and success (Nash 1978). While the increasing emergence of a social structure based on military hierarchy undoubtedly threatened to erode the perceived importance of the female "domestic" sphere, it is important to recognize that military success was seen as a collective responsibility.

Although the battlefield itself was a male domain, warfare was central to the lives of all Aztecs, both men and women (Burkhart 1997). Women were honored in military language as the mothers of future warriors, heralded for carrying "the small shield" and "capturing" a baby; the afterlife of a woman who died in childbirth parallels that of a man who died in battle or as a sacrifice. Possessing a direct conduit to the divine, women engaged in symbolic struggles that were believed to have concrete consequences on the battlefield: a wife who carelessly allowed food to stick to the pot could cause her husband's arrow to miss his mark (Sahagún 1979, Book V). Triumph in war was dependent on women's diligent performance of domestic rituals and prayers, which preserved the safety of their menfolk, as well as their practical responsibilities for sustaining the city and provisioning the army. Although women physically fought only in the most dire circumstances, they were seen as strong, effective, and independent partners in the most fundamental of Aztec activities: the practice of war.

So central was the Aztec emphasis on individuals' value and effectiveness in their designated roles that gender distinctions appear to have been lessened in old age. Past their prime as warriors, mothers, and workers, old men and women saw their significance pass away, as the specific values of their sexes became less relevant to their daily experience. These elders were respected as models for behavior, as ancestors, and as guardians of tradition, but, with the passing of their vitality, so masculinity and femininity too seem to have been diminished. An old woman might remain a homemaker, an old man a political advisor, but their gender identities ebbed along with their fertility and energy, until they blurred into the "forefathers, the old men, the old women, the white haired ones" who watched over the words "to live by" which guided the next generation (Sahagún 1969, Book VI).

References Cited

Berdan, Frances F., and Patricia Rieff Anawalt (editors)
1992 *Codex Mendoza*. University of California Press, Berkeley.
Bourdieu, Pierre
1977 *Outline of a Theory of Practice*. Cambridge University Press, Cambridge, UK.
Brown, Betty Ann
1985 Seen But Not Heard: Women in Aztec Ritual—The Sahagún Texts. In *Text and Image in Pre-Columbian Art: Essays on the Interrelationship of the Verbal and Visual Arts*, edited by Janet Catherine Berlo, pp. 119–153. British Archaeological Review, Oxford, UK.
Brumfiel, Elizabeth M.
1991 Weaving and Cooking: Women's Production in Aztec Mexico. In *Engendering Archaeology: Women and Prehistory*, edited by Joan M. Gero and Margaret W. Conkey, pp. 224–251. Wiley Blackwell, Oxford, UK.

Burkhart, Louise M.

1997 Mexica Women on the Home Front: Housework and Religion in Aztec Mexico. In *Indian Women of Early Mexico*, edited by S. Schroeder, S. Wood, and R. Haskett, pp. 25–54. University of Oklahoma Press, Norman.

Clendinnen, Inga

1991 *Aztecs: An Interpretation*. Cambridge University Press, Cambridge, UK.

Dodds Pennock, Caroline

2008 *Bonds of Blood: Gender, Lifecycle and Sacrifice in Aztec Culture*. Palgrave Macmillan, Basingstoke, UK.

Kellogg, Susan

1995 *Law and the Transformation of Aztec Culture*. University of Oklahoma Press, Norman.

1997 From Parallel and Equivalent to Separate But Unequal: Tenochca Mexica Women, 1500–1700. In *Indian Women of Early Mexico*, edited by S. Schroeder, S. Wood, and R. Haskett, pp. 123–143. University of Oklahoma Press, Norman.

Klein, Cecelia F.

2001 None of the Above: Gender Ambiguity in Nahua Ideology. In *Gender in Pre-Hispanic America: A Symposium at Dumbarton Oaks, 12th and 13th October 1996*, edited by Cecelia F. Klein, pp. 183–253. Dumbarton Oaks Research Library and Collection, Washington, DC.

León-Portilla, Miguel

1999 Ometeotl, el supremo dios dual, y Tezcatlipoca "Dios Principal." *Estudios de Cultura Náhuatl* 30:133–152.

McCafferty, Sharisse D., and Geoffrey D. McCafferty

1991 Spinning and Weaving as Female Gender Identity in Post-Classic Mexico. In *Textile Traditions of Mesoamerica and the Andes: An Anthology*, edited by Margot Blum Schevill, Janet Catherine Berlo, and Edward B. Dwyer, pp. 19–44. Garland, New York.

Nash, June

1978 The Aztecs and the Ideology of Male Dominance. *Signs* 4(2):249–262.

Quiñones Keber, Eloise

1995 *Codex Telleriano-Remesis*. University of Texas, Austin.

Read, Kay A.

2000 More Than Earth: Cihuacoatl as Female Warrior, Male Matron, and Inside Ruler. In *Goddesses Who Rule*, edited by Elisabeth Benand and Beverly Moon, pp. 51–68. Oxford University Press, Oxford, UK.

Read, Kay A., and Jane Rosenthal

2006 The Chalcan Woman's Song: Sex as a Political Metaphor in Fifteenth-Century Mexico. *The Americas* 62(3):313–348.

Rodríguez-Shadow, María J.

1991 *La mujer azteca*. Universidad Autónoma del Estado de México, Toluca.

Sahagún, Fray Bernardino de

1969 *Florentine Codex, General History of the Things of New Spain: Book V, The Omens*. Translated and edited by A. J. O. Anderson and C. E. Dibble. School of American Research, Santa Fe, NM, and University of Utah Press, Salt Lake City.

1979 *Florentine Codex, General History of the Things of New Spain: Book VI, Rhetoric and Moral Philosophy*. Translated and edited by A. J. O. Anderson and C. E. Dibble. School of American Research, Santa Fe, NM, and University of Utah Press, Salt Lake City.

Schroeder, Susan

1997 Introduction. In *Codex Chimalpahin, Society and Politics in Mexico Tenochtitlan, Tlatelolco, Texcoco, Culhuacan, and Other Nahua Altepetl in Central Mexico*, edited and translated by Arthur J. O. Anderson and Susan Schroeder, pp. 3–13. University of Oklahoma Press, Norman.

Sigal, Pete
2007 Queer Nahuatl: Sahagún's Faggots and Sodomites, Lesbians and Hermaphrodites. *Ethnohistory* 54(1):9–34.
Smith, Michael E.
2012 *The Aztecs*. Wiley-Blackwell, Oxford, UK.
Townsend, Camilla
2006 "What in the World Have You Done to Me My Lover?" Sex, Servitude, and Politics among the Pre-Conquest Nahuas as Seen in the *Cantares Mexicanos*. *The Americas* 62(3):349–389.
Zorita, Alonso de
1965 *The Lords of New Spain: The Brief and Summary Relation of the Lords of New Spain*. Translated and edited by Benjamin Keen. Phoenix, London.

CHAPTER 27

THE HUMAN BODY IN THE MEXICA WORLDVIEW

ALFREDO LÓPEZ AUSTIN

THE TWO MEXICA CITIES

ACCORDING to Mexica sources, a group set out from Aztlan[1] in the early twelfth century A.D. under the tutelage of their patron god in search of their promised land. Once they started their journey, their god instructed his chosen people, the *Aztec*, to hereafter refer to themselves as *Mexitin*, which would later become *Mexica*. In A.D. 1325, after traveling for more than two centuries, the pilgrims arrived at the site chosen by their god, where they founded Mexico-Tenochtitlan. A few short years later, a dissenting group established itself nearby, founding the sister city of Mexico-Tlatelolco. At the time of the Spanish Conquest, Mexico-Tenochtitlan was the most powerful city in Mesoamerica. Thus the European campaign focused on gaining control of the capital, a goal they achieved in 1521. This chapter is based primarily on historical sources written by authors in both cities. The texts offer a glimpse of indigenous traditions from the eve of the Conquest through the first decades of the Colonial period.

The Mexica understanding of the human body is similar to ideas held by other Mesoamerican peoples of the era. The former are often used as a prototype, largely because the ancient and early Colonial sources, both in Nahuatl and in Spanish, tend to focus on them. Mexica ideas were rooted in contemporary cultural traditions; thus sources referencing synchronous groups can be used as supplemental information. In addition, and with appropriate caution, some ethnographic data may also be used to complement our understanding, offering important details on the indigenous ideas and practices that survived the long process of colonization.

Research on ideas about the constitution and functioning of the human body as conceptualized by a given group of people should focus on the social, economic, political, and religious setting of the time. Thus such research may explore both how the cultural context affects people's perceptions of themselves and how concepts of the body guide all human activities.

The most important sixteenth-century Mexica documents regarding the body include Fray Bernardino de Sahagún's (2000) *General History* and Fray Alonso de Molina's (1944 [1571]) impressive dictionary. Other authors have also offered important information, permitting us to assemble a coherent picture of these complex concepts (López Austin 1988).

THE COMPOSITION OF THE HUMAN BODY

One of the central precepts of both ancient and contemporary indigenous worldviews is that all creatures are composed of two types of substances. The first is heavy, dense, visible, and subject to the ravages of time. The other is light, subtle, and undetectable (Figure 27.1). The heavy part of the human body also contains a set of light substance entities that approximate our modern concept of "souls," taking appropriate precautions not to blindly equate the two. Within each individual reside several such entities, each

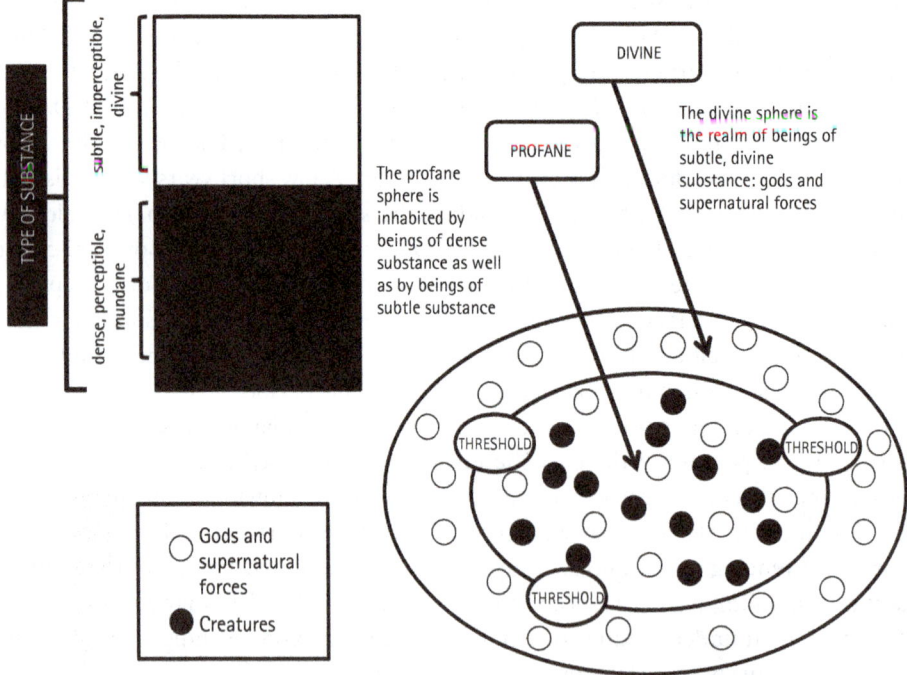

FIGURE 27.1 The cosmos is divided into two time-space realms. The divine is the realm of the gods and supernatural forces and is composed of subtle substance. The profane realm is inhabited by beings (composed of dense substance) as well as the gods and supernatural forces. Thresholds between the realms permit communication. Drawn by author and Kristin Sullivan.

with different, and often complementary, characteristics. The heterogeneity of these souls lies partly in the diversity of their origin. They are also unique in how they enter or leave the body, the dangers to which they are exposed, and the degree of comfort or discomfort they may cause to humans. In particular, their specific functions set them apart in terms of what we today conceptualize as physiological, psychological, moral, social, parental, religious, and so on. Importantly, these souls possess free will. Thus we must consider the harmony or cacophony of the whole, as the individual's health depends, in part, on maintaining good relations between the various components of the body.

The Heavy Substance of the Human Body

The heavy and dense part of the body deteriorates and is eventually destroyed in this life by the effects of time and wear. This part of the body is sustained by the bounty of the earth, and each individual's destiny is to settle his or her debt, offering his or her body to the earth goddess. Thus the heavy substance of the body returns to the earth. This idea, in particular, exemplifies a religion that revolved around intense reciprocity between men and gods.

The body's fuel, par excellence, was corn. To obtain the grain, specifically chosen by the gods to form and later sustain their human creations, the gods had to break the stone enclosure that prevented the corn from leaving the divine sphere in order to come into contact with the surface of the earth ("Leyenda de los soles" 1945:21).

The soft part of the body was metaphorically referred to as "the earthen or muddy" part and included adipose tissue, striated muscles, skin, organs, hair, and semen, all covering the bones. The various components were linked at the joints, weak points that could be penetrated by the invisible agents visiting the body in order to cause harm. Usually, the invaders were cold beings generically referred to as "airs."

The nerves, ligaments, and tendons bound the various bodily components, concentrating the vital forces in them. Blood vessels were distributed uniformly throughout the body, preventing the liquid's retention in any one place; while lubricating the muscles, strengthening, revitalizing, and allowing them to grow. Any change in the blood's density was considered very negative.

The head was the center of all major psychological functions, coordinating organs like the eyes and ears, which were attributed the powers of both perception and reasoning.

The viscera formed an interconnected web through which fluids circulated freely. Some of its functions, such as digestion or respiration, were conceived of as generating heat, which materialized as waste or steam. Food was cleansed and purified as it descended into the heat of the stomach and spleen. The heart was the vital center and the organ of consciousness; the liver was a reservoir for blood, while the gall bladder housed anger. Both the kidneys and the testes generated sexual joy. Semen was produced in the bone marrow, and procreation required that the father's semen mix with an equivalent fluid donated by the mother.

Souls

Souls can be roughly divided into organic entities making up the human body and those that, being contingent, invade the body to transform, sicken, alter the consciousness, inspire positive or negative passion, or grant extraordinary powers (Figure 27.2). The former are integrated into the body before birth or soon thereafter and perform their duties from the shelter of the heavy and dense part of the body, though remaining distinct thanks to their supernatural origin. In the Mesoamerican worldview, *supernatural* refers to all that is imperceptible, having originated before the creation of the world, acting on the everyday with results that can be perceived by humans. Some souls also have a personality, allowing them to achieve divine status.

To understand the supernatural quality of the Mexica soul and its place in the human body, one must first understand that within the Mexica worldview the supernatural

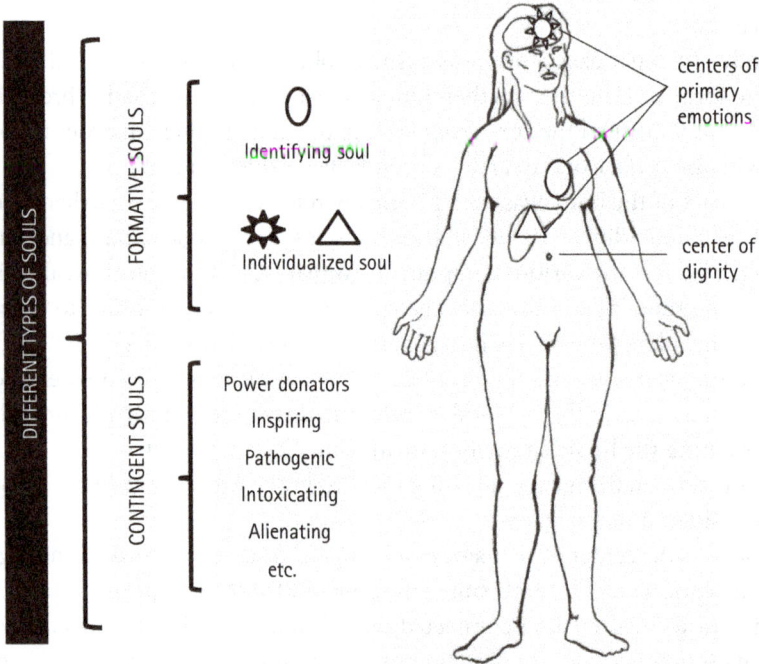

FIGURE 27.2 The body is composed of dense and subtle substance. The different souls are composed of subtle substance. Formative souls are necessary for human existence. In contrast, humans can survive without the different contingent souls. Prepared by author and redrawn by Kristin Sullivan.

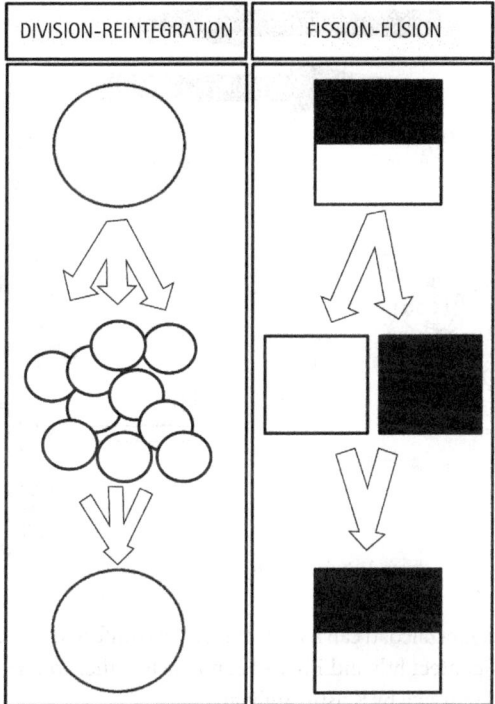

FIGURE 27.3 Each god can separate into two or more different gods, and two or more different gods can join together to form a single god. These two processes are known as fission and fusion. The gods can also separate into multiple gods, which can join together again. These two processes are known as division and reintegration. Prepared by author and redrawn by Kristin Sullivan.

substance was divisible, and its constituent parts could disperse throughout the world and later return to their point of origin (Figure 27.3). Moreover, souls could, and often did, enter different bodies. Thus an entity deriving from a god or creature could be shared by several individuals or might invade other beings on either a temporary or permanent basis.

Thus, for the Mexica, the human body was not a simple amalgamation of heterogeneous elements. These elements were not exclusive to any one body; rather, they could be shared with other beings, both supernatural and earthly. It was also a dynamic system, constantly transformed by time and permanently or temporarily possessed by invasive souls.

THE *TEYOLIA*

For the Mexicas, all creatures had a unique soul known as the "heart." Not to be confused with the organ of the same name that formed part of the heavy substance of the body, this soul was of divine origin. Originally, many gods transformed themselves in order to create the world. Covering themselves in a detectable layer made of a dense and heavy

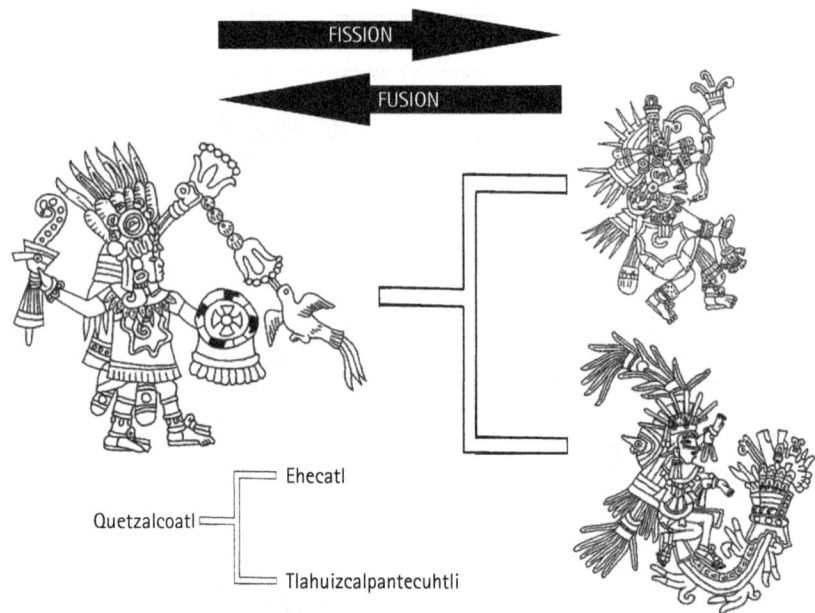

FIGURE 27.4 The god Quetzalcoatl can fission to form two different gods: Tlahuizcalpantecuhtli and Ehecatl. Tlahuizcalpantecuhtli and Ehecatl can fuse together to form the god Quetzalcoatl. Prepared by author and redrawn by Kristin Sullivan.

substance, the gods became creators-beings, maintaining their divine immortality within their light substance but entering the cycle of life/death via the heavy substance now covering them. When the heavy substance layer died or was destroyed, the exposed souls were stored inside the hollow Sacred Mountain, where they were prepared to be recycled and sent to form another being of the same class or species. Within these souls lie the essential characteristics of the different classes of the earthly entities: stars, elements, meteors, minerals, plants, animals, and humans.

The *teyolia*, the center of the light substance in humans, resided in the perceptible organ known as the heart, or *yóllotl*. It joined the child before birth and remained with the individual until his or her death. The *teyolia* was composed of the essential characteristics of human beings. However, within the complexity humans attributed themselves, the heart was conceived of as being composed of divine levels. Mesoamerican deities could fission, or split into heterogeneous components, so that the same god could be transformed into multiple gods (Figure 27.4).

Thus each human heart possessed the characteristic features that the patron god, or one of the god's component parts, had contributed when donating its own substance during creation (López Austin 1997:36–39). The patron god of all humanity endowed humans with an anthropomorphic essence; all of the gods that successively split from the original god possessed the latter's essential characteristics: ethnicity, town, *calpolli* group, or larger familial group, and so on in descending order (Figure 27.5). Thus humans considered essential their anthropomorphic qualities, such as their language,

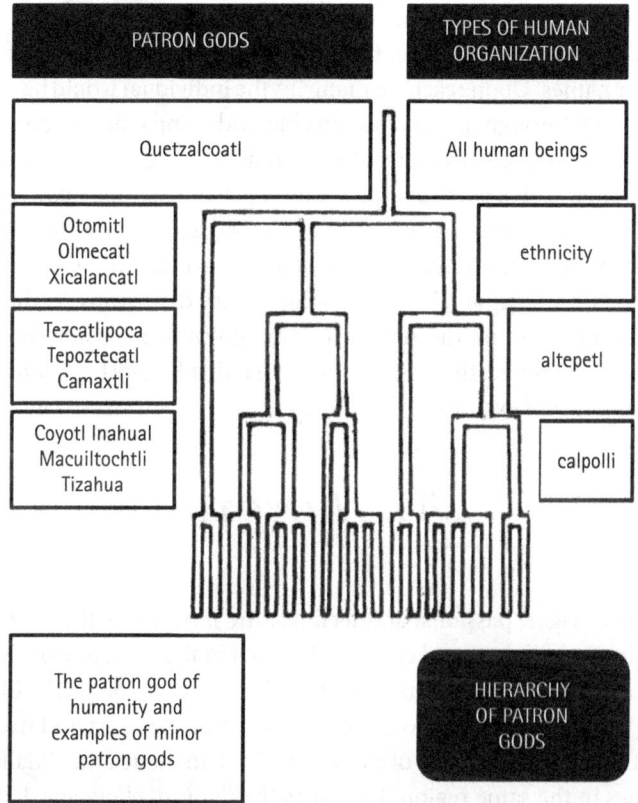

FIGURE 27.5 Patron gods belong to distinct hierarchies, presiding over the different *calpollis*, cities, ethnicities, and of all humankind. Prepared by author and redrawn by Kristin Sullivan.

customs, and economic specialization. The human being belonged, by participating in the collective *teyolia*, to different groups of varying sizes.

The main functions of the *teyolia* were to provide life to the body and serve as the center of thought and emotional well-being for the individual, coordinating the activities of the other components. The greatest threats were illness or madness stemming from the individual's immoral behavior.

The *Tonalli*

As with the *teyolia*, the *tonalli* was of divine origin. During the 13-day period in which a child was born, a ritual would be performed in which the newborn was presented with sunlight reflected in a water-filled vessel. A part of the god-day was bestowed upon the child shortly after birth.

While pouring water over the infant's head during the ritual, the priest infused the child with some of the qualities of the god-day selected. The sunlight's "soul" was dispersed throughout the body but concentrated at the top of the head. From that point onward, the child was considered a "carrier" of that particular god-day, the name of which became one of his or her names. Upon reaching maturity, the individual would be expected to care for his or her *tonalli* through upright, responsible, and compassionate behavior. Failure to do so would have serious consequences for the individual's very existence. This soul provided the individual with a particular physique, a personality that allowed the individual to develop skills, virtues, vices, and what can be likened to one's destiny.

Unlike the *teyolia*, the individual's *tonalli* could leave and did so freely during sleep or intercourse. Any strong shock was considered very dangerous, as the *tonalli* left the body unexpectedly, running the risk of becoming trapped outside the body where it might be captured by the earth gods. An individual that had lost his or her *tonalli* would become seriously ill and eventually die.

The *Ihiyotl*

As the nucleus of vigor, passions, and feelings, the *ihiyotl* was the soul that produced appetites, desires, greed, lust, and courage. Located in the liver, one of its functions was the administration of bile. Its origin was external as it was introduced—like the *tonalli*—through the ritual bath, which also dampened areas of the heart and liver. The gift was requested of the goddess and god of the stellar sky, Citlalicue and Citlallatónac, as well as minor deities in the same region, known as the *ilhuícatl chaneque*. In the prayer, the individual requested that the power develop by uttering the same coupled metaphor used for plant germination: *inic titzmoliniz, inic ticeliaz*, "may [the creature] grow and flourish."

Parts of this soul could leave the body as emissions expressing vigor, moderating pain, or inflaming courage. Often gaseous moods, smelly and evil, harmed the people, animals, plants, and objects they came in contact with. During sleep, for example, shamans could send their *ihiyotl* to invade other beings in a phenomenon known as *nahualismo*, or shape shifting.

The proper functioning of the *ihiyotl* depended on the maintenance of good relations with other souls, a life of controlled emotions, and sexual balance. Excesses and sexual sins damaged it, leading to emissions that would seriously harm family, neighbors, crops, and other aspects of an individual's life.

Secondary Souls

Humans with power, particularly rulers and shamans, received additional souls from various deities, and with this gift did their bidding on earth. It was common for the *tlahtoque*, Mexica kings, to display images of their associated gods on their attire. Today it is common for shamans to be attributed dual souls, which allow them to act upon supernatural forces.

Such divine possession could be of varying intensity. In some cases, it was permanent and of such strength that the possessed would become a living image of the invading god. An example of one of these human-gods is the Feathered Serpent (*Quetzalcoatl* in Nahuatl).

Other possessions, however, were shorter in length, such as those provoked by the "hearts" of psychoactive substances or intoxicants. Many diseases, artistic inspiration, criminal impulses, lewd desires, and madness were often interpreted as more or less fleeting divine possessions.

Health, Illness, and Health Care

The correct functioning of the body was due largely to balance, primarily between the two complementary yet opposing principles that produced cosmic movement. The opposing forces were commonly identified as either cold or hot. While these states did not refer to actual thermal qualities, they could manifest themselves as such, causing chills or fever. Moreover, there were exceptions, like fevers caused by dental ailments, which were considered cold in nature.

In very general terms, balance could be achieved by controlling the emotions, leading a righteous life, maintaining proper relationships with peers, nourishing ties to the gods (including, above all, the timely performance of rituals), and consuming a balanced diet. These also were classified as hot or cold in nature, meanings that stretched beyond the thermal states themselves.

As an example of an imbalance of hot and cold in the body, the ancient Nahuas considered anger and shame to be particularly dangerous. In anger, heat was concentrated in the innermost part of the body while cold inhabited the exterior of the body. On the other hand, shame involved a concentration of heat on the skin, outside the body, while cold inhabited the body itself. The imbalance was not only dangerous per se, but it favored the loss of important bodily elements or invasion by harmful invisible beings, including the so-called "airs," often from the underworld.

The same principle of balance ruled much of therapeutic medicine: drugs were classified based on the nature of their active ingredients, cold or hot, while particular foods were also prescribed based on their corrective powers.

Given the characteristics of the etiology, the doctor had to perform the duties of moral, family, social, and ritual advisor.

Human Sacrifice

To understand the concept of human sacrifice and self-sacrifice, we must first make a prior classification of the types of sacrifices made. Reciprocity, fundamental to

Mesoamerican religious beliefs, imposed on human beings the terrible obligation to repay the gods for the effort they exerted in creating humans. Since the gods were subjected in this world to the laws imposed by the Sun at the time of creation, their work resulted in fatigue. The god's fatigue was mitigated by offerings of food. Humans fed the tired gods, offering them their property and lives, bodily substance and energy. Thus the gods were compensated for their divine labor from which health, fertility, welfare, rainfall, soil fecundity, crop maturity, and many other prized goods derived.

Some of the human victims offered in sacrifice were called *nextlahualtin*, literally "payments," which crudely identifies their destiny. Another large group of sacrificial victims where known as the *teteo imixiptlahuan*, or "images of the gods." They were human-gods; their bodies had been occupied by the gods during a ritual, converting them into the living vessels of the gods. Thus because the gods had to be reinvigorated periodically, as any weakness was considered extremely dangerous because it reduced their effectiveness. The gods underwent a bodily death that liberated them from their worn-out shell and, through sacrifice, were "reborn" into the world with their initial energy restored.

Ritual cannibalism, also common among the Mexicas, has been interpreted, based on the contemporary description of the practice, as a communion with the ingested god.

Death

Death was considered the payment due to the gods for donating the materials necessary for human life. It was the final installment: heavy substance and bodily energy. Death meant the disintegration of the human being as the parts that had formed the whole began to fall apart. Molina's Spanish-Nahuatl dictionary includes several synonyms for death: *onacico in nacian, in nopoliuhya, in noxamanca, in nopoztequia* (1944 [1571], S-N:fol. 86v); literally, "I've reached my end, my destruction, my breaking point, my fragmentation." Every part of the human being would follow the path of his or her particular destiny. The *ihiyotl*, for example, would wander the earth as a fearsome *yohualehécatl*, or "night air."

The main soul, or *teyolia*, continued to fulfill its destiny after death. As the essence of the human host, and with humans essentially having been created to complement divine efforts through work, the *teyolia* retained its duties even after death.

Sources mention four regions: Mictlan, the underworld, for the common dead; Tonatiuhilhuícatl or "heaven of the Sun," for those killed during military service or as sacrificial victims, as well as women who died during their first childbirth; Tlalocan, the "place of the god of rain," a green paradise populated by those who died by drowning, by being struck by lightning, or suffered from "water diseases"; and Chichihualcuauhco, inhabited by children who passed away before they were old enough to consume corn.

We know little about the beliefs of the life in the hereafter. The dead continued assisting their families for some time, receiving offerings in return. It was not an eternal existence; the trip to the deepest part of Mictlan took four years. The hardships of the journey cleansed the individual's history. Even today, the Nahua consider death a process that cleanses the soul (Signorini and Lupo 1989:48). Following this cleansing process, the *teyolia* lost all vestiges of its former worldly individuality. The *Florentine Codex* says that, in the deepest level, "in the ninth Mictlan, was complete loss" *(Códice Florentino* [Sahagún 1979], Lib. III:fol. 26v). One of the names for Mictlan, *Ximoayan*, is clear on this: *xim* means to "polish, scrape, shave." The *teyolia* was left empty, devoid of history; all that remained was enough human essence to permit the soul to join another newly begotten human (López Austin 1997:263–267).

NOTE

1. The word *Aztlan*, as most terms in Nahuatl, is pronounced with the stress on the penultimate syllable and not as we often pronounce it today, stressing the final syllable. The same rule applies to Mexico. In this latter toponym, the "x" is pronounced like the English "sh."

REFERENCES CITED

"Leyenda de los soles"
1945 Leyenda de los soles. In *Códice Chimalpopoca*, translated by Primo Feliciano Velázquez, pp. 119–164. Instituto de Investigaciones Históricas, Universidad Nacional Autónoma de México, Mexico City.

López Austin, Alfredo
1988 *The Human Body and Ideology: Concepts of the Ancient Nahuas.* 2 vols. Translated by Thelma Ortiz de Montellano and Bernard R. Ortiz de Montellano. University of Utah Press, Salt Lake City.
1997 *Tamoanchan, Tlalocan: Places of Mist.* Translated by Bernard R. Ortiz de Montellano and Thelma Ortiz de Montellano. University Press of Colorado, Niwot.

Molina, Fray Alonso de
1944 [1571] *Vocabulario en lengua castellana y mexicana.* Cultura Hispánica, Madrid.

Sahagún, Fray Bernardino de
1979 *Códice Florentino: manuscrito 218-20 de la Colección Palatina de la Biblioteca Medicea Laurenziana* [Facsimile]. 3 vols. Secretaría de Gobernación, Archivo General de la Nación, Mexico City.
2000 *Historia general de las cosas de Nueva España.* 3 vols. Consejo Nacional para la Cultura y las Artes, Mexico City.

Signorini, Italo, and Alessandro Lupo
1989 *Los tres ejes de la vida: almas, cuerpo, enfermedad entre los nahuas de la Sierra de Puebla,* Universidad Veracruzana, Xalapa, Mexico.

CHAPTER 28

NAHUA ETHNICITY

JAMES M. TAGGART

ETHNICITY is the classification of self and others that develops among groups occupying the same region and sometimes competing for the same scarce resources (Lomnitz-Adler 1991; Stark and Chance 2008:2–12). Scholars of the ancient as well as contemporary Nahuas have found evidence of ethnicity in material artifacts, stone monuments, pictorial manuscripts, prose manuscripts created under the direction of the Spanish friars, Colonial period wills, notarized documents, court petitions, testimony, and parish records, and contemporary ethnographic observations. Implicit or sometimes explicit in their investigations is the question of how Nahua ethnicity changed after the fall of the Aztec Empire in 1521. There is little doubt that the Nahua concepts of ethnicity changed in the centuries following the Spanish Conquest, but there is also considerable evidence that the Nahuas did not adopt and in some cases actively resisted the Spanish concept of ethnicity hinged to race.

An examination of the prehispanic material artifacts reveals some of the ways the ancient Nahuas marked differences between themselves and others prior to the arrival of the Spaniards. Ethnic distinctions appeared in figurines adorned with distinctive styles of clothing, implements for the preparation and preservation of food, and differences in settlement patterns and ceremonial architecture (Stark 2008). To take just one example of ethnic distinctions in monumental sculpture, the sacrificial Tizoc Stone, created in Tenochtitlan before 1481, featured carvings of 15 pairs of captors, each of which have "title glyphs" that identify the representatives of polities and ethnic groups that fell to the Tenochca (Umberger 2008:66, 90–91, 93–94). Hicks (2001:390–391) named 27 ethnic groups that lived in central Mexico during the late prehispanic period.

Early Colonial era prose documents created by Nahuas under the direction of the Spanish friars hint at some of the ways that Nahua ethnicity differed markedly from the European concept of race with its "emphasis on innateness" and "inbred nature" (Chance 2008:147). The members of ancient Nahua ethnic groups had a connection to a place and a common history, interest, enemies, and destiny (Berdan 2008:108–112). They appear to have placed more emphasis on human activity in particular localities than on inherent characteristics passed through blood. The Nahuas marked differences between themselves and others by language, clothing, hairstyles, food preferences, distinctive technologies, and stereotypical behavior. For example, they said that the Matlatzinca, Totonac, Yopime, and Olmeca spoke barbarous tongues, although the Nahua did learn the languages of others. They remarked that the Tamime wore tattered capes, the Teochichimeca wore animal skins, the Matlatzinca wore coarse maguey fibers, Totonacas wore elegantly embroidered clothing, the Olmeca wore bark paper breech clouts, the Huaxtec wore no breech clouts, and the Otomi were vain and gaudy dressers. They reported that the Otomí shaved men's foreheads leaving the hair long in the back, and Totonac and Huaxtec women wore long hair braided with colorful strips of cloth and feathers. The Nahuas said that the Otomí had good food and drink, but the Matlatzinca did not use chile or salt and drank too much pulque, as did the Huaxtecs, and the Totonacs made very good tortillas, but Michoaque were bad cooks. Mixtecs were good metalworkers, the Xochimilca were skilled stoneworkers, and the Totonacs and Huaxtecs were excellent weavers. The Mexicas could find something valuable in groups whose behavior they also judged negatively. For example, by Nahua standards, the Huaxtec were imprudent, untrained, and too scantily dressed, and yet the Mexica ruler presented Huaxtec-style warrior costumes to accomplished warriors (Berdan 2008:111, 115, 117–127).

Nahua ethnicity and ethnic relations were linked to social and political organization in complex ways. The *altepetl*, or city-state, was sometimes a multiethnic political unit, and the constituent ethnic units were the *calpolli*, or land-holding wards, and the *tecalli*, or noble houses (Berdan 2008:109; Carrasco 1976; Chance 2008:135; Lockhart 1992:116). Some *calpolli* were stratified conical clans (Kierchoff 1955; Wolf 1959:136), and the *tecalli* consisted of "related landholding nobles and their commoner dependents who tilled the soil ... and were mindful of their own histories" (Chance 2008:135). Members of different ethnic groups within and between *altepetl* sometimes cooperated with each other by carrying out trade, joining in rituals, and intermarriage. Cloaks made in one location and appearing in other locations are evidence of tribute, trade, and migration between *altepetl* and their constituent units (Berdan 2008:124–125, 128–129). The Nahuas included other ethnicities in their rituals such as when they invited the Huaxtecs to accompany the goddess Toci (or Teteo inana) during the Mexica monthly festival of Ochpaniztli (Berdan 2008:113; Graulich 1999:92, 95). There is considerable evidence of intermarriage and trade across ethnic lines; Iztcoatl, the leader of the Tenochtitlan, was the son of a slave woman, and Nezahualcoyotl of Texcoco had Alcohua and Chichimeca ancestry, although ethnic mixing was probably more frequent among commoners than among the elite (Ward 2001:427).

The Spanish Conquest changed Nahuat ethnicity in some ways but not all. Chance (2008:138) contends that the most obvious change in the Basin of Mexico "was the decline of the principal regional identities." Most were gone by 1650 as "the focus of ethnicity scaled down to the *altepetl* and its constituent parts: the colonial Indian community" (Chance 2008:138; see also Gibson 1964:30). Chance asserts that "the race concept and the value placed on racial 'purity' were clearly present in early colonial Mexico as the framework of the *sociedad de castas* took shape in the seventeenth century" (Chance 2008:147). However, Colonial Nahuas did not adopt the Spanish category of *indio* designating a "biologically distinct ethnic group vis-à-vis Europeans or people of mixed heritage" (Chance 2008:139). Despite the rigidity of European racism, Nahuas managed ethnic categories in order to secure personal advantage. For example, *caciques*, or political leaders of the colonial *altepetl*, maintained "'Indianness' to hold on to their legal privileges, but they also had to distinguish themselves from the *macehuales* of the Indian commoners" (Chance 2008:147).

Cross-ethnic mating, common prior to the arrival of the Spaniards, also played a very important role in the creation of the ethnic landscape of Mexico after the Conquest (Carrasco 1975; Ward 2001). During the Colonial period, a few Nahua noblemen married Spanish women, but many more marriages involved Spanish men and noble Aztec women (Carrasco 1975:182-183). Most cases of mixing Indian with Spanish blood, or *mestizaje*, involved Spanish men and their colonial-born descendants who fathered children with Nahua women by sex outside of marriage and sometimes by rape (Lavrin 1989:79; Ward 2001:445). In some cases, *mestizaje* took place in the context of slavery. The ancient Nahuas had practiced a form of slavery prior to the arrival of the Spaniards, but it is not clear if their slaves were vulnerable to sexual exploitation. We know that slaves could get married, and their children sometimes rose to prominence: the Aztec king, Itzcoatl, the son of a slave woman, is one example (Ward 2001:435-436). Slavery during the Colonial period involved Spaniards who controlled the labor and probably exploited sexually the women of *encomiendas*, or trusteeships (Ward 2001:437). Spaniards promoted interethnic mating by legislating "ethnic reshuffling among the lower classes through resettlement, the *congregación*" and by enforcing the Church's idea of incest as marriage among kin (Gibson 1964:28, 368; Ward 2001:443-445).

Eric Wolf (1959:233-256) considered the creation of the *Mestizos* one of the most important social and demographic transformations in modern Mexican history. The Nahuas could change into *mestizos* by dressing differently, learning to speak Spanish, moving to a city and away from the place of one's birth, and taking up a profession generally not associated with the indigenous population (Ward 2001:448). Nevertheless, Indians, *mestizos*, and other non-Indians tended to live in separate but overlapping social worlds, and occasionally problems arose along ethnic lines. For example, there is a long history of agrarian struggle where Nahuas rose up in rebellion in order to gain or regain rights to land acquired by Spaniards or *mestizos*. Ethnic conflicts erupted in the Nahua area around Cuetzalan in the Sierra Norte de Puebla when, in the last half of the nineteenth century, the Nahuat Pala Agustin Dieguillo led an insurgency movement against *mestizo* settlers who took advantage of the Ley de Lerdo to buy land once held corporately by the community (Thomson 1991). The Colonization Laws of 1883 and 1894, which were specific applications of the Ley de Lerdo, were also the cause rebellions in the area around Papantla (Velasco Toro 1979).

Some interethnic conflicts came about because of the reorganization of regional government after Independence in 1820. The Mexican government "replaced the semi-autonomous *repúblicas (de indios)* with 'ethnically blind municipal governments'"

(Ducey 2001:528). The 1824 federal constitution allowed states to set population limits when forming municipalities, and one consequence was the creation of communities (*sujetos*) inhabited by Indians subordinated to head towns (*cabeceras*) dominated by non-Indians. The so-called Caste Wars that erupted in 1848 and 1849 in the Huasteca region of Veracruz started as an agrarian protest in 1845 but turned into efforts "demanding the rights to control the appointment of local officials" (Ducey 2001:544). Driving this effort was the frustration of the Indians in the *sujeto* communities who wanted more cultural autonomy (Ducey 2001:528–529, 543–544).

Scholars differ as to whether the image of Indians in Mexico improved after the Mexican Revolution of 1910–1920. The nineteenth and twentieth centuries were a time of privileging the values and culture of the white race, Western civilization, liberal democracy, the Christian religion, and the cultural legacy of the Greco-Roman civilization (Stavenhagen 1984:128). To be identified as an Indian meant being part of an inferior culture and race in the eyes of the European-oriented elite. The post-Revolutionary Mexican government adopted the policy of *indigenismo*, which, on the surface, appeared to be a change from the earlier image of the Indian. Dawson (1998:282) names several prominent scholars such as Antonio Warman (1970), Marjorie Becker (1995), Claudio Lomnitz-Adler (1992), and Mary Kay Vaughn (1997) who criticized the policy for holding the *mestizo* up as the model for the nation. Dawson (1998:284) adds that the *indigenistas* also believed that "the Mexican Indian possessed certain inherent or essential qualities which made Indians a superior national 'stock.'" Among those qualities were "communal traditions" that include a form of "agrarian communism," which, according to the Cardenista discourse, were cultural resources for a "new ethos of collectivity" (Dawson 1998:288–289).

Nevertheless, ethnographers such as Judith Freidlander (1975) concluded that there was only class, not ethnic consciousness, among the Nahuatl of Hueyapan in Morelos, a little over 30 years after the end of the Cardenas regime. Her findings resemble those of Oscar Lewis (1964) who wrote a biography of Pedro Martinez, the Nahuatl speaker from Tepoztlan and who had fought in Emiliano Zapata's agrarian army but did not value his Nahuatl ancestry. Other anthropologists and linguists, however, found ethnic consciousness among contemporary speakers of Nahua languages living in other parts of Mexico, such as the Rio Balsas region of Guerrero, Tlaxcala, the Northern Sierra of Puebla, and the Huasteca of Veracruz and Hidalgo. When making their ethnic judgments (Barth 1969:14), many Nahuas today, like their ancient ancestors, appear to focus on how one does work (*tequitl*) or carries out life activities in a particular place. The Nahuas living in the Rio Balsas region of Guerrero say that *tequitl* refers to activities as diverse as working a *milpa*, preparing *nixtamal*, grinding dough for tortillas, speaking with others, giving advice, persuading or convincing others, sharing knowledge, teaching others, curing, making offerings, praying, singing, dancing, playing musical instruments, and doing just about anything else one can imagine (Good 2005:91). The work connected with *milpa* agriculture is an important aspect of the group identity of the Nahuas of the Veracruz Huasteca, who say that corn is their blood. (Sandstrom 1991, 2008) The Nahuas generally value cooperative work, and they, like other indigenous groups (Ariel de Vidas 2007:224, 2008:187), project onto *mestizos* negative character traits, such as envy that disrupts cooperation.

Ethnic consciousness can also be present below the surface and reflect conditions that lead one to value one's membership in a particular ethnic group when modernization threatens the culture. Jane Hill and Kenneth C. Hill (1980) found evidence of subtle ethnic consciousness in language use among Nahuas in Tlaxcala who live in communities relying heavily on the national economy. The classical Nahuatl language had four levels of honorifics, and these Nahuas paradoxically reduced their use of honorifics in an effort to promote ethnic solidarity while also monitoring the grammar of numeral noun constructions in an effort to hold on to their language and their culture (Hill and Hill 1980:333–339). Kristina Tiedje (2002) discovered increased ethnic consciousness and revitalization among Nahua women in the Huasteca of San Luis Potosí, which she attributes to grassroots organization. Nuns started consciousness-raising among poor Nahua farmers in the 1970s as part of their program of Liberation Theology. Caciques expelled the nuns between 1978 and 1981, but a young priest continued their work, and, in 1994, women formed a union as part of the Organizing Committee of Indigenous and Rural Organizations of the Huasteca Potosina in the community of Xilitla. They opened a restaurant, and the Nahuas among them showed pride in their cultural heritage. Maria de Jesús told Kristina Tiedje that she felt ashamed to speak Nahuatl before joining the union in Xilitla. Afterward, she began to feel better and said, "The indigenous people are the real Mexicans" (Tiedje 2002:272, 279, 281, 295).

Today in Mexico there is an emerging Indian movement, marked most spectacularly by the Zapatista rebellion of 1994, which, among other things, is a struggle for cultural autonomy (Collier and Quaratiello 1999 [1994]). Cultural autonomy is a complicated issue because, as María Teresa Sierra (1995:228) has shown for the Nahuas of the Sierra de Puebla, state and customary law are "interrelated and mutually determining." Although the Nahuas have received horrible treatment in the criminal justice system, they nevertheless take cases to the district courts. Some of the disputes involve changing attitudes toward customs with long traditions such as paying bride-wealth and polygamy. The reification of customary law can create problems when there are disputes over its legitimacy; when customs work against the interests of some, such as when women are barred from inheriting land; when the codification of customary law creates rigidity; and when there are clashes between individual and collective rights such as occur with the killing of witches (Sierra 1995:228, 233–234, 240–246, 248).

One can see many of these aspects of ethnicity in particular cases such as in the Nahuat community of Huitzilan de Serdán. The Nahuat were the original and only inhabitants of Huitzilan until the 1880s when the first *mestizo* settlers appeared, apparently fleeing from the problems that arose during Pala Agustin Dieguillo's uprising in the late 1860s (García Martínez 1989:163–164, 169; Taggart 2007:36). Taking advantage of the Ley de Lerdo and the Colonization Laws, the *mestizos* acquired the vast majority of the arable land, which they converted from milpas to cattle pastures, sugar cane fields, and eventually coffee orchards. Huitzilan became a biethnic community of Nahuat, who comprised 90 percent of the population, and *mestizos*, who had acquired ownership of

FIGURE 28.1 Nahuat woman. Photo by author.

90 percent of the land. *Mestizos* referred to themselves as *gente de razón*, or "people of reason," and considered themselves a racially distinct and superior group. The Nahuat called themselves the people *de calzón*, referring to their loose-fitting white cotton trousers that many indigenous language men wore in the Northern Sierra de Puebla. Women wore blouses with a distinctive style of embroidery, long, flowing white cotton skirts, and aprons (Figures 28.1 and 28.2). The *razónes* marked differences between themselves and the Nahuat in many ways, including by regulating marriage and sexual behavior, particularly of their daughters, sisters, and wives. Marriage between a *razon* woman and a Nahuat man did not take place, but many *razon* men fathered children with Nahuat women who were not their wives. The *razones* make a point of referring to the children of a Nahuat woman and a *razón* man with the mother's surname to deny their legitimacy and their right to inherit the father's property.

In the late 1970s, a wave of agrarian insurgency swept through many Nahua communities (Schryer 1993), including Huitzilan (Taggart 2007, 2008), and many issues connected with Nahua ethnicity came to the surface in the years during and after the conflict. In 1977, 40 Nahuat men from Huitzilan invaded two cattle pastures that were the objects of a dispute between two prominent families of the *gente de razón* and planted them with corn. They called themselves the UCI, an acronym for the Unión

FIGURE 28.2 Nahuat men. Photo by author.

Campesina Independiente or Independent Farmers Union. The UCI originated with radicals who became disenchanted with the labor movement in Puebla and "decided to reorient their fight for the redistribution of land" in the Sierra Norte de Puebla (Beaucage 1994:39). Their movement in Huitzilan was crushed in October of 1983 when the Antorcha Campesina took over the *ayuntamiento* (municipal government). The Nahuat as well as the *gente de razón* who live in Huitzilan today remember the time of the UCI as a period of horrific violence and talk about the land at the center of the conflict in ways that express how they also think differently about ethnicity and descent. The *gente de razon* talked about who actually owned the land and recited the lines of patrilineal descent from the first ancestor who bought the land to the *gente de razón*, who fought over it 100 years later because the original order did not leave a will. The Nahuat, by contrast, talked about who had worked (*tequit*) the land, what crops they had grown, and who had converted it into cattle pastures.

One's own ethnicity for a Nahuat is the sum total of work (*tequit*) with particular people, especially including kin, in localities within Huitzilan There is a direct relationship between reckoning kinship and reckoning ethnicity. A Nahuat man described his kinship connection to another man in the following way: "He was our relative. From where I came, he was from where my grandmother came, from where my father came. We were from one stalk" (Taggart 2008:187). The man used the word *tactzon,* which is a combination of *tac-ti,* or torso, and *tzon-ti,* or head of hair (Karttunen 1983:256). He defined *tactzon* as the stalk of a plant because he, like the ancient (López Austin 1988:I:162) as well as contemporary Nahuas (Sandstrom 1991), identifies the human body with the corn plant. Regarding the ancient Nahuas, López Austin (1988:I:162) notes that the word *tonacayo* ("the whole of our flesh") "is applied to the fruits of the earth, especially to the most important one, corn, thus forming a metaphoric tie between man's corporeal being and the food to which he owed his existence."

At first glance, it might appear that the Nahuat think of kinship in terms of blood descent, as do the *mestizos* who also live in Huitzilan, because he invoked the image of a family tree when talking about his kinship with another Nahuat man. However, his image of the stalk refers to some of the ways he and other Nahuat think about kinship as activity. He alluded to the equation between planting and procreation, which runs through many of his stories and which are forms of *tequit* or work. When referring to his field of social relations, he traced many connections to different ancestors in particular places, to describe his ties not only to the place where he himself was born but also to many other named localities. For example, he was born in *Calyecapan* ("The place of the last house in the community"), and his relative was born in *Talcuaco* ("Land above the community"), but they have a common connection to *Taltzintan* ("Land at the foot "of *Talcuaco*) because their common ancestors were a brother and sister who were born in that locality. The sum total of his ties to people and places are what make him a *Huitzilteco,* or someone from the community of Huitzilan de Serdán. To consider oneself a *Huitzilteco* is the subjective notion of Nahuat ethnicity.

As the UCI era was coming to an end in Huitzilan, some Nahuat in the nearby Cuetzalan area of the Northern Sierra of Puebla formed the cooperative *Tosepan Titataniske* (Together We Shall Triumph) to improve their economic condition and raise ethnic consciousness with more peaceful means. (Bartra et al. 2004) The cooperative buys, at lower prices, the basic necessities, such as corn, beans, and sugar, directly from government stores and seeks higher prices for export crops such as coffee. (Beaucage 2010:15) To raise ethnic consciousness and preserve their culture, members of the cooperative formed the Taller de Tradición Oral (1994), whose members collect and archive the stories of their elders. The cooperative has expanded to include members in at least 50 communities and hamlets (Beaucage 2010:15), including Huitzilan.

References Cited

Ariel de Vidas, Anath
2007 The Symbolic and Ethnic Aspects of Envy among a Teenek Community (Mexico). *Journal of Anthropological Research* 63:215–237.
2008 What Makes a Place Ethnic? The Formal and Symbolic Manifestations of Teenek Identity (Mexico). *Anthropological Quarterly* 81:161–205.

Barth, Fredrik
1969 Introduction. In *Ethnic Groups and Boundaries: The Social Organization of Cultural Difference*, edited by Fredrik Barth, pp. 9-38. Little, Brown, Boston.

Bartra, Armando, Rosario Cobo, and Lorena Paz Paredes
2004 *Tosepan Titataniske. Abriendo horizontes: veintesiete años de historia*. Sociedad Cooperative Regional Tosepan Titataniske/Centro de Formación Kaltaixpetaniloyan, Cuetzalan, Mexico.

Becker, Marjorie
1995 *Setting the Virgin on Fire*. University of California Press, Berkeley.

Berdan, Frances F.
2008 Concepts of Ethnicity and Class in Aztec-Period Mexico. In *Ethnic Identity in Nahua Mesoamerica: The View from Archaeology, Art History, Ethnohistory, and Contemporary Ethnography*, edited by Frances F. Berdan, John K. Chance, Alan R. Sandstrom, Barbara L. Stark, James M. Taggart, and Emily Umberger, pp. 105-132. University of Utah Press, Salt Lake City.

Beaucage, Pierre
1994 Los estudios sobre los movimientos sociales en la Sierra Norte de Puebla (1969-1989). *Revista Mexicana de Sociología* 56:33-55.
2010 Representaciones y conductas: un repertorio de la violencia entre los nahuas de la Sierra Norte de Puebla. *Trace* 57:9-32.

Carrasco, Pedro
1975 La transformación de la cultura indígena durante la colonia. *Historia Mexicana* 25:175-203.
1976 The Chiefly Houses (Teccalli) of Ancient Mexico. *Actes XLII Congrès International des Américanistes* 9B:177-185.

Chance, John K.
2008 Indigenous Ethnicity in Colonial Central Mexico. In *Ethnic Identity in Nahua Mesoamerica: The View from Archaeology, Art History, Ethnohistory, and Contemporary Ethnography*, edited by Frances F. Berdan, John K. Chance, Alan R. Sandstrom, Barbara L. Stark, James M. Taggart, and Emily Umberger, pp. 133-149. University of Utah Press, Salt Lake City.

Collier, George A., with Elizabeth Lowery Quaratiello
1999 [1994] *Basta! Land and the Zapatista Rebellion in Chiapas*. Food First Books, Oakland, CA.

Dawson, Alexander S.
1998 From Models for the Nation to Model Citizens: *Indigenismo* and the "Revindication" of the Mexican Indian. *Journal of Latin American Studies* 30:279-308.

Ducey, Michael T.
2001 Indian Communities and Ayuntamientos in the Mexican Huasteca: Sujeto Revolts, Pronunciamentos and Caste War. *The Americas* 57:525-550.

Friedlander, Judith
1975 *Being Indian in Hueyapan: A Study of Forced Identity in Contemporary Mexico*. St. Martin's Press, New York.

García Martínez, Bernardo
1987 *Los pueblos de la sierra: el poder y el espacio entre los intios del norte de Puebla hasta 1700*. Colegio de México, Mexico City.

Gibson, Charles
1964 *The Aztecs under Spanish Rule: A History of the Indians of the Valley of Mexico, 1519-1810*. Stanford University Press, Palo Alto, CA.

Good Eshelman, Catharine
2005 Ejes conceptuales entre los nahuas de Guerrero: expresíon de un modelo fenomenológico mesoamericano. *Estudios de Cultura Nahuatl* 36:87–113.

Graulich, Michel
1999 *Ritos Aztecas: las fiestas de las veintenas*. Instituto Nacional Indigenista, Mexico City.

Hicks, Frederic
2001 Ethnicity. In *The Oxford Encyclopedia of Mesoamerican Cultures: The Civilizations of Mexico and Central America,* edited by Davíd Carrasco, pp. 390–392. Oxford University Press, Oxford.

Hill, Jane H., and Kenneth C. Hill
1980 Mixed Grammar, Purist Grammar, and Language Attitudes in Modern Náhuatl. *Language in Society* 9(3):321–348.

Karttunen, Frances
1983 *An Analytical Dictionary of Nahuatl*. University of Oklahoma Press, Norman.

Kierchoff, Paul
1955 The Principles of Clanship in Human Society. *Davidson Journal of Anthropology* 1:1–10.

Lavrin, Asunción
1989 Sexuality in Colonial Mexico: A Church Dilemma. In *Sexuality and Marriage in Colonial America*, edited by Asunción Lavrin, pp. 47–95. University of Nebraska Press, Lincoln.

Lewis, Oscar
1964 *Pedro Martínez: A Mexican Peasant and His Family*. Vintage, New York.

Lockhart, James
1992 *The Nahuas after the Conquest: A Social and Cultural History of the Indians of Central Mexico, Sixteenth Through Eighteenth Centuries*. Stanford University Press, Palo Alto, CA.

Lomnitz-Adler, Claudio
1991 Concepts for the Study of Regional Culture. *American Ethnologist* 18:195–214.
1992 *Exits from the Labyrinth: Culture and Ideology in the Mexican National Space*. University of California Press, Berkeley.

López Austin, Alfredo
1988 [1980] *The Human Body and Ideology: Concepts of the Ancient Nahuas* Translated by Thelma Mortiz de Montellano and Bernard Ortiz de Montellano. University of Utah Press, Salt Lake City.

Sandstrom, Alan
1991 *Corn in Our Blood: Culture and Ethnic Identity in a Contemporary Aztec Indian Village*. University of Oklahoma Press, Norman.
2008 Blood Sacrifice, Curing, and Ethnic Identity Among Contemporary Nahua of Northern Veracruz, Mexico. In *Ethnic Identity in Nahua Mesoamerica: The View from Archaeology, Art History, Ethnohistory, and Contemporary Ethnography,* edited by Frances F. Berdan, John K. Chance, Alan R. Sandstrom, Barbara L. Stark, James M. Taggart, and Emily Umberger, pp. 150–182. University of Utah Press, Salt Lake City.

Schryer, Fran J.
1993 *Ethnicity and Class Conflict in Rural Mexico*, Princeton University Press, Princeton, NJ.

Sierra, María Teresa
1995 Indian Rights and Customary Law in Mexico: A Study of Nahuas in the Sierra de Puebla. *Law & Society Review* 29:227–254.

Stark, Barbara
2008 Archaeology and Ethnicity in Postclassic Mesoamerica. In *Ethnic Identity in Nahua Mesoamerica: The View from Archaeology, Art History, Ethnohistory, and Contemporary*

Ethnography, edited by Frances F. Berdan, John K. Chance, Alan R. Sandstrom, Barbara L. Stark, James M. Taggart, and Emily Umberger, pp. 38-63. University of Utah Press, Salt Lake City.

Stark, Barbara, and John K. Chance
2008 Dichronic and Multidisciplinary Perspectives on Mesoamerican Ethnicity. In *Ethnic Identity in Nahua Mesoamerica: The View from Archaeology, Art History, Ethnohistory, and Contemporary Ethnography*, edited by Frances F. Berdan, John K. Chance, Alan R. Sandstrom, Barbara L. Stark, James M. Taggart, and Emily Umberger, pp. 38-63. University of Utah Press, Salt Lake City.

Stavenhagen, Rodolfo
1984 Notas sobre la cuestión étnica. *Estudios Sociológicos* 2:135-167.

Taggart, James M.
2007 *Remembering Victoria: A Tragic Nahuat Love Story*. University of Texas Press, Austin.
2008 Nahuat Ethnicity in a Time of Agrarian Conflict. In *Ethnic Identity in Nahua Mesoamerica: The View from Archaeology, Art History, Ethnohistory, and Contemporary Ethnography*, edited by Frances F. Berdan, John K. Chance, Alan R. Sandstrom, Barbara L. Stark, James M. Taggart, and Emily Umberger, pp. 183-203. University of Utah Press, Salt Lake City.

Taller de Tradición Oral
1994 *Tekintenkakiltiayaj in toueytatauan/Les oíamos contar a los abuelos*. Instituto Nacional de Antropología e Historia, Mexico City.

Thomson, Guy P. C.
1991 Agrarian Conflict in the Municipality of Cuetzalan (Sierra de Puebla): The Rise and Fall of "Pala" Agustín Dieguillo, 1861-1894. *The Hispanic American Historical Review* 71 205-258.

Tiedje, Kristina
2002 Gender and Ethnic Identity in Rural Grassroots Development: An Outlook from the Huasteca Potosina, Mexico. *Urban Anthropology and Studies of Cultural Systems and World Economic Development* 31:261-316.

Umberger, Emily
2008 Ethnicity and Other Identities in the Sculptures of Tenochtitlan. In *Ethnic Identity in Nahua Mesoamerica: The View from Archaeology, Art History, Ethnohistory, and Contemporary Ethnography*, edited by Frances F. Berdan, John K. Chance, Alan R. Sandstrom, Barbara L. Stark, James M. Taggart, and Emily Umberger, pp. 64-104. University of Utah Press, Salt Lake City.

Vaughn, Mary Kay
1997 *Cultural Politics in Revolution: Teachers, Peasants and Schools in Mexico, 1930-1940*. University of Arizona Press, Tucson.

Velasco Toro, José
1979 Indigenismo y rebelión totonaca de Papantla, 1885-1896. *America Indígena* 39:81-105.

Ward, Thomas
2001 Expanding Ethnicity in Sixteenth-Century Anahuac: Ideologies of ethnicity and Gender in the National-Building Process. *MLN* 116:419-452.

Warman, Arturo, Margarita Nolasco, Guidlermo Bonfil, Mercedes Olivera, and Enrique Valencia
1970 *De eso que llaman antropología Mexicana*. Editorial Nuestro Tiempo, Mexico City.

Wolf, Eric
1959 *Sons of the Shaking Earth: The People of Mexico and Guatemala—Their Land, History, and Culture*. University of Chicago Press, Chicago.

CHAPTER 29

INEQUALITY AND SOCIAL CLASS IN AZTEC SOCIETY

MICHAEL E. SMITH AND FREDERIC HICKS

LIKE any complex state-organized society, Aztec society was marked by social inequality. Some people were rich and powerful, while others were poor and powerless. In line with other premodern state societies, the most conspicuous manifestation of social inequality in the Aztec world was the difference between the social classes of noble and commoner. This was a distinction based on birth: a noble was one who had been born into a noble lineage, whereas a commoner was someone without noble parentage. Although each of these two social classes encompassed considerable variation in wealth, power, freedom, and lifestyle, the noble–commoner distinction was a fundamental chasm that cut through Aztec society.

We follow Gerhard Lenski (1966:74–75) in defining social class as "an aggregation of persons in a society who stand in a similar position with respect to some form of power, privilege, or prestige." Although all scholars agree that nobles and commoners were the primary Aztec social classes, some have argued for the emergence of a third, intermediate class during the century prior to Spanish conquest (Hicks 1999; Sanders 1992). Although we discuss five "special nonelite categories" in Aztec society, we agree with Bruce Trigger (2003:154) that the term "middle class" is best avoided because of its association with the rise of capitalism in western Europe.

Information on Aztec inequality is scattered among many different sources and types of data, and this has been a difficult topic for scholars to address. The standard accounts of the chroniclers—such as the works by Friars Bernardino de Sahagún (1950–1982) and Diego Durán (1994)—contain much information about inequality and class, but these accounts are highly biased and have to be carefully analyzed. For example, the chroniclers obtained most of their information from nobles and had little contact with Aztec commoners. Noble life is described at length in these sources, but descriptions of commoner affairs tend to be superficial, almost cartoon-like, sketches. A second type of bias is ideological. Aztec class distinctions were closely bound up with both religious ideals and political realities. Patterns of social class were projected onto the gods and the cosmos, and religion served to justify inequality and political domination. Needless to say, it can be difficult to sort out truth from ideology in official accounts.

Two types of data are largely free of these biases, but they tend to be fragmentary and rare. Administrative documents describing households, landholdings, and taxes can be highly informative about actual, on-the-ground conditions in particular places. Such sources sometimes contain quantitative data on demography and wealth. Archaeological excavations of houses and domestic contexts (see De Lucia this volume) are now starting to contribute information about wealth inequality, some of which can also be quantified to illuminate patterns of class and inequality.

The Aztec Nobility

A nobility is an elite class that is hereditary and legally defined (Bloch 1961:283), and this definition fits the Aztec case. Aztec nobles carefully traced their genealogy, claiming that all nobles were descendants of the earliest Aztec kings. Aztec kings claimed descent from the Toltec kings of Tula. While such links may have been more imagined than real, the notion that genealogical origin provided legitimacy was a basic concept in Aztec thought. Because of its strict hereditary definition, there was no way for commoners to enter the noble class. The Mexica king Motecuhzoma Ilhuicamina (r. 1440–1468) created a special title (*quauhpilli*) for the most accomplished warriors that is sometimes called "nobles by achievement." This did not involve full entry into the noble class, however, and later his great-grandson, the king Motecuhzoma Xocoyotzin (r. 1502–1520), abolished the category (Smith 2012:143).

Evidence for the legal definition of the Aztec nobility comes from descriptions of sumptuary laws—rules that limited consumption of certain goods to the noble class. Friar Diego Durán (1994:209–210) recorded a list of these laws established by Motecuhzoma Ilhuicamina. They grant certain privileges to kings and nobles, including the right to wear cotton clothing (forbidden to commoners), to wear certain types of jewelry, and to build houses on elevated platforms.

Ethnohistorical sources describe four grades of nobles. A *pilli* was a full member of the nobility but lacked a position of power and wealth; most nobles were *pillis*. *Teuctli* are often described as lords, or high lords. They occupied important offices in the city-state government and typically controlled large and wealthy estates. A *tlahtoani* (plural, *tlatoque*) was a king who ruled a city-state, and the wealth and power of a *tlahtoani* varied with the size and power of his realm. At the top of the scale were the *huey tlatoque*, the emperors of the Triple Alliance empire.

The hierarchy of nobles was expressed in the size and opulence of palaces (Evans this volume; Smith 2008:117). The palaces of the kings of Tenochtitlan were between 8,000 m² and 25,000 m² in area, and that of king Nezahualcoyotl of Texcoco was described as covering over 800,000 m². The documented palaces of city-state kings were between 2,000 m² and 7,000 m², while the palaces of the lowest-ranking nobles fell between 200 m² and 600 m² (Smith 2008:117). Several such palaces are shown in Figure 29.1. The Cuexcomate palace is that of a provincial rural *pilli*; the others are royal palaces.

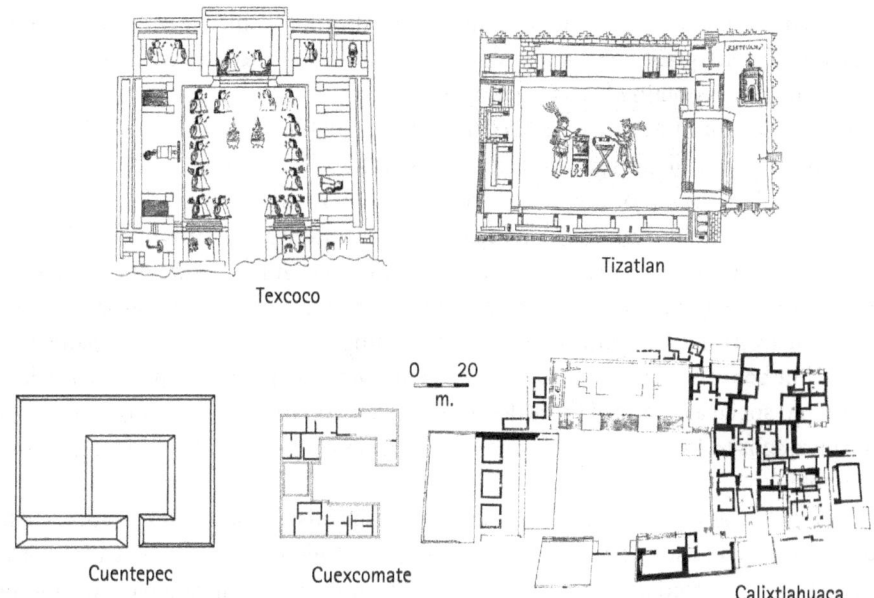

FIGURE 29.1 Palaces of Aztec nobles. The Texcoco and Tizatlan examples are from codices, and their size is unknown; the others are archaeological plans. See Smith (2008:ch. 4) for discussion and citations. Graphic by Michael E. Smith.

Although data are fragmentary, it appears that the Aztec nobility comprised approximately 2 percent of the population. Census lists made shortly after the Spanish conquest include counts of nobles and commoners at several communities in Morelos; nobles comprised 1.0 percent of the population in Yacapixtla (Carrasco 1976a:110), 1.4 percent in Huitzillan, and 1.8 percent in Quauhchichinollan (Cline 1993:103–104). On the basis of other records, Hicks (1999:411) estimated the Aztec nobility in the Basin of Mexico at approximately 2 percent, a figure accepted by Nutini and Isaac (2009:22–28). This figure fits well with comparative data on agrarian societies from around the world; Gerhard Lenski (1966:219), for example, notes that in agrarian societies the governing class, "rarely contained more than 2 per cent of the population, and sometimes appreciably less" (see also Bodley 2003:91–101). Early colonial records from the Huexotzinco region report that nobles in some communities formed between 4 and 14 percent of the population (Dyckerhoff and Prem 1976), a discrepancy with other regions that scholars have yet to account for (Carrasco 1974).

Farmers and Urban Commoners

Just as the noble class contained considerable variation in wealth, so too did the category of commoners. Wealth variation among commoners was associated with differences in the quality of life and in the extent of personal or household freedom. The vast majority of Aztec commoners were farmers, including most urban commoners, and the source of much of the inequality within the commoner class was the varying mechanisms by which commoners obtained land to cultivate.

Commoners could not own land (Cortés 1865; Lockhart 1992:141–155). There were three primary ways farmers gained access to fields to cultivate: membership in a *calpolli*, membership in a *tecalli*, or direct service to a noble. A *calpolli* was an organization of commoner households residing in a single rural community or an urban neighborhood. After a century of fruitless debate about the significance and structure of the *calpolli*, its organization was greatly illuminated by study of a series of Nahuatl-language census documents from six communities in Morelos, compiled shortly after the Spanish conquest (Cline 1993; Díaz Cadena 1978; Hinz et al. 1983). In a series of pioneering demographic and social analyses of these documents, Pedro Carrasco (1964, 1971, 1972, 1976a, 1976b) brought to light the structure and operation of the *calpolli* and its relationship with nobles.

The *calpolli* was a basic unit of residence and administration for taxes, corvée labor, and vital records (Hicks 2012; Reyes García 1996). *Calpolli* officials kept track of this information in painted documents. Members of rural *calpolli* farmed plots of land provided by a local noble landowner. They paid rent to the noble in the form of cotton textiles, foodstuffs, and labor service (scholars often call these payments "tribute"), and in return the *calpolli* council was allowed to allocate plots of land to the members and make other decisions about land use and membership. *Calpolli* members could count on continued access to their plots year after year, so long as they continued to farm them. Abandoned fields would revert to the *calpolli* council, where they would be reallocated. The picture painted by the Morelos censuses and other Nahuatl-language documents (Lockhart 1992:15–20) contradicts older claims that *calpollis* owned land collectively and that they were somehow free of noble control. In the words of Carrasco (1976a:116), "nobles are found within the structure of the *calpolli*, and as an important part of that structure" (author's translation).

Calpolli were prevalent in the Basin of Mexico and Morelos, but they were largely absent in the eastern Nahua region (in the modern states of Puebla and Tlaxcala), where an institution known as the *teccalli* served to regulate access to land (Chance 2000; Hicks 2009). The *teccalli*, or "noble house," consisted of a group of related nobles and a number of commoner villages. The land was held collectively by the *teccalli*, which was governed by a high lord. The nobles usually owned additional plots of their own. The commoners were granted access to farmland based on their residence in the *teccalli*'s villages, and they provided rent and various services to the nobles and to the overall *teccalli* organization.

The third way farmers obtained access to land was through direct dependence on a noble. These "dependent commoners" lacked the level of freedom and self-determination afforded by the *calpolli* (and, to a lesser extent, the *tecalli*). They had no regular claim to land beyond what their noble patron decided. They made payments of goods and labor services to their noble, and these services included agricultural and other types of work (Carrasco 1964; Hicks 1974; Lockhart 1992:96–100). Scattered information suggests that these dependent laborers had a harder lot in life than the commoners who belonged to a *calpolli* or a *tecalli*.

Some writers have compared Aztec dependent commoners to medieval European serfs. Unlike medieval Europe, however, Aztec dependent commoners were not bound to the land. They could move if they found a better situation, such as a less repressive lord or a more prosperous community that would accept them. Unlike European serfs, their former lord lacked any right to track them down and force them to return (Hicks 1974). Sixteenth-century rosters and censuses often include a category of refugees (*huidos*), and the pictorial versions show footprints of those leaving (Williams and Harvey 1997). There are also accounts of families arriving at a lord's land and asking the supervisor for land on which they could settle, and their request seems usually to have been granted. Often these mobile laborers moved in with commoner *calpolli* households, where they boarded and worked the household's lands. Carrasco (1976a:107) reports that up to 16 percent of commoners in some of the Morelos census communities were dependent commoners working on the lands of other commoner households who belonged to a *calpolli*.

Most urban commoners were farmers who cultivated either infield plots within the city or outfields in the countryside (Isendahl and Smith 2013). This situation may explain archaeological results showing that commoner life at sites in Morelos varied little between rural and urban contexts. Commoner houses were almost identical at rural and urban sites (Figure 29.2), and basic domestic activities and conditions were quite similar (Smith 2016). Another factor that may have contributed to rural–urban similarities was the prevalence of residential movements among Aztec commoners. Dependent commoners often moved among regions, and they probably moved between rural and urban settings.

FIGURE 29.2 Urban commoner residence at Yautepec, Morelos. The dimensions of this structure (unit 517) are approximately 7 m × 5 m. Photograph by Michael E. Smith.

Special Nonelite Categories

Aztec society included a number of special categories of commoners who stood apart from others in terms of wealth and prestige. Five of these categories—*pochteca* (guild merchants), luxury artisans, top warriors, high priests, and *calpixque* (officials)—occupied positions "above" farmers and most urban commoners, whereas one category—slaves—stood at the bottom of the social scale.

Pochteca and Luxury Artisans

The first two categories of wealthy commoners are economic specialists who took advantage of the commercial economy to accumulate sizable fortunes. The professional guild-based merchants known as the *pochteca* (see Hirth and Nichols this volume could assemble considerable personal fortunes. They worked both for the king and as entrepreneurs for themselves. Wealthy Aztec commoners refrained from showing off their wealth, both because of sumptuary laws and because they did want to draw the attention of nobles who might be jealous. Accordingly, *pochteca* built tall walls around their yards to keep people from seeing in, and when they returned to Tenochtitlan from a successful expedition they entered the city and unloaded their cargos at night (Sahagún 1950–1982, Book 9:31). Successful *pochteca* were probably the wealthiest Aztec commoners. They lived in specific neighborhoods in Tenochtitlan and several other cities in the Basin of Mexico (Rojas 2012).

Like the *pochteca*, the artisans who produced luxury goods such as featherwork, sculpture, and jewelry combined work for noble patrons with independent entrepreneurial activities (see Hosler this volume; Otis Charlton and Pastrana this volume). They worked on their craft full-time, their labor was highly specialized, and their products were the most valuable objects in Aztec society; as a result, many of these artisans grew to be quite wealthy. Many or most worked directly for the king or a high noble, in a workshop in the palace, but they also sold their products in the marketplace; others worked independently (Berdan 2014).

High Priests and Warriors

The next categories of commoners with elevated wealth and status describe those who occupied the top positions in two hierarchical organizations that were linked to the state. The Aztec priesthood is very poorly understood. The terms for priestly offices, however, suggest a hierarchical structure to the priesthood. Most priests were called *tlamacazqui;* novices had the title *tlamacazton* ("little priest"); and the highest priests were called *tlenamacac* ("fireseller"). Only the latter could officiate at certain important sacrificial ceremonies. It seems logical that the high priests had more power and prestige than the others, but there is little firm information (Nicholson 1971).

The military was another hierarchical organization, somewhat better documented than the priesthood (see Cevera Obregón this volume). All males served as soldiers, and they could move up in rank by capturing enemy prisoners and performing other battlefield feats. Each rank was a named category that came with increased power, prestige, and privileges. Members of a given rank wore special haircuts and had permission to wear specific types of clothing and jewelry, practices that emphasized the prestige of military success and its hierarchical organization (Bueno Bravo 2007; Hassig 1988).

Calpixque

The term *calpixqui* (plural, *calpixque*) is often translated as "imperial tax collector," but in fact this term was applied to a range of officials who collected taxes and organized other tasks at both the city-state and the imperial level. In a study of Aztec taxation, Smith (2015) identified five types of *calpixqui* (Table 29.1). The head imperial *calpixque* were nobles, but the officials who actually assembled tax goods in the imperial provinces (*calpixqui* type C) were commoners. They "reported to the accountants and stewards of the king on what they had collected and the people they had registered in the towns under their care" (Carrasco 1999:224, paraphrasing Torquemada 1975–1983:4:334).

At the city-state level, both types of *calpixqui* were commoners (Hicks 1978). The lowest level officials (type E), who were responsible for taxes, labor, and record-keeping in their neighborhood are often called "barrio heads" in the sources. They may have been wealthier, perhaps with larger houses, than other commoners (Hicks 2012). It seems

Table 29.1 Types of *Calpixque* (Tax Collectors)

Type	Duties	Class
Imperial Level:		
A	Receive and organize goods in Tenochtitlan	noble
B	Ship goods from provincial capital	noble
C	Collect goods in provincial city-states	commoner
City-State Level:		
D	Receive and organize goods at the royal palace	commoner
E	Collect tax and carry out other official tasks in the *calpolli*	commoner

Slaves

The category of *tlacotli* ("slave") occupied the lowest position in the Aztec social hierarchy. Slavery was not a hereditary category; people became slaves through debt (often from gambling) or punishment for theft. In times of famine or crisis, people sometimes sold themselves into slavery so that their owner would be responsible for their care and feeding. Slaves were generally used for household labor, and their overall contribution to the economy was minimal (Shadow and Rodríguez V. 1995).

PATTERNS OF WEALTH INEQUALITY

The distinction between nobles and commoners would have been quite obvious to a foreign visitor to an Aztec city. The houses of nobles were considerably larger and more sumptuous than commoner houses. Sumptuary laws on clothing and jewelry, coupled with wealth differences, made it easy to tell nobles from commoners in the street or the market (Olko 2005). A visit to the royal palace would reveal nobles in the high positions of city-state government (the king, royal council, and the top war leaders and priests) and commoners the lower positions (servants, tax collectors, guards, and other bureaucrats). But the noble–commoner distinction went beyond their public faces and influenced diet, health, and life chances.

The *Relaciones Geográficas* from central Mexico (Acuña 1984–1988:vol. 6) are a collection of several hundred local questionnaires that include information about life and conditions prior to the Spanish conquest. These documents consistently describe differences in the diets of nobles and commoners. It seems that each city-state had its own specific sumptuary rules for diet, but they all suggest that nobles ate more meat than commoners. In Tepoztlan, for example, nobles ate tortillas, tamales, chiles, turkey, deer, and rabbit, while commoners ate tortillas, chiles, atole, beans, chia, and an occasional rabbit. In Yacapitztlan, nobles ate turkey, deer, and rabbit, while commoners consumed maize and dogs. In addition, commoners in Ixcateopan were not allowed to hunt or eat turkey; if they killed a game animal, they had to give it to the king or nobles. While archaeologists have not yet excavated enough burials of nobles and commoners to investigate dietary distinctions as revealed in the human skeleton, the available evidence points to likely distinctions in health and longevity arising from the differences in diet and lifestyle.

Some idea of the magnitude of class-based wealth variation can be gleamed from census documents and archeological excavations of residences (Table 29.2). Quantitative data in this table are scaled so that the commoner values equal 1 and the other values are multiples of the commoner level. For example, context A depicts

Table 29.2 Wealth Differences among Social Categories[a]

Category	Context				
	A	B	C	D	E
Commoners	1	1	1	1	1
Calpixque, type E		17			2
Nobles	16	51	29	34	14
Rulers		149			197

Context A:	Landholdings within a *calpolli*, Morelos (Carrasco 1972:341–343)
Context B:	Landholdings in six communities, Morelos (Smith et al. 2014)
Context C:	Houselot size in Tenochtitlan (unpublished data from Edward Calnek)
Context D:	Size (area) of residences, Cuexcomate (Olson and Smith 2016)
Context E:	Size (area) of residences, Yautepec (Olson and Smith 2016)

[a] Quantities scaled so that commoner levels equal 1.

landholdings within the *calpolli* of Molotla, a neighborhood of Yautepec, Morelos (Carrasco 1972). The noble (named Molotecatl) controlled 16 times as much land as the average commoner household. Molotecatl in fact owned *all* of this land, but his own portion (worked by dependent labor) was 16 times the size of the average plot worked by a commoner household in his *calpolli*. Similarly, the excavation of commoner and elite houses at the sites of Cuexcomate and Yautepec in Morelos reveal a similar level of elite–commoner differentiation (Olson and Smith 2016). The data in Table 29.2 reveal significant noble–commoner wealth differences as expressed in the domains of land and housing.

Another perspective on patterns of inequality is provided by research on the cumulative distribution of household wealth within a community, irrespective of social class. The extent of inequality can be measured by the Gini index, whose values can run from 0.0—complete equality in the distribution of wealth—to 1.0, meaning complete inequality, whereby one household owns *all* of the wealth (Milanovic 2011). Smith et al. (2014) measured house size at archaeological sites in Morelos and agricultural field size of households in the Morelos census documents, revealing Gini scores between 0.33 and 0.49 for towns and cities and 0.10 for the peasant village of Capilco. After Mexica conquest, the noble compound at Cuexcomate was abandoned and, in spite of the continued presence of a noble household, the Gini index dropped to 0.19. In comparison to broader patterns of premodern wealth patterns, these data suggest a moderate level of inequality prior to Mexica conquest. A Gini value of 0.45 characterizes the United States today.

Explaining Aztec Inequality

Although all ancient states had elite classes and wealth inequality (Lenski 1966; Trigger 2003), these societies differed greatly in the nature and extent of these phenomena and in their linkages to other social processes. A powerful framework for explaining such patterns is Charles Tilly's (1998, 2001) model of durable social inequality. It sheds light on how Aztec society operated and, in particular, how a small group—the nobility—was able to control the political apparatus, appropriate much of the wealth, and ensure its continued privileged existence, even into the Spanish period.

For Tilly (1998:10), the most important social mechanism underlying systems of durable inequality is exploitation, "which operates when powerful, connected people command resources from which they draw significantly increased returns by coordinating the efforts of outsiders whom they exclude from the full value added by that effort." For the Aztec nobility, the key resources were land, labor, and the city-state government. Law and custom prevented commoners from owning land, yet they had to work the land to survive. By requiring payment of rent to noble landowners and taxes to the local city-state, the Aztec nobility enlisted commoners to increase the returns on their land; these practices exemplify Tilly's definition of exploitation.

Payments from commoners to nobles are illustrated in the *Codex Kingsborough* (Valle 1995), a portion of which is shown in Figure 29.3. Two nobles sit on the right side, identified by their name glyphs. The first commands the corvée labor of six communities and the second receives labor from three communities. Each community is shown with its name glyph positioned above a kneeling male with a digging stick, which is a symbol of corvée labor. The actual number of laborers for the community is shown by numerical symbols above the worker; the first community sent 15 workers (15 vertical lines), and the second sent 20 (the flag glyph). To the right of the labor quantities are bundles of cotton textiles owed to the lord.

FIGURE 29.3 Labor and goods (left), often incorrectly called "tribute," paid by commoners to two nobles (right). Each box shows the number of laborers from a named community; to their right are bundles of cotton cloth (money). The nobles are identified by their name glyph. Redrawn from the *Codex Kingsborough*, lám. 5A (Valle 1995).

There are countless other records of such payments in Conquest-period central Mexico, including both pictorial documents and textual accounts. Although textual sources—and scholars—tend to use the term "tribute" for such payments, that label is imprecise and inadequate as a comparative concept. In fact, these payments can be considered as both rent and taxes. They are rent in that commoners make payments to a landlord in exchange for using the lord's land. But a portion of these payments was passed on (by the landlord) to the local king as a form of land tax (Smith 2015). "Tribute" is defined in economics as a lump-sum payment made after a conquest or a threat of conquest. Tax, on the other hand, refers to payments from individuals to states that have a regular schedule and fixed amounts, are collected by professional tax collectors, and are recorded in writing (Tarschys 1988). It is quite clear from the historical record that "tribute" in the comparative sense was rare in the Aztec world, whereas everyone except kings (i.e., both nobles and commoners) paid a variety of types of tax (Smith 2015). In summary, taxes and rent were primary mechanisms by which commoners supported nobles, and they provide the key to the system of inequality and social class in Aztec central Mexico.

Author's Note

When Frederic Hicks died in 2013, he had begun writing this chapter. Before his death, he asked Smith to join as a co-author. Smith wrote the chapter after Hicks's death, incorporating text and notes from Hicks, including material from the latter's papers on the subject.

References Cited

Acuña, René
1984–1988 *Relaciones geográficas del siglo XVI*. 10 vols. Universidad Nacional Autónoma de México, Mexico City.
Berdan, Frances F.
2014 *Aztec Archaeology and Ethnohistory*. Cambridge University Press, New York.
Bloch, Marc
1961 *Feudal Society*. 2 vols. University of Chicago Press, Chicago.
Bodley, John H.
2003 *The Power of Scale: A Global History Approach*. M. E. Sharpe, Armonk, NY.
Bueno Bravo, Isabel
2007 *La guerra en el imperio azteca: expansión, ideología y arte*. Editorial Complutense, Madrid.
Carrasco, Pedro
1964 Family Structure of Sixteenth-Century Tepoztlan. In *Process and Pattern in Culture: Essays in Honor of Julian H. Steward*, edited by Robert A. Manners, pp. 185–210. Aldine, Chicago.

1971 Las clases sociales en el México antiguo. In *Proceedings of the 38th International Congress of Americanists, Stuttgart-Munich, 1968*, Vol. 2, pp. 371–376. International Congress of Americanists, Stuttgart.

1972 La casa y hacienda de un señor tlahuica. *Estudios de Cultura Náhuatl* 10:235–244.

1974 Introducción: la Matrícula de Huexotzinco como fuente sociológica. In *Matrícula de Huexotzinco: Ms. mex. 387 del Bibliothèque Nationale Paris*, edited by Hanns J. Prem, pp. 1–16. Akademische Druck-u. Verlagsanstalt, Graz.

1976a Estratificación social indígena en Morelos durante el siglo XVI. In *Estratifiación social en la Mesoamérica prehispánica*, edited by Pedro Carrasco and Johanna Broda, pp. 102–117. Instituto Nacional de Antropolgía e Historia, Mexico City.

1976b The Joint Family in Ancient Mexico: The Case of Molotla. In *Essays on Mexican Kinship*, edited by Hugo Nutini, Pedro Carrasco, and James M. Taggert, pp. 45–64. University of Pittsburgh Press, Pittsburgh, PA.

1999 *The Tenochca Empire of Ancient Mexico: The Triple Alliance of Tenochtitlan, Tetzcoco, and Tlacopan*. University of Oklahoma Press, Norman.

Chance, John K.

2000 The Noble House in Colonial Puebla, Mexico: Descent, Inheritance, and the Nahua Tradition. *American Anthropologist* 102:485–502.

Cline, S. L.

1993 *The Book of Tributes: Early Sixteenth-Century Nahuatl Censuses from Morelos*. University of California Latin American Center, Los Angeles.

Cortés, Fernando

1865 Carta de Hernan Cortés, al Consejo de Indias . . . Sobre la Constitución de la Propriedad de las tierras entre los Indios (1538). In *Colección de Documentos Inéditos . . . de Indias*, Vol. 3, pp. 535–543. Real Academía de la Historia, Madrid.

Díaz Cadena, Ismael

1978 *Libros de Tributos del Marquesado del Valle: texto en español y náhuatl*. Cuadernos de la Biblioteca, Investigación. Museo Nacional de Antropología e Historia, Mexico City.

Durán, Fray Diego

1994 *The History of the Indies of New Spain*. Translated by Doris Heyden. University of Oklahoma Press, Norman.

Dyckerhoff, Ursula, and Hanns Prem

1976 Aspectos generales y reigonales de la estratificación social (en Huexotzinco). In *Estratifiación social en la Mesoamérica prehispánica*, edited by Pedro Carrasco and Johanna Broda, pp. 157–177. Instituto Nacional de Antropolgía e Historia, Mexico City.

Hassig, Ross

1988 *Aztec Warfare: Imperial Expansion and Political Control*. University of Oklahoma Press, Norman.

Hicks, Frederic

1974 Dependent Labor in Prehispanic México. *Estudios de Cultura Náhuatl* 11:243–266.

1978 Los calpixque de Nezahualcoyotl. *Estudios de Cultura Náhuatl* 13:129–152.

1999 The Middle Class in Ancient Central Mexico. *Journal of Anthropological Research* 55:409–427.

2009 Land and Successsion in the Indigenous Noble Houses of Sixteenth-Century Tlaxcala. *Ethnohistory* 56:569–588.

2012 Governing Smaller Communities in Aztec Mexico. *Ancient Mesoamerica* 23(2):47–56.

Hinz, Eike, Claudine Hartau, and Marie Heimann-Koenen
1983 *Aztekischer Zensus: Zur Indianischen Wirtschaft und Gesellschaft im Marquesado um 1540*. Verlag fur Ethnologie, Hanover.

Isendahl, Christian, and Michael E. Smith
2013 Sustainable Agrarian Urbanism: The Low-Density Cities of the Mayas and Aztecs. *Cities* 31:132–143.

Lenski, Gerhard E.
1966 *Power and Privilege: A Theory of Social Stratification*. McGraw-Hill, New York.

Lockhart, James
1992 *The Nahuas After the Conquest: A Social and Cultural History of the Indians of Central Mexico, Sixteenth Through Eighteenth Centuries*. Stanford University Press, Stanford, CA.

Milanovic, Branko
2011 *The Haves and the Have-Nots: A Brief and Idiosyncratic History of Global Inequality*. Basic Books, New York.

Nicholson, H. B.
1971 Religion in Pre-Hispanic Central Mexico. In *Archaeology of Northern Mesoamerica, Part 1*, edited by Gordon F. Ekholm and Ignacio Bernal, pp. 395–446. Handbook of Middle American Indians, Vol. 10. University of Texas Press, Austin.

Nutini, Hugo G., and Barry L. Isaac
2009 *Social Stratification in Central Mexico, 1500–2000*. University of Texas Press, Austin.

Olko, Justyna
2005 *Turquoise Diadems and Staffs of Office: Elite Costume and Insignia of Power in Aztec and Early Colonial Mexico*. Polish Society for Latin American Studies, Warsaw.

Olson, Jan Marie, and Michael E. Smith
2016 Material Expressions of Wealth and Social Class at Aztec-Period Sites in Morelos, Mexico. *Ancient Mesoamerica* 27:133–147.

Reyes García, Luis
1996 El término calpolli en documentos del siglo XVI. In *Documentos nahas de la Ciudad de México del siglo XVI*, edited by Luis Reyes García, Celestino Eustaquio Solís, Armando Valencia Ríos, Constantino Medina Lima, and Gregorio Guerrero Días, pp. 21–68. Centro de Investigaciones y Estudios Superiores en Antropología Social, Mexico City.

Rojas, José Luis de
2012 *Tenochtitlan: Capital of the Aztec Empire*. University Press of Florida, Gainesville.

Sahagún, Fray Bernardino de
1950–1982 *Florentine Codex: General History of the Things of New Spain*. 12 books. Translated and edited by Arthur J. O. Anderson and Charles E. Dibble. School of American Research, Santa Fe, NM, and University of Utah Press, Salt Lake City.

Sanders, William T.
1992 Ranking and Stratification in Prehispanic Mesoamerica. In *Mesoamerican Elites: An Archaeological Assessment*, edited by Diane A. Chase and Arlen F. Chase, pp. 278–291. University of Oklahoma Press, Norman.

Shadow, Robert D., and María J. Rodríguez V.
1995 Historical Panorama of Anthropological Perspectives on Aztec Slavery. In *Arqueología del norte y del occidente de México: Homenaje al Doctor J. Charles Kelley*, edited by Barbro Dahlgren de Jordán and María de los Dolores Soto de Arechavaleta, pp. 299–323. Instituto de Investigaciones Antropológicas, Universidad Nacional Autónoma de México, Mexico City.

Smith, Michael E.
2008 *Aztec City-State Capitals*. University Press of Florida, Gainesville.
2012 *The Aztecs*. 3rd ed. Blackwell, Oxford.
2015 The Aztec Empire. In *Fiscal Regimes and the Political Economy of Premodern States*, edited by Andrew Monson and Walter Scheidel, pp. 71–114. Cambridge University Press, New York.
2016 *At Home with the Aztecs: An Archaeologist Uncovers Their Domestic Life*. Routledge, New York.

Smith, Michael E., Timothy Dennehy, April Kamp-Whittaker, Emily Colon, and Rebecca Harkness
2014 Quantitative Measures of Wealth Inequality in Ancient Central Mexican Communities. *Advances in Archaeological Practice* 2(4):311–323.

Tarschys, Daniel
1988 Tributes, Tariffs, Taxes and Trade: The Changing Sources of Government Revenue. *British Journal of Political Science* 19:1–20.

Tilly, Charles
1998 *Durable Inequality*. University of California Press, Berkeley.
2001 Relational Origins of Inequality. *Anthropological Theory* 1(3):355–372.

Torquemada, Fray Juan de
1975–1983 *Monarquía indiana*. 7 vols. Edited by Miguel León-Portilla. Universidad Nacional Autónoma de México, Mexico City.

Trigger, Bruce G.
2003 *Understanding Early Civilizations: A Comparative Study*. Cambridge University Press, New York.

Valle, Perla (editor)
1995 *Códice de Tepetlaoztoc (Códice Kingsborough), Estado de México: edición facsimilar*. 2 vols. El Colegio Mexiquense, Toluca, Mexico.

Williams, Barbara J., and Herbert R. Harvey
1997 *The Códice de Santa María Asunción: Facsimile and Commentary: Households and Lands in Sixteenth-Century Tepetlaoztoc*. University of Utah Press, Salt Lake City.

PART V
AZTEC PROVINCES, FRIENDS, AND FOES

CHAPTER 30

STRUCTURE OF THE TRIPLE ALLIANCE EMPIRE

FRANCES F. BERDAN

THE year was One Flint Knife, 1428 in the Christian calendar. The place was the densely populated and politically fragmented Basin of Mexico. In that time and place, a rebellion was fomented and an alliance forged that was to largely prescribe the political and economic makeup of central Mexico until the arrival of the Spaniards 91 years later. This was the inception of the Triple Alliance or Aztec Empire, composed of the powerful and growing city-states of Tenochtitlan and Texcoco and the somewhat less powerful city-state of Tlacopan. Each of these polities was ruled by an established dynasty and represented a recognized ethnic tradition: the Mexica at Tenochtitlan, the Acolhua at Texcoco, and the Tepaneca at Tlacopan. This chapter provides a discussion of how this tripartite organization was structured and how its three component polities juggled their relations with one another and managed to dominate and control local as well as distant subjects through conquest, intimidation, and diplomacy. The Triple Alliance was complex, volatile, and documented by contradictory historical sources. To add to the complications in unraveling this story, the alliance itself lasted only about three generations, during which dramatic changes occurred both internally among the alliance leaders and externally with neighboring and distant friends and foes. This is essentially a top-down perspective; the bottom-up view is offered in the next several chapters.

TRIPLE ALLIANCE PREMISES

The Aztec Triple Alliance was born in a political climate of uncertain and sometimes devastating warfare, opportunistic rebellions, and unstable alliances. The forging of alliances for political and military advantage was not a new idea in central Mexico but rather was an institution well-grounded in established political tradition. Nigel Davies (1977:297–302) supports the possibility of tripartite alliances preceding the one formed in 1428: a triple alliance of Tula, Otompan, and Culhuacan, followed by a coalition of Azcapotzalco, Coatlichan, and Culhuacan. In these arrangements, Tula was replaced by Coatlichan (an Acolhua center) and Otompan by Azcapotzalco (a Tepaneca powerhouse). It was a history of power shifts, eventually leading to the violent overthrow of Azcapotzalco and the ascendancy of Tenochtitlan (supplanting Culhuacan, with the Tenochtitlan people sometimes called Culhua-Mexica), Texcoco (an Acolhua center replacing Coatlichan), and Tlacopan (enjoying the Tepaneca power vacuum left by the defeated and razed Azcapotzalco). In other words, the general idea of a tripartite structure representing significant ethnic groups was developed and implemented through several centuries, with shifts only in the specific actors dominating the political landscape.

While we know little of the specifics of the early tripartite alliances, considerable information is available on the essentials of the Aztec Triple Alliance structure. These fundamentals consisted of political segmentation and autonomous control of defined territories, intermingling of territories and subjects, and asymmetrical hierarchies. We perceive these fundamentals through the lens of contradictory and often partisan documentary sources, most notably those of Durán (1994) and Alvarado Tezozomoc (1975) favoring Tenochtitlan and Alva Ixtlilxochitl (1965) elevating the role of Texcoco in the alliance.

Segmentation and Autonomous Territories

In 1428 the building blocks of political organization in central Mexico were the many *altepetl*, or city-states. An *altepetl* encompassed the people of a defined place and presumably the place itself (Lockhart 1992:14). Settlements that qualified as *altepetl* were headed by a legitimate ruling dynasty, enjoyed a sense (if not the actuality) of political autonomy, controlled local lands and labor, were validated by a well-established founding legend, and were sanctified by a patron deity complete with temple and specified ceremonies. Many *altepetl* exhibited predominant ethnicities; some enjoyed renown as production centers of specialized crafts, as sites of celebrated markets, or as pilgrimage destinations. Tenochtitlan itself became recognized (and feared) as a military force, and Texcoco enjoyed renown as a center for engineering, philosophy, poetry, and law.

Each of the Triple Alliance capitals was an *altepetl*, and each directly controlled other *altepetl* in their immediate Basin of Mexico region and somewhat farther afield. In the earliest years of the Triple Alliance, the lords (*huey tlatoque*) of each of the three capital cities held sway over lords (*tlatoque*) of other less powerful city-states. Reportedly, Itzcoatl of Tenochtitlan ruled 9 city-states, mostly to the south of his capital; Nezahualcoyotl of Texcoco ruled 14 to the northeast in and beyond the Basin of Mexico; and Totoquihuatzin of Tlacopan ruled 7 toward the northwest (Alva Ixtlilxochitl 1965) (Figure 30.1).

These might be considered "core dependencies," since their rulers (or the rulers' sons) directly served the Triple Alliance king in his capital city and were expected to

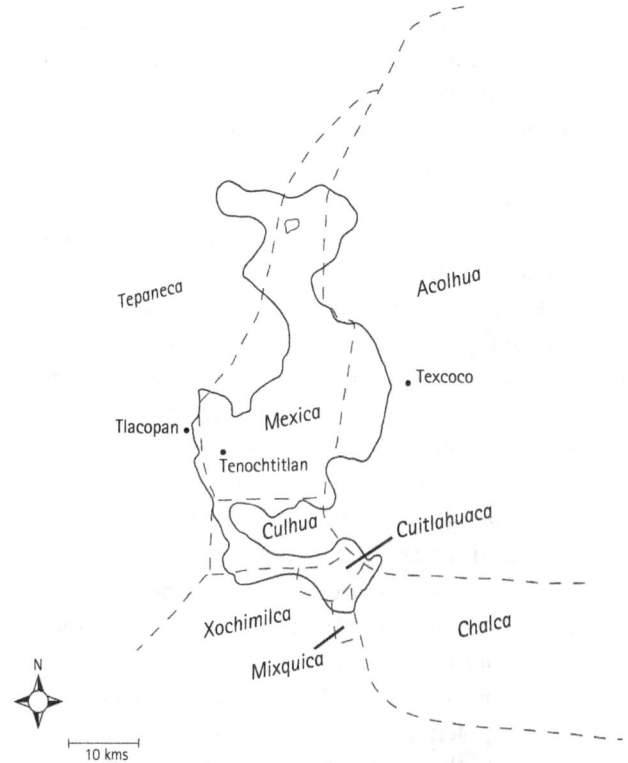

FIGURE 30.1 The Triple Alliance capitals and their domains in the Basin of Mexico. Map drawn by Jennifer B. Lozano.

be unhesitatingly available for service in war, major construction projects, or any other demand made by their overarching lord. As the coalition evolved into an expansionist empire, these three powerful entities continued to control these and additional subject city-states, demanding their obeisance and tributes without interference from their allies—thus the principle of segmentation and autonomous territories.

Intermingling of Territories and Subjects

A second fundamental principle guiding the activities of the Triple Alliance was the "intermingling of territories" (to borrow a term from Pedro Carrasco [1999]). The principle of segmentation and autonomous territories references exclusive dominion over certain "core dependencies" in each of the Triple Alliance regions. That said, each of the three capitals also controlled territories and demanded tributes from city-states within the other two capitals' regions. This practice yielded, on the surface, a complex geographic and administrative web that became more intricate as the empire matured. As an example, Charles Gibson (1971:390) summarizes the complicated situation of Cuauhtitlan on the northwestern edge of Lake Texcoco in the early 1500s: this city (or perhaps different subjects within the city) paid tribute to their own local ruler, to the rulers of Tlacopan and Tenochtitlan, and to other undefined "owners" in Texcoco, Tlatelolco, Culhuacan, Ixtapalapa, Mexicaltzinco, and Azcapotzalco. Much as this appears to deplete the Cuauhtitlan ruler's local resources, it is noteworthy that he himself held additional lands in Chalco and Matlatzinco (Carrasco 1999:124). In the Texcoco domain, "the intermingling of tribute-paying lands among rulers reached the point where it is difficult to determine the actual boundaries of city-states" (Hodge 1996:43). Viewing this situation from the bottom up, it would have been fairly common for the various residents of any one town to owe allegiance and pay tribute to more than one lord (see Carrasco 1999:38). Intricate webs of homage, political control, and tribute obligations permeated the three patrimonial domains of the Triple Alliance capitals by the time of the Spanish arrival. This was complicated by the occasional practice of the conquerors' replacing local rulers with their own selection of a favored relative or other worthy noble.

This complex intermingling, largely within and adjacent to the Basin of Mexico, derived from several related dynamics. First, one aftermath of conquest was the distribution of vanquished lands and subjects not only to the *huey tlahtoani* but also to his close relatives, other prominent nobles, and achieved warriors. This was standard practice and resulted in considerable fragmentation of conquered lands and subjects as they were dispersed among a number of high-status victors often from several allied victorious city-states. This practice of rewards also enhanced the recipients' wealth and cemented their allegiance to their paramount ruler. Second, the Triple Alliance rulers engaged in a diplomacy that involved the mutual granting of lands in each other's territories, "comparable to a trading contract or an exchange of gifts between allied rulers" (Carrasco 1999:35; see also Hodge 1996:21, 42). A third dynamic was the steady erosion of rights to Tlacopan lands and subjects in favor of Tenochtitlan. Texcoco, the second-ranked kingdom in the alliance, lost less political ground as Tenochtitlan incessantly solidified its preeminence in the alliance.

Asymmetrical Hierarchies

The principle of asymmetrical hierarchies permeated the Triple Alliance at all levels, although it appears that Late Postclassic central Mexican social and political dynamics occasionally tolerated power equivalencies. For instance, some city-states in the Basin of Mexico (such as Xochimilco and Cuitlahuac) were governed fairly equally by more than one *tlahtoani*, and Tenochtitlan's perpetual rival Tlaxcallan was ruled by four supreme kings (although two of these apparently were more supreme than the others). That said, the basic world of the Aztecs and their neighbors was a hierarchical one.

It did not take long for Tenochtitlan to exercise its military might and demonstrate its supremacy within the Triple Alliance. Indeed, it can be argued that Tenochtitlan was preeminent from the very beginning of the alliance. Texcoco enjoyed second place: "Itzcoatl, as he was dying, ordered that the king of Tetzcoco should be the second king of the land" (Carrasco 1999:43). But it was probably a close second, as even pro-Mexica Diego Durán (1994:344, 345) stressed that Nezahualcoyotl, the *tlahtoani* of Texcoco, was "always the first to speak, his words were respected, and during elections his vote was decisive," and the other kings "dared not contradict him." Nezahualcoyotl was a particularly charismatic individual, and such respect may have been due as much to his personal stature as to his lofty title. Tlacopan, the third alliance partner, was clearly the weakest and politically the least significant partner.

These hierarchical relationships were intensified as the empire grew and the Tenochtitlan *tlatoque* took charge of military engagements. Vertical chains of command were mirrored throughout the Triple Alliance realm, where each of these capitals dominated less powerful city-states, which sometimes in turn ruled over even smaller and weaker *altepetl*. It was a fairly steep hierarchy (Hodge 1996:42). These were the principles on which the alliance was ideally built. But how, we may ask, did these fundamentals hold up as the alliance evolved and the empire expanded?

Tricky Politics at the Highest Level

Sharing power is frequently an awkward business, especially when a great deal is at stake—in this case, control of an empire and its immense wealth. It is no surprise, then, that the leading rulers of the tripartite alliance were conspicuously and unmistakably ranked. These rankings, on the loftiest rung of the political ladder, were somewhat unstable in the beginning and required repeated reinforcement. Fortified by recurrent behaviors in social, political, military, and ceremonial events, these relations became relatively stabilized by the time of the Spanish arrival. We can see these relationships played out as the primary member, Tenochtitlan, variously made demands and requests of its partners and other lesser allies, and Texcoco and Tlacopan positioned themselves as favorably as they could in this fluid and dynamic political world.

Demands and Requests: Balance and Imbalance of Power

Hierarchical power structures and relations were established in the early years of the alliance. Jockeying for power between Tenochtitlan and Texcoco is revealed in a pair of contrasting stories from partisan sources. One tells of moves by Nezahualcoyotl of Texcoco (r. 1418–1472) to solidify his lands in the eastern sector of the Basin of Mexico by negotiating a north–south territorial "dividing line" with Itzcoatl of Tenochtitlan (r. 1426–1440) and then assuming the exalted title of Chichimecatl Teuctli, although the title actually applied only to the Acolhua domain and nowhere else. These moves culminated in a military conflict between Nezahualcoyotl and Itzcoatl whereby the former reportedly emerged victorious and gained some valuable tributary territories at the expense of the latter and Tlacopan; these lands were located around the lakeshore and in the rich *chinampa* regions of the southern Basin of Mexico (Alva Ixtlilxochitl 1965:158, 162–164). If this encounter did indeed occur, its consequences were perhaps short-lived or piecemeal. Part I of the *Codex Mendoza* records conquests of many of these communities by Tenochtitlan rulers, including several by Itzcoatl himself (Berdan and Anawalt 1992, Vol. III:folios 5v–6v). In this same pictorial, Itzcoatl's conquests also included Acolhuacan, perhaps referring to Texcoco. To complicate matters further, an earlier Tenochtitlan ruler, Huitzilihuitl (r. 1391–1415) is recorded as conquering Texcoco and four of Texcoco's "core dependencies" (Berdan and Anawalt 1992, Vol. III:folios 3v–4r).

These reported early conquests do not align well with yet another conquest story. This account pitted Itzcoatl's successor Motecuhzoma Ilhuicamina (r. 1440–1468) against the long-lived Nezahualcoyotl in an elaborate mock battle. Reportedly the Texcocan ruler acquiesced to the plan by feigning defeat, professing servitude to Motecuhzoma, and declaring perpetual peace with Tenochtitlan (Durán 1994:125–129). Only two of Texcoco's core dependencies are listed in the *Codex Mendoza* as paying tribute to Tenochtitlan, so perhaps Texcoco retained much of its patrimony despite its sworn subordinate status to Tenochtitlan. Whether or not these tales are true, they symbolize the early unsettled relations between these two superpowers; over time, the dominance of Tenochtitlan became unquestioned. Throughout, Tlacopan became more and more subsumed under Tenochtitlan's dominion. Tlacopan's integration into Tenochtitlan's sphere is also suggested by its *pochteca* accompanying Tenochtitlan *pochteca* in extra-empire economic and diplomatic missions (Sahagún 1950–1982, Book 9) (Figure 30.2).

Hierarchical relationships were reinforced in every collaborative effort undertaken by the three allies. *Tlahtoani* elections in one capital city were necessarily affirmed by the *tlatoque* of the other two cities. In Tenochtitlan, lengthy speeches made at elections as well as at coronations and royal funerals followed strict protocol with the Texcoco ruler speaking first, the Tlacopan ruler second, and other allied rulers following in turn. The rulers of Texcoco and Tlacopan (as well as the rulers of Tenayuca, Chiconauhtla, and Colhuacan), all "friends" of Motecuhzoma Xocoyotzin (r. 1502–1520), were housed in the Tenochtitlan royal palace when they visited; a similar courtesy was extended to the Tenochtitlan and Tlacopan rulers or their representatives in at least Texcoco (Berdan and Anawalt 1992, Vol. III:folio 69r; Douglas 2010:87).

These relationships were further reinforced on occasions when the Tenochtitlan ruler needed support in far-flung military ventures and large-scale work projects. Success in warfare depended to a large extent on amassing and coordinating enormous, motivated armies. As the empire expanded beyond the Basin of Mexico, the Mexica of Tenochtitlan obtained this military support from their allies. An ambitious or affronted Mexica ruler summoned his allied rulers to Tenochtitlan to discuss an upcoming war, ordering them to join him in his enterprise. The allied rulers uniformly agreed (or acquiesced) to participate, certainly calculating the rewards they would gain in a successful war in distant, rich territories. These allies included not only Texcoco and Tlacopan but also frequently Xochimilco (and other *chinampa* cities) and Chalco (after its conquest in 1465), as well as Tlalhuicas, Otomís, other Tepanecas, and people from the "Hot Countries"

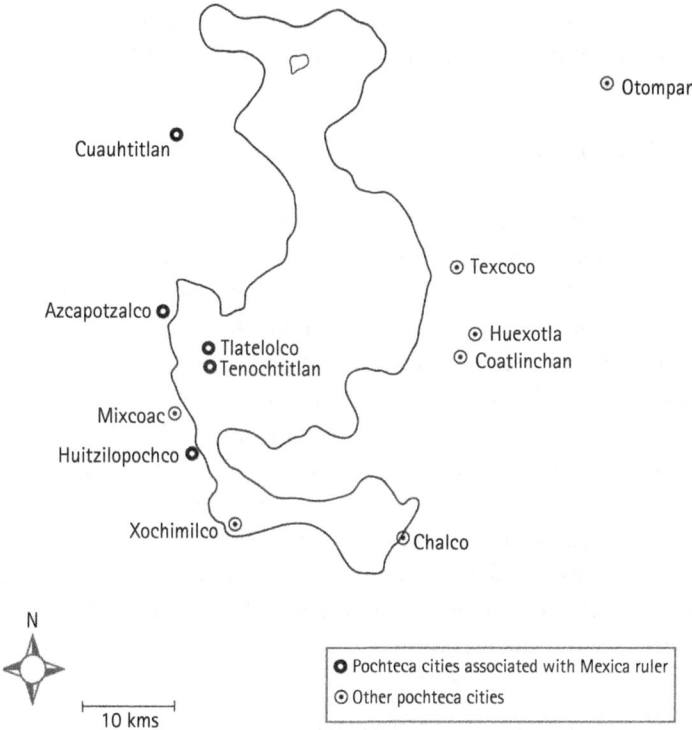

FIGURE 30.2 *Pochteca* cities in the Basin of Mexico. Map drawn by Jennifer B. Lozano.

(Cuauhnahuac and environs). The primacy of Tenochtitlan was further reaffirmed when the allied troops returned from battle, all marching into a celebrating Tenochtitlan and then required to wait to be dismissed by the Mexica ruler.

Similarly, some labor projects were simply too ambitious and massive for the Mexica to handle alone. One of these was the renovation of the Tenochtitlan Templo Mayor by Motecuhzoma Ilhuicamina, who called on ("ordered") his allies for assistance; they were reportedly willing to contribute since "this was expected of them" (Durán 1994:226). The work was divided among the allied cities, with Texcoco responsible for constructing the front of the temple, Tlacopan the back, Chalco the right side, and the people of Xochimilco and the *chinampa* area the left side. Other allied city-states provided and transported necessary raw materials (Durán 1994:224–226). Whether or not this arrangement actually materialized (Doris Heyden [see Durán 1994:225], doubts it), it expresses the obligations understood between the dominant Tenochtitlan and its allied city-states. Another interesting event was the moving of a rather difficult and verbose rock from Chalco to Tenochtitlan. The job turned out to be too much for the Mexica alone, leaving Motecuhzoma Xocoyotzin to call on his allies to move the rock by brute force. He dealt with each polity differently, "begging" the Texcocan *tlahtoani*, "requesting" help from the Azcapotzalco (Tepaneca) ruler, "summoning" the Otomí, and "ordering" the cities of the *chinampa* district. While one perhaps should not read too much into these terms, they may nonetheless suggest the different ways in which the Tenochtitlan ruler perceived and orchestrated his relations with his allied and subject city-states.

Elite Intermarriages

Much about high-level power relations can be gleaned from a look at patterns of elite intermarriages. Arranged marriages at the highest political levels sent important political messages and set the stage for the assumption of subordinate rulerships. A usual pattern was for a superordinate ruler to give a daughter in marriage to a subordinate ruler. This was the case between Tenochtitlan and Texcoco, where the Tenochtitlan king Huitzilihuitl gave his daughter to king Ixtlilxochitl of Texcoco; their child, Nezahualcoyotl, inherited the Texcocan rulership and was Itzcoatl's nephew and contemporary. This type of arrangement continued until the time of the Spanish arrival, whereby Texcocan rulers were sons of Mexica princesses (Carrasco 1999:43). For their part, the Texcocan kings offered daughters to their subordinate lords, cementing supremacy and establishing dynastic ties to succeeding rulers in their dependent city-states. Thus throughout the imperial realm these interconnected hierarchies served as integrative devices at the highest political levels.

Ceremonies in the Service of Politics

The hierarchical ordering of the three allied kings was reinforced during specified ceremonial occasions. One particularly spectacular event was the dedication of a further expansion of the Tenochtitlan Templo Mayor by the ruler Ahuitzotl in 1487. This ritual extravaganza included sacrifices of large numbers of warriors seized in recent wars by the Mexica and their allies. The captives from each of the participating city-states were lined up separately so an accurate count could be made—thus credit was given where due. The three Triple Alliance rulers, along with the Tenochtitlan Cihuacoatl (second-in-command) then personally began the sacrifices until they tired (Alvarado Tezozomoc 1975:499–509). The participation by rulers and captives from the allied cities in a distinctly Tenochtitlan ceremony further reaffirmed Tenochtitlan's supremacy in the alliance. This extraordinary event aside, other politico-ceremonial events such as royal funerals and coronations took place in each ruler's city.

IMPERIAL GOALS: EXPANDING AND MANAGING AN EMPIRE THROUGH ALLIANCE

Things became a bit more complicated when the Triple Alliance conquered city-states beyond its established core region in and around the Basin of Mexico. Some of these conquests were undertaken by one of the allies alone, but many were joint efforts. In these cases, the allies' well-established relations played out predictably as the coalition expanded, conquering distant city-states and demanding immediate and periodic tributes from their new subjects. Vanquished rulers were typically allowed to retain their eminent positions, although the conquerors uniformly assigned tribute collectors in all provinces and established governors and military garrisons where they considered it necessary. The empire employed military force and subtler, nonviolent negotiation strategies to control far-flung regions (Berdan et al. 1996) (Figure 30.3).

The intermingling of territories and subjects appears as a factor in faraway subject regions: in some conquered territories, tribute collectors (*calpixque*) and occasionally other officials were installed in a single province by more than one Triple Alliance ruler, suggesting that each imperial polity was extracting resources from the same area (but perhaps different individual subjects). Similarly, repopulation of specific war-devastated regions was shared by the three allies, along with several of their neighbors. Beyond such administrative matters, the Triple Alliance powers developed workable cooperative strategies of benefit to each member; these arrangements can be seen especially in the manner in which they combined their military forces for conquest and the rules surrounding the distribution of the considerable spoils of war.

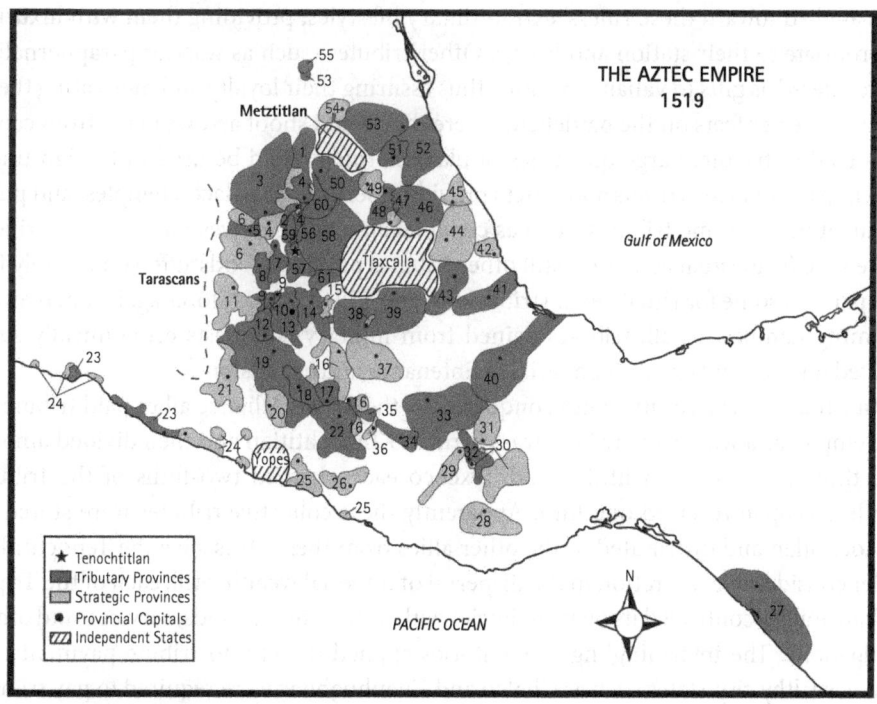

FIGURE 30.3 The Triple Alliance or Aztec Empire, 1519. Map drawn by Jennifer B. Lozano.

The Conduct of War

Principles of segmentation and hierarchy were evident in war preparations and battlefield engagements. Each allied city-state prepared and equipped its own troops and usually traveled to the battlefield site independently. Once all were assembled, the Tenochtitlan ruler or his designated general took charge as supreme commander of the overall campaign. Prior to and during the battle, each city-state contingent set up its own camp, was exorted by its own leader, carried its own banner, and passionately yelled "Texcoco!," "Tenochtitlan!," or some other city as they advanced on the enemy. Importantly, warriors from each city-state took and retained rights to their own prisoners. Nonetheless, "the Aztecs always were in the lead" (Durán 1994:266).

Tribute and Imperial Finance in the Triple Alliance

Tributes were paid on regular schedules from conquered tributary provinces (see Figure 30.3) or delivered to the imperial cities to support unscheduled ritual or social occasions such as a temple dedication or a royal coronation. These vast quantities of raw materials and luxury and utilitarian goods supported elite lifestyles, imperial growth, and urban sustenance (Berdan 2005:44–47). All three of the *huey tlatoque* maintained expensive palaces and enjoyed lavish feasts and other extravagances. Some of the tribute income (such as fine clothing, precious gems, shimmering feathers, jaguar pelts, and cacao) was applied toward these rulers' extraordinary lifestyles, providing them with luxuries appropriate to their station and image. Other tributes (such as warrior paraphernalia) were offered as gifts to valiant warriors, thus assuring their loyalty and motivating them to even greater feats on the battlefield where they could shoot arrows made from canes also paid in tribute. Large quantities of plain clothing could be used in foreign trade and in payments to artisans and others providing services to palaces, temples, and public institutions. Some tributes, such as copal incense and captives for human sacrifice, were specific to ritual activities. Still other tributes provided foodstuffs, some surely for the palaces, some for ritualized distributions, and still others as stores against perceived looming famines. In all, tributes gained from military conquests economically supported internal and external imperial maintenance and expansion.

In situations where city-states conquered by the Triple Alliance allies paid tribute to the empire as a whole, the tribute was carried to Tenochtitlan and then divided among the three capitals; Tenochtitlan and Texcoco each claimed two-fifths of the tribute while Tlacopan received one-fifth. Apparently these collective tributes were stored in Tenochtitlan and distributed to the other allies from there. This gave the Tenochtitlan ruler considerable discretion in the dispersal of imperial wealth. Still, each of the Triple Alliance allies controlled its own territories with its tributes in goods, services, and other obligations. The intermingling of territories applied directly to tribute payments, as some wealthy city-states such as Chalco and Cuauhnahuac were required to pay tribute to all three allies; apparently these were separate, not shared collections since tributes from these subject city-states were stored in at least Tenochtitlan and Texcoco, with the status of Tlacopan undocumented (Berdan and Anawalt 1992, Offner 1983:107–108). Overall, tribute income for all three allies contributed heavily to the maintenance and expansion of their imperial ambitions.

THE TRIPLE ALLIANCE IN 1519: STRENGTHS AND WEAKNESSES

The Triple Alliance *huey tlatoque* spent considerable time and energy ruling their own domains as conquest states. However, certain occasions warranted the mobilization of allied efforts. Warfare was preeminent among these. The Tenochtitlan ruler would call on his allies to contribute their military forces to ambitious and lucrative wars of conquest, many of them at considerable distances from the Basin of Mexico. Allied commitments also were animated for special work projects requiring extraordinary amounts of labor. These allies, in both war and peace, included not only Tenochtitlan, Texcoco, and Tlacopan but also other loyal city-states in and beyond the Basin of Mexico. These situational mobilizations of forces and labor for mutual benefit and gain amassed huge and highly effective armies and workforces over the brief time span of the empire.

Yet the entire arrangement was also loosely structured and competitive at all political levels. Subject polities calculated the benefits and risks of their current and future allegiances and sometimes took measures to direct their political fortunes accordingly. This appears to have been the case with Tepechpan (a Texcocan dependency), which manipulated its own fate at one time by ignoring its subservience to Texcoco and throwing in its lot with Tenochtitlan, solidifying that association with a marriage alliance (Diel 2008:56, 61). Instability in alliances was probably more the rule than stability. In the end, even Texcoco abandoned its avowed ally Tenochtitlan to the ravages of conquest led by the Spanish siege in 1521.

REFERENCES CITED

Alva Ixtlilxochitl, Fernando de.
1965 *Obras Históricas*. 2 vols. Editora Nacional, Mexico City.
Alvarado Tezozomoc, Hernando
1975 *Crónica Mexicana*, 2nd ed. Editorial Porrua, Mexico City.
Berdan, Frances F.
2005 *The Aztecs of Central Mexico: An Imperial Society*. 2nd ed. Wadsworth, Belmont, CA.
Berdan, Frances F., and Patricia Rieff Anawalt (editors)
1992 *The Codex Mendoza*. 4 vols. University of California Press, Berkeley.
Berdan, Frances F., Richard E. Blanton, Elizabeth Hill Boone, Mary G. Hodge, Michael E. Smith, and Emily Umberger

1996 *Aztec Imperial Strategies*. Dumbarton Oaks Research Library and Collection, Washington, DC.

Carrasco, Pedro
1999 *The Tenochca Empire of Ancient Mexico: The Triple Alliance of Tenochtitlan, Tetzcoco, and Tlacopan*. University of Oklahoma Press, Norman.

Davies, Nigel
1977 *The Toltecs Until the Fall of Tula*. University of Oklahoma Press, Norman.

Diel, Lori Boornazian
2008 *The Tira de Tepechpan: Negotiating Place Under Aztec and Spanish Rule*. University of Texas Press, Austin.

Douglas, Eduardo
2010 *In the Palace of Nezahualcoyotl*. University of Texas Press, Austin.

Durán, Diego
1994 *The History of the Indies of New Spain*. University of Oklahoma Press, Norman.

Gibson, Charles
1971 Structure of the Aztec Empire. In *Handbook of Middle American Indians*, Vol. 10, edited by Robert Wauchope, pp. 376–394. University of Texas Press, Austin.

Hodge, Mary G.
1996 Political Organization of the Central Provinces. In *Aztec Imperial Strategies*, edited by Frances F. Berdan, Richard E. Blanton, Elizabeth Hill Boone, Mary G. Hodge, Michael E. Smith, and Emily Umberger, pp. 17–45. Dumbarton Oaks Research Library and Collection, Washington, DC.

Lockhart, James
1992 *The Nahuas After the Conquest*. Stanford University Press, Stanford, CA.

Offner, Jerome
1983 *Law and Politics in Aztec Texcoco*. Cambridge University Press, Cambridge.

Sahagún, Fray Bernardino de
1950–1982 *Florentine Codex: General History of the Things of New Spain*. Edited by Arthur J. O. Anderson and Charles E. Dibble. 12 vols. University of Utah Press, Salt Lake City.

CHAPTER 31

MEXICA WAR

New Research Perspectives

MARCO ANTONIO CERVERA OBREGÓN

PRECOLUMBIAN studies focused on the Mexica have proliferated in recent years. The Mexica world is well documented by data from multiple sources, including ethnohistoric documents, the Spanish chronicles, and archaeological studies. However, not all aspects have been adequately addressed: such is the case for warfare.

GENERAL HISTORIOGRAPHY OF MEXICA WARFARE

Following on the heels of the chroniclers and subsequent researchers of the seventeenth and eighteenth centuries, some of the first outstanding examples of early research on Mexica warfare were published during the late nineteenth century. For example, Adolphus Bandelier (1877), in particular, marks the beginning of a much deeper concern with the study of warfare as part of the Mexica world.

During the first half of the twentieth century, important researchers, such as Pedro Armillas (1942), Eduardo Noguera (1945), Celia Nuttal (1891, 1892), Antonio Peñafiel (1903), and Eduard Seler (1960), offered some precursor proposals in the topic. By the middle of the twentieth century, the first synthetic works began to emerge; these are considered complete works, devoted entirely to this topic. One important example is Jorge Canseco's (1966) *La guerra sagrada*, in which the author offers a vision of what he calls "The Sacred War." Some of the works that formally give rise to the historiography of Mexica warfare include those by José Lameiras, which are primarily based on written sources and codices, including *Los déspotas armados, un espectro de la guerra prehispánica* (1985) and *El encuentro de la piedra y el acero* (1994).

Of all the books published to date on warfare in the Mexica world, none has had as much impact on the academic world as the work of Ross Hassig. However, while Hassig's pioneering work continues to be indispensable, it is not definitive. With a mature and focused theoretical basis, Hassig's (1988) *Aztec Warfare Imperial Expansion and Political Control* as well as his second work, *War and Society in Ancient Mesoamerica* (Hassig 1992) present a basic outline of our knowledge of prehispanic warfare. These works also provided future researchers (e.g., Bueno 2005, 2007; Cervera 2007, 2011; Pohl 1991) a solid basis for developing some of the finest studies based on this initial framework.

MILITARY ARCHAEOLOGY: A NEW DISCIPLINE IN MEXICO

Studies on Mesoamerican warfare have always been dominated by explanations based on the ritual functions of this activity. Unfortunately, such studies almost completely ignore the other side of the coin: human involvement in warfare. Hassig (2000:169) warned of this epistemological limitation:

> This is true regardless of whether the society in question creates Jehovah, Allah, Huitzilopochtli, or Chac. The army can only advance a set number of miles, every soldier consumes a certain amount of food and drink each day, and these supplies must be provided if the war is to be won, regardless of ideology.... I believe that the knowledge of what happens on earth is an essential requirement.

The words of Fernando Quesada (2006), another great scholar of warfare in antiquity, offer a revealing glimpse into the topic. Championing the need to address the problems of military history, from the perspective of military history and archeology, Quesada (2006:149) warned against viewing this approach as archaic or outmoded, urging rather that "Unapologetically, military history must be focused on the military."

This is likely one of the main factors preventing a more balanced view of the subject. This does not mean that the religious and symbolic aspects of warfare, which of course are many (González 2011:317), should be minimized but rather that alternatives on the other end of the spectrum should also be considered. The goal is to eventually achieve a balance that permits us to consider all possible angles and mechanisms, whether religious or mundane, related to the phenomenon of warfare in the Mexica world.

Starting with Carlos Brokmann's (2000:261–286) work, we begin to see the development of research with a more mature perspective of concepts of warfare in the Mexican school. Some of these new ideas derive from the discipline of military archaeology (Gracia 2011). Thus military archeology, also known as conflict archaeology—with strong proponents in England, France, Spain, and the United States—has allowed us to understand more fully how warfare is conducted and what that meant for the armies of antiquity (Gracia 2011:3). Although not without limitations, the application of these

FIGURE 31.1 Experimental reconstruction of a *macuahuitl* by Marco Cervera and Marco Antonio de la Cruz. (Photo: Marco Antonio Cervera File).

theoretical models to data from a variety of Mexica sources has painted a different picture of this subject. Military archeology is concerned with the painstaking task of creating a scientific typology of weapons based on the available iconography (i.e., sculptures) (Trejo 2000:221) and the recovery of weapons from archaeological contexts. This permits morpho-functional studies of these artifacts in order to identify their defensive or offensive uses in the battlefield. Recently, such studies have included experimental archeology of Mesoamerican weapons (Cervera 2006:34–35, 2011:118–125) (Figures 31.1 and 31.2).

From the Aztecs we have mostly obsidian artifacts, although there are also a few examples of wooden weapons, such as the recently published *macuahuitl* uncovered in Mexico City by Juana Moreno Hernández of the Subdirection of Archaeological Studies at the National Institute of Anthropology and History (Instituto Nacional de Antropología e Historia).

Military archaeology has also been concerned with the identification and excavation of battlefields as part of a subdiscipline known in the English-speaking world as battlefield archaeology (Gracia 2011:14). For various reasons related to conservation, it has been very difficult to take a similar approach to the study of Mexica warfare. Mexican military archeology (Cervera and Bueno 2014) has been under development for, at

FIGURE 31.2 Experimental reconstruction of a *teputopilli* by Marco Cervera and Marco Antonio de la Cruz. (Photo: Marco Antonio Cervera File).

most, a decade. Future generations of researchers will secure the place of this discipline and ensure its development in Mexico.

WAR IN THE MEXICA WORLD: TWO PERSPECTIVES

The driving force behind the expansion of the empire and the development of the Mexica civilization was war, which therefore must be considered with great care and consideration. Much of the political, economic, and religious foundations were thoroughly saturated by the Mexican military phenomenon, and therefore the problem and its explanation become increasingly complex.

To facilitate analysis, I delineate two types of Mexica warfare: wars of conquest and the "flowery" wars. The difference between the two is obvious from their names. The former was the real engine of expansion for the empire, with the primary objectives of obtaining tribute and economic resources and ensuring territorial expansion. Although not the primary objective, no doubt war captives were also obtained, as is the case in any military conflict.

The latter, which are the source of considerable debate among researchers, are better known as the holy wars. This type of warfare had as its primary objectives the capture of prisoners for sacrifice and the advent of mobility within the Mexica military structure, which was particularly important for the *macehualtin* who had few other options for advancement (Cervera 2012b:36). Various authors, including Hassig (1998:54) and Isabel Bueno (2007:158), argue that these wars were part of a political strategy to keep subjected nobles at bay, as it was difficult to truly subjugate them and far easier to simply keep them in a state of constant exhaustion from defending themselves against the Mexica military. Sometimes these two types of wars could merge into a single vision or be modified as political and military processes developed, as was the case with the war waged against Chalco.

Note that these two basic types of war are specific to the Mexica world—it would be wrong to apply them to all Mesoamerican societies, as often happens when trying to explain this phenomenon in other societies that were contemporary with or even preceded the Mexica. The flowery or ritual warfare was a Mexica invention, and warfare did not take on the same form in other Mesoamerican cultures (e.g., Teotihuacan or Tula).

Each type of warfare has its respective implications; that is, how they were carried out was distinct. Thus the number of troops assembled for combat, tactical maneuvers, the use of weapons, and the forms of combat were likely very different. Different objectives clearly marked the strategies and logistics of each campaign.

Generally, a war began with a request from the Mexican state for a particular kind of tribute, which, depending on the area, might be different manufactured items or raw materials, among other things. Many such demands were recorded in documents like the *Matrícula de Tributos* or the second part of the *Codex Mendoza*. Should the towns in question refuse this request (which they did on two occasions), the Mexica army could declare war (Berdan 1978:78; Carrasco 1994:186).

Typically, the Mexica sent an emissary to carry out the ritual of declaring war. The representative, sent on behalf of the ruling aggressor, offered the following gifts: a lead carbonate ointment, feathers, a shield, and darts for armed conflict. If the opponent accepted the military dispute, the Mexica representative offered him a *macuahuitl* and a shield decorated with a flower (Durán 1967, Vol. II:ch. IX). It was understood that this initiated the preparations for war. The next step involved the provisioning of armies, which included corn-based food items like tortillas, tamales, cornmeal, and, as mentioned in written sources, tortilla chips, which were easier to preserve and transport, as well as weapons (Hassig 1988:73).

Much discussion has focused on how to use the written sources to distinguish between wars of conquest and the flowery wars. This is significant because, in many cases, the sources contradict each other. In fact, some sources mention that the flowery wars were "agreed upon" with six specific adversaries. According to Durán (1967, Vol. II, ch. XXVIII): "And it would be very strategic to have our market and festival in the six cities I have mentioned: Tlaxcala, Huexotzingo, Cholula, Atlixco, Tliluhquitepec, and Tecoac, as the people of those towns will accept our god as they would bread hot from the oven, soft and tasty." Thus, theoretically, any other campaigns mentioned in the Spanish documents were wars of conquest, and their development was different. Of course operating a campaign with the nearly exclusively goal of transporting captives to Tenochtitlan was strategically more convenient than having adversaries located in the Basin of Mexico.

THE STRUCTURE OF THE ARMY

By the "structure" of the Mexican army I mean in particular the bureaucratic body and the chain of command in which it was established. Elsewhere I have proposed that Mexica warfare be understood in terms of three stages: origins, mercenaries, and imperial stages. The Mexica army changed considerable during its history (Cervera 2011:62). Thus, during the Imperial period, the Mexica social and military structures were better developed (López Austin 1985:215) and could sustain a true control system, which is hotly debated today.

The eagle and jaguar warriors were the most emblematic aspects of this typically Mesoamerican control system. They were present at least from Teotihuacan times (Cabrera 2002:137; Cervera 2012a:21), and their symbiotic relationship with these predatory animals is undeniable. The capture of prisoners, particularly as part of the flowery wars, was the main mechanism for mobility within the Mexica chain of command. Captives were more important than the number of enemies killed. This is a rather contradictory situation where warfare is concerned (*Codex Mendoza*, Plate 67r). Mobility within the control system was reflected by the diversity of uniforms available, each very ornate and adorned with very specific symbols (Broda 1978:120).

The flowery wars were an important route, in particular for the *macehualtin*, for gaining access to military rank, prestige, and some privileges. However, the most important ranks were reserved only for *pipilltin*. In many cases, the ranks are identified by Nahuatl words that do not necessarily correspond to a logical and consecutive chain of command, such as *Yaoquiscayacanqui, yaoquiscatepacho, yaociscatachcahu, yaotachcahu,* and *yaotequihua*, terms that are simply translated as "commander of men" or "men of war" (Lameiras 1985:173–174). Therefore, it is not entirely clear which ranks correspond to the modern military ranks of general, captain, and lieutenant. In addition, other systems such as weaponry and communications were also intimately linked with warfare.

There has been considerable discussion of how many troops the Mexican army could muster to do combat on the battlefield. Estimates are calculated as a percentage of the total population. The inherent military probability (IMP), a concept coined by military historian A. H. Bume (Quesada 2006:151), is often used by archaeologists and military historians. The IMP permits estimation of the number of troops available to ancient armies based on population estimates. It is estimated that between 6 percent and 10 percent of the population, excluding the disabled, children, women, and the elderly, would be available for combat and able to wield a weapon. Most authors consider that, at its height, the city of Tenochtitlan housed an estimated 200,000 people (Hassig 1990:67), thus a total of 20,000 troops for the armies of Tenochtitlan alone and around 60,000 soldiers if the other members of the Triple Alliance are included would have been available. There were also auxiliary troops, many of which were provided by subjected cities. When the Mexican army passed by such towns or initiated a campaign, the townspeople had an obligation to provide troops, food, and weapons (Hassig 1990:107). Estimates based on the IMP agree somewhat with the figures cited in the Spanish sources. For example, for the war against the Tarascans, the armies numbered 40,000 and 25,000 warriors for the Tarascans and Mexicas, respectively.

The size of an army is often an important element in terms of winning or losing a battle, though it is not the only factor. In the battle between the Tarascans and the Mexicas, however, it was a determining factor. The larger Tarascan army defeated the Mexicas, who, until that moment:

> had never feared that any army would attack them, nor had they ever faced weapons or other war supplies of higher quality, were concerned what other nations would say that if they returned now, having arrived without being summoned or provoked [Durán 1967, Vol. II:ch. XXXVII].

The communication system (the way the Mexica army transmitted and received orders) is well-known. Written sources, like Torquemada (1975), Durán (1967), and Sahagún (1997), as well as iconographic sources, such as the *Codex Ixlilxóchitl*, Folio 106r, report that information could be transmitted by audio or visual means. The former was achieved through two basic instruments, the conch shell and a small drum that generals carried on their backs (Figure 31.3).

In contrast, the visual transmission of information typically involved the use of flags carried by soldiers on their backs. Each of the flags represented either the *calpolli* or the village of origin, to facilitate organization on the battlefield (Durán 1967, Vol. II:ch. XXXVII).

Weapons, Weapon Systems, and Tactical Approaches

Much has been said about the basic typology of Mexica weapons, both offensive and defensive arsenals. In *El armamento entre los mexicas* (Cervera 2007), I attempt to establish the origins, types, functions, and various roles of these in the Mexica world. Using a variety of data sources, I outline our basic knowledge on the topic. However, this earlier work did not include experimental archaeology, which has since revolutionized what we know about Mexica weapons.

Thus Mexica weaponry has drawn more attention over the past decade. On the one hand, we have passive defensive weapons, such as the *ichcahuipill* cotton breastplate and

FIGURE 31.3 Nezahualcoyotl as a soldier, with weapons that include a *macuahuitl* and *chimalli*. He carries a small drum on his back to transmit orders on the battle field. *Codex Ixtlilxóchitl*, Folio 106r.

helmets, while on the other were active defense weapons that included shields or *chimalli*. Offensive weapons may be divided into two types: long-distance weapons such as the *atlatl*, sling, throwing darts, and bow and arrow, and weapons for hand-to-hand combat, such as the *quauholloll* (mace or club), *macuahuitl* (hand spear or sword), and *teputzopilli* (similar to both a halberd and a spear).

The best way to understand the functional aspects of these devices is through experimental archeology. In terms of analyzing weapons, this school of thought has only recently garnered interest in Mexico. However, new generations of researchers, in particular, have successfully employed this analytical method. Among the researchers who have generated experimental results are Bob Perkins, Ross Hassig, Alfonso Garduño, Alejandro Pastrana, and Marco Cervera. Many of these studies have yet to be published in scientific journals or books (Cervera 2006, 2011:118), although some television networks have aired segments involving re-creations. In fact, tests have been carried out in order to examine the lethality of the weapons used by the Mexica against the Spanish.

The structure of these weapons systems, that is, the balance between offensive and defensive weapons, can be divided—with all the epistemological problems that entails—into two segments: light infantry units with throwing weapons and heavy infantry, such as *ichcahuipilli* and spears, *macuahuitl*, and shields (Cervera 2011:110).

The Future of Research on Mexica Warfare

Among new topics only recently receiving attention, Isabel Bueno (2005, 2007:175) has recently offered important new interpretations of naval warfare. Moreover, as mentioned previously, experimental archeology involving Mexica weapons is still an area of active investigation. This is apparent in the discussions generated by the recently recovered *macuahuitl*. Detailed analyses of historical sources shed light on the tactical approaches and details of the major battles fought by the Mexica while also offering specific details on their weapon systems and combat patterns (Cervera 2011:185). All of these aspects, of course, are related to control systems, an area ripe for future investigation.

Case studies accompanied by experimental archeology will allow us to approach these topics in an even more didactic manner (Cortadella 2011:91) (Figure 31.4).

The clearest examples of this new interest in prehispanic military archeology and history are the different symposia and conferences that have been held in Mexico over the past decade, starting with FES-Acatlan, Universidad Nacional Autónoma de México in 2008

FIGURE 31.4 Resin replica of a Mexica soldier, dressed as *Tzitzimitl*. First hyperrealistic reconstruction developed in Mexico for artistic and scientific purposes by *Caronte Lab* in consultation with Marco Cervera. (Photo: Marco Antonio Cervera File)

and followed by the *Primer coloquio sobre la Guerra en el México Antiguo*, which was held at the Museo del Carmen in 2009 and another conference at the Museo del Templo Mayor in 2010. Various meetings have also been organized by the Escuela Nacional de Antropología e Historia in 2012 and 2013. Such displays of interest, particularly among younger generations and in conjunction with the increase in graduate theses on the subject, have greatly advanced our knowledge of warfare in the Mexica world. The future of Mexica warfare studies has much to offer.

Dedication

In memory of Felipe Solís Olguín.

References Cited

Armillas, Pedro
1942 Oztuma, Gro, fortaleza de los mexicanos en la frontera de Michoacán. *Revista Mexicana de Estudios Antropológicos* 6:165–175.

Bandelier, Adolphe
1877 On the Art of War and Mode of Warfare of the Ancient Mexicans. *Peabody Museum of American Archeology and Ethnology, Annual Report* 2(10):95–161.

Berdan, Frances
1978 Tres formas de intercambio en la economía Azteca. In *Economía, política e ideología en el México prehispánico*, edited by Pedro Carrasco and J. Broda, pp. 77–94. Instituto Nacional de Antropología e Historia, Mexico City.

Broda, Johanna
1978 El tributo en trajes y la estructura del sistema tributario mexica, guerreros. In *Economía, política e ideología en el México prehispánico*, edited by Pedro Carrasco and J. Broda, pp. 115–146. Instituto Nacional de Antropología e Historia, Mexico City.

Brokmann, Carlos
2000 Armamento y tácticas: evidencia lítica y escultórica de las zonas Usumacinta y Pasión. In *La guerra entre los antiguos mayas: memoria de la Primera Mesa Redonda de Palenque*, edited by Silvia Trejo, pp. 263–286. Instituto Nacional de Antropología e Historia, Mexico City,

Bueno, Isabel
2005 La guerra naval en el Valle de México. *Estudios de Cultura Náhuatl* 36:199–223.
2007 *La guerra en el Imperio Azteca: expansión ideología y arte*. Ed. Complutense, Mirada de la Historia, Madrid.

Cabrera, Rubén
2002 La expresión pictórica de Atetelco, Teotihuacan: su significado con el militarismo y el sacrificio humano. In *Ideología y política a través de materiales, imágenes y símbolos: memoria de la primera Mesa Redonda de Teotihuacan*, edited by Maria Elena Ruiz Gallut, pp. 137–164. Instituto Nacional de Antropología e Historia, Mexico City.

Canseco Vincourt, Jorge
1966 *La Guerra Sagrada*. Instituto Nacional de Antropología e Historia, Mexico City.

Carrasco, Pedro
1994 La Triple Alianza: organización política y estructura territorial. In *Temas mesoamericanos*, edited by Sonia Lombardo, pp. 167–209. Instituto Nacional de Antropología e Historia, Mexico City.
Cervera Obregón, Marco Antonio
2006 The *Macuáhuitl:* An Innovative Weapon of the Late Post-Classic in Mesoamerica. *Arms and Armour: Journal of the Royal Armouires* 1(3):107–128.
2007 *El armamento entre los mexicas.* Anejos de Gladius 11. Consejo Superior de Investigaciones Científicas, Polifemo, Madrid.
2011 *Guerreros aztecas.* Nowtilus, Madrid.
2012a La guerra compleja, posibles alcances de conflictos armados en Teotihuacan, *Revista El Humanista* 3(3):10–26.
2012b La guerra florida en el mundo azteca-mexica. *Desperta Ferro* 9:36–39.
2014 La Arqueología e historia militar en México y el conocimiento de los ejércitos prehispánicos, una visión panorámica. In *Historia de los ejércitos mexicanos.* Secretaría de la Defensa Nacional, Secretaría de Educación Pública, pp. 33–41. Instituto Nacional de Estudios Históricos de las Revoluciones de México, Mexico City.
Codex Mendoza
1995 *The Codex Mendoza.* 4 vols. Edited by F. F. Berdan and P. R. Anawalt. University of California Press, Berkeley.
Códice Ixtlilxóchitl
1996 Papeles y pinturas de un historiador/Geert Bastiaan van Doesburg—México: FCE, Akademische Druck-und Verlagsanstalt.
Cortadella, Jordi
2011 Los grupos de recreación histórica (Historical Re-Enactment). In *La Guerra en la antigüedad desde el presente,* edited by Jordi Vidal and Borja Antela Barcelona, 91–139. Libros Pórtico, Zaragoza, Spain.
Durán, Diego
1967 *Historia de las Indias de la Nueva España.* 2 vols. Editorial Porrúa, Mexico City.
Gracia, Alonso Francisco
2011 La arqueología e historia militar antigua en Europa y Estados Unidos: situación actual y perspectivas. In *La Guerra en la antigüedad desde el presente,* pp. 1–36. Ariel, Barcelona.
González, Carlos Javier
2011 *Xipe Tótec: guerra y regeneración del maíz en la religión Mexica.* Fondo de Cultura Económica, Mexico City.
Hassig, Ross
1988 *Aztec Warfare: Imperial Expansion and Political Control.* University of Oklahoma Press, Norman.
1990 *Comercio, tribute y transportes: la economía política del Valle de México en el siglo XVI.* Alianza editorial, Mexico City.
1992 *War and Society in Ancient Mesoamerica.* University of California Press, Berkeley.
2000 La guerra maya vista a través del Altiplano Posclásico. In *La guerra entre los antiguos mayas: memoria de la Primera Mesa Redonda de Palenque,* edited by Silvia Trejo, pp. 157–173. Instituto Nacional de Antropología e Historia, Mexico City.
Lameiras, José
1985 *Los déspotas armadas, un espectro de la Guerra prehispánica.* Colegio de Michoacan, Mexico City.
1994 *El encuentro de la piedra y el acero.* El Colegio Michoacano, Zamora Michoacan, Mexico.
López, Austin Alfredo

1985 Organización política en el Altiplano Central de México durante el Posclásico. In *Mesoamérica y el Centro de México*, compiled by Jesús Monjarás Ruiz, Rosa Brambilia, and Emma Pérez-Rocha, pp. 197–234. Instituto Nacional de Antropología e Historia, Mexico City.

Noguera, Eduardo

1945 "El *átlatl*" en *Anales del Museo Nacional*. ep. 5 v. III, Mexico.

Nuttall, Celia

1891 The *Átlatl* or Spear-Thrower of the Ancient Mexicans. *Peabody Museum of American Archeology and Ethnology Papers* 3:169–199.

1892 On Ancient Mexican Shields. *Internationales Archiv für Ethnographie* 5:34–53.

Peñafiel, Antonio

1903 *Indumentaria ntigua—armas, vestidos guerreros y civiles de los antiguos mexicanos*. Secretaría de Fomento, Mexico City.

Pohl, John

1991 *Aztec, Mixtec and Zapotec Armies*. Osprey, London.

2001 *Aztec Warrior, 1325–1521*. Ospray, London.

Quesada Sanz, Fernando

2006 La Celtiberia y la Guerra. In *Segeda y su contexto histórico, entre Catón y Nobilor, (195 al 153)*, edited by Francisco Burillo, pp. 149–167. Fundación Segeda, Centro de Estudios Celtibéricos, Zaragoza, Spain.

Sahagún, Fary Bernardino de

1997 *Historia General de las Cosas de la Nueva España*, Porrúa Sepan Cuantos n. 300. Mexico.

Seler, Eduard

1960 *Gesammelte Abhandlungen zur Amerikanischen Sprach-und Altertumskunde*. 5 vols. Akademishe Drunck-und Verlagsanstalt, Graz.

Torquemada, Fray Juan

1975 *Monarquía Indiana*, Instituto de Investigaciones Históricas, UNAM, Mexico.

Trejo, Silvia

2000 La imagen del guerrero victorioso en Mesoamérica. *Estudios de Cultura Náhuatl* 31:221–222.

CHAPTER 32

AZTEC PROVINCES OF THE CENTRAL HIGHLANDS

MAËLLE SERGHERAERT

After securing its core (Anahuac) between A.D. 1428 and 1430, the Aztec Triple Alliance, formed by the rulers (*tlatoque*) of Tenochtitlan, Texcoco, and Tlacopan, began to expand outside the Basin of Mexico. The Aztec Empire grew gradually—mostly via military conquests—to extend over a large part of northern Mesoamerica until the Spanish Conquest in 1521.

Many of the conquered city-states were organized into 38 tributary provinces whereas others played more of a role in the defense of the empire. They have been categorized as "strategic" provinces by some scholars (Smith, 1996:ch. 6). The areas included in the provinces are shown on the map in Figure 32.1, which encompasses an area of 135,000 km².

Aztec Expansion in the Central Highlands

Being the closest to the Basin of Mexico, the Central Highlands provinces were the first to be conquered by imperial forces, mostly between 1430 and 1481. In Figure 32.1, Central Highlands are divided into 14 tributary provinces (Axocopan, Atotonilco de Pedraza, Xilotepec, Xocotitlan, Cuahuacan, Tollocan, Ocuilan, Malinalco, Tlachco, Cuauhnahuac, Huaxtepec, Quiauhteopan, Tlacozauhtitlan, and Tepequacuilco) and 5 strategic provinces (Chiapan, Ixtlahuacan, Temazcaltepec, Ocuituco, and Chiauhtlan).

The Triple Alliance counted on strong military forces, and most of the new territories were subjugated during military campaigns. The Aztec strategy involved targeting the major city-states (*altepetl*) of each region, because when an *altepetl* capital was subdued, imperial rule was initiated over the entire area of the *altepetl* and all

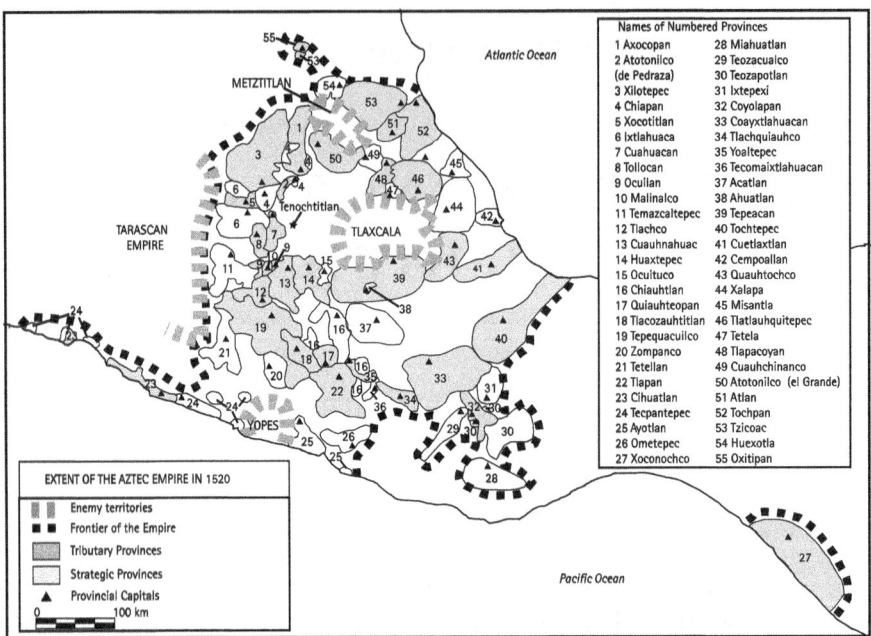

FIGURE 32.1 Map of the Aztec Empire. Based on Berdan et al. (1996:Fig. 11.1); redrawn by Marion Forest, Maëlle Sergheraert, and Kristin Sullivan.

its population, not just the capital city that was defeated. This principle is illustrated in many of the depictions of conquest found in Aztec pictorial histories, where the name of the defeated city is generally tied to a symbol for *altepetl* (a hill sign in most of them). Figure 32.2 shows the conquest of Xiquipilco in the year 12 rabbit, or 1478 (Xiquipilco is in province 6 in Figure 32.1). The Mexica warrior is on the right, linked to the glyph for Tenochtitlan (a cactus growing out of a rock). He defeats a warrior whose domain is the entire *altepetl* (the hill emblem, *tepetl*) of Xiquipilco (symbolized by the incense bag).

The information on capitals given by the codices allows us to understand the expansion dynamic and its efficiency: the Aztecs did not have to conquer all the towns and villages—only the most important towns in each province—to subjucate large portions of them. This is related to Mesoamerican patterns of political control. The extent of a polity was defined not in terms of a border surrounding an area of territory but rather as the area in which the people subject to the king lived (Smith 2008:89–91).

Tribute/Taxes

The tax system was the most important mechanism by which the imperial capitals obtained resources from the provinces. Although scholars have traditionally used the

FIGURE 32.2 Conquest of Xiquipilco by Tenochtitlan. *Codex Telleriano-Remensis*, folio 37v; redrawn by Maëlle Sergheraert.

term "tribute" for these payments, they in fact correspond more closely to the definition of "taxes" in economic history: payments were regularly scheduled, recorded in official documents, and collected by teams of professional tax collectors (Smith 2014, 2015). "Tribute," from a comparative perspective, refers to single lump-sum payments made by subject polities to their conquerors or overlords. Aztec tax obligations were assessed by province and recorded in pictorial documents (Berdan 1996; Berdan and Anawalt 1992).

The *Matrícula de Tributos* is a surviving pre-Spanish tax record, and its early colonial copy, the *Codex Mendoza*, is the clearest and most heavily studied tax roll (Berdan and Anawalt 1992). The taxes for each tributary province in the *Codex Mendoza* (Figure 32.1) are listed in these documents. The page for the province of Huaxtepec (Figure 32.3) shows how the taxes were recorded. The towns that made up this province are listed down the left side and bottom of the page, starting with the provincial capital, Huaxtepec. At the top are images of 10 cotton textiles, each with a feather that indicates 400 items. These were paid twice a year, for an annual total of 8,000 textiles. Next are 46 warrior costumes with shields, two large bins of grain, and finally 2,000 gourd bowls and 8,000 pieces of bark paper (for painting codices). When the annual income in the *Codex Mendoza* is added up, the totals are impressive.

FIGURE 32.3 Imperial taxes paid by the Huaxtepec Province. *Codex Mendoza*, folio 24v–25r; from Berdan and Anawalt (1992:4:54–55). Reproduced with permission.

Taxes were collected by a battery of officials called *calpixque*. There were several types of *calpixque*, from low-level officials who ran errands and organized labor on public works for local *tlatoque* to the heads of the imperial tax system. Tax records such as the *Matrícula de Tributos* were probably kept by the highest level of *calpixque* in Tenochtitlan. Each province had two high-level *calpixque*, one in Tenochtitlan and one in the provincial capital, who was aided by a series of lower-ranking tax collectors.

Imperial Control in the Central Highlands Provinces

Although scholars have traditionally emphasized the indirect nature of control of the provinces (Berdan et al. 1996; Hassig 1988), recent research suggests that the empire wielded more power in provincial areas than was previously thought (Sergheraert 2009). The nature and the degree of imperial control varied considerably among the cities of the empire, ranging from indirect to strong, direct control. Historical sources detail four types of cases:

Indirect Control

In certain conquest cities, local kings (*tlatoque*) were left in power. Nevertheless, they had to show their obedience to the Triple Alliance through several actions such as paying tribute; providing food, men, and supplies when the Aztec army passed by; or attending imperial ceremonies in Tenochtitlan. In order to strengthen their ties and avoid rebellions, the Aztecs developed relationships with provincial elites by several means: gift exchanges, marriage alliances, and education of the sons in Tenochtitlan (Berdan et al. 1996:122, 211).

Light Control

In other cities where local kings remained in power, imperial forces sent Aztec tax collectors (*calpixque*). Besides assuming their specific task—insuring imperial tribute payment and transport—they also embodied imperial authorities, which explains why rebellions against the Triple Alliance could begin with the murder of Aztec tax collectors, as in Cuetlaxtlan located in the state of Veracruz (Durán 2002:ch. XXIV; Tezozomoc 1992:ch. 34). In such cases, imperial armies were first launched to quell the rebellion; imperial tribute was raised as a punishment, and Aztec authorities imposed a stronger control afterward.

Military Control

Aztec military leaders and soldiers were sometimes sent to strategic areas to defend imperial borders or maintain internal control in resistant areas. In these cases, they settled garrisons next to or directly in the cities. For example, a garrison was settled in Oztuma, in the modern state of Guerrero on the Tarascan border. Two military governors were appointed to rule over the soldiers and the settlers sent from the Basin of Mexico (*Codex Mendoza* folio18r in Berdan and Anawalt 1992; Durán 2002:chs. XLIV, XLV; Silverstein 2001; Tezozomoc 1992:chs. 72–74).

Direct Control

Finally, in some cities, Aztec governors were sent to replace local kings and rule. In the Central Highlands, Aztec governors were sent to the cities of Chiapan, Tlalatlauhco, Malinalco, Zumpahuacan, Xochitepec, Huaxtepec, Tepoztlan, Cuauhnahuac, Xilotepec, Tollocan, and Calixtlahuaca (Berdan et al. 1996:Appendix 4; Sergheraert 2009). Frequently, Aztec governors were not sent alone to a city; they could be accompanied by a *calpixque*, military chiefs, soldiers, or even Aztec settlers. Sending an Aztec governor to a city was the strongest degree of imperial control.

Imperial authorities strategically adapted the degree of control they exercised in each city. In nearby regions and in places where they previously entertained good elite relationships, an indirect or light control was sufficient to ensure the respect of their authority. But in more distant areas, in cases where local kings showed resistance to imperial authority or in the regional city-states capitals, they generally opted for strong, direct control. The degree of imperial control in a city could also evolve over time. In the following, we discuss three concrete examples: Cuauhnahuac, Malinalco, and Calixtlahuaca.

Cuauhnahuac

Cuauhnahuac, the capital city of the eponym tributary province in Morelos, had good relations with Tenochtitlan going back to A.D. 1395 (before Aztec expansion). Over time, at least four marriage alliances were sealed between Cuauhnahuac's princesses and Tenochtitlan's *tlatoque*, with their heirs becoming the next Aztec rulers (Smith 1986:76–82). Besides these strong family ties, Cuauhnahuac and Tenochtitlan engaged with each other in other ways. Cuauhnahuac's nobles were always invited and attended imperial ceremonies in Tenochtitlan, they participated in the election of the new rulers in Tenochtitlan, and they received gifts from imperial authorities. Good relationships also spread over trade via common expeditions of long-distance merchants from Cuauhnahuac and Tenochtitlan (Berdan et al. 1996:271).

At first these ties were probably considered strong enough by the Aztecs that representatives were not sent to Cuauhnahuac, despite the city's importance in the region. However, in 1487 they appointed an Aztec governor in Cuauhnahuac for a short time (*Codex Aubin*, folio 38v [Dibble 1963]). This reinforcement of their authority occurred precisely when there was no ongoing marriage alliance between the elites of these two cities (the last heir born from such an alliance had died five years earlier) and just after the election of a new *tlahtoani* in Tenochtitlan (a period when imperial authority was always challenged through rebellions). Sending an Aztec governor at such a moment appeared to be a good strategy to remind the people of Cuauhnahuac of imperial authority and strength.

Malinalco

Archaeological remains (carved temple and monumental buildings) of ancient Malinalco still exist in the state of Mexico. An Aztec governor was appointed in Malinalco shortly after its conquest by the armies of Axayacatl (who ruled in Tenochtitlan between 1469 and 1481; Gerhard 2000:170–171). To signify this change of authority, the Aztecs took control over the core area main buildings as evidenced by elements in Aztec architectural style. Recognizing Aztec-style buildings outside of the Basin of Mexico is challenging, because Aztec architecture was deeply influenced by former civilizations, especially Teotihuacan and Tula. Even its double-temple pyramids or pyramids presenting specific types of ramps (*alfardas* with *doble rematos*) were proved not to be typically Aztec. Since 1993, only one thing has been agreed upon in the literature as typically Aztec (López Luján 1998; Umberger and Klein 1993): an architectural ornament called "binder molding." More recently, other diacritic ornaments of the Aztec style have been identified: *clavos* or stone tenons; different kinds of *almenas* (merlons); one of them in the form of a shell transect (*tipo caracol cortado*); and skulls in the round, which were also used as tenons and certain kinds of braziers (Ohnersorgen 2006; Sergheraert 2009).

These specific ornaments, especially stone tenons (*clavos*), have been identified in several buildings at Malinalco, related to Structures II and V. Besides these, several Aztec-style sculptures have been found around these buildings (*temalacatl, cuauhxicalli, tlalpanhuéhuetl*), and mural paintings of Structure III also appear to be Aztec. Moreover, the *Codex Aubin* (Figure 39-e; Dibble 1963) informs us that the construction of the famous main temple, carved in the rock, was directly ordered by the Mexica ruler Ahuizotl (a successor of Axayacatl). All of these elements are evidence of how the Aztec governor appropriated the core of Malinalco.

Calixtlahuaca

Calixtlahuaca—the former city of Matlatzinco—was located in the tributary province of Toluca. Several sources indicate that the Aztecs conquered Calixtlahuaca around 1476 (*Codex Telleriano-Remensis* 1995, folio 37v; Durán 2000:ch. XXXV). The local king was killed, and part of the population migrated west. After some time, an Aztec tax collector (*calpixque*) and even an Aztec governor were sent to the city to replace the local authority. In addition, given the strategic position of the site, an Aztec garrison settled there.

Archaeological data show Aztec presence at the site through imperial sculptures and architectural style, especially around the main buildings of the city. At Calixtlahuaca, it is hard to identify a monumental center: Calixtlahuaca's 16 main monuments are spread out over the Cerro Tenismo hill (foot, slopes, and top).

Four construction stages can be recognized at the site. The first, second, and third construction stages used local materials (directly from the hill), and architectural traits that are found elsewhere in the region. But the fourth construction stage is very distinct and presents several characteristics indicating a clear Aztec architectural style. Local grey andesite stone from previous construction stages is replaced by small *tezontle* (volcanic rock) quarried blocks (from a mine 4 km away) covered with stucco, which are very common in Aztec buildings. Specific construction techniques, widespread in Aztec architecture, can also be observed in the corners and stairs of the structures. In addition, many Aztec architectural ornaments have been found embedded in the walls, along with Aztec-style sculptures.

More precisely, we can still observe *clavos* and skulls in the round in the walls of the cruciform building (Structure 20), and, according to García Payón's (1979:190) excavation notes, 469 clavos were found next to the structure, 56 of them still on the walls and 9 skulls in the round still inserted in the circular east wall. García Payón also reported 123 clavos found in a residential room and several others next to the grand platform of Structure 17, called the *Calmecac* ("school of priests"), which was more likely a palace. Moreover, several fragments of shell transect ornaments and an entire shell were found in the central patio and in the pyramid rubble. There are no drawings or photographs of these elements, but their description and their localization tend to indicate that there were *almenas tipo caracol cortado*, which probably decorated the roof of the temple on top of the large platform. Thus we can assume that certain rooms of the palace and the temple of the principal platform were decorated in the Aztec style.

In Structure 3, better known as the Ehecatl temple, there are disappointingly no remains or mention in García Payón's (1979) notes of architectural ornaments; however, other typical Aztec elements are associated with the building: the Ehecatl sculpture (clearly Aztec) and a sacrificial stone with *chalchihuite* (jade symbol) designs.

It is very probable that Structure 4 was decorated with a Tlaloc (rain deity) brazier (a fragment was found not too far from it during recent excavations led by Michael E. Smith in 2007). Interestingly, this structure was named the "Tlaloc temple" by García Payón (1979:188), due to several objects found during the excavation of the pyramid. García Payón indicates that there was a brazier at the bottom of the pyramid, as well as a Tlaloc head and a jaw fragment of the same deity. Unfortunately, again, we do not have any drawings or photographs of the artifacts. Finally, an Aztec Cihuateotl (goddess representing a woman who died in childbirth) sculpture was found on top of the hill associated with one of the structures. From these data, it clearly appears that Aztec officials used Calixtlahua's main building to symbolize their imperial authority.

Conclusion

Detailed comparisons of written, pictographic, and archaeological data reveal the specific ways in which the Aztecs targeted the most important *altepetl* in each region in order to achieve strong control with minimal effort. In this strategy, Aztec administrative governors were sent to rule directly the principal *altepetl* of the outer provinces (often the provincial capital). They were typically accompanied by military forces, settlers, and/or tax collectors to reinforce Aztec presence. When available, archaeological data attest to a strong presence, with significant concentrations of Aztec artifacts in the capitals of the major *altepetl*: temples and palaces were often redecorated with Aztec architectural ornaments; Aztec sculptures were displayed in visible areas; and imported Aztec censers, temple-models, and other ritual paraphernalia were used in religious ceremonies.

In dealing with important but less powerful *altepetl*, the Aztecs tended to establish good relationships with local authorities (through gift-giving, attendance at imperial celebrations) and to encourage their cooperation with a slighter Aztec presence (perhaps a tax collector or small garrison). Finally, they focused on controlling larger *altepetl* that dominated smaller ones. This mechanism facilitated control of the outer territory at a minimal expense. Imperial impact on the local area was low, but control was maintained.

In 90 years, the Aztecs built an extensive empire through the strategic use of existing political organization in each *altepetl*, both for expanding their territories and maintaining control. The empire grew gradually and was progressively organized in order to ensure various incomes to the imperial capital. Imperial strategy generated the cohesion of the empire, even if the Aztecs did not have total control over their territories. Rebellions happened each time subjected people had the feeling that the empire was weakened (e.g., at times of *tlatoque* succession). But the Aztecs were fast to respond and put down these rebellions. The arrival of the Spaniards in 1519 presented a new occasion for the subjected people to rebel against the Aztecs, allying themselves with the Spanish forces, and, this time, they were stronger. The Aztec Empire fell at the hands of its Spanish and native enemies on August 13, 1521.

References Cited

Berdan, Frances F.
1996 The Tributary Provinces. In *Aztec Imperial Strategies*, by Frances Berdan, Richard E. Blanton, Elizabeth H. Boone, Mary G. Hodge, Michael E. Smith, and Emily Umberger, pp. 115–135. Dumbarton Oaks Research Library and Collection, Washington, DC.

Berdan, Frances F., and Patricia Rieff Anawalt (editors)
1992 *The Codex Mendoza*. University of California Press, Berkeley.

Berdan, Frances F., Richard E. Blanton, Elizabeth H. Boone, Mary G. Hodge, Michael E. Smith, and Emily Umberger
1996 *Aztec Imperial Strategies*. Dumbarton Oaks Research Library and Collections, Washington, DC.

Dibble, Charles E.
1963 *Historia de la nación Mexicana: reproducción a todo color del codice de 1576 (Códice Aubin)*. Ediciones José Porrua Turanzas, Madrid.

Durán, Fray Diego de
2002 *Historia de las Indias de Nueva España e islas de la Tierra Firme*. Cien de México, Mexico City.

García Payón, José
1979 *La zona arqueológica de Tecaxic-Calixtlahuaca y los matlatzincas*. Talleres gráficos de la Nación, Mexico City.

Gerhard, Peter.
2000 *Geografía histórica de la Nueva España, 1519–1821*. Universidad Nacional Autónoma de México, Mexico City.

Hassig, Ross.
1988 *Aztec Warfare: Imperial Expansion and Political Control*. University of Oklahoma Press, Norman.

López Luján, Leonardo.
1998 *Anthropologie religieuse du Templo Mayor*. Ph.D. dissertation, Université Paris X, Paris.

Ohnersorgen, Michael
2006 Aztec Provincial Administration at Cuetlaxtlan, Veracruz. *Journal of Anthropological Archaeology* 25:1–32.

Sergheraert, Maëlle
2009 *L'expansion mexica (1430–1520 après J.-C.): la question du contrôle impérial dans les provinces extérieures de l'Empire.* Ph.D. dissertation, Department of Archaeology, Université Paris 1, Panthéon-Sorbonne.

Silverstein, Jay
2001 Aztec Imperialism at Oztuma, Guerrero: Aztec-Chontal Relations during the Late Postclassic and Early Colonial Periods. *Ancient Mesoamerica* 12:31–48.

Smith, Michael E.
1986 The Role of Social Stratification in the Aztec Empire: A View from the Provinces. *American Anthropologist* 88:70–91.
1996 The Strategic Provinces. In *Aztec Imperial Strategies,* edited by Frances Berdan, Richard E. Blanton, E. H. Boone, Mary G. Hodge, Michael E. Smith, and Emily Umberger, pp. 137–150. Dumbarton Oaks Research Library and Collection, Washington, DC.
2008 *Aztec City-State Capitals.* University Press of Florida, Gainesville.
2014 The Aztecs Paid Taxes Not Tribute. *Mexicon* 36:19–22.
2015 The Aztec Empire. In *Fiscal Regimes and the Political Economy of Premodern States,* edited by Andrew Monson and Walter Scheidel, pp. 71–114. Cambridge University Press, Cambridge, UK.

Tezozomoc, Fernando Alvarado.
1992 *Cronica Mexicayotl.* Universidad Nacional Autónoma de México, Mexico City.

Umberger, Emily, and Cecilia F. Klein
1993 Aztec Art and Imperial Expansion. In *Latin American Horizons,* edited by Don Stephen Rice, pp. 295–336. Dumbarton Oaks Research Library and Collection, Washington, DC.

CHAPTER 33

AZTEC PROVINCES OF THE SOUTHERN HIGHLANDS

GERARDO GUTIÉRREZ

THE objective of this chapter is to address the Aztec provinces of the Southern Highlands of Mexico, in particular a group of six provinces in the middle Balsas River basin of Guerrero: Tlachco, Tepequacuilco, Tlapan, Tlalcoçauhtitlan, Quiauhteopan, Yoaltepec; three provinces in the highlands of western Oaxaca: Coayxtlahuacan, Coyolapan, Tlachquiauco; and one province in the Pacific coastal plain: Cihuatlan. The latter is included given its symbiotic relationship with the Tepequacuilco region (Litvak 1971). Together these 10 provinces were structured by 95 native states depicted as tributaries of the Aztec Empire in the *Codex Mendoza*. These states were composed of smaller segments or parts (*parcialidades*) dotting an intricate political landscape, likely comprising between 1,000 to 2,000 settlements of varying sizes that remain to be studied. For historical information about these provinces see Acuña (1982–1988), Barlow (1949), Berdan et al. (1996), Carrasco (1999), Gerhard (1972), Gonzáles de Cosío (1952), Paso y Troncoso (1905–1906, 1939–1942), and Vera Cruz (1904). These 10 provinces embraced a tract of land of 500 km by 200 km, running from the border of the Tarascan Empire to the valley of Oaxaca.

Here I present the most recent information on the geographic location of the places mentioned in the *Codex Mendoza* (Figure 33.1 and Table 33.1), with an emphasis on archaeological settlements associated with the *Codex Mendoza* and not merely the locations of modern towns, as has been customarily done in previous studies. Traditional interpretations provide the basic framework for our understanding of the provinces. Nonetheless, work in the region over the past 15 years, incorporating new information from remote sensing (aerial photography 1:20,000; Digital Globe satellite imagery), the Integración Territorial of the 2010 Mexican Census, 1:50,000 maps of Mexico, and archaeological surveys of provinces located in modern-day Guerrero and along the border with Oaxaca, together with a reanalysis of ethnohistorical sources, now offers greater insights and corrections to earlier scholarly assessments of the composition and administration of the Aztec provinces of the Southern Highlands.

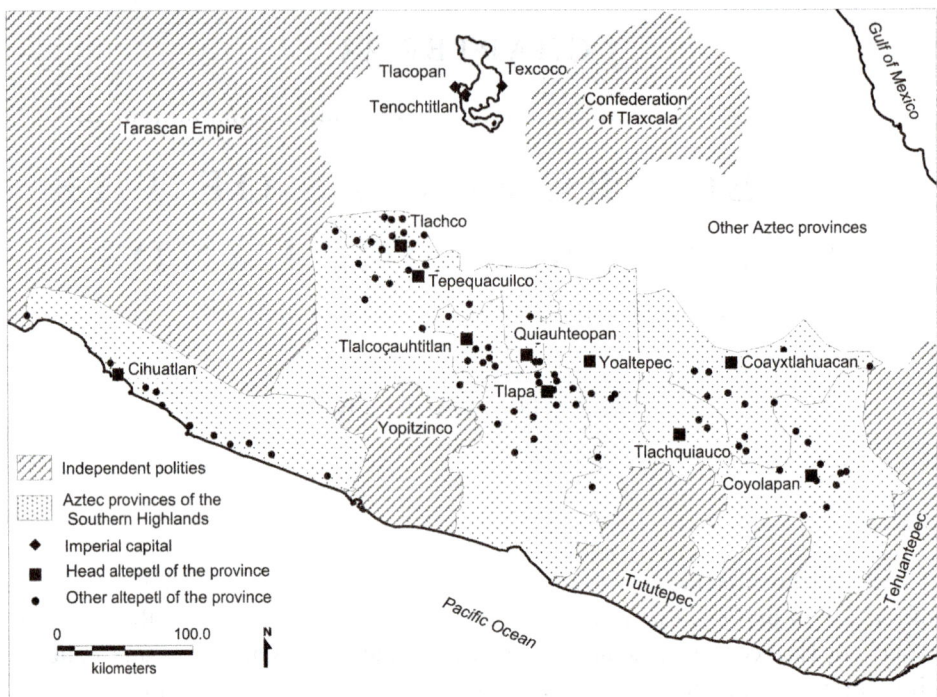

FIGURE 33.1 Map of the southern highlands of Mexico showing areas that were Aztec provinces and other independent political entities. Map by author.

I define the Aztec Empire as the complex political-spatial entity created by the confederation of Tenochtitlan, Texcoco, and Tlacopan (Tacuba) and the relations of subordination, cooperation, or resistance that it developed with the hundreds of other Mesoamerican political systems between A.D. 1428 and 1521 (Berdan et al. 1996; Berdan and Anawalt 1992; Carrasco 1999; Davies 1968, 1987). Specialists in Aztec studies have referred to the basic building blocks that formed the economic, political, and ideological networking of the empire as either (a) city-states, comparing them to the ancient Greek *poleis*; (b) *señoríos*, or "Lordships," from the Latin *dominium* and *dominatus*, which refers to the dignity, authority, and domain exercised by a regional nobility over people and territories through an assumed natural right or by the right of conquest; or (c) *altepetl*, or "water-mountain," metaphorically referring to the native state and its network of rulers and territories (Fargher et al. this volume; Gutiérrez 2003b; Hirth 2003; Hodge 1984; Lockhart 1992). *Altepetl* was translated by sixteenth-century Spaniards as "pueblo" to refer to both the place and the people who shared similar cultural practices and identified themselves, or were identified by others, as belonging to a particular political space (Gutiérrez 2012).

The Spanish conquistador Andrés de Tapia (1971:592) stated during the sixteenth century that the Aztec triumvirate had two types of political relations with other indigenous polities depending on the circumstances in which they had been incorporated into the

Table 33.1 Aztec Provinces of the Southern Highlands

Province	Altepetl	Modern Town	Type of Settlement
Tlachco	Tlachco	Tlaxco El Viejo	Ridgetop
Codex Mendoza: Folio 36r	Acamilyxtlahuaca	Acamixtla	Fortified hilltop
State of Guerrero	Chontalcoatlan	Chontalcuatlan	Terraces on slopes
	Teticpac	Tetipac	Fortified ridgetop
	Nochtepec	Noxtepec	Terraces on slopes
	Teotl iztacan	Teusisapan?	Terraces on a plain
	Tlamacazapa	Tlamacazapa	Terraces on slopes
	Tepexahualco	Tepetlapa?	Terraces on slopes and alluvial plain
	Tzicapuçalco	Ixcapuzalco	Fortified hilltop
	Tetenanco	Tenango del Paraiso	Fortified ridgetop
Tepequacuilco	Tepequacuilco	Tepecoacuilco de Trujano	Terraces on alluvial plain
Codex Mendoza: Folio 37r	Chilapan	Chilapa de Alvarez	Terraces on slopes and plain
State of Guerrero	Ohuapan	San Agustin Oapan	Terraces on alluvial plain
	Huitzoco	Huitzuco de los Figueroa	Terraces in enclosed valley
	Tlachmalacac	Tlaxmalac	Terraces in enclosed valley
	Yoallan	Iguala	Terraces in broad valley
	Cocolan	Cocula	Terraces on alluvial plain
	Atenanco	Atenango del Rio	Terraces on slopes and alluvial plains
	Chilacachapan	Chilacachapa	Terraces on slopes
	Teloloapan	Teloloapan	Fortified ridgetop
	Oztoma	Ixtepec	Fortified ridgetop
	Ychcateopan	Ixcateopan de Cuauhtemoc	Fortified ridgetop
	Alahuiztlan	Alahuixtlan	Terraces on slopes
	Cueçalan	Cuetzalan del Progreso	Terraces on slopes

(continued)

Table 33.1 (Continued)

Province	Altepetl	Modern Town	Type of Settlement
Cihuatlan	Cihuatlan	Zihuatanejo?	Site in protected valley and bay
Codex Mendoza: Folio 38r	Colima	San Jeronimito?	Site on coastal plain
State of Guerrero	Panotla	San Luis, San Pedro?	Site on coastal plain
	Nochcoc	Nuxco	Site on coastal plain
	Yztapan	La Salitrera-Ixtapa	Site on coastal plain
	Petlatlan	Petlatlan	Site on coastal plain
	Xihuacan	Tecpan de Galeana?	Site on coastal plain
	Apancalecan	Papanoa	Site in protected valley and bay
	Coçohuipilecan	San Jeronimo?	Site on coastal plain
	Coyucac	Coyuca de Benitez	Site on coastal plain
	Çacatulan	Zacatula	Site on coastal plain
	Xolochiuhyan	Joluchuca	Site on coastal plain
Tlapan	Tlapan	Tlapa de Comonfort	Terraces on slopes and plain
Codex Mendoza: Folio 39r	Xocotla	San Jose Buena Vista	Fortified hilltop
State of Guerrero	Ychcateopan	Ixcateopan	Terraces on slopes and alluvial plain
	Amaxac	Atlamaxac	Terraces on slopes and alluvial plain
	Ahuacatla	Aguacatitlan & Mexquititlan	Fortified ridgetop
	Acocozpan	Alcozauca	Terraces on slopes
	Yoalan	Igualita	Fortified ridgetop
	Ocoapan	Ocoapa & Ocotequila	Terraces on slopes
	Huitzamola	Huitzapula	Fortified hilltop
	Acuitlapan	Teocuitlapan & Texmelincan	Fortified ridgetop
	Malinaltepec	Malinaltepec	Colonial site only
	Totomixtlahuacan	Totomixtlahuaca	Terraces on alluvial plain

(continued)

Table 33.1 (Continued)

Province	Altepetl	Modern Town	Type of Settlement
	Tetenanco	Hueycatenango	Fortified ridgetop
	Chiepetlan	Chiepetlan	Fortified ridgetop
Tlalcoçauhtitlan	Tlalcoçauhtitlan	Tlacozotitlan	Terraces on slopes and alluvial plain
Codex Mendoza: Folio 40r	Tolimani	Tuliman	Terraces on slopes
State of Guerrero	Quauhtecomaçinco	San Antonio Tecomatlan	Fortified ridgetop
	Ychcatlan	Ixcatla	Terraces on slopes
	Tepoztitlan	Tepoztlan	Terraces on slopes
	Ahuaçiçinco	Ahuacuotzinco	Fortified hilltop
	Mitzinco	Mitlacingo	Terraces on slopes and alluvial plain
	Çacatla	San Juan de las Joyas & Zicapa	Fortified ridgetop
Quiauhteopan	Quiauhteopan	Xochimilco & Rodrigo Gonzaga	Terraces on slopes
Codex Mendoza: Folio 40r	Olinalan	Olinala	Terraces in enclosed valley
State of Guerrero	Quauhtecomatla	Cantecomatlan	Fortified ridgetop
	Qualac	Cualac	Terraces on slopes
	Ychcatla	Ixcamilpa de Guerrero	Terraces on slopes and alluvial plain
	Xala	Xolmolapa?	Terraces on the Slope
Yoaltepec	Yoaltepec	San Juan Igualtepec	Fortified ridgetop
Codex Mendoza: Folio 40r	Ehuacalco	Santa Maria Calihuala	Terraces on slopes and alluvial plain
States of Oaxaca & Guerrero	Tzilaca apan	Villa de Silacayoapan	Terraces on slopes and alluvial plain
	Patlanalan	Santiago Platanala	Fortified hilltop
	Yxicayan	Xicayan de Tovar	Terraces on slopes and alluvial plain

(continued)

Table 33.1 (Continued)

Province	Altepetl	Modern Town	Type of Settlement
	Ychca atoyac	San Isidro, Tlacoachistlahuaca?	Terraces on slopes and alluvial plain
Coayxtlahuacan	Coayxtlahuacan	San Juan Bautisat Coixtlahuaca	Terraces on slopes and alluvial plain
Codex Mendoza: Folio 43r	Texopan	Tejupan	Terraces on slopes and alluvial plain
State of Oaxaca	Temaçolapa	Villa de Tamazulapan	Terraces on slopes and alluvial plain
	Yancuitlan	Santo Domingo Yanhuitlan	Terraces on slopes and alluvial plain
	Tepuzcululan	San Pedro Teposcolula	Fortified hilltop and alluvial plain
	Nochiztlan	Asuncion Nochixtlan	Fortified hilltop and alluvial plain
	Xaltepec	Magdalena Jaltepec	Fortified hilltop
	Tamaçolan	San Juan Tamazola	Fortified hilltop
	Mictlan	Santiago Mitlatongo	Terraces on slopes
	Coaxomulco	Guadalupe Cuazimulco?	Terraces on slopes and alluvial plain
	Cuicatlan	San Juan Bautista Cuicatlan	Fortified hilltop
Coyolapan	Coyolapan	Cuilapan de Guerrero	Terraces on alluvial plain
Codex Mendoza: Folio 44r	Etlan	San Pedro y San Pablo Etla	Terraces on slopes and alluvial plain
State of Oaxaca	Quauxilotitlan	San Pablo Huitzo	Hilltop and terraces on alluvial plain
	Guaxacac	Oaxaca de Juarez	Broad valley and alluvial plain
	Camotlan	Santiago Camotlan	Terraces on slopes
	Teocuitlatlan	Santa Ana Tlapacoyan	Terraces on slopes and alluvial plain
	Quatzontepec	Santiago Tlazoyaltepec, Loma Mecate	Fortified hilltop
	Octlan	Ocotlan de Morelos?	Broad valley and alluvial plain
	Teticpac	San Juan Teitipal	Terraces on slopes and alluvial plain

(continued)

Table 33.1 (Continued)

Province	Altepetl	Modern Town	Type of Settlement
	Tlalcuechauhuayan	San Jeronimo Tlacochahuaya	Terraces on slopes and alluvial plain
	Macuilxochic	San Mateo Macuilxochitl	Terraces on slopes and alluvial plain
Tlachquiauco	Tlachquiauco	Santa Maria Asuncion Tlaxiaco	Hilltop and terraces on alluvial plain
Codex Mendoza: Folio 45r	Achiotlan	San Miguel Achiutla	Fortified hilltop and alluvial plain
State of Oaxaca	Çapotlan	El Zapotito	Terraces on slopes

empire. All of the political systems that had voluntarily integrated themselves and offered no resistance to Aztec expansion were considered "friends" and enjoyed a "peaceful" domination; this meant the Aztecs did not impose heavy tributary obligations. Instead, these friends gave "gifts" to Aztec rulers based on their own will and capacity to do so. In turn, the Aztecs did not interfere in their internal affairs, and they were not monitored by imperial agents. In contrast, all the political systems annexed to the empire by military force endured harsh tributary demands based on a strict cycle of payments and were constantly visited by tribute collectors; their political affairs were tightly monitored by Aztec governors who in some cases resided permanently in the defeated polities, as was the case for the province of Tlapan (also known as Tlapa) (Gutiérrez 2013:150). Tapia's comments coincide with other observations preserved in European and indigenous chronicles and administrative records created by the Spanish bureaucracy to govern the former Aztec provinces (*Codex Chimalpahin* 1997; Cortés 1988; Díaz del Castillo 1986; Durán 1994; León-Portilla 1969; Miranda 1952; Torquemada 1969; Zorita 1999; see also documents in Scholes and Adams 1958). Modern scholars refer to Aztec imperial control as "hegemonic"—based on indirect rule with a strategic use of economic and political resources to co-opt local rulers and elites. This contrasts with what has been defined as a "territorial" imperial administration—direct rule over conquered regions by imperial governors using military force, transplanted colonies, and the imposition of a metropolitan ideology (Doyle 1984; Hassig 1988; Smith and Berdan 1996b). This conceptual dichotomy, while useful for some analyses, should not be applied perfunctorily.

Geographic and Cultural Settings of the Southern Highlands: Huiztlampa

Because the island of Mexico was the symbolic center of the Aztec Empire, and the Viceroyalty of New Spain perpetuated and expanded the same political and economic functions for the metropolitan core, it is not surprising that any description of Mexican geography is based on the relative position of specific regions to the symbolic location culturally assigned to Tenochtitlan/Mexico City (Gutiérrez 2015). Therefore, all lands located to the south of the Basin of Mexico, between the valley of Morelos and the Pacific Ocean, and from western Guerrero to eastern Oaxaca, including southern Puebla, are considered to be part of southern Mexico. The Aztec called these southern regions *Huitztlampa* or "thorny place" (Zantwiijk 1985:154).

Southern Mexico comprises the physiographical region of the Sierra Madre del Sur (Southern Sierra Madre), consisting of the subregions of the Balsas-Mezcala basin, the highlands of Oaxaca, and the southern slope and Pacific Coastal plain (Servicio Geológico México 1998). Elevations throughout the Southern Sierra Madre range between 300 m, along the banks of the Balsas River in the municipality of Totolapan, Guerrero, to 3000 m, in the mountains of Juxtlahuaca, Oaxaca. Climatic gradients due to topographic variability produce three main ecological tiers: the Tierra Caliente (0–1000 m of elevation), Tierra Templada (1000–2000 m) and Tierra Fría (2000 m or more). Rainfall variability due to leeward and windward adiabatic processes impacts vegetation: the Balsas-Mezcala basin is mainly low deciduous forest with a predominance of thorny vegetation adapted to arid conditions. Slopes throughout the Tierra Templada are covered mainly in oak, while pine-oak forest predominates on the summits of the Tierra Fría of Guerrero and Oaxaca. Along the southern slope and the Pacific Coastal plain (the windward Tierra Caliente), the primary vegetation is medium semi-deciduous forest and savanna. This vegetation cover has been deeply affected by human activities since early times, especially by prehispanic agriculture and later by European cattle-ranching practices.

The political systems of the Southern Highlands were multiethnic and multilingual. At least three linguistic families were present from the Michoacan-Guerrero border to the valley of Oaxaca: Tarascan, Uto-Aztec, and Macro-Otomangue. The Purepecha, Nahuatl, Tlapanec, Mixtec, Amuzgo, Popoloca, Ixcateco, Chocho, Triqui, Zapotec, and Cuicatec languages survived into the Colonial period and their villages are relatively well documented (Hendrichs 1939). Although other languages and groups are mentioned in ethnohistoric sources, they have since disappeared without a trace, thus their linguistic and ethnic affiliations are unclear. Among these are Apaneca, Tolimeca, Chumbio, Panteca, Cuitlateca, Chontal, Cuyumateca, Itzuco, Texome, Matlame, Tlacotepehua, Cuyumateca, Tepetixteca, Texcateca, Tlatzihuizteca, and others (Figure 33.2). Notably, all of these linguistic and ethnic labels are reported in the Nahuatl language. The Aztec Empire was the primary disseminator of ethnic labels, and it disregarded how different groups identified themselves (Hill this volume). The practice of using Nahua concepts to refer to the other native groups of central and southern Mexico was continued by the Spanish Colonial system and later by the nation-state of Mexico.

A variety of Nahua groups arrived in central Mexico after the collapse of Teotihuacan and competed for settlements and lands with Macro-Otomaguean linguistic groups (Beekman and Christensen 2003; Gutiérrez 2003a). During the Epiclassic period (A.D. 600–900), eastern Guerrero presented a local material culture similar to that found in western Oaxaca, but by the end of that period, and during the Early Postclassic period,

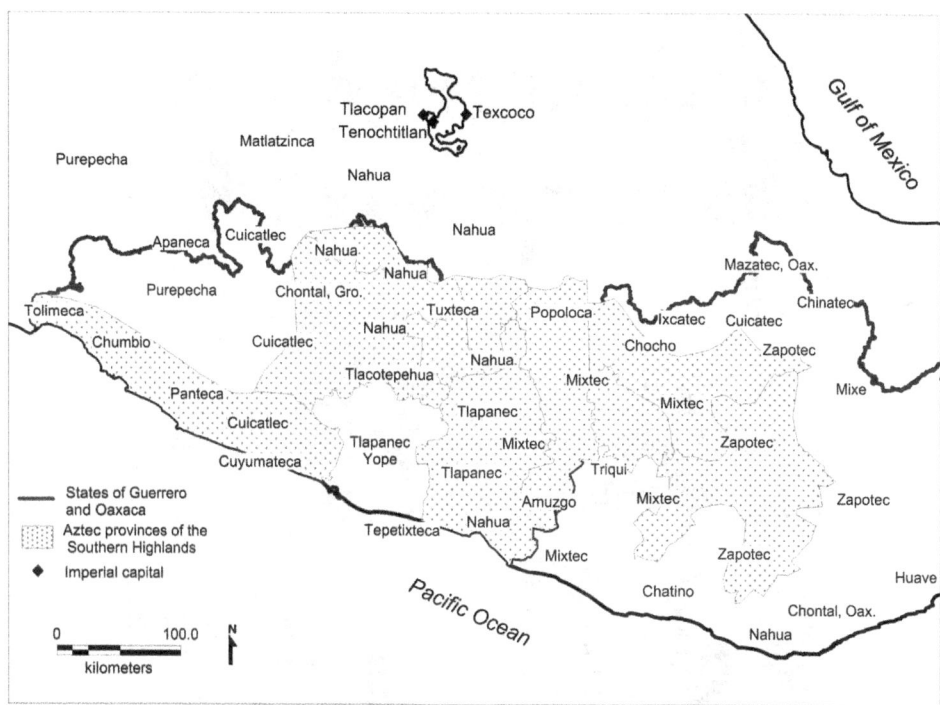

FIGURE 33.2 Language group distributions at the time of the Aztec Empire (after Barlow 1949). The area shown includes the modern states of Guerrero and Oaxaca, Map by author.

material culture typically associated with the Nahua groups of central Mexico became more frequent (Gutiérrez 2008). The Cohuixca-Nahuatl–speaking group dominated all of northern Guerrero from Tlachco to Quiauhtepec prior to the fifteenth-century Aztec expansion. The Cohuixca people claimed political relations with the Nahua polities of Morelos (Smith and Berdan 1996a:270). Intermarriage between these pre-Aztec Nahuas of Guerrero with local non-Nahuatl elites occurred perhaps as early as the twelfth century. One of these interethnic marriages was likely recorded in the political history of Tlapa. The ethnic label of *Cohuixca* comes from *tecuixin*, which was a small alligator with a white neck, and the locative *co* literally means "the people of the place where alligators are abundant." Indicative of the Nahuatization process of the Postclassic period, Lord Couixcal married a local woman named Matlatli Oçomaxoch (10 Monkey-Flower) and became ruler of Tlapa-Tlachinollan around A.D. 1398 (Figure 33.3) (Gutiérrez and Brito 2014). The women of the dynastic lines of Tlapa came from an original marriage alliance between the Tlapanec rulers of Acuitlapan and Tlapa with the Mixtec ruling houses of the valleys of Igualita and Alcozauca, a tradition that may date back to the early thirteenth century. Interethnic elite marriages between Tlapanecs, Mixtecs, and Nahuas of eastern Guerrero lasted until the eighteenth century, when a large percentage of Nahua grooms and brides were still brought to Tlapa from the Morelos Valley, as I have been able to document in ecclesiastical records from the parish of Alcozauca.

FIGURE 33.3 The union of Lord Couixcal and Matlatli Oçomaxoch from the Lienzo de Tlapa. By permission of Biblioteca Nacional de Antropología e Historia, Mexico.

As a general trend, the Nahua presence became more dominant during the fifteenth century in Guerrero and spread into Oaxaca, beginning with the rule of the emperor Moteuczoma Ilhuicamina.

Approaches to the Study of the Aztec Southern Highlands Provinces

In 1949 Robert H. Barlow published the first modern analysis of the structure of the Aztec provinces based on a geographic, political, and economic interpretation of the *Matrícula de Tributos*, complemented by information from the *Codex Mendoza*, the two pictographic tributary tallies of the empire. His provincial map drawn on the "Millionth Map" of the American Geographical Society, sheet "Ciudad de México," continues to be the standard for comparison and a heuristic tool to locate, describe, collect, and correct data on the tributary political systems and their aggregation into "provinces." Barlow decided to group all the Aztec tributary provinces into eight regions according to geographic, ethnic, and historical attributes. Three of the provinces I analyze here were allocated to the Tarascan Frontier: Çihuatlan, Tepecualcuilco. and Tlachco; two provinces were included in the southwest Old Acolhua Domain: Tlacoçauhtitlan and Quiauhtepan; and the remaining five provinces were assigned to the Mixtec-Zapotec Zone: Yoaltepec, Tlapan, Tlachquiauco, Coayxtlahuacan, and Coyolapan. Barlow also located 54 out of 95 place names in these provinces and provided historical data that has been useful for later researchers to locate some of the missing pueblos. Moreover, he identified in other ethnohistorical sources a number of pueblos whose authorities declared themselves to have been subject to the Aztec Empire but were not painted in the *Matrícula de Tributos* or the *Codex Mendoza*. Anderson and Barlow (1943) were also pioneers in performing spatial analyses of imperial activities, with the creation of thematic maps showing the geographic distribution of tributary goods.

The publication of the *Información de 1554* (Rojas 1997; see also Scholes and Adams 1957), the *Matrícula de Tributos* (Reyes 1997), and the breathtaking facsimile edition of the *Codex Mendoza* by Berdan and Anawalt (1992), as well as the availability of new Mexican cartography printed at 1:250,000 scale, promoted a major revision of Barlow's original research. One of these reconsiderations materialized in *Aztec Imperial Strategies* (Berdan et al. 1996), particularly with the redrawing of provincial boundaries to differentiate between two types of provinces: (a) "tributary provinces," those formed by the pueblos painted in the *Codex Mendoza*, and (b) "strategic provinces," those associated somehow with the empire but not painted in the *Codex Mendoza*. Other than the 10 original tributary provinces of the *Codex Mendoza*, Smith and Berdan (1996a:265–349) further proposed the existence of 12 strategic provinces in the Southern Highlands of the Aztec Empire: Temazcaltepec, Chiauhtlan, Zompanco, Tetellan, Tecpantepec, Ayotlan, Ometepec, Miahuatlan, Teozacualco, Teozapotlan, Ixtepexi, and Acatlan, which in turn were formed by 90 pueblos (Figure 33.4). These proposed strategic provinces are subtractive when compared to the original provincial polygons drawn by Barlow (1949), and their proposed tributary provinces are also greatly diminished in geographic extent (see Berdan et al. 1996:324, Figure A4-1). This dichotomy (tributary/strategic provinces) permitted a novel reanalysis of the Aztec Empire in relation to loosely controlled areas, especially those located along frontiers with independent polities such as the Tarascan Empire, Yopitzinco, and Tututepec.

Nonetheless, this dichotomy may potentially mislead researchers into a false sense of surety in defining the provinces. Apart from "spatial propinquity," we do not know what criteria the Aztecs themselves used to group specific pueblos into tributary units as represented in the pages of the tribute tallies. If this uncertainty is patent in the folios of the *Matrícula de Tributos*, the *Codex Mendoza*, and the *Información de 1554*, the same holds true for the hypothesized creation of strategic provinces based on grouping pueblos that are poorly defined entities with problematic geographic locations. The province of Tlapan, in eastern Guerrero, offers a case study demonstrating the difficulties in spatially defining the actual nature of a tributary unit (Gutiérrez 2009). Table 33.1 presents the Tlapan province, composed of 14 *altepetl*, according to the *Codex Mendoza*. Based on this list, Barlow (1949:108) added the pueblos of Ayutla, Cintla,

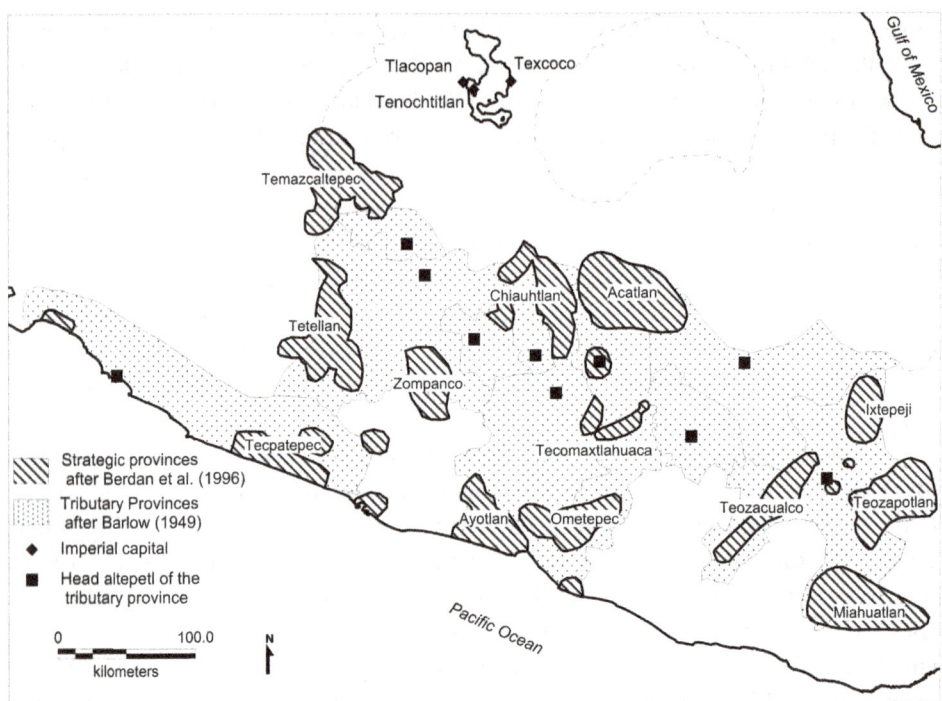

FIGURE 33.4 Regions reported as under the control of the Aztecs but that do not appear in the *Codex Mendoza*. These regions were organized into 12 "strategic" provinces by Berdan et al. (1996). Map by author.

Copalitech, and Tototepec (the latter not to be confused with the independent *señorío* of Tututepec in coastal of Oaxaca), extending the limits of the province from the valley of Huamuxtitlan in the Southern Sierra Madre to the Pacific coast of the State of Guerrero. Similarly, Smith and Berdan (1996a:300–301) added three pueblos to the list from the *Codex Mendoza* (Atliztacan, Petlacallan, and Tlachinollan) and remapped the province by encapsulating the assumed locations of these 17 pueblos. The result that Smith and Berdan present is a Tlapan tributary province 63 percent smaller than the province depicted by Barlow. At the same time, they proposed the existence of two strategic provinces from the pueblos around Ayotlan (Ayutla de los Libres) and Ometepec, Guerrero.

Because the Aztec Empire covered such a vast area, even minor misidentifications of individual tributary components can modify the geographic extent and strategic relevance of particular provinces. In the case of Tlapan, Carrasco (1999:276–278) noted errors of interpretation reproduced from earlier works. For example, Barlow (1949) could not locate at least seven of the provincial pueblos, while Smith and Berdan (1996a) misplaced the pueblos of Acuitlapan, Tetenanco, and Tlanchinollan. More problematic in the analysis of Smith and Berdan (1996a:329, 331, 339) is the formation of the strategic province of Chiautlan by taking large components of the actual province of Yoaltepec, including the head town of that province (Igualtepec) and misplacing Caltitlan. This revision of the province of Yoaltepec renders it difficult to understand its key importance or explain the large, fortified ridgetop used to deter attacks from the independent Tututepec *Señorío*, which extended into the neighboring Mixtec highlands. Reanalysis and remapping of the provinces of Tlapan and Yoaltepec demonstrate that the strategic province of Ometepec, as proposed by Smith and Berdan, did not exist (Figure 33.1).

An ethnohistoric source from 1571 captures the extent of the Tlapan tributary province; it describes a spatial entity composed of 123 pueblos that still survived at that date (Carta de Religiosos 1904:97–106). I have located and registered the archaeological sites for 74 of the places mentioned in the *Carta de Religiosos* and inferred the proximate location of the missing locales based on their relative distances from known places (Gutiérrez 2009, 2010; Gutiérrez and Medina Luna 2008). Using this information, I plotted a more nuanced configuration of the province of Tlapan that deviates considerably from the proposals of Barlow (1949) and Smith and Berdan (1996a). This interpretation offers a yardstick to evaluate the strengths and weaknesses of other researchers' assumptions in their reconstructions of the political and economic geography of the Aztec Empire. As is evident in Figure 33.5, Barlow tended to propose overextended provinces, while Smith and Berdan were conservative in their mapping of the provinces, at the expense of the

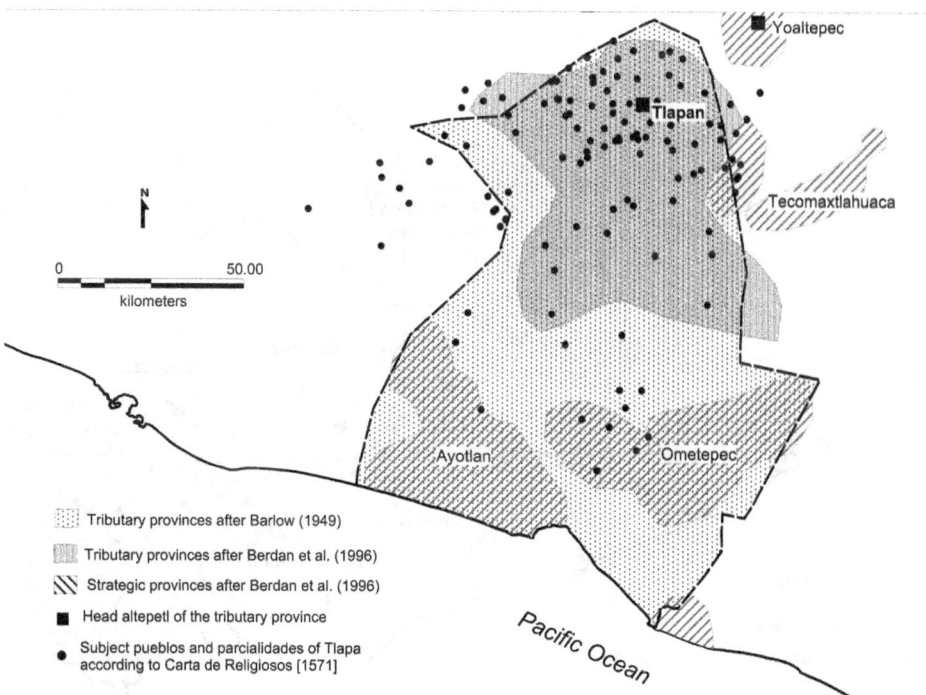

FIGURE 33.5 Map showing the deviations in shape and area of the interpretations of the Tlapan province (Barlow [1949] versus Berdan et al. [1996]). Note that the two graphic interpretations do not match the actual extent of the Tlapan province according to the *Cartas de Religiosos* (1904). Map by author.

complexity of the large networks of rulers and territories comprising each province. Importantly, the pueblos mentioned in the Aztec tallies were composed of a myriad of complementary *parcialidades* and subjects that were not necessarily recorded in other ethnohistorical sources. Moreover, spatial intermingling of the *parcialidades* and subject settlements continues to be a challenge for archaeological modeling (Gutiérrez 2012).

THE CONQUEST OF HUITZTLAMPA AND THE NAHUATIZATION PROCESS

It is no surprise that after the conquest of Cuauhnahuac (Cuernavaca), during the reign of Itzcoatl, the first Aztec incursion into the southern provinces was directed toward Tepecuacuilco, Teloloapan, and Yoallan (Iguala) (Figure 33.6). This region was easily accessed from the Morelos valley and was populated with large settlements located in broad intervalley systems between the Tierra Templada and Tierra Caliente ecological tiers (Hassig 1988:155; Kelly and Palerm 1952:287). Also, the Cohuixca people of the Middle Balsas River associated themselves with the Tlahuicas of Morelos, a relationship perhaps exploited by the Aztecs in their southward expansion (Gutiérrez and Brito 2014:100–101).

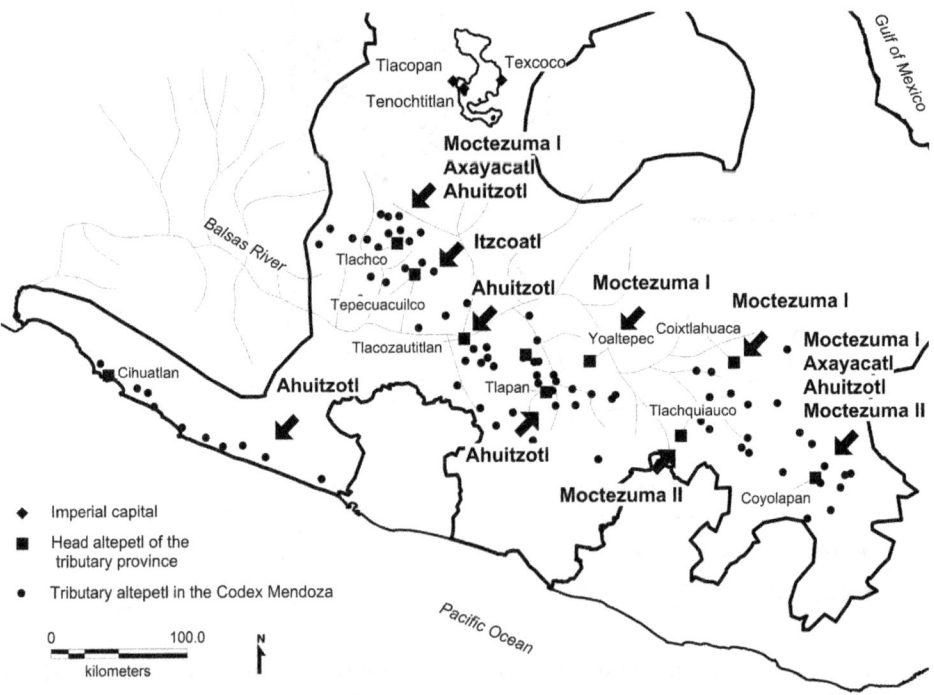

FIGURE 33.6 Map showing the military campaigns of Aztec emperors in the southern highlands. Map by author.

This first encounter with the Cohuixco pueblos seems to have been short-lived, because Moteuczoma Ilhuicamina (aka Moteuczoma I or Huehue Moteuczoma) had to reconquer the area after 1440, annexing the region west of Tlachco, a rugged area with well-fortified hilltops. Moteuczoma Ilhuicamina vigorously pursued a southern expansion, obtaining some control over the dry valleys of Piaxtla-Chinantla and Acatlan in the Mixteca-Poblana, even though this large region was not included in the *Codex Mendoza*. This omission has left a large, poorly understood gap in the geography of the empire. Perhaps the most renowned victory of Moteuczoma Ilhuicamina in the Mixtec region was the conquest and punishment of the ruler of Coayxtlahuacan after that political entity decided to attack an Aztec caravan. The impressive fortified ridgetop of Yoaltepec (Igualtepec, Oaxaca) was also conquered at this moment (Carrasco 1999:280–283, 299). Interestingly, as part of the proposed Nahuatization process, colonial Mixtec caciques of Yoaltepec adopted the last name of Moteuczoma and used it proudly until the eighteenth century, when the famous cacica Doña Lucia Terrazas y Moteuczoma litigated land boundaries along the borders of Oaxaca with modern Guerrero and Puebla (Archivo General de la Nación 1724–1733). Huaxyacac (Oaxaca City) was also conquered by this emperor and became the core of the Aztec domain in the state of Oaxaca. Axayacatl then pushed toward Tehuantepec, but control over that region is not well understood, and Tehuantepec constantly rebelled. Along the Tarascan border, Axayacatl had to shore up Aztec presence in Chontalcoatlan and Acapetlahuaya—an exercise that Ahuitzotl was forced to repeat in Teloloapan, Alahuiztlan, and Oztuma. This last intervention in Guerrero resulted in the establishment of the celebrated Aztec military garrison of Oztuma used to contain the expansion of the Tarascan Empire (Armillas 1944; Carrasco 1999:39). Aztec colonies then complemented and reinforced the continuous flows of Nahua migration into northern Guerrero and the Balsas basin. The Nahuatization of this vast area was consolidated when Ahuitzotl finally conquered Tlacozautitlan and the rich *Señorío* of Tlapa-Tlachinollan, which reached into areas of coastal Guerrero (Gutiérrez 2014). Ahuitzotl also consolidated the passage of Aztec traders through central Oaxaca and Tehuantepec, but again it remains unclear the degree of control the Aztecs had over Oaxaca apart from the primary communication routes that crossed through the state (Pye and Gutiérrez 2007). This uncertain control forced Moteuczoma Xocoyotzin (aka Moteuczoma II) to launch a new campaign in Oaxaca, capturing Tlachquiaco in this later engagement.

Huitztlampa was not easy to conquer and required the combined efforts of all the Aztec emperors to maintain and achieve cumulative gains (Figure 33.6). The region of Yopitzinco and the *Señorío* of Tututepec remained independent and forced the Aztecs to be vigilant throughout these regions. The Tarascan Empire was also pushing eastward toward the middle Balsas, and it is uncertain whether the Aztecs would have been able to stop them at Oztuma. Overall, the 10 provinces of Huitztlampa covered 38 percent of the land surface under some kind of Aztec control and yet provided only 21 percent of the tributary revenue of the empire, based on conversion rates in the *Información de 1554* (see Gutiérrez 2015; Gutiérrez et al. 2009). Perhaps more important, the southern provinces of the Aztec Empire provided much-needed space to accommodate Nahua migrations (Gutiérrez 2014). Given these patterns, I argue that the provinces in Guerrero underwent an intense process of Nahuatization as part of the constant flow of Nahuatl speakers into the Balsas River basin, resulting in interethnic marriages between Nahuas and non-Nahuas. In the case of the provinces located in Oaxaca, Aztec influence seems less intense, and Nahua ways of life were diluted by local political systems and cultures. Although the Aztec presence in the Southern Highlands of Mesoamerica altered previous ways of governance, ethnicity, and material culture, these influences were diverse and dependent on regional dynamics and local historical circumstances.

By analyzing Aztec expansion and administration of the southern provinces, it is possible to review the intellectual traditions that different generations of scholars have used to approach this complex indigenous political system. An early generation of scholars, beginning with Peñafiel (1885) and continued by Clark (1938) and later by Corona Nuñez (1964–1967), was primarily interested in publishing key pictorial sources with the correct deciphering of glyphic place names and their approximate geographic locations. Given the economic nature of the Aztec tributary tallies, it is not surprising that this early approach gave way to the study of the economic and ecological geography of the empire by mapping the provenience and flow of tribute (Anderson and Barlow 1943; Barlow 1949; Kelly and Palerm 1952; Litvak 1971). These early descriptive phases were followed by the development of two analytical approaches based on anthropological theory: one directed to the study of what might be called imperial geopolitics (Berdan and Anawalt 1992; Berdan et al. 1996; Davies 1968; Hassig 1988; Zantwijk 1985) and the other rooted in Marxist political economy (Carrasco and Broda 1978; Carrasco 1999). Regardless of all the advances in our knowledge, we continue to suffer from the same problems faced by earlier scholars: (a) an overreliance on a handful of ethnohistoric sources and (b) the use of simplistic assumptions in nomothetic deductive modeling, based on dichotomous categories (e.g., hegemonic vs. territorial; tributary vs. strategic). On the one hand, the Aztec polity continues to be an empire "on paper": meaning that, without ethnohistory, it would be very difficult to address an Aztec Empire relying solely on archaeological evidence. On the other hand, the models constructed so far, based on assumed but not demonstrated universal imperial "drives," continue to be mechanistic. Perhaps more than trying to reconstruct Aztec imperial strategies, which imply teleological explanations, we need to focus on an empire formed by reactive responses and opportunistic tactics, attempting to fulfill a divine promise in which economic gains came after the fact.

References Cited

Acuña, René
1982–1988 *Relaciones geográficas del siglo XVI*. Universidad Nacional Autónoma de México, Mexico, C.F.

Anderson, Edgar, and Robert H. Barlow
1943 The Maize Tribute of Moctezuma's Empire. *Annals of the Missouri Botanical Garden* 30(4):413–420.

Archivo General de la Nación
1724–1733 *Ramo de tierras del Archivo General de la Nación*, Vol. 494, Expediente 5: *Huajapan po.—Lucia de Terrazas y Moctezuma, cacica del pueblo de San juan Igualtepec, contra Pedro de Alvarado y Juan Maldonado Morales y Alvarado, caciques de los de Tlapa y Santa Mónica Alcozauca, sobre propiedad de los sitios de nombrados Tlalixtaquilla o Atlistaquilla y Huajolotitlan o Huajilotitlan.*

Armillas, Pedro
1944 Oztuma, Gro. *Revista Mexicana de Estudios Antropológicos* 6:165–174.

Barlow, Robert H.
1949 *The Extent of the Empire of the Culhua Mexica.* Ibero-Americans No.28. University of California Press, Berkeley.

Beekman, Christopher S., and Alexander F. Christensen
2003 Controlling for Doubt and Uncertainty through Multiple Lines of Evidence: A New Look at the Mesoamerican Nahua Migrations. *Journal of Archaeological Method and Theory* 10(2):111–164.

Berdan, Frances F., and Patricia Rieff Anawalt (editors)
1992 *The Codex Mendoza.* 4 vols. University of California Press, Berkeley.

Berdan, Francis F., Richard E. Blanton, Elizabeth Hill Boone, Mary G. Hodge, Michael E. Smith, and Emily Umberger (editors)
1996 *Aztec Imperial Strategies.* Dumbarton Oaks Research Library and Collection, Washington, DC.

Carrasco, Pedro
1999 *The Tenochca Empire of Ancient Mexico: The Triple Alliance of Tenochtitlan, Tezcoco, and Tlacoapan.* University of Oklahoma Press, Norman.

Carrasco, Pedro, and Johanna Broda
1978 *Economía política e ideología en el México prehispánico.* Nueva Imagen, Mexico City.

Cartas de Religiosos
1904 Cartas de reliogiosos: Tlapa. In *Relación de los obispos de Tlaxcala, Michoacan, Oaxaca y otros lugares en el siglo XVI: manuscrito de la colección del señor don Joaquin García Icazbalceta*, edited by Luis García Pimental, pp. 97–107. Casa del Editor, Mexico City, Casa de A. Donnamettte, Paris, and Librería de Gabriel Sánchez, Madrid.

Clark, James Cooper
1938 *Codex Mendoza: The Mexican Manuscript Known as the "Collection of Mendoza" and Preserved in the Bodleian Library, Oxford.* 3 vols. Translated and edited by James Cooper Clark. Waterlow & Sons, London.

Codex Chimalpahin
1997 *Codex Chimalpahin: Society and Politics in Mexico Tenochtitlan, Tlatelolco, Texcoco, Culhuacan, and other Nahua Altepetl in Central Mexico. The Nahuatl and Spanish Annals and Accounts Collected and Recorded by Don Domingo de San Antón Muñon Chimalpahin Quautlehuanitzin.* Edited and translated by Arthur J. O. Anderson and Susan Schroeder. University of Oklahoma Press, Norman.

Corona Núñez, José (editor)
1964–1967 *Antigüedades de México, basadas en la recopilación de Lord Kingsborough.* 4 vols. Secretaría de Hacienda y Crédito Público, Mexico, D.F.

Cortés, Hernán
1988 *Cartas de relación.* 15th ed. Editorial Porrúa, Mexico City.

Davies, Nigel

1968 *Los señoríos independientes del imperio azteca*. Instituto Nacional de Antropología e Historia, Mexico City.

1987 *The Aztec Empire: The Toltec Resurgence*. Oklahoma Press University, Norman.

Díaz del Castillo, Bernal

1986 *Historia verdadera de la conquista de la Nueva España*. 14th ed. Editorial Porrúa, Mexico City.

Doyle, Michael W.

1984 *Empires*. Cornell University Press, Ithaca, NY.

Durán, Diego

1994 *The History of the Indies of New Spain*. Translated by Doris Heyden. University of Oklahoma Press, Norman.

Gerhard, Peter

1972 *A Guide to the Historical Geography of New Spain*. Cambridge University Press, New York.

González de Cossío, Francisco

1952 Prólogo. In *El libro de las tasaciones de los pueblos de la Nueva España, siglo XVII*, pp. xi–xiv. Archivo General de la Nación, Mexico City.

Gutiérrez, Gerardo

2003a Interacción de grupos lingüísticos en la costa del golfo de México: el caso de la separación geográfica del idioma huasteco del resto de las lenguas mayas. In *¡Viva la Huaxteca! Jóvenes Miradas Sobre la Región*, edited by Juan Pérez Zevallos and Jesus Ruvalcaba Mercado, pp. 25–39. Centro de Investigaciones y Estudios Superiores en Antropología Social, Mexico City.

2003b Territorial Structure and Urbanism in Mesoamerica: The Huaxtec and Mixtec-Tlapanec-Nahua Cases. In *El urbanismo en Mesoamérica = Urbanism in Mesoamerica*, edited by William Sanders, Guadalupe Mastache, and Robert Cobean, pp. 85–118. Pennsylvania State University, University Park, and Instituto Nacional de Antropología e Historia, Mexico City.

2008 Four Thousand Years of Communication Systems in the Mixteca-Tlapaneca-Nahua Region: From the Archaic Cauadzidziqui Rock Shelter Murals to the Colonial Codices of Azoyú. In *The Native Community and its Records: Historical Transformations in Southern Mexico*, edited by Maarten Jansen and L. Van Broekhoven, pp. 71–107. Royal Netherlands Academy of Arts and Sciences, Amsterdam.

2009 La organización político-territorial del reino de Tlapa, siglos XV y XVI: elementos empíricos para entender la estructura espacial de la unidad política mesoamericana. In *Bases de la complejidad social en Oaxaca: memoria de la Cuarta Mesa Redonda of Monte Albán*, edited by Nelly M. Robles García, pp. 309–378. Instituto Nacional de Antropología e Historia, Mexico City.

2010 *Arqueología de la antigua provincia de Tlapa: desde el periodo Arcaico hasta la Independencia de México*. Municipio de Tlapa de Comonfort y Letra Antigua, Mexico.

2012 Hacia un modelo general para entender la estructura político-territorial del estado nativo mesoamericano (*altepetl*). In *El poder compartido: ensayos sobre la arqueología de organizaciones políticas segmentarias y oligárquicas*, edited by Annick Daneels and Gerardo Gutérrez, pp. 27–67. Centro de Investigaciones y Estudios Superiores en Antropología Social and El Colegio de Michoacán, Mexico.

2013 Negotiating Aztec Tributary Demands in the Tribute Record of Tlapa. In *Merchants, Markets, and Exchange in the Pre-Columbian World*, edited by Kenneth G. Hirth and

Joanne Pillsbury, pp. 141–167. Dumbarton Oaks Research and Library Collection, Washington, DC.

2014 Aztec Battlefields of Eastern Guerrero: An Archaeological and Ethnohistorical Analysis of the Operational Theater of the Tlapanec War. In *Conflict, Conquest, and the Performance of War in Pre-Columbian America*, edited by Andrew Scherer and John Verano, pp. 143–170. Dumbarton Oaks Research Library and Collection, Washington, DC.

2015 Mexico-Tenochtitlan: Origin and Transformations of the Last Mesoamerican Imperial City. In *The Cambridge World History*, Vol. 3: *Early Cities in Comparative Perspective, ca. 4000 BCE–CE 1200*, edited by Norman Yoffee. Cambridge University Press, Cambridge, UK.

Gutiérrez, Gerardo, and Baltazar Brito

2014 *El códice Azoyú 2: política y territorio en el señorio de Tlapa-Tlachinollan. Siglo XIV–XVI*. Secretaría de Educación Pública, Consejo Nacional para la Cultura y las Artes, Instituto Nacional de Antropología e Historia y Raíz de Sol S.A. de C.V., Mexico.

Gutiérrez, Gerardo, Viola Koenig, and Baltazar Brito

2009 *Códice Humboldt Fragmento 1 (Ms. Amer. 2) y Códice Azoyú 2 Reverso: nómina de tributos de Tlapa y su provincia al Imperio Mexicano*. Bilingual edition. Centro de Investigaciones y Estudios Superiores en Antropología Social and Stiftung Preussischer Kulturbesitz, Mexico.

Gutiérrez, Gerardo, and Constantino Medina Luna

2008 *Toponimia náhuatl en los códices de Azoyú 1 y 2: un estudio crítico*. Centro de Investigaciones y Estudios Superiores en Antropología Social, Mexico City.

Hassig, Ross

1988 *Aztec Warfare: Imperial Expansion and Political Control*. University of Oklahoma Press, Norman.

Hendrichs, Pedro R.

1939 Un estudio preliminar sobre la lengua cuitlateca de San Miguel Totolapan, Guerrero. *El Mexico Antiguo* 4:329–362.

Hirth, Kenneth G.

2003 The Altepetl and Urban Structure in Prehispanic Mesoamerica. In *El urbanismo en Mesoamérica Urbanism in Mesoamerica*, edited by William Sanders, Guadalupe Mastache, and Robert Cobean, pp. 57–84. Pennsylvania State University, University Park, and Instituto Nacional de Antropología e Historia, Mexico City.

Hodge, Mary G.

1984 *Aztec City-States*. Memoirs of the Museum of Anthropology No. 18. University of Michigan, Ann Arbor.

Kelly, Isabel T., and Angel Palerm

1952 *The Tajin Totonac*. Institute of Social Anthropology No. 13. Smithsonian Institution, Washington, DC.

León-Portilla, Miguel

1969 Ramírez de Fuenleal y las antigüedades mexicanas. *Estudios de Cultura Náhuatl* 8:32–33.

Litvak King, Jaime

1971 *Cihuatlán y Tepecoacuilco: provincias tributarias de México en el siglo XVI*. Universidad Nacional Autónoma de México, Mexico City.

Lockhart, James

1992 *The Nahuas after the Conquest: A Social and Cultural History of the Indians of Central Mexico, Sixteenth through Eighteenth Centuries*. Stanford University Press, Stanford, CA.

Miranda, José
1952 *El tributo indígena en Nueva España durante el siglo XVI.* Colegio de México, Mexico City.

Paso y Troncoso, Francisco del (editor)
1905–1906 *Papeles de Nueva España. Segunda serie: geografía y estadística.* 9 vols. Tipografico "Sucesores de Rivandeneyra," Madrid.
1939–1942 *Epistolario de Nueva España (1505–1818).* 16 vols. Antigua librería Robredo, de J. Porrúa e hijos, Mexico City.

Penafiel, Antonio
1885 *Nombres geográficos de México.* Secretaría de Fomento, Mexico City.

Pye, Mary E., and Gerardo Gutiérrez
2007 The Pacific Coast Trade Route of Mesoamerica: Iconographic Connections between Guatemala and Guerrero. In *Archaeology, Art, and Ethnogenesis in Mesoamerican Prehistory: Papers in Honor of Gareth W. Lowe,* edited by Lynneth S. Lowe and Mary E. Pye, pp. 229–236. Papers of the New World Archaeological Foundation No.68. Brigham Young University, Provo, UT.

Reyes García, Luís
1997 *Matrícula de tributos o códice Moctezuma.* Akademische Druck-und Verlagsanstalt, Graz, and Fondo de Cultura Económica, Mexico City.

Rojas, José Luís de
1997 *Información de 1554 sobre los tributos que los indios pagaban a Moctezuma.* Secretaria de Educación Pública and Centro de Investigaciones e Estudios Superiores en Antropología Social, Mexico City.

Scholes, France V., and Eleanor B. Adams
1958 *Sobre el modo de tributar los indios de Nueva España a su Majestad 1561–1564.* Documentos para la historia del México colonial V. José Porrúa e Hijos, Mexico City.

Servicio Geológico México
1998 *Carta Geológico-Minera Chilpancingo E14-8, Guerrero, Oaxaca, Puebla, escala 1:250,000.* Servicio Geológico México, INEGI, Pachuca.

Smith, Michael E., and Frances F. Berdan
1996a Appendix 4: Province Descriptions. In *Aztec Imperial Strategies,* edited by Frances Berdan, Richard E. Blanton, Elizabeth H. Boone, Mary G. Hodge, Michael E. Smith, and Emily Umberger, pp. 265–349. Dumbarton Oaks Research Library and Collection, Washington, DC.
1996b Introduction. In *Aztec Imperial Strategies,* edited by Frances Berdan, Richard E. Blanton, Elizabeth H. Boone, Mary G. Hodge, Michael E. Smith, and Emily Umberger, pp. 1–9. Dumbarton Oaks Library and Research Collection, Washington, DC.

Tapia, Andres de
1971 Relación sobre la conquista de México. In *Colección de documentos para la historia de México,* Vol. 2, edited by Joaquín García Icazbalceta, pp. 554–594. Editorial Porrúa, Mexico City.

Torquemada, Juan de
1969 *Monarquía Indiana.* 3 vols. Editorial Porrúa, Mexico City.

Vera Cruz, Bartolomé de la
1904 Relación verdadera hecha por el P. Prior Fray Bartolomé de la Vera Cruz, fraile agustino, del pueblo y provincia de Chiautlan, que está en la corona real, de los tributantes vecinos y casados, casas y estancias que tiene toda la provincia hecha a 18 de Hebrero de 1571 años. In *Relación de los obispos de Tlaxcala, Michoacan, Oaxaca y otros lugares en el siglo*

XVI: manuscrito de la colección del señor don Joaquin García Icazbalceta, edited by Luis García Pimental, pp.109–115. Casa del Editor, Mexico City, Casa de A. Donnamettte, Paris, and Librería de Gabriel Sánchez, Madrid.

Zantwijk, Rudolph van

1985 *The Aztec Arrangement: The Social History of Pre-Spanish Mexico*. University of Oklahoma Press, Norman.

Zorita, Alonso de

1999 *Relación de la Nueva España*. 2 vols. Conaculta, Mexico City.

CHAPTER 34

AZTEC PROVINCES OF THE GULF LOWLANDS

MARCIE L. VENTER

Introduction

THE Gulf Lowland provinces of the Aztec Empire were among the richest provinces incorporated into the empire (Berdan 1996). The provinces from this region supplied large quantities of several varieties of cotton, tropical bird feathers, cacao, rubber, liquidambar, and other exotic resources (Berdan and Anawalt 1992; Stark 1978). The diversity of items produced in the Gulf Lowlands was due to the ecological variability that characterized the zone, which consists of areas falling between the 1000 m interval and the Gulf of Mexico (Stark and Arnold 1997:4). Many of the Gulf Lowland provinces were also located along strategic political boundaries and both coastal and overland trade routes.

The Gulf Lowlands consist of a mosaic of alluvial savannah-like plains, meandering rivers and streams, mangroves, coastal estuaries, low hills, salt domes, deeply incised river valleys, and cloud forests (Stark 1978; Stark and Arnold 1997). The region's geology is characterized by sedimentary bottomlands and volcanic massifs. The Sierra de Chiconquiaco and the Sierra de los Tuxtlas (Tuxtla Mountains) punctuate the plains of the central and southern Gulf Lowlands (Figure 34.1).

This long stretch of *tierra caliente* from southern Tamaulipas in the north to western Tabasco in the south was also characterized by variable patterns of precipitation that made some areas especially productive (Stark and Arnold 1997:6). Because of this high productivity and the wealth derived from it, Smith and Berdan (2003:28) considered the Gulf Lowlands to be one of several Affluent Production Zones in the Postclassic Mesoamerican World System.

The Gulf Lowlands were also ethnolinguistically heterogeneous (Daneels 2012). Several Postclassic settlements that eventually became provincial towns had hosted waves of Nahuat-speaking groups that settled alongside native Chinantec, Huastec,

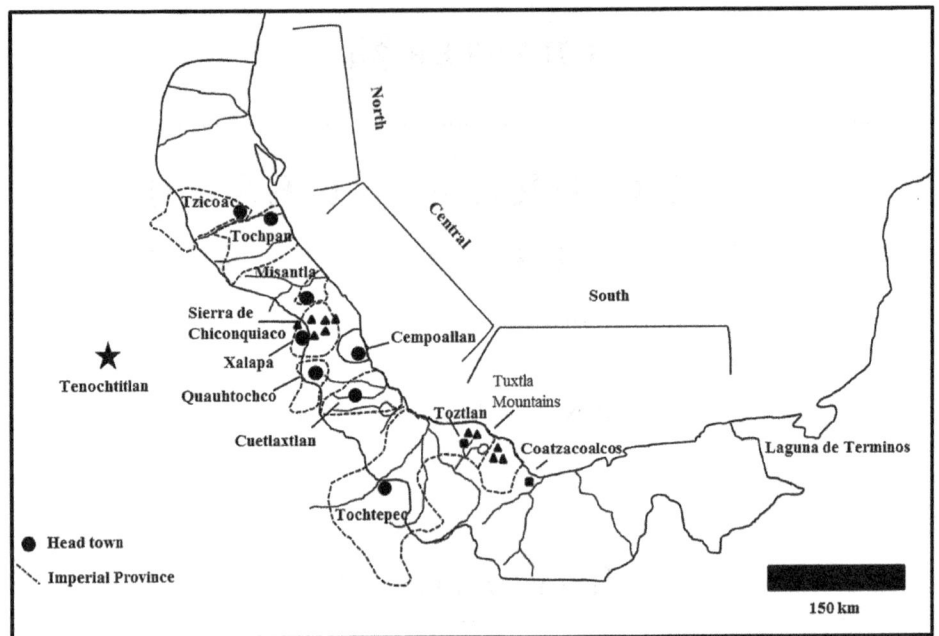

FIGURE 34.1 Mesoamerican Gulf Lowlands showing conventional divisions and imperial provinces (Divisions within the Gulf Lowlands following Daneels 2012:25.1 and Stark and Arnold 1997:Figure 1; provincial boundaries adapted from Berdan et al. 1996:Figure II-1; Carrasco 1999; Gerhard 1993; Killion and Urcid 2001:Figure 9). Prepared by Marcie Venter.

Totonac, and Sierra Popoluca (Mixe-Zoque) populations (Berdan 2003; Kauffman 2001; Umberger 1996). Some of these immigrants probably arrived during the Early to Middle Postclassic periods, and others may have arrived during the Late Postclassic (Daneels 2012; Kauffman 2001; Ohnersorgen 2006; Stark 2008; Umberger 1996; Venter 2010, 2012). Late Postclassic arrivals from the highlands would have probably been Nahuatl-speakers. Chontal Maya groups also occupied portions of the southern Gulf Lowlands, although most were probably outside of the Aztec imperial boundary (Daneels 2012).

Aztec Interests and Strategies in the Gulf Lowlands

Aztec interest in the Gulf Lowlands was apparent in the empire's economic, elite, and frontier strategies (Berdan and Smith 1996). Interactions between the central Mexican highlands and the Gulf Lowlands followed a long tradition of mutual material exchange and symbolic communication that began by at least the Early Formative period (e.g., Covarrubias 1943; Grove 1968; Piña Chan 1951; Pires-Ferreira 1976; Rattray 1987; Pool

1992; Santley 1994). The importance of the Gulf Lowlands to the empire was ongoing, requiring consistent attention due to the need for new sources of tribute (taxes), access to markets, the volatile character of imperial–provincial relationships, and ongoing conflicts between neighboring communities within and straddling the imperial boundary (Berdan 2003:76; Berdan et al. 1996:285–286; Carrasco 1999; Esquivias 2003; Killion and Urcid 2001; Venter 2008).

Different parts of the Gulf Lowlands were incorporated following varying schedules; some were added decades prior to Spanish arrival, whereas others were new in 1519. New areas were often attached to previously established provinces (Berdan 2003). For example, at the time of the Spanish invasion, Motecuhzoma II had recently appended new city-states to existing provinces (Berdan et al. 1996:284–292; see also Duran 1994).

The incorporation of new areas was one of the outcomes of new reigns. The status of towns conquered by preceding *tlahtoanis* also had to be constantly renegotiated or reinforced at the transition from one ruler to another (Berdan and Anawalt 1997:19, 23). The case of the rebellious Cuetlaxtlan province is one of the best examples of ongoing imperial intervention in the Gulf Lowlands. Relationships between the Basin of Mexico and other Gulf Lowland communities (e.g., Toztlan) may have been less volatile (Carrasco 1999; Venter 2008, 2012).

For a detailed examination of conquest dates, see the syntheses by Berdan and Anawalt (1992, 1997) and Carrasco (1999). Although documentation regarding conquest and subsequent administration is poor for some parts of the Gulf Lowlands (e.g., Tochtepec [Berdan and Anawalt 1997:113]), most city-states were incorporated or reconquered during the reigns of Motecuhzoma Ilhuicamina (ca. 1440/1441–1469), Axayacatl (ca. 1469–1481), Ahuitzotl (ca. 1487/1486–1502), and Motecuhzoma Xocoyotzin (ca. 1502/1503–1520).

IMPERIAL STRATEGIES IN THE GULF LOWLANDS

The nodes in the imperial framework were the many constituent city-state capitals and their territories. In addition to variability in their duration of incorporation, city-states differed greatly in size and type of imperial interaction (Berdan and Smith 1996; Garraty and Stark 2002; Ohnersorgen and Venter 2012; Skoglund et al. 2006; Venter 2012). As a result, the pattern of conquest was discontinuous (Berdan and Smith 1996; Smith and Sergheraert 2012), to a degree that was perhaps even greater than that drawn in depictions of the empire's provincial boundaries (Berdan and Smith 1996:112; Venter 2012) (Figure 34.1).

Berdan and Smith (1996) categorized regional groupings of city-states whose primary imperial relationships were economic as "tributary provinces" (Berdan and Smith 1996:110, 2003; Berdan 1996). One of the primary functions of tributary provinces was the payment of taxes through a dendritic network of regional collection points. City-states that were located along important political frontiers and whose inclusion in the empire did not appear directly related to the flow of goods were referred to as "strategic provinces" (Berdan and Smith 1996:110, 2003; Smith 1996). Both economic/tributary and frontier/strategic interests were represented in the Gulf Lowland provinces.

The Gulf Lowland provinces accounted for much of the eastern Aztec boundary (Berdan 2003:74; Ohnersorgen and Venter 2012). In addition to the resources these provinces contained, or the boundary functions they served, city-states within the eastern Aztec boundary were also important for their convenient locations along natural transportation arteries that connected the highlands to the lowlands. Other incorporated towns were situated at important starting points for expeditions to international trade centers (Carrasco 1999; Gasco and Berdan 2003; Ohnersorgen and Venter 2012).

Aztec provinces in the Gulf Lowlands included (from north to south) Tochpan (tributary), eastern portions of Tzicoac (tributary), Misantla (strategic), eastern portions of Xalapa (strategic), Cempoalla (strategic), Quauhtochco (tributary), Cuetlaxtlan (tributary), and Tochtepec (tributary) (Berdan 1996; Smith 1996). Despite the principal functions of these provinces, some were sites for both economic and frontier strategies (e.g., Tochtepec, characterized as a tributary province, also had a garrison; Berdan and Anawalt 1997; Carrasco 1999).

The empire employed a third strategy that pertained to the Gulf Lowland provinces: the elite strategy (Berdan and Smith 1996). This strategy relied on the integration of local city-state leaders, their constituents, and networks through alliance-building and mutual gift-giving to provide the cohesive glue for economic exchanges, boundary maintenance, and cross-boundary diplomacy (Berdan and Smith 1996; Smith et al. 2003). The success of these strategies, and the degree of provincial investment, was affected, in part, by the reception of the empire's overtures by these local elites (Garraty and Ohnersorgen 2009; Ohnersorgen 2006; Ohnersorgen and Venter 2012; Skoglund et al. 2006; Venter 2012). When resistance was mounted, exceptions were made to the empire's generally indirect style of administration (Garraty and Ohnersorgen 2009; Ohnersorgen 2006).

Archaeological Evidence for Aztec Imperialism in the Gulf Lowlands

Because of the diversity of strategies employed during incorporation and subsequent administration, as well as the duration of inclusion, the amount of preexisting infrastructure, and level of cooperation within the Gulf Lowland provinces, the material correlates recovered archaeologically are similarly varied (Ohnersorgen and Venter 2012). Umberger (1996) and others (e.g., Curet et al. 1994; Daneels 2012; Ohnersorgen 2006;

Umberger and Klein 1993; Venter 2012) have presented case studies illustrating some of the diversity in Gulf Lowland material patterns associated with Aztec imperialism.

Direct Administration

Aztec-style material components documented in the Gulf Lowlands include sculpture (Umberger 1996), architecture and architectural components (Ohnersorgen 2006; Umberger 1996), pottery (Aztec III Black-on-Orange-style vessels and Texcoco molded-style censers; Garraty and Ohnersorgen 2009; Garraty and Stark 2002; Ohnersorgen 2006; Ohnersorgen and Venter 2012; Skoglund et al. 2006; Umberger 1996), figurines (Garraty and Ohnersorgen 2009; Miller et al. 2005; Ohnersorgen 2006), and temple models (Ohnersorgen 2006). Settlements containing all or most of these elements have been interpreted as having frequent interactions with the empire, a result of a more direct style of imperial control (Ohnersorgen 2006). The amount of imperial investment may also reflect the prior existence of state infrastructure (Ohnersorgen and Venter 2012). Ohnersorgen (2006) has also inferred the presence of particular Aztec-style figurines to reflect the presence of Aztec colonists (Ohnersorgen 2006; see also Miller et al. 2005), perhaps as a consequence of famine in the highlands.

Indirect Administration

Two regions of the Gulf Lowlands located at some distance from their respective provincial capitals (i.e., Cuetlaxtlan and Tochtepec) have recently been the subject of systematic analysis: the Mixtequilla region of the Rio Blanco and the western Tuxtla Mountains. Sites in the Mixtequilla (Garraty and Stark 2002; Skoglund et al. 2006) and in the Tuxtlas (Arnold and Venter 2004; Venter 2008; Venter and Stoner 2009) that contained primarily ceramic components of this material style set have been interpreted as reflecting less direct imperial control (Ohnersorgen and Venter 2012).

Assessments of the directness of imperial control in these two regions have been balanced with considerations of local group agency (Ohnersorgen and Venter 2012; Skoglund et al. 2006; Stark 1990; Venter 2008, 2012). The selective incorporation of Aztec-style materials may have been related to the frequency and intensity of interactions within this distant corner of the empire, but it also may represent more specific attempts by local elites or others to bolster or somehow negotiate their own status, to minimize the effects of imperial overtures, and to reject a large-scale Aztec presence (i.e., public architectural footprints) (Ohnersorgen and Venter 2012).

Skoglund et al. (2006:557; see also Ohnersorgen and Venter 2012) have suggested that the emulation of imperial-style Aztec III Black-on-Orange pottery and Texcoco Molded ritual censers (Minc this volume) may represent efforts by local elites and others to engage in the widespread Mesoamerican practice of foreigner "quotation," whereby groups in the Mixtequilla region attempted to acquire prestige by association. Perhaps because of local demand, imperial-style ceramics were market-distributed throughout that region and adopted by elites and nonelites alike.

Aztec III Black-on-Orange pottery was absent or extremely rare in the Tuxtla Mountains (Arnold and Venter 2004; Arnold 2007; Venter 2008). Instead, Texcoco Molded censers were the primary imperial symbol adopted at several settlements. Molds recovered from the region suggest that some of these censers were made locally (Venter 2008, 2012). The comparatively low frequency and diversity of Aztec materials in the Tuxtlas may in part relate to Toztlan's status as an important but less powerful city-state (e.g., Smith and Sergheraert 2012:457). Toztlan, like Tlacotalpan (also Tochtepec), had a resident imperial tax collector (Berdan and Anawalt 1992; Paso y Troncoso 1905).

In contrast to economic emulation of Aztec symbols in the Mixtequilla, Venter (2008, 2012) has suggested that elites in the Tuxtlas willingly incorporated Texcoco Molded censers into community rituals as a way of mediating the potentially conflicting interests of local constituents and imperial overlords. This strategy was at least partly successful because Texcoco Molded censers were incorporated into the household rituals of several residents at Totogal who had otherwise local material inventories (i.e., it is unlikely that they represent highland immigrants).

One of the perks of imperial affiliation throughout the Gulf Lowlands may have been preferential access to green Pachuca obsidian (Daneels 2012; Pastrana and Dominguez 2009), but this was not directly related to a community's location within the empire, as high proportions are reported for areas beyond imperial boundaries, even hostile ones (Braswell 2003). For example, despite frequent battles between Toztlan and independent Coatzacoalcos (Medel y Alvarado 1993; Paso y Troncoso 1905), investigations at Villa del Espiritu Santo (in Coatzacoalcos) contained high percentages of green obsidian (Arellanos and Beauregard 2001).

Finally, imperial expansion into some parts of the Gulf Lowlands may have affected transformations of local settlement hierarchies, even when other permanent footprints, such as imperial style temples or garrisons, were absent (Garraty and Ohnersorgen 2009; Venter 2008, 2012, 2013; Venter and Stoner 2009). Settlement pattern evidence from the Mixtequilla suggests that incorporation of that area into the Cuetlaxtlan province resulted in a power shift from the Middle Postclassic center of El Sauce, which was abandoned, to the new Late Postclassic center Callejón del Horno (Garraty and Ohnersorgen 2009; Garraty and Stark 2002).

Late Postclassic settlement shifts also characterized the southwest Tuxtlas. Maxayapan, the Early to Middle Postclassic center, was abandoned. It was supplanted by Totogal (a large village during the Early to Middle Postclassic) during the Late Postclassic (Venter 2013; see also Stoner 2011; Venter and Stoner 2009). This change of capitals also resulted in a shift of the polity boundary (Venter 2013; Venter and Stoner 2009).

Callejón del Horno's founding represented a complete break from the material traditions and political leadership at El Sauce (Garraty and Ohnersorgen 2009). Much greater continuity is reflected in the Tuxtlas case. The direct role of the empire or its provincial administrators in the establishment of a center at Callejón del Horno and the promotion of Totogal is not clear. However, both centers were probably local focal points for the operation of the imperial provincial networks even though many of the more monumental symbols listed previously were absent (Garraty and Ohnersorgen 2009; Garraty and Stark 2002; Skoglund et al. 2006; Stark 2008; Venter 2008, 2012, 2013; Venter and Stoner 2009). Callejón del Horno was located in prime agricultural land where cotton harvests were particularly successful. Totogal was located at a nexus of overland routes connecting the interior Tuxtlas and its resources (e.g., liquidambar, feathers, cotton) with the bottomlands of the Eastern Lower Papaloapan Basin. The Tuxtlas were also importantly located at the west end of isthmian trade corridors (Carrasco 1999:343).

Role of the Gulf Lowland Provinces in the Transformation from Aztec to Spanish Administration

Of the Gulf Lowland Aztec provinces, those in the central region have received the most attention by Contact era historians: Cempoallan, with its "Fat Cacique," and Cuetlaxtlan. The ruler of Cotaxtla, the capital of Cuetlaxtlan, figures prominently in initial encounters. This ruler, Teniltzin, was a *calpixqui* installed to oversee the collection of taxes from Cuetlaxtlan by Motecuhzoma II after its capital rebelled. Paintings that Teniltzin had commissioned provided the Aztec hierarchy in Tenochtitlan some of their first credible information about the newcomers (Díaz 1956:72).

The colonial trajectory of Cuetlaxtlan was intertwined with that of Toztlan to the south. In 1529, Charles V granted both areas, along with Rinconada, to Cortés as parts of his marquisate (Bermudez Gorrochotegui 1978; Gerhard 1993). One of the earliest sugar mills on the mainland of New Spain was established within the boundaries of the colonial Tuxtla province and governed from the headtown, which had been recently relocated from Totogal to Santiago Tuxtla (Gerhard 1993; Rivas Castellanos 1999; Venter 2008, 2012). The Tuxtla mill was located at the juncture of the western Tuxtlas piedmont and the coastal plain (Barrett 1970; Bermudez Gorrochotegui 1978; García Martínez 1969; Venter 2008). That initial Tuxtla mill lasted only a short time and had far less output than Cortés' Cuernavaca endeavor. But the impact of sugar was tremendous on the Gulf Lowlands, both economically and socially, and it remains a cornerstone of the regional economy.

Cempoallan also had a crucial role in initial Spanish encounters. The region was home to initial Spanish settlements north of modern Veracruz City. When Cortés landed on the shores of the province, it was governed by the Fat Cacique and Aztec *calpixque*. According to Bernal Diaz del Castillo (1956:88), the Fat Cacique notoriously "complained bitterly of the great Moteuczoma and his governors saying that he had recently been brought under his yoke; that all his golden jewels had been carried off, and he and his people were so grievously oppressed, that they dared do nothing without the

Moteuczoma's orders." Later that week, Díaz (1956:89) describes the arrival of Aztec tax collectors and their attendants who "came to the place where we were assembled... and approaching us with the utmost assurance and arrogance without speaking to Cortés, or to any of us, they passed us by." The aloofness of the *calpixque*, their subsequent response to the Spaniards' presence (the sacrifice of 20 victims), and Spanish revulsion (expressed through the imprisonment of the tax collectors) and diplomatic maneuvering set the tone for subsequent Aztec–Spanish encounters, targeted alliances meant to undermine Motecuhzoma's authority, and political conquest (Evans 2008:524).

Additional details of Spanish exploits along the Gulf Coast are presented in Bernal Díaz del Castillo's (1956) firsthand account of the Grijalva and Cortés expeditions and in Cortés' (1986) own recounting of the conquest (Evans 2008:521). Of particular interest in these documents are the encounters between Spaniards and groups in the Coatzacoalcos region of the southern Gulf Lowlands, not only because this region was just outside of the eastern boundary of Tochtepec and had engaged in consistent conflicts with Toztlan (Berdan and Anawalt 1997; Carrasco 1999; Paso y Troncoso 1905; Venter 2008) but because Malinalli, the key interpreter between Spaniards and Aztecs and consort of Cortés, was from this area (Duran 1994; Evans 2008:522).

Conclusions

The relationships between the Aztec Empire and the Gulf Lowland provinces were complicated and variable, not only spatially but temporally. Documentary resources such as the *Codex Mendoza* (Berdan and Anawalt 1992), the *Memorial de Tlacopan* (Carrasco 1999), and eye-witness accounts of first encounters have informed the better part of our understanding of imperial–provincial interactions, as well as Contact era events.

Until recently, archaeological research pertaining to this period and region was conducted from a culture historical perspective or within the context of cultural resource management salvage projects. The findings of past projects (e.g., Brüggemann 1991; Medellin Zenil 1960) were important for the construction of regional chronologies and were sometimes used to define internal cultural boundaries (Huaxteca, Totonacapan, Olman) (Daneels 2012). Researchers did not devote much time to directly addressing imperial–local relationships, even if data could be later mined in order to attempt reconstructions (e.g., Smith 1990).

That situation is changing. The past 15 years have seen at least six projects in the south-central and southern Gulf Lowlands alone that have specifically attempted to characterize Aztec provincial relationships and the place of the Gulf Lowlands in the Late Postclassic Mesoamerican world (Arnold and Venter 2004; Daneels 1997, 2012; Esquivias 2003; Garraty and Stark 2002; Killion and Urcid 2001; Lira Lopez 2010; Ohnersorgen 2006; Ohnersorgen and Venter 2012; Maldonado Vite 2010; Skoglund et al. 2006; Venter 2008, 2012). As these and other new studies are published, they will permit the Gulf Lowland provinces of the Aztec Empire to demand inclusion in archaeological syntheses of Late Postclassic Mesoamerica. The importance of the region, often considered peripheral to broader Mesoamerican trends, will no doubt become more evident in advance of 2019, the quincentennial of Cortés' landing at La Villa Rica de la Vera Cruz and the transformative events that precipitated from those encounters.

REFERENCES CITED

Arellanos Melgarejo, Ramón, and Lourdes Beauregard García
2001 *La Villa del Espiritu Santo y sus materiales culturales*. Ediciones Cultura de Veracruz, Mexico City.

Arnold, Philip J.
2007 *Isla Agaltepec: ocupaciones posclásicas en la Sierra de los Tuxtlas, Veracruz, México, reporte final del Proyecto Arqueológico de la Isla Agaltepec*. Instituto Nacional de Antropología e Historia, Mexico City.

Arnold, Philip J.III, and Marcie L. Venter
2004 Postclassic Occupation at Isla Agaltepec, Southern Veracruz, Mexico. *Mexicon* 16(6):121–126.

Barrett, W.
1970 *The Sugar Hacienda of the Marqueses del Valle*. University of Minnesota Press, Minneapolis.

Berdan, Frances F.
1996 The Tributary Provinces. In *Aztec Imperial Strategies*, edited by Frances F. Berdan, Richard E. Blanton, Elizabeth H. Boone, Mary G. Hodge, Michael E. Smith, and Emily Umberger, pp. 115–135. Dumbarton Oaks Research and Library Collection, Washington, DC.
2003 Borders in the Eastern Aztec Empire. In *The Postclassic Mesoamerican World*, edited by Michael E. Smith and Frances F. Berdan, pp. 73–77. University of Utah Press, Salt Lake City.

Berdan, Frances F., and Patricia Anawalt
1992 *The Codex Mendoza*. University of California Press, Berkeley.
1997 *The Essential Codex Mendoza*. University of California Press, Berkeley.

Berdan, Frances F., Richard E. Blanton, Elizabeth H. Boone, Mary G. Hodge, Michael E. Smith, and Emily Umberger
1996 *Aztec Imperial Strategies*. Dumbarton Oaks Library and Research Collection, Washington, DC.

Berdan, Frances F., and Michael E. Smith
1996 Imperial Strategies and Core-Periphery Relations. In *Aztec Imperial Strategies*, by Frances F. Berdan, Richard E. Blanton, Elizabeth H. Boone, Mary G. Hodge, Michael E. Smith, and Emily Umberger, pp. 209–217. Dumbarton Oaks Research and Library Collection, Washington, DC.

Bermudez Gorrochotegui, Gilberto
1978 *La Caña de azúcar y Santiago Tuxtla*. Instituto Nacional de Antropología e Historia, Mexico City.

Braswell, Geoffrey
2003 Obsidian Exchange Spheres of Postclassic Mesoamerica. In *The Postclassic Mesoamerican World*, edited by M. Smith and F. Berdan, pp. 131–158. University of Utah Press, Salt Lake City.

Brüggemann, J. K. (editor)

1991 *Zempoala: el estudio de una ciudad prehispánica.* Instituto Nacional de Antropología e Historia, Mexico City.

Carrasco, Pedro

1999 *The Tenochca Empire of Ancient Mexico: The Triple Alliance of Tenochtitlan, Tetzcoco, and Tlacopan.* University of Oklahoma Press, Norman.

Covarrubias, Miguel

1943 Tlatilco, Archaic Mexican Art and Culture. *Dyn, the Review of Modern Art* 4–5:40–46.

Curet, L. Antonio, Barbara L. Stark, and Sergio Vásquez Zarate

1994 Postclassic Changes in Veracruz, Mexico. *Ancient Mesoamerica* 5:13–32.

Daneels, Annick

1995 La Cerámica postclásica de la Cuenca Baja del Jamapa-Cotaxtla. *Arqueología* 13–14:85–88.

1997 Settlement History in the Lower Cotaxtla Basin. In *Olmec to Aztec: Settlement Patterns in the Ancient Gulf Lowlands,* edited by Barbara L. Stark and Philip J. Arnold III, pp. 206–252. University of Arizona Press, Tucson.

2012 Development Cycles in the Gulf Lowlands. In *The Oxford Handbook of Mesoamerican Archaeology, Part III: Villages, Cities, States, and Empires,* edited by Deborah L. Nichols and Christopher A. Pool, pp. 348–371. Oxford University Press, New York.

Díaz del Castillo, Bernal

1956 *The Discovery and Conquest of Mexico, 1517–1521.* Farrar, Straus, and Cudahy, New York.

Durán, Fray Diego

1994 *The History of the Indies of New Spain.* Translated by Doris Heyden. University of Oklahoma Press, Norman.

Esquivias, Chantal

2003 *On the Edge of Empire? Settlement Changes in Chacalapan, Southern Veracruz, Mexico during the Classic and Postclassic Periods.* BAR International Series 1053, Archaeopress, Oxford.

Evans, Susan T.

2008 *Ancient Mexico and Central America: Archaeology and Culture History.* Thames & Hudson, London.

García Martínez, Bernardo

1969 *El Marquesado del Valle.* Nueva Serie 5. Centro de Estudios Históricos, El Colegio de México, Mexico.

Garraty, Christopher P., and Michael A. Ohnersorgen

2009 Negotiating the Imperial Landscape: The Geopolitics of Aztec Control in the Outer Provinces of the Empire. In *The Archaeology of Meaningful Places,* edited by B. J. Bowser and M. Nieves Zedeño, pp. 107–131. University of Utah Press, Salt Lake City.

Garraty, Christopher P., and Barbara L. Stark

2002 Imperial and Social Relations in Postclassic South-Central Veracruz, Mexico. *Latin American Antiquity* 13(1):3–33.

Gasco, Janine, and Frances F. Berdan

2003 International Trade Centers. In *The Postclassic Mesoamerican World,* edited by Michael E. Smith and Frances F. Berdan, pp. 109–116. University of Utah Press, Salt Lake City.

Gerhard, Peter

1993 *A Guide to the Historical Geography of New Spain.* Rev. ed. University of Oklahoma Press, Norman.

Grove, David C.

1968 The Pre-Classic Olmec in Central Mexico. In *Dumbarton Oaks Conference on the Olmec,* edited by Elizabeth P. Benson, pp. 179–185. Dumbarton Oaks Research Library and Collection, Washington, DC.

Kaufman, Terrence
2001 The History of the Nawa Language Group from the Earliest Times to the Sixteenth Century: Some Preliminary Results. Electronic document: http://www.albany.edu/pdlma/Nawa.pdf, accessed November 26, 2010.

Killion, Thomas W., and Javier Urcid
2001 The Olmec Legacy: Cultural Continuity in Mexico's Southern Gulf Coast Lowlands. *Journal of Field Archaeology* 28(1):3-25.

Lira López, Yamile
2010 *Tradición y cambio en las culturas del Valle de Maltrata, IIA/UNAM—IAUV*. S y G Editores, Mexico City.

Maldonado Vite, María Eugenia
2010 Una visión de la provincia tributaria de Cuetlachtlan. *Perspectivas* 4:131–152.

Medel y Alvarado, León
1993 *Historia de San Andrés Tuxtla (1525–1975)*. Fascimile of 1963 edition. Estado de Veracruz, Veracruz, Mexico.

Medellin Zenil, Alfonso
1960 *Cerámicas de Totonacapan: exploraciones en el Centro de Veracruz*. Instituto de Antropología, Universidad Veracruzana, Xalapa, Mexico.

Miller, R. Neil, Christopher Garraty, Barbara L. Stark
2005 Local and Imperial Identities at the Edge of the Empire. Paper presented at the 70th Annual Meeting of the Society for American Archaeology, Salt Lake City.

Ohnersorgen, Michael A.
2006 Aztec Provincial Organization at Cuetlaxtlan, Veracruz. *Journal of Anthropological Archaeology* 25:1–32.

Ohnersorgen, Michael A., and Marcie L. Venter
2012 Aztec Boundary Interactions. In *The Oxford Handbook of Mesoamerican Archaeology, Part III: Villages, Cities, States, and Empires*, edited by Deborah L. Nichols and Christopher A. Pool, pp. 525–535. Oxford University Press, New York.

Paso y Troncoso, Francisco
1905 *Papeles de Nueva España*. 2nd series, 7 vols. Suc. de Rivadeneyra, Madrid.

Pastrana, Alejandro, and Silvia Dominguez
2009 Cambios en la estrategia de la explotación de la obsidiana de Pachuca: Teotihuacan, Tula y la Triple Alianza. *Ancient Mesoamerica* 20(1):129–148.

Piña Chan, Román
1951 El Horizonte preclásico del Valle de México. Master's Thesis No. 35. Escuela Nacional de Antropología e Historia, Mexico City.

Pires-Ferreira, Jane W.
1976 Obsidian Exchange in Formative Mesoamerica. In *The Early Mesoamerican Village*, edited by Kent V. Flannery, pp. 292–306. Academic Press, New York.

Pool, Christopher A.
1992 Strangers in a Strange Land: Ethnicity and Ideology at an Enclave Community in Middle Classic Mesoamerica. In *Ancient Images, Ancient Thought: The Archaeology of Ideology*, edited by A. S. Goldsmith, pp. 43–55. Archaeological Association, University of Calgary, Calgary.

Rattray, Evelyn
1987 Evidencias de un grupo étnico de la costa del Golfo en Teotihuacan. Paper presented at the first meeting of Balance y Perspectivas de la Antropología en Veracruz, Jalapa, Veracruz, Mexico.

Rivas Castellanos, Eneas
1999 *La Real Villa de Tuxtla*. 2nd ed., rev. and exp. Rescate Municipal de IVEC, Veracruz, Mexico.

Santley, Robert S.
1994 The Economy of Ancient Matacapan. *Ancient Mesoamerica* 5:243–266.

Skoglund, Thanet, Barbara L. Stark, Hector Neff, and Michael D. Glascock
2006 Compositional and Stylistic Analysis of Aztec-Era Ceramics: Provincial Strategies at the Edge of Empire, South-Central Veracruz, Mexico. *Latin American Antiquity* 17(4):542–559.

Smith, Michael E.
1990 Long-Distance Trade under the Aztec Empire: The Archaeological Evidence. *Ancient Mesoamerica* 1:153–169.

1996 The Strategic Provinces. In *Aztec Imperial Strategies*, by Frances F. Berdan, Richard E. Blanton, Elizabeth H. Boone, Mary G. Hodge, Michael E. Smith, and Emily Umberger, pp. 137–150. Dumbarton Oaks Research and Library Collection, Washington, DC.

Smith, Michael E., and Francies F. Berdan
2003 Spatial Structure of the Mesoamerican World System. In *The Postclassic Mesoamerican World*, edited by M. Smith and F. Berdan, pp. 20–31. University of Utah Press, Salt Lake City.

Smith, Michael E., and Maelle Sergheraert
2012 The Aztec Empire. In *The Oxford Handbook of Mesoamerican Archaeology, Part III: Villages, Cities, States, and Empires*, edited by Deborah L. Nichols and Christopher A. Pool, pp. 449–458. Oxford University Press, New York.

Smith, Michael E., Jennifer Wharton, and Jan M. Olson
2003 Aztec Feasts, Rituals, and Markets: Political Uses of Ceramic Vessels in a Commercial Economy. In *The Archaeology and Politics of Food and Feasting in Early States and Empires*, edited by Tamara Bray, pp. 235–270. Klewer Academic/Plenum, New York.

Stark, Barbara L.
1978 Ethnohistoric Model for Native Economy and Settlement Patterns in Southern Veracruz, Mexico. In *Prehistoric Coastal Adaptations: The Economy and Ecology of Maritime Middle America*, edited by Barbara L. Stark and Barbara Voorhies, pp. 211–238. Academic Press, New York.

1990 The Gulf Coast and the Central Highlands of Mexico: Alternative Models for Interaction. *Research in Economic Anthropology* 12:243–285.

2008 Archaeology and Ethnicity in Postclassic Mesoamerica. In *Ethnic Identity in Nahua Mesoamerica*, edited by Frances Berdan, John Chance, Alan Sandstrom, Barbara Stark, James Taggert, and Emily Umberger, pp. 38–63. University of Utah Press, Salt Lake City.

Stark, Barbara L., and Philip J. Arnold III
1997 Introduction to the Archaeology of the Gulf Lowlands. In *Olmec to Aztec: Settlement Patterns in the Ancient Gulf Lowlands*, edited by Barbara L. Stark and Philip J. Arnold III, pp. 3–32. University of Arizona Press, Tucson.

Stoner, Wesley D.
2011 Disjuncture among Classic Period Cultural Landscapes in the Tuxtla Mountains, Southern Veracruz, Mexico. Unpublished Ph.D. dissertation, Department of Anthropology, University of Kentucky, Lexington.

Umberger, Emily
1996 Aztec Presence and Material Remains in the Outer Provinces. In *Aztec Imperial Strategies*, by Frances F. Berdan, Richard E. Blanton, Elizabeth H. Boone, Mary G. Hodge, Michael E. Smith, and Emily Umberger, pp. 151–179. Dumbarton Oaks Research and Library Collection, Washington, DC.

Umberger, Emily, and Cecilia F. Klein
1993 Aztec Art and Imperial Expansion. In *Latin American Horizons*, edited by Don S. Rice, pp. 295–336. Dumbarton Oaks Research and Library Collection, Washington, DC.

Venter, Marcie L.
2008 Community Strategies in the Aztec Imperial Frontier: Perspectives from Totogal, Veracruz, Mexico. Unpublished Ph.D. dissertation, Department of Anthropology, University of Kentucky, Lexington.
2010 Innovations in Cooking Technology: The Implications of Comal Use in the Late Postclassic Tuxtla Mountains. Paper presented at the 75th annual meeting of the Society for American Archaeology, St. Louis, MO.
2012 A Reassessment of the Extent of the Eastern Aztec Empire in the Mesoamerican Gulf Lowlands. *Ancient Mesoamerica* 23(2):235–250.
2013 After Teotepec: Framing Intraregional Interaction in the Western Tuxtlas. Paper presented at the 78th annual meeting of the Society for American Archaeology, Honolulu, HI.

Venter, Marcie L., and Wesley D. Stoner
2009 Classic to Postclassic Changes in the Tepango Valley of Southern Veracruz, Mexico. Poster Presented at the 74th annual meeting of the Society for American Archaeology, Atlanta, GA.

CHAPTER 35

TUTUTEPEC

A Mixtec Imperial Capital in Southern Oaxaca

MARC N. LEVINE

Aztec imperial expansion in Oaxaca led to the establishment of tributary provinces in the Northern Highlands, the central Valley of Oaxaca, and the eastern Isthmus of Tehuantepec regions (Figure 35.1). Imperial pursuits to the south, however, were thwarted by Tututepec, the largest and most powerful Mixtec polity of the Late Postclassic. This chapter synthesizes data from historic documents, indigenous pictorial manuscripts, and recent archaeological work to present our current understanding of Tututepec—an important player in the geopolitical landscape of Late Postclassic Mesoamerica.

THE MIXTEC CAPITAL OF TUTUTEPEC

Tututepec, also referred to as *Yucu Dzaa* in the Mixtec language, grew from its capital in the lower Río Verde region to conquer a broad area of southern Oaxaca during the Yucudzaa phase (A.D. 1100–1522). The capital of the ancient center lies in the foothills approximately 20 km north of the Pacific Ocean and overlooking the Río Verde floodplain, one of the largest and most fertile tracts of land in Oaxaca (Joyce 1991, 2010) (Figure 35.1). Apart from its proximity to excellent farmland, Tututepec also enjoyed access to a bounty of resources associated with nearby rivers, estuaries, marshes, lagoons, and the sea. These resources included valuable lowland trade goods, such as high-quality sea-salt, dried fish, dyes, cotton, feathers, cacao, and animal pelts (e.g., jaguar). Tututepec's tributary empire—described later—institutionalized resource extraction from vassal communities located along the coast and beyond, funneling goods to the capital and ultimately fueling trade with highland centers. Tututepec appears to have been a regional entrepôt that served as the critical southern node of a lucrative

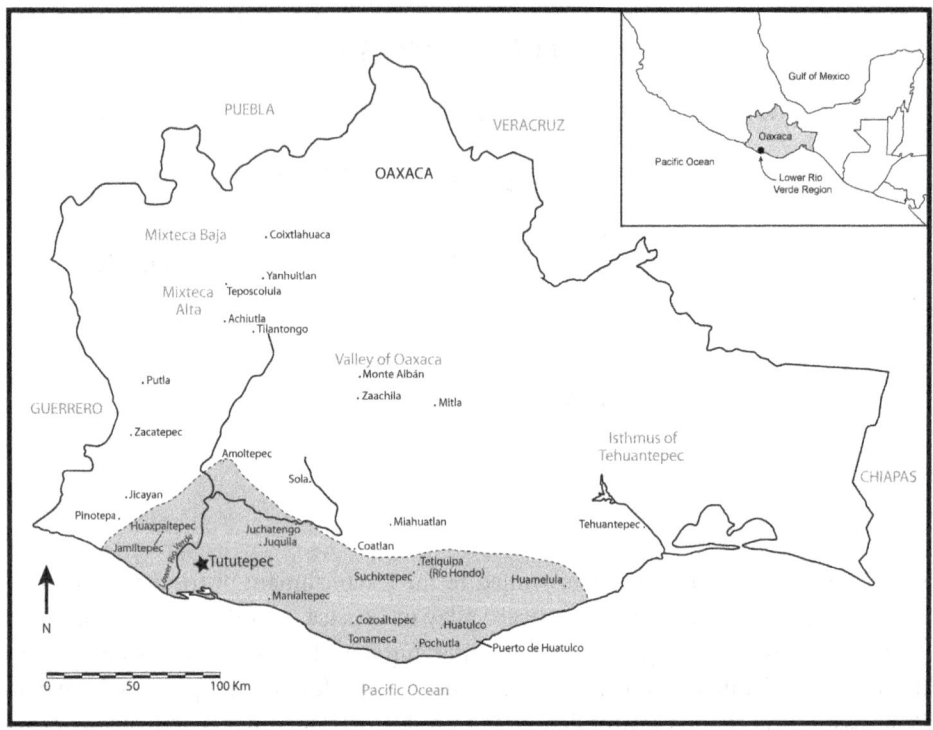

FIGURE 35.1 Map of Oaxaca highlighting estimated boundaries of Tututepec Empire. (Based on Smith 1973:Map 4; Spores 1993:Figure 1). Drawn by author.

highland–lowland Mixtec trade circuit (Joyce et al. 2004; Levine 2007; Monaghan 1994; Pohl 1994; Spores 1993).

Arthur Joyce and colleagues' (2004) ongoing full-coverage archaeological survey of the lower Río Verde region included extensive investigations at Tututepec that expanded on earlier work (see O'Mack 1990; Workinger 2002). The results indicate very limited evidence of settlement at Tututepec immediately prior to the Yucudzaa phase, when it became a regional political and economic capital. At this time, the site's occupational area grew to 2185 hectares, comprising over 94 percent of the region's total. This increase signified both regional population growth and nucleation at Tututepec, yet Joyce and colleagues (2004:288) estimate the capital's population was only 11,000 to 22,000 people. This relatively low estimate reflects the fact that settlement outside of Tututepec's central urban area was variable, including many areas of dispersed settlement. These areas were generally characterized by artifact scatters associated with small-scale architectural features, including residential and agricultural stone terrace walls and ancient footpaths.

Tututepec's ancient civic-ceremonial core has been obscured by historic and modern settlement, although a prehispanic platform mound approximately 2.9 ha in area and 5 m to 10 m high survives beneath a Colonial Period church (Joyce et al. 2004:289). The church has suffered through a series of earthquakes over the centuries, yet its masonry preserves a number of prehispanic "disk-frieze" architectural elements borrowed from earlier structures. The church platform was likely the heart of the ancient center, supporting the royal palace and temple complex. Just south of the site center, a low platform and ballcourt lie on a hill known as *Cerro de los Pajaros*, and a second ballcourt sits at Tututepec's northeastern boundary (Joyce et al 2004:284). Two additional locales with low mounds, the "La Maquina Group" and "South Platform," were found at the southern end of the site and may represent the remains of high-status residences.

Several carved stone monuments and sculptures have been recovered at Tututepec, and most are housed in the Museo Yucusaa, the town's community museum (Levine 2007:430–440). Monuments 3, 4, and 8 are carved with serpent or crocodilian heads at one end, while the opposite ends are uncarved tenons for mounting the stones. Though lacking precise provenience information, the carved stones resemble those from other sites in Oaxaca associated with ballcourts, suggesting a similar context at Tututepec. Most intriguing is Monument 6, reportedly excavated by a priest from on top of the church platform in 1830 (Maler 1883) (Figure 35.2).

This finely carved stela depicts an individual who makes an enigmatic gesture, drawing the hands in front of the torso with the thumbs together and palms against the body. The individual is gendered female, based on the braided hairstyle, triangular blouse (*quechquemitl*), and skirt with step-fret motif. She wears a large beaded necklace,

FIGURE 35.2 Tututepec Monument 6. Photograph by author.

composite ear ornaments, a prominent mirror on her back, and face paint around the eyes in a mask-like pattern associated with central Mexican deities (Joyce et al. 2004). Pohl (1999:184) suggests that Monument 6 may depict *Itzpapalotl*, the "Obsidian Butterfly." This identification is bolstered by reports that Itzpapalotl was worshipped in Pochutla, a tribute-paying vassal of Tututepec (Acuña 1984:193). Pochutla's citizens, who spoke an isolated dialect of Nahuatl known as *Pochutecan* (Kroefges 2004:89), reportedly made a variety of offerings to the goddess, including incense, animals, blood, and human sacrificial victims. Monument 6 bears a general resemblance to Central Mexican styles (cf. Umberger 1996:Figure 7-17), yet remains distinct from Aztec sculptural traditions.

Intriguingly, Tututepec's early history is also chronicled in three of the surviving indigenous painted manuscripts, including the *Codices Bodley, Colombino-Becker,* and *Nuttall* (Joyce et al. 2004). The *Codex Colombino* was preserved by the native rulers of Tututepec and did not come to light until presented as evidence in a court case in 1717 (Smith 1973:13, 15). All three codices chronicle the life of the legendary Lord 8 Deer "Jaguar Claw," who was born in Tilantongo, an important capital located in the Mixteca Alta region (Figure 35.1). Although Lord 8 Deer did not have royal bloodlines, the codices track his emigration from Tilantongo and his ambitious rise as a successful warrior, priest, and statesman (Joyce et al. 2004). Of particular interest here, the codices recount Lord 8 Deer's migration to the southern coast where he performed a sacred ballcourt ritual associated with the founding of Tututepec in A.D. 1083 (Figure 35.3). This date fits well with archaeological evidence for occupation at Tututepec at the onset of the Yucudzaa phase (A.D. 1100–1522; see Joyce et al. 2004).

Linguistic studies of the coastal Mixtec dialect also suggest that it branched off from a highland variety at approximately the same time (Josserand et al. 1984:154). Though it is unclear to what extent Lord 8 Deer's narrative melds historical fact with mythological

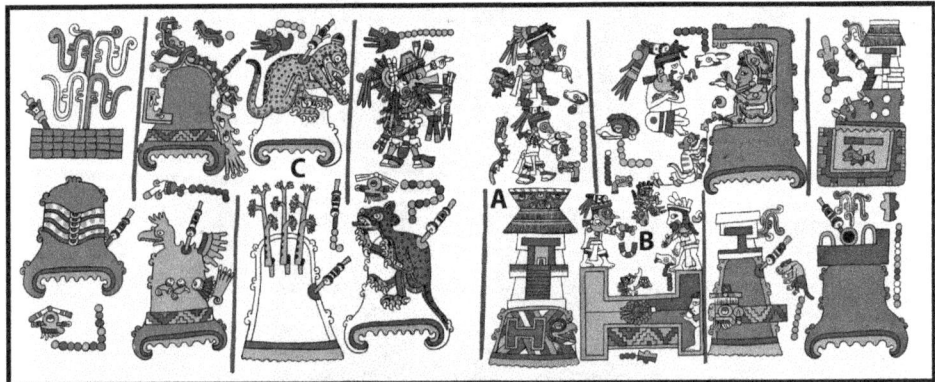

FIGURE 35.3 *Codex Nuttall*, pages 45 (right) and 46 (left); (A) indicates the toponym for Tututepec or Yucu Dzaa ("Hill of the Bird"); while (B) shows Lord 8 Deer conducting a ballcourt ritual with a "Toltec" official; and (C) indicates a series of seven conquered place names pierced by spears. Copyright Dover Publications, used with permission.

embellishment (see Jansen and Perez 2007:33–37; Joyce et al. 2004), the weight of evidence indicates Tututepec was founded by a foreign contingent of highland Mixtecs by the turn of the twelfth century.

SOCIOPOLITICAL ORGANIZATION

The surviving *Relaciones geográficas* from Tututepec's subject communities provide vital information regarding sociopolitical organization of the Mixtec polity, although the *Relación* from Tututepec itself was lost. Based on these documents and other ethnohistoric sources, Spores (1993:167) estimates that at the time of the Spanish Entrada, Tututepec controlled a tributary empire covering 25,000 km^2 of southern Oaxaca—an area larger than the modern state of Belize (Joyce et al. 2004; Smith 1973:84–88; Spores 1993:167) (Figure 35.1).

The *Relaciones* from Tututepec's subjects record a range of tribute in goods and services paid to the capital by Mixtec, Amuzgo, Chatino, Chontal, Nahua, and Zapotec communities. Although Tututepec's core territory was the coastal region, the *Relaciones* explain that they regularly raided and warred with polities throughout Oaxaca, including Miahuatlan, Tehuantepec, Achiutla, Tlaxiaco, Mitla, Zaachila, and others (Acuña 1984; Berdan 1996:Table 5-2; Davies 1968; Spores 1993:172).

Tututepec's expansion into central and northern Oaxaca in the early sixteenth century was impeded by the Aztecs, who competed for control of these same tributary communities. It is unclear whether the two imperial powers ever clashed directly, but there is evidence that they fought proxy wars. Tututepec sent warriors to aid Yanhuitlan, for instance, when they were attacked by the Aztecs.

Tututepec's eastward expansion was limited by its longstanding rivals at Tehuantepec, who fought off the Aztecs for a time before joining forces with the Triple Alliance (Zeitlin 2005). Though Tututepec's expansion to the west is less well understood, its territory went beyond the Río Verde and probably as far as the border with Guerrero. Importantly, Tututepec's territorial boundaries, like those of the Aztecs, were not entirely contiguous and continually ebbed and flowed through time with changing political circumstances.

The codices provide a record of Tututepec's early conquests using recognizable graphic conventions common to this medium. Lord 8 Deer stands dressed as a warrior before a series of toponyms or distinct place-names representing conquered communities (Byland and Pohl 1994:65; Joyce et al. 2004; Smith 1973:36). In the *Codex Nuttall*, more than 20 toponyms are pierced with a spear or dart, which signifies their conquest by Tututepec and conversion into tributaries (Figure 35.3). The codices also indicate that Lord 8 Deer brokered an alliance with a group of foreign Tolteca-Chichimeca, who appear in distinctive top-knot hairstyle and black face paint. Whether these visitors came from Cholula (Caso 1960; Jansen and Perez 2007:222), San Miguel Tulancingo in the Mixteca Alta (Pohl 1994:83), or Tula (Jansen

1989) remains undetermined, but it is clear that their meeting served to legitimize Lord 8 Deer's authority. In fact, the highlanders pierced Lord 8 Deer's nose with a turquoise jewel, awarding him the title of *teuctli* and inducting him into the Tolteca-Chichimeca royal house. In return for this honor, Joyce and colleagues (2004:285) contend that the "Toltecs" were able to secure greater access to valuable lowland goods under Lord 8 Deer's command.

Lord 8 Deer's founding of Tututepec and political consolidation of the coast served as a prelude to his eventual return to Tilantongo, where he ascended to the throne and established a new ruling dynasty in A.D. 1098 (Joyce et al. 2004:286). Lord 8 Deer's codical narrative suggests that, for a time, he may have ruled over a Mixtec empire spanning the highlands and coast, from Tilantongo to Tututepec (Smith 1973:68). If such an empire ever existed, it may not have survived much longer than Lord 8 Deer himself, who was assassinated and sacrificed in A.D. 1115.

Regarding Tututepec's imperial governance, information gleaned from the *Relaciones* suggests a combination of both indirect and direct modalities of control (Spores 1993:170). Following the conquest of a given community, local nobles could retain leadership roles but only at the discretion of the lords of Tututepec. The *Relación* from the subject community of Pochutla, for instance, indicates that Tututepec sent officials to serve as tribute collectors and judges, yet they selected a governor from among the local nobility (Acuna 1984:193).

We have only limited information regarding the nature of political organization and rulership at Tututepec itself. But given that the coastal capital was established by highland Mixtec migrants, it likely conserved many features of the more well-known but smaller highland Mixtec city-states or *yuhuitayu* (Lind 2000; Spores 1993:172; Terraciano 2001). This Mixtec term refers to the institution of joint political rulership consisting of a married couple and their combined holdings, including structures, land, resources, and relatives (Terraciano 2001:158). Ideally, the married couple came from separate communities so that the *yuhuitayu* represented an interdynastic marriage alliance and an actual place (Terraciano 2001:173). The rulers, or *yya*, lived in the *aniñe* ("palace"), which served as the royal household but was also the symbolic representation of the *yuhuitayu*. The *yya* wielded absolute authority, yet Pohl (1994) finds evidence in the codices for an institution of councilor priests, who were guardians of sacred bundles and served both religious and administrative roles. Pohl furthermore identifies an additional office held by the *yaha yahui* priest, who was responsible for human sacrifice and necromancy but may have also been an economic manager and tribute collector.

Tututepec's rulers likely expanded on this highland Mixtec tradition, delegating authority to administrator-priests with secular and religious roles. Far larger than the typical *yuhuitayu*, Tututepec's imperial dimensions would have demanded additional governors, adjudicators, tribute collectors, and lesser officials (Spores 1993:172). At the capital itself, it is unclear to what extent distinct communities (*ñuu*) or smaller neighborhoods (*siqui*) governed their own affairs. Far more archaeological research is needed at Tututepec to clarify the nature of its internal governance.

Economic Organization

Tututepec was largely agrarian-based, reaping agricultural surpluses from the fertile lower Verde floodplain. In addition, terrace walls interspersed among the remains of residences in the hills of the capital itself suggests that in-fields, gardens, and orchards were also important to local subsistence. Recent excavations at three household areas (Residence A, B, and C) at Tututepec provide greater detail regarding domestic economy among the capital's urban commoners (Levine 2007, 2011). Residences A, B, and C were located among a cluster of households approximately 1.25 km northwest of the site's civic-ceremonial center. Residences A and B date to the fourteenth and fifteenth centuries, respectively, while Residence C dates more generally to the Yucudzaa phase. Analysis of the domestic architecture and household artifact inventories indicate that these were not high-status residences but rather those of relatively affluent commoners (Levine 2011:31).

The household excavations reveal that textile production was crucial to the local economy and an important component of Tututepec's long-distance trade. Excavations recovered dozens of ceramic spindle whorls at Residences A ($n = 79$), B ($n = 39$), and C ($n = 16$), indicating surplus cotton thread production (Levine 2011:31) (Figure 35.4). A ceramic spindle whorl mold recovered at Residence B demonstrates that some whorls were homemade.

Apart from a handful of bone awls, no weaving-related tools or equipment, such as battens, were recovered. The Yucudzaa-phase spindle whorls are small and lightweight, similar to those utilized in coastal communities where cotton-spinning traditions persist today (Avila 1997; Heijting 2006). Yucudzaa phase whorls are distributed broadly across Tututepec's surface, indicating that spinning was a widespread practice in the Postclassic period. Cotton crops would have flourished in the well-watered lower Verde floodplain, which was in fact a center of industrial cotton production until the early 1980s, when plagues shifted local agricultural interests to citrus and other cash crops

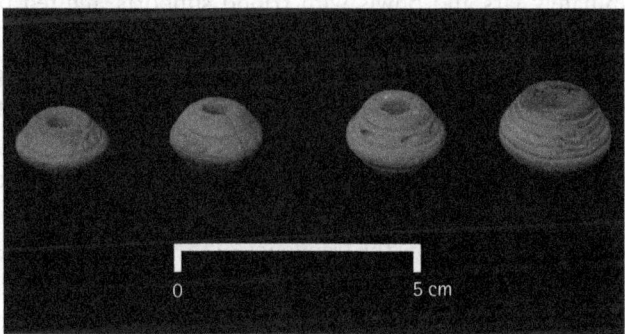

FIGURE 35.4 Ceramic spindle whorls used for spinning cotton from household excavations at Tututepec. Photograph by author.

(Rodríguez Canto 1996). The *Relaciones* from Early Colonial Period communities in the valley of Oaxaca also confirm that Tututepec was a cotton exporter (Acuña 1984:220, 272). The Mixtec capital was clearly an important supplier of cotton, and there was no shortage of demand for raw and woven cotton products throughout Mesoamerica because of its multiplicity of uses.

Although more costly to obtain than more locally available chert, obsidian represented over 96 percent of the Tututepec household chipped-stone assemblages (Levine 2014; Levine et al. 2011). Obsidian artifacts were imported from six highland Mexican sources, but the vast majority came from Pico de Orizaba (54 percent) and Pachuca (43 percent). A small amount of blade production debris at Residence B suggests very limited household blade production, perhaps generated by an itinerant blademaker. Most obsidian tools were made from blade blanks and probably acquired through Tututepec's central marketplace. A host of lowland goods, many of them perishable and thus invisible archaeologically, may have been exchanged for the obsidian. The ubiquity of spindle whorls at the households, however, points to the likelihood that cotton thread was traded for obsidian brought from highland areas where textiles were in great demand.

The Tututepec households were not self-sufficient but instead relied on exchange to obtain both everyday items and social valuables. Local items included utilitarian and decorated pottery, groundstone axes, ceramic figurines, and stamps, while imported material consisted of obsidian, milling stones, and copper implements. The considerable amount and diversity of goods acquired by Tututepec commoners suggests that they were closely linked to a reliable nexus of trade: a central marketplace. Early Spanish accounts provide corroborating evidence, albeit brief, for the presence of markets at Tututepec (Levine 2011:29).

Tututepec's role as a regional trade center, with an influx of goods from the coastal region and beyond, may have presented novel economic opportunities for its local commoners (Levine 2013). Judging by their household possessions, the commoners from Residences A, B, and C appear to have been relatively wealthy. They had access to a range of social valuables, including imported obsidian, copper bells, and relatively high quantities of Mixteca-Puebla polychrome pottery. These exquisitely painted polychrome vessels, predominately jars and bowls with tripod supports, figured prominently in frequent household rituals and feasting contexts (Forde 2006) (Figure 35.5). Ceramic sourcing studies indicate that the Tututepec polychromes were produced at a number of workshops located within the Lower Río Verde region or adjacent areas (Levine et al. 2015).

Tututepec's rulers generated revenue from a variety of sources. Principal among these was tribute from vassal communities and, to a lesser extent, taxation of the local populace (Levine 2011). We do not know the frequency of these tribute payments, but we do know that they provided an array of both commodities (e.g. corn, firewood, clothing) and social valuables (e.g., cacao, feathers, gold). Attendant labor payments were allocated to service royal households or to work their fields and other land holdings, such as cacao orchards, saltworks, and fish ponds (Fernández de Recas 1961:194). Furthermore,

FIGURE 35.5 Mixteca-Puebla polychrome pottery bowl with tripod supports from household excavations at Tututepec. Photograph by author.

subject communities also provided warriors to fight in Tututepec's wars. Finally, the Mixtec rulers may have taxed commerce at the capital and probably sponsored foreign trade expeditions, combining mercantile and diplomatic functions to advance their economic and political aims.

Tututepec's Interaction Sphere

Ethnohistoric and archaeological data affirm that Tututepec's interregional affiliations were most closely linked to points north, especially the Mixtec polities of greater highland Oaxaca and, to a lesser extent, groups in central Mexico (Gutiérrez this volume; Joyce et al 2004; Levine 2007; Levine et al. 2011; Spores 1993). Historical ties to the Mixteca Alta persisted through time via warfare, trade, diplomacy, and interelite gift-giving and marriage (Pohl 2003; Spores 1993). Regarding the latter, Tututepec's royal offspring strategically intermarried with their counterparts from a host of polities, including Zacatepec, Tilantongo, and as far away as Cholula (Pohl 2003; Smith 1973).

Archaeologically, these links are most clearly manifest in Yucudzaa polychrome pottery (Figure 35.5), a coastal variant of the codex-style Mixteca-Puebla Polychrome that proliferated in the greater Puebla and Oaxaca regions during the Late Postclassic (Hernandez 2010; Nicholson and Quiñones Keber 1994). Yucudzaa Polychromes bear a close resemblance to Pilitas Polychromes from the Mixteca Alta (Forde 2006; Lind 1987). Yet Tututepec's ceramic assemblage is otherwise stylistically distinct from surrounding regions, and no imported potsherds from distant lands have yet been identified among the more than 83,000 fragments recovered in household excavations (Levine 2007:248). Apart from ceramic material, well-hewn three-legged metates made from nonlocal vesicular basalt may have been imported from highland Oaxaca, but this awaits further confirmation (Levine 2007:232).

Ethnohistoric records also reveal Tututepec's central Mexican connections. The surviving *Relaciones* from Pochutla and Tonameca, for instance, indicate that these Nahuatl speakers living within Tututepec's realm celebrated religious cults of central Mexican deities such as Itzpapalotl and Tezcatlipoca (Acuña 1984; Olivier 2003:25–28). As described previously, the identification of Monument 6 as Itzpapalotl suggests that this cult was also active at Tututepec. At a minimum, this stela's general form and style evokes that of central Mexico and has been compared to the Atlantid warriors from Pyramid B at Tula (Pohl 1999:184).

As discussed earlier, the *Codices Nuttall, Colombino-Becker,* and *Bodley* also record a historic alliance struck between Lord 8 Deer and a group of Tolteca-Chichimeca. Their precise origin remains in question, but the meeting bespeaks Tututepec's incorporation into an alliance network of Mixtec, Eastern Nahua, and other groups stretching well beyond Oaxaca's northern border (see Joyce et al. 2004; Pohl 2003).

Archaeological evidence for contact with highland Mexico is demonstrated by the proliferation of Pachuca and Pico de Orizaba obsidian imports (Levine et al. 2011). Tututepec commoners clearly preferred obsidian tools and had the means to obtain a regular supply. A slight drop in the frequency (46 percent to 32 percent) of Pachuca imports at Tututepec from the fourteenth to fifteenth centuries indicates a change in the availability of this material, perhaps resulting from the Aztecs seizing control of the mines in the latter period (Pastrana 2007; Pastrana and Carballo this volume). More direct forms of trade with highland Mexico may have been possible in the fourteenth century, whereas the growing rivalry between these two imperial powers in the fifteenth century would have necessitated trade through intermediaries or neutral markets, such as those known from highland Oaxaca (see Pohl et al 1997). In any case, no clear Aztec or Aztec-style archaeological material has yet come to light at Tututepec. The archaeological data supports ethnohistoric evidence that Tututepec was never conquered by the Aztecs, but they did eventually meet the same fate as their rivals in the early sixteenth century.

Shortly after their conquest of Tenochtitlan, the Spanish marched on Tututepec in early 1522 with a force of 40 horsemen and 200 well-armed foot soldiers (Cortés 1986:275–276, 286). Pedro de Alvarado captured Tututepec's ruler Coaxintecuhtli, and his subjects paid a ransom in gold before ceding control of the capital. This marked the fall of Oaxaca's largest and most dominant polity of the Late Postclassic period.

References Cited

Acuña, René
1984 *Relaciones geográficas del siglo XVI: antequera*. Vol. 1. Universidad Autónoma de México, Mexico.

Avila Blomberg, Alejandro de
1997 Threads of Diversity: Oaxacan Textiles in Context. In *The Unbroken Thread: Conserving the Textile Traditions of Oaxaca*, edited by Kathryn Klein, pp. 87–151. Getty Conservation Institute, Los Angeles.

Berdan, Frances F.
1996 The Tributary Provinces. In *Imperial Strategies and Core-Periphery Relations*. In *Aztec Imperial Strategies*, edited by Frances F. Berdan and Michael E. Smith, pp. 115–135. Dumbarton Oaks Research Library and Collection, Washington, DC.

Byland, Bruce, and John M. D. Pohl
1994 *In the Realm of 8 Deer: The Archaeology of the Mixtec Codices*. University of Oklahoma Press, Norman.

Caso, Alfonso
1960 *Interpretation of the Codex Bodley 2858*. Sociedad Mexicana de Antropología, Mexico City.

Cortés, Hernán.
1986 *Letters from Mexico*. Yale University Press, New Haven, CT.

Davies, Nigel
1968 *Los Señoríos Independientes del Imperio Azteca*. Instituto Nacional de Antropología e Historia, México, D.F.

Fernández de Recas, Guillermo S.
1961 *Cacicazgos y nobilario indegena de la Nueva España*. Biblioteca Nacional de México, Instituto Bibliográfico Mexicano 5. Universidad Nacional Autónoma de México, Mexico City.

Forde, Jamie E.
2006 Ideology, Identity, and Icons: A Study of Mixtec Polychrome Pottery from Late Postclassic Yucu Dzaa (Tututepec), Oaxaca, Mexico. Master's thesis, Department of Anthropology, University of Colorado, Boulder.

Heijting, Femke
2006 Cotton Thread Production in Late Postclassic Tututepec: A Study of Excavated Spindle Whorls, Tututepec Archaeological Project 2005. Master's thesis, University of Leiden, Leiden.

Hernández Sánchez, Gilda
2010 Vessels for Ceremony: The Pictography of Codex-Style Mixteca Puebla Vessels from Central and South Mexico. *Latin American Antiquity* 21:252–273.

Jansen, Maarten
1989 Nombres históricos e identidad étnica en los Códices Mixtecos. *Revista Europea de Estudios Latinoamericanos y del Caribe* 47:65–87.

Jansen, Maarten, and Gabina Aurora Pérez Jiménez
2007 *Encounter with the Plumed Serpent: Drama and Power in the Heart of Mesoamerica*. University Press of Colorado, Boulder.

Josserand, J. Kathryn, Maarten Jansen, and Maria de los Angeles Romero
1984 Mixtec Dialectology: Inferences from Linguistics and Ethnohistory. In *Essays in Otomanguean Culture History*, edited by J. K. Josserand, M. Winter, and N. Hopkins,

pp. 141–163. Vanderbilt University Publications in Anthropology No. 31, Vanderbilt University, Nashville, TN.

Joyce, Arthur A.

1991 Formative Period Occupation in the Lower Río Verde Valley, Oaxaca, Mexico: Interregional Interaction and Social Change. Unpublished Ph.D. dissertation, Department of Anthropology, Rutgers University, New Brunswick, NJ.

2010 *Mixtecs, Zapotecs, and Chatinos: Ancient Peoples of Southern Mexico.* Wiley-Blackwell, Malden, MA.

Joyce, Arthur A., Andrew G. Workinger, Byron Hamann, Peter Kroefges, Maxine Oland, and Stacie M. King

2004 Lord 8 Deer "Jaguar Claw" and the Land of the Sky: The Archaeology and History of Tututepec. *Latin American Antiquity* 15:273–297.

Kroefges, Peter

2004 Sociopolitical Organization in the Prehispanic Chontalpa de Oaxaca, Mexico: Ethnohistorical and Archaeological Perspectives. Ph.D. dissertation, Department of Anthropology, State University of New York, Albany.

Levine, Marc N.

2007 Linking Household and Polity at Late Postclassic Yucu Dzaa (Tututepec), a Mixtec Capital on the Coast of Oaxaca, Mexico. Ph.D. dissertation, Department of Anthropology, University of Colorado, Boulder.

2011 Negotiating Political Economy at Late Postclassic Tututepec (Yucu Dzaa), Oaxaca, Mexico. *American Anthropologist* 113:22–39.

2013 La cerámica polícroma, el mercado, y el ritual domestico en Tututepec posclásico. Paper presented at the Décimo Simposio Internacional de Estudios Oaxaqueños, Oaxaca, Mexico.

2014 Obsidian Obsessed? Examining Patterns of Chipped-Stone Procurement at Late Postclassic Tututepec, Oaxaca. In *Obsidian Reflections: The Symbolic and Ritual Dimensions of Obsidian in Ancient Mesoamerica*, edited by Marc N. Levine and David M. Carballo, pp. 159–191. University Press of Colorado, Boulder.

Levine, Marc N., Lane Fargher, Leslie Cecil, and Jamie E. Forde

2015 Polychrome Pottery Economics and Ritual Life in Postclassic Oaxaca, Mexico. *Latin American Antiquity* 26:319–340.

Levine, Marc N., Arthur A. Joyce, and Michael D. Glascock

2011 Shifting Patterns of Obsidian Exchange in Postclassic Oaxaca, Mexico. *Ancient Mesoamerica* 22:123–133.

Lind, Michael D.

1987 *The Sociocultural Dimensions of Mixtec Ceramics.* Vanderbilt University Publications in Anthropology No. 33. Vanderbilt University, Nashville, TN.

2000 Mixtec City-States and Mixtec City-State Culture. In *A Comparative Study of Thirty City-State Cultures: An Investigation Conducted by the Copenhagen Polis Centre*, edited by Mogens Herman Hansen, pp. 567–580. Royal Danish Academy of Sciences and Letters, Copenhagen.

Maler, M. T.

1883 Notes sur la Basse Mixtéque. *Revue d'ethnologie* 2:154–161.

Monaghan, John

1994 Irrigation and Ecological Complementarity in Mixtec Cacicazgos. In *Caciques and Their People: A Volume in Honor of Ronald Spores*, edited by Joyce Marcus and Judith Zeitlin, pp. 143–161. University of Michigan, Ann Arbor.

Nicholson, Henry B., and Eloise Quiñones Keber (editors)
1994 *Mixteca-Puebla: Discoveries and Research in Mesoamerican Art and Archaeology.* Labyrinthos, Culver City, CA.

Olivier, Guilhem
2003 *Mockeries and Metamorphoses of an Aztec God: Tezcatlipoca, "Lord of the Smoking Mirror."* University Press of Colorado, Boulder.

O'Mack, Scott
1990 Reconocimiento arqueológico en Tututepec, Oaxaca. *Notas Mesoamericanas* (12):19–38.

Pastrana, Alejandro
2007 *La distribución de obsidiana de la Triple Alianza en la Cuenca de México.* Colección Científica 519. Instituto Nacional de Antropología e Historia, México, D.F.

Pohl, John M. D.
1994 *The Politics of Symbolism in the Mixtec Codices.* Vanderbilt University Publications in Anthropology 46. Vanderbilt University, Nashville, TN.
1999 The Lintel Paintings of Mitla and the Function of the Mitla Palaces. In *Mesoamerican Architecture as a Cultural Symbol*, edited by Jeff Karl Kowalski, pp. 176–197. Oxford University Press, New York.
2003 Royal Marriage and Confederacy Building among the Eastern Nahuas, Mixtecs, and Zapotecs. In *The Postclassic Mesoamerican World*, edited by Michael E. Smith and Frances F. Berdan, pp. 243–248. University of Utah Press, Salt Lake City.

Pohl, John M. D., John Monaghan, and Laura R. Stiver
1997 Religion, Economy, and Factionalism in Mixtec Boundary Zones. In *Códices y documentos sobre México: Segundo Simposio*, edited by Salvador Rueda Smithers and Constanza Vega Sosa, pp. 205–232. Instituto Nacional de Antropología e Historia, México, D.F.

Rodríguez Canto, Adolfo
1996 *Historia Agrícola y Agraria de la Costa Oaxaqueña.* Universidad Autónoma de Chapingo, Mexico.

Smith, Mary Elizabeth
1973 *Picture Writing from Ancient Southern Mexico: Mixtec Place Signs and Maps.* University of Oklahoma Press, Norman.

Spores, Ronald A.
1993 Tututepec: A Postclassic-Period Mixtec Conquest State. *Ancient Mesoamerica* 4:167–174.

Terraciano, Kevin
2001 *The Mixtecs of Colonial Oaxaca: Ñudzahui History, Sixteenth Through Eighteenth Centuries.* Stanford University Press, Stanford, CA.

Umberger, Emily
1996 Aztec Presence and Material Remains in the Outer Provinces. In *Aztec Imperial Strategies*, edited by Frances F. Berdan, Richard E. Blanton, Elizabeth Hill Boone, Mary G. Hodge, Michael E. Smith, and Emily Umberger, pp. 151–179. Dumbarton Oaks Research Library and Collection, Washington, DC.

Workinger, Andrew
2002 Coastal/Highland Interaction in Prehispanic Oaxaca, Mexico: The Perspective From San Francisco de Arriba. Ph.D. dissertation, Department of Anthropology, Vanderbilt University, Nashville, TN.

Zeitlin, Judith
2005 *Cultural Politics in Colonial Tehuantepec: Community and State Among the Isthmus Zapotec, 1500–1750.* Stanford University Press, Stanford, CA.

CHAPTER 36

CHOLULA IN AZTEC TIMES

PATRICIA PLUNKET AND GABRIELA URUÑUELA

LOCATED in the western half of the Puebla-Tlaxcala Valley, *Tollan Cholollan Tlachihualtepetl*, the "city of flowing water and the man-made mountain" (González-Hermosillo and Reyes 2002:110) was the Postclassic name of one of Mesoamerica's most venerable metropolises. It was the capital of an 800 km² kingdom with 49 subject communities that was bordered on the north by Tlaxcala, on the east by Tepeaca, on the south by Quauhquechollan, and on the west by Huejotzingo (Lind 2008:68) (Figure 36.1).

The area was first inhabited by the beginning of the Middle Formative period, and the population eventually coalesced into an important urban center during the Formative/Classic transition as geopolitical shifts associated with Teotihuacan's expansion and a major volcanic eruption of Popocatépetl led to significant transformations in settlement patterns and the built landscape (Uruñuela et al. 2009). Then, after 500 years of affluence, in the seventh century A.D., Cholula, like Teotihuacan, suffered an important demographic decline. During the Early Postclassic, however, Cholula was revitalized, first by the Olmeca-Xicalanca who became the overlords of the region in the eighth century after the eclipse of the Teotihuacan world, and subsequently by the Nahuatl-speaking Tolteca-Chichimeca who usurped political power in the Puebla-Tlaxcala Valley after the downfall of Tula. Thus, Cholula was a famous and well-established center long before the rise of the Triple Alliance in the neighboring Basin of Mexico.

According to the sagas recorded in the Mixtec codices, Toltec-style investiture ceremonies were already being held in Cholula toward the end of the eleventh century. The *Codex Bodley*, for example, narrates how Lord 8 Deer, the celebrated warrior from the Mixtec kingdom of Tilantongo in Oaxaca, traveled to Cholula in A.D. 1097; he met first with Lord 4 Jaguar in front of the Sacred Bundle to present his sacrificial captive and subsequently received the turquoise nose ornament used by Toltec rulers after having his nasal septum pierced by Lord 8 Death in the city's temple precinct (Jansen and Pérez 2007:221–224; Oudijk 2008:126–127). The enactment of this induction ceremony was the cornerstone of Cholula's Postclassic prominence. Sixteenth-century sources (e.g., Las Casas 1971:5, 54; Rojas 1985:130–131) stress the fact that nobles from surrounding

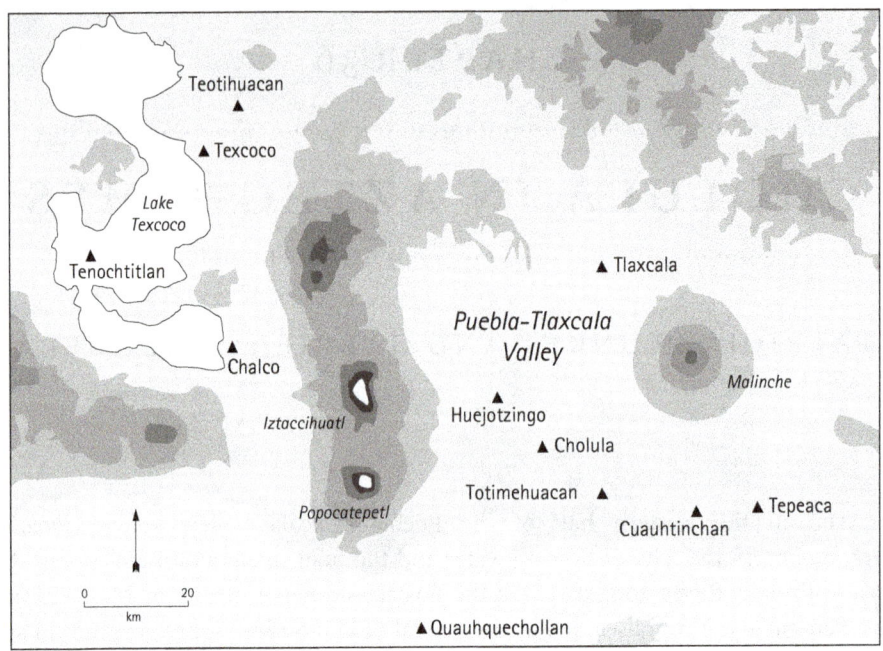

FIGURE 36.1 Map of the Puebla-Tlaxcala. Drawing by Patricia Plunket.

areas came to the city to receive the emblems of rulership and then be escorted back to their homelands by representatives of Cholula's two high priests in order to leave no doubt that they were now the legitimate lords of their kingdoms.

Cholula's ninth-century revitalization included the partial restoration of its massive Classic-period Great Pyramid, the Tlachihualtepetl, seat of ancient authority linked to the Teotihuacan world order. Its damaged facades were shorn up (Marquina 1970:40), and elegant residences were constructed on the eastern corners of its first tier (Noguera 1937). Although the Olmeca-Xicalanca leaders of the restored city capitalized on the mystique of this ancient monument (Kirchhoff et al. 1989:141–146), the conquering Tolteca-Chichimeca relocated the main temple about 500 m to the northwest of the Tlachihualtepetl and, like the Olmeca-Xicalanca before them (Muñoz Camargo 1984:133), dedicated their shrine to the cult of Quetzalcoatl.

This new temple was said to have housed the relics of the mortal Quetzalcoatl, whom Maarten Jansen (2006:203) identifies as the historical Lord 4 Jaguar of the Mixtec codices. Some legends hold that Quetzalcoatl fled from Cholula to the Gulf Coast to escape from the aggressions of Huemac, the Toltec ruler of Tula (Kirchhoff et al. 1989:133). After he died in Nonhualco Teotlixco, Muñoz Camargo (1984:132) tells us that his cremated remains were mixed with the blood of four sacrificed children and placed in a jar along with precious stones to symbolize his heart; this reliquary supposedly was returned to Cholula and stored in a wooden box inside the temple until the Spaniards burned this building in October 1519.

The Late Postclassic City

Today, there are few visible remains of Postclassic Tollan Cholollan or of the first century of colonial rule. The Spaniards sacked and burned the city, and although many of its upper-class houses later were refurbished, its temples were subsequently razed or left to decay. According to the *Relación de Cholula* (Rojas 1985:126), in 1519 the urban core and its surrounding area had about 40,000 households, but by 1581, only 9,000 of these had survived the plagues of the late 1540s and 1576, a population decline of over 75 percent.

Our knowledge of the Postclassic city comes primarily from sixteenth-century manuscripts, not archaeological evidence. The most important documents are the *Historia Tolteca-Chichimeca* (Kirchhoff et al. 1989) (Figure 36.2), the *Mapas de Cuauhtinchan* 1 and 2 (Carrasco and Sessions 2007; Yoneda 1991), the *Relación de Cholula* (Rojas 1985), and the *Códice de Cholula* (González-Hermosillo and Reyes 2002). All of them include a map of the city, but each presents its own version of the urban landscape. Most of this cartography sought to describe the social order of the community (Carrasco 1971:57; Kubler 1968:124) and illustrate elaborate foundational narratives written to legitimate the Toltec heritage and territorial claims of specific lineages; thus, none of it constitutes a precise rendition of the city's physical geography.

Political, Social, and Economic Structures

Cortés (1928:36–37) portrays Cholula as an independent kingdom governed by a Venetian-style council rather than a single supreme ruler. These noblemen, referred to as *caciques* or "captains" by soldiers like Bernal Díaz del Castillo (1956:172–173) and Andrés de Tapia (Schwartz 2000:117), elected a principal *cacique* or "captain general" (Cervantes de Salazar 1914:258), who seems to have been charged with the administration of the city's internal affairs. Cholula's foreign relations and ceremonial life were handled by its two high priests, the *Aquiach* and the *Tlalchiach* (Rojas 1985:130–131); no military obligations are recorded for these two offices, but their symbols, the eagle and the jaguar, respectively, were emblematic of military orders throughout central Mexico.

In the eyes of the conquistadors, Tollan Cholollan was a city fit for a Spaniard (Cortés 1928:36–37), a wealthy cosmopolitan community that attracted long-distance trade, pilgrims, and foreign royalty. Its six districts were subdivided into *calpolli* (Lind 2008:68), social segments that were bound together in endless cycles of ritual events, civic duties, and rotational tribute obligations. The number of *calpolli* noted in the *Historia Tolteca-Chichimeca* is 12, but more are listed in other sources; these inconsistencies perhaps reflect the sixteenth-century reorganization of the population as the community weathered a series of devastating epidemics.

The four *calpolli* in the center of the city—the Xiuhcalca, the Uitziluaque, the Chimalzolca, and the Tianquiznahuaca—included the civil and religious authorities

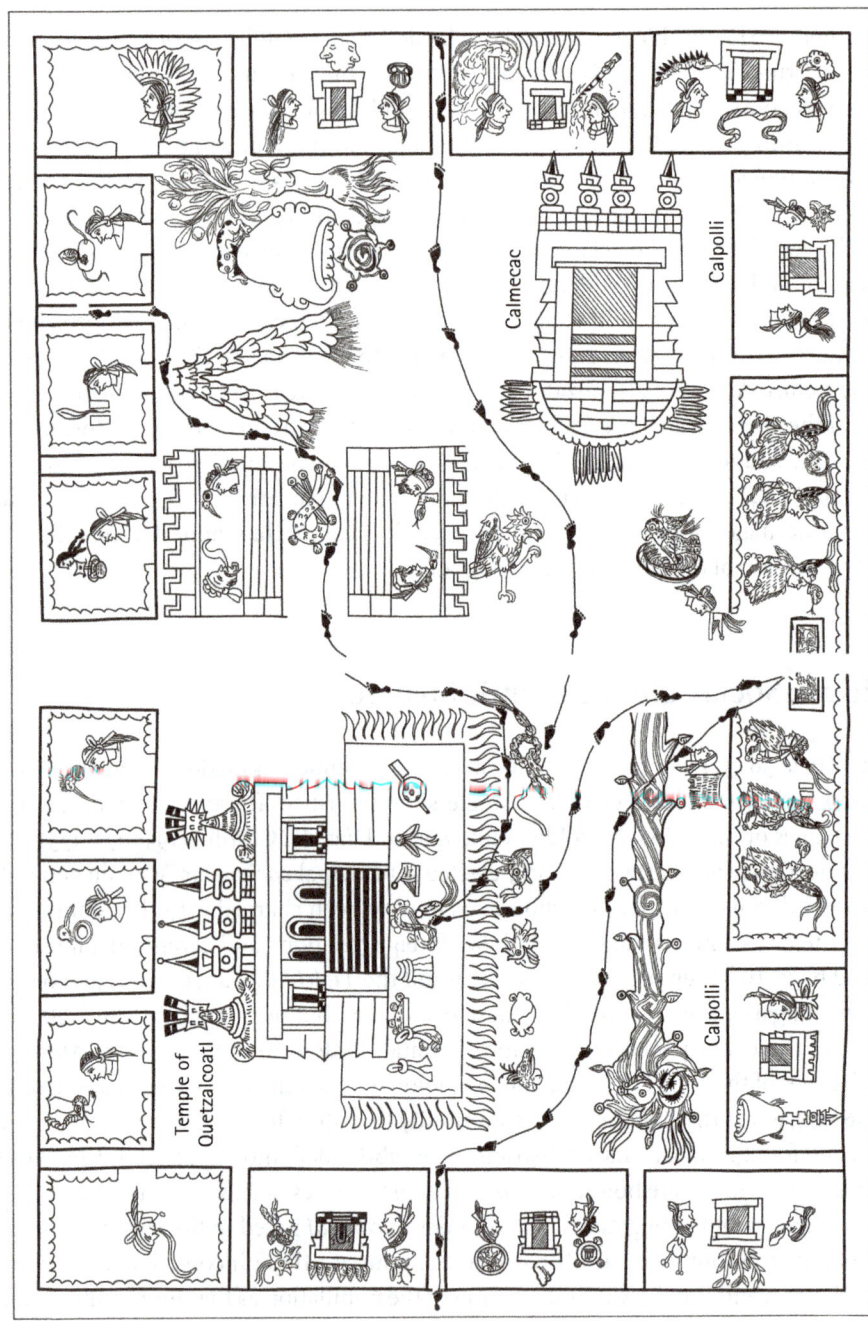

FIGURE 36.2 Map of Tollan Chollollan. Redrawn by Gabriela Uruñuela from the *Historia Tolteca-Chichimeca* ca. 1550:26v–27r.

(Kirchhoff et al. 1989:148, n.2). Nobles and prosperous merchants lived in Tianquiznahuac, the highest ranked *calpolli*, and it was from here that the priests of Quetzalcoatl were chosen (Rojas 1985:130). The remaining eight *calpolli* were outlying communities known as the "hands and feet" of the urban core (Kirchhoff et al. 1989:148, n.2). This core-periphery structure probably accounts for Cortés' (1963:37) eyewitness description of 20,000 houses in the city proper and another 20,000 in the hinterland.

Cholula's market, situated to the west of the religious precinct in the city center, was one of the most important venues for buying and selling in central Mexico. Transactions probably took place outdoors in the plaza just as they did until the middle of the twentieth century. Gabriel de Rojas (1985:143–144) provides a colorful description of the market. Wealthy merchants, both men and women, were said to be the greatest traders of the highlands, traveling up to 1500 km to bring back cacao, feathers, shells, gold, copper, mineral and plant pigments, jade, incense, cotton, salt, bitumen, obsidian, and other commodities. The market was also the place to acquire local products like elaborately painted codex-style pottery, ritual paraphernalia, jewelry, featherwork, elegant clothing made from spun rabbit fur, fine embroidery, tools, weapons, pulque, cochineal, rope, and shoes. The city's merchants used cacao beans as their medium of exchange and were able to amass huge quantities of them during a day's work.

The Holy City

Tollan Chololan's status as a holy city, often compared to Rome or Mecca (Motolinia 1914:46; Rojas 1985:131–132), rested partially on its association with Teotihuacan's legacy, a privileged heritage that underpinned its right to confirm kings and rulers (Boone 2000). The iconic symbol of the city, the ancient Tlachihualtepetl, stood as a constant reminder of that illustrious history, while the relics stored in the Postclassic temple of Quetzalcoatl established its authority among the kingdoms of the Central Highlands and beyond who sought to validate their Toltec affiliation. Cholula's economy was energized not only by its renowned market but also by the steady flow of pilgrims, both noble and commoner, to visit its venerable shrine. Highly trained scholars and craftsmen turned out illuminated manuscripts, ceremonial ceramics, costume elements, and numerous other cult items and souvenirs that were in demand by both religious practitioners and devout visitors. Indeed, it is likely that much of the city's business was in pilgrimage, providing food, sanitation, shelter, and offerings in addition to religious services, including divination and curing, for large numbers of travelers.

The Temple of Quetzalcoatl

Since Cholula's main temple was destroyed in 1519 and by 1529 the Franciscans had initiated the construction of their monastery over its ruins (Oroz et al. 1947:166), we are left with few eyewitness descriptions of this structure. During their short stay, the conquistadors were lodged in buildings set within a spacious court, with a single gate and high double walls, that probably formed part of the religious precinct; the Temple of

Quetzalcoatl itself had 120 steps, making it six steps higher than the Great Temple of Tenochtitlan, but it was built according to a different plan (Díaz del Castillo 1956:172, 224). Not only did this temple house the relics of the city's patron god, but his anthropomorphic statue, wearing a richly decorated feather cape and the insignia of Quetzalcoatl-Ehecatl, stood on an elaborate altar in its main chamber (Durán 1971:130–139). Pilgrims from all over Mesoamerica came here to worship and consult the highly revered idol.

The Calmecac

The religious school where young men trained for the priesthood and learned the scribal arts, the *calmecac*, also was located southwest of the main temple (see Figure 36.2) (Kirchhoff et al. 1989:183). Here students mastered the complex iconography used to represent Postclassic Mesoamerica's esoteric knowledge. The only archaeological evidence of this activity, however, is the abundant corpus of codex-style ceramics (Hernández 2010) (Figure 36.3) and, perhaps, the *Codex Borgia* (Uruñuela et al. 1997). Cholula's elegant scribal production belongs to the Postclassic International Style and emphasizes bloody sacrificial rites and their corresponding cult objects—maguey thorns, bone awls, and flint knives (Lind 1994:94–97)—in addition to military emblems like jaguars and birds of prey, shields and darts, and the symbols of Xipe-Totec (Solís et al. 2006; Uruñuela 2011). For the most part, Cholula's polychrome ceramics present themes that underscore the ritual

FIGURE 36.3 Codex-style polychrome vessel from Cholula. Drawing by Gabriela Uruñuela.

and military interests of the holy city while the genealogical concerns of political elites, so often portrayed on similar wares from the Mixtec area, are absent (Lind 1994).

Minor Shrines

Cholula had hundreds of secondary shrines (Cortés 1928:36–37). Scattered throughout the city, many of these turreted white-washed buildings were *barrio* temples where *calpolli* members "carried out their rites and ceremonies, adorations, and sacrifices of men accorded to each district from war" (Rojas 1985:132); these war captives were held in wooden prisons as they awaited sacrifice on the altars of the *barrio* temples (Díaz del Castillo 1956:181–182). Other large chapels belonged to nobles and kings from other provinces who maintained residences in the holy city in order to attend the many festivals held throughout the year (Las Casas 1971:54; Motolinia 1914:46). Vestiges of these minor sanctuaries were still visible in 1581, but during the following centuries their remains were dismantled and reused in new building projects.

A House Divided: Cholula and the Aztec Empire

Geopolitical relations among the Late Postclassic kingdoms of Puebla-Tlaxcala were complicated, and warfare was a common condition (Motolinia 1914:46). After the defeat of Chalco in 1465 (Chimalpahin 1965:204), the Mexica and their allies advanced into the region from the south, placing military outposts at both Quauhquechollan and Tepeaca (Dyckerhoff 1988:20–21, 26), as they began to encircle the "Independent Kingdoms" of Tlaxcala, Huejotzingo, and Cholula. Imperial provinces bordering these realms, like the conquered Tepeaca, were required to supply high-value captives from these independent polities for the altars of Tenochtitlan (Berdan and Anawalt 1997:30, 99, 100, 192, n. 3). This tactic, along with the introduction of a type of ceremonial warfare known as the *Xochiyaoyotl*, or "Flowery War" (Cervera Obregón this volume), was designed to weaken the Puebla-Tlaxcala states by decimating their troops (Plunket and Uruñuela 1994). Indeed, Tlacaelel, counselor to the Aztec emperor, is reported to have said, "The people from these places [the independent kingdoms] will come to our god like warm breads, soft, tasty, straight from the fire" (Durán 1994:232). Cholula's status as a holy city does not appear to have insulated it from these predations, and the tensions between Cholula and its neighbors inhibited the formation of a successful defensive alliance against the Aztecs.

Although Black-on-Orange Aztec I–like ceramics are a hallmark of the Early Postclassic in Cholula, Aztec II and III sherds are extremely rare. There may have been little reason to bring pottery from the Basin of Mexico to the Puebla Valley, since Cholula was a major producer of terracotta so fine that it was used at Motecuhzoma's table (Díaz del Castillo 1956:210), but the absence of Aztec II and III ceramics might indicate that these were not highly valued by the local population, not even the residents of the Mexico-Tenochtitlan colony located in the southern part of the city (González-Hermosillo 2001:100).

In October 1519, when the Spaniards entered Tollan Chololan, Motecuhzoma's messengers were already there, preparing a report for their emperor on the foreigners' activities (Cortés 1928:57). This has led some to assume that the kingdom was either an Aztec ally or a vassal state, a position advanced to Cortés (1928:53) by Cholula's mortal enemies, the Tlaxcalans (Sahagún 1975:29). Indeed, the night before the Spanish-Tlaxcalan alliance destroyed the city and massacred thousands in the precinct of the Temple of Quetzalcoatl, two of Cholula's priests informed Cortés that Motecuhzoma had sent 20,000 soldiers, half of whom were already in the holy city, to kill or imprison them (Díaz del Castillo 1956:174). On the other hand, in 1581 Rojas (1985:129), the city's *corregidor*, or "chief magistrate," recounts that Chololan was a sovereign kingdom that acknowledged obedience to no external authority.

Several sources indicate that there was a fundamental schism among Cholula's social segments. Both Francisco Cervantes de Salazar (1914:258) and Fray Juan de Torquemada (1969:438) state that in 1519 half of the districts sided with Tenochtitlan while the other half were friendly to the Tlaxcalans and in opposition to the pro-Aztec stance. Cervantes de Salazar (1914:251, 258) elaborates further that Motecuhzoma had sent rich presents to the three loyal lords who imprisoned the leaders of the rival faction, effectively suppressing their participation in deciding how best to deal with the Spaniards and the pressure from the Aztec Emperor.

The *Códice de Cholula* shows that, during the massacre, most of the killing took place in the district of Tianquiznahuac, where the nobles and high priests lived, but heavy fighting and casualties also are displayed in the districts to the southwest, where colonies from Mexico-Tenochtitlan had been established; conversely, little combat appears in the northern districts (González-Hermosillo 2001:100). This might indicate that the pro-Aztec faction was centered among the nobles residing in the city core and in the southern *calpollis*. In contrast, the Tlaxcalan-allied faction probably was concentrated in the northern partiality of Tenanquiahuac—whose leader Tequahuehuetzin perished during the massacre and whose heirs later were given lands and privileges—in addition to what was to become the *cabecera* of San Andrés Collomochco, which included Tlaxcalan colonies (González-Hermosillo 2001:97–106). This rift may underpin Cholula's modern division into two antagonistic municipalities, San Andrés and San Pedro, although anthropologists have tended to attribute it to ethnic differences dating back to the Tolteca-Chichimeca conquest of the Olmeca-Xicalanca in the Early Postclassic (e.g., Dyckerhoff 2002–2003:191, n. 86; Olivera and Reyes 1969).

References Cited

Berdan, Frances F., and Patricia R. Anawalt
1997 *The Essential Codex Mendoza*. University of California Press, Berkeley.
Boone, Elizabeth H.
2000 Venerable Place of Beginnings: The Aztec Understanding of Teotihuacan. In *Mesoamerica's Classical Heritage: From Teotihuacan to the Aztecs*, edited by David Carrasco, Lindsay Jones, and Scott Sessions, pp. 371–396. University Press of Colorado, Boulder.

Carrasco, Davíd, and Scott Sessions (editors)
2007 *Cave, City, and Eagle's Nest: An Interpretive Journey through the Mapa de Cuauhtinchan No. 2.* University of New Mexico Press, Albuquerque.

Carrasco, Pedro
1971 Los barrios antiguos de Cholula. *Estudios y documentos de la región de Puebla-Tlaxcala* 3:9–88.

Cervantes de Salazar, Francisco
1914 *Crónica de Nueva España*, Vol. 1. Edited by Francisco del Paso y Troncoso. Papeles de la Nueva España. Estudio Fotográfico Hauser y Menet, Madrid.

Chimalpahin Quauhtlehuanitzin, Don Francisco de San Antón Muñón
1965 *Relaciones originales de Chalco Amequemecan escritas por Don Francisco de San Antón Muñón Chilapahin Cuauhtlehuanitzin.* Edited and translated by Sylvia Rendón. Fondo de Cultura Económica, Mexico City.

Cortés, Hernán
1928 *Five Letters 1519–1526.* Translated by Bayard Morris. George Routledge and Sons, London.
1963 *Cartas de Relación.* 2nd ed. Editorial Porrúa, Mexico City.

Díaz del Castillo, Bernal
1956 *The Discovery and Conquest of Mexico, 1517–1521.* Translated by Alfred P. Maudslay. Farrar, Straus and Cudhay, New York.

Durán, Fray Diego
1971 *The Book of the Gods and Rites and the Ancient Calendar.* Translated and edited by Fernando Horcasitas and Doris Heyden. University of Oklahoma Press, Norman.
1994 *History of the Indies of New Spain.* Translated by Doris Heyden. University of Oklahoma Press, Norman.

Dyckerhoff, Ursula
1988 La época prehispánica. In *Milpa y hacienda: tenencia de la tierra indígena yespañola en la cuenca del Alto Atoyac, Puebla, México (1520–1650)*, edited by Hanns J. Prem, pp. 18–34. Centro de Investigaciones y Estudios Superiores en Antropología Social, Instituto Nacional de Antropología e Historia, Secretaría de Educación Pública, Mexico City.
2002–2003 Grupos étnicos y estratificación socio-política: tentativa de interpretación histórica. *Indiana* 19–20:155–196.

González-Hermosillo, Francisco
2001 El sometimiento del señorío indígena de Cholula ante la Corona española. *Signos Históricos* 6:95–114.

González-Hermosillo, Francisco, and Luis Reyes García
2002 *El Códice de Cholula: la exaltación testimonial de un linaje indio.* Gobierno del Estado de Puebla. Centro de Investigaciones y Estudios Superiores en Antropología Social, Conaculta, Instituto Nacional de Antropología e Historia and Miguel Angel Porrúa, Mexico City.

Hernández, Gilda
2010 Vessels for Ceremony: The Pictography of Codex-Style Mixteca-Puebla Vessels from Central and South Mexico. *Latin American Antiquity* 21:252–273.

Jansen, Maarten
2006 Los señoríos de Ñuu Dzaui y la expansión tolteca. *Revista Española de Antropología Americana* 36(2):175–208.

Jansen, Maarten, and Gabina Aurora Pérez Jiménez
2007 *Encounter with the Plumed Serpent: Drama and Power in the Heart of Mesoamerica.* University Press of Colorado, Boulder.

Kirchhoff, Paul, Lina Odena Güemes, and Luis Reyes García
1989 *Historia Tolteca-Chichimeca*. 2nd ed. Centro de Investigaciones y Estudios Superiores en Antropología Social, Estado de Puebla, and Fondo de Cultura Económica, Mexico City.

Kubler, George
1968 La traza colonial de Cholula. *Estudios de Historia Novohispana* 2:111–127.

Las Casas, Fray Bartolomé de
1971 *Los indios de México y Nueva España: antología*. 2nd ed. Edited by Edmundo O'Gorman and Jorge A. Manrique. Editorial Porrúa, Mexico City.

Lind, Michael
1994 Cholula and Mixteca Polychromes: Two Mixteca-Puebla Regional Sub-Styles. In *Mixteca-Puebla: Discoveries and Research in Mesoamerican Art and Archaeology*, edited by H. B. Nicholson and Eloise Quiñones-Keber, pp. 79–99. Labyrinthos, Culver City, CA.

2008 La Gran Cuadra de la ciudad: el gobierno prehispánico de Cholula. *Arqueología* 39:65–76.

Marquina, Ignacio
1970 Pirámide de Cholula. In *Proyecto Cholula*, edited by Ignacio Marquina, pp.31–45. Serie Investigaciones 19. Secretaría de Educación Pública, Instituto Nacional de Antropología e Historia, Mexico City.

Motolinia [Benavente], Fray Toribio de
1914 *Historia de los indios de la Nueva España*. Herederos de Juan Gil Editores, Barcelona.

Muñoz Camargo, Diego
1984 *Descripción de la ciudad y provincia de Tlaxcala. Relaciones geográficas del siglo XVI: Tlaxcala*, Vol. 1, edited by René Acuña. Universidad Nacional Autónoma de México, Mexico City.

Noguera, Eduardo
1937 *El altar de los cráneos esculpidos de Cholula*. Talleres Gráficos de la Nación, Mexico City.

Olivera, Mercedes, and Cayetano Reyes
1969 Los choloques y los cholultecas: apuntes sobre las relaciones étnicas en Cholula hasta el siglo XVI. *Anales del Museo Nacional de México* 1:247–274.

Oroz, Pedro Fray, Fray Jerónimo de Mendieta, and Fray Francisco Suárez
1947 *Relación de la descripción de la provincia del Santo Evangelio que es en las Indias Occidentales que llaman La Nueva España, hecha el año de 1585*. Introduction and notes by Fray Fidel de J. Chauvet. Imprenta mexicana de Juan Aguilar Reyes, Mexico City.

Oudijk, Michel R.
2008 De tradiciones y métodos: investigaciones pictográficas. *Desacatos* 27:123–138.

Plunket, Patricia, and Gabriela Uruñuela
1994 The Impact of the Xochiyaoyotl in Southwestern Puebla. In *Economies and Polities in the Aztec Realm*, edited by Mary G. Hodge and Michael E. Smith, pp. 433–446. Institute for Mesoamerican Studies, State University of New York, Albany.

Rojas, Gabriel de
1985 Relación de Cholula (1581). In *Relaciones geográficas del siglo XVI*, Vol. II, edited by René Acuña, pp. 121–145. Instituto de Investigaciones Antropológicas, Universidad Nacional Autónoma de México, Mexico City.

Sahagún, Fray Bernardino de
1975 *Florentine Codex: General History of the Things of New Spain, Book 12: The Conquest of Mexico*. Edited and translated by Arthur J. D. Anderson and Charles E. Dibble. University of Utah Press, Salt Lake City, and School of American Research, Santa Fe, NM.

Schwartz, Stuart B.
2000 *Victors and Vanquished: Spanish and Nahua Views of the Conquest of Mexico.* Bedford/St. Martin's, Boston.

Solís, Felipe, Verónica Velasquez, and Roberto Velasco
2006 Cerámica policroma de Cholula y de los otros valles de Puebla. In *Cholula: la Gran Pirámide*, edited by Felipe Solís, Gabriela Uruñuela, Patricia Plunket, Martín Cruz, and Dionisio Rodríguez, pp. 78–129. Conaculta and Grupo Azabache, Mexico City.

Torquemada, Fray Juan de
1969 *Monarquía Indiana.* Introduction by Miguel León-Portilla. Editorial Porrúa, Mexico City.

Uruñuela, Gabriela
2011 Polychrome Bowl. In *100 Selected Works: National Museum of Anthropology*, edited by Mónica del Villar, pp. 158–159. Conaculta and Artes de México, Mexico City.

Uruñuela, Gabriela, Patricia Plunket, Gilda Hernández, and Juan Albaitero
1997 Bi-Conical God Figurines from Cholula and the Codex Borgia. *Latin American Antiquity* 8(1):63–70.

Uruñuela, Gabriela, Patricia Plunket, and Amparo Robles
2009 Cholula: Art and Architecture of an Archetypal City. In *The Art of Urbanism: How Mesoamerican Kingdoms Represented Themselves in Architecture and Imagery*, edited by William L. Fash and Leonardo López Luján, pp. 135–171. Dumbarton Oaks Research and Library Collection, Washington, DC.

Yoneda, Keiko
1991 *Los mapas de Cuauhtinchan y la historia cartográfica prehispánica.* 2nd ed. Centro de Investigaciones y Estudios Superiores en Antropología Social, Estado de Puebla, and Fondo de Cultura Económica, Mexico City.

CHAPTER 37

THE INDEPENDENT REPUBLIC OF TLAXCALLAN

LANE F. FARGHER, RICHARD E. BLANTON, AND VERENICE Y. HEREDIA ESPINOZA

THE Terminal Postclassic (A.D. 1350–1521) was an era of conquest states and large empires in western Mesoamerica. In West Mexico, the Tarascan Empire (Fisher this volume) controlled a large part of Michoacan, Jalisco, Guanajuato, Colima, and Guerrero. Much of Central Mexico (Basin of Mexico, Puebla, Morelos), the Gulf Coast (Veracruz), sections of the Pacific Coast, and Highland Oaxaca had been conquered by the Aztec Triple Alliance (Berdan et al. 1996). On the Pacific Coast of Oaxaca, Tututepec reigned supreme (Joyce et al. 2004). Yet, near the very center of this region, a scant 100 km from Tenochtitlan, the tiny state of Tlaxcallan successfully resisted repeated attempts by the Aztec Triple Alliance to force it into submission and remained the only fully autonomous polity in Central Mexico despite being completely surrounded by the Aztec Triple Alliance (Berdan et al. 1996:Figure II-1; Cortés 1963:44). How could a state that covered less than 2500 km^2, with maybe 100,000 to 200,000 inhabitants, resist the mighty Aztec Triple Alliance (Figure 37.1)?

Residents resisted by building an entirely new sociopolitical order that mobilized the hearts, souls, and bodies of the Tlaxcaltecan body politic in a way that allowed them to accomplish the improbable (see Fargher et al. 2010). Throughout the prehispanic era, the region that would become the state of Tlaxcallan maintained a strongly independent character ("local chauvinism"; Gibson 1952) through decentralization and dispersion (García Cook and Merino Carrión 1991). Up until the Terminal Postclassic, the Tlaxcalteca had neither unified into a single state nor been conquered by an imperial power (e.g., Teotihuacan, Cholula) (García Cook and Merino Carrión 1991). The Tlaxcalteca of the eastern subregion even remained independent and dispersed in the face of centralization at Xochitecatl-Cacaxtla during the Epiclassic (García Cook and Merino Carrión 1991). Thus, at the onset of the Terminal Postclassic, Tlaxcaltecan state-builders faced two important dilemmas. On the one hand, imperial power in the Basin

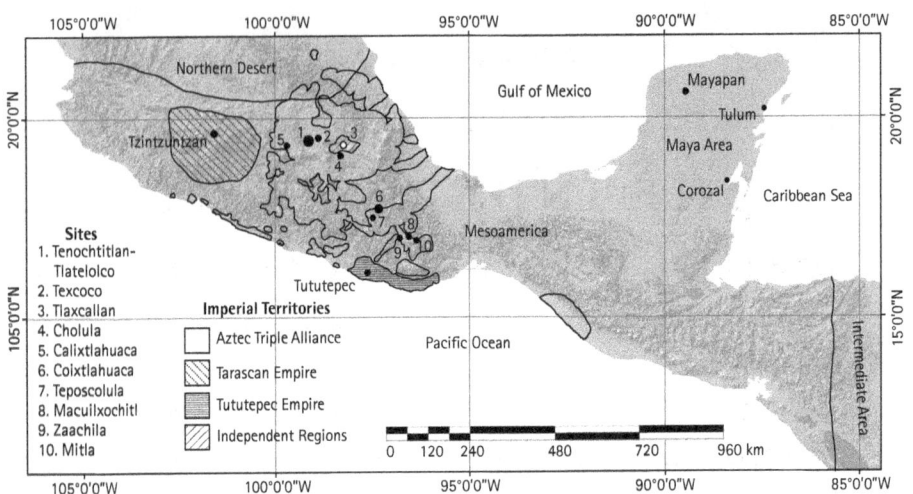

FIGURE 37.1 Map Showing the geopolitical position of Tlaxcallan in the Postclassic Mesoamerican world. Prepared by Lane F. Fargher, Kristin Sullivan, and David Romero.

of Mexico was being consolidated (first at Azcapotzalco and shortly thereafter in the Aztec Triple Alliance) with an eye toward expansion into the Puebla-Tlaxcala Valley, which posed a clear and present danger for Tlaxcallan. On the other hand, they faced the deeply rooted parochial character of the Tlaxcaltecas, which posed a strong barrier to uniting to defend the region. Under these conditions, the political architects devised an ingenious plan that promoted unification through collective action.

COLLECTIVE ACTION THEORY AND THE POLITICAL ORDER OF STATES

Collective action theory proposes that states emerge through cooperation among individuals or factions that make up a polity (the following is summarized from Blanton and Fargher 2008). Because these individuals or factions have divergent goals and diverse revenue endowments, principals (the chief governing agents of a state, e.g., kings, presidents, senators) must strike bargains with them to achieve stable political formations. Where a large constituency (e.g., commoners) controls revenues needed by the state (in the case of Tlaxcallan this was primarily military corvée), principals must make concessions with them to gain compliance with revenue demands. Cross-cultural research shows that principals interested in these types of revenues (known as internal revenues) implement a number of strategies to cultivate quasi-compliance with tax demands. They build trust among taxpayers by accepting limits on their personal power and consumption and by controlling the agency of their officials to demonstrate that they are committed to achieving collective agreements. They also employ strategies to identify and castigate free-riders or individuals that seek to benefit from collectivity without paying the requisite costs. Finally, they distribute public goods (e.g., public security, water management, road building and maintenance, food security) in exchange for compliance with tax payments. Conversely, where principals maintain direct control over revenue sources (e.g., patrimonial estates, mines, monopolies on long-distance exchange, etc.), they do not need to negotiate with constituents to achieve compliance and are, thus, largely free to behave despotically as well as to plow resources into conspicuous consumption and the construction of personal networks of power.

Tlaxcaltecan Collective Action

Recent research indicates that Tlaxcaltecan political architects employed collective strategies to achieve the degree of compliance with military corvée demands necessary to remain independent (Fargher et al. 2010; Fargher, Heredia Espinoza, and Blanton 2011). Specifically, they devised a multipronged strategy that included the construction of a new political configuration, the founding of a new capital, territorial reorganization, and strategies to develop trust and credibility among constituents.

Political Reorganization

The traditional political structure of the Puebla–Tlaxcala Valley, built around patrimonial estates (*teccalli*) and intense competition among powerful nobles (*teteuctin*) (see Fargher, Heredia Espinoza, and Blanton 2011:314–315), was ripped down to its foundation and reconstructed. The political apparatus that emerged in Tlaxcallan consisted of a ruling council that oversaw a newly bureaucratized administrative structure. First, supreme political authority was vested in a ruling council that consisted of somewhere between 50 and 200 titled officials. Together they reached decisions and set policy through debate and consensus (Fargher et al. 2010:238). Extant information indicates that the council had the power to declare war and peace, engage ambassadors, form alliances, and appoint and remove any political agent, including principals (*teteuctin*) (Fargher et al. 2010:237).

Second, the *teccalli* (or heritable patrimonial estate) was retasked as a territorial administrative unit (Fargher et al. 2010:237). Access to these new administrative positions was opened to individuals from across social sectors, and selection criteria included merit and were no longer based solely on ascription (Fargher et al. 2010:235–237). Thus, the ruling council raised to the status of *teuctli* individuals who had provided exceptional service in trade, religion, and, especially, warfare, regardless of social status. These persons were awarded a title, an administrative district (*teccalli*) from which revenue was drawn to offset administrative costs associated with governing it, and a seat on the ruling council (Fargher et al. 2010:237). Importantly, the lands of the *teccalli* were "attached" to the political office and were not the personal property of the official, which provided the state with more control over governing officials (Fargher et al. 2010:237). In exchange, the official agreed to provide military leadership and governing services under a strict behavioral code.

Ideological Reorganization

This new political order was undergirded by a radical change in ideology that replaced the traditional political ideology, that focused on Quetzalcoatl and elite status, with an emphasis on Tezcatlipoca as the linchpin of an egalitarian ideology (Fargher et al. 2010:239–244). The ideology associated with Tezcatlipoca foregrounded the value of individuals regardless of social status, making it possible to earn merit instead of just inheriting it through noble birth. Thus, the adoption of Tezcatlipoca and his cult paved the way for the recruitment of commoners and members of diverse ethnic groups (especially the Otomi) to governing positions, including positions on the ruling council, as a reward for service to the state. But it was also employed to legitimize an egalitarian legal philosophy in which all Tlaxcaltecas received equal treatment under the law regardless of social status.

Finally, this ideology played a key role in a grueling initiation rite associated with the promotion of individuals to *teuctli* status by the governing council (Fargher et al. 2010:238–239). First, the candidate's septum was pierced and he received an eagle's claw and a jaguar's bone signifying that he had accumulated great merit in military service to the state. From there, the candidate was presented to the public, who tore the clothes from his body, pushed him about, and insulted him. If the candidate remained calm, he then proceeded, naked, to the temple and lived there for one to two years. During this period of "penance" he fasted, was deprived of sleep for extended periods, received thrashings from priests wielding ropes lined with maguey spines, engaged in autosacrifice, and was instructed in a rigid code of moral behavior that stressed responsibility to the state and its people. At the end of this period, the candidate was dressed in rich cloth and given a bow, which represented his responsibility to lead in war, and a scepter, which represented his role as administrator and judge. Now clothed, the candidate officially received his title and lands and began his period in office by hosting a massive investiture feast attended by large numbers of nobles and commoners.

The Tezcatlipoca cult also acted as the basis for an inclusive Tlaxcaltecan identity that transcended ethnic divisions. All members of Tlaxcaltecan society participated in the induction rituals, as well as a statewide ritual cycle dedicated to Tezcatlipoca that took place every four years (described in Motolinía 1950:78–83). During the Tezcatlipoca festival, every adult, regardless of ethnic origin or gender, fasted for the 20 days leading up to the event. Then on the designated day, everyone descended on his or her local temple, where (s)he offered blood through autosacrifice to Tezcatlipoca and participated in extensive state-funded festivals and pageants. Such large-scale inclusive rituals helped sustain a strong sense of a Tlaxcaltecan identity as well as stout patriotic sentiments. Inclusiveness is also indicated by the promotion of ethnic minorities (e.g., Otomi) to the ruling council and intermarriage among ethnic groups (e.g., Nahua–Otomi marriage).

Public Goods

Compliance with this new political system was rewarded with a rich supply of public goods. The state codified legal equality by developing a judiciary that offered impartial justice across social sectors. Descriptions from Spanish conquistadors indicate that the state effectively maintained public security and had the capacity to catch and punish criminals (Cortés 2007:64). Archaeological data and historic descriptions suggest that the state also invested in building and maintaining roads and highways (Fargher, Blanton, Heredia Espinoza, Millhauser, et al. 2011; Muñoz Camargo 1999). The multitude of public ceremonies also functioned to redistribute large amounts of foodstuffs and goods among citizens. For example, Toribio Motolinía (1971:341–343) describes public festivals (including induction ceremonies) where approximately 1,500 turkeys were consumed, along with *pulque*, cacao, and tortillas, indicating that thousands of Tlaxcaltecas participated in these state-sponsored prestational events. Although only cloth is mentioned, these events probably involved significant distributions of other goods (e.g., pottery, obsidian, baskets, etc.). Finally, and most importantly, the state provided effective military leadership, protecting Tlaxcallan from attacks by the Aztec Triple Alliance and its allies.

A New Capital

Concurrently with the reorganization of the political structure, Tlaxcaltecan state-builders established a new capital in a previously unoccupied location near the geographical center of the prehspanic state in Tizatlan (Fargher, Blanton, Heredia Espinoza, Millhauser, et al. 2011). The selection of a neutral location without a history of occupation was vital to the new political formulation because it provided a symbolic break with previous political ideologies that were associated with other geographic location (e.g., Xochitecatl-Cacaxtla), and it did not preferentially empower any *teuctli* by locating the capital in his *teccalli* (see Blanton 1976). The state constructed a massive platform at this site, which (we suspect) supported an immense plaza and public buildings, but residences (especially palaces) were not built at this location. Thus Tizatlan was founded as a true disembedded capital and remained so throughout the prehispanic era.

As part of this strategy, urban settlement was apparently displaced to a zone about 1 km from the site of the capital, and as a result no single *teuctli* could accrue political benefits by controlling the capital (Fargher, Blanton, Heredia Espinoza, Millhauser, et al. 2011). Furthermore, the massive urban settlement constructed on the hills of Quiahuixtlan, Ocotelulco, and Tepeticpac was organized heterarchically, and no single plaza or monumental complex dominated the site. Archaeological research on this city also indicates that public building programs emphasized the construction of highly accessible plazas and low, open platforms with small temples, not elaborate private residences (palaces) or grandiose tombs.

Regional Reorganization

Using a collective strategy, Tlaxcaltecan state-builders were able to bring the entire territory of Tlaxcallan (an area covering 1500 - 2500 km^2) under a single political structure for the first time in history (Fargher et al. 2010; García Cook and Merino Carrión 1991; Gibson 1952). They were successful, in part, in incorporating this territory because they offered the dominant *teuctli* (or *tlahtoani*) of settlements located outside the core of the polity a seat on Tlaxcallan's ruling council. Such an inclusive strategy and the ideology associated with it not only brought these settlements into the system, but it also provided for the successful military mobilization of the populations in outlying settlements in defense of the Tlaxcaltecan republic. Descriptions from Early Colonial chroniclers reveal the fierce loyalty of Otomi settlements situated between the Tlaxcaltecan core and Acolhuacan, as well as their willingness to fight and die for Tlaxcallan (Durán 1994:453–458; Muñoz Camargo 1998:136–137, 1999:182). Despite being located on the edge of its territory and belonging to an ethnic minority, these Otomi claimed Tlaxcallan as their own and did not consider themselves as tributaries or vassals of the core Nahua population.

Discussion—The Collective Action Payoff

The multipronged strategy employed by Tlaxcaltecan state-builders was very costly both in terms of administrative expenditures and the loss of personal income and reduced conspicuous consumption on the part of the "élite" that had formerly controlled large personal estates. However, despite this, the payoff was enormous for both commoners and nobility. By developing trust and credibility among constituents through opportunities to advance socially and politically, the distribution of public goods, the fair treatment commoners and ethnic minorities in judicial matters, and placing limits on conspicuous consumption, Tlaxcaltecan state-builders achieved compliance levels with respect to tax and corvée demands that were probably unrivaled anywhere in Terminal Postclassic Mesoamerica. Compliance translated into the flow of enormous amounts of goods, foodstuffs, and corvée into state coffers despite a comparatively small population and the economic strains associated with Aztec embargos. The collective strategy employed in this case also provided a mechanism for integrating refugee Otomi who were fleeing oppression by the Aztec Triple Alliance, settling them along the frontier, and deploying their military prowess and anger against the Aztec. All of this translated into the construction of a powerful and motivated military force that was able to fend off repeated conquest attempts by the mighty Aztec Triple Alliance. Commoner and noble, Nahua and Otomi alike offered themselves up as sacrifices in temples to Tezcatlipoca and, most importantly, on the battlefield to the idea of an independent, just, and egalitarian Tlaxcallan. Commoners for their part enjoyed a rich supply of public goods and the possibility to rise socially, conditions that they would have been keen to defend. At the same time, the nobility did not have to face a military defeat that would have reduced their private land holdings and forced them to pay large amounts of tribute to the Aztec Triple Alliance.

References Cited

Berdan, Frances F., Richard E. Blanton, Elizabeth Hill Boone, Mary G. Hodge, Michael E. Smith and Emily Umberger
1996 *Aztec Imperial Strategies*. Dumbarton Oaks Research Library and Collection, Washington, DC.
Blanton, Richard E.
1976 Anthropological Studies of Cities. *Annual Review of Anthropology* 5:249–264.
Blanton, Richard E., and Lane F. Fargher
2008 *Collective Action in the Formation of Pre-Modern States*. Springer, New York.
Cortés, Hernán
1963 *Cartas y documentos*. Editorial Porrúa, Mexico City.
2007 *Cartas de Relación*. Grupo Editorial Exodo, Mexico City.
Durán, Diego
1994 *The History of the Indies of New Spain*. University of Oklahoma Press, Norman.
Fargher, Lane F., Richard E. Blanton, and Verenice Y. Heredia Espinoza
2010 Egalitarian Ideology and Political Power in Prehispanic Central Mexico: The Case of Tlaxcallan. *Latin American Antiquity* 3:227–251.
Fargher, Lane F., Richard E. Blanton, Verenice Y. Heredia Espinoza, John Millhauser, Nezahualcoyotl Xiuhtecutli, and Lisa Overholtzer
2011 Tlaxcallan: The Archaeology of an Ancient Republic in the New World. *Antiquity* 85:172–186.
Fargher, Lane F., Verenice Y. Heredia Espinoza, and Richard E. Blanton
2011 Alternative Pathways to Power in Late Postclassic Highland Mesoamerica. *Journal of Anthropological Archaeology* 30:306–326.
García Cook, Angel, and Beatriz L. Merino Carrión
1991 *Tlaxcala: textos de su historia*, Vol. 3: *Los orígenes: arqueología*. Consejo Nacional para la Cultura y las Artes y Gobierno del Estado de Tlaxcala, Tlaxcala, Mexico.
Gibson, Charles
1952 *Tlaxcala in the Sixteenth Century*. Yale University Press, New Haven, CT.
Joyce, Arthur, Andrew Workinger, Byron Hamann, Peter Kroefges, Maxine Oland, and Stacie King

2004 Lord 8 Deer "Jaguar Claw" and the Land of the Sky: The Archaeology and History of Tututepec. *Latin American Antiquity* 15:273–97.

Motolinía, Toribio

1950 *History of the Indians of New Spain.* Cortés Society, Berkeley, CA.

1971 *Memoriales.* Instituto de Investigaciones Históricas, Universidad Nacional Autónoma de México, Mexico City.

Muñoz Camargo, Diego

1998 *Historia de Tlaxcala.* Gobierno del Estado de Tlaxcala, Centro de Investigaciones y Estudios Superiores en Antropología Social Universidad Autónoma de Tlaxcala, Tlaxcala, Mexico.

1999 *Relaciones geográficas de Tlaxcala (descripción de la ciudad y provincia de Tlaxcala de las Indias y del mar).* El Colegio de San Luis, San Luis Potosí, and Gobierno del Estado de Tlaxcala, Tlaxcala, Mexico.

CHAPTER 38

THE TARASCAN (PURÉPECHA) EMPIRE

ANNA S. COHEN AND CHRISTOPHER T. FISHER

At the time of European contact, western Mexico was dominated by a population known as the Tarascos with a distinctive language (Purépecha), customs, and centralized sociopolitical system that is best characterized as an empire. During the two centuries prior to European Conquest, the Purépecha Empire at times controlled more than 75,000 km² of the modern state of Michoacán as well as parts of Guerrero, Jalisco, Colima, and Guanajuato (Figure 38.1). The supreme ruler (*cazonci*) operated from the imperial capital of Tzintzuntzan in the Lake Pátzcuaro Basin, Michoacán. Never defeated by the bordering Aztec Empire, the Purépecha instituted a bureaucratic system that was designed to extract tribute from subjects and control political, economic, and social life throughout their territory.

Current archaeological research in the region centers on identifying social and environmental processes that allowed Purépecha elite to consolidate political and economic power during the Late Postclassic period (A.D. 1350–1522) to become the dominant force in western Mexico. Ethnohistoric investigation suggests that existing sociopolitical heterogeneity in western Mexico was co-opted by Purépecha tribute-based and ideological systems (Gorenstein and Pollard 1983; Pollard 2008; Warren 1985), but this remains to be tested archaeologically (Figure 38.2). According to the official Purépecha history documented in the *Relación de Michoacán* (RM) (2000 [1541]), by A.D. 1350 leader Taríacuri and his descendants had successfully subjugated and consolidated small polities in the Lake Pátzcuaro Basin. This was followed by territorial conquest in western Mexico through ideological manipulation, intermarriage, and control of resources.

In this chapter we review archaeological and ethnohistoric evidence for Purépecha Empire development both from the LPB core region and elsewhere in the empire. These data suggest that there was a spectrum of state–local relations that were more complex than that shown by ethnohistory alone. We conclude with a discussion of recent models of Purépecha complexity, including data from archaeological work within the LPB. Emerging research shows how the Purépecha regime developed over a long trajectory in

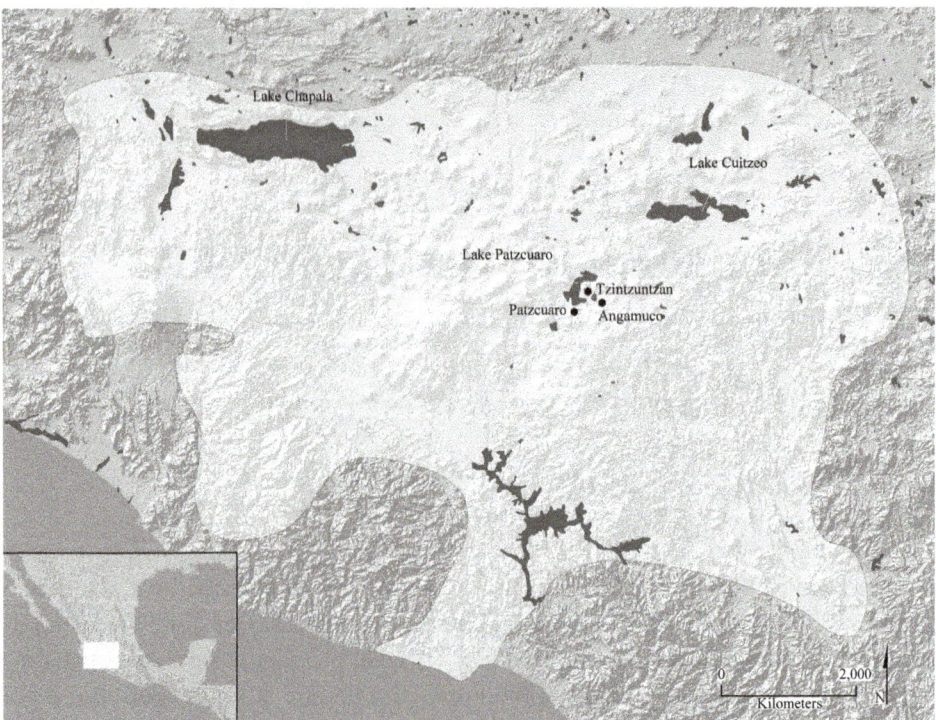

FIGURE 38.1 Map of the Tarascan Empire showing major archaeological sites within the Lake Pátzcuaro Basin, Michoacán, Mexico. Drawing by author.

western Mexico, engaging in a series of negotiations that can be documented over multiple centuries of social, political, and economic change.

Purépecha Governance in Ethnohistory

Between the fourteenth and early sixteenth centuries, the Purépecha are thought to have established the most consolidated and centralized empire in Postclassic Mesoamerica (A.D. 1000–1522) (Beekman 2010; Pollard 2012; Smith and Berdan 2003). This was due in part to the highly centralized bureaucratic system instituted by the Purépecha elite that is described in the partially preserved RM. As told to Franciscan priest Fray Jeronimo de Acalá by Purépecha noblemen around A.D. 1539, this official history of the Purépecha describes how the seminomadic *uacúsecha* ("eagle") lineage migrated from the Zacapu Basin to the Pátzcuaro Basin in the early 1300s (see also Beaumont 1932:ch. 7). After defeating several chiefdoms in the region, leader Taríacuri ruled from the city of Pátzcuaro and installed his newphews Híripan and Tángaxoan as lords of

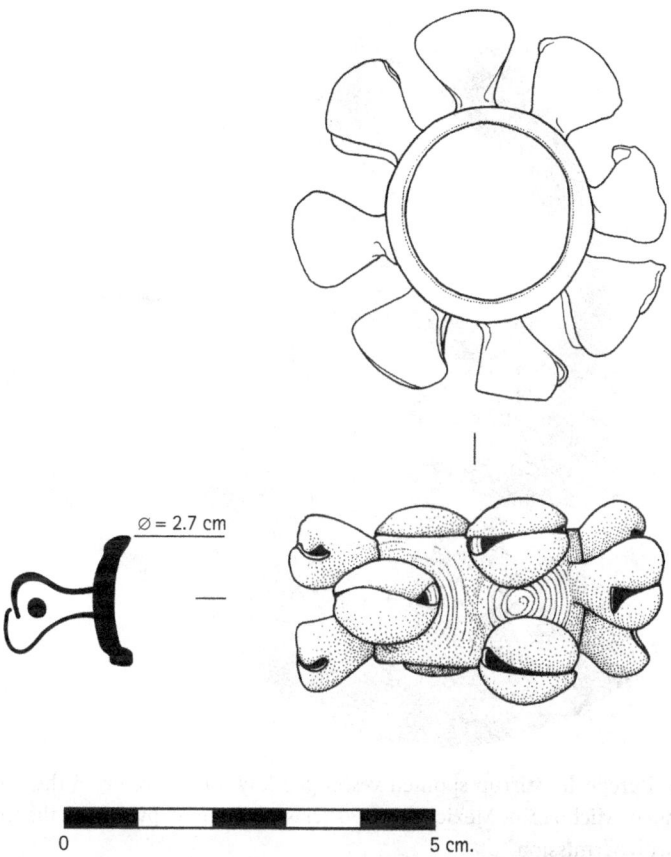

FIGURE 38.2 Rattle for a Purépecha thunderstick composed of multiple bells around a central ring. From the cemetery at the site of Angamuco, Michoacán, Mexico, Late Postclassic. Drawing by Daniel Salazar Lama for the LORE-LPB project.

the cities of Ihuatzio and Tzintzuntzan. Their descendants expanded the Purépecha Empire throughout western Mexico, instituting a tributary system and an administrative bureaucracy centered in the Pátzcuaro Basin. This system functioned by appointing a tribute collector (*ocámbecha*) for every 25 households who then submitted payments to the central authority in Tzintzuntzan (Beltrán 1994). Tribute largely varied by settlement. For example, at the high-ranking site of Acámbaro located on the northeastern border of the empire, inhabitants paid corn, food stuffs, and blankets to Tzintzuntzan while Pátzcuaro Basin residents may have paid tribute in labor (Aguilar González 2005; Beaumont 1932:64–69). The RM also lists numerous officials who were in charge of each aspect of craft production and resource procurement, ranging from hunting, woodwork, and pottery production to *pulque* and honey processing (RM 2000:558–572). In other words, this coordination of tax collection, leadership, and political economic activity throughout the empire was controlled by a highly centralized system.

FIGURE 38.3 Purépecha stirrup spouted vessel possibly for cacao. From the cemetery at the site of Angamuco, Michoacán, Mexico, Late Postclassic. Photo copyright of the the LORE-LPB project, used with permission.

Aspects of Purépecha social and religious life are illustrated in the RM, including architecture, social organization, customs, and material culture. For example, distinctive "Purépecha-style" ceramic artifacts such as Polychrome spouted vessels, miniatures, elaborate pipes, and animal effigy vessels called *patojas* appear in the RM and have been documented archaeologically in the Pátzcuaro Basin and elsewhere in Late Postclassic contexts in western Mexico (Figure 38.3) (e.g. Arnauld et al. 1993; Castro Leal 1986; Hernández 2000; Macias Goytia 1989, 1990; Pollard 1993; Porter 1948; Ramírez and Cárdenas 2006).

Metallurgy, which also appears in the RM, was strongly associated with elite culture and played a significant role in the structure of political economic power. For example, copper ingots and items such as tweezers and bells were given as gifts to foreign visitors and by regional elites to the king, and as tribute to state storehouses in the Pátzcuaro Basin (Pollard 1993:119).

The Purépecha were associated with distinctive architecture, such as the *yácata*, which was a semicircular rubble-filled pyramid faced with dressed stone slabs that sometimes had petroglyphs and a perishable structure on top (Figure 38.4). These pyramids were devoted to the main deity Curicuaeri and were related to religious practices

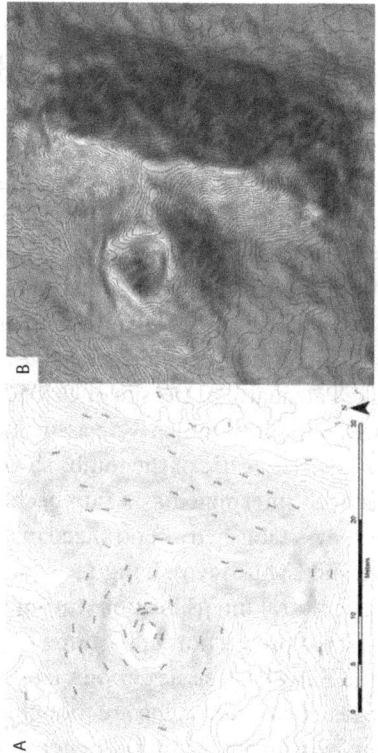

FIGURE 38.4 Traditional *yácata*-style pyramid composed of a rectilinear and circular element, from the site of Angamuco, Michoacán, Mexico. (A) Shows a plan view of this feature as a 5 cm contour map; (B) shows a perspective view of this same feature using the same contour map overlain on a hillshade. All features derived from a 0.25 cm digital elevation model created from high resolution LiDAR data. Prepared by author

such as human sacrifice in major settlements. The recovery of several elite individuals exhibiting dental modification and grave goods associated with the Tzintzuntzan *yacatas* indicate that they were also used in mortuary contexts (Moedano 1941; Rubín de la Barbolla 1939, 1941).

During the fifteenth and sixteenth centuries, the Purépecha fought a number of wars against the Aztecs and their allies, but they never lost against the larger empire (Durán 1967:282; Garcia Payón 1941:80). Purépecha rulers were aware of Spanish presence due to an intricate network of spies in Aztec territories and later due to several Aztec emissaries sent to Tzintzuntzan requesting aid. The Purépecha refused to help their enemies against the Europeans. Around this time, political in-fighting in the Purépecha capital weakened the king, which led him to secretly escape the city to regain control of his territory (Pollard 1993; Warren 1985). When Spanish general Cristóbal de Olid arrived at Tzintzuntzan in A.D. 1522, *cazonci* Tangáxuan II submitted to the Spanish without resistance and ruled with partial independence until his execution in A.D. 1530 (Beaumont 1932:ch. 5).

Archaeological Perspectives in the Imperial Core and Beyond

Archaeological research has examined this ethnohistoric model by looking at how the Purépecha regime controlled elite identity, economy, and border zones to the north. In the Pátzcuaro Basin, scholars have argued that political changes were facilitated by environmental fluctuations and associated population growth (Fisher et al. 2003; Gorenstein and Pollard 1983; Pollard 2008). The development and consolidation of the Purépecha Empire was visible in the construction of *yácatas*, elite artifacts, and increasing populations around Lake Pátzcuaro. At the site of Urichu, Pollard and Cahue (1999) argued that Lupe phase (A.D. 600–900) tombs were associated with imported and luxury grave goods while later Postclassic use of the tombs shows localized exploitation of upper-class items. This has been interpreted as a Purépecha elite emphasis on home-grown symbols of power as they established a centralized imperial base in the Pátzcuaro Basin (Pollard 2008; Pollard and Cahue 1999). Long-term landscape modification in the Pátzcuaro area included agricultural intensification during the Late Postclassic, which is understood as state-sponsored production in part due to population growth (Fisher 2005). During the Classic and Early Postclassic periods, landscape degradation and subsequent recuperative strategies such as terracing are thought to be a result of increasing populations and social complexity in the region (Fisher et al. 2003).

Resource Extraction and Production

Research into resource exploitation and production shows that while the Purépecha Empire may have exacted tribute from its subjects, craft production was not under direct state control. For example, the primary supplier of copper was the central Balsas Basin in the southern portion of Purépecha territory, but there is evidence that smelting—one of several key production steps—occurred in other areas such as the Zirahuén Basin (south of Pátzcuaro) (Hosler and MacFarlane 1996; Maldonado and Rehren 2009). After copper ingots were produced, they were sent to yet another location for final processing. This means that intermittent specialists, who carried out copper production steps such as smelting in addition to other activities such as farming, were probably key players in the broader political economic system (Maldonado 2009). Moreover, imperial involvement in production varied and economic integration was probably very local.

Lithic and ceramic production studies reflect a similar pattern. Obsidian, which is not local to the imperial core, was primarily exploited during the Late Postclassic from the Ucareo-Zinapecuaro source in Michoacán (Rebnegger 2013). This source was used throughout central and western Mexico during the preceding time periods but was largely limited to the Purépecha territories during imperial consolidation (Pollard and Vogel 1994). This may have been because the Purépecha wanted direct control over the

Ucareo-Zinapecuaro source area, which was in a strategic region near the Aztec Empire (Healan 2009; Hernández and Healan 2008). Importantly, however, the empire did not control all aspects of production since obsidian items continued to be processed by part-time specialists and in households throughout western Mexico (Darras 2008, 2009). Pottery manufacture at sites in the Pátzcuaro Basin may also have been local though with clear stylistic changes during the Late Postclassic. Comparison of ceramics between the Classic and Postclassic periods at the site of Urichu and Postclassic ceramics from Tzintzuntzan suggest that Purépecha pottery emerged from a long tradition of local forms and motifs rather than from top-down, state-controlled production (Hirshman et al. 2010; Hirshman and Ferguson 2012).

The Zacapu Basin

Work in the Zacapu Basin—ancestral home of the *uacúsecha* lineage—has sought to establish a model of long-term occupation before and during early Purépecha Empire formation (Arnauld et al. 1993; Darras 1998; Michelet 1992). Excavations at the site of Loma Alta have documented a Preclassic and Classic period (100 B.C.–A.D. 550) ancient island cemetery and ceremonial center with square and circular platforms and sunken plazas (Carot 2001, 2013). Loma Alta artwork included rounded-base figurines, polychrome ceramic vessels, and over 40 motifs that influenced art throughout Michoacán during the Classic period (Filini 2004; Macías Goytia 1990; Manzanilla López 1988; Pollard 2003). These motifs also appear in Postclassic contexts suggesting that the Purépecha used earlier designs as symbols of past local societies, possibly in an effort to perpetuate sociopolitical legitimacy in the region (Carot 2013). During the Later Classic and Epiclassic periods, Zacapu Basin art was influenced by Teotihuacan and Tula workmanship, including depictions of warfare and pyrite discs (the *tezcacuitlapilli*) (Pereira 1999; cf. Kelly 1947:125–127; Piña Chan and Oí 1982:Figure 25). Around this time, existing communities and new migrants began to build cities on raised lava flows (*malpaís*), eventually creating an urban zone that extended more than 4 km². Movement to these inhospitable settlements may have been due to population growth and for defense, though there is no evidence for warfare (Michelet 2000). Artifacts from these urban sites show pre-Purépecha vessel forms and styles that may have been precursors to Late Postclassic Purépecha artifacts elsewhere (Forest 2014; Jadot 2016). By the mid-fifteenth century, the *malpaís* sites were abandoned for environmental and political economic reasons (Michelet 2010; Migeon 2003).

The Imperial Borderlands

Settlements along the Purépecha border regions reveal a mixed picture of imperial consolidation and porosity. Along the regime's northeastern border, between the states of Michoacán, Hidalgo, Querétaro, and México, there is evidence for different ethnic communities (e.g. Otomí, Matlatzinca, Nahuatl, and Purépecha speakers) throughout the Postclassic who may have served as a "buffer" between the warring Aztecs and Purépecha (Hernández 2000; Hernández and Healan 2008). Borderland fortress communities retained distinct practices despite allegiance to their respective kings in Tzintzuntzan or Tenochtitlan (Gorenstein 1985; Lefebvre 2012; Silverstein 2001). In northern Michoacán in the Cuitzeo Basin, Purépecha objects and local ceramics have been recovered in association with temples and tombs, indicating contemporaneous Purépecha and non-Purépecha populations (Macías Goytia 1989, 1990). In the Sayula Basin, Jalisco, Purépecha elite ceramics and other artifacts were found exclusively in local elite burials, suggesting that Purépecha symbols were exported and used to constitute authority in heterogeneous border regions (Acosta Nieva 1996; Ramírez and Cárdenas 2006).

Recent Perspectives on Purépecha Development

Archaeological work over the past few decades has sought to problematize the limited ethnohistorical accounts of Purépecha development and governance (Arnauld et al. 1993; Carot 2013; Darras 1998; Gorenstein 1985; Fisher 2005; Fisher et al. 2003; Hernández and Healan 2008; Michelet 1992, 2000, 2010; Pereira 1999; Pollard 1993, 2008). One perspective that has become increasingly clear is that the Purépecha Empire did not emerge in a vacuum during the Late Postclassic but was rather the product of long-term changes throughout western Mexico. Postclassic artifact styles and motifs have their roots in earlier Preclassic- to Classic-period Chupicuaro and Loma Alta traditions, and artifact changes do not reflect significant ruptures over time (e.g. Carot 2013; Michelet 2013; Pollard 2003, 2008, 2012). A long-term model of Purépecha complexity and change provides an important foundation for understanding localized practices in both the Pátzcuaro area and elsewhere in the Late Postclassic imperial territories. Less clear, however, is the mechanisms for empire formation and the changes in internal social, political, and economic structure that must have occurred in preimperial contexts. How did Purépecha leadership subjugate existing local communities? How were particular domestic and social practices affected during subject incorporation, and when did this occur?

In the imperial core region, recent work at the ancient city of Angamuco is providing information about such local changes during the Postclassic period. Located on a *malpaís* land form approximately 9 km southeast of Tzintzuntzan, Angamuco was occupied from at least the Early to Late Postclassic periods (A.D. 900–1522), with a primary occupation before and during imperial changes in the Postclassic. Full-coverage pedestrian survey and Light Detection and Ranging (LiDAR) data have aided in the documentation of over 7,000 architectural features in recent years (Fisher and Leisz 2013). The LiDAR analysis shows that the city was at least 12 km² and comprised of over 20,000 stone architectural features such as *yácatas*, roads, terraces, and domestic structures (Chase et al. 2012; Fisher et al. 2011; Fisher and Leisz 2013). The discovery of this previously unknown city demonstrates that complex urban centers existed in the core region before the Purépecha established their empire. This is particularly significant because if a large population of people was living in the Pátzcuaro area before imperial consolidation, this means that the path to imperial development must have occurred earlier than previously thought.

Based on research at Angamuco since 2009, a working model of site occupation has been established (Fisher and Leisz 2013). During the Early Postclassic (A.D. 900–1200), inhabitants lived in sunken plaza complexes and consumed artifacts that are similar to those documented in the Bajío region and elsewhere in Michoacán during the Classic to Epiclassic periods (Cárdenas 1999; Piña Chan and Oí 1982; Pomédio et al. 2013). This was followed by major growth and expansion during the Middle Postclassic (A.D. 1200–1350) when building platforms and walls were clustered in distinct areas with rectilinear or semicircular pyramid complexes and ceramic artifacts are similar to those documented at the *malpaís* sites in the Zacapu Basin (Arnauld et al. 1993; Michelet 2000; Pereira and Forest 2011; Pereira et al. 2012). The final phase of occupation is represented by a contraction of the settlement area during the Late Postclassic (A.D. 1350–1522) with a focus around Purépecha imperial-style architecture such as large *yácatas* and plazas. A high degree of social differentiation and an emphasis on public ritual activities suggests that Angamuco at this time was organized like other Late Postclassic sites in the Pátzcuaro Basin, such as Ihuatzio (Acosta 1939).

As these data show, the origins of the Purépecha Empire were significantly more complex than the narrative described in ethnohistoric texts. If the Purépecha did emerge from a long trajectory of social, economic, and material practices in the Pátzcuaro Basin, then they had to negotiate with existing cities with complex bureaucratic systems and large populations. Ongoing archaeological research at sites like Angamuco will investigate these negotiations in an effort to document the alternative pathways to political control in western Mexico.

References Cited

Acosta Nieva, Rosario
1996 Los patrones de enterramiento en la cuenca de Sayula a través de tiempo. In *Estudios de Hombre*, No. 3, edited by Otto Schondude Baumbach, pp. 65–80. Universidad de Guadalajara, Guadalajara.

Aguilar González, José
2005 *Tzintzuntzan irechequa: política y sociedad en el estado Tarasco*. Tesis de Licenciatura, Facultad de Historia, Universidad de Michoacana, Morelia, Mexico.

Arnauld, Charlotte, Patricia Carot, and Marie-France Fauvet-Barthelot (editors)
1993 *Arqueología de las lomas en la cuenca lacustre de Zacapu, Michoacán, México*. Centro de Estudios Mexicanos y Centroamericanos, Mexico City.

Beaumont, Pablo
1932 *Crónica de Michoacán*, Vol. 2. Talleres gráficos de la nación, Mexico City.

Beekman, Christopher
2010 Recent Research in Western Mexican Archaeology. *Journal of Archaeological Research* 18:41–109.

Beltrán, Ulises
1994 Estado y sociedad tarascos en la época prehispánica. In *El Michoacán Antiguo*, edited by B. Boehm de Lameiras, pp. 29–163. El Colegio de Michoacán/Gobierno del Estado de Michoacán, Mexico.

Cárdenas García, Efraín
1999 *El Bajío en el Clásico: análisis regional y organización política*. El Colegio de Michoacán, Zamora, Mexico.

Carot, Patricia
2001 *Le Site de Loma Alta, Lac de Zacapu, Michoacan, Mexique*. Paris Monographs in American Archaeology 9. Archaeopress, Oxford.
2013 La large historia purépecha. In *Miradas renovadas al occidente indígena de México*, edited by Ángel Aedo, Patricia Carot, Verónica Hernández, and Marie Areti Hers, pp. 133–214. Conaculta, Institute Nacional de Antropologia e Historia, Centro de Estudios Mexicanos y Centroamericanos, Mexico City.

Castro Leal, Marcia
1986 *Tzintzuntzan, Capital de los Tarascos*. Gobierno del Estado de Michoacán, Morelia, Mexico.

Chase, Arlen, Diane Chase, Christopher Fisher, Stephen Leisz, and John Weishampel
2012 The Geospatial Revolution Mesoamerican Archaeology. *Proceedings of the National Academy of Sciences* 109(32):12916–12921

Darras, Véronique
2008 Estrategias para la producción de navajas en la región de Zacapu y la Vertiente del Lerma (Michoacan, México) entre el Epiclásico y el Posclásico Tardío. *Ancient Mesoamerica* 19:243–264.
2009 Peasant Artisans: Household Prismatic Blade Production in the Zacapu Region, Michoácan (Milpillas Phase 1200–1450 AD). *Archaeological Papers of the American Anthropological Association* 19(1):92–114.

Darras, Véronique (editor)
1998 *Génesis, culturas y espacios en Michoacán*. Centro de Estudios de Mesoamericano y Centroamericano, Mexico City.

Durán, Fray Diego
1967 *Historia de las Indias de Nueva España e Islas de Tierra Firme*, Vol. II. Translated by Angel Garibay K. Editorial Porrua, Mexico City.

Filini, Agapi
2004 *The Presence of Teotihuacan in the Cuitzeo Basin, Michoacán, Mexico: A World-Systems Perspective*. British Archaeological Reports International Series 1279. Archeopress, Oxford.

Fisher, Christopher T.
2005 Demographic and Landscape Change in the Lake Patzcuaro Basin, Mexico: Abandoning the Garden. *American Anthropologist* 107(1):87–95.

Fisher, Christopher T., and Stephen J. Leisz
2013 New Perspectives on Purépecha Urbanism through the Use of LiDAR at the Site of Angamuco, Mexico. In *Space Archaeology: Mapping Ancient Landscapes with Air and*

Spaceborne Imagery, edited by Douglas Comer and Michael Harrower, pp. 199–210. Springer, New York.

Fisher, Christopher T., Stephen J. Leisz, and Gary Outlaw

2011 LiDAR: A Valuable Tool Uncovers an Ancient City in Mexico. *Photogrammetric Engineering and Remote Sensing* 77(1):963–967.

Fisher, Christopher T., Helen P. Pollard, Isabel Israde-Alcántara, Victor H. Garduño-Monroy, and Subir Banerjee

2003 A Reexamination of Human-Induced Environmental Change within the Lake Patzcuaro Basin, Michoacan, Mexico. *Proceedings of the National Academy of Sciences* 100(8):4957–4962.

Forest, Marion

2014 L'Organisation Sociospatiale des Sites Urbains du Malpaís Zacapu, Michoacan, Mexique [1250–1450 après J.-C.]. Ph.D. dissertation, Université de Paris I, Paris.

Garcia Payón, José

1941 *Matlatzincas o Pirindas*. Ediciones Encuademables de El Nacional, Mexico City.

Gorenstein, Shirley

1985 *Acámbaro: Frontier Settlement on the Aztec-Purépecha Border*. Vanderbilt University Publications in Anthropology No. 32. Vanderbilt University, Nashville, TN.

Gorenstein, Shirley, and Helen P. Pollard

1983 *The Purépecha Civilization: A Late Prehispanic Cultural System*. Vanderbilt University Publications in Anthropology No. 28. Vanderbilt University, Nashville, TN.

Healan, Dan M.

2009 Ground Platform Preparation and the Banalization of the Prismatic Blade. *Ancient Mesoamerica* 20(1):103–111.

Hernández, Christine L.

2000 A History of Prehispanic Ceramics, Settlement, and Frontier Development in the Ucareo-Zinapécuaro Obsidian Source Area, Michoacán. Ph.D. dissertation, Tulane University, New Orleans.

Hernández, Christine L., and Dan Healan

2008 The Role of Late Pre-Contact Colonial Enclaves in the Development of the Postclassic Ucareo Valley, Michoacán, Mexico. *Ancient Mesoamerica* 19(1):265–282.

Hirshman, Amy, and Jeffrey R. Ferguson

2012 Temper Texture Models and Assessing Ceramic Complexity in the Emerging Purépecha State. *Journal of Archaeological Science* 39(10):3195–3207.

Hirshman, Amy, William A. Lovis, and Helen P. Pollard

2010 Specialization of Ceramic Production: A Sherd Assemblage Based Analytical Perspective. *Journal of Anthropological Archaeology* 29(3):265–277.

Hosler, Dorothy, and Andrew MacFarlane

1996 Copper Sources, Metal Production, and Metals Trade in Late Postclassic Mesoamerica. *Science* 273:1819–1824.

Jadot, Elsa

2016 Productions Céramiques et Mobilités dans la Région Tarasque de Zacapu (Michoacán, Mexique), Continuités et Ruptures Techniques entre 850 et 1450 après J.-C. Ph.D. dissertation, Université de Paris I, Paris.

Kelly, Isabel

1947 *Excavations at Apatzingan, Michoacan*. Wenner-Gren, Johnson, NY.

Lefebvre, Karine
2012 L'Occupation du Sol dans la Région d'Acámbaro entre le Postclassique Récent et le XVIe siècle. Ph.D. dissertation, Université de Paris I, Paris.

Macías Goytia, Angelina
1989 La Cuenca de Cuitzeo. In *Historia General de Michoacán*, Vol. 1, edited by Enrique Florescano, pp. 171–190. Gobierno del Estado de Michoacán, Morelia, Mexico.
1990 *Huandacareo: Lugar de Juicios, Tribunal*. Colección Científica No. 34. Instituto Nacional de Antropología e Historia, Mexico City.

Maldonado, Blanca
2009 Metal for the Commoners: Purépecha Metallurgical Production in Domestic Contexts. *Archaeological Papers of the American Anthropological Association* 19(1):225–238.

Maldonado, Blanca, and Thilo Rehren
2009 Early Copper Smelting at Itziparátzico, Mexico. *Journal of Archaeological Science* 36:1998–2006.

Manzanilla López, Rubén
1988 Salvamento arqueológico en Loma de Santa María, Morelia, Michoacán. In *Primera Reunión sobre las sociedades prehispánicas en el centro occidente de México*, pp. 151–160. Centro Regional de Querétaro, Instituto Nacional de Antropología e Historia, Mexico City.

Michelet, Dominique
2000 "Yácatas" y otras estructuras ceremoniales tarascas en el Malpaís de Zacapu, Michoacán. In *Arqueología, historia y antropología*. In memoriam *José Luis Lorenzo Bautista*, edited by Jaime Litvak K. and L. Mirambell, pp. 117–137. Colección Científica 415. Instituto Nacional de Antropología e Historia, Mexico City.
2010 De palabras y piedras: reflexiones en torno a las relaciones entre arqueología e historia en el Michoacán protohistórico, sector de Zacapu. *Revista de Historia Internacional* 11(43):27–43.
2013 Cerámicas del centro-norte de Michoacán entre el clásico y el posclásico. In *Tradiciones cerámicas en al Bajío y regiones aledañas: cronología e interacción*, edited by Cholé Pomédio, Grégory Pereira, and Eugenia Fernández-Villaneuva, pp. 91–103. British Archaeological Reports International Series, Paris.

Michelet, Dominique (editor)
1992 *El Proyecto Michoacán 1983–1987. Medio Ambiente e Introducción a los Trabajos Arqueológicos*. Centre Français d'Études Mexicaines et Centraméricaines, Mexico City.

Migeon, Gerard
2003 Abandonos programados, rituales de "matanza" o de terminación, y reocupaciones: los casos de los sitios del Cerro Barajas, Guanajuato y de Milpillas en el Malpaís de Zacapu, Michoacán. *Trace* 43:97–115.

Moedano, Hugo
1941 Estudio preliminar de la cerámica de Tzintzuntzan, Temporada III: 1939–1940. *Revista Mexicana de Estudios Antropológicos* 5(1):21–42.

Rubín de la Borbolla, Daniel F.
1939 Antropología Tzintzuntzan-Ihuatzio: Temporadas I y II. *Revista Mexicana de Estudios Anthropológicas* 3(2):99–121.
1941 Exploraciones arqueológicas en Michoacán: Tzintzuntzan Temporada III. *Revista Mexicana de Estudios Antropológicas* 5(1):5–20.

Pereira, Grégory
1999 *Potrero de Guadalupe: a Anthropologie funéraire d'une communauté pré-tarasque du nord du Michoacán, Mexique*. British Archaeological Reports International Series 816. Archaeopress, Oxford.

Piña Chan, Román, and Kuniaki Oí
1982 *Exploraciones arqueológicas en Tingambato, Michaocán*. Instituto Nacional de Antropología e Historia, Mexico City.

Pollard, Helen P.
1993 *Taríacuri's Legacy*. University of Oklahoma, Normal.
2003 La fase de Loma Alta en la cuenca de Pátzcuaro: unas raíces de la puebla Purépecha. In *Tradiciones Arqueológicas del Occidente de México*, edited by Efraín Cárdenas García, pp. 183–193. El Colegio de Michoacán, Zamora, Mexico.
2008 A Model of the Emergence of the Purépecha State. *Ancient Mesoamerica* 19:217–230.
2012 La economía política del almacenaje en el estado tarasco prehispánico. In *Almacenamiento prehispánico del norte de México al altiplano central*, edited by Séverine Bortot, Dominique Michelet, and Véronique Darras, pp. 131–144. Laboratoire Archaéologie des Amériques, Universidad Autónoma de San Luis Potosí, Université de Paris 1, Panthéon-Sorbonne, and Centro de Estudios Mexicanos y Centroamericanos, Mexico City.

Pollard, Helen P., and Laura Cahue
1999 Mortuary Patterns of Regional Elites in the Lake Patzcuaro Basin of Western Mexico. *Latin American Antiquity* 10(3):259–280.

Pollard, Helen P., and Thomas Vogel
1994 Implicaciones políticas y económicas del intercambio de obsidiana dentro del Estado Tarasco. In *Arqueología del Occidente de México*, edited by Eduardo Williams and Robert Novella, pp. 159–182. El Colegio de Michoacán, Zamora, Mexico.

Pomédio, Chloé, Grégory Pereira, and Eugenia Fernández-Villanueva (editors)
2013 *Tradiciones cerámicas del Epiclásico en el Bajío y regiones aledañas. Cronología e Interacción*. British Archaeological Reports International Series 2519. Paris Monographs in American Archaeology 31, Paris.

Porter, Muriel N.
1948 *Pipas precortesianas. Introducción de chita de la calle*. Acta Anthropologica 3, Vol. 2. Escuela Nacional de Antropología e Historia, Mexico City.

Ramírez Urrea, Susana, and Cinthya Cárdenas
2006 Análisis de la cerámica del postclásico. In *Transformaciones socioculturales y tecnológicas en el sitio de La Peña, Cuena de Sayula, Jalisco*, edited by Catherine Liot, Susana Ramírez, Javier Reveles, and Otto Schöndube, pp. 307–372. Instituto Nacional de Antropología e Historia, Universidad de Guadalajara, Guadalajara.

Rebnegger, Karin J.
2013 Obsidian Consumption and Production in the Tarascan State. Ph.D. dissertation, Michigan State University, East Lansing.

Relación de Michoacán
2000 *Relación de las ceremonias y rictos y población y gobernación de los indios de la provincia de Michoacán*. Edited by Moisés Franco Mendoza. El Colégio de Michoacán, Gobierno del Estado de Michoacán, Zamora, Mexico.

Silverstein, Jay
2001 Aztec Imperialism at Oztuma, Guerrero: Aztec-Chontal Relations during the Late Postclassic and Early Colonial Periods. *Ancient Mesoamerica* 12(1):31–48.

Smith, Michael E., and Frances F. Berdan
2003 Postclassic Mesoamerica. In *The Postclassic Mesoamerican World*, edited by M. E. Smith and F. F. Berdan, pp. 3–13. University of Utah Press, Salt Lake City.

Warren, J. Benedict
1985 *The Conquest of Michoacán*. University of Oklahoma Press, Norman.

CHAPTER 39

AZTEC EMPIRE IN COMPARATIVE PERSPECTIVE

R. ALAN COVEY AND AMANDA S. ALAND

THE Europeans who brought devastation to the Aztec Empire struggled to describe the civilization that they encountered in the Mexican highlands. Some, like the Anonymous Conqueror (1917:ch. 16), drew comparisons with the Iberian world, mentioning cities such as Granada, Segovia, Valladolid, Burgos, and Salamanca as parallels for the *altepetl* societies of Tlaxcalla and the Basin of Mexico. By contrast, Bernal Díaz del Castillo (1956:ch. 61) expressed a sense of bedazzlement that evoked medieval legends such as *Amadís de Gaula*—on the approach to the Basin, "we were amazed and said that it was like the enchantments they tell of in the legend of Amadis [sic], on account of the great towers and cues and buildings rising from the water and all built of masonry." Cortés himself compared the Aztec realm to the world of Islamic empires ("Moors"), whereas subsequent Spanish discourse on the legitimacy of American conquests introduced a Roman referent for indigenous empires that were not Christian but had not explicitly rejected Christianity (e.g., Pagden 2001).

Today, Aztec scholars have established a sound foundation for making much better comparisons, and it is possible for researchers working in other times and places (such as ourselves) to engage with the rich body of evidence to speak in general terms about how the realm of the Triple Alliance compares with other imperial societies. This chapter focuses on different sources of imperial power and the extent to which other empires employed comparable institutions and administrative strategies to increase or redirect power from other social structures. To this end, we discuss the relative size of the territory and population under imperial rule; the degree to which the state monopolized violence internally and served as the exclusive agent of offensive and defensive military force; the extent to which local societies embraced the state religion; the role of the empire in intensifying economic production, constructing, or maintaining infrastructure to facilitate the distribution of staple and wealth goods and in overseeing economic transactions; and the extent to which political hierarchies "governed down" to subsume the responsibilities of local rulers, kin groups, and families. We begin by comparing the

Aztec Empire with its contemporaries and then take the contrasts that emerge to draw parallels between the Aztec Triple Alliance and the Athenian Empire, which emerged in the fifth century B.C. from a regional military alliance among Greek city-states (*poleis*). We conclude with a few words comparing the Aztec order with Spain, an expanding state that was forced to confront its own imperial identity in the aftermath of the invasion of the Mesoamerican highlands.

The Aztecs and the Age of Empires

The Mexica and their allies achieved a degree of power that was unprecedented in Mesoamerica, at a time when many other imperial societies were creating macroregional networks or binding existing ones under the rule of new dynasties. The traditional dates for the Aztec dynasty (A.D. 1428–1521) overlap with several other empires—including the Inca, Songhay, Ottoman, Safavid, Vijayanagara, and Ming—and their final years overlap with the early period of expansion of several European empires, including Russia and Spain. Recognizing the vastness of the scholarship that exists on these empires, we focus on very coarse-grained aspects of imperial power.

Scale

Imperial scale can be approximated in terms of territory and population, and each of these metrics involves a different degree of speculation to assess a distinct aspect of imperial power. In terms of territory alone, the Aztecs dominated a fairly modest domain (Figure 39.1). Many contemporary empires annexed large territories, although these included vast areas that were too marginal for agriculture.

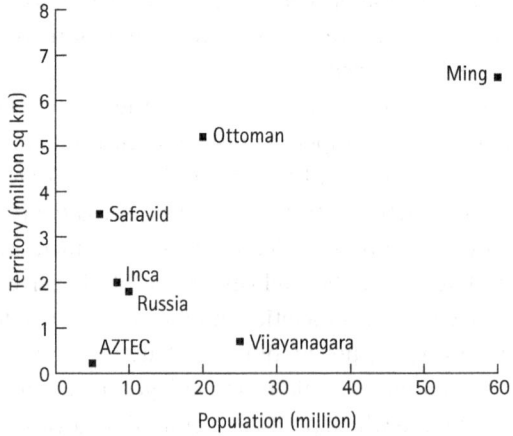

FIGURE 39.1 Imperial territory sizes and populations. Prepared by R. Alan Covey.

These regions often had low population densities interrupted in places by archipelagoes of towns and cities built in the oases along strategic exchange routes. Safavid and Inca territory contained areas of desert, steppe, and tundra that were not intensively populated or administered (Streusand 2011:182). The Ottoman and Ming empires ruled over large and densely settled regions, but both benefited from regional traditions of local statecraft, urbanism, and imperial administration that extended millennia into the past (Dale 2010; Twitchett and Mote 1998; cf. Cline and Graham 2011; Lewis 2007). The Aztecs were an empire in a part of the world where the state was a younger social phenomenon, and they also faced significant challenges as they expanded beyond the Basin of Mexico, including cultural boundaries, marginal environments, and high transportation costs (Nichols and Evans 2010:265).

Ancient populations are notoriously difficult to state with precision. Estimates of world empires around the start of the sixteenth century suggest that the Triple Alliance dominated a population that was probably comparable with that of the Safavid (Streusand 2011:182) and Inca empires (Cook 1980) and greater than the Songhay Empire (Gomez 1990:8). The Ottoman and Vijayanagara empires had subject populations several orders of magnitude larger (Dale 2010; Stein 1990), whereas the population of the Ming Empire was at least 60 million (Bannister 1987:4). With the exception of Vijayanagara (Sinopoli and Morrison 1995), the empires that had the largest populations tended to be dynasties that united kingdoms and city-states that had deeply entrenched practices of civic governance and agrarian economies that were geared toward surplus production and commodity exchange. The distribution of population across an empire's territory is probably more significant than absolute counts of people or square kilometers claimed by a central government. The Aztec and Vijayanagara empires stand out for their overall population density, which reflects the ability to unify very large populations in relatively constrained territories. Population estimates for Tenochtitlan and the Basin of Mexico at the time of the European invasion (Márquez Morfín and Storey this volume) put the population size and density of the Aztec heartland on par with the largest metropolitan areas in the world at the time—Beijing and Vijayanagara—and much larger than imperial capitals such as Cuzco or Gao.

Military Organization

The Triple Alliance used warfare as a means of establishing and maintaining political hegemony and promoting Mexica ideological power. Participation in military campaigns also sustained gender identities and differences in social status (Oudijk and Castañeda de la Paz this volume; Cervera Obregón this volume). Aztec military service was simultaneously a civic duty, a vehicle for social advancement, and a means of reinforcing the power of men in the inner elite. Large-scale conflicts between polities relied on the use of conscripted forces from each allied city-state (Berdan this volume), which sets Aztec military power apart from contemporary empires that maintained professional forces at the expense of the state or the ruler. The Ottoman, Vijayanagara, Safavid, Songhay, and Ming empires all had standing military forces, and the Inca Empire had begun to transition from conscript armies to long-term deployment of specialized soldiers fighting at its frontiers. Each supplemented its core troops in unique fashion with allies, mercenaries, slaves, and citizens (e.g., Dale 2010; Streusand 2011). Aztec warfare did not include powerful rapid response forces such as cavalry (horses, camels, elephants), and the projectile weapons that most foot soldiers carried with them lacked the lethal power that firearms were beginning to introduce into Old World fighting (Streusand 2011:82–84, 182, 293).

During the expansion of the Triple Alliance, military force was determined primarily by sheer numbers of troops (rather than advantages in tactics, training, or weaponry), and the destruction of enemy troops and resources ran counter to the imperial goal of increasing its military and economic power using indirect rule. This might explain the choice not to invest in fortifications the way that many Old World empires did—defensive works would contribute to less effective diplomacy and more destructive siege warfare. For defensive power, the Aztecs preferred, in many instances, to delegate the costs of frontier defense to strategic provinces.

The Imperial Economy

The Aztec imperial core was remarkably integrated economically, and the promotion of marketplace exchanges helped to establish a lively trade of local commodities and craft goods made of exotic materials from across Mesoamerica (Nichols and Evans 2010). The exchange system was not monetized to the degree that many Old World empires were, but the role of trade contrasts strongly with the Inca imperial economy, where labor undergirded the political economy and barter dominated economic exchanges (D'Altroy and Earle 1985). Indirect rule provided the Aztec inner elite with exotic materials that buttressed the power of military elites and connected the ruling families of city-states across the imperial core. Sumptuary laws kept the long-distance *pochteca* merchants from challenging the social power of these elites. The Aztec accentuation of the economic gulf between elites and commoners helped to bind regional networks of *tlahtoani* rulers and minor nobles. Such practices differ from contemporaneous Inca strategies designed to remove wealth from provincial regions and to concentrate exotic goods, production expertise, and finished craft goods at the capital, where they were distributed by the ruler as a gift economy.

Aztec marketplace activity resembled many Old World empires that focused externally on access to exotic raw materials and trade routes while using connections to long-distance networks to export fine trade goods (silk, textiles, pottery). The Old World dynasties possessed economies where currency and shared units of measure had considerable antiquity and where hierarchical modes of production were well established in core areas. Marketplaces permitted a degree of state economic supervision and served as places where tax collection could potentially take place (Dale 2010:110, 182; Gomez 1990:21; Hunwick 1996:181; McKissack and McKissak 1994:102; Streusand 2011:182). The Aztec state focused more on how goods changed hands than on modes of production, and the central administration made limited investments in agricultural intensification or the construction of transportation infrastructure that could facilitate the flow of goods and information.

Official Religion

The Mexica promoted the cult of their religious patron, Huitzilopochtli, as central to universal maintenance and the productivity of maize agriculture, although they did so most prominently at the capital, leaving other city-states to propitiate their own patrons (Olivier this volume; Matos Moctezuma this volume). Rather than attempt to establish their solar deity in local contexts, the Mexica packaged the cult within broadly shared cosmological beliefs. The human sacrifices offered to Huitzilopochtli at the main temple in the capital permitted the military ideology that extended the power of the Triple Alliance to be treated as essential to the broader ritual project of ensuring subsistence success and staving off cosmological disaster. Tenochtitlán was the site of the most explicit expressions of dominant Mexica beliefs, but it was also a place for the accumulation of cults to other deities—the empire recognized an extensive pantheon and the capital became a repository of sacred power under state patronage.

In many ways, Aztec religious power resembled that of the Inca Empire, where the worship of what Spanish priests called a "second cause"—an entity that was created but exerted power over lesser supernatural forces—allowed the state to insert itself into many local religious systems (e.g., Cobo 1990 [1653]). The Incas experienced difficulty in co-opting broader beliefs and practices regarding creation, but they were effective at acquiring religious power from provincial groups by serving as patrons to local shrines and requiring portable sacred objects to be carried to the capital. The Incas expended far more resources than the Aztecs in constructing facilities for the state religion in provincial contexts and in sending human sacrifices from the capital to important mountains and other shrines (Covey 2006). Inca religion could not supersede creator worship in some parts of the empire, and it could not supplant local ritual practices, but it was integral to communicating state patronage and maintaining the imperial administrative hierarchy.

The Vijayanagara and Ming empires were home to world religions that were practiced beyond their borders (Hinduism and Buddhism, respectively), and rulers engaged in co-opting local sacred forces into an official pantheon or corpus of state-approved rituals (Taylor 1998; Verghese 2004). Vijayanagara rulers were religious patrons and used temples as an institution for expanding economic production that made elite donors both righteous and rich (Morrison 2001). In the Ming Empire, the emperor exerted control over ecclesiastical religion (Buddhist and Taoist) by requiring approval for temple construction and the ordination of priests, and the ruler's central cosmological role was essential for the well-being of the imperial society (Taylor 1998). The plural and international nature of religious power in these empires might have limited their contributions to expansionist ideologies, but religion helped to buttress other forms of imperial power, including the maintenance of order in directly ruled territories. Like Inca Cuzco, Vijayanagara and Beijing were cosmic centers where monumental constructions attested to the supernatural authority of the ruling dynasty (e.g., Farrington 2013; Fritz 1986; Zhu 2003).

By contrast, monotheism presented different opportunities and constraints for the Songhay, Ottoman, and Safavid empires, all of which embraced a particular form of Islam as an official religion. These empires were tolerant of other faiths to varying degrees but did not allow for the official acquisition of new cults alongside their own—in fact, a sense of religious unity helped to justify military actions against outside groups, including adherents of other Islamic sects. The Muslim empires embraced official variants of Islam that promoted a specific identity and centered religious practices under the political authority of the ruling dynasty (Dale 2010; Hunwick 1996; Streusand 2011). To varying degrees, monotheism helped to substantiate military expansion, the implementation of direct rule, and the promotion of a shared imperial identity that could delineate imperial geography (core/periphery/exterior) and hierarchy (rulers/subjects/infidels).

Central Legal Authority

If military force represents the state's outward expression of violence, a system of laws and punishments (and the personnel required to carry them out) constitutes its internal counterpart. Aztec law was based on common-law practices that probably varied between city-states and was applied in different ways to elites and commoners. The heterarchical nature of Aztec legal power contrasts with the Ming and Inca empires, where law emanated from the emperor, who delegated the power to judge and punish criminals (Langlois 1998; MacCormack 1997). Law in these empires represented a way for the ruler to manage the behavior of the inner elite, and for royal appointees to monopolize the judicial power existing outside of households and local kin networks. In other contemporary empires, legal practices were tied more explicitly to expectations laid out by the official religion, as refracted through the interpretation of the ruling elite (e.g., Gerber 1994; McKissack and McKissack 1995). Although it is difficult to build a solid comparative context for Aztec legal practice, it appears that most legal power and authority resided outside of the inner elite of the Triple Alliance. Such an arrangement could be seen in a positive sense—as a governing cost that the central administration did not need to incur—but also a potential constraining factor for consolidation and centralization of the empire over time.

The Reach of Political Power

The Postclassic *altepetl* was governed by its *tlahtoani* and a noble advisory council, and the imperial expansion of the Triple Alliance did not result in widespread restructuring of local administrative organization. Imperial growth generally focused on controlling *tlahtoani* offices and worked through regional alliance networks that served to connect the city states socially, politically, and economically (Nichols and Evans 2010:268; also see Berdan this volume). The absence of an extensive imperial court and corresponding civil service contrasts with the Ming and Inca empires, where many thousands of officials governed down toward subject populations, invoking the authority of the ruler as their source of power (Hucker 1998; Julien 1988). This is not to say that these empires imposed a more intensive form of local political power; although Inca decimal administration reached units of 10 households in some provincial areas, and in many parts of China, the lowest officials oversaw populations in the tens of thousands. Like the Aztecs, many contemporary empires found it effective to leave client rulers in place and were content with indirect rule as long as it provided strategic access to resources and trade routes. For example, the Ottoman Empire maintained clerical and bureaucratic hierarchies but also used the policy of *mudarra* (moderation, friendship) to leave conquered local rulers in place (Streusand 2011:80).

The Triple Alliance lacked an imperial bureaucracy and did not have a well-developed articulation of provincial rule, relying instead on the *altepetl* as an ideal administrative unit that could be governed indirectly (see Fargher et al. this volume). This contrasts with other empires that developed provincial institutions that were seen as distinct from existing social and political orders. The Inca *hunu* (D'Altroy 2002) and the Ottoman *timar* system (Streusand 2011:80) represent clear contrasts with Aztec provincial strategies. It should be noted that the Songhay and Safavid empires also lacked a strong bureaucratic reach and were less urbanized than the Aztecs, relying far more on clans and local tribes to maintain political order (Gomez 1990:910; Streusand 2011:180). The Triple Alliance built on a clearly articulated model of local statecraft but did little to establish an imperial system that would restructure or transcend it in most instances.

Resistance and Rebellion and Dynastic Duration

No discussion of imperial power would be complete without acknowledging the interior and exterior limits to imperial power. In a rough sense, territorial size speaks to the power of the expanding empire relative to unconquered groups lying beyond the most distant frontier, although measuring the high-water mark of an empire fails to take into consideration the internal frontiers that many empires possessed. Any close assessment of imperial trajectory encounters the fact that empires faced considerable resistance within the regions over which their rulers proclaimed dominion. This could include groups that the state found difficult to administer directly—for example, unassimilated minorities or nomadic groups (pastoralists, hunter-gatherers) (e.g., Barfield 2001)—but there were also places and times where people stood opposed to the imperial order due to belief, identity, or out of desperation or frustration (Morrison 2001). Imperial policies could create a sense of disenfranchisement, but other phenomena, such as natural disasters, often played a role in serious uprisings against the government (e.g., White 2011).

The Triple Alliance possessed an internal frontier and unhappy subjects who aided the European invasion, as did the Inca Empire (D'Altroy 2002). Provincial rebellions were common in the Andes, and harsh Inca reprisals remained in provincial minds when the Pizarro expedition reached the region in the 1530s (Murra 1986). Other empires struggled with groups living in their territories who challenged their power in ideological ("heretics"), economic ("bandits"), military ("warlords"), and political ("anarchists") domains, although it is problematic to read state accounts without some skepticism (Robinson 2001). Climatic disruptions and unruly subjects threatened the resources that funded imperial institutions, whereas factionalism, ambition, and corruption among the inner elite destabilized empires from the top down. The Aztec focus on regional economic integration and local *altepetl* self-rule might have promoted greater overall protection against these kinds of pressures, although the empire clearly experienced its own internal threats and disruptions.

Overall, Aztec imperial power was modest by design, harnessing the destructive military potential of the Triple Alliance to establish a new status quo where elite populations in the growing core benefited from strong economic interactions among themselves and with groups living beyond the Basin of Mexico. The empire promoted the growth of economic power across many local city-states without centralizing that power or diverting it to costlier ruling strategies. By comparison, the success of dispersed empires lay in establishing working administrative linkages across space, often through the construction of infrastructure to bind the imperial network more securely. Conversely, empires with very large populations faced a greater degree of scalar stress among the populations they ruled, and they succeeded to the extent that they were able to sustain intricate and costly governing hierarchies.

The Triple Alliance and the Delian League

The Aztecs grew unprecedented power from existing models of civic order and by reducing the destruction of military engagements and channeling them outward toward rival groups. This promotion of imperial identity through the identification of barbarians or rival empires is reminiscent of the strategies of coeval empires in other parts of the world. However, the creation of an imperial order from a military alliance among city-states sharing the same broad cultural identity might find a useful analogue in the Delian League, which many scholars call the Athenian Empire (Low 2008). The league was a military alliance among Greek city-states that was established in 478 B.C. to expel the Persians from the Aegean. Membership initially required city-states to provide ships or to make monetary payments, but over time Athens established military superiority and levied tribute payments on its erstwhile allies. Over several decades, Athens emerged from the position of *primus inter pares* to be the dominant power in an emerging empire, and its former allies were acknowledged as "the cities over which the Athenians rule."

Athens attempted to formalize its power through the establishment of colonies (*apoikia*) founded by its citizens, as well as cleruchies, which were settlements of Athenian lot-holders who retained their citizenship rights in Athens. These new settlements could be established in the territory of Athenian allies, as well as in that of non-Greek peoples, and they tended to redistribute resources away from local populations to wealthier Athenians (Zelnick-Abromovits 2004). Overall, Athenian imperialism enhanced the military and economic power of one city-state, which attempted to capitalize on its dominance by establishing its own people in new communities that remained politically dependent. In the absence of external threats, these imperial ambitions led to rival alliance building that culminated in the Peloponnesian War, and Athenian colonization efforts proved to be unsustainable. Although the Aztec case exhibits some important differences with the Athenian one, the two provide comparative ground for considering the efforts of empire-building in a context of shared cultural identity, as well as the limitations presented by attempting to build an empire through a network of city-states.

The Aztecs and "Early Modern" Spain

Having looked broadly at non-Western empires contemporaneous to the Aztecs, and at the Delian League as an ancient European analogue for the Triple Alliance, it is appropriate to close with a few words on the empire that destroyed the Aztec order. Spain arguably became an empire during the process of conquering the Aztecs and Incas (cf. Kamen 2004:87ff.). In 1519, it was an uneven conglomeration of Iberian kingdoms under the growing central power of the Castilian crown but lacking a large population or significant resources (Elliott 1963). The conquest of small-scale societies in the Canary Islands and the Caribbean employed a feudal conquest model that prevailed during the *Reconquista*, and it was not until the mid-sixteenth century that Habsburg rulers began to develop an imperial ideology and the administrative institutions to match. When Cortés arrived in Tenochtitlán, Castile ruled a smaller population than the Aztec Empire, had a more modest urban tradition, and lacked a strong presence in the international trade driven by non-Western empires. The Inquisition had begun to serve as a tool for imposing an orthodox state religion and expelling peripheral populations, but in the early sixteenth century Spain was still poised between the twin crusades of the *Reconquista* and the Counter-Reformation. Spain grew into an empire as its orgy of plunder in the Aztec world enabled it to act like one in Europe, and it developed institutions for peripheral government only after its ruthless extraction failed to destroy the entirety of the native populace. This is especially true in places like Mesoamerica and the Andes, where indigenous empires demanded that Spain put forth at least the semblance of "good governance" if it would claim the mission of bringing civilization and salvation.

References Cited

Anonymous Conquerer
1917 *Narrative of Some Things of New Spain and of the Great City of Temestitan Mexico*. Translated by Marshall H. Saville. The Cortés Society, New York.

Bannister, Judith
1987 *China's Changing Population*. Stanford University Press, Stanford, CA.

Barfield, Thomas J.
2001 The Shadow Empires: Imperial State Formation along the Chinese-Nomad Frontier. In *Empires: Perspectives from Archaeology and History* edited by Susan E. Alcock, Terence N. D'Altroy, Kathleen D. Morrison, and Carla M. Sinopoli, pp. 10–41. Cambridge University Press New York.

Cline, Eric H., and Mark W. Graham
2011 *Ancient Empires: From Mesopotamia to the Rise of Islam*. Cambridge University Press, New York.

Cobo, Bernabé
1990 *Inca Religion and Customs*. Translated by Roland Hamilton. University of Texas Press, Austin.

Cook, Noble David.
1980 *Demographic Collapse: Indian Peru, 1520–1620*. Cambridge University Press, Cambridge, UK.

Covey, R. Alan
2006 *How the Incas Built Their Heartland: State Formation and the Innovation of Imperial Strategies in the Sacred Valley, Peru*. University of Michigan Press, Ann Arbor.

Dale, Stephen F.
2010 *The Muslim Empires of the Ottomans, Safavids, and Mughals*. Cambridge University Press, New York.

D'Altroy, Terence N
2002 *The Incas*. Blackwell, New York.

D'Altroy, Terence N., and Timothy K. Earle
1985 Staple Finance, Wealth Finance, and Storage in the Inka Political Economy (With Comments). *Current Anthropology* 26:187–206.

Díaz del Castillo, Bernal
1956 *The Discovery and Conquest of Mexico*. Translated by A. P. Maudslay. Farrar, Straus & Cudahy, New York.

Elliott, J. H.
1963 *Imperial Spain 1469–1716*. Penguin, New York.

Farrington, Ian S.
2013 *Cusco: Urbanism and Archaeology in the Inka World*. University Press of Florida, Gainesville.

Fritz, John M.
1986 Vijayanagara: Authority and Meaning of a South Indian Imperial Capital. *American Anthropologist* 88:44–55.

Gerber, Haim
1994 *State, Society, and Law in Islam: Ottoman Law in Comparative Perspective.* State University of New York Press, Albany.

Gomez, Michael
1990 Timbuktu under Imperial Songhay: A Reconsideration of Autonomy. *The Journal of African History* 31:5–24.

Hucker, Charles O.
1998 Ming Government. In *The Cambridge History of China*, Vol. 8: *The Ming Dynasty, 1368–1644, Part 2*, edited by Denis Twitchett and Frederick W. Mote, pp. 9–105. Cambridge University Press, Cambridge, UK.

Hunwick, John
1996 Secular Power and Religious Authority in Muslim Society: The Case of the Songhay. *The Journal of African History* 37:175–194.

Julien, Catherine J.
1988 How Inca Decimal Administration Worked. *Ethnohistory* 35(3):257–279.

Kamen, Henry
2004 *Empire: How Spain Became a World Power 1492–1763.* HarperCollins, New York.

Langlois, John D. Jr.
1998 Ming Law. In *The Cambridge History of China*, Vol. 8: *The Ming Dynasty, 1368–1644, Part 2*, edited by Denis C. Twitchett and Frederick W. Mote, pp. 172–220. Cambridge University Press, Cambridge, UK.

Lewis, Mark E.
2007 *The Early Chinese Empires: Qin and Han.* Stanford University Press, Stanford, CA.

Low, Polly (editor)
2008 *The Athenian Empire.* Edinburgh University Press, Edinburgh, UK.

MacCormack, Sabine G.
1997 History and Law in Sixteenth-Century Peru: The Impact of European Scholarly Traditions. In *Cultures of Scholarship*, edited by S. C. Humphreys, pp. 277–310. University of Michigan Press, Ann Arbor.

McKissack, Patricia, and Frederick McKissack
1994 *The Royal Kingdoms of Ghana, Mali, and Songhay: Life in Medieval Africa.* Henry Holt, New York.

Morrison, Kathleen D.
2001 Coercion, Resistance, and Hierarchy: Local Processes and Imperial Strategies in the Vijayanagara Empire. In *Empires: Perspectives from Archaeology and History*, edited by Susan E. Alcock, Terence N. D'Altroy, Kathleen D. Morrison, and Carla M. Sinopoli, pp. 252–278. Cambridge University Press, New York.

Mote, Frederick W., and Denis Twitchett (editors)
1988 *The Cambridge History of China*, Vol. 7: *The Ming Dynasty, 1368–1644, Part 1.* Cambridge University Press, Cambridge, UK.

Murra, John V.
1986 The Expansion of the Inca State: Armies, Wars, and Rebellions. In *Anthropological History of Andean Polities*, edited by John V. Murra, Nathan Wachtel, and Jacques Revel, pp. 49–58. Cambridge University Press, New York.

Nichols, Deborah L., and Susan T. Evans
2010 Aztec Studies. *Ancient Mesoamerica* 20(2):265–270.

Obregón, Marco A. Cervera
2017 Aztec Warfare. In press. In *Oxford Handbook of the Aztecs*, edited by Deborah L. Nichols and Enrique Rodríguez-Alegría, pp. 451–462, Oxford University Press, New York.

Pagden, Anthony
2001 Introduction. In *Hernán Cortés: Letters from Mexico*, edited by Anthony Pagden, pp. xxix–lxxx. Yale Nota Bene, New Haven, CT.

Robinson, David M.
2001 *Bandits, Eunuchs, and the Son of Heaven: Rebellion and the Economy of Violence in Mid-Ming China*. University of Hawaii Press, Honolulu.

Sinopoli, Carla M., and Kathleen D. Morrison
1995 Dimensions of Imperial Control: The Vijayanagara Capital. *American Anthropologist* 97(1):83–96.

Stein, Burton
1990 *The New Cambridge History of India: Vijayanagara*. Cambridge University Press, Cambridge, UK.

Streusand, Douglas E.
2011 *Islamic Gunpowder Empires: Ottomans, Safavids, and Mughals*. Westview Press, Boulder, CO.

Taylor, Romeyn
1998 Official Religion in the Ming. In *The Cambridge History of China*, Vol. 8: *The Ming Dynasty, 1368–1644, Part 2*, edited by Denis Twitchett and Frederick W. Mote, pp. 840–892. Cambridge University Press, Cambridge, UK.

Twitchett, Denis, and Mote, Frederick W. (editors)
1998 *The Cambridge History of China*, Vol. 8: *The Ming Dynasty, 1368–1644, Part 2*. Cambridge University Press, Cambridge, UK.

Verghese, Anila
2004 Deities, Cults and Kings at Vijayanagara. *World Archaeology* 36(3):416–431.

White, Sam
2011 *The Climate of Rebellion in the Early Modern Ottoman Empire*. Cambridge University Press, Cambridge, UK.

Zelnick-Abramovitz, R.
2004 Settlers and Dispossessed in the Athenian Empire. *Mnemosyne* 57:325–345.

Zhu, Jianfei
2003 *Chinese Spatial Strategies: Imperial Beijing 1420–1911*. Routledge Curzon, New York.

PART VI
RITUAL, BELIEF, AND RELIGION

CHAPTER 40

HUMANS AND GODS IN THE MEXICA UNIVERSE

GUILHEM OLIVIER

Shortly before the fall of the Mexica Empire and the capture of their king (*tlahtoani*), Cuauhtemoc, by the Spanish on August 13, 1521, the Mexicas made one last attempt to fight off the invaders. The brave warrior Tlapaltecatl Opochtzin was outfitted with the weapons and insignia of their patron god, Huitzilopochtli, and sent to battle the Spanish. Wearing a quetzal owl costume and armed with the powerful arrow of Huitzilopochtli, the brave warrior did some damage; unfortunately, his heroic intervention did not incite as much panic among Cortés' troops as the Mexicas had hoped (Sahagún 1950–1982:12:117–118).

This tragic episode in the Conquest of Mexico clearly illustrates how, in a moment of extreme crisis, the Mexicas reenacted the myth in which their solar deity was born fully armed on Coatepec Hill—model for the Templo Mayor—and defeated his stellar enemies (Sahagún 1950–1982:3:1–5). With its structured pantheon, temples of worship, and complex priestly hierarchy, the Mexica religious sphere extended past the boundaries we impose today between the "sacred" and the "profane" (Nicholson 1971). Thus, any activity, from the most important—the enthronement of a king—to the most trivial—harvesting honey or going fishing—had a religious dimension, based on myths, which required that the appropriate rites be performed. It bears mentioning that the Mexicas were heirs to a religious tradition dating to at least the first millennium B.C. and extending throughout the broad geographical area known as Mesoamerica—from the Sinaloa, Lerma, and Panuco rivers to Costa Rica (López Austin and López Luján 1996). Finally, the continuity of certain rites or religious symbols over time should not obscure the extraordinary diversity and complex evolution of ancient Mesoamerican religion.

Conception of Time and the Universe

To better understand their religion, we must first examine how the Mexicas conceived of the universe. Broadly speaking, the Mexicas thought the earth was a flat surface, either rectangular or round, surrounded by the sea, which extended toward the heavens. These heavens were held up by four or five trees or gods (one in each of the four corners and one in the middle). In the *Codex Borgia* (1963:49–52), for example, Tlahuizcalpantecuhtli (god of the planet Venus), Xiuhtecuhtli (god of fire), Quetzalcoatl (god of wind), and Mictlantecuhtli (god of death) held up the heavens; each god was associated with a particular cardinal point and a specific calendrical sign. Vertically, the cosmos were divided into 13 celestial layers plus an underworld composed of nine layers. Gods, stars, and other mythological creatures inhabited each layer (López Austin 1980:1:58–68) (Figure 40.1).

The Mesoamerican concept of time is also important in order to better understand the religious tradition (Caso 1967). Time was measured using two different calendars: a

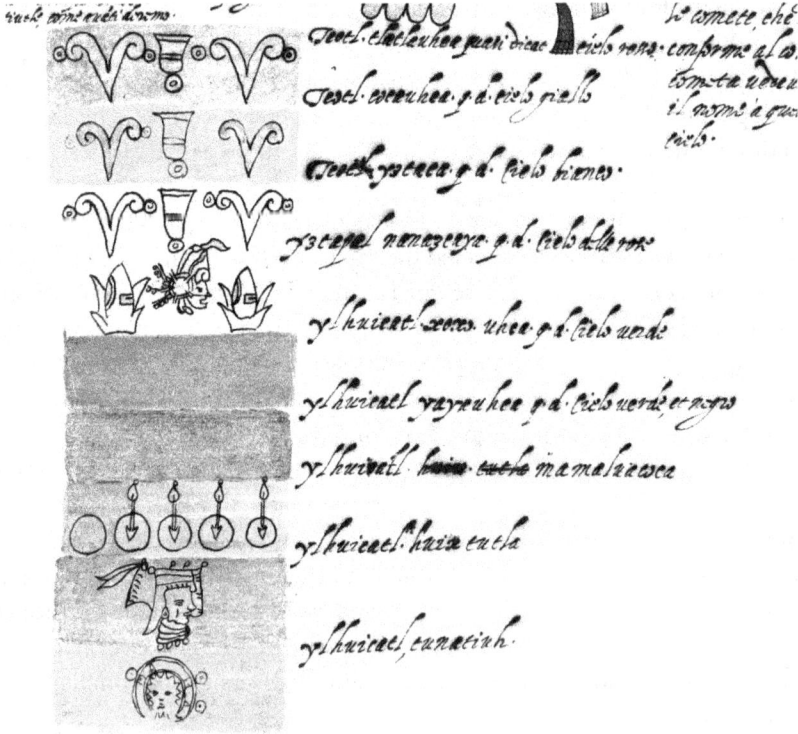

FIGURE 40.1 The 13 layers of heaven and the nine layers of the underworld based on beliefs from the Postclassic-period Central Highlands (*Códice Vaticano-Latino 3738* 1996:fol. 1v-2r). Reproduced with permission.

solar calendar consisting of 365 days (*xiuhpohualli*) divided into 18 "months" of 20 days plus five "unlucky" days, and a ritual calendar of 260 days (*tonalpohualli*) formed by combining 20 day signs with 13 numbers. To designate a solar year, the initial day that corresponded to the ritual calendar was used: these first days were the so-called year bearers. Each solar year consisted of 360 days plus five days; thus the first day each year was displaced by five days with reference to the previous year. After four years, the displacement was then 20 days and the cycle began again on the initial day. Therefore, only four days—*acatl* (reed), *tecpatl* (flint), *calli* (house), and *tochtli* (rabbit)—could serve as "bearers" with progressive numbers (from 1 to 13). The "indigenous century" was composed of 52 (4 × 13) different years.

Certain dates also had symbolic and mythological significance (López Austin 1973:79–106). For example, the year *Ce Tecpatl* (1 Flint), in addition to being equivalent to a given date in the calendar, also symbolized a beginning. Thus the Mexica migration from Aztlan starts, according to many sources, in the year *Ce Tecpatl*. The date also corresponds to the birth of the god Huitzilopochtli, who used it as a calendar name. In addition, an individual's date of birth influenced his or her personality and destiny (and also that of the gods), and the positive or negative connotations of different dates were considered when planning certain activities like sowing, harvesting, taking a trip, hunting, marriage, performing a healing ceremony, blessing a home, electing a king, and other endeavors. The *tonalpouhque* (specially trained priests) were consulted, as they could read and interpret the divinatory codices that explained the different calendrical signs and the specific gods associated with them (Boone 2007; Seler 1963) (Figure 40.2).

Mexica Myths

Although Spanish chroniclers such as Fray Bernardino de Sahagún qualified indigenous stories as "ridiculous fables," various sources recorded a significant corpus of myths, some in the original Nahuatl. Here I focus on the myths that tell of the creation of the heavens and earth, the birth of the sun and moon, the origin of mankind, and the "Legend of the Suns."

The first act of creation was attributed to the supreme couple, Ometecuhtli and Omecihuatl, whose four children were gods: Tlatlauhqui Tezcatlipoca (also known as Mixcoatl, Cloud Serpent), Yayauhqui Tezcatlipoca (the Black Tezcatlipoca, Smoking Mirror), Quetzalcoatl (Quetzal Serpent), and Huitzilopochtli (Hummingbird of the Left). Those gods decided to create the heavens and the earth from a being known as Tlalteotl—the earth deity—floating on the primeval waters. Quetzalcoatl and Tezcatlipoca entered the body of Tlalteotl and split it in two, thus creating heaven and earth. They erected four posts to prevent Tlalteotl from reconstituting himself. The supreme couple were angered by this insult to Tlalteotl (Quetzalcoatl and Tezcatlipoca had, in a sense, violated Tlalteotl) and, to make amends, caused plants to grow out of his

FIGURE 40.2 A *tonalpouhque* ("He who possesses the count of days") uses a codex to show a woman on the day ("10 Rabbit") on which her child will be baptized (Sahagún 1959–1982:I, Book 4; fol. 34 v°). Reproduced with permission.

body and ordered that the blood of sacrificial victims be used to nourish his body/the land (*Historia de los mexicanos por sus pinturas* 1941:209–214; Thévet 1905:25–26).

The birth of the sun and the moon is another myth fundamental to the Mexica worldview. The gods gathered at Teotihuacan to choose two from among them to be transformed into these celestial bodies. Hoping to become the sun, the rich and proud Tecuciztecatl could not bring himself to jump into the fire. Meanwhile, the poor but brave Nanahuatzin courageously threw himself in. Tecuciztecatl followed him but fell into the ashes and was transformed into the moon. Both stars sat motionless in the sky. The sun then demanded the sacrifice of the other gods in order to set the stars in motion. Quetzalcoatl was elected to sacrifice the gods, after which he blew on the sun and moon to set them in motion (Sahagún 1950–1982:7:3–8).

Other important myths tell of the creation of humans. One in particular stands out: the story that describes how Quetzalcoatl descended to the underworld where the god Mictlantecuhtli stored the bones of the giants who had inhabited the earth during an earlier era. After several tests, like blowing into a sealed shell that had been perforated by bees, Quetzalcoatl gained access to the bones and brought them to the surface of the earth. However, he stumbled along the way, and the bones shattered; thus humans of the current era are smaller than the giants who preceded them. The bones were ground like corn by the goddess Quilaztli, while Quetzalcoatl contributed blood from his penis; from this mixture were born the humans that currently inhabit the earth (*Leyenda de los Soles* 1992:145–146).

The myth of the origin of prayers and music is invaluable in illustrating the complex relationships that existed between humans and gods. Following the death of their gods at Teotihuacan, humans wrapped their relics in blankets, forming what would later be known as *tlaquimilolli*, or sacred bundles. Humans were still unable to worship their creators. Thus Tezcatlipoca intervened, sending his double, Night Wind, to the house of the sun, where musicians of four colors could be found. Upon arriving, Night Wind used a ruse: he intoned a "mellifluous song" that elicited, despite the warning of the sun, the immediate response of the forgetful musicians. Thus Tezcatlipoca's envoy enticed the solar musicians to come down to earth, and humans were granted the ability to pray and sing to appease their gods (Thévet 1905:32–33).

Another myth tells of the different eras that preceded our own. The different versions that have survived consistently mention four or five eras, also known as Suns (Graulich 1997:63–95). Each of these eras ended in a great cataclysm, and the last era, the one in which we currently live, is destined to end with an earthquake. Some sources mention that humans were transformed based on the particular type of destruction that befell them: they became fish during the flood, monkeys during the hurricane, then butterflies, dogs, and turkeys during the rain of fire. Each Sun was dominated by a deity; the *Codex Vaticano A* (1996:fols. 4v–7r) associates Chalchiuhtlicue, Quetzalcoatl, Xiuhtecuhtli, and Xochiquetzal—gods representing water, wind, fire, and earth, respectively—with different eras. Important mythological data indicate that Tezcatlipoca and Quetzalcoatl took turns as the Sun (*Historia de los mexicanos por sus pinturas* 1941:212–214). The struggle between these two deities is highlighted in the story of the fall of Tula, where Quetzalcoatl—as the Fourth Sun—was defeated by Tezcatlipoca (Graulich 1997:117–206; Olivier 2003:125–164). The Fifth Sun of the Mexicas was naturally dominated by Huitzilopochtli, their tutelary god, who also shared some characteristics with Tezcatlipoca. It is no wonder, then, that at the end of the fifth era (i.e., the Spanish Conquest), Tezcatlipoca appeared drunk (as Quetzalcoatl was at the end of the Toltec era), fleeing from the Spanish, whose arrival was interpreted by the Mexicas as the return of the Feathered Serpent (Olivier 2003:159–160; Sahagún 1950–1982:12:33–35).

The Mexica Pantheon

Both numerous and multifaceted, Mexica gods could take on a variety of forms: elements such as water, air, earth, and fire; places like hills or rivers; phenomena such as lightning or rain; animals, plants, and even objects like musical instruments could be gods or receptacles for divine forces. Some individuals, slaves, or war captives as well as priests or leaders "possessed" by a particular deity could become *ixiptla*, meaning an "image" or "representative" of that god. At the same time, a god like Quetzalcoatl could manifest himself as a natural element (air) or as a planet (Venus), or appear as an animal (monkey, opossum), a captive slave (his "image" in Cholula), or a political leader (Topiltzin Quetzalcoatl at Tula) (Carrasco 1992; López Austin 1990; Nicholson 2001) (Figure 40.3).

Statues of wood, clay, stone, and even copal and rubber were used by the ancient Mexicas to physically represent their gods. For example, the Tepictoton, the gods of the mountains, Popocatepetl, Iztaccihuatl, Tlaloc, Poiauhtecatl, and others were represented by statues of amaranth seeds adorned with beans for eyes and pumpkin seeds for teeth. Moreover, after the sacrifice of the gods at Teotihuacan, people began to wrap their relics—ashes, glass, jade stones, sticks, obsidian fragments, arrows, and so on—in blankets, thus forming "sacred bundles" (*tlaquimilolli*). As symbols of identity for the people who worshiped them, the sacred bundles acted as witnesses to their history (they often appear in the stories of migration and the founding of cities) and contained the relics that had been given to the people by their patron god to commemorate their divine selection. Significantly, the sacred bundles were prominent in the enthronement ceremonies of kings (Olivier 2006).

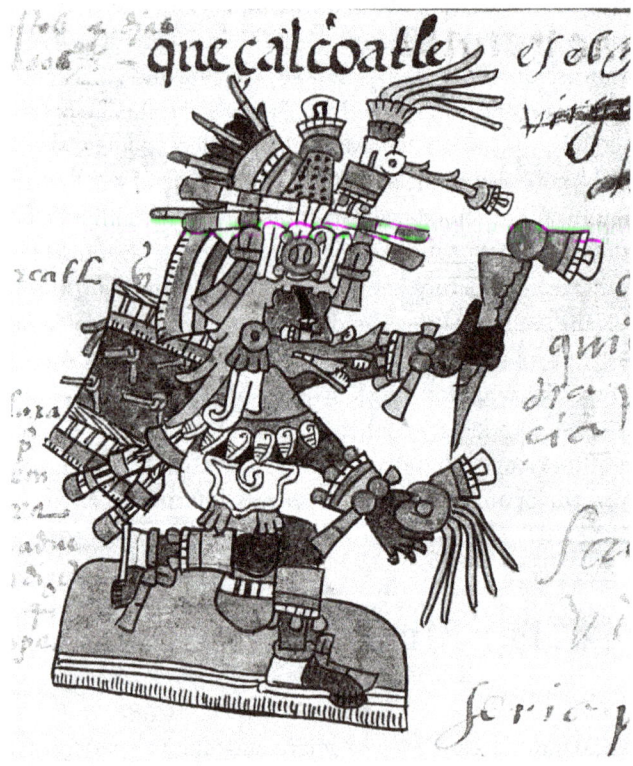

FIGURE 40.3 Quetzalcoatl, with a mouth mask identifying him in his manifestation as Ehecatl, god of wind (*Codex Telleriano-Remensis* 1995:fol. 8 v°). Reproduced with permission.

Rituals in Ancient Mexico

Undoubtedly, public and private rituals were prominent in the lives of the ancient Mexicas. Each stage of life—for example, birth, marriage, death—required the fulfillment of specific rites. Moreover, different social groups, communities, or states had their own rituals to worship their patron gods or ensure the success of different activities. All of the various ritual activities had to be conducted at precise moments determined through calculations involving the solar and ritual calendars (Aveni this volume).

The practice of ritual sacrifice has received top billing from those who discuss Mexica religion (Carrasco 1999; Graulich 2005; López Luján and Olivier 2010). In their stories, the chroniclers describe in terrifying detail the human sacrifices, ritual activities that, incidentally, along with idolatry, became one of the main "arguments" used to justify the Spanish Conquest. As in many other belief systems throughout the world, the sacrifice of animals and humans was essential to ancient Mesoamerican religion. Traditionally, immolation rituals were seen as practices characteristic of the Postclassic period. However, archaeological discoveries in Teotihuacan and the Maya area, for example, suggest the practice was much older. For the Postclassic period, however, we have detailed descriptions of the rituals that culminated in human sacrifice. Most of the sacrifices were intended to nourish the sun and the earth, the very gods who sacrificed themselves at Teotihuacan in order to set the stars in motion. In fact, in ancient Mesoamerican thought, the idea that life is born of death was essential, as expressed by various creation myths.

We can distinguish two types of sacrificial victims: the prisoners of war who served as food for the gods—men were regarded as beings of corn with which the gods were nourished—and *ixiptla*, or representatives of the gods. Children, unmarried men, young girls, adult women, and even elderly men could be the "images" of different deities for a given time, at the end of which they were sacrificed. These ritual sacrifices of divine representatives were thought to permit the periodic rebirth of the gods.

An example is the 20-day *Toxcatl*, the main festival dedicated to Tezcatlipoca, during which a young man represented that god (Sahagún 1950–1982:2:66–77). His selection from among a group of prisoners of war followed very strict rules, and Nahuatl texts describe a long list of necessary physical traits, which together represented a true image of idealized beauty among the ancient Nahuas. For a year, the young man was treated like a god; as he passed through the streets, playing his flute, smelling flowers, and smoking tobacco, people bowed and ate earth as a sign of respect and women introduced their children to him. Shortly before the festival, the representative of Tezcatlipoca was married to four women, images of the goddesses Xochiquetzal, Xilonen, Uixtacihuatl, and Atlatonan. Twenty days later the young man—who had been dressed by the king himself—traveled by canoe to a small temple accompanied by his four wives. The representatives of the goddesses then abandoned the young man to his tragic fate. Willingly, the representative of Tezcatlipoca slowly climbed the steps of the pyramid; as he climbed, he broke a flute on each step. At very top of the structure, the priests opened his chest with precision to remove his heart then threw his body down the stairs (Figure 40.4). Unfortunately, there is only room here for a cursory examination. To summarize, the representative of Tezcatlipoca was the substitute for the king or *tlahtoani*, who sacrificed himself symbolically through this young man. Thus this young man represented the protective deity of the king and acted on his behalf on earth during the *Toxcatl* feast (Olivier 2003:193–230).

In another account, we again find the *tlahtoani*, this time leading a great collective hunt during the 20-day month of *Quecholli* (*Códice Tudela* 1980:fol. 24r; Sahagún 1950–1982:2:134–140). Dressed and adorned as Mixcoatl, the god of the hunt, the Mexica king instructed hunters around Zacatepetl Hill—in the southern part of Mexico City—to gather at the peak with various animals such as rabbits, coyotes, and particularly deer. These prey were then sacrificed "in the manner of men," that is, by removing their hearts. In addition, the sources describe the sacrifice of war captives who were carried as if they were hunting trophies. These interconnected immolations, of deer and war captives, reflect the equivalence of hunting and war in Mesoamerican thought (Olivier 2010, 2015). Furthermore, during *Quecholli*, the myth that tells of the encounter between Mixcoatl and Chimalma, which resulted in the birth of Quetzalcoatl, was also reenacted.

FIGURE 40.4 Sacrifice of the young man representing the god Tezcatlipoca during the 20-day *Toxcatl* festival (Sahagún 1959–198:I, Book 2:fol. 30 v°). Reproduced with permission.

That is, the Mexica hunters, led by their king—Mixcoatl's *ixiptla* ("impersonator")—symbolically impregnated the goddess of the earth (Chimalma, also known as Coatlicue) during this 20-day ritual month. During the following 20-day ritual month (known as *Panquetzaliztli*), the birth of Quetzalcoatl was logically celebrated. Such was the case, for example, among the Yucatecan Maya, who honored Kukulkan, the Maya equivalent of the Feathered Serpent, during that month. In contrast, during *Panquetzaliztli*, the Nahua celebrated the birth of Huitzilopochtili, the god who took the place of Quetzalcoatl as patron god of the Mexica (Graulich 2005:109–112). Thus during *Quecholli* the Mexica hunters and their king served as the "ritual generators" of Huitzilopochtli, their tutelary god. By reenacting the impregnation of the goddess of the earth, who ultimately gave birth to Huitzilopochtli, they thus begat their own god (Olivier 2015:417–421, 653).

Although hunting at that time did not represent an important economic activity, hunting ideology remained extremely important to support the practice of war (i.e., hunting for men) and human sacrifice. Moreover, one of the mythic models for rites commemorating access to power (i.e., enthronement ceremonies) was the sacrifice of Mimixcoa—prototypes of sacrificial victims similar to deer—by the Mexicas during their migration. Indeed, the future rulers performed various rituals during which they symbolically died. In one example, the leader was stretched over a sacrificial stone while the septum of his nose was pierced. This act signified at once his status as a potential sacrificial victim—like the Mimixcoa of myth—and also his transformation into *tlahtoani* (Olivier 2015).

Parallel to all of these majestic public rites, many private rites were conducted at different venues. They were carried out in private homes to recognize a birth, in the cornfields to promote the fertility of the land, in caves to give thanks to the owners of the mountains, and so on. Many of these rites have survived, of course with some changes, and are practiced today in contemporary indigenous communities.

Mexica Gods and Society

Throughout this chapter I have repeatedly mentioned the ties that existed between gods and different social groups (Broda and Carrasco 1978). Most of the deities were closely linked to specific people: for example, Huitzilopochtli with the Mexicas, Mixcoatl with Tlaxcala, Quetzalcoatl with the inhabitants of Cholula. In addition, every village and neighborhood had its own temple to venerate its divine protector. Similarly, groups of people engaging in the same activity also had a patron deity, such as Yacatecuhtli for merchants, Quetzalcoatl for priests, Coyotl Inahual for feather artisans, and Xipe Totec for goldsmiths. Even the most downtrodden, slaves (*tlatlacotin*) were protected by a deity as powerful as Tezcatlipoca. On the day 1 Death (*Ce Miquiztli*), owners removed their slaves' collars and treated them with the utmost respect; if they failed to do so, Tezcatlipoca would reverse the roles of master and slave (Sahagún 1950–1982:4:34–35).

In Mexico-Tenochtitlan, although the *tlahtoani* was the supreme leader, he shared power with the *cihuacoatl* ("serpent woman")—whom the Spanish called the "viceroy." In the most general terms, the king associated with the Sun focused on "foreign policy" (particularly war), while the *cihuacoatl*—named after the goddess of the earth—was in charge of internal affairs. This dualism is reflected in the Great Temple of Tenochtitlan, which was also a double building: the southern part was dedicated to Huitzilopochtli, the sun god of war, and the northern section to Tlaloc, god of the earth and rain (López Austin and López Luján 2009).

Destiny and Reciprocity

In exchange for prayers, chants, offerings, and sacrificial victims, the gods provided the Mexicas with life and sustenance, as well as cultural heritage. This strong dependence on divine beings resulted from the intense devotion of the indigenous people who carried out bloody self-sacrifice and rituals. While testimony exists regarding captives or slaves

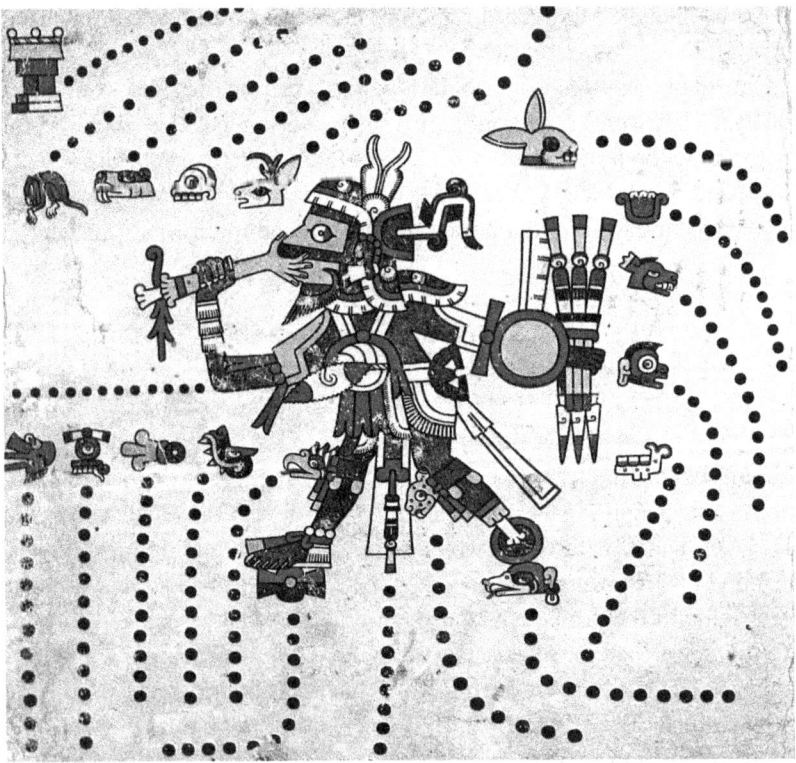

FIGURE 40.5 Tezcatlipoca, god of destiny, surrounded by the signs of the divinatory calendar (*Códice Fejérváry-Mayer* 1994:44). Reproduced with permission.

who resisted being sacrificed, other reliable sources assert that many of those destined to be sacrificed—like the representative of Tezcatlipoca described earlier—accepted their deaths. This is consistent with the importance of the particular destiny assigned to each person based on his or her date of birth. As a result, many reference the "fatalistic" character of the ancient Mexicas. However, this characterization should be qualified. The *tonalpouhque* assigned a particular destiny (*tonalli*) to each newborn based on his or her day of birth; however, for those born on an unlucky day, one option was to postpone the baptism ceremony in order to associate the child with a more favorable *tonalli* (Figure 40.2). Moreover, divinatory practices—some based on consulting codices—far from simply revealing an immutable destiny, represented a means of communicating with the gods and the opportunity for the gods to intervene, since the gods could be directed and even manipulated in a positive manner for humans (Olivier 2012). Finally, considering the nocturnal apparitions of Tezcatlipoca that used to taunt humans, in reality, these taunts were tests meant to reveal different individuals' destinies. Here it was even possible for confrontations to occur in which daring individuals were able to defeat Tezcatlipoca himself (Sahagún 1950–1982:5:151–159) (Figure 40.5). Thus, and without underestimating the importance of one's destiny, the winners of these contests would have been born on "strong" *tonalli*; an individual's attitude also played a role in his or her relationship with the gods.

As mortals in the world of the gods, the ancient Mexicas created complex divine figures with which they established a subtle yet permanent dialogue, a dialogue that also highlights the principles of reciprocity and hierarchy that structured their own society.

References Cited

Boone, Elizabeth H.
2007 *Cycles of Time and Meaning in the Mexican Books of Fate*. University of Texas Press, Austin.
Broda, Johanna, and Pedro Carrasco (editors)
1978 *Economía política e ideología en el México Prehispánico*. Nueva Imagen, Mexico City.
Carrasco, Davíd
1992 *Quetzalcoatl and the Irony of Empire*. University Press of Colorado, Boulder.
1999 *City of Sacrifice: The Aztec Empire and the Role of Violence in Civilization*. Beacon Press, Boston.
Caso, Alfonso
1967 *Los calendarios prehispánicos*. Universidad Nacional Autónoma de México, Instituto de Investigaciones Históricas, Mexico City.
Codex Telleriano-Remensis
1995 *Ritual, Divination, and History in a Pictorial Aztec Manuscript*. Edited by Eloise Quiñones Queber. University of Texas Press, Austin.
Códice Borgia
1963 [1904] *Códice Borgia*. Edited by Eduard Seler. Fondo de Cultura Económica, Mexico City.
Códice Fejérváry-Mayer
1994 *El libro de Tezcatlipoca, Señor del tiempo. Libro explicativo del llamado Códice Fejérváry-Mayer*. Edited by Ferdinand Anders, Maarten Jansen, and Gabina Aurora Pérez Jiménez.

Akademische Druck-u. Verlagsanstalt, Graz, and Fondo de Cultura Económica, Mexico City.

Códice Florentino

1979 *El manuscrito 218-220 de la colección Palatina de la Biblioteca Medicea Laurenziana.* 3 vols. Giunti Barbéra and Archivo General de la Nación, Florencia, Mexico City.

Códice Tudela

1980 *Códice Tudela.* Edited by José Tudela de la Orden. Ediciones Cultura Hispánica del Instituto de Cooperación Iberoamericano, Madrid.

Códice Vaticano-Latino 3738

1996 *Religión, costumbres e historia de los antiguos mexicanos. Libro explicativo del llamado Códice Vaticano A.* Edited by Ferdinand Anders and Maarten Jansen. Akademische Druck-u. Verlagsanstalt, Graz, and Fondo de Cultura Económica, Mexico City.

Graulich, Michel

1997 *Myths of Ancient Mexico.* University of Oklahoma Press, Norman.

2005 *Le sacrifice humain chez les Aztèques.* Fayard, Paris.

Historia de los mexicanos por sus pinturas

1941 In *Nueva colección de documentos para la historia de México*, edited by Joaquín García Icazbalceta, pp. 209–240. Salvador Chavez Hayhoe, Mexico City.

Leyenda de los Soles

1992 Leyenda de los Soles. In *History and Mythology of the Aztecs: The Codex Chimalpopoca*, edited by John Bierhorst, pp. 139–162. University of Arizona Press, Tucson.

López Austin, Alfredo

1973 *Hombre-dios: religión y política en el mundo náhuatl.* Universidad Nacional Autónoma de México, Instituto de Investigaciones Históricas, Mexico City.

1980 *Cuerpo humano e ideología: las concepciones de los antiguos nahuas.* 2 vols. Universidad Nacional Autónoma de México, Instituto de Investigaciones Antropológicas, Mexico City.

1990 *Los mitos del tlacuache: caminos de la mitología mesoamericana.* Alianza Editorial Mexicana, Mexico City.

López Austin, Alfredo, and Leonardo López Luján

1996 *El pasado indígena.* Fondo de Cultura Económica, El Colegio de México, Mexico City.

2009 *Monte Sagrado-Templo Mayor.* Instituto Nacional de Antropología e Historia, Universidad Nacional Autónoma de México, Instituto de Investigaciones Antropológicas, Mexico City.

López Luján, Leonardo, and Guilhem Olivier (editors)

2010 *El sacrificio humano en la tradición religiosa mesoamericana.* Instituto Nacional de Antropología e Historia, Universidad Nacional Autónoma de México, Instituto de Investigaciones Históricas, Mexico City.

Nicholson, Henry B.

1971 Religion in Pre-Hispanic Central Mexico. In *Archaeology of Northern Mesoamerica*, edited by Gordon F. Ekholm and Ignacio Bernal, pp. 395–446. Handbook of Middle American Indians, Vol. 10, Robert Wauchope, General Editor, University of Texas Press, Austin.

2001 *Topiltzin Quetzalcoatl: The Once and Future Lord of the Toltecs.* University Press of Colorado, Boulder.

Olivier, Guilhem

2003 *Mockeries and Metamorphoses of an Aztec God. Tezcatlipoca, "Lord of the Smoking Mirror."* University Press of Colorado, Boulder.

2006 The Sacred Bundles and the Coronation of the Aztec King in Mexico-Tenochtitlan. In *Sacred Bundles. Ritual Acts of Wrapping and Binding in Mesoamerica*, edited by Julia Guernsey and F. Kent Reilly, pp. 199–225. Ancient America Special Publication No. 1. Boundary End Archaeology Research Center, Barnardsville, NC.

2010 El simbolismo sacrificial de los Mimixcoa: cacería, guerra, sacrificio e identidad entre los mexicas, In *El sacrificio humano en la tradición religiosa mesoamericana*, edited by López Luján and Guilhem Olivier, pp. 453–482. Instituto Nacional de Antropología e Historia, Universidad Nacional Autónoma de México, Instituto de Investigaciones Históricas, Mexico City.

2012 Divination, manipulation du destin et mythe d'origine chez les anciens Mexicains. In *Deviner pour agir: regards comparatifs sur des pratiques divinatoires anciennes et contemporaines*, edited by Jean-Luc Lambert and Guilhem Olivier, pp. 145–172. École Pratique des Hautes Études, Paris.

2015 *Cacería, sacrificio y poder en Mesoamérica: tras las huellas de Mixcóatl, "Serpiente de Nube."* Instituto de Investigaciones Históricas, Universidad Nacional Autónoma de México, Fondo de Cultura Económica, Centro de Estudios Mexicanos y Centramericanos, Mexico City.

Sahagún, Fray Bernardino de

1950–1982 *Florentine Codex: General History of the Things of New Spain*. 12 vols. Edited by Arthur J. O. Anderson and Charles E. Dibble. School of American Research, Santa Fe, NM, and the University of Utah, Salt Lake City.

Seler, Eduard

1963 *Comentarios al Códice Borgia*. Fondo de Cultura Económica, Mexico City.

Thévet, André

1905 Histoyre du Mechique, manuscrit français inédit du XVIe siècle. *Journal de la Société des Américanistes* 2:1–41.

CHAPTER 41

AZTEC ART, TIME, AND COSMOVISIÓN

WILLIAM L. BARNES

INTRODUCTION

IN Aztec Mexico, the visual arts were employed to make manifest the ties that bound together natural and supernatural worlds. Particularly in the imperial center of Tenochtitlan, the arts were often used to cast the polity as the center of both realms. The visual was used to record historical events as well, and because the Aztecs believed that the hands of various supernaturals directed the history of the polity, even those records were infused with aspects of the divine. Conversely, works of art that might be viewed today as grand symbols of religious devotion were usually commissioned with contemporary political expediency in mind and hence often have references to historical events couched within their predominantly religious iconography.

For the Aztecs, the sacred and the profane were indivisible, and the most tangible evidence of divine action in the world was the Mesoamerican calendar with its interlocking 260-day and 365-day cycles. Aside from marking time, the calendar was also used to both name Aztec deities and regulate their worship. The calendrical name of a deity, painted on a support or carved in stone, was enough to invoke that particular supernatural, and calendrical coincidences were seen as acts of divine providence. Was it, after all, simply chance that the Tenochca defeated Azcapotzalco in the *Year 1* Flint, a victory that essentially gave birth to the Aztec Empire, when the *Day 1* Flint also served as the name-day of their tutelary god Huitzilopochtli?

The divine most often became manifest in the natural world at calendrically regulated theophanic festivals. In these, the raiment of the deity, his or her costume, and related iconography that transformed deity impersonators (*teixiptla*) into the divine incarnate. To the Aztecs, the visual was not simply descriptive; by conflating the iconic and the indexical, Aztec artists and artisans could call forth the gods.

Aztec Art, Artists, and the Divine

The Aztecs had a clearly defined notion of the visual arts as a discrete phenomenon and, not surprisingly, attributed a temporal quality to it. They cultured an awareness of the deep history of art in Mesoamerica, and they sought out examples of past peoples' works to appropriate and, at times, emulate with newer works of their own. Most people of Postclassic central Mexico identified the preeminent artists of the past, the ideal artists, as "Toltecs." The term *Toltec* today usually refers to the people who lived at the archaeological site of Tula, Hidalgo. And while the Aztecs used this term to reference those past peoples as well, they employed it in a broader sense to reference most admirable ancients, including those from Xochicalco, Classic Veracruz, and Teotihuacan, among others (López-Luján 2002; Umberger 1989). This perception of those past peoples' expertise in the visual arts was such that, in Nahuatl, the closest approximation to the English term "art" is *toltecayotl*, or "Toltec-ness." If mentioning artisans and craftsmen generally, as Fray Bernardino de Sahagún does in his sixteenth-century *Florentine Codex* (Sahagún 1950–1982:10:25), they are simply called *toltecatl*, or Toltecs.

Aztec *toltecatl* usually specialized in a particular media (Figure 41.1). While they were most often identified by the media with which they worked as goldsmiths, lapidaries, featherworkers, stone carvers, painters, and the like, it appears that they were also thought of as a collective whole in the same manner that we talk of "artists" today. This greater group of artists, and in particular scribes and weavers (notably women weavers and embroiders), shared the divine patronage of Chicome Xochitl (7 Flower). Sahagún (1950–1982:2:35–36, 1979:4:7) notes that this calendrical supernatural, along with his female counterpart Xochiquetzal (see also Durán 1971:244), was venerated by artists on his name-day festival that occurred every 7 Flower. Particularly fortuitous, claims Sahagún (1950–1982:4:7), were the artists who had 7 Flower as their own name-day, for "he who was born on it would perform all crafts well, he would be a good craftsman; he would plan well great works."

This passage in Sahagún is telling, for it illustrates how even the act of creation could be seen as an aspect of divine providence. And while *all* artisans may have venerated Chicome Xochitl for the gifts he or his consort might bestow, there were also a host of other supernaturals regularly venerated and invoked by practitioners of specific crafts. For example, goldworkers paid reverence to the fearsome deity Xipe Totec (Sahagún 1950–1982:9:69), particularly during his spectacular *veintena* festival of Tlacaxipehualiztli. The lapidaries honored a group of four deities led by the calendrically named goddess Chiconahui Itzcuintli (9 Dog). A version of the goddess Chantico (Nicholson 1971:Table 3, 413–414), she was said to have invented the lapidary arts along with three collaborators: Naualpilli, Macuilcalli (5 House), and Centeotl (the corn-god) (Sahagún 1950–1982:9:79). The featherworkers had a group of patrons led by Coyotl Inaual (He of the Coyote Disguise) and included six male (Tiçaua, Macuil Ocelotl [5 Jaguar], Macuil Tochtli [5 Rabbit], Tepoztecatl) and two female (Xiuhtlati and Xilo) deities (Sahagún 1950–1982:9:83–84).

FIGURE 41.1 Images of goldsmiths at work. From the *Florentine Codex* 9, f52. Reproduced with permission.

The concern of these various artists with their patron deities, the majority of which have calendrical names (the other deities mentioned likely had specific feast days in the calendar as well), illustrates how religion and the calendar were pervasive in both Aztec life and art. Aztec artists venerated their patron calendrical deities, and the work that they produced—as evidenced from surviving objects—directly addressed the calendar in both the depictions of various deities, dates, and events and for their prescribed use during specific festivals, celebrations, and rites. This concern was so ubiquitous that even historical events were referenced using a visual language of supernatural actors and religiously significant calendrical dates (Olivier and López Luján 2009), as can be seen in works such as the great *Tizoc Stone* and the *Teocalli of Sacred Warfare*.

THE DESIGN OF THE COSMOS

One of the best-known works of Aztec art, the Aztec Calendar Stone (also called the *Piedra del Sol*, Stone of the Sun) illustrates how Aztec artists could masterfully blend mythic/religious and calendrical/historical concerns (Figure 41.2).

FIGURE 41.2 The Aztec Calendar Stone, or Stone of the Sun. Drawing courtesy of Emily Umberger.

This enigmatic monument has been the subject of both wild theories and serious study since the fall of Tenochtitlan (see Villela and Miller 2010). The Calendar Stone is, as Emily Umberger (2010 [1988]) pointed out, one in a series of sun-stones commissioned by Aztec rulers, and just as the Aztecs referenced past cultures in their eclectic art, they also referenced past rulers and those past rulers' great commissions.

The patron of the Calendar Stone, likely Motecuhzoma II, used his version of a sun-stone to integrate mythic and dynastic histories by combining calendrical data and religious iconography. The central portion of the stone is comprised of a large calendrical name-glyph of the current sun, the fifth in a series of creations: 4 Movement (4 Ollin). This complex glyph takes the form of an X pierced through the center by a triangular dart. At the crux of the X is the circular face of a deity, likely Nahui Ollin (4 Movement). Within that large glyph, artists also couched mention of the previous four eras, or suns, using their own respective day-names. The first sun, 4 Jaguar (4 Ocelotl) is in the upper right quadrant, with its successors placed counterclockwise around the central face of the sun (4 Wind, 4 Rain, and 4 Water).

This group of symbols that references the grand ages of creation is surrounded by a circular band of 20 symbols, each representing a day-sign in the central Mexican divinatory calendar. The order of the days begins with *cipactli* (crocodilian), just to the left of the central diadem of the large 4 Movement glyph, and continues counterclockwise around the central group. These signs were used to delineate quotidian time in the 260-day calendar (*tonalpohualli*), and, in conjunction with the 365-day count (*xihuitl* [year] or *xiuhtlapohualli* [year count]), they served to name each day in the 52-year calendar round (Caso 1967, 1971; Tena 1987; see also Aveni this volume). As employed in the *tonalpohualli*, these 20 signs were used to name humans and gods and allowed priests to divine the significance of past, present, and future events (Boone 2007).

Placed in the interstices between the day-names and the names of the mythic ages is an enigmatic grouping of glyphs carved in lower relief. They are not sequential like the others, nor are they all date-glyphs. To the left of the triangular diadem of the 4 Movement glyph is a small symbol that, in the main, has been interpreted as the name-glyph of Motecuhzoma II (Olivier and López Luján 2009:78–92; Umberger 1981:66–71, 199; 2010 [1988]:241–255; Villela and Miller 2010). Facing it across the diadem is the date 1 Flint (1 Tecpatl) which serves, among other things, as the name-glyph of Huitzilopochtli. These two glyphs have counterparts below the central group, the Day 1 Rain (1 Quiahuitl) on the left, a glyph comprised of the face of the rain deity Tlaloc, and the date 5 Monkey (5 Ozomatli) on the right. These lower glyphs have been interpreted a number of different ways over the years, with scholars suggesting that they might reference the four directions, various supernaturals, and feast days of unknown relevance (see Villela and Miller 2010). More recently it has been suggested that they reference periods of time that link the reigns of Axayacatl (r. 1468–1481) with that of his son, the work's patron, Motecuhzoma II (Barnes 2015).

Such a dynastic concern is not unexpected, as the emperor's name-glyph is a fairly prominent feature of the work, yet it is also telling in how these glyphs rank, in a hierarchical fashion, to the other glyphs on the stone. They occupy an intermediate space and are of an intermediate size. With their royal and divine associations, they would then rank somewhat below the grand mythic dates of the five ages and yet rank higher than the surrounding smaller 20 day-signs of the *tonalpohualli*.

While debate surrounding the identification of the various supernaturals depicted on the stone, including the central face, continues to this day, one can still discern the underlying message of the stone by looking to the calendrical information, for couched within it is a clear attempt to link together the cosmic eras and their divine actors, the dynasty of Tenochtitlan, and the sacred passage of time.

Indeed, we can glimpse within the design of the Calendar Stone a version of the Aztec conception of the cosmos, or *cosmovisión*. This is a pervasive design that even informs the layout of the Aztec capital city of Tenochtitlan (see Luis de Rojas this volume). As noted by Michael Smith (2003:185), the Aztecs borrowed from the urban layout of both Teotihuacan and Tula to construct their own sacred city, particularly in the creation of a ceremonial core. At the center of the city, walled off with a serpent wall, or *coateopantli*, were numerous temples, shrines, and sacred structures surrounding the great Templo Mayor, a multistepped pyramid with twin shrines at its top dedicated to the ancient central Mexican rain deity Tlaloc and the tribal deity of the Aztecs, Huitzilopochtli. The surrounding structures were each dedicated to a particular deity or designated for a specific ritual purposes.

In its organization, the central ceremonial precinct echoed the sacred landscape of Nahua creation mythology (López Austin and López Luján 2009), and the Templo Mayor, in particular, served to reify the divine narrative of Huitzilopochtli's birth (Matos Moctezuma 1987). The tutelary deity of the Aztecs, Huitzilopochtli sprang forth from his mother's womb fully grown and fully armed to slay his sister and disperse his other siblings who had gathered to kill him and his mother. Upon defeating his sister Coyolxauhqui, he cast her body down from the summit of Coatepec (Serpent Hill) whereupon it landed dismembered at the base of the mountain. This same fate then awaited the captured warriors of rebellious provinces or those from polities who declined to submit to Aztec hegemony, for when they were sacrificed atop the Templo Mayor in Tenochtitlan, their bodies were cast down from the top of that serpent-studded "mountain" (a Coatepec itself) to land ignobly atop or aside any number of Coyolxauhqui monuments that Aztec rulers installed at its base (López Luján 2010). The most famous of these, discovered in 1979 (Figure 41.3), depicts a mostly nude woman, wearing both male warrior costume elements and solar deity iconography, splayed and dismembered.

FIGURE 41.3 The Coyolxauhqui Stone. Drawing courtesy of Emily Umberger.

This version was likely meant to remind its viewers of the recent conquest of Tlatelolco, Tenochtitlan's sister city (Graulich 2000; Klein 1994; Umberger 1996, 2007). Indeed, in accounts of the defeat of Tlatelolco, that city's ruler was cast down from Tlatelolco's own main temple by the Aztec *tlahtoani* Axayacatl in the same way that Huitzilopochtli had done with his doomed sister.

In its design, the city and its central precinct follows the layout of the Calendar Stone in echoing the Aztec conception of the cosmos. The ceremonial core was the domain of the deities and was filled with religious and ceremonial structures that made reference to past and present divine action. Surrounding this sacred core, just outside the *coateopantli*, were structures of dynastic significance: the palaces of past and present Aztec rulers. This placement of the palaces, then, echoes the interstitial location of the more dynastic glyphs on the Calendar Stone. Enclosing these mythic and dynastic glyphs on the stone is the band of 20 day-signs, the fundamental building blocks of the Mesoamerican calendar. Likewise, then, in the city of Tenochtitlan, the central divine and royal nucleus was surrounded by the houses and *chinampas* of the city's more common inhabitants, all of which were organized into *calpolli* (Calnek 1976; Lockhart 1992; van Zantwijk 1976) that had at their centers myriad temples (*teocalli*) dedicated to members of the Aztec pantheon—members whose name-days and festivals essentially populate the Mesoamerican calendar.

Art and Cosmovisión

While imperial works and civic design could be expected to have some relation to conceptions of the cosmos, these same concerns pervade almost every aspect of Aztec artistic production. Aztec artists made reference to sacred or mythic concerns when crafting almost every work of art. The manuscripts and even maps created by Aztec *tlacuilo* (see Boone this volume) were almost entirely devoted to the depiction of sacred time and/or space. When looking at a calendar page from the *Codex Borbonicus*, an early colonial manuscript likely copied from a prehispanic original similar to the *Codex Borgia*, we find even the most simple depiction of a 13-day *trecena* is rife with supernatural concerns, from the patron deities and ritual paraphernalia that occupy the largest portion of the page to the small, cellular depictions of specific days with their divine lords of the day and nighttime hours and the sacred birds by which one could take auguries. The message here is that time itself was a sacred substance, and one could not move along its path without interacting with the various supernaturals who ruled its every moment.

Hence even the more mundane production of Aztec artists, the crafting of jewelry and even more utilitarian ceramic objects, resulted in objects that were adorned with sacred imagery, from the skulls of sacrifice (as with the Dumbarton Oaks Skull Necklace [PC.B.083]) to the geometric and stylized designs on plates and cups (see Minc this volume). The challenge for current scholars of Aztec art is to then divine the significance of these sometimes obscure references, placing them in some approximation of their original context.

Conclusion

Art, time (calendrical, cultural), and space all intertwined in the imperial art of Tenochtitlan, from the deities honored by the artists to the deities adopted from foreign lands. The calendar was seen as a complex intertwined system that allowed insight into the will of the gods. Aztec rulers, working in the same manner as their artists and artisans, saw the stuff of the world—its natural features, politics, and peoples—as the raw materials they could work and form in order to achieve the divine directives discernable within the calendar. In each depiction of the gods, even as the most abstracted motif, some stuff of the divine could be reified in this world and serve to remind people of their sacred obligations and the gods' designs for both man and empire.

References Cited

Barnes, William L.
2015 Divine Reckoning: The Calendrical Ground of Mexican Dynastic Imagery. In *The Measure and Meaning of Time in the Americas*, edited Anthony F. Aveni. Dumbarton Oaks Research and Library Collection, Washington, DC.

Boone, Elizabeth H.
2007 *Cycles of Time and Meaning in the Mexican Books of Fate*. University of Texas Press, Austin.

Calnek, Edward
1976 The Internal Structure of Tenochtitlan. In *The Valley of Mexico*, edited by Eric R. Wolf, pp. 287–302. University of New Mexico Press, Albuquerque.

Caso, Alfonso
1967 *Los calendarios prehispánicos*. Intituto de Investigaciones Históricas, Universidad Nacional Autónoma de México, Mexico City.
1971 Calendrical Systems of Central Mexico. In *Handbook of Middle American Indians*, Vol. 10, edited by Robert Wauchope, Gordon F. Ekholm, and Ignacio Bernal, pp. 333–348. University of Texas Press, Austin.

Durán, Diego
1971 *Book of the Gods and Rites and the Ancient Calendar*. Translated and edited by Fernando Horcasitas and Doris Heyden. University of Oklahoma Press, Norman.

Graulich, Michel
2000 Más Sobre La Coyolxauhqui y Las Mujeres Desnudas de Tlatelolco. *Estudios de Cultura Náhuatl* 31:77–94.

Klein, Cecelia F.
1994 Fighting with Femininity: Gender and War in Aztec Mexico. *Estudios de Cultura Náhuatl* 24:219–253.

Lockhart, James

1992 *The Nahuas after the Conquest: A Social and Cultural History of the Indians of Central Mexico, Sixteenth through Eighteenth Centuries.* Stanford University Press, Stanford, CA.

López Austin, Alfredo, and Leonardo López Luján

2009 *Monte Sagrado-Templo Mayor.* Universidad Nacional Autónoma de México Instituto de Investigaciones Antropológicas, Mexico City.

López Luján, Leonardo

2002 The Aztec's Search for the Past. In *Aztecs,* edited by Eduardo Matos Moctezuma and Felipe Sólis Olgúin, pp. 22–29. Royal Academy of Arts, London.

2010 Los otras imágines de Coyolxauhqui. *Arqueología Mexicana* 17(102):48–59.

Matos Moctezuma, Eduardo

1987 *Great Temple of Tenochtitlan: Center and Periphery in the Aztec World.* University of California Press, Berkeley

Nicholson, H. B.

1971 Religion in Pre-Hispanic Central Mexico. In *Handbook of Middle American Indians,* Vol 10, edited by Robert Wauchope, Gordon F. Ekholm, and Ignacio Bernal, pp. 91–134. University of Texas Press, Austin.

Olivier, Guilhem, and Leonardo López Luján

2009 Images of Moteuczoma and his symbols of power. In *Moctezuma: Aztec Ruler,* edited by Colin McEwan and Leonardo López Luján, pp. 78–91. British Museum Press, London.

Sahagún, Fray Bernardino de

1950–1982 *Florentine Codex: General History of the Things of New Spain.* 13 vols. Edited and translated by Arthur J. O Anderson and Charles E. Dibble. School of American Research, Santa Fe, NM, and University of Utah Press, Salt Lake City.

Smith, Michael E.

2003 *The Aztecs.* 2nd ed. Blackwell, Malden MA.

Tena, Rafael

1987 *El calendario mexica y la cronografía.* Colección Científica 161. Instituto Nacional de Antropología e Historia, Mexico City.

Umberger, Emily G.

1981 *Aztec Sculptures, Hieroglyphs, and History.* Ph.D. dissertation, Columbia University, New York. University Microfilms, Ann Arbor.

1996 Art and Imperial Strategy in Tenochtitlan. In *Aztec Imperial Strategies,* edited by Francis F. Berdan, Richard Blanton, Elizabeth H. Boone, Mary Hodge, Michael E. Smith, and Emily Umberger, pp. 85–108. Dumbarton Oaks Research and Library Collection, Washington, DC.

2007 The Metaphorical Underpinnings of Aztec History: The Case of the 1473 Civil War. *Ancient Mesoamerica* 18:11–29.

2010 [1988] A Reconsideration of Some Hieroglyphs on the Mexica Calendar Stone. In *The Aztec Calendar Stone,* edited by Khristaan D. Villela and Mary Ellen Miller, pp. 238–257. Getty Research Institute, Los Angeles.

Villela, Khristaan D., and Mary Ellen Miller (editors)

2010 *The Aztec Calendar Stone.* Getty Research Institute, Los Angeles.

van Zantwijk, Rudolf

1976 La Organizacion social de la Mexico-Tenochtitlan Naciente. *Actas del XLI Congreso Internacional de Americanistas, México, 1974* 2:188–208.

CHAPTER 42

THE AZTEC RITUAL LANDSCAPE

LEÓN GARCÍA GARAGARZA

... motepeyocpa mitzvalitta moteua ...
("Your god watches you from your mountains.")
Hymn to Centeotl (Sahagún, *Primeros Memoriales*, Folio 280v)

A veritable world navel, the Basin of Mexico dramatically lies at the knot of the Trans-Mexican Volcanic Belt, which links the Eastern and Western Sierras that run along Mesoamerica. Surrounded by Sierras and majestic peaks and blessed with abundant water and agricultural fertility, the Basin has been the nucleus for the development of urban life in central Mesoamerica since antiquity. The Mesoamerican cosmovision was based on real geographic features, symbolically reinterpreted in myth and ritual (Broda 2009:47). The fundamental tropes of this cosmovision were set during the rise of the first agricultural communities, ca. 2500 B.C. Based on the productive dynamics of the cultivation of corn, these tropes form what Alfredo López Austin (2005:69) has termed the "hard nucleus" of Mesoamerican cosmovision, since they are enormously resistant to change and, moreover, have been—up to our own day—the "structuring center" of each successive historical transformation. At the very basis of this cosmovision was the perception of the world as a living entity, whose processes were assimilated to the physiology of the human body. The gods were the hidden cause of all phenomena, so everything in nature was but an envelope, a disguise of the deities, who constituted the heart, or inner essence, of every single existing thing. Each god was capable of fragmenting into multiple personae, each with its own avocation. Realistically perceived as both bountiful, dangerous, and capricious, gods were the *Teteuctin* ("lords," "proprietors") of their respective spheres: mountains, stars, rivers, fire, animals, ethnic groups, clouds, individual human beings, and so on. In a world saturated with divine presences, human life was framed by a continuous series of performative rituals. From awakening, to eating, to working, to going to sleep, every human activity was given significance by its conscious reference to the supernatural, divine person ruling it. Lapses in ritual recognition to the powers that animated each act of individual and social life resulted in illness and collective calamity, which again were to be ritually healed or corrected.

According to myth, the earth was itself the body of Tlalteotl, a female monster torn apart and separated from the sky *ab initio* by the gods Quetzalcoatl and Tezcatlipoca. From the sacrificial dismemberment of Tlalteotl the features of the earth were born: her hair became plants, her eyes became springs and fountains, her mouths became rivers and caves, and her noses became mountains and valleys (Tena 2002:147). Tlalteotl devoured her creatures at the same time that she spawned them. Her sacrifice inaugurated an agrarian economy of reciprocal violence, as humans ensured their sustenance by ritually feeding her with their own blood.

A prominent and central element of the Mesoamerican ritual landscape since ancient times was the cult of *Itecouh Tepetl*, the divine Owner of the Mountain, called *Tlaloc* by the Nahuatl-speaking peoples of the late Postclassic era. God of the earth, rain, thunder, and fertility, Tlaloc "literally embodied the Mexican landscape" (Arnold 1991:219). During the Late Postclassic era, the worship of Tlaloc was universal, and the god was considered the oldest in the land (Glockner,2012:108). From his mountainous abode, the deity gave life to the community and granted his children the right to settle at his feet. The orographic configurations of the landscape rendered a symbolic landscape of gendered and hierarchical relations: mountains were seen as male or female—like the pair Popocatepetl (male)–Iztaccihuatl (female), or Mount Tlaloc (male)–Matlacueye (female), and many other such couples—while minor hills were conceived as Tepictoton deities, junior members of these divine earthly families. The mythical adjudications and power struggles between the peaks of the landscape reflected the shifting hegemonic status of the numerous ethnic communities of central Mexico (Broda 2009:41). Serving as patrons of distinct ethnic communities, mountains marked the territorial borders of states.

As the Nahua word for "city" indicates, the *altepetl* ("Water/Mountain") was the reiteration of a divine order that allowed for the sustenance and successful reproduction of any human settlement. The design of the *altepetl* replicated the cosmic layout of the quadripartite horizon surrounded by water, with the Axial Mountain (and its analogue, the Flowery Tree of Tamoanchan), at its center. As Sacred Center, the *altepetl* integrated in its body the time of origins with the present: Tenochtitlan, for instance, reiterated Aztlan, the original abode of the Aztecs, surrounded by water and crowned by the Mountain of the Ancestors, Colhuatepec. Mountains were seen as the living deposits of all earthly wealth and fertility. The gods of rain, the Tlaloqueh, resided there, ruling the growth of all life on the surface of the earth (*Tlalticpac*). Their abode was called Tlalocan, a paradisal realm of unparalleled fertility. Projected to the four corners of the world, the Axial Mountain was the privileged channel communicating the three levels of the vertical world (Heaven, Earth, and the Land of the Dead). A universal generator, the mountain signified the place where everything was born, including the Sun, the father of the present era, born in the Eastern Mountain, called Coatepec by the Mexicas. In a society that homologated the life processes of the sun, corn, and human beings, Tlaloc's patronage was indispensable. The tutelary mountain was the abode of the parental deities who engendered the members of the *altepetl*, sustained them, and granted them the rights to appropriate a given territory. Every *altepetl* thus had a neighboring tutelary mountain.

In the Postclassic era, the archetypal *altepetl* was Tollan, founded by the creator god Quetzalcoatl, a heroic deity who ordained the fundamental mechanisms of the world through the establishment of penitential self-sacrifices. To give movement to the Sun (*id est*, to the present era), the gods died, giving their own blood. Quetzalcoatl also stole from Mictlan the seeds to create the present humanity and broke open the mountain of Tlaloc, snatching away from Tlalocan the seeds of corn that would nourish his human children. In his guise as Wind (Ehecatl), Quetzalcoatl manifested a brotherly activity with Tlaloc, purifying the land with his breath and bringing in his wake the rain clouds from Tlalocan's summit. As the creator of humanity, Quetzalcoatl was considered the tutelary deity of humanity at large—even as he also had particular tutelage over specific cities, such as Cholula and Cempoala—so his cult became integrated into the life of every altepetl during the Postclassic era. His cult was indeed acclimated to the demands of the ethnic groups that established dominance in central Mexico after the fall of Tollan—these were collectively known as Chichimecas, nomadic groups who gradually acculturated and appropriated the models of territorial legitimacy and cultural hegemony inherited from Tula. The Tolteca-Chichimecas shared the common creation myth of Chicomoztoc, in which the gods begat their respective human descendants in groups of seven, who emerged from a uterine cave to wander the land as hunter-gatherers in search of a permanent agricultural settlement. Like other peoples before them, the Tolteca-Chichimecas expanded the elements of the hard nucleus of the Mesoamerican cosmovision into a new historical synthesis. Several colonial sources—such as Alva Ixtlixochitl (1975) and the *Códice Xólotl* (1951)—indicate that the Chichimecas, led by Xolotl (ca. A.D. 1244), successfully reformulated the protocols of land appropriation inherited from Tula by performing ritual perambulations across several prominent mountain peaks around the Basin of Mexico, the most significant of which was Mount Tlaloc, east of Lake Texcoco. Xolotl established his capital at Tenayuca, where he built a temple astronomically aligned with Mount Tlaloc. Xolotl's model perambulation over symbolic mountains, as well as his recognition of Mount Tlaloc as the preeminent site on which to establish hegemonic status in the region, would remain as important features of the Aztec ritual landscape.

The shape of the Aztec main temple (*Huey Teocalli*) manifested the persistence of the ancient agricultural cult of Tlaloc side by side with the cult to the particular tutelary deity of the city—Huiztilopochtli in Mexico, Camaxtli in Tepeaca, and so on. In Mexico, the main Teocalli was crowned by two parallel altar-houses, one dedicated to the terrestrial rain deity and the other to the bellicose solar deity that ruled the city. This symbolic model was reproduced in other cities in the region. The coexistence of Tlaloc and the local ethnic deity not only articulated well the hierarchical status of Postclassic society but also fit well with the structure of the shared underlying cosmovision, with its notion of a living world made dynamic by the constant interaction of complimentary opposites: hot/cold, wet/dry, above/below, male/female, life/death, and so on. The pyramidal shape of the Aztec temples replicated the cosmic shape of the World Mountain, and their disposition in the ceremonial center may have also reflected the local orography (López Austin 2005:77).

Just as the world was the projection of the World Mountain into the four quarters, the Aztec *altepetl* was ideally divided into four wards, or *calpolli s*, each with its own patron deity. The result was a complex web of ritual interactions throughout the *altepetl*, as the hierarchical relations between the cults of the different *calpolli s* with the coalescing cult of the *altepetl* were symbolically accommodated throughout the calendar year. In turn, the relationship between the *altepetl* and the surrounding territory had a specular character, for the city integrated in its main temple the power emanating from the tutelary mountain at its margins. As an early chronicler writes, "every mountain had its *tetelli*" ("stone altar") (Ponce 2007:15), and many had more elaborate temples called *Ayauhcalco* ("On the House of Mist"). The real mountain and its human epigone, the Teocalli in the city, were mirror pivots of the world.

This spatial relation is most clearly seen in the main Teocalli of Cholula, which clearly duplicates the shape of majestic Popocatepetl to the east, but the same process happened all over central Mexico: with Tetzcoco and its tutelary Mount Tlaloc, for example, or with Tlaxcala and Mount Matlacueye. For this reason, the relation between center and periphery expressed in the Mesoamerican cosmovision had a specific ritual manifestation: rather than a marginal status, the periphery of the *altepetl* in central Mesoamerica was constantly recentered during the frequent pilgrimages to the mountains and hills that characterized the religious life of the people. It was from these that power flowed to the *altepetl*. In fact, the Nahua term for ritual pilgrimages, *Tlayahualoliztli*, emphasizes the circuitous nature of religious pilgrimages (the verbal stem *Yahualoa* means "to circle, to go around in procession") (Molina 1970:66) The map of the Aztec ceremonial landscape was drawn by the collective movement of the people, who closed with their ritual pilgrimages the circuit of the sacred from the temples in the city to the sanctuaries in the countryside, and back. The reciprocity of offerings was also a reciprocity of space, sacralizing the landscape and the heart of the participants by circulating the god's presence in a loop that tied the home and the *teocalli* in the *altepetl* to the deity's home in the landscape outside.

Collective rituals had an extraordinary frequency and intensity during the Postclassic era. The members of the *calpolli* and the *altepetl* articulated their sense of social cohesion through the regular celebration of magnificent festivals (*ilhuitl*). As stated by the Nahuas themselves, during the celebration of festivals, "every person went in procession, either before dawn or at sundown; [only] later everyone scattered" (Sahagún 1997:76) Participation in these religious processions often involved considerable discomfort and suffering, but these dangers only bolstered the resolve of the people, convinced as they were that the ordeals were fundamental elements of the cosmic economy of divine reciprocity, where gods and creatures gave and received life through reciprocal exertion and sacrifice. As the *tlahtoani* of Cuetlaxxochitla stated in a speech to his people, recalling the religious life of their altepetl before the conquest,

> We have heard from our grandfathers, from our grandmothers, the old men and women, how they used to make their offerings on the heights of the hills, at the mounds of stones (*teocalco*), at the piles of stone (*teolocholco*), even in the dark of night, when it was pitch black, even if thundering or even if raining very hard, they did not fail to make their sacrificial offerings; rather, they would carry them out successfully to the very end [Ruiz de Alarcon 1984:58].

The expenses dedicated to the collective rituals regulated in great part the flow and distribution of goods. It was also during these festivals that the state articulated its policies and justified the existence of social hierarchies. But these economic and political considerations were made intelligible by the performative rituals that made the landscape a meaningful, orienting cosmic body. In the words of Davíd Carrasco (1991a:xxiv), the Aztec "ceremonial landscape" was "marked, mapped, and rejuvenated by complex sets of performances that communicated knowledge about the social and symbolic order of the Aztec world and its sacred foundation."

The Mesoamerican collective rituals of this era can be divided into two categories: calendrical and noncalendrical. The first corresponded to the 18 months (*Meztli*) of the solar year, when every 20 days the community as a whole worshipped specific deities. There were also 16 moveable festivals (*Ilhuitl*) linked to the divinatory calendar of 260 days (*Tonalpohualli*), as well as other festivals held every four years. (Sahagún 1981:35–41). An important festival, the "Tying of the Years" (*Xiuhmolpilli*) was held every 52 years. The 18 regular festivals of the solar calendar (*Xiuhpohualli*) were linked to the seasonal rhythms of agricultural production—including those that emphasized the pursuit of war and conquest, activities that were pursued most vigorously after the harvest, when armies could be properly supplied (Hassig 1988:53). Other collective rituals were not tied to the solar calendar but celebrated the life stages of the individuals and their inscription into different institutions, or were organized to respond to natural calamities, warfare, and other ominous signs (López Austin and López Luján 1996:248–249). The signs inscribed on the ceremonial landscape necessarily marked as well the geography of private rituals, such as healing and divination, or even the apotropaic rituals that individuals performed in their daily lives as they moved about a world saturated by gods. As integral parts of a living world permeated by the perceptible transformations of sacred personae, where "the nature of the power of spirit [was] present in all animals and elements" (Aveni 1991:59), the Aztecs saw the landscape as a dramatic stage where the manifestation of the sacred "was not concentrated, limited, or restricted to one or several locations" (Carrasco 1991b:40). As Carrasco has shown, the Aztec ritual landscape was a dynamic map of symbols connected by the people who traversed it, performing rituals. In many of these, the participation of the *teixiptlahuan* (sing.: *teixiptla*)—human impersonators of deities, some of whom were sacrificed at the culmination of several rituals—reinforced a coextensive hierarchy between the temple, the altars, and the space traversed by the living deity in the person of the *teixiptla*.

Of course a number of symbolic places were more definitely invested with ritual meaning than others; in these places the presence of the deities was most clearly manifested. These consecrated places were natural—mountains, rivers, lakes, whirlpools, springs, caves, and prominent boulders—, and they were also humanly built, since every human construction was equally "owned" by a recognizable numen: the cultivated field (*milli*) and the house (*calli*), for example, reiterated the fourfold cosmogram, so each of their spatial and architectural features had discernible mythico-ritual referents. Other manmade territorial features, like the road and the crossroads, also represented a particular numinous imprint, linked to the cosmos at large. The crossroads (*Omaxac*), for instance, metaphorically referred to the vagina, so altars to the ominous *Cihuateteoh* (Goddesses) were erected there, where the goddesses issued to afflict humanity. The crossroads still serves as a liminal space par excellence in indigenous communities across Mexico—it is a dangerous point, where many ritual offerings are left (Sandstrom 1978:36).

The landscape formed an intelligible text, shared by all the members of the *altepetl*. Religious pilgrimages to the sacred sites in the wilderness were performed both collectively and individually. Often enough, the individual religious pilgrims willingly confronted the dangers of a living landscape as they traveled from the safety of their home to the abode of the deities in the wild, seeking direct communication with them through penitential ordeals involving fasts, bloodletting, and ingestion of psychoactive drugs, like mushrooms, peyote, and *ololiuhqui*. Initiatory ordeals in the hills were obligatory for all novice priests and regularly pursued by senior priests, the *tlamacazqueh* ("Knowledgeable ones," a title shared with the god Tlaloc himself, the patron of all ritual specialists, who commonly acted as rain-makers). Hernando Ruiz de Alarcón describes one such penitential ordeal in which, after surviving the supernatural attacks of sorcerers and spirits of the wild (*chanequeh*), the penitent (*tlamaceuhqui*) would offer his own blood to the "Owner of the Earth" (*Tlalticpaque*), whose abode was marked by a pile of stones called *Teocalco* ("Place of the house of the deity"). Falling into a deep trance, the penitent then heard the voice of Tlalticpaque and—if he survived the ordeal—went back to the *altepetl* carrying the penitential branches for bloodletting and the conviction that his house would be blessed with the bounty of the deity: good health and a prosperous family life (Ruiz de Alarcon 1984:57). This pattern was reproduced and magnified in other, state-sponsored rituals that involved the participation of the community as a whole. Bodies of water were generally conceived as female deities and consorts of the male Tlaloqueh, like Chalchiuhtlicue and Matlacueye. Rivers, springs, beaches, lakes, and whirlpools were important ritual scenarios. The whirlpool of Pantitlan in Lake Texcoco, for instance, owned by Matlacueye, was considered the mouth of Mictlan and was the site of many important sacrificial offerings.

The political economy of Postclassic Mesoamerica was articulated by the recognition that each *altepetl* controlled a territory granted by particular tutelary mountains, so hegemonic claims were symbolically consolidated by the ritual appropriation of specific hills and mountains. Upon their arrival in the Basin in the early fourteenth century, the Mexica-Tenochca attempted to occupy the fertile terrain next to the hill of Chapultepec and appropriate the hill's tutelage, but they were chased away by the combined forces of the Tepanecas and Culhuas. Later, when the Mexica-Tenochca legitimized their territorial establishment in the Basin by assuming the royal lineage of the *altepetl* of Culhuacan, they became inscribed in the ritual circuit, linking their *altepetl* to the hill of Huixachtecatl, the tutelary patron of the Colhuas, south of the Basin. The foundational ritual of Mexico would from then on be performed every 52 years in the ceremony of the Tying of the Years (*Xiuhmolpilli*), an eschatological ritual that reiterated a new cosmic cycle by lighting the New Fire at the summit of Huixachtecatl. During the nocturnal Xiuhmolpilli ceremony, all fires were extinguished, symbolizing the end of the world. Four priests slowly proceeded from the temple of Huitzilopochtli in Mexico south to Huixachtecatl. At midnight they lit the New Fire on the chest of a sacrificial victim. This fire was then transferred to all the hearths and temple braziers throughout the territory dominated by Mexico. The Xiuhmolpilli ritual periodically delineated the limits of the city and the renewal of its regional hegemony (Florescano 2009:75).

Like other powers before them, the Mexica rulers reiterated their territorial dominance through the performance of other pilgrimages and perambulations across the hills and islands of the Basin, appropriating their tutelage (see Arnold 1991; Aveni 1991; Broda 1991, 2003; Townsend 1992). For instance, in the festival of Huey Tozoztli, the Mexica ruler asserted his universal hegemony by ritually investing the ancient statue of Tlaloc on the sanctuary atop Mount Tlaloc. The rulers of Tetzcoco, Tlacopan, and Xochimilco then followed in the investiture, thereby fulfilling their role as representatives of the four Tlaloqueh dispensing food and fertility to the whole world. The festival included a parallel ritual in which a maiden impersonator of Tlaloc's consort, the goddess Matlacueye, was sacrificed and offered to the whirlpool of Pantitlan down in the lake, while four cosmic trees were erected in the center of Tenochtilan. The ritual expressed the gendered notion of landscape and communicated the fertilizing powers of the earth deities to the people via their rulers.

The ritual landscape also consecrated preagricultural institutions, such as warfare and hunting. For example, during the festival of Quecholli, the Mexicans reasserted the patronage of the hunting god Mixcoatl by performing a pilgrimage to the hill of Zacatepec, on the southern Basin, and offering sacrifices in the city (Broda 1991:107–112; Sahagún 1981:134–140) (Figure 42.1).

Huey Tozoztli and other rituals to the rain deities generally included the sacrifice of children and women, who were magically assimilated to corn, and to the Tlaloqueh deities themselves. The Festival of Mountains (*Tepeilhuitl*), held at the end of the rainy season, revealed in its structure the intimate relationship between the common people and the local geography. During this "General Festival of all the Lands" (Durán 1967:I:267), each family built an edible map of the ritual landscape on the domestic altar. Miniature figures of mountains were made with amaranth paste (*tzoalli*) and were dedicated to the Tepictoton, deified ancestors killed by the rain deities, who now belonged to the mountainous Tlalocan. The *tzoalli* figures were given faces and were arrayed with the paraphernalia of specific mountain deities. Those who wished to obtain the protection of the Tepictoton offered for edible consumption as many images of as many mountains as they wished (Sahagún 1997:113). While the resulting displays included distinct divine mountains

FIGURE 42.1 Aerial Projection of Lake Texcoco from the West. Image used with permission of Thomas Filsinger.

according to the locality, in the Basin of Mexico the *tzoalli* representation of Popocatepetl, arrayed as Tlaloc, was usually placed at the center of the altar, followed by his consorts: Iztaccihuatl, Matlacueye, and Chalchiuhtlicue. A fifth *tzoalli* figure—of Quetzalcoatl, bringer of food from Tlalocan—was added to the display. While at home the *tzoalli* gods were ritually decapitated and eaten, on the temples female representatives of the mountains (*ixiptlaoan tetepe*) were sacrificed, also by decapitation (Sahagún 1981:II:132). During Tepeilhuitl the geography of the Anahuac was ritually built in every household as a model with discernible features. The three-dimensional *tzoalli* map became the living territory and was ritually decapitated and eaten. The ritual landscape—composed of gods, active dead ancestors, and the living—was thus reborn in the heart, and in the stomach, of every person.

References Cited

Alva Ixtlixóchitl, Fernando de
1975 *Obras Históricas*. Edited by Edmundo O'Gorman. Universidad Nacional Autónoma de México, Mexico City.
Arnold, Philip P.
1991 Eating Landscape: Human Sacrifice and Sustenance in Aztec Mexico. In *To Change Place: Aztec Ceremonial Landscapes*, edited by Davíd Carrasco, pp. 219–232. University Press of Colorado, Boulder.
Aveni, Anthony F.
1991 Mapping the Ritual Landscape: Debt Payment to Tlaloc during the Month of Atlcahualo. In *To Change Place: Aztec Ceremonial Landscapes*, edited by Davíd Carrasco, pp. 58–73. University Press of Colorado, Boulder.
Broda, Johanna

1991 The Sacred Landscape of Aztec Calendar Festivals: Myth, Nature and Society. In *To Change Place: Aztec Ceremonial Landscapes*, edited by Davíd Carrasco, pp. 74–120. University Press of Colorado, Boulder.

2003 El culto mexica de los cerros de la cuenca de México: apuntes para la discusión sobre graniceros. In *Graniceros: cosmovisión y meteorología indígenas de Mesoamérica*, edited by Beatriz Albores and Johanna Broda, pp. 49–90. El Colegio Mexiquense, Mexico City.

2009 Simbolismo de los volcanes: los volcanes en la cosmovisión mesoamericana. In *Arqueología Mexicana* 16(95):41–47.

Carrasco, Davíd

1991a Introduction: Aztec Ceremonial Landscape. In *To Change Place: Aztec Ceremonial Landscapes*, edited by Davíd Carrasco, pp. xix–xxviii. University Press of Colorado, Boulder.

1991b The Sacrifice of Tezcatlipoca: To Change Place. In *To Change Place: Aztec Ceremonial Landscapes*, edited by Davíd Carrasco, pp. 31–57. University Press of Colorado, Boulder.

Códice Xólotl

1951 *Códice Xólotl*. 2 vols. Edited by Charles E. Dibble. Universidad Autónoma de México, Mexico City.

Durán, Fray Diego

1967 *Historia de las Indias de la Nueva España e islas de la tierra firme*, Vols. I and II. Porrúa, Mexico City.

Florescano, Enrique

2009 *Los orígenes del poder en Mesoamérica*. Fondo de Cultura Económica, Mexico City.

Glockner, Julio

2012 *Los volcanes sagrados: mitos y rituales en el Popocatépetl y la Iztaccíhuatl*. Punto de Lectura ediciones, Mexico City.

Hassig, Ross

1988 *Aztec Warfare: Imperial Expansion and Political Control*. University of Oklahoma Press, Norman.

Hodge, Mary G.

1991 Land and Lordship in the Valley of Mexico: The Politics of Aztec Provincial Administration. In *Land and Politics in the Valley of Mexico: A Two Thousand Year Perspective*, edited by H. R. Harvey, pp. 113–139. University of New Mexico Press, Albuquerque.

López Austin, Alfredo

2005 Modelos a distancia: antiguas concepciones nahuas. In *El modelo en la ciencia y la cultura*, edited by Alfredo López Austin, pp. 68–93. Siglo XXI, Mexico City.

López Austin, Alfredo, and Leonardo López Luján

1996 *El pasado indígena*. Fondo de Cultura Económica, Mexico City.

2009 *Monte Sagrado-Templo Mayor: el cerro y la pirámide en la tradición religiosa mesoamericana*. Universidad Nacional Autónoma de México, Instituto Nacional de Antropología e Historia, Mexico City.

Molina, Fray Alonso de

1970 *Vocabulario en lengua castellana y mexicana*. Porrúa, Mexico City.

Ponce, Pedro

2007 *Breve relación de los dioses y ritos de la gentilidad*. Linkgua ediciones, Barcelona.

Ruiz de Alarcón, Hernando

1984 *Treatise on the Heathen Superstitions that Today Live Among the Indians Native to This New Spain*. Edited and translated by J. Richard Andrews and Ross Hassig. University of Oklahoma Press, Norman.

Sahagún, Fray Bernardino de
1981 *Florentine Codex, Book 2: The Ceremonies*. Edited and translated by Arthur J. O. Anderson and Charles E. Dibble. Salt Lake City, University of Utah Press.
1997 *Primeros Memoriales*. Paleography of Nahuatl Text and English Translation by Thelma D. Sullivan. University of Oklahoma Press, Norman.

Sandstrom, Alan R.
1978 *The Image of Disease: Medical Practices of Nahua Indians of the Huasteca*, Vol. 3. University of Missouri Monographs in Anthropology, University of Missouri, Columbia.

Tena, Rafael
2002 *Mitos e historias de los antiguos Nahuas*. Conaculta, Mexico City.

Townsend, Richard F.
1992 Landscape and Symbol. In *The Ancient America: Art from Sacred Landscapes*, edited by Richard F. Townsend, pp. 27-49. Art Institute of Chicago, Chicago, and Prestel Verlag, Munich.

CHAPTER 43

STATE RITUAL AND RELIGION IN THE SACRED PRECINCT OF TENOCHTITLAN

ALFREDO LÓPEZ AUSTIN
AND LEONARDO LÓPEZ LUJÁN

MYTH AND REALITY

AROUND 1-Flint and 2-House (A.D. 1324–1325), a series of miraculous signs led the Mexica to the location where they would found the city of Mexico-Tenochtitlan.[1] A tiny island in the middle of Lake Texcoco in the Basin of Mexico, the place was specifically chosen for them by Huitzilopochtli, their solar god of war (Alvarado Tezozómoc 1949:62–63; Chimalpahin 1965:55; *Códice Aubin* 1902:95; Durán 1994:2:40–43). The new arrivals immediately thanked their patron god by building a modest earthen altar above the threshold between the human world and that of the gods (Carrasco 1981:180–282, 1987:130; Reyes García 1979:34). Considered the entrance to the afterlife, it has been variously described as an anthill, a juniper tree, a two-cavern cave, or a double spring by different sources (Alvarado Tezozómoc 1944:8, 16, 1949:4, 62–63, 73; Durán 1994:40; "Historia de los mexicanos por sus pinturas" 1965:51). During the next 200 years, this primeval altar would be enlarged repeatedly, each time using even more sumptuous materials. By the early sixteenth century, it had become the great Coatepec ("Hill of the Serpents"), an imposing, 45 m tall dual pyramid presiding over the island city's Sacred Precinct (Figure 43.1) (Boone 1987; León-Portilla 1978, 1987; López Austin and López Luján 2009; Marquina 1960; Matos 1987, 1988).[2]

Huitzilopochtli appeared in a dream to the priest Cuauhtlequetzqui (Alvarado Tezozómoc 1949:74–75; Durán 1994:41), decreeing that the altar would also mark the

FIGURE 43.1 The Sacred Precinct of Mexico-Tenochtitlan according to Sahagún (1993:fol. 269r). Drawing by Fernando Carrizosa, courtesy of the Templo Mayor Project.

intersection of the two horizontal axes that would guide the future urban expansion of the imperial capital, extending onto the mainland in the form of avenues: Tepeyacac, Iztapalapan, and Tlacopan. Thus Mexico-Tenochtitlan was divided into four large quadrants, or *nauhcampan*: Atzacualco, Cuepopan, Moyotan, and Teopan. This division was the earthly embodiment of the great cosmic cross, with the Sacred Precinct as the very *heart* of the city, since the heart in Mesoamerican symbolism was equivalent to the essential center of all animate beings (Calnek 1976; Heyden 1988:51–54; Nicholson 1971:403; van Zantwijk 1964:198). Much later and when they had already attained power, the Mexica would conceive of this temple complex as the heart of the world they had conquered by force.

The Sacred Precinct was the center par excellence of divine atonement and one of the most prominent centers of liturgy in Mesoamerican history (López Luján 2001). Clearly separated from the profane space of Mexico-Tenochtitlan, it was delimited on all four sides by a wide rectangular platform composed of alternating walls, balustrades, and stairways on both the interior and exterior (López Austin and López Luján 2009:223–228; López Luján and López Austin 2011; Marquina 1960). This platform, which would have measured 340 m north-south and 360 m east-west, was interrupted three or four times by the main entryways (Durán 1984:1:22; López Austin and López Luján 2009:215–219; López de Gómara 1985:122–124; Oviedo 1945:10:53; Sahagún 1951:165). The interior space of nearly 20 ha. was occupied by pyramids of all sizes crowned by temples; *momoztli* (small ritual platforms); priestly quarters; oratories (areas devoted to fasting and penance by the most important people); *calmecac* (temple-schools for the nobility); *tlachtli* (ballcourts); *tzompantli* (palisades where the skulls of sacrificial *victims* were displayed); *tlacochcalco* (storehouses where weapons acquired sacred powers); *Yopilcalco* (the temple where visiting foreign sovereigns stayed when they traveled to Tenochtitlan to witness the great ceremonies); ritual monoliths like the *techcatl, temalacatl*, and *cuauhxicalli* (for the sacrifice and the offering of blood and hearts); and springs and other replicas of the sacred geography (including a grove), all separated by wide plazas or smaller patios (Acosta 1962:238; Durán 1984:1:20–30; López Austin and López Luján 2009, 2012; López Luján and Barrera 2011; Matos 1999, 2001; Matos and López Luján 2009; Sahagún 2000:1:271–281).

Historical data regarding the number of buildings vary greatly from one source to another. Hernán Cortés (1994:64) recorded "40 very tall and well-wrought towers," while the Anonymous Conqueror (1941:45) speaks of more than 20. Motolinia (Benavente 1995:51) mentioned 12 to 15 *teocalli* (temples), while Gonzalo Fernández de Oviedo (1945:53) identified more than 60 *cus* (religious buildings of various types) (Figure 43.2).

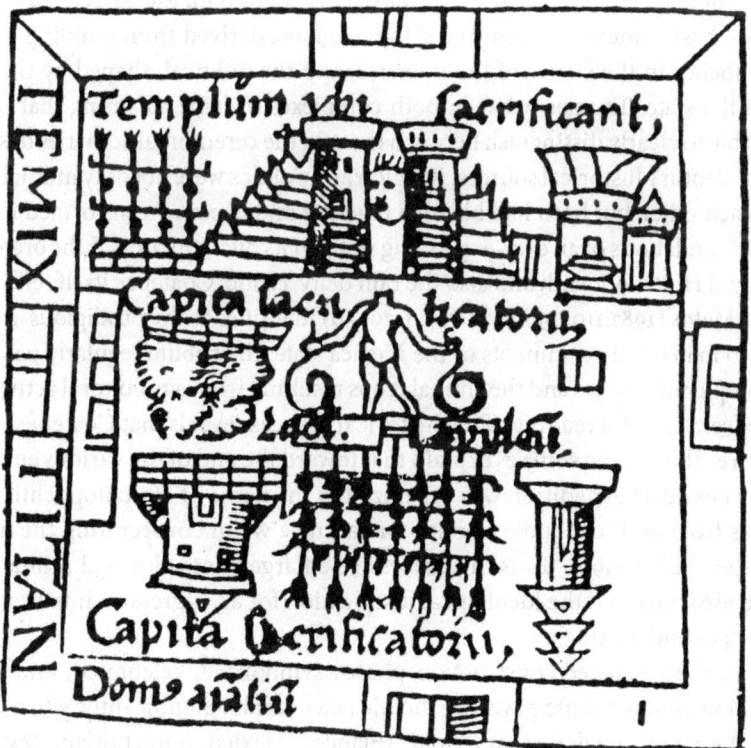

FIGURE 43.2 The Sacred Precinct of Mexico-Tenochtitlan according to Cortés (1994: second letter). Drawing by Fernando Carrizosa, courtesy of the Templo Mayor Project.

Meanwhile, Fray Diego Durán (1984:1:20–21) mentioned eight or nine groups of temple buildings that provided lodging for ministers, each with its own roof emblems, patio, and steps. In contrast, the indigenous informants consulted by Fray Bernardino de Sahagún (1951:165–180) described 78 buildings of varying sizes and functions (Couvreur 2002; López Austin 1965; Matos 2001). Whatever the case, many other temples were scattered around the city, beyond the limits of the Sacred Precinct and as a means of paying homage to it. They were located in "the parishes and neighborhoods; with towers and sanctuaries with altars where the idols are kept and images of their gods, and which serve as mausoleums for the nobles who own them" (López de Gómara 1985:122). Thus the Sacred Precinct became the nerve center of the capital and the Mexica Empire, a symbol of power embodying the hegemony of Mexico-Tenochtitlan.

The Functional Centrality of the Sacred Precinct

Playing on the importance of security and glory to society, and combined with the gradual economic and military rise of Mexico-Tenochtitlan, the Sacred Precinct articulated two basic functional complexes: the religious, derived from building a shrine to Huitzilopochtli in the center of the universe, and the political, shaped by the growing needs of the state. The ties between both complexes became so strong that today it is not possible to clearly distinguish between them in the ceremonial activities described in sixteenth-century historical sources. Religion and politics were not only mutually dependent of each other, but both had blended together and become transformed in order to form the foundations of an ever-expanding state. In its dual function as the oratory of the warrior god Huitzilopochtli and also the rain deity Tlaloc, Coatepec itself reflected what Eduardo Matos (1982:110, 1990:22–23, 26, 29–30) identifies as the prodigious appearance of the two material determinants of the Mexica state: the tribute regularly paid by militarily conquered peoples and the annual crops resulting from agricultural activities.

Moreover, a careful reading of the historical sources reveals that Coatepec grew with the empire. These same sources explain that toward the end of the various enlargement phases, a conquest expedition was organized in the name of Huitzilopochtli to obtain prisoners from an independent polity for sacrifice when consecrating the new pyramid (López Luján 1999). Thus the successive enlargements glorified military expansion and also provided the ideological justification for an aggressive imperialist policy (Figures 43.3 and 43.4).

Each of the Coatepec construction phases symbolized, celebrated, and sanctified the addition of new tribute payers to the Mexica domain. Significantly, when the members of the *excan tlatoloyan*, or Triple Alliance—Mexico-Tenochtitlan, Texcoco, and Tlacopan—could not subjugate an independent polity (e.g., the unsuccessful campaign against the Purepecha of Michoacan), they postponed the building's inauguration until

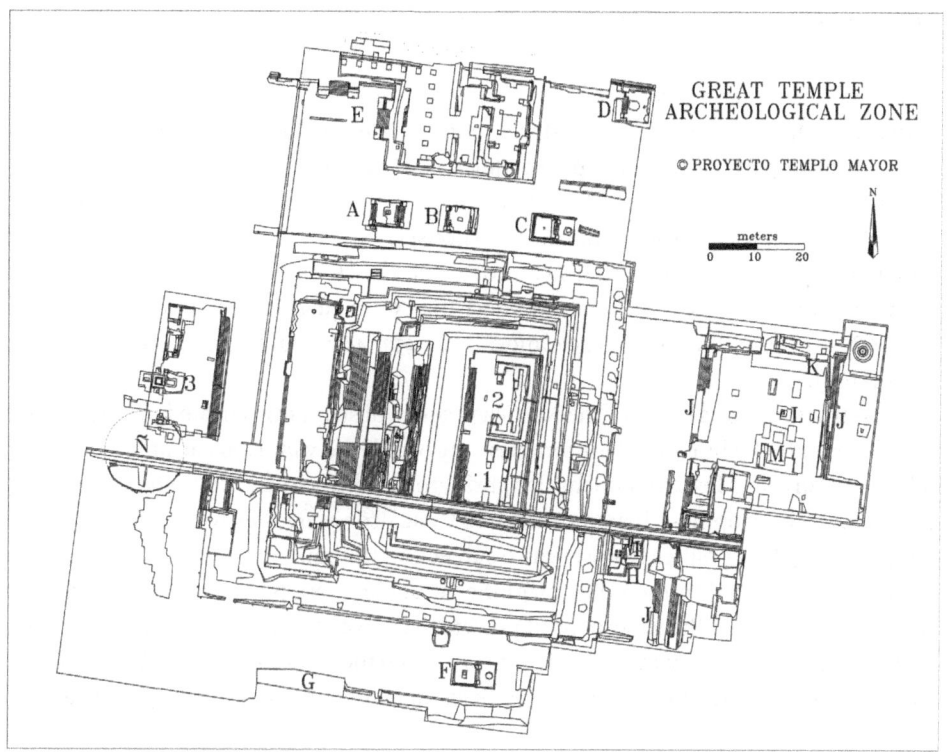

FIGURE 43.3 The archaeological zone of the Templo Mayor, Mexico City. Drawing by Leonardo López Luján, Saburo Sugiyama, and Michelle De Anda, courtesy of the Templo Mayor Project.

FIGURE 43.4 The archaeological zone of the Templo Mayor, Mexico City. Photograph by Leonardo López Luján, courtesy of the Templo Mayor Project.

a successful conquest was achieved. This helps us understand why the archaeological ruins of Coatepec, located in the historic center of Mexico City, provide evidence for at least 13 total or partial expansion phases during just 130 years (Figure 43.5).

Contained within the temple of Huitzilopochtli was the celebrated Coateocalli or Coacalco ("temple" or "place of the meeting house"), which "here dwelt the gods of cities which, in all places which the Mexicans overran, they took captive. They then carried them back and shut them in here. And here they were guarded at Coacalco" (Sahagún 1951:168; see also Alvarado Tezozómoc, 1944:457–461; Durán 1994:431–437; López Austin 1965:82).

This structure was a result of the Mexica practice of stripping defeated people of their divine strength: by burning their temples; afterward, the victorious armies made their jubilant return to Mexico-Tenochtitlan, bringing with them the cult effigies captured in battle. As war trophies, they were taken to Coacalco where they were displayed along with those of other polities that were also subjects of the empire.

Temples dedicated to the other magnificent deities were built near Coatepec, from which also emanated the supernatural powers that gave the Mexica people the strength and protection necessary to prevail militarily in the most remote places. Among them, the pyramid dedicated to the god of fate, Tezcatlipoca, stood out for being "very tall and

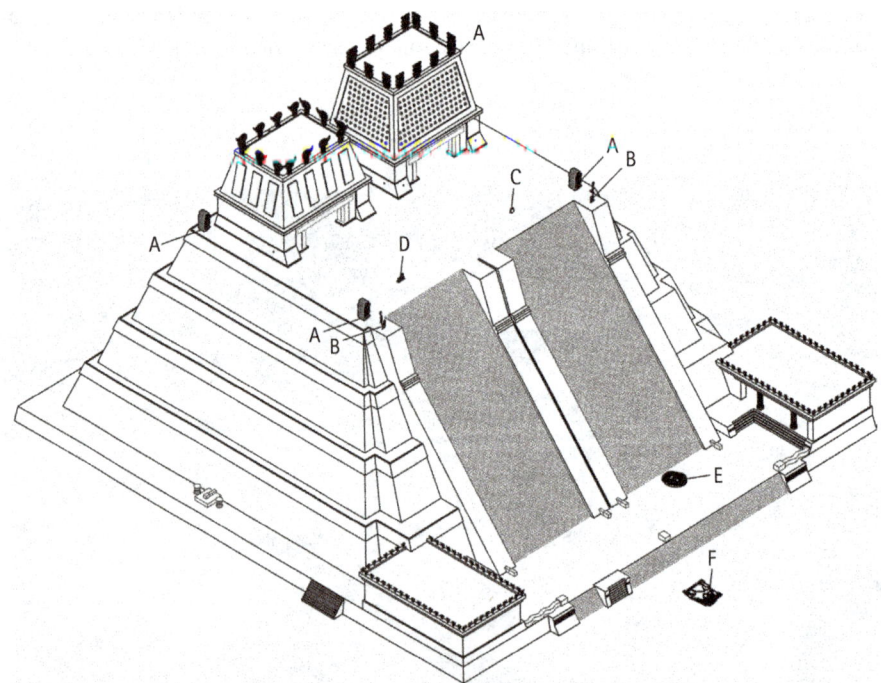

FIGURE 43.5 Hypothetical reconstruction of the Templo Mayor. (A) sculptures of the goddess Coatlicue, (B) standard bearers, (C) geometric sacrificial stone, (D) Chacmool sacrificial stone, (E) Coyolxauhqui monolith, (F) Tlaltecuhtli monolith and Offering 126. Drawing by Tenoch Medina, courtesy of the Templo Mayor Project.

very beautifully constructed" (Acosta 1962:238; López Luján 2015; Matos 1997; Olivier 1997), while the temple dedicated to the god of wind, Ehecatl-Quetzalcoatl, was built in the form of truncated cone "because of the form air takes on as it swirls around in the sky, they made his temple round;" and "the entrance was a door in the form of a serpent's mouth, and devilishly painted. Its fangs and teeth in relief, amazing all who came there, particularly Christians, who imagined they were seeing hell before them" (López de Gómara 1985:123; Matos and Barrera 2011).

Archaeology has revealed several buildings in an archaic style associated with these three great pyramids, which evoked in their profiles and decorative art two renowned civilizations by then long disappeared: Teotihuacan and Tula. Indeed, four neo-Teotihuacan shrines have been unearthed, three of which are now known as the "red temples." They were dedicated to Xochipilli-Macuilxochitl, the solar god of music and dance (Batres 1902:47–49; Gussinyer 1979; López Luján 1989; Olmedo 2002). Oriented toward the rising sun, its colors, images, and symbols related to the sun, while offerings of musical instruments allude to the beginning of a new era in the mythical Teotihuacan, the creation of the Fifth Sun. Two neo-Toltec portico precincts have been uncovered as well. One is the great *calmecac* associated with the temple of Ehecatl, the god of the wind and one of the many manifestations of Quetzalcoatl, patron god of this noble educational institution and the legendary ruler of Tula. Archaeologists have named the other the House of the Eagles, a ritual setting for the transmission of power from the deceased *tlahtoani* (supreme ruler) to his newly elected successor (Barrera and López Arenas 2008; López Luján 2006, 2013; López Luján and López Austin 2009:403–411). Mexica power was based on two factors: (a) the direct descent of the ruling lineage from the god Quetzalcoatl and (b) the link to ancient Tula through the blood ties of Acamapichtli, founding *tlahtoani* of the royal dynasty (López Luján and López Austin 2009:391–392).

Through this tremendous concentration of the powerful forces of ancestors and gods—both their own and those of other groups—the Sacred Precinct linked the preservation of the well-being of the Mexican people and the fertility of the land to the achievement of state cohesion, the sacralization of centralized government power, and military domination over other peoples. Obviously, all of this was subordinate to religious discourse; however, this discourse held that the supreme divinities were represented not by priests but by the *tlahtoani* himself.

Large Public Rituals

In terms of daily religious activities in Mesoamerican cities, community life in the *calpultin* or neighborhoods contrasted with that of the large public precincts—mainly markets and temple complexes—controlled by the state government. The temples were of considerable capacity because religious architecture is distinguished precisely by the predominance of open spaces on roofs and plazas on the massive pyramidal temples. Regarding the Sacred Precinct of Mexico-Tenochtitlan, Cortés (1994:64) mentioned that the area could accommodate 500 people, while Andrés de Tapia (1963:65, 67) cited just 400. Meanwhile, Francisco López de Gómara (1985:122–124) claimed that the precinct permanently housed some 5,000 people performing various services and whose primary mission was to maintain the order of this space. José de Acosta (1962:637) noted that on holidays between 8,000 and 10,000 people would congregate there to dance without hindrance.

Those attending the ceremonies ranged from large local crowds to the few and very select dignitaries from other political entities (Sahagún 1951:177). The former included inhabitants not only from the island but also from the whole region, as mentioned regarding "gladiatorial" combat between sacrificial victims and Mexica warriors (Sahagún 1951:176) or the *tlahtoani*'s redistribution of food to the poor during eight days of the 20-day period known as *hueytecuhilhuitl* (Sahagún 1951:91–92). Regarding foreign dignitaries, presumably only those from allied polities visited Tenochtitlan; however, historical sources report that the Mexica *tlahtoani* also invited some hostile counterparts, who were hidden behind screens so they could witness the ritual performances without being seen by the other spectators (Sahagún 1951:53). This political maneuver was obviously meant to discourage and intimidate, as it was not uncommon for attendees to witness the sacrifice of their own warriors who had previously been captured in battle.

Centralized Liturgy

The contrasting spheres of religion (i.e., daily life in the *calpultin* vs. at large public venues) are clearly perceptible in the historical sources (López Austin and López Luján 2005:211–215, 240–246). On the one hand was the communitary worship in each of the small urban districts that were like neighborhoods where groups of relatives and people dedicated to the same productive tasks resided. There they worshipped the *calpulteotl*, or local patron, who had delegated a specific profession to his followers. They dedicated prayers and offerings in the hopes of meeting the needs of the *calpolli* : family, school, career, and so on. On the other hand, the state cult, as we have seen, was sponsored by the supreme government to promote the great divinities, like Huitzilopochtli, Tlaloc, Quetzalcoatl, Tezcatlipoca, and Xipe Totec, to ensure the wellbeing of all people living under the empire as well as its agricultural and military success (Figure 43.6).

The two forms of worship were subject to the overarching ritual calendar. The community cult of the *calpultin* largely followed the *tonalpohualli* (divinatory cycle of 260 days divided into 20 periods of 13 days each). Meanwhile, the state religion followed the *xiuhpohualli* (agricultural cycle of 365 days organized into 18 periods of 20 days each plus five unlucky days), with the priest Epcoacuacuilli leading liturgy from the Sacred Precinct (Sahagún 1951:194). Even though the *calpultin* and the state religion followed

FIGURE 43.6 Templo Mayor Offering 126 was discovered under the monolith of the earth goddess Tlaltecuhtli. Photograph by Jesús López, courtesy of the Templo Mayor Project.

For example, certain precinct temples, like the Tetlanma, Chicomecoatl Iteopan, and Tulnahuac, were clearly linked to the *tonalpohualli*; the names of other temples, like the Macuilcipactli, Macuilcalli, Macuilmalinalli, and Macuilquiahuitl, refer to specific days of that cycle (Sahagún 1951:166, 170, 175).

Outside the regular progression of the calendrical cycles, the state hosted lavish rituals in the Sacred Precinct for royal and noble funerals—including burial in the complex itself—the election and enthronement of rulers, the recognition of newly elected *tlahtoque* of allied political entities, the arrival of triumphant armies, and the parading of captives before sacrificing them to the gods (Alvarado Tezozómoc 1944:26–27, 175, 245–248, 269–337, 393–399; Chávez 2007; Durán 1994:58–60, 65–66, 70–72, 123, 247–248, 295–298, 309–313, 355–360, 387–393, 417–424; López Austin and López Luján 2009:403–407; López Luján 2005:172–183; 2006:1:244–253; Olivier 1997:94–103; Townsend 1987). In addition, both the inauguration of the sacrificial monoliths as well as the continuous building and enlargement of the pyramid temples warranted lavish celebrations and the burning and burial of sumptuous offerings (Alvarado Tezozómoc 1944:114–121, 132–141, 153–166, 202–222, 494–499; Broda 1987; Durán 1994:182–193, 223–232, 234–235, 272–277, 286–290, 335–341, 479–482; López Luján 2005:183–225; 2006:1:225–255; Matos 1988).

Finally, the Sacred Precinct was also the stage for grand ceremonies dedicated to seeking relief from the great misfortunes inflicted by the gods to punish humans: agricultural disasters, famines, and epidemic diseases (Chimalpahin 1965:99–100; Durán 1984:238–241; López Luján 2005:148–157).

The Transmission of Ideology through the Temple-Schools

We have already mentioned that the *calmecac* in the Sacred Precinct served as both priestly residences for those directing liturgy at the temples and as centers for the formation of new officiants. Usually these buildings were dedicated to the worship of specific deities: the so-called Mexico Calmecac-revered Tlaloc; meanwhile, the Tetlanman Calmecac was dedicated to Chantico, the goddess of hearth fires and volcanoes; the Puchtlan to Yacatecuhtli, patron god of trade; the Atlauhco to the enigmatic goddess Huitzilincuatec, and so on (Durán 1984:1:21; Sahagún 1951:168, 170, 174). Some *calmecac* offered specialized education in specific skills, such as the Mecatlan, where students learned to play the trumpet (Sahagún 1951:172–173). Individuals attending these temple-schools from early childhood were considered priests from the time of admission; they were both male and female (Cortés 1994:64). *Calmecac* education was extremely strict. Students practiced self-sacrifice on a daily basis in order to obtain blood to offer to the divine images. The punishment for young people who failed at this or any other obligation was harsh. For example, upon failing to fulfill part of their obligations, the students in charge of the temple of the rain god Epcoatl (Sahagún 1951:80–81) were taken to the swamps, where they were beaten and submerged in water until they nearly drowned during the 20-day period of *etzalcualiztli*.

The other *calmecac* distributed throughout the city and in the towns subject to the empire were controlled from the Sacred Precinct. The top position was held by the priest Mexicatl Teohuatzin, who was personally responsible for punishing the transgressors of ecclesiastical rules. He was assisted in his duties by Huitznahuatl Teohuatzin and Tepan Teohuatzin (Sahagún 1951:193).

Giving and Receiving Gifts

The religion of the Mexica and their contemporaries was characterized by the practice of reciprocity, which not only created an ethos of exchange between individuals but also governed the essential everyday interactions between the living and dead and between humans and the divine. All economic production was seen as a joint effort in which both the mundane and the divine made a contribution, and thus the fruits of any labor were shared by both.

In the great cosmic apparatus, exchange was consummated through the *axis mundi*, composed of, from the bottom up, the Place of the Dead, the Holy Mountain (the large storehouse of potential goods), and the Tree of Life. This great structure, which animated the world and propelled different cycles, was projected onto the main pyramid of the Sacred Precinct: Coatepec. Indeed, the building itself brought together the two fundamental forces of movement in the cosmos: fire and water, personified by the gods Huitzilopochtli and Tlaloc (López Luján 1999; López Austin and López Luján 2009).

The Sacred Precinct thus became the model of reciprocity, where men offered members of their own species as sacrificial victims: as containers for the gods or as food for them (López Austin 1980:1:432–436, 1988:1:375–379; González 1985; Carrasco 1987, 1999; Graulich 2005; López Austin and López Luján 2008). In the first case, the victims were *teteo imixiptlahuan*, or living representatives of the divinities, who were reborn through the death of their human representatives. The second were the *nextlahualtin* or "payments," sustenance required by the gods to recover the energy lost doing their part in the world. In the Sacred Precinct, the gods were paid with the labor via prayers, music, dancing, and singing, as well as the physical effort involved in performing the required rituals for the ball game, races, and skirmishes that were part of the festivities (López Austin 1967).

Also presented periodically to the divine images were the bodies and blood of animals (i.e., quail, raptors, felines, and canines), food, copal incense smoke, flowers, and rubber. During the most solemn moments, rich offerings were interred in religious buildings and under platforms and plazas (López Arenas 2003; López Luján 2005:81–353, 2006:1:225–256; Nagao 1985). About 80 percent of the materials offered at Coatepec were allochthonous, derived mostly from territories that had become tributaries of the *excan tlatoloyan*. Faunal remains are the most abundant (López Luján et al. 2014). To date, we have identified over 300 species from temperate ecosystems in the Central Highlands, tropical rainforests, coral reefs, and coastal estuaries and lagoons. In sharp contrast, flora and crude minerals are less common. The former includes maguey, copal, coniferous wood, and rubber; the latter is characterized by marine sands and fragments of jet, turquoise, and greenstone. Human skeletal remains are also widely represented in the sample. Some belong to very high-ranking individuals who were ritually buried following cremation; the vast majority, however, were victims of sacrifice by slitting the throat or extracticing the heart. Imported goods that arrived in Tenochtitlan via tribute, trade, gift, or plunder stand out among the artifacts recovered by archaeologists. These include obsidian from the Sierra de las Navajas and Otumba, Mixteca-style sculptures made of green marble, urns from Veracruz, pottery and travertine objects from the Puebla-Tlaxcala region, as well as a large quantity of copper bells and metamorphic greenstone ornaments of diverse origins. An impressive number of antiques belonging to cultures that were not contemporaneous with the Mexica, including a mask, a sacrificial spoon, a pendant, and several anthropomorphic figurines of Olmec style; and several fragments hundreds of Mezcala-style greenstone figurines and masks; dozens of Teotihuacan lapidary and pottery complete objects and fragments; several Classic Maya jade ornaments; and a Toltec imitation of a plumbate ceramic vessel. Surprisingly, Mexica goods are not as common.

complete objects and fragments; several Classic Maya jade ornaments; and a Toltec imitation of a plumbate ceramic vessel. Surprisingly, Mexica goods are not as common.

In exchange for these offerings, the gods delivered their gifts to the Sacred Precinct itself. Thus political power was sacralized; the fruits of the fields were turned into fertile seeds in the temples (Sahagún 1951:7, 60–63, 116); there consumption was consecrated (Sahagún 1951:99); weapons received divine strength in buildings known as the Tlacochcalco Acatl Yiacapan and Tezcacoatl Tlacochcalco (Sahagún 1951:179), and the faithful ingested pieces of *tzoalli*, divine images formed from amaranth dough (Durán 1984:1:28–30) or drank holy water from the Tozpalatl spring (Sahagún 1951:178). Moreover, in one of the temples of the great complex—the Tlillan Calmecac—the goddess Cihuacoatl miraculously appeared outside the confines of the temple (Sahagún 2000:1:274).

All this was carried out ritually throughout the 18 periods of 20 days that divided the year, dedicated to the major gods in the form of 18 festivals of considerable complexity. Documentary sources detail the diversity of rites; the magnificent garments worn by priests, nobles, and warriors; the richness of the divine images (Carrasco 1999; Durán 1984:1:18–20, 39, 47; Graulich 1999; Sahagún 1951:1–216); and the time and effort required for the celebration. It was, indeed, an alienating complexity whose varied ritual details held the attention of any spectator.

CENTER-PERIPHERY

The Sacred Precinct was not only the largest place of worship but also the point of origin for ceremonial processions to the lake, swamps, fountains, fields, forests, hermitages, and, importantly, the neighborhoods and homes of ordinary people (Carrasco 1981, 1987). For example, the "Painal race," held during the month of *panquetzaliztli*, covered a considerable radius (Durán 1984:1: 28–29; Sahagún 1951:133–135). Conversely, all *capultin* in the city participated in the great festivals, and on the platform surrounding the Sacred Precinct were buildings known as *Calpolli* (Sahagún 1951:179–180), which may have served as meeting places for the people coming from the different neighborhoods of the city. The Sacred Precinct was therefore the center of a huge network that directed all members of the state in support of a government that sought to integrate a huge population and weaken, through ostentatious demonstrations of its greatness and glory, the resistance of those who opposed its hegemony.

NOTES

1. Based on the *Historia de los mexicanos por sus pinturas* "*Historia de los mexicanos por sus pinturas*" (1965:56), Cuauhmixtitlan, or the "Cloudy Place of the Tree," was the name originally given by the Mexica to Mexico-Tenochtitlan. However, it is possible that the name Cuauhmixtitlan was derived much later considering the religious tie to the cosmic axis.

"Templo Mayor" (Great Temple), which has led to considerable confusion. Coatepec pyramid was enlarged thirteen times. Its last building phase measured 84.47 from North to South and 77.24 meters from East to West.

References Cited

Acosta, José de
1962 *Historia natural y moral de las Indias, en que se tratan de las cosas notables del cielo, elementos, metales, plantas y animales dellas, y los ritos y ceremonias, leyes y gobierno de los indios.* Fondo de Cultura Económica, Mexico City.

Alvarado Tezozómoc, Fernando
1944 *Crónica Mexicana.* Editorial Leyenda, Mexico City.
1949 *Crónica Mexicáyotl.* Universidad Nacional Autónoma de México, Instituto Nacional de Antropología e Historia, Mexico City.

Anonymous Conquerer
1941 *Relación de algunas cosas de la Nueva España y de la gran ciudad de Temestitán México, escrita por un compañero de Hernán Cortés.* Editorial América, Mexico City.

Barrera Rodríguez, Raúl, and Gabino López Arenas
2008 Hallazgos en el recinto ceremonial de Tenochtitlan. *Arqueología Mexicana* 93:18–25.

Batres, Leopoldo
1902 *Excavations in Escalerillas Street, City of Mexico: Year 1900.* Aguilar Vera & Co., Mexico City.

Benavente, Fray Toribio de (Motolinia)
1995 *Historia de los indios de Nueva España: Relación de los ritos antiguos, idolatrías y sacrificios de los indios de Nueva España, y de la maravillosa conversión que Dios en ellos ha obrado*, 2nd ed. Porrúa, Mexico City.

Boone, Elizabeth H.
1987 Templo Mayor Research, 1521–1978. In *The Aztec Templo Mayor*, edited by Elizabeth H. Boone, pp. 5–69. Dumbarton Oaks Research Library and Collection, Washington, DC.

Broda, Johanna
1987 The Provenience of the Offerings: Tribute and Cosmovision. In *The Aztec Templo Mayor*, edited by Elizabeth H. Boone, pp. 211–256. Dumbarton Oaks Research Library and Collection, Washington, DC.

Calnek, Edward
1976 The Internal Structure of Tenochtitlan. In *The Valley of Mexico*, edited by Eric Wolf, pp. 287–302. University of Mexico Press, Albuquerque.

Carrasco, Davíd
1981 Templo Mayor: The Aztec Vision of Place. *Religion* 11:275–297.
1987 Myth, Cosmic Terror, and the Templo Mayor. In *The Great Temple of Tenochtitlan, Center and Periphery in the Aztec World*, by Johanna Broda, Davíd Carrasco, and Eduardo Matos Moctezuma, pp. 124–169. University of California Press, Berkeley.
1999 *City of Sacrifice. The Aztec Empire and the Role of Violence in Civilization.* Beacon Press, Boston.

Chávez Balderas, Ximena
2007 *Rituales funerarios en el Templo Mayor de Tenochtitlan.* Instituto Nacional de Antropología e Historia, Mexico City.

Chimalpahin Cuauhtlehuanitzin, Francisco de San Antón Muñón
1965 *Relaciones originales de Chalco Amaquemecan.* Fondo de Cultura Económica, Mexico, D.F.

Chimalpahin Cuauhtlehuanitzin, Francisco de San Antón Muñón
1965 *Relaciones originales de Chalco Amaquemecan*. Fondo de Cultura Económica, Mexico, D.F.
1902 *Códice Aubin, manuscrito azteca de la Biblioteca Real de Berlin, anales en mexicano y geroglíficos desde la salida de Aztlan hasta la muerte de Cuauhtemoc*. Secretaría de Fomento, Mexico City.

Cortés, Hernán
1994 *Cartas de relación*. Porrúa, Mexico City.

Couvreur, Aurélie
2002 La description du Grand Temple de Mexico par Bernardino de Sahagún (Codex de Florence, Annexe du Livre II). *Journal de la Société des Américanistes* 88:9–46.

Durán, Fray Diego
1984 *Historia de las Indias de Nueva España e islas de tierra firme*, 2nd ed. 2 vols. Porrúa, Mexico City.
1994 *The History of the Indies of New Spain*. Translated by Doris Heyden, University of Oklahoma Press, Norman.

González Torres, Yolotl
1985 *El sacrificio humano entre los mexicas*. Fondo de Cultura Económica, Instituto Nacional de Antropología e Historia, Mexico City.

Graulich, Michel
1999 *Ritos aztecas: Las fiestas de las veintenas*, Instituto Nacional Indigenista, Mexico City.
2005 *Le sacrifice humain chez les aztèques*. Fayard, Paris.

Gussinyer, Jordi
1979 La arquitectura prehispánica en los alrededores de la catedral. In *El Recinto Sagrado de Mexico-Tenochtitlan, Excavaciones 1968-69 y 1975-76*, edited by Constanza Vega, pp. 67–74. Instituto Nacional de Antropología e Historia, Mexico City.

Heyden, Doris
1988 *México, orígenes de un símbolo*. Instituto Nacional de Antropología e Historia, Mexico City.

Historia de los mexicanos por sus pinturas
1965 Historia de los mexicanos por sus pinturas. In *Teogonía e historia de los mexicanos: Tres opúsculos del siglo xvi*, edited by Ángel María Garibay K., pp. 21–90. Porrúa, Mexico City.

León-Portilla, Miguel
1978 *México-Tenochtitlan: Su espacio y tiempo sagrados*, Instituto Nacional de Antropología e Historia, Mexico City.
1987 The Ethnohistorical Record for the Huey Teocalli of Tenochtitlan. In *The Aztec Templo Mayor*, edited by Elizabeth H. Boone, pp. 71–96. Dumbarton Oaks Research Library and Collection, Washington, DC.

López Arenas, Gabino
2003 *Rescate arqueológico en la Catedral y el Sagrario metropolitanos: estudio de ofrendas*, Instituto Nacional de Antropología e Historia, Mexico City.

López Austin, Alfredo
1965 El Templo Mayor de Mexico-Tenochtitlan según los informantes indígenas. *Estudios de Cultura Náhuatl* 5:75–102.
1967 *Juegos rituales aztecas*. Universidad Nacional Autónoma de México, Mexico City.
1980 *Cuerpo humano e ideología: Las concepciones de los antiguos nahuas*, 2 vols., Universidad Nacional Autónoma de México, Mexico City.
1988 *The Human Body and Ideology. Concepts of the Ancient Nahuas*. Translated by Thelma Ortiz de Montellano and Bernard Ortiz de Montellano. University of Utah Press, Salt Lake City.

2008 The Aztec Human Sacrifice. In *The Aztec World*, edited by Elizabeth Brumfiel and Gary Feinmann, pp. 137–152. Harry N. Abrams, New York.

2009 *Monte Sagrado-Templo Mayor: El cerro y la pirámide en la tradición religiosa mesoamericana*. Instituto Nacional de Antropología e Historia, Universidad Nacional Autónoma de México, Mexico City.

2012 The Posthumous History of the Tizoc Stone. In *Fanning the Sacred Flame: Mesoamerican Studies in Honor of H.B. Nicholson*, edited by Matthew A. Boxt and Brian D. Dillon, pp. 439–460. University Press of Colorado, Boulder.

López de Gómara, Francisco
1985 *Historia general de las Indias (Segunda parte: Conquista de México)*. Orbis, Barcelona.

López Luján, Leonardo
1989 *La recuperación mexica del pasado teotihuacano*. Instituto Nacional de Antropología e Historia, GV Editores, Mexico City.

1999 Water and Fire: Archaeology in the Capital of the Mexica Empire. In *The Archaeology of Mesoamerica. Mexican and European Perspectives*, edited by Warwick Bray and Linda Manzanilla, pp. 32–49. British Museum Press, London.

2001 Tenochtitlan: Ceremonial Centers. In *Archaeology of Ancient Mexico and Central America: An Encyclopedia*, edited by Susan T. Evans and David L. Webster, pp. 712–717. Garland, New York.

2005 *The Offerings of the Templo Mayor of Tenochtitlan*. University of New Mexico Press, Albuquerque.

2006 *La Casa de las Águilas: Un ejemplo de la arquitectura religiosa de Tenochtitlan*. 2 vols. Instituto Nacional de Antropología e Historia, Fondo de Cultura Económica, Mexico City.

2013 Echoes of a Glorious Past: Mexica Antiquarianism. In *World Antiquarianism: Comparative Perspectives*, edited by Alain Schnapp, pp. 273–294. Getty Research Institute, Los Angeles.

2015 Ruinas sobre ruinas: de los aposentos de Tezcatlipoca a las aulas de la Universidad. In *Fundación Herdez, una restauración ejemplar*, written by Luis Ortiz Macedo, pp. 21–50 and 134–135. Fundación Herdez, Mexico City.

López Luján, Leonardo, and Alfredo López Austin
2009 The Mexica in Tula and Tula in Mexico-Tenochtitlan. In *The Art of Urbanism: How Mesoamerican Cities Represented Themselves in Architecture and Imagery*, edited by William L. Fash and Leonardo López Luján, pp. 384–422, Dumbarton Oaks Research and Library Collection, Washington, DC.

2011 El coatepantli de Tenochtitlan: Historia de un malentendido. *Arqueología Mexicana* 111:64–71.

López Luján, Leonardo, and Raúl Barrera Rodríguez
2011 Hallazgo de un edificio circular al pie del Templo Mayor de Tenochtitlan. *Arqueología Mexicana* 112:17.

López Luján, Leonardo, Ximena Chávez Balderas, Belem Zúñiga Arellano, Alejandra Aguirre Molina, and Norma Valentín Maldonado
2014 Entering the Underworld: Animal Offerings at the Foot of the Great Temple of Tenochtitlan. In *Animals and Inequality in the Ancient World*, edited by Benjamin S. Arbuckle and Sue Ann McCarty, pp. 33–61. University Press of Colorado, Boulder.

Marquina, Ignacio
1960 *El Templo Mayor de México*. Instituto Nacional de Antropología e Historia, Mexico City.

Matos Moctezuma, Eduardo
1982 El Templo Mayor: Economía e ideología. In *El Templo Mayor: Excavaciones y estudios*, edited by Eduardo Matos Moctezuma, pp. 109–118. Instituto Nacional de Antropología e Historia, Mexico City.

1987 The Templo Mayor of Tenochtitlan: History and Interpretation. In *The Great Temple of Tenochtitlan, Center and Periphery in the Aztec World*, by Johanna Broda, Davíd Carrasco, and Eduardo Matos Moctezuma, pp. 15–60. University of California Press, Berkeley.

1988 *The Great Temple of the Aztecs: Treasures of Tenochtitlan*, Thames & Hudson, London.

1990 El Proyecto Templo Mayor: Objetivos y programas. In *Trabajos arqueológicos en el centro de la ciudad de México*, 2nd ed., edited by Eduardo Matos Moctezuma, pp. 17–39. Instituto Nacional de Antropología e Historia, Mexico City.

1997 Tezcatlipoca, espejo que humea. In *Antiguo Palacio del Arzobispado, Museo de la Secretaría de Hacienda y Crédito Público*, Miguel León-Portilla, pp. 27–41. Secretaría de Hacienda y Crédito Público, Mexico City.

1999 Sahagún y el recinto ceremonial de Tenochtitlan. *Arqueología Mexicana* 36:22–31.

2001 The Ballcourt in Tenochtitlan. In *The Sport of Life and Death: The Mesoamerican Ballgame*, edited by E. M. Whittington, pp. 89–95. Thames & Hudson, New York.

Matos Moctezuma, Eduardo, and Leonardo López Luján

2009 *Escultura monumental mexica*. Fundación Conmemoraciones 2010. Fondo de Cultura Económica, Mexico City.

Matos Moctezuma, Eduardo, and Raúl Barrera Rodríguez

2011 El Templo de Ehécatl-Quetzalcóatl del recinto sagrado de México-Tenochtitlan. *Arqueología Mexicana* 108:72–77.

Nagao, Debra

1985 *Mexica Buried Offerings. A Historical and Contextual Analysis*. British Archaeological Reports, Oxford.

Nicholson, H. B.

1971 Religion in Pre-Hispanic Central Mexico. In *Handbook of Middle American Indians*, vol. 10, edited by Robert Wauchope, pp. 396–446. University of Texas Press, Austin.

Olivier, Guilhem

1997 *Moqueries et métamorphoses d'un dieu aztèque : Tezcatlipoca, le "Seigneur au miroir fumant."* Institut d'Ethnologie, Paris.

Olmedo Vera, Bertina

2002 *Los templos rojos del recinto sagrado de Tenochtitlan*. Instituto Nacional de Antropología e Historia, Mexico City.

Oviedo y Valdés, Gonzalo Fernández de

1945 *Historia general y natural de las Indias, islas y tierra firme del mar océano*. 14 vols. Editorial Guarania, Asunción.

Reyes García, Luis

1979 La visión cosmológica y la organización del imperio mexica. In *Mesoamérica: Homenaje al Doctor Paul Kirchhoff*, edited by Barbro Dalhgren, pp. 34–40. Instituto Nacional de Antropología e Historia, Mexico City.

Sahagún, Fray Bernardino de

1951 *Florentine Codex: Book 2, The Ceremonies, Part III of General History of the Things of New Spain*. Translated by Arthur J. O. Anderson and Charles E. Dibble. School of American Research, Santa Fe, and University of Utah, Salt Lake City.

1993 *Primeros memoriales*. Patrimonio Nacional y la Real Academia de la Historia. University of Oklahoma Press, Norman.

2000 *Historia general de las cosas de Nueva España*. 3 vols. Consejo Nacional para la Cultura y las Artes, Mexico City.

Tapia, Andrés de
1963 Relación de Andrés de Tapia. In *Crónicas de la Conquista*, 3rd ed., edited by Agustín Yáñez, pp. 25–78. Universidad Nacional Autónoma de México, Mexico City.
Townsend, Richard F.
1987 Coronation at Tenochtitlan. In *The Aztec Templo Mayor*, edited by Elizabeth H. Boone, pp. 371–409. Dumbarton Oaks Research and Library Collection, Washington, DC.
van Zantwijk, Rudolf
1963 Principios organizadores de los mexicas, una introducción al estudio del sistema interno del régimen azteca. *Estudios de Cultura Náhuatl* 4:187–222.

CHAPTER 44

AZTEC DOMESTIC RITUAL

LISA OVERHOLTZER

THE Aztec house, or *calli*, with its four sides and center point, was a microcosm of the universe. As Louise Burkhart (1997:30) argues, the house "was not a tranquil refuge from the significant currents of cosmos and history but a place where those currents intersected forcibly with human existence." Within the house many quotidian tasks, such as weaving, sweeping, and disposing of domestic refuse, were ritualized: they were structured, subject to taboos, and associated with deities (Burkhart 1997:34). Fray Bernardino de Sahagún (1950–1982, Book 4:7) describes fasting, offerings, and bathing as ritual practices that ensured that "their embroidery or design might be a work of art, well fabricated, and well painted." Brooms were given to baby girls at their naming ceremony (Sahagún 1950–1982, Book 4:93–94), carried by deities Tlazolteotl and Toci (*Codex Magliabecchiano*: fol. 27r; Sahagún 1950–1982, Book 1:Figures 8 and 12) and left outside so that they would not bring dirt, and therefore strife, into the home (Garibay 1967:36–37). Just as sweeping was an essential task of temple priests designed to maintain cosmic order (DiCesare 2009), so too women in their homes were exhorted to "be diligent with the sweeping" (Sahagún 1950–1982, Book 6:95). Women were tasked with sweeping up *tlazolli*—a Nahuatl term referring to worn-out things and connoting actively polluting and powerful filth—and thus constantly maintaining order and protecting against dangerous forces (Burkhart 1989:117–124; see also Hamann 2008). Documentary sources stress the role of women in household ritual—Diego Durán mentioning that women maintained the household altar (Durán 1994:164–165), for example—though children and men also actively participated in ritual activities. For example, the Florentine Codex details the many life cycle rituals that made properly socialized boys and girls out of the metaphorical chips and flakes of their ancestors (Joyce 2000). In addition, old men, who may have symbolized the elderly fire god, were required to be present when a house was founded and the new fire was drilled (Sahagún 1950–1982, Book 5:194). The historic record therefore suggests that domestic ritual and ritualized household practice, though often carried out in what would today be considered private space, were thoroughly enmeshed in broader cosmological concerns.

Unfortunately, colonial documents mention Aztec household ritual only occasionally (Smith 2002). Sahagún (1997:69–75; also see Brown 1983) ascribes several temple and household ritual practices to women: burning incense, letting blood, sweeping, and making offerings of food and other items. Fray Diego Durán (1971:463, 1967:1:289) indicates that families made offerings at home in conjunction with the monthly *veintena* temple ceremonies. However, Spanish priests generally avoided talking to native women and did not enter their homes (Burkhart 1997), and thus many ritual practices were unknown to and omitted by the friars. In addition, there is a heavy Tenochtitlan bias in the work of chroniclers that might lead us to underestimate the variation in household ritual across the Aztec Empire. Fray Ruiz de Alarcón (1984) offers an exceptional account from his own observations of the "idolatry" he sought to eliminate in Guerrero and Morelos. However, scholars have been hesitant to use this rich source because it was written in the early seventeenth century.

Analyses of household ritual objects found in museums, archaeological survey, and excavations of domestic contexts at heartland and hinterland sites have complemented the written record. This research demonstrates that domestic ritual practice was not only intimately connected to broader cosmologies but also served as political action and social commentary. It has also indicated significant variability in some rituals, especially burials, though more extensive household excavations are needed to fully characterize those differences. This chapter focuses on ritual practices as they have been reconstructed archaeologically via burials, figurines, feasting ceramics, trash dumps, and musical instruments.

Scholars often compare and contrast household and state-sponsored rituals. As Michael Smith (2002) notes, some religious themes were shared, including the maintenance of cosmic order, fire worship, and agricultural fertility. Moreover, some ritual implements, such as long-handled censers, were similar in imperial Tenochtitlan and Aztec households (Figure 44.1).

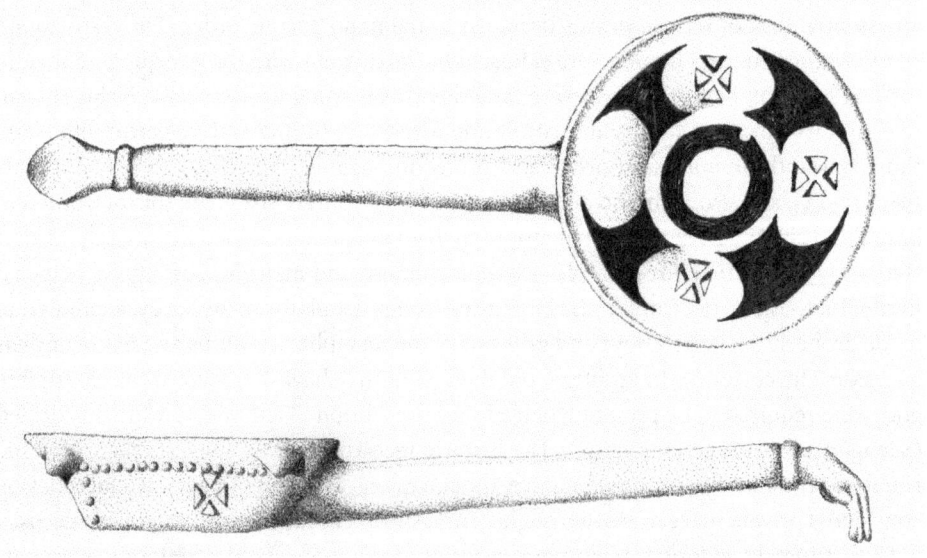

FIGURE 44.1 Long-handled censer recovered from Xaltocan house. Drawing by Viveros Sánchez.

However, scholars have more frequently examined objects such as ceramic figurines that are largely absent in monumental contexts and that reflect ancient Mesoamerican rituals that "flourished largely outside of the control of the state" (Smith 2002:93). Smith frames state and household-level rituals in terms of Robert Redfield's great and little traditions, while Elizabeth Brumfiel (1996) uses domestic ritual objects as evidence for household rejection of imperial dominant ideology. More recent scholarship has found that many imperial Aztec rituals likely represent widespread pre-Aztec commoner household rituals that were appropriated and modified for imperial ideological purposes (Brumfiel 2007; De Lucia 2014; Smith 2002). Many Aztec household rituals thus have great chronological depth and were intimately connected to state-sponsored rituals in complex ways.

Funerary Rites

Documentary sources cite cremation as the primary Aztec funerary treatment, with exceptional deaths, such as those from childbirth and drowning, given a primary interment (Sahagún 1950–1982, Book 3:41–43). Excavations at the Templo Mayor of Tenochtitlan have yielded cremated remains in urns (Chávez Balderas 2007), but archaeological examples outside the imperial capital are rare (but see Sisson 1973:31, 37). For example, excavations of a palace at Cihuatecpan did not recover any cremated remains (Evans 1988). At Calixtlahuaca, García Payón excavated many elite, primary burials in a civic-ceremonial patio group (Garcia Payón 1941a, 1041b; cited in Smith et al. 2013). Thus cremation may not have been common outside of Mexica ruling and noble classes (Brundage 1985:193–194; see also Smith 2002). Household excavations have demonstrated that across much of the Aztec Empire primary interment was the most common burial within household space. However, not all household members were selected for such a practice, and there is a significant amount of variation that has to date bewildered archaeologists.

Many excavations of Aztec and pre-Aztec central Mexican household contexts have yielded few burials. Smith's (1992; Smith et al. 1999) partial excavations in Morelos of more than 50 domestic structures at rural sites and seven urban houses yielded only nine burials, all juveniles. Similarly, Mary Hodge (2008) found no Late Aztec burials and only one Early Aztec juvenile burial in excavations of domestic contexts on Mound 65 at Chalco, and Susan Evans (1988:35) encountered only two burials—both juveniles—in extensive excavations of nine houses at Cihuatecpan. At Early Postclassic Xaltocan, excavations have consistently recovered infant and child burials in each house (De Lucia 2010). However, between sites, the context of these interments varies. In Morelos, children were found under house floors and in outside space, while at Early Postclassic Xaltocan, they were always interred under house floors. Excavations at Early Postclassic Cholula similarly recovered a large number of juveniles, but few adults, interred inside and outside the house, though many of these seem to have been placed shortly post-abandonment or termination (McCafferty 2007). Smith (1992:259, 2002:109) speculated that adults were buried in cemeteries, but these have rarely been found. The lack of adult household burials led Smith (2002:109) to suggest that the Aztecs did not practice ancestor veneration. Kristin De Lucia (2010), on the other hand, has argued for the importance of children in the social memory and perpetuity of the house as a corporate structure.

Other excavations have recovered men, women, and children interred in outside household space. At Tula, the arrival of Aztec III Black-on-Orange pottery was associated with a shift in burial practices to this pattern (Gómez Serafín et al. 1994). Similarly, in the Middle Postclassic, some Xaltocan residents began to bury some residents of all ages under the patio (Overholtzer 2012a). Overholtzer and De Lucia (2016; see also De Lucia and Overholtzer 2014) determined that this burial pattern was spatially segregated to the edges of the former island, where they argue people with ceramic consumption patterns distinct from existing residents settled in the mid-13th century. Burying deceased family members of all ages in exterior patio space may have served as a way for new settlers to stake a claim to land, they suggest, a tradition not shared with existing residents who continued to inter only infants within household space in the center of the island. This variation in burial practice could also reflect a more active relationship of new settlers with household ancestors. For example, Sahagún (1950–1982, Book 1:167) relates that on the eighth day of Izcalli, family members buried within the house were each given offerings of tamales before the feast began. Thus, variation in burial patterns across central Mexico in the Middle and Late Postclassic may reflect efforts to define and display differing social identities, between and even within regions and sites.

Interestingly, during the Middle and Late Postclassic at both Tula and Xaltocan—in households where adults and children were buried together outside the house—infants were often buried inside cooking jars covered with upturned decorated serving vessels. Such a pattern finds parallels in other central Mexican contexts. The Early Postclassic UA-1 house at Cholula also contained the remains of fetuses, infants, and children interred inside jars and bowls (McCafferty 2007). And 17 of the 30 juveniles (and one adult) sacrificed to Ehécatl-Quetzalcóatl at the civic ceremonial complex at Tlatelolco during the 1454–1457 drought were buried inside large cooking jars that were often covered with upturned Aztec III dishes and basins and sometimes comals, similar to the residential pattern at Tula and Xaltocan (Guilliem Arroyo 1999). Documentary sources suggest the Aztecs believed that deceased infants went to *Chichihuacuauhco*, the Place of the Nursemaid Tree, where they sipped milk that dripped from the tree and waited to be reborn (*Codex Ríos* 1964; López Austín 1988; Sahagún 1950–1982, Book 6:115). Burial in household space, particularly inside cooking jars—hollow, dark, and humid places akin to wombs and caves—may have meant to ensure such a fate by keeping the souls close by (De Lucia 2010; Overholtzer 2012a).

Aztec Figurines

Whereas excavations have encountered significant variability in burial practices in Aztec Mexico, ceramic figurines reveal remarkable continuity of tradition across space and time (Figure 44.2). Many Aztec figurine types are iconographically identical across the entire Postclassic and, in some cases, into the Early Colonial period (Brumfiel and Overholtzer 2009). Aztec-style figurines (both imported and imitated) appear outside of the Basin of Mexico at Yautepec, Morelos, as early as the Middle Postclassic (Smith 2005:45). Aztec figurines followed the expansion of the Aztec Empire and possibly colonists to reach some cities farther from the Aztec heartland (Ohnersorgen 2006), although this acceptance was not universal (Venter 2012).

Aztec figurines are the most thoroughly researched of all domestic ritual artifacts (see Overholtzer [2016] for more in-depth treatment). Early research devoted to creating typologies and identifying deity representations (Kaplan 1958; Millian 1981; Parsons 1972) has given way to investigations of household ideologies, ritual use, and materialities. Brumfiel largely initiated this shift in 1996 by comparing the iconography of Aztec figurines and monumental sculpture to assess whether commoner households accepted imperial gender ideologies. Differences in the presentation of men and women in these two media, and the intensification of use of female figurines that reflected concerns with female reproduction and curing rituals, led her to conclude that commoners contested the male dominant ideology of the Aztec elite.

FIGURE 44.2 Aztec rattle figurines and figurine mold. Drawings by Juan Joel Viveros Sánchez (left, center) and Tom Quinn (right).

Following Brumfiel, other scholars have used figurines for emic understandings of rituals relating to fertility and health and curing. Household archaeology has enabled a contextual understanding of figurine use. Susan Evans's (1990, 2001) excavations at Cihuatecpan found that 90 percent of the figurines with good behavioral context were recovered in habitation and sweatbath areas; of these, most were female. The association with sweatbaths—locations of healing rituals often performed by women and midwives—confirms that some figurines were used by women for household social reproduction. Overholtzer (2012b) combines iconographic, archaeological, and ethnohistoric evidence of Aztec rattle figurines to suggest that this type, in particular, was used in healing rituals. These smooth, three-dimensional musical instruments were designed to be held and shaken, in stark contrast to the plaque-like figurines with undecorated backs and large bases that likely stood on household altars. Overholtzer argues that as percussion instruments used by midwives in the sweatbath, rattle figurines may have encouraged pregnant mothers to focus on rhythmic sound and relax, thereby alleviating pain and facilitating labor. As depictions of women as mothers and healers, rattle figurines presented an image of the female body that reinforced women's active roles in the production and reproduction of the house and society.

Brumfiel and Overholtzer (2009) also use theories of embodiment to examine the variety of social issues that diverse figurine forms might have addressed. They distinguish between hollow rattle and dog effigy vessels that encouraged consideration of interior spaces and the flat-backed figurines and large braziers affixed with human figures that demonstrated attention to bodily class and status difference. A final category includes crude "mud men-and-women" and Formative and Classic period–style "curated" figurines that depicted alien representations of bodies and bodies of earth spirits and predecessors.

Discard location has allowed examination of variability in figurine use along class and age lines. In elite and nonelite households in Morelos, Jan Olson (2007) found that commoners consumed more figurines overall, while temple models were restricted to elite households. From the Middle to Late Postclassic, in association with an increase in long-distance market trade, there was a reduction in consumption differences between urban and rural residents and between elites and commoners (e.g., more imported goods in urban areas and in elite houses). De Lucia (2010) argues that adults were the primary users of the Aztec mold-made figurines that tend to be found in middens and ritual deposits, while children may have been the producers of crude figurines often left on house floors. Brumfiel and Overholtzer (2009), on the other hand, contend that the widespread, conventionalized form of the crude "mud men-and-women" type belies adult manufacture, and that their crude form represents an intentional design feature of these representations of earth beings. Though not strictly within the Aztec figurine tradition, McCafferty (2007) suggests that some Early Postclassic figurines at Cholula may have had a more secular role, since figurines recovered at the UA-1 household were particularly concentrated in porches where children would have played.

Finally, Overholtzer and Stoner (2011) reconstruct the biographies of curated figurines from Xaltocan in order to better understand their ritual meaning. They combine provenance data from instrumental neutron activation analysis; archaeological evidence for figurine production, use, and disposal in the Formative and Classic periods; and data on their disposal context in Postclassic households. They argue that curated figurines were produced, used, and disposed of at Teotihuacan and that Xaltocan residents collected them while on pilgrimage to the sacred site. As pieces of that place, the figurines carried the power of the "place of the birth of the gods," as the site was named in Nahuatl, and enchained their users to the people and history of Teotihuacan.

Ritual Feasting

While household burials and figurines relate primarily to household concerns, archaeological evidence for ritual feasting and the New Fire ceremony demonstrates interest in broader cosmological phenomena previously thought to have been the domain of the elite. Likewise, household ritual practices can highlight the construction of identity and the negotiation of social relations within and between elite and commoner households (see Brumfiel 2011:245–249). Feasting, or "household consumption rituals" (Smith 1987), represents one such politically significant ritual practice, and elites at many frontier sites selectively consumed Aztec-style pottery, including decorated serving vessels and incense burners, for use in such feasts (Ohnersorgen 2006; Venter 2012; see also Brumfiel 1987).

Colonial documents suggest that household feasts were held to commemorate life history events, such as births, marriages, and deaths, as well as achievement in warfare, religious vows, and trade expeditions (Durán 1967:II:123, 1971:122; Sahagún 1950–1982, Book 2:chs. 21, 25, 35, 37, Book 4:37:chs. 15, 23, 25, Book 6, Book 9:10; cited in Brumfiel 2011:261). Prehispanic household feasts involved music, dancing, incense burning, and eating and drinking from tripod vessels, bowls, *pulque* jars and bowls, and cacao jars and goblets (Smith et al. 2003). These events and associated feasts were scheduled after consultation with specialists in the 260-day ritual calendar (Durán 1971:395–399; Sahagún 1950–1982, Book 4:chs. 8, 19, Book 5:ch. 1, Book 6:ch. 23, Book 9: chs. 3, 7, Book 10:chs. 8, 12). Households also feasted in conjunction with some state rituals associated with the 365-day calendar (see Brumfiel 2001). For example, in months Tlacaxipehualiztli and Ochpaniztli, a man who had offered a captured enemy for temple sacrifice was celebrated with a household feast in which the captive's femur was hung in the captor's courtyard (Sahagún 1950–1982, Book 2:60). Feasting was such an important part of Aztec political negotiations that it continued long after the Spanish Conquest (Rodríguez-Alegría 2005).

Most feasting remains are mixed in middens with more quotidian serving wares (Smith et al. 2003:259–260), but scholars have examined decorated pottery from household contexts under the assumption that fancier wares were used for special occasions. Aztec ceramic production workshops and the highly developed market system operated largely outside of state control, and thus households of all classes had access to almost all

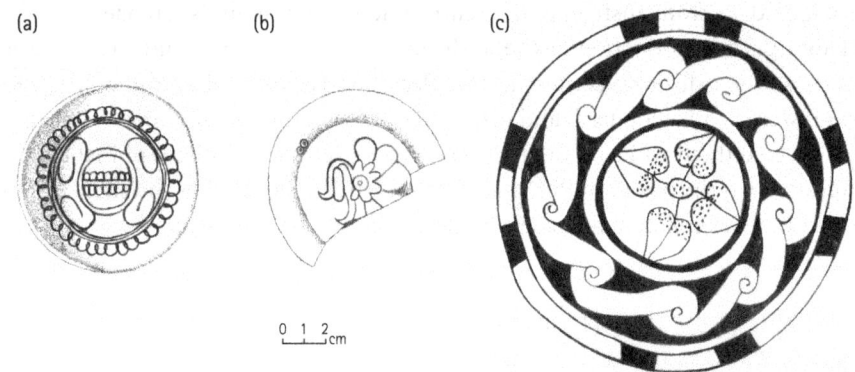

FIGURE 44.3 Calendrical design motifs on household feasting pottery from Xaltocan: (a) Quadripartite design; (b) Cipactli motif; (c) spiral or oscillating motion motif. Drawings by Juan Joel Viveros Sánchez.

of these wares (Blanton 1996; Hodge and Minc 1990; Olson 2001; Smith 1999; Smith and Heath-Smith 1994). Class purchasing power determined frequencies of serving vessels and imported wares, but overall Aztec households of all social statuses engaged in feasts involving the same pottery (Smith et al. 2003:260).

The visual symbolism presented in Aztec household feasts is evident in the design motifs, composition, and color of elaborately decorated serving vessels (Brenner 1931; Forde 2006; Hernández Sánchez 2005; Lind 1987; Solís et al. 2005; Vega Sosa 1984). Many vessels have quadripartite motifs, which represent the four quarters of the universe, the points where the sun rises and sets at the solstices (Vega Sosa 1984). Design motifs such as flowers, spirals, and concentric circles also referred to solar cycles (Figure 44.3). Brumfiel (2004, 2011) found a symbolic opposition between Late Postclassic Black-on-Orange and Red Ware vessels, associated with the sun and the night, respectively. These feast ceramics allude to cosmic warfare and, when used together, "rehearse the narrative of opposition between the orderly, life-giving sun and the destructive forces of darkness" (Brumfiel 2004:252). Finally, Aztec I Black-on-Orange serving vessels from commoner contexts at Xaltocan had flower, *cipactli*, and oscillating motion motifs, all associated with calendrical cycles (Brumfiel 2011). Brumfiel argues that as early as the tenth century, commoner households consulted calendrical specialists to time feasts in congruence with cosmic forces and demonstrated this practice to others with feasting pottery.

New Fire Ceremony

For the Aztecs, the 365-day secular calendar and the 260-day ritual calendar combined every 52 years to create a "bundle" similar to our century. The transition from one cycle to the next was marked by uncertainty and trepidation, for the current age would be destroyed at the end of one such cycle. To ensure the renewal of the world, the Aztecs carried out the *Xiuhtlalpilli*, or New Fire ceremony. Colonial chroniclers described this ceremony as necessitating both imperial and household-level ritual practices (Sahagún 1950–1982, Book 7:25–32; see also *Códice Tudela* 1980:folio 83v–84r; Durán 1967:Book II:453–454; Gómez de Orozco 1945; Motolinía 1951). Five days prior to the end of a cycle, the fires in all Aztec temples and houses were extinguished. People swept out their homes and hearths, made offerings, and discarded all of their household goods, such as ceramic cooking and serving vessels and figurines (Figure 44.4). On the last day of the cycle, imperial priests drilled a new fire on the chest of a sacrificial victim. This new fire was distributed to the temples, religious schools, and households throughout the empire, symbolizing the imperial hierarchy and the authority of the capital over the provinces (Carrasco 1999:96–114). In their houses, people rejoiced and replaced the goods they had broken.

George Vailliant (1937, 1938) first suggested that the New Fire ceremony would have created archaeologically recognizable middens consisting of nearly reconstructable vessels deposited simultaneously. Christina Elson and Michael Smith (2001) added the expectation that New Fire ceremony deposits would be located near houses and reflect typical household assemblages in type and proportions of objects. They found

FIGURE 44.4 Disposal of household goods for the New Fire ceremony, Sahagún 1950-1982, Book 7:Figure 19 Florence, The Biblioteca Medicea Laurenziana, ms. Med. Palat. 220, f. 21r. Reproduced with permission of MiBACT. Further reproduction by any means is prohibited.

archaeological evidence of New Fire ceremonies at Nonoalco and Chiconauhtla in the Basin of Mexico and Cuexcomate in Morelos, indicating that this ceremony took place widely across the Aztec Empire. Elson and Smith (2001) cite New Fire iconography at Epiclassic Xochicalco (Sáenz 1967) and Mixtec codex depictions of new fires being drilled in rituals celebrating a town's founding (Boone 2000:94–160) as evidence that the New Fire ceremony was a widespread, popular pre-Aztec ritual. Rather than the imposition of Aztec imperial ideology, they argue the New Fire ceremony demonstrates imperial appropriation of an ancient ritual and the imposition on conquered subjects of a version adorned with imperial pomp and circumstance. This argument is supported by De Lucia's (2014) excavations of a twelfth- or thirteenth-century house at Xaltocan featuring a ritual deposit of smashed complete ceramic objects. Aztec ritual practices were thus developed "through a dialectic between traditional local and household practices . . . and innovative imperial policies" (Elson and Smith 2001:172).

Ritual Music

Many, if not all, of the household ritual practices described earlier would have been accompanied by music, and yet Aztec music has only rarely been investigated (Both 2002, 2005, 2007; Stevenson 1968). Nonetheless, musical instruments are often recovered in household excavations, and here I present data from excavations of Middle to Late Postclassic houses at Xaltocan (Overholtzer 2012; see De Lucia 2014 for complementary Early to Middle Postclassic household data). In decreasing order of abundance, the instruments found include rattles (including rattle figurines, round forms with small handles, and incense burners with rattle handles), flutes, whistles, bone rasps, and copper bells (Figure 44.5). These houses likely also had perishable gourd rattles and drums, the most important of which was the *huehuetl*, a vertical hand drum made of wood covered in stretched animal hide.

Aztec ceramic flutes from Xaltocan houses often have flowers on the end, alluding to instrumental music understood as a "flowery song," or *xochicuicatl*. Both sound and scent—similarly invisible but sensual—were sacrificial offerings through which one communicated with the gods (Both 2002:281). Rattles and rasps were often used to petition earth, water, and rain deities for help (Both 2007:95; Stevenson 1968:38). Finally, excavations have recovered *omechicahuaztli*, bone rasps worked from human femurs, in finished and unfinished form, indicating household production of these ritual implements (Overholtzer 2012a:224–225). Such bone rasps have a long history of use at Xaltocan, as they have also been recovered in Early Postclassic household contexts (De Lucia 2014:394).

Ethnohistoric documents associate human femurs with captured warriors, and, as discussed earlier, the captor was given the femur to hang in his patio. Fray Diego Durán (1994:161–162) mentions the inclusion of these femurs in household rituals women carried out while their husbands were away at war. It is plausible that some femurs from

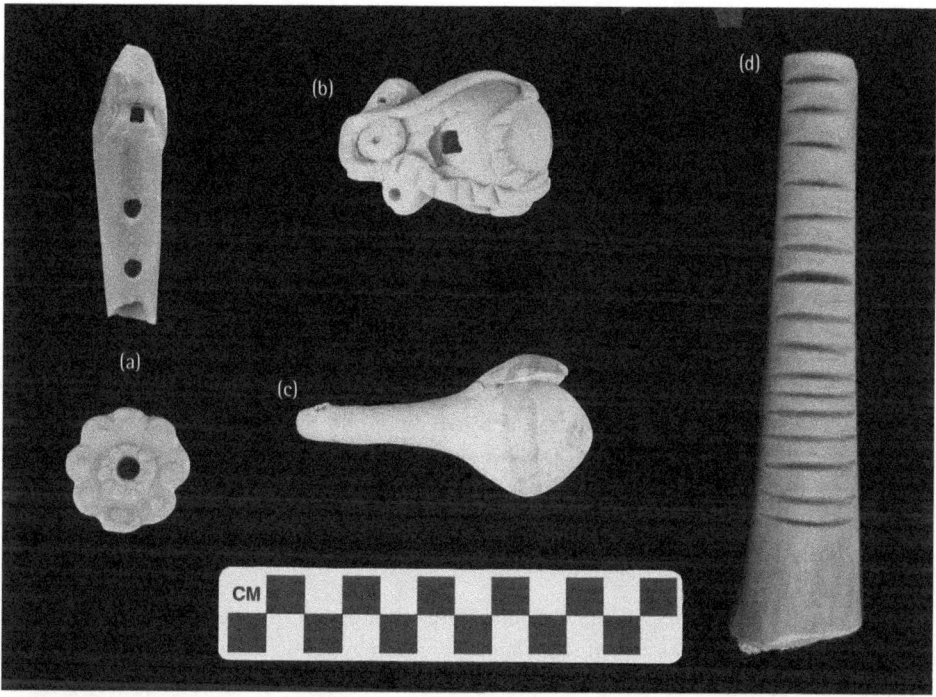

FIGURE 44.5 Household musical instruments recovered from Xaltocan house: (a) flute and flower from end of flute, (b) whistle, (c) rattle, (d) bone rasp or *omechicahuaztli*. Photograph by the author.

sacrificed enemy warriors were carved into bone rasps (Overholtzer 2012a:224–225). Durán (1994:151) describes dancing to the sound made by bone rasps at funerals for dead warriors, and a taphonomic analysis of a collection of bone rasps from Zacapu, Michoacan, revealed wear patterns consistent with such use (Pereira 2005:299–305). Bone rasps were thrown away in middens at Xaltocan and buried with the deceased at Maztlazinco Calixtlahuaca and Valle de Bravo (García Payón 1941b; Reinhold 1981). *Omechicahuaztli* thus seem to be associated with funerals and rites of passage for the dead, though there may have significant differences in their use and disposal (McVicker 2005).

Conclusion

In sum, household ritual in the Aztec Empire was concerned not only with household maintenance or reproduction, but also with broader cosmologies and political negotiations. Household ritual was not simply a way for individuals or families to petition deities. It was also how families related with each other and asserted their status, claims to property, or relationship with past peoples and places; how men and women contested gender ideologies; and how people ensured the continuity of their world. Archaeological research suggests a complex and often bidirectional relationship between ritual at the domestic and imperial levels. Finally, the limited extensive household excavations that have been carried out hint at significant variation within funerary rituals, variation that is not apparent within the elite-centered, Tenochtitlan-biased documentary record.

References Cited

Blanton, Richard E.
1996 The Basin of Mexico Market System and the Growth of an Empire. In *Aztec Imperial Strategies*, edited by F. F. Berdan, R. E. Blanton, E. H. Boone, M. G. Hodge, M. E. Smith, and E. Umberger, pp. 47–84. Dumbarton Oaks Research and Library Collection, Washington, DC.

Boone, Elizabeth Hill
2000 *Stories in Red and Black: Pictorial Histories of the Aztecs and Mixtecs*. University of Texas Press, Austin.

Both, Arnd Adje
2002 Aztec Flower-Flutes: The Symbolic Organization of Sound in Late Postclassic Mesoamerica. In *Studien zur Musikarchäologie*, edited by E. Hickmann, A. D. Kilmer, and R. Eichmann, pp. 279–289. Verlag Marie Leidorf, Rahden, Germany.
2005 *Aerófonos Mexicas de las Ofrendas del Recinto Sagrado de Tenochtitlan*. Lateinamerika-Institut, Freie Universität Berlin.
2007 Aztec Music Culture. *The World of Music* 49(2):91–104.

Brenner, Anita
1931 *The Influence of Technique on the Decorative Style in the Domestic Pottery of Culhuacan*. Columbia University Press, New York.

Brown, Betty Ann
1983 Seen But Not Heard: Women in Aztec Ritual—The Sahagun Texts. In *Text and Image in Pre-Columbian Art: Essay on the Interrelationship of the Verbal and Visual Arts*, edited by J. C. Berlo, pp. 119–153. BAR International Series 180. British Archaeological Reports, Oxford.

Brumfiel, Elizabeth M.
1987 Consumption and Politics at Aztec Huexotla. *American Anthropologist* 8:676–686.
1996 Figurines and the Aztec State: Testing the Effectiveness of Ideological Domination. In *Gender and Archaeology*, edited by R. P. Wright, pp. 143–166. University of Pennsylvania Press, Philadelphia.
2001 Aztec Hearts and Minds: Religion and the State in the Aztec Empire. In *Empires: Perspectives from Archaeology and History*, edited by S. E. Alcock, T. N. D'Altroy, K. Morrison, and C. Sinopoli, pp. 283–310. Cambridge University Press, Cambridge, UK.
2004 Feasting and Figured Worlds in Postclassic Mexico. In *Mesoamerican Archaeology: Theory and Practice*, edited by J. A. Hendon and R. A. Joyce, pp. 239–264. Blackwell, Oxford.
2007 Solar Disks and Solar Cycles: Spindle Whorls and the Dawn of Solar Art in Postclassic Mexico. In *Interpreting Household Practices: Reflections on the Social and Cultural Roles of Maintenance Activities*, edited by S. Monton Subías, P. González-Marcén, M. Picazo, and M. Sánchez-Romero, pp. 91–113. Treballs d'Arqueologia 13. Universidad Autónoma de Barcelona, Barcelona.

2011 Toward a Middle Range Theory of Household Politics: The Standardization of Decorative Motifs in Middle Post-Classic Mexico. In *The Archaeology of Politics: The Materiality of Political Practice and Action in the Past*, edited by P. G. Johansen and A. M. Bauer, pp. 245–282. Cambridge University Press, Cambridge, UK.

Brumfiel, Elizabeth M., and Lisa Overholtzer

2009 Alien Bodies, Everyday People, and Internal Spaces: Embodiment, Figurines and Social Discourse in Postclassic Mexico. In *Mesoamerican Figurines: Small-Scale Indexes of Large-Scale Phenomena*, edited by K. A. F. Christina, T. Halperin, and Rhonda Taube, pp. 297–323. University Press of Florida, Gainesville.

Brundage, Burr C.

1985 *The Jade Steps: A Ritual Life of the Aztecs*. University of Utah Press, Salt Lake City.

Burkhart, Louise M.

1989 *The Slippery Earth: Nahua-Christian Moral Dialogue in Sixteenth-Century Mexico*. University of Arizona Press, Tucson.

1997 Mexica Women on the Home Front: Housework and Religion in Aztec Mexico. In *Indian Women of Early Mexico*, edited by S. Schroeder, S. Wood, and R. Haskett, pp. 25–54. University of Oklahoma Press, Norman.

Carrasco, Davíd

1999 *City of Sacrifice: The Aztec Empire and the Role of Violence in Civilization*. Beacon Press, Boston.

Chávez Balderas, Ximena

2007 Los rituales funerarios en el Templo Mayor de Tenochtitlan. Mexico City: Instituto Nacional de Antropología e Historia.

Codex Magliabecchiano

1903 *The Codex Magliabecchiano: The Book of Life of the Ancient Mexicans*. University of California Press, Berkeley.

Codex Ríos

1964 *Codex Ríos* (Vaticanus A or Vaticanus 3738). Facsimile edition. In *Antigüedades de México*, Vol. 3, edited by J. Corona Nuñez, pp. 7–313. Secretaría de Hacienda y Crédito Público de México, Mexico City.

Códice Tudela

1980 *Códice Tudela*. 2 vols. Edited by José Tudela de la Orden. Ediciones Cultura Hispánica, Madrid.

De Lucia, Kristin

2010 A Child's House: Social Memory, Identity, and the Construction of Childhood in Early Postclassic Mexican Households. *American Anthropologist* 112(4):607–624.

2014 Everyday Practice and Ritual Space: The Organization of Domestic Ritual in Pre-Aztec Xaltocan, Mexico. *Cambridge Archaeological Journal* 24(3):379–403.

De Lucia, Kristin, and Lisa Overholtzer

2014 Everyday Action and the Rise and Fall of Ancient Polities: Household Strategy and Political Change in Postclassic Xaltocan, Mexico. *Ancient Mesoamerica* 25(2):441–458.

DiCesare, Catherine

2009 *Sweeping the Way: Divine Transformation in the Aztec Festival of Ochpaniztli* University Press of Colorado, Boulder.

Durán, Fray Diego

1967 *Historia de las Indias de Nueva España*. 2 vols. Porrúa, Mexico City.

1971 *Book of the Gods and Rites and the Ancient Calendar*. Translated and edited by Fernando Horcasitas and Doris Heyden. University of Oklahoma Press, Norman.

1994 *The History of the Indies of New Spain*. University of Oklahoma, Norman.

Elson, Christina M., and Michael E. Smith

2001 Archaeological Deposits from the Aztec New Fire Ceremony. *Ancient Mesoamerica* 12(2):157–174.

Evans, Susan T.

1988 *Excavations at Cihuatecpan: An Aztec Village in the Teotihuacán Valley*. Vanderbilt University Publications in Anthropology No. 36. Vanderbilt University, Nashville, TN.

1990 Household Ritual in Aztec Life. Paper presented at the annual meeting of the Society for American Archaeology, Las Vegas, NV.

2001 Aztec Noble Courts: Men, Women, and Children of the Palace. In *Royal Courts of the Ancient Maya*, edited by T. Inomata and S. Houston, pp. 237–273. Westview Press, Boulder, CO.

Forde, Jamie E.

2006 *Ideology, Identity, and Icons: A Study of Mixtec Polychrome Pottery from Late Postclassic Yucu Dzaa (Tututepec), Oaxaca, Mexico*. Ph.D. dissertation, University of Colorado, Boulder.

García Payón, José

1941a La cerámica del Valle de Toluca. *Revista Mexicana de Estudios Antropológicos* 5:209–238.

1941b Manera de disponer de los muertos entre los matlatzincas del Valle de Toluca. *Revista Mexicana de Estudios Antropológicos* 5:65–78.

Garibay K., Angel María

1967 Códice Carolino: Manuscrito anónimo del siglo XVI. *Estudios de Cultura Náhuatl* 7:11–58.

Gómez de Orozco, F.

1945 Costumbres, fiestas, enterramientos y diversas formas de proceder de los indios de Nueva España. *Tlalocan* 2(1):38–63.

Gómez Serafín, Susana, Francisco Javier Sansores, and Enrique Fernández Dávila

1994 *Enterramientos humanos de la época prehispánica en Tula, Hidalgo*. Colección Científica, Instituto Nacional de Antropología, Mexico, D.F.

Guilleim Arroyo, Salvador

1999 *Ofrendas a Ehécatl-Quetzalcoatl en Mexico-Tlatelolco: Proyecto Tlatelolco, 1987–1996*. Colección Científica 400. Instituto Nacional de Antropología e Historia, Mexico City.

Hamann, Byron E.

2008 Chronological Pollution: Potsherds, Mosques, and Broken Gods before and after the Conquest of Mexico. *Current Anthropology* 49(5):803–836.

Hernández Sánchez, Guilda

2005 *Vasijas para Ceremonia: Iconografía de la cerámica Tipo Códice del estilo Mixteca-Puebla*. CNWS Publications, Leiden.

Hodge, Mary G.

2008 *Place of Jade: Society and Economy in Ancient Chalco*. University of Pittsburgh Press, Pittsburgh, PA, and Instituto Nacional de Antropología e Historia, Mexico City.

Hodge, Mary G., and Leah D. Minc

1990 The Spatial Patterning of Aztec Ceramics: Implications for Prehispanic Exchange Systems in the Valley of Mexico. *Journal of Field Archaeology* 17(4):415–437.

Joyce, Rosemary A.

2000 Girling the Girl and Boying the Boy: The Production of Adulthood in Ancient Mesoamerica. *World Archaeology* 31(3):473–483.

Kaplan, Flora
1958 *The Post-Classic Figurines of Central Mexico*. Ph.D. dissertation, Columbia University, New York.
Lind, Michael D.
1987 *The Sociocultural Dimensions of Mixtec Ceramics*. Vanderbilt University Publications in Anthropology Vol. 33. Vanderbilt University, Nashville, TN.
López Austin, Alfredo
1988 *The Human Body and Ideology: Concepts of the Ancient Nahuas*. 2 vols. University of Utah Press, Salt Lake City.
McCafferty, Geoffrey G.
2007 Altar Egos: Domestic Ritual and Social Identity in Postclassic Cholula, Mexico. In *Commoner Ritual and Ideology in Ancient Mesoamerica*, edited by N. Gonlin and J. C. Lohse, pp. 213–250. University Press of Colorado, Boulder.
McVicker, Donald
2005 Notched Human Bones from Mesoamerica. *Mesoamerican Voices* 2:1–31.
Millian, Alva Clarke
1981 *The Iconography of Aztec Ceramic Figurines*. Ph.D. dissertation, Department of Art History and Archaeology, Columbia University, New York.
Motolinía, Fray Toribio de
1951 *Motolinía's History of the Indians of New Spain*. Translated by F. Borgia Steck. Academy of American Franciscan History, Washington, DC.
Ohnersorgen, Michael A.
2006 Aztec Provincial Administration at Cuetlaxtlan, Veracruz. *Journal of Anthropological Archaeology* 25:1–32.
Olson, Jan
2001 *Unequal Consumption: A Study of Domestic Wealth Differentials in Three Late Postclassic Mexican Communities*. Ph.D. dissertation, State University of New York, Albany.
2007 A Socioeconomic Interpretation of Figurines Assemblages from Late Postclassic Morelos, Mexico. In *Commoner Ritual and Ideology in Ancient Mesoamerica*, edited by N. Gonlin and J. C. Lohse, pp. 251–279. University Press of Colorado, Boulder.
Overholtzer, Lisa
2012a *Empires and Everyday Material Practices: A Household Archaeology of Aztec and Spanish Imperialism at Xaltocan, Mexico*. Ph.D. disseration, Northwestern University, Evanston, IL.
2012b So That the Baby Not Be Formed Like a Pottery Rattle: Aztec Rattle Figurines and Household Social Reproductive Practices. *Ancient Mesoamerica* 23(1):69–83.
In press Aztec Figurines. *In Oxford Handbook of Prehistoric Figurines*, edited by T. Insoll. Oxford University Press, Oxford.
Overholtzer, Lisa and Kristin De Lucia
2016 A Multiscalar Approach to Migration and Social Change at Middle Postclassic Xaltocan. *Ancient Mesoamerica* 26(1): 163–182.
Overholtzer, Lisa, and Wesley D. Stoner
2011 Merging the Social and the Material: Life Histories of Ancient Mementos from Central Mexico. *Journal of Social Archaeology* 11(2):171–193.
Parsons, Mary H.
1972 Aztec Figurines from the Teotihuacán Valley, Mexico. In *Miscellaneous Studies in Mexican Prehistory*, edited by M. W. Spence, J. R. Parsons, and M. H. Parsons, pp. 81–164. Anthropological Papers Vol. 49. Museum of Anthropology, University of Michigan, Ann Arbor.

Pereira, Grégory
2005 The Utilization of Grooved Human Bones: A Reanalysis of Artificially Modified Human Bones Excavated by Carl Lumholtz at Zacapu, Michoacán, Mexico. *Latin American Antiquity* 16(3):293–312.

Reinhold, Manfred
1981 *Exploraciones Arqueológicas en el Valle de Bravo*. Biblioteca Enciclopedica del Estado de México, Mexico, D.F.

Rodríguez-Alegría, Enrique
2005 Eating Like an Indian: Negotiating Social Relations in the Spanish Colonies. *Current Anthropology* 46(4):551–573.

Ruíz de Alarcón, Hernando
1984 *Treatise on the Heathen Superstitions that Today Live among the Indians Native to This New Spain, 1629*. University of Oklahoma Press, Norman.

Sáenz, César A.
1967 *El Fuego Nuevo*, Vol. 18. Instituto Nacional de Antropología e Historia, Mexico City.

Sahagún, Friar Bernardino de
1950–1982 *The Florentine Codex: General History of the Things of New Spain*. Translated by A. Anderson and C. E. Dibble. School of American Research, Santa Fe, NM, and University of Utah Press, Salt Lake City.
1997 *Primeros Memoriales*. Edited by T. D. Sullivan. University of Oklahoma Press, Norman.

Sisson, Edward B.
1973 *First Annual Report of the Coxcatlan Project*. Phillips Academy, Andover, MA.

Smith, Michael E.
1987 Household Possessions and Wealth in Agrarian States: Implications for Archaeology. *Journal of Anthropological Archaeology* 6:297–335.
1992 *Archaeological Research at Aztec-Period Rural Sites in Morelos, Mexico*, Vol. 1: *Excavations and Architecture*. Instituto Nacional de Antropología e Historia, Mexico City, and University of Pittsburgh Press, Pittsburgh, PA.
2002 Domestic Ritual at Aztec Provincial Sites in Morelos. In *Domestic Ritual in Ancient Mesoamerica*, edited by P. Plunket, pp. 93–114. Cotsen Institute of Archaeology, Los Angeles.
2005 Aztec-Style Ceramic Figurines from Yautepec, Morelos. *Mexicon* 27:45–55.

Smith, Michael E., Aleksander Borejsza, Angela Huster, Charles D. Frederick, Isabel Rodríguez López, and Cynthia Heath-Smith
2013 Aztec Period Houses and Terraces at Calixtlahuaca: The Changing Morphology of a Mesoamerican Hilltop Urban Center. *Journal of Field Archaeology* 38(3):227–243.

Smith, Michael E., and Cynthia Heath-Smith
1994 Rural Economy in Late Postclassic Morelos: An Archaeological Study. In *Economies and Polities in the Aztec Realm*, edited by M. G. Hodge and M. E. Smith, pp. 349–376. Institute for Mesoamerican Studies, Albany, NY.

Smith, Michael E., Cynthia Heath-Smith, and Lisa Montiel
1999 Excavations of Aztec Urban Houses at Yautepec, Mexico. *Latin American Antiquity* 10(2):133–150.

Smith, Michael E., Jennifer B. Wharton, and Jan Marie Olson
2003 Aztec Feasts, Rituals, and Markets: Political Uses of Ceramic Vessels in a Commercial Economy. In *The Archaeology and Politics of Food and Feasting in Early States and Empires*, edited by T. L. Bray, pp. 235–268. Kluwer Academic/Plenum, New York.

Solís, Felipe, Verónica Velasquez, and Roberto Velasco
2005 Cerámica polícroma de Cholula y de los otros valles de Puebla. In *La Gran Pirámide Cholula*, edited by F. Solís, G. Uruñuela, P. Plunket, M. Cruz, and D. Rodríguez, pp. 78–129. Conaculta, Instituto Nacional de Antropología e Historia, Mexico City.

Stevenson, Robert
1968 *Music in Aztec and Inca Territory*. University of California Press, Berkeley.

Vaillant, George C.
1937 History and Stratigraphy in the Valley of Mexico. *Scientific Monthly* 44:307–324.
1938 A Correlation of Archaeological and Historical Sequences in the Valley of Mexico. *American Anthropologist* 40:535–573.

Vega Sosa, Constanza
1984 El curso del sol en los glifos de la cerámica azteca tardía. *Estudios de Cultura Náhuatl* 17:125–170.

Venter, Marcie L.
2012 Negotiating Aztec Imperialism: Late Postclassic Ceramic Evidence from Totogal. Veracruz. *Mexicon* 34(3):58–63.

PART VII
AZTECS AFTER THE CONQUEST

CHAPTER 45

POST-CONQUEST RURAL AZTEC ARCHAEOLOGY

PATRICIA FOURNIER G. AND CYNTHIA L. OTIS CHARLTON

INTERDISCIPLINARY approaches are employed to investigate urban and rural post-Conquest Aztec sites in central Mesoamerica by integrating archaeological, ethnohistorical, historical, and ethnographic information to provide the basis for understanding Early Colonial (A.D. 1521–1620) developments in areas formerly under Aztec rule in central Mexico (e.g. Charlton 1981; Charlton and Fournier G. 1993; Charlton et al. 2005).

Thomas Charlton's pioneering Colonial study was in the Otumba region, located in the Basin of Mexico's Teotihuacan Valley (e.g. Charlton 1972, 1986; Charlton and Otis Charlton 1998) (Figure 45.1).

The results derived from that project contribute to the definition of the nature and organization of rural indigenous communities from the Aztec Postclassic through the post-Conquest era and provide insights into different aspects of their reorganization and transformation during the Colonial and Republican periods addressing demography, landscape, ecological changes, and settlement patterns.

Additional case studies that have used this type of integrated research include those in the Otomí region of the Mezquital Valley, Hidalgo (Fournier G. and López Aguilar 2015; Fournier G. and Mondragón 2003; López Aguilar 2009; Mondragón et al. 1997; Parsons and Parsons 1990) and ongoing studies in Xaltocan, in the Basin of Mexico (e.g. Brumfiel 2005; Millhauser 2012; Overholtzer 2012; Rodríguez Alegría 2010). These examples, based on surveys, excavations, detailed documentary analyses, and occasional ethnoarchaeological approaches, illustrate that post-Conquest archaeology is a logical extension of research programs originally implemented to study the Aztec Postclassic period.

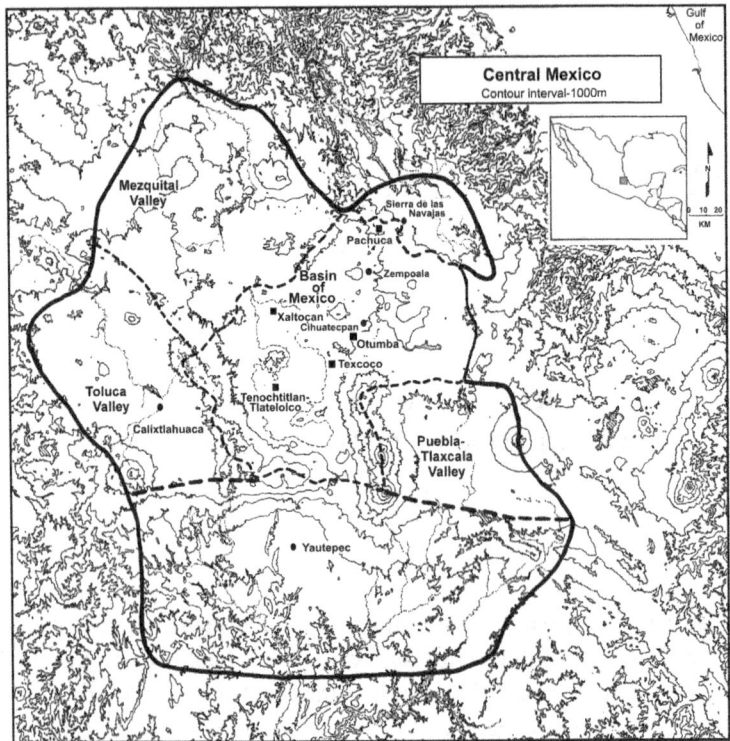

FIGURE 45.1 Map of central Mexico with locations mentioned in the text (base map adapted from Detenal 1:250,000 series 1970/1977: Cynthia Otis Charlton).

THE LATE PRE-CONQUEST PERIOD

The Late Postclassic Aztec imperial structure is treated more extensively elsewhere (see Blanton et al., this volume). Those dimensions most relevant to Early Colonial period changes in rural areas located in central Mexico are noted here.

The Aztec Triple Alliance city of Tenochtitlan was the dominant political, ideological, social, and economic center of a vast multiethnic tributary empire. Initial Aztec expansion first consolidated its hold on nearby areas within the Basin of Mexico and subsequently expanded militarily into adjacent areas outside the Basin (see Blanton et al., this volume). All subordinates within the immediate hinterlands of the core of the Aztec Empire were variably linked to the Triple Alliance centers and to other subordinate communities through market and tribute systems, in which agricultural products, raw materials, and partially finished and unfinished noncomestibles moved in and out of Tenochtitlan and Texcoco and the central cities, and also through horizontal market networks to and from other communities (see Hirth and Nichols, this volume). These economic and political structures were not only imposed through military might but were also underwritten by cross-cutting shared religious and political ideologies. Regional, ethnic, and social class distinctions are marked archaeologically in ceramic styles and design preferences (Charlton 1994; Garraty 2006; Hodge and Minc 1990; Hodge et al. 1993).

The inner core of Aztec hegemony linked communities to a system that brought them into contact, albeit usually indirectly, with other state systems and nonstate systems in Mesoamerica (Blanton and Feinman 1984), and these societies were closely connected in a vigorous and dynamic macroregional economy (Alexander and Kepecs 2005). Of particular importance in this interaction was the trade in luxury goods that was related to elite power and ethnic self-definition. The artisans producing goods were dependent on the elite for raw materials as well as for the distribution and consumption of the products of their workshops (e.g. Otis Charlton 1994). The impact of the Spanish Conquest on this system can be seen in the studies of four areas outside the Triple Alliance centers: Xaltocan (Nahuatl and Otomí speakers) in the northern Basin of Mexico lakebed; Otumba (Nahuatl and Otomí speakers), one of six city states in the Teotihuacan Valley in the eastern Basin; Zempoala-Pachuca (Nahuatl, Otomí, and Pamé speakers) in the region of the Sierra de Las Navajas obsidian mines to the northeast of the Basin; and the Mezquital Valley (Otomí and Nahuatl speakers) to the north of the Basin.

THE EARLY COLONIAL PERIOD, A.D. 1521–1620

The Conquest of the Aztec Empire by the Spanish in A.D.1519–1521 had a wide impact, but it was felt earlier and in differing degrees in the core compared to the periphery and rural areas (see also Barrera Rivera and Rodriguez-Alegría, this volume). The Early Colonial period in the Basin of Mexico began with a devastating military conquest at the center of the Triple Alliance, but outlying areas saw changes only gradually. Tribute and labor obligations that were distinctly defined for people and communities prior to the Conquest transferred to a new set of rulers but with changes. Under the *encomienda*, or land grant system established by the Spanish, the tribute obligations of the indigenous population included familiar comestibles such as salt, corn, and beans, as well as introduced cultivars such as wheat and barley. Noncomestibles included familiar materials such as textiles and ceramics, such as comales, ollas, jars, and goblets, among other items, but with some design variations to fit differing Spanish needs. Under the *repartimiento*, or labor draft system, individuals and communities were also required to provide labor to work in Spanish homes; on farms, ranches, and haciendas, once these appeared; and in mines (Acuña 1985, 1986a, 1986b; González de Cosío 1952; Paso y Troncoso 1905; Valle 1993). Work was also required on an irregular basis on the flood mitigation structures for Mexico City-Tenochtitlan (Gibson 1964:236–243).

Continuities and modifications that took place in the Early Colonial period must be understood as occurring against a backdrop of devastating epidemics brought about by European diseases, which by the mid-1600s reduced the indigenous population to about 10 percent of pre-Conquest levels in the Basin of Mexico (Gibson 1964:136–148). This much-reduced population was no longer capable of providing the necessary tribute or labor. The Spanish response to the loss was a series of *congregación* orders that concentrated the decimated and scattered rural population into centralized towns in each area. A majority of Aztec towns in the Basin and its hinterlands ceased to be occupied between the end of the sixteenth century and 1625 (Charlton 1986; Charlton et al. 2005; Gibson 1964).

The Spanish Conquest that devastated the prehispanic cultures, over a relatively short space of time, realigned or replaced religious ideologies, political organization, and economic systems. The new system was integrated beyond the dimensions of the prehispanic Mesoamerican world system (e.g. Blanton and Feinman 1984). Mexico-Tenochtitlan remained at the top, but not only at the top of a regional hegemony. The region was linked, as the capital of the Viceroyalty of New Spain, formally established in 1535, to a Spanish worldwide empire. Through Mexico-Tenochtitlan flowed the dominant, strongly structured religious, political, economic, and class components that impacted the communities of the former Aztec Empire during the Early Colonial period. The new class system archaeologically fell roughly into the categories of Hispanic urban, indigenous urban, Hispanic rural, and indigenous rural as determined by material culture. Archaeological studies in rural sites indicate aspects of both continuity and change in settlement systems, land use, and material culture as manifested in structures, ceramics, and obsidian.

Settlement Patterns, Land Use, and Resources

Outside of Mexico-Tenochtitlan and other large cities, the obvious archaeological markers of conquest and incorporation into the new world system are few. They include, as in the urban centers, the destruction of indigenous religious structures and their replacement by church-monastery-cemetery complexes. Less elaborate structures with non-resident clergy such as chapels and *visitas* also occur (Genotte 2001).

With the abandonment of large tracts of land due to the population decline and the *congregaciones* of the remaining residents, small ranch structures began to appear in open areas. *Encomienda* land grants gave rise to ranch sites beginning in about 1535 in the Mezquital Valley and by about 1580 in the Otumba area. These raised introduced livestock such as cattle and sheep and cultivated wheat and other cereal crops (Charlton et al. 2005; Fournier G. and Mondragón 2003; Hunter 2014). Indigenous communities practicing traditional agriculture either for their subsistence or to pay tribute continued to occupy terraces and valleys into the early seventeenth century, by which time the major *congregación* orders had been implemented as the population rapidly declined. The surviving rural populations of the Basin of Mexico, the Mezquital Valley, and the

Pachuca-Zempoala area were relocated into a few regionally based larger communities that were retained as centers (Charlton 1991; Charlton et al. 2005; Gerhard 1986; Gibson 1964; López Aguilar 2009). In some cases, those communities whose populations were moved did retain their identities in the new location, in, near, or between the designated *congregación* centers, often named *barrios* within those centers (e.g. Charlton 1991; Gerhard 1986).

Agricultural soil suffered degradation and severe erosion as the result of deforestation and recurrent flooding episodes during the post-Conquest period in the Lake Texcoco Basin (Gibson 1964). The demographic decline and shift of most of the surviving indigenous population also resulted in the lack of maintenance of terraces and irrigation systems (Córdova and Parsons 1997). In the Mezquital Valley, native agriculture persisted in the lowlands where livestock were initially generally excluded, but deforestation of the region was the inevitable result of the introduction of large flocks of sheep that even the local indigenous population began to raise, resulting in drastic erosion of the thin soils of this arid area (Fournier G. and Mondragón 2003; Hunter 2014; Melville 1994).

In the Pachuca-Zempoala area, the introduction of silver mining and extraction began to produce the piles of contaminated waste that resulted from mining and refining in the area (e.g. Carrillo-González 2005; Mondragón Romero 2008).

Ceramics

The effects of the Spanish Conquest on material culture were varied, often gradual, and unequal, depending on a number of factors including location and access. In the case of indigenous ceramics, two parallel effects were the continuation for some time of essentially unchanged indigenous ceramic types, particularly in the more rural areas, while at the same time in other locations, stylistic, technological, and formal modifications were being made to native types in response to Spanish preferences and use. The degree of fusion and convergence with Hispanic ceramic traditions found in urban areas prior to 1620, such as the use of the wheel in manufacture of Hispanic forms and the use of glaze on indigenous wares, was small in the rural areas until the middle of the seventeenth century (Charlton and Fournier G. 1993; Charlton et al. 2007; Rodríguez-Alegría et al. 2013).

Paralleling this, other more traditional Spanish ceramics such as majolica began to appear, first imported from Spain and then increasingly manufactured in the New World (e.g. Fournier, Blackman, et al. 2009). The most common indigenous ceramic type, Aztec Orange Ware, experienced a florescence in decorative Black-on-Orange designs that early on became extremely elaborate in the urban centers of Tenochtitlan and Tlatelolco (Charlton et al. 2007) (Figure 45.2).

In Otumba, in stratigraphic excavations, the pre-Contact Aztec III Black-on-Orange designs seem to coexist with new Colonial Aztec IV Black-on-Orange design variants, but they are generally not nearly as elaborate as those from the major cities (Charlton 1996; Charlton et al. 2007). A slow decline in the numbers of decorated pieces continued

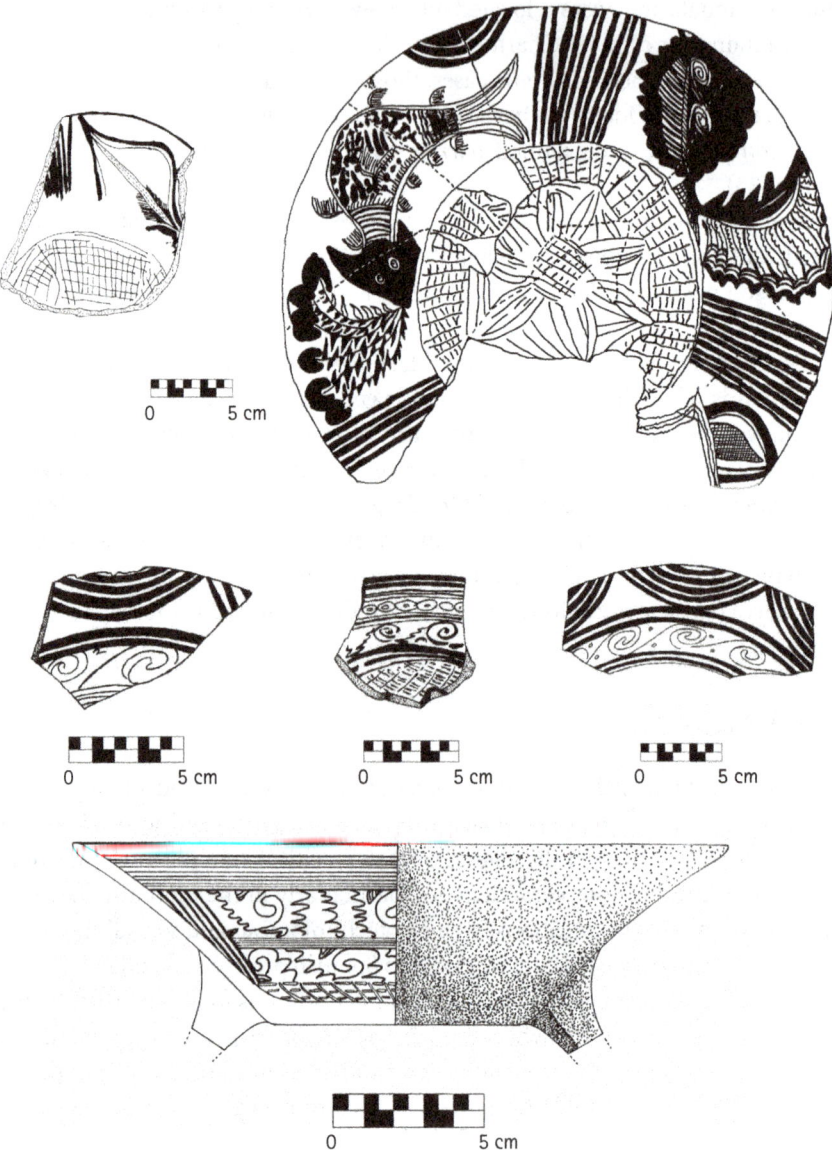

FIGURE 45.2 Aztec IV Black-on-Orange *molcajetes* from the Alameda district in Mexico City (upper row) and the Sierra de las Navajas obsidian source (lower rows). Adapted from Charlton et al. 2007:443–444.

through the Early Colonial period. One innovation that does appear to have been adopted in the rural Otumba area and seems to be a Spanish introduction is the use of cattail fluff in the pastes of Colonial wares, apparently to lighten the pieces in weight after firing (Charlton et al. 2007).

In excavations at Cihuatecpan in the Teotihuacan Valley and at the Sierra de Las Navajas obsidian mines near Pachuca-Zempoala, Aztec III Black-on-Orange vessels persist into the Early Colonial period mixed with low percentages of Aztec IV Black-on-Orange pots and a limited number of plain glazed sherds (Evans and Freter 1996; Pastrana and Fournier 1998). At Zempoala in the Santa Inés site, life after the Conquest appears to have continued without major changes in pre-Conquest ceramic traditions other than the introduction of a few plain glazed vessels (Fournier G. and Charlton 2012). In the Xaltocan area and the Mezquital Valley to the north of the Basin of Mexico, a few examples of Aztec IV Black-on-Orange have been identified either from surface collections or excavations (Gamboa Cabezas and Vélez Saldaña 2011; Millhauser 2012; Overholtzer 2012; Rodríguez-Alegría 2010).

Prehispanic Aztec Red Ware also continues after the Conquest, first with a burst of design elaboration, particularly in the Black-on-Red, but with an increasing decline in surface finish (Figure 45.3).

A new form—the shallow, flat-bottomed plate or bowl—was developed for use with some Spanish cuisine. Aztec Red Ware, which probably seemed familiar to the Spanish in that it resembled a red ware from Spain (Charlton and Fournier 2010), took on a great many new forms, designs, and finishes, and 80 to 90 percent of the Colonial Red Ware from Tlatelolco appears to exhibit these innovations (Charlton et al. 2007). Early Colonial period burnished Red Ware made in the Basin of Mexico is uncommon at rural sites however, but has been found in low percentages at Xaltocan, in the Mezquital Valley, at the Sierra de Las Navajas obsidian mines (Gamboa Cabezas and Vélez Saldaña 2011; Overholtzer 2012; Pastrana and Fournier 1998; Rodríguez-Alegría et al. 2013), and at the Santa Inés (Zempoala) site.

Spanish technological innovations that appeared early include the pottery throwing wheel—entirely for Spanish ceramic forms—and the application of glazes. Glazes primarily appear on plain-bodied local Orange Wares, the pastes generally indistinguishable from Aztec Plain Orange, though on some rare occasions a few pieces of Black-on-Orange ceramics have been found that are glazed, a type sometimes referred to as Aztec V (Charlton et al. 2007). These have also been found at Xaltocan (Overholtzer 2012). One glazed zoomorphic tripod support was found during excavations at Tlatelolco. At Otumba, Xaltocan, the Sierra de Las Navajas, the Santa Inés (Zempoala) site, and the Mezquital Valley, glazed wares were plain.

Whereas indigenous ceramic forms and designs became less variable and complex in urban contexts as the sixteenth century progressed, the reduction in complexity of the indigenous ceramic complex was gradual in rural settings where it was less complex to begin with, and the wares were almost entirely plain by the end of the Early Colonial period, around 1620 (Charlton 1996).

Majolica tableware produced in Spain and Italy, and later in Mexico City and Puebla, was fairly common in Mexico-Tenochtitlan, the urban center of Spanish occupation, and less so at Tlatelolco, the city designated early on to contain an indigenous community (Charlton et al. 2007). Imported majolica as well as majolica made in New Spain was rare this early at Otumba and in the Mezquital Valley. From the 1530s to

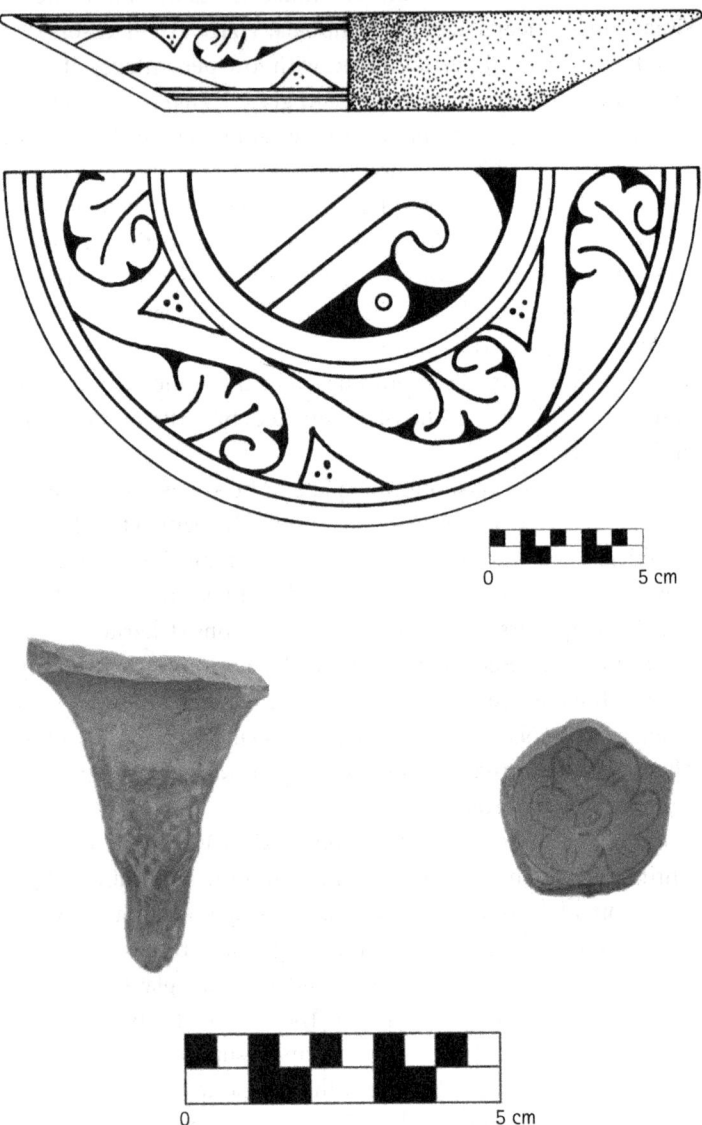

FIGURE 45.3 Colonial Red wares. Top row: plate from Tlatelolco (adapted from Charlton et al. 2007:449). Bottom row: molded zoomorphic support from a tripod plate and a decorated spinning bowl from the Santa Inés site. Photos by Patricia Fournier G.

the 1580s, small ranches begin to appear in the Otumba region and in the Mezquital Valley, perhaps occupied by Spanish or indigenous *cacique* local rulers (Charlton 1986; Fournier G. and López Aguilar 2015), but their pottery is little different from other households, though some small amounts of majolica may be present (Charlton 1976) that can date the sites. In Xaltocan, it has been suggested that the use of Early

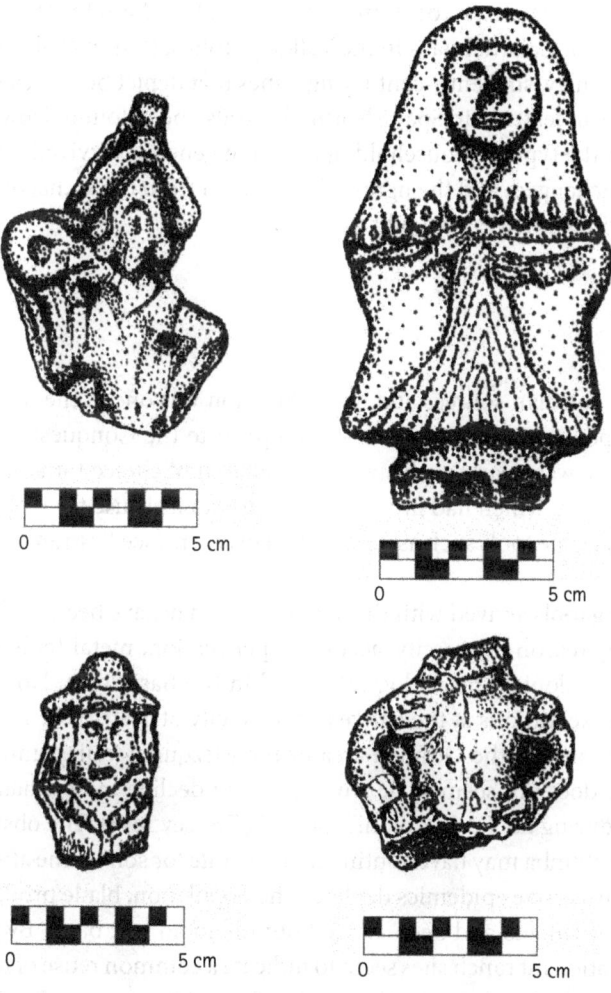

FIGURE 45.4 Colonial figurines from the Otumba site. Illustrations by Cynthia Otis Charlton.

Colonial period majolica by some members of the indigenous population may mark status distinctions and the aspiration to power by people of lesser rank than the elites (Rodríguez-Alegría 2010).

Another ceramic object in the archaeological record that is an indicator of change is the figurine. After centuries of relatively unchanging figurine style in the Late Postclassic Aztec complex, figurines showing males and females in contemporary Spanish dress appear quite quickly after the Conquest at Tlatelolco in the heart of the former Aztec Empire (Otis Charlton 1995). At Otumba, where the Battle of Otumba gave the local population an early firsthand look at Spaniards in full armor, the local ceramic workshops almost immediately turned out copies of armored figures and then Spaniards in more common European clothing (Otis Charlton and Charlton 2007, 2011) (Figure 45.4).

In Xaltocan (Overholtzer 2012), the Yautepec Valley, Morelos (Smith 2005), at the Matlaltzinca site of Calixtlahuaca in the Valley of Toluca (Smith et al. 2013), as well as in the Mezquital Valley, sixteenth-century figurines that depict both locals as well as people with European features in Spanish attire have also been found. However, there is no indication that the type, or household figurines in general, survived for long. The style of dress was unchanged, and the figures disappeared from the archaeological record, as their original ritual use was no doubt discouraged.

Obsidian

The control of obsidian sources and its exploitation was one of the marks of the whole succession of powers in the Basin of Mexico prior to the Conquest. Obsidian with its fine cutting edge was nearly exclusively the material of choice for cutting tools during the prehispanic era, which had little metal and found little use for it beyond decorative objects and a few fine tools such as needles and tweezers (see Pastrana and Carballo, this volume).

Metal cutting tools arrived with the Spanish and may have been held in high esteem, but whether by reason of scarcity, access, or permission, metal tools are rare to nonexistent in the Colonial archaeological record in the Basin area. No metal tools have been found in excavations at the native occupied city of Tlatelolco, and metal does not show up commonly in the Otumba area or the Mezquital Valley until the nineteenth century. There does not seem to be any significant decline in obsidian working in the Otumba area during the Early Colonial period (Cressey 1974). The obsidian core-blade workshops at Otumba may have continued to operate for some time after the Conquest, though after successive epidemics depleted the population, blade production may have moved into households and been carried out on an ad hoc basis. By the seventeenth century, excavations at ranch sites seem to indicate a common reuse of found blades that are heavily retouched and smaller than earlier forms (Parry 1990). During the sixteenth century at Xaltocan as well, flaked obsidian artifacts appear to have been produced and used instead of metal tools (Rodríguez-Alegría 2008).

The obsidian prismatic blade that had been ubiquitous prior to the Conquest no doubt continued to be in common use as a cutting tool in all native areas. Obsidian tools also evolved to some extent to meet new uses. At the Sierra de Las Navajas obsidian mines, a new form of large, high-backed scraper is found in association with Colonial ceramics, including regionally made plain Red Ware and the remains of a small Franciscan shrine dated to about 1528 (Pastrana and Fournier 1998) (Figure 45.5).

The workshops are associated with a group of residences and a plaza occupied by Colonial craftspeople. The scrapers were probably used on hides as cattle became more common. Hides were one of the few materials exported to Spain in the Early Colonial period (Pastrana and Fournier 1998). Obsidian tools may have also been used to process cordage required for silver and gold mining operations in the same area (Pastrana and Fournier 1998).

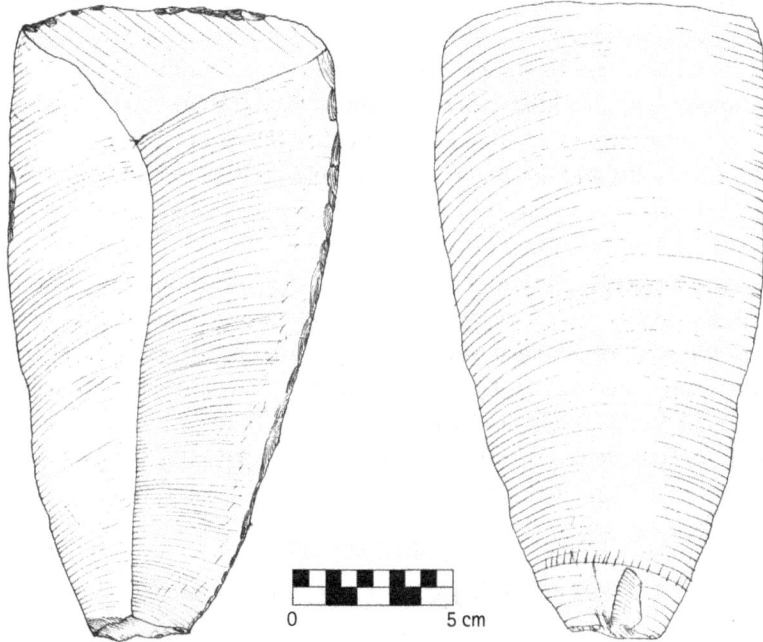

FIGURE 45.5 Colonial high-backed scraper from the Sierra de las Navajas obsidian source. Adapted from Pastrana and Fournier 1998:491.

Trade

By the mid-1500s, the huge native market at Tlatelolco had declined and most sales had moved off to other markets throughout the city of Mexico-Tenochtitlan, often targeted toward a specific ethnic group and specialized in goods offered (Gibson 1964; Lockhart 1992). However, at the native market of San Hipólito, located north of the center of the city and founded in 1540, Indians, *mestizos*, *criollos*, and *peninsulares* all traded (Gibson 1964).

Some of the goods crafted by indigenous and *mestizo* or mixed-race workers were traded freely at markets, including pottery vessels and spindle whorls, though their makers and distributors had to pay fixed local taxes during the Early Colonial period (Anderson et al. 1976; Gibson 1964). Some towns offering goods for which there was a continuing demand, including ceramic vessels, maintained specialized markets such as the pottery *tianguis*, or market, at Cuauhtitlán (Gibson 1964), where Red Wares were extensively produced (Charlton and Fournier 2010).

Probably by the early 1600s, Mexico City became the center of an informal but widespread trading system with the emergence of small manufacturing enterprises, including pottery workshops where majolica and glazed wares were produced prior to the establishment of guild regulations in the late 1600s (e.g. Fournier, Castillo, et al. 2009; Gage 1838; Olvera Ramos 2007), which partially reinforced this centralization process.

Ceramics and other goods were distributed at markets, but there were also retailers, *tratantes* (wholesalers), peddlers, as well as shopkeepers or provincial agents of *almaceneros* (warehouse owners). By the 1680s more than 600 people were classified as merchants in Mexico City, and these were only the Spaniards. About 180 were wholesalers (Schell Hoberman 1977; Studnicki-Gizbert 2000). The wholesale organization probably started in the 1550s or earlier in the capital.

Still, despite the centralization of much trade and production of noncomestibles to the city, rural areas, as evidenced by their archaeological remains, still appear to have maintained the same or similar trade as their prehispanic predecessors through their local markets, thus there was little change to the material culture that remained. Early Colonial period Orange Ware, Red Ware, and eventually glazed ware were either produced locally or traded to rural settlements from different production centers located in the Basin of Mexico (e.g. Carrillo Ruiz 2011; Rodríguez-Alegría et al. 2013).

Conclusion

For at least a time following the Conquest, indigenous and Hispanic cultures existed side by side in the urban areas in what was designed to be a compromise of separate but more or less equal conditions, with separate occupation zones, markets, and, to some extent, local autonomy and with interaction but not intermixing of the two groups (Gibson 1964). This produced the separate cities of Mexico-Tenochtitlan as the occupation zone for the Hispanic settlers and Tlatelolco as the occupation zone for indigenous urban inhabitants and a marked contrast between the material culture of the newcomers against the backdrop of the existing one.

In the rural areas there was, in general, little early direct contact and little evidence of this in an archaeological context. Early on there were very few Spaniards living in the rural areas, at least on a full-time basis. The most obvious Colonial religious structures were served by a small number of resident clergy who would have used familiar materials from local residents. What little majolica and glazed ware may have been associated with members of the native elite may represent either patron–client relationships with urban-dwelling Spaniards or an elevated socioeconomic status that somehow gave them access to nonlocal goods. The absence of significant examples of major ceramic changes in the indigenous tradition might indicate a continuation of the indigenous population expressing group membership through traditional ceramic forms and designs, or their lack of interest in changing their life ways. The extensive population decline that continued through the Early Colonial period may have helped erase native memory of earlier ways of life. As population decline and relocation began to open up large tracts of land, ranches began to move into the empty areas. Those who were farming small ranches displayed a somewhat increased level of use of majolica and glazed ware, but the contrast is not so great as to determine adequately whether these farmers were perhaps Spanish or *mestizo* mixed-race inhabitants or if they were slightly more prosperous indigenous households that were able or inclined to purchase a few more expensive or higher status goods.

Even in a rural area such as Pachuca-Zempoala with its change to intensive silver mining and changes in the output of the Sierra de Las Navajas obsidian mines, all under close Spanish influence, the most obvious archaeological evidence of contact is the Franciscan chapel at the obsidian source (Pastrana and Fournier 1998). Change in one obsidian tool type is obvious, but ceramic evidence of contact is still scarce.

If we view the connections between central Mexico and the Hispanic worldwide empire as hierarchical and dendritic in nature, the differences between urban and rural populations and Hispanic and indigenous populations might be understood as reflections of the degree to which each ethnic-residential group was attached to the empire. The ceramics of the Hispanic populations in the few large urban centers marked their distinctiveness and reflected their wealth and importance in New Spain. In the same urban centers, the indigenous population identified themselves with their own ceramic tradition, for a time with a great florescence of design, marking themselves distinct from the Spanish. Then again, other materials may not have been available due to access or expense.

In rural areas, both indigenous and Spanish or *mestizo* residents were part of the empire but distant from it. Their incorporation into the system is barely reflected in the ceramics present or in other archaeologically visible material culture. Thus, although there is evidence of religion spreading far and wide, the social, economic, and political integration of central Mexico during the Early Colonial period with the worldwide empire would seem to be extremely variable, depending on the locus and the ethnic group under discussion.

Colonization, transculturation, ethnic, and to some extent social borders were part of the new order during the Early Colonial period. A new or evolving material culture derived from the combination of pre-Conquest traditions and Hispanic technologies ultimately did develop, demonstrating that the indigenous and Hispanic economic, social, and aesthetic values eventually crossbred. This cultural *mestizaje* produced syncretic or hybrid traditions that appealed both to the conquerors and to the conquered in urban settings. In contrast however, in rural indigenous regions such as Otumba, Xaltocan, the Zempoala-Pachuca region, and the Mezquital Valley, material culture transformations were slow, and the impact of the new order eventually took place only after the devastation of repeated epidemics had drastically reduced the local population.

References Cited

Acuña, René (editor)
1985 *Relaciones geográficas del Siglo XVI: México, Part 1*. Universidad Nacional Autónoma de México, Mexico City.

1986a *Relaciones geográficas del siglo XVI: México, Part 2*. Universidad Nacional Autónoma de México, Mexico City.

1986b *Relaciones geográficas del siglo XVI: México, Part 3*. Universidad Nacional Autónoma de México, Mexico City.

Alexander, Rani T., and Susan Kepecs

2005 The Postclassic to Spanish-Era Transition in Mesoamerica. In *The Postclassic to Spanish-Era Transition in Mesoamerica: Archaeological Perspectives*, edited by Susan Kepecs and Rani T. Alexander, pp. 1–12. University of New Mexico Press, Albuquerque.

Anderson, Arthur J. O., Frances Berdan, and James Lockhart

1976 *Beyond the Codices: The Nahua View of Colonial Mexico*. University of California Press, Berkeley.

Blanton, Richard, and Gary Feinman

1984 The Mesoamerican World System. *American Anthropologist* 86:675–682.

Brumfiel, Elizabeth M.

2005 *Production and Power at Postclassic Xaltocan*. University of Pittsburgh, Pittsburgh, PA, and Instituto Nacional de Antropología e Historia, Mexico City.

Carrillo-González, Rogelio

2005 Breve descripción de la minería en México. In *El sistema planta-microorganismo-suelo en áreas contaminadas con residuos de minas*, edited by M. C. González-Chávez, J. Pérez-Moreno, and R. Carrillo-González, pp. 137–152. Colegio de Postgraduados, Montecillo, Estado de México, Mexico.

Carrillo Ruiz, Erika

2011 Producción de cerámica de contacto en Atetelco. In *Investigaciones recientes en el conjunto arquitectónico de Atetelco, Teotihuacan*, coordinated by Rubén Cabrera Castro and Verónica Ortega Cabrera, pp. 169–179. Instituto Nacional de Antropología e Historia, Mexico City.

Charlton, Thomas H.

1972 *Post-Conquest Developments in the Teotihuacán Valley, Mexico, Part 1: Excavations*. Report 5. Office of the State Archaeologist of Iowa, Iowa City.

1976 Contemporary Central Mexican Ceramics: A View from the Past. *Man* (n.s.)11:517–525.

1981 Archaeology, Ethnohistory, and Ethnology: Interpretive Interfaces. In *Advances in Archaeological Method and Theory*, Vol. 4, edited by Michael B. Schiffer, pp. 129–176. Academic Press, New York.

1986 Socioeconomic Dimensions of Urban-Rural Relations in the Colonial Period Basin of Mexico. In *Ethnohistory, Supplement to the Handbook of Middle American Indians*, Vol. 4, edited by Ronald Spores and Patricia Andrews, pp. 122–133. University of Texas Press, Austin.

1991 Land Tenure and Agricultural Production in the Otumba Region, 1785–1803. In *Land and Politics in the Valley of Mexico: A Two Thousand Year Perspective*, edited by Herbert R. Harvey, pp. 223–263. University of New Mexico Press, Albuquerque.

1994 Economic Heterogeneity and State Expansion: The Northeastern Basin of Mexico during the Late Postclassic Period. In *Economies and Polities in the Aztec Realm*, edited by Mary G. Hodge and Michael E. Smith, pp. 221–256. Studies on Culture and Society Vol. 6. Institute for Mesoamerican Studies, State University of New York, Albany.

1996 Early Colonial Period Ceramics: Decorated Red Ware and Orange Ware Types of the Rural Otumba Aztec Ceramic Complex. In *Arqueología Mesoamericana, Homenaje a William T. Sanders*, coordinated by Alba Guadalupe Mastache, Jeffrey R. Parsons, Robert S. Santley, and Mari Carmen Serra Puche, pp. 461–479, Instituto Nacional de Antropología e Historia and Arqueología Mexicana, Mexico City.

Charlton, Thomas H., and Cynthia L. Otis Charlton
1998 Continuidad y cambio después de la conquista: hallazgos recientes en la ciudad–estado Azteca de Otumba, Estado de México. In *Primer Congreso Nacional de Arqueología Histórica: Memoria*, coordinated by Enrique Fernández Dávila and Susana Gómez Serafín, pp. 458–467. Instituto Nacional de Antropología e Historia, Mexico City.

Charlton, Thomas H., Cynthia L. Otis Charlton, and Patricia Fournier G.
2005 The Basin of Mexico A.D. 1450–1620: Archaeological Dimensions. In *The Postclassic to Spanish-Era Transition in Mesoamerica. Archaeological Perspectives*, edited by Susan Kepecs and Rani T. Alexander, pp. 49–63. University of New Mexico Press, Albuquerque.

Charlton, Thomas H., and Patricia Fournier G.
1993 Urban and Rural Dimensions of the CONTACT period: Central México, 1521–1620. In *Ethnohistory and Archaeology: Approaches to Postcontact Change in the Americas*, edited by J. Daniel Rogers and Samuel M. Wilson, pp. 201–220. Plenum Press, New York.
2010 Pots and Plots: The Multiple Roles of Early Colonial Red Wares in the Basin of Mexico. In *Enduring Conquests: Rethinking the Archaeology of Resistance to Spanish Colonialism in the Americas*, edited by Matthew Liebmann and Melissa S. Murphy, pp. 127–148. SAR Press, Santa Fe.

Charlton, Thomas H., Patricia Fournier, and Cynthia L. Otis Charlton
2007 La cerámica del periodo Colonial Temprano en la cuenca de México: permanencia y cambio. In *La producción alfarera en el México antiguo*, Vol. V, edited by B. Leonor Merino and Angel García Cook, pp. 429–496. Colección Científica 208. Instituto Nacional de Antropología e Historia, Mexico City.

Córdova, Carlos E., and Jeffrey R. Parsons
1997 Geoarchaeology of an Aztec Dispersed Village on the Texcoco Piedmont of Central Mexico. *Geoarchaeology* 12:177–210.

Cressey, Pamela J.
1974 *Post-Conquest Developments in the Teotihuacan Valley, Mexico, Part 4: The Early Colonial Obsidian Industry*. Research Report No. 1. Mesoamerican Research Colloquium, Department of Anthropology, University of Iowa, Iowa City.

Evans, Susan Toby, and AnnCorinne Freter
1996 Teotihuacan Valley, Mexico, Postclassic Chronology. Hydration Analysis of Obsidian from Cihuatecpan, an Aztec-Period Village. *Ancient Mesoamerica* 7:267–280.

Fournier G., Patricia, M. James Blackman, and Ronald L. Bishop
2009 Empleo de análisis instrumentales de activación neutrónica (INAA) en el estudio del origen de la mayólica en México. *Arqueología* 42:151–165.

Fournier G., Patricia, Karime Castillo, Ronald L. Bishop, and M. James Blackman
2009 La loza blanca novohispana: Tecnohistoria de la mayólica en México. In *Arqueología Colonial Latinoamericana: modelos de estudio*, edited by Juan García Targa and Patricia Fournier G., pp. 99–114. BAR International Series 1988. Archaeopress, Oxford.

Fournier G., Patricia, and Thomas H. Charlton
2012 Historical Archaeology in Central and Western Mesoamerica. In *The Oxford Handbook of Mesoamerican Archaeology*, edited by Deborah L. Nichols and Christopher A. Pool, pp. 916–932. Oxford University Press, New York.

Fournier G., Patricia, and Fernando López Aguilar
2015 El camino real, la minería y la producción de carbón entre los otomíes del Valle del Mezquital. In *Patrimonio e identidad en el Camino Real de Tierra Adentro y el camino nacional*, edited by Luis Carlos Quiñones, pp. 21–63. Universidad Juárez del Estado de Durango, Durango, Mexico.

Fournier G., Patricia, and Lourdes Mondragón
2003 Haciendas, Ranches, and the Otomí Way of Life in the Mezquital Valley, Hidalgo, Mexico. *Ethnohistory* 50(1):47–68.

Gage, Thomas
1838 [1625] *Nueva relación que contiene los viages de Tomas Gage en la Nueva España*. Librería de Rosa, Imprenta de Everat, Paris.

Gamboa Cabezas, Luis M., and Nadia V. Vélez Saldaña
2011 Arqueología Histórica en el Antiguo Convento de San Francisco, Tepeji del Río de Ocampo, estado de Hidalgo, Mexico. *ArqueoWeb* 13:32–54.

Garraty, Christopher P.
2006 The Politics of Commerce: Aztec Pottery Production and Exchange in the Basin of Mexico, A.D. 1200–1650. Unpublished Ph.D. dissertation, Department of Anthropology, Arizona State University, Tempe.

Genotte, Jean-Francoise
2001 The Mapa de Otumba. *Ancient Mesoamerica* 12(1):127–147.

Gerhard, Peter
1986 *Geografía histórica de la Nueva España*. Universidad Nacional Autónoma de México, Mexico City.

Gibson, Charles
1964 *The Aztecs under Spanish Rule: A History of the Indians of the Valley of Mexico*. Stanford University Press, Stanford, CA.

González de Cosío, Francisco (editor)
1952 *Libro de las Tasaciones de los Pueblos de la Nueva España*. Archivo General de la Nación, Mexico City.

Hodge, Mary G., and Leah D. Minc
1990 The Spatial Patterning of Aztec Ceramics: Implications for Prehispanic Exchange Systems in the Valley of Mexico. *Journal of Field Archaeology* 17(4):415–437.

Hodge, Mary G., Hector Neff, M. James Blackman, and Leah D. Minc
1993 Black-on-Orange Ceramic Production in the Aztec's Empire Heartland. *Latin American Antiquity* 4(2):130–157.

Hunter, Richard
2014 Land Use Change in New Spain: A Three-Dimensional Historical GIS Analysis. *The Professional Geographer* 66(2):260–273.

Lockhart, James
1992 *The Nahuas after the Conquest: A Sociocultural and Cultural History of the Indians of Central Mexico, Sixteenth through Eighteenth Centuries*. Stanford University Press, Stanford, CA.

López Aguilar, Fernando
2009 Fundación y colapso: El altépetl de Ixmiquilpan entre los siglos X y XVIII. In *Arqueología Colonial Latinoamericana: modelos de estudio*, edited by Juan García Targa and Patricia Fournier G., pp. 17–36. BAR International Series 1988. Archaeopress, Oxford.

Melville, Elinor G. K.
1994 *A Plague of Sheep: Environmental Consequences of the Conquest of Mexico*. Cambridge University Press, Cambridge, UK.

Millhauser, John K.
2012 Saltmaking, Craft, and Community at Late Postclassic and Early Colonial San Bartolome Salinas, Mexico. Unpublished Ph.D. dissertation, Northwestern University, Evanston, IL.

Mondragón, Lourdes, Patricia Fournier G., and Nahúm Noguera
1997 Arqueología histórica de Sta. María del Pino, Hgo., Mexico. In *Approaches to the Historical Archaeology of Middle and South America*, edited by Janine Gasco, Greg Ch. Smith, and Patricia Fournier G., pp. 17–28. Monograph 38. Institute of Archaeology, University of California, Los Angeles.

Mondragón Romero, Emmanuel
2008 Caracterización de un jal de mina con fines de restauración ecológica en Pachuca, Hidalgo. Unpublished B.S. thesis, Universidad Autónoma Chapingo, Chapingo, Estado de México, Mexico.

Olvera Ramos, Jorge
2007 *Los mercados de la Plaza Mayor en la ciudad de México*. Cal y Canto, Centro de Estudios Mexicanos y Centroamericanos, Mexico City.

Otis Charlton, Cynthia L.
1994 Plebeians and Patricians: Contrasting Patterns of Production and Distribution in the Aztec Figurine and Lapidary Industries. In *Economies and Polities in the Aztec Realm*, edited by Mary G. Hodge and Michael E. Smith, pp. 195–219. Institute of Mesoamerican Studies, State University of New York, Albany.
1995 Las figurillas prehispánicas y coloniales de Tlatelolco. In *Presencias y encuentros: investigaciones arqueológicas de salvamento*, pp. 157–175. Dirección de Salvamento Arqueológico, Instituto Nacional de Antropología e Historia, Mexico City.

Otis Charlton, Cynthia L., and Thomas H. Charlton
2007 Artesanos y barro: figurillas y alfarería en Otompan, estado de México. *Arqueología Mexicana* 14(83):71–76.
2011 Sociocultural Evolution and Craft Specialization: The Case of the Household-Based Fired Clay Industries of Otompan. In *Producción artesanal y especializada en Mesoamérica: áreas de actividad y procesos productivos*, edited by Linda R. Manzanilla and Kenneth G. Hirth, pp. 227–259. Instituto Nacional de Antropología e Historia, Universidad Nacional Autónoma de México, Mexico City.

Overholtzer, Lisa
2012 Empires and Everyday Material Practices: A Household Archaeology of Aztec and Spanish Imperialism at Xaltocan, Mexico. Unpublished Ph.D. dissertation, Northwestern University, Evanston, IL.

Parry, William J.
1990 Analysis of Chipped Stone Artifacts from Otumba (TA-80) and Neighboring Rural Sites in the Eastern Teotihuacan Valley of Mexico. In *Early State Formation Processes: The Aztec City-State of Otumba, Mexico, Part 1, Preliminary Report on Recent Research in the Otumba City State*, Vol. 1, edited by Thomas H. Charlton and Deborah L. Nichols, pp. 73–88. Research Report No. 3. Mesoamerican Research Colloquium, Department of Anthropology, University of Iowa, Iowa City.

Parsons, Jeffrey R., and Mary H. Parsons
1990 *Maguey Utilization in Highland Central Mexico: An Archaeological Ethnography*. Anthropological Papers No. 82. Museum of Anthropology, University of Michigan, Ann Arbor.

Paso y Troncoso, Francisco del
1905 Suma de visitas de pueblos por orden alfabético, manuscrito 2,800 de la Biblioteca Nacional de Madrid, anónimo de la mitad del siglo XVI. In *Papeles de la Nueva España*. Segunda Serie. Geografía y Estadística Vol. I. Est. Tipográfico "Sucesores de Rivadeneyra," España, Madrid.

Pastrana, Alejandro, and Patricia Fournier
1998 Explotación colonial de obsidiana en el yacimiento de Sierra de las Navajas. In *Primer congreso nacional de arqueología histórica: memória*, coordinated by Enrique Fernández Dávila and Susana Gómez Serafín, pp. 486–496. Instituto Nacional de Antropología e Historia, Mexico City.

Rodríguez-Alegría, Enrique
2008 Narratives of Conquest, Colonialism, and Cutting-Edge Technology. *American Anthropologist* 110(1):33–43.
2010 Incumbents and Challengers: Indigenous Politics and the Adoption of Spanish Material Culture in Colonial Xaltocan, Mexico. *Historical Archaeology* 44(2):51–71.

Rodríguez-Alegría, Enrique, John K. Millhauser, and Wesley D. Stoner
2013 Trade, Tribute, and Neutron Activation: The Colonial Political Economy of Xaltocan, Mexico. *Journal of Anthropological Archaeology* 32:397–414.

Schell Hoberman, Louisa
1977 Merchants in Seventeenth-Century Mexico City: A Preliminary Portrait. *The Hispanic American Historical Review* 57(3):479–503.

Smith, Michael E.
2005 Aztec Style Ceramic Figurines from Yautepec, Morelos. *Mexicon* 27:45–55.

Smith, Michael E., Aleksander Borejsza, Angela Huster, Charles D. Frederick, Isabel Rodríguez López, and Cynthia Heath-Smith
2013 Aztec Period Houses and Terraces at Calixtlahuaca: The Changing Morphology of a Mesoamerican Hilltop Urban Center. *Journal of Field Archaeology* 38(3):227–243.

Studnicki-Gizbert, Daviken
2000 From Agents to Consulado: Commercial Networks in Colonial Mexico, 1520–1590 and Beyond. *Anuario de Estudios Americanos* 57(1):41–68.

Valle, Perla
1993 *Memorial de los Indios de Tepetlaóztoc o Códice Kingsborough*. Colección Científica 263. Instituto Nacional de Antropología e Historia, Mexico City.

CHAPTER 46

A CITY TRANSFORMED

From Tenochtitlan to Mexico City in the Sixteenth Century

ENRIQUE RODRÍGUEZ-ALEGRÍA

MEXICO-TENOCHTITLAN, the Mexica capital that fascinated the Spaniards with its beauty and monumentality, underwent a series of changes during and after the Conquest of 1521. These changes were both demographic and material, and they are the result of the political, social, and economic strategies of different groups, as well as patterns of health, migration, and socialization. The transformation of the city, as much as the factors that caused it, defy any attempt to explain the process as either imposition or domination by the colonizers, or simply the result of indigenous resistance or cooperation. Barbara Mundy (2015:3) has argued that "while the Conquest changed an indigenous New World capital ... it did not destroy indigenous Tenochtitlan, either as an ideal, as a built environment, or as an indigenous population center. Instead, indigenous Tenochtitlan lived on."

In this chapter, I focus on documenting the transformation of the city as well as the continuities that followed the conquest of Tenochtitlan. I examine both historical sources and data obtained from decades of archaeological research in Mexico City. Archaeology has offered us a window into Colonial houses, churches, convents, hospitals, mortuary practices, and countless aspects of daily life that enrich our understanding of the era. In this analysis, I focus specifically on the patterns that transformed the historic center of the city, including destruction, appropriation of space, continuity, reconstruction, and changes in the use of space. It can be difficult to separate these patterns analytically, given that they are not mutually exclusive. Nevertheless, it is useful to examine each pattern in turn in order to more fully understand how Mexico City emerged. To illustrate the transformation of the city, I close with a brief discussion of the consumption patterns in some of the Colonial households that have been excavated in the city center.

Destruction

The first transformative process to affect Tenochtitlan as a built space was the destruction of architecture, monuments, and portable cultural materials. The destruction began with the war of conquest, in which an army composed of Spaniards and indigenous people besieged the Mexica and waged a full-out battle against them (Oudijk and Castañeda, this volume). The Templo Mayor was practically destroyed, and we now know that many of the temple's construction stages were demolished partially. Only Phases 1 and 2 of the Templo Mayor remain. Phase 1 has not yet been excavated (Matos Moctezuma 1987, 1990). Of course, the Templo Mayor was not the only Mexica structure that was destroyed. Since 1991, the Templo Mayor Museum's Urban Archaeology Program (*Programa de Arqueología Urbana*) has uncovered new evidence of the destruction incurred during the Conquest and throughout the Colonial period in excavation in several urban blocks surrounding the Templo Mayor (Figure 46.1). Items recovered include sculptures, stone floors, stones carved with glyphs, various architectural elements, and the remains of a cosmic tree associated with Mexica rituals (Barrera Rodríguez et al. 2012), among an endless number of examples of the partial destruction of the area around the Templo Mayor at the time of contact. Research is ongoing, and each project offers new data on the city during historically significant moments (Barrera Rodríguez et al. 2012; Matos Moctezuma 1999, 2003). After the Conquest, the city was partially destroyed and the indigenous population had been decimated by epidemics and war.

Appropriation and Continuity

Two patterns that are difficult to separate in this analysis are appropriation and continuity; the distinction between them depends on our ability to understand the intentions of those involved in these processes. *Appropriation* is defined here as the act of taking over a space and continuing its previous function for personal gain or for the advantage of one group over another. An example of appropriation would be building the Metropolitan Cathedral in an area previously used for Mexica rituals. There was continuity in the use of space, as the area continued to be used for public religious rituals; however, the intent was that these rituals benefit the colonists' interests of domination and religious conversion.

Continuity can be defined as the existence and persistence of any space, in the absence of major changes in use. Unlike appropriation, continuity does not imply the intent of a group of people to benefit from the use of an area to the exclusion of people who previously used the area. When colonizers laid out their streets following the prehispanic

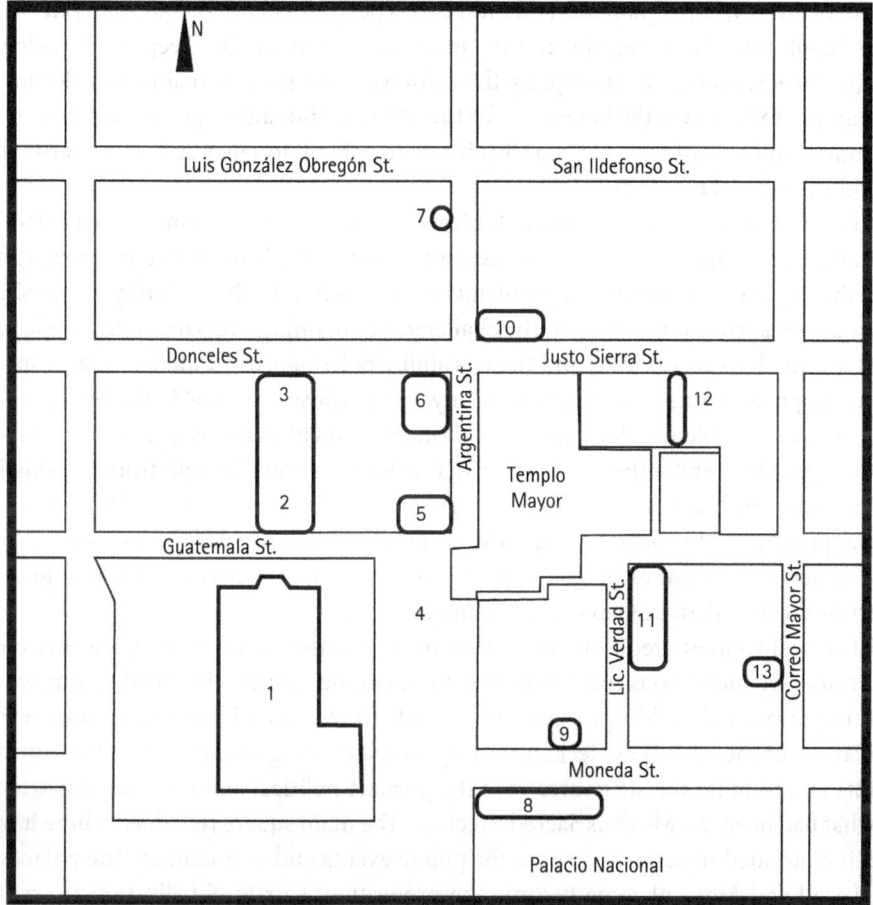

FIGURE 46.1 Some of the house lots excavated by the Programa de Arqueología Urbana in the historic center of Mexico City. Drawn by the author, based on maps published in Matos Moteuczoma 1999:12, 2003:9).
1. Metropolitan Cathedral and Tabernacle.
2. Centro Cultural de España.
3. Donceles #97.
4. Plaza Manuel Gamio.
5. Guatemala #38.
6. Palacio del Marqués del Apartado.
7. Luis González Obregón #25.
8. Palacio Nacional.
9. Moneda #11.
10. Argentina #15, Librería Porrúa.
11. Licenciado Verdad #2-8.
12. Justo Sierra #33.
13. Correo Mayor #11.

layout of the city, both Spaniards and indigenous people benefitted; thus this is an example of continuity. However, the argument can also be made that keeping the orientation of the streets was an attempt by the colonists to impose or maintain order in the colony and to take over the house lots for themselves. Thus although they are important to understanding Colonial Mexico City, it can be difficult to separate both patterns analytically (see also Low 1995).

After the Conquest of 1521, some colonizers were opposed to making Tenochtitlan the capital of New Spain. After all, they had looted and partially destroyed it. They argued that the city posed a number of problems, including floods, the difficulty of transiting the marshes surrounding the city, the challenge of obtaining drinking water, the lack of land on which to graze cattle, and the possibility of being surrounded by a large indigenous population that could attack at any time (Gibson 1964:368; Kubler 1948:69). Despite these problems, Hernán Cortés thought Tenochtitlan was a great city and saw that keeping the capital there was a way that colonizers could benefit from the existing tax system, which was already bringing revenue and food into the city. He also hoped that appropriating the power of the Mexica capital would have such a strong psychological impact on indigenous people as to discourage future rebellions (de Gante 1954:45; Martínez 1988; Valero de García Lascuráin 1991:143).

Historical sources credit one of Cortés' men (Alonso García Bravo), another colonizer, and two indigenous collaborators with designing the new city and deciding where streets, plazas, and buildings would be located. The team took advantage of the existing layout of the city. They decided to respect the existing orientation to the cardinal points and to build the structures with the greatest political and religious importance in what had been the Mexica's Sacred Precinct. The main square remained where it was, and it continued to serve as a space for public events and as a market. The palaces of Axayacatl and Motecuhzoma became the property of Cortés. Finally, the city center, and the seat of religious and political power, remained, an example of appropriation by the colonists (de Gante 1954:47; Kubler 1948:75; Morales Padrón 1989:34; Rubial García 2012). Archaeologists in Mexico City identified several religious structures under the Metropolitan Cathedral and Tabernacle, including the Temple of the Sun, a temple dedicated to Ehecatl, god of wind, and part of a ballcourt, among other structures (Barrera Rivera 1999; Islas Domínguez 1999). Architectural remains are a dramatic example of the appropriation of Mexica religious spaces to serve Christian goals.

The colonists designated an area of approximately 100 city blocks in the city center exclusively for the residences of Spaniards, known as *la traza*. This exclusive area occupied approximately a quarter of Tenochtitlan. Four residential areas around this exclusive zone were designated for indigenous residents: Santa María Cuepopán to the northwest, San Sebastián Atzacoalco to the northeast, San Pablo Zoquipan (Teopan) to the southeast, and San Juan Moyotlan to the southwest (Gibson 1964:370; Martínez 1988:27; Mundy 2015:73). These four areas were based on prehispanic use of space and place-names (Mundy 2015:58, Figure 1.10). However, the attempt to make it an area of exclusive Spanish residence was not entirely successful, as some indigenous people lived in *la traza* during the sixteenth century. Spaniards also lived in areas that had been set aside for indigenous residences (Rodríguez-Alegría 2002:166–168; Valero de García Lascuráin 1991:183). In addition, it is estimated that there were at least 8,000 Africans in Mexico City by 1555 (Meza 2013:43). Many of them were slaves in colonists' homes. If we add to this demographic pattern the biological mixing between people of different ethnic groups, it is clear that in Mexico City in general, and in *la traza* in particular, there was a mix of different groups of people; thus any segregation was only partial, never complete. Indigenous, Spanish, African, and other groups of people interacted in public places in *la traza* as well as in domestic contexts, living and working together, sometimes in harmony, sometimes in discord. The city remained primarily indigenous in terms of its demography and built space (Mundy 2015).

The work of Alfonso Caso (1956) highlights the many continuities in the use of space in Mexico City after the Conquest. A good example of continuity evident in the historical sources is the continued use of the main plaza as a market, albeit with some changes (Cervantes de Salazar 2001:26–27). In prehispanic times, the southern end of the main plaza served as the receiving area for goods that arrived in the city by canoe. The products were sold in the large open air market, or *tianguis*, in the main plaza (Matos Moctezuma 2012). Recent excavations, as well as explorations during the early twentieth century, uncovered two fragments of stone sculptures with the *tianguis* glyph in the main plaza of Tenochtitlan (Barrera Rodríguez et al. 2012). Indigenous people continued to sell their agricultural products, food, mats, wood, and water and offering their services as porters and barbers in the southern portion of the square. The Manila Market or *Parián*, was located to the west, and it sold all kinds of imported goods brought by the colonists from Asia, including clothing, jewelry, pottery, and a host of luxury items. The third space designated for exchange in the main plaza was the *Baratillo*, or flea market, where used clothing, tools, stone, and pottery, as well as stolen goods and contraband, were sold (Katzew 2004:56; Rubial García 2012:40). The main plaza was also used to host festivities in which all segments of Colonial society interacted.

Reconstruction

Immediately following the Conquest, the colonizers began rebuilding the city, with indigenous laborers carrying out most of the work. Historical sources indicate that Don Fernando Ixtlilxochitl, lord of Texcoco, and Tlacotzin, the *cihuacoatl* or high priest of Tenochtitlan, managed most of the indigenous labor force participating in the reconstruction of the city. The first generation of colonizers brought neither architects nor books to plan and refine the structures (Kubler 1948:109). Therefore, the initial constructions were simple and generally lacked any decoration (de Gante 1954:163–167; Kubler 1948:109, 120). Archaeological evidence indicates that indigenous knowledge was crucial in the reconstruction process. Some Colonial structures were built with huge vertical piles or wooden stakes to provide support for the structure and avoid, or at least mitigate, subsidence resulting from soil compaction and changes in the water table. This construction technique was known in prehispanic times and was adopted in the Colonial era thanks to indigenous knowledge (Barrera Rivera 1999:25, 35, 45; Barrera Rodríguez 2002:70; Barrera Rodríguez et al. 2008:65).

Those reconstructing the city occasionally took advantage of the ruins of prehispanic architecture, both as the foundations of new houses and also for construction materials. Hernández Durán (this volume) examines how the process of using Mexica architecture and monuments as building material was motivated by both practical and ideological concerns; that is, the material was used because of availability, but sometimes the use of prehispanic material in the Colonial era also served to demonstrate the imposition of Spanish power. Monuments were reused as column bases and other architectural elements, as was the case of an image of Tlaltecuhtli, which later became part of a Colonial column (Figure 46.2). At Donceles Street #97, archaeological excavations have uncovered pillars from a Colonial house that were constructed using a prehispanic wall as the foundation (Berrera Rivera et al. 2008:85). Materials from different local structures were used, sometimes to build or repair a single architectural element. Also at Donceles #97, Colonial flooring was made of basalt slabs, andesite blocks, and ceramic bricks. Unfired adobe was also discovered in one Colonial floor (Barrera Rodríguez et al. 2008:37, 82).

Later, in the eighteenth century, stones that had been carved by the Mexica before the arrival of the Spanish were used for decoration or as construction material in Colonial homes. Unlike during previous centuries, instead of destroying or concealing

FIGURE 46.2 Colonial Column Base with Tlaltecuhtli, ca. 1525–1537, stone. Courtesy Instituto Nacional de Antropología e Historia, Museo Nacional de Antropología, Mexico City.

sculptures, the Spanish incorporated them into structures (López Luján and Sánchez Reyes 2012). In other instances, all throughout the Colonial period, the sculptures were used as bases for Christian crosses (e.g., Fauvet-Berthelot and López Luján 2012), baptismal fonts, and other Christian religious items (e.g., Baudez 2013); as foundations for Colonial architecture (e.g., López Luján 2005); and for countless decorative, symbolic, and architectural functions. Many of the sculptures were buried during the Colonial era, and today we have little information regarding their use or outright destruction at the time of contact. For example, two monumental sculptures of Mexica deities (*Xiuhtecuhtli* and *Mictlantecuhtli*) were found buried among Colonial pottery fragments, including majolica and Chinese porcelain, at Donceles #97. Therefore, it is clear that they were buried during Colonial times, although we do not know if they were used for some period of time or buried immediately after they were found or after building the Colonial house (Barrera Rodríguez and López Arenas 2008).

Changes in the Use of Space

In addition to the patterns of continuity previously discussed, there were also changes in the use of space beginning in prehispanic times and continuing into the Colonial era and even today. One of the important changes was the transformation of domestic religious spaces. Several of the plots excavated by the Programa de Arqueología Urbana included Colonial houses built on religious architecture or architecture that previously belonged to the Mexica state. For example, at Donceles #97, archaeologists excavated Colonial residences that were built on a structure believed to be the *calmecac*, a school where elite children studied to become priests and received military training (Barrera Rodríguez and López Arenas 2008). Mexica ritual spaces have also been found under Colonial houses at Guatemala Street #38, including impressive offerings and the now-famous Tlaltecuhtli monolith (Gallardo Parrodi 2011; López Luján 2009). Colonial houses have been excavated in the northern portion of the Templo Mayor's Eagle Warrior Precinct, at Argentina #15 (Rivas Barrera García and Rodríguez 1997). In many of the areas that have been excavated, Colonial houses have been discovered on top of spaces previously used for rituals or set aside for public use.

Nevertheless, it would be a mistake to think that changes in the use of space occurred only at the beginning of the Colonial era; many changes also occurred over the centuries following the Conquest. For example, excavations in the Plaza Gamio, in front of the Templo Mayor, have revealed that, prior to the Conquest, some Mexica buildings were partially destroyed to expand the forecourt of the Templo Mayor. After the Conquest, first Colonial houses were built there; then, in 1688, the Conciliar Seminary, which was later used as a hotel and for commercial stalls, was constructed. The Conciliar Seminary building was demolished in 1933. The space was later used for public roads; then public bathrooms were built there. At the time of this writing, the space is being prepared to serve as the new entrance to the Templo Mayor (Barrera Rodríguez and Martínez Meza

2010; Barrera Rodríguez et al. 2012). At first glance we see simple continuity in its use as a plaza, but in fact it has undergone many changes over time.

Some of the changes that took place in the Colonial period were related to the search for power among colonizers, who wanted to establish themselves as a dominant new class. They violently put an end to many of the public rituals of the Mexica state, appropriated tribute and labor, and created their own structures of power. However, indigenous people also searched for power and even began new architectural programs to reestablish themselves as a powerful class in Colonial Mexico City. Barbara Mundy (2015:108–111) has argued that the center of indigenous power moved from the area around the Templo Mayor, where the new Spanish traza was located, to the area south of the main plaza, directly west of the indigenous tianguis. Indigenous rulers established their *tecpan*, or governmental palace, there and created a new center for the indigenous city. Thus changes in the layout, architecture, and centers of power in the city were in part related to competition for power between both Spaniards and indigenous lords, as well as demographic change and a long period of interaction between Spaniards, Indians, Africans, and other groups of people in Mexico City.

Daily Life in the Colonial City

In this section, I focus on key aspects of daily life in the Colonial city, including food, the use of pottery, and the adoption of indigenous lithic technology. These are just three of many aspects of daily life that can be studied. While focusing on just three aspects limits my approach somewhat, I have chosen these particular aspects because considerable evidence is available from archaeological contexts and because these aspects are also important to understand the interaction between colonists and indigenous people, as well as to examine basic aspects of daily life in a city in transition.

Diet and all matters related to food are important to understanding daily life and revealing aspects of survival and cultural preferences, taboos, production, and countless other factors. Archaeological evidence makes it clear that the diet of the colonists integrated local and imported ingredients. Among the faunal remains excavated in the Colonial residences at Justo Sierra #33, there was a notable preference for imported mammals, including cattle (*Bos taurus*), pig (*Sus scrofa*), goats (*Capra* sp.), sheep (*Ovis aries*), and cats (*Felis domesticus*), the latter being the only animal not used as food. Fewer than half of the animals identified at Justo Sierra #33 were local and could easily be obtained in the markets, including rabbit, turkey, and waterfowl. In general, the colonists preferred animals similar to those consumed in Iberia at the time (Valentin Maldonado 2003). At Donceles #97, a similar preference for mammals brought by the colonists was found, although turkey was also consumed by residents. Turkey was the preferred source of protein for the Mexica, who discarded the remains within the prehispanic archaeological contexts at Donceles #97. However, in Colonial times, turkey became the least common among the animals consumed, although it was nearly as common as chicken (Barrera Rodríguez et al. 2008:24). In the Colonial residences at Licenciado Verdad #2, the preference for birds in prehispanic times was replaced by a penchant for imported mammals (Barrera Rivera 2002:251).

Botanical remains provide evidence of the consumption of imported and native plants. The imported botanical remains excavated at Justo Sierra #33 include olives, grapes, cantaloupe, and peaches, while endemic plants include corn, chili, amaranth, tomatoes, black cherry, Mexican hawthorn, prickly pear fruit, and pine nuts. In general, the botanical remains reflect a mixture of imported and local ingredients that, as with the faunal remains, were available in local markets (Montúfar López 2003).

In addition to importing plants and animals, the colonists also brought pottery from Europe; they soon began to produce ceramics in New Spain and by 1573 were importing pottery from Asia. Among the imported wares were lead-glazed pottery (used both for cooking as well as for storing and serving food), majolica (lead and tin glazed pottery used mostly for serving food), and Chinese porcelain (Deagan 1987:96; Fournier García 1990; Hernández Sánchez 2012; Kuwayama 1997; Lister and Lister 1982; Rodríguez-Alegría 2005a, 2005b). In the Central Highlands, indigenous artisans produced a variety of pottery types, including monochrome ceramics, Black-on-Orange bowls, and Texcoco Red pottery (Fournier and Otis Charlton this volume; Minc this volume). In Colonial times, the colonists used a combination of imported ceramics and goods made locally by indigenous potters.

Researchers have made several attempts to explain why, if the colonists imported pottery, they also used indigenous pottery for serving food. Some researchers have argued that the colonists simply appreciated the Mexica pottery tradition, particularly Red Ware pottery, which was similar to European *terra sigilatta* (Fournier 1997:134). Indeed, Hernán Cortés' son Martín sent for pottery from Cuauhtitlán for his son's christening (Charlton et al. 1995; Fournier García 1990; Suárez de Peralta 1990 [1589]:185). Others see the phenomenon as an economic one (Charlton and Fournier 2011; Fournier García 1990:33; Fournier 1998; Lister and Lister 1982; critiques by Rodríguez-Alegría 2005a and Voss 2012). There are also political and social explanations regarding the use of local pottery among colonists (Rodríguez-Alegría 2005a, 2005b; critiqued by Charlton and Fournier 2011). Although researchers disagree regarding the relationship between political strategies, socioeconomic factors, and patterns of consumption of local pottery and different types of Colonial imports or locally made goods, it is clear that indigenous pottery was among the possessions of the Spaniards from the beginning of the viceroyalty. Local pottery appears in both historical documents and archaeological contexts, leaving no doubt regarding its widespread use among colonists.

Finally, indigenous people used both obsidian and polished stone tools after the Conquest, despite the importation of knives and other metal tools by the Spaniards (Pastrana 1998; Pastrana and Carballo this volume; Pastrana and Fournier García 1998; Rodríguez-Alegría 2008a, 2008b, 2014). Historical sources indicate that the colonists appreciated and preferred obsidian for cutting, particularly for shaving (Clark 1989; Saunders 2001). Although obsidian is mentioned in some sources as an instrument used for shaving, it must have been used for other functions to supplement the use of metals the colonists' homes. Future archaeological investigations may provide more information by paying particular attention to the very small finds recovered from Colonial contexts, as these micro-artifacts can provide more details on the prevalence or rarity of obsidian use in the homes of the colonists.

Discussion

With the arrival of the Spaniards, Mexico-Tenochtitlan underwent a series of changes that also included considerable continuity. The changes were not only the direct result of Colonial imposition but also arose from the labor management practices of indigenous leaders, indigenous building techniques and engineering knowledge, and commercial and social interaction between Spaniards, Africans, and indigenous people. The design of the exclusive zone was based on the layout that already existed, as well as the contributions of two indigenous consultants to the plans designed by Alonso García Bravo.

We still have much to learn about the indigenous presence in the exclusive zone during the Colonial era. Not all contexts can be associated with the Spanish, and in the future, both historical as well as archaeological evidence will allow us to identify both Indians and Spaniards in archaeological contexts of the exclusive zone. Future work will also allow us to associate contexts with the presence and activities of Africans. Africans lived in Mexico City, worked as slaves in Spanish homes, and lived as free colonizers (Zabala Aguirre 2013:37). African burials have also been found in the city's cemeteries (Meza 2013). To better understand their presence and its effects on the Colonial city, we must fortify our empirical knowledge regarding the various groups in the city and also develop theoretical approaches that can be used to identify and include them in analyses. Another step will involve eliminating distinctions between Spaniards, indigenous people, and Africans and including in our thinking the presence of different groups of people. The identification and inclusion of a wider range of people in the Colonial city is just one step we can take in our research. In this chapter, I have only touched the surface of the wealth of archaeological, historical, and artistic evidence regarding the transformation of the city, and certainly there is much to learn in the future.

References Cited

Barrera Rivera, José Alvaro
1999 El rescate arqueológico en la Catedral y el Sagrario metropolitanos de la Ciudad de México (1991–1996). In *Excavaciones en la Catedral y el Sagrario Metropolitanos, Programa de Arqueología Urbana*, edited by Eduardo Matos Moctezuma, pp. 21–30. Instituto Nacional de Antropología e Historia, Mexico City.

Barrera Rodríguez, Raúl
2002 El Antiguo Palacio de Odontología de la UNAM a Través de su Espacio y Tiempo Arqueológicos. B.A. thesis, Escuela Nacional de Antropología e Historia, Mexico City.

Barrera Rodríguez, Raúl, and Gabino López Arenas
2008 Hallazgos en el recinto ceremonial de Tenochtitlan. *Arqueología Mexicana* 93:18–25.

Barrera Rodríguez, Raúl, Gabino López Arenas, Cristina Cuevas Carpintero, Rocío Morales Sánchez, Ulises Lina Hernández, and Alejandro Funes Salazar
2008 *Informe final del salvamento arqueológico en el predio de Donceles No. 97, Centro Histórico de la Ciudad de México* (Centro Cultural de España en México), Vol. I. Report submitted to the Instituto Nacional de Antropología e Historia, Mexico City.

Barrera Rodríguez, Raúl, and Roberto Martínez Meza
2010 Informe final del proyecto "Programa de Investigación Frente Principal del Templo Mayor de Tenochtitlán (Plaza Manuel Gamio)." Report submitted to the Instituto Nacional de Antropología e Historia, Mexico City.

Barrera Rodríguez, Raúl, Roberto Martínez Meza, Rocío Morales Sánchez, and Lorena Vázquez Vallin
2012 Espacios rituales frente al Templo Mayor de Tenochtitlan. *Arqueología Mexicana* 116:18–23.

Baudez, Claude François
2013 La conversión de los ídolos. *Arqueología Mexicana* 122:18–29.

Caso, Alfonso
1956 Los barrios antiguos de Tenochtitlan y Tlatelolco. *Memorias de la Academia Mexicana de la Historia* 15:7–62.

Cervantes de Salazar, Francisco
2001 *México en 1554*. Edición facsimilar. Universidad Nacional Autónoma de México, Mexico City.

Charlton, Thomas, and Patricia Fournier
2011 Pots and Plots: The Multiple Roles of Early Colonial Red Wares in the Basin of Mexico. In *Enduring Conquests: Rethinking the Archaeology of Resistance to Spanish Colonialism in the Americas*, edited by Matthew Liebmann and Melissa Scott Murphy, pp. 127–148. School for Advanced Research, Santa Fe, NM.

Charlton, Thomas H., Patricia Fournier, and J. Cervantes
1995 La cerámica del periodo Colonial Temprano en Tlatelolco: El caso de la Loza Roja Bruñida. In *Presencias y Encuentros Investigaciones arqueológicas de salvamento*, pp. 135–155. Dirección de Salvamento Arqueológico, Instituto Nacional de Antropología e Historia, Mexico City.

Clark, John E.
1989 Obsidian: The Primary Mesoamerican Sources. In *La obsidiana en Mesoamerica*, edited by Margarita Gaxiola and John E. Clark, pp. 299–319. Instituto Nacional de Antropología e Historia, Mexico City.

de Gante, Pablo C.
1954 *La arquitectura de México en el siglo XVI*. Editorial Porrúa, Mexico City.

Deagan, Kathleen
1987 *Artifacts of the Spanish Colonies of Florida and the Caribbean 1500–1800, Vol. I: Ceramics, Glassware, and Beads*. Smithsonian Institution Press, Washington, DC.

Fauvet-Berthelot, Marie-France, and Leonardo López Luján
2012 Édouard Pingret, un coleccionista europeo de mediados del siglo XIX. *Arqueología Mexicana* 114:66–73.

Fournier, Patricia
1990 *Evidencias arqueológicas de la importación de cerámica en México, con base en los materiales del Ex-Convento de San Jerónimo.* Instituto Nacional de Antropología e Historia, Mexico City.
1997 Símbolos de la conquista hispana: hacia una interpretación de significados de artefactos cerámicos del periodo Colonial Temprano en la cuenca de México. In *Simbológicas*, edited by Marie-Odile Marion, pp. 125–138. Consejo Nacional para la Ciencia y la Tecnología y Plaza y Valdés, Mexico City.
Gallardo Parrodi, María de Lourdes
2011 Conservación del material orgánico de la ofrenda 102 del Templo Mayor de Tenochtitlan. *Arqueología Mexicana* 108:61–65.
Gibson, Charles
1964 *The Aztecs under Spanish Rule: A History of the Indians of the Valley of Mexico, 1519–1810.* Stanford University Press, Stanford, CA.
Hernández Sánchez, Gilda
2012 *Ceramics and the Spanish Conquest.* Leiden: Brill.
Islas Domínguez, Alicia
1999 El Templo del Sol en el centro ceremonial mexica. In *Excavaciones en la Catedral y el Sagrario Metropolitanos: Programa de Arqueología Urbana,* edited by Eduardo Matos Moctezuma, pp. 51–62. Instituto Nacional de Antropología e Historia, Mexico City.
Katzew, Ilona
2004 *Casta Painting: Images of Race in Eighteenth-Century Mexico.* Yale University Press, New Haven, CT.
Kubler, George
1948 *Mexican Architecture of the Sixteenth Century,* Vol. I. Yale University Press, New Haven, CT.
Kuwayama, George
1997 *Chinese Ceramics in Colonial Mexico.* University of Hawaii Press, Honolulu.
Lister, Florence C., and Robert H. Lister
1982 *Sixteenth Century Maiolica Pottery in the Valley of Mexico.* University of Arizona Press, Tucson.
López Luján, Leonardo
2005 La piedra de la Librería Porrúa y los orígenes de la arqueología mexica. *Arqueología Mexicana* 76:18–19.
2009 La Tlalteccuhtli. In *Escultural Monumental Mexica*, edited by Eduardo Matos Moctezuma and Leonardo López Luján, pp. 381–447. Funcación Cnmemoracion, Mexico D.F.
López Luján, Leonardo, and Gabriela Sánchez Reyes
2012 El jaguar mexica de la calle Emiliano Zapata en la ciudad de México. *Arqueología Mexicana* 115:78–81.
Low, Setha
1995 Indigenous Architecture and the Spanish American Plaza in Mesoamerica and the Caribbean. *American Anthropologist* 97(4):748–762.
Martínez, José Luis
1988 Construcción de la nueva ciudad. *El Centro Histórico de la Ciudad de México. Artes de México* 1:22–29.
Matos Moctezuma, Eduardo
1987 The Templo Mayor of Tenochtitlan: History and Interpretation. In *The Great Temple of Tenochtitlan, Center and Periphery in the Aztec World,* by Johanna Broda, Davíd Carrasco, and Eduardo Matos Moctezuma, pp. 15–60. University of California Press, Berkeley.

1990 El Proyecto Templo Mayor: Objetivos y programas. In *Trabajos arqueológicos en el centro de la ciudad de México*, 2nd ed., edited by Eduardo Matos Moctezuma, pp. 17–39. Instituto Nacional de Antropología e Historia, Mexico City.

1999 *Excavaciones en la Catedral y el Sagrario Metropolitanos: Programa de Arqueología Urbana*. Instituto Nacional de Antropología e Historia, Mexico City.

2003 *Excavaciones del Programa de Arqueología Urbana*. Colección Científica 452. Instituto Nacional de Antropología e Historia, Mexico City.

2012 La Plaza Mayor o Zócalo en tiempos de Tenochtitlan. *Arqueología Mexicana* 116:24–27.

Meza, Abigail

2013 Presencia africana en el cementerio del Hospital Real de San José de los Naturales. *Arqueología Mexicana* 119:40–44.

Montúfar López, Aurora

2003 Arqueobotánica de un basurero colonial. In *Excavaciones del Programa de Arqueología Urbana*, edited by Eduardo Matos Moctezuma, pp. 75–84. Colección Científica 452. Instituto Nacional de Antropología e Historia, Mexico City.

Morales Padrón, Francisco

1989 *La Ciudad del Quinientos*. University of Seville, Seville.

Mundy, Barbara E.

2015 *The Death of Aztec Tenochtitlan, the Life of Mexico City*. University of Texas, Austin.

Pastrana, Alejandro

1998 *La explotación azteca de la obsidiana en la Sierra de las Navajas*. Colección Científica 383. Instituto Nacional de Antropología e Historia, Mexico City.

Pastrana, Alejandro, and Patricia Fournier García

1998 Explotación colonial de obsidiana en el yacimiento de Sierra de las Navajas. In *Primer Congreso Nacional de Arqueología Histórica, Memoria 1996*, edited by Enrique Fernández Dávila and Susana Gómez Serafín, pp. 486–496. Instituto Nacional de Antropología e Historia, Mexico City.

Rivas García, Flor, and Raúl Barrera Rodríguez

1997 *Informe Preliminar del rescate arqueológico Argentina #15 Librería Porrúa*. Report on file at the Programa de Arqueología Urbana, Museo del Templo Mayor, Instituto Nacional de Antropología e Historia, Mexico City.

Rodríguez-Alegría, Enrique

2002 *Food, Eating, and Objects of Power: Class Stratification and Ceramic Production and Consumption in Colonial Mexico*. PhD dissertation, Department of Anthropology, University of Chicago.

2005a Consumption and the Varied Ideologies of Domination in Colonial Mexico City. In *The Late Postclassic to Spanish-Era Transition in Mesoamerica: Archaeological Perspectives*, edited by Susan Kepecs and Rani Alexander, pp. 35–48. University of New Mexico Press, Albuquerque.

2005b Eating Like an Indian: Negotiating Social Relations in the Spanish Colonies. *Current Anthropology* 46(4):551–573.

2008a De la Edad de Piedra a la Edad de más Piedra. *Cuadernos de Arqueología Mediterránea*. 17:15–30.

2008b Narratives of Conquest, Colonialism, and Cutting-Edge Technology. *American Anthropologist* 110(1):33–41.

Rubial García, Antonio

2012 La Plaza Mayor de la ciudad de México en los siglos XVI y XVII. *Arqueología Mexicana* 116:36–43.

Saunders, Nicholas J.
2001 A Dark Light: Reflections on Obsidian in Mesoamerica. *World Archaeology.* 33(2):220–236.

Suárez de Peralta, Juan
1990 *Tratado del Descubrimiento de las Indias*. Consejo Nacional para la Cultura y las Artes, Mexico City.

Valentín Madonado, Norma
2003 Análisis del material zoológico. In *Excavaciones del Programa de Arqueología Urbana*, edited by Eduardo Matos Moctezuma, pp. 27–37. Instituto Nacional de Antropología e Historia, Mexico City.

Valero de García Lascuráin, Ana Rita
1991 *Solares y conquistadores: orígenes de la propiedad en la ciudad de México*. Instituto Nacional de Antropología e Historia, Mexico City.

Voss, Barbara
2012 Status and Ceramics in Spanish Colonial Archaeology. *Historical Archaeology* 46(2): 39–54.

Zabala Aguirre, Pilar
2013 Esclavitud, asimilación y mestizaje de negros urbanos durante la colonia. *Arqueología Mexicana* 119:36–39.

CHAPTER 47

THE AZTECS AND THE CATHOLIC CHURCH

LOUISE M. BURKHART

BECOMING COLONIAL, BECOMING CHRISTIAN

As the Spanish king replaced the Mexica emperor as the highest political authority in formerly Aztec territories, the Mexica and other Nahua groups found they were expected to embrace a new set of religious beliefs and practices. For Spain, the cross justified the sword: the spread of Christianity into pagan or infidel lands provided moral validation for conquest, forced labor, and the extraction of tribute. New Spain would be a Roman Catholic land, just like Spain. Indeed, as the Protestant Reformation swept through much of Europe, Spain and its American territories stood firm as a principal stronghold of the Catholic Church. Indigenous people had no choice but to come to terms, both as individuals and as corporate communities, with Catholicism.

The systematic introduction of Christianity was entrusted to friars—priests and some unordained, or lay, brothers—of the Mendicant religious orders. In the Nahuatl-speaking areas of central Mexico, the Franciscan Order predominated, but Dominicans and Augustinians served some communities. These men were street preachers, not cloistered monks, and they depended on alms for their livelihood. Some were highly educated "Renaissance men"; some were mystics who saw the conquest of America as a harbinger of the apocalypse. Many were favorably impressed by aspects of indigenous lifestyle, religious devotion, and moral philosophy; none had any tolerance for practices they viewed as idolatry or devil worship—categories into which they placed all pre-Conquest gods and rites (Figure 47.1). They strove, with mixed success, to alter not only the objects of indigenous worship but people's worldview and concepts of selfhood (Díaz Balsera 2005; Gruzinski 1988). Their own chronicles present lively accounts of their evangelization strategies, experiences, and attitudes (Motolinia 1979; Mendieta 1980).

FIGURE 47.1 Franciscan friars burn temples in the city of Tlaxcala, driving out gods whom the indigenous artist, working later in the sixteenth century, depicts as devils. Drawing in Diego Muñoz Camargo's *Descripçíon de la çiudad y prouincia de Tlaxcala*, f. 240v. Courtesy of the University of Glasgow Library, Special Collections.

Fanning out across the landscape, the friars founded establishments in larger communities and visited smaller ones on a rotating basis. Unlike in Europe, they acted as parish priests, living among the native people, performing masses, and administering the sacraments. The plan was that the friars would be replaced by secular, or diocesan, parish priests—clergymen who were not members of religious orders—once the native people were adequately Christianized. In practice, although some communities were "secularized" by the late sixteenth century, Mendicant orders managed to maintain their position in some Nahua communities to the end of the colonial era (Taylor 1996:83–86, 426–427).

All the religious orders placed a high priority on learning Nahuatl and other indigenous languages, though of course some of their members acquired new tongues more easily than others. From the beginning they depended on indigenous students to help them learn Nahuatl, find ways to express Christian ideas in Nahuatl, and write sermons and other texts. Thus Christianity as presented to the Nahuas was already a collaborative product, dependent on approximations and compromises forged as alien ideas, such as "sin," "hell," or "devil," were adapted to familiar categories (Burkhart 1989).

Nahuas joined the Christian ranks through the sacrament of baptism, which followed upon a rudimentary education in the basic precepts of Christian doctrine. Baptism was

FIGURE 47.2 A Franciscan friar joins a Nahua couple in marriage. The groom wears a traditional indigenous man's cloak; his adoption of European style hat, shoes, and pants suggests he is of high social rank. Woodcut in Fray Alonso de Molina, *Confessionario mayor, en lengua mexicana y castellana* (Antonio de Espinosa, Mexico, 1565:f. 57r). Courtesy of the John Carter Brown Library at Brown University.

voluntary but did not indicate a complete change of beliefs and attitudes. Many people followed the example of their leaders and neighbors, with little knowledge of Christian theology. As late as 1540, many people remained unbaptized, but eventually this ritual incorporation into the church became a nearly universal experience (Pardo 2004 offers an extensive study of this sacrament).

A baptized person was expected also to marry via the Roman Catholic sacrament. For the first generation of Christianized nobility, the suppression of polygyny caused much disruption. Noblemen who complied with the Christian rules lost a key means of forging alliances and expanding their households, while some women, legally married under the old customs, lost their homes and husbands (Figure 47.2).

Some friars were skilled preachers, persuading by word and by example. Others impressed the native people with their otherworldly mysticism. Some gained allies by teaching people to read and write, master Spanish and Latin, or earn a living using European tools and technologies. Some sided with indigenous people against excessive tribute and labor requirements and other colonial abuses. But the persuasiveness of the Christian gospel and the personal qualities of its bearers only partly explain why so many Nahuas joined the new faith.

One motivation was political. Native elites could not continue to govern their communities and claim other privileges unless they were Christians. Any petition they brought before Spanish authorities was sure to fail if the nobles could not credibly claim loyalty to God as well as to the Spanish crown. The *altepetl*—the indigenous corporate community—could survive under colonial rule as a self-governing entity with a recognized territory, but only if it publicly presented itself as a Christian polity (Lockhart 1992). As early as 1560, indigenous leaders emphasized their Christian identity when seeking assistance from the king (Lockhart 1993:288–297).

Another motivation was religious. Destruction of temples and suppression of public rituals left a hole in the lives of people accustomed to a lively religious life, to diverse sacred beings who manifested themselves in elaborately costumed images and impersonators, and to monumental architecture that expressed their communities' collective identity and divine affiliations. The obvious and easiest way to rebuild a religious life was to turn Christianity to their own purposes: to build a church on or near the old temple platform, to accept a calendar of saints' festivals, to erect crosses and statues of saints, to stage processions and plays instead of the old sacrificial rites. Communities channeled significant resources into these activities.

For the most part, Nahuas did not overtly resist the new faith, a strategy that would only bring persecution. But acceptance of a new god, however sincere, did not automatically discredit other manifestations of sacred forces. People learned to be discreet about practices that Catholic priests would not tolerate, and the church only occasionally cracked down on these clandestine traditions with campaigns to extirpate what they viewed as idolatry (Tavárez 2011). While many pre-Conquest ideas and actions can be tracked into the Colonial period and beyond, neither Colonial nor contemporary indigenous religion can be neatly broken down into "pre-Conquest" and "Christian" components: older ones took on Christian attributes, and the Christian ones were adapted according to indigenous concepts and values.

Native Christianity was not uniform (Klor de Alva 1982; Christensen 2013). People in some remote areas were barely affected. Only men of the nobility had access to higher education and alphabetic literacy. Different people developed distinctive local devotions. Christianity as practiced by colonial Nahuas is best viewed as, simply, diverse varieties of Christianity, appropriated and reinterpreted by Nahua people to express their own worldview and their own concerns and to allow them to function within the new, colonial order. However, the hierarchical structure of the colonial system meant that native Christianity could never be granted the same legitimacy as the religion of Spaniards. It was, indeed, different and would always be judged as inferior (Burkhart 1998).

Churches and Church People

Most central Mexican towns with histories that go back to Aztec times have a sixteenth-century church, monumental in scale, simple in design, and often still functioning as the community's sacred center. The church-building fervor that swept

FIGURE 47.3 The sixteenth-century church at Tepoztlán, Morelos. Photograph by the author.

through indigenous civilization in the mid-1500s demanded an enormous marshalling of labor and materials, overseen by friars but financed by the communities and carried out by native artisans and workers. The buildings testify to some sort of religious revitalization movement that occurred as communities, adjusting to colonial rule and shaken by the first epidemics of Old World diseases, expeditiously reorganized themselves around a new kind of sacred center that renewed each *altepetl*'s covenant with the divine. Each community now had a new patron: a saint or an aspect of the Virgin Mary. The new temple was dedicated to this personage, and his or her name was prefixed to the Nahuatl name of the *altepetl*: San Juan Tenochtitlan, Santiago Tlatelolco (Figure 47.3).

Pre-Conquest pyramids replicated mythical mountains. Often constructed atop existing raised platforms, the tall churches were like both mountains and sacred caves: their large, barrel-vaulted interior spaces were something indigenous people had never before known how to build. Positioned to align with mountains, water sources, or other sacred features of the landscape, or along astronomical sightlines, sometimes with older carved stones incorporated into the building in accordance with these alignments, the churches shared more than their name, *teopan* or *teocalli*, "holy place" or "deity house," with the old temples (Wake 2010).

Outside each church a four-sided patio or atrium hosted open-air religious activities, including masses celebrated from an outdoor chapel. The four sides replicated the quadrilateral Mesoamerican cosmos. A stone cross carved with bleeding wounds, a crown of thorns, and other symbols of the crucifixion of Christ typically stood at the center of this courtyard, a world tree linking earth to heaven in a manner appropriate to the Christian era. Next to the church a spacious porch or portal gave access to a *convento*, enclosed spaces arranged around a cloister, where friars resided and some community meetings and religious activities took place.

The atrium crosses are but one component of an astonishing artistic project, now recognized as a distinctive "Indo-Christian" or *tequitqui* (from the word for "tribute") style of art (Reyes-Valerio 1978; Aguilar-Moreno 2005). Drawing on Renaissance-era religious imagery and design elements introduced via European woodcuts, native artists adorned the exteriors of the new religious buildings with relief sculpture and plastered their interiors with cycles of mural paintings. The murals alone once covered 300,000 or more square meters of wall (Reyes-Valerio 1989:10). Murals could transform a cloister into a sacred garden, depict Christianized native warriors conquering pagan enemies, or graft sacred features of the local landscape onto a scene from the life of Christ or a saint (Peterson 1993; Vergara Hernández 2010; Wake 2010). Flowers and other vegetation line walls and climb archways, bringing stone to life. Architectural elements imitating buildings in Jerusalem reflect utopian ideas of the friars as well as indigenous assertions of community eminence (Lara 2004). Each *altepetl* saw itself as the center of the world, a sacred Jerusalem inscribed upon the local terrain, its church symbolizing its corporate identity and its legitimacy as a part of the colonial order. And the bigger and better adorned the church, the more prestige it bestowed on the community and the individuals who paid for its enhancements.

Only a handful of native men were ever ordained as Roman Catholic priests. However, since priests were always too few to supervise native religious life very closely, Nahuas were in charge of most of their own religious affairs apart from the performance of mass and the administration of sacraments—though lay people could baptize an infant in danger of death. The principal indigenous church official was the *fiscal*, who oversaw the day-to-day running of the religious complex and its economic affairs. Under him were choirmasters or *cantores, cuicanime* ("singers") in Nahuatl, in charge of organizing choral and instrumental music and other aspects of religious festivities. Other *teopantlaca*, or "church people," taught catechism classes, maintained the church building and grounds, collected the bodies of the dead for burial, rang the bell, or made sure that everyone showed up at church on Sunday or, in smaller communities, on those days that a priest actually visited. A notary kept records of baptisms and marriages and took down the testaments of the dying. Confraternities (*cofradías*), voluntary religious organizations that planned processions and other devotional activities and served as mutual aid societies, proved immensely popular, providing indigenous men and women with a means to exercise leadership and serve their community (on these offices and institutions see Lockhart 1992:ch. 6).

Books and Manuscripts

As the first friars learned Nahuatl, they also worked with their Nahua students to write the language using the Roman alphabet, giving rise to a new, alphabetic literacy that the Nahuas embraced more enthusiastically and effectively than any other Mesoamerican people. The first books printed in Mexico were Nahuatl-language catechisms. Over a hundred Nahuatl works were published during the Colonial era, overwhelmingly Christian religious texts (Sell 1993). These range from simple booklets listing the components of the catechism that native people were expected to memorize—the Lord's Prayer, Ten Commandments, and so forth—to complex theological treatises, works of contemplative spirituality, and, in one notable case, a book of songs (Sahagún 1993). These volumes were published under the names of friars and, later, Jesuits or diocesan clergy. Yet these men, unless they grew up speaking Nahuatl and were truly fluent, typically relied on indigenous co-authors or, at least, language consultants to prepare the Nahuatl text. Hence Nahuas had a significant influence on how Christianity was presented in their language, even in printed books, which went through a rigorous review process (Figure 47.4).

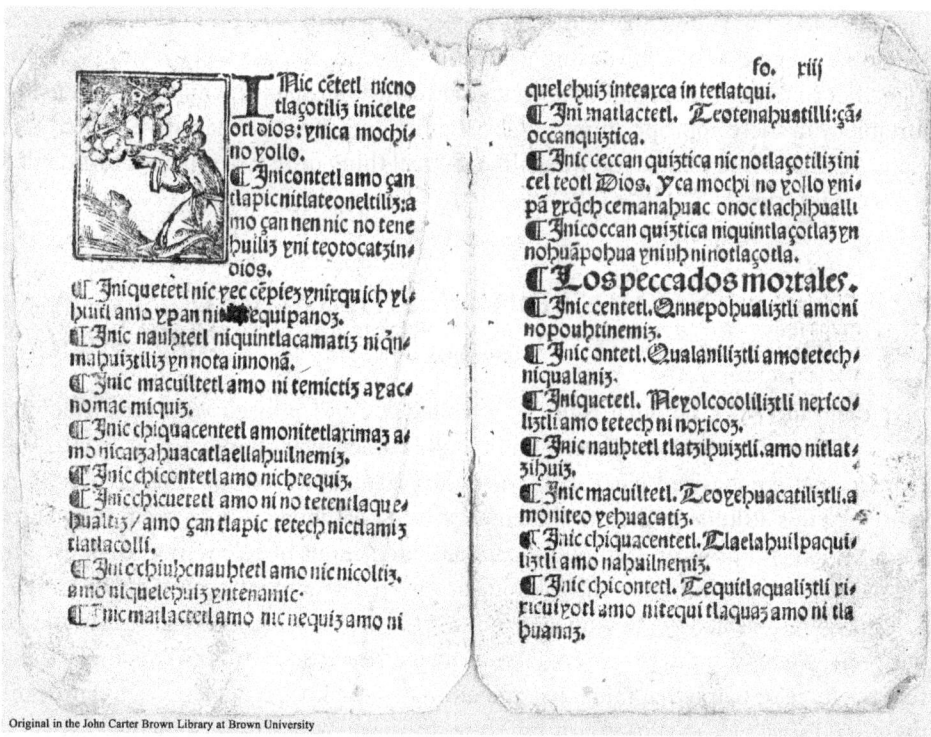

FIGURE 47.4 The Ten Commandments and the Seven Deadly Sins, adapted into the Nahuatl language in one of the earliest surviving Nahuatl books. Fray Pedro de Gante, *Doctrina christiana en lengua mexicana* (Mexico, 1547:f. 12v-13r). Courtesy of the John Carter Brown Library at Brown University.

Nahuas circulated many other Christian texts among themselves, copying them by hand. In this way they maintained access to works that would not pass review for publication, choosing stories or prayers they liked, such as legends about the Virgin Mary, and even developing markedly unorthodox versions of some Christian narratives (Burkhart 2001; Christensen 2013). The most interesting component of this literary underground is theater (Burkhart 1996, 2011). No Nahuatl plays were published in Colonial times, but a couple dozen surviving scripts illuminate a lively tradition in which Nahua boys, men, and—by the end of the seventeenth century, if not earlier—women brought Christian narratives to life with their own bodies, words, and gestures. Nahua and Franciscan sources indicate that plays began to be performed during the 1530s; extant scripts date from around 1590 through the mid-eighteenth century. A few were translated from Spanish plays, but most were Mexican creations. Morality plays encouraged people to participate in the annual, Lenten-season confession that was expected of them and to perform other pious deeds such as praying for the souls of the dead. Other plays enacted stories from the Bible or legends of the saints, including the Mexican story of Our Lady of Guadalupe, which became widely known after it was published in Nahuatl and Spanish in the mid-seventeenth century (Poole 1995; Taylor 2003). During Holy Week, Nahuas played Jesus, Mary, Judas, Pontius Pilate, and other roles as they acted out the events that culminated in the crucifixion. Scripts for these Passion plays show that partial manuscripts were passed from one community to another, such that two towns might use the same Last Supper scene or Judas monologue but different versions of other scenes. Meanwhile, Spanish churchmen, uncomfortable with these appropriations of Christianity's most central narrative, fretted that Nahua Christs were treated too much like the real thing or that drunken actors defiled the sacred stories.

Encountering the Sacred

Like their ancestors, colonial Nahuas inhabited a world infused with sacred powers that manifested themselves directly and tangibly. Their Christianity was a "hands-on" religion that emphasized participatory, sensory experience (Clendinnen 1990). They expressed this attitude in their treatment of images. Although miracle-working statues were a staple of European Catholicism as well, indigenous people were predisposed to see sacred beings as immanent in the stone or wood carvings that, according to Catholic priests, merely depicted a personage who resided, invisibly, in heaven. Priests chided native people for worshipping "idols" of wood and stone; Spaniards did not understand that the force or being that inhabited and animated the image made the wood or stone divine and alive, at least during a ritual. The enthusiasm with which Nahuas dressed and adorned their Christian images, offered them flowers and incense, kept their precincts neatly swept, and paraded them around the *altepetl* in feast-day or Holy Week processions signaled a devotion both intense and distinctively indigenous.

Miraculous images peppered the Colonial landscape, moving, speaking, weeping, sweating, bleeding, curing diseases, reviving dead children, saving people from floods and other dangers, spontaneously renovating themselves when shabby, or simply showing up in unexpected places—in a tree, on a kernel of corn. Among these, images of the Virgin Mary were the most numerous, followed by figures of Christ on the cross (Hughes 2010; Taylor 2010, 2011). Communities sought to propagate devotion to their own miraculous images, gaining prestige and pilgrim traffic. People, including women, would take miracle-working images on road trips, allowing members of other communities to reap blessings from their presence—and contribute money to their upkeep (Osowski 2010). Interethnic conflict sometimes arose when Spaniards sought to wrest a popular (or lucrative) devotion from native control or discredit indigenous visionaries who might undermine the authority of Catholic priests.

Some saints lived at church; others lived in people's homes. Nahuatl wills from the seventeenth and eighteenth centuries reveal an increasing attachment to Christian images that were kept on home altars, collectively called *santos* whether they represented a saint, an angel, or Jesus Christ on the cross. Men and women would pass these statues or pictures to their heirs, sometimes with instructions for the sweeping or other devotional behaviors the bequeathed treasures were to receive. Late-Colonial people apparently did understand that there was a distinction between the personage represented—say, Saint Catherine or Saint Francis—and their own manifestation of him or her but nevertheless viewed the images as integral members of the household and referred to them directly by name, not as an "image of" one saint or another (Pizzigoni 2012; Wood 1991a).

In the eyes of Catholic priests, not only were Nahuas overly credulous of miracles and prone to idolatry. They also partied too heartily at religious festivals. One aspect of this excess was alcohol. While many pressures led Nahuas, like other colonized Native Americans, toward drink, a ritual was a time when one sought to step outside the bounds of the normal, to open oneself to divine forces external to the body. Drunkenness was one way to do this, as was the consumption of hallucinogens. To Spaniards, the resulting loss of decorum debased the Christian sacred, though indigenous revelers generally intended no such disrespect. Another aspect of excess was the dances, mock battles, and fireworks that native communities sponsored along with the more sedate processions and masses. Again, the goal was to create ritual inversions, attract and entertain positive sacred powers while repelling evil ones, and fully experience the events by engaging the body and all the senses. These practices came under censure especially in the eighteenth century, as the European Enlightenment fostered a distaste for exuberant religious spectacles. Efforts to suppress them were partially successful, but similar celebrations continue to the present day.

The Dark Side

The friars viewed the Aztec gods as devils: actual beings, not figments of native imagination (Cervantes 1994). Throughout the Colonial period, Europeans, as well as the increasing numbers of Afro-Mexicans and people of mixed heritage, associated native religious practice with devil worship. This meant that native healers and diviners were thought to have real power: pacts with the devil that allowed them to tell fortunes, find lost objects or people, cure or cause illness, keep a lover faithful, or bewitch a client's enemies. The ancient Mesoamerican idea of the *nahualli*, the shaman who can transform into an animal alter-ego, retained its force, the shape-shifting now interpreted as a deception the devil worked on behalf of his devotees. Practitioners themselves were more likely to view their knowledge as the gift of a saint or the Virgin Mary than of the devil, but Catholic priests saw all native magic as diabolical witchcraft. Even so, plenty of non-Indians were willing to pay for charms or spells in an effort to solve their personal or financial problems. Indigenous healers charged much less than Spanish physicians, and their medicine was more effective (Lewis 2003; Ruiz de Alarcón 1984).

Since the Mexican Inquisition did not prosecute indigenous people, clients of native magicians might be punished while the practitioners themselves were not—though the practitioners might be hauled in to testify about these suspect transactions. Thus, Inquisition records reveal how indigenous specialists exercised their reputed skill at the dark arts to gain money and a shadowy prestige. Similarly, churchmen's efforts to document "idolatry" or "sorcery" detail colonial practices unacceptable to those priests but that coexisted comfortably with more overtly Christian ones. Continuities with pre-Conquest mythology can be striking: for example, a Nahua curer in seventeenth-century Guerrero imagined himself descending to the underworld to recover his patient's broken bone, like Quetzalcoatl retrieving the bones of the people from the fourth sun (Ruiz de Alarcón 1984:189–191).

Looking Back

However imperfect Nahua religion remained in Spanish eyes, later Colonial native elites presented the coming of Christianity as one of their *altepetl*'s primordial, foundational events. They wrote community histories, today called "primordial titles," that present their Conquest-era ancestors immediately allying themselves with the Spanish, welcoming the friars, and erecting churches. So predisposed were those ancestors to accept the new faith that the friars were hardly needed (Haskett 2005; Wood 1991b, 2003).

Another later Colonial textual strategy promoting the idea of a primordial conversion to Christianity was the use of pictographic catechisms, small booklets that present the Lord's Prayer, Hail Mary, and other basic texts of Christian doctrine as lines of pictures, each image corresponding to a word or phrase in Nahuatl or, in a few cases, Otomi or Mazahua. Tied to a fixed text, to be read word for word and in some cases captioned in Nahuatl, these are very different from pre-Conquest pictorial manuscripts. But people associated picture-writing with the ancestors, and the use of these catechisms could commemorate or replicate a primordial conversion to Christianity, so early that it preceded the adoption of alphabetic writing. One of these documents actually states that

FIGURE 47.5 The Hail Mary prayer in a pictographic catechism from 1714. A Nahua notary named don Lucas Mateo painted the images and wrote out the accompanying text of the prayer in Nahuatl. The kneeling figures in red cloaks represent indigenous men praising Mary and Jesus. (*Doctrina cristiana*, Egerton Ms. 2898, British Museum, f. 2v-3r). © Trustees of the British Museum.

don Pedro de Moteucçoma, a son of Emperor Moteucçoma II, was "the first Catholic" (at least in his own community) and learned the faith with these pictures when the first Franciscans came, in 1524 (Boone et al. 2017). Many scholars have assumed these books date to the early evangelization period, but their inclusion of a doctrinal text from 1644 shows that the surviving examples are from the seventeenth and eighteenth centuries (Burkhart 2014) (Figure 47.5).

As colonial noblemen petitioned for privileges and for the return of *altepetl* lands lost during the violence and plagues of the sixteenth century, it was to their benefit to present themselves and their communities as staunchly Christian, all the way back to the time of the Conquest. Yet this view of their past was more than a politically expedient fiction. Christianity—as Nahuas understood and practiced it—had become part of their identity, just as the church building embodied the collective identity of the *altepetl*.

References Cited

Aguilar-Moreno, Manuel
2005 *"Utopía de Piedra": El arte tequitqui de México*. Editorial Conexión Gráfica, Mexico City.

Boone, Elizabeth Hill, Louise M. Burkhart, and David Tavárez
2017 *Painted Words: Nahua Catholicism, Politics, and Memory in the Atzaqualco Pictorial Catechism*. Dumbarton Oaks Research Library and Collection, Washington, DC.

Burkhart, Louise M.
1989 *The Slippery Earth: Nahua-Christian Moral Dialogue in Sixteenth-Century Mexico*. University of Arizona Press, Tucson.
1996 *Holy Wednesday: A Nahua Drama from Early Colonial Mexico*. University of Pennsylvania Press, Philadelphia.
1998 Pious Performances: Christian Pageantry and Native Identity in Early Colonial Mexico. In *Native Traditions in the Postconquest World*, edited by Elizabeth Hill Boone and Tom Cummins, pp. 361–381. Dumbarton Oaks Research Library and Collection, Washington, DC.
2001 *Before Guadalupe: The Virgin Mary in Early Colonial Nahuatl Literature*. Institute for Mesoamerican Studies, State University of New York, Albany.
2011 *Aztecs on Stage: Religious Theater in Colonial Mexico*. University of Oklahoma Press, Norman.
2014 The "Little Doctrine" and Indigenous Catechesis in New Spain. *Hispanic American Historical Review* 94(2):167–206.

Cervantes, Fernando
1994 *The Devil in the New World: The Impact of Diabolism in New Spain*. Yale University Press, New Haven, CT.

Christensen, Mark Z.
2013 *Nahua and Maya Catholicisms: Texts and Religion in Colonial Central Mexico and Yucatan*. Stanford University Press, Stanford, CA.

Clendinnen, Inga
1990 Ways to the Sacred: Reconstructing "Religion" in Sixteenth-Century Mexico. *History and Anthropology* 5(1):105–141.

Díaz Balsera, Viviana
2005 *The Pyramid under the Cross: Franciscan Discourses of Evangelization and the Nahua Christian Subject in Sixteenth-Century Mexico*. University of Arizona Press, Tucson.

Gruzinski, Serge
1988 *La colonisation de l'imaginaire: Sociétés indigènes et occidentalisation dans le Mexique espagnol, XVIe–XVIIe siècle*. Gallimard, Paris.

Haskett, Robert
2005 *Visions of Paradise: Primordial Titles and Mesoamerican History in Cuernavaca*. University of Oklahoma Press, Norman.

Hughes, Jennifer Scheper
2010 *Biography of a Mexican Crucifix: Lived Religion and Local Faith from the Conquest to the Present*. Oxford University Press, Oxford.

Klor de Alva, J. Jorge
1982 Spiritual Conflict and Accommodation in New Spain: Toward a Typology of Aztec Responses to Christianity. In *The Inca and Aztec States 1400–1800: Anthropology and History*, edited by George A. Collier, Renato I. Rosaldo, and John D. Wirth, pp. 345–366. Academic Press, New York.

Lara, Jaime
2004 *City, Temple, Stage: Eschatological Architecture and Liturgical Theatrics in New Spain*. Notre Dame University Press, Notre Dame, IN.

Lewis, Laura
2003 *Hall of Mirrors: Power, Witchcraft, and Caste in Colonial Mexico*. Duke University Press, Durham, NC.

Lockhart, James
1992 *The Nahuas after the Conquest: A Social and Cultural History of the Indians of Central Mexico, Sixteenth through Eighteenth Centuries.* Stanford University Press, Stanford, CA.

Lockhart, James (editor and translator)
1993 *We People Here: Nahuatl Accounts of the Conquest of Mexico.* University of California Press, Berkeley and Los Angeles.

Mendieta, Fray Gerónimo de
1980 *Historia eclesiástica indiana.* Edited by Joaquín García Icazbalceta. Editorial Porrúa, Mexico City.

Motolinia, Fray Toribio de Benavente
1979 *Historia de los indios de la Nueva España.* Edited by Edmundo O'Gorman. Editorial Porrúa, Mexico City.

Osowski, Edward W.
2010 *Indigenous Miracles: Nahua Authority in Colonial Mexico.* University of Arizona Press, Tucson.

Pardo, Osvaldo F.
2004 *The Origins of Mexican Catholicism: Nahua Rituals and Christian Sacraments in Sixteenth-Century Mexico.* University of Michigan Press, Ann Arbor.

Peterson, Jeanette Favrot
1993 *The Paradise Garden Murals of Malinalco: Utopia and Empire in Sixteenth-Century Mexico.* University of Texas Press, Austin.

Pizzigoni, Caterina
2012 *The Life Within: Local Indigenous Society in Mexico's Toluca Valley, 1650–1800.* Stanford University Press, Stanford, CA.

Poole, Stafford
1995 *Our Lady of Guadalupe: Origins and Sources of a Mexican National Symbol, 1571–1797.* University of Arizona Press, Tucson.

Reyes-Valerio, Constantino
1978 *Arte indocristiano: escultura del siglo XVI en México.* Instituto Nacional de Antropología e Historia, Mexico City.

1989 *El pintor de conventos: los murales del siglo XVI en la Nueva España.* Instituto Nacional de Antropología e Historia, Mexico City.

Ruiz de Alarcón, Hernando de
1984 *Treatise on the Heathen Superstitions that Today Live among the Indians Native to This New Spain.* Edited and translated by Richard J. Andrews and Ross Hassig. University of Oklahoma Press, Norman.

Sahagún, Fray Bernardino de
1993 *Psalmodia Christiana (Christian Psalmody).* Edited and translated by Arthur J. O. Anderson. University of Utah Press, Salt Lake City.

Sell, Barry David
1993 *Friars, Nahuas, and Books: Language and Expression in Colonial Nahuatl Publications.* Ph.D. dissertation, Department of History, University of California, Los Angeles.

Tavárez, David
2011 *The Invisible War: Indigenous Devotions, Discipline, and Dissent in Colonial Mexico.* Stanford University Press, Stanford, CA.

Taylor, William B.
1996 *Magistrates of the Sacred: Priests and Parishioners in Eighteenth-Century Mexico.* Stanford University Press, Stanford, CA.

2003 Mexico's Virgin of Guadalupe in the Seventeenth Century: Hagiography and Beyond. In *Colonial Saints: Discovering the Holy in the Americas*, edited by Allan Greer and Jodi Blinkoff, pp. 277–298. Routledge, New York.

2010 *Shrines and Miraculous Images: Religious Life in Mexico Before the Reforma*. University of New Mexico Press, Albuquerque.

2011 *Marvels and Miracles in Late Colonial Mexico: Three Texts in Context*. University of New Mexico Press, Albuquerque.

Vergara Hernández, Arturo

2010 *Las pinturas del templo de Ixmiquilpan: ¿Evangelización, reivindicación indígena o propaganda de guerra?* Universidad Autónoma del Estado de Hidalgo, Pachuca, Mexico.

Wake, Eleanor

2010 *Framing the Sacred: The Indian Churches of Early Colonial Mexico*. University of Oklahoma Press, Norman.

Wood, Stephanie

1991a Adopted Saints: Christian Images in Nahua Testaments of Late Colonial Toluca. *The Americas* 47(3):259–294.

1991b The Cosmic Conquest: Late-Colonial Views of the Sword and Cross in Central Mexican Títulos. *Ethnohistory* 38(2):176–195.

2003 *Transcending Conquest: Nahua Views of Spanish Colonial America*. University of Oklahoma Press, Norman.

CHAPTER 48

AZTEC ART AFTER THE CONQUEST AND IN MUSEUMS ABROAD

RAY HERNÁNDEZ-DURÁN

MUCH of what we know about the so-called Aztec Empire comes from documents written during and after the Spanish Conquest of Mexico, and the archaeological remains do not match the expectations raised by the historical archive (Umberger 2012). Various distinctions have been noted between the kinds of information provided by ethnographic texts and that suggested by the material record, revealing a lack of correlation and even contradictions among primary and secondary sources (Pasztory 1987; Quiñones Keber 1992).

In this chapter, Aztec art is understood as the visual and material culture produced by members of the dominant Nahua group in what today is central Mexico, that is, the Aztec, Mexica, or Tenochca. It embraces the monumental architecture, sculpture, and works in other media produced in the imperial capital of Mexico-Tenochtitlan, as well as the material production that occurred outside of the imperial center in the provinces under the direction of imperial representatives and members of subject native groups.

The chapter's broad theme implies a diachronic perspective that requires the definition of Aztec art to not only include the kinds of objects produced before contact with Europeans but also the repurposing of Aztec art forms to serve new functions following the Conquest and the production of what can be regarded as a Colonial brand of indigenous esthetic expression. Over time, Aztec art forms have also been reproduced in diverse media, including prints, paintings, plaster casts, photographs, archaeological reconstructions, and exhibitions. Such iterations, indexing Aztec source material, must be considered in a historical discussion that traces the fate of Aztec art after the fall of the Aztec Empire.

Works of art were central to Aztec culture not only as signifiers of wealth, social status, and ethnic distinction but also as the primary material embodiments and conveyors of ideas and traditions in that society (Pasztory 1983; Pohl and Lyons 2010; Townsend

1979: Umberger 1996). From the Iberian perspective of the sixteenth century, Aztec art was to be admired for its technical skill and creative use of materials; however, in terms of religion and esthetics, it was incomprehensible. In the best of cases, Aztec art objects became curiosities worthy of admiration, but in the worst, they were vilified as demonic expressions and ugly monstrosities, a response exemplified by the extirpation of idols such as promoted by the first bishop in Mexico, Juan de Zumárraga (Baudot 1996; Feest 1995; Fernández 1972; Gómara 1943; Keen 1971; Motolinía 1971; Pasztory 1983; Sahagún 1992; Villela and Miller 2010).

Following the conquest of Tenochtitlan, a long process was initiated that entailed modifying the Aztec material presence, beginning with the Aztec capital's architectural landscape, to suit the visual, spatial, and signifying needs of the new sociopolitical order that was unfolding (Edgerton 2001; García Zambrano 1994; Kubler and Soria 1959; Kagan 2000; Mundy 1998). Such patterns of appropriation and defacement were not new or unique phenomena but can be seen as an extension of the kinds of practices conducted on the Iberian Peninsula in the latter part of the fifteenth century when Christians expelled the Moors and reclaimed territory that had been ruled by Muslims for centuries (Lafaye 1974; Harvey 1990; Mann et al. 1992; Mariejol 1961). The Christian appropriation of Muslim sites in Late Medieval Spain was a practice that continued in the Americas with the demolition of native shrines and the construction of churches over indigenous sacred sites (Bargellini 1997; Cortés 1986; Edgerton 2001; Fernández 1972; Keen 1971; Kubler 1948; McAndrew 1965; Toussaint 1967; Townsend 1992). The most dramatic example was the dismantling of the principal Aztec monument, the Templo Mayor and the reuse of its material in new construction (Díaz del Castillo 1972; Matos Moctezuma 1988a, 1988b; Quiñones Keber 1992; Ricard 1966).

The martial accomplishments of the conquistadors were compared to that of ancient Roman emperors. Julius Caesar and Titus were cited as predecessors, the former as the institutional ancestor of the king of Spain and the latter as the model for Hernan Cortés' victorious siege of Tenochtitlan, which was seen as echoing the Roman sack of Jerusalem (Cervantes de Salazar 1558–1566; Clavigero 1971; Díaz del Castillo 1972; Lupher 2003; Torquemada 1975–1979). This identification with Classical figures and events extended to include a broad range of references in other Colonial forms, among them literary sources, the visual arts, and public ceremonies (Cañeque 2004, 2010; Curcio-Nagy 2004; Greene 1995; Harris 2000; Kügelgen 1994; MacCormack 1995; Sigüenza y Góngora 2005).

The repurposing of Aztec building and sculptural materials, like *spolia* in other imperial contexts, may have been motivated by both ideological and pragmatic reasons (Brenk 1987; Kinney 2001, 2006). On one hand, given the location and need for expeditious construction, the recycling of local materials into usable forms was a necessity. On the other hand, making visible the defeat of the Aztec through the conspicuous reconstitution of the Mexica city and corresponding representational forms had to have been seen as a useful if not necessary tool as the power structure shifted and the formation of new loyalties became important. In addition to the dismantling of Aztec buildings, Aztec sculptures, if not destroyed, were reshaped to function in new capacities.

The results of this violent recontextualization are exemplified by a colonial column base with a relief of the Aztec earth deity, *Tlaltecuhtli*, on its underside and a millstone that retains vestiges of the same figure in relief on one of its faces, remnants suggesting each object's possible original form and function (Kubler 1948; Matos Moctezuma and Hecht 1990) (Figure 48.1).

In addition to considering post-Conquest responses to Aztec works of art, we must consider both the preservation of certain native forms, although altered, in the Early Colonial period (e.g. manuscripts and featherwork) and the presence of indigenous esthetics in Colonial art production (e.g., sculpture and wall painting).

Only 12 pre-Contact codices are known to have survived from central Mexico, with the majority of extant manuscripts dating from the Colonial period (Berdan and Anawalt 1999; Boone 1998, 2000; Robertson 1959). Across the range of Early Colonial manuscript production, a consistent element is the adaptation of Nahua forms to a written alphabet and the European book format, which differed from pre-Contact pictography and the native screenfold (*amoxtli* in Nahuatl). Aztec pictographic elements were accommodated to the segmented pagination of the European book, were translated via

FIGURE 48.1 Unidentified artist, Colonial column base with Tlaltecuhtli, ca. 1525–37, stone. Courtesy of Instituto Nacional de Antropología e Historia, Museo Nacional de Antropología, Mexico City.

glosses for a nonnative audience, and increasingly manifested naturalistic pictorial tendencies, revealing the influence of renaissance European ideas about images and their relationship to written text (Baird 1979; Berdan and Anawalt 1992; Lara 2008; Robertson 1954) (Figure 48.2).

By mid-century, Christianized natives had relinquished traditional religious books, but they continued to produce historical annals and cartographic histories, at least through the end of the sixteenth century (Boone 1998, 2000; Carrasco and Sessions 2007; Mundy 1996; Robertson 1959).

An Aztec art form that found new life during the Early Colonial period was featherwork, also identified as feather painting or feather mosaic. Featherwork (*amantecayotl* in Nahuatl) was highly prized by the Aztec and was originally used in the production of shields, wall coverings, cloaks, and banners, which were decorated with zoomorphic figures and nonobjective imagery (Dibble and Anderson 1967; Estrada de Gerlero et al. 1990b; Gómara 1979; Motolinía 1971; Pasztory 1983; Pohl and Lyons 2010; Sahagún 1992). Given the need for images to facilitate conversion and structure cult worship among natives in central New Spain, members of the religious orders who were directing the workshops in and around the capital, such as the Franciscan, Pedro de Gante at San

FIGURE 48.2 Unidentified artist, "The Founding of Tenochtitlan," Frontispiece: *Codex Mendoza*, ca. 1541, ink and watercolor on paper. Bodleian Library, Oxford University, Oxford. (Berdan and Anawalt, *Codex Mendoza* p.1r.). Reproduced with permission.

José de los Naturales in Tlatelolco, were impressed with the beauty and technical skill of Aztec featherwork and commissioned the production of Catholic cult objects and religious images in this medium (Estrada de Gerlero et al. 1990b; Fernández 1972; Lara 2008; Sahagún 1992; Toussaint 1967) (Figure 48.3).

Similar processes of transculturation are evident in Colonial sculptural production and wall painting, specifically that which was meant to ornament and/or accompany religious architectural complexes. The friars depended on native labor for construction, as well as for sculpting and painting. Although the degree to which Indian craftsmen retained an indigenous esthetic sensibility in their Colonial art production has been debated, non-European conceptual and stylistic influences have been noted in Early Colonial art production, a tendency that has been identified in certain cases by the term *tequitqui* (Bargellini 1997; Kubler 1948; Oles 2013; Toussaint 1967).

Atrial crosses with surfaces carved in relief depicting free-floating symbols of Christ's passion or with Christ's face emerging from the object, including examples that contain substances considered sacred by the Aztec, such as jade and obsidian, were common in the sixteenth century (Aguilar-Moreno 2006; Edgerton 2001; Estrada de Gerlero et al. 1990a; Kubler 1948; Toussaint 1967; Weismann 1950). Baptismal fonts display syncretic processes in the blending of Christian and Aztec forms, functions, and symbolism,

FIGURE 48.3 School of San José de los Naturales, "The Mass of St. Gregory," 1539, feathers on wood with paint. Musée des Jacobins, Auch, France. Reproduced with permission.

such as in the repurposing of an eagle-shaped *cuauhxicalli* (a vessel for sacrificial offerings) for use in the holy sacrament (Estrada de Gerlero et al. 1990a; Reyes Valerio 1978). Similarly, relief carving at sites, such as the Church of San Miguel at Huejotzingo, includes representations of flowers and hearts drawn from indigenous visual vocabularies and resembling glyphs associated with blood sacrifice, song, and dance (Edgerton 2001; Kubler 1948; McAndrew 1965).

The murals at the Church of San Agustín at Malinalco employ a variety of visual and thematic idioms that include biblical subjects, devotional images, and vegetal imagery. The garden scenes on the ground level of the cloistered courtyard consist of naturalistic depictions of local flora and fauna and Nahua pictographic forms, such as speech scrolls and flower motifs, including a pictographic reference to "tall grass," or *malinalli*, that is, the place name for Malinalco (Peterson 1993). At the Church of San Miguel at Ixmiquilpan, murals depict battle scenes between Aztec warriors and barbaric Chichimecas. Along with stylized European dragons and centaurs, the artists integrated images of eagles, jaguars, and speech scrolls (Carrillo y Gariel 1961; Pierce 1981).

Following the earliest contact between Europeans and Amerindians, various kinds of native artifacts were sent back to Europe as specimens of what the Europeans were encountering in the Americas. Many of these objects circulated throughout Europe and were added to royal collections and curiosity cabinets. In 1519, Cortés sent to Charles V, the king of Spain and Holy Roman emperor, a group of artifacts that included two codices and several costumes used in Aztec religious performances, which were given to him by the Aztec emperor Motecuhzoma II (Boone 2003; Feest 1995). Objects that were collected were obtained as loot, as ceremonial exchanges, and as evidence of natural resources, and were selected based on physical qualities (i.e., rarity or beauty), the distance of point of origin (historically or geographically), and/or their familiarity to Europeans (e.g., pipes; Feest 1995). Many objects made of perishable materials, such as wood, feathers, and paper, were lost early in the encounter, as were works made of gold, which were melted down and shipped to Europe as bullion (Feest 1995; Quiñones Keber 1992).

Many Aztec art objects that were added to European collections deteriorated, were forgotten, and/or were lost; thus the ethnographic and archaeological records are inconsistent and riddled with lacunae. The provenance of Aztec materials in foreign collections is also impeded due to misidentification. Often, the term "Moorish" is used as a descriptor for Mexican objects, along with "Indian" and "American"; interestingly, the term "Mexican" is rarely used as an attribution, although there are cases where Mexican artifacts are mislabeled as corresponding to other indigenous groups and non-Mexican native objects are identified as being from Mexico. Based on catalogues and inventories of Amerindian objects in European collections, numerous objects are listed without any identification at all (Feest 1995; Keen 1971; Nowotny 1960).

In Europe, Aztec artworks were greatly admired not only for their exotic qualities but also for their technical mastery and beauty. In 1520, the German artist, Albrecht Dürer (1971:53–54) viewed Aztec artifacts in Brussels. In his diary entry, dated August 27, 1520, he wrote:

> At Brussels is a very splendid Townhall ... I saw the things which have been brought to the King from the new land of gold ... all kinds of wonderful objects of human

use ... all so precious that they are valued at 100,000 florins [guilders]. All the days of my life I have seen nothing that rejoiced my heart so much as these things, for I saw amongst them wonderful works of art, and I marvelled at the subtle Ingenia of men in foreign lands. Indeed I cannot express all that I thought there.

In the late eighteenth century, archaeological activity developed and flourished in central New Spain. Several accidental discoveries in the Plaza Mayor of Mexico City during this period contributed to the interest in Aztec archeology and Mexican history. After claiming the Spanish throne in 1700, Bourbon officials began to implement a number of reforms intended to restructure educational, economic, and institutional practices; urban renovation was a central concern. In December 1790, as workers dug up pavement while repairing the main plaza of Mexico City, three monumental Aztec sculptures were unearthed: the Coatlicue, the "Calendar" Stone, and the Stone of Tizoc (Durán 1964; Fernández 1972; Miller and Villela 2010; Torquemada 1975–1979) (Figure 48.4). Drawings of archaeological sites, ancient architecture, and sculptural details were publicly disseminated via publication in periodicals, such as the *Gazeta de México* and the *Gazeta de Literatura*.

The work of Europeans, such as the Austro-Hungarian Guillermo Dupaix and the Prussian nobleman Alexander von Humboldt, contributed to the fascination with

FIGURE 48.4 Unidentified Artist, "Calendar Stone," ca. 1502–1520, stone. Photo taken by William T. Gassaway. Courtesy of Instituto Nacional de Antropología e Historia, Museo Nacional de Antropología, Mexico City.

Mexico's prehispanic past. Authorized by Charles IV, Dupaix arrived in New Spain in 1791 and led three royal expeditions between 1805 and 1807 to study and document ancient archaeological sites. Dupaix published a two-volume book, the second of which, titled, *Expediciones acerca de los antiguos monumentos de la Nueva España 1805–1808* (1969) includes archaeological information about Aztec sites, such as Xochicalco (Carrera 2011; Estrada de Gerlero 1994; Kingsborough 1830–1848; López Luján 2011). Similarly, Alexander von Humboldt received permission from Charles IV to travel through Spain's American territories from 1799 through 1804 with French naturalist, Aimé Bonpland (Carrera 2011; Rupke 1999, 2005). Humboldt returned to Europe and proceeded to publish the data he had gathered in several volumes, among them, *Vues de Cordillères et monumens des peuples indigenes de l'Amerique* (1810–1813), which included assorted maps and illustrations of, among other things, archaeological artifacts, such as the recently recovered Calendar Stone (Ades 1989; Humboldt 1810–1813; Villela and Miller 2010).

After 1821, the archaeological activity of the Late Colonial period languished for a period of time in light of the turmoil occasioned by Mexico's struggle for independence from Spain. By mid-century, however, the interest in the Aztec resurfaced in response to increased foreign fascination with Mexico's ancient civilizations and a developing local interest in defining a national history and cultural identity. The first national museum in Mexico was established in 1825 as a way to bring to light the achievements of ancient cultures and insure that Mexican antiquities continued to be collected, studied, and exhibited. In 1827, the museum published *Colección de las Antigüedades Mexicanas que existen en el Museo Nacional,* which highlighted its collection of ancient artifacts (Carrera 2011; Morales Moreno 2001).

Foreign travellers, among them scientists, businessmen, and artists, flooded into Mexico throughout the nineteenth century and contributed to the production of a large body of books and illustrated albums that documented Mexican history, flora, and fauna and included picturesque renditions of the landscape, its inhabitants, and ancient sites (Prescott 1843). One of the most successful publications that included illustrations of ancient Mexican sculpture and ruins was Carl Nebel's *Voyage pittoresque et archéologique dans la partie la plus intéressante du Mexique* (1836) (Ades 1989; Carrera 2011; Oles 2013; Quiñones Keber 1992; Villela and Miller 2010). Mexicans produced similar publications for local audiences in order to promote travel and learning about the country among its citizens. A collaborative publication by Mexican authors and lithographers exemplifying this practice is *México y sus alrededores: Coleccion de monumentos, trajes y paisajes* (1855–1864). A print from this publication, titled *Antigüedades Mexicanas que existen en el Museo Nacional de México* (1855–1856), illustrated by C. Castro and J. Campillo, depicts a random assortment of known monumental and small-scale Aztec sculpture, including the Coatlicue and the Stone of Tizoc (Berlo 1985; Carrera 2011; Gutiérrez Haces 1995; León y Gama 1792).

In 1822, the Englishman William Bullock traveled to Mexico to explore possible economic ventures in mining. Bullock toured the country and collected all manner of objects, including plaster casts of Aztec objects, such as the already iconic Calendar

Stone and the Stone of Tizoc. Following his return to England, he published his travelogue, titled *Six Months' Residence and Travels in Mexico* (1824), and he curated an exhibition of the material he had brought back to London. Accompanied by a catalogue, titled *Ancient and Modern Mexico*, the impressive display was exhibited in the Piccadilly Egyptian Hall and included dioramas, assorted maps, the plaster replicas of Aztec sculpture he had procured, and even a scale model of one of the pyramids from Teotihuacan (Carrera 2011) (Figure 48.5).

A popular early venue for the display of Mexican cultural material abroad included international expositions or world's fairs, which were held from the mid-nineteenth through the early twentieth century in Europe and the United States. Replicas of Aztec works of art were typically displayed as part of a Mexico pavilion that combined artwork with exhibitions of a more ethnographic nature. In 1867, during the end of the French intervention in Mexico, the Hapsburg emperor Maximilian sent a cast of the Calendar Stone to Paris to be installed as part of the Mexico building at the *Exposition universelle*, then again, at the 1889 expo in Paris, with the Palacio Azteca, which incorporated copies of Aztec sculptures (Jackson 2008; Tenorio 1996; Villela and Miller 2010).

In the latter part of the nineteenth century, academically trained artists in Mexico produced history paintings that depicted events both historically accurate and imagined corresponding to the period of Aztec rule. Although the subjects are prehispanic, the realist compositions follow classicizing, pictorial conventions, such as Rodrigo Gutiérrez's "Senate of Tlaxcala" (1875), which depicts Tlaxcalteca leaders debating in a dramatically illuminated architectural interior as if Roman senators. Landscape painters also referenced the Aztec past in their works, such as José María Velasco's "The Pyramid of the Sun at Teotihuacan" (1878), which depicts the ruins at the ancient site, or the panoramic "View of the Valley of Mexico from the Hill of Santa Isabel" (1875),

FIGURE 48.5 Agostino Aglio, "Mexican Exhibition at the Egyptian Hall, Piccadilly," 1824–1825, drawing and lithograph. With permission of Getty Research Institute, Los Angeles.

where an eagle and cactus, referencing the founding myth of Tenochtitlan, occupy the foreground with Mexico City in the distance (Ades 1989; Fernández 1993; Oles 2013; Widdifield 1996).

In the early twentieth century, growing US interest in Mexico was motivated, in part, by increased tourism following the construction of the railroad and the recognition of potential new economic ventures and later by a desire to fortify Pan-American relationships during the World Wars (Berlo 1992; Delpar 1992; Kelemen 1946). The first scholarly work in the United States that approached precolumbian objects as works of art was the doctoral dissertation produced in 1913 by anthropologist Herbert Spinden. Spinden's student, George Kubler continued his mentor's work, as did Kubler's protégé, Donald Robertson (Berlo 1985; Carrera 2011; Fernández 1972; Pasztory 1979; Paz 1990; Quiñones Keber 1992; Schreffler 1994). During this period, the Museum of Modern Art in New York became the site of two early exhibitions of prehispanic art. The first exhibition in 1933 focused specifically on prehispanic sculpture and included Aztec material; the next and much larger exhibition was in 1940 and was the first comprehensive exhibition of Mexican art in the United States, titled *Twenty Centuries of Mexican Art*, which included a precolumbian art section curated by Alfonso Caso (Museum of Modern Art 1940; Schreffler 1994; Villela and Miller 2010).

In Europe, the presence of prehispanic art in certain museum collections, such as at the Museo de América in Madrid, the Museum of Ethnology in Vienna, the Ethnological Museum in the Vatican, and Le Musée de Quai Branly in Paris, represents the legacy of earlier collecting practices with later additions acquired as purchases or as gifts from donors. The search for "new" formal idioms by modern artists working in Spain, France, and Germany in the early twentieth century contributed to the interest in collecting so-called tribal or primitive arts. Relevant European art historical studies of precolumbian art include such publications as the early *Handbuch des Kunstgeschichte* (1842) by Franz Kugler and later *Altmexikanische Kunstgeschichte* (1921) by Walter Lehman, *L'Art Precolumbien* (1928) by Adolphe Basler and Ernest Brummer, and *Medieval American Art: Masterpieces of the New World before Columbus* by Pál Kelemen (1943).

The earliest prehispanic art historical publication in Mexico, titled *Arte precolombino de México y de la América Central*, was written in 1944 by Salvador Toscano, one of the founders of the Instituto de Investigaciones Estéticas in 1934, along with colonial art historian Manuel Toussaint. Toussaint's student, Justino Fernández, then published the seminal art historical text, *Coatlicue: Estética del arte indígena antiguo* in 1954 (Berlo 1985; Fernández 1972; Klein 1982a, 1982b; Schreffler 1994). As had happened before whenever there had been any kind of excavation in the main plaza of Mexico City, in 1978, the monumental Coyolxauhqui relief was unearthed by construction workers in the Zócalo of the city, along with the remains of the Templo Mayor complex. Like the discoveries of the late eighteenth century, these finds greatly contributed to scholarly production and public interest in Aztec art. In Mexico, the majority of extant canonical Aztec artworks have been gathered and are exhibited in the Museo Nacional de Antropología in the Mexican capital. (Broda et al. 1987; Fernández 1972; Matos Moctezuma 1988).

References Cited

Ades, Dawn
1989 *Art in Latin America: The Modern Era 1820–1980*. Yale University Press, New Haven, CT.
Aguilar-Moreno, Manuel
2006 *Handbook to Life in the Aztec World*. Facts on File, New York.
2013 Transculturation in Art: Sculpture in the Posa Chapels at the Monastery of Calpan, Mexico. *Colonial Latin American Review* 22(1):39–66.
Baird, Ellen T.
1983 *Sahagun's "Primeros Memoriales": A Structural and Stylistic Analysis of the Drawings*. University of Oklahoma Press. Norman.
Bargellini, Clara
1997 Architecture: Colonial. In *Encyclopedia of Mexico: History, Society and Culture*, edited by Michael S. Werner, pp. 66–77. Fitzroy Dearborn, Chicago.
Basler, Adolphe, and Ernest Brummer
1928 *L'Art Precolumbien*, Librairie de France, Paris.
Baudot, Georges
1996 *México y los albores del discurso colonial*. Nueva Imagen/Editorial Patria, S.A. de C.V., Mexico City.
Berdan, Frances F. and Patricia Rieff Anawalt (editors)
1992 *The Codex Mendoza*. University of California Press, Berkeley.
Berlo, Janet Catherine
1985 The Art of Pre-Columbian Art History: An Historiographic Review. In *The Art of Pre-Hispanic Mesoamerica: An Annotated Bibliography*, edited by Janet Berlo, pp. 1–33. G. K. Hall, Boston.
Berlo, Janet Catherine (editor)
1992 *The Early Years of Native American History*. University of Washington Press, Seattle.
Boone, Elizabeth Hill
1998 Pictorial Documents and Visual Thinking in Postconquest Mexico. In *Native Traditions in the Postconquest World*, edited by Elizabeth Hill Boone and Tom Cummins, pp. 149–199. Dumbarton Oaks Research Library and Collection, Washington, DC.
2000 *Stories in Red and Black: Pictorial Histories of the Aztecs and Mixtecs*. University of Texas Press, Austin.
Brenk, Beat
1987 Spolia from Constantine to Charlemagne: Aesthetics versus Ideology. *Dumbarton Oaks Papers* 41:103–109.
Cañeque, Alejandro
2004 *The King's Living Image: The Culture and Politics of Viceregal Power in Colonial Mexico*. Routledge, New York.
2010 Imaging the Spanish Empire: The Visual Construction of Imperial Authority in Hapsburg New Spain. *Colonial Latin American Review* 19(1):29–68.
Carrillo y Gariel, Abelardo
1961 *Ixmiquilpan*. Instituto Nacional de Antropología e Historia, Mexico City.
Carrasco, Davíd, and Scott Session (editors)
2007 *Cave, City, and Eagle's Nest: An Interpretive Journey through the Mapa de Cuauhtinchan Mapa 2*. University of New Mexico Press, Albuquerque.

Carrera, Magali
2011 *Traveling from New Spain to Mexico: Mapping Practices of Nineteenth-Century Mexico.* Duke University Press, Durham, NC.

Clavigero, Francisco Javier
1971 *Historia Antigua de México.* Editorial Porrúa, S.A., Mexico City.

Cortés, Hernan
1986 *Letters from Mexico.* Edited and translated by Anthony Pagden. Yale University Press, New Haven, CT.

Couto, José Bernardo
1995 *Diálogo sobre la historia de la pintura en México.* Instituto de Investigaciones Estéticas, Universidad Nacional Autónoma de México, Mexico City.

Curcio-Nagy, Linda A.
2004 *Great Festivals of Colonial Mexico City: Performing Power and Identity.* University of New Mexico Press, Albuquerque.

Delpar, Helen
1992 *The Enormous Vogue of Things Mexican: Cultural Relations between the United States and Mexico 1920–1935.* University of Alabama Press, Tuscaloosa.

Díaz del Castillo, Bernal
1992 *Historia verdadera de la conquista de la Nueva España.* Edited by Joaquín Ramírez Cabaña. Editorial Porrúa, Mexico City.

Dibble, Charles.E., and Arthur J. O. Anderson
1967 Feather Merchants. *Craft Horizons* 27:18–23.

Dupaix, Guillermo
1969 *Expediciones acerca de los antiguos monumentos de la Nueva España 1805–1808.* Vol. 1. Ediciones José Porrua Turanzas, S.A., Madrid, Spain.

Durán, Diego
1967 *Historia de las Indias de Nueva España e islas de tierra firme.* Edited by Ángel María Garibay Kintana. Editorial Porrúa, S.A., Mexico City.

Dürer, Albrecht
1971 *Albrecht Dürer: Diary of His Journey to the Netherlands.* New York Graphic Society, Greenwich, CT.

Edgerton, Samuel Y.
2001 *Theaters of Conversion: Religious Architecture and Indian Artisans in Colonial Mexico.* University of New Mexico Press, Albuquerque.

Estrada de Gerlero, Elena Isabel
1994 La labor anticuaria novohispana en la época de Carlos IV: Guillermo Dupaix, precursor de la historia del arte prehispánico. In *Arte, Historia e Identidad en América: Visiones comparativas,* Vol. I, edited by Gustavo Curiel, Renato González Mello, and Juana Gutiérrez Haces, pp. 191–205. Instituto de Investigaciones Estéticas, Universidad Nacional Autónoma de México, Mexico City.

Estrada de Gerlero, Elena Isabel, and Marita Martínez del Río de Redo
1990a Baptismal Font. In *Mexico: Splendors of Thirty Centuries,* pp. 252–255. Metropolitan Museum of Art, New York.
1990b The Mass of St. Gregory. In *Mexico: Splendors of Thirty Centuries,* pp. 258–260. Metropolitan Museum of Art, New York.

Feest, Christian F.
1995 The Collecting of American Indian Artifacts in Europe 1493–1750. In *America in European Consciousness 1493–1750,* edited by Karen Kupperman, pp. 324–360. University of North Carolina Press, Chapel Hill.

Fernández, Justino
1972 *Estética del arte mexicano: Coatlicue. El retablo de los reyes. El hombre*. Universidad Nacional Autónoma de México, Instituto de Investigaciones Estéticas, Mexico City.
1993 *Arte moderno y contemporáneo de México: El arte del siglo XIX*. Universidad Nacional Autónoma de México, Mexico City.

García Zambrano, Angel J.
1994 Early Colonial Evidence of Pre-Columbian Rituals of Foundation. In *Seventh Palenque Round Table 1989*, edited by. Merle Greene Robertson and Virginia M. Fields, pp. 217–227. Pre-Columbian Art Research Institute, San Francisco.

Greene, Roland
1995 Petrarchism among the Discourses of Imperialism. In *America in European Consciousness 1493–1750*, edited by Karen Ordahl Kupperman, pp. 130–165 University of North Carolina Press, Chapel Hill.

Gutiérrez Haces, Juana
1995 Estudio preliminar. In *Diálogo sobre la historia de la pintura en México*, by José Bernardo Couto, pp. 9–64. Instituto de Investigaciones Estéticas, Universidad Nacional Autónoma de México, Mexico City.

Harris, Max
2000 *Aztecs, Moors, and Christians: Festivals of Reconquest in Mexico and Spain*. University of Texas Press, Austin.

Harvey, L. P.
1990 *Islamic Spain 1250–1500*. University of Chicago Press, Chicago.

Humboldt, Alexander von
1810–1813 *Vues de Cordillères et monumens des peuples indigenes de l'Amerique*. F. Schoell, Paris.

Jackson, Anna
2008 *Expo: International Expositions 1851–2010*. Harry N. Abrams, New York.

Kagan, Richard L.
2000 *Urban Images of the Hispanic World 1493–1793*. Yale University Press, New Haven, CT.

Keber, Eloise Quiñones
1992 (Re)discovering Aztec Images. In *Amerindian Images and the Legacy of Columbus*, edited by René Jara and Nicholas Spadaccini, pp. 132–162. University of Minnesota Press, Minneapolis.

Keen, Benjamin
1971 *The Aztec Image in Western Thought*. Rutgers University Press New Brunswick, NJ.

Kelemen, Pál
1943 *Medieval American Art: Masterpieces of the New World before Columbus*. Dover, New York.
1946 Pre-Columbian Art and Art History. *American Antiquity* 11:145–154.

Kingsborough, Lord Edward
1830–1848 *Antiquities of Mexico*. A. Aglio, London.

Kinney, Dale
2006 The Concept of Spolia. In *A Companion to Medieval Art: Romanesque and Gothic in Northern Europe*, edited by Conrad Rudolph, pp. 233–252. Oxford University Press, Oxford.
2001 Roman Architectural Spolia. *Proceedings of the American Philosophical Society* 145:138–161.

Klein Cecelia F.
1982a Arte precolombino y ciencias sociales. *Plural* 11:40–48.
1982b The Relation of Mesoamerican Art History to Archaeology in the United States. In *Pre-Columbian Art History: Selected Readings*, edited Alana Cordy-Collins. pp. 1–6. Peek Publications, Palo Alto, CA.

Kubler, George
1948 *Mexican Architecture of the Sixteenth Century*. Yale University Press, New Haven, CT.

Kubler, George, and Martin Soria
1959 *Art and Architecture in Spain and Portugal and their American Dominions 1500–1800*. Penguin Books, London.

Kügelgen, Helga von
1994 Así "repercute" la Gloria del mundo: Aproximación a la reconstrucción de los arcos de triunfo de Don Carlos de Sigüenza y Góngora y Sor Juana Inés de la Cruz. In *Arte, Historia e Identidad en América: Visiones comparativas*, Vol. III, edited by Gustavo Curiel, Renato González Mello, and Juana Gutiérrez Haces, pp. 707–718. Instituto de Investigaciones Estéticas, Universidad Nacional Autónoma de México, Mexico City.

Kugler, Franz
1842 *Handbuch der Kunstgeschichte*. Ebner and Seubert, Stuttgart, Germany.

Lafaye, Jacques
1974 Reconquest, Djihad, Diaspora: Three Visions of Spain at the Discovery of America. *Diogenes* 22(87):50–60.

Lara, Jaime
2008 *Christian Texts for Aztecs: Art and Liturgy in Colonial Mexico*. University of Notre Dame Press, Notre Dame, IN.

Lehman, Walter
1921 *Altmexicanische Kunstgeschichte*. W. Wasmuth Verlag, Berlin.

León y Gama, Antonio
1992 *Descripcion histórica y cronológica de las dos piedras que con occasion del Nuevo empedrado que se está formando en la plaza principal de México se hallaron en ella el año de 1790*. Imprenta de Don Felipe de Zúñiga y Ontiveros, Mexico City.

López de Gómara, Francisco
1943 *Historia de la conquista de México*. Editorial Porrúa, S.A., Mexico City.

López Luján, Leonardo
2011 El capitán Guillermo Dupaix y su album arqueológico de 1794. *Arqueología Mexicana* 19(109):71–81.

Lupher, David
2003 *Romans in a New World: Classical Models in Sixteenth-Century Spanish America*. University of Michigan Press, Ann Arbor.

MacCormack, Sabine
1995 Limits of Understanding: Perceptions of Greco-Roman and Amerindian Paganism in Early Modern Europe. In *America in European Consciousness 1493–1750*, edited by Karen Ordahl Kupperman, pp. 79–129. University of North Carolina Press, Chapel Hill.

Mann, Vivian B., Thomas F. Glick, and Jerrilyn D. Dodds (editors)
1992 *Convivencia: Jews, Muslims, and Christians in Medieval Spain*. George Braziller in association with The Jewish Museum, New York.

Mariejol, Jean-Hippolyte
1961 *The Spain of Ferdinand and Isabella*. Rutgers University Press, New Brunswick, NJ.

Matos Moctezuma, Eduardo
1990 Tlaltecuhtli. In *Mexico: Splendors of Thirty Centuries*, pp. 232–234. Metropolitan Museum of Art, New York.
1998a *The Great Temple of the Aztecs: Treasures of Tenochtitlan*. Translated by Doris Heyden. Thames & Hudson, London.

1998b The Templo Mayor of Tenochtitlan: History and Interpretation. In *The Great Temple of Tenochtitlan: Center and Periphery in the Aztec World*, edited by Johanna Broda, Davíd Carrasco, and Eduardo Matos Moctezuma, pp. 15–60. University of California Press, Berkeley.

Moctezuma, Eduardo, and Johanna Hecht
1990 Column Base with Earth Monster Relief. In *Mexico: Splendors of Thirty Centuries*, pp. 255–256. Metropolitan Museum of Art, New York.

McAndrew, John
1965 *The Open-Air Churches of Sixteenth-Century Mexico: Atrios, Posas, Open Chapels, and Other Studies*. Harvard University Press, Cambridge, MA.

Morales Moreno, Luis Gerardo
2001 El primer Museo Nacional de México (1825–1847). In *Hacia otra historia del arte en México: De la estructuración colonial a la exigencia nacional (1780–1860)*, edited by Esther Acevedo, pp. 36–60. Consejo Nacional para le Cultura y las Artes, Mexico City.

Motolinía, Fray Toribio de Benavente
1971 *Memoriales, o libros de las cosas de la Nueva España y de los naturales de ella*. Edited by Edmundo O'Gorman. Universidad Nacional Autónoma de México, Instituto de Investigaciones Históricas, Mexico City.

Mundy, Barbara E.
1998 Mapping the Aztec Capital: The 1524 Nuremberg Map of Tenochtitlan, Its Sources and Meanings. *Imago Mundi* 50:11–33.
1996 *The Mapping of New Spain: Indigenous Cartography and the Maps of the Relaciones Geograficas*. University of Chicago Press, Chicago.

Museum of Modern Art
1940 *Twenty Centuries of Mexican Art*. Museum of Modern Art in collaboration with the Mexican Government, New York.

Nowtony, Karl Anton
1960 *Mexikanische Kostbarkeiten aus Kunstkammern der Renaissance*. Museum für Völkerkunde, Vienna.

Pasztory, Esther
1987 Texts, Archaeology, Art, and History in the Templo Mayor: Reflections. In *The Aztec Templo Mayor*, edited by Elizabeth Hill Boone, pp. 451–462. Dumbarton Oaks Research and Library Collection, Washington, DC.

Pasztory, Esther
1976 Masterpieces in Pre-Columbian Art. In *Actes du XLII Congrès International des Amèricanistes, Congrès de Centenaire, Paris, 2–9, September 1976*, pp. 377–390. Sociéte des Américanistes, Paris.
1983 *Aztec Art*. Harry N. Abrams, New York.

Paz, Octavio
1990 The Power of Ancient Mexican Art. Translated by Anthony Stanton. *The New York Review* 6 December: 18–21.

Peterson, Jeanette Favrot
1993 *The Paradise Garden Murals of Malinalco: Utopia and Empire in Sixteenth-Century Mexico*. University of Texas Press, Austin.

Pierce, Donna
1981 The Identification of the Warriors in the Frescoes of Ixmiquilpan. *Research Center for the Arts Review* 4(4):1–8.

Pohl, John M. D., and Claire L. Lyons
2010 *The Aztec Pantheon and the Art of Empire* J. Paul Getty Museum, Los Angeles.

Prescott, William H.
1843 *The Conquest of Mexico, With a Preliminary View of the Ancient Mexican Civilization, and the Life of the Conqueror, Hernando Cortés*. Harper and Brothers, New York.

Reyes Valerio, Constantino
1978 *Arte indocristiano: escultural del siglo XVI*. Instituto Nacional de Antropología e Historia, Mexico City.

Ricard, Robert
1966 *The Spiritual Conquest of Mexico: An Essay on the Apostolate and the Evangelizing Methods of the Mendicant Orders in New Spain 1523–1572*. Translated by Lesley Boyd Simpson. University of California Press, Berkeley.

Robertson, Donald
1959 *Mexican Manuscript Painting of the Early Colonial Period: The Metropolitan Schools*. Yale University Press, New Haven, CT.

Rupke, Nicolaas
1999 A Geography of Enlightenment: The Critical Reception of Alexander von Humboldt's Mexico Work. In *Geography and Enlightenment,* edited by David N. Livingstone and Charles W. J. Withers, pp. 319–339. University of Chicago Press, Chicago.
2005 *Alexander von Humboldt: A Metabiography*. Peter Lang, New York.

Sahagún, Fray Bernardino de
1992 *Historia general de las cosas de Nueva España*. Edited by Ángel María Garibay K. Editorial Porrúa, Mexico City.

Schreffler, Michael
1994 The Making of an Aztec Goddess: A Historiographic Study of the Coatlicue. Unpublished M.A. thesis, Arizona State University, Tempe.

Sigüenza y Góngora, Carlos
2005 *Teatro de virtudes políticas que constituyen a un príncipe: advertidas en los monarcas antiguos del Mexicano Imperio, con cuyas efigies se hermoseó el Arco triunfal que la . . . Ciudad de México erigió para . . . recibimiento del . . . Virrey Conde de Paredes, Marqués de La Laguna . . . /ideolo entonces y ahora lo describe D. Carlos de Sigüenza y Góngora*. Biblioteca Virtual Miguel de Cervantes, Alicante, Spain.

Torquemada, Juan de
1975–1979 *Monarquía Indiana: De los veinte y un libros rituals y monarquía Indiana, con el origen y guerras de los indios occidentales, de sus poblazones, descrubimiento, conquista, conversion y otras cosas maravillosas de la misma tierra*. Edited by Miguel León-Portilla. Universidad Nacional Autónoma de México, Mexico City.

Toscano, Salvador
1944 *Arte precolombino de México y la América Central*. Univesidad Autónoma de México, Instituto de Investigaciones Estéticas, Mexico City.

Toussaint, Manuel
1967 *Colonial Art in Mexico*. University of Texas Press, Austin.

Townsend, Richard F.
1992 *The Aztecs*. Thames & Hudson, London.
1979 *State and Cosmos in the Art of Tenochtitlan*. Dumbarton Oaks Research Library and Collection, Washington, DC.

Umberger, Emily
1996 Art and Imperial Strategy in Tenochtitlan. In *Aztec Imperial Strategies,* edited by Frances Berdan, Richard E. Blanton, Elizabeth Hill Boone, Mary G. Hodge, Michael E. Smith, and Emily Umberger, pp. 85–106. Dumbarton Oaks Research Library and Collection, Washington, DC.

Villela, Khristaan D. and Mary Ellen Miller (editors)
2010 *The Aztec Calendar Stone.* Getty Research Institute, Los Angeles.

Widdifield, Stacie G.
1996 *The Embodiment of the National in Late Nineteenth-Century Mexican Painting.* University of Arizona Press, Tucson.

Weismann, Elizabeth Wilder
1950 *Mexico in Sculpture 1521–1821.* Harvard University Press, Cambridge, MA.

CHAPTER 49

THE AZTECS AND THEIR DESCENDANTS IN THE CONTEMPORARY WORLD

ALAN R. SANDSTROM

Introduction to the Problem of Tracing Descent

Tracing contemporary genealogical descendants of the ancient Aztec Empire (or, more accurately, the Triple Alliance) appears on the surface to be a straightforward task, easily accomplished by consulting historical documents and ethnographic reports, compiling demographic data, mapping population distributions, and interviewing people about their ancestry. In reality, determining what happened to the people of the Triple Alliance following the empire's collapse in 1521 is a problem of immense complexity that strikes at the heart of current crises in historiography and social science. Ascertaining descent implicates powerful contemporary struggles surrounding questions of ethnicity, the concept of culture, migration policy, and the role of art in identity politics. Despite these difficulties, it is a fact that Aztec culture is not dead—far from it. Perhaps most remarkable of all, given the tumultuous history of Mesoamerica, is the reality that many contemporary peoples continue to exhibit cultural patterns shared by the Aztecs that are deeply rooted in the prehispanic past. The persistence of these patterns amid some of the most cataclysmic changes experienced by a people anywhere teach us that culture is resilient, adaptable, and far from ephemeral.

Use of the Name *Aztec*

Use of the name *Aztec* to describe the Triple Alliance creates from the start a false impression. The designation was popularized 300 years after the conquest by

Alexander von Humboldt in the early nineteenth century, and many writers have pointed out that it has been applied ambiguously over the years (López Austin 2001:68). *Aztec* was not used as an ethnonym historically by the people of the Triple Alliance, or by anyone else for that matter. It derives from the name of the probably mythical homeland Aztlán, from which several ethnic groups who inhabited the Valley of Mexico at the time of the arrival of the Spaniards traced their origins (Lint-Sagarena 2001). The people who came to be labeled "Aztecs" in the published literature belonged to one of the three kingdoms comprising the Triple Alliance. Subjects of this kingdom called themselves *Mexica* to distinguish their group from others in the region and from inhabitants of the imperial kingdoms that were their allies. Adding to the confusion, *Aztec* has been applied by writers over the years to many different contemporary groups in Highland Mesoamerica. Furthermore, as discussed in this chapter, the term implies a coherence and central organization of the Triple Alliance that did not exist.

Nahuatl Language and the Nahua

Aztec has also been applied to *Nahuatl*, the language spoken by the Mexica and their imperial allies. This usage, too, is imprecise and confusing. Many people throughout Mesoamerica spoke the language, but not all of them were participants in the Triple Alliance. The Tlaxcalans, for example, were traditional enemies of the Triple Alliance, and yet they spoke Nahuatl. To avoid confusion, anthropologists call speakers of Nahuatl (or the related Nahuat dialect) *the Nahua,* and they are careful to point out that the Aztecs were simply one group of Nahua, among many (Taggart 2001). As a consequence of the power and extent of the empire, Nahuatl was becoming the lingua franca for the region by the time of the arrival of the Spaniards. It is likely that many people included in the empire were multilingual, speaking Nahuatl along with their own language and other languages of neighboring groups. In some communities, Nahuatl came to replace the predominant local languages. Largely due its imperial connections, Nahuatl continues to be the most widely spoken indigenous language in Mexico (Kaufman 1994:34). In sum, the fact that a certain group of people today speak Nahuatl does not necessarily confirm that they are descendants of the original members of the Triple Alliance.

Characterizing the Triple Alliance

The nature, structure, and history of the Triple Alliance constitute major obstacles in identifying its direct descendants today. The empire was centered in the Basin of Mexico, and over a period of about 100 years beginning in 1428, its power and influence spread over a large area of central Mexico, eventually reaching both Pacific and Gulf coasts (Berdan et al. 1996; Carrasco 2001). Power was divided among three constituent kingdoms, each representing an ethnic group with its own urban center, territorial domain, and ruler (*tlahtoani*). The three major cities were Tenochtitlan, Texcoco, and Tlacopan. Each kingdom had specific tasks to perform in running the empire, but the alliance came to be dominated by the Mexica, the ethnic group that ruled over Tenochtitlan and the nearby city of Tlatelolco. Despite their superordinate position, the Mexica actually occupied only a tiny slice of the Valley of Mexico and relied on intimidation and military force to exercise control over vast conquered territories, expand the empire, and extract tribute from the people they ruled (Gibson 1964:20). Subordinate to the three monarchs were lesser rulers of territories, towns (sing.: *altepetl*), and neighborhoods within towns (sing.: *calpolli*). In the Basin of Mexico alone there were at least 27 ethnic groups dispersed among the towns (Hicks 2001a), led by some 50 lesser rulers (also *tlahtoani* [sing.]) (Gibson 1964:34). Ethnic group affiliation, however, was not the primary focus of identity for people in the empire, nor was social class (or estate, in the class-like system) (Hicks 2001b). During prehispanic times, the *calpolli* was the center of social life, while the *altepetl* of which it was a part was the primary basis for individual and group identity (Berdan 2008:108–110). This is not to say, however, that ethnicity was unimportant. At no time did the Triple Alliance try to eliminate ethnic diversity, and, in fact, some of its policies encouraged identity based on ethnic group affiliation (Gibson 1964:22).

Political Structure and Identity

Most Triple Alliance towns (and certainly the capital cities themselves) were multiethnic in composition (Umberger 2008). For the majority of people, it was the *altepetl* that provided access to land for farming, protection from external threat, and lines of communication to the imperial political hierarchy. Despite their importance, towns throughout the empire were characterized by a high degree of instability with incessant wars waged among the leaders as they maneuvered to gain advantage over one another. Internal disputes flared on occasion as residents of each *calpolli* fought over access to resources. Not infrequently, nomadic and seminomadic peoples moved into settled territories, stirring hostilities. And the shifting of people and families from one locale to another to evade danger or exploit economic opportunities must have been common and surely disruptive to local farmers and town dwellers. War and famines were frequent during the period, creating large displaced populations (Berdan 2008:108). At the same time, the inhabitants of hundreds of towns throughout the conquered territories labored under the yoke of imperial oppression. Millions of subjects were forced to produce and transport articles of tribute to the towns and capitals (Berdan and Anawalt 1997). Instability characterized the empire, resistance was met with violence, rebellions were common in the conquered territories, and only force (or the threat of force) kept the system together.

By contemporary standards, the Triple Alliance appears to have been volatile and chaotic. With its unstable political structure, shifting populations, and lack of emphasis on ethnic solidarity, it is not surprising that identifying descendants of the Aztecs today is highly problematic. Should we count as a descendant anyone who can trace their ancestors to one of the three city kingdoms of the Triple Alliance, or should we instead restrict our criteria to include only the Mexica? Surely many of the people living in the three capitals did not identify as bona fide members of the empire. And should our focus be only on the Mexica who lived in a very restricted area of the Valley of Mexico centered on the imperial capital, Tenochtitlan, and its sister city, Tlatelolco? Presumably we should not, because there were numbers of people, including soldiers, merchants, and government officials, who lived outside of the imperial capitals in the conquered territories but who identified as Mexica.

Post-Conquest Demographic Collapse

Tracing descent from the Triple Alliance to modern-day peoples is complicated by yet another historical factor that constitutes one of the greatest disasters in all human history (see Márquez Morfín and Storey this volume). Following the dissolution of the empire in 1521, Spanish colonial policies and a series of epidemics caused the deaths of millions of people throughout Mesoamerica. We know that smallpox swept rapidly through the capital of Tenochtitlan during the Spanish siege of the city (Davies 1980 [1973]:273), with major epidemics of contagious diseases occurring in 1545–1548, 1576–1581, and 1736–1739 (Gibson 1964:137). The loss of human life was staggering, and subsequent social disorganization must have been severe. Peter Gerhard (1972:23–24) estimates that, of the 22 million people in the empire at its height, fewer than 1 million people survived the decades after the Conquest. Charles Gibson (1964:141) estimates that a population base of 1.5 million people living in the Valley of Mexico at the height of the empire had declined to 70,000 by 1650, the year of the lowest point of decline. We have no evidence about which groups survived or who were among those least affected by the disaster and consequently left descendants to carry on.

Colonial Policies and Identity

Spanish governmental programs further alienated subject populations from their own history, adding to the difficulties of accounting for their genealogical descendants. Anthropologist Edward Spicer showed that Spanish colonial (and later Mexican) policy aimed to remove people from their ancestral land, gather them into new communities, and then, under direction of missionaries and other representatives of the dominant culture, ease the entire community into the local version of European society. Spanish ranchers and hacienda owners recruited labor from these communities, and mixed populations of indigenous people became the major workforce in the national economy. At the same time, nonindigenous people were allowed by law to settle in indigenous territories, and over time they also mixed with the local population. The result of these colonial policies is that individual tribal and ethnic group identity never developed (to the extent that it did among indigenous populations in the United States), while nondifferentiated Indian identity persisted (Spicer 1962:463ff, 567ff). Spicer (1962:573) described this process as one of suspended assimilation. In place of a strong identity with a particular ethnic group, people continued the prehispanic pattern of directing their loyalty to the local community with its indigenous customs, language, and style of living. Ironically, Spanish policies designed to promote assimilation led to a generalized indigenous identity that is often in deliberate opposition to cultural patterns of the Hispanic elites (Sandstrom 2008). In sum, because links to their own history have been interrupted, the identification that contemporary indigenous people have with their own ethnic group is relatively undeveloped and weakened.

Establishing the ethnic identity of contemporary descendants of the Triple Alliance is further complicated by additional sixteenth-century colonial policies developed to establish and maintain order in New Spain. The initial plan of the conquerors was to keep much of the prehispanic political system in place, while Spaniards were to occupy the elite positions in the hierarchy. Spanish authorities thus recognized the indigenous nobility and accorded them privileges in the colonial system that were denied to the average person. Indigenous nobles were allowed to continue collecting tribute from their subjects, and many of the ancient sumptuary laws were maintained. A study of Nahua living in the Valley of Puebla by ethnohistorian John Chance (2008) shows that descendants of the original indigenous nobility expended considerable effort to convince Spanish authorities that they were the rightful heirs to positions of privilege in their respective communities. It can be assumed that the people in the Valley of Mexico and throughout the empire engaged in similar behavior following the Conquest. Chance reveals how strategies used by people aspiring to noble status changed over time to meet evolving conditions, causing the nature of Nahua ethnic identity to shift. Heirs provided documents, often of questionable accuracy, to Spanish courts purporting to trace their ancestry back to the original founders of a community and to noble lines that derived from them. This documentary evidence further complicates efforts to link descendants of the Triple Alliance to people today. However, there is at least one possible exception to these general statements. Following the Conquest, certain people were able to demonstrate their genealogical links the highest ranked prehispanic nobility. Some of the descendants of these ancient indigenous elites are important members of today's Mexican aristocracy (Nutini 1995).

Continuities and Discontinuities in Modern Mexico

As a product of colonialism, New Spain was composed of regions that were ecologically diverse, widely separated, and had little in common with each other. While indigenous people of Mexico shared certain common traditions, they had distinct histories and spoke more than 100 different languages. A few years after the war of independence from Spain (1810–1821), Mexico lost much of its territory to the United States and in the following decades was devastated by the revolution that gave birth to the modern nation. After the Mexican Revolution (1910–1920), government officials, artists, and writers embarked on a program of *indigenismo* to fashion a national identity for the nation. The fundamental strategy involved glorifying the Native American past of the country paying special attention to the Aztecs and, to a lesser extent, the Maya. The Triple Alliance and Maya civilizations were exalted in books, paintings and public murals, movies, dance, school curricula, and advertising, while Spaniards, represented by the figure of Hernán Cortés, were vilified and defined as imperialist usurpers. Indigenismo has undergone a complex history, but in its original conception, contemporary Indians were seen as a hindrance to modernization and economic progress (Barnet-Sanchez 2001:42–44). As a result of this effort at creating a national identity, many contemporary indigenous people in Mexico with no direct link to the Triple Alliance now claim to be descendants of the ancient Aztecs.

Survival of Cultural Antecedents

In the early 1930s, French historian Robert Ricard (1966[1933]) published a history of the Catholic Church's activities in Mexico beginning in the sixteenth century, titled in English *The Spiritual Conquest of Mexico*. Ricard claimed that in the areas where missionaries worked most intensely, such as the Central Highlands, the local populations cast off their ancient pagan religious beliefs and practices and embraced Christianity wholeheartedly. He was writing to counter the work of Mexican anthropologist Manuel Gamio, who had concluded that contemporary religion among indigenous people in Mexico was a syncretic blend of Spanish Catholicism and the prehispanic traditions. Scholars have known for years that aspects of the ancient traditions had survived the Conquest based on court proceedings and the testimony of Spanish chroniclers such as Ruíz de Alarcón (1984[1629]; Taggart 2001). Idolaters who were discovered in possession of ritual paraphernalia or conducting pagan rituals were brought before judges and their cases entered in court records. Ricard (1966[1933]:275ff) states that the heterodox beliefs and practices revealed in the documents can be explained in a number of ways: as reflecting various European origins, as the result of ignorance or errors perpetrated in missionary teachings, or as a product of what he termed "psychology," presumably the unconscious predispositions of native adherents to the old ways. He claimed that they do not, in any case, trace to prehispanic religious belief and worldview. However, in 1960, ethnographer William Madsen (1969[1960]) published a study of folk religion, *The Virgin's Children: Life in an Aztec Village Today*, focusing on the community of Tecospa, then outside of Mexico City and now completely surrounded by urban development. Madsen found, contrary to Ricard's conclusions, that many elements of beliefs, myths, and ritual practices survived from the days of the Aztecs (Stresser-Péan 2009 [2005]:546). He shows that although we cannot be certain that the people of Tecospa were the direct descendants of the Mexica or the other ethnic groups at the head of the Triple Alliance, elements of the ancient culture in the imperial heartland had most definitely persisted into modern times.

Ethnography at the Margins of Mesoamerica

Additional ethnographic research in the highlands of Mesoamerica and on the periphery of the culture area has repeatedly affirmed Madsen's findings. Ethnographers reporting on indigenous communities, located at the margins of Mesoamerica, including Guerrero (Broda and Good 2004; Dehouve 1974), the Huasteca Veracruzana (Gómez Martínez 2002; Sandstrom 1991), Nayarit (Furst and Schaeffer 1996; Neurath 2002), Oaxaca (Lipp 1991; Monaghan 1995), the Sierra de Puebla (Dow 1986; Ichon 1973 [1969]; Taggart 1997), Tlaxcala (Nutini 1968), as well as the Maya region (Vogt 1976) present copious evidence that ancient traditions and beliefs, although modified by time and distance, are still at the center of many people's lives. As Ricard (1966 [1933]:280–281) admitted, the greatest survival of Native American traditions has been in the regions furthest removed from direct Spanish influence. These areas for the most part were never urbanized and thus lack documents from the early chroniclers. The Spaniards were little interested in recording traditions from the empire's rural areas that contained fewer valuable minerals or trade goods and also lacked sufficient populations as sources of labor. It is in the realms of language and religion that the ancient beliefs are easiest to detect. Many of the religious beliefs, myths and oral histories, and ritual practices documented by anthropologists in these remote regions probably did not derive directly from urban centers. They undoubtedly originated instead from a time predating the appearance of cities and empires in the highlands. Ancient Mesoamerican traditions forged over the millennia and persisting today in small villages throughout the periphery likely provided the fundamental substrate upon which sophisticated urban dwellers and founders of empire elaborated their religious systems in the service of the emerging state.

Nahuas of the Huasteca and Cultural Continuity

An excellent case in point is the Nahua of the southern Huasteca, who live outside of the highlands in one of the most indigenous regions of Mexico. The people living in rural communities speak Nahuatl in everyday communication and call themselves Mexica, but whether they represent actual descendants of the inhabitants of the Valley of Mexico is difficult to prove (although Nahua from the Triple Alliance moved into the region prior to the coming of the Europeans) (Berdan, et al. 1996:291–293; Berdan and Anawalt 1997:131–141; Provost 1975:28–29). The Huastecan Nahua have also undergone a traumatic history, and their culture has undergone dramatic change over the centuries. What is clear, however, is that Nahua religious beliefs and rituals, as well as other aspects of their social life and customs, are rooted in the ancient traditions of Mesoamerica. A brief enumeration of beliefs and ritual practices illustrates the case for cultural continuity: a pantheistic religion (alien to Christianity), based on a single, sacred animating principle; a pantheon of spirit entities or aspects of the sacred principle that overlap with that recorded among the sixteenth-century Mexica, including spirits or personifications of water, clouds, rain, earth, sacred hills, sun, seeds, fire, death, and a host of underworld figures; belief in transforming sorcerers and disease-causing winds; extensive use of ritual paper-cutting involving the sprinkling of animal blood on paper images of the spirit entities, a practice specifically recorded among the Mexica by the chronicler Bernardino de Sahagún (1950–1969[1575–1580?], Part 10, Book 9:9–11); use of copal incense, flowers, cornmeal, and tobacco as offerings; elaborate pilgrimages to sacred mountains, caves, springs, and geographic anomalies; a well-developed cycle of myths that overlap significantly with those recorded in the sixteenth century; ritual observances tied to the calendrical cycle, which feature sacred music, dancing, chanting, spirit possession by male and female ritual specialists called people of knowledge, and construction of elaborate altars. The listing of religious beliefs and practices could be extended indefinitely and matched with cultural information recorded among the Mexica in Tenochtitlan; very few of these elements were introduced by the conquering Spaniards. What is impossible to determine from the historical records is whether the Nahua of the southern Huasteca inherited their religion from the ancient Mexica of the Valley of Mexico, or whether both religions simply partake of an older, widespread Pan-Mesoamerican tradition. In favor of the latter explanation, non-Nahua people in in the Huasteca region such as Otomí and Tepehua also exhibit these features in their beliefs and rituals.

Understanding Pan-Mesoamerican Religious Beliefs and Practices

Because the cultures of Mesoamerica are historically related and so intertwined, anthropologists and other researchers are wise to compare religious beliefs and practices among contemporary people with those recorded among the Mexica in the sixteenth century. The ancient religion has been well documented by the chroniclers, and their writings are sources of insight that aid in interpreting modern ethnographic data. Study of indigenous peoples today can likewise be an invaluable resource for ethnohistorians working to better understand these ancient cultures. Of course, such comparisons must be undertaken with great care. Furthermore, if there is historical evidence that people of the Triple Alliance occupied a given region, it appears legitimate to call their Nahua descendants living in the same region by the equivocal term *Aztec*. This practice is commonly used by researchers (e.g., Madsen 1969; Sandstrom 1991) and should not be a source of confusion for readers.

Aztec Historiography and Ethnography

Many Mexicans today identify very strongly with the Aztecs regardless of the ambiguous nature of that designation. They consider themselves descendants of the Aztec Empire, an identity that separates them from Spain and the rest of Europe and gives their nation a unique character. The federal government spends large sums in excavating Aztec archaeological sites almost as a sacred mission, the entire country is saturated with Aztec symbols, and children are taught to be proud of their Native American heritage. Aztec identity has spread beyond the border and has been taken up in the United States by Chicanos who proclaim that the American Southwest is the site of Aztlán, the mythic Aztec homeland (Fields and Zamudio-Taylor 2001). Half a millennium separates people today from the people of the Triple Alliance, who can be credited with founding the largest empire in the New World. But, as we have seen, history ultimately fails us when it comes to identifying their descendants in the contemporary world. The documentary record yields no clear answers. Ethnography—with its focus on culture—serves us better. While history records discontinuities, ethnography reveals continuities with the past. Ethnography may not connect the people of the sixteenth century with specific people living today through genealogical links, but it can show that Mexica of the Triple Alliance and contemporary Nahua (and other Native American groups as well) partake of a common prehispanic Mesoamerican cultural system tracing back thousands of years. It is testimony to the power of culture to survive and thrive under seemingly hopeless circumstances, given the devastating events that have befallen the people of this world region since the sixteenth century and that continue today in the struggle over indigenous people's rights to define their own identity and intellectual property (e.g., see Lupo 1998).

Ethnogenesis and the Creation of an Aztec Identity

Ethnic identity is now seen by many anthropologists as actively created by local people who find it in their interest to separate themselves from other groups in the society. In this view, identity is much more than simply a dead inheritance from the past (Stark and Chance 2008). A common term for this process is *ethnogenesis*—the creation of ethnic difference (Sandstrom 2008:150). Although biological relationships are commonly invoked in explaining ethnic difference, the sharing of biological substance among people is unrelated to ethnicity. For people engaged in ethnogenesis, what matters is the creation of difference from other groups, not historical accuracy or biological relatedness. Many markers of ethnic groups throughout the world have no historical salience. From this perspective we can see that the inability of contemporary people to trace genealogical links to the Aztecs does not invalidate the creation of Aztec identity. Ethnic difference is closely related to cultural difference, and herein lies a dilemma for social science. Culture increasingly appears to be contingent, based on opposition with other systems, founded on people's self-interest, and constantly in process—not the complex whole in its original modern definition by Edward B. Tylor (1871) in his classic work *Primitive Culture*. At the same time, all cultural and ethnic identities are authentic in that they provide meaning for people regardless of whether they are based on historical or biological facts. We require far more sophisticated theories to account for such a complex social phenomenon as ethnogenesis.

Authentic Descendants of the Aztec Empire

Who are the contemporary descendants of the Aztec Empire? Just as the historical Aztecs have receded into the mists of time, their authentic descendants are the people who invoke them in the creation of their own identity. They are to be found in Native American villages throughout Mexico, where people may or may not call themselves *Mexica* but have used their historical legacy to forge identities in opposition to the dominant Hispanic culture. They can be found among the Mexican citizens migrating to the United States and other countries in search of work, in the Chicano populations in the new Aztlán of the American West whose art celebrates their links to prehispanic civilizations, and anywhere people locate their identity in the historical legacy of ancient

Highland Mesoamerica. The Aztecs and their descendants are very much a part of the contemporary world.

References Cited

Barnet-Sanchez, Holly
2001 Indigenismo and Pre-Hispanic Revivals. In *The Oxford Encyclopedia of Mesoamerican Cultures*, Vol. 2, edited by David Carrasco, pp. 42–44. Oxford University Press, Oxford.

Berdan, Frances F.
2008 Concepts of Ethnicity and Class in Aztec-Period Mexico. In *Ethnic Identity in Nahua Mesoamerica: The View from Archaeology, Art History, Ethnohistory, and Contemporary Ethnography*, edited by Frances F. Berdan, John K. Chance, Alan R. Sandstrom, Barbara L. Stark, James M. Taggart, and Emily Umberger, pp. 105–132. University of Utah Press, Salt Lake City.

Berdan, Frances F., and Patricia Rieff Anawalt (editors)
1997 *The Essential Codex Mendoza*. University of California Press, Berkeley.

Berdan, Frances F., Richard E. Blanton, Elizabeth Hill Boone, Mary G. Hodge, Michael E. Smith, and Emily Umberger (editors)
1996 *Aztec Imperial Strategies*. Dumbarton Oaks Research Library and Collection, Washington, DC.

Broda, Johanna, and Catharine Good Eschelman (editors)
2004 *Historia y vida ceremonial en las comunidades mesoamericanas: Los ritos agrícolas*. Instituto Nacional de Antropológia e Historia; Universidad Nacional Autónoma de México, Mexico City.

Carrasco, Pedro
2001 Triple Alliance. In *The Oxford Encyclopedia of Mesoamerican Cultures*, Vol. 3. edited by David Carrasco, pp. 266–267. Oxford University Press, Oxford.

Chance, John K.
2008 Indigenous Ethnicity in Colonial Central Mexico. In *Ethnic Identity in Nahua Mesoamerica: The View from Archaeology, Art History, Ethnohistory, and Contemporary Ethnography*, edited by Frances F. Berdan, John K. Chance, Alan R. Sandstrom, Barbara L. Stark, James M. Taggart, and Emily Umberger, pp. 133–149. University of Utah Press, Salt Lake City.

Davies, Nigel
1980 [1973] *The Aztecs: A History*, 1st ed. University of Oklahoma Press, Norman.

Dehouve, Danièle
1974 *Corvée des saints et luttes des marchands*. Klincksieck, Paris.

Dow, James W.
1986 *The Shaman's Touch: Otomí Indian Symbolic Healing*. University of Utah Press, Salt Lake City.

Fields, Virginia M., and Victor Zamudio-Taylor
2001 *The Road to Aztlan: Art from a Mythic Homeland*. Los Angeles County Museum of Art, Los Angeles.

Furst, Peter T., and Stacy B. Schaeffer (editors)
1996 *People of the Peyote: Huichol Indian History, Religion, and Survival*. Albuquerque: University of New Mexico Press.

Gerhard, Peter
1972 *A Guide to the Historical Geography of New Spain*. Cambridge Latin American Studies Vol. 14. Cambridge University Press, Cambridge.

Gibson, Charles
1964 *The Aztecs Under Spanish Rule: A History of the Indians of the Valley of Mexico, 1519–1810*. Stanford University Press, Stanford, CA.

Gómez Martínez, Arturo
2002 *Tlaneltokilli: La espiritualidad de los nahuas chicontepecanos*. Ediciones del Programa de Desarrollo Cultura de la Huasteca, Conaculta, Mexico City.

Hicks, Frederic
2001a Ethnicity. In *The Oxford Encyclopedia of Mesoamerican Cultures*, Vol. 1, edited by David Carrasco, pp. 388–392. Oxford University Press, Oxford.
2001b Social Stratification. In *The Oxford Encyclopedia of Mesoamerican Cultures*, Vol. 3, edited by David Carrasco, pp. 152–155. Oxford University Press, Oxford.

Ichon, Alain
1973 *La religión de los Totonacas de la Sierra*. Colección SEP-INI No. 16. Instituto Nacional Indígena, Secretaría de Educación Pública, México, D.F. Originally published 1969, Centre National de la Recherche Scientifique, Paris.

Kaufman, Terrence
1994 The Native Languages of Meso-America. In *Atlas of the World's Languages*, edited by Christopher Moseley and R. E. Asher, pp. 34–41. Routledge, New York.

López Austin, Alfredo
2001 Aztecs. In *The Oxford Encyclopedia of Mesoamerican Cultures*, Vol. 1, edited by David Carrasco, pp. 68–72. Oxford University Press, Oxford.

Lint-Sagarena, Roberto
2001 Aztlán. In *The Oxford Encyclopedia of Mesoamerican Cultures*, Vol. 1, edited by David Carrasco, pp. 72–73. Oxford University Press, Oxford.

Lipp, Frank J.
1991 *The Mixe of Oaxaca: Religion, Ritual, and Healing*. University of Texas Press, Austin.

Lupo, Alessandro
1998 Los cuentos de los abuelos: Un ejemplo de construcción de la memoria entre los nahuas de la Sierra Norte de Puebla, México. *Anales de la Fundación Joaquín Costa* 15:263–284.

Madsen, William
1969 *The Virgin's Children: Life in an Aztec Village Today*. Greenwood Press, Westport, CT. Originally published 1960, University of Texas Press, Austin.

Monaghan, John
1995 *Covenants with Earth and Rain: Exchange, Sacrifice, and Revelation in Mixtec Sociality*. Civilization of the American Indian Series Vol. 219. University of Oklahoma Press, Norman.

Neurath, Johannes
2002 *Las fiestas de la Casa Grande*. Colección Etnografia en el Nuevo Milenio Serie Estudios Monográficos. Instituto Nacional de Antropológia e Historia, México, City, Universidad de Guadalajara, Guadalajara.

Nutini, Hugo G.
1968 *San Bernardino Contla: Marriage and Family Structure in a Tlaxcalan Municipio*. University of Pittsburgh Press, Pittsburgh, PA.
1995 *The Wages of Conquest: The Mexican Aristocracy in the Context of Western Aristocracies*. University of Michigan Press, Ann Arbor.

Provost, Paul Jean
1975 Culture and Anti-Culture Among the Eastern Nahua of Northern Veracruz, Mexico. Ph.D. dissertation, Department of Anthropology, Indiana University, Bloomington.

Ricard, Robert
1966 *The Spiritual Conquest of Mexico: An Essay on the Apostolate and the Evangelizing Methods of the Mendicant Orders in New Spain: 1523-1572*. Translated by Lesley Bird Simpson. University of California Press, Berkeley. Originally published 1933, *La Conquête spirituelle du Mexique*, Institut d'Ethnologie, Paris.

Ruíz de Alarcón, Hernando
1984 [1629] *Treatise on the Heathen Superstitions That Today Live Among the Indians Native to This New Spain, 1629*. Edited and translated by J. Richard Andrews and Ross Hassig. Civilization of the American Indian Series Vol. 164. University of Oklahoma Press, Norman.

Sahagún, Fray Bernardino de
1950-1969 [1575-1580?] *Florentine Codex: General History of the Things of New Spain*. Edited and translated by Arthur J. O. Anderson and Charles E. Dibble. Monographs of the School of American Research No. 14, Parts 1-13. School of American Research, Santa Fe, NM, and University of Utah Press, Salt Lake City.

Sandstrom, Alan R.
1991 *Corn is Our Blood: Culture and Ethnic Identity in a Contemporary Aztec Indian Village*. Civilization of the American Indian Series Vol. 206. University of Oklahoma Press, Norman.
2008 Blood Sacrifice, Curing, and Ethnic Identity Among Contemporary Nahua of Northern Veracruz, Mexico. In *Ethnic Identity in Nahua Mesoamerica: The View from Archaeology, Art History, Ethnohistory, and Contemporary Ethnography*, edited by Frances F. Berdan, John K. Chance, Alan R. Sandstrom, Barbara L. Stark, James M. Taggart, and Emily Umberger, pp. 150-182. University of Utah Press, Salt Lake City.

Spicer, Edward H.
1962 *Cycles of Conquest: The Impact of Spain, Mexico, and the United States on the Indians of the Southwest, 1533-1960*. University of Arizona Press, Tucson.

Stark, Barbara L., and John K. Chance
2008 Diachronic and Multidisciplinary Perspectives on Mesoamerican Ethnicity. In *Ethnic Identity in Nahua Mesoamerica: The View from Archaeology, Art History, Ethnohistory, and Contemporary Ethnography*, edited by Frances F. Berdan, John K. Chance, Alan R. Sandstrom, Barbara L. Stark, James M. Taggart, and Emily Umberger, pp. 1-37. University of Utah Press, Salt Lake City.

Stresser-Péan, Guy
2009 *The Sun God and the Savior: The Christianization of the Nahua and Totonac in the Sierra Norte de Puebla, Mexico*. Mesoamerican Worlds: From the Olmecs to the Danzantes. University Press of Colorado, Boulder. Originally published 2005, *Le Soleil-Dieu et le Christ*, L'Harmattan, Paris.

Taggart, James M.
1997 *The Bear and His Sons: Masculinity in Spanish and Mexican Folktales*. University of Texas Press, Austin.
2001 Nahua. In *The Oxford Encyclopedia of Mesoamerican Cultures*, Vol. 2, edited by David Carrasco, pp. 359-363. Oxford University Press, Oxford.

Tylor, Edward B.
1871 *Primitive Culture: Researches into the Development of Mythology, Philosophy, Religion, Language, Art and Custom*. John Murray, London.

Umberger, Emily
2008 Ethnicity and Other Identities in the Sculptures of Tenochtitlan. In *Ethnic Identity in Nahua Mesoamerica: The View from Archaeology, Art History, Ethnohistory, and Contemporary Ethnography*, edited by Frances F. Berdan, John K. Chance, Alan R. Sandstrom, Barbara L. Stark, James M. Taggart, and Emily Umberger, pp. 64–104. University of Utah Press, Salt Lake City.

Vogt, Evon Z.
1976 *Tortillas for the Gods: A Symbolic Analysis of Zinacanteco Rituals*. Harvard University Press, Cambridge, MA.

Index

Page numbers in italic indicate illustrations.

Acalá, Jeronimo de, 544
Acamapichtli, 63, 65, 59, 98, 99
Acámbaro, 545
Acapetlahuaya, 487
Acatetelco, 241
Acatlan, 483, 487
accession: rituals of, 120, 124, 166
Acequia Royal (Tenochtitlan), 240
Achiutla, 513
Acolco, 64
Acolhua, 3, 63, 94, 138, 150–151, 236, 237, 238, 239, 241, 443
Acolhuacan, 63, 150, 153, 444
Acolhua dynasty, 204
Acolman, 151
Acosta, José de, 34, 117, 612
  and Tula excavations, 53–54, 55, 56, 60
Acozac, 57
Acuitlapan, 481, 484
administrators, administration, 225, 229, 236, 429–430, 447, 466, 467, 514
  of Gulf Lowlands, 498–501
Africans, 9, 665, 670
agave. *See* maguey
Aglio, Agostino, 697
agriculture, 7–8, 83, 179, 181, 213, 263, 476, 646
  chinampa, 84–85, 182–185, 267–269
  intensification of, 264, 291
  landscape and, 180, 265–267
  land tenure and, 269–270
  market system and, 270–271
  terms for, 130, 137
Agua Bendita obsidian source, Valle de, 332
Aguilar, Francisco de, 34
Ahuitzotl, 25, 26, 27, 124, 286, 487, 497
Alahuitztlan, 487
Alcozauca, 481

algae, 304, 311
alliances, 93, 100, 235, 286
  tripartite, 439–440
  Tututepec, 513–514
  in warfare, 444–445
  See also Triple Alliance
alloys, 319, 320, 321, 322, 324
altars, 57, 58–59, 95, 210, 252, 638
altepetl (*altepeme*), 105, 201, 412, 563
  as capitals, 202–208
  in Central Highlands, 468–471
  Christianization of, 678–679
  churches in, 679–680
  conquests of, 463–464
  cosmological landscape of, 596–598
  evolution of, 146–148
  historical focus on, 121, 124
  marketplaces, 148–149
  and parks, 238–239
  public architecture in, 208–211
  and ritual, 598–599
  in Southern Highlands, 474–488
  and state formation, 149–150, 151
  structure of, 145–146
  territorial organization of, 211–212, 660–661
  and Triple Alliance, 440–441, 449, 470–471, 709
Alva Ixtlilxochitl, Fernando de, 34, 440, 597
Alvarado Tezozomoc, Hernando, 34, 440
Amadis de Gaula, 557
amanteca, 224, 289, 392, 586
amantecayotl, 304, 692–693
Amaquemecan, 150
amaranth (*Amaranthus* spp.), 265
  figures of, 601–602, 616
amate paper, 30

amber, 343, 344
Amecameca rock art, 59
Amuzgo, 480, 513
Anales de Cuauhtitlán, 34
Anales del Museo Nacional (journal), 24
ancestor veneration, 147
Ancient and Modern Mexico (exhibit catalog), 697
Angamuco, 550, 551
animals, 628
    Colonial period, 668–669
    sacrifices of, 578, 615
Antigüedades de la Nueva España (Hernández), 34
Antorcha Campesina, 417
Apaneca, 480
apartment compounds, 146–147
appanage system, 153
aquatic resources, 301–302
    exploitation of, 303–311
aqueducts, 219, 222, 239–240, 241
Aquiach, 525
archaeological materials: conservation of, 41, 44–45, 46–48
archaeology, 23, 177, 473, 510, 611, 625, 661, 695, 715
    Early Colonial period, 646–655
    experimental, 453, 454, 458, 459
    Gulf Lowlands, 502–503
    household, 250–254, 424
    on lake resources, 303–304
    Malinalco, 468–469
    military, 452–454
    of New Fire Ceremony, 631–632
    Purépecha, 548–551
    salt-making, 308–310
architecture, 114, 201
    Calixtlahuaca, 469–470
    conservation of, 45–46
    public, 208–211
    Purépecha, 546–547
    Spanish Colonial, 665–666
    Spanish repurposing of, 690–691
    tecpan, 233–234
    See also by type
Argentina #15 (Mexico City), 667
Armillas, Pedro, 451

army. *See* military
Arqueología Mexicana (journal), 7
arsenopyrite, 319, 322
art(s), 591, 680
    Christian, 682–683
    Colonial production of, 692–694
    role of, 689–690
    visual, 585–592
Arte precolombino de México y de la América Central (Toscano and Toussaint), 698
art history, 9, 698
artifacts: display and curation of, 694–695, 696–697
artisans, 224, 366, 392–393, 428
    patron deities of, 586–587
Art Precolumbien, L' (Basler and Brummer), 698
Asiatic mode of Production concept, 144
Atenco, 64
Athenian Empire, 564–565
Atizapan, 96
Atlantes (Atlantean figures), 53, 65
Atlapulco, San Gregorio, 179, 191, 192
    chinampa system in, 182–185
Atlatonan, 577
Atlauhco, 614
Atlicahualo, 109
Atliztacan, 484
Atotonilco de Pedraza, 463
Atotonilco de Tula, 64
Atzacualco (Tenochtitlan), 100, 606
Atzcapotzalco, 96, 98, 100, 112
Augustinians, 675
autosacrifice, 59, 407, 538, 600
Axayacatl, 27, 66, 103, 120, 205, 468, 487, 497, 591
    palace of, 236, 241, 664
axe-monies, 322
axis mundi, 180–181, 598, 615
Axocopan, 463
Ayauhcalco, 598
Ayotlan, 483
Ayutla, 483
Azcapotzalco, 63, 130, 150, 151, 152, 166, 236, 294n.2, 365, 440, 442, 445, 585
    and Tenochtitlan, 219, 239
Azcatzpozalco, 320

Aztec: use of term, 3, 707–708
Aztec Calendar Stone. *See* Sun Stone
Aztec I pottery, 77, 356, 357, 358, 529
Aztec II period, 149, 150, 253
    in Xaltocan, 254–256
Aztec II pottery, 56, 63, 77, 356, 358
Aztec III period, 149, 150, 256
Aztec III pottery, 56, 57, 60, 61, 77, 356–357, 358–359, 529, 649
    Gulf Lowlands, 499, 500
Aztec IV pottery, 60, 61, 77, 358, 359, 647–648, 649
Aztec Orange Ware, 647
Aztec period, 63–64, 149
Aztec Plain Orange, 649
Aztec Warfare Imperial Expansion and Political Control (Hassig), 452
Aztlán, 2, 95, 409n.1, 708
    migrations from, 3, 32, 94
    Tenochtitlan's reproduction of, 240, 596

ballcourts, 57, 58, 65, 210, 222, 511, 664
Balsas-Mezcala basin, 473, 480, 486, 488, 548
Bandelier, Adolphus, 451
baptism, 676–677
baptismal fonts, 693–694
Baratillo, 665
bark paper, 253
Barlow, Robert H., 482–483
baskets, 302, 304
Basler, A., 698
bathing ritual, *379, 390*
Batres, Leopoldo, 24, 204
Becker, Marjorie, 414
Belize, 320
bells: metal, 319, 320–321, 322
Benavente, Toribio de (Motolinía), 34, 114, 117, 607
biface preforms: obsidian, 337–338
Black-on-Orange (Black/Orange) pottery, 76, 77, *367*, 529, 630, 647, 669
    in Gulf Lowlands, 499–500
    sequence of, 356–359
Black-on-Red pottery, 649
blades: obsidian, 285–286, 290, 291, 337, 516
bloodletting, 600, 624
Boas, Franz, 76

bone tools, 254
book keepers, 225
books, 30
    Christian, 681–682
    history, 121–125
    painted, 117–118
    See also codices
Borgia Group documents, 31
botanical remains. *See* plants
Bourbon reforms, 695
Bravo, Valle de, 633
broad sword, *337, 453, 458*
Brokmann, Carlos, 452
bronze bells, 319, 322
Brumfiel, Elizabeth, 204
Brummer, E., 698
Brussels: Aztec artworks in, 694–695
Bullock, William, 696–697
bundles (*tlaxilacaltin*), 147, 576
bureaucratization, 152, 153
burials, 26, 59, 253, 376, 547, 613, 625–626, 633, 670
    household, 251, 252, 256
Burnt Palace (Tula), 55–56

Cacamatzin, 164, 166
cacao beans, 224
caches, 345–346. *See also* offerings
Calendar Round, 107, 109, 112
calendars, calendrical cycles, 23, 380, 572–573, 585
    codex descriptions of, 30, 31
    post-Conquest structure of, 114–*115*
    ritual, 599, 612–613
    structure of, 107–110
    See also by type
Calixtlahuaca, 204, 205, *209*, 212, 214, 266, *425*, 467, 625, 652
    monuments at, 469–470
Callejón del Horno, 500–501
Calligraphic Black/Orange pottery, 358
calmecac, 118, 153, 211, 225, 238, 390, 470
    ceramic merlons from, 45, *46*
    in Cholula, 528–529
    in Tenochtitlan, 611, 614
Calnek (Tenochtitlan), 191, 193
calpixque, calpixqui, 225, 429–430, 447, 466, 467

Calpulalpan, 241
calpolli, 94, 100, 118, 272, 289, 346, 392, 412, 616
   in *altepeme*, 206, 213
   Cholula, 525, 527
   commoners in, 426, 427, 428
   and ritual landscapes, 598–599
Caltitlan, 484
Camaxtli, 597
canals, 219–220, 240, 265
Canesco, Jorge, 451
cannibalism, 408
canoes, 222
capes, 376, 377
Capilco: houses in, 252–253, 431
captives, 101, 166, 379, 446, 577, 578, 629
cardinal directions, 104, 180–181, 249
Carta de Religiosos, 485
Cartas de relación (Cortés), 33
cartographies, 483
Casa de las Ajaracas, 47
Casa de las Campanas, 47
Casa de Morelos (Tula), 57
Caso, Alfonso, 665, 698
Caso correlation, 109–110
cassiterite, 319, 322
Caste Wars, 414
catechisms: pictographic, 684–685
cathedral: Mexico City, 241–242, 662
Catholic Church, 675;
syncretism, 712–713
causeways, 83, 222, 241
caves, 376
Ce Acatl Topiltizin Quetzalcóatl, 53, 59, 64, 98, 576
celestial phenomena, 112–113. *See also* Moon; Sun; Venus
Cempoala, 335, 498, 597. *See also* Pachuca-Zempoala region
Cempoallan, 501
Cenote of Sacrifice (Chichen Itza), 322
censers, 624
   elite production of, 287–288, 365
   Texcoco Molded, 499, 500
censuses, 189, 193, 196–197
Centeotl, 586
Central America: metallurgy from, 319, 320

Central Highlands
   city-states in, 468–471
   imperial control, 466–468
   tribute paid by, 464–466
ceramics, 10, 60, 149, 254, 615, 669
   Aztec period, 63–64
   Black/Orange sequence, 356–359
   Cholula polychrome ceramics, 528–529
   chronology of, 75–78
   Early Colonial period, 647–652
   Gulf Lowlands, 499–500
   organization of production, 364–368
   Otumba production of, 288–289, 290
   Purépecha, 546, 549
   for ritual feasting, 629–630
   technology, 359–364
   from Tula, 55, *61–63*
   from Tututepec, *517*, 518
   typologies, 355–356
ceremonies, 446
   public, 213, 611–612
   See also rituals; *by type*
Cervantes de Salazar, Francisco, 530
Ce Tecpatl, 573
chacmool sculptures, 56, 65, 66
chain of command, 456
Chalcas, 94
chalchihuites, 344
Chalchihuitl, 344
chalchihuitl disks, 233
Chalchiuhtlicue, *119*, 575, 600, 602
Chalco, 34, 60, 150, 151, 294n.2, 625
   ceramic production, 365, *367*
   tribute, 442, 448
   in Triple Alliance, 444, 445
Chalco, Lake, 269, 302, 303, 358
Chalco tradition, 357
Chantico, 586, 614
Chapultepec, 32, 59, 96, 600
Chapultepec aqueduct, 219, 222, 241
Chapultepec Park, 238–239
Charles IV, Emperor, 696
Charles V (Carlos V), King, 165, 501, 694
Charlton, Thomas, 643
Chatino, 513
Chiapan, 463, 467
Chiapas, 320, 344, 376

Chiauhtlan, Chiautlan, 463, 483, 484
Chichen Itza, 58, 93, 322
Chichihualcuauhco, 408, 626
Chīchīmēcah, 129–130
Chichimecas, Chichimecs, 94, 95, 98, 144, 146, 597
Chichimecatl Teuctli, 443
Chicomecoatl Iteopan, 613
Chicome Xochitl, 586
Chicomoztoc (Seven Caves), 32, 94, 95, 597
Chiconahui Itzcuintli, 586
Chiconautla, 239, 292, 310, 632
childbirth, 26, 379, 394–395
childcare, 388
children, 181, 390, 391, 408, 524, 625
Chimalhuacan, 150
Chimalhuacan Atenco, 239
chimalli, 166, 167, 379, *458*
Chimalma, 578, 579. *See also* Coatlicue
Chimalpopoca, 65
Chimalzolca (Cholula), 525
chinampas, 7–8, 153, 179, 182–*185*, 267–269
  Late Aztec period, 84–85
  in Tenochtitlan, 222, 224
Chinampeca, 63
Chinantec, 495
Chocho, 129, 480
Cholula, 93, 104, 165, 191, 252, 517, 596, 597, 598
  burials in, 625–626
  induction ceremonies at, 523–524
  Late Postclassic period, 525–530
  Quetzalcoatl's temple in, 527–528
  spindle whorls from, 376, 380, *381*
Chontal, 129, 480, 513
Chontalcoatlan, 487
Chontal Maya, 496
Christianity, 675, 678, 681–682
Christianization: of indigenous peoples, 162, 675–678, 684–685
chronicles: Spanish colonial, 33–35
chronology, 112
  ceramics and, 75–77, 355–359
  Tula, 55, 59, 60
Chumbio, 480
churches
  layout and placement of, 679–680
  Spanish Colonial, 678–679

syncretic art in, 693–694
Cihuacoatl, 378, *380*, 394–395, 446
cihuacoatl, 394, 579–580
Cihuacoatl Tlacaelel, 101
Cihuatecpan, 237, 238, 239, 253, 625, 628, 649
Cihuateotl, 470
Cihuateteo, *cihuateotl*, *395*, 600
Cihuatlan, 473, 483
cihuatlatoque, 393
Cintla, 483
Cipactónal, 180
cities, 202–204, 214
  public architecture, 208–211
  sizes of, 205–208
  See also altepetl (altepeme)
Citlalicue, 406
Citlallatónac, 406
Citlaltepec, 310
city-states, 84
  Greek, 564–565
  See also altepetl(altepeme)
clans, 93, 94, 412
Classic period, 143, 191
  Purépecha, 548, 549
  See also by subperiod
clay: characteristics and sources, 360–361, *362*
climate, 124
cloth: cotton, 224, 378, 424
Coateocalli (Coacalco), 610
coatepantli, 53–54, 65, 589
Coatepec, 21, 120, 571, 596
  Mexica at, 95–96
  Templo Mayor as, 605, 608, 610, 615, 616–617n.2
coatequitl, 213
Coatetelco, *202*, 210
Coatlicue, 6, 21, 23, 103, 579, 695, 696
Coatlicue: Estética del arte indígena antiguo (Fernández), 698
Coatlinchan, Coatlichan, 63, 100, 151, 294n.2, 440
Coatlinchan-Huexotla, 150
coats of arms: indigenous, 166–167
Coatzacoalcos, 500
Coaxintecuhtli, 518
Coayxtlahuacan, 473, 483
cochineal (*Dactylopus coccus*), 291

Codex Aubin (*Codex de 1576*), 32, 95, 125
Codex Azcatitlán, 59
Codex Bodley, 512, 518, 523
Codex Borbonicus, 30, 118, 591
Codex Borgia, 528, 572, 591
Codex Boturini, 96, 121
Codex Chimalpopoca, 34
Codex Colombino-Becker, 512, 518
Codex (Códice) de Cholula, 525, 530
Codex (Códice) de los Alfarreros, 365
Codex de tributos de Coyoacán, 32
Codex Fejérváry-Mayer, 113–114
Codex Florentino; Florentine Codex
    (Sahagún), 33, 138, 249, 389, 409, 623
  on art, 586, *587*
  ceramic production, 360, *363*, 365, 366
  obsidian source, 332, *333*
Codex Huitzilopochtli, 31
Codex Ixlilxóchitl, 457
Codex Kingsborough, 32, 432
Codex Magliabechiano, 31, 57
Codex Matritenses, 32
Codex Mendoza, 32, 113, 123, 270, 377, 444, 455, 465, 473, 502, 692
  on provinces, 482, 483–484
Codex Mexicanus, 32, 124–*125*
Codex Moteuczoma, 121
Codex Nuttall, 512, 513, 518
Codex Rios (*Codex Vaticano A*), 31, 575
Codex Saville, 121
Codex Telleriano-Remensis, 31, 32
Codex Tudela (*Codex del Museo de América*), 31
Codex Xolotl, 121, 150, 597
codices, 29, 691–692
  Colonial era, 30–31, 32–33
  history in, 31–32
  records in, 117–118
  See also by name
Cohuatitlan, 96
Cohuixca, 137, 481, 486
Cohuixco pueblos, 487
Colección de las Antigüedades Mexicanas que existen en el Museo Nacional, 696
Colhua, 96, 601
Colhuacan, 94, 100, 104, 120
  historic depictions of, *123*, 124

  Mexica as vassals to, 96, 98
Colhuatepec, 596
Colima, 321, 543
collaboration, 11
  in conservation efforts, 42–43, 48
collections, 43, 694–695, 696–697, 698
collective action theory, 10, 536–537
Colonial period, 11, 162, 365, 712
  assimilation policies, 710–711
  censuses, 189, 193
  codices, 30–32
  depopulation, 194–195
  Gulf Lowlands, 501–502
  household structure in, 248–249
  Mexico City, 661–670
  Nahua ethnicity, 411–412
  population recovery, 195–198
Colonization Laws, 415
commemorations, 9, 23
commerce, 10, 281
  agents of, 284–287
  and long-distance trade, 293–294
  markets and, 282–284
  in Otumba, 287–292
  Postclassic, 144, 148–149
  and tribute relationships, 292–293
  See also markets, marketplaces; trade
commoners, 100, 146, 147, 180, 181, 345, 423, 455
  agriculture, 271–272
  ceramic production, 364–365, 366
  dependent, 426–427
  households and commerce, 282, 283, 284
  houses of, 212–213, 249, 252–253
  wealth variation among, 425–426, 428–431
communities, 250
  lake resource specialization by, 310–311
  tecpans in, 233, 234
Conciliar Seminary (Mexico City), 667
concubines, 393
confederacies, 149–150
conflict: interethnic, 413–414
confraternities (*cofradías*), 680
congregaciones, 646–647, 711
conquests, 444, 456, 513
  of Central Highlands, 463–464
  of Huitzlampa, 486–488

of Tlatelolco, 590–591
by Triple Alliance, 446–447
conquistadors, 9, 232, 690
  indigenous, 162–163, 166–167
conservation
  of archaeological materials, 41, *44–45*, 46–48
  Templo Mayor, 45–46
  Templo Mayor Project, 42–43
Conservatorio de Antigüedades (Conservatory of Antiquities), 41
Convent of the Conception, 23
copal, 47
Copalitech, 484
Copil, 96
copper, 319, 320, 321, 322, 324–325, 548
core-blade workshops: at Otumba, 287–288, 290, 291
corn. *See* maize
corporate neighborhoods. *See calpolli*
corporate organization, 152, 251
Cortés, Hernán, 25, 33, 109, 229, 241, 530, 557, 694, 712
  and Gulf Lowlands, 501, 502
  Motecuhzoma Xocoyotzin's response to, 163–165
Cortés, Martín, 669
cosmogram: fourfold, 600
cosmology, cosmovision, 31, 108, 591, 595
  of Tenochtitlan, 104, 589–590, 606
  and time, 110–111
cosmos, 380, 394, 572–573, 624
  altepetl as model of, 596–598
  and creation cycle, 110–111
  design of, 587–591
  structure of, *111*–112
  time-space realms, *400*, 592
costumes, 377–378
Cotaxtla, 501
cotton, 224, 377, 378, 424, 515–516
Couixcal, Lord, 481, *482*
councils: Triple Alliance, 152–153
courtyards, 222, 234–235
Coyoacan, 167, 222
Coyoaco, 332
Coyolapan, 473, 483
Coyolxauhqui, 9, 21, 22, 23, 45, 96, *590*, 698

Coyotlatelco, 55, 235
Coyotl Inaual, 586
craft production, 545
  ceramic, 360–368
  household, 212, 253, 254–256
  lapidary objects, 345, 347, 350–352
  specialists, 284, 285–289, 290–292
  women and, 392–393
creation, 586, 590
  calendrical symbols of, 588–589
  cycles of, 110–111
  gendered pairs in, 393–394
  of humans, 574–575
  myths of, 573–574, 596
cremations, 524, 625
Crónica Mexicana (Alvarado Tezozomoc), 34
Crónica Mexicayotl (Alvarado Tezozomoc), 34, 100
crops, 265, 646
  in tribute and market system, *270–271*
crosses: atrial, 693
Cruz del Milagro (Sierra de Las Navajas), 330
Cuahuacan, 463
Cuauhnahuac, 445, 448, 463, 467, 468, 486
Cuauhtemoc, 65
Cuauhtitlan, 150, 292, 294n.2, 306, 365, 366, 669, 441–442
Cuauhtitlan River, 267, *268*
Cuauhtlecohuatzin, 65
Cuauhtlequetzqui, 605
Cuauhxicalco, 26, 27
Cuauhxicalli, 66
Cuautitlan, 64
Cubas, García, 59
Cuello volcano, 330
Cuepopan (Tenochtitlan), 100, 606, 664
Cuetlaxtlan, 467, 498, 499, 500, 501
Cuetlaxxochitla, 598–599
Cuetzalan, 413
Cueva y Valenzuela, Francisca de la, 65
Cuexcomate, 213, 252–253, 424, *425*, 431, 632
Cuicatec, 480
Cuitlahuac, 25, 3, 98, 149
Cuitlatec, 129
Cuitlateca, 480
Cuitzeo Basin, 550
Culhuacan, 149, 150, 235, 248, 440, 442, 601

Culhuacan phase, 356
Culhuacan tradition, 357
Culhua-Mexica, 440
Culhuaque, 235
cultivation. *See* agriculture
cultural ecology, 7, 8, 175–176
Curicuaeri, 546–547
curing rituals, 627, 628
Cuyumateca, 480
cypress trees (*ahuehuetl*), 241

Dani neighborhood (Tula), 58
Day Lords, 112
day names, 108, 589
day signs, *108*
death(s), 120, 181, 395, 408–409
deforestation, 647
deformed people, 223
deities, 137, 334, 378, 401, 575–576
  as devils, 683–684
  human impersonators of, 408, 577–578, 580–581, 585, 599, 615
  and landscape, 595–596, 600
  paired, 393–394
  patron, 145, 146, 310, 579–580, 586–587
  Purépecha, 546–547
  ritual cycles and, 180, 181
  rulers and, 406–407
  state promotion of, 612–613
  transformations of, 403–405
Delian League, 564–565
demography, 10–11, 196–*197*
dentists, 225
Department of Conservation: Templo Mayor Project, 42–43
depopulation: post-Conquest, 77–78, *192*, 194–195, 710
descendants
  authentic, 716–717
  cultural syncretism and survival, 712–713
Descripción de la ciudad y provincia de Tlaxcala (Muñoz Camargo), 34
Descripción histórica y cronológica de las dos piedras (Leon y Gama), 23
déspotas armados, un espectro de la guerra prehispánica, Los (Lameiras), 451

devils: Aztec deities as, 683–684
Díaz, Porfirio, 24
Diaz del Castillo, Bernal, 33–34, 163, 166, 225, 229, 270, 502, 525, 557
Dieguillo, Pala Agustin, 413, 415
diet, 430, 668–669
diseases, 194–195, 196, 225
divination, diviners, 118, 225, 573, 581, 684
divine realm, *400*, 585
DNA analysis, 11
documentary records, 6, 9, 161, 178–179
  chronicles, 33–35
  codices, 29–33
  on gender roles, 388–389
  painted books, 117–118
Dominicans, 675
Donceles Street #97 (Mexico City), 666–667, 668
Dresden Codex, 137
dress, 375–376, 394, 412, 651
drums, *458*, 632
drunkenness, 683
duality
  altepetl-park, 238–239
  gender and, 387–388, 393–394
  of human body, 400–401
Dueño, el, 189–191
Dupaix, Guillermo, 695, 696
Durán, Diego, 32, 33, 95, 424, 440, 443, 608
  on household ritual, 623, 624, 632–633
Dürer, Albrecht, 394–395

eagle-cactus foundation symbol, *113*
eagle-feline-serpent triad, 24
Eagle Warrior Precinct, 667
Eagle Warriors, 25, 45
Early Aztec period, 60, 76, 77, 78, 201
  Red wares, 359, *360*
  settlement pattern, 79, 85
Early Colonial period, 10, 643, 645
  ceramics, 647–652
  depopulation in, 194–195
  obsidian use, 652–653
  settlement patterns, 646–647
  trade, 653–654
Early Formative period: Gulf Lowlands, 496–497

Early Postclassic period, 10, 48, 55, 149, 251, 496, 632
  burials, 625–626
  Guerrero, 480–481
  Purépecha, 548, 551
earspools, ear plugs, 291, 338, 345, 351
earth: as body of Tlalteotl, 596
Ecatepec, 57, 96, 310
eclipses, 108, 113
ecology, 145
  Basin of Mexico, 302–303
  cultural, 7, 8, 175–176
  historical, 176–177
economic specialists, 428
economic system, economy, 7, 10, 32, 149
  in Tututepec, 515–517
education, 225, 390
Ehecatl (Ehecatl-Quetzalcoatl), 204, 210, 334, 470, 576, 597, 611, 626, 664
Ejido San Gregorio Altapulco, 182, *184–185*
Ejido Xochimilco, 182
El Canal site (Tula), 251–252
El Cielito (Tula), 58
elections: tlahtoani, 444
elites, 253, 292, 393, 446, 625
  censer production, 287–288, 365
  Christianization of, 677–678, 684–685
  Purépecha, 543, 546, 548
  See also nobility
El Llano (Tula), 58
El Pizarrín obsidian source, 332, 344
El Salitre (Tula), 58, 63–64
El Sauce, 500
El Tesoro, Cerro (Toltacatepetl), 54–55, 59
emotions, 401, *402*
empires
  economy, 560–561
  military, 559–560
  and official religions, 561–562
  Postclassic, 150–151
  resistance to, 563–564
  sizes of, 558–559
employees, 224–225
encomienda system, 64–65, 645, 646
encuentro de la piedra y el acero, El (Lameiras), 451
Epazoyuca, 335

Epcoacuacuilli, 612
Epiclassic period, 55, 147, 535, 549, 551
epidemics, 194–195, 196
Era of the Fifth Sun, 32
Escuela Nacional de Antropología e Historia, 6
estates, 232, 241
  patrimonial, 426, 427, 537–538
  See also palaces
ethnicity, ethnic identity, 2, 530, 545, 709, 711
  in Mexican republic, 413–414
  Nahua, 411–412, 414–415
  Spanish Colonial period, 412–413
ethnogenesis, 716
ethnography, 303, 713–714
  Aztec, 715–716
ethnohistories
  household structure, 248–250
  Postclassic, 143–144
  Purépecha, 544–547
Ethnological Museum (Vatican), 698
Europe: collections in, 696–697
events: and celestial phenomena, 112–113
exchange system, 84, 282, 293, 337. *See also* trade, traders; tribute
exhibits, 8, 696, *697*
Expediciones acerca de los antiguos monumentos de la Nueva España 1805–1808 (Dupaix), 696
Exploraciones en la calle de las Escalerillas (Batres), 24
Exposition universelle, 697

families, 226, 238, 250, 427
  assistance from dead, 408–409
  royal, 121, 144
farmers, 291
  as dependent commoners, 426–427
  land tenure and, 271–272
Fat Cacique, 501–502
faunal remains. *See* animals
feasting, feasts
  household ritual, 629–630
  xihuitl, 108–109
feathered serpent, 59
feathers, 304, 375, 377
featherwork (*amantecayotl*), 304, 692–693

featherworkers (*amanteca*), 224, 289, 392, 586
felines, 24
Felipe II, 65
femurs: as rasps, 632–633
Fernández, Justino, 698
Fernández de Oviedo, Gonzalo, 607
fertility, 181, 627, 628
FES-Acatlan, Universidad Nacional Autónoma de México, 459
Festival of Mountains (Tepeihuitl), 601
festivals, 577, 683
    and landscape, 598–599, 601–602
Fifth Sun, 23, 32, 102, 575
52-year calendrical cycle, 30, 630–631
    festival for, 599, 601
fig bark (*amatl*), 118
figurines, 47, 411
    Aztec, 626–629
    Early Colonial, 651–652
    Otumba production of, 288–289, 290
finance: Triple Alliance, 448–449
fish, fishing, 254, 301, 304, 306, 307, 310
flooding, 647
floors: painted plaster, 252, 253, 256
Flowery War (Xochiyaoyotl), 454–455, 529
flutes: ceramic, 632, 633
food, 412, 430, 455, 577, 624
    Colonial period, 668–669
footwear, 304
foreign travelers, 695–696
Franciscans, 242, 527, 675, 676, 677
Franco, Jose Luis, 56
funerary rites, 225, 625–626

Gabinete de Historia Natural (Department of Natural History), 41
Galindo y Villa, Jesús, 24
Gamio, Manuel, 24, 25, 76, 712
Gante, Pedro de, 692–693
García Bravo, Alonso, 670
García Payón, José, 205
gardens, 201, 229
    Spanish terms for, 232–233
    Tenochtitlan, 240–241, 242
    Texcotzingo, 239–240
Garibay, Ángel María, 162
garments, 375–376

Gazeta de Literatura, 695
Gazeta de México, 695
gendered pairs, 393–394
gender roles, 375, 387
    documentary sources on, 388–389
    life cycles and, 389–393
    warfare and, 395–396
gender systems, 387–388
genealogy, 424
General History of New Spain. See *Historia general de las cosas de Nueva España*
geography. See landscape
glaze wares, 649, 654–655, 669
glottographics, 120
glyphs: structure of, 119–120
gods. See deities
gold, 319, 320, 324, 652
goldworkers, 586, 587
Great Ballcourt (Chichen Itza), 58
Great Coatlicue, 6
Great Compound (Teotihuacan), 148
Great Pyramid (Cholula). See Tlachihualtepetl
green stone, 344, 345, 346, 615
Grijalva expedition, 502
Guanajuato, 543
Guatemala, 320, 344
Guatemala Street #38 (Mexico City), 667
guerra sagrada, La (Canesco), 451
Guerrero, 3, 129, 543, 624, 713
    metalwork from, 321–322
    Nahuatization in, 487–488
    Nahuatl in, 137, 414
    Triple Alliance and, 473, 475–477(table), 480–481, 484
Gulf Lowlands, 3
    administration of, 498–501
    archaeology, 502–503
    ethnic groups in, 495–496
    Spanish Colonial period, 501–502
    as tributary provinces, 497–498
Gutiérrez, Rodrigo, 697
Guzmán, Nuño de, 166

Habsburg/Hapsburg dynasty, 565, 697
hamlets, 80, 190
Handbuch des Kunstgeschichte (Kugler), 698
Hassig, Ross, 452

head, 406
health, 407, 430, 627, 628
heart: divine, 403, 404–405
heaven, 572
Hernández, Francisco, 34, 242
Hidalgo, 194
hide industry, 652
hieroglyphic writing, 30
Híripan, 544–555
Historia de la nación chichimeca (Alva Ixtlilxochitl), 34
Historia de las Indias de Nueva España e islas de Tierra Firme, 33
Historia de las Indias y conquista de México (López de Gómara), 34
Historia de los Indios de la Nueva España (Benavente), 34
Historia de los mexicanos por sus pinturas, 66
Historia general de las cosas de Nueva España (Sahagún), 32, 33, 53, 400
Historia natural y moral de las Indias (Acosta), 34
Historia Tolteca-Chichimeca, 525
Historia verdadera de la Conquista de la Nueva España (Diaz del Castillo), 33–34
historical ecology, 176–177
historiography, 162
  Aztec, 715–716
  of warfare, 451–452
history, histories, 112, 117, 118, 121
  in Colonial codices, 31–32
  local focus of, 124–125
  migration, 94–98, 122–123
  of Spanish Conquest, 161–162
  Toltec, 104–105
Hokan language family, 129
Holy Mountain, 615
Holy Week, 682
Honduras, 320
hospitality buildings, 225
Hot Countries: allies from, 444–445
house groups: in Tula, 251–252
households, 10, 11, 28, 247, 365, 394
  archaeological evidence, 250–254, 424
  figurine sin, 627–629
  markets and, 282, 283, 284

Otumba, 291–292
  ritual feasting, 629–630
  ritual music, 632–633
  rituals, 623–626, 633–634
  structure of, 248–250
  Tenochtitlan, 225, 226
  Tututepec, 515, 516
  urban, 212–213
  in Xaltocan, 254–256
house lots: Mexico City, 663, 664
House of the Eagles, 25, 66, 211, 611
houses, 211, 222, 424, 427, 430
  archaeological evidence, 250–254
  Colonial period, 248, 249–250
  ritual, 623–626
  in Xaltocan, 254–256
Huamuxtitlan, 484
Huapalcalco, 64
Huastec, 495
Huaxteca (Huasteca, Huastecans), 130, 412, 414, 415, 502, 713, 714
Huaxtepec, 240, 242, 463, 465, 466, 467
Huaxyacac (Oaxaca City), 487
huey tecuhihuitl, 612
Huejotzincas, 94
Huejotzingo, 529, 694
Huemac, 152, 153, 524
Huexotla, 61, 204, 212, 214, 271, 294n.2, 365
Hueyapan, 414–415
Huey Teocalli, 597
huey tlahtoani/tlatoque, 152, 424, 440, 448
Huey Tozoztli, 601
Huichilipochco, 310
Huitzilan de Serdán, 425
  insurgency in, 416–417
  Nahuat in, 415–416, 417–418
Huitzilhuitl, 96, 98, 99, 444, 446
Huitzilincuatec, 614
Huitzilopochco, 365
Huitzilopochtli, 3, 21, 32, 102, 379, 561, 571, 575, 589, 590, 591, 597, 610, 612
  birthdate of, 573, 579
  and Mexica migrations, 95–96
  Templo Mayor shrine to, 24, 114, 222–223
  and Tenochtitlan Sacred Precinct, 605–606, 608
Huitzilopochtli Group, 30, 31

Huitzilopochtli-Tonatiuh, 102
Huitzlampa, 480, 487–488. *See also* Southern Highlands
Huitznahuatl Teohuatzin, 614
Huixachtecatl, 601
human body, 399, 418
    duality of, 400–401
    heavy substance of, 401–402
    souls in, 402–407
human remains, 11, 615, 632–633
humans
    creation of, 574–575
    as divine representations, 577–578, 585, 599, 615
Humboldt, Alexander von, 23, 695, 696, 708
hunting, hunters, 310, 311
    ritual, 578–579, 601
    seasonal, 306, 307

identity, 2, 711, 716
    dual, 393–394
    Nahuat, 417–418
    occupation and, 412, 414–415
    residence and, 250, 253
    textile production and, 375, 392
    Toltec influence on, 102–103, 104
    Triple Alliance, 709–710
idols, 23, 344, 682, 690
Igualtepec, 484
ihiyotl, 406
Ihuatzio, 545
Ilhuitl Temoc, 65
illness, 407
images: Christian, 682–683
imago mundi, 104
IMP. *See* inherent military probability
imperialism, 10, 154n.2
Imperial Strategies (Berdan), 483
Inca Empire, 558, 559, 561, 562, 563, 564
incense burning, 624
Indian Movement, 415
indigenismo, 414, 712
indigenous peoples, 9, 196, 654
    Christianization of, 676–677, 680
    in Mexico City, 664–665, 669–670
    See also by group

inequality
    social, 423, 432–433
    wealth, 430–431
infants, 256, 379, 405–406
Información de 1554, 483
inherent military probability (IMP), 456, 457
Inquisition, 565, 684
Inspección de Monumentos, 24
institutional theory-building, 144
Instituto Nacional de Antropología e Historia, 6, 24, 61
insurgencies: agrarian, 415, 416–417
intermarriage, 12, 446
intoxicants, 407
irrigation systems, 7, 82, 182, 267, 647
Islam, 562
Itecouh Tepetl, 596
Iturbide, Agustín de, 41
Itzcoatl, 100, 101, 151, 321, 412, 413, 440, 442–443, 444, 486
Itzlacoliuhqui, 334
Itzli, 334
Itzpapalotl, 334, 512, 518
Itzuco, 480
Ixcateco, 480
Ixcateopan, 430
Ixmiquilpan, 694
Ixtapaluca, 57, 204, 205–206, 210, 442
Ixtepexi, 483
Ixtetes, Barranca de los, 330
Ixtlahuacan, 463
Ixtlilxochitl, 100, 446
Ixtlixochitl, Fernando, 665
Izcalli, 109, 626
Iztaccihuatl, 576, 602
Iztaccihuatl mountain, 596
Iztapalapa, 60, 222
Itztapalapan avenue, 606

jade/jadeite, 344, 345
Jalisco, 319, 321, 543, 550
jewelry, 291, 319, 320, 338, 344, 345, 351, 424
Jiménez Moreno, Wilberto, 54, 59
Justo Sierra #33 (Mexico City), 668, 669

Kelemen, Pál, 698
kilns, 363–364

kinship, 64, 94, 100, 248, 417–418
knives, 58, 59, 291, 329, 333, 338
knowledge
　indigenous, 665–666
　specialized, 237–238
Kubler, George, 698
Kugler, Fanz, 698

labor, 224, 364, 516
　agricultural, 264, 265, 271–272
　commoners, 180, 213, 426–427
　corvée, 100, 281, 432
　lake resource exploitation, 306–308
　Spanish colonial system, 645, 665
　for Triple Alliance, 445–446
laboresque capital, 265
La Dicha mine, 322
La Garrafa cave, 376
lake resources, 84, 301–302, 304
　extraction and processing of, 254–256
　specialized exploitation of, 306–308
lakes, 7, 8, 84, 96
　in Basin of Mexico, 75, 83, 301–303
La Malinche (Tula), 58
La Malinche, Cerro (Coayahualco), 59
Lameiras, José, 451
land, 87, 100, 263, 265, 413
　agriculture and, 269–270
　common, 271–272
　commoner access to, 426–427
　pictographic records of, 117–118
　Triple Alliance, 443–444
landesque capital, 264, 269–270
landscape, 177
　agricultural systems and, 180, 265–269
　paintings of historical, 697–698
　ritual/sacred, 179, 182–185, 589–590, 595–602, 607
landscaping: in Tenochtitlan, 229. *See also* parks
languages
　of Aztec Empire, 129–138, 412
　Southern Highlands, 480, *481*
lapidaries, lapidary art, 392, 586, 615
　materials used in, 343–345
　Otumba, 289, 290, 291, 350–352
　perceived attributes of, 345–346

Late Aztec period, 76, 77–78, 360
　city sizes, 207–208(table)
　population growth, 82–83
　pyramids, 208–209
　settlement pattern, 79, 80, *81–82*, 83–84, 85
Late Postclassic-Colonial transition, 178–179
Late Postclassic period, 3, 59, 191, 248, 271, 303, 308, 500
　Cholula, 525–530
　Purépecha Empire, 543, 548
　Triple Alliance of, 644–645
　Tula region, 60–63
Late Toltec period, 78
　settlement pattern, 80, *81–82*, 85
La Union mine, 322
leaders, 94, 100
　duality, 579–580
　See also nobility
lead-glazed pottery, 669
Lehman, Walter, 698
Leon de Gama, Antonio de, 23
León-Portilla, Miguel, 162
Lewis, Oscar, 414
Ley de Lerdo, 413, 415
Leyenda de los soles, 34
Liberation Theology, 415
libraries, 118
　in Tenochtitlan, 104–105
Lienzo de Tlapa, 482
Lienzo de Tlaxcala, 162
lienzos, 118, 162, 482
life cycles, 23
　gender and, 389–393
life expectancy, 197–198, 430
Light Detection and Ranging (LiDAR), 550–551
lineages, 93, 147–148
lingua franca: Nahuatl as, 137–138
livestock, 646, 647, 668
loan words, 130, 137
Lockhart, James, 162, 205–206
logographics, 120
Loma Alta, 549
Lomnitz-Adler, Claudio, 414
López, Jerónimo, 270
López de Gómara, Francisco, 34, 163, 612
Lopez de Velasco, 34

Lord 4 Jaguar, 523, 524
Lord 8 Death, 523
Lord 8 Deer (Jaguar Claw), *512*–513, 514, 518, 523
Lords of the Night, 112
Luz y Fuerza del Centro, 24

Macana red-on-brown, 55
Macayapan, 500
macehualtin. *See* commoners
Macro-Otomangue language, 480
macuahuitl, *337*, *453*, *458*
Macuilcalli, 586
Macuil Ocelotl, 586
Macuil Tochtli, 586
Madsen, William, 713
Magliabechiano Group, 30, 31
maguey (*Agave* spp.), 59, 84, 118, 265, 266, 375, 377, 378
   processing, 289, 290
maize (*Zea mays*), 23, 181, 265, 401, 418, 577
majolica: Colonial use of, 647, 649–651, 654–655, 669
Malinalcas, 94
Malinalco, 463, 467, 468–469, 694
Malinalxochitl, 95, 96
Malintzin, Malinalli, 376, 502
Manila Market (Parián), 665
manuscripts
Christian, 681–682
copying, 21
Mapa Quinatzin, 121
Mapas de Cuauhtinchan, 525
Mapa Sigüenza, 94, 121, *122*
Mapa Tlotzin, 121
maps, 118, *526*
   of Mexica migration, 94, *122*
   of Tenochtitlan, *103*, *113*
   of tributary provinces, 482–483, *484*, *485*, *486*
marble, 343, 344
markets, marketplaces, 10, 213, 263, 294, 345, *527*, 375, 393, 665
   ceramic distribution, 629–630
   commercial exchange and, 282–284
   empires, 560–561
   lake resources, 306, 307

Otumba, 291–292
peddlers, 286–287
Postclassic, 148–149
producer-sellers, 285–286
Tenochtitlan, 223–224
market system, 10, 145, 282
   agricultural products, 270–271
   Basin of Mexico, 84, 85, 644
   Colonial period, 653–654
marriages, 94, 238, 390, 392, 412, 446, *677*
   cross-ethnic, 413, 481, *482*
Martinez, Pedro, 414
matchmakers, 390
Matlacueye, 596, 598, 600, 601, 602
Matlame, 480
Matlatli Oçomaxoch (10 Monkey Flower), 481, *482*
Matlatzinca, 3, 94, 124, 130, 322, 412, 550, 652
Matlatzinco, 442. *See also* Calixtlahuaca
matlazahuatl (typhus), 196
Matos Moctezuma, Eduardo, 57–58, 608
Matrícula de Huexotzinco, 365–366
Matrícula de Tributos, 32, 455, 465, *482*, *483*
   tribute items in, 321–322
mats (*petates*), 254, 302, 304
Maximilian, Emperor, 697
Maxtla, 100, 151, 166
Maya, 104, 110, 713
Mayan language family, 129, 137
Mazahuas, 3
Mazapan tradition, 77
Mazatzin Moteuczoma, Gonzalo, 163
Mazatzintamalco, 241
Maztlazinco Calixtlahuaca, 633
medical practitioners, 225
medicines, 304
Medieval American Art: Masterpieces of the New World before Columbus (Kelemen), 698
Memorial de Tlacopan, 502
Memoriales (Motolinia), 34
men, 249, 375, 392
Mendoza, Antonio de, 166
mercenaries, 96, 98
merchants, 284, 286, 287, 291–292, 393, 527, 654. *See also pochteca*
merlons, 45, *46*

mestizos, *mestizaje*, 413, 414, 415–416
metallurgy, 289, 319, 546
　Spanish descriptions of, 323–324
　at Tenochtitlan, 320–323
metepantle, 266
Metropolitan Cathedral and Tabernacle
　(Mexico City), 22, 24, 241–242, 662,
　664
Mexicaltzingo, 253, 310, 442
"Mexican Exhibition at the Egyptian Hall"
　(Aglio), 697
Mexican Independence, 413–414, 696
Mexicanishe Kunstgeschichte (Lehman), 698
Mexican Revolution, 414, 712
Mexica phase, 60
Mexicas, 2–3, 104, 714
　migration of, 94–98, 399
　origin myth, 93, 94
　state structure, 101–*102*
　at Tula, 55–56
Mexicatl Teohuatzin, 614
Mexico: ethnic issues in, 413–414
Mexico, Basin of, 3, 5, 61, 97, 175, 189, 265
　depopulation of, 194–195
　lake resources, 301–302
　physical geography of, 74–75
　pre-Conquest population, 190–194
　ritual landscape of, 595–602
　settlement pattern, 78–85
　Settlement pattern survey, 7, 75–78
Mexico City, 21, 130, 645, *663*
　Colonial period life in, 668–670
　population recovery in, 195–198
　residential areas of, 664–665
　space use in, 667–668
　Spanish reconstruction of, 241–242, 661,
　662, 665–667
　trading system, 653–654
Mexico-Tenochtitlan. See Mexico City;
　Tenochtitlan
*México y sus alrededores: Coleccion de
　monumentos, trajes y paisajes en el
　Museo Nacional de México*, 696
Mezquital Valley, 643, 645, 646, 647, 649, 652
Miahuatlan, 483, 513
Michimaloya, 64
Michoacan, 319, 321, 543, 548–549, 550

Michoaque, 412
Mictlan, 26, 394, 408, 409, 597, 600
Mictlancihuatl, 394
Mictlantecuhtli, 25, 31, *44*, 45, 394, 572,
　574, 667
middens: New Fire ceremony, 631–632
Middle Formative period, 523
Middle Postclassic period, 496, 626, 632
　tecpan system, 235–236
midwives, 628
migrations, 2, 144, 196, 201, 412, 544, 549
　histories of, 32, 94–98, *122*–*123*
　Mexica, 93, 399
　to Southern Highlands, 480–481
milchimalli, 271
military, 98, 429, 455
　as leaders and conquerors, 93–94
　structure of, 456–457
　Triple Alliance, 101, 103, 443, 444–445,
　449, 467
minerals, 615. *See also by type*
mines, mining
　copper, 322, 324
　gold and silver, 652, 655
　obsidian, 330, 335–336
Ming Empire, 558, 559, 560, 561, 562, 563
miracles, 683
mirrors: obsidian, 329, 338, 344, *347*, 349
Misantla, 498
Mitla, 513
Mixcoatl, 573, 578
Mixe-Zoquean language family, 129, 496
Mixquiahuala, 64, 65
Mixquic tradition, 357
Mixtec, 480, 481, 512, 632
Mixteca, Mixtecs, 129, 412, 509–510,
　513, 514
Mixteca Alta, 163, 485, 517
Mixtecan, 130
Mixteca-Puebla Polychrome, 518
Mixtec regions, 487
Mixtec-Zapotec zone, 483
Mixtequilla region: Aztec ceramics, 499–500
Mixton, war of, 166
Mizquic, 63, 98
Moteuczoma, Isabel de, 65
Moteuczoma, Martín, 65

Moctezuma, Pedro (Tlacahuepantzin Yohualicahuacatzin; Pedro de Moteucçoma), 64–65, 685
Moctezuma Ilhuicamina. *See* Motecuhzoma Ilhuicamina
Moctezuma Ilhuitemotzin, Diego Luis de, 65
Moctezuma Xocoyotzin. *See* Motecuhzoma Xocoyotzin
Molina, Alonso de, 35, 400
Molotecatl, 431
Molotla (Yautepec), 431
Monarquía indiana (Torquemada), 34
Monoliths Gallery, 42
monumental art, 9, 45, 65
  Calixtlahuaca, 469–470
  Tenochtitlan, 666–667
  Tututepec, 511–512
Moon, 108, 574
moral code, 152
Morelos, 194, 425, 426, 624, 625, 628
  commoner houses in, 212–213
  rural houses in, 252–253
Motagua, Rio, 344
Motecuhzoma Ilhuicamina (Motecuhzoma I; Huehue Moctezuma), 66, 100, 103, 120, 151, 240, 424, 444, 482, 487
  state structure reform, 101–102
Motecuhzoma Xocoyotzin (Motecuhzoma II), 64, 103, 153, 223, 323, 424, 444, 445, 487, 497, 501, 694
  and Cortés, 163–164
  death of, 25–26, 31
  palaces of, 236, 242, 664
  speeches by, 164–165, 167n.2, 234
motlatocapaca, 166
Moyotan, Moyotlan (Tenochtitlan), 100, 606, 664
mud men-and-women, 628
Muerto, Barranca del, 330
multicrafting, 10, 291
Muñón Chimalpahin, Francisco de San Anton, 34
Muñoz Camargo, Diego, 34, 35
Musée de Quai Branly (Paris), 698
Museo de América (Madrid), 698
Museo del Templo Mayor. *See* Templo Mayor Museum

Museo Nacional (National Museum), 42, 696
Museo Nacional de Antropología, 6, 23–24, 42
Museo Yucusaa, 511
Museum of Ethnology (Vienna), 698
Museum of Modern Art, 698
museums, 696, 697, 698
music, 632–633
musical instruments, 290, 324, 545, 628, 632–633
myths, 21, 571
  birth of Quetzalcoatl, 578–579
  creation, 573–575, 596

Nahua, 3, 708, 714
  Christianization of, 677–683
  ethnicity, 412–413
  ethnic judgment, 414–415
  migration stories, 94, 147
  in Southern Highlands, 480–481, 513
Nahuat
  in Huitzilan de Serdán, 415–417
  kinship and work, 417–418
Nahuatization: Southern Highlands, 480–482, 486–488
Nahuatl, 3, 130, 414, 480, 550, 645, 676, 708
  books and manuscripts in, 681–682
  as lingua franca, 137–138
naming: children, 390, 623
Nanahuatzin, 574
Nappa teuctli, 310
Narvaez, Panfilo de, 33
natural phenomena, 124
Natural Protected Areas, 182
Naualpilli, 586
Navajas, Sierra de las (Hidalgo), 645, 649, 655
  high-backed scrapers from, 652, 653
  obsidian from, 330, 331, 332, 334, 335–338, 339, 344, 348, 349, 615
Nayarit, 321, 713
Nebel, Carl, 696
neighborhoods, 213, 365
  craft specialization in, 287–289
  Mexico City, 664–665
  See also calpulli, calpolli
neo-evolutionary theory, 7, 8
New Conquest History, 9, 162

New Fire ceremony, 107, 109, 601, 629, 630–632
New Spain, 501
Nexquipayac, 310
nextlahualtin, 408, 615
Nextlalpan, 64
Nezahualcoyotl, 100, 153, 204, 222, 289, 323, 412, 424, 444, 446, 458
  exile of, 150–151
  park design by, 238–239
  Texcoco palace of, *240, 241*
  and Triple Alliance, 440, 443
Nezahualtecolotl, 65
Night of Sorrows (Noche Triste), 65
nobility, 33, 34, 94, 100, 144, 146, 147, 423, 424–425, 426, 625, 711
  and Cholula, 523–524, 527
  Christianized, 677–678
  encomienda system, 64–65
  wealth variation, 430–431
Noche Triste (Night of Sorrows), 65
Noguera, Eduardo, 76, 451
Nonoalco, 632
Norte de Puebla, Sierra, 417
Nuttal, Celia, 451

Oaxaca, 480, 487, 516, 518, 713
  language families in, 129, 137, *481*
  metallurgy in, 320, 321
  and Triple Alliance, 473, 477–479(table), 509
obsidian, 287, 347, 453, 500, 516, 615
  artifacts made from, 329–330, 333–334
  Colonial period use, 652–653, 669–670
  lapidary art, 343, 344, 345, 350
  from Otumba, 290–291
  prismatic blades from, 285–286, *337*
  Sierra de Las Navajas production of, 335–338
  sources of, 330–333
  Ucareo-Zinapecuaro source, 548–549
occupation: and ethnicity, 412, 414–415, 418
Ochpaniztli, 412
Ocotelulco, 539
Ocuilan, 463
Ocuilteca, 3
Ocuituco, 463

offerings, 66, 181, 624, 632, 714
  lapidary objects used in, 345–346
  Pyramid C (Tula), 56–57
  Templo Mayor, 320–321, 322, *613*, 615–616
Old Acolhua Domain, 483
Olmec cosmology, 104
Olmeca, 129, 412
Olmeca-Xicalanca, 523, 524
Omaxac, 600
Omechicahuaztli, 633
Omecihuatl, 393–394, 573
Ometecuhtli, 393–394, 573
Ometeotl, 394
Ometepec, 483, 484, 485
Opochtli, 310
Orange ware, 355–356, 361, 366
  Early Colonial, 647–652
  See also Black-on-Orange
Organizing Committee of Indigenous and Rural Organizations of the Huasteca Potosina, 415
ornaments, 320, 329
Otomanguean language family, 129, 130
Otomí, 3, 64, 98, 130, 150, 412, 538, 550, 643, 645, 714
  and Tlaxcallan, 540–541
  and Triple Alliance, 444, 445
Otompan, 440
Otontecuhtli, 167
Ottoman Empire, *558, 559, 560, 562, 563*
Otumba, 151, 212, 214, 294n.2, 338, 378, 645, 646
  ceramic production, 365, 366, 647–648, 649, 650, *651*
  commerce in, 287–292
  Early Colonial period, 643, 652
  independent households, 291–292
  lapidary workshops at, 350–352
  obsidian source at, 330, 332, 344
Otumba Polished Tan, 290, 365
Our Lady of Guadalupe, 682
Ovando y Godoy, Juan de, 34–35
Oxomoco, 180
Oztlalpan, 64
oztomeca, 286
Oztuma, 467, 487

Pachuca obsidian source, 335, 500, 516, 518
Pachuca-Zempoala region, 645, 647, 649, 655
Pacific coast, 473
painters, 289, 392
paintings: of historical events, 697–698
paints: ceramic, 362–363
Pajaros, Cerro de los, 511
palaces, 229, 230–232(table), 242, 250, 664
   in *altepetl* capitals, 210–211
   at Ixtapaluca, 205–206
   Postclassic period, 148, 233–237
   social hierarchy and, 424–425
   Spanish terms for, 232–233
   Tenochtitlan, 224–225, 240
   Texcoco, 239, 241
Palacio del Marqués del Apartado, 24
Palacio Tolteca, 235
palma processing, 375
Pamé speakers, 129–130, 645
Panquetzaliztli, 579
Panteca, 480
Pantitlan, 600, 601
Papantla, 413
Paredón obsidian sources, 330, 332, 333, 344
parks, 229, 230–232(table), 238–239
Parsons, Jeffrey R., 60
Parsons, Mary: on whorls, 376–377
patio groups, 251–252, 626
Pátzcuaro, Lake, 95
Pátzcuaro Basin, Lake, 543, 544–545, 549
peasants, 269. *See also* commoners
peddlers, 284, 286–287, 294
Peña, Agustín, 58
Peñafiel, Antonio, 451
penitential rituals, 600
petates, 254, 302, 304
Petlacallan, 484
petroglyphs (rock art), 59
Piaxtla-Chinantla, 487
Pico de Orizaba obsidian source, 330, 516, 518
pictography
   historic and legal records, 117–118
   structure of, 119–121
pictures: Christian, 682–683
pilgrimages, 598, 600, 601, 714
Pilitas Polychrome, 518
Pinctada maztlanica, 45
pipiltin. *See* leaders; nobility

Pizarro expedition, 564
place names, 120, 137, 352, 512, 513
Place of the Dead, 615
plants, 615, 669
   lake-derived, 301, 304
platforms, 210, 510–511, 606, 679–680
plays: morality, 682
Plaza Gamio, 48, 667–668
plazas, 234, 242, 665
pleasure palaces and parks, 229, 240–241, 242, 319, 323
pochteca, 145, 284, 286, 288, 291, 292, 294n.2, 345, 428, 444
Pochutec, Pochutecan, 137, 512
Pochutla, San Pedro, 137, 512, 514, 518
Poiauhtecatl, 576
polishing sand, 345
Polychrome pottery, 356
polygyny, 39, 677
Pomar, Juan Bautista, 34, 35
Popocatepetl, 576
Popocatépetl volcano, 523, 596, 598
   tzoalli of, 601–602
Popoloca, 480
Popoloca, Sierra, 129, 496
Popotlan, 96
population, 10–11, 559
   Basin of Mexico, 7, 78, 82–83, 190–194
   Colonial period recovery and, 195–198
   Early Colonial period, 646–647
   Late Aztec, 82–83, 150, 151
   Spanish Conquest and, 194–195, 710
   and *tecpan* system, 235–236
   and Tenochtitlan, 219–220
porcelain: Chinese, 669
Portezuelo, Cerro, 143
Postclassic period, 629
   altepeme in, 145–149
   in Cholula, 525–530
   ethnohistories in, 143–144
   house forms in, 248–254
   pictography of, 119–121
   salt making in, 308–310
   social organization of, 93–94
   tecpan system in, 235–236
   Tula, 65–66
   See also by subperiod
potters: in Otumba, 288–289

pottery. *See* ceramics
precipitation, 75
Prescott, William H., 162
priests, priestesses, 118, 225, 394, 428–429, 600
Primer coloquio sobre la Guerra en el México Antiguo, 460
Primeros memoriales (Sahagún), 32–33, 378, 379
prismatic blades, 58, 290, 291, 333
prisoners. *See* captives
producer-sellers, 284, 285
profane realm, *400*
Programa de Arqueología Urbana, 25, 43–44, 210, 662, 663, 667
projectile points, 329, 338
prostitutes, 226
Proto-Aztecan, 130, 137
Proyecto de Rescate Arqueológico Boulevard Tula-Iturbide, 58–59
Proyecto Templo Mayor, 24, 25
Proyecto Tula, 56, 57–58
psychoactive substances, 407, 600
Puchtlan, 614
Puebla, 194, 417, 480, 487
Puebla, Sierra de, 713
Puebla-Tlaxcala Valley, 523, *524*, 529, 711
  political structure of, 537–538
pulque, 31
Purépecha, 480
  archaeology, 548–551
  architecture, 546–547
  history of, 544–545
Purépecha Empire, 543–551
purification rituals, 109
Pyramid B (Tula), 53, 57, 148
Pyramid C (Tula), 56–57
"Pyramid of the Sun at Teotihuacan, The" (Velasco), 697
pyramids, 469
  in *altepetl* capitals, 208–209
  Tenayuca, *203*, 204
  Tenochtitlan Sacred Precinct, 607, *609*, 610–611, 613, 616–617n.2
  yacata-style, 546–547
  See also by name
pyrite discs, 549

Qualpopoca, 164, 165
quarries, Sierra de Las Navajas, 335, 339
Quauhchichinollan, 425
quauholloll (mace or club), 458
quauhpilli, 424
Quauhquechollan, 529
Quauhtochco, 498
Quecholli: ritual hunting during, 578–579
Quesada, Fernando, 452
Quetzalcoatl, 23, 152, 164, 338, 407, 538, 572, 573, 576, 596, 597, 602, 612
  birth of, 578–579
  creation of humans, 574–575
  Ehecatl as avatar, 204, 210
  temples to, 222, 524, 527–528
Quetzaltepec, 345
Quiahuixtlan, 539
Quiauhteopan, Quiauhtepan, 321, 463, 473, 483
Quiauhtepec, 481
Quilaztli, 575
Quinatzin, 236, 241

racism, 413, 414
ranches, 646, 650, 54
rasps: bone, 632–633
rattles, 632, *633*
Real y Pontificia Universidad de México, 23
rebellions, 413, 439, 564
reciprocity, 180, 181, 598
  human sacrifice and, 407–408
  and Tenochtitlan Sacred Precinct, 614–616
Red Ware pottery, 290, 356, 359, *360*, *361*, 367, 630, *650*
  Early Colonial, 649, 669
  production areas, 366, 368
reed-processors, 307–308
reeds, 301–302, 304–305, 360
refugees, 427
Relación de Cholula, 525
Relación de las cosas notables de la Nueva España (Zorita), 34
Relación de Michoacan (RM), 283, 543, 545
Relación de Texcoco (Pomar), 34
Relaciones geográficas, 335, 430, 513, 516, 518
Relaciones geográficas del siglo XVI (Ovando y Godoy), 34–35, 310

Relaciones históricas (Alva Ixtlilxochitl), 34
Relaciones originales de Chalco Amaquemecan (Muñón Chimalpahin), 34
religion
  centralized, 612–614
  in codices, 30–31
  empires and, 561–562
  Mexica, 102, 571
  native, 713–714
  Pan-Mesoamerican, 714–715
  reciprocity and, 614–616
  syncretism, 712–713
  See also Christianity
religious orders: Christian, 675–676
reliquary: Quetzalcoatl's, 524, 527
repartimiento, 645
residences, 229, 250, 251. *See also* houses; palaces
resilience theory, 176, 177
resistance: to imperial authority, 498, 563–564
resource exploitation: Purépecha, 548–549
Revillagigedo, Viceroy, 21, 23, 196–197
revitalization, 524, 679
Reyes García, Luis, 162
Ricard, Robert, 712
Rinconada, 501
rituals, 31, 118, 166, 212, 304, 334, 412, 446, 538, 577–579, 683
  cyclical, 152, 180, 181
  fertility and curing, 627–628
  funerary, 625–626
  household, 623–625, 633–634
  household feasting, 629–630
  landscape and, 596–602
  music and, 632–633
  New Fire Ceremony, 630–632
  performative, 595–596
  warfare, 455–456
  See also sacrifice
roads, 219, 539
Robertson, Donald, 698
rock crystal, 343, 344, 345, 346
Rodríguez, María del Carmen, 58
Romans, 690
royalty, 121, 147–148, 229. *See also* nobility; rulers, rulership
Ruiz de Alarcón, Hernando, 600, 624

rulers, rulership, 120, 121, 271, 447, 514
  altepetl, 440–441
  histories of, 32, 33
  male and female, 393, 394, 579–580
  in Triple Alliance, 443–444
ruling councils, 525
rural areas: in Spanish Colonial period, 643–655
Russian Empire, 558

sacred bundles, 523, 575, 576
Sacred Mountain, 180–181, 182
Sacred Precinct (Tenochtitlan), 664
  design of, 606–608
sacrifice(s), 101, 109, 380, 561, 576, 629, 631
  child, 181, 524
  creation of time, 110–111
  human, 95, 96, 407–408, 577–578, 579, 580–581
  for Templo Mayor, 446, 615–616
Safavid Empire, 558, 559, 560, 562, 563
Sahagún, Bernardino de, 6, 32–33, 53, 250, 267, 360, 400, 586, 608, 623, 714
saints, 679, 682–683
salas claustros, 65
salt, salt making, 84, 292, 301, 305, 306, 307
  archaeological evidence for, 308–310
San Andrés Collomochco, 530
San Bartolomé Salinas, 308, 310
Sanders, William T., 60, 175
San Gregorio Atlapulco-Xochimilco, 191, 192. *See also* Atlapulco; Xochimilco
San Hipólito market, 653
San José de los Naturales, 693
San Juan Moyotlan, 664
San Luis Potosí, 322
San Pablo Zoquipan (Teopan), 664
San Sebastián Atzacoalco, 664
Santa Cecilia Acatitlan, 208
Santa Inés site, 649
Santa María Cuepopán, 664
Santiago Tulantepec obsidian source, 332
Santiago Tuxtla, 501
Santley, Robert S., 60
Sayula Basin (Cuenca de Sayula), 319, 324, 550
scent: as offering, 632
scepters, 338, 344, *347*, *348*

scholarship, scholars, 6–7
schools, 146, 211, 213, 225, 390, 614
scrapers, 291, 329, 333, 652, 653
scribes, 586
sculptures, 22, 53, 57, 242, 344, 469
    conservation of, 44–45
    monumental, 21, 23, 24, 42
    Spanish Colonial, 693–694
    Spanish repurposing of, 690–691
    Tenochtitlan, 666–667
    Tlaltecuhtli, 25, 26(fig.)–27
    Toltec-influenced, 65–66
    from Tututepec, 511–512
seasons, 181, 306
Seler, Eduard, 451
"Senate of Tlaxcala" (Gutiérrez), 697
serpentine/jadeite, 343
serpents, 24, 65
services sector, 224–225
settlement patterns
    Basin of Mexico, 78–85
    Early Colonial period, 646–647
    lake resource specialists, 310–312
shamans, 406, 407
sheep, 647
shell, 45, 344
shields, 166, 167, 379, *458*
shrines, 24, 25, 147, 210, 222–223, 524, 529, 611
Sigüenza Map, 94
silver, 319, 320, 652, 655
Six Months' Residence and Travels in Mexico
    (Bullock), 697
skull rack, 27, 57, 58, 65, 222
slaves, 413, 430, 665, 670
slips: ceramic, 362–363
smallholders: farmers as, 271–272
smallpox epidemics, 65, 194–195
small-scale producers, 284
social class, 414, 423–424, 646
social hierarchy, 73, 152
social inequality, 432–433
social organization, 250
    Central and Southern Highlands, 93–94
sociedad de castas, 413
Soconusco, 138
soils, 265
soldiers, 429, *459*

Songhay Empire, *558*, 559, 560, 562, 563
songs: flowery, 632
souls
    after death, 408–409
    in human body, 402–407
sound: as offering, 632
South America: metallurgy from, 319
Southern Highlands, 473
    Aztec provinces in, 474–479
    ethnic groups in, 480–481
    geography of, 479–480
    Nahuatization, 481–482, 486–488
    studies of, 482–486
Soyaltepec volcano, 330
space-time, 110–111, *113*, 592
Spain, *558*, 565–566, 690
Spaniards, 9, 664–665
Spanish Conquest, 9, 109, 153, 161, 189, 530, 547
    chronicles, 33–35
    death of Motecuhzoma II, 25–26
    Gulf Lowlands, 501–502
    indigenous conquerors, 162–163
    metalwork, 323–324
    Motecuhzoma Xocoyotzin's role in, 163–165
    and Nahua ethnicity, 412–413
    outlying areas, 645–655
    rebuilding of Mexico City, 241–242
    repurposing Aztec buildings and
        sculptures, 690–691
    space-time and, 114–115
speakers, 234–235
speeches: Motecuhzoma Xocoyotzin's, 164–165, 167n.2
Spicer, Edward, 710–711
Spinden, Herbert, 698
spindle whorls, 375, *515*
    analysis of, 376–378
    decorations on, 380–381
    Otumba production of, 290, 291
spinning and weaving, 290, 378
Spiritual Conquest of Mexico, The (Ricard), 712
springs, 239, 267, 302
state(s), 8, 10, 104
    altepetl structure, 145–149
    confederacies, 149–150
    power sharing, 144–145
    structure of, 101–102

statues: Christian, 682–683
stela: from Tututepec, 511–512
stone(s)
    physical and spiritual properties of, 344
    sacrificial, 380
See also obsidian
storage systems, 224, 249
Stoutamire, James, 60
street systems, 147, 220, 222
sugar production, 501
sumptuary laws, 424, 430
Sun, 574
    and *tonalli*, 405–406
Sun Stone, 6, 21, 22, 23, *111*, 380, 695
    design of, 587–590
    religious iconography of, 588–589
    replicas of, 696–697
supernatural beings, 180, 212, 585. *See also*
    deities
supernatural forces, 180, 402–403, 407, 682
survey: Basin of Mexico, 7, 75–78
sustenance, 181, 615
sweat baths, 57, 58, 222, 225, 252, 628
sweeping, 623
syncretism
    cultural and religious, 712–713
    in Spanish Colonial art, 693–694

tadpoles, 304
Tamazcaltepec, 322
Tamime, 412
Tángaxoan, 544–545
Tangáxuan II, 547
Tapia, Andrés de, 34, 474, 525, 612
Tarascan Empire, 487, 543, *544*
Tarascan Frontier, 483
Tarascan languages, 480
Tarascans, 129, 283, 324, 457, 543. *See also*
    Purépecha Empire
Tarascan State, 319
Taríacuri, 543, 544–545
tax collectors, 429, 447, 466, 467
tax system, 10, 96, 98, 118, 225, 270, 432, 464–
    466. *See also* tribute
Tazayulan, 64
teachers, 225
tecalli, teccalli, 426, 427, 537–538
Tecocomulco obsidian source, 332

Tecolote obsidian source, Cerro, 332
Tecospa, 713
Tecozautla, 65
tecpan, 146, 229
    Postclassic period, 235–237
    structure of, 233–235
    in villages, 237–238
tecpan glyph, 233
Tecpantepec, 483
tecpantlalli, 271
Tecpayocan, 96
Tecpilpan, 335
Tecuciztecatl, 574
teuctli, 424
tehcatl, 223
Tehuacan Valley, 376
Tehuantepec, 306, 487, 513
tehuehuelli, 379
Tehuetzquititzin, Diego de San Francisco, 166
teixiptla, texiptlahuan, 408, 577–578, 580–581,
    585, 599, 615
Teloloapan, 486, 487
telpochcalli, 146, 211, 213, 222, 225, 390
temalacatl, 380
Temazcalapa, 335
temazcales, 57, 58, 222, 225, 252, 628
Temezcaltepec, 463, 483
Temple of the Sun (Tenochtitlan), 664
temples, 239, 524
    in *altepeme*, 146, 147, 204
    circular, 204, 210, 222
    Ehecatl, 470, 664
    on pyramids, 208–209
    Quetzalcoatl's, 527–528
    in Tenochtitlan Sacred Precinct, 607,
        610–611, 613
Templo Mayor (Tenochtitlan), 9, 11, 26, 66, 114,
    222, 225, 242, 446, 580, *609*, 613, 625, 662
    architectural conservation, 45–46
    construction of, 608, *610*
    cosmology of, 104, 589–590
    excavation of, 24–25
    metalwork offerings in, 320–321, 322
    obsidian objects in, 347, 350
    and Plaza Gamio, 667–668
    as primordial mountain, 103, 104
    renovation of, 124, 445
    sacrifices and offerings in, 615–616

Templo Mayor Museum, 6, 25, 27, 41, 43
Templo Mayor Project, 42–43
Tenanco, 150
Tenango obsidian source, Rancho, 332
Tenayuca, 60, *123*, 124, 202, *203*, 204, 208, 209, 236, 597
Tenayuca phase, 356, 358
Tenayuca pottery, 56, 358
Teniltzin, 501
Tenime, 129
Tenismo, Cerro, 205, 469
Tenoch, *123*–124
Tenochca, 3, 103, 151, 235, 239, 240–241, 585
Tenochtitlan, 3, 7, 24, 34, 45, 60, 85, 99, 100, 109, 118, 137, 164, 195, 209, 219, 229, 292, 294n.2, 303, 334, 388, 390, 644, 662, 709
  Aztec map of, *113*, *123*
  and Central Highlands, 468–470
  ceramic production, 365, *367*
  cosmological structure of, 589–590, *591*
  founding of, 32, *123*, 236
  houses in, 212–213
  landscape of, 596–597
  market, 223–224, 283
  metallurgy, 320–321
  parks and palaces in, 240–241, 236–237
  population of, 191–193, 559
  reciprocity in, 614–616
  Sacred Precinct of, 605–614, 664
  size of, 219–220
  structure of, *103*–104, 114, 220–223
  supremacy of, 442–443
  tribute system, 84, 151, 448
  and Triple Alliance, 73, 101, 151, 440
  warfare, 444–445
  work in, 224–226
Tenochtitlan phase, 356, 358
Tenochtitlan-Tlatelolco, 153, 365
Teocalco, 600
Teocalli, 597, 598
Teocalli of Sacred Warfare, 59, 587
Teochichimeca, 3, 412
teomamaque, 94
Teopan (Tenochtitlan), 100, 606
Teopanzolco, 208
Teotihuacan, 23, 83, 98, 104, 137, 148, 191, 251, 330, 346, 376, 523, 574, 589, 611
  apartment compounds, 146–147

  collapse of, 143, 480
  relics, 575, 576
Teotihuacan Valley, 643, 645, 649
  market trade in, 291, 292
teotlalli (temple land), 271
Teotlalpan, 63, 64
Teoyaomiqui. *See* Coatlicue
Teozacualco, 483
Teozapotlan, 483
Tepanecas, 3, 94, 99, 440, 444
Tepanec Empire, 31, 32, 63, 96, 98, 100, 150–151, 236, 238
Tepanec War, 239
Tepan Teohuatzin, 614
Tepeaca, 529, 597
Tepechpan, 449
Tepecualcuilco, 483, 486
Tepeqoacuilco, 321, 322, 463, 473
Tepeticpac, 539
Tepetitlan, 64, 252
Tepetixteca, 480
Tepetlaoztoc, 365
Tepexic, 64
Tepeyacac avenue, 606
Tepeyac Hill, 222
Tepictoton, 576, 601
Tepozotlán, 150, 430, 467, *679*
Tepoztecatl, 586
teputopilli, 454
Tequahuehuetzin, 530
Tequistlatec, 129
tequitcatlalli, tequitcamilli, 271
tequitl relationships, 292–293
Terminal Formative period, 191
Terminal Postclassic, 535–536
terrace systems, 265–267
Terrazas y Moctezuma, Lucia, 487
territorial organization, 211–212
Tesifón de Moctezuma, Pedro, 65
Tesoro, 61
Tetellan, 483
Tetenanco, 484
teteo imixiptlahuan, 408, 615
Tetla, 252
Tetlanma, 613, 614
Tetlystaca, 335
teuctli, 537, 538
Texcateca, 480

Texcoco, Tetzcoco, 34, 98, 104, 118, 121, 130, 166, 191, 209, 222, 283, 289, 292, 294n.2, *425*, 448, 509, 601, 644
    Acolhua dynasty, 204, 236
    ceramic production, 366, *367*, 368
    Late Postclassic ceramics, 60, 61
    parks and palaces in, 239–*240*, 241
    in Triple Alliance, 73, 151, 440, 442–443, 444
    warfare, 100, 150, 151
Texcoco, Lake, 84, 222, 302, 647
Texcoco Fabric Mark pottery, 292, *308*, 310
Texcoco Molded; Texcoco Filleted censers, 365, 499, 500
Texcoco Red pottery, 669
Texcotzingo, 59, 238, 239–*240*, 242
Texome, 480
textiles, 212, 291, 304, 375–376, 381, 55
teyolia, 404–405, 408, 409
Tezcacoatl Tlacochcalco, 616
Tezcatlipoca, 148, 152, 334, 344, 518, 573, 575, 596, 612
    divine representative of, 577–*578*, 580–581
    Tenochtitlan temple to, 610–611
    Tlaxcaltecan cult of, 538–539
Tezontepec, 335
Tezoyuca, 61
Tezozomoc, 100, 151
Thomas, Hugh, 162
Tianquiznahuaca (Cholula), 525, 527, 530
Tiçaua, 586
Tierra Caliente, 480
Tierra Fria, 480
Tierra Templada, 480
Tilantongo, 512, 514, 517
Tillan Calmecac, 616
time, 592
    Aztec concepts of, 112–114
    Spanish interpretation of, 114–115
    and universe, 110–111, 572–573
time depth, 177
tin, 319, 322–323
Tira de la Peregrinación, 32
Tira de Tepechpan, 118, 125
Tizapan, 98
Tizatlan, *425*, 539–540
Tizoc, 27, 103, 124, *125*

Tizoc Stone, 21, 23, 66, 411, 587, 695
    replicas of, 696–697
Tlacaelel, 151, 152, 153, 529
Tlacahuapan, 65
Tlacahuepantzin Yohualicahuacatzin. *See* Moctezuma, Pedro
Tlacaxipeualiztli, Tlacaxipehualiztli, 109, 586
Tlachco, 463, 473, 481, 483, 487
Tlachihualtepetl (Cholula), 524, 527
Tlachinollan, 484
Tlachquiauco, Tlachquiaco, 473, 483, 487
Tlacoçautitlan. *See* Tlacozauhtitlan
Tlacochcalco Acatl Yiacapan, 616
tlacôcoalnamacac, 284, 286–287, 294
Tlacopan, 73, 100, 191, 222, 294, 440, 445, 601
    loss of power, 442, 443
    tribute system, 84, 448
Tlacopan avenue, 606
Tlacotepehua, 480
tlahtoani, 413, 430, 665, 670
Tlacozauhtitlan (Tlacozautitlan, Tlacoçautitlan), 463, 473, 483, 487
tlacuiloque (painters), 30, 118
tlahuehuetquei (land elders), 146
Tlahuelilpan, 65
Tlahuizcalpantecuhtli, 572
tlahuiztli, 166–167
Tlalatlauhco, 467
Tlalchiach, 525
Tlalhuicas, 444, 486
Tlalmanalco, 150
Tlaloc, 114, 209, 470, 576, 589, 600, 601, 602, 612
    patronage of, 596–597
    Templo Mayor shrine to, 24, 103, 222
    and Tenochtitlan Sacred Precinct, 608, 614
Tlaloc, Mount, 596, 597, 601
Tlalocan, 26, 114, 181, 408, 596, 597
Tlaloqueh, 596, 600, 601
Tlaltecuhtli, 25, *26*–27, 45, 103, 666, *691*
Tlalteotl, 573–574, 596
Tlalticpac, 596
Tlalticpaque, 600
tlamatinime, 118
Tlanchinollan, 484
Tlapa dynasty, 481
Tlapaltecatl Opochtzin, 571

Tlapan, 473, 479, 483–484, 485
Tlapanec, 480, 481–482
Tlapaneca, 129
Tlapa-Tlachinollan, 481, 487
Tlapizáhuac, 251
tlaquimilolli, 523, 575, 576
Tlataya, Sierra de, 322–323
Tlatelolco, 3, 9, 66, 151, 209, 294n.2,
    303, 334, 365, 376, 442, 626,
    654, 709
  conquest of, 590–591
  market in, 283, 285
Tlatelolco phase, 60
  pottery, 356, 358
Tlatilco, *190*
Tlatlauhqui Tezcatlipoca, 573
tlahtoani, tlahtoque, 33, 105, 147, 213, 223, 234–
    235, 394, 424, 444, 467, 497, 560
  Acamapichtli as first, 63, 98, 99
  and *altepeme*, 145, 146, 206,
    211–212, 440
  and *cihuacoatl*, 579–580
  ritual hunting, 578–579
  souls of, 406–407
  state formation and, 149–150
tlatocan, 152–153, 525
tlatocatlalli, teuctalli, 271
Tlatzihuizteca, 480
Tlaxcala, 3, 34, 144, 194, 529, 530, 590,
    676, 713
  Cortés in, 165, 166
  Nahuas in, 415, 708
Tlaxcallan, 442, 535–536
  political structure, 537–538, 539–540
  state building, 540–541
  Tezcatlipoca cult, 538–539
Tlaxcaltecans, 535–536, 537, 539–540
Tlaxcopan, 65
Tlaxiaco, 513
tlaxilacaltin, tlaxilacalli (corporate
    groups), 146–147, 149
tlayacatl, tlayacatin, 149–150
Tlayahualoliztli, 598
Tlazolteotl, 378, 623
Tochpan, 498
Tochtepec, 497, 498, 499, 502
Toci (Teteo inana), 412, 623

Tolimeca, 480
Tollan, 103, 152
  as archetypal *altepetl*, 597–598
  Tollan Chollollan Tlachihualtepetl, 523, 525,
    526, 530
  as holy city, 527–529
  See also Cholula
Tollan phase, 60
Tollan-Teotihuacan, 104–105
Tollan Xicocotitlan, 53, 54–55
Tollocan, 463, 467
Tōltēcah, 129
tolteca itzli, 332, 333
Tolteca-Chichimeca, 65, 513–514, 518,
    523, 597
Toltec Empire, 55
Toltec orange pottery, 55
Toltecs, 3, 98, 144, 148, 330, 424, 586
  heritage of, 65–66
  and Mexica identity, 102–103, 104
Toluca Valley: commoner households
    in, 212–213
Tonalamatl de Aubin, 31
tonalli, 405–406
tonalpohualli (260-day cycle), 30, 107–108,
    573, 585, 589, 612, 613
tonalpouhque, 573, 574, 581
Tonameca, 518
Tonatiuh, 102, 111
Tonatiuhilhuícatl, 408
toponyms, 137, 352, 512, 513
Torquemada, Juan de, 34, 241, 530
Toscano, Salvador, 698
Totogal, 500–501
Totolapan, 480
Totonac, 412, 496
Totonacan language family, 129, 130
Totonacapan, 344, 502
Totoquihuatzin, 440
Tototepec, 345, 484
Totozoquean, 129
tourism, 696–697, 698
Toussaint, Manuel, 698
Toxcati festival, 577–578
Tozpalatl spring, 616
Toztlan, 500, 501, 502

trade, traders, 10, 137, 393, 412
  Early Colonial period, 653–654
  lapidary objects, 344, 346
  long-distance, 282, 286, 293–294
  Mixtec, 509–510
  into Otumba, 291–292
  Tututepec, 515, 516
transportation, 223–224, 281, 284, 303
travel: promotion of, 696
traza, la (Mexico City), 664, 665
Tree of Life, 615
Tres Cabezas obsidian source, 332
tribute, 10, 64, 100, 117, 151, 193, 271, 284, 291, 292–293, 306, 364, 396, 412, 513, 545, 645
  agricultural products, 263, 270
  Aztec Empire, 84, 482–483, 644
  from Central Highlands, 463, 464–466
  from Gulf Lowlands, 497–498
  lapidary material, 344, 346
  metal objects as, 321–322
  vs. taxation, 432, 433
  textiles as, 375, 377–378, 381
  Triple Alliance, 441–442, 448–449, 488, 709
Triple Alliance, 3, 4(fig.), 73, 118, 219, 332, 439, 541, 557, 563, 644–645, 708–709
  and *altepeme*, 440–441
  asymmetry of, 442–443
  and Central Highlands, 463–471
  comparison to Delian League, 564–565
  conquests of, 446–447
  economy, 560–561
  and Gulf Lowland provinces, 495–503
  identity and political structure, 709–710
  intermingling among, 441–442
  languages spoken in, 130–138
  lapidary objects, 345–352
  as military power, 559–560
  obsidian sources, 335, 336–337, 338–339
  population, 191, 193
  power sharing in, 443–446
  in Southern Highlands, 473–488
  and Spain, 565–566
  structure of, 100–101, 151–153
  tribute and finance, 448–449
Triqui, 480

Tula, 66, 93, 98, 104, 148, 152, 164, 191, 202, 235, 440, 575, 589, 611, 626
  Aztec era, 63–64
  cultural sequence of, 55–58
  excavations of, 53–54, 60–61
  house groups in, 251–252
  post-Toltec materials and features at, 58–59, 61–63
  under Spanish rule, 64–65
  as Tollan Xicocotitlan, 54–55
Tula Chico, 60–61
Tula Grande, 54, 56, 63
Tulancingo obsidian, 330, 332, 333
tules: goods made of, 304–306
Tultengo (Tula), 58
Tumba Azteca (Tula), 56
turkeys, 111, 668–669
turquoise, 343, 344, 523, 615
Tututepec, 484, 487
  civic-ceremonial core, 510–511
  conquests and alliances, 513–514
  economic organization, 515–517
  interaction sphere, 517–518
  and Mixtec trade circuit, 509–510
  Monument 6, *511–512*
Tuxtla Mountains, 499, 500–501
Twenty Centuries of Mexican Art, 698
260-day calendrical cycle, 30, 107–108, 573, 585, 589, 612, 613
Tying of the Years festival (*Xiuhmolpilli*), 599, 601
typhus (*matlazahuatl*), 196
Tzicoac, 498
Tzihuacoyotllos, 65
Tzintzuntzan, 543, 545, 549
tzoalli, 601–602, 616
tzompantli, 27, 57, 58, 65, 222

uacúsecha lineage, 549
Ucareo-Zinapecuaro obsidian source, 548–549
UCI. *See* Unión Campesina Indpendiente
Uitziluaque (Cholula), 525
Uixachtecatl (Star Hill), 109
Uixtacihuatl, 577
Uixtoccihuatl, 310
Uixtoti, 129

underworld, 408, 572. *See also* Mictlan
Unidad Deportiva y Residencial Campestre Acozac, 204
Unión Campesina Indpendiente (UCI), 417
United States: tourism, 698
universe, 108, 110–111, 572–573
Universidad Nacional Autónoma de México (National Autonomous University of Mexico), 41
University of Missouri: Tula excavations, 60, 61
urban centers, 80, 83, 84, 427. *See also various cities*
urban planning, 201
Urichu, 548, 549
Uto-Aztecan language family, 129, 130, 480

Vaillant, George, 76, 631
Vaughn, Mary Kay, 414
Vázquez de Tapia, Bernardino, 34
Velasco, José María, 697
Venus, 108
Veracruz Huasteca, 414
Verde, Rio, 509, 510
Victoria, Guadalupe, 23
"View of the Valley of Mexico from the Hill of Santa Isabel" (Velasco), 697–698
Vijayanagara Empire, 558, 559, 560, 561–562
Villa del Espiritu Santo (Coatzacoalcos), 500
villages, 80, 190
  tecpans in, 237–238
Villagrán, Agustín, 59
Virgin's Children: Life in an Aztec Village Today, The (Madsen), 713
Vistas de las Cordilleras y Monumentos de los pueblos indigenas de América (Humboldt), 23, 696
Vocabulario en lengua castellana y mexicana (Molina), 35, 400
Vocabularios, 35
Voyage pittoresque et archéologique dans la partie la plus intéresante du Mexique (Nebel), 696
Vues de Cordilliéres et monumens des pueples indigenes de l'Amerique (Humboldt), 696

War and Society in Ancient Mesoamerica (Hassig), 452
warehouses: Tenochtitlan, 224
warfare, 9, 124, 166, 379, 456–458, 513, 529, 601
  archaeology of, 452–454
  Basin of Mexico, 63, 98
  flowery, 454–455, 529
  gender roles and, 395–396
  historiography of, 451–452
  and Mexica migrations, 96, 98
  Purépecha, 547, 549
  research on, 459–460
  Tepaneca, 150, 236, 238
  Tezozomoc-Texcoco, 100
  and Triple Alliance, 151, 444–445, 448, 559–560
Warman, Antonio, 414
warrior processions, 65
warriors, 424, 429, 517, 633
  houses for, 211, 390, 392
  women who die during childbirth as, 26, 379
water control, 83, 219, 239
  agriculture and, 266–267
  chinampas, 182–185
water folk, 310
waterfowl, 301, 304, 306
water sources, 182, 219, 222, 600, 616
wealth
  of commoners, 425–426
  inequality of, 430–431
weaponry, 457–458, 616
  obsidian used in, 333, 336–337
weaving, weavers, 254, 378, 379, 392, 586
whistles, 632, 633
women, 375, 376, 379, 396, 586
  during childbirth, 394–395
  household roles, 249, 392, 623, 624
work
  and ethnic identity, 412, 414–415, 418
  in Tenochtitlan, 224–226
work projects, 444, 445–446
workshops: household, 10, 212
World Mountain, 598
writing, 392

Xalapa, 498
Xaltocan, 7, 96, 150, 212, 214, 306, 310, 337, 365, 632, 633, 643, 645
  burials in, 625, 626
  curated figurines form, 628–629
  Early Colonial period, 649, 652
  households in, 251, 253–256
  majolica use, 650–651
Xaltocan, Lake, 84, 267, 302
xihuitl, 108–109, 110, 115
Xilitla, 415
Xilo, 586
Xilonen, 577
Xilotepec, 463, 467
Xipe Totec, 167, 528, 586, 612
Xippacoyan, 64
Xiquipilco, 464, 465
Xiuhcalca (Cholula), 525
xiuhmolpilli (52-year cycle), 30, 630–631
  festival for, 599, 601
xiuhpohualli (365-day cycle), 30, 573, 585
  festival for, 599, 612
Xiuhtecuhtli, 572, 575, 667
Xiuhtlalpilli, 601, 629, 630–632
Xiuhtlati, 586
Xochicalco, 104, 191, 632
Xochimilcas, 94, 412
Xochimilco, 63, 98, 149, 268, 269, 294n.2, 358, 365, 444, 445, 601
Xochimilco, Lake, 151, 269, 302, 303
Xochipilli-Macuilxochitl, 611
Xochiquentzin, Pablo, 166
Xochiquetzal, 575, 577
Xochitecatl-Cacaxtla, 535
Xochitepec, 467
Xochitlan, 64
Xocotitlan, 463
Xolotl, 204, 597
Xoxopehualoc, 65

Yacapixtla, 425
yacata, 546–547
Yacatecuhtli, 614
Yautepec, 212, 213, 427, 431
Yautepec Valley, 652
Yayauhqui Tezcatlipoca, 573
Year Bearers, 109–110, 180
Yehualican, 241
Yoallan (Iguala), 486
Yoaltepec, 473, 483, 484–485, 487
yóllotl, 404
Yopico, 320
Yopilcalco, 607
Yopime, 412
Yucu Dzaa. *See* Tututepec
Yucudzaa phase, 509
Yucudzaa Polychrome pottery, 518
yuhuitayu, 514

Zaachila, 513
Zacapu, 633
Zacapu Basin, 544, 549
Zacatecas, 319, 322
Zacatenco, 310
Zacatepec, 517
Zacatepetl Hill, 578
Zacualtipan, 344
Zapata, Emiliano, 414
Zapatista rebellion, 415
Zapotecan language, 130, 130, 480
Zapotecs, 513
Zempoala-Pachuca region. *See* Pachuca-Zempoala region
Zirahuén Basin, 548
Zompanco, 483
zoos, 223, 240–241, 242, 323
Zoquean language family, 129, 130
Zorita, Alonso de, 34, 35
Zumárraga, Juan de, 242, 690
Zumpahuacan, 467
Zumpango, 96, 267
Zumpango, Lake, 302